Roads to Paradise

Volume 2

Roads to Paradise

Eschatology and Concepts of the Hereafter in Islam

VOLUME 2

Continuity and Change
The Plurality of Eschatological Representations in the Islamicate World

Edited by

Sebastian Günther and Todd Lawson

With the Assistance of

Christian Mauder

TUTA SUB AEGIDE PALLAS 1683

BRILL

LEIDEN | BOSTON

Originally published in hardback in 2016 as Volume 136/2 in the series Islamic History and Civilization – Studies and Texts.

Cover illustration: *Ḥūrīs* in Paradise, *Miʿrājnāme*, Herat, 1430s. BnF Supplement Turc 190 – Fol. 49v.

The Library of Congress has cataloged the hardcover edition as follows:

Names: Gunther, Sebastian. | Lawson, Todd, 1948– | Mauder, Christian.
Title: Roads to paradise : eschatology and concepts of the hereafter in Islam / edited by Sebastian Gunther, Todd Lawson, with the assistance of Christian Mauder.
Description: Leiden ; Boston : Brill, [2017] | Series: Islamic history and civilization, ISSN 0929-2403 ; volume 136 | Includes bibliographical references and index. Contents: Volume 1. Foundations and the formation of a tradition. Reflections on the hereafter in the Quran and Islamic religious thought— Volume 2. Continuity and Change. The Plurality of Eschatological Representations in the Islamicate World (Set)
Identifiers: LCCN 2016046348 (print) | LCCN 2016047258 (ebook) | ISBN 9789004333130 (hardback : alk. paper) | ISBN 9789004330948 (hardback : alk. paper) | ISBN 9789004330955 (hardback : alk. paper) | ISBN 9789004333154 (E-book)
Subjects: LCSH: Islamic eschatology. | Future life—Islam. | Islamic eschatology—Qur'anic teaching. | Future life—Islam—Qur'anic teaching.
Classification: LCC BP166.8 .R63 2017 (print) | LCC BP166.8 (ebook) | DDC 297.2/3—dc23
LC record available at https://lccn.loc.gov/2016046348

Typeface for the Latin, Greek, and Cyrillic scripts: "Brill". See and download: brill.com/brill-typeface.

ISBN 978-90-04-72491-4 (paperback, set, 2024)
ISBN 978-90-04-71180-8 (paperback, vol. 1, 2024)
ISBN 978-90-04-71249-2 (paperback, vol. 2, 2024)
ISBN 978-90-04-33313-0 (hardback, set)
ISBN 978-90-04-33094-8 (hardback, vol. 1)
ISBN 978-90-04-33095-5 (hardback, vol. 2)
ISBN 978-90-04-33315-4 (e-book)

This book is printed on acid-free paper and produced in a sustainable manner.

Printed by Printforce, the Netherlands

Contents

VOLUME 1

Foundations and Formation of a Tradition: *Reflections on the Hereafter in the Quran and Islamic Religious Thought*

Zum Geleit xv
Josef van Ess

Acknowledgments xxvi
List of Illustrations xxix
Note on Transliteration and Style xxxii
Abbreviations xxxiv
List of Contributors xxxvii

1 Introduction 1
Sebastian Günther and Todd Lawson

PREPARING FOR THE JOURNEY – CONFERENCE OPENING ADDRESSES

The Paths to Reality are as Diverse as the Souls of Humanity

2 Paradise Lost 31
Tilman Nagel

3 The Path to Paradise from an Islamic Viewpoint 39
Mahmoud Zakzouk

PART 1

Paradise, Hell, and Afterlife in the Quran and Quranic Exegesis

4 Quranic Paradise: How to Get to Paradise and What to Expect There 49
Muhammad Abdel Haleem

5 Paradise as a Quranic Discourse: Late Antique Foundations and Early Quranic Developments 67
Angelika Neuwirth

6 Paradise in the Quran and the Music of Apocalypse 93
Todd Lawson

7 Paradise and Nature in the Quran and Pre-Islamic Poetry 136
Jaakko Hämeen-Anttila

8 Dying in the Path of God: Reading Martyrdom and Moral Excellence in the Quran 162
Asma Afsaruddin

9 The Poetics of Islamic Eschatology: Narrative, Personification, and Colors in Muslim Discourse 181
Sebastian Günther

PART 2
The Pleasures of Paradise

10 "Reclining upon Couches in the Shade" (Q 35:56): Quranic Imagery in Rationalist Exegesis 221
Andrew J. Lane

11 Delights in Paradise: A Comparative Survey of Heavenly Food and Drink in the Quran 251
Ailin Qian

12 Strategies for Paradise: Paradise Virgins and Utopia 271
Maher Jarrar

13 Beauty in the Garden: Aesthetics and the *Wildān, Ghilmān,* and *Ḥūr* 295
Nerina Rustomji

PART 3
The Afterlife in Sunni Tradition and Theology

14 "Are Men the Majority in Paradise, or Women?" Constructing Gender and Communal Boundaries in Muslim b. al-Ḥajjāj's (d. 261/875) *Kitāb al-Janna* 311
Aisha Geissinger

15 The 'Eight Gates of Paradise' Tradition in Islam: A Genealogical and Structural Study 341
Christian Lange

16 Temporary Hellfire Punishment and the Making of Sunni Orthodoxy 371
Feras Hamza

17 Paradise and Hell in the *Kitāb al-Jihād* of ʿAlī b. Ṭāhir al-Sulamī (d. 500/1106) 407
Niall Christie

18 Al-Ghazālī on Resurrection and the Road to Paradise 422
Wilferd Madelung

19 Sleepless in Paradise: Lying in State between This World and the Next 428
Dorothee Pielow

PART 4
A Wise Man's Paradise – Eschatology and Philosophy

20 Paradise in Islamic Philosophy 445
Michael E. Marmura

21 The Orthodox Conception of the Hereafter: Saʿd al-Dīn al-Taftāzānī's (d. 793/1390) Examination of Some Muʿtazilī and Philosophical Objections 468
Thomas Würtz

22 'Being-Towards-Resurrection': Mullā Ṣadrā's Critique of Suhrawardī's Eschatology 487
Hermann Landolt

23 A Philosopher's Itinerary for the Afterlife: Mullā Ṣadrā on Paths to Felicity 534
Mohammed Rustom

PART 5
The Path beyond this World – Vision and Spiritual Experience of the Hereafter

24 Muslim Visuality and the Visibility of Paradise and the World 555
Simon O'Meara

25 A Garden beyond the Garden: ʿAyn al-Quḍāt Hamadānī's Perspective on Paradise 566
Maryam Moazzen

26 Beyond Paradise: The Mystical Path to God and the Concept of Martyrdom in ʿAṭṭār's *Conference of the Birds* 579
Katja Föllmer

PART 6
Unity in Variety – Shiʿism and Other Muslim Identities

27 "And the Earth will Shine with the Light of its Lord" (Q 39:69): *Qāʾim* and *qiyāma* in Shiʿi Islam 605
Omid Ghaemmaghami

28 Paradise as the Abode of Pure Knowledge: Reconsidering al-Muʾayyad's "Ismaʿili Neoplatonism" 649
Elizabeth Alexandrin

29 Notions of Paradise in the Ismaʿili Works of Naṣīr al-Dīn Ṭūsī 662
S.J. Badakhchani

30 Apocalyptic Rhetoric and the Construction of Authority in Medieval Ismaʿilism 675
Jamel A. Velji

31 Just a Step away from Paradise: *Barzakh* in the Ahl-i Ḥaqq Teachings 689
Alexey A. Khismatulin

32 "Paradise is at the Feet of Mothers": The Ḥurūfī Road 701
Orkhan Mir-Kasimov

33 Which Road to Paradise? The Controversy of Reincarnation in Islamic Thought 735
Mohammad Hassan Khalil

VOLUME 2
Continuity and Change:
The Plurality of Eschatological Representations in the Islamicate World

PART 7
Paradise and Eschatology in Comparative Perspective

34 A Typology of Eschatological Concepts 757
Fred M. Donner

35 The "World" in its Eschatological Dimension in East-Syrian Synodical Records 773
Martin Tamcke

36 St. Ephraem the Syrian, the Quran, and the Grapevines of Paradise: An Essay in Comparative Eschatology 781
Sidney H. Griffith

37 Paradise? America! The Metaphor of Paradise in the Context of the Iraqi-Christian Migration 806
Martin Tamcke

PART 8
Eschatology and Literature

38 The Characteristics of Paradise (*Ṣifat al-Janna*): A Genre of Eschatological Literature in Medieval Islam 817
Waleed Ahmed

39 "Roads to Paradise" in *Risālat al-ghufrān* of the Arab Thinker al-Maʿarrī 850
Mahmoud Hegazi

40 Muslim Eschatology and the Ascension of the Prophet Muḥammad: Describing Paradise in *Miʿrāj* Traditions and Literature 858
Roberto Tottoli

41 An Islamic *Paradiso* in a Medieval Christian Poem? Dante's *Divine Comedy* Revisited 891
Samar Attar

42 Paradise, Alexander the Great and the *Arabian Nights*: Some New Insights Based on an Unpublished Manuscript 922
Claudia Ott

43 Paradise in an Islamic *ʿAjāʾib* Work: *The Delight of Onlookers and the Signs for Investigators* of Marʿī b. Yūsuf al-Karmī (d. 1033/1624) 931
Walid A. Saleh

44 Expulsion from Paradise: Granada in Raḍwā ʿĀshūr's *The Granada Trilogy* (1994–8) and Salman Rushdie's *The Moor's Last Sigh* (1995) 953
Suha Kudsieh

PART 9
Bringing Paradise Down to Earth – Aesthetic Representations of the Hereafter

45 Madīnat al-Zahrāʾ, Paradise and the Fatimids 979
Maribel Fierro

46 The *Chār Muḥammad* Inscription, *Shafāʿa*, and the Mamluk Qubbat al-Manṣūriyya 1010
Tehnyat Majeed

47 Visualizing Encounters on the Road to Paradise 1033
Karin Rührdanz

48 Images of Paradise in Popular Shiʿite Iconography 1056
Ulrich Marzolph

49 Where is Paradise on Earth? Visual Arts in the Arab World and the Construction of a Mythic Past 1068
Silvia Naef

PART 10
Heavens and the Hereafter in Scholarship and Natural Sciences

50 The Configuration of the Heavens in Islamic Astronomy 1083
Ingrid Hehmeyer

51 The Quadrants of *Sharīʿa*: The Here and Hereafter as Constitutive of Islamic Law 1099
Anver M. Emon

52 Perceptions of Paradise in the Writings of Julius Wellhausen, Mark Lidzbarski, and Hans Heinrich Schaeder 1127
Ludmila Hanisch

PART 11
Paradise Meets Modernity – The Dynamics of Paradise Discourse in the Nineteenth, Twentieth, and Twenty-First Centuries

53 Islam and Paradise are Sheltered under the Shade of Swords: Phallocentric Fantasies of Paradise in Nineteenth-Century Acehnese War Propaganda and their Lasting Legacy 1143
Edwin P. Wieringa

54 **Eschatology between Reason and Revelation: Death and Resurrection in Modern Islamic Theology** 1187
Umar Ryad

55 **Between Science Fiction and Sermon: Eschatological Writings Inspired by Said Nursi** 1222
Martin Riexinger

56 **Notions of Paradise and Martyrdom in Contemporary Palestinian Thought** 1267
Liza M. Franke

57 **Crisis and the Secular Rhetoric of Islamic Paradise** 1290
Ruth Mas

Bibliographical Appendix 1323

Indices

Index of Proper Names 1395
Index of Geographical Names and Toponyms 1414
Index of Book Titles and Other Texts 1417
Index of Scriptural References 1427
Ḥadīth Index 1440
Index of Topics and Keywords 1442

PART 7

Paradise and Eschatology in Comparative Perspective

CHAPTER 34

A Typology of Eschatological Concepts

Fred M. Donner

The present article offers a set of categorizations that will, it is hoped, offer a consistent, comprehensive, and unambiguous way to classify the many diverse concepts that flourish in eschatological thought. This classification emerged from my own frustration in trying to understand the existing scholarship on eschatology, much of which I found confusing and unclear because different scholars appear to use different terms to refer to comparable concepts or practices, or use the same term in divergent ways. Terms like "post-millennial" or "apocalyptic" often seem to be predicated on unspoken, or at least unclarified, assumptions about the groups and concepts to which they are applied.

The word *eschatology* (derived from Greek *ta eschata*, "the last things") developed in Western scholarship as a designation for those traditions that claim to know how things will "end up" at the end of normal life. That is, such traditions claim to describe the ultimate fate of an individual (or of the individual's soul), or of a community, or of the whole cosmos. Or, more simply put, they describe what happens after we die – which, of course, we the living cannot know from direct experience.

Although the concept of eschatology as a scholastic category has been used by Christian theologians since at least the seventeenth century, the term eschatology is a relatively recent coinage in English and most other modern languages. According to the *Oxford English Dictionary*, *eschatology* first appeared in print in English in 1844. It was first used in discussions of religious traditions, particularly Judaism and Christianity, that feature an explicitly articulated notion of an afterlife or comparable "other-worldly" realm that one can experience only after death. The term eschatology, however, sometimes came to be applied also to phenomena that are not linked to a time after the end of the world, but rather anticipated at some future time in the present world, such as expectations involving the raising (or restoration) of a community to a dominant or triumphant political position – often through the arrival of an earthly and this-worldly messiah who brings worldly salvation. In recent years, the term eschatology has even been extended into an entirely different context: that is, in discussions of "medical eschatology" – hospice or other care

 | DOI 10.1163/9789004333154_035

provided by health practitioners to the terminally ill at the end of life.[1] In the following pages, we focus on the more traditional notions of eschatology.

Eschatological concepts vary tremendously in content. Many, but not all, share the belief that in the fullness of time there will occur a fundamental *change* or *transformation* in the world, often described as the dawning of a "new era" or "new eon," in which conditions are in some way radically different from the (ordinary, present) era that preceded it. (This is especially true of the so-called "apocalyptic" eschatologies, on which we have more to say later.) The purpose of eschatological schemes is thus to situate the subject – whether it is the individual, community, or cosmos – in the context of the new era. In doing so, they invariably describe the status of the subject as markedly different from its status in the present: so, for example, the downtrodden in this era may become those in positions of authority and power in the new era. As Sigmund Mowinckel observed, eschatological schemes revolve around the perception of a profound duality.[2] This perceived duality may be either a distinction between the present time and a future eon or time, different from our own; or a distinction between the present world and some other world, a separate realm or space that is physically apart from our own world (but may coexist with it in time).

Beyond this common assumption of some kind of fundamental duality, the specific features of different eschatological schemas are structured around a limited repertoire of conceptual categories. The goal of this paper is to present, in preliminary form, a tentative catalog of these conceptual categories. We can thus describe specific eschatological schemas as being either *linear* or *cyclical*; or we can describe them as being *other-worldly, this-worldly*, or *composite*; they can be characterized as *religious* or *secular*; they can be *moral* or *amoral*; they can be *positive* or *negative*; they can be *individual, communal*, or *cosmic*; they can be *serial* or *catastrophic*; they can be *evolutionary* or *cataclysmic*; and they can be *future-oriented* or *realized*. It is of course possible that they can be characterized in other ways as well, but that must be left for future scholars to determine. The remainder of this essay is devoted to providing a very brief discussion and defense of the aforementioned categories, with a few examples to illustrate how they show up in known eschatological traditions.

---

1 I thank Dr. Gregor Prindull (Göttingen) for calling this usage to my attention.

2 Mowinckel, *He that cometh* 144, 263–6.

1 Linear vs. Cyclical Eschatologies

Perhaps the most basic conceptual distinction in eschatological schemes is between those whose cosmology is strictly *linear* and those that embrace a *cyclical* cosmology. A linear conception posits a single timeline for the world and for the life of the individual. The individual has a single birth and proceeds through life to a single death; the world as we know it proceeds from a single definite point of creation to a single definite end-time, when the world (and maybe time itself) will cease to exist, or be destroyed; there will be, as the phrase common to some such schemes has it, a "Last Day" after which there will be no further existence in the world. Christianity and Islam offer familiar examples of strictly linear eschatologies. Cyclical schemes, on the other hand, such as the *saṃsāra* chain of birth-life-death-rebirth in some forms of Hinduism and Buddhism, portray the individual as being repeatedly (and eternally) "recycled" into the world; in some forms of these traditions, there is no "end," as the world and universe, no less than the individual, are continually dying and being reborn. This recycling may continue until, through progressive enlightenment and the acquisition of sufficient *karma*, the individual attains – if he ever does – some permanent terminal state; this may be the *mokṣa* or "release," that is, the reunion of his soul with a perpetual "World of the Fathers," as in Vedic Hinduism or the Upanishads; or it may be the attainment of *nirvaṇa*, which is either release from the birth-life-death-rebirth cycle of *saṃsāra* (as in Theravāda Buddhism), or the realization of the interconnectedness of all things and the detachment from all desires, emotions, and ignorance (as in Mahāyāna Buddhism).[3]

While in the long run – the very long run – both linear and cyclical systems seem to share the idea that the individual will (or at least may) end up in some final state, so that in some sense the cyclical systems also have an underlying linearity, the two conceptualizations differ profoundly in the way the individual's life is construed within the respective systems. In linear systems, each of us has but one life, and our ultimate fate after death depends on what we do in this life: there is, in short, a kind of urgency because our single life has a definite and inescapable "deadline," namely our own ever-approaching death. In cyclical systems, on the other hand, the individual has "other chances" to attain escape from the troubles of this life – in future lives to which he may be reincarnated – although of course in those systems the way one behaves in

3 MacGregor, *Images* 64–6, 84–6, 90–2, 119–21; Moreman, *Beyond the threshhold* 97–137; Nattier, Buddhist eschatology; and Knipe, Hindu eschatology, offer good overviews of these concepts, much more complex than can be presented fully here.

this life determines how much *karma* one acquires and, therefore, is also crucial to whether one moves closer to escaping the cycle of *saṃsāra*/rebirth. We might therefore observe that, from the perspective of the individual, it matters little whether one chooses to pursue virtue in order to escape eternal damnation in hell (as in a linear eschatology) or in order to escape reincarnation in the next life as a lower being (as in some cyclical eschatologies). The matter is made more complex by the fact that in some cyclical systems, such as certain forms of Hinduism, there has developed the idea that the deceased may go to a heaven or vividly-described hell (perhaps on the way to eventual reincarnation?). This, too, seems to introduce an aspect of linearity in systems that are putatively cyclical.

2 Religious vs. Secular Eschatologies

Eschatologies can also be differentiated according to whether they are motivated by secular or by religious values. In religious eschatologies, the events that are predicted as part of the scenario leading to the end of time are decreed by God (or the gods); in secular eschatologies, on the other hand, the end is brought about by the workings of the blind forces of nature, which is not intentional and does not know or care about human existence; or it is brought about by human agency, which is intentional and ought to know better, but is heedless or ignorant and so fails to stave off the dire consequences.

The best example of a secular eschatology is, perhaps, Marxism-Leninism.[4] It rails against a present "sinful age," complete with corruption of the rulers/hegemons, oppression of the workers and poor, and other ills, and offers hope of a cataclysmic change ushering in a "new era" that will be marked by the overthrow of capitalist interests and the privileged classes, the end of capitalist exploitation, an egalitarian society, and the "dictatorship of the proletariat."

3 This-Worldly, Other-Worldly, and Composite Eschatologies

Eschatologies can be differentiated according to whether they describe the ultimate fate of the subject individual or group as belonging to this world or to some other world or realm. This-worldly eschatologies describe a new eon dawning here on earth, but at some time in the future through the normal passage of time – albeit, perhaps, a lot of time. Other-worldly eschatologies, on the

4 Cohn, *Pursuit of the millennium* 100–1, 307–10.

other hand, see either a new eon beginning with the end of time and history, so that, in effect, a new creation is inaugurated, different from this world; or else they see man's existence after death as taking place in some other realm spatially separated from the present world. This other realm may exist parallel to the normal world of eschatological hope in which we live. In some cases, the realm to which the deceased depart is separated from the present world both temporally (i.e., it begins with an end-time that marks the end of history) and spatially (i.e., in some non-terrestrial world).

3.1 *This-Worldly Eschatologies*

Zoroastrianism – Zoroastrian cosmology presents history as the struggle of Ahura Mazda, the god of good, against Aingra Mainyu, the god of evil. The goal of the individual believer is to strive in every way to free himself from the forces of evil (usually associated with materiality/the physical world), and to join the forces of good (associated with the spirit and symbolized by light). The culmination of normal history will be a final judgment, during which the earth will be purged by a flood of molten metal; those people who are evil will be scalded by it, but the righteous will walk through it "as though through warm milk." Evildoers will be subjected to a period of painful punishment, but will eventually repent and be rehabilitated, to join the righteous in a world now purified of all evil and disease, where everyone will live in peace, plenty and harmony. The world is certainly transformed beyond recognition by this process of purging and judgment, but it remains, in Zoroastrian cosmology, this same world we inhabit. The dead are not removed to an ideal paradise; rather the earth itself becomes paradise.[5]

Early Israelite messianism – Another this-worldly schema was found among the early Israelites. Some of the early Israelite prophets foretold a new age when a mighty king of Israel would deliver the Israelites from bondage and oppression by their enemies, and even subject their enemies to servile status. In early Israelite usage, the term *messiah* (Hebr. *māshīaḥ*) meant someone who was anointed by Yahweh – that is, recognized and commissioned by God to undertake a special task for God's people Israel – and early kings are usually styled *māshīaḥ*; but the term lacks at this early stage the transcendent, semi-divine overtones it would acquire in the intertestamental period (ca. 200 BCE–100 CE). In the early prophetic period, we find rather "a future hope of a coming kingdom ..." in David's line, "... an earthly kingdom, political

5 Ara, *Eschatology in the Indo-Iranian traditions* 195–217, offers a good survey.

in character, nationalistic in outlook and military in expression."[6] This is not, in fact, an eschatological concept properly speaking, in that it did not deal with the "end of the world," but only with a change of Israel's political situation in this world. Israel would no longer be a weak, oppressed, and reviled community, but would evolve into a powerful nation in this world and would prevail over all those enemies that had formerly oppressed it (there is a strikingly vindictive quality to this formulation). It seems to be only in the intertestamental period that the notion of *messiah* acquires its more supernatural qualities, as a redeemer who transcends time, space, and death and allows his people to enter a beatific afterlife; this is particularly prominent in Christianity, of course, and takes the notion of *māshīaḥ* into the realm of other-worldly eschatology.

Jehovah's Witnesses – The Protestant Christian sect known as Jehovah's Witnesses, which arose in the United States in the 1870s, teaches that in the eventual millennial kingdom, the majority of the righteous will live forever on earth. The Witnesses reject the idea of hell, preaching that deceased sinners simply cease to exist after death. They do not dispense entirely with the notion of other-worldly realms, however, for they also hold that a minority of the righteous will ascend to heaven to rule with Christ. The main emphasis of their doctrines, however, seems to be on a this-worldly future, eternal life on the earth we know for the majority of righteous people.[7]

Marxist eschatology – Certain secular ideologies foresee an ultimate fate for the world, or for a nation, in a manner that resembles closely the concepts we call eschatological in religious traditions. Marxism, as noted above, can be seen as a secular eschatological scheme that predicts a new era dawning in this world with the overthrow of capitalist society and its bourgeois manifestations. This would result in the creation of a universal classless society, marking the end of the present era of class struggle, capitalist oppression, poverty, etc. There is in such an ideology, of course, no hint that the "life to come" will be anywhere but on the earth we know, albeit one transformed in ways that would make it almost unrecognizable to us.

Doomsday predictions of various kinds sometimes also belong to the category of this-world eschatologies; for example, the warnings or predictions of global environmental disaster or of a global nuclear holocaust that will end life

---

6 Russell, *Method and message* 265; cf. also Arnold, Old Testament eschatology 25: "[Israelite eschatology] longs for, indeed expects, a period when Yhwh triumphs over evil, redeems his people Israel, and finally rules the world in peace and salvation." See also Mowinckel, *He that cometh*, esp. 122–4, 125–37.

7 A summary of these doctrines is presented in the Witnesses' newsletter, *The Watchtower* 130.21 (1 November 2009). They seem to be derived from a reading of Deutero-Isaiah (Isa. 40–55).

on earth "as we know it" (as the phrase usually has it) can be considered forms of this-worldly eschatology.

Hindu eschatology – The rebirth of the individual in this world as part of the *saṃsāra* chain of birth-life-death-rebirth is a basic concept of both Buddhist and Hindu thought. As noted above, however, Hinduism's rich traditions whereby individuals may escape the *saṃsāra* chain and (if virtuous) move to a permanent abode in heaven, or (if sinful) be consigned to horrible punishments in hell, introduces the notion of other-worldly realms in what seems to have begun as a cyclical and this-worldly eschatological scheme.

3.2 *Other-Worldly Eschatologies*

More familiar, perhaps, are other-worldly eschatologies. In the Ancient Near East several versions of the trope of the Underworld fit this description.

Ancient Near Eastern eschatologies – Sheol, the underworld of the ancient Hebrews referred to in the Hebrew Bible, seems to exist as a parallel universe where the *repa'īm* or shades of the dead lead a sad, shadowy, and unchanging existence. There can be no communication between the two worlds; when Joseph's father Jacob is told of Joseph's death (Genesis 37:35), he laments that he will have to "go down to Sheol to my son, mourning."[8] The implication is that he will spend eternity in Sheol unhappy. As Ecclesiastes 9:5, 10 describes it, "... the dead know nothing, and they have no more reward ... there is no work or thought or knowledge or wisdom in Sheol, to which you are going." The Homeric Tartarus or House of Hades, similarly, or the underworld of Mesopotamian myths, the "Land-of-no-return" where the dead exist in a state resembling sleep, seem similarly to be places where the shades of the deceased are "warehoused" indefinitely, distant realms that generally have no contact with the real world in which we live.[9]

Mainstream Christian eschatology derives from the Gospels' emphasis on Jesus as the messiah and on his resurrection to reign in heaven, as well as from elaborate scenarios for the end-time (as presented with pathological vengefulness, for example, in the Book of Revelation). These are shaped around a basic plot in which the "natural" world and time come to an end when God raises people for the last judgment.[10] The fate of individuals is then decreed by God

---

8 All quotations from the Bible follow the *Revised Standard Version*.

9 Albinus, *House of Hades* 41–2, 51–6; Cumont, *After life* 44–90; James, *The ancient gods*, 179–91.

10 Revelations 21:1 "Then I saw a new heaven and a new earth; for the first heaven and the first earth had passed away, and the sea was no more."

on the basis of their record in life; they go to hell or heaven, in either case not a place that is part of this world or of the normal continuum of time.

Muslim eschatology involves similar scenarios played out in a heavenly or other-worldly realm or realms. The ultimate destinations of individuals, "the garden" (*al-janna*)/paradise or hell depending on how they behaved in this life, is in neither case portrayed as being part of the natural world; rather, they are depicted as perfect utopias or dystopias – places either of endless pleasure and bliss, or of endless torment. In paradise, for example, righteous men are rewarded by, among other things, having a limitless supply of nubile sexual partners, ever-virginal, willing, with no complications of family ties or pregnancy – and enjoyment of them is guilt-free because God has provided them to the righteous for just this purpose, as a reward for their steadfastness in their former lives on earth. So this is obviously not some kind of purified real world, but a fantasy realm where the sometimes irksome realities of life in the natural world (such as menstruation and in-laws) simply do not exist.[11]

3.3 *Composite Eschatologies*

Some eschatological scenarios involve two or more phases, beginning in this world and ending up in some other world. Millenarian scenarios belong to this category of eschatology, which we can term *composite eschatologies*. The eschatological scheme presented in the Book of Revelations, for example, posits a first phase of cataclysmic wars and strife in this world, and unspeakably gruesome tribulations (Rev. 6–19), to be followed by a thousand-year period when Satan is locked up by an angel and the martyrs for Christ are resurrected and reign in glory with Christ – presumably reigning over a world in which peace prevails, as Satan is out of the picture. Upon Satan's release, however, the world is again plunged into tribulation; the evil "nations which are at the four corners of the earth, that is Gog and Magog," attempt to besiege the righteous, until their forces, and the devil with them are cast by God into a lake of fire and brimstone, to suffer forever, after which the last judgment ends the earth and consigns all resurrected souls to either heaven or hell (Rev. 20–21). All of these ultimate destinations seem to be other-worldly ones, beyond the realm of normal time and space.

Muslim eschatology also involves, in some cases, a kind of millenarian vision, according to which the actual last judgment is preceded by a lengthy period of wars, marked by the appearance of the Dajjāl or Antichrist and then the second coming of Jesus, who will vanquish the Dajjāl to inaugurate the millennium – a prolonged period of bliss on earth – which will eventually be

---

11 Smith and Haddad, *The Islamic understanding* 164–8.

followed by the judgment. Those Muslim traditions that speak of the *mahdī* or eschatological deliverer also belong to this category, for they foresee the arrival of the *mahdī* as marking the beginning of an expected era "when the world will be filled with justice as it had earlier been filled with injustice."[12] This preliminary, this-worldly phase will eventually give way to the end-time, last judgment, and final dispatch of all souls to heaven or hell.

While secular eschatologies are always this-worldly, we cannot say that religious eschatologies are always other-worldly. As noted above, the original idea of Jewish messianism was built around the notion of a triumphant restoration of the Kingdom of David in this world, not (or not only) in the next, and Zoroastrian visions of the period after the final judgment set it in this world, purified of all evil.

4 Moral vs. Amoral Eschatologies

Many eschatological schemes involve explicit or implicit moral judgments that determine the fate of the individual or community in the afterlife. The good will go to heaven, the wicked to hell, depending on their behavior in this life. Moral eschatologies involve some kind of final judgment, on the basis of which one's destination in the afterlife is determined. Obviously, such moral eschatological schemes constitute pseudo-narrative devices contributing powerfully to the maintenance of moral imperatives in the culture that produces the eschatology in question.

Not all eschatologies, however, are moral. If, for example, the eschatological schema portrays everyone as going to the same underworld after death, without any judgment, the eschatology is amoral, because one's fate in the afterlife is not portrayed as contingent upon one's moral behavior in this life. The examples from antiquity described earlier – early Israelite concepts of Sheol, or Homeric views on the underworld/Tartarus, or ancient Mesopotamian traditions about the underworld – can be classified as amoral eschatologies because everyone, whether prince or pauper, hero or traitor, eventually finds his way to the sad, shadowy realm of the underworld, and all are equally trapped and miserable there. It seems that in some schemes, the same kind of injustices and tensions that exist in this world may be replicated in the netherworld.[13] Similarly, predictions of global environmental disaster, which will destroy

---

12 See Madelung, al-Mahdī 1232–3. For specific references to prophetic *ḥadīths* with this phrase see Wensinck, *A handbook* 139, under "*mahdī*."

13 For a Roman example, see Cumont, *After life* 72.

everyone, are amoral in character (however much their proponents may moralize against those who fail to act to thwart the impending doom).

The amoral eschatologies of antiquity seem, however, to have been gradually modified in a number of instances, developing first certain exceptions to their amoral quality (that is, to their tendency to view everyone as having the same fate after death), and then a sometimes quite elaborate moralism. In Greek myth, even at a fairly early stage, the idea that individuals are not judged on their way to Tartarus and hence are treated the same there was modified slightly by the acknowledgment that certain individuals guilty of crimes especially hateful to the gods would be subjected by them to endless torture in the underworld; for example, Sisyphus was condemned to push a heavy rock up a steep hill, only to have it slip away near the top and roll to the bottom again, forcing him to repeat the chore endlessly throughout eternity. The ancient Egyptian concepts of the underworld, which seem originally also to have been essentially amoral, later developed an elaborate judgment scenario in which the soul of the deceased would be judged by Osiris, the god of the underworld, by placing it in a balance opposite a feather. If the deceased had, during his life, paid sufficient attention to the cult of the dead, then his soul would be light and would pass the test, allowing him to live a shadowy eternal existence in the underworld. If his soul failed the test, however, it would be devoured by the crocodile-headed Attim, resulting in the much-feared "second death," or total annihilation of the person's soul. "If condemned, the deceased could not become a transfigured spirit; rather, he had to vanish from the created cosmos, and **that** was the second death."[14]

5 Positive vs. Negative Eschatologies

Many eschatologies are a form of soteriology – that is, they predict and, it is thought, help to realize the salvation of the subject individual or group. As such, they can be called *positive eschatologies* in that they anticipate a positive fate for the subject individual or community. Some eschatologies, however, are negative; that is, they anticipate the destruction of the subject group or individual. Secular "doomsday" eschatologies, of course, such as those anticipating a nuclear holocaust, can be classified as negative eschatologies.

Of course, an eschatological scheme that must be considered positive from the perspective of the subject group or individual may contain negative predic-

14 Assmann, *Death and salvation* 76 and 73–7 on Egyptian judgment generally; Moreman, *Beyond the threshhold* 14–8.

tions about the eventual fate of others, particularly about the subject group's opponents. A good example is provided by the Quran, which describes how on the day of judgment Pharaoh will lead his unbelieving people down to hell, even as the believers find salvation (Q 40:45–50).

6 Individual, Communal, and Cosmic Eschatologies

An eschatology can be termed *individual* when it focuses on the fate of a single person (that is, of his or her soul), and describes or predicts whether, after death, that person attains salvation and how salvation is affected. The frequently heard pious comment that persons who have recently died have already gone to their appointed place in heaven (from which they are often described as "looking down on we who remain behind") or in hell, rests on the assumption that one's ultimate fate is determined solely by the belief and behavior of the individual. Ancient Near Eastern religious traditions (including early Israelite beliefs), which portray the individual as going after death to a gloomy existence in an underworld (in the early Israelite case, Sheol) can also be placed in this category of individual eschatologies. The final destination of the individual is not dependent on his or her membership in any larger community, but is simply a reality that must be accepted.

Some eschatologies, however, focus not on the fate of individuals per se, but on the fate of a whole community, and so can be termed *communal*. Messianic movements presaging the triumphant restoration of a people or nation or state in this world can be placed in this category. Although the community that is the subject of the eschatology is made up of many individuals, the presence or role of any particular individual in the community's anticipated fate is purely incidental; the point is that the community will be restored as a collectivity, not that any present individual will necessarily experience this event (although the expectation of such a prediction's imminent fulfillment can galvanize many individuals with hope that they will experience it).

Other-worldly eschatologies, too, can be communal; as noted above, in the Quran, all the dead are described as being raised on judgment day and judged by God *as communities*, and each community goes to its destined fate apparently as a community; thus one reads of Pharaoh leading his community down to hell, while the Prophet Muḥammad leads his followers to paradise.[15] Such

15 Q 11:97–8. Smith and Haddad, *The Islamic understanding* 26–9, discuss the tension between the individual and his community, and the idea of intercession as part of the Muslim community.

imagery, of course, raises the question of whether in eschatological schemas of this kind mere membership in the community outweighs the role of individual belief and behavior (virtue vs. sin) in deciding one's ultimate fate in the afterlife, a theological question that often generates heated debate. The focus of such debates is usually the two "problem cases," namely what is the fate of the sinful member of the subject ("righteous") community, or of the virtuous person belonging to the "wrong" (unbelieving) community.[16] Such deliberations often result in the creation of many nuances or degrees of "reward" and "punishment" in an eschatological system; so that, for example, sinful members of the subject community are described as enjoying a lesser level of bliss than righteous ones, but a higher level of bliss than righteous non-believers. In general, it seems that this tension between a focus on the individual as opposed to the community generates a great deal of complexity for eschatological systems.

Eschatologies can be called *cosmic* when they presage the ultimate fate of the entire world. Many communal eschatologies of a religious variety have a cosmic dimension, in that the salvation of the subject community is seen as part of a larger final end-time when the whole world as we know it comes to an end. But, as we have seen, not all communal eschatologies are necessarily cosmic (this-worldly messianism, for example), and some cosmic eschatologies, such as scenarios of environmental disaster (or plans for environmental salvation) take as their subject of salvation or destruction no particular human community, but rather the whole of humanity, or even all life on earth.

7 Serial vs. Catastrophic Eschatologies

Some eschatologies describe the ultimate fate of individuals as taking place independent of one another, so that the eschatological fate of various individuals who die at different times can be considered *serial*. For example, a system that posits that believers go to heaven, and unbelievers to hell, immediately upon their death, sees these events as separate consignments of individual souls to their fated places, and implies (if it does not state explicitly) that the judgment of each individual takes place separately, and that the afterlife realms to which the deceased are consigned exist forever in parallel with the natural world. Hence they are always available to receive new inmates. Ancient

---

16 A Muslim student once informed me that I had a positive reputation among his fellows at the university, who considered me a *kāfir ṭayyib*, "virtuous unbeliever." Although flattered, I did not press him to clarify for me what long-term implications this status might have.

Egyptian, Mesopotamian, and Greco-Roman eschatological schemes seem to follow this pattern.

Other eschatological schemes, however, anticipate a situation in which all souls are consigned at the same time, usually as communities of believers (destined for paradise or the "overworld") or unbelievers (destined for the underworld). Quranic judgment imagery, or that of the Book of Revelation, can be taken as an example. Such schemes assume that a single last judgment of souls will take place at the end of time, for which all dead souls are raised. Because this single last judgment by definition marks the end of the normal continuum of time, it is often described as taking place immediately following a cosmic cataclysm or series of catastrophes that end the world as we know it and inaugurate the events of the last judgment. For this reason, such schemes can be called *catastrophic eschatologies*. They include most eschatologies usually called "apocalyptic," although the most widely-accepted definition of "apocalypse"[17] does not explicitly include catastrophic events as a feature of such texts; nonetheless, many apocalypses contain visions of cataclysmic events (often, as noted with the Book of Revelation, imbued with a distinctly vengeful and sometimes sadistic quality).

The corollary of a single last judgment for which all souls are raised is that once people die, their souls must be stored somewhere, to be awakened at the end-time for the judgment; in Islamic tradition, which subscribes to the view of a single collective judgment, this generated many contradictory views on what the dead souls actually experience before finally being raised for the judgment at the end-time. The Quran itself states clearly that the deceased cannot hear anything the living may say to them (Q 27:82), and it also emphasizes the absolute impermeability of the *barzakh* or barrier that separates the world of the living from that of the dead, so that the existence of the deceased in the grave, before the judgment, seems conceptually analogous to that of the deceased in the underworld of ancient myth (Hebrew Sheol, Greek Tartarus). But later Islamic tradition developed various scenarios, sometimes elaborate ones, describing what happens to the souls of the deceased in the interim between death and judgment, including the ability to hear and observe the bereaved mourning over one's own body, terrifying inquests by examining

17 The definition, developed by a working group of the Society of Biblical Literature in the 1970s, defines apocalypse as "... a genre of revelatory literature with a narrative framework, in which a revelation is mediated by an otherworldly being to a human recipient, disclosing a transcendent reality which is both temporal, insofar as it envisages eschatological salvation, and spatial insofar as it involves another, supernatural world." See Collins, Introduction: Towards the morphology of a genre 9.

angels, the so-called *ʿadhāb al-qabr* or "punishment of the grave" (which seems to pre-judge the judgment), heavenly journeys during which the souls of the deceased obtain glimpses of paradise, the reunion of the soul with the body in the grave, favors enjoyed by the souls and bodies of the righteous during their wait for judgment day (such as a window in the coffin through which a refreshing breeze from paradise wafts), etc. On the other hand, some Muslim thinkers rejected categorically most such speculations on what happened to the souls of the deceased.[18]

The notion of a single last judgment sometimes clouds the distinction between this-worldly and other-worldly eschatologies. In Zoroastrianism, for example, the dead are apparently immediately required to cross over an abyss via the Chinvat Bridge, leading to a heavenly realm; the righteous do so with no problem, but the sinful find that the bridge narrows until they fall into the abyss and enter a hellish underworld, where they suffer grievously. Needless to say, this heaven and hell are both otherworldly realms. The deceased are then warehoused in these abodes until the final judgment, after which they return to the purified earth. While the scheme is thus this-worldly in the long term, in the middle term it involves other-worldly destinations – which appear, however, to be only temporary, and cease to be needed (or cease to exist?) after the final judgment and purification of the earth, to which all people belong.

8 Future-Oriented vs. Realized Eschatologies

Most eschatologies are explicitly *future-oriented*, that is, they anticipate final events that are destined to take place at some time in the future (whether determinate or indeterminate). All predictions of a last judgment, etc., obviously fall into this category.

Some eschatological schemes, however, see the fate of the subject group or individual as having taken place in the past. The Bible's or the Quran's descriptions of the destruction of various sinful communities, for example, such as the story of Sodom and Gomorrah, seem to be eschatologies oriented to the past rather than the future. We can call such stories eschatological because they are related as lessons meant to inform those who are still living, i.e., those to whom the stories are told, warning them to avoid the errors of these already "judged" communities. We can call such schemes exercises in *realized*

18 See Smith and Haddad, *The Islamic understanding* 31–61.

eschatology (following loosely the terminology of C.H. Dodd)[19] because the fate of the community in question has been realized. It goes without saying that a fully past-oriented eschatology implies a this-worldly eschatology (such as the fate of Sodom, in this world) because the end of time clearly has not yet come.

Most interesting are instances of *partly-realized eschatology*, that is, schemes in which the events of the present are portrayed as the beginnings of the end-time or cataclysmic events associated with the last judgment. Such eschatologies combine both an other-worldly orientation with the notion that the other-worldly fate of the subject group is not only imminent (i.e., in the near future) but already heralded (partly realized) by this-worldly events taking place in the present time. The early Christians seem to have understood Jesus' teachings within a framework of eschatological expectation prevalent in Judaism of the first century CE, and argued that with Jesus' death and resurrection the end-time had actually begun to be realized.[20] It has been suggested that certain groups in the earliest Islamic community also understood the dramatic events of the early Islamic conquests as evidence of the nearness of the last day, as "signs of the hour" marking the dawning of a new age presaging the last judgment.[21] These hypotheses are suggestive but remain to be more thoroughly tested.

The protean forms of eschatological concepts provide a rich field of study. It is hoped that the categories identified above can help provide compact and unambiguous descriptive terminologies that will facilitate comparative work by making it possible for scholars from diverse fields more readily to grasp the essential characteristics of various traditions' eschatological schemes.

Bibliography

Albinus, L., *The house of Hades: Studies in ancient Greek eschatology*, Aarhus 2000.

Ara, M., *Eschatology in the Indo-Iranian traditions: The genesis and transformation of a doctrine*, New York 2008.

Arnold, B.T., Old Testament eschatology and the rise of apocalypticism, in J.L. Walls (ed.), *The Oxford handbook of eschatology*, New York 2008, 23–39.

19 Dodd, *Parables of the kingdom* 51: "It represents the ministry of Jesus as 'realized eschatology,' that is to say, as the impact upon this world of the 'powers of the world to come' in a series of events, unprecedented and unrepeatable, now in actual process."

20 Aune, *The cultic setting of realized eschatology*.

21 Donner, Piety and eschatology.

Assmann, J., *Death and salvation in ancient Egypt*, Ithaca, NY 2005.
Aune, D.E., *The cultic setting of realized eschatology in early Christianity*, Leiden 1972.
Bible, *The holy Bible: Revised Standard Version containing the Old and New Testaments*, New York 1946–52.
Cohn, N., *The pursuit of the millennium*, London 1957.
Collins, J.J., Introduction: Towards the morphology of a genre, in J.J. Collins (ed.), *Apocalypse: The morphology of a genre*, issue of *Semeia* 14 (1979).
Cumont, F.V.M., *After life in Roman paganism*, New Haven, CT 1922.
Dodd, C.H., *Parables of the kingdom*, New York 1936.
Donner, F.M., Piety and eschatology in early Kharijite poetry, in M. al-Saʿafin (ed.), *Fī miḥrāb al-maʿrifa: Festschrift for Ihsan ʿAbbas*, Beirut 1997, 3–19 [English Section].
Fakhry, M. (trans.), *An interpretation of the Qurʾan: English translation of the meanings: A bilingual edition*, New York, 2000.
James, E.O., *The ancient gods: The history and diffusion of religion in the ancient Near East and the eastern Mediterranean*, New York 1960.
Knipe, D.M., Hindu eschatology, in J.L. Walls (ed.), *The Oxford handbook of eschatology*, New York 2008, 170–90.
MacGregor, G., *Images of afterlife: Beliefs from antiquity to modern times*, New York 1992.
Madelung, W., al-Mahdī, in *EI*², v, 1230–8.
Moreman, C.M., *Beyond the threshhold: Afterlife beliefs and experiences in world religions*, Plymouth (UK) 2008.
Mowinckel, S., *He that cometh*, New York and Nashville, TN, n.d. [ca. 1954].
Nattier, J., Buddhist eschatology, in J.L. Walls (ed.), *The Oxford handbook of eschatology*, New York 2008, 151–69.
Russell, D.S., *The method and message of Jewish apocalyptic*, Philadelphia 1974.
Smith, J.I. and Y.Y. Haddad, *The Islamic understanding of death and resurrection*, Oxford and New York 2002.
Walls, J.L. (ed.), *The Oxford handbook of eschatology*, New York 2008.
Watchtower Bible and Tract Society of New York, *The Watchtower* 130.21 (1 November 2009).
Wensinck, A.J., *A handbook of early Muhammadan tradition*, Leiden 1927, repr. 1971.

CHAPTER 35

The "World" in its Eschatological Dimension in East-Syrian Synodical Records

Martin Tamcke

It is clear that the texts which comprise the collection of East-Syrian synodical records beginning in 410 CE and ending with a synod in the early Islamic period, in 775–76 CE, do not reveal a uniform understanding of what the concept "world" stands for.[1] The world as the entirety of everything that exists can be understood in the texts as positive, negative, or neutral. However, in the early texts, the driving force of faith is understood in contrast with the world; and the world is understood as that which culturally, socially, and religiously determined the Iranian homeland of the East-Syrian Christians.

According to the writings of Catholicos Mar Abā (540–552), which were recorded in the synodical records, the good path begins with the fear of God. The wealth of this ephemeral world could never equal the fear of God and, without this, the beauty of man and the orders of angels would be "infinitely abhorrent."[2] Only he who is open to imagine the perfection amidst all imperfections creates a standard that allows everything to be questioned since the present world in the end does not guarantee satisfactory wealth or beauty. Human beings attain their splendor only through a splendor that exists outside them by keeping a higher or, so to speak, more forward-looking perspective in mind. It is by this perspective that human actions and behavior are judged.

The idea that even the hierarchy of angels receive their splendor and beauty only through the fear of God may have originated in the *vita angelica*. It is, moreover, also a substantial declaration about the core and the scope of what the fear of God means with regard to the world.

The fear of God alone is set apart from all of the interconnectedness in our present lives and actions. It bears witness to the eternal world in so far as it

1 Until a comprehensive critical edition of the *Synodicon orientale* is available, students of this text have to use the editions of Chabot (who offers an edition on the basis of several manuscripts with French translation) and Braun (who gives only a German translation, but based on a different manuscript and thus valuable for comparison).

2 Chabot, *Synodicon orientale* 80 (Syriac text) / 333 (French translation); Braun, *Buch der Synhados* 128.

 | DOI 10.1163/9789004333154_036

does not subject human beings to the laws of the ephemeral, but rather, on the contrary, immunizes them against them. This occurs with a proper dash of morality, and two ways and realities are set in contrast:

> And each desire that does not focus its ambition on this [fear of God] is completely disgraceful and the man condemned to hell is the one who did so and thereby caused his own pain. All wisdom and science that is not rooted in it [the fear of God] and whose aim is not guided by it is vain and tasteless and causes all sorts of harm to its possessor. All powers that are not supported by it and solidified by it are irrelevant. But, whoever focuses on it, lends it his 'mental ear,' and guides his will and his speech toward its community, plans nothing without it and regulates his entire behavior in the course of his temporal life according to it, in which there is space for everyone who wants to perform good deeds.[3]

The difference between a human being of this ephemeral world and a human being who lives in the fear of God – that is, a human being in the sphere of influence of the eternal world – is thus a difference in behavior and in the inner rationale behind human acts. In place of an undisguised desire that establishes itself, the act of a human being who fears God is not simply contrived from mechanisms in the world and used for its own establishment, but rather formed by an ethical purpose and related to an immovable, ethical standard. He who does good in this manner and is filled with the fear of God is, according to the explanations of Mar Abā, "living in truth in the house of Christ."[4] This world and the present life, however, are the only places in which justice and proper behavior and acts are practiced.

The idea which Mar Abā epitomizes in the metaphors of the ephemeral and eternal worlds is characterized by Catholicos Ezekiel (570–582) by using the image of successive temporal appearances, as can be seen when he speaks of the "future world" as opposed to the present world. To sell priesthood titles for payment, i.e., positions generally described as "noble" or as "the world and everything that is in it," means for those willing to be involved in such dealings that they are buying "the hell and the pain that is reserved for the godless in the future world."[5] Furthermore, this reflection about the future world as opposed

---

3 Chabot, *Synodicon orientale* 80 / 333; Braun, *Buch der Synhados* 128.

4 Chabot, *Synodicon orientale* 80 / 333; Braun, *Buch der Synhados* 128.

5 Chabot, *Synodicon orientale* 122–3 / 381; Braun, *Buch der Synhados* 181; cf. also the statements of Catholicos Ishōʿyahb I, who speaks of God as the wise regent "of this and the future world," Chabot, *Synodicon orientale* 193 / 452; Braun, *Buch der Synhados* 274.

to this present world serves to give special importance to ethically demanded behavior. Priesthood, always in danger of becoming estranged from its orientation toward the things to come, must therefore be regarded as "noble" in order to prevent it from being seen exclusively from a financial perspective. And this is precisely because an opposite reality attempts to turn it away from this orientation.

A third way in which the opposite poles of human existence can be understood is through reference to a higher and lower world (heaven and hell), both created by God. The good and the just, then, are associated with both the present and the future world. In this way of speaking about human existence, both the horizontal and vertical characterize the intellectual coordinates of the world.[6] This idea is found in the statements of Catholicos Ishōʿyahb I (582–596). In his introduction to the synodical records, he professes God as the

> founder and regulator of both worlds, the mortal world that was created with a beginning and has a temporal end, and the eternal world that is above the measurement of time, was created with a beginning (as though it were ephemeral) but that continues without end according to the will of the grand regulator who adorned man with the light of reason, which is supported, strengthened, and enlightened by the use of appropriate rules.[7]

The Church of the East does not recognize original sin as it is taught by the Western churches. The prominent place of reason (not only in this text) has consistently led to discussions regarding to what end church rules and regulations are needed. Their necessity is seen, for the most part, as due to the limitations of human reason with regard to responsible behavior. God created both worlds, but in the ephemeral world eternity is permitted to exist in the light of reason and its ancillary rules.

These rules are brought to life in the Bible, as Biblical books serve the world by providing guidance.[8] The prophets wrote of their affliction "so that the memory [about them] would not disappear from the world."[9] The canons of the church, which in the wake of the Biblical laws, claim the power to regulate

---

6 Chabot, *Synodicon orientale* 193 / 452; Braun, *Buch der Synhados* 273–4.

7 Chabot, *Synodicon orientale* 130 / 390; Braun, *Buch der Synhados* 192.

8 Chabot, *Synodicon orientale* 230 / 494; Braun, *Buch der Synhados* 352 (letter from Catholicos George to Mina).

9 Chabot, *Synodicon orientale* 204 / 466–7.; Braun, *Buch der Synhados* 292 (letter from Catholicos Sabrishōʿ I to the hermits from Barkitai).

the lives of those that are united here (in this world) as those that live for the future world and who thereby allow these rules to become actual in the present one as "high walls and impregnable castles that protect their observer from all harm."[10] Catholicos George I (661–680) says similarly that God gave the world "helpful laws" to test the volition of his creatures, indeed "so that we and the angels would like to prove our free will."[11] Monks comply with the orders given by those above them and do not act without their knowledge, "which would be not only inappropriate for monks and hermits but also for those that simply live in the world."[12] Even if this applies primarily to monks, in the end it applies to all human beings as well.

The stance toward monasticism in the Church of the East expressly documents how the policy of the church changed over the course of time. Originating from a proto-monastic tradition in which all members of the congregation lived like monks, the church's policy began to change in the fifth and the beginning of the sixth century until monasticism was relegated to the periphery of the church and it became a requirement that all representatives of the episcopate, even the catholicoi, be married. Then, at the beginning of the seventh century, monasticism regained its dominant position and bishops and catholicoi were once more required to be celibate. These changes in the policy of the church are reflected in the synodical records, and they are explainable by historical changes that demanded appropriate reactions from the church.

In the end, the only function of the world is to serve as a laboratory for man's reason, thereby making it possible for him to learn. The good Lord "created this world, rich in variety, change, and ordeals and full of contradictions in wisdom," for instruction, testing, differentiation, as well as a step by step proof "of the spiritual and physical beings of reason of this world, so that the autonomy and freedom of the will of all rational creatures would be recognized."[13] This strict division between the worlds implies that the present world must be overcome through means found in the present world, namely reason in autonomy and freedom of will. Faith is not the loss of free will nor of autonomy, it is rather what the will utilizes and what autonomy requires.

---

10 Chabot, *Synodicon orientale* 97 / 355; Braun, *Buch der Synhados* 148 (synod of the Catholicos Joseph).

11 Chabot, *Synodicon orientale* 231 / 495–6; Braun, *Buch der Synhados* 353–4 (letter from Catholicos George to Mina).

12 Chabot, *Synodicon orientale* 206 / 468–9; Braun, *Buch der Synhados* 295 (letter from Catholicos Sabrishōʿ I to the hermits from Barkitai).

13 Chabot, *Synodicon orientale* 230 / 494; Braun, *Buch der Synhados* 353 (letter from Catholicos George to Mina).

He who has knowledge of the other world sees to the material requirements of the church in this world with, for instance, donations for the construction and upkeep of the church. One lives symbolically in anticipation of the future world, and all deeds in this world will affect the future life. The theological rationale for such sponsoring is ambitious, direct, and deliberate. "Because the true believers know that there is a world of eternal reward for them, they give God gifts to construct, furnish, and preserve the holy temples, churches, convents, hospices, schools, and episcopal residences, so that they may conceal their sins, purify their souls, and preserve their race."[14] Such benevolence transforms the seemingly lost possession into an eternal possession, or as Catholicos Ishōʿyahb I said, "it makes, so to speak, the ephemeral possession into an eternal possession."[15]

In this way, from a certain perspective, belonging to the other world decreases one's margin of profit, because of the voluntary donation of gifts as a symbolic obtaining of (God's) love. It contains, however, a shockingly far-reaching soteriological message regarding the purposefulness of such behavior. With respect to the behavior that results from belonging to the eternal world there are two types of people: the man of the world (*Weltmensch*) and the man of spirit (*Geistmensch*). Affiliation with the future (eternal) world does not lead only to the willingness to donate, it also leads to behavior that establishes boundaries with respect to the rest of society. Thus, Canon 37 of the synods of Catholicos Ezekiel expressly commands "that, from now on, Christians should no longer send their daughters away to learn worldly music."[16] Clergymen were urged to stop educating 'worldly people' because this would belittle the dignity of the church.[17] Ethical behavior in the spirit of the future world was considered noble. The church's dignity is vulnerable to interactions in which those involved are not able to account for the motivation of the believers, especially the priests, because they, in their steadfast connection to this world, are blind to the fact that the others belong to a different, opposing world.

The synod of Catholicos Joseph (552–567, d. 576) describes the death of his predecessor Mar Abā in 551–2 with the words "[he] departed from this world."[18] One leaves this world and, thus, belonging to the future world becomes the

14 Chabot, *Synodicon orientale* 143 / 405; Braun, *Buch der Synhados* 209 (synod of Ishōʿyahb I, Canon 7).

15 Chabot, *Synodicon orientale* 143 / 405; Braun, *Buch der Synhados* 209 (synod of Ishōʿyahb I, Canon 7).

16 Chabot, *Synodicon orientale* 127 / 386; Braun, *Buch der Synhados* 187.

17 Chabot, *Synodicon orientale* 127 / 386; Braun, *Buch der Synhados* 187 (Canon 36).

18 Chabot, *Synodicon orientale* 96 / 353; Braun, *Buch der Synhados* 146.

only important goal. To what degree the symbols of Catholicos Ishō'yahb I show a self-countained theology of the Church of the East of the resurrection and a future life may be questioned. This is also due to the fact that the cited formulation is given as a quote from the west-Nicene tradition. However, it is now believed that this acknowledgment comes from the east-Syriac understanding of the world. From this understanding the ephemeral is differentiated from the eternal, the spiritual from the material, above from below, and that which belongs to the 'now' from that which belongs to the future. Non-Christian courts are to be avoided[19] and the same is true for the holidays of other religions: "no Christian is permitted to attend a non-Christian celebration or accept anything that is given to him as a result of it."[20] Pubs and picnics are also to be avoided altogether.[21] Instead, one is to practice a spiritual transformation for which the priests serve as examples. Consequently, priests are not allowed "to wear elegant clothing, lead a carnal lifestyle, live with a childish mentality capricious as the weather, or act like worldly people, but rather they must try to live as far as possible in accordance with the future life."[22]

Thus, 'world' can be understood horizontally or vertically with concept pairs such as above and below, ephemeral and eternal, temporal and non-temporal, present and future. To perceive responsibility in the world therefore means to distance oneself from the established societal, cultural, religious, and social life and instead dedicate oneself to the parallel church-society that in the form of the church is a stepping-stone to the future, eternal, or higher world. Thus, the future world is the guiding principle for the conduct of life in the present world. Human beings are, as it were, without splendor if they do not bear the splendor of the future world toward which they strive. In this way the future world influences the acts and behavior of human beings in the present. The future world contains the perfection that, because it is only *there* and can be experienced *here* only in the intention of reaching the future world, makes all life here a field of ethical probation and simultaneously frees the present world from attributions of "permanent" religious meaning and exaltation. Here, nothing equals that which becomes visible *there*; but in the best case there exists a non-thing, which exists as a potential completely free from religious attributions; and this non-thing corresponds either to the claim of belief, or it

19 Chabot, *Synodicon orientale* 155 / 415; Braun, *Buch der Synhados* 225.

20 Chabot, *Synodicon orientale* 158 / 417–8; Braun, *Buch der Synhados* 228.

21 Chabot, *Synodicon orientale* 158–9 / 418; Braun, *Buch der Synhados* 229; cf. Braun's note 142.

22 Chabot, *Synodicon orientale* 176 / 435–6; Braun, *Buch der Synhados* 252 (synod of Ishō'yahb I, Canon 7).

is simply filth. With respect to this world it is obsolete, ephemeral, lackluster, and low.

The separation of the worlds that is introduced from belief in the present world can originally be traced back to the experience of Christ:

> The entire world requires the appearance of our savior, but humankind requires this especially in that he lifts us from the guilt of sin, delivers us from the bondage of death, saves us from the indignation found in the slow decomposition we call death, and gives us the most splendid, eternal life, the complete knowledge of his divinity and the lasting attachment of being in the glory of his majesty born out of grace toward human beings and the spirits.[23]

In this way life in the world is determined as a life outside of the above, future, and unending world. Paul Tillich's primary claim – "The divine life participates in every life as its ground and aim"[24] – is actually taken up by the Church of the East but only as an entirely Christological claim that the divine life is, when it comes to acts grounded in reason, an internal driving force that allows human beings to remain human beings without allowing them to receive any amount of divinity. And so it naturally makes sense that the separation characterized by the Church of the East between the divine and human in Christology, in which the divine only exists in human beings as it exists in a temple, as it were, has a parallel in the separation from the divine world and this ephemeral world. Even if the ephemeral world is thought of as finite, even if it is only filth, the world here is still nothing other than the world here and in it nothing other than the laws of reason apply; these laws of reason, which indeed remain the medium for shaping the world, are taken from another world, as it were, and utilized in this one.

The synods of the Church of the East assume an already disenchanted world and make this disenchanted world into a test area, so to speak, where the present and future worlds of Christ find one another but do not unite nor simply remain separate, but rather exist in the acts and life that originate in the mind and aim toward the life ahead. But this ideal is no mere representation of the modern idea of withdrawing from the world. Even the disempowerment and relativization of the claim of this world aim at something else: A life lived within the borders of the material, economic, political and religious world here, but lived as a representation of an alternative, eternal, intrinsically

23 Chabot, *Synodicon orientale* 234 / 499; Braun, *Buch der Synhados* 357.

24 Tillich, *Systematic theology* i, 245.

spiritual world. Further to this, the deliberate disempowerment of this world from the beginning facilitates its role as a place of ethical probation and makes the way of life of the believers a permanent declaration of war against a world that follows rules that differ from the ethics established in the Bible. This alternative view scrutinizes the world so that it is seen as something temporary in which the final thing – the true "abode" or goal – is reflected in anticipation.

Bibliography

Braun, O. (trans.), *Das Buch der Synhados oder Synodicon Orientale: Die Sammlung der nestorianischen Konzilien*, Stuttgart and Vienna 1900, repr. Amsterdam 1974.

Chabot, J.B. (ed.), *Synodicon orientale ou recueil de synodes Nestoriens* (Notices et extraits des manuscrits de la Bibliothèque Nationale 37), Paris 1902.

Tillich, P., *Systematic theology*, 3 vols., London 1988[3].

CHAPTER 36

St. Ephraem the Syrian, the Quran, and the Grapevines of Paradise: An Essay in Comparative Eschatology

Sidney H. Griffith

1 Syriac and the Arabic Quran

For many years, scholars engaged in the study of the Quran and of Islamic origins have been aware of the fact that works written in pre-Islamic Late Antiquity, in the dialect of Aramaic known as Syriac, offer them one of several sure paths into the religious thought-world of Arabian Christianity. It was into this world that the Arabic Quran appeared of a sudden in the first third of the seventh Christian century. Historically speaking, this is only to be expected; the Arabic-speaking Christian communities in the milieu in which Islam was born, be they from Sinai, Palestine, Transjordan, Syria, lower Mesopotamia, or even southern Arabia, all belonged to communities whose liturgies, doctrines, and ecclesiastical associations were of primarily Aramaic expression.[1] As for Syriac itself, there is an interesting, if not a very compelling, reference to it already in early Islamic tradition to the effect that some Syriac books had come to Muḥammad's attention. According to the report deriving from his well-known secretary, the Prophet is alleged to have said to Zayd b. Thābit, "Do you know Syriac well? Some books have come to my attention. I said, 'No.' He said, 'Learn it.' So I learned it in nineteen days."[2]

Alphonse Mingana, writing in 1927, estimated that seventy percent of the "foreign influences on the style and terminology" of the Quran could be traced to "Syriac (including Aramaic and Palestinian Syriac)."[3] Noting this high incidence of Syriac etymologies for a significant portion of the Quran's 'foreign vocabulary,' Arthur Jeffrey wrote in 1938 that "one fact seems certain, namely that such Christianity as was known among the Arabs in pre-Islamic times was

1 See the helpful survey in Hainthaler, *Christliche Araber vor dem Islam*.

2 Ibn al-Ashʿath al-Sijistānī, *Kitāb al-Maṣāḥif* 6. I am grateful to Prof. David Powers of Cornell University for bringing the passage to my attention.

3 Mingana, Syriac influence.

 | DOI 10.1163/9789004333154_037

largely of the Syrian type, whether Jacobite or Nestorian."[4] He noted further that numerous early Islamic texts mention Muḥammad's contacts with both Syrian and Arabian Christians, and this observation prompted Jeffery to conclude that these texts "at least show that there was an early recognition of the fact that Muḥammad was at one time in more or less close contact with Christians associated with the Syrian Church."[5]

More radically, and most recently, Christoph Luxenberg has been exploring what he calls the 'Syro-Aramaic' reading of the Quran.[6] His method involves the use of the Syriac lexicon and the consultation of Syriac grammatical usages to help in the reading of certain passages in the Quran, to explore the possibility that a more historically intelligible reading of hitherto obscure passages might be attained, often found to be congruent with earlier, Aramaean Christian ideas and formulations.[7] Luxenberg's ongoing work has inspired a number of other researchers, who have pushed his ideas further, virtually re-inventing early Islamic history in ways that have evoked considerable controversy.[8] On the one hand, these inquiries have underlined the importance of Syriac for Quranic studies; on the other hand, in the enthusiasm for finding new readings and new interpretations, based on perceived grammatical and lexical possibilities, sometimes too little attention has been paid by these scholars to the usages of classical Syriac literature that underlay the religious idiom of Arabic-speaking Christians in the Quran's milieu. The present writer has undertaken cautious soundings in this area in previous essays[9] and now he approaches it again, this time in the context of the Quran's eschatology, and particularly in connection with Christoph Luxenberg's widely publicized reconstruction and

4 Jeffery, *Foreign vocabulary* 20–1.

5 Ibid., 22.

6 See Luxenberg, *Die syro-aramäische Lesart* (English trans., *Syro-Aramaic reading*, ed. Müke).

7 Luxenberg was preceded in this enterprise by Günter Lüling, who had argued that about a third of the Quran as we now have it is built on the foundation of an earlier Christian, strophic hymnody that was concealed under successive layers of text. According to him, this early Arabic, Christian hymnody, which celebrated an angel-Christology, was at home among the pre-Islamic Arabs and had a place in Christian liturgy in the then-Christian Kaʿba in Mecca. See Lüling, *Über den Ur-Qurʾān*; Lüling, *Der christliche Kult*; Lüling, *Die Wiederentdeckung des Propheten Muhammad*. For a more personal discussion of his idea and its reception among scholars see Lüling, Preconditions for the scholarly criticism.

8 See, e.g., Ohlig and Puin (eds.), *Die dunklen Anfänge*; Ohlig (ed.), *Eine historisch-kritische Rekonstruktion*; Ohlig and Gross (eds.), *Schlaglichter*.

9 See Griffith, Syriacisms in the 'Arabic Qurʾān'; Griffith, Christian lore and the Arabic Qurʾān; Griffith, *An-Naṣārā* in the Qurʾān, forthcoming.

reinterpretation of the Quran's thrice repeated phrase *ḥūr ʿīn*[10] to mean 'white, crystal(-clear), (grapes)' instead of the traditional 'wide-eyed/dark-eyed *ḥūrīs*.'[11] In the process, Luxenberg puts some stress on the importance of the proper understanding of a passage in one of Ephraem the Syrian's (c. 306–373) Syriac *madrāshê* 'On Paradise,' and it is precisely in connection with these Syriac liturgical poems that the present study unfolds.

2 The Quran and Ephraem the Syrian's *Madrāshê* 'On Paradise': The Views of Modern Scholars

2.1 *Tor Andrae*

The late Swedish scholar Tor Andrae (1885–1947) is undoubtedly the modern researcher who has, to date, most systematically investigated what he considered to be Muḥammad's and the Quran's indebtedness to Christian eschatology in its Syriac expression.[12] In his seminal study, *Der Ursprung des Islams und das Christentum*, he specifically draws attention to the importance in this connection of Ephraem's *madrāshê* 'On Paradise' and he spends some time unfolding the connecting themes between these Christian, liturgical compositions and the Quran. What Andrae perceived was not a direct literary connection between Syriac texts and the Quran. Rather, he spoke of "one and the same homiletic scheme," and he offered it as his opinion that "whatever Muhammad received from Christianity, he got from oral preaching and personal contacts."[13] More specifically in regard to the works of Ephraem, and taking his cue from a remark made by Hubert Grimme to the effect that in his descriptions of paradise, Muḥammad "must have benefited much from recalling images used by Ephrem,"[14] Andrae averred that "in fact, on this point, there is a surprising

10 See Q 44:54; 52:20; 56:22.

11 See Luxenberg, *Syro-Aramaic reading* 247–83.

12 Andrae first published the results of his research on this theme in a series of three long articles: Andrae, Der Ursprung des Islams, in *Kyrkohistorisk Årsskrift* 23, 149–206; 24, 213–92; 25, 45–112. Subsequently the articles were collected into the volume, Andrae, *Der Ursprung des Islams*. This volume has been translated into French in Andrae, *Les origines de l'islam*. In later works Andrae continued to appeal to Syriac sources, most notably in Andrae, *Mohammed, sein Leben und sein Glaube* (English trans., *Mohammed: The man and his faith*). See also Andrae, *I Myrtenträdgården* (English trans., *In the garden of myrtles*).

13 Andrae, Der Ursprung des Islams 45–6; Andrae, *Les origines de l'islam* 145–6.

14 Grimme, *Mohammed* ii, 160 note 9.

relationship between Muhammad and the Syrian preacher."[15] And Andrae proceeds to list a number of convergences between the very concrete, even sensual descriptions of the garden of paradise in Ephraem's *madrāshê* and passages in the Arabic Quran. It is at this juncture in his discussion that Tor Andrae made the very controversial observation that in a stanza of one of Ephraem's *madrāshê*, "one can even point out in his words a hidden allusion to Paradise's virgins."[16] Andrae quotes the passage in his own German translation from Ephraem's *madrāshâ* VII:18:

> Wer bis zu seinem Hingang sich des Weines enthalten hat, wird von den Weinstöcken des Paradieses sehnsüchtig erwartet. Jeder von ihnen reckt ihm seine hängende Traube entgegen. Und wenn jemand in Virginität gelebt hat, den empfangen sie (fem.) in ihrem reinen Schoße, weil er als Mönch nicht in dem Bette und Schosse irdischer Liebe fiel'. Von den Weinstöcken, deren Trauben sich herabsenken, sodass sie bequem zu erreichen sind, spricht auch Muhammed (Q 76:14).[17]

In his later publication, *Mohammed, sein Leben und sein Glaube*, Andrae expanded on this passage to say:

> To be sure, Afrem occasionally points out that this is only an attempt to give some idea of a joy which no earthly mind is able to grasp. But most of his listeners and readers no doubt remained quite oblivious to his feeble attempts to spiritualize his sensual images. Popular piety certainly

---

15 Andrae, Der Ursprung des Islams 52; Andrae, *Les origines de l'islam* 151. It is interesting to note that in his later book on Muḥammad, Andrae makes this point more apodictically. He says, "Christians have often pointed out that Mohammed depicts eternal bliss merely as an endless and unrestricted satisfaction of extremely primitive sensual desires. The polemical ardour should be damped by what seems to me to be the irrefutable fact that the Koran's descriptions of Paradise were inspired by the ideas of this Christian Syrian preacher." Andrae, *Mohammed: The man and his faith* 87.

16 "Der Wein, den die Seligen genießen, fehlt auch nicht bei Afrem, selbst eine versteckte Anspielung auf die Paradiesjungfrauen könnte man in seinen Worten hineindeuten," Andrae, Der Ursprung des Islams 54; "Même une allusion caché aux vierges du Paradis pourrait être trouvée dans ses paroles," Andrae, *Les origines de l'islam* 153.

17 Andrae, Der Ursprung des Islams 54; *Les origines de l'islam* 153–4. The Quranic verse quoted speaks of the garden's "low-hanging, pickable [fruit] (*quṭūfuhā*)" (Q 76:14). The Arabic word *qiṭf* (pl. *quṭūf*) is normally understood to mean a bunch of grapes. See Lane, *An Arabic-English lexicon* viii, 2991. All translations from the Quran are based on Fakhry (trans.), *Interpretation.*

interpreted this daring imagery in a crass and literal sense, and under such circumstances one cannot blame a citizen of pagan Mekka for doing the same thing.[18]

2.2 *Dom Edmund Beck, OSB*

Two modern scholars in particular have contested Tor Andrae's view that Ephraem the Syrian's words can be taken to prefigure in any way the 'wide-eyed/dark-eyed *ḥūrīs*' of Islamic tradition; both the Syriac-scholar, Dom Edmund Beck OSB (1902–91), and Christoph Luxenberg have opposed it. Beck made his critique from the perspective of the proper understanding of Ephraem's stanza in its context in *madrāshâ* VII 'On Paradise.'[19] In particular, he proposed that Andrae had been misled in his interpretation by a faulty reading in the text of the *madrāshâ* as it appears in the *Editio Romana* of Ephraem's complete works.

As it happens, the Syriac word for 'grapevine,' *gupnâ* (pl. *gupnê*), is grammatically feminine, a point that, according to Beck, escaped the attention of both the editor of Ephraem's text of *madrāshâ* VII:18 'On Paradise' in the *Editio Romana* and Tor Andrae. Specifically, in the first half of the stanza, quoted above in Andrae's German version, when the text says of the one who in this life abstained from wine, that he "wird von den Weinstöcken des Paradieses sehnsüchtig erwartet," the Syriac participle translated as 'he is eagerly awaited' by the grapevines was wrongly written in the Roman text in the masculine form, i.e., *sāwḥîn*[20] instead of the correct, feminine form, *sāwḥān*. This error in turn, according to Beck, prompted Andrae to look for an un-expressed, feminine antecedent for the third person feminine plural suffix attached to the term 'bosom'/ '*Schosse*' (*'ûbheyn*) in the second part of the stanza, when the text speaks of the one who had lived in virginity, and characterizes him as the one "den emfangen sie (fem.) in ihrem reinen Schosse." Not recognizing that the grapevines (fem.) were the ones who, according to Ephraem, would then receive such a one into their pure bosom, Andrae was misled to think the text was discreetly speaking of some unmentioned, pure virgins, on the order of the Quran's 'dark-eyed *ḥūrīs*,' who would be awaiting the monk in paradise. Along the way, Beck also corrects what he perceives to be inexact renderings of

---

18 Andrae, *Mohammed: The man and his faith* 88.

19 See Beck, Eine christliche Parallele; a précis of the article appeared in a French translation in Beck, Les Houris du Coran. See also Beck, *Hymnen über das Paradies* 16–8. Subsequently Beck published a critical edition of Ephraem's *madrāshê* 'On Paradise,' along with a German translation, in Beck, *Hymnen de Paradiso*.

20 See the Syriac text translated by Andrae in Mobarak and Assemani, *Opera omnia* iii, 584.

the Syriac in Andrae's version of the stanza, but these are minor matters.[21] The important point for Beck was his satisfaction that he had successfully removed the textual basis for Tor Andrae's suggestion that Ephraem had anticipated the *ḥūrīs*. What is more, Beck also showed that, as in other passages of the *madrāshê* 'On Paradise,' so in this one, Ephraem was evoking the imagery of a lush garden and speaking of the over-hanging trees and grapevines of paradise that offer their bunches of grapes to the blessed. As a case in point, he cited the example of *madrāshâ* IX: 3 & 4, where Ephraem uses much the same imagistic language.

Should you wish
  to climb up a tree,
with its lower branches
  it will provide steps before your feet,
eager to make you recline
  in its bosom above,
on the couch of its upper branches.
  So arranged is the surface of these branches,
bent low and cupped
  – while yet dense with flowers –
that they serve as a protective womb
  for whoever rests there.
Who has ever beheld such a banquet
  in the very bosom of a tree,
with fruit of every savor
  ranged for the hand to pluck.
Each type of fruit in due sequence approaches,
  each awaiting its turn:
fruit to eat,
  and fruit to quench the thirst;
to rinse the hands there is dew,
  and leaves to dry them with after
a treasure store which lacks nothing,
  whose Lord is rich in all things.[22]

21 Beck's own version of the stanza is as follows: "Wer des Weines * in Klugheit sich enthielt, – dem eilen freudiger * die Weinstöcke des Paradieses entgegen – und jeder wird seine Trauben * ihm darreichen. – Lebte er auch noch jungfräulich, * dann führen sie ihn ein – in ihren reinen Schoss, * weil er als Asket – nicht gefallen ist in den Schoss * und in das Bett der Ehe." Beck, *Hymnen de Paradiso* clxxv, 28, VII:18.

22 Translated by Brock, *Hymns on paradise* 137.

2.3 *Christoph Luxenberg*

Christoph Luxenberg, who paid close attention to Beck's refutation of Tor Andrae's suggestion that the 'dark-eyed *ḥūrīs*' of Islamic tradition were anticipated in Ephraem the Syrian's *madrāshê* 'On Paradise,' argues that in fact there are no such things as *ḥūrīs* in the Quran at all.[23] After a brief review of the standard scholarship, including the view that the notion of the 'virgins of paradise' is due to Persian influence on the later exegetical tradition, Luxenberg, who pledged to proceed on 'purely philological' grounds in his examination of the matter, nevertheless begins his examination with the re-affirmation of his basic, non-philological, and presumed operating principle. He says it is not the case that "the Prophet had misunderstood Christian illustrations of Paradise, but rather that the later Islamic exegesis had misinterpreted the Koranic paraphrase of Christian Syriac hymns." And he goes on at the same place to say: "The Koran takes as its starting point the axiom that the *Scripture* preceding it (the Old and New Testament) has been revealed. Understanding itself as a component of this *Scripture*, to be consistent it derives from this the claim that it itself has been revealed."[24] From this premise, and the corollary that the Quran "takes the *Scripture* as its model," Luxenberg observes that "there would be such an *inconsistency*, if the likes of the *ḥūrīs* ... were not to be found in the *Scripture*. Then the Koran, against its usual assertion, would have thus produced proof that it had not come from God."[25] But, says Luxenberg, "The Koran is not to blame if, out of ignorance, people have read it so falsely and projected onto it their subjective, all too earthly daydreams."[26] And with this assertion, having on a priori, hermeneutical grounds ruled out any interpretation of the Quran's words and phrases that would admit of any hint of *ḥūrīs*, or any other explicit sexual imagery in its depiction of the joys of paradise, Luxenberg applies his signature philological method not only to the *rasm* of the phrase *ḥūr ʿīn*, but to all the passages in which the Quran's language has been thought to evoke just such imagery.

In the most notable instance of the application of his philological method, which has even attracted the attention of the popular press far and wide, Christoph Luxenberg first of all attended to the enigmatic phrase at the heart of the matter, the canonical Quran's twice repeated utterance, "*wa-zawwajnāhum bi-ḥūrin ʿīnin*" (Q 44:54 and 52:20). Stripping away the customary vowel markings and diacritical points from the basic Arabic script, and presuming the Arabic scripture's original intention to yield a 'Syro-Aramaic' reading, with

---

23 See the long discussion in Luxenberg, *Syro-Aramaic reading* 247–83.
24 Ibid., 249.
25 Ibid., 250.
26 Ibid., 250.

attention to other Quranic passages, and the reminder that "with the supposed *ḥūrīs* the Koran would be contradicting *Scripture*,"[27] Luxenberg delves into the Syriac grammar and lexicon for a likely alternative reading consistent with the prominent imagery of grapes and grapevines. But first, on Arabic lexical and grammatical grounds he argues that the conventional reading is impossible and having thus disposed of the 'imagined *ḥūrīs*,' which, he says, "disappear *ipso facto* into thin air," he says:

> Thus, too, would be removed the related contradictions in the Koran and objectivity would be restored to the Koranic statement cited above to the extent that the claim, documented in the *Scripture*, according to which one is neither *married* nor *given in marriage* in Paradise (Mt 22:30; Mk 12:25; Lk 20:35) is now confirmed.[28]

With the *ḥūrīs* thus removed, Luxenberg then moves to the task of putting what seems to him to be the proper construction upon the Quran's words in the problematic, key phrase under consideration, i.e., *ḥūr ʿīn*. It is at this juncture that he recalls Edmund Beck's rejection of Tor Andrae's suggestion that the *ḥūrīs* might have been adumbrated in Ephraem the Syrian's *madrāshê* 'On Paradise'[29] and Beck's further indication of the prominence of the imagery of grapes and grapevines in Ephraem's depiction of the garden. Taking his cue from here, Luxenberg found his interpretive frame of reference for the enigmatic Arabic phrase in the realm of viticulture, and with this insight in mind he explored the orthographic, grammatical, and lexical possibilities of the bare Arabic *rasm*, the un-vowelled, un-pointed, original script. After some detailed grammatical and lexical explorations, and with the image of garden bowers in mind, construed of grapevines, with their over-hanging clusters of grapes, Luxenberg proposed the now famous 'Syro-Aramaic' reading, "We will make you comfortable under white, crystal(-clear) (grapes)."[30]

Against the background of this signal accomplishment, and still deploying his usual philological method, Luxenberg proceeds to re-adjust the understanding of other Quranic passages that have been read in connection with

27 Ibid., 254.

28 Ibid., 256–7.

29 Citing Beck's rejection of Andrae's mistaken understanding of the feminine referent in Ephraem's stanza, Luxenberg makes the curious remark, "In the end it was also this that led the Arabic exegetes of the Koran to this fateful assumption." Luxenberg, *Syro-Aramaic reading* 259.

30 Ibid., 251.

the *ḥūrīs* or with reference to other women in paradise, so that their hitherto unrecognized evocations of the imagery of grapes and grapevines might come to light. But for the present purpose one might let the review of this 'Syro-Aramaic' re-reading of these Quranic passages rest here for the moment. It remains only to mention that at least one other scholar has sought to further adjust Luxenberg's re-construction of this imagery.

In an interesting review of Christoph Luxenberg's work, along with a number of suggestions of his own for consulting possible early Christian antecedents for a number of other Quranic phrases, Jan M.F. van Reeth suggested an alternative to Luxenberg's reading of the phrase, "*wa-zawwajnāhum bi-ḥūrin ʿīnin*."[31] Against the background of a deep study of the development of the 'grapes and grapevine' motif in Biblical and patristic sources, which he suggests is lying behind the passages in Ephraem the Syrian's *madrāshê* 'On Paradise,' van Reeth proposed that the Quranic phrase in question might better be read as a calque on the Syriac phrase, *kūrâ dəʿenbên*, attested in the Syriac of *Second Baruch* "which could be rendered into Arabic as *kūr ʿ-n-b* or *khūr ʿ-n-b*: a certain measure of grapes, of wine."[32] In a long footnote in a later edition of his work, Luxenberg rejected van Reeth's suggestion,[33] but the latter's sketch of the early development of the 'grapes and grapevines' motif in early Christian literature nevertheless remains a valuable contribution to the discussion.

On the one hand, while Christoph Luxenberg's philological soundings are impressive in their ingenuity, if not always in their verisimilitude, he neglects finding instances of the actual currency in Syriac literature of phrases like his postulated "white, crystal(-) (grapes),"[34] construed on the basis of grammatical and lexical possibilities alone. And on the other hand, he does not consider the full context of the passages to which he refers in Ephraem the Syrian's *madrāshê* 'On Paradise,' where marital metaphors definitely do appear, as we shall see, along with the 'grapes and grapevines' motif in the author's depiction

31 See van Reeth, Le vignoble du paradis. See also van Reeth, L'Évangile du Prophète.

32 Van Reeth, Le vignoble du paradis 515.

33 See Luxenberg, *Syro-Aramaic reading* 263 note 324.

34 At one point in defense of his suggestion that the Syriac feminine adjective *ḥewwārtâ* 'white' has been used in Syriac to apply to grapes, Luxenberg cites the authority of R. Payne-Smith's *Thesaurus Syriacus*. But the reference is not in fact to grapes but to a white grapevine, in a Syriac translation of a phrase in the Greek *Geoponica*, viz., η λευκη αμπελος. See Payne-Smith, *Thesaurus Syriacus*, col. 1230. Similarly, the citation from the dictionary of Manna actually refers to a grapevine. See Manna, *Vocabulaire Chaldéen-Arabe* 229a. What is more, the only instance of the appearance of the adjective 'white' (*ḥewwārê*) in Ephraem the Syrian's *madrāshê* 'On Paradise' is in reference to the "new, white garments" of the just in the garden. See Beck, *Hymnen de Paradiso*, VI:9.6.

of the joys and pleasures of the garden of paradise. What is more, it appears from his own words, quoted above, that it was not philology in the first place, but a pre-conceived line of *scriptural* reasoning, and an idiosyncratic view of the Quran's origins, that first prompted Christoph Luxenberg to reject the *ḥūrīs* of the Islamic exegetical tradition; he then used 'Syro-Aramaic' philology to produce another reading of the Arabic phrases actually appearing in the Quran.

3 Ephraem the Syrian's Syriac *Madrāshê* 'On Paradise'

While they have often been mentioned in the present discussion, in fact not much attention has actually been paid in the studies we have reviewed to Ephraem the Syrian's *madrāshê* 'On Paradise' and their multiple images of the joys and pleasures of the garden of paradise. The collection of fifteen *madrāshê* 'On Paradise' are preserved in an early sixth-century manuscript, written in the city of Edessa in the year 519 CE by an otherwise unknown scribe named Julian.[35] In the manuscript, they are all presented in the same meter-melody, with the exception that *madrāshê* XIII and XIV appear in a continuous, alphabetical, acrostic pattern of stanzas, a feature that binds these two pieces together, somewhat out of step with the presentation of the other *madrāshê* in the collection. This arrangement suggests that in spite of the fact that they are now presented as separate compositions, numbers XIII and XIV must once have circulated as a single composition. And it is quite possible that they and other parts of the collection were not originally by Ephraem, but were later included in the portfolio.[36]

The Syriac *madrāshâ* is a genre of liturgical poetry set to music. In Ephraem's hands it also became the literary genre of choice for winning and holding the allegiance to Nicene orthodoxy of the Syriac-speaking Christians in Syria/Mesopotamia and the frontier regions between the Roman and Persian empires in the fourth and fifth centuries.[37] It is a 'teaching song,' a distinctive genre in its own right; it is not just hymnody,[38] nor is it simply a poetic

35 See Beck's discussion of British Library Ms. add. 14571 in Beck, *Hymnen de Paradiso* clxxiv, 3. Beck's edition and German translation are now standard. The *madrāshê* have been translated into both English and French, in English in Brock, *Hymns on paradise*, and in French in Lavenant and Graffin, *Hymnes sur le paradis*.

36 See Palmer, Restoring the ABC 147–94; Palmer, Nine more stanzas.

37 See Griffith, The clash of *Madrāshê* in Aram.

38 See Lattke, Sind Ephräms *Madrāshê* Hymnen?

recitative. Rather, the *madrāshê* composed by Ephraem the Syrian were poetically metered recitatives set to music.[39] In the Divine Liturgy, they were publicly performed after the solemn reading from the scriptures; they explored the scriptural themes meditatively and they were sung by trained choirs, with congregational responses after each stanza. In all likelihood their tunes were catchy and their words and phrases would have been eminently memorable.

In Ephraem's *madrāshê* 'On Paradise,' the point of departure seems to have been a passage from the Gospel according to Luke:[40]

> One of the robbers who were hanged railed at him, saying, "Are you not the Christ? Save yourself and us!" But the other rebuked him, saying, "Do you not fear God, since you are under the same sentence of condemnation? And we indeed justly; for we are receiving the due reward of our deeds; but this man has done nothing wrong." And he said, "Jesus, remember me when you come in your kingly power." And he said to him, "Truly, I say to you, today you will be with me in Paradise." (Luke 23:39–43)

Ephraem says he heard this passage proclaimed in the liturgy. He put it this way at the beginning of one of the *madrāshê*:

> A statement that delighted me
>   shone forth in my ears
> from the text that was read
>   about the story of the robber.
> It gave consolation to my soul,
>   due to the multitude of her faults,
> that the One pitying the robber
>   would lead her
> to the very garden (*gantâ*) whose name
>   I had heard and was overjoyed.
> My mind cut loose its reins
>   and proceeded to meditate on it.[41]

Ephraem described the manner of his meditation on paradise in other songs in the collection. In the first one, he speaks of his reading about paradise in the Torah, "the treasury of revelations," as he styled it, in which "the story of the

39 See McVey, Songs or recitations.
40 See Griffith, Syriac/Antiochene exegesis.
41 Beck, *Hymnen de Paradiso*, VIII:1.

garden is revealed." Here in the Torah, Moses, "who teaches all men his celestial texts, the master of the Hebrews taught us his doctrine." And Ephraem goes on to sing:

> Gladly did I come to
>   the story of Paradise,
> which is short to read
>   but rich to investigate.
> My tongue read the stories,
>   clear in the account of it,
> and my mind flew up to soar
>   in awe.
> It searched out its glory,
>   not indeed as it is,
> but as it is given,
>   to mankind to apprehend.
> In my mind's eye
>   I saw Paradise.[42]

In yet another song in the collection, Ephraem very evocatively describes his first-person journey to paradise, led there by the lines of the book of Genesis. With the Quran and later Islamic tradition in mind, one might even think of Ephraem's adventure as a spiritual *miʿrāj* avant le lettre.[43] He says:

> I read the opening of this book
>   and was filled with joy,
> for its verses and lines
>   spread out their arms to welcome me;
> the first rushed out and kissed me,
>   and led me on to its companion;
> and when I reached that verse
>   wherein is written
> the story of Paradise,
>   it lifted me up and transported me
> from the bosom of the book
>   to the very bosom of Paradise.

---

42 Ibid., I:1, 3–4.1.

43 On the importance of this event in the development of Islamic theology, see van Ess, *The flowering of Muslim theology* 45–77.

The eye and the mind
  traveled over the lines
as over a bridge, and entered together
  the story of Paradise.
The eye as it read
  transported the mind;
in return the mind, too,
  gave the eye rest
from its reading,
  for when the book had been read
the eye had rest,
  but the mind was engaged.
Both the bridge and the gate
  of Paradise
did I find in this book.
  I crossed over and entered;
my eye indeed remained outside
  but my mind entered within.
I began to wander
  amid things not described.
This is a luminous height,
  clear, lofty and fair:
Scripture named it Eden,
  the summit of all blessings.[44]

As he came down from his mental journey amid the glories and wonders of the garden, Ephraem reflected:

I was in wonder as I crossed
  the borders of Paradise
at how well-being, as though a companion,
  turned round and remained behind.
And when I reached the shore of earth,
  the mother of thorns,
I encountered all kinds
  of pain and suffering.

44 Beck, *Hymnen de Paradiso*, V:3–5, in the English translation of Brock, *Hymns on paradise* 103–4.

I learned how, compared to Paradise,
our abode is but a dungeon;
yet the prisoners within it
weep when they leave it.[45]

In the course of his meditation on the story of paradise in the Bible, Ephraem conjures up in his *madrashê* a kaleidoscopic, verbal icon of the joys and pleasures of human destiny in the hereafter. He envisions the scriptural account of the garden of Eden as embodying a typological sketchbook of paradise in the end time. As Dom Edmund Beck put it, in these *madrāshê* 'On Paradise,' Ephraem "umfasst das Thema *de Paradiso* 'Primordiologie' und Eschatologie zugleich."[46]

As Tor Andrae and others have mentioned, a notable feature of Ephraem's descriptions of the after-world in the garden of paradise is their appeal to the senses, albeit for him, as one scholar has put it, "The bodily senses become symbols of another kind of perception, namely spiritual perception."[47] However that may be, in the travelogue of his mind's journey into the garden of paradise, Ephraem describes the beauties of Paradise Mountain in terms of vision, taste, and even scent. He speaks of a beauty that "no paints can portray,"[48] where "scented breezes blow with varied force" over a banquet "where those who minister never weary in their service."[49] The trees, with their branches form a bower that invites the blessed to recline in their bosom, and "as the saints recline; below them are blossoms, above them fruit."[50] Ephraem envisions each season as yielding its best produce in paradise and he uses an earthy image to make the point. He says,

45 Beck, *Hymnen de Paradiso*, V:13, in the English translation of Brock, *Hymns on paradise* 106–7. Note that Ephraem, like Muḥammad after him, had companionship in paradise, but unlike Gabriel as Muḥammad's guide, Ephraem speaks of "well-being, as though a companion," in Brock's translation. A more literal rendering might be: "The company of the wholesome stayed and turned back." One notices here the counterpoint between the Islamic concreteness and the Syrian Christian abstraction.

46 Beck, *Hymnen über das Paradies* ix.

47 Botha, The significance of the senses 28. See also Botha, Honour and shame.

48 Beck, *Hymnen de Paradiso*, IV:9.

49 Ibid., IX:7.

50 Ibid., IX:5.

The air of this earth
  is as wanton as a prostitute
with whom the twelve months
  consort:
each one in turn
  makes her comply with its own whims
while she produces fruits
  from them all;
whereas the chaste and pure air
  of Paradise
is unpolluted in its purity
  by the dalliance of the months.
There the abundant flow
  of their produce is ceaseless,
for each month bears its own fruit,
  its neighbor, flowers.
There the springs of delights
  open up and flow
with wine, milk, honey
  and cream.[51]

Ephraem makes a major point of the fact that not only the souls of the just, but their bodies, too, are destined to enjoy the delights of paradise. He says, "The soul cannot have any perception of Paradise without its mate, the body, its instrument and lyre."[52] And so, in a beautiful stanza he envisions the following scenario unfolding:

In the delightful mansions
  on the borders of Paradise
do the souls of the just
  and righteous reside,
awaiting there
  the bodies they love,
so that, at the opening
  of the Garden's gate,

51 Ibid., X:5–6, in the translation of Brock, *Hymns on paradise* 149–50.

52 Beck, *Hymnen de Paradiso*, VIII:2, in the translation of Brock, *Hymns on paradise* 132.

both bodies and souls might proclaim,
amidst Hosannas,
"Blessed is He who has brought Adam from Sheol
and returned him to Paradise in the company of many."[53]

In one of the most poignant of the *madrāshê* 'On Paradise,' Ephraem turns his attention to the many classes of people in the church's congregations, who will also be represented among the blessed in paradise, and he describes the conditions of their bliss. He speaks of the 'mourners,' who were a special order of ascetic hermits in the Syriac-speaking communities, the poor, baptized men and women, virgins, youth, married people, children, the elderly, the lame, those who fast, the saints who abstain from wine and from marriage, and finally the martyrs.[54] And as if to recognize that most people in the Christian congregations were married, in one stanza of another *madrāshâ* he likens the perennial fruit of the trees of paradise in the several seasons to the extended human family, and to the perennial productivity of the institution of marriage in human society. He says,

That cornucopia full of fruits
in all stages of development
resembles the course
of human marriage;
it contains the old,
young, and middle-aged,
children who have already been born,
and babies still unborn;
its fruits follow one another
and appear
like the continuous succession
of human kind.[55]

In fact, with this image of marriage in mind, on a broader reading of Ephraem's *madrāshê* it emerges that much of the lush imagery, the grapes and the grape-vines, the fruits and the flowers, the trees and the fragrances, all go together in Ephraem's imagination to furnish paradise as a setting for what he calls the

53 Beck, *Hymnen de Paradiso*, VIII:11, in the translation of Brock, *Hymns on paradise* 135.
54 See Beck, *Hymnen de Paradiso*, VII:3–19.
55 Beck, *Hymnen de Paradiso*, X:12, in the English translation of Brock, *Hymns on paradise* 152.

'bridal chambers' (*gnānê*) of the blessed, bridal chambers "of glory (*shubḥâ*),"[56] "of light (*zaliqâ* and *nuhrâ*),"[57] and even "of joys (*ḥadwāthâ*)."[58] In paradise, Ephraem says that one sees the disciples, "On high in their bridal chambers,"[59] where God also gave Adam "a chaste bridal chamber."[60] Ephraem says further, in paradise, "The virgin who rejected the marriage crown that fades, now has the radiant marriage chamber that cherishes the children of light."[61] And referring in broad strokes to the happiness of the blessed in paradise, Ephraem wrote:

> There all fruit is holy,
> all raiment luminous,
> every crown glorious,
> every rank the most exalted –
> happiness without toil,
> delight that knows no fear,
> a marriage feast (*ḥlūlâ*) which continues
> forever and ever.[62]

From the broader perspective of Syriac literature, it emerges that in terms of the marital imagery of paradise, with its bridal chambers and banquets, Ephraem in fact is reflecting an ancient tradition that dates from at least as early as the early third century and reaches well beyond Ephraem's own time in the liturgies of the Syriac-speaking Christian communities.[63] As "one of the most common terms used as a metaphor for the Kingdom of Heaven," Sebastian Brock concludes:

> One could fairly say that the image of the Bridal Chamber permeates Syriac liturgical poetry, serving essentially as a metaphor for the place of union between the divine and the human realms. The eschatological Bridal Chamber of Light/Joys represents the fulfillment of the potential Bridal Chamber of Adam and Eve.[64]

---

56 Beck, *Hymnen de Paradiso*, XIII:10.
57 Ibid., VII:15 and 24.
58 Beck, *Hymnen de Virginitate*, XXIV:3.
59 Beck, *Hymnen de Paradiso*, I:6.
60 Ibid., XIII:3.
61 Ibid., VII:15.
62 Ibid., XIV:8, in the translation of Brock, *Hymns on paradise* 8.
63 See Brock, The bridal chamber.
64 Ibid., 179 and 189.

Brock's mention of "the potential Bridal Chamber of Adam and Eve" refers to the view of Ephraem and other early Syriac-speaking Christians that had they not sinned, Adam and Eve would have been united in a Bridal Chamber in primordial paradise. This view seems to have been elaborated by Christian exegetes in contrast to a view espoused in Jewish circles, according to which "Adam and Eve were united in a Bridal Chamber in Paradise before the fall."[65] In one of his verse homilies 'On Creation,' the Syriac poet Jacob of Serugh (c. 451–521) portrayed the aborted marital consummation vividly. He wrote:

> God made Adam a bridegroom in this great Bridal Chamber that He had decorated,
> He adorned Eve as a virgin bride, and gave her to Adam,
> providing, in her dowry, the sea, dry land and air.
> All the Ages gathered for the great wedding feast He had made,
> the bridal couple were radiant in their crowns and their garments;
> He had covered them with glorious light and splendid radiance.
> He left them on their own among the trees with their fruits,
> having given them as a wedding present every kind of tree and fruit.
> The Garden rejoiced at the beloved bride and groom.
> As for the Tree of Life, He had hidden it in Eden's great Bridal Chamber,
> to be there for the bridal couple of light once they had been fulfilled.
> But the Tree of Knowledge, full of death, stood beautifully outside.
> And so that they would know who was the Lord who had honored them,
> He established the law that they should not eat of the tree.
> He gave the whole Garden to the new children He had acquired;
> He appointed only one tree to test them.
> The mischief-maker barged in and sowed discord in that banquet;
> he stole the bride, he whispered his lie, he deceitfully led her astray.
> The wretched little hawk came to stand among the innocent doves;
> he chased them out of the wide nest of Eden.[66]

One notices the prominence of light, and the related concept of glory, in the passages that speak of the Bridal Chambers of paradise in the Syriac texts, a feature that recalls the importance in the Syriac exegetical tradition of the originally Jewish idea of Adam's 'robe of glory/light' in paradise.[67] This luminous

65 See Brock, The bridal chamber 184. See also Anderson, Celibacy or consummation.

66 De Saroug, *Quatre homélies métriques*, text IV ll. 156–79, in the English translation of Brock, The bridal chamber 185, augmented by the present author.

67 See Brock, Clothing metaphors; Kronholm, *Motifs from Genesis*.

dimension of the imagery serves the purpose of reminding the reader that in the view of Ephraem, and of the other Syriac writers in whose works the theme appears, the sensual images of paradise are meant as metaphors. As P.J. Botha put it,

> The reason why Ephrem perceives Paradise in such dazzling colours, scents, sights and delights is that this is a place that is so intimately associated with the presence, and therefore the honour, of God. The 'awe' he experiences for Paradise, is the same 'awe' one should have for God.[68]

Nevertheless, when all is said and done, in the writings of Ephraem the Syrian and the Syriac liturgical tradition in general one does find, contrary to Christoph Luxenberg's views, an abundance of marital and sexual imagery in the descriptions of the joys of the garden of paradise. What relation this lush imagery in Syriac literature might have to the depictions of paradise in the Arabic Quran is another matter.

4 Paradise, Ephraem the Syrian, and the Arabic Quran

The Quran's evocations of the beauties and delights of the garden of paradise are *sui generic*; they stand on their own,[69] yet in many features they are hauntingly familiar to readers of eschatological poetry in Syriac. It is for this reason that Tor Andrae, whose hermeneutical approach to the Quran included a search for what he considered to be the sources of the Arabic scripture, turned to Ephraem the Syrian's *madrāshê* 'On Paradise' to look for narrative parallels. He found them in a number of places, but he was particularly drawn to the passage in *madrāshâ* VII:18 that speaks of the clusters of grapes and the grapevines that in paradise would, as it were, stretch out their arms to draw the earthly ascetic into the bosom of their embrace. In the text, as Tor Andrae mistakenly read it, there seemed to him to be no immediate antecedent for the feminine plural pronoun that identified the ones into whose bosom in the garden the celibate ascetic would be enfolded, so, as we have seen, it put Andrae in mind of the Quran's 'dark-eyed *ḥūrīs*,' and he wondered if in this particular passage (i.e., *madrāshâ* VII:18.5) Ephraem might be indirectly alluding to a similar reward in the afterworld for the life-long, sober ascetic in this world. Andrae further opined that most of Ephraem's listeners and readers "no doubt

68 Botha, Honour and shame 54.

69 See Rustomji, *The garden and the fire*.

remained quite oblivious to his feeble attempts to spiritualize his sensual images.... and under such circumstances one cannot blame a citizen of pagan Mecca for doing the same thing."[70] While Dom Edmund Beck rightly pointed out that the pronoun in question actually refers to the preceding 'grapevines' (*gupnê*), feminine in Syriac, and not to some subliminally summoned female companions, who, therefore cannot be the literary ancestors of the *ḥūrīs* of Islamic tradition,[71] he did not call attention to the imagery of the 'bridal chambers of light,' embowered within the garden's canopy of trees and grapevines, with their dangling grape clusters, that awaited the blessed in Ephraem's vision of paradise. So, as we have seen, marital bliss does in fact figure in Ephraem's *madrāshê* as a metaphor for heavenly joy, albeit not in the Quran's vivid and fetching descriptions of the *ḥūrīs*.

But what is one to make of the echoes of Syriac eschatological visions and parallel imagery that so readily seem to the readers of Syriac to shine through the Quran's Arabic diction? It is basically a question about Quranic hermeneutics. And one principle that should certainly apply is that the meaning of the Arabic Quran cannot authentically be reduced to the parameters of its presumed conceptual background in the language of one of its predecessor narratives; it has its own textual integrity and frames of reference.[72] Nevertheless, the Arabic Quran did not come down into a religious or scriptural vacuum. The Arabic scripture clearly presents itself in dialogue with both the canonical and apocryphal scriptures of the earlier communities of Jews and Christians, and with much Jewish and ecclesiastical lore. In all likelihood, Arabic-speaking Jews and Christians were in fact in the Quran's original audience. And in the Christian instance, as one has argued elsewhere, it is becoming increasingly evident that the theological and liturgical heritage of these Arabic-speaking Christians lay in Syriac sources, a situation that in some instances has even left its traces in the 'Syriacisms' to be found in the Quran's evocation of Christian lore and Arabic usage.[73]

But there are no 'Syriacisms,' either linguistic or thematic, in the Quran's eschatology, yet it is still hauntingly familiar. Ephraem's and Jacob of Serugh's Syriac descriptions of the garden of paradise, right down to and including the marital and sexual imagery, are in part from the same thought-world as the descriptions in the Arabic Quran, revealing at the very least the latter's inten-

70 Andrae, *Mohammed: The man and his faith* 88.
71 See Beck, Eine christliche Parallele.
72 See Saleh, The etymological fallacy.
73 See the studies mentioned in note 9 above.

tion to address an audience within that same frame of reference. It is not, as Tor Andrae supposed, a matter of finding in these Syriac texts the sources of Muḥammad's or the Quran's language and imagery. Rather, the coincidence of image and expression bespeaks the Quran's familiarity with the imaginative world of its Arabic-speaking audience, living within the range of the Syriac-speaking churches of Late Antiquity, to whose liturgies and modes of expression Arabic-speaking Christians were manifestly indebted. What is different, and comparative eschatology reveals many differences, is basically the difference between Christianity and Islam. For the Christians, paradise is paradise restored and the just are led into its lush garden by the crucified and risen Messiah, Jesus, Mary's son and son of God, the new Adam, who will have harrowed Hell to lead the old Adam and the blessed, whom the Messiah has redeemed, to their eternal reward, themes that are everywhere in the Christian texts. By way of contrast, for Muslims, whose Quran critiques these Christian beliefs as "going beyond the bounds of religion" (Q 4:171) and "transgressing the bounds of the truth" (Q 5:77), the garden of paradise is for "those who have believed and have done good works" (Q 2:25; 4:57), for "those who are God-fearing (*muttaqīn*)" (Q 3:15; 44:51; 52:17; 78:31), for "the true servants of God" (Q 37:43; 38:49), and for "those who believe in Our signs and are submissive (*muslimīn*)" (Q 43:69).

Furthermore, by comparison with the images of paradise as we find them in Syriac Christian texts written before the time of Islam, and which doubtless circulated at least partially in oral translation in the milieu of the Arabic-speaking Christians of Arabia, there is an enhanced concreteness in the Arabic Quran's descriptive language, not least in the marital imagery. In addition to the "chaste spouses" (Q 3:15; 4:57), for example, there are also in the Quran's garden those described as *ḥūr ʿīn* (Q 44:54; 52:20), for whom, it is true, there are no exact analogues in the earlier scriptural traditions.[74] This is an instance in which the Quran has given further development and specificity to a narrative motif that appeared metaphorically and in a different guise in the Christian imagination, reflecting at the very least a different anthropology, a different view of human bodiliness, and a different conception of ultimate human happiness. Ephraem put it this way:

74 In this connection, Walid Saleh has called attention to the intriguing idea that in addition to earlier scriptural traditions, the Quran might also reflect images found in Hellenic mythology that might also have been current in its milieu, such as the image of Ganymede and of the goddess Hera, the *boōpis*, the 'oxen-eyed.' See Saleh, The etymological fallacy 39–40.

Far more glorious than the body
  Is the soul,
And more glorious still than the soul
  Is the spirit,
But more hidden than the spirit
  Is the Godhead.
At the end
  The body will put on
The beauty of the soul,
  The soul will put on that of the spirit,
While the spirit shall put on
  The very likeness of God's majesty.[75]

In terms of Late Antique depictions of the afterworld, Ephraem's *madrāshê* 'On Paradise' and the Arabic Quran can both be seen to have chosen their colors from virtually the same imagistic palette to portray somewhat different models of ultimate human happiness. Reading the eschatological passages in the Arabic Quran against the background of widely circulated Syriac liturgical texts such as Ephraem's *madrāshê* or Jacob of Serugh's *mêmrê* allows one to bring into focus not only the Quran's close familiarity with the religious discourse of others in its own milieu, but all the better, by way of comparison and contrast, to discern the new, Islamic turn given to earlier eschatological themes. Ephraem's imaginative journey to paradise, led by scripture's verses to contemplation's luminous, divine beauty, stands in contrast to Muḥammad's bodily Night Journey and Ascension into the heavens.

As for the grapes and the grapevines of paradise, it is interesting to observe that according to their respective traditions both Ephraem the Syrian and the Prophet Muḥammad had visions of the heavenly vines with their clusters of grapes, reaching into their daily lives. Envisioning the church, with its daily Eucharistic liturgies, Ephraem wrote:

The assembly of the saints
  is the type of Paradise. [cf. Q 89:29–30]
Its fruit, which enlivens all,
  is plucked in it every day;
in it, my brothers, there is pressed out,
  the clustered grapes [of Paradise], the enlivener of all.[76]

75 Beck, *Hymnen de Paradiso*, IX:20, in the translation of Brock, *Hymns on paradise* 143.
76 Beck, *Hymnen de Paradiso*, VI:8.

In the Islamic community, an early prophetic tradition reports Muḥammad's account of his vision of paradise in the context of what is called the Eclipse Prayer. The Prophet said: "I saw the Garden and I reached out for a bunch of grapes from it, and if I had taken it you would have been able to eat from it for as long as this world lasted."[77]

These two passages, with their common imagery of the grape cluster, when read together reveal both the Christian's conception of a realized eschatology, disclosed in the church's sacramental liturgy in this world, and the Muslim's act of envisioning the garden materially and concretely as a defining feature of Islam's own distinctive, eschatological vision,[78] according to which neither lifelong virginity nor celibacy, as in the Christian view, would epitomize or signify human striving for perfection.

Bibliography

Anderson, G., Celibacy or consummation in the garden? Reflections on early Jewish and Christian interpretations of the garden of Eden, in *The Harvard Theological Review* 82 (1989), 121–48.

Andrae, T., *I Myrtenträdgården: Studier I Tidig Islamisk Mystik*, Lund 1947.

———, *In the garden of myrtles: Studies in early Islamic mysticism*, Albany, NY 1987.

———, *Mohammed, sein Leben und sein Glaube*, Göttingen 1932.

———, *Mohammed: The man and his faith*, trans. T. Menzel, New York 1936.

———, *Les origines de l'islam et le christianisme*, trans. J. Roche, Paris 1955.

———, Der Ursprung des Islams und das Christentum, in *Kyrkohistorisk Årsskrift* 23 (1923), 149–206; 24 (1924), 213–92; 25 (1925), 45–112.

———, *Der Ursprung des Islams und das Christentum*, Uppsala 1926.

Beck, E., Eine christliche Parallele zu den Paradiesesjungfrauen des Korans?, in *Orientalia Christiana Periodica* 14 (1948), 398–405.

———, *Ephraems Hymnen über das Paradies: Übersetzung und Kommentar*, Rome 1951.

———, *Des heiligen Ephraem des Syrers Hymnen de Paradiso und contra Julianum*, Leuven 1957.

———, *Des heiligen Ephraem des Syrers Hymnen de Virginitate*, Leuven 1962.

———, Les Houris du Coran et Ephrem le Syrien, in *MIDEO* 6 (1959–61), 405–8.

Botha, P., Honour and shame as pivotal values in Ephrem the Syrian's vision of paradise, in *Acta patristica et byzantina* 10 (1999), 49–65.

---

77 A tradition recorded in the *Muwaṭṭaʿ* of Malik Ibn Anas, *al-Muwaṭṭaʿ of Malik ibn Anas*, no. 12.1.2, as quoted by Rustomji, *The garden and the fire* 23.

78 In this connection, see also M. Jarrar's contribution to this publication.

———, The significance of the senses in St. Ephrem's description of paradise, in *Acta patristica et byzantina* 5 (1994), 28.

Brock, S., The bridal chamber of light: A distinctive feature of the Syriac liturgical tradition, in *The Harp* 18 (2005), 179–91.

———, Clothing metaphors as a means of theological expression in Syriac tradition, in M. Schmidt and C. Geyer (eds.), *Typus, Symbol, Allegorie bein den östlichen Vätern und ihren Parallelen im Mittelalter*, Regensburg 1982, 11–38.

——— (trans.), *Saint Ephrem: hymns on paradise*, Crestwood 1990.

Fakhry, M. (trans.), *An interpretation of the Qur'an: English translation of the meanings, a bilingual edition*, New York 2000.

Griffith, S., Christian lore and the Arabic Qur'ān: The 'companions of the cave' in *Sūrat al-Kahf* and in Syriac Christian tradition, in G. Reynolds (ed.), *The Qur'ān in its historical context*, London and New York 2008, 109–37.

———, An-Naṣārā in the Qur'ān: Some hermeneutical reflections and a working hypothesis, in *The Qur'ān in its historical context* 2, forthcoming.

———, St. Ephraem, Bar Dayṣān and the clash of *Madrāshê* in Aram: Readings in St. Ephraem's *Hymni contra Haereses*, in *The Harp* 21 (2006), 447–72.

———, Syriac/Antiochene exegesis in Saint Ephrem's teaching songs *De Paradiso*: The 'types of paradise' in the 'treasury of revelations,' in R. Miller (ed.), *Syriac and Antiochian exegesis and Biblical theology for the 3rd millennium*, Piscataway NJ 2008, 27–52.

———, Syriacisms in the 'Arabic Qur'ān': Who were 'those who said, 'Allāh is third of three' according to *al-Mā'idah* 73?, in M. Bar-Asher et al. (eds.), *A word fitly spoken: Studies in mediaeval exegesis of the Hebrew Bible and the Qur'ān; Presented to Haggai Ben-Shammai*, Jerusalem 2007, 83–110.

Grimme, H., *Mohammed*, 2 vols., Munster 1892–5.

Hainthaler, T., *Christliche Araber vor dem Islam: Verbreitung und konfessionelle Zugehörigkeit: Eine Hinführung* (Eastern Christian studies 7), Leuven 2007.

Ibn Anas, M., *al-Muwatta of Malik ibn Anas: The first formulation of Islamic law*, trans. A. Abdurrahman Bewley, London 1989.

Jeffery, A., *The foreign vocabulary of the Qur'ān*, Baroda 1938.

Kronholm, T., *Motifs from Genesis 1–11 in the genuine hymns of Ephrem the Syrian with particular reference to the influence of Jewish exegetical tradition*, Uppsala 1978.

Lane, E., *An Arabic-English lexicon*, xviii, London 1863–93, repr. Beirut 1968.

Lattke, M., Sind Ephräms *Madrāshê* Hymnen?, in OC 73 (1989), 38–43.

Lavenant, R. and F. Graffin (trans. and intro.), *Éphrem de Nisibe: hymnes sur le paradis*, Paris 1968.

Lüling, G., *Der christliche Kult an der vorislamischen Kaaba als Problem der Islamwissenschaft und christlichen Theologie*, Erlangen, 1977.

———, Preconditions for the scholarly criticism of the Koran and Islam, with some autobiographical remarks, in *Journal of higher criticism* 3 (1996), 73–109.

———, *Über den Ur-Qur'ān: Ansätze zur Rekonstruktion vorislamischer christlicher Strophenlieder im Qur'ān*, Erlangen 1974.

———, *Die Wiederentdeckung des Propheten Muhammad: Eine Kritik am 'christlichen' Abendland*, Erlangen 1981.

Luxenberg, C., *The Syro-Aramaic reading of the Koran: A contribution to the decoding of the language of the Koran*, ed. T. Müke, Berlin 2007.

———, *Die syro-aramäische Lesart des Koran: Ein Beitrag zur Entschlüsselung der Koransprache*, Berlin 2000, 2004^2 (rev. ed.).

Manna, J., *Vocabulaire Chaldéen-Arabe*, Mosul 1900.

McVey, K., Were the earliest *Madrāshê* songs or recitations, in G. Reinink and A. Klugkist (eds.), *After Bardaisan: Studies on continuity and change in Syriac Christianity in honour of Professor Han J.W. Drijvers* (Orientalia Lovaniensia Analecta 89), Leuven 1999, 185–99, 213–36.

Mingana, A., Syriac influence on the style of the Qur'ān, in *Bulletin of the John Rylands Library of Manchester* 11 (1927), 77–98.

Mobarak, P. and S. Assemani, *Sancti patris nostri Ephraem Syri opera omnia quae exstant Graece, Syriace, Latine*, 6 vols., Rome 1732–46.

Ohlig, K. (ed.), *Eine historisch-kritische Rekonstruktion anhand zeitgenössischer Quellen*, Berlin 2007.

——— and M. Gross (eds.), *Schlaglichter: Die beiden ersten islamischen Jahrhunderte*, Berlin 2008.

——— and G. Puin (eds.), *Die dunklen Anfänge: Neue Forschungen zur Entstehung und frühen Geschichte des Islam*, Berlin 2005.

Palmer, A., Nine more stanzas to be banished from Ephraim's paradise, in A. Drost-Abgarjan, J. Tubach, and J. Kotjatko (eds.), *Vom Nil an die Saale: Festschrift für Arafa Mustafa zum 65. Geburtstag am 28. Februar 2005*, Halle-Wittenberg 2008, 301–57.

———, Restoring the ABC in Ephraim's cycles on faith and paradise, in *The Journal of Eastern Christian Studies* 55 (2003), 147–94.

Payne-Smith, R., *Thesaurus Syriacus*, 2 vols., Oxford 1879.

Rustomji, N., *The garden and the fire: Heaven and hell in Islamic culture*, New York 2009.

Saleh, W., The etymological fallacy and Qur'ānic studies: Muḥammad, paradise and late antiquity, in A. Neuwirth, *The Qur'ān in context: historical and literary investigations into the Qur'ānic milieu*, Leiden 2009, 1–47.

Saroug, J. de, *Quatre homélies métriques sur la creation*, trans. K. Alwan, Leuven 1989.

al-Sijistānī, Ibn al-Ashʿath, D., *Kitāb al-Maṣāḥif*, Cairo 1936.

van Ess, J., *The flowering of Muslim theology*, trans. J. Todd, Cambridge 2006.

van Reeth, J., L'Évangile du Prophète, in D. De Smet et al. (eds.), *Al-Kitāb: La sacralité du texte dans le monde de l'Islam*, Brussels 2004, iii, 155–74.

———, Le vignoble du paradis et le chemin qui y mène; la thèse de C. Luxenberg et les sources du Coran, in *Arabica* 53 (2006), 511–24.

CHAPTER 37

Paradise? America! The Metaphor of Paradise in the Context of the Iraqi-Christian Migration

Martin Tamcke

For sixteen hundred years, Christian authors from the Mesopotamian area have been thinking about paradise in various contexts. The metaphor, even when it takes effect in eminently theological writings, is open to many interpretations and is used in very different contexts. Behind supposedly Christian-theological terms there may loom ideas from other religious traditions including the pagan.[1] In fact, the metaphor of paradise was soon used in non-theological contexts as well. Nowhere is this more apparent than in the works of the most important representative of the Syrian Renaissance[2] in the realm of eastern Syrian culture, ʿAḇdīshōʿ bar Berīkā (d. 1318),[3] whose influential poetic work – the Paradise of Eden[4] – was conceived as a deliberately artistic challenge to Arabic poetry and was meant to demonstrate the artistry and superiority of the Syriac language over the Arabic.

As it has happened in European and widely secularized societies, in the Christian orient the use of the metaphor of "paradise" is no longer exclusively theological but it has been adapted to carry religious connotations sometimes only as distant memories.[5] Just like in Western societies, the metaphor is used

1 See the controversy between Carl Brockelmann and Paul Krüger. Brockelmann believed he could find traces of pre-Christian, pagan practices in the Christian sources of that area; Krüger on the other hand vehemently rejected this approach. He pointed to the distinctly theological character of the writings and their roots in the life of the church (cf. Brockelmann, Ein syrischer Regenzauber; Krüger, Die Regenbitten Aphrems. For a discussion of this controversy see Tamcke, *Die Christen vom Tur Abdin* 121–51).

2 Cf. Teule, *The Syriac renaissance*.

3 Cf. Tamcke, Ebedjesus (ʿAbdisoʿ Bar Berika); previously published as Tamcke, Ebedjesus.

4 Cf. Tamcke, ʿAbdiso Bar Brika, Paradaisa da- ʿden.

5 Cf. Ebel, Das versprochene Paradies; Buschmann, Religiöse und biblische Motive in der Werbung; Buschmann and Pirner, *Werbung, Religion, Bildung*; Klie, *Spiegelflächen*; Börner: *Auf der Suche nach dem irdischen Paradies*; for more on the changing ideas of paradise in the course of history see Krauss, *Das Paradies*.

 | DOI 10.1163/9789004333154_038

in connection with wholesome and pleasant or beautiful things such as milk with honey. This drink is traditionally considered the "food of paradise."[6]

1 Paradise between Reality and Unreality

From the last quarter of the twentieth century as Christian oriental communities have come under more pressure, their tendency to migrate to other continents that seem to promise better living conditions has increased.[7] Their longing to live in these countries and enter these societies was so strong that the promised way of life was imagined as "paradise." For several Christian authors of eastern Syrian heritage in Iraq, looking to America has become so much a part of their thinking and their strategies for survival that as soon as they are exposed to actual interaction with American reality their perspective is inevitably challenged.

Such is the case with Sargon Boulus.[8] Born into a family of Assyrian refugees on 19 February 1944 close to Lake Habbaniyya near Baghdad, he later moved with his family to Kirkuk in northern Iraq. In 1962 he went to Baghdad, in 1967 he crossed the Iraqi-Syrian border on foot and – with no money or identification – reached Beirut, where he took an active part in the revival of the leading Arabic literary magazine *Shiʿr*. From 1969 on he lived in the United States of America most of the time. After a long illness he died on 22 October 2007 in Berlin.[9] Sargon Boulus wrote his poems in Arabic, a language he had learned from his mother amidst a family speaking "Syriac." His life was marked by seemingly incompatible contradictions even before his arrival in America. On one hand there was the early suffering when he and his family were refugees (his father was a carpenter, ironed laundry, and worked as a traditional healer), and living in a makeshift clay and tin hut, in which four families lived separated only by sheets hanging on ropes. This stood in stark contrast to the professional who translated the works of poets of the Beat generation (Plath and Lowell) into Arabic and who could plainly say about his emigration to the United States that America was to him the opportunity for a new dream. With

6 Khoury, *Königreich der Fremdlinge* 60.

7 After the Russo-Persian War (1826–8) and especially in the aftermath of the pogroms against the Assyrians in the Hakkari Province, the first Assyrian migrations began already around the middle of the nineteenth century, cf. Tamcke, Nach Russland.

8 For biographies of Sargon Boulus see Boulus, *Mittenaus, Mittenein*, 115–6; Taufiq, Über den Autor und sein Werk; Nijland, Sargon Boulus.

9 Cf. Naggar, Generation Zufall.

his migration to America, however, the past did not end; home did not simply stay behind in Iraq. "I never left Iraq. As far as you may go, you will return to the same sources, to their origins in childhood and in relatives, to drink from them. You do not stop returning to the past while living in the present."[10]

A key incident during childhood was his first encounter with English women. The British occupation troops in Iraq had gathered the Assyrians close to their military basis in al-Habbaniyya, after these had repeatedly become victims of pogroms. Sargon Boulus' father was among those working for the English. He often brought his son with him into the English camp.

> My father used to work for the English and one of my first and very cherished memories is when as a kid my father used to take me to the place of his work, which was a camp where only the English lived with the Iraqi workers (mostly Assyrian). We used to see these English ladies in summertime among their flowers and lawns, a totally different woman from the women that I knew like my mother, my sisters and the other women in my family. Here was another type of image of humanity, let's say, and I was like sneaking a view through the trees, from far away into these gardens. For me, I think now, that's a vision of paradise, paradise meaning something very flowery, full of colour.[11]

What he describes here in an interview with Margaret Obank can be found in similar form in his autobiographical text "Poetry and Other Mysteries":

> My father used to work for the English, and one of my first and very cherished memories is when as a kid my father used to take me to the place of his work, which was a camp where only the English lived, surrounded by an enormous fence. We used to see these English ladies in summertime having their tea, half naked, among their flowers and well kept lawns, a totally different kind of female from our mothers and sisters who were wrapped in black most of the time, and looked as if they had just returned from a funeral. It was like sneaking through a chink in the wall of paradise, finding yourself in another world. Of course I wasn't aware at the time that they were occupying the country, I was too young to know.[12]

---

10 Quoted from Tamcke, Die konfessionelle Dimension 168, taken up again in a shorter form in Tamcke, *Christen in der islamischen Welt* 140–1.

11 Obank, Sargon Boulus talks about his life in poetry.

12 Forum Internationale Zusammenarbeit für Nachhaltige Entwicklung (ed.), f.ize-Geburtstagsparty.

The cultural distinctness of the West fascinated him and found his approval. While his own Christian oriental culture, surrounded by Islamic culture, was restrictive, the Western world seemed liberated. And exactly in what was possible in the Western world, he found himself. What is interesting about the two texts is that despite the differences in the two versions of the same situation, not only the event is clearly the same, but also the metaphor for what was seen: namely, paradise as metaphor for the observed reality of European existence that was so different from the reality of his own Assyrian-Arabic existence in Iraq. What he saw there as a European alternative to his own world was so extraordinary that he could not grasp it without recourse to the term "vision." He was looking at an unfamiliar reality that he nevertheless felt close to. He had had, speaking in terms of classic mysticism, a revelation, a vision.

Paradise, located this way between reality and unreality, is described by Boulus only vaguely in character as "very flowery, full of colour." This rich coloring contrasts with the colorless monotony of his own culture. Things have a different, richer taste and are full of color. Sargon Boulus was not only one of "the most important Arabic poets of the present,"[13] he acted as an unremitting advocate and mediator for Western authors, mainly modern authors, in the Arabic world. His emotional ties to the West led him to follow his yearning for paradise. Through the desert on foot, without a passport he was incarcerated as an illegal migrant in Beirut, but finally departed, with the help of the American embassy there, for America, never to return permanently to Iraq or the Middle East. Asked about how he could just leave his Arab home, he replied "I believe it is the imagination. When I read something, I can imagine it. My reading has filled me with dreams. I followed my imagination."[14] Belonging to two worlds is a familiar feeling for oriental Christians from early childhood on. It has turned them into driving forces for the modernization of their home countries.[15] But it also led to a situation in which the majority of the population among which they lived continued to slander them as a fifth column of the West. And when the dynamics of their mediative role are impeded too much, they emigrate.

2 Escaping from a 'Lost' Paradise

The inclination to migrate to America, and to Europe as well, has increased even after the American occupation of Iraq, despite the fact that the coincident

13 Naggar, Generation Zufall.

14 Ibid.

15 Cf. Tamcke, Die orientalischen Christen und Europa.

disillusion with America has become apparent among Christians all over the country. The will to emigrate has not decreased. The difficult situation for Christians in the Middle East and their looking to America now explicitly finds its expression in terms of hell and paradise. Hell, that is Baghdad, the Iraqi home. Paradise, that is America.

In his book on the situation of Christians in his country, Jean Benjamin Sleiman, the Latin archbishop in Baghdad (born in 1946 in Lebanon), uses the metaphor "paradise" repeatedly. On the one hand there is a simple line from the admired West to the metaphor. "Since ancient times the West has been taken for a kind of paradise, a place of retreat and refuge."[16] Even if the duration of Western orientation is enhanced by Sleiman into an almost mythical dimension of an unimaginable time frame, the modern kind of Western orientation is relatively recent; it begins with the failing Ottoman Empire, and becomes more genuine still with the taking over of the mandate by Great Britain after the defeat of the Ottomans.

Ever since the Christians in Iraq have been afflicted by measures against the people of the Middle East, this treatment has put a damper on their traditional ties to the West, which they demonstrated several times during the last century: they are now met, according to Baghdad archbishop Sleiman, with the same distrust by the West as the Muslims in their country and consider this, as those do, to be a "degradation."

The move to a distant country, to America most of all, has become increasingly difficult. Hope that often survived only because of the thought of a possible emigration dwindles. The pressure against Christians in the country, however, who are seen as the secret allies of the Americans, is increasing. "While Christians in Iraq are being discriminated against ever more vehemently, the 'paradise,' into which they want to emigrate, moves further and further away from them every day."[17] Nevertheless, exactly because it has become more and more difficult to leave the country and head for the West, the hope to be among the few who succeed in emigrating increases. "To escape the 'lost paradise,' one is willing to use all means necessary to reach a new 'paradise' like the USA, considered the 'promised land' par excellence."[18]

Paradise is far away, in a world that is believed to be ideal. Paradise is almost unattainable, but it is real. Paradise is that world in which desperately missed freedom is to be found – freedom that has not materialized despite all the promises made surrounding the new constitution of Iraq.

---

16 Sleiman, *Der Aufschrei des Erzbischofs von Bagdad* 95.

17 Ibid., 98.

18 Ibid., 115.

Indeed, this idealization of America is tied to an almost religious belief which, regardless of all the frustrating experiences with Americans, seems to be without alternative the driving source of future plans made by Iraqi Christians. Only the idealization of the Iraqi past as a lost paradise counteracts the lure of a paradise named America. But this paradise of Iraq is already only an object of nostalgia, an act of looking back; it is tied to past times that are forever gone. The future is not something their own country's lost paradise can still offer. The future only beckons from outside and beyond the ocean in that other world, where the burden of social and religiously sanctioned humiliation no longer has to be carried.

From there lure freedom and equality, there is a society that one can be an integral part of without carrying the yoke of an ostracized and marginalized minority.

3 Immigration to a 'New' Paradise?

The lost paradise: that is Iraq; but the paradise which all hope lies upon: that is still America. The fact that very real aspirations of Christian existence in Iraq are tied to America, which is attributed with the metaphor of paradise, seems at first to imply an empty use of the metaphor. The unreal that is also part of the metaphor is doubled in the non-perception of the by no means simple shining American reality. It is not paradise itself that unleashes the strength to leave home for the unfamiliar, and yet, the appropriation of the unfamiliar takes place exactly because in light of its religious connotation the unfamiliar is turned into something already familiar, into the always already alluring unreal-real. Where life is only determined by terror and unrest, the foreign and, in terms of civilization, seemingly superior is seen as paradise, as promising as a world in complete contrast to daily oppression. All this may not have much to do with theological teachings or religious imagery, but a reality is enhanced and removed from the reality of conflict, such that movement results. That movement, while it might not lead to paradise, will end in the departure from a world in which the realization of one's own values and wishes become increasingly difficult to attain and at times even the hope for them is lost.

If America wasn't paradise it might lose its respectability. As it is, as paradise it can overcome the sobering reality of the encounter with the Americans in Iraq, "in the middle of hell."[19]

---

19 Ibid., 77.

Sleiman surely did not intend to simply comply with this belief of his fellow believers and countrymen; rather he fought for Christians to stay in Iraq. However, he testifies to those mechanisms he cannot control when he cannot express the continued attractiveness of America for his people in any other way than with a comparison to paradise.

Bibliography

Börner, K.H., *Auf der Suche nach dem irdischen Paradies: Zur Ikonographie der geographischen Utopie*, Frankfurt am Main 1984.

Boulus, S. et al., *Mittenaus, Mittenein: Lyrik aus dem Irak*, ed. K. al-Maaly, S. Taufiq, and S. Weidner, Berlin 1993.

———, *Ein unbewohnter Raum: Erzählungen*, trans. S. Taufiq, Meerbusch 1996.

Brockelmann, C., Ein syrischer Regenzauber, in *ARW* 9 (1906), 518–20.

Buschmann, G., Religiöse und biblische Motive in der Werbung: Herausforderung und Chance christlicher Verkündigung, in *Deutsches Pfarrerblatt* 104 (2004), 409–12.

——— and M.L. Pirner (with the collaboration of T. Bickelhaupt, U. Böhm, and J. Mühleisen), *Werbung, Religion, Bildung: Kulturhermeneutische, theologische, medienpädagogische und religionspädagogische Perspektiven* (Beiträge zur Medienpädagogik 8), Frankfurt am Main 2003.

Ebel, A., Das versprochene Paradies: Das erste Gebot des Marktes: Religion in der Werbung, in *Sonntagsblatt. Evangelische Wochenzeitung für Bayern* 59 (2003), 4–5.

Forum Internationale Zusammenarbeit für Nachhaltige Entwicklung (ed.), Veröffentlichung anlässlich der Großen f.ize-Geburtstagsparty am 10.07.2003, http://www.fize.de/gaeste.boulos_sargon.htm (accessed 30 May 2010).

Khoury, E., *Königreich der Fremdlinge*, Berlin 1998.

Klie, T., *Spiegelflächen: Phänomenologie – Religionspädagogik – Werbung*, Munster 1999.

Krauss, H., *Das Paradies: Eine kleine Kulturgeschichte*, Munich 2004.

Krüger, P., Die Regenbitten Aphrems des Syrers. Ihre Überlieferung unter besonderer Berücksichtigung des nestorianischen Officiums der Ninivitenfasten und ihre religionsgeschichtliche Bedeutung, in *Oriens Christianus* 8 (1913), 13–61 and 144–51.

Naggar, M., Generation Zufall: Nachruf auf den irakischen Dichter Sargon Boulus, http://de.qantara.de/webcom/show_article.php/_c-299/_nr-494/i.html (accessed 30 May 2010).

Nijland, K., Sargon Boulus: Iraq, 1944–2007, http://iraq.poetryinternationalweb.org/piw_cms/cms/cms_module/index.php?obj_id=9402 (accessed 30 May 2010).

Obank, M., Sargon Boulus talks about his life in poetry, http://www.sargonboulus.com/wp/?p=70 (accessed 30 May 2010).

Sleiman, J.B., *Der Aufschrei des Erzbischofs von Bagdad: Christliche Kirchen im Irak*, Würzburg 2009 (previously published as *Dans le piège irakien: Le crie du cœur de l'archevêque de Bagdad*, Paris 2006).

Tamcke, M., 'Abdiso Bar Brika, Paradaisa da- 'den, in H.L. Arnold (ed.), *Kindlers Literatur-Lexikon*, i, 3, Stuttgart and Weimar 2009, 21.

———, *Christen in der islamischen Welt: Von Mohammed bis zur Gegenwart*, Munich 2008, 140–1.

———, *Die Christen vom Tur Abdin: Hinführung zur Syrisch-Orthodoxen Kirche*, Frankfurt 2009.

———, Ebedjesus ('Abdiso' Bar Berika), in M. Vinzent (ed.), *Theologen: 185 Porträts von der Antike bis zur Gegenwart*, Stuttgart 2004, 97–8.

———, Ebedjesus, in M. Vinzent (ed.), *Metzler Lexikon christlicher Denker*, Stuttgart and Weimar 2000, 216–7.

———, Die konfessionelle Dimension in der "assyrischen" Migrationsliteratur in Deutschland: "Unwissenschaftliche" Lesefrüchte, in M. Tamcke (ed.), *Daheim und in der Fremde: Beiträge zur jüngeren Geschichte und Gegenwartslage der orientalischen Christen* (Studien zur Orientalischen Kirchengeschichte 21), Hamburg 2002, 163–75.

———, Nach Russland, Deutschland, „Ja über den Ozean in das Land der Freiheit und des Dollars:" Streiflichter aus deutschen Akten zur ersten Migrationswelle der Ostsyrer (Assyrer/„Nestorianer"), in *Journal of Eastern Christian Studies* 54 (2002), 25–38.

———, Die orientalischen Christen und Europa, "Motor der Modernisierung" oder "fünfte Kolonne des Westens"?, in *Theologische Literaturzeitung* 134 (2009), 139–52.

Taufiq, S., Über den Autor und sein Werk, in S. Boulus, *Ein unbewohnter Raum: Erzählungen*, trans. S. Taufiq, Meerbusch 1996, 106–7.

Teule, H.G.B. et al. (eds.), *The Syriac renaissance*, Leuven 2010.

PART 8

Eschatology and Literature

CHAPTER 38

The Characteristics of Paradise (*Ṣifat al-Janna*): A Genre of Eschatological Literature in Medieval Islam

Waleed Ahmed

Modern scholarship has paid considerable attention to the themes and formulations of Islamic eschatology in the Quran, Muslim traditions (*ḥadīths*), and a range of classical Islamic works. Thus far, however, there has been virtually no interest in analyzing the various categories of Muslim eschatological literature as literary genres. A group of works usually entitled *Ṣifat al-janna* (The characteristics of paradise) represents, as I propose here, one of these genres. It includes:

- *Waṣf al-firdaws* (The description of paradise) by Abū Marwān ʿAbd al-Malik b. Ḥabīb b. Sulaymān al-Sulamī (d. 238/853), hereafter referred to as Ibn Ḥabīb,
- *Ṣifat al-janna* by Ibn Abī l-Dunyā (d. 281/894),
- *Ṣifat al-janna* by Abū Nuʿaym al-Iṣfahānī (d. 430/1038),
- *Ḥādī l-arwāḥ ilā bilād al-afrāḥ* (The guide of souls to the land of delights) by Ibn Qayyim al-Jawziyya (d. 751/1350)
- and *Ṣifat al-janna* by Ibn Kathīr (d. 774/1373).[1]

1 Ibn Ḥabīb's *Waṣf al-firdaws*, despite its title, incorporates two short chapters on the departure of the soul from the body and the torment of the grave. The two chapters appear at the end of the book and it is not clear whether they belong to *Waṣf al-firdaws* or to another work that was copied along with it. Manuscripts of this work were not available to the author. The work is mentioned in al-Ziriklī, *al-Aʿlām* 157–8 and a Spanish edition of one of its manuscripts is also available, see Ibn Ḥabīb, *Kitāb Waṣf al-firdaws*. Since the section on paradise constitutes by far the largest portion of *Waṣf al-firdaws* and, as will be clear in the next few pages, it shares the genre's defining features, it was decided to include it in the present study. Ḍiyāʾ al-Dīn Abū ʿAbdallāh Muḥammad b. ʿAbd al-Wāḥid b. Aḥmad b. ʿAbd al-Raḥmān al-Ḥanbalī (d. 643/1245), known as al-Ḍiyāʾ al-Maqdisī, is recorded in *Siyar aʿlām al-nubalāʾ* to have written a certain *Ṣifat al-janna* work of two volumes (al-Dhahabī, *Siyar* iii, 3544–5). Neither an edited copy nor a manuscript of this work has been available to the author, except for an incomplete electronic version circulating on the Internet. The work is thus not included in the present study. *Ṣifat al-janna* by Ibn Kathīr is originally a chapter in his book *al-Nihāya*

 | DOI 10.1163/9789004333154_039

The principal aim of the present study is to demonstrate that these works share definable formal characteristics and goals and thus constitute a distinctive literary genre. In so doing, I also offer an account of this genre's development and significance in the scholarly and socio-cultural context of Sunni Islam.[2]

The notion of genre has a long and convoluted history during which its definition and even its validity have been contested. Shared conventions of form and content have been traditionally acknowledged as defining aspects of literary genres and since the 1920s, owing to the scholarship of the Russian formalists,[3] shared function has also become widely recognized as a core element in identifying genres. Modern scholarship has also identified and explored some principal dimensions of genre, of which the socio-cultural, ideological, and historical dimensions appear particularly promising for our analysis.[4]

By being instruments of action in their context, genres are not only distinctive ways of responding to social conditions or situations they at the same time influence their social context.[5] Genres are also cultural; as Deborah Dean maintains, "genres are cultural in the sense that they occur in and respond to what [Amy J.] Devitt calls a 'macro level of context' – a context broader than the immediate situation of the genre – or culture."[6] Not detached from the socio-cultural dimension of genres is their ideological dimension, first articulated by Mikhail Bakhtin particularly with reference to the genre's content.[7] As David Duff asserts, paraphrasing Bakhtin's view, "all genres, of literature and speech, are not simply sets of devices and conventions, but 'forms of seeing and interpreting particular aspects of the world,' ways of 'conceptualising reality' that are stored within the 'genre memory.'"[8] Recognizing these dimensions has at least one clear implication: genres, studied carefully, could offer significant insights into many facets of their context. In this regard, we are not

---

fī l-fitan wa-l-malāḥim with the title *Ṣifat ahl al-janna wa-mā fīhā min al-naʿīm*. It exhibits, as I demonstrate below, the genre's function and features and therefore has been considered in the analysis.

2 The scope of the present study does not include Shiʿi scholarship. Further research is certainly needed on Shiʿi works on paradise that could be considered instances of the genre of *ṣifat al-janna*.

3 Duff, *Modern* 7.

4 Ibid., 1–19; Dean, *Genre* 3–26.

5 Dean, *Genre* 11.

6 Ibid., 16.

7 Duff, *Modern* 10.

8 Ibid.

discussing origins of content. We are examining how the connotations of the genre's textual substance bear witness to its function.

As for the relationship of genres (and their development) to history, despite the fact that this has long been identified, it is still frequently debated in literary criticism.[9] The debate seems to center on how to delimit the synchronic, diachronic, continuous, and discontinuous in the historical development of genres.[10] As opposed to outlining a comprehensive literary history of the emergence and development of the genre of *ṣifat al-janna* we are interested in the more modest task of merely identifying this historical genre. We mainly focus on describing the continuous aspects in the genre's history, from a synchronic perspective, without however failing to note its discontinuous and diachronic development. This will be demonstrated in the course of this study and in its final section where we attempt to make the distinction between *ṣifat al-janna* works as a genre and some other typical examples of works on paradise in Sunni Islam, specifically: the chapters on paradise in Muslim b. al-Ḥajjāj's (d. 261/875) *Ṣaḥīḥ* and al-Tirmidhī's (d. 279/892) *al-Jāmiʿ al-ṣaḥīḥ, Daqāʾiq al-akhbār fī dhikr al-janna wa-l-nār* attributed to ʿAbd al-Raḥīm b. Aḥmad al-Qāḍī, *al-Durar al-ḥisān fī l-baʿth wa-naʿīm al-jinān* attributed to al-Ṣuyūṭī (d. 911/1505), and the chapter on paradise in *al-Targhīb wa-l-tarhīb* (The [moral] suasion and exhortation) of Abū Muḥammad Zakī l-Dīn al-Mundhirī (d. 656/1258). The first two steps of our inquiry are dedicated to the examination of the form(s) through which *ḥadīth*s and Quranic material, respectively, are utilized in *ṣifat al-janna* works. The content and function of these works are dealt with in the study's third section. Adopting this order of presentation is necessary; as will be clear in the following pages, the distinctive approach to *ḥadīth*s and Quranic material evident in *ṣifat al-janna* works has bearing on their content and function.

Before proceeding to the first section of the study, note should be taken of some general qualities of the composition of *ṣifat al-janna* works. The compilers of these works belong to the Sunni branch of Islam, specifically to the Mālikī, Ḥanbalī, and Shāfiʿī schools of jurisprudence (*madhhab*s) of this tradition.[11]

---

9 According to Duff, the historical nature of genres was first recognized in the Romantic period. See Duff, *Modern* 4.

10 See for instance Jauss, Theory 127–47. These issues seem to be particularly pressing for those who see genres as the principal dynamics through which literary history unfolds.

11 Ibn Ḥabīb was a Mālikī and a zealous advocate of this school of law (*madhhab*) in Muslim Spain (Ibn al-Faraḍī, *Tārīkh* i, 459–62; Huici-Miranda, Ibn Ḥabīb 775), Ibn Abī l-Dunyā and Ibn al-Qayyim were Ḥanbalīs (see respectively, Ibn Abī Yaʿlā, *Ṭabaqāt* ii, 36–42; Dietrich, Ibn Abi ʾl-Dunyā 684; Ibn Rajab, *al-Dhayl* v, 170–9; Laoust, Ibn Ḳayyim al-Dj̲awziyya 821–2), and Ibn Kathīr and al-Iṣfahānī were Shāfiʿīs (see respectively Ibn al-ʿImād, *Shadharāt* viii,

They were all prominent scholars of their time, erudite in a wide range of Islamic sciences (particularly jurisprudence and theology). Perhaps even more informative, all of these scholars, with the exception of Ibn Ḥabīb, were acknowledged as prominent traditionists (i.e., *ḥadīth* scholars) and authorities on the sciences of *ḥadīth* and its transmission. Consistent with these affiliations, the material in *ṣifat al-janna* works is exclusively culled from the Quran and the vast depository of traditions attributed to the Prophet Muḥammad, his companions, and the generation of their successors (*al-tābiʿūn*). It is also not surprising that the compilers of *ṣifat al-janna* works do not present any allegorical or mystical commentary on the body of material they cite.[12] In fact, there is virtually no explication of the content (*matn*) of the traditions in *ṣifat al-janna* works. That is to say, meaning is almost exclusively communicated through the traditions' content, not the compilers' own words.[13]

1 The Literary Genre of *Ṣifat al-Janna* and *Ḥadīth* Sciences

Without exception, the compilers of *ṣifat al-janna* works cite multiple traditions in relation to every theme they discuss. They also mention the chains of transmission (*isnād*s) of all these traditions. The work of Ibn Ḥabīb is, to some extent, an exception here. It contains, alongside the traditions with complete *isnād*s, many traditions with partial or no *isnād*s.[14] Nevertheless, bearing in

---

397–9; Laoust, Ibn Kat͟hīr 817–8; al-Subkī, *Ṭabaqāt* iv, 18–25; al-Dhahabī, *Siyar* i, 816–8; Pedersen, Abū Nuʿaym al-Iṣfahānī 142–3).

12 Neither does al-Iṣfahānī present this material in his *Ṣifat al-janna*. Besides being a jurist and a traditionist, Abū Nuʿaym al-Iṣfahānī has also been described as a Sufi. One of his most popular works, *Ḥilyat al-awliyāʾ wa-ṭabaqāt al-aṣfiyāʾ*, comprises a rich collection of sayings by Muslim mystics of earlier generations, see al-Subkī, *Ṭabaqāt* iv, 18–25; al-Dhahabī, *Siyar* i, 816–8.

13 It should be noted that Ibn al-Qayyim does not completely adhere to this scheme; he comments on the content of several traditions in his *Ḥādī l-arwāḥ*. See for example Ibn al-Qayyim, *Ḥādī* 69, 87. It is not clear why there has been no contribution by Ḥanafīs to the genre of *ṣifat al-janna*. This might relate to the Ḥanafīs limited use – compared to scholars of other Sunni *madhhab*s – of prophetic traditions in their scholarship, being traditionally classified among the proponents of individual reasoning (*ahl al-raʾy*). On points of doctrine, Ḥanafīs also differ slightly from other Sunni *madhhab*s (see below).

14 See for example Ibn Ḥabīb, *Waṣf* 9–12, 15, 30–1. Ibn Ḥabīb's *Waṣf al-firdaws* was in all probability written between 195/810 and 238/853, around the period when the mention of complete *isnād* chains had become a necessary scholarly practice. Authors of Muslim biographical dictionaries criticized Ibn Ḥabīb for his deficient knowledge of *ḥadīth* and

mind that Ibn Ḥabīb's *Waṣf al-firdaws* emerged during the formative period of *ḥadīth* sciences, I propose that the citation of *isnāds* represents the first formal characteristic of the genre of *ṣifat al-janna*.

Muslim scholars came to classify traditions, primarily, into three main categories based on authenticity and authority: sound (*ṣaḥīḥ*), accepted (*ḥasan*), and weak (*ḍaʿīf*). Traditions that were frequently assessed as weak are abundant in *ṣifat al-janna* works, alongside sound and accepted traditions. Several examples of this category of traditions are adduced in the different sections of the article and in footnotes below. Due to space limitations, I only discuss two examples here.

The compilers of *ṣifat al-janna* works transmit a lengthy tradition attributed to the Prophet which touches on, among other themes, the following: a tree in paradise called *ṭūbā*, the believers' vision of God in paradise, and paradise's luxurious palaces. Ibn Abī l-Dunyā and Abū Nuʿaym al-Iṣfahānī transmit this tradition through two different *isnād* strands which nevertheless originate from Muḥammad b. ʿAlī b. al-Ḥusayn (d. 114/732–118/736), known as al-Bāqir and recognized as the fifth *imām* by the Shiʿites. Al-Bāqir is, to use Joseph Schacht's term, the common link in the *isnād* chain of this tradition.[15] No intermediary transmitters from the generation of the companions or their successors are named in the two *isnād* strands as al-Bāqir's informants.[16] Ibn al-Qayyim and Ibn Kathīr both transmit the tradition and criticize its *isnād* extensively.[17] Ibn al-Qayyim concludes his critique by asserting that the tradition should not be attributed to the Prophet. He states that it should only be considered as Muḥammad al-Bāqir's own speech and that some weak transmitters erred and attributed it to the Prophet (*wa-ḥasbuhu an yakūna min kalām Muḥammad ibn ʿAlī fa-ghalaṭa fīhī baʿḍ hāʾulāʾi al-ḍuʿafāʾ fa-jaʿalahu min kalām al-nabī*).[18] In his evaluation of the tradition, Ibn al-Qayyim transmits the views of scholars such as Ibn ʿAdī l-Jurjānī (d. 363/974) and al-Dāraquṭnī (d. 385/995) on the unreliability of its *isnād* strands.[19] Ibn Kathīr considered this tradition weak as well. He explicitly asserts that the tradition is *mursal* (i.e., narrated from the successor directly on the authority of the Prophet without mentioning a companion),

its sciences, see Ibn al-Faraḍī, *Tārīkh* i, 459–62. The criticism is late and was most likely rooted in the clumsiness of Ibn Ḥabīb's *isnāds*.

15 Schacht, *The origins* 171–2.

16 Ibn Abī l-Dunyā, *Ṣifat* 80–3; al-Iṣfahānī, *Ṣifat* iii, 242–8.

17 Ibn al-Qayyim, *Ḥādī* 193–5; Ibn Kathīr, *Ṣifat* 216–8.

18 Ibn al-Qayyim, *Ḥādī* 195.

19 Ibid.

odd (*gharīb*), and weak.[20] Ibn Ḥabīb also transmits the tradition but through an incomplete *isnād* chain that does not reach the authority the tradition supposedly originates with, Muḥammad b. al-Ḥanafiyya (16–81/637–701) in this case. Moreover, in his *isnād* Ibn Ḥabīb does not name an intermediary transmitter, a companion of the Prophet, from whom Muḥammad b. al-Ḥanafiyya would have received the tradition. Ibn Ḥabīb's tradition is thus also weak by Sunni Muslim scholars' standards; it is at best *mursal*.[21]

Another example of weak traditions transmitted in *ṣifat al-janna* works is the tradition stating that the width of the gates of paradise, or the gate from which the Muslim nation will enter, is three days' journey.[22] Except for al-Tirmidhī's *al-Jāmiʿ al-ṣaḥīḥ*, the six Sunni canonical *ḥadīth* books (*al-kutub al-sitta*) do not transmit this tradition. Al-Tirmidhī actually comments negatively on the authenticity of this tradition's *isnād*, mentioning that, according to al-Bukhārī (d. 256/870), a certain Khālid b. Abī Bakr in the lower segment of the *isnād* chain is reputed to have transmitted objectionable (*munkar*)[23] traditions from

20 Al-Mundhirī, *al-Targhīb* 797–8; Ibn Kathīr, *Ṣifat* 218. The term *gharīb* could signify a critique of the *isnād* and/or the *matn* of a tradition. According to Ibn al-Ṣalāḥ, when it pertains to both it means that the tradition was transmitted from an earlier authority (a companion or a successor) through a single narrator from the later generations (if this narrator is unreliable then the tradition should be considered weak). When the term *gharīb* pertains to a critique of the *isnād* only, it means that the content of the tradition is known through other *isnād* chains originating from different companions but the particular *isnād* chain under scrutiny is unique because it transmits the tradition on the authority of a companion that no other transmitter had related. See Ibn al-Ṣalāḥ, *ʿUlūm* 270–1.

21 Ibn Habib, *Waṣf* 86–9. The tradition mentioned above is neither transmitted in the so-called six canonical *ḥadīth* collections nor in the vast majority of the *ḥadīth* reference collections reputable among Sunni Muslims, such as that of Ibn Ḥibbān, *Ṣaḥīḥ*; Ibn Khuzayma, *Ṣaḥīḥ*; al-Dāraquṭnī, *Sunan*; al-Dārimī, *Sunan*; al-Bayhaqī *al-Sunan*; al-Ṭabarānī, *al-Muʿjam*; al-Baghawī, *Sharḥ*; al-Bayhaqī, *Shuʿab*; ʿAbd al-Razzāq, *Muṣannaf*; Mālik, *Muwaṭṭaʾ*. This tradition represents a case in which a report attributed to Shiʿi figures is discredited. In this particular case, we have a broken link in the tradition's *isnād* (in all of its transmission strands) and this justifies considering the tradition weak according to Sunni *ḥadīth* criticism criteria. Whether there are other traditions attributed to Shiʿi figures in *ṣifat al-janna* works and how these traditions are presented and evaluated are issues that need further investigation.

22 Ibn Abī l-Dunyā, *Ṣifat* 167–8; al-Iṣfahānī, *Ṣifat* ii, 26–7; Ibn al-Qayyim, *Ḥādī* 55; Ibn Kathīr, *Ṣifat* 20–1.

23 The *munkar* category is defined by Jonathan Brown: "in the 3rd/9th and 4th/10th centuries to criticize a report attributed to the Prophet, … [as] (*munkar*), could mean that the report was reliable but was narrated by only one chain of transmission, that this version

Sālim b. ʿAbdallāh b. ʿUmar (the successor who is the transmission source of Khālid).[24] The tradition is transmitted in the *ṣifat al-janna* works of Ibn Abī l-Dunyā and Abū Nuʿaym al-Iṣfahānī, with the same *isnād*, without any comment on its *isnād* or *matn*.[25] Ibn al-Qayyim transmits the tradition as well, but his collective commentary on the traditions concerning the width of the gates of paradise indicates that it also has problems of reliability.[26] Ibn Kathīr also transmits this tradition but criticizes it, transmitting al-Tirmidhī's opinion.[27] Other reputable Muslim scholars criticized this tradition as well. For instance, Ibn al-Jawzī al-Tamīmī (d. 597/1201) reproduced al-Tirmidhī's assessment concerning the tradition[28] and al-Dhahabī (d. 748/1348 or 753/1352–3) singled out this particular tradition as being among Khālid b. Abī Bakr's objectionable traditions (*manākīr*).[29] Abū Bakr al-Bayhaqī (d. 458/1066) also transmitted this tradition but immediately contrasted it with the *ḥadīth* transmitted in the *ṣaḥīḥ* books.[30] In contrast, Aḥmad b. ʿAlī al-Tamīmī (known as Abū Yaʿlā l-Mawṣilī) (d. 307/919) transmitted the tradition without any comment on its *isnād* or *matn* and Ibn Ḥibbān (d. 354/965) in his *Kitāb al-Thiqāt* mentioned Khālid among the trustworthy transmitters of *ḥadīth*.[31]

This last example bears witness to the fact that there is no complete consensus among Muslim scholars that a certain body of traditions is weak. Not only because there is no consensus on all classification criteria but also because when agreement on a particular criterion exists the scholars' assessment may differ; the aforementioned appraisal of the reliability of Khālid b. Abī Bakr as a *ḥadīth* transmitter is a case in point. There have been, however, traditions that a majority of Muslim scholars criticized (although they were not necessarily in full agreement) for problems such as those identified above, for example for having weak links. My purpose in pointing to this type of *ḥadīth* here is to draw attention to one of the main characteristics of *ṣifat al-janna* works that stem

of the ḥadīth narrated through a certain *isnād* was unreliable but other authentic versions existed, or that the report was entirely forged." See Brown, How we know 174. In cases of *ḥadīth* criticism, the particular significance of the term *munkar* can be recognized by reading the scholar's critique of the tradition in question.

24 Al-Tirmidhī, *al-Jāmiʿ al-ṣaḥīḥ* iv, 684.

25 Ibn Abī l-Dunyā, *Ṣifat* 167–8; al-Iṣfahānī, *Ṣifat* ii, 26–7.

26 Ibn al-Qayyim, *Ḥādī* 55.

27 Ibn Kathīr, *Ṣifat* 20–1.

28 Ibn al-Jawzī, *al-ʿIlal* ii, 930.

29 Al-Dhahabī, *Mīzān* ii, 409.

30 Al-Bayhaqī, *Kitāb al-Baʿth* 168.

31 Al-Tamīmī, *Musnad* ix, 407; Ibn Ḥibbān, *Kitāb al-Thiqāt* vi, 245. Ibn Ḥibbān also stated that Khālid b. Abī Bakr sometimes errs (*yukhṭiʾu*).

from the conventions of the scholarly tradition within which they emerged. Ibn al-Ṣalāḥ (d. 643/1245) in his *ʿUlūm al-ḥadīth* (widely known as *Muqaddimat Ibn al-Ṣalāḥ* – The introduction of Ibn al-Ṣalāḥ) states that *ḥadīth* scholars have generally allowed the narration of weak traditions in matters of *moral suasion* (*targhīb*), dissuasion (*tarhīb*), anecdotes (*qiṣaṣ*), and commendable behavior (*faḍāʾil al-aʿmāl* or *adab*), as long as they were not deemed forged (*mawḍūʿ*) and did not conflict with the precepts of the law (the forbidden and the allowed) or matters of religious doctrine (*ʿaqīda*) established by sound and accepted traditions.[32] Paradise, as the reward of righteous beliefs and actions, belongs to the *targhīb* category and *ṣifat al-janna* works clearly reflect this license articulated by Ibn al-Ṣalāḥ. It is the proliferation of weak traditions in *ṣifat al-janna* works that, I suggest, gives them their second constitutive characteristic as a literary genre.[33]

The *ṣifat al-janna* works of Ibn Ḥabīb, Ibn Abī l-Dunyā, and Abū Nuʿaym al-Iṣfahānī reflect yet another scholarly convention articulated in Ibn al-Ṣalāḥ's *ʿUlūm al-ḥadīth*. Ibn al-Ṣalāḥ states that *ḥadīth* scholars have also allowed the narration of weak traditions on the above-named group of topics without pointing out their weakness.[34] In these three works one invariably finds no criticism of the *isnād*s, be they reliable or weak. Thus, effectively, weak traditions are presented on an equal standing with *ṣaḥīḥ* and *ḥasan* traditions. As the preceding examples show, in the late works of Ibn al-Qayyim and Ibn Kathīr we see a clear break with this attitude. While Ibn al-Qayyim and Ibn Kathīr still transmit most of the weak traditions transmitted by their predecessors they prefer to assess their *isnād*s; in fact they do so with virtually all the traditions they transmit. These two scholars indicate, for example, whether the tradition has been transmitted in one or more of the six canonical *ḥadīth*

---

32 Ibn al-Ṣalāḥ, *ʿUlūm* 103.

33 The tradition stating that the lowest in rank in paradise is in the sixth stratum below the seventh is another example of weak traditions in *ṣifat al-janna* works. This tradition is transmitted by Abū Nuʿaym al-Iṣfahānī without any comment on its *isnād* or *matn* (al-Iṣfahānī, *Ṣifat* iii, 290). Ibn Kathīr criticized it as *inqitāʿ* (i.e., a discontinuous *isnād* chain) and *gharīb* (Ibn Kathīr, *Ṣifat* 104). Ibn al-Qayyim also criticized it for *isnād* and *matn* problems and considered it *munkar* (Ibn al-Qayyim, *Ḥādī* 116–7). In the vast majority of *isnād* criticism cases, including the above mentioned examples, Ibn al-Qayyim and Ibn Kathīr usually transmit the opinions of different *ḥadīth* scholars concerning the *isnād*s under scrutiny, thus substantiating their critique of these *isnād*s and confirming that the tradition is regarded weak by various authorities. Ibn Ḥabīb does not provide full *isnād*s for many of the traditions he transmits and this renders them weak traditions (see n. 14).

34 Ibn al-Ṣalāḥ, *ʿUlūm* 103.

books (usually by naming the compiler). In many cases, they explicitly assess the overall value of the *isnād* (e.g., *ṣaḥīḥ*, corresponding to the *ṣaḥīḥ* valuation criteria of al-Bukhārī or Muslim, *mursal*, or *munkar*). In their works Ibn al-Qayyim and Ibn Kathīr also identify the unreliable and uncreditable *ḥadīth* transmitters.[35]

When we turn to the *matn* of the traditions, specifically to the issue of *matn* criticism, it is somewhat surprising that Ibn Ḥabīb transmits a very limited number of traditions with conflicting *matn*s in his *Waṣf al-firdaws*.[36] On the other hand, judging from their *ṣifat al-janna* works, it seems that Ibn Abī l-Dunyā and Abū Nuʿaym al-Iṣfahānī were not overly concerned with the issues of *matn* criticism. As the examples adduced below demonstrate, the traditions with problematic *matn*s that they transmit could be classified into two categories: weak traditions that conflict with traditions considered authentic and weak traditions that conflict with each other.[37] In either case, *matn* conflicts do

---

35 See for example Ibn al-Qayyim, *Ḥādī* 89–90, 136, 168–9; Ibn Kathīr, *Ṣifat* 80, 100, 104. It is worth mentioning that Muslim scholars believe that weak traditions can be used to substantiate other weak traditions, and consequently elevate their degree of authenticity. A good example of this process is the presence of *mutābaʿāt* (sing. *mutābaʿa*, lit., tracking or continuation). A *mutābaʿa* for a weak tradition would be another identical tradition, in *matn*, transmitted through a different *isnād* strand that originates from the same trustworthy persons (*thuqāt*) at the root of the *isnād* of the weak tradition under consideration, i.e., it originates from the same transmitter from the generation following the successors, the same successor, or the same companion of the Prophet (see Ibn al-Ṣalāḥ, *ʿUlūm* ii, 82–5). The works of Ibn Ḥabīb and Ibn Abī l-Dunyā do not reflect this method of reevaluation, or, in fact, other methods of reevaluation. Abū Nuʿaym al-Iṣfahānī on the other hand transmits additional *isnād* strands for several weak traditions; some of which could be interpreted as *mutābaʿāt* (e.g., the *ḥadīth* stating that the first to be called to paradise are those who thank God in good and bad circumstances [*al-sarrāʾ wa-l-ḍarrāʾ*] in al-Iṣfahānī, *Ṣifat* i, 107–8). Ibn Kathīr also cites additional *isnād* strands for some traditions as evidence of *mutābaʿāt*; Ibn al-Qayyim does this much less (see for instance Ibn Kathīr, *Ṣifat* 34–5; Ibn al-Qayyim, *Ḥādī* 116 (the *ḥadīth* reporting that the lowest in rank in paradise could wander in his domains for two thousand years) and Ibn Kathīr, *Ṣifat* 144–5 (the tradition on the believer wishing for a son in paradise)).

36 An example of the few traditions with conflicting *matn*s in his *Waṣf al-firdaws* is the tradition on the number of levels of paradise (Ibn Ḥabīb, *Waṣf* 20).

37 Several of the traditions that are considered reliable and that conflict with weak traditions in *ṣifat al-janna* works have been transmitted in the six canonical *ḥadīth* collections. They are thus considered to have the rank of *ṣaḥīḥ* or *ḥasan* by way of scholarly consensus (*ijmāʿ*). As erudite scholars, Ibn Abī l-Dunyā and Abū Nuʿaym al-Iṣfahānī were certainly aware of these authentic traditions, whether they transmitted them in their *ṣifat al-janna* works or not. It would hence be implausible to ascertain that the *ḥadīth*s with conflicting *matn*s in their *ṣifat al-janna* works lie outside the criteria of *matn* criticism, which

not provoke any response on the part of these two authors, either on the *matn* or the *isnād* level. An important question now is whether Ibn Ḥabīb utilized *matn* criticism. One certainly cannot dismiss the possibility that Ibn Ḥabīb was particularly attentive to *matn* problems. It is, on the other hand, possible to argue that the limited instances of *matn* conflicts in his *Waṣf al-firdaws* is an accidental consequence of the relatively modest number of traditions he acquired (compared to later compilers of *ṣifat al-janna* works) that relate to paradise.[38] Add to this the clumsiness of Ibn Ḥabīb's *isnād*s, the absence of any commentary on the traditions he transmits, and the nature of the *ṣifat al-janna* works of Ibn Abī l-Dunyā and Abū Nuʿaym al-Iṣfahānī, and with regard to *matn* criticism we might be more likely to believe that Ibn Ḥabīb did not engage in systematic *matn* criticism. In contrast, in their *ṣifat al-janna* works Ibn al-Qayyim and Ibn Kathīr offer several cases of implicit and explicit *matn* criticism, in which they criticize many traditions with problematic *matn*s transmitted by Ibn Abī l-Dunyā and Abū Nuʿaym al-Iṣfahānī (or Ibn Ḥabīb).

Ibn al-Qayyim criticizes, for example, the *matn* of a tradition which reports on the number of wives for the man with the lowest rank in paradise. The tradition mentions that the width of the seat (*miqʿad*) of any of these wives will be one mile. Ibn al-Qayyim takes issue with this detail. He asserts that the authentic tradition (transmitted in the *ṣaḥīḥ* books) reports that the height of men and women in paradise is sixty cubits.[39] According to Ibn al-Qayyim, it is improbable that the seat of a person of this height would be one mile. Ibn al-Qayyim then criticizes the *isnād* of the problematic tradition by indicating that two of its transmitters are considered unreliable by several scholars. He then concludes that the tradition should be regarded as *munkar*.[40] Ibn Abī

---

requires the scrutiny of weak traditions against *ḥadīth*s acknowledged as authentic by scholarly *ijmāʿ*.

38 Ibn Ḥabīb transmits 256 traditions in his *Waṣf al-firdaws*. Ibn Abī l-Dunyā transmits a higher number, 364 traditions. Abū Nuʿaym al-Iṣfahānī's work comprises 454 traditions and Ibn Kathīr's work 446. Ibn al-Qayyim transmits more or less a similar number of traditions as Abū Nuʿaym al-Iṣfahānī and Ibn Kathīr (these numbers are based on the editors numbering of the traditions in the contemporary editions of these works and include the repeated traditions). We should bear in mind that Ibn Ḥabīb was a scholar from Islamic Spain. Acquiring knowledge at his time required traveling to the Islamic East and staying there for a period of time. It is possible therefore that he was not able to collect as many traditions as his eastern peers. The biographical data available concerning him indicates that he learned many traditions through acquired written material only, not by listening to *ḥadīth* transmitters, see Ibn al-Faraḍī, *Tārīkh* i, 460–1.

39 See for example al-Bukhārī, *Ṣaḥīḥ* 817–8; Muslim, *Ṣaḥīḥ* xvii, 251–2.

40 Ibn al-Qayyim, *Ḥādī* 116–7.

l-Dunyā and Abū Nuʿaym al-Iṣfahānī transmit both the problematic tradition and the one that mentions sixty cubits without any comment on their *isnād*s or *matn*s.[41] Furthermore, both transmit other weak traditions (also without any comment on their *isnād*s or *matn*s) that report that the height of men and women in paradise is seventy or ninety miles, thus directly contradicting the *ṣaḥīḥ* tradition that notes sixty cubits.[42]

Other examples of *matn*-problematic traditions are those that report the number of wives that every man will marry in paradise.[43] The tradition indicating that every man in paradise will have two paradisal female companions (*ḥūrī*s) and seventy women from "*ahl mirāthihi min al-dunyā*" (lit., the people of his inheritance from the people of this world) is a good point with which to begin. Ibn Kathīr transmits this tradition but also states that it is very odd (*gharīb jiddan*).[44] In an unmistakable instance of *matn* criticism, he asserts that this *ḥadīth* contradicts a reliable tradition – committed to the traditionists' memory (*maḥfūẓ*) – concerning the number of paradisal wives assigned to the believer in paradise, that is, seventy *ḥūrī*s and two earthly wives.[45] He then points out that a certain Khālid b. Yazīd b. Abī Mālik in the *isnād* chain of this *ḥadīth* was criticized by Aḥmad b. Ḥanbal (d. 241/855) and Yaḥyā b.

---

41 Ibn Abī l-Dunyā, *Ṣifat* 53, 194; al-Iṣfahānī, *Ṣifat* 99–100, 109.

42 Ibn Abī l-Dunyā, *Ṣifat* 194; al-Iṣfahānī, *Ṣifat* ii, 109. A similar case of *ḥadīth*s with problematic *matn*s in *ṣifat al-janna* works is reflected in the traditions that report on the width of the gates of paradise. Traditions report the following different values: the distance between Mecca and a city called Hajar (probably an ancient city in the Arabian Peninsula), forty years', three days', or seven years' journey. Ibn Kathīr does not address this particular *matn* criticism case. On the other hand, Ibn al-Qayyim offers a detailed *isnād-matn* critique of these traditions, the result of which is that he considers the Mecca-Hajar tradition the ultimate authority on the width of the gates of paradise. Ibn al-Qayyim utilizes *matn* criticism when he concludes that the tradition of three days', although he must have been aware of the critique of its *isnād*, agrees with the *matn* of the Mecca-Hajar tradition. Ibn al-Qayyim states that the horseman riding a fast horse and traveling continuously would take, more or less, three days to travel the distance between these two cities. While Ibn Ḥabīb only transmits the version that states that it is forty years' (with a different *isnād*), Ibn Abī l-Dunyā and Abū Nuʿaym al-Iṣfahānī transmit the four traditions. They comment neither on their *isnād*s nor on their conflicting *matn*s. See respectively Ibn al-Qayyim, *Ḥādī* 54–5; al-Iṣfahānī, *Ṣifat* ii, 21–3, 25, 26–7; Ibn Kathīr, *Ṣifat* 18–22; Ibn Abī l-Dunyā, *Ṣifat* 168–9; Ibn Ḥabīb, *Waṣf* 9.

43 Ibn Ḥabīb mentions only one value concerning the number of paradisal wives assigned to the believer (seventy-two). See Ibn Ḥabīb, *Waṣf* 79.

44 Ibn Kathīr, *Ṣifat* 131. On the issue of the *ḥūrī*s see also S. Griffith's contribution to the present publication.

45 Ibn Kathīr, *Ṣifat* 131.

Maʿīn (d. 233/847).[46] The problematic *ḥadīth* is transmitted in Abū Nuʿaym al-Iṣfahānī's *Ṣifat al-janna* without any comment despite the fact that it contradicts another tradition on the issue that Abū Nuʿaym al-Iṣfahānī also transmits (assigning seventy-three *ḥūrī* wives to the believer in paradise).[47]

Ibn Kathīr also transmits a tradition which assigns the following number of wives to the believer in paradise: four thousand virgins, eight thousand single/widowed women (*ayyim*), and a hundred *ḥūrīs*.[48] He asserts that this tradition is also *gharīb jiddan*.[49] Ibn Kathīr's critique of this tradition is largely formed with respect to its *isnād*. Nonetheless, he probably considered that the number of wives reported in it contradicts the number he considers more authentic (as above). Ibn Abī l-Dunyā relates two traditions similar to this exaggerated report criticized by Ibn Kathīr, both offering incompatible numbers.[50] Moreover, they conflict with another tradition that he transmits which states that the lowest in rank in paradise will have seventy-two wives.[51] The exaggerated report criticized by Ibn Kathīr, with the same *isnād* but with the slight change, from *ḥūrīs* to *jawārin* (slave girls/maids), is also transmitted by Abū Nuʿaym al-Iṣfahānī.[52] In Abū Nuʿaym al-Iṣfahānī's work it conflicts with the number of wives mentioned in two other reports that he cites in the same chapter.[53] Neither Ibn Abī l-Dunyā nor Abū Nuʿaym al-Iṣfahānī comment on the *matn* or the *isnād* of any of these traditions. In contrast, Ibn al-Qayyim transmits many of them but criticizes their *isnād*s and considers them of uncertain reliability.[54] For Ibn al-Qayyim, the only authentic reports concerning the number of wives of the believer in paradise are those transmitted in the *ṣaḥīḥ* books. The number mentioned there is two wives only. Ibn al-Qayyim, however, does not proceed to critique the conflicting *matn*s of the wives traditions with reference to the *ṣaḥīḥ* reports of two wives, probably because there is a qualification for the two wives mentioned in the latter which does not allow the exclusion of the possibility that the believers might have more wives in paradise.[55]

---

46 Ibid.

47 Al-Iṣfahānī, *Ṣifat* ii, 205.

48 Ibn Kathīr, *Ṣifat* 195.

49 Ibid.

50 Ibn Abī l-Dunyā, *Ṣifat* 194–5, 201.

51 Ibid., 161, 194–5, 201.

52 Al-Iṣfahānī, *Ṣifat* iii, 212–3.

53 Ibid., iii, 206, 218.

54 Ibn al-Qayyim, *Ḥādī* 168–70.

55 Ibid. The tradition of two wives is also cited in Ibn Abī l-Dunyā, *Ṣifat* 195–6; al-Iṣfahānī, *Ṣifat* ii, 83–5; and Ibn Kathīr, *Ṣifat* 132–3. In this regard, Ibn Ḥabīb only relates the

2 The Genre of *Ṣifat al-Janna* and Quranic Exegesis

Quranic material and the exegetical traditions are only marginally present in *ṣifat al-janna* works compared to non-exegetical traditions. Not only because of the copiousness of the latter but also because the compilers of *ṣifat al-janna* works mostly quote selected Quranic verses in relation to the themes they discuss (if Quranic descriptions are available). The interpretation of these selected verses is usually accomplished by citing traditions in which the verses occur alongside their interpretation. This is particularly the case in Ibn Abī l-Dunyā and Abū Nuʿaym al-Iṣfahānī's works. In Ibn Ḥabīb's *Waṣf al-firdaws*, alongside this type of tradition, there is also a section dedicated to the explication of Quranic verses relevant to paradise. Ibn al-Qayyim and Ibn Kathīr also transmit exegetical traditions of this sort but cite a number of Quranic verses independently as well. In Ibn Kathīr's work, these verses figure frequently at the beginning of his chapters; on occasion, they appear with very brief paraphrastic commentary. Compared to Ibn Kathīr, Ibn al-Qayyim presents a considerably lengthier commentary on such verses (frequently of a philological nature). The following examples are intended to help us fathom the approach to Quranic exegesis employed in *ṣifat al-janna* works.

Q 13:29 reads: "(As for) those who believe and do good, a *felicitous* final state (*ṭūbā*) shall be theirs and a goodly return."[56] The word *ṭūbā* mentioned in this verse has prompted varying interpretations in Muslim exegetical literature. Al-Ṭabarī reports that ʿIkrima (d. 105/723–4), among others, considered "*ṭūbā* shall be theirs" to mean blessings, or good things, are theirs (*niʿma mā lahum*).[57] Al-Ṭabarī also mentions two views attributed to Qatāda b. Diʿāma al-Sadūsī (d. 117/735): one indicates that *ṭūbā* means *ḥusnā* (which could be translated "a pleasant outcome") and the other asserts that *ṭūbā lak* means *aṣabta khayran* (i.e. [you] acquired good things).[58] In addition, al-Ṭabarī reports that Ibn ʿAbbās

traditions which indicate that the believers will have seventy-two wives in paradise (Ibn Ḥabīb, *Waṣf* 79).

56 Unless otherwise indicated, all translations of the Quran are according to Muḥammad Ḥabīb Shākir (trans.), *The Qur'an*. The translation of this verse is Shākir's with my minor modification (the italicized word).

57 Al-Ṭabarī, *Tafsīr* xiii, 519–20. Al-Ṭabarī's *Tafsīr* has been chosen as a *tafsīr* reference in the present study because it transmits one of the most comprehensive collections of views with regard to any verse. The views al-Ṭabarī cites are frequently transmitted in later exegetical works, with more or less variety. For the interpretation of the verses discussed in this paper, the reader may also consult the following medieval Muslim *tafsīrs*: al-Thaʿlabī, *al-Kashf*; al-Qurṭubī, *al-Jāmiʿ*; and al-Rāzī, *Tafsīr*.

58 Al-Ṭabarī, *Tafsīr* xiii, 521.

(d. 68/687–8) interpreted *ṭūbā* to mean delight and solace for the eyes (*faraḥ wa-qurrat ʿayn*).[59] The above-mentioned views indirectly assert the Arabic origin of the word *ṭūbā*. The reports attributed to Qatāda do so explicitly, stating: "it is a word from the speech of the Arabs" and "it is an Arabic word" (*wa-hiya kalima min kalām al-ʿArab* and *hādhihi kalima ʿarabiyya*).[60] Other reports suggested that *ṭūbā* may be the name of paradise in the Abyssinian language (*al-ḥabashiyya*) or the Hindi language (*al-hindiyya*).[61] Al-Ṭabarī also gives a lengthy list of reports which assert that *ṭūbā* is a great tree in paradise. At the end of the list, he adduces some traditions attributed to the Prophet that confirm this view.[62]

Commenting on *ṭūbā* in their *ṣifat al-janna* works, Ibn Ḥabīb, Abū Nuʿaym al-Iṣfahānī, Ibn al-Qayyim, and Ibn Kathīr present only the prophetic traditions which indicate that it is a tree in paradise.[63] Ibn Abī l-Dunyā cites these traditions along with one additional view which indicates that *ṭubā* is the name of paradise in Abyssinian.[64]

The interpretation of Q 108:1 is offered in a similar fashion. The verse speaks of *al-kawthar* as being given to the Prophet by God. Again, in the exegetical literature there are several interpretations of *al-kawthar*. It is interpreted as great wealth (*khayr kathīr*), as a basin in paradise, or as a river in paradise.[65] Ibn Ḥabīb, Ibn Abī l-Dunyā, and Abū Nuʿaym al-Iṣfahānī opt to present the interpretation of *al-kawthar* as a paradisal river and neglect the other views.[66] Ibn al-Qayyim and Ibn Kathīr transmit one additional interpretation: *al-kawthar* as *al-khayr al-kathīr*.[67] It must be noted here that some of the prophetic traditions interpreting *al-kawthar* as a river and *ṭūbā* as a tree were considered reliable by scholarly consensus (*ijmāʿ*).[68] The next example is different insofar as there are no prophetic traditions that pertain to the verse in question.

Q 36:55 reads: "*inna aṣḥāba al-janna al-yawm fī shughul fākihūn*" which may be translated "the people of Paradise have joy in all that they do." The sexual

---

59 Ibid. Other reports that interpret *ṭubā* in the same vein are also transmitted in al-Ṭabarī's *tafsīr*. See al-Ṭabarī, *Tafsīr* xiii, 519–22.

60 Ibid., xiii, 521.

61 Ibid., xiii, 522.

62 Ibid., xiii, 523–9.

63 Ibn Ḥabīb, *Waṣf* 36–8; al-Iṣfahānī, *Ṣifat* iii, 241, 248; Ibn Kathīr, *Ṣifat* 89–91; Ibn al-Qayyim, *Ḥādī* 125–6.

64 Ibn Abī l-Dunyā, *Ṣifat* 83–6.

65 Al-Ṭabarī, *Tafsīr* xxiv, 679–90.

66 Ibn Ḥabīb, *Waṣf* 27–8; Ibn Abī l-Dunyā, *Ṣifat* 89–90; al-Iṣfahānī, *Ṣifat* iii, 168–71.

67 Ibn Kathīr, *Ṣifat* 68–75; Ibn al-Qayyim, *Ḥādī* 134.

68 Ibn al-Qayyim, *Ḥādī* 125–6, 134; Ibn Kathīr, *Ṣifat* 89–91.

intercourse between men and women in paradise (*jimāʿ ahl al-janna*) is not discussed at any point in the Quran. The Quran simply mentions *zawwajnāhum* (lit., we joined them in pairs).[69] In the exegetical literature there are several interpretations of Q 36:55; for example, Mujāhid b. Jabr (died between 100/718 and 104/722) and al-Ḥasan al-Baṣrī (d. 110/728) are reported to have asserted that *fī shughul fākihūn* means *fī niʿma* (that is, enjoying good things or good fortune). Another view, attributed to al-Ḥasan al-Baṣrī and others, asserts that *fī shughul fākihūn* means that the believers will be fully occupied with the blessings of paradise and not be thinking of those in hellfire and their torment.[70] The compilers of *ṣifat al-janna* works, however, cite only one exegetical view with regard to Q 36:55. It explains the phrase "*fī shughul fākihūn*" to mean that the people of paradise will be busy with the deflowering of virgins.[71]

The preceding examples epitomize the distinctive exegetical approach employed in *ṣifat al-janna* works. There is a tendency in these works to present a very limited range of interpretations for the Quranic verses related to paradise, even for those that prompt multiple interpretations in the exegetical literature. In fact, it is not uncommon to find a single interpretation adduced with regard to such verses in *ṣifat al-janna* works. It could not possibly be a coincidence that this attitude is evident in the works of Ibn Ḥabīb, Ibn Abī l-Dunyā, Abū Nuʿaym al-Iṣfahānī, and Ibn Kathīr.[72] Ibn al-Qayyim's *Ḥādī l-arwāḥ* again is something of an exception. Ibn al-Qayyim not infrequently presents several interpretations of the verses he cites, particularly when there are no prophetic traditions concerning their interpretation that could be considered reliable.[73] Sometimes he also utilizes philology and cites poetry as explicative evidence; both are exegetical approaches not attested to in the *ṣifat al-janna* works of his peers.

The *ṣifat al-janna* works of Ibn Ḥabīb and Ibn Abī l-Dunyā emerged during the formative stage of Quranic exegesis, the pre-Ṭabarī period. Abū Nuʿaym al-Iṣfahānī, Ibn al-Qayyim, and Ibn Kathīr on the other hand operated in the context of the mature scholastic tradition of Quranic exegesis that was largely

69 See Q 44:54; 52:20.

70 See the various interpretations of the verse in al-Ṭabarī, *Tafsīr* xix, 459–64.

71 Ibn Ḥabīb, *Waṣf* 77; Ibn Abī l-Dunyā, *Ṣifat* 193–4; al-Iṣfahānī, *Ṣifat* iii, 209–10; Ibn al-Qayyim, *Ḥādī* 174–5; Ibn Kathīr, *Ṣifat* 141.

72 See for example, Ibn Ḥabīb, *Waṣf* 16 (the interpretation of Q 93:5); Ibn Abī l-Dunyā, *Ṣifat* 138, 152–3, 182 (respectively, the interpretations of Q 56:15; 8:4; 19:85); al-Iṣfahānī, *Ṣifat* i, 40–1 (the interpretation of Q 21:105); al-Iṣfahānī, *Ṣifat* ii, 115–6 (the interpretation of Q 35:34); and Ibn Kathīr, *Ṣifat* 56, 191 (respectively, the interpretation of Q 32:17 and 30:15).

73 See for example his interpretation of Q 55:54, 76 (Ibn al-Qayyim, *Ḥādī* 152–4).

defined by al-Ṭabarī's seminal work *Jāmiʿ al-bayān*. The citation of multiple interpretations for any verse from a multitude of exegetical traditions, usually alongside the author's own preference or interpretation, is characteristic of the classical Muslim exegetical tradition. This suggests that the tendency to offer a single interpretation for each verse in *ṣifat al-janna* works is intrinsic. Notwithstanding the relative divergence of Ibn al-Qayyim from the norm thus described, it constitutes the third distinctive characteristic of *ṣifat al-janna* works as a literary genre.

Before we proceed to examine the content and function of *ṣifat al-janna* works, we should take stock of the previous analyses and the implications of the features thus far identified in these works in terms of the significance of the material they transmit. Clearly, the works of *ṣifat al-janna* maintain a high degree of uniformity but also exhibit variation. This is all too natural otherwise works belonging to a certain genre would be dull copies of each other and would not exhibit authors' ingenuity. The keenness of Ibn al-Qayyim and Ibn Kathīr in identifying the degree of reliability of the traditions' *isnād*s and the considerable attention they pay to *matn* criticism could be for a variety of reasons, one being that both were working within a fully mature and reformed scholarly tradition of *ḥadīth* criticism.[74] Such innovative manipulations of the material do not detract from Ibn al-Qayyim and Ibn Kathīr's participation in the genre. For, in their works, they principally maintain the three defining characteristics of the genre I suggested above. It becomes even clearer that

74 In the centuries separating Ibn al-Qayyim and Ibn Kathīr from Abū Nuʿaym al-Iṣfahānī, works by scholars such as al-Khaṭīb al-Baghdādī and Ibn al-Ṣalāḥ significantly contributed to advancing, refining, and stabilizing technical criteria of *ḥadīth* criticism and its terminology. On the issue of *matn* criticism especially, the earliest extant work that offers a "systematic discussion and application" of *matn* criticism (titled, *al-Manār al-munīf fī l-ṣaḥīḥ wa-l-ḍaʿīf*) was actually an achievement of Ibn al-Qayyim himself (Brown, How we know 145). It is also evident that compendia of forged *ḥadīths* first appeared late in the fourth/tenth century (Brown, How we know 145). Thus, seemingly, the lack of attention to issues of *matn* criticism evident in the *ṣifat al-janna* works of Ibn Abī l-Dunyā and Abū Nuʿaym al-Iṣfahānī, in contrast to those by Ibn al-Qayyim and Ibn Kathīr, lends support to the position that systematic *matn* criticism, at least in explicit form, was a late development in *ḥadīth* sciences. This contention however sets aside Ibn al-Ṣalāḥ's two statements (mentioned above) concerning the early scholarly permission to narrate weak traditions on the topic of *targhīb* without pointing out their weakness. We need not achieve a resolution for this problem here; I should nonetheless suggest that the findings offered in this study might add to the discussion on the development of *matn* criticism in Islam.

their works belong squarely to the genre of *ṣifat al-janna* when we discuss the content and function of these works in the next section.

It was pointed out earlier in this study that *ṣifat al-janna* works were composed by scholars of great stature who were considered authorities in a range of Islamic sciences. These scholars culled their material exclusively from authoritative texts, the Quran and *ḥadīth*s. If we couple this with some of the recurrent features in *ṣifat al-janna* works, such as the citation of *isnād*s and the common absence of commentary on or provision of allegorical meanings for the *matn*s of the traditions, it is fairly plausible to conclude that these works present their content as authoritative and literal. It must also be noted that the compilers of *ṣifat al-janna* works effectively suppressed the diversity of interpretations available for many of the Quranic verses they quote. That is to say, the multitude of interpretations available for these verses and the criteria according to which the selection(s) from among these interpretations were made were concealed from the users of these works. It should be conceded, too, that all the traditions in the *ṣifat al-janna* works of Ibn Ḥabīb, Ibn Abī l-Dunyā, and Abū Nuʿaym al-Iṣfahānī were in effect presented as genuine. This includes the doubtful information conveyed by the weak traditions. In theory, of course, interested or specialist Muslims had the opportunity to examine, for instance in works of *tafsīr*, the other interpretations available for the Quranic verses interpreted in *ṣifat al-janna* works. The presence of the *isnād* chains also meant that a user of a *ṣifat al-janna* work, if he had the knowledge and the resources required, could scrutinize the authenticity of the quoted traditions on his own. Nevertheless, one could certainly argue that the majority of believers, those without significant training in the Islamic sciences, still had access to the material transmitted in *ṣifat al-janna* works, directly or through sermons by public preachers, storytellers and the like,[75] and were unsuspecting and willing recipients of the works. The overall corollary therefore is that a gap between the scholars and the general public was inevitable; the scholars' assessment of the nature of the exegetical material and the veracity of the traditions they transmitted in their *ṣifat al-janna* works were, on many occasions, not disclosed to the genre's audience.

---

75 The *wuʿʿāẓ* (public preachers) and storytellers were repeatedly criticized by medieval Muslim scholars for propagating false *ḥadīth*s and for having no knowledge of *ḥadīth* sciences, and thus being unable to differentiate between authentic, weak, and forged traditions. See, for instance, Pedersen, The criticism 215–31.

3 The Content and Function of *Ṣifat al-Janna* Works

There is remarkable consistency in *ṣifat al-janna* works in terms of the themes they deal with;[76] attested to not only in the wide overlap in the material transmitted in these works but also in the titles of their various chapters.[77] It was remarked that the prophetic traditions constitute the most sizeable part of the content of *ṣifat al-janna* works. Nonetheless, it is not only this extensive use of traditions (epitomized in the citation of multiple traditions for every theme and the inclusion of a multitude of weak traditions) that gives these works a distinctive nature in terms of content. It is also that these works are keen to draw on the Quran and by necessity its exegesis (the exegetical traditions). The essential disposition of the works of *ṣifat al-janna* is a concern to offer the most comprehensive exposition of paradise possible based on Islam's most authoritative sources: the Quran and the Sunna (the teachings of the Prophet). This gives these works their fourth and perhaps most distinguishing characteristic as a literary genre.

The largest thematic group of material in *ṣifat al-janna* works correlates explicitly with their titles; it deals with the depiction of paradise proper as well as the many felicities its inhabitants will enjoy. This group comprises a wide range of themes: for instance, paradise's vegetation, rivers, animals, and atmosphere.[78] Paradise's human inhabitants as well as their food, drink, clothing, palaces, and social life are also described in considerable detail.[79] The vast

---

76 Despite the wide time frame over which these works were produced, it is rare to find a theme or an issue that is not common to them. One such case is *al-aʿrāf* (the heights), which is only present in Ibn Ḥabīb (*Waṣf* 51–2). Since al-Aʿrāf is identified as a location between hellfire and paradise, it is probable that later authors of *ṣifat al-janna* works did not include it in their works because they did not believe that it belongs to the subject of paradise proper. Despite this remarkable topical unity in the genre, there are some differences with regard to the variety of traditions cited in relation to each theme in *ṣifat al-janna* works. As we would expect, not every compiler possessed the exact collection of traditions the others had or, equally, desired to transmit the same traditions his peers transmitted.

77 There is great similarity in the organization of *ṣifat al-janna* works. For instance, all these works have chapters on the gates of paradise, its trees, rivers, the *jimāʿ ahl al-janna* (sexual relationships in paradise), the food of the people of paradise, and the paradisal wives.

78 Ibn Ḥabīb, *Waṣf* 24–31, 36–41, 66–8, 73–5; Ibn Abī l-Dunyā, *Ṣifat* 73–98, 109–19, 180–1; al-Iṣfahānī, *Ṣifat* i, 148–51; al-Iṣfahānī, *Ṣifat* ii, 52–4; al-Iṣfahānī, *Ṣifat* iii, 151–71, 180–3, 185–94, 261–7; Ibn al-Qayyim, *Ḥādī* 122–38, 186–7, 195–6; Ibn Kathīr, *Ṣifat* 63–102, 172–81, 203–08.

79 Ibn Ḥabīb, *Waṣf* 14–7, 32–41, 45–7, 57–65, 68–72, 80–93; Ibn Abī l-Dunyā, *Ṣifat* 42–70, 80–4, 109–46, 155–66, 177–200, 214–21; al-Iṣfahānī, *Ṣifat* i, 124–30, 135–47, 157–9; al-Iṣfahānī,

majority of these descriptions are offered by traditions that go significantly beyond the Quranic descriptions, when the latter are available. Several studies have examined this material in terms of the various characteristics of paradise narratives in Islam.[80] Our concern here is to illustrate the overall significance conveyed by this material; the next few examples should suffice for this purpose.

Ṣifat al-janna works inform us that every other brick (*labina*) in the structures of paradise is made of gold or silver. The mortar of paradise is musk, its sand is saffron, and its pebbles are pearls.[81] Its palaces, rooms, and tents are beyond count, grand, and extraordinarily luxurious.[82] The believer will dwell therein in extreme comfort served by a multitude of servants and will enjoy endless sustenance of food and drink.[83] And despite variations in the believers' rewards, everyone will be content with their lot for there is no distress, envy, or hatred in paradise.[84] Paradise is hence represented as a place with everlastingly and perpetually abundant beauty, pleasures, and fulfillment, where all phenomena, spaces, and structures are grand in scale and supernaturally luxurious. This portrayal of paradise reflects an afterlife where comforts, abundance, and felicities replace toil, and a state of perfect and peaceful existence prevails. This first type of material does not merely describe paradise and life in it, above all it communicates to the believers a particular formulation of salvation, its meaning and its worth.[85]

Ṣifat ii, 78–135; al-Iṣfahānī, *Ṣifat* iii, 141–50, 172–85, 194–231, 249–95; Ibn al-Qayyim, *Ḥādī* 107–19, 138–57, 187–90. Ibn Kathīr, *Ṣifat* 35–59, 103–122, 167–71, 209–22. On the issue of food in paradise see also A. Qian's contribution to the present publication.

80 See for example al-Azmeh, Rhetoric; Rustomji, *The garden and the fire*.

81 Ibn Ḥabīb, *Waṣf* 7; Ibn Abī l-Dunyā, *Ṣifat* 43–4; al-Iṣfahānī, *Ṣifat* i, 157–9; Ibn al-Qayyim, *Ḥādī* 103–4; Ibn Kathīr, *Ṣifat* 43–4.

82 Ibn Ḥabīb, *Waṣf* 14–7; Ibn Abī l-Dunyā, *Ṣifat* 80–3, 144, 210–3; al-Iṣfahānī, *Ṣifat* ii, 230, 242–8, 252; Ibn al-Qayyim, *Ḥādī* 108–10; Ibn Kathīr, *Ṣifat* 51–9.

83 Ibn Ḥabīb, *Waṣf* 58–9; Ibn Abī l-Dunyā, *Ṣifat* 146; al-Iṣfahānī, *Ṣifat* iii, 210–1; Ibn al-Qayyim, *Ḥādī* 168; Ibn Kathīr, *Ṣifat* 55.

84 Ibn Ḥabīb, *Waṣf* 21–2; Ibn Abī l-Dunyā, *Ṣifat* 151–2; al-Iṣfahānī, *Ṣifat* iii, 146–7; Ibn al-Qayyim, *Ḥādī* 90, 115.

85 Sebastian Günther insightfully points out the importance of taking into consideration the "mode of statement" and the "character of portrayal" exhibited by traditions when reflecting on their significance, see Günther, Modern 172. The traditions in *ṣifat al-janna* works present their content predominantly as a record of non-fictional narratives.

The second theme we can identify here consists of a group of traditions which addresses the status of the Prophet Muḥammad[86] and the Muslim community in the afterlife. Traditions report that the gates of paradise will only open for the Prophet Muḥammad and that he will be the first to enter paradise.[87] The intercession of the Prophet is also affirmed. God will grant him the right to intercede in favor of the believers and he is the first among God's prophets to be granted this right.[88] Also, several traditions relate that the Prophet asked the believers to pray that God will grant him *al-wasīla* (lit., medium or instrument) or that he hoped that God will grant it to him. *Al-wasīla* is identified in these traditions as the highest place in paradise, only one of God's servants is entitled to it.[89] As for the Prophet's community, various traditions report that the majority of the people of paradise will be Muslims, specifically two-thirds of its inhabitants.[90] Other traditions assert that Muslims will enter paradise before all other nations[91] and that the language spoken in paradise is Arabic.[92] Overall, the excellence of the medieval Muslim community is noticeably reflected and affirmed in the traditions describing the Prophet and his community's status in paradise.

The third thematic group of material I was able to isolate has conspicuous theological connotations. Some of the traditions in this group revolve around the question of whether paradise has already been created. These unequivocally express the Sunni view in this regard; paradise has already been created and it awaits the believers.[93] The beliefs and actions that lead to paradise are

86 It is worth noting that the status of the Prophet Muḥammad is the subject of several groups of Muslim traditions. For instance, Sebastian Günther has identified several traditions on the Prophet's night journey and ascension (*al-isrāʾ wa-l-miʿrāj*) that describe the Prophet's status in relation to previous prophets (see Günther, Paradisevorstellungen 40). On the Prophet's night journey see also the contributions by R. Tottoli and K. Ruehrdanz in the present publication.

87 Ibn Ḥabīb, *Waṣf* 41; Ibn Abī l-Dunyā, *Ṣifat* 172–3; al-Iṣfahānī, *Ṣifat* ii, 33–4; Ibn al-Qayyim, *Ḥādī* 87–8; Ibn Kathīr, *Ṣifat* 13–5.

88 Al-Iṣfahānī, *Ṣifat* ii, 30–1; Ibn al-Qayyim, *Ḥādī* 88; Ibn Kathīr, *Ṣifat* 15.

89 Ibn Ḥabīb, *Waṣf* 22–3; Ibn Abī l-Dunyā, *Ṣifat* 154; Ibn al-Qayyim, *Ḥādī* 68–9; Ibn Kathīr, *Ṣifat* 40–2.

90 Ibn Ḥabīb, *Waṣf* 43–4; al-Iṣfahānī, *Ṣifat* ii, 75; Ibn al-Qayyim, *Ḥādī* 95–6; Ibn Kathīr, *Ṣifat* 233–4, 242.

91 Ibn Ḥabīb, *Waṣf* 41; al-Iṣfahānī, *Ṣifat* i, 101–2; Ibn al-Qayyim, *Ḥādī* 88–9; Ibn Kathīr, *Ṣifat* 233.

92 Ibn Abī l-Dunyā, *Ṣifat* 162–3; al-Iṣfahānī, *Ṣifat* ii, 112–3; Ibn al-Qayyim, *Ḥādī* 280; Ibn Kathīr, *Ṣifat* 253.

93 Ibn Ḥabīb, *Waṣf* 5–6, 10–3; Ibn Abī l-Dunyā, *Ṣifat* 57, 62, 72; al-Iṣfahānī, *Ṣifat* i, 41–8; Ibn al-Qayyim, *Ḥādī* 18–27, 45–9; Ibn Kathīr, *Ṣifat* 226–9, 245–50.

mentioned in some traditions as well. The Ḥanbalī, the Shāfiʿī, and the Mālikī *madhhab*s, to which the compilers of our *ṣifat al-janna* works adhered, came to adopt the view that faith (*īmān*) is believing by verbal confession (*bi-l-qawl*) and inward certitude (*taṣdīq*, or *iʿtiqād bi-l-qalb*). They also believed that faith increases and decreases through actions (*ʿamal*).[94] Besides this, there is a wide belief in Sunni Islam that those who profess faith by verbal confession and inward belief will eventually enter paradise.[95] The traditions in *ṣifat al-janna* works convey to us a picture that is in accordance with these precepts. It is reported that those who confess the *shahāda*, i.e., there is no god but God, will (eventually) enter paradise, for the price of paradise (*thaman al-janna*) is the belief in God's unity.[96] Other traditions clearly differentiate between the believers who will enter paradise; they will dwell in different levels or attain special rewards and merits in paradise according to their deeds (corresponding to the *ʿamal* component of faith).[97] There are also traditions which bring together the "belief and deeds" components of faith. They emphasize the idea of adhering to Islam (as traditions sometimes call it, [dwelling in] *al-dār* "the house").[98] Here the price of paradise (*thaman al-janna*) is the belief in God, the Prophet Muḥammad as His messenger, God's revelations, and acting on those beliefs by practicing the rituals, avoiding what God has forbidden, and embracing what He has commanded. Belonging to this group also are the traditions which interpret "and more" (*wa-ziyāda*) in Q 10:26 ("For those who do good is the best [reward] and more [thereto]. Neither dust nor ignominy cometh near their faces. Such are rightful owners of the Garden; they will abide therein") and "more" (*mazīd*) in Q 50:35 ("There [i.e., in paradise] they have all that they desire, and there is more with Us") as denoting the believers' vision of God in paradise, a theological view held by mainstream Sunni Muslims.[99]

---

94 For a comprehensive study of the conception of *īmān* in the four Sunni *madhhab*s consult al-Khamīs, *Iʿtiqād*. On the Ḥanbalī and the Mālikī view that *īmān* increases and decreases and the contrary beliefs of the Ḥanafīs regarding this issue see Watt, *The formative* 131–5.

95 Watt, *The formative* 127.

96 Al-Iṣfahānī, *Ṣifat* i, 71–4; Ibn al-Qayyim, *Ḥādī* 71–2; Ibn Kathīr, *Ṣifat* 15, 23.

97 Ibn Ḥabīb, *Waṣf* 20, 22; Ibn Abī l-Dunyā, *Ṣifat* 143, 151, 173–4; al-Iṣfahānī, *Ṣifat* i, 104; Ibn al-Qayyim, *Ḥādī* 65–8; Ibn Kathīr, *Ṣifat* 30–2.

98 Ibn Ḥabīb, *Waṣf* 20; al-Iṣfahānī, *Ṣifat* i, 30–2; Ibn al-Qayyim, *Ḥādī* 64, 70–3; Ibn Kathīr, *Ṣifat* 182–3.

99 Ibn Ḥabīb, *Waṣf* 92; Ibn Abī l-Dunyā, *Ṣifat* 105; al-Iṣfahānī, *Ṣifat* iii, 225–9; Ibn al-Qayyim, *Ḥādī* 206–9, 221–2, 234–9, 243; Ibn Kathīr, *Ṣifat* 158–66. The interpretation of these two verses is another example of the univalent mood of Quranic exegesis evident in *ṣifat al-janna* works.

Usually, there is commentary on this third type of material in the *ṣifat al-janna* works of Ibn al-Qayyim and Ibn Kathīr. This commentary reflects their theological pertinence unequivocally and in some instances it is explicitly polemical, for example against the Muʿtazilīs who held different views concerning the creation of paradise and the definition of faith.[100] Ibn al-Qayyim has even dedicated one of the longest chapters in his *Ḥādī l-arwāḥ* to marshal evidence in support of the doctrine of the vision of God in paradise and to censure the various Muslim factions denying it.[101]

The fourth, and last, group of materials I highlight here consists of *ḥadīth*s with patent social undertones. Traditions from this group give assurances of entrance to paradise or ascribe privileged status in it to certain moral models: The just arbiter (*ḥakam ʿadl*),[102] the just ruler (*imām ʿadl* or *sulṭān muqṣiṭ*),[103] charitable persons (*al-mutaṣaddiqūn*),[104] those who treat other Muslims with compassion and maintain good relations with their relatives (*rajul raḥīm raqīq al-qalb li-kull dhī qurbā wa-muslim* and *al-wāṣilūn* [*al-raḥim*]),[105] those who spread peace (*man afshā l-salām*) and talk kindly to others (*alāna al-kalām*),[106] the slave not hindered by slavery from obeying God, and the poor with chil-

---

100 See for example Ibn al-Qayyim, *Ḥādī* 18–27, 46–9, 70–2; Ibn Kathīr, *Ṣifat* 226–7. In contrast to the Sunnis, the Muʿtazilīs believed that paradise has not been created yet. For them *īmān* was neither the inner nor outward confession of belief; it is nothing but "the performance of all religious duties, obligatory and supererogatory." Cf. Watt, *The formative* 134–5. *Ṣifat al-janna* works convey the following perception regarding the "road to paradise": Inward and outward confessions of faith are essential to enter paradise which is above all obtained by God's grace and forgiveness. Deeds, while still affecting faith (they decrease or increase its amount), mainly decide the Muslim's rank in paradise. Ibn al-Qayyim conveys this perception in his work explicitly, see Ibn al-Qayyim, *Ḥādī* 72–3. On the other hand, in the Muʿtazilīs' view actions are decisive with regard to one's admittance to paradise. Cf. Watt, *The formative* 138, 229.

101 See Ibn al-Qayyim, *Ḥādī* 204.

102 Ibn Abī l-Dunyā, *Ṣifat* 143; Ibn al-Qayyim, *Ḥādī* 109.

103 Ibn Ḥabīb, *Waṣf* 14; Ibn al-Qayyim, *Ḥādī* 94; Ibn Kathīr, *Ṣifat* 236.

104 Ibn Ḥabīb, *Waṣf* 66; Ibn Abī l-Dunyā, *Ṣifat* 173–4, 180; Ibn al-Qayyim, *Ḥādī* 94.

105 Ibn Ḥabīb, *Waṣf* 71; Ibn Abī l-Dunyā, *Ṣifat* 173–4; Ibn al-Qayyim, *Ḥādī* 94; Ibn Kathīr, *Ṣifat* 236, 238–9.

106 Ibn Ḥabīb, *Waṣf* 15; Ibn al-Qayyim, *Ḥādī* 108–10; Ibn Kathīr, *Ṣifat* 53–5. Ibn al-Qayyim transmits that *ifshāʾ al-salām* (i.e., spreading peace) means "shaking the hand of one's brother [in Islam] and greeting him" (*muṣāfaḥat akhīka wa-taḥīyyatuhu*), see Ibn al-Qayyim, *Ḥādī* 108–10. Ibn Kathir provides a similar interpretation; see Ibn Kathīr, *Ṣifat* 54–5. For Ibn al-Qayyim, *aṭyaba al-kalām* (another expression of *alāna al-kalām*) is to say: "God is exalted, praise to God, and there is no God but God" (*subḥān Allāh wa-l-ḥamd li-llāh wa-lā ilāha illā llāh*), see Ibn al-Qayyim, *Ḥādī* 108–10.

dren who are still virtuous (*muta'affif*).[107] The Muslim duty of *jihād* (the duty to participate in military service to defend Islam) and the status of the *jihād* martyrs (*al-shuhadā'*) in paradise is the subject of some traditions as well. The distinguished reward of *al-mujāhidīn* (those who take part in *jihād*) is articulated clearly.[108] Likewise the status and reward of the *shuhadā'* in paradise is clear: they are among the first to enter paradise, they enter paradise from an exclusive entrance (*bāb al-jihād*), they have exclusive access to a certain palace in paradise, and, along with the prophets and righteous men, they belong to the highest ranks of paradise.[109]

Belonging to this fourth group as well are the traditions that denounce certain moral behavior: for instance, severing one's relationship with his relatives (*qāṭi' al-raḥim*),[110] disobeying one's parents (*al-'āqq*, pl. *al-'āqqūn*),[111] falsely claiming a man as one's father (*man idda'ā ilā ghayr abīhi*),[112] and killing *dhimmīs* (the people of the book living under Muslim governments) or members of groups in alliance with Muslims (*nafsan mu'āhida*).[113] The individual who commits any of these lapses is described as not being able to smell the fragrance of paradise (*lam yuriḥ rā'iḥat al-janna*), a metaphor for a diminished prospect of admittance to paradise. It is also reported that the woman who causes pain to or troubles her husband (*tu'dhī zawjahā*) will be the subject of the prayers of her husband's paradisal wife; she will call on God to fight her (*qātalaki Allāh*).[114] Most of the moral precepts described in this fourth group are not concerned with an individual's self-improvement, rather they pertain to the individual's relationships with others; they are in essence social.

It would certainly be inaccurate to consider *ṣifat al-janna* works as being dedicated to the description of paradise only, as a cursory reading of their titles may indicate. The examples adduced above reveal that a significant portion of the traditions cited in these works do not pertain to the description of paradise proper. Yet, these traditions figure consistently in the genre. In light of the preceding content analysis, *ṣifat al-janna* works are better described as

---

107 Al-Iṣfahānī, *Ṣifat* i, 104; Ibn al-Qayyim, *Ḥādī* 90, 94; Ibn Kathīr, *Ṣifat* 220, 236.

108 Ibn Ḥabīb, *Waṣf* 61; Ibn Abī l-Dunyā, *Ṣifat* 151, 170, 173–4; al-Iṣfahānī, *Ṣifat* i, 50; Ibn al-Qayyim, *Ḥādī* 65; Ibn Kathīr, *Ṣifat* 17, 23, 29.

109 Ibn Ḥabīb, *Waṣf* 14, 20, 22, 66; Ibn Abī l-Dunyā, *Ṣifat* 143, 150–1, 170, 173–4; al-Iṣfahānī, *Ṣifat* i, 104; Ibn Kathīr, *Ṣifat* 132, 162–3, 220–1; Ibn al-Qayyim, *Ḥādī* 65, 68, 90, 190, 193, 213.

110 Al-Iṣfahānī, *Ṣifat* ii, 42–3; Ibn Kathīr, *Ṣifat* 177; Ibn al-Qayyim, *Ḥādī* 120.

111 Al-Iṣfahānī, *Ṣifat* ii, 42–3; Ibn Kathīr, *Ṣifat* 177.

112 Al-Iṣfahānī, *Ṣifat* ii, 43–7; Ibn al-Qayyim, *Ḥādī* 120; Ibn Kathīr, *Ṣifat* 172–3.

113 Al-Iṣfahānī, *Ṣifat* ii, 45; Ibn al-Qayyim, *Ḥādī* 119; Ibn Kathīr, *Ṣifat* 173–5.

114 Ibn Abī l-Dunyā, *Ṣifat* 206; al-Iṣfahānī, *Ṣifat* i, 114; Ibn al-Qayyim, *Ḥādī* 172; Ibn Kathīr, *Ṣifat* 136.

compilations on paradise, in which the subject of paradise is both a religious ideology, pertaining to salvation and theological dogma, and an index of social relevance.

The main function of the genre is certainly didactic: first, it imparts to believers a description of paradise and its many felicities, thereby conveying a certain formulation of salvation. Second, it indoctrinates believers with the ideology of mainstream Sunni Islam (beliefs and dogma) insofar as it concerns the topic of paradise. Third, but no less important, it instructs the believers on the salvific worth of actions in accordance with faith and certain behavioral models.

The genre's social function is closely interwined with these didactic purposes. In medieval Muslim societies, knowledge, culture, law, institutions, and the individuals' morality and functioning within the community were largely articulated through the prism of religion. In such contexts, religious ideology is of course not separate from social reality, nor is the topic of paradise. The reward of salvation (the first thematic group) is closely tied to right belief and dogma (the third group) as well as to right actions (the third and fourth). The particular formulation of the concept of faith in the traditions of the third group and the emphasis on the Prophet's intercession in the second assure the believer admittance to paradise, however without encouraging moral laxity. The incentive to moral excellence is attested in the emphasis of many traditions of the third group on actions in accordance with faith. Moreover, social moral prescriptions, as precepts from the *sunna*, and their salvific worth came to be the subject of a fair number of traditions in the genre (the fourth group of material).

With all these traditions considered, the genre certainly seems to affirm and sustain several social structures, particularly behavioral ones. Concomitantly, by propagating a unified set of theological beliefs and guidelines as regards paradise the genre promotes unity and harmony. Equally important, the genre affirms the community's self-image as a whole, its righteousness and excellence among the nations (the second group of material). Overall, thus, the genre of *ṣifat al-janna* could be viewed as a vehicle that stabilizes both the ideological and socio-cultural context within which it emerged.[115]

---

115 It is worth mentioning also that several traditions in *ṣifat al-janna* works explicitly confirm that the Prophet's immediate successors, the caliphs Abū Bakr (d. 13/634) and ʿUmar (d. 23/644), are granted a place in paradise, thereby confirming the legitimacy of the institution of the caliphate as opposed to the imamate ideology of the Shiʿites. This could also be seen as an ideological connotations of the *ṣifat al-janna* genre. See Ibn Ḥabīb, *Waṣf* 9;

The combination of the four characteristic conventions of *ṣifat al-janna* works, their distinctive content, and their function represents a process for treating the topic of paradise that is unique to these works. In my view, it indubitably sets them apart as a literary genre distinctive from other works on paradise in Sunni Islam.

4 The Genre of *Ṣifat al-Janna* and Other Works on Paradise in Sunni Islam

The chapters on paradise in Muslim's *Ṣaḥīḥ* and al-Tirmidhī's *al-Jāmiʿ al-ṣaḥīḥ* were compiled with different criteria than the genre of *ṣifat al-janna*.[116] Muslim and al-Tirmidhī were principally interested in transmitting prophetic *ḥadīth*s that pertain to paradise. Thus, in their chapters on paradise they do not attest the Quranic verses that relate to paradise and the associated exegetical traditions, most of which are not attributed to the Prophet. Furthermore, Muslim was interested in transmitting *ḥadīth*s from the *ṣaḥīḥ* category and al-Tirmidhī was interested in transmitting *ḥadīth*s from the *ṣaḥīḥ* and *ḥasan* categories. Therefore, the whole host of weak traditions that constitute a significant bulk of the traditions adduced in *ṣifat al-janna* works were simply rejected by Muslim and al-Tirmidhī.[117] These are not the only reasons that make their chapters on paradise distinct from *ṣifat al-janna* works. Several traditions that appear consistently in *ṣifat al-janna* works are transmitted by Muslim and al-Tirmidhī, but not in chapters related to paradise. For example, in his *Ṣaḥīḥ* Muslim relates a *ḥadīth* concerning *al-kawthar*; it appears in the chapter on prayer (*Kitāb al-Ṣalāt*). In *al-Jāmiʿ al-ṣaḥīḥ* by al-Tirmidhī only one tradition

Ibn Abī l-Dunyā, *Ṣifat* 142, 169–71; al-Iṣfahānī, *Ṣifat* ii, 35–6; al-Iṣfahānī, *Ṣifat* iii, 180–1, 251; Ibn al-Qayyim, *Ḥādī* 87, 109; Ibn Kathīr, *Ṣifat* 16–7, 248.

116 Ibn Māja dedicates a very small subchapter (*bāb*) to paradise in his *Sunan* (under the chapter entitled *al-zuhd*). It is too short and "thin" to warrant a comparison with *ṣifat al-janna* works, see Ibn Māja, *Sunan* ii, 1447–53. On the chapter on paradise in Muslim's *Ṣaḥīḥ* see also A. Geissinger's contribution to the present publication.

117 There are numerous examples of weak traditions on paradise absent from the chapters on paradise in Muslim's *Ṣaḥīḥ* and al-Tirmidhī's *al-Jāmiʿ al-ṣaḥīḥ*. For instance, the *ḥadīth*s reporting the height of the inhabitants of paradise in miles (Ibn Abī l-Dunyā, *Ṣifat* 194; al-Iṣfahānī, *Ṣifat* ii, 109) and also the *ḥadīth*s reporting the number of the paradisal wives of the believers in thousands (Ibn Abī l-Dunyā, *Ṣifat* 201; al-Iṣfahānī, *Ṣifat* iii, 212–3). For the exegetical tradition concerning Q 36:55 (*inna aṣḥāba al-janna al-yawm fī shughul fākihūn*), see Ibn Ḥabīb, *Waṣf* 77; Ibn Abī l-Dunyā, *Ṣifat* 193–4; al-Iṣfahānī, *Ṣifat* iii, 209–10; Ibn al-Qayyim, *Ḥādī* 174–5; Ibn Kathīr, *Ṣifat* 141.

on *jihād* and *shuhadāʾ* is transmitted in the chapter on paradise (*Kitāb Ṣifat al-janna ʿan rasūl Allāh*).[118] The rest of the traditions on *jihād* and *shuhadāʾ*, while consistently cited in the genre of *ṣifat al-janna*, are either absent or transmitted in chapters other than those on paradise. The chapters on paradise in Muslim's *Ṣaḥīḥ* and al-Tirmidhī's *al-Jāmiʿ al-ṣaḥīḥ* cannot be considered part of *ṣifat al-janna* genre, which has a narrower purpose and scope.

The chapters on paradise in the hyperbolic eschatological treatises, of which *Daqāʾiq al-akhbār fī dhikr al-janna wa-l-nār* by ʿAbd al-Raḥīm b. Aḥmad al-Qāḍī and *al-Durar al-ḥisān fī l-baʿth wa-naʿīm al-jinān* attributed to al-Suyūṭī are examples, cannot be considered instances of the *ṣifat al-janna* genre either. First, the authors of these treatises discuss at length the torment of the grave, the details of the day of reckoning, and hellfire (among other themes). They only touch on paradise in the closing sections of their works. Second, the Quran figures very rarely in these works and the exegetical traditions are virtually nonexistent. Third, the groups of traditions of theological and social connotations discussed above are also virtually absent from the sections dedicated to paradise in these works. Fourth, and perhaps most important, the traditions transmitted in these two works are, by the standards of Muslim *ḥadīth* scholars, of very dubious origins. The embroidered accounts, at times quite fanciful, given in these traditions betray their purpose: attracting the audiences' attention. Compared to the traditions adduced in the works of *ṣifat al-janna*, it is quite clear that most of those transmitted in *Daqāʾiq al-akhbār* and *al-Durar al-ḥisān* are of different intensity in respect to fantastic descriptions. Given the lack of *isnād*s, save a few direct attributions to the Prophet and certain companions, it is not surprising that Muslim *ḥadīth* scholars considered the traditions cited in such treatises equivalent to those of the much-criticized *quṣṣāṣ* (storytellers).[119]

The chapter on paradise in *al-Targhīb wa-l-tarhīb* by al-Mundhirī on the other hand bears the greatest resemblance to the works of *ṣifat al-janna*.[120] Like the compilers of these works, al-Mundhirī cites, alongside *ṣaḥīḥ* and *ḥasan* *ḥadīth*s, numerous weak traditions. Citations from the Quran and exegetical traditions are also attested in his chapter on paradise and these resemble those

118 Muslim, *Ṣaḥīḥ* iv, 148–9; al-Tirmidhī, *al-Jāmiʿ al-ṣaḥīḥ* iv, 697, 698.

119 Al-Qāḍī, *Daqāʾiq* 103–15; al-Suyūṭī, *al-Durar* 33–49.

120 Abū l-Qāsim al-Jawzī l-Aṣbahānī (d. 535/1140) dedicates a very small subchapter to paradise (*bāb fī l-targhīb fī l-janna wa-l-tashmīr li-ṭalabihā*) in his work *Kitāb al-Targhīb wa-l-tarhīb*, widely known as *Qawām al-sunna*. It is quite short, consisting of only thirty traditions, and too incomprehensive to warrant a comparison to *ṣifat al-janna* works, see al-Aṣbahānī, *Kitāb al-Targhīb* i, 537–50.

in Ibn Abī l-Dunyā and Abū Nuʿaym al-Iṣfahānī's *ṣifat al-janna* works. Moreover, al-Mundhirī touches on virtually all the themes pertaining to the description of paradise and its felicities. Altogether, al-Mundhirī adduces around one hundred fifty traditions in his chapter on paradise, considerably fewer than those transmitted in the earliest example of the genre, that of Ibn Ḥabīb, and one-third of those transmitted by Abū Nuʿaym al-Iṣfahānī (see note 38). Several of al-Mundhirī's traditions are considerably lengthier and multi-thematic compared to those transmitted in *ṣifat al-janna* works. This compensates, in part, for the deficiency in the number of traditions he adduces. Still, in comparison to the works of *ṣifat al-janna*, he offers a very poor presentation of some themes: for instance, the theme of paradise's rivers and the theme of paradisal chanting.[121]

The purpose of al-Mundhirī's work is, however, very different from the genre of *ṣifat al-janna*. Al-Mundhirī aspires to cultivate commendable behavior and to warn against deplorable behavior, all based on the *sunna*. This orientation dictates that he divide his work, voluminous in nature, into chapters, each of which is dedicated to a particular issue of *targhīb* and *tarhīb*. The result is that many of the traditions frequently transmitted in *ṣifat al-janna* works appear in his *al-Targhīb wa-l-tarhīb* in chapters other than that on paradise. For example, virtually all of the traditions on the distinguished status of the Prophet Muḥammad and the Muslim community in the hereafter are absent from his chapter on paradise,[122] as are the traditions on the conception of faith.

---

121 Four thematic traditions about the rivers of paradise are absent from al-Mundhirī's work: the tradition mentioning that four rivers on earth originate from paradise, the traditions concerning a river called *al-baydakh* or *al-baydaḥ*, the traditions speaking of rivers in paradise that produce slave maidens, and the traditions which indicate that the rivers of paradise spring from *al-firdaws* (the highest stratum of paradise). Compare al-Mundhirī, *al-Targhīb* 784–5 to Ibn Abī l-Dunyā, *Ṣifat* 89–98; al-Iṣfahānī, *Ṣifat* ii, 151–71; Ibn Kathīr, *Ṣifat* 63–81; and Ibn al-Qayyim, *Ḥādī* 131–8. Ibn Ḥabīb's account of the rivers of paradise is richer than that of al-Mundhirī, particularly because he combines both traditions and Quranic verses in his presentation, see Ibn Ḥabīb, *Waṣf* 27–31. For the theme of paradisal chanting, compare al-Mundhirī, *al-Targhīb* 793–4 to Ibn Ḥabīb, *Waṣf* 73–5; Ibn Abī l-Dunyā, *Ṣifat* 187–90; al-Iṣfahānī, *Ṣifat* ii, 268–73; Ibn Kathīr, *Ṣifat* 191–200; Ibn al-Qayyim, *Ḥādī* 182–6.

122 The traditions concerning the following themes are absent from al-Mundhirī's chapter on paradise (entitled *al-Targhīb fī l-janna wa-naʿīhā*): The gates of paradise will open first to the Prophet Muḥammad; the Prophet is the first to enter paradise; the Prophet is the first to be granted the right to intercede on behalf of the believers; Muslims will be the majority of the inhabitants of paradise; Muslims will enter paradise before all other nations; and the language spoken in paradise is Arabic, see al-Mundhirī, *al-Targhīb* 776–803.

Moreover, al-Mundhirī adduces only one tradition from the type prescribing the salvific worth of certain social moral models in his chapter on paradise.[123] The vast majority of the traditions of this type are cited in other chapters of his work.

It should be noted also that al-Mundhirī does not mention the full *isnād*s of the traditions he transmits. He predominantly cites the final two authorities to which the tradition is attributed and the reputable authority (Muslim, or al-Bukhārī, etc.), if any, that transmitted it. He uses keywords at the beginning of the traditions together with brief notes on their *isnād*s to indicate his assessment of their reliability.[124] Al-Mundhirī asserts that he adopted this scheme based on a request from some of his pious students that he compile a comprehensive work on *targhīb* and *tarhīb* not congested with lengthy *isnād*s and their criticism.[125] In his view, the purpose of citing *isnād*s is to differentiate between traditions in terms of their reliability, a task which is only possible for erudite scholars. Citing full *isnād*s is thus meaningless to the inexpert and it obscures the edifying purpose of the traditions.[126]

We should take into consideration that al-Mundhirī was writing in the seventh/thirteenth century, at which point there existed a well-established scholarly *ḥadīth* tradition and three examples of the genre; one of which, that of Abū Nuʿaym al-Iṣfahānī, was among the most comprehensive of *ṣifat al-janna* works in terms of the scope of traditions. In terms of technical conventions, al-Mundhirī's scheme of treating *isnād*s is certainly exceptional. It circumvents the long-established scholastic tradition of citing *isnād*s that had long been honored by the compilers of *ṣifat al-janna* works.[127] When compared to Ibn Abī l-Dunyā's and Abū Nuʿaym al-Iṣfahānī's *ṣifat al-janna* works, al-Mundhirī's chapter on paradise represents a regression, particularly in terms of richness and comprehensiveness. Though it is still possible to argue that it belongs to the genre of *ṣifat al-janna*, albeit a somewhat poor and deviant example of it. I am, however, inclined to consider it on or outside the genre's boundaries.

---

123 Ibid., 784.

124 See al-Mundhirī's introduction, *al-Targhīb* 23–4.

125 Ibid.

126 Ibid.

127 It should be mentioned that al-Mundhirī lists his sources as books not as *isnād* chains, and provides a list of the controversial transmitters included in his compilation. See al-Mundhirī, *al-Targhīb* 8–25.

5 Conclusion

The analysis presented in this study demonstrates that the *ṣifat al-janna* genre was amenable to the conventions and developments of the scholastic tradition from which it emerged. But regardless of whether there was commentary on the authenticity of the *isnāds* or critique of the *matns* of the traditions in *ṣifat al-janna* works, they continued to serve their function. The commentaries on the *isnāds* and *matns* in the late *ṣifat al-janna* works should be analyzed within the frame of a culture adjusting itself from within, without losing its fundamental structures. These developments were certainly informative for the users of the genre; especially with regard to differentiating between weak and reliable traditions. They continue in today's works on the topic of *al-targhīb wa-l-tarhīb*. In the introduction of his *Ṣaḥīḥ al-targhīb wa-l-tarhīb* (The sound [traditions] of moral suasion and exhortation), the renowned modern traditionist Muḥammad Nāṣir al-Dīn al-Albānī (d. 1999) insists that for the sake of presenting the *sunna* to the nation well (*nuṣḥan lahā*), it is imperative to make clear distinctions between sound and weak traditions.[128] This trend is also reflected in the modern editions of *ṣifat al-janna* works, in which the majority of editors provide extensive evaluation of the authenticity of the traditions, from which the present author has benefited.

The research objective of this paper was not to investigate whether the material transmitted in the genre of *ṣifat al-janna* is a byproduct of its ideological or social connotations and function, nor has this paper intended to imply any sort of appraisal of such issues of provenance. This analysis only demonstrates that a significant part of the content of this genre is certainly germane to the ideological and socio-cultural systems within which it transpires; put differently, it demonstrates that the consistent inclusion of certain characteristic content in the genre defines major aspects of its function. It might be worthwhile to assess the representation of paradise conveyed by traditions, or by non-*ṣaḥīḥ* traditions, in comparison to that in the Quran. One of the recurrent shortcomings of modern scholarship on Muslim paradise narratives has been to overlook such distinctions, particularly the distinctions between the various categories of Muslim traditions that Muslim scholars themselves have made. This study points out that a contextual analysis of Muslim paradise narratives and an appreciation of their significance requires attention to such distinctions. For instance, in terms of authenticity, irrespective of the lingering skepticism in certain Western – and for that matter "Eastern" – scholarly

128 Cf. al-Albānī, *Ṣaḥīḥ al-targhīb* i, 15.

quarters as to the value of *isnāds*,[129] the classfication of traditions that Muslim scholars established based on this technical device, although it sometimes led to conflicting results, has a central value to Muslims and should be considered in any serious contextual analysis. Above I have paid attention to such issues. Nonetheless, given the sizeable content of *ṣifat al-janna* works and the extended historical period over which they were produced, it was not feasible to present a comprehensive account of their form and content within the confines of a single paper. The analysis I presented is only intended to offer an adequate characterization of their value as representative of a distinctive genre. Future studies will certainly present further refinements.

Bibliography

'Abd al-Razzāq, Abū Bakr, *al-Muṣannaf*, ed. A. Ḥabīb al-Raḥmān, Beirut 1970.

al-Albānī, M.N., *Ṣaḥīḥ al-targhīb wa-l-tarhīb*, 3 vols., Riyadh 2000.

al-Aṣbahānī, Abū l-Qāsim al-Jawzī, *Kitāb al-Targhīb wa-l-tarhīb*, ed. A. Sha'bān, 3 vols., Cairo 1993.

al-Azmeh, A., Rhetoric for the senses: A consideration of Muslim paradise narratives, in *JAL* 3 (1995), 215–31.

al-Baghawī, Abū Muḥammad, *Sharḥ al-sunna*, ed. Sh. al-Arna'ūṭ and M. al-Shāwish, 16 vols., Beirut 1983.

al-Bayhaqī, Abū Muḥammad, *al-Jāmi' li-shu'ab al-īmān*, ed. A. Ḥāmid, 14 vols., Riyadh 2003.

———, *Kitāb al-Ba'th wa-l-nushūr*, ed. A.A. Ḥaydar, Beirut 1986.

———, *al-Sunan al-kubrā*, ed. M.A. 'Aṭa, 11 vols., Beirut 2003.

al-Bukhārī, Muḥammad b. Ismā'īl, *Ṣaḥīḥ al-Bukhārī*, Beirut 2002.

Brown, J., How we know early ḥadīth critics did *matn* criticism and why it's so hard to find, in *Islamic Law and Society* 15 (2008), 143–84.

Calder, N., Tafsīr from Ṭabarī to Ibn Kathīr: Problems in the description of a genre, illustrated with reference to the story of Abraham, in G.R. Hawting and A.A. Shareef (eds.), *Approaches to the Qur'ān*, Oxford 1988, 101–40.

al-Dārimī, 'Abdallāh, *Sunan al-Dārimī*, ed. F.A. Zamurlī and Kh.S. al-'Alamī, 2 vols., n.p. 1986.

al-Dāraquṭnī, 'Alī b. 'Umar, *Sunan al-Dāraquṭnī*, ed. A. 'Ādil and A.M. Mu'awwaḍ, 3 vols., Beirut 2001.

129 This is despite the work of scholars such as Harald Motzki and Gregor Schoeler. See for instance, Motzki, *The origins*; Motzki, Muṣannaf; Schoeler, Schreiben und Veröffentlichen; Schoeler, Mündliche; Schoeler, Weiteres zur Frage; Schoeler, Die Frage.

Dean, D., *Genre theory: Teaching, writing, and being*, Urbana IL 2008.

al-Dhahabī, Abū ʿAbdallāh Muḥammad, *Mīzān al-iʿtidāl fī naqd al-rijāl*, ed. A.M. Muʿawwaḍ and A.A. ʿAbd al-Mawjūd, 8 vols., Beirut 1995.

———, *Siyar aʿlām al-nubalāʾ*, ed. Ḥ. ʿAbd al-Mannān, 3 vols., Amman 2004.

Dietrich, A., Ibn Abi ʾl- Dunyā, Abū Bakr ʿAbd Allāh b. Muḥammad b. ʿUbayd b. Sufyān al-Ḳurashī al-Baghdādī, in *EI*², iii, 684.

Duff, D. (ed.), *Modern genre theory*, London 2000.

Günther, S., « *Gepriesen sei der, der seinen Diener bei Nacht reisen ließ* » (Koran 17:1): Paradiesvorstellungen und Himmelsreisen im Islam – Grundfesten des Glaubens und literarische Topoi, in E. Hornung and A. Schweizer (eds.), *Jenseitsreisen: ERANOS 2009 und 2010*, Basel 2011, 15–56.

———, Modern literary theory applied to classical Arabic texts: Ḥadīth revisited, in V. Klemm and B. Gruendler (eds.), *Understanding Near Eastern literatures: A spectrum of interdisciplinary approaches*, Wiesbaden 2000, 171–6.

Huici-Miranda, A., Ibn Ḥabīb, Abū Marwān ʿAbd al-Malik b. Ḥabīb al-Sulamī, in *EI*², iii, 775.

Ibn Abī l-Dunyā, Abū Bakr ʿAbdallāh, *Ṣifat al-janna wa-mā aʿadd Allāh li-ahlihā min al-naʿīm*, ed. A.A. al-ʿAsāsla, Beirut and Amman 1997.

Ibn Abī Yaʿlā, Muḥammad, *Ṭabaqāt al-ḥanābila*, ed. A. al-ʿUthaymīn, 3 vols., Mecca 1998.

Ibn al-Faraḍī, Abū l-Walīd, *Tārīkh ʿulamāʾ al-Andalus*, ed. I. al-Ibyārī, 2 vols., Cairo and Beirut 1989.

Ibn Ḥabīb, Abū Marwān ʿAbd al-Malik, *Kitāb Waṣf al-firdaws*, ed. J.P. Sala, Granada 1997.

———, *Waṣf al-firdaws*, ed. S.K. al-Darʿamī, Alexandria n.d.

Ibn Ḥanbal, Aḥmad, *al-Musnad*, ed. A. Shākir, 20 vols., Cairo 1995.

Ibn Ḥibbān, Muḥammad, *Kitāb al-Thiqāt*, ed. M.A. Khān, 9 vols., Hyderabad 1973.

———, *Ṣaḥīḥ Ibn Ḥibbān*, ed. A.M. Shākir, Cairo 1952.

Ibn al-ʿImād, Abū l-Falāḥ, *Shadharāt al-dhahab fī akhbār man dhahab*, ed. A. al-Arnāʾūṭ and M. al Arnāʾūṭ, 10 vols., Damascus and Beirut 1986.

Ibn al-Jawzī, Jamāl al-Dīn, *al-ʿIlal al-mutanāhiya fī l-aḥādīth al-wāhiya*, ed. Kh. al-Mīs, 2 vols., Beirut 1983.

Ibn Kathīr, Ismāʿīl b. ʿUmar, *al-Nihāya fī l-fitan wa-l-malāḥim*, ed. A. al-Ṣabābṭī, 2 vols., Cairo n.d.

———, *Ṣifat al-janna*, ed. A. al-Dimashqī, Beirut 1993.

Ibn Khuzayma, Muḥammad b. Isḥāq, *Ṣaḥīḥ Ibn Khuzayma*, ed. M.M. al-Aʿẓamī, 4 vols., Beirut 1980.

Ibn Māja, Abū ʿAbdallāh, *Sunan*, ed. M. ʿAbd al-Bāqī, 2 vols., Cairo n.d.

Ibn Qayyim al-Jawziyya, Muḥammad, *Ḥādī l-arwāḥ ilā bilād al-afrāḥ*, Beirut 1983.

Ibn Rajab, Abū l-Faraj, *Kitāb al-Dhayl ʿala ṭabaqāṭ al-ḥanābila*, ed. M.H. al-Fiqī, 2 vols., Cairo 1952.

Ibn al-Ṣalāḥ, Abū ʿAmr ʿUthmān, *ʿUlūm al-ḥadīth*, ed. N. ʿItir, 2 vols., Damascus 1986.
al-Iṣfahānī, Abū Nuʿaym, *Ḥilyat al-awliyāʾ wa-ṭabaqāt al-aṣfiyāʾ*, 10 vols., Beirut 1988.
———, *Ṣifat al-janna*, ed. A.A. ʿAlī Riḍa, 3 vols., Damascus 1995.
Jauss, H.R., Theory of genres and medieval literature, in D. Duff (ed.), *Modern genre theory*, London 2000, 127–47.
Juynboll, G.H.A., Munkar, in EI², vii, 575–6.
al-Khamīs, M., *Iʿtiqād al-aʾimma al-arbaʿa: Abī Ḥanīfa wa-Mālik wa-l-Shāfʿī wa-Aḥmad*, Riyadh 1992.
Laoust, H., Ibn Kat͟hīr, ʿImād al-Dīn Ismāʿīl b. ʿUmar b. Kat͟hīr, in EI², iii, 817–8.
———, Ibn Ḳayyim al-D̲jawziyya, S̲hams al-Dīn Abū Bakr Muḥammad b. Abī Bakr al-Zarʿī, in EI², iii, 821–2.
Mālik, Ibn Anas, *al-Muwaṭṭaʾ*, ed. M.F. ʿAbd al-Bāqī, 2 vols., Beirut 1985.
Motzki, H., Muṣannaf of ʿAbd al-Razzāq al-Sanʿānī as a source of authentic *aḥādīth* of the first century A.H., in JNES 50 (1991), 1–21.
———, *The origins of Islamic jurisprudence: Meccan fiqh before the classical schools*, Leiden, Boston MA and Cologne 2002.
al-Mundhirī, ʿAbd al-ʿAẓīm, *al-Targhīb wa-l-tarhīb*, ed. A. al-Karmī, Amman n.d.
Muslim, Ibn al-Ḥajjāj, *Ṣaḥīḥ Muslim bi-sharḥ al-Nawawī*, 18 vols., Cairo 1994.
al-Nasāʾī, Aḥmad b. Shuʿayb, *Sunan*, ed. A. Abū Ghudda, 9 vols., Aleppo n.d.
Pedersen, J., Abū Nuʿaym al-Iṣfahānī, Aḥmad b. ʿAbd Allāh b. Isḥāḳ b. Mūsā b. Mihrān al-S̲hāfiʿī, in EI², i, 142–3.
———, The criticism of the Islamic preacher, in WI 4 (1953), 215–31.
al-Qāḍī, ʿAbd al-Raḥīm b. Aḥmad, *Daqāʾiq al-akhbār fī dhikr al-janna wa-l-nār*, ed. D.M. Wolf, Leipzig 1872.
al-Qurṭubī, Abū ʿAbdallāh Muḥammad, *al-Jāmiʿ li-aḥkām al-Qurʾān*, ed. A. Iṭfīsh, 24 vols., Cairo 1967.
al-Rāzī, Fakhr al-Dīn, *Tafsīr al-Fakhr al-Rāzī al-mushtahir bi-l-tafsīr al-kabīr wa-mafātīḥ al-ghayb*, ed. Kh. al-Mays, 32 vols., Beirut 1981.
Robson, J., Ḥadīth, in EI², iii, 23–8.
Rustomji, N., *The garden and the fire: Heaven and hell in Islamic culture*, New York 2009.
Schacht, J., *The origins of Muhammadan jurisprudence*, Oxford 1979.
Schoeler, G., Die Frage der schriftlichen oder mündlichen Überlieferung der Wissenschaften im frühen Islam, in *Der Islam* 62 (1985), 201–30.
———, Mündliche Thora und Ḥadīth: Überlieferung, Schreibverbot, Redaktion, in *Der Islam* 66 (1989), 213–51.
———, Schreiben und Veröffentlichen: Zu Verwendung und Funktion der Schrift in den ersten islamischen Jahrhunderten, in *Der Islam* 69 (1992), 1–43.
———, Weiteres zur Frage der schriftlichen oder mündlichen Überlieferung der Wissenschaften im Islam, in *Der Islam* 66 (1989), 38–67.

Shākir, M.H. (trans.), *The Qur'an*, New York 2002.
al-Subkī, Tāj al-Dīn, *Ṭabaqāt al-shafiʿiyya al-kubrā*, ed. M. al-Ṭanāḥī and A. al-Ḥilw, 10 vols., Cairo n.d.
al-Suyūṭī, Jalāl al-Dīn, *al-Durar al-ḥisān fī l-baʿth wa-naʿīm al-jinān*, Egypt 1870.
al-Ṭabarānī, Sulaymān b. Aḥmad, *al-Muʿjam al-kabīr*, ed. Ḥ. al-Salafī, 25 vols., Cairo 1983.
al-Ṭabarī, Abū Jaʿfar Muḥammad, *Tafsīr al-Qur'ān: Jāmiʿ al-bayān ʿan ta'wīl āy al-Qur'ān*, ed. A. al-Turkī, 26 vols., Cairo n.d.
al-Tamīmī, Aḥmad b. ʿAlī, *Musnad Abī Yaʿlī al-Mawṣilī*, ed. Ḥ.S. Asad, 13 vols., Beirut 1989.
al-Ṭayālisī, Abū Dāwūd, *Musnad Abī Dāwūd al-Ṭayālisī*, ed. M. al-Turkī, 4 vols., Cairo 1999.
al-Thaʿlabī, Aḥmad b. Muḥammad, *al-Kashf wa-l-bayān al-maʿrūf bi-tafsīr al-Thaʿlabī*, ed. A. ʿAshūr and N. al-Sāʿidī, 10 vols., Beirut 2002.
al-Tirmidhī, Muḥammad b. ʿĪsā, *al-Jāmiʿ al-ṣaḥiḥ*, ed. A. Shākir, 5 vols., Cairo 1978.
Watt, M., *The formative period of Islamic thought*, Edinburgh 1973.
al-Ziriklī, Khayr al-Dīn, *al-Aʿlām*, 8 vols., Beirut 2002.

CHAPTER 39

"Roads to Paradise" in *Risālat al-ghufrān* of the Arab Thinker al-Maʿarrī

Mahmoud Hegazi

Abū l-ʿAlāʾ al-Maʿarrī (d. 449/1057) was one of the most important figures in the history of Arabic literature.[1] His concept of religion, however, was a matter of dispute in classical Arabic biographical works because of some isolated critical verses. Ibn al-Jawzī (d. 654/1257) wrote in his *Mirʾāt al-zamān* (The mirror of the age) a detailed biography of al-Maʿarrī, in which some skeptical statements and several verses about his religious belief were given.[2] Ibn al-Jawzī's judgment about al-Maʿarrī refers to his uncertain belief, doubts, and some Brahmanical, Manichean, and atheistic points of view, as expressed in a few of his verses. It is noteworthy that al-Maʿarrī's *Risālat al-ghufrān* (The epistle of forgiveness)[3] was not mentioned in that text.[4] In this connection, the Arab historian Ibn al-ʿAdīm (d. 660/1262) wrote his book *al-Inṣāf* (The just treatment).[5] In modern studies such as that of the Egyptian scholar Shawqī Ḍayf an evaluation has been attempted through al-Maʿarrī's poetic works.[6] Moreover, the Egyptian scholar Ḥāmid ʿAbd al-Majīd, who has published many works of al-Maʿarrī, wrote on this topic in his critical edition of *Sharḥ al-mukhtār min Luzūmiyyāt Abī l-ʿAlāʾ* (The explanation of selections from Abū l-ʿAlāʾ's "*Luzūmiyyāt*").[7]

This paper aims to analyze the *Risālat al-ghufrān* in respect of views relevant to the theme "roads to paradise." There are several writings in Arabic-

1 Brockelmann, *Geschichte* i, 295–7; Suppl. i, 449–54.

2 Al-Maʿarrī, *Taʿrīf* is a collective volume containing most biographies of al-Maʿarrī in classical Arabic works. For the text of Ibn al-Jawzī, see 143–81.

3 Al-Maʿarrī, *Risālat al-ghufrān* 21–68.

4 Most biographies of him contain excerpts from his poetry.

5 Ibn al-ʿAdīm, *al-Inṣāf*. See al-Maʿarrī, *Taʿrīf* 384–578.

6 Ḍayf, *al-Baḥth al-adabī* 42–60.

7 ʿAbd al-Majīd in Ibn al-Sayyid al-Baṭalyawsī, *Sharḥ al-mukhtār*. The statements "*man sallama al-amra lil-bārī fa-qad salima*," "*maghfirat Allāhi marjuwwatun*" and "*majjadtu wāḥidan*" (543–4) lead to the conclusion that al-Maʿarrī confessed to the rightness of religion and devotional worship. In this dispute, the text of *Risālat al-ghufrān*, which contained in a literary form discussions and quotations of several persons about roads to paradise, has not been dealt with. For more studies on al-Maʿarrī, see Badran, Vernunft 61–84.

 | DOI 10.1163/9789004333154_040

Islamic culture on the life in the hereafter from various points of view. The importance of the *Risālat al-ghufrān* in this regard lies in its various dialogues in paradise and in hell about creeds and deeds in life, which lead to specific consequences in the hereafter.[8]

The *Risālat al-ghufrān* was written by al-Maʿarrī as a response to the *Risāla* of his friend Ibn al-Qāriḥ. Al-Maʿarrī described it as preaching the acceptance of the Islamic *sharīʿa* and blaming those who deviate from a major principle (*aṣl*), or who diverge widely from a minor aspect of Islamic law (139).[9]

The terms used in the *Risālat al-ghufrān* for forgiveness and mercy are *ghufrān* and *maghfira* (177, 185, 251, 286, 218). These are explained as *al-khalāṣ min al-nār* (178), i.e., freedom from hell. These are closely related to *raḥmat Allāh* (the mercy of God, 219), *raḥmat rabbinā* (our Lord's mercy, 182), or *raḥma dāʾima* (everlasting mercy, 344). Forgiveness is a consequent result of good manners, characterized as *mūjib lil-raḥma* (185, literally "leading to forgiveness"). The main concepts of forgiveness and mercy are explained in *Risālat al-ghufrān* with the support of many Quranic verses: one ought not despair of God's mercy and should be sure that God forgives all wrong deeds. God, however, does not forgive polytheism even though other mistakes/sins may be forgiven. Only *kuffār* (unbelievers) have no hope of God's mercy. In this context the repentance (*tawba*) of any person combined with *shafāʿa* (intercession) leads to forgiveness (203, 228, 447, cf. Q 39:53; 4:116; 7:87).

Many terms are in diametric opposition, such as those pertaining to earthly life on the one hand and the life in the hereafter on the other, such as the days of life (*ayyām al-ḥayāt*) on the one side and eternity (*baqāʾ, al-taʾbīd,* and *al-khulūd,* 185, 186, 296) on the other. Earthly life has many names, the most frequent are *al-dār al-ʿājila* (201, 254, 260, 268, 279, 286, 288, 293, 338), *al-fāniya* (153, 175, 191, 231, 288, 257, 355), *al-khādiʿa* (164, 216, 280, 358), and *al-dhāhiba* (251, 257, 280, 293), meaning that life is short, vanishing, misleading, and fleeting. Several words for this concept are used only once: *al-dār al-mākira, al-gharūra,* and *al-sākhira* (362, 358, 147, 181) to mean the cunning, the deceptive, and the mocker, and also *al-sābiqa, al-khāliya,* and *al-māḍiya* (181, 293, 395) to mean the last and previous. Earthly life is also *dār al-shaqwa* (241), i.e., the home of hardship. These words are used many times in combination with the noun *al-dār* or *al-dunyā,* so *al-dār al-fāniya* or *al-dunyā al-fāniya.*

8 It is not our aim here to select specific items that are parallel to that in other creeds, such as Greek mythology or the Brahmanic religion, rather it is to know al-Maʿarrī's views through a synchronic approach.

9 All numbers given in brackets designate pages of the *Risālat al-ghufrān.*

The term used in the *Risālat al-ghufrān* to express the concept of life in the hereafter is the Quranic *al-ākhira* (216). A distinction is then made between one's fate in paradise or in hell, with regard to several levels or "sub-paradises": *firdaws* (272, 364), *al-janna* (373), *al-jinān* (372), *al-naʿīm* (237), *al-khuld* (296) and *baqāʾ al-taʿabbud* (185), i.e., eternity and eternal abode on the one hand. Other persons, however, are in hell, called *al-nār* and *al-jaḥīm*. The constructions used for the first were *ahāḍīb al-firdaws* (372), *ghīṭān al-janna* (372) and *rimāl al-janna* (372), to mean plateaus of paradise, parks of paradise, and sands of paradise. It was also called *jannat ʿadn* (218) as in the Quran and *al-naʿīm al-dāʾim* (238), i.e., permanent bliss or pleasure. There are, conversely, a few constructions combined with words for hell: *aṭbāq al-jaḥīm* (298), *ahl al-nār* (289, 351, 389), *aṣḥāb al-nār*, and *khazanat al-nār* (352) to mean levels of hell, people in hell, and wards of hell.

A distinction is made between people of this earthly life, *ahl al-ʿājila* (521, 629) on the one hand, and people of the life hereafter, *ahl al-ākhira* (521), on the other. The persons in paradise are named *al-shukhūṣ al-firdawsiyya* (206) or *ahl al-khulūd* (185), meaning paradise persons, people in paradise, or people of eternity. The groups represented in paradise according to *Risālat al-ghufrān* are prophets, their followers, angels, poets, scholars, writers, singers, servants, martyrs, paradise virgins – called *al-ḥūr al-ʿīn* (284), *ḥūr al-jinān* (286) or *ḥūriyyat al-jinān* (288) – and also some supernatural creatures – *jinn* – who confessed to the truth of Islam. In this context, monotheism is the religion of all prophets; the basic religious problem is that of paganism (186). Moreover, people in paradise are described as intelligent and as having no interaction with stupid people (185). No discrimination because of color is attested. The high status of several Afro-Arab poets is elaborated. Also, a black slave woman who served, during her earthly life, in the famous Dār al-ʿIlm ('House of Knowledge') in Baghdad, is placed in paradise as a reward for her help to scribes (287). No discrimination because of gender is attested. Many women, accordingly, have places in paradise, for example the poetess al-Khansāʾ, while her brother Ṣakhr is consigned to hell (308–9). Contrary to various views about blind people in our present world, some of them are able to see in the hereafter, for example, the controversial poet Bashshār b. Burd (d. 168/784) is described as being able to see his own suffering in hell (310). Persons in paradise are described as young and vital in spite of their age at death, as is the case with the pre-Islamic and early Islamic poet Labīd (d. ca 31/661) who was very old when he died (215). There is no use of force – described as a *jāhiliyya* trait – in paradise. No hatred continues in the hereafter, so in the next world there is no rivalry between the philologists Sībawayhi (d. ca 180/796) and al-Kisāʾī (d. 189/805) or between the grammarians al-Mubarrad (d. 286/900) and Thaʿlab (d. 291/904). The contrast between our world and paradise is also aesthetic; so there, ugly women become beautiful (287).

The dialogues, verses and stories illustrate al-Maʿarrī's concept of salvation. The main concept is *al-tuqā*, piety (187). There are stories about the possibility of prophetic *shafāʿa* (intercession) on the day of judgment for some persons because of good deeds. Khadīja (d. 620 CE), the Prophet's first wife, his sons and daughters, his cousin ʿAlī (d. 40/661) and his descendants are placed in paradise. The relevance of good expression, i.e., *al-kalim al-ṭayyib* or *al-kalima al-ṭayyiba* (cf. Q 35:10; 14:24–5), is emphasized in paradise; it is described in the Quran as a good fruitful tree. In this respect, the image of the pre-Islamic sacred tree *dhāt al-anwāṭ* is given (140, 142). Good expression is more important for the salvation of any person than even the character and behavior of his own children.

Al-ṣidq, that is, telling the truth, is a road to paradise and is at the same time most uncommon in earthly life. Faithful sincere people are fortunate in the hereafter. So the poet al-Ḥuṭay'a (d. after 41/661) is in paradise because of his *ṣidq*. Good behavior is a prerequisite for admittance to paradise. This includes the avoidance of unlawful food such as carrion and of unacceptable sexual relations, i.e., adultery (178). The road to paradise is presented in various stories in a way that emphasizes the importance of asceticism, worship, and hard work (287).

Faith in monotheism is, according to al-Maʿarrī, a prerequisite for admittance to paradise. The pre-Islamic poets such as Zuhayr and Labīd are described as having two palaces in paradise because they avoid *bāṭil*, wrong things, and they believe in God and the day of judgment (183, 184, 186). The pre-Islamic poet Nābighat Banī Jaʿda has a place in paradise because he confessed to the creed of the *ḥanīfiyya*, the pre-Islamic Arabian monotheism attributed to the preaching of Abraham (202). Thus, in one of the above-mentioned dialogues, some verses on drinking are said to have been falsely attributed to him (208–9).

The pre-Islamic poet ʿAdī b. Zayd (d. ca. 600 CE) is described as being in paradise, because – as a result of his Christian faith – he praised morality, trust, and sincerity in one of his poems (188). Al-Nābigha al-Dhubyānī, the pre-Islamic poet, believed in monotheism and performed the pilgrimage (*ḥajj*) to Mecca (202). The pre-Islamic poet Aʿshā Qays believed in God, resurrection, and judgment, and intended to be a Muslim (180–1).

To be a poet, however, is not enough for salvation. Tamīm b. Muqbil (d. after 37/657) is reported to have had no excuse for his poetry or *rajaz* (247). His problem is clear in the aim of some of his poems, where the objective was to have access to kings; as such it is a condemned craft (309). The late Umayyad and early ʿAbbasid poet Bashshār b. Burd is assigned a place in hell; he was good in verbal art (*maqāl*) but deficient in creed (*muʿtaqad*). Al-Maʿarrī, as a fellow poet, wished *tawba*, repentance, for him because of some of his fine verses (310).

Contrary to the popular view favoring the pre-Islamic poet and hero ʿAntara (fl. in the sixth century CE), he is assigned his place in hell (322), mainly because he drank and denied the possibility of innovation in poetry (323). Al-Maʿarrī comments that, even so, it is difficult to imagine him in hell (324). The same fate is shared by the pre-Islamic poet and tribal knight ʿAmr b. Kulthūm (fl. in the sixth century CE, 329). The pre-Islamic poet Ṭarafa (fl. most probably in the sixth century CE) has the same infernal fate; he regretted being a poet and wished to be in paradise with the common people.

The Christian Umayyad poet al-Akhṭal (d. 92/710) is described to be also in hell because of his poems (345), his frequent encounters with Yazīd, the son of the Caliph Muʿāwiya (d. 39/680) and also because of his sarcastic verses about some Islamic rituals (350). Yazīd is described as *safīh*, i.e., "a fool." In hell, al-Akhṭal regretted his attitude in life (350).

The early Muslim Ḥassān b. Thābit (d ca. 40/659) was famous as the first poet to praise the Prophet, so his place is in paradise, in spite of his "free" verses (235).

Many philologists are depicted in paradise. Among them are those concerned with the transmission of classical Arabic poetry, the *ruwāt* (206). These are examined about various textual issues, their attribution, and explanation (207–8). To write such a good book as *al-Ḥujja* (The proof, on Quranic readings) was the achievement of Abū ʿAlī al-Fārisī (d. 377/987); for this he is in paradise, despite those few questionable remarks in this otherwise excellent book on morphological items (255). He is praised also because he refrained from bloodshed. Great respect is expressed by Ibn al-Qāriḥ and al-Maʿarrī for those philologists of that time (56, 531).

The contrast between good and bad deeds can be deduced from a poem attributed to a *jinn*. He pretends to commit many sins: he is not ascetic, he scorns religion, has no respect for the great institution of Sunday, he defaces the Pentateuch, destroys crosses, opposes God, praises the rule of the sinful and unwise, promotes religious deviation, brings charges of adultery against chaste women, and tempts priests (300). Devilish actions are illustrated in poems: uncontrolled sexual behavior with and to women, participation in drinking sessions, the encouragement of injustice, the denial of truth, the misleading of wise people and so on (294–5). However, it is emphasized that *tawba* is in all cases possible (296).

To avoid drinking in this world is a cause for salvation. *Khamr* (wine) is available in paradise only for those who have avoided it in life (181) and for other persons before *taḥrīm al-khamr*, i.e., the prohibition of wine in Islam (184). One problem discussed in *Risālat al-ghufrān* is that of the different names for drinks, such as *qahwa* (here: wine), *nabīdh* (an intoxicating drink, wine), and *ṭilāʾ* (grape syrup, 512, 556).

Al-Maʿarrī's refusal and condemnation of drinking is attested also in various non-Muslim creeds. The Indians, for example, do not accept a king who drinks (555). The use of the word *khamr* and similar words is differentiated with regard to their usage in life or the hereafter, to express two distinct concepts (142–53). It is precisely the "honey of paradise": *ʿasal al-janna* (166) and *ʿasal al-jinān* (164), which is different from the *khamr* of earthly life.

Ethical dangers are described in *Risālat al-ghufrān*: hypocrisy (381–2), committing serious mistakes in writing and orthography (412), and pretending religious affiliation without belief (420).

Zanādiqa (freethinkers, apostates, also dualists) and atheists (*mulḥidūn*) invent doubts and are fond of criticizing the mission of prophets (30, 434), they pretend to know the future (450–1), pretend to have special spiritual power (452–3), believe in *tanāsukh*, the transmigration of the soul from one creature to another (458–9), believe in incarnation as some Sufis pretend (454–5), and exaggerate in their praise of Ismaʿili *imāms* (461).

The second part of *Risālat al-ghufrān* is a literary response to the epistle of Ibn al-Qāriḥ. Both he and the author, it is pointed out, have significant things in common, such as attitudes toward some specific persons and creeds. The problem of politically motivated groups hiding behind religious slogans or nomenclature is discussed in a large number of cases. Al-Manṣūr al-Ṣanādīqī's preaching in the third/ninth century in Yemen encouraged uneducated people to abandon Islamic rites in order to have free access to sex and drinking (438–9). Some leaders of those groups proclaimed themselves *imāms* and prophets, others gods (439–41).

The materialistic aim of such people is expressed through the words *mutakassib bi-l-tadayyun* (442), i.e., profiting through pretended religiosity. They aim at *jibāyat al-māl*, i.e., collecting money through tricks and deceit (442), and they attempt to rule and to mislead. In this context al-Maʿarrī offers some stories about the Ismaʿili group of the Qarmatians in al-Aḥsāʾ (442–3).

The importance of peace is stressed by reference to the poem of the pre-Islamic Zuhayr who praises the two men who put an end to tribal wars (388).

The ethical aspect is illustrated in several verses with examples: one should have a testament with God (389), not insult any Muslim (389), and not give any false statement (389).

In this respect, it is noteworthy that the concept and terms of violence, aggression, and war do not exist in *Risālat al-ghufrān*; in fact they do not figure in the roads to paradise. Most of the people in paradise were *aṣḥāb qalam*, men of letters and scholarship, and not *aṣḥāb khayl*, men of horses – i.e., soldiers (195).

Al-Maʿarrī's view of life and people is rather pessimistic (477). Every individual who concentrates on the affairs of our world regrets it later on (491). Salvation is possible through *tawba* (508). Faith and spirituality are for God and not for people (516). Al-Maʿarrī's point of view recognizes that religiosity in general is a human instinct, but reason can decide (464). Theoretical knowledge is not an end, but deeds in life situations are the most important (464).

The importance of the *Risālat al-ghufrān* lies – as far as our topic is concerned – in dealing with the roads to paradise. Other authors have a different approach. For example, in Ibn Shuhayd's (d. 426/1035) *al-Tawābiʿ wa-l-zawābiʿ* (The familiar spirits and demons) poems are cited, but no discussion on salvation is offered. Like al-Maʿarrī's *al-ghufrān*, Ibn al-Qāriḥ's *Risāla* also emphasizes that real *adab* is *adab al-nafs*, i.e., the training of the soul/self, not *adab al-dars*, i.e., the rules of book learning (292, 309, 314, 268, 272, 267, 410). Both works were written as moral reactions to events, conspiracies, politically motivated groups, and other creeds. They share, therefore, similar themes and concerns. Both are against hypocrisy (24, 515), *zanādiqa* (30, 428), atheists (30, 428), the Qarmatians (34, 442) and the mystic al-Ḥallāj who died in 309/922 (36, 452). Moreover, both refer to famous poets and freethinkers such as al-Mutanabbī (28, 29, 414, 424), al-Walīd b. Yazīd (32, 443), Ibn al-Rāwandī (38, 467), al-Shalmaghānī (38, 463), Ibn al-Rūmī (40, 476), and Abū Tammām (41, 483). Both have great respect for philologists (169–74). The problem of concepts, terms, and views of *khamr* is discussed in both works (52, 142, 555, 558). The main difference between the components of these works concerns Ismaʿilis, who are criticized only in *Risālat al-ghufrān* by the poet al-Ḥasan b. Hāniʾ (461). It was not proper for Ibn al-Qāriḥ, who was in close relation with the Ismaʿili rulers, to pen such a critique (58, see also 21).

The interest of al-Maʿarrī's contribution to Arabic and Islamic eschatological thought lies in his citations of a large amount of poetry and other material in a new narrative form; he frankly describes people mentioned partly in paradise and partly in hell. A textual comparison with books of Islamic theology, such as those of famous scholars such as al-Ashʿarī (d. 324/935–6) and al-Ghazālī (d. 505/1111), reveals a significant difference.[10] They concentrate on death, suffering, the burial, the tomb, the resurrection, and judgment. They mainly cite religious texts and not poetry as such. They contain statements, but no dia-

10 Books of Muslim theologians consulted include al-Ghazālī, *Iḥyāʾ ʿulūm al-dīn*; as well as al-Ashʿarī's books, *al-Lumaʿ*; *al-Ibāna*; and *Māqālāt al-islāmiyyīn*.

logues similar to that in al-Maʿarrī's *Risālat al-ghufrān*, which is thus significant to our general theme in aim, content, and literary form.

Bibliography

al-Ashʿarī, Abū l-Ḥasan ʿAlī b. Ismāʿīl, *al-Ibāna ʿan uṣūl al-diyāna*, Beirut 1397/1979.

———, *Kitāb al-Lumaʿ fī l-radd ʿalā ahl al-zaygh wa-l-bidaʿ*, Beirut 1952.

———, *Kitāb Maqālāt al-islāmiyyīn wa-khtilāf al-muṣallīn*, ed. H. Ritter, Istanbul 1929.

Badran, M.A., ... denn die Vernunft ist ein Prophet: Zweifel bei Abū l-Aʿlāʾ al-Maʿarrī, in F. Niewöhner and O. Pluta (eds.), *Atheismus im Mittelalter und in der Renaissance*, Wiesbaden 1999, 61–84.

al-Baṭalyawsī, ʿAbdallāh Ibn al-Sayyid, *Sharḥ al-mukhtār min Luzūmiyyāt Abī l-ʿAlāʾ*, ed. Ḥ. ʿAbd al-Majīd, Cairo 1998.

Brockelmann, C., *Geschichte der arabischen Litteratur*, Leiden 1943.

Ḍayf, S., *al-Baḥth al-adabī*, Cairo 1979.

al-Ghazālī, Abū Ḥamīd, *Kitāb Iḥyāʾ ʿulūm al-dīn*, 4 pts. in 2 vols., Cairo 1306/1888.

Ibn al-ʿAdīm, ʿUmar, *Kitāb al-Inṣāf wa-l-taḥarrī fī dafʿ al-ẓulm wa-l-tajarrī ʿan Abī l-ʿAlāʾ al-Maʿarrī*, ed. ʿA. Ḥarfūsh, Damascus 2007.

al-Maʿarrī, Abū l-ʿAlāʾ, *Risālāt al-ghufrān*, ed. A. ʿAbd al-Raḥmān, Cairo 1997.

———, *Taʿrīf al-qudamāʾ bi-Abī l-ʿAlāʾ*, ed. M. Saqqā and T. Ḥusayn, Cairo 1944.

CHAPTER 40

Muslim Eschatology and the Ascension of the Prophet Muḥammad: Describing Paradise in *Miʿrāj* Traditions and Literature

Roberto Tottoli

Paradise and hell on the one hand and the ascension (*miʿrāj*)[1] of the Prophet Muḥammad on the other are two main chapters of Muslim belief and major subjects of many traditions. Along with these traditions, both general topics gave rise to two distinct literary genres over the centuries and throughout Muslim cultures. This is not surprising given the relevance and prominence of eschatological themes in the Quran and the importance of the experience of the night journey and the ascension in the sacred biography of the Prophet.

Even more significant in this regard is the fact that some traditions and literary works combine aspects of these differing topics and make reference to the ascension of the Prophet in eschatological descriptions or, vice versa, insert eschatological hints into *miʿrāj* narratives. In a recent publication I reviewed the significance of the mention of categories of damned people in hell which Muḥammad saw during his ascent to heaven in some of these traditions, and I pointed out how the insertion of these descriptions of the damned emerged and were included or excluded in different versions throughout the literary genre of the *miʿrāj*.[2] The same can also be done with regard to paradise and its descriptions since some *miʿrāj* traditions and narratives state that Muḥammad was not shown only the damned and hell but also made a proper tour of paradise during his ascent. The insertion and use of paradise descriptions into *miʿrāj* narratives and literature, and how and when this happened constitutes the subject of this contribution.

There are a number of issues that arise in addressing this topic. First, I hope to provide more evidence pertaining to the development of the literary genre of the *miʿrāj*, so as to show how the elaboration of motifs and narrative details

---

* My thanks are due to Todd Lawson for reading a first draft of this paper and for his suggestions.

1 Though *miʿrāj* means only ascension/ladder, I use the term throughout the article to indicate both the night journey (*isrāʾ*) and the ascension and to make reference to traditions and literature including both.

2 See Tottoli, Tours of hell.

 | DOI 10.1163/9789004333154_041

burgeoned in the Middle Ages, thus evidencing the significance of the topic and, consequently, of the literature about it. Along with this I wish to give further testimony to the relevance of the *miʿrāj* narratives in the context of the eschatological traditions and narratives and to see how these narratives preserved and included particulars of some relevance to eschatology as a whole. The results expected are thus twofold. First, to analyze the growing proliferation over time of eschatological material and in particular of traditions on paradise from early *ḥadīth* reports to the late medieval literature (after the fifth/eleventh century). Second, to discuss how the description of paradise as included in the *miʿrāj* literature contributed to the eschatological reports and even added a significant re-elaboration of the details on the description and landscape of paradise.[3]

1 Paradise in Early *Miʿrāj* Traditions

The night journey and the ascension to heaven of the Prophet Muḥammad are the topic of many traditions and substantial literary works. Though a vision of paradise and hell are usually considered a fundamental part of this experience, the situation in Arabic sources is not so clear-cut. As a matter of fact, only a few early traditions on the *miʿrāj* include a description of paradise and hell, and further, only some of them include eschatological details.

The first topic is thus the relation between *miʿrāj* narratives and eschatology. When Quranic exegesis started to connect the ascension of Muḥammad to Q 53:1–18, where there are some verses introducing the lote-tree of the boundary and other elements pointing to the heavens and paradisal abodes, a vision of paradise could be read into the experience of the *miʿrāj* and pave the way for the insertion of eschatological elements into it. This could have somehow constituted a pretext for relating eschatological descriptions of paradise, on one side, and *miʿrāj* narratives on the other. But this was not always the case as is clear if we address the question from two perspectives: first, that of the *miʿrāj* in Muslim literature on paradise as a whole and, second, that of paradise and eschatology in early *miʿrāj* traditions and literature.

Eschatological literature as a whole devotes little space to traditions and statements connected to the night journey or the ascension of the Prophet. For instance, if we take into consideration a number of statements of the Prophet

3 I deal only with verses and reports discussing or even picturing the structure of paradise and its contents and not with what is said about the moral related to paradise when describing people destined to it.

describing visits to paradise or visions of it, we notice that only a few of them make explicit mention of the fact that the visit took place during the ascension to heaven, and not, for instance, during a dream or in another unspecified situation.[4] Further, although an examination of a large body of texts shows that a number of reports explicitly relates the night journey or ascension to heaven to the fact that Muḥammad entered paradise and saw or did something, the number of texts that do so is rather limited.[5] Thus, interestingly enough, it can be safely stated and stressed that eschatological literature displays little interest in these traditions.[6] Also, it seems that though paradise is mentioned in various reports as a place Muḥammad entered, early *ḥadīth*s seem to treat the question with care when coming to a possible connection with his ascension. For this reason eschatological discussions mostly avoid references to the *miʿrāj*, or when they do mention it, it is clear that the question is evoked as a testimony to the real and present existence of paradise. Indeed, it is this problem of the existence of paradise which emerges as the main question and which in turn suggests prudence on the topic of the actual ascension.[7] This is the

4 On these traditions see Rustomji, *The garden and the fire* 36–9.

5 A long list of references, coming also from Shiʿi literature, can be easly traced through the libraries of texts now stored electronically. I limit myself to quoting the main sources, see for instance al-Tirmidhī, *al-Jāmiʿ al-ṣaḥīḥ*, no. 3159: "(Muḥammad and Gabriel) did not abandon the back of Burāq until they saw paradise, hellfire ..." (trans. by Colby, *Constructing an Islamic ascension narrative* 130); al-Bayhaqī, *Kitāb al-Baʿth wa-l-nushūr* 112, nos. 118 and 146, no. 188. On the topic more generally and from the literature I have taken into consideration, see also Ibn Māja, *Sunan* ii, 812, no. 2431; al-Qurṭubī, *Kitāb al-Tadhkira* 960; al-Ṭabarānī, *al-Muʿjam al-awsaṭ* vii, 16; al-Muttaqī l-Hindī, *Kanz al-ʿummāl* vi, 210, no. 15374; al-Suyūṭī, *al-Budūr al-sāfira* 397: "during the *miʿrāj* Muḥammad saw on the gate of paradise ..." and 438: "during the *miʿrāj* he entered paradise ..."; Abū Nuʿ aym, *Ṣifat al-janna* i, 168, no. 151; cf. also al-Ṭabarānī, *al-Muʿjam al-kabīr* xxii, 137. There are many more examples. For instance, a version of the report about the castle seen by Muḥammad and destined for ʿUmar is introduced by the statement that Muḥammad saw it during the *miʿrāj*, see al-Ṭabarī, *Jāmiʿ al-bayān* xx, 153. Other reports connect the visit to other episodes: him hearing Bilāl or on the night Muḥammad entered paradise, he ate its fruits and drank its water etc., see Ibn ʿAsākir, *Taʾrīkh madīnat Dimashq* 35, 40.

6 See, for instance, Ibn Abī l-Dunyā's *Ṣifat al-janna* 103, no. 341, where the short description of a vision of paradise at the end of a long *miʿrāj* narrative is mentioned with the *isnād*, but with no mention of the ascension or where this vision took place. There is also an explicit tradition, not included in canonical traditions and mostly excluded by eschatological tracts, in which the Prophet simply states that the night of the night journey he saw paradise and hell in heaven, see Ibn Rajab, *al-Takhwīf min al-nār* 68.

7 Ibn Qayyim al-Jawziyya, *Ḥādī l-arwāḥ* 18 and all of the chapter on the topic: 18–25; see also Ibn Kathīr, *Nihāya* 448, 450, and above all 520, in a chapter dedicated to *wujūd al-janna*.

procedure, for instance, in works such as those of al-Qurṭubī (d. 671/1272) or ʿAbd al-Raḥīm al-Qaḍī (fl. sixth/twelfth century) which include no more than a couple of references when dealing with eschatological details of things that happened to – or were seen by – the Prophet during his night journey or his ascension.[8]

If, however, we take into consideration the traditions of the night journey and the ascension and thus include early long and short reports about it, the situation appears a bit more complex. If only the so-called canonical collections of *ḥadīth*s or works mostly relying upon these materials are taken into consideration, it can be firmly stated that the majority of the reports included in these works does not mention eschatological abodes and limits the question to the mention of the lote-tree of the boundary or some other supposedly paradisal elements but does not explicitly address paradise as such. References to eschatology and to paradise in particular in reports about the *miʿrāj* of Muḥammad are few and of little relevance to the details that are mentioned. In relation to hell and the description of the damned we have already discussed the question and suggested that for some reason the inclusion of this topic was a point at issue and a sensitive question to be touched in subsequent reports and later longer literary versions in connection with the obvious moral questions indicated by the categories of sinners mentioned and included.[9]

The case of paradise, instead, appears more problematic and elusive. What is more significant, to begin with, is that only one of the long sayings of Muḥammad included in al-Bukhārī and Muslim's works mentions anything at all about this event, and it only adds a few words stating clearly that Muḥammad was made to enter paradise. From Ibn Shihāb al-Zuhrī (d. 124/742) through Anas b. Mālik (d. most probably 91–3/709–11), the report tells us that after meeting the various prophets in the seven heavens, and after visiting the lote-tree of the boundary, we learn that the Prophet stated: "Finally I was led into paradise, there were pearly cupolas and its earth was musk" and nothing more.[10] Though short, at the end, and isolated, since most of the other reports

---

8 See for instance al-Qurṭubī, who introduces an eschatological tradition with no mention of paradise and states that it is "in the *ḥadīth al-miʿrāj*" (*Kitāb al-Tadhkira* 935, and cf. 960 quoting Ibn Māja above and ʿAbd al-Raḥīm al-Qaḍī, *Daqāʾiq al-akhbār* 76: on the night of the night journey he "was shown all the paradises" (*jamīʿ al-jinān*)).

9 Tottoli, Tours of hell.

10 Al-Bukhārī, *Ṣaḥīḥ* i, 116, no. 349; Muslim, *Ṣaḥīḥ* i, 149, no. 263; Ibn Ḥanbal, *Musnad* iv, 144; Ibn Ḥibbān, *Ṣaḥīḥ* ix, 249, no. 7363; al-Isfarāyīnī, *Musnad* 120; Ibn al-ʿArabī, *Aḥkām al-Qurʾān* iii, 180; Ibn Kathīr, *Tafsīr* iii, 11; Ibn ʿAsākir, *Taʾrīkh madīnat Dimashq* iii, 491, 492; al-Muttaqī l-Hindī, *Kanz al-ʿummāl* xi, 387, no. 31839; al-Suyūṭī, *al-Durr al-manthūr* v, 195; see the discussion in Juynboll, *Encyclopedia* 692. Many other sources could be added,

do not include this, it is indeed a relevant sentence, pointing to the *imaginaire* we discuss later on in connection with paradise. It is not much when compared to the lists of sinners and the damned included in early reports, nor to later extensive tours of paradise, but it constitutes definite evidence that according to some early narratives on the *miʿrāj* a visit to paradise was included. Of course, along with this, there are also, in the *ḥadīth* literature, some other short reports, mentioned above, where a vision of paradise or something in it is connected to the night journey or the ascension. But these, as we have seen above, are relatively few in the corpus of eschatological literature and of less significance with regard to the history of the literature on the night journey and ascension where the early long *ḥadīth* reports are more important.

Of further significance in this connection is that of other early works that also attest to the circulation of narratives mentioning paradise and which ultimately did not find, apart from the one just discussed, their way into *ḥadīth* collections. The example of Ibn Saʿd (d. 230/845) and his *Kitāb al-Ṭabaqāt* is significant in this regard. He introduces the paragraph on the topic stating that the Prophet "used to ask his Lord to show him paradise and hell" followed by a pair of traditions with their *isnāds*.[11] In the same way, some of early works of Muslim literature, though not properly considered *ḥadīth* collections, are nonetheless equally important; these include, for instance, the biography of the Prophet by Ibn Hishām (d. 218/833) and early Quranic commentaries. Ibn Hishām includes a long report according to which the Prophet stated that Gabriel made him enter paradise where he saw a servant girl awaiting and destined for Zayd b. Ḥāritha. This detail is recalled also in eschatological reports and it constitutes the only reference to what Muḥammad saw in paradise according to the *Sīra*.[12] A similar situation also emerges in early commentaries of the Quran, for instance those which we have already discussed in relation to the description of sinners and punishments, which also include a vision or a visit to paradise and thus display a general interest in eschatological elements.[13]

---

for instance the works on the life of Muḥammad, such as those of Ibn Sayyid al-Nās or al-Ḥalabī, where they deal with the *miʿrāj* of the Prophet.

11 Ibn Saʿd, *Kitāb al-Ṭabaqāt al-kubrā* i, 213; on the relevance of this passage, see also Colby, *Narrating Muḥammad's night journey* 58.

12 Ibn Hishām, *al-Sīra al-nabawiyya* i, 272; see on this Colby, *Narrating Muḥammad's night journey* 56; and for other traditions including this motif see Colby, *Constructing an Islamic ascension narrative* 194, 212.

13 It is not necessary here to discuss all these sources at length. See the sources mentioned in Tottoli, Tours of hell; and the commentaries, for instance, by Muqātil and al-Qummī.

This evidence shows that in early Islam along with the reports quoted in *ḥadīth* collections, most of which do not include any hint of the eschatological abodes, some other reports that do mention a visit to paradise circulated and found their way into major literary works. The reasons for this situation are probably related to a general, fundamental conception of the experience of the Prophet which was slightly different from that of critics and collectors of the sayings of the Prophet. On the one hand, the visits to hell and paradise gave the story the outline of an apocalypse according to Near Eastern religious concepts and expectations, thus introducing the Prophet Muḥammad to a well-known genre of religious narratives in which the vision of hell and paradise was a fundamental element in such an experience or story. On the other hand, Muslim scholars of traditions for some reason had difficulty with this story, difficulties that may have been connected to theological questions which were likewise probably related to intramural Muslim debates, such as the question of the actual existence of paradise and also questions related to the problem of the vision of God. In this context, the exclusion of *miʿrāj* versions that included eschatology was also to avoid directly addressing certain sensitive issues in Muslim theological debates and, more indirectly, to take, at the same time, a position in these debates.

Later authors who collected these *ḥadīth* reports on the topic show, though sometimes with slightly differing attitudes, how this body of literature – or at least those traditions deemed to belong to this genre – displays a general reluctance to mention paradise and hell as a feature of Muḥammad's ascension. If we take into consideration the example of three long collections of *ḥadīth* reports on the *miʿrāj*, such as those found in the Quranic commentary of al-Ṭabarī (d. 310/923), the history of Damascus of Ibn ʿAsākir (d. 571/1175), and the work on the signs of the prophecy by al-Bayhaqī (d. 458/1066), we notice that no useful details on the structure of paradise can be found and that in general the shorter reports relating visions of paradise with this episode of Muḥammad's life are not addressed. All of them quote the *ḥadīth* with the brief mention of paradise from Ibn Shihāb mentioned above; it constitutes the major evidence for the question of the visit to paradise during the *miʿrāj*.[14] Other hints are also brief, such as one in which Adam is described as being on the right of the gate of paradise and laughing when looking at it, or simple statements to the effect that Muḥammad also entered paradise, but these statements give no more detail.[15] Something more can be found in a later

14 Al-Bayhaqī, *Dalāʾil al-nubuwwa* ii, 382; Ibn ʿAsākir, *Taʾrīkh madīnat Dimashq* iii, 491, 493.

15 Al-Ṭabarī, *Jāmiʿ al-bayān* xvi, 13, 20; Ibn ʿAsākir, *Taʾrīkh madīnat Dimashq* iii, 505; al-Bayhaqī, *Dalāʾil al-nubuwwa* ii, 371, 401.

commentary such as that of al-Suyūṭī (d. 911/1505), who included more *miʿrāj* reports mentioning paradise. Along with the usual quotation of the *ḥadīth* going back to Ibn Shihāb al-Zuhrī, we find mention of the story of Adam, a pair of other references, and a final section in which some of the shorter visions are collected.[16] Further, in al-Suyūṭī and also in some other sources, we find a version of the report going back to Abū Saʿīd al-Khudrī (d. ca. 74/693) that contains the description of the damned and which mentions that Muḥammad entered paradise.[17]

This detail is significant: it verifies that the version typified by the inclusion of the eschatological details on hell and the damned also includes mention of paradise. But along with this, it shows that the simple mention of paradise was deemed enough in the wide context of the long *miʿrāj* reports. It means that according to these few versions Muḥammad also entered and visited paradise but no detail is given. But that reports including it and also including and displaying longer treatments of the motif of the tour of paradise existed quite early is attested to by Ibn Saʿd, Ibn Hishām, and the well known long tradition quoted by al-Suyūṭī in his *al-Laʾālī l-maṣnūʿa fī l-aḥādīth al-mawḍūʿa* (The artificial pearls on the fabricated *ḥadīth*s).[18] We thus understand that for some reason paradise as a place that exists and was seen by Muḥammad during the historical experience of the night journey and the ascension was a controversial theme. And above all there was no space for reports insisting on this description that involved a long visit and a visualization of the eternal abode. The writers of canonical collections preferred to avoid the question as much as possible, but the circulation of other reports including this motif prompted some versions to include at least a brief mention of a visit to paradise.

16 Al-Suyūṭī, *al-Durr al-manthūr* v, 189, 190, 195 (Ibn Shihāb), 200 (the voice of paradise), 206, 214, 218–89 (shorter visions).

17 Al-Suyūṭī, *al-Durr al-manthūr* v, 197; see also al-Bayhaqī, *Dalāʾil al-nubuwwa* ii, 394.

18 Al-Suyūṭī, *al-Laʾālī l-maṣnūʿa* i, 62–74. This tradition was first noted by M. Asín Palacios (*La escatologia musulmana* 23–30) and was recently discussed further. For its relevance to the evolution of the tour of paradise in *miʿrāj* traditions and literature, see Colby, *Constructing an Islamic ascension narrative* 167. On paradise see 73–4, where there is a long description of what Muḥammad saw in paradise, thus attesting that a *ḥadīth* or at least a narrative in *ḥadīth* style had a comprehensive section on this. What is more relevant is that the details of this long description are all taken from eschatological short *ḥadīth*s on castles, mansions, tents, and trees of paradise. That is, it is nothing new but it is evidence of how details scattered in sound eschatological sayings of the Prophet could constitute a problem for authors of works on *ḥadīth* or *ḥadīth*-oriented literature, when these details are inserted in the long narratives on the *miʿrāj* of the Prophet Muḥammad.

2 Elements for a Description of Paradise from the Quran and *ḥadīth*s

What early *miʿrāj* narratives could not include – i.e., a description of paradise giving a perception of its architecture and permitting a proper visit from Muḥammad – should be first of all sought in the Quran and eschatological literature as a whole, where a lot of space is dedicated to the paradise that awaits Muslims. It is indeed necessary to examine these sources and note what emerged along with early *miʿrāj* narratives and thus determine if *miʿrāj* narratives could have known of other contemporary reports useful for introducing a visit to paradise in the experience of the Prophet.

The question of the description of paradise that emerges from early Muslim traditions has been recently dealt with by Nerina Rustomji in her monograph on paradise and hell. She speaks of an architecture of paradise originating from the literature, and I also touch on this briefly below. There the main feature is the display of the various elements mentioned in the traditions, where the most relevant particulars are gates, mansions, and layers of paradise along with major physical elements such as rivers, trees, and so on. Muslim *ḥadīth*-oriented[19] literature thus contains a description or even a real topography, since "by following the progression from throne to rivers, readers would be able to create a map of the garden."[20] Literature of traditions on paradise, as Rustomji rightly asserts in her work, in fact introduces a series of motifs related to the objects mentioned in connection to paradise according to the different purposes of the various texts. In some cases it is a chronological listing of them so as to deal with them in the order given by the sequence of eschatological times, some others are actual tours of paradise.[21] What Rustomji asserts is indeed the significant question for our topic and the question that we try to answer: can motifs and scattered elements in single units of the early traditions and then the later works that collect them prompt a proper tour of paradise including an idea of its architecture?

2.1 *The Quran*

Let us start from the beginning, the Quran. Given the centrality of the eschatological themes in the holy text, many indications and suggestions relating to an architecture of paradise can be found, though, according to Quranic style, they

19 With "*ḥadīth*-oriented" I mean literature that relies mainly on *ḥadīth*s (sayings of the Prophet), but also includes reports and statements going back to Companions and Successors, and literature constructed mainly from their literal quotations.

20 Rustomji, *The garden and fire* 115–7, in part. quotation from 117.

21 Ibid., 106–7.

are not organized in a coherent picture. Notwithstanding this, we learn from it that the term most often used to mention paradise is *janna* meaning "garden" and it occurs more than eighty times. This is no doubt a first and fundamental indication inasmuch as it defines paradise first of all as a place with, for example, trees and that which is "naturally" found in a garden. A few passages among the many specify something of special relevance to our discussion: the Quranic paradise has gates and gatekeepers (Q 39:50, 73; cf. 13:23 one gate), and there is a mention of two (Q 34:15; 55:46, 62) or more gardens (*jannāt*), with the plural term occurring over forty times. Some passages name the people destined for paradise and state that there will be "mid thornless lote-trees, serried acacias, and spreading shade and outpoured waters" (Q 56:28–31). One specific tree is indeed mentioned, though context and contents of the verses are not completely clear. It is the lote-tree of the boundary (Q 53:14–5), a mysterious tree that apparently demarcates the boundary of the heavenly abode. Shades and fountains appear together in another verse (Q 77:41) to indicate where godfearing people will dwell. In fact, along with trees, various bodies, and "modes" of water (and whatever is connected to this), another major feature appears in the Quranic description of paradise: various fountains and springs which in some cases are even given specific names in the text (see Q 76:18; 83:27; 108:1). Rivers in paradise are also often mentioned and evocated as one of the major rewards awaiting those destined for it. The most relevant passage in this regard is that which mentions rivers of water, milk, wine, and rivers of honey (Q 47:15).[22] In this connection, many other frequent passages simply mention a garden or gardens underneath which rivers flow (Q 2:25, passim, more than thirty times).

The Quranic picture of paradise thus has both clear and scattered elements, and this prompts subsequent exegetical elaboration. According to the contents of the holy text only, paradise is a garden or gardens, and as such it contains a profusion of trees with sheltering shade and above all lasting waters such as flowing springs and rivers as the reward for believers. The mention of gates suggests that it is also somehow enclosed and protected, but no details of its dimensions, the nature of the enclosure or other more specific elements are given. Further, other names such as *firdaws*, *ʿadn*, or expressions denoting paradise are of less importance in this regard, since they bear no further information on the true nature of paradise, though later exegetical literature

22 See on this Tottoli, Due fiumi 1225–8.

sometimes interprets these somewhat obscure Quranic designations to distinguish various paradises from others.[23]

2.2 *The* Ḥadīth *Literature*

With regard to the picture presented by the sayings of Muḥammad, the main data reveals that it is not typologically different than that of the Quran, since it follows the Quranic line of thought strictly, though it adds bountiful details and images. Though this is not the place to discuss at length *ḥadīth* reports about paradise, it is necessary to provide some information. The most important feature, as already stated, is that *ḥadīth* literature as a whole works like an expansion of the Quranic data, strictly following the Quranic parallel between paradise and a garden. Thus, the mention of paradise in the Quran, or paradises through the use of the singular, dual, and plural (*janna, jannatān, jannāt*), along with the other names and expressions such as *firdaws* and *ʿadn* became the key point in the description of the gardens of paradise.[24] A saying going back to the Prophet through Abū Mūsā l-Ashʿarī states, for instance, that paradise comprises two silver gardens and two golden gardens wherein everything is made of silver or gold.[25] According to some versions, these four gardens/paradises are those of *firdaws*.[26] *Firdaws* appears in one other significant report, where it is affirmed that it is the navel (*surra*) of the paradise,[27] along with other reports that stress its position among all the paradises.[28]

Ḥadīth reports take Quranic data and add some elements that align with them in small narratives. One major element already explicitly mentioned in the Quran is the gates (*bāb*, pl. *abwāb*), thus recalling paradise as an enclosed space with few access points. *Ḥadīth* reports insist on this and also state that

---

23 On all of them see Kinberg, Paradise 12–5. About the Quran and later exegetical and traditional additions, see also El-Ṣaleḥ, *La vie future* 15–8, 29–43; Rustomji, *The garden and the fire* 63–76, 83–97.

24 See for example, Ibn Ḥibbān, *Ṣaḥīḥ* ix, 242, no. 7348, from Umm Ḥāritha.

25 Ibn Ḥanbal, *Musnad* vii, 162, no. 19702; Ibn Ḥibbān, *Ṣaḥīḥ* ix, 240, no. 7343; al-Baghawī, *Sharḥ al-sunna* vii, 541, no. 4276; Ibn Abī ʿĀṣim al-Shaybānī, *al-Sunna* i, 420; al-Tirmidhī, *al-Jāmiʿ al-ṣaḥīḥ* iv, 674, no. 2528. See on this tradition Juynboll, *Encyclopedia* 20.

26 Ibn Abī Shayba, *al-Muṣannaf* viii, 90; al-Ṭayālisī, *Musnad*, 73, no. 529; al-Dārimī, *Sunan* ii, 790, no. 2718; al-Haythamī, *Majmaʿ* x, 397–8; al-Thaʿlabī, *al-Kashf wa-l-bayān* vi, 202.

27 Hannād b. al-Sarī, *Kitāb al-Zuhd* i, 67, no. 49, Mujāhid, *Tafsīr* i, 382; al-Thaʿlabī, *al-Kashf wa-l-bayān* vi, 202, where among the various interpretations it is also stated that *firdaws* is a garden full of trees.

28 Fakhr al-Dīn al-Rāzī, *Mafātīḥ al-ghayb* xxi, 149; cf. Yaḥyā b. Sallām, *Tafsīr* i, 211: it is a mountain in paradise from where the rivers of paradise originate.

they are eight;[29] or, they mention a gate of paradise or one or more specific gates destined for specific pious believers, while others add other details.[30] Additional information on the nature of paradise as a space and a place can be argued by collating and juxtaposing various reports. In a report in which Abū Hurayra is asked about the structure (*binā'*) of paradise, he answers that it is made of one golden brick and one silver brick, with a pavement of perfumed musk with pebbles of pearl and jacinth and the dust of saffron.[31] Some reports are quite significant because they make use of the term *ḥā'iṭ*, a term usually indicating a "wall," a "wall of enclosure," i.e., a walled fence surrounding a garden or an orchard.[32] Walls are also evoked and numbered in other reports that note this detail.

Mention of buildings or similar references to what exists inside these gardens is of great relevance for a reconstruction of its architecture. We come to know that paradise also includes or will include buildings of various kinds. There is, for instance, frequent mention of a castle or castles in paradise, or

---

29 On all this see Ibn Ḥanbal, *Musnad* vi, 132, no. 17368; al-Dārimī, *Sunan* ii, 788–9, no. 2714; al-Ḥākim al-Naysābūrī, *al-Mustadrak ʿalā l-ṣaḥīḥayn* iv, 607; al-Bukhārī, *Ṣaḥīḥ* iv, 427, no. 3257; Ruwaynī, *Musnad* ii, 200, no. 1034; al-Maqdisī, *Kitāb Ṣifat al-janna* 51; al-Bayhaqī, *Shuʿab al-īmān* iii, 296–7, no. 3084: al-Rayyān is the gate for those who fast. Ibn Ḥanbal, *Musnad* vi, 464, no. 18818. The tradition stating that paradise has eight gates while *jahannam* has seven is the most attested one on this point. A further detail is given by al-Suyūṭī, *al-Budūr al-sāfira*, 393: seven gates are closed and one open. There is one version stating that paradise has seven gates, see al-Muttaqī l-Hindī, *Kanz al-ʿummāl* xiv, 452, no. 39220; on seven, eight or even ten gates in Muslim traditions, see the discussion by J.P. Monferrer Sala in ʿAbd al-Malik b. Ḥabīb, *Kitāb Waṣf al-firdaws: La descripción del paraíso* 53, note 57; and cf. also al-Qurṭubī, *Kitāb al-Tadhkira* 957: gates are more than eight. See also C. Lange's contribution to the present publication.

30 Ibn Abī Shayba, *al-Muṣannaf* viii, 81–2; Ibn Ḥibbān, *Ṣaḥīḥ* ix, 241, nos. 7345–6; al-Haythamī, *Majmaʿ* x, 397; dimensions of the gates are discussed by Ibn Kathīr, *Tafsīr* iv, 73–5.

31 Ibn Ḥanbal, *Musnad* iii, 452, no. 9750; Hannād b. al-Sarī, *Kitāb al-Zuhd* i, 106, no. 130; al-Tirmidhī, *al-Jāmiʿ al-ṣaḥīḥ* iv, 672, no. 2526; al-Dārimī, *Sunan* ii, 789, no. 2717; al-Haythamī, *Majmaʿ* x, 396–7; cf. also Ibn Abī Shayba, *al-Muṣannaf* viii, 67; al-Baghawī, *Maṣābīḥ* ii, 372, no. 2298; Ibn Ḥibbān, *Ṣaḥīḥ* ix, 241, no. 7344. According to a report in ʿAbd al-Raḥīm al-Qaḍī, *Daqā'iq al-akhbār* 80, the Prophet saw angels in paradise building castles made of golden and silver bricks.

32 ʿAbd al-Razzāq, *al-Musannaf* xi, 416–7, no. 20875; Ibn al-Mubārak, *Kitāb al-Zuhd*, 428, nos. 251–2; al-Baghawī, *Sharḥ al-sunna* vii, 549, no. 4287; al-Muttaqī l-Hindī, *Kanz al-ʿummāl* xiv, 494, no. 39401; see also al-Bayhaqī, *Kitāb al-Baʿth wa-l-nushūr* 157, no. 214: "*inna Allāh aḥāṭa ḥā'iṭ al-janna ...*"

mention that paradise is indeed a castle itself.[33] These castles are described with many prodigious details and fantastic dimensions.[34] In other instances Muḥammad sees a castle in paradise, but, e.g., it awaits ʿUmar b. al-Khaṭṭāb;[35] the same may be said of other structures destined for other main characters of early Islamic history. Other traditions mention rooms or chambers in paradise (*ghurfa*, pl. *ghuraf*), and also tents. However paradise does not only include buildings and constructions thought to be destined for humans, there are also other elements relating more to its geographical extent. There is mention of a sea or seas in paradise, which are connected to the rivers already mentioned in the Quran, though some reports state that in paradise there are also gulfs or abysses (*qīʿān*), and even ships with golden oars.[36]

Trees play a major role, following the importance accorded to this feature in the Quran itself. The reports on the topic are many; suffice it here to mention the one most frequently affirmed: there is even a tree so huge that a rider can travel under its shade for a hundred years.[37] Along with the Quranic trees such

33 See, for example, Ibn Abī Shayba, *al-Muṣannaf* viii, 79 (there are many golden, silver, jacinth castles, etc., quoted also by al-Suyūṭī, *al-Durr al-manthūr* iv, 238); this is indeed the report discussed by Ibn al-Jawzī, in his *Kitāb al-Mawḍūʿāt* ii, 424; and al-Suyūṭī, *al-Laʾālī l-maṣnūʿa* ii, 376; Ibn Ḥibbān, *Ṣaḥīḥ* ix, 238, no. 7337; and al-Ṭabarānī, *al-Muʿjam al-awsaṭ* vi, 329, no. 6543.

34 Ibn Abī Shayba, *al-Muṣannaf* viii, 80; al-Muttaqī l-Hindī, *Kanz al-ʿummāl* xv, 834, no. 43316; al-Haythamī, *Majmaʿ* x, 420; al-Ṭabarānī, *al-Muʿjam al-awsaṭ* ix, 164, no. 9430; al-Ṭabarī, *Jāmiʿ al-bayān* xiii, 142: here this castle is called *ʿadn* (see also various versions in x, 179, 181–2, commenting on *jannāt ʿadn* in Q 9:72; see in fact al-Thaʿlabī, *al-Kashf wa-l-bayān* v, 68, Ibn Kathīr, *Tafsīr* ii, 789; al-Suyūṭī, *al-Durr al-manthūr* iv, 237), and later on, still commenting on the same Q 13:23, it is stated that *ʿadn* is the name of the town (*madīna*) of paradise, see al-Ṭabarī, *Jāmiʿ al-bayān* xiii, 142.

35 Al-Bukhārī, *Ṣaḥīḥ* iv, 424, no. 3242; Hannād b. al-Sarī, *Kitāb al-Zuhd* i, 104–5 nos. 127–8; Ibn Ḥanbal, *Musnad* ii, 339.

36 Ibn al-Mubārak, *Kitāb al-Zuhd* 431, no. 272.

37 ʿAbd al-Razzāq, *al-Musannaf* xi, 417 nos. 20876–8 (no. 20878 connects the report with the exegesis of Q 56:30, in fact see al-Tirmidhī, *al-Jāmiʿ al-ṣaḥīḥ, tafsīr* of Q 56:30); al-Bukhārī, *Ṣaḥīḥ* iv, 426, nos. 3251–2; Muslim, *Ṣaḥīḥ* iv, 2175–6, nos. 2826–8; Ibn Abī Shayba, *al-Muṣannaf* viii, 71; Ibn Ḥanbal, *Musnad* iii, 370, no. 9254, passim; iv, 220, no. 12071 passim; Hannād b. al-Sarī, *Kitāb al-Zuhd* i, 97, no. 113; al-Dārimī, *Sunan* ii, 795, nos. 2733–4; Ibn Māja, *Sunan* ii, 1450, no. 4335; Ibn Ḥibbān, *Ṣaḥīḥ* ix, 250, no. 7369; al-Ḥumaydī, *al-Musnad* ii, 479, no. 1131; al-Baghawī, *Maṣābīḥ* ii, 370, no. 2284; al-Tirmidhī, *al-Jāmiʿ al-ṣaḥīḥ* iv, 671, nos. 2523–4; cf. also al-Suyūṭī, *Jāmiʿ al-aḥādīth* iii, 12, no. 7637, 14, no. 7644 (different versions); see also al-Haythamī, *Majmaʿ* x, 414. The explanation given by Nuʿaym b. Ḥammād is quite interesting, see Ibn al-Mubārak, *Kitāb al-Zuhd* (*ziyādāt* by Nuʿaym b. Ḥammād) 430, no. 266: it is the *shajarat al-khuld* (Q 20:120, the tree of eternity), i.e., the tree

as the lote-tree of the boundary (Q 53:14) and the mysterious *ṭūbā* (Q 13:29), which are also treated in *ḥadīth* literature, golden date palms are also mentioned. A complete list of the places or geographical details included in this literature would be very long: in paradise in fact there are markets, mountains, hills, and also animals, especially horses.[38]

Thus, strictly following the Quran, *ḥadīth* literature adds elements to the description of paradise, but we have no comprehensive, lengthy description of the nature of paradise. To be sure, all the elements serve the purpose of conveying a sense of the place,[39] but this is achieved by detailing the prodigious dimensions of its various features, mostly Quranic, rather than by describing the organic architecture of a place awaiting faithful inhabitants. Traditional literature based upon *ḥadīth* reports cannot but try to give a list of Quranic verses and single sayings of the Prophet, rich in detail but not really yet a proper organic description of what is in paradise and how it appears. Early Muslim beliefs and traditions did not build a proper description of the abode of paradise. Such a description emerges neither from the Quran nor from the *ḥadīth* and those single reports referred to above, notwithstanding the vast amount of pertinent material attested in this regard.[40]

3 Collecting and Ordering *Ḥadīth*s as a Way of Describing Paradise

There is a way for traditional literature, i.e., literature relying upon the reworking of *ḥadīth*s and *ḥadīth*-oriented material, to mark their specific outlook and thus justify the need for new works: to choose among the existing materials and versions, to include or to exclude and, when needed, to add some words to explain choices. In terms of our topic, to understand the way eschatological works organize their descriptions of paradise by collecting small eschatological units is a way to analyze and describe the literary genre, and thus to observe whether or not the emerging landscape is actually constructed through the literary activity of collecting, collating, and assessing *ḥadīth*s.

---

connected with the creation and fall of Adam and Eve (and cf. another tradition about a tree in paradise: 429–30, no. 263). According to al-Muṭahhar b. Ṭāhir al-Maqdisī, *al-Badʾ wa-l-taʾrīkh* i, 183, this tree is indeed the lote-tree of the boundary.

38 See, for example, al-Tirmidhī, *al-Jāmiʿ al-ṣaḥīḥ* iv, 681, nos. 2543–4. On the topic see the materials collected and discussed by Canova, Animals in Islamic paradise and hell.

39 As stated by al-Azmeh, Rhetoric for the senses 222. A brief summary of this description of paradise is given in Reinhart, The here and the hereafter 16–7.

40 See in fact also El-Ṣaleḥ, *La vie future* 35.

Much eschatological material is quoted in *tafsīr*s but it is obviously scattered among the comments on the various verses relating to paradise described above. Only some of the longest commentaries have long parts of relevance, such as, for instance, the work of al-Ṭabarī, who compiled more than ten reports focused upon *firdaws* mentioned in Q 18:107.[41] But in general, exegetes reproduced the material discussed above and tried to identify the various expressions found in the Quran, such as the meaning of *firdaws*, *jannāt ʿadn*, and others. The case of *ḥadīth* works is different and more interesting, as is assessing how they organize material and how they treat questions related to paradise.

A major concern in this literature is evidently the theological questions connected to paradise.[42] Some of the *ḥadīth* collections of the *muṣannaf* type – i.e., those that organize reports according to topic and divide them into various chapters (usually named *kitāb*, lit., "book") and paragraphs (usually named *bāb*, lit., "chapter") – mention a description of paradise similar to other debated topics, such as the description of hell, the question of temporary punishment for Muslim sinners in hell, the basin (*ḥawḍ*) of the Prophet, or the meaning of the Quranic term *kawthar* (Q 108:1). For this reason, a major author such as al-Bukhārī (d. 256/870) quoted the various sayings on the topic, but did not collect all of them in a specific chapter. In fact he included them in the chapter on the creation of the world, in a short paragraph on "what is reported in description of paradise and that it is created" and later on, in the *Kitāb al-Riqāq*, in another paragraph on the "description of paradise and hell" (*bāb ṣifat al-janna wa-l-nār*)[43] where some of the sayings quoted above are also repeated. A similar intent, but one served by a greater interest in the topic is displayed by Muslim (d. 261/875), whose work is among the so-called canonical collections; he dedicates to the topic a single book including more than eighty reports, though most are devoted to moral questions rather than a physical description of the eternal abode.[44]

These two differing positions well represent the relevance of the topic for the collection of sayings of the Prophet: the question to be dealt with is the characteristics/description (*ṣifa*) of paradise and thus most of the collections must touch the topic, though some dedicate more space to it than others, and others, instead, limit their interest to the simple mention of a few major reports.

---

41 Al-Ṭabarī, *Jāmiʿ al-bayān* xvi, 37–8.

42 On these, along with the perceived conceptions of other religions, see Muṭahhar b. Ṭāhir al-Maqdisī, *al-Badʾ wa-l-taʾrīkh* i, 183–200; and El-Ṣaleḥ, *La vie future* 29–31.

43 Al-Bukhārī, *Ṣaḥīḥ* iv, 423–7; vii, 255–61.

44 Muslim, *Ṣaḥīḥ* iv, 2174–206.

The first type, along with Muslim, is well represented by Ibn Ḥibbān (d. 354/965), who devoted a long chapter to the description of paradise, a chapter that displays a clear organization in the materials included: it begins with reports on its physical description (i.e., on *ṣifat al-janna*), and then addresses moral questions about the inhabitants (*ahl al-janna*) and those who will deserve it.[45] Similarly, Ibn Abī Shayba (d. 235/849) has a specific chapter on paradise (*Kitāb al-Janna*), and al-Tirmidhī (d. 279/892) also has a chapter on the description of paradise (*Kitāb Ṣifat al-janna*), together with some early *zuhd* works that focus on the topic.[46] Among later works, al-Haythamī entitled a chapter the "Book of the people of paradise" (*Kitāb Ahl al-janna*).[47] ʿAbd al-Razzāq (d. 211/827) includes, in apparently no order, a few reports on the topic in a paragraph in his final long general chapter. Among the others, al-Dārimī (d. 255/869) has a short paragraph in the *Kitāb al-Riqāq*, Ibn Māja (d. 273/887) in the *Kitāb al-Zuhd*, and al-Baghawī (d. 516/1122) in several paragraphs in various chapters in his *ḥadīth* collections.[48] Needless to say, apart from these works, there are also works in which these reports are not collected in a specific unit, but are included among other topics. Finally, the state of the question is well exemplified by the way the two major later works on forged *ḥādīth*s by Ibn al-Jawzī (d. 597/1201) and al-Suyūṭī treat the subject. Ibn al-Jawzī highlights the topic by giving it a specific chapter titled *Kitāb Ṣifat al-janna*, while al-Suyūṭī collects some reports in the chapter on resurrection.[49]

From this cursory portrait it is clear that, as might be expected, the major concern of *ḥadīth* works is theological; the attitude toward paradise relates to the relevance alloted to the topic of the actual existence of paradise and its creation, and this is in accordance with the attitude of each author and with the fact that, whatever the position of a given author, there are Quranic verses and sayings of the Prophet deemed trustworthy such that these reports must be included.

---

45 Ibn Ḥibbān, *Ṣaḥīḥ* ix, 238–75. This is made explicit also in al-Muttaqī l-Hindī, *Kanz al-ʿummāl* xiv, which includes a chapter on *ṣifat al-janna* (451–64) and then one on *ahl al-janna* (464–514); on this see also al-Bayhaqī, *Kitāb al-Baʿth wa-l-nushūr* 164f.

46 Ibn Abī Shayba, *al-Muṣannaf* viii, 67–90; al-Tirmidhī, *al-Jāmiʿ al-ṣaḥīḥ* iv, 671–700; see also Hannād b. al-Sarī, *Kitāb al-Zuhd* i, 47–136; Ibn al-Mubārak, *Kitāb al-Zuhd* 424–32 (*Fī ṣifat al-janna*).

47 Al-Haythamī, *Majmaʿ* x, 396–422.

48 ʿAbd al-Razzāq, *al-Musannaf* xi, 413–21; al-Dārimī, *Sunan* ii, 788–97; Ibn Māja, *Sunan* ii, 1447–53; al-Baghawī, *Maṣābīḥ* ii, 370–6; al-Baghawī, *Sharḥ al-sunna* vii, 530–52 (consisting of various paragraphs in the *Kitāb al-Fitan*).

49 Ibn al-Jawzī, *Kitāb al-Mawḍūʿāt* ii, 423–32; al-Suyūṭī, *al-Laʾālī l-maṣnūʿa* ii, 376–80.

Something more can be argued from eschatological literature, i.e., those collections of traditions on paradise or on related topics such as death, or the end of the world. There are indeed some significant points in this regard: first, we must take into consideration the fact that a number of specific works are dedicated to the description of paradise and mostly titled *Ṣifat al-janna* (Characteristic(s) of paradise). A tendency displayed in the early collection activity is evidenced by the monograph of ʿAbd al-Malik b. Ḥabīb (d. 238/853) – it is rich in alternative reports (amounting to a total of 317) – and the narrower work by Ibn Abī l-Dunyā (d. 281/894) who did not organize or divide the materials into those offering a proper description of the physical elements in paradise and those details pertaining to the people living therein.[50] This is the tendency followed, for instance, by Abū Nuʿaym, who includes quite a number of reports (454), but gives canonical and non-canonical reports on the same topics although not in a strict order. And the same is true of the monograph on the subject by Ibn Qayyim al-Jawziyya (d. 751/1350), who makes theological arguments the main focus of a discussion based on quotations and comments on traditions on the main questions related to the description of paradise.[51] The fact that traditions could be ordered in the way we have discussed above is attested by some other works. Ḍiyāʾ al-Dīn al-Maqdisī (d. 643/1245), for instance, collected 212 *ḥadīth*s and organized them in a perfectly perceptible order: first the *bināʾ* (structure) of paradise, starting with gates and stopping with paradise markets, then he proceeded to traditions on the people of paradise. A major eschatological treatment such as the *Nihāya* by Ibn Kathīr (d. 774/1373) organizes the reports in the same way, starting from the gates and then, later on, moving to the traditions dedicated to the food of people in paradise, and coming finally in the long second part to a description of the people of paradise.[52] Though not so strictly organized, this broad outline is also followed by al-Suyūṭī in his lengthy final part on paradise in his eschatological treatise.[53]

Some of these tendencies are also displayed in the major work on eschatological traditions, i.e., the *Tadhkira* by al-Qurṭubī (d. 671/1272), who describes paradise after hell and, like some of the sources quoted above, inserts a paragraph between the two when they are discussed in this order, i.e., a chapter on the last to leave hell and to enter paradise. Though quoting various *ḥadīth* reports to substantiate his argument, the work of al-Qurṭubī displays his major

50 Ibn Ḥabīb, *Kitāb Waṣf al-firdaws*; Ibn Abī l-Dunyā, *Ṣifat al-janna*.

51 Abū Nuʿaym, *Ṣifat al-janna*; Ibn Qayyim al-Jawziyya, *Ḥādī l-arwāḥ*.

52 Ibn Kathīr, *Nihāya* 433–522.

53 Al-Suyūṭī, *al-Budūr al-sāfira* 375–495.

interest as an exegete. The chapter on paradise covers many pages;[54] it begins with the Quranic quotations, in particular with the question of the number of paradises – one, two, or several – according to the Quranic data, before reaching the issue of the *ṣifat al-janna*. The organization is, broadly speaking, common, it displays the distinction between the *ṣifa* and the reports of the benefits that await believers, and then it includes paragraphs on what can be considered more in line with *ahl al-janna*.[55] Though it offers various comments and explanations on the reports, it is evident that al-Qurṭubī follows the Quranic and traditional data to substantiate a description that combines various scattered elements but he does not provide an organized description of how paradise is built. His major concern is to explain the numerous reports and data, giving preference to the exegetical discourse rather than offering a critical discussion of the contents and versions of the traditions.

Many other works on eschatology dedicate chapters and paragraphs to the description of paradise, but they do not change the portrait given thus far. And this picture is no different if we examine other literary genres. Abū l-Shaykh al-Iṣfahānī (d. 396/1006), in his *Kitāb al-ʿAẓama* (The book of the sublime), dedicates a number of pages, including forty-one reports, under the title "mention of [various Quranic] paradises (*jannāt*) and their description." The emphasis here is on the vastness of the paradise "system" in relation to God's creation. This is indeed the topic of the work itself. What is more relevant is the first long report, which can be traced back to Wahb b. Munabbih, that lists the various paradises in a sort of cosmology rich in colorful and stereotyped descriptions.[56] What follows is a collection of *ḥadīth*s, partly from canonical works and partly not.

We can add a few words at the end of the discussion of the way *ḥadīth*-oriented works quote and organize traditions and reports on the architecture of paradise. Only a broad division between the proper description of paradise and the traditions on the people destined for paradise can be seen in later works and thus considered the result of an evolution in the literary genre.

54 Al-Qurṭubī, *Kitāb al-Tadhkira* 929–1053.

55 Al-Qurṭubī (*Kitāb al-Tadhkira*) deals with the first people to enter paradise (974f.), *ḥūrī*s (985f.), food for people there (994f.), wives in paradise, birds and animals therein (997f.). At the end another long paragraph discusses the exegesis of some Quranic verses on the topic. In the part on the description of paradise we find the usual paragraphs on the rivers (938f.), trees (944f.), gates (953f.), grades (960f.), rooms (963f.), castles (968f.) etc.

56 Abū l-Shaykh, *Kitāb al-ʿAẓama* 202–5, no. 575.

4 The Tour of Paradise in Late *Miʿrāj* Literature

Apart from *ḥadīth* and exegetical reports and related traditions, the topic of the night journey and the ascension of the Prophet is touched upon in a number of literary works sufficient to constitute a proper literary genre, one which emerged from and was based on these traditional reports but which added to and treated all the early formative elements differently. These later literary works on the *miʿrāj* add further relevant particulars and reflect a clear tendency to literary creativity, remaking, and enlarging. They represent a collection of numerous works dedicated to the *miʿrāj*, works of varying length and mostly unpublished and in some cases reaching hundreds of pages. These works emerged and spread from the fifth/eleventh century onwards, with the ninth/fifteenth and tenth/sixteenth centuries as particularly productive. A look at the manuscript holdings in the National Library (Dār al-Kutub) in Cairo or in Al-Azhar Library shows, for instance, that hundreds of copies preserve some forty or fifty works on the *miʿrāj*, attesting to the relevance of the theme in this period. Thus far, this literature has not received specific attention by researchers on the topic nor have students of literature paid it much attention, apart from the recent studies by Frederick Colby.[57] It is indeed a significant body of literature, displaying some specific features and attesting to a peculiar evolution in the treatment and discussion of the question of the night journey and ascension and specifically the matter of the ensuing visit to paradise and hell.

I am not going to give a comprehensive description of this literature, but only a survey based upon fifteen works, some published and some other still in manuscript form, ranging from the work by al-Qushayrī (d. 465/1072) to a few unpublished and anonymous late works on the *miʿrāj*. These works are evidence of different attitudes and are all reworkings of the story which likely relies on rich evidence from early *ḥadīth*s and other reports. According to the way authors include and treat the motifs constituting the story some peculiarities of these works and their relation to the preceding traditions and narratives can be ascertained or at least suggested. It is easy to detect a major division between the works considered, one that is quite common in medieval religious literature, namely the division between strictly *ḥadīth*-oriented literature and those works that display a more narrative or even popular character (I use the

57 See above all his dissertation: Colby, *Constructing an Islamic ascension narrative*, where other late medieval literature on the *miʿrāj* is discussed in a part that was not included in his monograph (Colby, *Narrating Muḥammad's Night Journey*). See also S. Günther's contribution to this publication.

word "popular" for the sake of simplicity and with full caution, knowing the manifold problems inherent in the use of such a term).

In *ḥadīth*-oriented literature, we find a variety of attitudes toward the topic of paradise. Some works give space to the motif of the tour of paradise and others do not. These different attitudes attest once more to the problems related to the description of paradise that derives from Muḥammad's ascension, in line with the problems already displayed in early reports, but here, where they appear in larger and more elaborate retellings, the narrative setting gives us further information on the question. Here the mention of paradise is a question of quotation or omission: sometimes reports on this are chosen and inserted, sometimes they are omitted. Whatever the different attitudes of these authors might be, *ḥadīth*-oriented works give less space to paradise.

Most typical of this attitude are a number of works, such as the one by Najm al-Dīn al-Ghayṭī (d. 984/1576), the author of the most widely-diffused work on the topic of the ascension of the Prophet, as attested by the many extant manuscripts. His version of the *miʿrāj* mentions the usual references to paradise or paradisal elements: the gate of paradise (and that of hell) in relation to Adam, the lote-tree of the boundary, the river al-Kawthar. These come just before a short mention of Muḥammad entering paradise and a very short description of what was inside, that which the "eye has not seen, nor ear heard."[58] Here it is remarkable that the structure and disposition of elements are similar to that of the more popular narratives which will be described below, but without physical details. He, in a certain way, absorbed the scheme but not the contents. Though quite short, the indication that Muḥammad entered paradise is a clear attestation that *ḥadīth*-oriented works could not but include explicit mention of the tour of paradise. Along the same lines is the work of Abū l-Khaṭṭāb b. Diḥya (d. 635/1236) which follows strictly whatever the *ḥadīth*s say on the question: paradise was shown to Muḥammad. This is clear in various passages of the work, which does not include any organic narrative describing the tour of paradise, though it obviously accepts that the tour of paradise was an established part of the ascension.[59] Similarly, Zayn al-ʿĀbidīn al-Barzanjī (d. 1103/1691) includes a brief description of paradise in which he provides a few particulars including the mention of the maiden promised to Zayd b. Ḥāritha.[60] There is also Muḥammad b. Yusūf al-Ṣāliḥī al-Shāmī (d. 942/1536)

58 Al-Ghayṭī, *Qiṣṣat al-miʿrāj* 20–2; on his treatment of the topic, see Colby, *Constructing an Islamic ascension narrative* 383.

59 Ibn Diḥya, *al-Ibtihāj fī aḥādīth al-miʿrāj* 23, 43, 49–50, 111, 137, 148–52; on his treatment of the topic, see Colby, *Constructing an Islamic ascension narrative* 266.

60 Al-Barzanjī, *al-Isrāʾ wa-l-miʿrāj* 22.

who dedicated three works to the theme. In his *Khulāṣat al-faḍl al-fāʾiq fī miʿrāj khayr al-khalāʾiq*, the main intent is exegetical and the discussion centers, for instance, on the location of *jannat al-maʿwā*, in which the "heaven paradise' is found, along with a comprehensive analysis of other related terms and questions. Thus the narrative construction of the whole story is not addressed, nor is there mention of the tour of paradise.[61] In this kind of work the exegetical or the *ḥadīth*-oriented contents are strictly related to theological concerns and a general, though implicit, criticism of popular narratives. Abū l-Irshād al-Ujhurī (d. 1066/1656), for instance, who produced another long work on the ascension of Muḥammad, is interested first of all in the identification, description, and explanation of the various details and elements, mainly those which are Quranic, scattered throughout the work and not those restricted to the section on paradise.[62]

Perhaps one exception to this situation is found in the *Kitāb al-Miʿrāj* by al-Qushayrī, which is a collection of *ḥadīth*s followed by a few chapters dedicated to specific topics related to theological and exegetical issues. In one of these al-Qushayrī explicitly states that one of the purposes of the *miʿraj* was to make it possible for God to show Muḥammad paradise and hell with his eyes.[63] Among those works where scant attention is given to the topic, al-Qushayrī appears as the more sensible author. He includes a report of a short tour of paradise in which Muḥammad enters and leaves along with Gabriel, and a longer one that describes paradise as comprising four paradises with its degrees, rivers, eight gates, and other details.[64] Colby defined the long narrative that includes this description as a "revised Ibn Isḥāq version," rightly pointing out its similarity to the report on the question in Ibn Hishām's *Sīra* and underlining that al-Qushayrī's version adds some popular details.[65] With regard to the facts of its description, the version of the tour of paradise mentioned in it is more in line with later popular versions since it includes some details as later developed, though not yet fully elaborated. This attests to al-Qushayrī's striking and perhaps unusual interest in the general question and in the various

61 Al-Shāmī, *Khulāṣat al-faḍl al-fāʾiq*, cf. 118, 172, 178, 183, 184, 266, 284, 343.

62 Al-Ujhurī, *al-Nūr al-wahhāj* 149, 151, 191, 223, 280, 299–304, 315.

63 Al-Qushayrī, *Kitāb al-Miʿrāj* 26, 69, cf. 108.

64 Ibid., 51–3, 61–2.

65 Colby, *Constructing an Islamic ascension narrative* 236–7. This is indeed the same report which al-Samarrai, *The theme of the ascension in mystical writings* 247–8, considers as probably interpolated into the work because of the "contradictions between this and what al-Qushayrī states in another part of the work" (247). And this is mainly because of the "incredible and fanciful description of Heaven and Hell" (248).

details found outside the "canonical" sayings. In fact, though basing his discussion on the *ḥadīth* literature and further introducing those transmitted by Anas b. Mālik as the most sound, he adds some popular narratives.

Instead, what we called above popular retellings are for the most part not strictly *ḥadīth*-oriented narratives, and though they are no doubt based upon the contents of traditional reports they do not simply quote them, rather they rework them in a continuous narrative setting. Later narratives, though displaying differing attitudes and adding versions of the same motifs, share some common features. First of all those mentioning a tour of paradise usually include long treatments of the topic. This body of literature states simply that Muḥammad entered paradise and saw many wondrous things; these things were all seen by the eye of the Prophet. This is one major common point in the later narrations of the *miʿrāj*: the architecture of paradise appears as the Prophet reviews what he saw while proceeding through paradise: prodigies are enhanced and described as something never before seen or never heard of, yet encountered during Muḥammad's procession. That is, they are given in specific, circumscribed spatial dimensions. As a result of this, a set of narrative possibilities emerges to introduce these descriptions.

A key work in this process of enriching and enhancing the narrative stabilization of motifs constituting the *miʿrāj* story is no doubt the differing versions on the *miʿrāj* attributed to the mysterious Abū l-Ḥasan al-Bakrī (fl. sixth/twelfth century?). While the short version of his *Ḥadīth al-miʿrāj* includes only a brief visit to paradise, one which states that Gabriel took Muḥammad to paradise and that he saw there various castles including the one destined for the first four caliphs, the longer version dedicates more space to the topic.[66] Though not as long as those in Ibn ʿAbbās' versions, here we find that Gabriel comes with the Prophet to the gate of paradise and a voice from inside asks who is at the gate. What is peculiar here, especially in relation to the other versions discussed below, is that the voice is not yet identified. In other versions, such as the Ms. Cairo Dār al-Kutub, Taʾrīkh Taymūr 205 (Anonymous, *Qiṣṣat al-miʿrāj*), the voice is simply identified as belonging to the guardian (*khāzin*) of paradise.[67] Someone aswered and opened the gate, then Muḥammad was

66 Al-Bakrī, *Ḥadīth al-miʿrāj* (short version) 177a; al-Bakrī, *Ḥadīth al-miʿrāj* (long version) 88a–89a. On the relevance of al-Bakrī's texts expanding narremes of the story of the ascension, see Colby, *Narrating Muḥammad's night journey* 128.

67 Anonymous, *Qiṣṣat al-miʿrāj*, Ms. Cairo Dār al-Kutub, Taʾrīkh Taymūr 205, fols. 67b–71a on the tour of paradise. In this version Muḥammad enters paradise and first describes its floor, more white than milk, with prodigious particulars. Tents, castles, rooms, and rivers are listed according to what the Prophet sees while entering; and there is a large space to

brought by Gabriel to see castles and other buildings, rivers, and trees in great number.

The same or similar or even expanded details in the motifs included in the tour of paradise are further reworked by the various other sources. One major feature, the fact that the description is given by Muḥammad while traveling through paradise, has been already mentioned. One other useful example of the dynamics at work in the elaboration of the tour of paradise which offers something new can be found in the formulas introducing the description of paradise. While the work by al-Bakrī introduces Muḥammad and Gabriel through the unnamed figure answering and opening the gate, a number of other works identify this anonymous agent as the angel Riḍwān, the custodian of paradise; his is the voice they heard, who opens the gate and then escorts Muḥammad on this tour. The so-called "Modern Standard"[68] version of the *miʿrāj* ascribed to the Prophet's cousin Ibn ʿAbbās (d. ca. 68/687–8) and its related versions include this detail. The longer description of paradise among the versions ascribed to Ibn ʿAbbās is given in the *Miʿrāj al-nabī*. Here Gabriel accompanies Muḥammad to the gate of paradise and calls to Riḍwān who bids them enter and then, following Gabriel's order, takes Muḥammad by the hand and shows him paradise. What follows, then, is a version of the various details giving substance to the prodigious contents of paradise, in line with elements from traditions and other literature: cupolas, gates, eight hundred million castles, *ḥūrīs*, trees, and rivers, all before arriving at the explicit Sunni

---

visit which is further enhanced by a shift in the narration when it is stated that Gabriel brings him [Muḥammad] inside to go around (*yaṭūfu*) paradise. Here, as in the manuscript above, a long description of the *ḥūrīs* underlines the benefits awaiting the believers, while at the end of this long section, Gabriel opens the gate of a tent and further shows him prodigious elements, so that Muḥammad asks him to let him in paradise.

68 The so-called Modern Standard version is what Colby (see in particular his *Constructing an Islamic ascension narrative*) calls the version that has been printed several times and diffused in modern Arab world. A comprehensive study of the origins of this edition, its relation to the extant manuscripts, and its various versions, thus a combination of textual criticism and bibliographical studies, has yet to be undertaken. It appears that this version was first printed at the beginning of the twentieth century in Damascus or Cairo, and from there taken and printed in many Arab and Muslim countries, but mostly in Egypt. It became a sort of major version of the story of the *miʿrāj*, mostly discussed and criticized by authors of modern works on the topic, and translated in other languages (Turkish, English, Spanish, and most recently also Italian). The recent publication or discussion of other versions of this work (for example, Ibn ʿAbbās, *Miʿrāj al-nabī*; the relation of this version to the Modern Standard printed version is discussed in Tottoli, Two *Kitāb al-miʿrāj* 708–9) indicates clearly that the Modern Standard edition was one of the versions circulating under the name of Ibn ʿAbbās.

characterization that emerges from the list of the four castles which Abū Bakr, ʿUmar, ʿUthmān, and ʿAlī (the first four "rightly guided caliphs") are destined for.[69] The so-called Modern Standard version contains the same introductory role for Riḍwān but omits the second half of the description; the longer version introduces the gates and what is written on them.[70] A work relying on Ibn ʿAbbās' long version, such as the Ms. Cairo Dār al-Kutub, Majmūʿa 9684 (Anonymous, *al-Miʿrāj al-sharīf*) follows the short description of the Modern Standard version but adds quotations of some *ḥadīth* reports which no doubt served the anonymous author to enhance the trustworthiness of his narration.[71] The various versions of this work, such as those attributed to al-Bakrī, are indeed significant case studies that show, better than works by different authors, how the various motifs and the tour of paradise were reworked.

The introductory detail in which Riḍwān appears can be also found in the story of the *miʿrāj* written by Mūsā b. Ḥājjī Ḥusayn al-Iznīqī (d. 833/1430). Here Riḍwān also leads Muḥammad to a visual perception of the eternal abode, full of prodigies but now in a comprehensive picture. In this case, specific dimensions are given for the wall of paradise: it is seventy years (of walking) wide. Then the narration of Ibn ʿAbbās' versions is followed, or at least the clear reference to the list of castles, rivers, and trees, and further also we find the pro-Sunni mention of the four *rāshidūn*.[72] Along these lines there is also Muḥammad b. Aḥmad al-Mālikī's unpublished and long *Kitāb Miʿrāj al-nabī* which collects and repeats the various details. Muḥammad and Gabriel knock on the gate of paradise and Riḍwān opens and bids them enter, then Gabriel tells Riḍwān that God ordered him to show Muḥammad paradise. The visual perception of paradise is enhanced by the dimensions given: the length of the walls of paradise are one thousand years of walking, and, in another passage, seventy parasangs; the gates are listed with the writing that adorns them. The usual prodigies follow: castles, rivers, horses, tents, trees, various animals, and finally the *ḥūrīs*, their creation, then the names of the eight paradises with castles, trees, and fruits in each. And after all this Muḥammad even asks Gabriel

---

69 Ibn ʿAbbās, *Miʿrāj al-nabī*, ed. Ṣalībā, 291–8.

70 Ibn ʿAbbās, *al-Isrāʾ wa-l-miʿrāj* 40–3; this printed version abruptly interrupts the narration; it adds a few lines on the rivers and then comes suddenly to the descent to earth.

71 Anonymous, *al-Miʿrāj al-sharīf*, Ms. Cairo Dār al-Kutub, Majmūʿa 9684, 27b–30b. This work is also preserved in Anonymous, *al-Miʿrāj*, Ms. Riyadh King Saud University 7514, see in part. 30b–33b.

72 Al-Iznīqī, *Kitāb al-Miʿrāj*, fols. 19b–21b. On the same line we also find Zayn al-Dīn (d. 1002/1594), who follows Ibn ʿAbbās including the introduction of Riḍwān, see Zayn al-Dīn, *al-Najm al-wahhāj* 24b–25b.

to allow him to stay there.[73] This feature is further enhanced in one other version which we mention as our last example. Ms. Cairo Dār al-Kutub, Taʾrīkh 748 (Anonymous, *Qiṣṣat al-miʿrāj*), introduces the tour of paradise with Riḍwān, and states that he (Riḍwān), Muḥammad, and Gabriel walked through paradise. After the names of the eight paradises, he adds that in paradise there are towns (*madāʾin*) built with high walls (*aswār*) with castles inside, along with tents and domes. One further significant feature, also attested in other versions, is the description of the wall of paradise, which is made up of bricks not only of gold and silver, but also of gemstone and jacinth, and which is ninety thousand parasangs long.[74] Something similar can be found in other versions which, though not so explicit in the visual description of paradise, nevertheless, dedicate a long chapter to the vision of paradise.

It is interesting to note that the various *miʿrāj* works show how the motif of Riḍwān is the result of a specific development of a detail introduced in later reports. As in the case of al-Bakrī introduced above, some versions display a sort of middle version: Muḥammad comes to the gate of paradise, knocks and an unanamed angel answers so that Gabriel and Muḥammad enter. Here the angel is not identified as Riḍwān.[75] The most significant work attesting to how this motif emerged and was inserted into narratives, is the well-known *Book of the Ladder*, containing a long description of paradise.[76] It is indeed a double description of paradise thus evidencing how the translator from the Arabic (the Jew Abraham) relied on differing sources and combined some of them to formulate a new text on the *miʿrāj*. In the case of the tour of paradise, there is first a description starting from the wall with many details that emerge from Muḥammad's questions to Gabriel. The rivers, the seven (*sic*) paradises and their walls, towns, castle, *ḥūrīs*, food, the *ṭūbā* tree (chaps. XXX–XLIV) are all mentioned. Then Muḥammad meets Riḍwān (chaps. XLV–XLVIII) who takes him by the hand through all the paradises with their rivers, trees, fruits, and

73 Muḥammad b. Aḥmad al-Mālikī, *Kitāb Miʿrāj al-nabī* fols. 65b–77b. Probably similar to this work is *al-Sirāj al-wahhāj fī laylat al-isrāʾ wa-qiṣṣat al-miʿrāj* by Muḥammad Ẓalam al-Bābilī (Aleppo n.d.) used by Bencheikh, *Le voyage nocturne de Mahomet*, in his reworking of the story (81–119); it contains – according to Bencheikh – a long chapter on the description of paradise.

74 Anonymous, *Qiṣṣat al-miʿrāj*, Ms. Cairo Dār al-Kutub, Taʾrīkh 748, fols. 12b–16a. This is only a small sample from later mostly anonymous works dedicated to the topic which display the same features. A comprehensive inquiry into the rich collections of manuscripts is necessary to establish how paradise is described in *miʿrāj* literature.

75 See on this regard Scherberger, *Das Miʿrāǧnāme* 105–6.

76 Cerulli, *Il "Libro della scala"* 101–45, nos. XXX–XLVIII.

women, in a narrative reprise of the visual review of the main features of paradise typical of later *miʿrāj* works.[77]

But the motif of Riḍwān opening the gate and showing Muḥammad paradise is just a small sample of how an original element emerged and was introduced into the motif and thus the whole story. Other details give a further taste of novelties introduced by later versions. For instance, the well-known description of the wall as made of golden and silver bricks was attested in sound *ḥadīths* and from there repeated in all *miʿrāj* literary traditions and works. Some of these versions add that along with golden and silver bricks, there are also gemstones, jacinth, and green chrysolite,[78] or pearl, red jacinth, and green chrysolite, or other similar lists.[79] The point is clear: the *ḥadīth* report establishes the content of the description of the wall, and later reports enhance the details of it, adding new particulars that deviate somewhat from the literal contents of the sayings of Muḥammad though following the same general drift. Further particulars could be added; these not only enrich the description with prodigious details but also add others with a view to giving a more factual verisimilar description, when, for instance, some sources state that the mortar (*ṭīn*) between the bricks is musk. The fantastic dimension of the prodigies

77 The two narratives are evidently taken from two different sources. Apart from the detail of Riḍwān, the first description is evidently remade by the translator who underlines specific points in Muslim beliefs, as displayed through the question-answer construction of the narrative. The second seems to be a tour of paradise, including Riḍwān, which follows those described above and bears the signs of a more integrated narration. It is interesting to note that similar variants of the role of Riḍwān and the constructions of narrative can be seen in Aljamiado literature. Though some versions do not include this motif, others do and give a visual description similar to the popular Arabic narratives just discussed, see for example, Anonymous, *Ḥadīš de cuando subió el-annabī Muḥammad a los cielos*, Ms. Madrid Junta 9, fols. 31a–33b. I am indebted to Juan Carlos Villaverde for providing me with a transcript of this manuscript taken from a PhD dissertation (Laureano García, *Tradiciones musulmanas* 232–6) and for a number of other Aljamiado manuscripts including differing versions of apparently the same dynamics and elaboration of the motifs of the tour of paradise, quite similar to the Arabic sources but also with the introduction of original details. The question requires further inquiry to enrich the knowledge of the Muslim *miʿrāj* literature and, above all, underline the relevance of Aljamiado testimonies for the study of Muslim literature and Islamic studies in general. On Aljamiado versions of the *miʿrāj*, see Rueter, *Aljamiado narratives of Muhammad's ascension*.

78 See for example al-Mālikī, *Kitāb Miʿrāj al-nabī* fol. 68a.

79 Al-Iznīqī, *Kitāb al-Miʿrāj* fol. 20a; see for example already in al-Qushayrī, *Kitāb al-Miʿrāj* 51–2: bricks of gold, silver, pearl, red jacinth, green gemstone, yellow jacinth, and green chrysolite; cf. Anonymous, *Ḥadīš de cuando subió el-annabī Muḥammad a los cielos*, Ms. Madrid Junta 9, fol. 31a: gold, silver, and pearl.

described is enriched along with the addition of details pertaining to human experience and as such constituting a sort of "domesticated" imagination.

Along with this, the visual landscape encountered by this prophetic entrance to paradise and his traveling through it with Gabriel or with Gabriel and Riḍwān is the most significant novelty introduced by the *miʿrāj* literature, a novelty which offers a distinctive elaboration of the structure of paradise. The tour of paradise in late *miʿrāj* narratives represents a further step in the collection and elaboration of the description of paradise, different from that offered by *ḥadīth*-oriented literature and, no less relevant, from the testimonies of eschatological literature. In fact, a narrative reconstruction of paradise is given in some other texts. The anonymous *Kitāb al-ʿAẓama* published recently by K. Abu-Deeb,[80] but known under different titles with differing versions, such as *Kitāb al-ʿAjāʾib wa-l-gharāʾib* (The marvels of unfamilar things) ascribed to ʿAbdallāh b. Salām (d. 43/663),[81] for instance, includes a narrative description of paradise. Notwithstanding this and although given in a continuous narration, this long description includes mostly if not only particulars taken from the Quran and *ḥadīth*s: paradise is under the throne, there are several gardens with different names, there are rivers, tents, walls, castles – all of them described with numerous prodigious particulars in line with what is already known from traditional literature.[82] It is really a *ḥadīth*-oriented description of paradise without ever quoting specific *ḥadīth*s and without the comprehensive description of the ascension of Muḥammad.

5 Conclusions

A few conclusions can be drawn after this review of traditions on paradise and the *miʿrāj* literature. The Quran and *ḥadīth* literature do not contain an all-inclusive description of paradise, though both sources mention many physical details, with the purpose, usually, of emphasizing the marvelous elements which are in paradise or for the moral message vis-à-vis the people destined for it. Some *miʿrāj* traditions and *ḥadīth*s include the mention and a limited description of paradise, mostly in accord with what is found in other sayings

---

80 Abu-Deeb, *The imagination unbound*; he simply revised and published a text from a manuscript in Oxford, Bodleian Library (Hunt 353).

81 See for example Ms. Gotha A745. On this work, see the description by Raven, A *Kitāb al-ʿaẓama*.

82 See Abu-Deeb, *The imagination unbound* 141–60. Wim Raven is working on a critical edition published and updated on-line: see http://kitabalazama.wordpress.com.

of the Prophet. But in general, these do not allot much space to the question, generally less than to the description of hell and sinners. Notwithstanding this, the inclusion of the mention of paradise and hell is attested early in *miʿrāj* traditions, though later canonical collections came to include only one long version and a few details of Muḥammad's visit to paradise during his ascension to heaven. Some hypotheses may be suggested to help explain this. Most probably the relevance of the story of the night journey and ascension of the Prophet and its contents prompted, early on, the inclusion of eschatological details so as to build a proper apocalypse connected with the figure of Muḥammad. Such an apocalypse would require a vision of paradise and hell, in line with contemporary cultural and religious expectations.[83] This, however, came to constitute a problem, and, especially with regard to the vision of paradise which, for theological reasons, was related to the problem of the actual existence of paradise and its location. On a second level, other problems arose in regard to the related question of the meeting with God. For this reason canonical collections of *ḥadīth* most probably preferred not to include longer reports on the *miʿrāj* and rarely mention eschatological details.

There is another factor which could have prompted the inclusion or at least mention of the visit to paradise and hell. This factor relates to popular taste, which was no doubt much interested in eschatological details, a taste which the authors and compilers of our sources may have sought to address directly. Other recent works on the *miʿrāj* literature underlined the function of some late literary versions as proselytizing texts aimed to inspire or prompt conversion to Islam.[84] This also could have been a function of these reports: the more complete the description of the Prophet's apocalypse, the more entertaining would be the resulting portrait of the Prophet Muḥammad, which would then correspond more closely to existing Near and Middle Eastern religious beliefs and literary motifs. Such a context helps us understand how the insertion of eschatological traditions into early versions of the *miʿrāj* reports later came to be handled with care for theological reasons.

Later on, the picture changes. It seems clear that after the fifth/eleventh century, and mostly in the ninth/fifteenth and the tenth/sixteenth centuries,

83 Or said differently: "the night journey and ascension discourse became widely circulated and discussed partially because it was an entertaining tale, but also partially because of what was at stake, namely the empowerment that one gains by controlling the content of otherworldly secrets." Colby, *Narrating Muḥammad's night journey* 166.

84 See for example Gruber, *The Prophet Muḥammad's ascension* 108–239; Colby, *Narrating Muḥammad's night journey* 172–3; Scherberger, The Chagatay *Miʿrājnāma* attributed to Ḥakīm Süleymān Ata 87–8.

the *miʿrāj* of the Prophet became the topic of many literary works. These works have not been the subject of particular interest by researchers on this topic. Notwithstanding, they are relevant as a distinct body of literature since they attest to a further elaboration of the story of Muḥammad's ascent to heaven. Along with this, as regards a specific topic such as the description of paradise, they attest to the emergence and insertion or exclusion of a comprehensive description of paradise granting a sort of visual definition that complies more with the need for a simple, clear-cut, and popular image in place of the simple repetition of well-known Quranic and *ḥadīth* material. The many *ḥadīth*-oriented works written in the same centuries bear witness that some other authors tried to counterbalance this tendency and to impose a reconstruction of paradise more in line with traditional reports.

Thus some works avoided even the mere mention of the vision of paradise, let alone prolonged treatment of the description of the *miʿrāj*. Some others offered something more, thus showing their own characteristic attitude toward the topic and underlining a specific stand in relation to the question of the function of paradise during the ascension of the prophet. Needless to say this is not only related to the question of eschatology in *miʿrāj* narratives, but as already emphasized in studies by Colby, it can be seen at work with regard to all the topics or better, as Colby himself has it, the various narremes constituting the story of the ascension. In this regard the most significant aspect of some of these later remakings of the story of the ascension of Muḥammad is that they go a step further in the description of paradise during the *miʿrāj* and give a first notion of the interconnected and harmonious architecture of paradise, i.e., a full description of its physical dimensions and landscape.

At this point there is only one thing to ponder, and this is why all this happened in these later times. This is not an easy question to answer. The study of many other examples from different genres has recently underlined how literature after the fifth/eleventh century displays new sensibilities and a distinct development in the elaboration of traditional elements. The case at hand could be another one of these, further strengthened by the fact that Quranic and traditional accounts had already paved the way for an organic description of paradise as a garden or an orchard. Whatever the reason and the historical motivations behind the evolution of the eschatological description of paradise and its insertion in *miʿrāj* narratives, in the above we have seen a clear testimony to the richness of Muslim literary elaboration in the late Middle Ages. The importance of eschatology and of the ascension of the Prophet and the rich early literary portrayals did not stop later authors from reworking existing narrations and creating new literary elaborations whatever theological or exegetical concerns may have prompted them to write anew on these subjects.

Bibliography

ʿAbd al-Raḥīm al-Qāḍī, *Daqāʾiq al-akhbār fī dhikr al-janna wa-nār*, Beirut 1984.

ʿAbd al-Razzāq b. Hammām, *al-Muṣannaf*, ed. Ḥ al-Raḥmān al-Aʿẓamī, 11 vols., Beirut 1983.

Abu-Deeb, K., *The imagination unbound: Al-adab al-ʿajaʾibi and the literature of the fantastic in the Arabic tradition*, London 2007 (including an edition of Anonymous, *Kitāb al-ʿAẓama*, 67–163).

Abū Nuʿaym al-Iṣfahānī, *Ṣifat al-janna*, ed. ʿA.R. b. ʿAlī Riḍā, Beirut 1995.

Abū l-Shaykh al-Iṣfahānī, ʿAbdallāh, *Kitāb al-ʿAẓama*, ed. M. Fāris, Beirut 1994.

Afsaruddin, A., Garden, in *EQ*, ii, 282–87.

Anonymous, *Ḥadīš de cuando subió el-annabī Muḥammad a los cielos*, Ms. Madrid Junta 9.

Anonymous, *al-Miʿrāj*, Ms. Riyadh King Saud University 7514.

Anonymous, *al-Miʿrāj al-sharīf*, Ms. Cairo Dār al-Kutub, Majmūʿa 9684.

Anonymous, *Qiṣṣat al-miʿrāj*, Ms. Cairo Dār al-Kutub, Taʾrīkh 748.

Anonymous, *Qiṣṣat al-miʿrāj*, Ms. Cairo Dār al-Kutub, Taʾrīkh Taymūr 205.

Asín Palacios, M., *La escatologia musulmana en la Divina Comedia*, Madrid 1919.

al-Azmeh, A., Rhetoric for the senses: A consideration of Muslim paradise narratives, in *JAL* 26 (1995), 215–31.

al-Baghawī, Abū Muḥammad, *Maṣābīḥ al-sunna*, ed. Y. ʿAbd al-Raḥmān al-Marʿashlī, M. Salīm Ibrāhīm Samāra, and J. Ḥamdī al-Dhahabī, 4 vols., Beirut 1998.

———, *Sharḥ al-sunna*, ed. S. al-Laḥḥām, 8 vols., Beirut 1992.

al-Bakrī, Ḥasan, *Ḥadīth al-miʿrāj*, Ms. Istanbul, Ayasofya 867, 170a–178b (short version); Ms. Paris Bibliothéque Nationale ar. 1931 (long version).

al-Barzanjī, Zayn al-ʿĀbidīn, *al-Isrāʾ wa-l-miʿrāj*, Cairo 1973.

al-Bayhaqī, Aḥmad, *Dalāʾil al-nubuwwa*, ed. ʿA. al-Qalʿajī, 7 vols., Beirut 1985.

———, *Kitāb al-Baʿth wa-l-nushūr*, ed. ʿĀ. Aḥmad Ḥaydar, Beirut 1986.

———, *Shuʿab al-īmān*, ed. M. b. Basyūnī Zaghlūl, 7 vols., Beirut 1990.

Bencheikh, J.E., *Le voyage nocturne de Mahomet*, Paris 1988.

al-Bukhārī, Muḥammad b. Ismāʿīl, *Ṣaḥīḥ*, 8 vols., Beirut 1992.

Canova, G., Animals in Islamic paradise and hell, in *The Arabist. Budapest Studies in Arabic* 28–9 (2008), 55–81.

Cerulli, E., *Il "Libro della scala" e la questione delle fonti arabo-spagnole della Divina Commedia*, Vatican City 1949.

Colby, F.S., *Constructing an Islamic ascension narrative: The interplay of official and popular culture in pseudo-Ibn ʿAbbas*, PhD dissertation, Duke University 2002.

———, *Narrating Muḥammad's night journey: Tracing the development of the Ibn ʿAbbās ascension discourse*, Albany, NY 2008.

al-Dārimī, ʿAbdallāh, *Sunan*, ed. M. Dīb Bughā, 2 vols., Damascus 1991.

El-Ṣaleḥ, Ṣ., *La vie future selon le Coran*, Paris 1986.

al-Ghayṭī, Najm al-Dīn, *Qiṣṣat al-miʿrāj*, publ. in margin of al-Dardīr, *Ḥāshiyat ʿalā qiṣṣat al-miʿrāj li-Najm al-Dīn al-Ghayṭī*, Cairo 1948.

Gruber, C., *The Prophet Muḥammad's ascension (miʿrāj) in Islamic art and literature, ca. 1300–1600*, PhD dissertation, University of Pennsylvania 2005.

Günther, S., « *Gepriesen sei der, der seinen Diener bei Nacht reisen ließ* » (Koran 17:1): Paradiesvorstellungen und Himmelsreisen im Islam – Grundfesten des Glaubens und literarische Topoi, in E. Hornung and A. Schweizer (eds.), *Jenseitsreisen: ERANOS 2009 und 2010*, Basel 2011, 15–56.

al-Ḥākim al-Naysābūrī, Abū ʿAbdallāh, *al-Mustadrak ʿalā l-ṣaḥīḥayn*, ed. M. ʿAbd al-Qādir ʿAṭā, 4 vols., Beirut 1990.

Hannād b. al-Sarī, *Kitāb al-Zuhd*, ed. ʿA. ʿAbd al-Jabbār al-Faryawāʾī, 2 vols., Kuwait 1985.

al-Haythamī, *Majmaʿ al-zawāʾid wa-manbaʿ al-fawāʾid*, 10 vols., Beirut 1967.

Horovitz, J., Das koranische Paradies, in R. Paret (ed.), *Der Koran*, Darmstadt 1975, 53–73 (and in *Scripta Universitatis atque Bibliothecae Hierosolymitanarum*, Jerusalem 1923).

al-Ḥumaydī, Abū Bakr, *al-Musnad*, ed. Ḥ. al-Raḥmān al-Aʿẓamī, 2 vols., Beirut 1988.

Ibn ʿAbbās, ʿAbdallāh, *al-Isrāʾ wa-l-miʿrāj*, Cairo n.d.

———, *Miʿrāj al-nabī*, in L. Ṣalībā, *al-Miʿrāj fī l-wijdān al-shaʿbī*, Jubayl 2008, 139–310; and Ms. Turin, Dip. di Orientalistica, P. Kahle collection no. 180.

Ibn Abī l-Dunyā, ʿAbdallāh b. Muḥammad, *Ṣifat al-janna*, ed. Ṭ. al-Ṭanṭāwī, Cairo 1994.

Ibn Abī Shayba, ʿAbdallāh b. Muḥammad, *al-Muṣannaf*, ed. S. al-Laḥḥām, 9 vols., Beirut 1989.

Ibn al-ʿArabī, Abū Bakr, *Aḥkām al-Qurʾān*, 4 vols, Beirut 1988.

Ibn ʿAsākir, ʿAlī, *Taʾrīkh madīnat Dimashq*, ed. ʿA. b. Gharāma al-ʿUmrawī, 80 vols., Beirut 1995–6..

Ibn Diḥya, ʿUmar, *al-Ibtihāj fī aḥādīth al-miʿrāj*, ed. R. Fawzī ʿAbd al-Muṭṭalib, Cairo 1996.

Ibn Ḥabīb, ʿAbd al-Malik, *Kitāb Waṣf al-firdaws*, Beirut 1987.

———, *Kitāb Waṣf al-firdaws* (*La descripción del paraíso*), trans. and comm. J.P. Monferrer Sala, Granada 1997.

Ibn Ḥanbal, Aḥmad, *Musnad*, ed. ʿA.M. al-Darwīsh, 10 vols., Beirut 1991.

Ibn Ḥibbān al-Bustī, *Ṣaḥīḥ* = Ibn Balabān al-Fārisī, *al-Iḥsān bi-tartīb ṣaḥīḥ Ibn Ḥibbān*, ed. K. Yūsuf al-Ḥūt, 9 vols., Beirut 1987.

Ibn Hishām, ʿAbd al-Malik, *al-Sīra al-nabawiyya*, ed. S. Zakkār, 2 vols, Beirut 1992.

Ibn al-Jawzī, Abd al-Raḥmān, *Kitāb al-Mawḍūʿāt*, ed. T. Ḥamdān, 2 vols., Beirut 1995.

Ibn Kathīr, Ismāʿīl, *Nihāya al-bidāya wa-l-nihāya*, ed. I. b. Muḥammad al-Anṣārī, Cairo n.d.

———, *Tafsīr*, 4 vols., Cairo n.d.

Ibn Māja, Muḥammad, *Sunan*, ed. M.F. ʿAbd al-Bāqī, 2 vols., Cairo n.d.
Ibn al-Mubārak, ʿAbdallāh, *Kitāb al-Zuhd*, Alexandria 1994.
Ibn Qayyim al-Jawziyya, Muḥammad, *Ḥādī l-arwāḥ ilā bilād al-afrāḥ*, ed. Z. ʿUmayrāt, Beirut 2002.
Ibn Rajab al-Ḥanbalī, *al-Takhwīf min al-nār*, ed. al-S. al-Jumaylī, Damascus 1984.
Ibn Saʿd al-Zuhrī, Muḥammad, *Kitāb al-Ṭabaqāt al-kubrā*, ed. I. ʿAbbās, 9 vols., Beirut n.d.
al-Isfarāyīnī, Abū ʿAwāna, *Musnad*, Beirut n.d.
al-Iznīqī, Mūsā b. Ḥājjī, *Kitāb al-Miʿrāj*, Ms. Marmara Üniversitesi, Ilahiyat Oğüt 1229.
Juynboll, G.H.A., *Encyclopedia of canonical ḥadīth*, Leiden 2007.
Kinberg, L., Paradise, in EQ, iv, 12–8.
al-Kisāʾī, Muḥammad, *Qiṣaṣ al-anbiyāʾ*, ed. I. Eisenberg, 2 vols, Leiden 1922–3.
Laureano García, G.S., *Tradiciones musulmanas* (*Ms. IX de la Biblioteca de la antigua Junta para la Ampliación de Estudios de Madrid*), PhD dissertation, Universidad de Oviedo 2008.
al-Majlisī, Muḥammad Bāqir, *Biḥār al-anwār*, 110 vols., Beirut 1993.
al-Mālikī, Muḥammad b. Aḥmad, *Kitāb Miʿrāj al-nabī*, Ms. Turin, Dip. di Orientalistica, P. Kahle collection no. 179.
al-Maqdisī, Ḍiyāʾ al-Dīn, *Kitāb Ṣifat al-janna*, ed. Ṣ. b. Salāma Shāhīn, Riyadh 2002.
Mujāhid b. Jabr, *Tafsīr*, ed. ʿA. al-Ṭāhir b. Muḥammad al-Suwartī, 2 vols., Beirut n.d.
Muslim b. al-Ḥajjāj, *Ṣaḥīḥ*, ed. M. Fuʾād ʿAbd al-Bāqī, 5 vols., Cairo 1991.
al-Muṭahhar b. Ṭāhir al-Maqdisī, *al-Badʾ wa-l-taʾrīkh*, ed. C. Huart, Paris 1899–1919.
al-Muttaqī l-Hindī, *Kanz al-ʿummāl fī sunan al-aqwāl wa-l-afʿāl*, ed. B. Ḥayyānī and Ṣ. al-Saqā, 18 vols., Beirut 1989.
al-Qurṭubī, Abū ʿAbdallāh, *Kitāb al-Tadhkira bi-aḥwāl al-mawtā wa-umūr al-ākhira*, ed. al-Ṣ. b. Muḥammad b. Ibrāhīm, 3 vols., Riyadh 2005.
al-Qushayrī, ʿAbd al-Karīm, *Kitāb al-Miʿrāj*, ed. ʿA. Ḥasan ʿAbd al-Qādir, Cairo 1964.
Raven, W., A *Kitāb al-ʿaẓama*: On cosmology, hell and paradise, in F. de Jong (ed.), *Miscellanea arabica et islamica*, Leuven 1993, 135–42.
al-Rāzī, Fakhr al-Dīn Abū ʿAbdallāh, *Mafātīḥ al-ghayb*, 32 vols., Beirut 1990.
Reinhart, A.K., The here and the hereafter in Islamic religious thought, in S.S. Blair and J. Bloom (eds.), *Images of paradise in Islamic art*, Hanover NH 1991, 15–24.
Rueter, W.M., *Aljamiado narratives of Muhammad's ascension to heaven: The Moriscos and the miʿraj*, Ann Arbor MI 2009.
Rustomji, N., *The garden and the fire: Heaven and hell in Islamic literature*, New York 2009.
al-Ruwaynī, Muḥammad b. Hārūn, *Musnad*, ed. A. ʿAlī Yamānī, 2 vols., Cairo n.d.
al-Samarrai, Q., *The theme of the ascension in mystical writings*, i, Baghdad 1968.
al-Shāmī al-Ṣāliḥī, *Khulāṣat al-faḍl al-fāʾiq fī miʿrāj khayr al-khalāʾiq*, ed. Ḥ. Aḥmad Isbir, Beirut 2003.

Scherberger, M., The Chagatay *Miʿrājnāma* attributed to Ḥakīm Süleymān Ata: A missionary text from the twelfth or thirteenth century preserved in modern manuscripts, in C. Gruber and F. Colby (eds.), *The Prophet's ascension: Cross-cultural encounters with the Islamic* miʿrāj *tales*, Bloomington IN 2010, 78–96.

———, *Das Miʿrāğnāme: Die Himmel- und Höllenfahrt des Propheten Muḥammad in der osttürkischen Überlieferung*, Würzburg 2003.

al-Shaybānī, Abū Bakr b. Abī ʿĀṣim, *al-Sunna*, ed. M. Nāṣir al-Dīn al-Albānī, 2 vols., Riyadh 1998.

Sperl, S., Man's "hollow core": Ethics and aestetics in *Ḥadīth* literature and classical Arabic *adab*, in BSOAS 70 (2007), 459–86.

al-Suyūṭī, Jalāl al-Dīn, *al-Budūr al-sāfira fī umūr al-ākhira*, ed. M. ʿĀshūr, Cairo 1990.

———, *al-Durr al-manthūr fī l-tafsīr al-maʾthūr*, 8 vols., Beirut 1983.

———, *Jāmiʿ al-aḥādīth*, 13 vols., Cairo n.d.

———, *al-Laʾālī l-maṣnūʿa fī l-aḥādīth al-mawḍūʿa*, ed. Ṣ. b. Muḥammad b. ʿUwayḍa, 2 vols., Beirut 1996.

al-Ṭabarānī, Abū l-Qāsim, *al-Muʿjam al-awsaṭ*, ed. Ṭ. b. ʿAwḍ Allāh b. Muḥammad and ʿA. b. Ibrāhīm al-Ḥusaynī, 10 vols., Cairo 1995.

———, *al-Muʿjam al-kabīr*, ed. Ḥ. ʿAbd al-Majīd al-Salafī, 25 vols., Beirut n.d.

al-Ṭabarī, Muḥammad b. Jarīr, *Jāmiʿ al-bayān ʿan taʾwīl āy al-Qurʾān*, 30 vols., Cairo 1968.

Tamari, S., *Iconotextual studies in the Muslim vision of paradise*, Wiesbaden 1999.

al-Ṭayālisī, Abū Dāwūd, *Musnad*, Cairo 1904.

al-Thaʿlabī, Aḥmad b. Muḥammad, *al-Kashf wa-l-bayān*, ed. A.M. b. ʿĀṣhūr, 10 vols., Beirut 2002.

al-Tirmidhī, Muḥammad b. ʿĪsā, *al-Jāmiʿ al-ṣaḥīḥ*, ed. A. Muḥammad Shākir and M. Fuʾād ʿAbd al-Bāqī, 5 vols., Cairo 1962.

Tottoli, R., "Due fiumi sono credenti e due miscredenti ...": Una geografia fluviale sacra in un detto di Muḥammad?, in M. Bernardini and N.L. Tornesello (eds.), *Scritti in onore di Giovanni M. D'Erme*, Napoli 2005, 1221–35.

———, Muslim eschatological literature and Western studies, in *Der Islam* 83 (2006), 449–74.

———, Tours of hell and punishments of sinners in *miʿrāj* narratives: Use and meaning of eschatology, in C.C. Gruber and F. Colby (eds.), *The Prophet's ascension: Cross-cultural encounters with the Islamic* miʿraj *tales*, Bloomington IN 2010, 11–26.

———, Two *Kitāb al-miʿrāj* in the manuscripts collection of the Paul Kahle Library of the University of Turin, in P.G. Borbone, A. Mengozzi and M. Tosco (eds.), *Loquentes linguis: Studi linguistici e orientali in onore di Fabrizio A. Pennacchietti*, Wiesbaden 2006, 703–10.

al-Ujhurī, ʿAlī, *al-Nūr al-wahhāj fī l-kalām ʿalā l-isrāʾ wa-l-miʿrāj*, ed. F. ʿAbd al-Raḥmān Aḥmad Ḥijāzī, Beirut 2003.

Vuckovic, B.O., *Heavenly journeys, earthly concerns: The legacy of the miʿrāj in the formation of Islam*, New York and London 2005.
Yaḥyā b. Sallām al-Baṣrī, *Tafsīr*, ed. H. Shalabī, 2 vols., Beirut 2004
Zayn al-Dīn, *al-Najm al-wahhāj fī l-masrā wa-l-miʿrāj*, Ms. Cairo Dār al-Kutub, Majāmīʿ 829.

Internet Sources

http://kitabalazama.wordpress.com (accessed 1 July 2012).

CHAPTER 41

An Islamic *Paradiso* in a Medieval Christian Poem? Dante's *Divine Comedy* Revisited

Samar Attar

God is the Light
Of the heaven and the earth,
The parable of His Light
Is as if there were a Niche
And within it a Lamp
The Lamp enclosed in Glass
The glass as it were
A brilliant star
Lit from a blessed Tree,
An olive, neither of the East
Nor of the West,
Whose Oil is well-nigh
Luminous,
Though fire scarce touched it;
Light upon Light!
God doth guide
Whom He will
To His Light.

Q 24:35[1]

∴

In his article "Dante and Islam" which was published in 1973, Sir Richard William Southern, a notable English medieval historian, argued that

> Medieval Europe was extremely resistant to cultural influences except in the single area in which Islam acted as a link with ancient Greek thought.

1 Ali (trans.), *Kur'an.*

 | DOI 10.1163/9789004333154_042

> Nothing that has a specifically Islamic inspiration took root in the west. The west had enough of its own. That was all ... [Miguel Asín Palacios] was wrong to think that Dante's mind especially was filled with images drawn from Islamic sources ... [Dante] was a wholly western man.[2]

Southern's argument is certainly not unique in this regard. It may represent the attitude of many western scholars who believe that the West differs from other civilizations not only in the way it has developed but also in the distinctive character of its values and institutions. Westerners are indebted only to other Westerners. They constitute a unique breed of human beings.[3] Unfortunately, once the distinction between the Orient and the Occident is accepted as a starting point in research, the notion of the encounter between Islamic civilization and the West, particularly in the medieval period, is either marginalized, or ignored.

Asín Palacios was a Catholic priest and Professor of Arabic at the University of Madrid. In 1919 he published a monumental book entitled *La Escatologia musulmana en la Divina Comedia* (Muslim Eschatology and the Divine Comedy) in which he traced the influence and religious thought of medieval Islam on Dante's *Divine Comedy*. Asín considered Muḥammad's nocturnal journey and ascension from Jerusalem to the throne of God as the basic models that had influenced the great Florentine poet. But he also referred to other Muslim journeys and traced in particular the influence of some Neoplatonic mystics, such as the Spanish Muslim Ibn ʿArabī on Dante's allegory. The book was abridged and translated into English by Harold Sutherland and published in London in 1926, and then reprinted in 1968. Although there was heated argument among scholars at the time concerning the validity of Asín's thesis and the emergence of a trickle of studies since then, there is no doubt that Dante's scholars have largely ignored these claims and continued to teach and write on Dante either as the perfect embodiment of Christian Western culture, or as the ultimate rebel against religious authority and the corruption of the pastors of the church.[4] But in either case, Dante remains a unique 'western man,' absolutely oblivious to foreign Islamic ideas during his troubled age.

---

2 Southern, Dante and Islam 143–4.

3 The most prominent advocate of this position is Samuel P. Huntington in his book *The clash of civilizations and the remaking of world order*.

4 See for instance what Harold Bloom writes on Dante's *Divine Comedy* in his book, *The western canon*. Bloom criticizes American professors who teach the *Comedy* as something religious. "The theological Dante of modern American scholarship," he observes, "is a blend of Augustine, Thomas Aquinas, and their companions. This is a doctrinal Dante, so absolutely

My aim in this paper is twofold: first, to show that Dante may have used other Islamic sources beside the ones mentioned by Asín, with special reference to Ibn Ṭufayl's *Ḥayy Ibn Yaqẓān* (composed most probably between 1177 and 1182); and second, to explore why the majority of Western scholars still turn a blind eye to the issue of Islamic and Arabic influence on the culture of Christian Europe.

It is true that Dante lived in Florence from the year he was born in 1265 to January 1301 when he was exiled, and as a result became a wandering intellectual till he died in Ravenna, Italy, in 1321. But the very air he breathed wherever he lived was heavily impregnated with the influences of Islamic culture. The university professors in Europe, the clergy, regardless of their religious order, and the emerging European intellectuals were all engaged in reading, discussing, or contesting Islamic ideas not only in philosophy, but also in literature, theology, and science. Many Arabic and Islamic sources became available in Latin translations. Thanks to Alfonso the Wise (1221–84) King of Castile and Leon from 1252, many Arabic books were translated into Spanish, then Latin. But other sources were transmitted orally for decades. Europeans used them without even being aware of their origin most of the time. It is true, as critics maintain, that Dante had European models for his various books, but these models were not enough to fully enrich his imagination. During his lifetime, Dante would have had many opportunities to get to know firsthand or through friends and mentors a variety of Arabic-Islamic sources for eschatological, literary, philosophical, or mystic journeys to heaven and hell. In 1264 the Italian Bonaventura of Siena made a French and Latin translation of the Prophet Muḥammad's nocturnal journey to the throne of God from a Spanish version, which was based on an Arabic manuscript. A copy of this translation is preserved in the Bibliothèque Nationale. Another entitled *Liber scale Machemeti* can be found in the Vatican Library. R. W. Southern dismisses the idea that the manuscript had any possible influence on Dante. He argues that even if it

> came into Dante's hands he would no doubt have thought it a very poor thing. Yet in its general plan of Heaven and Hell it is a good deal nearer

learned and so amazingly pious that he can be fully apprehended only by his American professors … An alternative to the Eliot-Singleton-Freccero Dante emerges, a prophetic poet rather than a theological allegorist" (Bloom, *Western canon* 78, 80). Consult also Barolin, *Undivine*; Havely, *Dante and the Franciscans*; Scott, *Understanding Dante*. Arabists, or Islamists, such as Max Scherberger (*Das Mi'rāğname* 26–31), might still stir up the issue of Dante's debt to Islamic sources but Dante's scholars are largely oblivious to the argument of their Orientalist colleagues.

> to the plan of the *Divine Comedy* than any existing Christian vision. It has more order, more discussion, more geographical exactitude, and though highly inartistic, it is 'literary' in the sense that no Christian reader would be inclined to take the journey as a genuine revelation.[5]

Of course, this manuscript is only one version of Muḥammad's nocturnal journey.[6] There are many more and richer versions, but perhaps still not discovered in European languages. This does not mean that they did not exist. The topic was of extreme interest, particularly to Christian theologians who were engaged at the time in translating the Quran and everything related to the Muslim prophet.[7] It was the Spaniard Paulo Alvaro (died about 862) who once complained that his

> fellow Christians delight in the poems and romances of the Arabs; they study the works of Muhammadan theologians and philosophers, not in order to refute them, but to acquire a correct and elegant Arabic style. Where today can a layman be found who reads the Latin commentaries on the Holy Scriptures? Alas! The young Christians who are most conspicuous for their talents have no knowledge of any literature of language save Arabic: they read and study avidly Arabic books; they amass whole libraries of them at vast cost, and they everywhere sing the praises of Arabic lore.[8]

This comment, which was made in ninth-century Cordoba, Spain, could be applied to a certain extent over the following centuries, and to the years in which Dante lived in Italy. We have no proof that Dante knew Arabic, but we do know from his works that he must have been very familiar with some aspects of Arabic and Persian poetry. He certainly did not learn his craft as a poet only from Ovid, or other Western masters, but also from the infidels, his own enemies, and the troubadours who were deeply influenced by them. Even his

---

5 Southern, Dante and Islam 141.

6 The narrative of Muḥammad's ascension developed from the first verse of Sura 17 of the Quran. The prophet was carried from Mecca to the Dome of the Rock in Jerusalem. It was the Sufis who used this verse along with other stories on Muḥammad's journey to create numerous legends dating back to the ninth century.

7 The first translation of the Quran into Latin was commissioned by Peter the Venerable and was done by the Englishman Robert of Ketton in the first half of the twelfth century. Other translations followed.

8 Alvaro, *Indiculus luminosus*. Quoted in English by Desmond, *Early Islam* 143. Cf. Hitti, *History of the Arabs* 515–6.

greatest creation, Beatrice, may be linked to the long series of exalted women in Arabic history and literature. Dante's familiarity with Islamic philosophy, particularly the daring philosophical notions about the significance of reason and the irrelevant role of conventional religions, the Illuministic school, and theories in optics, astrology, and astronomy is very evident in his work, but particularly in the *Comedy* that was called *Divine* some 200 years after his death.

Thus Southern's thesis, which confidently asserts that no specific Islamic inspiration has ever taken root in the West because the West has enough native inspiration of its own, must be carefully scrutinized. People of all races and religions have always lived in a global village, throughout history. Ideas, or images, or songs, or poems may not have traveled as quickly, or on such a large scale as they do nowadays, but nevertheless they did manage to infiltrate other places. There were always enough travelers, merchants, missionaries, diplomats, scholars, students, prisoners of war, and warriors to carry these ideas, or tunes to distant shores. No nation can totally resist the cultural influences of other nations.

1 Historical Background

1.1 *The Crusades and Dante's Ancestor: 1097–1291*

Whether as merchants, or as Christian warriors, the Italians participated in the crusades from the outset. On 26 November 1095 Pope Urban called the faithful from the city of Claremont, in the southeast of France to wrest the Holy Sepulcher in Jerusalem from the Muslims. Most participants of the first crusade who rushed to please the Pope were Franks and Normans. On 15 July 1099 Jerusalem fell. Horrible massacres took place there.[9] Dante assigns Duke Godfrey, the commander-in-chief of the Christian armies who was crowned King of Jerusalem, to the abode of the just in Canto XVIII along with Robert Guiscard, Duke of Apulia and Calabria who triumphed over the Saracens and Greeks in Sicily and southern Italy.[10] But Dante highlights the second crusade in particular in his *Paradise*, because a certain ancestor of his had joined the troops led by Conrad III of Germany and Louis VII of France between 1147 and 1149. In Canto XV where the warriors of God are to be found, Cacciaguida, Dante's ancestor, describes his own death.

---

9 For historical information on the crusades consult Runciman, *History*; Maalouf, *Arab eyes*; Mayer, *Crusades*.

10 Dante, *Comedy: Paradise*, Canto XVIII, 46–48.

Later, I rode at Emperor Conrad's side,
Who belted me among his chosen knights,
My service left him so well satisfied;
And in his train I marched to foreign fights
Against those infidels that, through the sin
Of the Chief Pastors, have usurped your rights.

There was I reft by the vile Saracen
From this deceitful world whose vanities
Win many souls and ruin all they win;

And came from martyrdom unto this peace.[11]

In sum, Dante's *Paradiso* is heavily populated with warriors against Islam and Muslims not only during the crusades, but in earlier times as well. Roland and Charlemagne soar like falcons in the abode of the just. Both are venerated as the champions of Christendom and the enemies of Islam in the second half of the eighth century. William, Count of Orange, known as Guillaume au Curb Nes and Reynald, or Reneward, called "Rainouart au tinel," a converted Saracen, also feature in this paradise. Both men are important figures in the medieval French narrative epics.

Then Roland on the track of Charlemayne
Sped and my keen eye following – as it does
The flight of one's own falcon – watched the twain;

After, my sight was drawn along the cross
By William, Reynald, and Duke Godfrey – three
Fires, and a fourth, which Robert Guiscard was;

Whereon the soul that had discoursed with me,
Moving and mingling with those myriads bright,
Showed me his art of heavenly minstrelsy.[12]

On the contrary, men who tarry in their fight against Saracen and carry on wars at home with Christians, or play the role of evil counselors in this matter are placed in hell. Count Guido da Montefeltro, a Lord of the Romagna, refers to

11 Ibid., Canto XV, 139–148.

12 Ibid., Canto XVIII, 43–51.

the loss of Acre and accuses Pope Boniface VIII of not devoting his complete resources to the recovery of the important city-port.[13]

1.2 *Norman Sicily: 1060–1250*

Although the relationship between Europe and the Arab-Muslim world was very tense during the twelfth century as a consequence of the crusades, Norman Sicily continued to play an important role as a transmitter of Arabic culture. The Norman kings adopted methods of toleration, almost unknown at that period, in ruling a population composed of races differing in language, customs, and religion. Greek, Latin, and Arabic were used in official circles simultaneously. Arab and Muslim scholars thrived in the kingdom. Trade between the island and the Muslim world was at its peak. Although Jerusalem was recaptured by Saladin (Ṣalāḥ al-Dīn al-Ayyūbī) in July 1187, that is, seventy-eight years before Dante's birth, Norman Sicily continued to act as a medium for the transmission of ancient and medieval learning not only to Italy, but also to the rest of Europe.[14]

Only fifteen years before Dante's birth Syrian and Iraqi scholars flourished in the court of the semi-Oriental Emperor, Frederick II of Hohenstaufen (1215–50), who ruled both Sicily and Germany and held the title of emperor of the Holy Roman Empire. Arabic was one of his official languages. He himself was able to read and write Arabic. Philosophers, mathematicians, astronomers, writers, poets, singers, dancers, craftsmen, and translators filled his court. The twice-excommunicated emperor also patronized Provençal troubadours. In 1224 he founded the University of Naples, the first such university established by a definite charter in Europe. In it he deposited hundreds of Arabic manuscripts in different fields, some of which he had his own translators render into Latin. Aristotle and Ibn Rushd (Latinized: Averroes) were taught there. Thomas Aquinas, who was later to influence Dante's work, was a student at the university for six years. One of the most prominent translators for Frederick II was Michael Scot, a scholar who made a Latin summary of Aristotle's biological and zoological works for the emperor from Arabic; he also served as the astrologer of the court. Dante condemns him with the magicians and soothsayers in the

---

13 It was then the Prince of the New Pharisees drew * his sword and marched upon the Lateran – * and not against the Saracen or the Jew, * for every man that stood against his hand * was a Christian soul: not one had warred on Acre, * nor been a trader in the Sultan's land. Dante Aligheri, *Comedy: Inferno*, Canto XXVII, Circle Eight: Bolgia Eight, 82–87.

14 For historical information on Norman Sicily consult Hitti, *History of the Arabs*.

Inferno and accuses him of mastering every trick of magic fraud.[15] Frederick II also maintained some relationships with an Andalusian Murcian by the name Abū Muḥammad ʿAbd al-Ḥaqq b. Sabʿīn (1217–69), who wrote *Asrār al-ḥikma al-mashriqiyya*, or *The Mysteries of Illuministic Philosophy*. The emperor wished to know from this prominent Sufi, who was residing at the time at Ceuta in Morocco, something about the eternity of matter, the nature and immortality of the soul, the object of theology, and other such issues. In Sicily Ibn Sabʿīn's answers became known as *al-Ajwiba ʿan al-asʾila al-Ṣiqilliyya* (The responses to the Sicilian questions) and were given to the emperor between 1232 and 1242. The subject matter would have greatly interested and perhaps was even known to Dante when he began writing his *Comedy*.

On the political and commercial fronts, Frederick II kept his interest in the world of Islam, particularly through his strong ties with the sultan of Egypt, al-Kāmil Muḥammad (1218–38), a nephew of Saladin. With the help of the latter, Frederick II even reclaimed Jerusalem after his marriage with the heiress, Isabelle of Brienne. He went on a crusade in 1228 against the will of the pope, Gregory IX, who had previously excommunicated him. The peace treaty signed at Jaffa on 18 February 1229 between al-Kāmil and his friend Frederick II was supposed to help both rulers: Al-Kāmil would have more time to settle his internal and external affairs, while Frederick II would enhance his reputation in Europe. On 18 March 1229 the emperor walked into the Church of the Holy Sepulcher and put the crown on his own head since the patriarch refused to crown him as king of Jerusalem. But the treaty angered both Christians and Muslims. The pope in Rome condemned it.[16]

Dante placed Frederick II in *The Inferno* with the 'Heretics.'[17] For him the emperor was reputed to be an Epicurean who was solely interested in temporal

---

15 The other there, * the one beside him with the skinny shanks * was Michael Scott, who mastered every trick * of magic fraud, a prince of mountebanks. Dante Aligheri, *Comedy: Inferno*, Canto XX, 114–117.

Scot is a scholar of the first half of the thirteenth century. He was from the British Isles, though his exact place of birth is not known. His reputation as a wizard entered into the myths and legends of Europe, particularly in the border area of Scotland. He learned Arabic at Toledo in Spain and gained sufficient knowledge to translate important works from Arabic into Latin. He then went to Sicily and was known in papal circles. Eventually, around 1220, Frederick II invited him to his court. In his ballad "The Lay of the Last Minstrel" (1805), Sir Walter Scott immortalized the translator's reputation. For more information on Michael Scot, Alfonso X of Castile, Averroes and Dante, see Watt, *Influence* 61–79. Cf. also Metlitzki, *Matter* 41–54.

16 For more information on the crusade of Frederick II see Mayer, *Crusades* 219–30.

17 Dante Aligheri, *Comedy: Inferno*, Canto X, Circle Six, 119.

happiness and consequently denied eternal life. Yet in Canto XIII, Dante has Pier della Vigne, who is placed with 'The Violent Against Themselves,' speak of Frederick II as one worthy of honor.[18]

It is no wonder that until now the Italian nationalists think of Dante as their hero. Islam, Muslims, and the crusades dominated his world. The crusaders were still there on the Syrian coast in Tarsus, Tripoli, Beirut, Sidon, Tyre, and Acre when he was an adult and still living in Florence, not only as a writer and poet, but also as a politician. Only in 1291 did the last crusader city, Acre, fall to the Muslims. As a result of the crusades, Italian ports flourished and the norms of life in general began to change. The influence of the Norman kings on Italy in particular and on the rest of Europe in general is immense.

1.3 *Muslim Spain: 710–1492*

The Muslim presence in the Iberian Peninsula lasted for nearly eight centuries, from 710 to 1492. Like Sicily, Spain was an important transmitter of Muslim learning and culture even after the Christian re-conquest was almost complete by the middle of the thirteenth century. But during Dante's life, Muslim Granada, the jewel of Europe, still flourished.[19] A large number of Arabic philosophical, scientific, and literary works were translated into Spanish and Latin, particularly during the reign of Alfonso the Wise (1252–84) and transmitted to Europe.[20] One such literary manuscript was a collection of fables of Indo-Persian origin, *Kalīla wa-Dimna*, which later became the main source for La Fontaine's (1668–94) *Fables*. In 1264 Alfonso the Wise also ordered *The Book of the Ladder*, or *al-Miʿrāj* to be translated into French and Latin from an existing Castilian version. The translator was a Sienese notary called Bonaventura da Siena. Dante's mentor, Brunetto Latini, happened to visit Toledo at the time of the translation.

In Muslim Spain, poets celebrated earthly, erotic, or divine love. One of the most important voices was Ibn Ḥazm (994–1064) who was born in Cordoba into a family that had recently converted from Christianity to Islam. He was imprisoned several times for his political associations. By the end of his life he had abandoned politics and led a life of seclusion. His most popular work is

18 I am he who held both keys to Frederick's heart ... * I swear to you that never in word or spirit * did I break faith to my lord and emperor * who was so worthy of honor in his merit. Dante Aligheri, *Comedy: Inferno*, Canto XIII, Circle Seven: Round Two, 58, 73–75. Note that Frederick's mother the Empress Constance is placed in *Paradise*, Canto III.

19 For historical information on Muslim Spain consult Hitti, *History of the Arabs* 493–591; Dozy, *Spanish Islam*; Chejne, *Islam and the West.*

20 See Procter, *Alfonso X of Castile.*

Ṭūq al-ḥamāma (*The Dove's Necklace*), a treatise on courtly and Platonic love. Written many decades before the first troubadour lyrics of Provence, it may have served as a useful textbook for emerging poets in southern France. Ibn Ḥazm also includes in his treatise his own poetry that extols Platonic love.[21] Another poet and politician was Ibn Zaydūn (1003–71) who wrote the most sensitive lyrics about the loss of his beloved Wallāda, the daughter of the king of Cordoba, a distinguished poet herself and a beautiful woman. There were many more love poets in Muslim Spain who undoubtedly influenced Romance vernacular lyrics in southern Europe and beyond: Ibn Quzmān (d. 1160), the wandering minstrel of Cordoba and al-Tuṭīlī, a blind poet who invented new forms in poetry and died as a young man in 1129.

But, perhaps, it was Ibn ʿArabī (1165–1240), who was born in Murcia and flourished mainly in Seville (until 1202) that was likely to have inspired Dante the most. He died in Damascus twenty-five years before Dante was born. Ibn ʿArabī was a mystic poet who had his Beatrice, too: A beautiful Persian woman and a learned religious scholar by the name Niẓām. He met her in Mecca along with a group of Persian mystics. His love poems dedicated to her describe his symbolic rendering of the path of the mystic. Her beauty was related to the divine reality. Ibn ʿArabī's *Tarjumān al-ashwāq* (The Interpreter of Longing) is an allegory that could be read on different levels. But his critics accused him of heresy and of composing erotic poetry. As a result, he felt obliged to write a commentary on his deep religious experience and show how truth may be expressed in different ways.

His most influential book is *al-Futūḥāt al-Makkiyya* (*The Meccan Revelations*). In a chapter entitled "The Alchemy of Happiness," there is an esoteric allegory of the ascension of man to heaven. Another book by the name *al-Isrāʾ ilā maqām al-asrā* (The nocturnal journey toward the station of the most magnanimous one), Ibn ʿArabī develops the theme of the Prophet's ascension to the seventh heaven. Asín refers to these books as possible sources for Dante's vision of paradise. He argues that Christian theologians, such as the Spaniards Raymond Lull and Raymond Martin, were very familiar with Ibn ʿArabī's concept of this spiritual paradise at the time Dante was composing his *Comedy*.[22] Furthermore, he observes:

---

21 Ibn Ḥazm, *Ring*, trans. Arberry.

22 Asín Palacios, Islam and the Divine Comedy, trans. Sutherland 140. Note that Dante's notion of paradise as pure light may be also borrowed from Ibn Masarra (883–931) of Cordoba who is the founder of the Illuministic school, or pseudo-Empedoclean philosophy. According to this school, God should be interpreted as light and our process of

> In the Moslem world two antithetical ideas flourished almost simultaneously – the coarse and sensual paradise of the Koran, and the spiritual picture of the philosophers and the mystics. In the Christian world, the same two ideas existed – the materialistic conception, equivalent to that of the Koran, which flourished prior to the *Divine Comedy*, and the spiritual picture, which was solely the work of the Florentine poet.[23]

Dante himself professed to have created new means, unknown to other Christians, to behold God:

> ... I make my way above
> still in these swathings death dissolves. I came here
> through the Infernal grief. Now, since God's love
> incloses me in Grace so bounteous
> that he permits me to behold His court
> by means wholly unknown to modern use.[24]

Dante's new heaven has nothing to do with the earthly paradise of other Christians who preceded him. It is the heaven where rational souls reside according to their understanding.[25] In this sense, it is akin to that of Ibn ʿArabī, al-Ghazālī (Latinized: Alghazel, 1058–1111),[26] and Ibn Rushd (Latinized: Averroes, 1126–98). Furthermore, Dante's astronomical paradise is related to the Sufi mystical treatment of astronomy and astrology. Beatrice, the lost beloved, does not symbolize the sinful and the forbidden as one would expect in the literature of the Christian Middle Ages. Rather, she can easily be categorized with the long list of female guides clad in mantles that seem as if made of

---

cognition as an illumination from above through the intermediary of the spirits of the spheres. Ibn Masarra's ideas were transmitted to the Augustinian scholastics.

23 Asín Palacios, *Islam and the Divine Comedy*, trans. Sutherland 141.

24 Dante Aligheri, *Comedy: Purgatorio*, Canto XVI, 37–42.

25 Compare with the Muslim mystic interpretation of the Verse of Light (Q 26:35) contrasted with Darkness, Q 26:40 in Ali (trans.), *Kur'an*. Also consult *Mishkāt al-anwār* (*Niche for Light*) by al-Ghazālī, ed. ʿAfīfī', and the English translation by Gairdner.

26 Note that al-Ghazālī was partly translated into Latin before 1150. He exerted a great influence on Jewish and Christian scholasticism. See for instance his book *al-Durra al-fākhira* (The precious pearl), an eschatological treatise on death, translated into French by Gautier. The Arabic original is also included. Here the heavenly maiden is to accompany the virtuous dead until judgment day. On this issue see also S. Günther's contribution to the present publication.

light in Muslim mystic poetry. All these females are instructors along the path to union with God.

It is not only through books, or discussions with Italian university professors, or theologians, or poets that Dante might have accumulated some knowledge of Arabic and Islamic sources, but also through contact with his mentor Brunetto Latini (1220–94) who was sent to Seville on an embassy to Alfonso el Sabio of Castile to seek help for Florence against the Sienese. Like Dante, Latini was born in Florence.[27] He was a prominent Florentine Guelph and the author of various works in prose and verse that Dante admired. Latini would have had firsthand knowledge of Islamic philosophy and literature in Spain.

2 Visions of the Afterworlds

There is no doubt that Dante modeled his own journey to the afterworlds on that of Virgil's Aeneas, at least in part. Both travel down through hell accompanied by a guide until they reach Satan himself in the lowest pit. Both are ferried across a river to the kingdom of the dead. Both converse with sinners guilty of various crimes. But Dante lingers more in that gloom-hidden abode than Aeneas and gives us more detail about his journey using certain Islamic eschatological motifs and ideas. *Purgatory* and *Paradise*, however, owe little to Virgil's *Aeneid*. Another source that might have inspired Dante is *De Consolatione Philosophiae* (*On the Consolation of Philosophy*) written in the sixth century by a Christian Roman statesman and philosopher, Boethius, who was imprisoned at Pavia, and finally tortued to death in 525. In his book Boethius represents philosophy as a gracious and beautiful woman. It is likely that this figure partly

27 As a result of the defeat of the Guelphs at the battle of Montaperti, Latini was exiled from his native city. He took refuge for some years (1260–6) in France. When he returned to Tuscany in 1266 he held high offices for some twenty years. He was interested in philosophy in particular and was a great orator. His two principal works were *The book of the treasure* and *The little treasure*. From the latter poetic allegorical journey Dante learned a number of his devices. Although Latini was Dante's mentor and friend, he was condemned in the *Inferno* to eternal suffering, scorched by fire from above and below, in the seventh circle of hell. Grouped with the sodomites who committed violence against nature, Latini ran in endless circles. But Dante's reunion with his mentor and friend was very warm, as the following lines indicate: 'O my son! May it not displease you,' he cried, * 'if Brunetto Latino leave his company * and turn and walk a little by your side.' * And I to him: 'With all my soul I ask it * Or let us sit together, if it please him * Who is my Guide and leads me through this pit.' Dante Aligheri, *Comedy: Inferno*, Canto XV, 31–36.

inspired Dante to create Beatrice, who is a very different woman. Furthermore, Boethius' attitude toward Neoplatonism may have fascinated Dante.[28] For all these reasons, perhaps, Boethius, the persecuted philosopher, was placed in *Paradise* in Canto X. But many other Islamic sources may have supplemented the *Aeneid*, and *On the Consolation of Philosophy*, and consequently helped Dante enrich his imagination and create his national Christian poem that became canonical throughout western history.

In his article "Dante and Islam: History and Analysis of a Controversy" Vicente Cantarino argues that

> the diffusion of the Mohammedan legend in Christian Europe has been proved by literary documents, namely the *Libro della Scala*. To reject a priori any other contacts between Christian and Muslim lore, through literary or oral channels, would be to adopt a position that can hardly be reasonable. For we know now that toward the end of the 12th century, there was written an allegorical and philosophical treatise on the soul's journey into the Other World. It was composed in either Sicily or Catalonia, and shows an obvious and deep influence of Avicenna's philosophy and also of Ibn Gabriol. This proves that by the beginning of the 'Duecento' such philosophical allegories of Arabic descent were known in Christian Europe.[29]

3 Echoes from *Ḥayy b. Yaqẓān*

Although the first translation that we know of *Ḥayy b. Yaqẓān* into Latin and other European languages was completed after Dante's death, it is likely that the story of the boy born on a desert island had been orally transmitted

---

28 Many critics suggest the comparison between Book VI of the *Aeneid* and Dante's *Comedy*. See for instance Gilson, *Dante and philosophy*, trans. D. Moore 66. Others refer to the influence of Boethius and the philosophy of Neoplatonism on Dante. Consult, for instance, Holmes, *Dante* 19, 39.

29 Cantarino, Dante and Islam 187. Note that here Cantarino is referring to Ibn Sīnā, or Avicenna, the most illustrious Persian physician and philosopher (980–1037); Dante places him in limbo along with Aristotle, Plato, Empedocles, and Averroes. As for Solomon ben Gabriol (Avicebron, Avencebrol), he was an Arab Jew who died in Valencia, Spain in 1058. He was a teacher of Neoplatonism in the West. His book, *Yanbūʿ al-ḥayāt* (*The fountain of life*) was translated into Latin in 1150 and inspired the Franciscan school. See Hitti, *History of the Arabs* 580–1.

throughout Spain and Italy, or even summarized, or translated in one way or another during the twelfth, the thirteenth, or the early first half of the fourteenth century.[30] At times the similarities between Ḥayy and Dante are very striking. Although Ḥayy does not understand the relevance of hell and paradise, reward and punishment, or why the prophets have to create such concepts, he himself embarks on a journey to see the Mover of the Universe, or the Ultimate Truth.[31]

Dante was thirty-five years old when he felt the urge to seek the True Way and cleanse himself from worldliness and errors. This was Ḥayy's exact age when he turned his gaze toward heaven. Both men highlight the inner light that shines on them and helps them see their way. But while Ḥayy journeys alone and depends on his own reason, Dante needs a guide who symbolizes reason, and this he finds in the celebrated pagan Roman poet, Virgil. Ḥayy attempts alone to ascend from earth to heaven, but realizes that there are prerequisites for such ascension, and that human reason has its limitations. In order to reach the very throne of the Mover of the Universe, one has to cleanse one's self of earthly desires and be guided by intuition and the inner light. Dante, too, attempts to reach the pinnacle of joy and come to the Light of God. Virgil offers to guide him but only as far as Human Reason can go. The sinner has to recognize his sins and those of others. He must renounce his sins by ascending through purgatory, and only then may he reach his goal. Another guide, Beatrice, symbol of divine love, must take over for the final ascent, for Human Reason is limited. Finally, St. Bernard, the symbol of Contemplation, will help the seeker fix his gaze on the intense light and behold God. But regardless of how much the two men differ in approaching their ascent, both are endowed with free will and immense capacity for compassion and love.

In Dante's *Comedy*, there are seven distinct heavens, that is, seven stars in the Ptolemaic system: The Moon, Mercury, Venus, the Sun, Mars, Jupiter, and Saturn. In addition there are the spheres of the Fixed Stars, the Crystalline Heaven, and finally the Empyrean, or the abode of God. In each heavenly

---

30 In 1349 Moses of Narbonne translated Ibn Ṭufayl's *Ḥayy Ibn Yaqẓān* into Hebrew. During the second half of the fifteenth century Pico Della Mirandola, one of the most significant figures of the Renaissance, translated *Ḥayy* into Latin. Dante could not have seen the Hebrew translation because he died in 1321. But he is likely to have known something about *Ḥayy* through oral channels, or perhaps some written abstracts of the novel. See Attar, *Roots*.

31 I have consulted the Arabic versions of *Ḥayy Ibn Yaqẓān* published by Dār al-Mashriq, ed. Nādir; Dār al-Āfāq, ed. Saʿd; the 5th edition published by Damascus University, ed. Ṣalībā and ʿAyyād; and the English translations of Goodman and Kocache.

sphere, Dante meets a variety of souls and converses with them. Then Beatrice disappears. St. Bernard of Clairvaux, the Abbot of the Benedictine Order, comes to lead him to the vision of God. Through contemplation, Dante reaches the state of ecstasy in which the souls of the blessed gaze directly upon God. It is important to remember however that in 1144 St. Bernard, the symbol of contemplation and piety, had preached a new crusade against the Muslim infidels. Ḥayy, on the other hand, refers only to the Moon, Saturn, the Sun, the Fixed Stars, and the Highest Celestial Sphere, or what he calls *al-falak al-aʿlā*.[32] He does not speak of specific souls on his journey to the Mover of the Universe. He has no need for any guide except himself. Eventually, he recognizes the existence of one true being – this he does without the help of prophets, or religious institutions, or men who may be viewed as very objectionable to some of us today – and succeeds in glimpsing the divine world.

Light metaphors are abundant in both allegories. It is by the illumination of the mind rather than by sense impressions that Dante ultimately comes to know God. His ascent beyond the senses symbolizes the progress of the soul in its advance toward knowledge of the Ultimate Truth. The sun is the symbol of intellectual illumination and ultimately of God Himself. In *Ḥayy*, light metaphors are used in reference to this perfect, beautiful, omniscient, and omnipotent Being. They are associated with the science of optics. The properties and phenomena of both visible and invisible light are carefully examined. In his yearning to see the divine light, Ḥayy realizes that reason alone is not enough, it must be supplemented with intuition. It is only when he experiences total annihilation that he sees the highest sphere that has no physical body.

> It could be compared to the image of the sun as seen in a polished mirror. It is neither the sun nor the mirror nor is it anything other than them. He saw signs of such perfection, glory and beauty in the essence of that non-material sphere so great as to be beyond description … In a state of ultimate pleasure, happiness … and joy, his vision showed him the essence of Truth …[33]

Ḥayy endeavored to see the divine light, which shines within each one of us. His story shows how an individual can progress to perfection if he so desires.

---

32 We know that Ibn Ṭufayl had very advanced and useful theories in astronomy unlike those of Ptolemy and al-Biṭrūjī, his own pupil (d. 1185–86); unfortunately his manuscripts are lost.

33 Ibn Ṭufayl, *Journey*, trans. Kocache 48.

The concept of equating joy and happiness to brilliant light in both Dante's and Ibn Ṭufayl's works is very striking. Dante, too, speaks of

> Pure intellectual light, fulfilled with love,
> Love of the True Good, filled with all delight,
> Transcending sweet delight, all sweet above.[34]

But the progress to perfection is arduous. One of the many stages of the spiritual journey involves the renunciation of one's worldly possessions. In *Paradise* St. Thomas Aquinas tells the story of St. Francis who declared himself to be 'the bridegroom of poverty.' Later Dante sees Francis himself among the ranks of the blessed in the Empyrean. It is important to note that the Italian St. Francis of Assisi (Francesco Bernardone: 1182–1226), who once lived comfortably as the son of a rich wool merchant, was one of Dante's heroes. He "spoke Provençal, the language used by the troubadours ... His own poetry" as Idries Shah suggests, "... strongly resembles in places that of the love poet Rūmī ..."[35] At the age of twenty-five, Francis became seriously ill and vowed to devote himself to a life of religion. He renounced all his worldly possessions. In 1219, Francis went to Egypt in a vain attempt to convert the Muslim sultan to Christianity. Espousing poverty like St. Francis, Dante attacked the excessive wealth of the church in his *Comedy* and did not hesitate to put some of the popes in hell.[36] Nick Havely writes in his book *Dante and the Franciscans*:

> Soon after the death of Clement v on 20 April 1314, Dante wrote a letter to the Italian cardinals assembled at Avignon to elect the next Pope. Accusing them repeatedly of abusing the 'bride of Christ', of leading the chariot of the church astray, and of failing to act as true pastors; he cited, as the root cause of their betrayal, their pharisaical greed and their 'marriage' to avarice.[37]

---

34 Dante Aligheri, *Comedy: Paradise*, Canto XXX, 40–42.

35 Shah, *The Sufis* 228. Shah relates "'The Song of the Sun', hailed as the first-ever Italian poem ... composed after the saint's journey to the East" to the numerous poems written by Rūmī and dedicated to the sun (see 231–4). Note that St. Francis was one of the first poets to encourage popular hymn singing in the vernacular. See Jacobs, *Music* 23–4.

36 See Dante Aligheri, *Comedy: Inferno*, Canto XIX, Circle Eight: Bolgia Three. The Simoniacs (sellers of ecclesiastic favors and offices).

37 Havely, *Dante and the Franciscans* 1.

Ḥayy, on the other hand, espoused poverty as a principle, both on his desert island and in society. He was content with very little; he ate 'no more than just what would satisfy his hunger.' He even formulated a thesis about the preservation of plants, animals, and water. In society, Ḥayy observed that many people were greedy and loved to amass excessive fortunes. Buying and selling were the major activities in their cities. Passion controlled men's lives. No one was interested in learning or using reason. Everyone was seeking pleasure, or satisfying some lust. Religion was understood literally and religious rites were performed mechanically. Ḥayy saw a potential hazard in commerce. Wealth is not only likely to create conflicts in society, it also creates masters and slaves. For Ḥayy, man is born equal to his other fellowmen. Commerce only disrupts this notion of equality and subsequently destroys human freedom. He himself owned nothing and had no desire to own anything. Nevertheless, he came to understand the craving of some men for buying and selling when he lived among other human beings. His conclusion was that commerce, if not regulated by a just king, would lead to greed and moral corruption.

Abstinence, renunciation, poverty, patience, and trust in God are stages in the journeys of both Ḥayy and Dante. But there are also literary devices that unite both of them: Reality and mirrors, faint and intense light, visions that disappear in a flash, the perpetual motion of the lovers/seekers who continuously circle, from their own free will, as heavenly stars around the Prime Mover. The differences between the two men are obvious.

According to one version of the story concerning his birth, Ḥayy was born on an island that enjoyed the most perfect temperature on earth and received its light from the highest possible point in heaven. He had no parents and no religion. He did not know humans. Nevertheless he managed to survive in a natural state, free of society, history, and tradition. He invented his own tools, clothed himself, tamed animals, and fortified his dwelling against possible attacks from wild beasts. Eventually, and after being occupied with such earthly matters – gathering food, building shelter, preserving natural resources, observing, and experimenting – Ḥayy began to turn his gaze toward heaven. Dante, on the other hand, was an Italian Christian soldier, poet, and politician. His great-great grandfather was a crusader who died in a foreign land fighting against the Muslims. He was thirty-seven years old when he was exiled from Florence and sentenced to be burnt alive should he ever return to the city of his birth. His enemies accused him of corruption. It was the appropriate time for him to think seriously about his own spiritual failure, and the active pursuit of the love of good.

Ḥayy believed that the body would perish after death. But Dante adhered to the notion that the body would be united with the soul after the last judgment whether we are assigned to heaven, or hell. In *Paradise*, Canto XIV, Solomon explains to Dante the relationship between grace, vision, love, and radiance. He assures him that

> ... when we put completeness on afresh
> All the more gracious shall our person be,
> Reclothed in the holy and glorious flesh[38]

Ḥayy's journey through heaven concentrates on the One True Being and the desire of the traveler to meet Him face to face. Dante, on the other hand, populates all the heavens with souls representing the stages of spiritual attainment both in the active and contemplative life. Along with Beatrice, he moves from heaven to heaven. Emperors, warriors, politicians, and theologians who dabbled in politics are to be found bathed in light: Justinian, Emperor of Constantinople who is chiefly renowned for his great codification of the Roman Law; Dante's ancestor who marched to foreign lands; Charlemagne, the Emperor of the Franks and his nephew Roland; Robert Guiscard, Duke of Apulia and Calabria; Duke Godfrey, the commander-in-chief of the Christian armies in the First Crusade, and many more. Most of them have some relation to the Arabs, or the Muslim infidels. But there are also troubadour poets (Foulquet of Marseilles who repented for his worldly life), mystics (the Scottish Richard of St. Victor), and professors of philosophy who admired Averroes, or disagreed with him (Albertus Magnus, St. Thomas Aquinas, and Sigier of Brabant) among many others. The majority, of course, are Christians, both men and women, but there are a few Jews and some virtuous pagans as well.

In sum, the journey of Ḥayy and Dante to the abode of the Mover of the Universe describes a significant shift from the collectivity and group values of medieval culture to the recognition of individual needs and possibilities. The personal search for the Ultimate Truth is highlighted in both allegories. In Dante's case, the church helps in this personal quest, but the traveler's own reason and love are indispensable for salvation. In this context the journey is not performed as an act of obedience to please ecclesiastic authority. Rather, it is enacted as a personal drive for perfection.[39] But Ḥayy, who is a natural man free of religion and history, is bound to fix his gaze on heaven after he solves his daily problems. This is the logical consequence of growing up entirely alone on a desert island.

---

38 Dante Aligheri, *Comedy: Paradise*, Canto XIV, 43–45.

39 See Cantor and Klein (eds.), *Dante and Machiavelli* 3–9.

In his book *The Mystics of Islam*, Reynold A. Nicholson observes that

> mystics of every race and creed have described the progress of the spiritual life as a journey or a pilgrimage … The *Sufi* who sets out to seek God calls himself a "traveler" …; he advances by slow "stages" … along a "path" … to the goal of union with Reality.[40]

The Sufi passes seven stages before he journeys in the Real, by the Real, to the Real and becomes himself a reality. According to the author of the *Kitāb al-Lumaʿ* (lit., The book of flashes) the Sufi must traverse all the stages of repentance, abstinence, renunciation, poverty, patience, trust in God, and finally satisfaction; he should experience whatever states it pleases God to bestow upon him, otherwise he will never become a 'knower' or 'Gnostic,' and will never realize that knowledge, knower, and known are One.[41]

Both Ḥayy and Dante choose to forsake their earthly abode in search of the Divine Light. The journey toward the Prime Mover of the Universe means above all journeying away from all sins. At every stage where they halt they traverse a station on the way to the Light. Ḥayy violates the mystic code when he decides to go alone without a guide, while Dante adheres to the rites of the journey.

4 Divine Beatrice

No real Western model for Beatrice was ever discovered by Dante's scholars. There are numerous suggestions, but none are totally satisfactory. George Holmes, who is oblivious to any Islamic influence on Dante, argues that Boethius' "'Lady Philosophy' was probably the inspiration for Dante's new lady, a very different figure from Beatrice."[42] Karl Vossler on the other hand suggests something more feasible. He believes that Guido Cavalcanti (1257–1300), Dante's personal friend, a noted poet whose poetry exalts women, and a reputed heretic known to be an Averroist, influenced Dante's literary and intellectual development. He cites Cavalcanti's last song, addressed to his beloved from exile, as an example of mystical tenderness.[43] Another critic, John A.

40 Nicholson, *Mystics of Islam* 28.

41 Ibid., 29.

42 Holmes, *Dante* 19.

43 Vossler, *Medieval culture*, trans. Lawton ii, 146–8.

Scott, is puzzled to see learned Beatrice attack the follies of preachers and considers her truly astonishing for Dante's age. He argues,

> St. Paul had forbidden women to teach (1 Tim. 2.12): They were to be subject to men especially to priests ... Instead, as Joan Ferrante has brilliantly documented 'only Beatrice and God are infallible in the *Commedia* ... Dante gives the office of major theologians in his heaven to someone whose sex would have shocked virtually all the doctors of the church.'[44]

But had Dante's scholars looked elsewhere to Muslim Spain and Norman Sicily they might have discovered many Arab and Muslim women who were very alive in the popular imagination, not only as a means to reach the Divine, but in certain cases as the Divine themselves. Also, women teachers/preachers were abundant in Muslim history. The most illustrious mystic poet, Ibn ʿArabī (1165– 1240), who is believed to be among those who influenced Dante, had "studied under the Spanish woman Sufi Faṭima b. Waliyya";[45] in his love poems he emphasized the connection between human beauty and divine reality. Like other Muslim mystics and love poets, Ibn ʿArabī was able to perceive the beautiful woman, his muse, and the divinity at the same time. Another poet, Ibn Ḥazm led a life of exile not very different from that of Dante, wrote a treatise on love and lovers in which he included his own love poetry. His beloved was not an ordinary human being, but the light that helped him reach the ultimate Light.[46] Love here becomes a redeeming religious force. It is an ennobling experience. The beloved is a saint, and through love the lover is able to understand hidden truths and behold the Divine.

Sigrid Hunke refers briefly to an old Arabic attitude to love, whereby women are worshiped as divine objects, she states that this notion traveled to Europe in the Middle Ages, and even elevated Mary, the mother of Christ, from the servant of God to someone associated with Him. She argues that these new ideas invaded France, Italy, Sicily, Austria, and Germany from Muslim Spain. But according to her, the poets who later became known as Troubadours, or courtly love poets, did not seriously believe in these ideas and used them only to attract women. Thus, Ovid's views on the female as a vain, frail, and inconstant creature whose main goal in life is to deceive men and be deceived by

---

44 Scott, *Understanding Dante* 331.

45 Shah, *The Sufis* 140.

46 Hunke, *Allahs Sonne über dem Abendland*, trans. Baydūn and Dasūqī 521.

them remain the cornerstone in treating women in the West to this day.[47] But Dante is the exception to the rule. His Beatrice evokes the memory of sacred women, such as Laylā, ʿAbla, Buthayna, Rābiʿa al-ʿAdawiyya, Niẓām, and many other unnamed women in Arabic or Persian love poetry.[48] In numerous Islamic works the mystic heavenly bride is a spiritual being who has surely anticipated Dante's lost beloved. In her book *Spain To England*, Alice Lasater observes that

> In two ... major medieval eschatological works, the *Commedia* of Dante and the fourteenth-century Middle-English vision *The Pearl*, with the introduction of a lost beloved female as a guide through paradise, appears a tradition which the Islamic Sufis had developed from the ninth century. The female guide as conceived by the Islamic mystics and as found in *The Pearl* and Dante's *Paradiso* in no way resembles the Celtic fairy mistress who lures mortal heroes into a never-never land, but rather fills the role played in other Christian visions by various saints and angels in guiding and instructing the dreamer.[49]

5 Conflicting Views on Dante's *Commedia*

In his dismissal of Asín's thesis that Dante may have had a sympathetic attitude to Islamic culture for placing important figures from Islamic history in limbo and not in hell, Richard Southern minimizes the significance of such a scheme. He argues that Ibn Sīnā (Avicenna) and Ibn Rushd (Averroes) are

---

47 Ibid., 523–4.

48 Laylā is usually referred to in the epithet Majnūn Laylā (lit., the man who is crazy about Laylā). This ancient Arabic legend has spread to different parts of the world. It extols the power of undying love. Laylā's father gives her away in marriage to another man. Consequently, her lover becomes insane and sets out to wander half-naked in the desert living among wild animals. His poems about Laylā, whom he transforms from an ordinary being into something extraordinary – a goddess – have influenced not only the Persians and the Turks, but also the Hungarians, among others. However, love that enters through the eyes, attacks the heart, and destroys the lover's strength is viewed as something destructive, for it leads the lover to sheer madness. Buthayna is another example of an idolized woman. She is the beloved of Jamīl al-ʿUdhrī (d. 701); she too is married to another man. But her lover remains loyal to her until death. His poetry exalts chaste and unrequited love. Poems by both Majnūn and Jamīl are set to music and sung to this day in the Arab world. Rābiʿa al-ʿAdawiyya (717–801) of Basra was a famous mystic woman and a revered guide along the mystic way.

49 Lasater, *Spain to England* 61.

not considered simply Muslims, but scholars who figure among the ancients. As for Saladin, however, who captured Jerusalem in October 1187 and defeated the crusaders, Dante preferred to portray him not as a historical figure, but as a character found in popular romances. Southern believes that Dante detested Islam – not only because he placed its Prophet and his son-in-law with 'The Sowers of Discord' at the bottom of hell, but also because of the death of Dante's ancestor in the land of the infidels. As for the praise of the modesty of Muslim women by Dante's friend Forese in *The Purgatorio*, Southern claims that Dante's aim is to show that even barbarians and Saracens are more modest than those in Florence. On the whole, Southern sees *The Divine Comedy* as an outcry against corruption in Italy and a passionate hatred of the vices of Florence in particular. For him, Dante is outraged not so much by the existence of Islam as a religion, but against the Christian church that refuses to be reformed and the clergy who failed to convert Saladin and other Muslims to Christianity. This interpretation leads Southern to believe that "Nothing that has a specifically Islamic inspiration took root in the west. The west had enough of its own."[50]

Other critics oblivious to the influence of Islamic sources on the *Comedy* suggest different interpretations. In his book *Medieval Culture: An Introduction to Dante and His Times*, Karl Vossler argues that

> *The Divine Comedy* ... is evidently intended to convert no heathen, to refute no heretic, to convince no doubter ..., to carry on no battle for the faith. Here and there polemic and didactic intentions emerge from it, but they run their course, one and all, within the Christian community, and never is there to be noted an assault or sally against the heathen. There is not even a rallying-cry for a crusade against Islam.[51]

Yet one wonders why Dante seems to be so confused and confusing at times. Does he admire Muslim civilization? Or does he detest it? Is he attracted to Arabic poetry or philosophy? Or is he repulsed by it? Does he accept Averroes' teaching? Or does he reject it? Does he support more crusades to the East? Or is he sick of wars and conflicts? Does he side with his friends and mentors who admire Muslim civilization? Or is he totally on the opposite side? Who is this Dante that so many scholars wrote about? Is he the true Christian believer they depicted? Or is he masquerading as a firm supporter of the crusades and the enemy of Islam? Why does he not acknowledge any Arabic influence? Yet,

50 Southern, Dante and Islam 143.

51 Vossler, *Medieval culture* 211.

he enumerates endless Western sources? What is puzzling is that one can find proofs for each side of the argument. Those who think that Dante is the model Christian and the enemy of Islam cling to the story of his ancestor who died in the Holy Land fighting the Muslims. The reward of the 'righteous' warrior was paradise. On the other hand, the lower part of hell is a city of mosques where heretics are severely punished. They are the skeptics who deny the soul's immortality and are associated in one way or another with Averroes and Islamic philosophy. Here one finds Cavalcanti, the father of Dante's friend Guido, and Frederick II, Emperor of the Holy Roman Empire. In the lower hell one also meets Dante's mentor Brunetto Latini among the violent against nature. Latini, too, had something to do with the learning of the Muslims. But it is Michael Scot, the translator of Arabic books, who languishes further down in hell among the fortune-tellers. He is referred to as the "wizard," never to be trusted; he tricked people and associated with a heretical emperor who admired Arabic science and literature and encouraged its dissemination all over Europe. Just one circle above Satan, one meets Muḥammad, the Prophet of Islam, and his son-in-law ʿAlī. Both men are condemned to hell for causing religious discord in the world. In sum, all traitors of the Christian church, or traitors of the empire are condemned to eternal hell. Aldo Bernardo suggests that Dante's ultimate goal is

> to depict as vividly as possible how man can be saved and become eternal through the use of his free will ... To achieve his goal Dante had to undertake a reproduction of the entire universe, of the senses and of the spirit. What's more, he had to create an impression of infallibility which in his day meant simply abiding by the teachings of the Church and of the Church Fathers. By taking these teachings and using them as foundations for a portrayal of the universe as presumably seen through the eyes of the Christian code, Dante hoped to help lead Mankind from the miseries of this world to salvation and true happiness.[52]

But those who believe that Dante either admires Muslim civilization, or is simply a heretic himself who masquerades behind a true Christian face, cite other proofs. Averroes and Avicenna who have supposedly created havoc in the medieval Christian mind are not suffering in hell. They are placed in limbo where there is no pain, or real punishment. The most conspicuous example of those who are spared from hell is the Muslim king and warrior Saladin. Although he is placed by himself apart from others, such as "the good Brutus"

52 Bernardo, Dante's Divine Comedy 47–8.

who once conspired to murder Caesar, and below Aristotle, he does not seem to be suffering from anything in limbo. Supporters of this theory argue that Dante was suspected of being a heretic in his own religious views during his lifetime, and that he had to be very careful in presenting these views. Heretics were usually punished, not only in Italy but also in the Islamic world. It is likely that Dante's contradictions stem from this fear of being branded as a heretic. Thus, Averroes is referred to in limbo as the philosopher "of the Great Commentary." But in *The Purgatorio* he is criticized for his views on the unity of the Possible Intellect by Statius who nevertheless still calls him "a wise head." Other scholastics were less generous in their criticism, but were not cited in Dante's *Commedia*. Indeed Averroes' views on the Possible Intellect enraged both Albertus Magnus and Thomas Aquinas such that the latter accused the Muslim philosopher of being the "perverter" of Aristotle's philosophy.[53] Paul A. Cantor argues that Dante is an Averroist, although modern Dante scholars disagree. He suggests that "Limbo is precisely an allegorical representation of Averroes's idea of the Possible Intellect. The eternal conversation of the philosophers in Dante's Limbo is a metaphor for what Averroes meant by the immortality of human thought."[54] Supporters of an uncanonical Dante raise many other issues to prove their point. What is Sigier of Brabant, the notorious Averroist professor at the University of Paris, doing in paradise? How can Dante beatify and glorify an Averroist, while he himself is supposedly a confirmed Thomist? At the end of his life did the professor really regret his opposition to his bitter opponent St. Thomas Aquinas in their dispute over the teaching of Aristotle in the light of the commentary by Averroes, as Abbé F. Van Steenberghen claims?[55] Or did St. Thomas seem to forget his foe by calling him "That's the eternal light of Sigier, who,/ Lecturing down in Straw Street, hammered home/ Invidious truths, as logic taught him to"?[56] The list of controversial people in the *Commedia* seems to be endless. But it is Beatrice, the ordinary woman from Florence who was transformed into a divine being that seems to excite the imagination of the supporters of this theory the most.

---

53 For Statius' criticism of Averroes, see Dante Aligheri, *Comedy: Purgatorio*, Canto XXV, 61–66. For the criticism by prominent Christian scholastics consult Zedler's preface to her translation of St. Thomas Aquinas's *On the unity of the intellect against the Averroists*. Note that Dante was publicly accused of being an Averroist in 1327, six years after his death. On this topic see Fortin, Dante and Averroism.

54 Cantor, The uncanonical Dante 147.

55 See Gilson, *Dante and philosophy*, trans. Moore 225–81, 317. See also Kibre, Dante and the universities 367–71.

56 Dante Aligheri, *Comedy: Paradise*, Canto X, 136–138.

Elevating the status of a woman to that of God is something unheard of in the Christian medieval world. Harold Bloom argues that Dante's

> heretical intensity has been masked by scholarly commentary which even at its best frequently treats him as though his *Divine Comedy* was essentially versified Saint Augustine. But it is best to begin by marking his extraordinary audacity, which is unmatched in the entire tradition of supposedly Christian literature, including even Milton. Nothing else in Western literature ... is as sublimely outrageous as Dante's exaltation of Beatrice, sublimated from being an image of desire to angelic status, in which role she becomes a crucial element in the church's hierarchy of salvation.[57]

6 Conclusion

Unfortunately, Dante scholars, or American comparatists who believe that Dante is either a true Christian believer, or a heretic, often turn a blind eye to the possible Islamic sources or resonances in the *Commedia*. For them it is absolutely irrelevant to delve into such an esoteric subject.[58] The fact that any aspiring intellectual in thirteenth- or fourteenth-century Europe might have been familiar with some aspects of Arabic and Islamic literature, philosophy, and science and thus flourished, seems to be of no interest to them. Thus Dante is not studied in a proper historical context. Rather, he is examined within his own narrow circle in Florence. When citing important contemporary and literary events, scholars may refer to St. Thomas Aquinas, Brunetto Latini, Guido Cavalcanti, Roger Bacon, St. Francis, or even some English and French monarchs, but their comments always remain exclusively Western. One will never know that these figures had anything to do with Islamic learning, or the East. Even the names that Dante himself mentions in his *Comedy*, such as Averroes,

57 Bloom, *Western canon* 76.

58 See, for instance, Gilson, *Dante and philosophy* 66. In a footnote Gilson writes, "There has been a suggestion of Muslim sources with regard to this point (Señor Asín Palacios). It goes without saying that I do not intend here to express any opinion on a thesis which this is not the place to examine. I endeavor to confine myself to what is certain. Now it is certain that Dante was long familiar with Virgil, and whatever we may think of the thesis of Señor Asín Palacios, we cannot ascribe to it a comparable degree of certainty." Other scholars do not even refer to Asín's thesis or include his book in their bibliography.

Avicenna, Saladin, Mahomet, and ʿAlī are usually omitted from the glossary as insignificant.[59]

Arabic and Islamic visions of the afterworld were familiar in Europe as early as the eleventh century. But modern Dante scholars and American comparatists do not concern themselves with the seventh-century Muḥammad's journey to hell and heaven, or with other literary journeys such as that of Ibn Shuhayd's (992–1035) travel through the valley of the demons,[60] or al-Maʿarrī's (973–1057) humorous and controversial journey to paradise and the abode of Satan.[61] Mystical journeys to heaven by mystic poets, such as Ibn ʿArabī, Farīd al-Dīn al-ʿAṭṭār (1145–1221),[62] Jalāl al-Dīn al-Rūmī (1207–1273),[63] or by rationalist philosophers, such as Ibn Ṭufayl are also out of the range of their studies. Even love poetry and poets like Ibn Ḥazm, Ibn Zaydūn, Ibn Quzmān, and al-Tuṭīlī are totally ignored. The founder of the Illuministic school in Cordoba, Ibn Masarra, the philosopher al-Suhrawardī, or the scientist Ibn al-Haytham, the principal Muslim physicist and student of optics are also ignored.[64] For them Dante did not acknowledge any debt to anyone of them in his *Commedia*. Therefore, according to this logic, they do not have to pay any attention to those

---

59 See, for instance, the "Glossary of Proper Names" in *Comedy: Paradise*, trans. Sayers and Reynolds, 356–394. Cf. Bernardo and Pellegrini, *A critical study*. This latter publication is meant to help generations of American students to appreciate Dante, the Italian poet who thoroughly absorbed the thought of Greco-Roman antiquity and the Judeo-Christian world. It is noteworthy that *Islam and the Divine Comedy* by Asín Palacios is not even mentioned in the "Selected Criticism." One has to read *A dictionary of proper names and notable matters in the works of Dante*, compiled by Paget Toynbee and revised by Charles S. Singleton in order to find Arabic and Islamic names, such as Alghazel, Alfagrano, Alfarabio among others. The author, however, states that Dante does not always acknowledge his debt as in the case, for instance, of Alfraganus on "the projection of the shadow of the earth as far as the sphere of Venus, *Paradise*, ix, 118–19" (Toynbee, *A dictionary* 27).

60 Ibn Shuhayd, *Risālat al-tawābiʿ wa-l-zawābiʿ*, trans. Monroe.

61 Al-Maʿarrī, *Risālat al-ghufrān*.

62 Farīd al-Dīn al-ʿAṭṭār, *Conference*, trans. Nott.

63 Jalāl al-Dīn al-Rūmī, *Poems*, trans. Nicholson; Jalāl al-Dīn al-Rūmī, *Tales*, trans. Arberry.

64 In 1191 at the age of thirty-six al-Suhrawardī, a celebrated Persian mystic, was executed as a heretic in Aleppo, Syria. His major work was *Ḥikmat al-ishrāq*, or *Wisdom of Illumination*. Ibn al-Haytham (Latinized: Alhazen), the principal Muslim physicist and student of optics, was born in Basra, about 965 and died around 1039. He wrote more than one hundred books on mathematics, astronomy, philosophy, and medicine. His most important book is on optics. It is entitled *Kitāb al-Manāẓir*. The Arabic original is lost, but the twelfth-century Latin translation has survived. Almost all medieval writers on optics base their works on Alhazen's *Opticae thesaurus*.

foreign poets, thinkers, or scientists. Dante most likely had not heard of all of them, but he certainly would have known bits and pieces about some of them since the period in which he lived was saturated with Arabic lore. American comparatists either deny or marginalize any interaction between cultures that seems to them irreconcilable. This is mainly due to their neglect of the study of history. Thus Dante could understandably learn from his Roman ancestors and other Europeans, but certainly not from the Arabs and Muslims even though the latter were the dominant players on the cultural and political stage in the medieval world. In this sense, American comparatists hardly differ from a British medievalist historian such as Sir Richard William Southern who propagates Kipling's ideas that East is East and West is West, and the two can never meet.[65] But when making some concessions, Southern accepts the borrowing theory only as long as it relates to original Greek sources transmitted to and by alien cultures to Europe.

Maria Rosa Menocal, a Spanish comparatist and a rare sympathizer with the interaction theory between Islamic culture and the West, suggests that she knows the answer to the riddle of the "Arabic influence" on Dante. She argues that Dante is

> a true believer and a true defender of the faith. He finds himself in the most embattled position imaginable, that of seeing his most respected elders, the most prestigious intellectuals of the time, and even his own best friends, won over to a philosophical system that, in his own view, can only lead to ultimate perdition. Thus the 'Arabic influence' on Dante's work is an overwhelmingly negative one, representing an intellectual and artistic revolution that would undermine everything he believed was important and redeeming in Christian society. In this context, and understanding his belief that he was, as the pilgrim, the model Christian and the scribe of Christ, it is not incongruous to imagine that in setting out to write an apologia he hoped would stem the tide of defections, in making his case for the benefits of fundamental Christianity, he would, consciously or not, have chosen to write a countertext to the *miʿrāj*, which he believed was part of Islamic sacred writings and which described a sensuous and self-fulfilling paradise in which the prophet of that religion had the mysteries of his faith explained to him by his guide, a text replete with both astonishing similarities to Dante's *Commedia* and, perhaps more significant, important counterpoints.[66]

65 Cf. Bassnett, *Comparative literature* 17–20.
66 Menocal, *Role* 130.

Menocal believes that Dante suppressed the Arabic influence on him, mainly because he felt threatened. She never doubts that he must have known the story of the *miʿrāj*, i.e., Muḥammad's ascension to the throne of God either through "Peter the Venerable's allusions to it or through one of the translations by Bonaventura da Siena."[67] She also cites Dante's knowledge of some of the Muslim and Arab philosophers. According to her, Dante was utterly revolted by what he saw and heard, whether in terms of Averroist philosophy, or un-Christian poetry of selfish love, or of excommunicated emperor and dangerous heresies. All these factors supposedly created a challenge for the Florentine poet. His anxiety becomes apparent and as a result he has no choice but to suppress his original sources and thus he prefers to be silent about them. Indeed, she argues that "The repression of the influence of the Arab world on the rest of Europe may well be dated to Dante, and, among other things, it may supply part of the answer to the question of why formative influences on the courtly poetry of Provence and Sicily are left conspicuously unaddressed."[68]

Dante may have detested everything about Islam and Muslim learning as Menocal and other scholars argue. But he also seems to have admired everything about Islam and Muslim learning, in spite of having placed the city of mosques in the lower part of hell and imagined the torture of the prophet Muḥammad and his son-in-law. There is no doubt that Dante was familiar with some Islamic visions of the afterworld, including Muḥammad's ascension to the throne of God. He also must have heard about this un-Christian love poetry coming from Sicily and Muslim Spain. But at the same time, he ought to have heard of a different kind of poetry, that is, the mystical one that was dedicated to the love of God. He would certainly have read something about the sensuous Muslim paradise, but equally he would have known something else about this other paradise that the Sufis described in detail. As for why he preferred to suppress his Arabic and Islamic sources in the *Commedia*, this can likely be attributed to his love-hate relationship with the enemy. Avicenna, Averroes, Saladin, Michael Scot, and Frederick II are either in limbo, or hell, but they are all splendid models in their respective fields. Thomas Aquinas, St. Francis, and St. Bernard who reside in heaven have torn themselves away from the enemy and managed to find their true selves at the end of their ordeal. But they had to absorb the enemy and his learning first, before liberating themselves from him. Dante would love to follow their path. His long poem would be his difficult trial. He would endeavor first to resemble the enemy to the point of disappearing in him. But along the way he would gradually shed his love-hate

67 Ibid., 127.

68 Ibid., 131.

complex and be his own self. Eventually he would walk once more beneath the stars. His love would move the sun and other celestial bodies. No one then would dare to say that his *Divine Comedy* is an example of the imitation of an enemy's journey to hell and heaven. He would create his Beatrice emulating the mystic female guide, emphasizing the connection between human beauty and divine reality, but he would camouflage her origin. He would use the mystics' numbers in structuring the *Comedy* and play on the metaphors of darkness and light throughout the poem. His heaven, too, would have echoes from al-Ghazālī, Ibn Ṭufayl, Ibn ʿArabī, and other Muslim mystics and philosophers. Its most learned inhabitants would be the nearest to the Ultimate Light. In his search for happiness he would have to be transformed into a new being, a purified and complete soul. Endowed with free will, love, and understanding, and purged of sin he would be drawn upwards to the abode of God. Like Ibn Ṭufayl, he, too, would speak about the inadequacy of language, of his own human power to express what he saw on his miraculous journey. But at the end he would produce an Italian nationalist Christian vision of the afterworld expressed in a new language through which he would regain total possession of himself.

Bibliography

Ali, Y.A. (trans.), *The glorious Kur'an*, Riyadh 1938[3].

Aquinas, T., *On the unity of the intellect against the Averroists*, trans. B. Zedler, Milwaukee WI 1968.

Asín Palacios, M., *Islam and the Divine Comedy*, trans. H. Sutherland, London 1968.

al-ʿAṭṭār, F.A., *The conference of the birds: A translation of the Persian poem Mantiq ut-tair*, trans. S.C. Nott, London 1954.

Attar, S., *The vital roots of European Enlightenment: Ibn Tufayl's influence on modern Western thought*, Lanham MD 2007.

Barolin, T., *The undivine comedy: Detheologizing Dante*, Princeton, NJ 1992.

Bassnett, S., *Comparative literature: A critical introduction*, Oxford, 1993.

Bernardo, A.S., Dante's Divine Comedy: The view from God's eye, in W. De Sua and G. Rizzo (eds.), *Dante symposium: In commemoration of the 700th anniversary of the poet's birth (1265–1965)*, Chapel Hill, NC 1965, 45–58.

——— and A.L. Pellegrini, *A critical study to Dante's Divine Comedy*, Totowa NJ and Los Angeles n.d.

Bloom, H., *The western canon: The books and schools of the ages*, New York 1994.

Cantarino, V., Dante and Islam: History and analysis of a controversy, in W. De Sua and G. Rizzo (eds.), *Dante symposium: In commemoration of the 700th anniversary of the poet's birth (1265–1965)*, Chapel Hill, NC 1965, 175–98.

Cantor, N.F. and P.L. Klein (eds.), *Renaissance Thought: Dante and Machiavelli*, Waltham, MA 1969.

Cantor, P.A., The uncanonical Dante: The Divine Comedy and Islamic philosophy, in *Philosophy and Literature* 20.1 (1996), 138–53.

Chejne, A.G., *Islam and the West: The Moriscos a cultural and social history*, Albany, NY 1983.

Dante Aligheri, *The Divine Comedy: 3 Paradise*, trans. D.L. Sayers and B. Reynolds, Harmondsworth 1962, repr. Baltimore 1967.

———, *The Inferno*, trans. J. Ciardi, New York 1954.

———, *The Purgatorio*, trans. J. Ciardi, 1957, repr. New York 1961.

Desmond, S., *Early Islam*, New York 1967.

Dozy, R., *Spanish Islam: A history of the Muslims in Spain*, trans. F.G. Stokes, London 1913.

Fortin, E., Dante and Averroism, in *Actas del V congreso international de filosofia medieval*, ii, Madrid 1979, 739–46.

al-Ghazālī, Abū Ḥāmid, *al-Durra al-fākhira*, trans. L. Gautier, Geneva 1878.

———, *Mishkāt al-anwār*, ed. A. ʿAfīfī, Cairo 1963.

———, *Niche for light*, trans. W.H.T. Gairdner, London 1924.

Gilson, E., *Dante and philosophy*, trans. D. Moore, New York 1963.

Havely, N., *Dante and the Franciscans*, Cambridge 2004.

Hitti, Ph., *The history of the Arabs*, London 1970[10].

Holmes, G., *Dante*, Oxford 1980.

Hunke, S., *Allahs Sonne über Dem Abendland: Unser Arabisches Erbe*, trans. F. Baydūn and K. Dasūqī, Beirut 1993.

Huntington, S.P., *The clash of civilizations and the remaking of world order*. New York 1996.

Ibn Ḥazm, Abū Muḥammad, *The ring of the dove*, trans. A.J. Arberry, London 1953.

Ibn Shuhayd, Abū ʿĀmir, *Risālat al-tawābiʿ wa-l-zawābiʿ: The treatise of familiar spirits and demons*, trans. J.T. Monroe, Berkeley 1971.

Ibn Ṭufayl, Abū Bakr, *Ḥayy Ibn Yaqẓān*, ed. A.N. Nādir, Beirut 1968.

———, *Ḥayy Ibn Yaqẓān*, ed. F. Saʿd, Beirut 1980.

———, *Ḥayy Ibn Yaqẓān*, ed. J. Ṣalībā, and K. ʿAyyād, Damascus 1962[5].

———, *Ḥayy Ibn Yaqẓān*, trans. L.E. Goodman, New York 1972.

———, *The journey of the soul: The story of Hai bin Yaqzan*, trans. R. Kocache, London 1982.

Jacobs, A., *A short history of Western music*, Harmondsworth 1972, repr. 1973.

Kibre, P., Dante and the universities of Paris and Oxford, in G. Di Scipio and A. Scaglione (eds.), *The Divine Comedy and the Encyclopedia of Arts and Sciences*, Amsterdam 1988, 367–71.

Lasater, A.E., *Spain to England: A comparative study of Arabic, European, and English literature of the Middle Ages*, Jackson MS 1974.

Maalouf, A., *The crusades through Arab eyes*, trans. J. Rothschild, London 1984.
al-Maʿarrī, Abū l-ʿAlāʾ, *Risālat al-ghufrān*, Beirut 1985.
Mayer, H.E., *The crusades*, trans. J. Gillingham, Oxford 1972.
Menocal, M.R., *The Arabic role in medieval literary history: A forgotten heritage*, Philadelphia 1987.
Metlitzki, D., *The matter of Araby in medieval England*, New Haven, CT 1977.
Nicholson, R.A., *The mystics of Islam*, London 1963.
Procter, E.S., *Alfonso X of Castile: Patron of literature and learning*, Oxford 1951.
al-Rūmī, Jalāl al-Dīn, *Selected poems from the Divan-i Shams-i Tabriz*, trans. R.A. Nicholson, Cambridge 1898.
———, *Tales from the Masnavi*, trans. A.J. Arberry, London 1961.
Runciman, S., *A history of the crusade*, 3 vols., 1951, repr. London 1991.
Scherberger, M., *Das Miʿrāğname: Die Himmel- und Höllenfahrt des Propheten Muhammad in der osttürkischen Überlieferung*, Würzburg 2003.
Scott, J.A., *Understanding Dante*, Notre Dame, IN 2004.
Shah, I., *The Sufis*, London 1977.
Southern, R.W., Dante and Islam, in D. Baker (ed.), *Relations between East and West in the Middle Ages*, Edinburgh 1973, 133–45.
Toynbee, P. (comp.), *A dictionary of proper names and notable matters in the works of Dante*, rev. C. Singleton, Oxford 1968.
Vossler, K., *Medieval culture: An introduction to Dante and his times*, trans. W.C. Lawton, 2 vols., New York 1929, repr. 1958.
Watt, W.M., *The influence of Islam on medieval Europe*, Edinburgh 1972.

CHAPTER 42

Paradise, Alexander the Great and the *Arabian Nights*: Some New Insights Based on an Unpublished Manuscript

Claudia Ott

> ... and behind them there is nobody else and nothing else but high mountains,
> and above the peaks of the high mountains is paradise hanging between heaven and earth
> like a huge town which God bordered from every side with winds and storms.[1]

The Arabic Alexander tradition consists of a heterogeneous group of texts which share only one feature: their protagonist is Alexander the Great, in Arabic (al-)Iskandar/Dhū l-Qarnayn. Among them we find texts belonging to the tradition of Pseudo-Callisthenes, i.e., the late classical Greek Alexander Romance, based on its Syriac translation. Other Arabic Alexander books can be classified as wisdom literature, still others as an independent branch of the Dhū l-Qarnayn traditions, while a fourth and quite large group of manuscripts contains texts of the semi-oral genre of the *sīra shaʿbiyya*, the Arabian epic.[2]

One of the most important witnesses of the Arabic Pseudo-Callisthenes tradition is a text preserved in a unique manuscript in Paris, dated 1104/1693.[3] Its title is *Sīrat al-malik Iskandar Dhū l-Qarnayn*.[4] The author of the work remains anonymous, but the copyist of this particularly beautiful manuscript has left

1 "*Wa-laysa warāʾahum aḥadan* (sic!) *illā l-jibālu l-shāmikhatu wa-l-jannatu fawqa ruʾūsi l-jibāli l-ʿāliyati l-shāmikhati wa-hiya bayna l-samāʾi wa-l-arḍi wa-hiya shibhu l-madīnati l-ʿaẓīmati qad ḥaffahā llāhu bi-l-riyāḥi l-ʿawāṣifi min kulli jānibin.*" *Sīrat al-malik Iskandar Dhū l-Qarnayn*, Ms. Paris BN Arabe 3687, fol. 74b, lines 10–2 (see figure).

2 Cf. Doufikar-Aerts, *Alexander Magnus Arabicus* passim.

3 The date is given in both the Islamic and the Coptic Calender: "the 18th of Dhu ʾl-Ḥijja, the holy month of the Arabic year 1104, equivalent to the 18 Misrā of the Coptic year 1409"; see Doufikar-Aerts, *Alexander Magnus Arabicus* 58.

4 According to Faustina Doufikar-Aerts, *Alexander Magnus Arabicus* 60, note 178, two more manuscripts of the same text could be traced. A critical edition of all three manuscripts is in preparation.

© KONINKLIJKE BRILL NV, LEIDEN, 2017 | DOI 10.1163/9789004333154_043

us his name: Yūsuf Ibn ʿAṭīya, known as Quzmān. Several Christian-Arabic manuscripts of the last decades of the seventeenth century originate from the same scribe, who was apparently a Coptic Christian.[5] Moreover, the contents of this manuscript show a moderate, but not exclusive Christian influence. As Faustina Doufikar-Aerts puts it: "Christian and Islamic elements alternate in a 'brotherly' fashion."[6] According to Doufikar-Aerts, this manuscript is not only the most important exponent of the Alexander Romance in Arabic, but can also be characterized as a missing link between the Syriac and the Ethiopian Alexander Romance.[7]

1 Alexander and Paradise

In this manuscript, we find an unexpected piece of information about paradise. It is related to Alexander's exploits to the boundaries of the world and the wall against Gog and Magog, both of which form major motifs in the Arabic Alexander tradition: Alexander the Great erects a barrier in order to protect mankind from the apocalyptic hordes of Gog and Magog who were believed to live in the extreme north.[8] The Arabic text is quoted above in transliteration and English translation; the original is displayed in the photograph of the manuscript.[9] It is a short but nevertheless most interesting passage. Alexander the Great has just asked his messengers about the remotest edges of the earth in the North and East, beyond Persia and China. And the messengers report to him that nothing other than paradise lies beyond them, "hanging between heaven and earth."

2 The Arabian Nights

In this passage of the Alexander Romance, paradise is located "beyond Persia and China," which is almost the same exotic, fascinating, and dangerous region where the *Arabian Nights* have their origin. This may be pure coincidence – it

5 On the name Quzmān and its linkage to Coptic circles see Doufikar-Aerts, *Alexander Magnus Arabicus* 58, note 173.
6 Ibid., 71–2.
7 Ibid., 59–66.
8 See van Donzel and Schmidt, *Gog and Magog*, passim.
9 *Sīrat al-malik Iskandar Dhū l-Qarnayn*, Ms. Paris BN Arabe 3687, fol. 74b, lines 11–3 (see figure).

seems interesting anyway to have a closer look at this analogy. The *Arabian Nights* explicitly mention "the islands of India and China"[10] or otherwise "the peninsulas of India and Indochina"[11] as the location of the frame story of Shahriyār and Shahrazād; besides that, the main literary motifs of the frame story of the *Arabian Nights* are rooted in Indian literature. The basic idea of the *Arabian Nights* is expounded in the frame story, which consists of the so-called prologue, the night formulas, and the various endings. In our context, the prologue is the most interesting. It is made up of three parts, all of which have their roots in Old Indian – Pali and Sanskrit – literature, but which are first woven into one single story in the *Arabian Nights*. The partition into three parts goes back to the French folklorist, Emmanuel Cosquin, who first published his ideas in 1909.[12] Cosquin's analysis was discussed by Enno Littmann in the afterword to his German translation of the *Arabian Nights*.[13] In their fundamental study on the *Arabian Nights*, Heinz and Sophia Grotzfeld give another detailed record of these ideas.[14] According to Grotzfeld, the first part of the prologue tells the story of two kings and brothers, who are betrayed by their wives and who give up their rule because of their disappointment at this betrayal. This motif is found more than once in the *Tipiṭaka*, a Buddhist collection of stories, part of which was translated into Chinese in 251 CE. The second part of the prologue is the story of the ʿIfrīt and the Maiden: a Demon keeps a young woman captive in a glass case to prevent her from being unfaithful to him. She, however, betrays him whenever he is asleep. Two men, who are traveling the world to find someone who was more cruelly tested and abused than themselves, are witnesses to this scene. The story can be found in *Jātaka* No. 436, which is similarly a part of the Pali Buddhist Canonical tradition. The third part of the prologue, which forms the actual setting of the *Arabian Nights*, is the story of a young woman who, night after night, tells stories to a cruel king, in order to put off her own execution. To do this, she enlists the help of a woman – Shahrazād's younger sister Dīnār(a)zād (or Dunyāzād) in the *Arabian Nights*. For this part of the prologue, Sanskrit prototypes can be found in the commentaries on the canonical Jaina texts. Apart from the frame story,

10 *"Jazāʾir al-Hind wa-l-Ṣīn." Alf layla wa-layla*, ed. Būlāq 3; Lyons and Lyons (trans.), *The Arabian nights* i, 3.

11 *"Jazāyir* (sic!) *al-Hind wa-Ṣīn al-Ṣīn,"* Mahdi (ed.), *The thousand and one nights* i, 56; Haddawy (trans.), *The Arabian nights* 3.

12 Cosquin, Prologue-cadre.

13 Littmann (trans.), *Erzählungen* vi, 666–7.

14 Grotzfeld, *Erzählungen* 50–67.

parallels to Indian literature can also be traced in many of the stories told by Shahrazād in the course of the *Arabian Nights*.[15]

Several works of old Indian literature have been transmitted to "the West," i.e., into Arabic, through Middle Persian Literature. Perhaps the most important of these is the *Pañcatantra*, which, by order of the Sassanian king Khusraw I. Anushirwān, was translated from Sanskrit into Pahlavi by the royal physician Burzōye (or Barzūya, Barzawayhi) around 570 CE and from Pahlavi into Arabic by ʿAbdallāh b. al-Muqaffaʿ (d. 139/756) under the new title of *Kalīla wa-Dimna*. If we trust Ibn al-Nadīm and the other Arabic literary sources, the frame story of the *Arabian Nights* went the same route. Its main motifs were collected for the first time in Persia in a book entitled *Hazār afsān* (*A Thousand Tales*),[16] then translated from Pahlavi into Arabic under the new title of *Alf layla* (*A Thousand Nights*), later *Alf layla wa-layla* (*A Thousand and One Nights*).[17] Although it is not clear whether the work called *Alf layla* is a direct translation of *Hazār afsān* or rather a kind of transformation of the latter, there is no doubt that these two works are very closely related to each other. Astonishingly, a source from the middle of the third/ninth century, ʿAbdallāh b. ʿAbd al-ʿAzīz al-Kātib – whose work on secretaries and scribes was quoted by Ibn Qutayba and printed as early as 1973, but only recently discovered as a source for the history of the *Arabian Nights* – ascribes the translation of the *Kitāb hazār afsān* to the above-mentioned famous translator of Middle Persian literature, Ibn al-Muqaffaʿ.[18]

3 Paradise in the Nights

As we have seen, the *Arabian Nights* (Middle Persian *Hazār afsān*, Arabic *Alf layla*) and the concept of paradise (Old Persian *pairi-daeza*, Arabic *firdaws*)[19] appear to follow similar historical trans-cultural trajectories, both moving from pre-Islamic Persian culture to that of the pre-modern Arabic-Islamic world. But are there other links between paradise and the *Nights*, with regard to the contents?

15 See Alsdorf, Belege; and Marzolph and van Leeuwen, *Encyclopedia* ii, 603–4 with further bibliographical references.

16 The Persian title *Hazār afsān* is commonly quoted in Arabic literary sources up to the fourth/tenth century. The content of *Hazār afsān* is recorded in detail at the end of the fourth/tenth century in the *Fihrist* of Ibn al-Nadīm: Cf. Ott (trans.), *Tausendundeine Nacht* 643–4 and Pellat, Alf layla wa layla.

17 The complete title *Alf layla wa-layla* is documented for the first time in 1155 CE. See Goitein, Evidence, reprinted in Marzolph, *Reader* 83–6.

18 Cf. Chraïbi, *Nuits* 24–6.

19 Cf. Leisten, Gärten 47.

Although the setting of most of the stories takes place either in the city or the desert, the *Arabian Nights* evoke almost every possible association of garden and paradise.[20] Some gardens are explicitly compared with paradise, as is the case with Hārūn al-Rashīd's garden on the bank of the Tigris, where a pair of lovers crept in unnoticed. In the description of this garden, the quotation of Q 13:4 emphasizes the association with paradise:

> They entered through a vaulted gateway that looked like a gateway in Paradise and passed through a bower of trellised boughs overhung with vines bearing grapes of various colors, the red like rubies, the black like Abyssinian faces, and the white, which hung between the red and the black, like pearls between red coral and black fish. Then they found themselves in the garden, and what a garden! There they saw all manner of things, "in singles and in pairs." The birds sang all kinds of songs: the nightingale warbled with touching sweetness, the pigeon cooed plaintively, the thrush sang with a human voice, the lark answered the ringdove with harmonious strains, and the turtledove filled the air with melodies. The trees were laden with all manners of ripe fruits: pomegranates, sweet, sour, and sour-sweet; apples, sweet and wild; and Hebron plums as sweet as wine, whose color no eyes have seen and whose flavor no tongue can describe.[21]

Paradise-like gardens serve as the setting for many a love episode in the *Arabian Nights*. The first rendezvous of Nūr al-Dīn and Shams al-Nahār, the favorite mistress of the caliph, takes place in the palace Qaṣr al-Khuld, the name of which derives from the Quranic term for paradise: *jannat al-khuld* (Q 25:15).[22] And when the lovers Anīs al-Jalīs and Nūr al-Dīn b. Khāqān sail from Basra to Baghdad, even the "City of Peace" itself gleams like paradise in the light of their love:

> A place whose citizens are subject to no fear[23]
> And safety is the master there.
> For its people it is a decorated paradise,[24]
> Its wonders being plain to see.[25]

---

20 Cf. Ott, Paradies; and Marzolph and van Leeuwen, *Encyclopedia* ii, 561–3.

21 Haddawy (trans.), *The Arabian nights* 365.

22 Cf. Haddawy (trans.), *The Arabian nights* 301.

23 This wording is also a part of the Quranic description of paradise, cf. e.g., Q 2:274.

24 "*Ka-annahū jannatan muzakhrafatan* (sic)." Mahdi (ed.), *The thousand and one nights* i, 456.

25 The English translation – except for the word "paradise" – has been quoted here after Lyons and Lyons (trans.), *The Arabian nights* i, 72.

Even unrequited love provokes associations of paradise. The harsher the rejection of the beloved, the more likely his or her favorable qualities are to be a paradise-like oasis in the midst of a dry and barren desert:

> You have a hidden secret in men's hearts,
> Folded away, concealed and not spread out.
> Your beauty puts to shame the gleaming moon
> While your grace is that of the breaking dawn.
> The radiance of your face holds unfulfillable desires,
> Whose well-known feelings grow and multiply.
> Am I to melt with heat, when your face is my paradise,
> And shall I die of thirst when your saliva is Kauthar?[26]

Paradise as a metaphor is particularly interesting in those stories of the *Arabian Nights* where the relation between two lovers is secret, forbidden or impossible. To these lovers, the fulfillment of their love seems like paradise on earth. And if, however rarely, they manage to be united like Nūr al-Dīn and Anīs al-Jalīs, whom we find sleeping on a bench in the park with their arms wrapped round each other, their union is a real Eden:

> Glory to God who caused this moon to rise,
> Bringing together lover with lover.
> For who has seen the sun and moon at once
> In Eden or on earth; who has ever?[27]

Certainly, these few and scattered observations cannot provide a comprehensive understanding of paradise in the *Arabian Nights*. Nevertheless, we see that paradise seems to be a (somewhat) natural element of the stories. Within the stories, the main connotation of paradise is love, no matter whether love is fulfilled, rejected or merely a wishful desire, or whether a love episode takes place in a paradise-like setting.

As we have already seen, the literary history of the *Nights* is also connected with paradise, both ideas following the same route of transmission. But at the end of the day, the genesis of the *Nights* still seem as mysterious as the location of paradise. This mystery causes even Alexander the Great to stop short and check with his messengers:

---

26 Ibid., i, 162–3.

27 Haddawy (trans.), *The Arabian nights* 300.

But how, then, can the four rivers flow from paradise
Shayḥān, Jayḥān, al-Dijla and al-Furāt,
if this paradise is suspended
between heaven and earth?[28]

Bibliography

Alf layla wa-layla, Būlāq 1252/1836–7; repr. Cairo 2010.

Alsdorf, L., Zwei neue Belege zur "indischen Herkunft" von 1001 Nacht, in *ZDMG* 89 (1935), 276–314.

Chraïbi, A., *Les mille et une nuits: Histoire du texte et classification des contes*, Paris 2008.

Cosquin, E., Le proloque-cadre des mille et une nuits, in *Revue Biblique* 6 (1909), 7–49; repr. in E. Cosquin, *Études folkloriques*, Paris 1922, 265–347.

Doufikar-Aerts, F., *Alexander Magnus Arabicus: A survey of the Alexander tradition through seven centuries: from Pseudo-Callisthenes to Suri*, Paris, Leuven, and Walpole 2010.

Goitein, S.D., The oldest documentary evidence for the title *Alf laila wa-laila*, in *JAOS* 78 (1958), 301–2.

Grotzfeld, H., Zu den vor- und außerislamischen Quellen von 1001 Nacht, Vortragsmanuskript im Rahmen der Konferenz *"Tausendundeine Nacht. Islam im Spiegel der Weltliteratur" vom 10.-12. März 2006 auf Burg Rothenfels am Main* (unpublished manuscript).

Grotzfeld, H. and S. Grotzfeld, *Die Erzählungen aus "Tausendundeiner Nacht,"* Darmstadt 1984.

Haddawy, H. (trans.), *The Arabian nights: Based on the text of the fourteenth-century Syrian manuscript edited by Muhsin Mahdi*, New York and London 1990, 1995².

Leisten, T., Die Gärten des Islam: Das islamische Paradies als Idealbild des Gartens, in H. Forkl, J. Kalter, T. Leisten, and M. Pavaloi (eds.), *Die Gärten des Islam*, Stuttgart 1993, 47–55.

Littmann, E. (trans.), *Die Erzählungen aus den Tausendundein Nächten: Nach dem arabischen Urtext der Calcuttaer Ausgabe aus dem Jahre 1839 übertragen*, Frankfurt am Main 1976.

Lyons, M.C. and U. Lyons (trans.), *The Arabian nights: Tales of 1001 nights, introduced and annotated by Robert Irwin*, 3 vols., Cambridge 2009.

---

28 *"Fa-qāla lahum Dhū l-Qarnayni kayfa khurūju l-anhāri min al-jannati aʿnī l-anhāra l-musammāta Shayḥān wa-Jayḥān wa-l-Dijla wa-l-Furāt wa-hiya hādhihi l-jannatu l-muʿallaqatu bayna l-samāʾi wa-l-arḍi?" Sīrat al-malik Iskandar Dhū l-Qarnayn*, Ms. Paris BN Arabe 3687, fol. 74b, lines 11–3.

Mahdi, M. (ed.), *The thousand and one nights (Alf layla wa-layla): From the earliest known sources, Arabic text edited with introduction and notes*, Leiden 1984.

Marzolph, U. (ed.), *The Arabian nights reader*, Detroit 2006.

——— and R. van Leeuwen, *The Arabian nights encyclopedia, with the collaboration of Hassan Wassouf*, Santa Barbara CA 2004.

Ott, C. (trans.), *Tausendundeine Nacht: Nach der ältesten arabischen Handschrift in der Ausgabe von Muhsin Mahdi erstmals ins Deutsche übertragen*, Munich 2004; 2009[10].

———, Das Paradies in den Erzählungen aus Tausendundeiner Nacht, in A. Müller and H. Roder (eds.), *1001 Nacht – Wege ins Paradies*, Mainz 2006, 11–8.

Pellat, C., Alf layla wa layla, in *EIr*, i, 831–5.

Sīrat al-malik Iskandar Dhū l-Qarnayn, Ms. Paris BN Arabe 3687.

van Donzel, E. and A. Schmidt, *Gog and Magog in early Eastern Christian and Islamic sources: Sallam's quest for Alexander's wall*, Leiden 2010.

ولا عصاة فزعًا من خلقتهم المفزعة ورويتهم الشنعة
وان هذه الحصون الخربة الذى تراها فى ارضنا وهذه
التلال العظام الذى تراهم اخربوهم وقتلوا اهلها ولاء
القتلة كلهم واما ارض فارس فهم فتحوا حصونهم
الكبار المنيعة وبادوا ملوكها وجبابرتها وسبوا
بنيهما وبناتها الكبار واخربوها كلهم فقال لهم الملك
ذو القرنين فهل رايتم وراهم احدًا من الانام فقالوا راينا
وراهم النفايس يعني النجايس روس الكلاب اناسًا
لا يدري ما عددهم واسماهم اسما لا نقدرون عليها
وليس وراهم احد الا الجبال الشامخة والجنة فوق
روس الجبال العالية الشامخة وهي بين السما والارض
وهي شبه المدينة العظيمة قد حفها الله بالرياح
العواصف من كل جانب فقال لهم ذو القرنين
كيف خروج الانهار من الجنة اعني الانهار المسماه
سيحان وجيحان والدجلة والفرات وهي هذه الجنة
المعلقة بين السما والارض وما رايتكم تذكرون انكم
رايتموها فقالوا له ان الله تعالى قادر ان يخرج
الانهار

FIGURE 42.1 Sīrat al-malik Iskandar Dhū l-Qarnayn, *Paris, BNF, Ms. Arabe 3687, fol. 74b.*
COURTESY OF THE BIBLIOTHÈQUE NATIONALE DE FRANCE.

CHAPTER 43

Paradise in an Islamic *ʿAjāʾib* Work: *The Delight of Onlookers and the Signs for Investigators* of Marʿī b. Yūsuf al-Karmī (d. 1033/1624)*

Walid A. Saleh

In researching the influence of the Nishapuri school of *tafsīr* on subsequent Islamic intellectual history, I encountered an unpublished and unstudied work by Marʿī b. Yūsuf al-Karmī (d. 1033/1624).[1] One of the leading Ḥanbalī scholars of eleventh/seventeenth-century Cairo, Marʿī l-Karmī was originally a native of Ṭūl Karm in Palestine. This work, *Bahjat al-nāẓirīn wa-āyāt al-mustadillīn* (The delight of onlookers and the signs for investigators), was clearly popular, given the number of extant copies available in library collections.[2] My initial interest in this work was motivated by Marʿī l-Karmī's extensive use of Aḥmad al-Thaʿlabī's (d. 427/1035) Quran commentary, *al-Kashf wa-l-bayān ʿan tafsīr al-Qurʾān* (Investigation and explanation of the exegesis of the Quran). Soon, however, I developed an appreciation of this work that goes beyond its relationship to *tafsīr*.

This article is both a study of the function and place of paradise in *Bahjat al-nāẓirīn* and an introduction to the work. Its aim is to draw attention to this fascinating work and to highlight its significance. In my opinion it is one of the most important works of *ʿajāʾib* (the marvel of creations genre) from the post-classical period (fourteenth to eighteenth century CE).[3] Since Marʿī l-Karmī relies heavily on an earlier *ʿajāʾib* work (*Kanz al-asrār wa-lawāqiḥ al-afkār* – Treasure of secrets and the harbingers of thoughts), itself still unpublished and much less well known to modern scholarship than Marʿī l-Karmī's, this chapter

* Research for this work was made possible by a generous grant from the Social Sciences and Humanities Research Council of Canada (SSHRC) to research the history of *tafsīr*.

1 On the Nishapuri school of *tafsīr* which consisted mainly of al-Thaʿlabī and al-Wāḥidī (d. 468/1076), see Saleh, The Nishapuri school.

2 We are extremely fortunate to have an autograph copy of this work. The copy is Gotha Manuscript Orient A-746, which was written in 1022/1613. My edition of the introduction uses also British Library manuscript Or. 5948. A large number of copies of the work are also available at Princeton University Library.

3 I am preparing a critical edition of this work.

is also an indirect introduction to this early work (see below). The *ʿAjāʾib al-makhlūqāt* of al-Qazwīnī (the use of the term *ʿajāʾib* in this title is clearly defined and discussed below) is still by far the best known specimen of this genre, despite the eagerness with which scholars have treated the category of *ʿajāʾib* in histories of Arabic literature. Moreover, *Bahjat al-nāẓirīn* is a work that is both literary and religious at the same time. This is a consciously constructed work that uses the tropes and methods of secular belles-lettres to construct an Islamic literary text. Islamic religious literature is the least researched of genres, lying as it does between two worlds (Arabic belles-lettres and Islamic studies), with the result that this literature is not assigned a role when we configure Islamic intellectual history. Recently Roberto Tottoli has reawakened the interest of scholars in this type of Islamic literature, and this article attempts to build on his work.[4]

1 Marʿī b. Yūsuf al-Karmī's Biography

Marʿī b. Yūsuf al-Karmī (d. 1033/1624) was a leading intellectual figure of the Arab Ottoman period. Because Marʿī l-Karmī stemmed from the dark centuries of Arabic Islamic cultural life, the Arab Ottoman centuries, until recently he has not garnered any serious attention. Indicative of his previous marginality is the fact that he has no entry in the second edition of the *Encyclopaedia of Islam*. Marʿī l-Karmī is, however, not an unknown figure. As one of the chroniclers of Ibn Taymiyya's merits he has secured for himself a position in the secondary literature, and, inadvertently, the dedication of Salafī editors who will soon make all of Marʿī l-Karmī's works available.[5] Thanks to the concerted

4 Tottoli, Muslim eschatological literature 452–77. A remark is in order about the significance of basing our work on more than the available published material from the Middle East. My investigation of manuscript library collections in Istanbul, Cairo, London, Berlin, Paris, and Dublin has radically altered my perception of my work as a scholar of medieval Islam. For despite the tremendous endeavor of Arab and Muslim scholars in publishing this corpus, most of it is still unpublished. Utilizing this unpublished corpus is essential if our work is to escape the constraints of the publishing politics of the Middle East. A fuller picture of Islamic intellectual history is impossible without incorporating manuscript works side by side with what is available in print. Needless to say, my awareness is accompanied by a deep appreciation for the editors of the vast extant library of Islamic literature and their tireless efforts.

5 Marʿī l-Karmī wrote two books on Ibn Taymiyya, both of which are published: *al-Kawākib al-durriyya fī manāqib al-mujtahid Ibn Taymiyya* (Beirut 1986) and *al-Shahāda al-zakiyya fī thanāʾ al-aʾimma ʿalā Ibn Taymiyya* (Beirut 1985).

efforts of these Salafī scholars we are now more aware of his scholarly output. Most critical editions of Marʿī l-Karmī's works contain studies on the man and his works, which have increased in detail as more and more of them are made accessible.[6] Michael Winter, to his credit, is the only scholar to have dedicated an article in English to one of the works of Marʿī l-Karmī.[7] Thus, despite the availability of many of his works, there is so far no comprehensive study of Marʿī l-Karmī's intellectual output.

If modern scholars are finding their way back to Marʿī l-Karmī, his contemporaries were fully aware of his significance. Al-Muḥibbī (d. 1111/1699), the chronicler of the eleventh/seventeenth century, was laudatory in his biography of Marʿī l-Karmī, describing him as "one of the great scholars of the Hanbalites in Egypt."[8] Al-Muḥibbī assures us that no scholar could find a flaw in Marʿī l-Karmī's scholarship, despite his many enemies. Marʿī l-Karmī taught at al-Azhar and became a professor at Sultan Ḥasan Mosque in Cairo. Most of al-Muḥibbī's biography is devoted to listing the titles of Marʿī l-Karmī's works – at least 70 in number.[9] The range of topics Marʿī l-Karmī covers is unusually varied, from legal *fatwās* to an epistle on the new habit of smoking; from textbooks on law to two works on plagues. Some of Marʿī l-Karmī's works were translated into Ottoman Turkish and one of his *inshāʾ* works was published early on in Istanbul in Arabic.[10]

2 The Conundrum of the *ʿajāʾib* Category

Thanks to the pioneering work of Syrinx von Hees, we are now aware that it is problematic to use the term *ʿajāʾib* in literary studies of medieval Arabic and Islamic literature.[11] The most famous of the titles that come to mind bearing this term is of course *ʿAjāʾib al-makhluqāt* of al-Qazwīnī (d. 682/1262), yet that work is not a work of *ʿajāʾib*, if by *ʿajāʾib* we understand fantastic or unreal features and characters.[12] As von Hees has clearly demonstrated in several

6 The most detailed of these introductions is by Shuʿayb al-Arnaʾūṭ, the editor of *Aqāwīl al-thiqāt* 29–43.
7 Winter, Seventeenth-century Arabic panegyric 130–56; see also Melchert, Marʿī ibn Yūsuf.
8 Al-Muḥibbī, *Khulāṣat al-athar* iv, 358–61; the quotation is on page 358.
9 For a detailed list of the works of al-Karmī see the introduction of *Shifāʾ al-ṣudūr* 10–6.
10 See Winter, Seventeenth-century Arabic panegyric 133, for the Ottoman translation and the *inshāʾ* collection.
11 See von Hees, The astonishing 101–20, for references to her other works on the subject.
12 Von Hees, *Enzyklopädie als Spiegel*.

of her publications, this is an encyclopedic scientific work that attempts to categorize the entities in existence in the world into an organized compendium of knowledge.[13] The term *ʿajāʾib* as used in the title of al-Qazwīnī has little to do with the fantastic or unreal or the unscientific: the word is used to invoke the wondrous nature of creation as demonstrating the majesty of God. And although in this title the word certainly *does not* refer to the fantastic or unreal, secondary literature has taken it to mean exactly that.

There is thus a real confusion in the secondary literature which, thanks to von Hees, is now resolved. It is because of this confusion that von Hees implores scholars to stop using the term altogether. Yet, the term *ʿajāʾib* is too useful to discard (although I am in full agreement with von Hees' analysis), and may be used as long as we realize that it was a term with a variety of meanings. Von Hees rightly takes C.E. Dubler, the writer of the *ʿajāʾib* entry in the second edition of the *Encyclopaedia of Islam*, to task for not mentioning any work of literature that fits his description of the genre as developing from a literature concerned with "tangible reality to the realm of fancy."[14] In his defense, there is actually a body of literature that does constitute what I would call Islamic *ʿajāʾib* literature – works that do cover the intangibles; this is the Islamic cosmological and eschatological literature that was available from early on in Islam and was, unlike what Dubler surmised, a constitutive element of Islamic culture and not a later degeneration.[15] The problem with Dubler's statement, apart from the fact that he produced no evidence to support this (faulty) historical evolutionary analysis, is that it is a value judgment and not a reflection of the facts; he valorized the early, supposedly scientific, phase of the literature and decried the subsequent decadence it allegedly suffered, although one is left with little information about what he meant by this.

There was actually a parallel world of *ʿajāʾib* Islamic literature, one that mirrored the Hellenistic heritage of the *ʿajāʾib* which was cultivated by the literati in Islamic culture (i.e., the Qazwīnī-type material). The two functioned in two different realms and the *ʿajāʾib* of al-Qazwīnī made no room for the *ʿajāʾib* of Islamic cosmography. The Islamic cosmographic and Islamic *ʿajāʾib* material were moreover a tradition searching for a form. One can document several forms that this material inhabited, from eschatological literature to *miʿrāj* narratives, from *ḥadīth* collections to cosmological tractates. Yet it did not find a full articulation in a single form until the work of Marʿī l-Karmī (although the work of Muḥammad al-Ṣinhājī (d. ca. 798/1393) needs to be investigated

13 Von Hees, al-Qazwīnī's *ʿAjāʾib al-makhlūqāt* 171–86.

14 Von Hees, The astonishing 103.

15 As demonstrated in Heinen, *Islamic cosmology*.

in more detail).[16] A complete history of the development of this material has yet to be documented, but Marʿī l-Karmī's *Bahjat al-nāẓirīn* represents a major development in this genre, a coming together of the different strands of Islamic material, whether from the high cultural sphere of the Islamic sciences (*tafsīr, ḥadīth*, scholarly commentaries, and related works) or from popular works (of the type studied by Tottoli), to fashion a comprehensive presentation of Islamic "folk" cosmological and *ʿajāʾib* material.[17]

One of the main characteristics of al-Qazwīnī's work is its total disregard of Islamic cosmology and its entities.[18] The only common denominator between the two is the angelic world. This is not a capitulation to Islamic cosmology on the part of al-Qazwīnī's scientific paradigm, so much as a coincidence of material: al-Qazwīnī's world could accommodate angels as it accommodated a single God. Otherwise Islamic entities were simply inadmissible in this world. Al-Qazwīnī, devout as he was, was in no mood to give his readers the dimensions of the throne of God (*al-ʿarsh*) or the magnitude of His chair (*al-kursī*).[19]

---

16 In this case I think a fuller analysis of al-Ṣinhājī's work *Kanz al-asrār* might alter my historical analysis. My only defense is that I intend to carry out a fuller analysis of *Kanz al-asrār* and am fully cognizant of the situation.

17 There are already some studies that help us grasp the outlines of *ʿajāʾib* material. Anton Heinen's work, *Islamic cosmology*, which documents the Islamicization of cosmological treatises, has unfortunately never been carried further. Meanwhile Roberto Tottoli's work on the eschatological treatise *Aḥwāl al-qiyāma* (The circumstances of resurrection, which is the same work as pseudo-Ghazālī's *al-Durra al-fākhira – The Precious Pearl*) shows how little we know about this material. I am hoping that by bringing attention to *Bahjat al-nāẓirīn* I can contribute to the attempts of scholars working on Islamic literature to outline the development of this genre. I also hope to draw attention to the close relationship between the cosmological Islamic literature (such as that studied by Heinen) and the *ʿajāʾib* eschatological literature (such as that studied by Tottoli).

18 The term "Islamic cosmology" is understood here to denote discourses influenced by Islamic religious concepts that address the origins and eventual fate of the universe, paying special attention to supernatural elements, entities, and powers such as angels, demons, and miraculous aspects of the landscape of paradise and hell. It is not intended to refer to the more scientific or philosophical studies produced by Muslim scholars.

19 See al-Qazwīnī's dismissive remarks about the fact that some early Muslims have equated *al-kursī* with the eighth sphere, while *al-ʿarsh* was equated with the ninth sphere. He is deferential to this effort, but hardly able to take it seriously; his tone betrays a determination not to contaminate his cosmology with Islamic entities: "wa-qad aḥabb baʿḍ al-salaf al-tawfīq bayna al-āyāt wa-l-akhbār wa-qawl al-ḥukamāʾ fa-zaʿam anna al-kursī huwa al-falak al-thāmin alladhī dhakarnā siʿatahu wa-ʿajāʾibahu, wa-l-ʿarsh huwa al-falak al-tāsiʿ alladhī huwa aʿẓam al-aflāk. Wa-Allāh taʿālā aʿlam bi-ṣiḥḥat hādhā al-qawl aw fasādih. …" al-Qazwīnī, *ʿAjāʾib al-makhlūqāt* 87–9.

The pious might talk about these things, and one might be forced to admit their existence, but they are hardly a fit subject for a scholarly work; hence al-Qazwīnī leaves them out. Al-Qazwīnī describes nothing that philosophy could not countenance. In many ways, Marʿī l-Karmī was left with no option but to fashion an *ʿajāʾib* work in which the Islamic "entities" are re-embedded in the world and "science."

3 *Bahjat al-nāẓirīn wa-āyāt al-mustadillīn*

Although Marʿī l-Karmī never deigns to mention al-Qazwīnī nor uses the word *ʿajāʾib* in the title of his work, there is no doubt about what he was attempting to do, or rather undo, in his *Bahjat al-nāẓirīn*. His was both a continuation and a refutation of al-Qazwīnī's work, and as such, it inserts itself in a deliberate manner in the genre of *ʿajāʾib*. *Bahjat al-nāẓirīn* fashioned itself as a refutation and rehabilitation of the philosophical scientific mode of writing about the wonders of creation. The beings that al-Qazwīnī left out of his catalogue of the various components of the universe, paradise, hell, God's throne, His celestial chair, His book of records, the primordial pen, the day of judgment, death, the events of the apocalypse – the host of beings that were part and parcel of the mythical world of the Quran and the world it generated – these beings were given center stage in *Bahjat al-nāẓirīn*. The world that al-Qazwīnī denied by not describing or refusing to include in his book *ʿAjāʾib al-makhlūqāt* were now given an existence that was independent of the usual genres in which such Islamic entities usually appeared. Thus instead of *ḥadīth, tafsīr*, or eschatological treatises where such a cosmology was elaborated, Marʿī l-Karmī used the form of the *ʿajāʾib* genre to fashion an Islamic cosmological world. The framework of *Bahjat al-nāẓirīn* is that of the wonders of creation genre, but the content has been thoroughly Islamized, perhaps as a way of harmonizing "science and religion."

Bahjat al-nāẓirīn is divided into ten chapters.[20] The sum total of the information presented in these ten chapters is found in one form or another in previous works. Indeed, Marʿī l-Karmī stated that he used at least 500 sources for his book (which is most certainly an exaggeration). Two books deserve special mention because of the frequency with which they were quoted, *al-Kashf wa-l-bayān ʿan tafsīr al-Qurʾān* of al-Thaʿlabī and *Kanz al-asrār wa-lawāqiḥ al-afkār* of Muḥammad al-Ṣinhājī.[21] *Kanz al-asrār*, a still unedited work, is beyond

20 See Appendix I for the content of *Bahjat al-nāẓirīn*.

21 The relationship of Marʿī l-Karmī's work to that of al-Ṣinhājī's *Kanz al-asrār* is a topic for another article. It is clear that Marʿī l-Karmī modeled his work after that of al-Ṣinhājī.

doubt the work most heavily utilized by Marʿī l-Karmī. Marʿī l-Karmī, moreover, mentions a long list of authors and book titles including *al-Durra al-fākhira* of al-Ghazālī (pseudo-Ghazālī; as I mentioned, it is the same as *Aḥwāl al-qiyāma* mentioned above) and *al-Hayʾa al-saniyya* of al-Suyūṭī (d. 911/1505).[22] It is however important to emphasize that Marʿī l-Karmī has assembled material not usually gathered together in order to fashion a new form of writing. Chapter 1, "On the Higher Spheres," and chapter 2, "On the Lower Spheres," are the only material from *ʿajāʾib* works proper (although here the Islamic cosmological elements dominate the presentation). The remaining eight chapters are what we usually encounter in eschatological treatises or *ḥadīth* collections. The arrangement of this disparate material and its presentation transforms Marʿī l-Karmī's work into something new.

If we analyze the sources of Marʿī l-Karmī we can document that he was tapping into several Islamic literary genres. There were the Quran commentaries; the *ḥadīth* collections and their commentaries (*shurūḥ*); ascension narratives; eschatological and apocalyptic works (he highlights two in particular, the already mentioned *al-Durra al-fākhira*, and Nuʿaym b. Ḥammād's *Kitāb al-Fitan*); history books; cosmological treatises; and theological treatises. The inclusion of the apocalyptic material (*ashrāṭ al-sāʿa*, i.e., the signs of the hour literature), a genre that early in Islam grew to be an independent form of writing, proves that Marʿī was attempting to fashion a world of seamless continuation, from the creation to the end of the world, passing through the events of the apocalypse.[23] Not only was he reformulating the *ʿajāʾib* genre, he was expanding its content by including (historical) events instead of only "spiritual" or "supra-rational" entities.

It should be evident that the genre of *ʿajāʾib* was unsuitable for an Islamic cosmographic outlook.[24] How did Marʿī l-Karmī then reconceptualize the genre? The introduction of *Bahjat al-nāẓirīn* plays a fundamental role in refashioning and repositioning the Islamic material into the mold of *ʿajāʾib*

Kanz al-asrār was as popular as *Bahjat al-nāẓirīn*, if not more so, given the high number of manuscripts of the work. I used manuscript Bibliothèque Nationale de France, Arabe 1400. One hopes that an edition of *Kanz al-asrār* will resolve many issues regarding the consolidation of this genre as a literary form.

22 On *al-Durra al-fākhira* see Tottoli, Muslim eschatological literature; on *al-Hayʾa* see Heinen, *Islamic cosmology*.

23 For a preliminary classification of this literature, see S. Günther's contribution to this publication. See, moreover, Saleh, Woman.

24 The term "cosmographic" is understood here to denote a discourse that maps the general features of the universe, using methods that are considered scientific by those who employ them.

works.[25] Marʿī l-Karmī used several stratagems to align his work with the marvels of creations genre. First, although Marʿī l-Karmī did not use the word *ʿajāʾib* in the title of his book, he could hardly wait to use it in a phrase in the work itself. His first sentence is, "we thank the Lord that expanded our breasts and enlightened our hearts to contemplate (*naẓar*) the wonders of His kingdom (*ʿajāʾib al-malakūt*)." The claim here is that this book is about "looking" at the marvels of the created entities. Soon the introduction discusses the science of observation (*ʿilm al-naẓar*) and induction (*al-istidlāl*) as being the highest ranks of science. Marʿī l-Karmī informs the reader that one ought to study the created beings (*maṣnūʿāt al-ṣāniʿ*) in the world in order to understand the wisdom and perfection of God. Only through personal individual endeavor could one attain certitude in faith, which allows one to reflect on this world and its marvels. These statements are much in line with what one finds in the introduction of al-Qazwīnī's *ʿAjāʾib al-makhlūqāt*, where investigation and observation are the basis of our acquired knowledge of the world. This appeal to the science of observation is carried out to align the book with al-Qazwīnī's book. Here, however, it is employed for a different purpose: the same act of "observation" according to Marʿī l-Karmī allows the observer to eventually discern divine secrets (*al-asrār al-ilāhiyya*), and this results in an increased capacity for revelatory knowledge (or knowledge attained through mystical experience, *kashf*). The term *al-kashf* is the ubiquitous Islamic term for acquiring knowledge through non-sensory means. This acquired revelatory knowledge transports the observer to a state of certitude (*yaqīn*), the highest level of knowledge, where one knows that what one knows is true. The introduction thus mixes two sets of technical terminology, the philosophical (natural history) and the mystical; this admixture allows the author an entry into the structure and form of a genre that has so far been the domain of natural sciences.

The second stratagem is genealogical. Marʿī l-Karmī informs the reader that he is aware that there is a long tradition of marvels of creation (*ʿajāʾib*) works, and that he has looked at many such works. The implication is that the reader should think of Marʿī l-Karmī's work as descending from this line of works. These works were, however, according to the author, unsatisfactory for several

---

25 See Appendix II for an edition of the introduction of *Bahjat al-nāẓirīn*. The long excursus into jealousy between scholars, a feature of the professorial compositions of the Islamicate world, is probably directed against the scholar al-Maymūnī (Ibrāhim b. Muḥammad b. ʿĪsā, d. 1079/1669); on him see al-Ziriklī, *al-Aʿlām* i, 67. Marʿī l-Karmī does not mention him by name but we know of the rivalry between the two from al-Muḥibbī, *Khulāṣat al-athar* iv, 360.

reasons. They were either too short and thus left out material, or they were too long, causing the reader to be bored and lose interest; others had faulty information. The main reason for Marʿī l-Karmī's dissatisfaction with previous works, however, was the fact that they did not follow the methodology of scholars who work on prophetic traditions (*sunan al-muḥaddithīn*). The authors of these works followed the methods of historians (*al-muʾarrikhūn*) and what he calls fabricators (*al-waḍḍāʿūn*). Here is the parting of the ways between the older form of *ʿajāʾib* works and Marʿī l-Karmī's work. He bases his work on the Quran, Quran commentaries, traditionalist material, and the prophetic Sunna. Marʿī l-Karmī informs the reader that he avoids the material from historians and fabricators. The Quran and the Sunna are thus positioned as counter-sources for the information provided by "mere" human agency. Despite this negative assessment of the previous *ʿajāʾib* genre of works, Marʿī l-Karmī nonetheless positions himself as continuing this genre – however flawed it is, according to him. The implied model of his work is thus made known only in negative terms. He still refuses to mention al-Qazwīnī by name, yet it is clear that he wants to write a work in the same style. It is this implicit connection Marʿī l-Karmī draws to *ʿajāʾib* literature that makes me hesitant to discard the term. Thus we should all take heed of von Hees' work when we approach *ʿajāʾib* works, but still use the term now that we know its various definitions.

The third stratagem Marʿī l-Karmī uses to align his work with the *ʿajāʾib* genre is his deployment of the fundamental division of the world into the higher realm (*al-ʿālam al-ʿulwī*) and the lower realm (*al-ʿālam al-suflī*). This traditional division is exactly the division offered by al-Qazwīnī in his *ʿAjāʾib al-makhlūqāt*. The outer garb of Marʿī l-Karmī's work is thus the same as the *ʿajāʾib* genre.

4 Paradise in *Bahjat al-nāẓirīn*

The study of a work that stems from the post-classical period presents the investigator with interesting problems. How does one approach such a text, a text of compounded genealogy, when much of its material is already centuries older? One might be tempted to dismiss the work as derivative, especially since this is the usual reaction to such material. Its collage-like nature is thus used against the work. The exemplars and sources for many of the texts from the post-classical periods are available, staring us in the eye, increasing the urge to go back to the originals. In the case of *Bahjat al-nāẓirīn* the author himself, Marʿī l-Karmī, admits to his indebtedness to the *Kashf al-asrār* of al-Ṣinhājī and *al-Durra al-fākhira*. The first implication of the nature of *Bahjat al-nāẓirīn* is that a purely descriptive discussion of its contents is out of the question as the details of the Islamic concept of paradise, to which Marʿī l-Karmī adds almost nothing new, are already well-known.

Fortunately, these post-classical texts present a great opportunity for studying the context in which they functioned and thus for re-examining the content as constitutive of new meanings. What we lack in the area of "originality" in subject matter is made up in the wealth of information that we have about the context of the text and, therefore, about the transformation of the old into something new. We know the author, we have an autograph copy of the work and the copies made of it; we have its sources, and we know much about the political and intellectual atmosphere of the period. The problem is thus one of research priorities and methodological approach.[26]

My approach to *Bahjat al-nāẓirīn* has been to contextualize the text and reinterpret its content, and to describe it intellectually and historically. In the first part of this chapter I have shown how the text was original insofar as it transformed and appropriated a genre of writing to create a new form, an Islamicized *ʿajāʾib* format. In the remaining part of this chapter I now attempt to understand what function such a text was fulfilling and in what way its content was indicative of its function and thus new insofar as it was a transformation.

Chapter 8 of *Bahjat al-nāẓirīn* is dedicated to paradise (*al-janna*), coming before chapter 9, which is dedicated to hell. This positioning of paradise is peculiar. Paradise in previous works was usually discussed last.[27] Far more intriguing is the fact that Marʿī l-Karmī added a new chapter (chapter 10) after his discussion of paradise and hell, a theological chapter on the implications of the existence of paradise and hell. The previous literature that dealt with paradise and hell did not usually engage in theological discussions of this nature, these being confined to theology works proper. Is hell eternal – meaning is paradise the only merciful option for a merciful God? Theodicy was the central

---

26 Today it is sometimes almost forgotten that most of the manuscripts of the Islamic world were written and copied in what we call the post-classical period. Most of them are actually from the Arab-Ottoman centuries. Yet, even in collections in European countries and North America, thousands of manuscripts from this period languish uncatalogued. Ironically, the fact of the matter is that the two centuries immediately following the conquest of the Near East by the Ottomans are still understudied, although they are amply documented.

27 Thus, for example, in Wolff's edited text of *Aḥwāl al-qiyāma*, paradise comes last. See Wolff (ed. and trans.), *Muhammedanische Eschatologie*. The same is true of al-Ṣinhājī's *Kanz al-asrār*, where paradise is the last item in the book; see Bibliothèque nationale de France Arabe 1400, fols. 8a–9a.

issue raised in chapter 10. The question is thus: how do we understand this work at this particular moment in the Arab-Ottoman East?

First, I see *Bahjat al-nāẓirīn* as a bold reaffirmation of the visionary understanding of existence and of history; more importantly it is the triumph of the state of *al-kashf* (unveiling), which I discussed before. Here is a world presented as it ought to be, or as it is really is, described through a quasi-visionary means. The world, what really matters of the world, is its eternal entities, those that will abide in existence, not the created realm that will be annihilated when the world ends. The *ʿajāʾib* that one should thus marvel at is the *ʿajāʾib al-malakūt*, i.e., of the divine realm, not the *ʿajāʾib al-makhlūqāt*, i.e., of the created beings. This is divine geography. What counts of the world is precisely what we are unable to confirm the existence of through sensory processes or through the mental activities of the philosophers or the rationalists, a clear rebuttal to al-Qazwīnī's world.

To appreciate this work, however, we have to see it as the product of the passing of the first Muslim millennium and of the intellectual and political situation of the Arab-Ottoman East at the beginning of the eleventh/seventeenth century. The anxiety over the coming of the apocalypse had abated, and the fact that the world did not end when the year 1000/1591 came to pass was a relief. Muslim scholars had, by the beginning of the tenth century (around 911 *hijrī* or so) agreed, after much wrangling, that the world would end around 1500 of the *hijrī* calendar.[28] Yet this anxiety did not come to an end – if one takes into consideration the amount of apocalyptic writing stemming from the eleventh/seventeenth century. There were two visions of human history that were based on the apocalyptic paradigm. The first, which can be described as the more traditional vision, saw human history and in particular the history of the Muslims as culminating in a total disintegration of the social fabric of the Muslim polity. In this view Islamic history was reaching its lowest point. Marʿī l-Karmī, however, was unique in proposing a radically alternative vision: for him, Islamic history was reaching its zenith.[29] Muslims were living in the

---

28 The story of the debate about the coming of the year 1000 *hijrī* is yet to be written. The most important treatise on the topic is al-Suyūṭī's *al-Kashf ʿan mujāwazat hādhihī l-umma al-alf*, which settled the debate about the issue. For the significance of this treatise see my forthcoming study *The coming of the first Muslim millennium*. On al-Suyūṭī's treatise see *al-Ḥāwī lil-fatāwī* ii, 86–92. On the influence of contemporary apocalyptical and messianic expectations on Ottoman concepts of political rule, see Fleischer, The lawgiver 160–71. On the influence of apocalyptic and messianic expectations on ʿAbbasid political culture, see Yücesoy, *Messianic beliefs*.

29 See the treatise studied by Michael Winter. Winter, however, misses the apocalyptic significance of this "historical" document. To Marʿī l-Karmī, Ottoman dynastic history was

fullness of time, in the shadow of the glorious Ottomans, the embodiment of history and the dynasty that would see the Muslims delivered to God. His small treatise on the Ottomans was one of the few, if not the only treatise, of a Muslim utopian vision of history offering a radical understanding of the meaning of the Islamic apocalypse. Marʿī l-Karmī was, however, still convinced that the world would end soon. A utopian apocalyptic vision is still an apocalyptic one, and Marʿī l-Karmī did write on the coming of the apocalypse.[30] Indeed chapter 5, the middle chapter of *Bahjat al-nāẓirīn*, is about the signs of the hour and chapter 6 covers the end of the world.

In this light, *Bahjat al-nāẓirīn* is a summation of history. It is a summary of the world and of human history from the first moment of creation to the beatific vision. This is a universal history starting from the creation of the very first thing and ending with the very last state of the human condition. It is a record of the things of significance, a parallel world to the perishable universe.

Scholars of the late Mamluk and early Ottoman Arab provinces have long noticed the decline in the art of historical writing after the Ottoman conquest. The destruction of an independent state based in Cairo with Arabic as its official language and the use of Persian and Ottoman Turkish, so the analysis went, caused a serious blow to the art of historiography in the Arab East. The evidence for this view so far is formidable. The last century of Mamluk rule in the Near East witnessed a proliferation of historical writings unprecedented in the Muslim world (the famous Ibn Khaldūn belongs to that century). One looks in vain for any comparable historical writings in Arabic from the time after the demise of the Mamluks and the coming of the Ottomans. There is much to recommend an analysis that sees in the demise of the Mamluks the main reason for the decline in the tenth/sixteenth and eleventh/seventeenth centuries of Arabic historiography.[31]

Yet I would like to propose another way of understanding the situation. It is not that scholars stopped being concerned with history, but rather that what history meant then underwent a major transformation. History in the shadow of the apocalypse is apocalyptic history. Thus understood, the Arab-Ottoman

---

the apogee of Islamic dynastic history precisely because he had a utopian vision of the Islamic apocalypse. Things were improving as the Muslims approached the end of times, not deteriorating.

30 See his treatise *Farāʾid al-fikr fī l-imām al-mahdī l-muntaẓar*, Princeton Garret Collection no. 1006H. The treatise was written the same year as *Bahjat al-nāẓirīn*.

31 However, it should be noted that there existed a robust tradition of vivid historiographical writing in Ottoman Turkish during these centuries, on which cf. e.g., Fleischer, The lawgiver 172–3; Fleischer, Royal authority 199–217; Fleischer, *Bureaucrat* 7–8, 44–6, 235–307. Cf. on early Ottoman historiography also Meier, Perceptions of a new era.

scholars were rather busy writing historical works, but these were now of a different order. The measure of history was now cosmic, not dynastic. It is this vision that allowed Marʿī l-Karmī to mix genres, to attempt to create a new form of writing where marvel at creation means seeing the unseen, and where human history is cosmic history. Paradise (*al-janna*) in this sense is more than a promise; paradise is the meaning of history and its culmination. Paradise and paradisal life become central, and *Bahjat al-nāẓirīn* mirrors the concerns of the Quran. Paradise is the only central abiding entity in this world.

Bibliography

Fleischer, C.H., *Bureaucrat and intellectual in the Ottoman Empire*, Princeton, NJ 1986.

———, The lawgiver as messiah: The making of the imperial image in the reign of Süleyman, in G. Veinstein (ed.), *Soliman le magnifique et son temps*, Paris 1992, 159–77.

———, Royal authority, Dynastic Cyclism, and "Ibn Khaldûnism" in sixteenth-century Ottoman letters, in *Journal of Asian and African Studies* 18 (1983), 198–220.

Hees, S. von, The astonishing: A critique and re-reading of ʿaǧāʾib literature, in *Middle Eastern Literatures* 8 (2005), 101–20.

———, *Enzyklopädie als Spiegel des Weltbildes: Qazwīnīs Wunder der Schöpfung – eine Naturkunde des 13. Jahrhunderts*, Wiesbaden 2002.

———, al-Qazwīnī's *ʿAjāʾib al-makhlūqāt*: An encyclopaedia of natural history?, in G. Endress (ed.), *Organizing knowledge: Encyclopaedic activities in the pre-eighteenth century Islamic world*, Leiden 2006, 171–86.

Heinen, A.M., *Islamic cosmology: A study of as-Suyūṭī's al-Hayʾa as-sanīya fī l-hayʾa as-sunnīya, with critical edition, translation, and commentary*, Wiesbaden 1982.

al-Karmī, Marʿī b. Yūsuf, *Aqāwīl al-thiqāt fī taʾwīl al-asmāʾ wa-l-ṣifāt wa-l-āyāt al-muḥkamāt wa-l-mutashābihāt*, ed. Sh. al-Arnaʾūṭ, Beirut 1985.

———, *Bahjat al-nāẓirīn wa-āyāt al-mustadillīn*, Gotha Manuscript Orient A-746; British Library manuscript Or. 5948.

———, *Farāʾid al-fikr fī l-imām al-mahdī l-muntaẓar*, Princeton Garret Collection no. 1006H.

———, *al-Kawākib al-durriyya fī manāqib al-mujtahid Ibn Taymiyya*, ed. N.ʿA. Khalaf, Beirut 1986.

———, *al-Shahāda al-zakiyya fī thanāʾ al-aʾimma ʿalā Ibn Taymiyya*, ed. N.ʿA. Khalaf, Beirut 1983.

———, *Shifāʾ al-ṣudūr fī ziyārat al-mashāhid wa-l-qubūr*, ed. ʿĀ. al-Jutaylī, Kuwait 1991.

Meier, A., Perceptions of a new era? Historical writing in early Ottoman Damascus, in *Arabica* 51 (2004), 419–34.

Melchert, C., Marʿī ibn Yūsuf, in J.E. Lowry and D.J. Stewart (eds.), *Essays in Arabic literary biography 1350–1850*, Wiesbaden 2009, 289–94.
al-Muḥibbī, Muḥammad, *Khulāṣat al-athar fī aʿyān al-qarn al-ḥādī ʿashar*, 4 vols., Beirut 1966.
al-Qazwīnī, Zakariyyā, *ʿAjāʾib al-makhlūqāt wa-gharāʾib al-mawjūdāt*, ed. F. Saʿd, Beirut 1981.
Saleh, W., The Nishapuri school of tafsir, in *EIr*, forthcoming.
———, The woman as a locus of apocalyptic anxiety in medieval Sunni Islam, in A. Neuwirth et al. (eds.), *Myths, historical archetypes and symbolic figures in Arabic literature: Towards a new hermeneutic approach*, Beirut 1999, 123–45.
al-Ṣinhājī, Muḥammad, *Kanz al-asrār wa-lawāqiḥ al-afkār*, Bibliothèque nationale de France Arabe 1400.
al-Suyūṭī, Jalāl al-Dīn, *al-Ḥāwī lil-fatāwī*, 2 vols., Cairo 1958.
Tottoli, R., Muslim eschatological literature and western studies, in *Der Islam* 83 (2006), 452–77.
Winter, M., A seventeenth-century Arabic panegyric of the Ottoman dynasty, in *Journal of Asian and African Studies* 13 (1980), 130–56.
Wolff, M. (ed. and trans.), *Kitāb Aḥwāl al-qayyima: Muhammedanische Eschatologie*, Leipzig 1872.
Yücesoy, H., *Messianic beliefs and imperial politics in medieval Islam: The ʿAbbāsid caliphate in the early ninth century*, Columbia SC 2009.
al-Ziriklī, Khayr al-Din, *al-Aʿlām: Qāmūs tarājim li-ashhar al-rijāl wa-l-nisāʾ min al-ʿarab wa-l-mustaʿribīn wa-l-mustashriqīn*, 8 vols., Beirut 1984.

Appendix 1: Marʿī's *Bahjat al-nāẓirīn's* Contents in Detail

1- Chapter One: Higher Spheres
   - a- What was Created First?
   - b- The Pen
   - c- Table of Records
   - d- Throne
   - e- Throne Carriers
   - f- *Kursī* (Celestial Chair)
   - g- The Cosmic Trumpet
   - h- Paradise (deferred to Chapter Eight)
   - i- The Cosmic Tree
   - j- Heavens
   - k- Sun
   - l- Moon

m- Planets
n- Angels
o- Major Angels
p- Rain
q- Clouds
r- Thunder and Lightening
s- Winds
t- Day and Night

2- Chapter Two: Lower Spheres
a- Seven Earths
b- The Qāf Mountain
c- The Measure of the Circumference of the Earth
d- The Seven Climes of the Earth
e- On the Seas
f- On Some Major Islands
g- Rivers and Springs

3- Chapter Three: The Creation of Human Beings and the *Jinn*
a- Ensoulment
b- On the Whisperings of the Devil
c- On the Descent to Earth
d- On the Primordial Covenant
e- The Lifespan of Adam
f- Eve
g- The Progeny of Adam
h- The Creation of the *Jinn*
i- The Progeny of Satan
j- Why do Amulets and Talismans have an Effect on *Jinn*?
k- Are *Jinn* Morally Responsible for their Actions?

4- Chapter Four: On Death
a- What is the Soul?
b- What is Sleep?
c- On Dreams
d- Does One's Lifespan Change according to God's Will?
e- On the Proper Attitude to Death and Asceticism
f- The Angel of Death
g- The Experience of Dying and the Woes that Accompany Death
h- The "Pulling" of the Soul from the Body

i- The Manner in which the Souls of the Unholy are Dealt With
j- The Grave
k- The First Inquisition by the Two Angels of the Graves
l- The Torments and the Pleasures of the Grave
m- On Souls, or, What Experiences Pleasure and Pain?
n- On Visitations to Cemeteries

5- Chapter Five: The Harbingers of the Apocalypse
a- The Age of the Universe
b- The Minor Signs that Herald the End
c- The Major Signs: Ten of Them

6- Chapter Six: The End of the World and the Destruction of the Universe
a- The First Blast of the Trumpet
b- Transformation of the Universe
c- The Death of all Creatures
d- General Resurrection

7- Chapter Seven: On Judgment and the Assembly of Human Beings
a- Standing in Attendance Waiting for God
b- The Humiliation of Humanity
c- On Intercession
d- The Coming of God
e- The Dragging of Paradise and Hell
f- Humanity Paraded before God
g- Books of Deeds
h- The Balance
i- On the Judgment of Humanity
j- On the Judgment of the Beasts
k- On the Testimony of Inanimate Beings against the Transgressions of Humanity
l- The Judgment on Believers
m- The Duration of the Judgment
n- Those who Escape Judgment
o- The Rich and the Poor
p- Igniting Hell
q- The Well of Water
r- The Bridge over Hell into Paradise
s- Disputes and Injustices among Human Beings

t- The Dismissal of Humanity from the Audience
u- Private Intercession
v- Intercession
w- God's Mercy

8- Chapter Eight: Paradise
a- Descriptions of the Inhabitants of Paradise
b- Descriptions of Paradise; Where is it?
c- The Maidens of Paradise (*Ḥūrī* Eyed)
d- The Lowest Rank in Paradise

9- Chapter Nine: Hell
a- Describing Hell
b- Gates of Hell/Levels of Hell
c- Valleys and Mountains
d- Snakes and Scorpions
e- Chains and Fetters
f- Garments of the Residents of Hell
g- Food of Hell
h- Drinks of Hell
i- The Custodians of Hell (*Zabāniya*)
j- The Cries of Humanity
k- Claustrophobia
l- The Least Tormented
m- The Most Tormented

10- Chapter Ten: Miscellaneous
a- Is Hell Eternal?
b- The Slaughter of Death
c- How do the Monotheists Suffer?
d- Sinners from among the Believers do not Suffer Eternally
e- The Limbo (*al-Aʿrāf*)
f- The Children of Believers Who Die Young
g- Nations who did not have Prophets; the Fool, the Deaf and the Decrepit
h- *Jinn* and Their Judgment
i- The Names of the Day of Resurrection
j- On Harmonizing Contradictory Reports about the World to Come
k- The Beatific Vision

Appendix 11

كتاب بهجة الناظرين وآيات المستدلّين
تصنيف الشيخ الإمام والعالم العلاّمة والبحر الحبر الهمام
المغترف من فيض ربّه العليّ
الشيخ مرعي بن يوسف المقدسيّ الحنبليّ
غفر الله له ولوالديه ومشايخه
وإخوانه وسائر
المسلمين والمسلمات
والمؤمنين
والمؤمنات
آمين [١و]

بسم الله الرحمن الرحيم وصلّى الله على سيّدنا وصحبه وسلم . ربّنا آتنا في الدنيا حسنة و في الآخرة حسنة . ربّنا آتنا من لدنك رحمة وهيّئ من أمرنا رشدا . نحمد من شرح صدورنا ونوّر قلوبنا للنظر في عجائب الملكوت . ونوحّد من توحّد في ملكه فأوجد العالم وجعل أوّله إيجاد أنوار سيّد بني آدم وخلق الموت والحياة . ولا يلحقه العدم والموت . ونمجّد من خلق اللوح والقلم ونقدّس من أوجد العرش والكرسيّ وغيرهما من العدم . ونتوكّل على الحيّ الذي لا يموت ونشهد بالربوبية لخالق الأرض والسماء ومسخّرا السحاب ليحمل الماء . ومرسل الرياح لواقح للمزن والشجر والنبات والقوت . ونشهد بالرسالة لسيّد العالمين وأشرف المرسلين المخبر لنا بما غاب عنّا من حشر ونشر وجنّة ونار إخبار كشف ويقين وثبوت . صلّى الله عليه وعلى آله وأصحابه أولي البصيرة والحقيقة والشريعة الذين حازوا أجلّ الأوصاف وأشرف النعوت وسلّم تسليما كثيرا.

وبعد فيقول أحقر الورى وأذلّ الفقراء مرعي بن يوسف المقدسيّ الحنبليّ : اعلم أنّ من أجلّ العلوم في القدر والشأن وأعظمها في السرّ والبرهان علم النظر في مصنوعات الصانع يستدلّ عليه والنظر في عجائب الملكوت يرشد إليه . فالناظر يطّلع على الأسرار الإلهيّة والبدائع الربّانيّة ويحصل له زيادة الكشف واليقين والمعارف الجمّة والخير المبين . ويرتقي من عالم الأكدار إلى عالم الأنوار ولا يصير مقلّدا في معرفة الواحد القهّار . والمقلّد قد اختلف في صحّة إيمانه وتكلّم أهل الكلام في حاله وشأنه.

وقد صنّف الأئمّة في عجائب الملكوت كتبا جمّة وأبدعوا فيها الغرائب إرشادا للأمّة . وقد وقفت منها على ما يسّر الوقوف عليه مولاي المعين وتأمّلت معانيها فإذا هي بدور

سوافر للناظرين . إلّا أنّ منها ما هو [١ظ] الموجز المخلّ والمطنب المملّ ، لم يف بالمقصود ولم يستوعب المطلوب المحمود . ومنها ما فيه المقبول والمردود . ولم يجروا فيها غالبا على سنن المحدّثين ويتمسّكون بنقول المؤرّخين وأقوال الوضّاعين . فلمّا رأيت ذلك ووقفت على ما هنالك دعاني داعي المشيئة والإلهام إلى جمع مؤلّف فريد في هذا المقام متكلّما فيه على العالم العلويّ والسفليّ من لدن مبتداه إلى آخر منتهاه وماذا يصير له أولى وأخرى . ليكون بالقبول أولى وأحرى . جانحًا في ذلك لنقول المفسّرين وأقوال المحدّثين وسنّة سيّد المرسلين . ومجانبا غالبا لأقوال المؤرّخين ونقول الوضّاعين.

وقد نقل ما في هذا المؤلّف الفريد والجمع الحسن المفيد من نحو خسماية مؤلّف أو يزيد باعتبار مواد أصوله . وقد اجتهدت في تحرير نقوله وبيان طريق تسهيله وإيضاح أبوابه وفصوله . فأصبح كاسمه بهجة الناظرين وآيات المستدلّين . فهاك كتابا لم يسمح الزمان في هذا الفنّ بمثله ولم ينسج ناسج على منواله وشكله . ودونك مؤلّفا يوضح المسائل ، محرّر الدلائل ، سهل العبارات ، بيّن الإشارات ، عبارته فائقة ، وألفاظه رائقة . جمع الفوائد من الكتب الصحيحة فأوعى وأبدع الغرائب ، وترك الأقوال المرجوحة فصار من أكثر كتب هذا الفنّ نفعا . ولعمري إنّه لجدير بأن يرسم بماء العيون ومداد الذهب . وأن يرقم في صحائف الورق فضلا عن الورق بأحسن خطّ من كتب . فإنّه جنّة فيها ما تشتهي الأنفس وتلذّ الأعين وروضة يكلّ عن وصفها الشفاه والألسن . وليس الخبر كالعيان . وستقرّ به بعد التأمّل العينان . فما كلّ من صنّف أجاد ولا كلّ من قال وفّى بالمراد . والفضل مواهب والناس في الفنون مراتب . والخلائق يتفاوتون في الفضائل . وقد تظفر الأواخر بما ترك الأوائل . وكم لله على خلقه من لطف وجود ، وكلّ ذي نعمة محسود والحسود لا يسود . هذا والفقير معترف بقصر الباع مغترف من بحر غيره [٢و] للانتفاع . مقرّ بقصور عبارته وحجاه . وسماعك بالمعيديّ خير من أن تراه.

وهذا المؤلّف في الحقيقة لا بدّ أن يقع لأحد رجلين . إمّا عالم محبّ منصف فيدعو لي بالحسنى ويدفع بالتي هي أحسن بما هو من صفته . وإمّا جاهل مبغض متعسّف فلا اعتبار بموافقته ولا بمخالفته . وإنّما الاعتبار بموافقة المحبّ المنصف لا بالمبغض المتعسّف.

إذا رضيت عنّي كرام عشيرتي   فلا زال غضبانا عليّ لئامها

وسميّته بهجة الناظرين وآيات المستدلّين . جعله الله خالصا لوجهه الكريم . وسببا للفوز لديه بجنّات النعيم . وصبّ عليه قبول القبول فإنّه أكرم مسؤول وأعزّ مأمول . وقد جعلته في عشرة أبواب ليكون أسهل لطرائق الصواب . وعلى الله اعتمادي وركوبي . وإليه فوّضت أمري في حركتي وسكوني.

تنبيه : نقل هذا الكتاب من كتاب الله الذي جمع علم الأوّلين والآخرين . ومن تفسير الثعلبيّ، وتفسير الزمخشريّ، وتفسير الإمام فخر الدين الرازيّ، وتفسير مكّيّ، وتفسير ابن عطيّة ,وتفسير الكواشيّ . ومن البخاريّ، ومسلم، والترمذيّ، والنسائيّ، وابن ماجه، وابن حبّان، وابن مندة، وابن منصور، وابن جرير، وابن المبارك، وابن راهويه، وابن عساكر، وابن المنذر، وابن مردويه، والطبرانيّ، والبيهقيّ، والحاكم، والبزار، والدارقطنيّ . ومسند أحمد، والطيالسيّ، وابن أبي شيبة، وابن أبي حاتم، وابن أبي الدنيا . والموطأ، وأبي داود، وأبي يعلى، وأبي الفرج، وأبي [الشيخ، وأبي نعيم،][32] ونعيم بن حمّاد، والديلميّ، وهنّاد، والأصبهانيّ، والخطّابي، والخطيب . والإحياء للغزاليّ، والدرّة الفاخرة له . ومن كتب التواريخ كمسالك البكري، وبهجة النفوس، والجغرافية، وخريدة العجائب . ومن الهيئة السنيّة للحافظ السيوطيّ، وشرح الصدور له، والبدور السافرة له . ومن شرح البخاريّ للحافظ ابن حجر، والروح لابن القيّم، وبحر الكلام للنسفيّ، [٢ظ] وشرح العقائد للسعد، ومن تذكرة القرطبيّ . ومن كنز الأسرار ولواحق الأفكار، وهو أجلّ هذا الفنّ إلى غيره من التصانيف المفيدة والرسائل العديدة . فصار مجتمعا في هذا المؤلّف ما هو متفرّقا في كتب كثيرة غيره . والله أسال لا ينساني من مزيدة وخير إنّه على ما يشاء قدير وبالإجابة جدير .

لطيفة : ما ورد في الأحاديث في الحسد وذمّ الحسود : قد أحببت أن أذكر في صدر هذا الكتاب ما يسرّ ذوي الفضائل والألباب ممن بلغ في الرتبة لأن يحسد وبما يرتدع به الحسود ويكمد . روى القاسم بن أصبع وأبو بكر بن أبي شيبة بإسنادهما عن الزبير بن العوّام رضي الله عنه أنّ رسول الله صلى الله عليه وسلم قال: "دبّ إليكم داء الأمم قبلكم الحسد والبغضاء - البغضاء هي الحالقة لا أقوال أنّها تحلق الشعر ولكن تحلق الدين - والذي نفسي بيده لا تدخلوا الجنّة حتّى تؤمنوا ولا تؤمنوا حتّى تحابّوا ألا أنبّئكم بما يثبت ذلك افشوا السلام بينكم ." وفي الحديث "أن الغلّ والحسد يأكلان الحسنات كما تأكل النار الحطب ." وعن أبي هريرة رضي الله عنه أنّ النبي صلّى الله عليه وسلم قال: "لا تباغضوا ولا تحاسدوا ولا تناجسوا وكونوا عباد الله إخوانا ." وفي الحديث إنّ لنعم الله تعالى أعداء قيل من أعداء نعم الله يا رسول الله قال "الذين يحسدون الناس على ما أتاهم الله من فضله ." وعن معاوية أنه قال لابنه "يا بني إيّاك والحسد فإنّه يبيّن فيك قبل أن يبيّن في حاسدك ." وقال بعض الحكماء إيّاكم والحسد فإنّ الحسد أوّل ذنب عصي الله به في السماء وأوّل ذنب عصي الله به في الأرض يشير إلى إبليس وقابيل . وروى عن الأحنف بن قيس قال "لا راحة لحسود ولا وفاء لبخيل ولا صديق لملوك[33] ولا مروّة لكذوب ولا سؤدد لسيّئ الخلق ." وقال ابن سيرين

32 الزيادة من مخطوطة المتحف البريطاني.
33 في مخطوطة المتحف البريطاني: لمملوك.

"ما حسدت أحدا على شيء من الدنيا فإن كان من أهل الجنّة فكيف أحسده وهو صائر إلى الجنّة وإن كان من أهل النار فكيف أحسده وهو صائر إلى النار." وقال الحسن البصريّ "يا بن آدم لم تحسد أخاك فإن كان الذي أعطاه الله عزّ وجلّ لكرامته عليه فلم تحسد من أكرمه الله وإن كان غير ذلك فلا ينبغي لك أن تحسد من مصيره إلى النار." وقال بعضهم ليس [٣و] شيء أضرّ من الحسد يصل إلى الحاسد خمس عقوبات قبل أن يصل إلى المحسود: غمّ لا ينقطع، ومصيبة لا يؤجر عليها، ومذمّة لا يحمد بها، ويسخط عليه الرب، ويغلق عليه أبواب التوفيق.

وقد ورد في ذمّ الحاسد آثار كثيرة وأخبار شهيرة ولقد أحسن بعض الفضلاء حين قال:

ألا قل لمن كان لي حاسدا أتدري على من أسأت الأدب
أسأت على الله في فعلة لأنّك لم ترض لي ما وهب
فجازاك منه بأن زادني وسدّ عليك وجوه الطلب

وأعلم أنّ من أشدّ الناس تحاسدا العلماء لا سيّما في زماننا هذا. ابتلاهم الله بذلك نعوذ بالله من ذلك. وروى ابن السكن بإسناد عن ابن عبّاس "قال استعلموا علم العلماء ولا تصدّقوا بعضهم على بعض فوالذي نفسي بيده لهم أشدّ تغايرا من التيوس في زربها." وروى مقاتل بن حيّان وعطاء الخراسانيّ عن سعيد بن المسيّب عن ابن عبّاس قال "خذوا العلم حيث وجدتم ولا تقبلوا أقوال الفقهاء بعضهم على بعض فإنّهم يتغايرون تغاير التيوس في الزريبة." وعن مالك بن دينار قال "يؤخذ بقول القرّاء والعلماء في كلّ الأقوال إلّا قول بعضهم في بعض. فلهم أشدّ تحاسدا من التيوس تنصب لها الشاة الصارف فيقتلها هذا من هنا وهذا من هنا." وعن ابن وهب أنّه قال "لا يجوز شهادة القرّاء بعضهم على بعض يعني العلماء لأنّهم أشدّ تحاسدا وتباغضا." وعن مالك بن دينار قال "أجيز شهادة القرّاء على جميع الخلق ولا أجيز شهادة بعضهم على بعض." وكذلك قال سفيان الثوريّ. وروى سحنون عن ابن وهب عن عبد العزيز بن أبي حازم قال سمعت أبي يقول "العلماء كانوا يقولون فيما مضى من الزمان إذا لقي من هو فوقه كان ذلك يوم غنيمة وإذا لقي من هو مثله ذاكره وإذا لقي من هو دونه لم يزه عليه. حتّى إذا كان هذا الزمان، فصار الرجل يعيب من هو فوقه ابتغاء أن ينقطع عنه الناس حتّى يروا أنّه ليست بهم حاجة إليه، ولا يذاكروا[34] ويزهوا على من هو دونه فهلك الناس."

34 في مخطوطة المتحف البريطاني: ولا يذاكر من هو مثله.

فإذا وقع [٣ظ] مثل هذا في زمانهم و زمن السلف فلأن يقع مثله في الخلف أجدر سيّما لما جبل عليه أبناء هذا الزمان من الأتراب والأقوال من مجد الفضائل مع قيام الدلائل ويحبّون لأنفسهم دون غيرهم الرئاسة والتعظيم ويسارعون إلى نبذ من تلوح عليه شواهد العلم بالقول الذميم . وينتقدون على من صنّف كتابا ويلتهبون بانتقادهم العثرات ويحسبون السيّأت حسابا ويضربون صفحا عن الحسنات . فأصبحت أعراض المصنّفين أغراض سهام ألسنة الحسّاد ، ونفائس تصانيفهم معرضة بأيدهم ، تنتهب فرائدها ثمّ ترميها بالكساد ، ولقد أحسن الإمام أبو حنيفة رضي الله عنه حيث حسدوه فقال :

إن يحسدوني فإنّي غير لائمهم قبلي من الناس أهل الفضل قد حسدوا
فدام لي ولهم ما بي وما بهم ومـات أكثـرنا غيظـا بما يجـد

إذا تقرّر ذلك فلنشرع في المقصود من الكتاب بعون الملك الوهّاب :

الباب الأوّل في ذكر العالم العلويّ . الباب الثاني في ذكر العالم السفليّ . الباب الثالث في ذكر خلق الإنس والجنّ . الباب الرابع في ذكر الموت وما يتعلّق به . الباب الخامس في أشراط الساعة . الباب السادس في قيام الساعة وخراب العالم وتغيّر نظامه . الباب السابع في ذكر الحشر والموقف والحساب وما يتعلّق بذلك . الباب الثامن في ذكر الجنّة ونعيمها . الباب التاسع في ذكر النار وعذابها . والباب العاشر في ذكر مسائل متفرّقة . وقد ذكرت في كلّ باب عدّة فصول كما ستراها فيما سيأتي إن شاء الله تعالى .

CHAPTER 44

Expulsion from Paradise: Granada in Raḍwā ʿĀshūr's *The Granada Trilogy* (1994–8) and Salman Rushdie's *The Moor's Last Sigh* (1995)[1]

Suha Kudsieh

The legacy of al-Andalus and its romanticized *convivencia* has proven versatile enough to accommodate recent reinterpretations by a wide variety of authors, including Amin Malouf (*Leo Africanus*, 1986), Antonio Gala (*La pasión turca*, 1993), Tariq Ali (*Shadows of the Pomegranate Tree*, 1993), Raḍwā ʿĀshūr (*Thulāthiyyat Gharnāṭa*, in English: *The Granada Trilogy*, 1994–8),[2] Salman Rushdie (*The Moor's Last Sigh*, 1995), and Diana Abu-Jaber (*Crescent*, 2003), among many others. Miguel Angel de Blunes observes that the reinterpretations are informed by present-day sensibilities more than historical fact.[3] Modern authors typically build on the allegorical depiction of al-Andalus as an earthly paradise, epitomized by the beautiful gardens of al-Ḥamrāʾ (Alhambra) Palace, where people of various religions, ethnicities, and languages coexisted in harmony; hence, the loss of al-Andalus mirrors the loss of Eden, and the fall of Granada in 897/1494, with the subsequent expulsion of Jews and Muslims, is akin to the fall of Adam and Eve and their expulsion from paradise.

The allegorical depiction of al-Andalus can express Spain's desire to assert national difference from the rest of Europe,[4] as well as from the Orient, by stressing its unique Islamic heritage and civilization. This difference attains a more poignant value for modern Muslims who hold out the Andalusian *convivencia* as a model that epitomizes Islam's tolerance and acceptance of diversity, refuting the current stereotypical depiction of Muslims in Western

1 I would like to thank Umar Ryad for his helpful comments and the audience's feedback in the panel entitled "Paradise meets Modernity" in *The Roads to Paradise* conference, held 27–31 May 2009 at the University of Göttingen. I also would like to thank the editorial team and John Detre for his editorial comments and suggestions.

2 Raḍwā ʿĀshūr's name also appears as Radwa Ashour, especially in English. I have opted to write it as it is pronounced in Arabic. The first part of the trilogy was published in 1994, the second in 1995, and the third in 1998.

3 Blunes, Introducción x.

4 Gilmour, Turkish delight 79.

 | DOI 10.1163/9789004333154_045

media as hard-line fanatics. For Arab literati, the waning of al-Andalus and the expulsion of its citizens foreshadows the loss of Palestine and the exile of its people; while the gradual elimination of the party kingdoms in al-Andalus by the united Christian-Spanish front, which are reincarnated today in the powerful West and its local allies, is seen as an ominous precursor of the disintegration of the Arab world into puppet states engaged in petty quarrels with their neighbors.[5]

In this paper, I focus on two novels that depict the moment of loss, that is to say, the fall from grace that led to the expulsion of Muslims from Spain's earthly paradise: *Thulāthiyyat Gharnāṭa*, written by the Egyptian novelist Raḍwā ʿĀshūr (b. 1946) in Arabic and published in 1994–8; and *The Moor's Last Sigh*, composed by the British-Indian writer Salman Rushdie (b. 1947) in English and published in 1995. Both novels grapple with the thorny issues of hybridity, cultural diversity, and ineffective heroes, themes that occur frequently in postcolonial literature. Moreover, although ʿĀshūr and Rushdie draw on works written by their literary predecessors, both authors break away from previous literary traditions. ʿĀshūr is the first Arab author to move the setting of her novel from the courts and palaces of the city, where the rulers and aristocracy reside, to the streets of Granada to examine the travails and responses of the ordinary people who bore the brunt of the tragic events that unfolded after the ruling elites surrendered the city to the Spaniards.[6] Similarly, Rushdie is the first South Asian author to depart from the literary tradition established by his forerunners,[7] which venerated the glorious legacy of al-Andalus, and

5 Gana, Search 229.

6 The Andalusian topos is more deeply entrenched in Arabic literary tradition than in its South Asian counterpart. It goes back to the late nineteenth century when several Arab writers, such as ʿAlī b. Salīm al-Wardanī (1861–1915), Aḥmad Zakī (1867–1934), and Muṣṭafā Farrūkh visited Spain and published their accounts (see Granara, Extensio animae 50–1). The short stories, poetry collections, and novels written in Arabic are too numerous to survey in this brief note, but Granara provides an excellent overview in his article entitled "Extensio animae." Al-Juʿaydī examines the work of several Palestinian poets whose poems retell the fall of al-Andalus as an allegory for the loss of Palestine. Regarding novels, it should be noted that almost all the relevant novels in Arabic depict events that take place in palaces or royal courts.

7 The well-known Muslim poet and philosopher, Muḥammad Iqbāl, who was born in British India (1877–1938), wrote a collection of quatrains, *ghazals*, and poems inspired by his visit to Spain in 1933. It was entitled *Bāl-i Jibrīl* (*Gabriel's Wing*) and was published in 1935, cf. Nourani, Garden. Unlike Iqbāl's earlier works, which were written in Farsi, *Bāl-i Jibrīl* was written in Urdu. One of the most celebrated poems in the collection is the *Masjid-i Qurtuba* poem, in which Iqbāl describes his feelings when he visited the mosque of Cordoba, which reminded

to foreground the complex socio-religious forces that have shattered India's image as an emblem of tolerance and pluralism.

Both authors move away from the poetics of Andalusian nostalgia. Unlike their predecessors who were captivated by the myth of al-Andalus as an interfaith paradise, they invoke the past to question why current Eastern societies are plagued by fanaticism and radicalism. Thus, while previous authors indulged in *restorative* nostalgia, ʿĀshūr and Rushdie engage in *reflective* nostalgia. According to Boym, the former reconstructs "emblems and rituals of home" to restore the past, whereas reflective nostalgia "cherishes shattered fragments of memory and temporalizes space."[8] From a reflective stance, al-Andalus is a convenient metaphor for exploring the cultural and religious crises in Egypt and India, where the mythic past is juxtaposed with a polarized present dominated by menacing discourses of ethnic and religious exclusion.

For Boym, "Restorative nostalgia evokes national past and future; reflective nostalgia is more about individual and cultural memory."[9] In a sense, ʿĀshūr and Rushdie fuse individual and cultural memory together. For example, ʿĀshūr married the well-known Palestinian refugee and poet Murīd al-Barghūtī (1944–present) in 1970. She opposed Anwar Sadat's peace negotiations with Israel in the late 1970s. In 1977 and on the day of his visit to Israel, al-Barghūtī was deported from Egypt due to his political activism. He was not allowed to return to Egypt until 1994, which meant he was separated from his wife and son for almost twenty years.[10] ʿĀshūr's novel bears the imprint of those personal

---

him of the grandeur of the Mughal Empire. The collection articulates Iqbāl's pan-Islamic vision, according to which all Muslims share one civilization and are united by the same culture. Another South Asian author who was inspired by the legacy of al-Andalus is Tariq Ali (1943–present). His historic novel *Shadows of the pomegranate tree*, written in English and published in 1992, depicts the struggle of the Hudayl clan after the fall of Granada. At first, they carry on with their carefree pursuits, but the Spaniards and the Inquisition's radical policies compel them to rebel, albeit belatedly. The uprising is quickly crushed and the family are expelled from their idyllic homeland. Ali stresses the legacy of al-Andalus as an Islamic oasis where different religions co-existed peacefully. He also attempts to dismantle stereotypes associated with current Muslims in Britain and in the West, namely that they are fanatical, terrorists, narrow minded, and anti-women, by depicting the Hudayl family as tolerant and liberal, almost secular.

8 Boym, Nostalgia 49.

9 Ibid.

10 Al-Barghūtī lived in Budapest, Hungary, as a PLO (Palestinian Liberation Organization) representative. It was the couple's decision that ʿĀshūr stay in Cairo so that their son, Tamīm, would grow up fluent in Arabic (see http://weekly.ahram.org.eg/Archive/2003/622/profile.htm).

trials: Salīma, the educated daughter of Abū Ja'far, is married to Sa'd, a poor refugee from Malaga who lost contact with his family after escaping to Granada. Sa'd decides to join the ranks of the revolutionaries, spending most of his time hiding in the mountains, away from Salīma and their daughter, 'Ā'isha. Malaga in the novel corresponds to Palestine, and Granada to Cairo. The novel's pervasive pessimism suggests 'Āshūr's disillusionment with the signing of the Peace Treaty of Camp David in 1978 and the Egyptians' passive acceptance of the treaty.

Rushdie's personal journey takes a different course. His earlier novel *The Satanic Verses*, published in 1988, caused a major controversy among Muslims in Britain and elsewhere. The title refers to an incident reported by Ibn Isḥāq and al-Ṭabarī, the two well-known historians and exegetes from the eighth and ninth century, respectively, regarding the Quranic verses that Muḥammad, the Prophet of Islam, retracted because they were inspired by Satan and not by God.[11] The controversy triggered a series of demonstrations and public burnings of Rushdie's novel in Britain, where he resided, and in India, where he was born. Ironically, these acts echoed the burning of Islamic and Arabic books at the hands of the Spaniards in al-Andalus. In 1989, Ayatollah Khomeini (1902–89), the Supreme Leader of Iran, announced a *fatwā* (an Islamic juristic ruling or edict) that declared Rushdie an apostate, exhorting Muslims to kill him. The *fatwā* forced Rushdie into hiding for several years. *The Moor's Last Sigh* was the first novel he published after the controversy. It was the product of exile, "of not being able to visit India for eight years since the Iranian *fatwā* sent him into hiding."[12] Another event that influenced Rushdie was the destruction of the Babri Mosque[13] in Ayodhya, Uttar Pradesh, in 1992 at the hands of Hindu extremists. The demolition triggered huge riots in India, leaving more than 2,000 people dead. Rushdie's cynicism toward religions that stake a claim about tolerance is reflected in *The Moor's Last Sigh*. Following this brief overview of the circumstances behind the writing of each novel, I examine the themes of paradise and the fall from grace as they unfold through the actions

11 Sawhney, Satanic 263.

12 Narain, Histories 56.

13 The mosque was built around 934/1528 at the behest of Sultan Bābur (888–937/1483–1530), the first Mughal emperor, on a site where an ancient Hindu temple was demolished. Hindus believe that Lord Rām, one of the Hindu deities, was born in that location. For more details about the history of the mosque and the controversy surrounding it, refer to Arshad Islam's article, Babri Mosque. Salman Rushdie discusses the politics surrounding the mosque and the rise of Hindu extremism in *Homelands* 26–33.

of ineffective and anti-heroic characters, whose failures rupture their families and destroy their communities.

One striking aspect in ʿĀshūr's novel is the paucity of accurate historical details. She utilizes the rough outlines of the fall of Granada to investigate current events in Egypt without explicitly recalling the brilliant history of al-Andalus. According to ʿĀshūr, all her novels are attempts to cope with defeat.[14] Her decision to steer away from writing a historical novel is intentional because, "Historical novels have a bad reputation: The imaginative recreation of an earlier period has often been problematic. This genre is traditionally associated with propaganda values and the romantic glorification of the past."[15] ʿĀshūr is referring here to nationalist propaganda, to the historical interpretations produced by Jurjī Zaydān, Aḥmad Shawqī, and ʿAlī al-Jārim, early twentieth-century writers whose works rallied readers to embrace Arab nationalism and celebrated the diversity of al-Andalus as a political model.[16] The story of al-Andalus also served as a moral lesson, an exemplum, warning readers against the grave consequences of separatism and political in-fights: divisions would lead to the downfall of Arabs, as it happened during the reign of the Petty Kings (*mulūk al-ṭawāʾif*) in al-Andalus (423–53/1031–61). However, the political and social conditions in Egypt and the Middle East changed after 1960s such that by the end of the twentieth century, Arab nationalism became a dead end for Arab literati rather than a *raison d'être*.[17] Therefore, ʿĀshūr chooses a different approach to narrating the events that led to the fall of Granada.

ʿĀshūr does not dwell on the glorious past or depictions of an idyllic Granada; instead, she focuses on how ordinary people reacted to the treaty and the loss of the city. Overall, they received the news rather passively, entrusting the task of resistance to their defeated Muslim rulers. In the novel, the residents of Granada exchange rumors and gossip about the fate of the rulers but are loath to join the guerrilla fighters who attack the Christian Castilians from their mountain base. One group of onlookers comments,

14 Ashour, Eyewitness 87.

15 Ibid., 90.

16 Granara, Nostalgia.

17 Rashid Khalidi differentiates between "Arabism," a popular concept among the masses in the Middle East, and "Arab nationalism," an ideology that Arab regimes manipulated to entrench their totalitarian governments. He adds that the humiliating defeat of the Arab forces in 1967, and Sadat's break up with the Arab block, after signing the peace treaty with Israel, tarnished the nationalist ideology and weakend it, cf. Khalidi, Demise 265–6.

> It does not matter what happened to Ibn Abī Ghassān [the last defender of the city]; this is not his time or ours. Let us carry what we can of our belongings and roam God's vast lands, or we surrender our fate to God and to our new masters in order to survive.[18]

The reaction is defeatist: the Muslims of Granada appear eager to abandon their Eden without waiting for an eviction order. When the treaty is signed, they draw solace from traditional sayings regarding the inescapability of God's decree, convinced that the stipulations of the treaty are the best that could be hoped for under the circumstances. Thus, "they wept and signed (*bakaw wa-waqqaʿū*)."[19] Another group is in denial. Since they could not avert the fall of the city, they comfort themselves with dreams of divine intervention. For instance, Abū Jaʿfar blames the last sultan for igniting the war between the Muslims and the Spaniards, musing to himself, "Who knows what will happen tomorrow?…Granada will remain protected, by God's permission and his will."[20]

ʿĀshūr plunges her readers into the moment of the fall by depicting a cocooned community that relies on superstition and hearsay, passively awaiting divine intervention. The community bears a striking resemblance to current Egyptian society, especially since a considerable segment of the population is illiterate. For example, slaves and concubines are missing from the novel, and the attitude toward women is extremely traditional. Most women in the novel direct their energies toward cooking, rearing their children, and looking after the men. The only exception is Salīma, who is preoccupied with pursuing her education and copying scientific and medical treatises. When Saʿd, Salīma's husband, complains to Ḥasan, her brother, about the way his sister neglects him, Ḥasan advises him to beat her: "Beat her, Saʿd. Beat her harshly until she comes to her senses! (*Iḍribhā yā Saʿd. Iḍribhā ḍarban mubriḥan ḥattā tafīqa.*)"[21] After following Ḥasan's advice and drawing tears from Salīma,[22] Saʿd realizes the importance and the value of the books to his wife. The fact that the two male figures who are closest to Salīma are unable to fathom the significance of her efforts to preserve al-Andalus' repository of scientific and medical knowledge demonstrates women's marginalization within their families, especially when they break the traditional roles assigned to them by a patriarchal society.

18 ʿĀshūr, *Gharnāṭa* 11. All translations from Arabic into English are mine.

19 Ibid., 12.

20 Ibid., 13.

21 Ibid., 124.

22 Ibid., 125.

The incident also illustrates the couple's inability to communicate and express their opinions to each other, even as they struggle to resist the draconian decrees imposed upon them by the Spaniards. Furthermore, it highlights the plight of female literati within traditional societies, and the ebbing importance of education.

Several decades later, in the isolated village of Jaʿfariyya, the men vent their anger over the grim political prospects and their paralysis to act by regularly beating the women (*yatafashshashūn fī zawjātihim*). Hearing the cries of their female neighbors, women feel lucky because they were not the ones being beaten, knowing however that their turn would soon come.[23] The vicious cycle of violence against women illustrates the fragmentation of the family unit and, ultimately, Muslim society.

By portraying the abuse of women, ʿĀshūr dismantles the myth of gender equality in al-Andalus. According to Nada Mourtada-Sabbah and Adrian Gully, Andalusian women are thought to have enjoyed a certain level of general emancipation and a great degree of personal freedom when compared with their medieval counterparts elsewhere; nevertheless, the balance of evidence is inconclusive because the details about those women as narrated by historians and anthologists are sparse. Pierre Guichard is of the opinion that the apparent emancipation of Andalusian women demonstrates society's schizophrenia regarding the position of women rather than "a particular emancipation stemming from the atmosphere of the time."[24] ʿĀshūr's depiction of the treatment of women points not only to a patriarchal society, but also to a regressive, phobic society that shuns strangers, including Muslims who do not share the same blood ties.

In a revealing incident that exemplifies the hardening of Muslim society in al-Andalus, ʿAlī, the grandchild of Salīma and Saʿd, stumbles upon the village of al-Jaʿfariyya while searching for his aunts, who were married off to Muslims from Valencia several decades earlier. The village and its closely-knit tribal community, which practice female honor killing, represent ultra conservative enclaves in the Middle East, like Upper Egypt. ʿAlī falls in love with Kawthar, whose name alludes to a lake or river in paradise.[25] Kawthar's family does not marry their daughters off to strangers, even if they happen to be

---

23 Ibid., 420.

24 Mourtada-Sabbah and Gully, High positions 184.

25 *Al-Kawthar* is the title of the Sura 108 of the Quran. Addressed to the Prophet Muḥammad, the first verse states that God has given al-Kawthar to Muḥammad, meaning he will enter paradise. It may also mean that God has given the Prophet great "abundance," meaning great progeny or great faculties, that is to say, abilities to reason.

Muslims. When Salsabīl, Kawthar's sister, whose name also refers to a spring in paradise,[26] falls in love with a Muslim who is not a member of her clan, her father and brothers covertly kill her. Kawthar informs the Spanish commissioner of the murder, thus endangering her own life. Instead of supporting Kawthar and protecting her, the Muslim community ostracizes her. She eventually marries Sancho Lopez and becomes pregnant. When ʿAlī questions Sancho's religion and asks whether he is a Christian, Kawthar replies, "Haven't we also become Christians? (*A-lam naʿud naḥnu ayḍan naṣārā?*)"[27] She reminds ʿAlī of the unacknowledged truth, which he cannot perceive, that the Muslims' identity has been twisted and deformed: although they practice their traditions in secret, they are officially Christians. Moreover, Kawthar's decision to marry a good man who happens to be a Christian instead of a Muslim (and her subsequent death) hint at the erosion of diversity within the remaining pockets of Muslim communities, which have become increasingly withdrawn. This is further evidenced when Kawthar's family manages to track her whereabouts and kills her. The elimination of both girls by their family illustrates the self-destructiveness of the remnants of Andalusian society. Their close-mindedness precipitates their inevitable fall. The aggression against women and fear of diversity, even among Muslims, challenges the idyllic myth of al-Andalus and invites readers to reflect on the erosion of hybridity and cosmopolitanism in modern Arab societies.

Another issue that ʿĀshūr puts into relief is the destructive influence of the weakened political leaders who betray the Muslims in Granada. For example, Abū ʿAbdallāh, who rose to power in Granada with the support of the people al-Bayasīn, signs the treaty of surrender with the Spaniards in return for thirty thousand pounds.[28] Some members of the Muslim nobility, including the sultan's sons, convert to Christianity. Yūsuf, the minister who negotiated in the name of the people and prepared the official and secret treaties, decides to convert and become a monk.[29] The famed warrior and fighter al-Thaghrī is jailed and eventually acquiesces and converts to Christianity.[30] Those events have abysmal consequences for the defeated community. The account of betrayals and secret treaties is reminiscent of how Egyptians felt when President Sadat signed the peace treaty with Israel. The importance of strong political leadership is underscored when Roberto informs ʿAlī, "The problem, lad,

26 See Q 76:18, which refers to a spring called Salsabīl.
27 ʿĀshūr, *Gharnāṭa* 444.
28 Ibid., 23 and 26.
29 Ibid., 27.
30 Ibid., 47.

is that our leaders were smaller than us. We were more mature, tolerant and able, but they were our leaders. When they broke, so did we (*Al-mushkila yā walad anna qādatanā kānū aṣghara minnā. Kunnā akbara wa-aʿfā wa-aqdara wa-lākinnahum al-qāda, inkasarū fa-inkasarnā*)."[31] Without a strong leader, the community edges closer toward the fall.

The elders in the novel, such as Abū Jaʿfar and Abū Manṣūr, belong to an older, dying breed of heroes. They remember Granada at its height, as a magnificent, enchanted city, bustling with energy, culture, knowledge, and learning. They would fight to defend it were they physically able, but their advanced age prevents them from bearing arms and joining the rebels. The death of the elders devastates the community, especially since their children are unable to fill the void. The younger generation is impotent even though it is educated and is physically strong enough to join the rebels' ranks. The generation gap points to the disintegration of the Arabs' moral and heroic *ethos*. Family ties are ruptured, underscoring the breakdown of the Muslim community in general: according to tradition, fathers take on their sons as apprentices and groom them to take over the family business, but Abū Manṣūr and Abū Jaʿfar choose to apprentice two orphaned lads, Naʿīm and Saʿd, who lost their homes and cities to the advancing Spanish armies, instead of teaching their offspring. Saʿd eventually marries Abū Jaʿfar's granddaughter Salīma and joins the resistance in the mountains of Bisharrāt.

William Granara observes that Ḥasan and Salīma, Abū Jaʿfar's grandchildren, represent binary opposites:[32] whereas Ḥasan devotes his energy to protecting his extended family and keeping its members safe, Salīma pursues esoteric knowledge and medicinal remedies that prolong life. The two siblings bicker constantly about their opposed priorities and have difficulty communicating with each other. The familial squabbles point to a weakened, besieged Muslim community rather than usher in the birth of a new, brave society. Salīma's devotion to the pursuit of knowledge may signify the liberation of women in a futuristic society, but her esoteric quest, which seeks answers to questions such as why people die, appears impractical when her community is in crisis. At the same time, Ḥasan's determination to safeguard his family at all costs curtails his ability to aid his community or his sister: he remains silent when Salīma is led to prison and then burnt alive.

Ḥasan's inaction signals a major theme in the novel, namely, the fragmentation of family structure, which mirrors the fragmentation of Arab society. When Saʿd accuses Ḥasan of being indifferent to the rebels, he replies that he

---

31 Ibid., 373.

32 Granara, Nostalgia 70.

is protecting the family's women and children.[33] Not only does Ḥasan ask Saʿd to leave his household and fails to help his sister, but he also refuses to offer refuge to Maryama's brothers,[34] his brothers-in-law, when they are released from prison, lest their presence should put the household under the Spaniards' watch. As the oppression increases, Ḥasan offers to marry his daughters off to wealthy suitors from Valencia. Consequently, the next generation of the family grows up scattered, without knowing the whereabouts of their aunts and cousins. The weakening of the family ties illustrates the fragmentation of the Islamic-Arabic society as a whole, divided among interest groups and split along class lines. For instance, ʿUmar and ʿAbd al-Karīm, the two brothers who marry Ḥasan's daughters, align themselves with the Christian nobility of Valencia. According to the brothers, when the Spanish fanatics attack Arabs, their real aim is to strike at the Spaniard nobility. The brothers also dislike the *mujāhidūn* among the Muslims (such as Saʿd) because their rebellion confirms the Spaniards' perception that Muslim Arabs are disloyal to the kingdom, leaving the Spanish with no choice but to Christianize them or drive them out. Both options complicate the lives of Valencian Muslims.[35]

Following the sisters' wedding, the conditions in Valencia deteriorate for Muslims there;[36] the husbands are accused of conspiring with the French and the Protestants against the Spaniards, and are thrown in jail.[37] Ḥasan never sees or hears from his daughters after their marriages. Thus, his efforts to protect his family eventually fail. He loses Saʿd, his best friend, his sister, his daughters, and their families.

ʿĀshūr is not the first author to dwell on the theme of Arab disunity. Many Arab writers, especially Palestinian poets, regard the fall of al-Andalus as a transhistoric image[38] that evokes the loss of Palestine in 1948, and the ensuing wars. ʿĀshūr alludes to this structure when she remarks:

> To me Granada was the Granada of the Moriscos, defeated men and women whose resistance was doomed to failure. It was a correlative of my experience of the bombing of Baghdad, a bombing which brought with it the 1967 bombing of Sinai, the 1982 bombing of Beirut, and the persistent bombing of southern Lebanon. It was a means to explore my

33 ʿĀshūr, *Gharnāṭa* 143.

34 Ibid., 211.

35 Ibid., 180–2.

36 Ibid., 196.

37 Ibid., 382.

38 Granara, Extensio animae 160.

> fears, impotence and also the chances of survival through resistance. Maybe the present was too difficult to handle as present, too scorching. I find myself going to the past which, however painful, was not as painful as the present.[39]

In the novel, the Spaniards acquire multivalent meanings. Sometimes, they stand for Western colonizers or Israelis, at other times for religious fanaticism. They are sometimes referred to as *al-Ikhwān* (Brethren), a term currently used to refer to the Muslim Brotherhood.[40] The Spanish inquisition represents the *mukhābarāt*, that is to say, the state intelligence services. The parallel is made clear when, for example, Salīma is strip-searched, interrogated, and tortured to confess that she practices witchcraft:

> Before they brought her before the three interrogators, they brought a woman who was as huge as a giant (*ka-l-ʿimlāq*), whose offense was great and whose face was stern. She cut her hair and ordered her to take off her clothes, all her clothes, until she was naked (*ʿāriya*) like the day when her mother gave birth to her. Then the woman searched with her hands (*tajūsu bi-yadayhā*) under her [Salīma's] armpits, between her thighs, her nostrils, mouth, ears, vagina and anus. Searching for what? Is this an absurdity or madness?[41]

Salīma is also tortured with hot iron and tested:

> When Salīma clutched (*qabaḍat*) the iron rod (*qaḍīb al-ḥadīd*) heated by fire (*al-maḥmī bi-l-nār*) in her hands, and walked with it along the assigned path, the interrogators did not conclude, as expected after passing a test of this type, that the accused was stating the truth. Instead, they were more certain that she drew strength from a Satan whose immense might enabled her to withstand the pain.[42]

Salīma's torture and her swollen feet[43] are reminiscent of the various methods the *mukhābarāt*, i.e., the secret agency, employs to torment innocent people

---

39 Ashour, Eyewitness 91.
40 ʿĀshūr, *Gharnāṭa* 181, 190.
41 Ibid., 235.
42 Ibid., 241.
43 Ibid., 243.

and extract confessions to deeds they did not commit. These types of torture were common during the Sadat and Mubarak eras in Egypt.[44]

Salīma's quest for knowledge jeopardizes her family's safety, but she is preoccupied with copying and cataloguing the books bequeathed to her by her father and collecting new ones. Despite her education and knowledge, she uses neither to help the rebels. When she was accused of practicing witchcraft and black magic, she could not save herself or convince her accusers of her innocence. Salīma's ineffectiveness and failure brings to mind the isolation of modern Arab intellectuals, who are aloof and disconnected from their societies despite their extensive knowledge and learning.

Salīma's knowledge stems from copying and memorizing the books she owns, not from innovation. William Granara thinks she is the voice of change and individualism,[45] but she does not conduct new experiments or make discoveries. When Ḥaṣan and Saʿd's friend Naʿīm shows Salīma a magnifying glass that belongs to Priest Miguel, she asks him to leave it with her for one night. Instead of trying to understand how it works so that she can make a similar instrument, she decides to lie to Naʿīm the next day, telling him she broke it, and keeps it.[46] Salīma does not mingle with her community because she has limited social skills. Her disheveled hair and her unkempt appearance strike fear in onlookers. When ʿUmar and ʿAbd al-Karīm's mother falls ill during the preparation for the wedding of Ḥaṣan's daughters, Salīma examines her. The old woman is so frightened by her that she refuses to take the medicine Salīma prepared.[47] These shortcomings render Salīma as ineffective as her brother.

As the novel progresses, the lines separating good and evil, which were clearly drawn at the beginning, become blurred. A cycle of violence sets in, making it difficult to assign the blame to any one group: every attack on the Castillians leads to an attack on the Bayasīn, the Granadan neighborhood where Muslims are holed up, which in turn pushes the Muslims to treason in Valencia and other cities, which provokes the Spaniards to harsher measures forcing Muslims to assimilate and convert to Christianity. Furthermore, when the next generations of Muslims start adopting Spanish names, identifying who is a friend (presumably a co-religionist) and who is a foe becomes rather confusing. To further complicate matters, the religious identity of some of the people who help the rebels and Muslim runaways is sometimes ambiguous. For instance, when ʿAlī is on the run, the identity of the woman who offers him

---

44 Esposito, *Islam and politics* 239–45 and 256.

45 Granara, Nostalgia 70.

46 ʿĀshūr, *Gharnāṭa* 135–6.

47 Ibid., 187–8.

refuge is hinted at but not stated;[48] by contrast, the man who betrays ʿAlī is José, his Muslim friend. Although the novel does not assign blame, it criticizes tribalism and blind loyalty to a community that has become aggressive and intolerant. The murder of Kawthar and her sister are testimony to its decline.

The vanquished Muslims are unable to foresee the long-term consequences of their actions, or make wise decisions regarding their loyalties. For example, when the people of Jaʿfariyya celebrate the victory of the English over the Spaniards, ʿAlī inquires who the British are. A man replies, "They are not better than our Spanish rulers. They quarrel over sovereignty and rulership, each hoping for the lion's share."[49] ʿĀshūr reminds her readers in this instance that all rulers are the same, regardless of their ethnicity or religion. The pilgrim who returned from his travels explains:

> I was as surprised as you were when I found out that Egyptians hate their rulers as we hate our Spanish rulers. And I became more surprised when I saw with my own eyes and heard how a Turk or a Mamlūk points to one of the natives and says, haughtily and disdainfully, 'Egyptian peasant!', as if he was one of the Spaniards calling one of us 'Arab dog'![50]

The abandonment of Muslims in al-Andalus by their Middle Eastern brethren prompts ʿAlī to ask, "Why did the scales weigh in favor of the East [during the crusades], and here they are light? Is there a defect in us, which they [those who fought the crusaders] did not have, or is our misfortune that we are separated by sea, that Egypt is not our neighbor and Iraq and Damascus do not border us?"[51] ʿAlī's questions resonate for today's Muslims and Arabs, for their predicament is the same.

ʿĀshūr is critical of the Andalusians' inaction while awaiting the assistance of Muslims and European rulers or divine intervention (i.e., the hand of fate). When all the Muslims are expelled from Spain, they passively line up at the harbor praying and reciting traditional sayings by the Prophet. When ʿAlī proposes that they disobey the order of expulsion, he is told that resistance is futile because the Spaniards are stronger, and it will only lead to a pointless bloodbath. Another voice suggests waiting for outside help. Eventually, the

48 Ibid., 352–3.

49 Ibid., 452–3.

50 Ibid., 469.

51 Ibid., 473.

crowds decide it is their fate to leave their olive trees and their lands. It is, after all, God's decree.[52] Thus, they passively accept expulsion from paradise.

While 'Āshūr is disillusioned by the resurgence of radical Islam in Egypt, associating it with the destruction of an Andalusian utopia, Salman Rushdie starts with the premise that al-Andalus was not real; it was a myth right from the start, just like Indian nationalism and interfaith coexistence. In his novel *The Moor's Last Sigh*, he sets out to prove this point of view.

Unlike 'Āshūr who eschews historical details, Rushdie's novel is replete with them. History for Rushdie is a technique for questioning and subverting nationalist narratives to uncover the suppressed narratives that were expunged from the official version of the birth of India. 'Āshūr achieves similar ends by different means: by refusing to join the chorus of authors who sing the praises of al-Andalus, she deconstructs the official history and brings buried stories to the light of day.

In *The Moor's Last Sigh*, Moraes Zogoiby ("the Moor"), the son of Abraham, a Bombay business mogul, and Aurora, modern India's most illustrious artist, leads a sheltered, carefree life with his family on Malabar Hill in Bombay (as Mumbai was known until 1947), until the day when he is hurled from the "Fabulous garden and plunged towards pandaemonium."[53] Moraes' maternal and paternal lineages are both distinguished. His mother Aurora is a descendent of Vasco da Gama, the Portuguese explorer who commanded the first ships that reached India, initiating the Western colonization of the subcontinent. Aurora's family built their fortune in the pepper trade by bullying the planters and monopolizing the market. Moraes' father, Abraham, traces his lineage to Boabdil, the last ruler of Granada, and to the Jews of al-Andalus. He is the descendent of the illegitimate child of a Spanish Jew who took refuge under Boabdil's roof. According to the story, the Jewish courtesan betrayed the deposed king and ran away taking with her Boabdil's crown.[54] Abraham was the Gamas' business manager when Aurora saw him and decided to marry him. Despite their difference in age, religion, and wealth, they build a secular Eden on Malabar Hill: Their marriage and union epitomizes the triumph of secularism in India. Consequently, Moraes, the only son of Abraham and Aurora and the narrator of the story, is of mixed blood and heritage, much like Bombay, the city of his birth: "I, however, was raised neither as Catholic nor as Jew. I was

52 Ibid., 495–7.

53 Rushdie, *Sigh* 5.

54 Ibid., 82.

both, and nothing: a jewholicanonymous, a cathjew nut, a stewpot, a mongrel cur. I was – what's the word these days? – *atomised*. Yessir: a real Bombay mix."[55]

Moraes' hybrid lineage is not analogous to the mythic *convivencia* of al-Andalus; it is a source of confusion rather than ethnic fusion. Like Bombay with its "uncontrollable increases" and its mushrooming urban sprawls, the Moor ages twice as fast as a normal person "without time for proper planning, and without any pauses."[56] His aging body and deformed hand, with its fingers fused together like a clenched fist, are a fitting metaphor for Bombay's asymmetrical "mix."

On account of his poor health, Moraes does not attend school or have friends.[57] His paradise is silent, lonely, full of deceivers whom he trusts (his parents, the women he loved, and Vasco Miranda) and people who make him feel ashamed because he is different. Moraes is forced to be deceptive in turn: "All this, too, I conquered. The first lessons of my Paradise were educations in metamorphosis and disguise."[58] However, the earthly paradise was neither diverse nor tolerant enough to accept all, including the deformed. To an outsider "it could have looked a great deal more like hell."[59]

Although the Zogoiby family, like Abū Jaʿfar's family, appears united, the veneer quickly disintegrates before the surmounting challenges and tensions. The theme of family, a collection of individuals united by blood ties despite their opposed interests and temperaments, functions as an allegory for communal unity in Rushdie's novel as in ʿĀshūr's. Aurora, the matriarch, is an artist, a creator, a mother, a goddess, and India itself. Moraes describes her as irresistible, the spark of her children's imaginations, the beloved of their dreams. They love her even as she destroys them: "If she trampled on us, it was because we lay down willingly beneath her spurred-and-booted feet; if she excoriated us at night, it was on account of our delight at the sweet lashings of her tongue."[60]

55 Rushdie, *Sigh* 104. Moraes' outburst echoes a verse that appears in Sura *Āl ʿImrān* ("The People of ʿImrān") in the Quran, which translates into English as "Abraham was neither a Jew nor a Christian, but turned away from all that is false, having surrendered himself to God" (Q 3:67). However, Rushdie reverses those qualities by depicting Abraham, Moraes' father, as a secular businessman, who accumulates his riches by engaging in shady deals and reigns over Bombay's underworld uncontested.

56 Ibid., 161–2.

57 Ibid., 221.

58 Ibid., 153–4.

59 Ibid., 198.

60 Ibid., 172.

The god-like matriarch also represents uncontested secularism: "God was absent" in her paintings.[61]

Abraham manages to salvage Aurora's family business despite the World War II blockade against Indian ships, but he is not a typical hero. The patriarch of the Zogoiby family is also the godfather of Bombay's underworld, kingpin of the city's gangs, drug dealers, and exploiters of indentured labor, overlord of all kinds of shady businesses. While Aurora, whose name means light, devotes her attention to art, lofty pursuits, and accumulating a succession of lovers, Abraham rules over the underworld like Hades in Greek mythology. The unity of opposites, light and darkness, adulterous mother and corrupt father, subverts the celebrated motto of Jawaharlal Nehru (1889–1964), India's first prime minister after its independence from Britain in 1947, "Unity among diversity."[62] This unity, which never was, is explicitly challenged after the assassination of Indira Gandhi (1917–1984), India's second prime minister, in 1984, and the rise of Hindu fundamentalism. Gandhi's assassination coincides with Aurora's sudden death, signaling the end of the secular state. When the Moor reflects on those events, he reminisces, "After the [Emergency Laws imposed in India by Gandhi] people started seeing through different eyes. Before the Emergency we were Indians. After it we were Christian Jews."[63]

Although Aurora represents absolute matriarchy and secularism in the novel, her character is too complex to fit within that category. Justyna Deszcz notes that Aurora's art is comprised of "three levels of utopian activity: it is a tale of her own family, of the nation's destiny, as well as of the East in the global context, seen not as traditionally passive and malleable, but as the locus of powerful intermingling stories, imaginations, and fantasies."[64] The malleability of Aurora's secularist art is contrasted with the work of an antipodal character, the artist Uma Saraswati's colossal and hard edged sculptures.[65] Contrary to Aurora, Uma embodies rigid Hindu fundamentalism. The undeclared war that ensues between the two women unfolds through their relationship with Moraes. For the Moor, Aurora was at first an irresistible, domineering goddess,[66] but when Uma appears in his life, he is consumed with passion for her. From that moment on, the mother-son relationship deteriorates. Uma snares Moraes and plots the destruction of the family and her artistic rival Aurora.

---

61 Ibid., 60.

62 Gabriel, Homeland 74.

63 Rushdie, *Sigh* 235.

64 Deszcz, Kingdom 43.

65 Almond, Mullahs 6.

66 Rushdie, *Sigh* 172.

While making love to Uma, and in the throes of passion, Moraes denounces his mother. Uma records his words and sends the tape to the family. Moraes is expelled from the family home. The betrayal effects Moraes' downfall and the demise of Bombay's hybrid *mix*.

Moraes cast himself as the hero of the story, but his attempts are foiled at every turn. Unaware of Uma's hidden agenda or the danger she represents, he assumes he was expelled from his paradise because his mother disapproved of Uma.[67] Betrayal is a cyclical theme in the novel: like Boabdil, who was deceived by his Jewish lover, and Abraham, whom Aurora is unfaithful to, the Moor is betrayed by Uma, who plots to kill him by persuading him to join her in a suicide pact. However, it is she who dies when she accidentally drops the two suicide pills on the floor, and swallows the pill meant for Moraes. When Moraes realizes the truth about Uma, he simply declares that she was an "*Insaan*, a human being."[68]

Deserted and alone after his fall, Moraes joins a gang led by Ram Fielding, also known as Mainduck. Fielding's character parodies Bal Thackeray, the Hindu fundamentalist leader in Bombay. Moraes is aware that Fielding is his father's underworld rival. Abraham and Fielding represent two sides of the same coin: one is secular, the other is religious, and both are corrupt. Moraes accepts to work for Fielding. Thus, not only does he betray his mother, but also his father. As a gangster, the Moor thrives. He easily makes the transition from a would-be-hero to a gangster, bludgeoning Fielding's foes with his fused fist. During his service to Fielding, Moraes learns that "Muslim conquerors had deliberately built mosques on the birthplaces of various Hindu deities." Fielding's young followers agree to liberate Hindu sites "hogged by minarets and onion domes"[69] and, as a result, they agree to join their boss's campaign, while ironically reciting Urdu poetry and admiring Mughal landmarks:

> Yes, indeed, a campaign for divine rights! What could be smarter, more *cutting edge*? – But when they began, in their guffawing way, to belittle the culture of Indian Islam, that lay palimpsest-fashion over the face of Mother India, Mainduck rose to his feet and thumbed at them until they shrank back in their seats. Then he would sing ghazals and recite Urdu poetry – Faiz, Josh, Iqbal – from memory and speak of the glories of Fatehpur Sikri and the moonlit splendour of the Taj.[70]

---

67 Ibid., 278.

68 Ibid., 313.

69 Ibid., 299.

70 Ibid.

Moraes is unperturbed, unaware that Fielding will eventually extend his campaign to target him because he is part of the "mix." The battle between Fielding and Abraham mirrors to some extent the battle between Uma and Aurora. In retrospect, as Moraes narrates the events that led to his fall, he is able to comprehend that people align themselves with others not on the basis of religion or ideals, but rather self-interest.

Meanwhile, Abraham, the Cochin Jew, manages to unite all the Muslims under his banner against Fielding and his gang:

> It occurred to me that my father's pre-eminence over Scar [the Muslim] and his colleagues was a dark, ironic victory for India's deep-rooted secularism. The very nature of this inter-community league of cynical self interest gave the lie to Mainduck's vision of a theocracy in which one particular variant of Hinduism would rule, while all India's other people bowed their beaten heads.[71]

Rushdie is critical of India's dark secularism, led by figures tainted by corruption, crime, and with links to the underworld; at the same time, he objects to any religion that becomes a theocracy. The rivalry between Abraham (Muslims) and Fielding (Hindus) spirals out of control, leading to the destruction of the Babri Mosque. Suddenly, the Muslims who lived in India for centuries are threatened to be "erased"[72] just as the Muslims were erased from Spain. Witnessing the mayhem, Moraes resolves to accede to his father's request to eliminate Fielding. When he smashes Fielding in the face with a green phone, he thinks he has succeeded but later realizes that someone else had beat him to the deed and that Fielding was already dead. The revelation renders Moraes an inept, frustrated hero. His failure is a central theme in the novel: whenever he is called upon to act like a hero, a voice within him stops him from fulfilling his expected role.

Fielding's death causes the destruction of Bombay, Abraham, Elephanta (the family's estate), and all the city's "mix." As Moraes hops on a plane to Spain, he laments:

> Bombay was central; had always been. Just as the fanatical 'Catholic Kings' had besieged Granada and awaited Alhmbra's [sic] fall, so now barbarism was standing at our gates. O Bombay! *Prima in Indis! Gateway to India! Star of the East with her face to the West!* Like Granada – al-Gharnatah of the Arabs – you were the glory of your time. But a darker time came upon

---

71 Ibid., 332.

72 Ibid., 364.

> you, and just as Boabdil, the last Nasrid Sultan, was too weak to defend his great treasure, so we, too, were proved wanting. For the barbarians were not only at our gates but within our skins. We were our own wooden horses, each one of us full of our doom… these fanatics of those, our crazies or yours; but the explosions burst out of our very own bodies. We were both the bombers and the bombs. The explosions were our own evil – no need to look for foreign explanations, though there was and is evil beyond our frontiers as well as within. We have chopped away our own legs, we engineered our own fall. And now we can only weep, at the last, for what we were too enfeebled, too corrupt, too little, too contemptible to defend.[73]

In the above passage, Rushdie faults Indians themselves for the destruction of their paradise. Both authors, ʿĀshūr and Rushdie, blame their respective communities for their fall from grace. The cities they depict may bear different names (Granada, Cairo, Bombay), but the process is the same: the diversity that used to exist in Cairo and Bombay, Egypt and India, is vanishing under the tide of religious fundamentalism. By employing the theme of al-Andalus as a vehicle for their criticism of the present, the authors subvert the romanticized vision of the past. For instance, in the series of paintings entitled *The Moor's Last Sigh*, Aurora superimposes her vision of a thriving, multi-cultural Bombay on al-Andalus and its celebrated *convivencia*, conjoining all those diverse elements together under the strokes of her brush: "The Alhambra quickly became a not-quite-Alhambra; elements of India's own red forts, the Mughal palace-fortresses in Delhi and Agra, blended Mughal splendours with the Spanish building's Moorish grace."[74] Against the idyllic notions of al-Andalus, Rushdie paints a more turbulent picture. The world of the painting, Aurora explains to her son is a place "where worlds collide, flow in and out of another, and washofy away. [It is one] universe, one dimension, one country, one dream, bumpo'ing into another, or being under, or on top of."[75] The suppressed narrative of this "one country," be it al-Andalus or India, is that it did not come into being *because of* communal co-existence, but *in spite of* ethnic and religious upheaval.

Aurora describes her painting as "a Palimpstine,"[76] a reference to the multi-layered history of India, where great kingdoms were built on the ruins of fallen dynasties. The term palimpsest originally refers to a parchment on which writ-

73 Ibid., 372–3.
74 Ibid., 226.
75 Ibid.
76 Ibid.

ing is barely visible under a more recent text. Parchment was expensive writing material; therefore, texts written on them were often erased so that the parchment could be reused. Since ink was made of strong dyes in the past, the original text was not always entirely effaced; it lingered, visible between the lines of the newer text. Rushdie neatly structures his novel as a palimpsest that mirrors India's complex history. The Moor is Bombay, Bombay is Granada, and the Moor is also Granada. All of them are mixed and have diverse roots. The demise of one entity triggers the fall of the next, and so on. Therefore, the collapse of al-Andalus foreshadows the demise of Bombay and Moraes.

Another important function of palimpsest in the novel is to reveal suppressed narratives of the past, since communities privilege certain histories over others. The psychoanalyst Sigmund Freud discusses a devise called the Mystic Pad that cleans a surface by erasing words. As on a palimpsest, the words are not erased completely and may be legible under suitable light. Freud draws parallels between those barely visible words and the unconscious, and between the new text and consciousness.[77] Viewed through this lens, the erased narratives on the palimpsest constitute India's suppressed narratives (the unconscious), and the recent narratives represent the official stories that are imposed by the government and society (the conscience). Jean Jacques Derrida builds on Freud's work by adding that the imposition of the conscience is sometimes disrupted when it experiences "cathectic innervations"[78] that emanate from within, from the unconscious, to the outside, to the conscious. These disruptions allow the suppressed narratives to surface and come into the open, if only briefly. Rushdie's novel functions similarly: it disturbs the official story, revealing the cracks through which the suppressed story can be discerned.

One aspect of Aurora's wild behavior is that she acquired a series of lovers, whom she later rejected. One of the lovers is Vasco Miranda, whom Moraes remembers fondly because of his joyful and fantastic paintings, which decorated the Moor's nursery room. When Vasco lived in the house of the Zogoibys, he was kind and nice to the ultra-normal Moor. However, Aurora's repulsion unleashes Vasco's dark side. He steals the last four paintings of Aurora's series *The Moor's Last Sigh* and leaves for Spain, where he builds his Little Alhambra and starts dressing like an Eastern Sultan. He builds a world that parallels Aurora's fantastic Mooristan.

Toward the end of the novel, the Moor follows Vasco to retrieve the paintings, thinking his daring plan would lay his mother's ghost to rest. However, Vasco imprisons him and commands him to write his story. Like Scheherazade,

---

77 Freud, *Works* 230–1.

78 Derrida, *Painting* 225.

the Moor's life will end the minute his story ends. Vasco also imprisons Aoi Uë, an art restorer whom he commands to remove the first layer of paint from Aurora's paintings. Vasco believes that Aurora's paintings are coded: under the palimpsest painting, she painted her murderer. When Aoi Uë is about to finish her task, Vasco aims his gun at her. Moraes tries to save her, but he is hampered by his advanced age and is unable to protect her. Once again, Moraes proves to be an ineffective hero. He saves his skin but not the hapless woman. Through Aoi Uë's efforts, Aurora's original painting is revealed, and the Moor is able to see that the murderer was his father, Abraham. At this moment, the Moor realizes that he, too, was duped by his father, and his ineptness as a hero is brought home to him again.

At the end, the Moor is not quite sure what story to tell. He even questions his lineage. Among the conundrum of hybridity, all interpretations are possible and nothing is certain. According to Rushdie, "India was uncertainty. It was deception and illusion."[79] Nevertheless, for him, the confusion of hybridity is preferable to fundamental rigidity and intolerance. At the end of the novel, the Moor is the only survivor of the Zogoiby family. His new mission is to spread the histories of his family, and his fall from India's earthly paradise. Predictably, he fails in that mission when he experiences an asthma attack.

Both novels end when the two protagonists ('Alī and Moraes), who are the last descendants of Granada, see a vision of idyllic Granada before they die, as if to stress the message that the celebrated al-Andalus is a mirage. It can only be seen by people who are leaving this world and entering the next.

At the end of *Thulāthiyyat Gharnāṭa*, 'Alī falls asleep. In his dream, he sees himself descending into the heart of the earth (*bāṭin al-arḍ*), as if there were seven levels underground like those in heaven.[80] He reaches a wide cave in which a river runs. The river leads him to an elaborately decorated palace. He enters and walks through a grand, royal parlor with walls made of beautiful mosaics. On a high bed, he finds Maryama sleeping peacefully, and the birds of paradise perched at her head. When 'Alī wakes up, the Elysian vision makes him wonder why he should leave his homeland; "death might lie in leaving, not in staying (*al-mawt fī l-raḥīl wa-laysa fī l-baqāʾ*)."[81] He turns his back to the sea and runs away from the coast and its crowds. As he makes his way inland, he is reminded that "there is no loneliness in Maryama's grave (*lā waḥsha fī*

79 Rushdie, *Sigh* 95.

80 The seven layers correspond to the seven heavens as mentioned in the Quran; see for example Q 2:29; 23:17; and 17:44, among many others.

81 'Āshūr, *Gharnāṭa* 501.

qabr Maryama)."[82] ʿAlī chooses to listen to his intuition rather than follow the wisdom of his community. However, his return is not triumphant: without a family or descendents, it is the homecoming of a battered hero returning to die peacefully in the family crypt. Thus, ʿAlī's return closes the final chapter on the myth of al-Andalus.

Likewise, Moraes has a vision. Gasping his last breath, his last sigh, he experiences an epiphany and sees:

> The Alhambra, Europe's red fort, sister to Delhi's and Agra's – the palace of interlocking forms and secret wisdom, of pleasure-courts and water gardens, that monument to a lost possibility that nevertheless has gone on standing, long after its conquerors have fallen; like a testament to lost but sweetest love, to the love that endures beyond defeat, beyond annihilation, beyond despair; to the defeated love that is greater than what defeats it, to the most profound of our needs, to our need for flowing together, for putting an end to frontiers, for the dropping of the boundaries of the self.[83]

To conclude, ʿĀshūr and Rushdie reinterpret the Andalusian topos and the vanishing of its legendary hybridity and cosmopolitanism by tracing the sagas of two families to warn their respective communities against the rise of fundamentalism. ʿĀshūr decries the passivity of common people and their dependence on inept leaders. She also criticizes Egyptians who are engulfed in simplistic binaries and cannot tolerate difference in opinion or religion. Similarly, Rushdie laments the rise of fundamentalism in the land of diversity, the nation of multi-headed gods and goddesses. Both authors depict communities that are caught up in religious and political turmoil, whose fall is guaranteed by the acts of inept heroes.

Whereas earlier authors hoped to resurrect the golden era of al-Andalus in their works, ʿĀshūr and Rushdie subvert that myth by rewriting the history of Granada. By dwelling on the issue of weakened nationalism, and the ensuing political traumas in their respective countries, the authors call on their readers to rethink and reevaluate the myth of earthly paradise, because questioning it may open up the opportunity to build a better world, and maybe a better paradise.

---

82 Ibid., 502.

83 Rushdie, *Sigh* 433.

Bibliography

Ahmad, D., This fundo stuff is really something new: Fundamentalism and hybridity in The Moor's Last Sigh, in *The Yale Journal of Criticism* 18.1 (2005), 1–20.
Ali, T., *Shadows of the pomegranate tree*, London 1992.
Almond, I., Mullahs, mystics, moderates and Moghuls: The many Islams of Salman Rushdie, in *English Language History* (ELH) 70.4 (2003), 1137–51.
Ashour, R., Eyewitness, scribe and story teller: My experience as a novelist, in *The Massachusetts Review* 41.1 (Spring 2000), 85–92.
ʿĀshūr, R., *Thulāthiyyat Gharnāṭa*, Cairo 2008[6].
Blunes, M.A. de, Introducción, in M. García Arenal: *Los moriscos*, Granada 1974, ix–xxvii.
Boym, S., *The future of nostalgia*, New York 2001.
Coetzee, J.M., Palimpsest regained: Review of *The Moor's Last Sigh* by Salman Rushdie, in *The New York Review of Books* (21 March 1996), 13–6.
Derrida, J., *The truth in painting*, trans. G. Bennington and I. McLeod, Chicago 1987.
Deszcz, J., Salman Rushdie's magical kingdom: The Moor's Last Sigh and fairy-tale utopia, in *Marvels & Tales* 18.1 (2004), 28–52.
Esposito, J., *Islam and politics*, Syracuse, NY 1998.
Freud, S., *The complete psychological works of Sigmund Freud: Standard edition*, London 1976.
Gabriel, S.P., "Imaginary homeland" and diaspora: History nation and contestation in Salman Rushdie's *The Moor's Last Sigh*, in M.K. Ray and R. Kundu (eds.), *Salman Rushdie: Critical essays*, ii, New Delhi 2006, 71–123.
Gana, N., In search of Andalusia: Reconfiguring Arabness in Diana Abū-Jaber's *Crescent*, in *Comparative Literature Studies* 45.2 (2008), 228–47.
Gilmour, N., Turkish delight: Antonio Gala's La pasión turca as a vision of Spain's contested Islamic heritage, in *Arizona Journal of Hispanic Cultural Studies* 10.1 (2006), 77–94.
Granara, W., Extensio animae: The artful ways of remembering "Al-Andalus", in *Journal of Social Affairs* 19.75 (Fall 2002), 45–74.
———, Nostalgia, Arab nationalism, and the Andalusian chronotope in the evolution of the modern Arabic novel, in *JAL* 36.1 (2005), 57–73.
Iqbal, M., *Bāl-i Jibrīl*, Lahore 1959.
Islam, A., Babri Mosque: A historic bone of contention, in *Muslim World* 97 (2007), 260–86.
al-Juʿaydī, M.ʿA., *A-ʿindakum nabaʾ? Istidʿāʾ al-Andalus: al-adab al-Filasṭīnī al-ḥadīth*, Beirut 2002.
Khalidi, R., The 1967 war and the demise of Arab nationalism, in W.R. Louis and A. Shlaim (eds.), *The 1967 Arab-Israeli War: Origins and Consequences*, Cambridge 2012, 264–84.

Mourtada-Sabbah, N. and A. Gully, 'I am, by God, fit for high positions': On the political role of women in al-Andalus, in *British Journal of Middle Eastern Studies* 30.2 (2003), 183–209.

Narain, M., Re-imagined histories: Rewriting the early modern in Rushdie's *The Moor's Last Sigh*, in *Journal for Early Modern Cultural Studies* 6.2 (2006), 55–68.

Nourani, Y., The lost garden of al-Andalus: Islamic Spain and the poetic inversion of colonialism, in *IJMES* 31.2 (1999), 237–54.

Rushdie, S., *Imaginary homelands: Essays and criticisms 1981–1991*, London 1992.

———, *The moor's last sigh*, Toronto 1996.

Sawhney, S., Satanic choices: Poetry and prophecy in Rushdie's novel, in *Twentieth Century Literature* 45.3 (1999), 253–77.

Internet Sources

http://weekly.ahram.org.eg/Archive/2003/622/profile.htm (accessed 1 September 2016).

PART 9

Bringing Paradise Down to Earth – Aesthetic Representations of the Hereafter

CHAPTER 45

Madīnat al-Zahrā', Paradise and the Fatimids*[1]

Maribel Fierro

1 The Building of Madīnat al-Zahrā'

Madīnat al-Zahrā'[2] stands on a site located on the side of the foothills of the Sierra Morena near Cordoba, a site which was set out in terraces in order to build the city of 'Abd al-Raḥmān III. At the highest point of this terraced site can be found what is considered to be a residential area. Further down is the 'official' area, with the reception hall known as the Hall of 'Abd al-Raḥmān III (previously known as the Salón Rico), while at the bottom are found the remaining

* [The original version of this chapter was published in Spanish in the journal *Al-Qanṭara* 25 (2004), 299–327, which has granted permission for its reprint here in English. Additions are indicated by square brackets. The English translation was made by Jeremy Rogers and financed by the Instituto de Lenguas y Culturas del Mediterráneo y de Oriente Próximo.

Regarding the paradise symbolism of Madīnat al-Zahrā', in an interview with Antonio Vallejo Triano in the Spanish journal ABC (28/02/2005), the director of the archeological complex of the town pointed out that epigraphical materials with Quranic verses describing paradise had been found outside the mosque. See http://www.abc.es/hemeroteca/historico-28-02-2005/abc/Cultura/medina-azahara-la-ciudad-mas-grande-jamas-levantada-en-occidente_20900171890.html.]

1 This is an expanded and modified version of a lecture given on 23 February 2004 in the Department of Arab Studies of the Institute of Philology of the CSIC. This lecture arose from the research I did for my biography of 'Abd al-Raḥmān III, published in the series *Makers of the Muslim World* (Oneworld, [2007]) and, more particularly, from a conversation I had with Julio Escalona. Attendance at the Fourth Madīnat al-Zahrā' Conference (held in Cordoba in November 2003) and the papers presented there (particularly that of María Antonia Martínez Núñez) undoubtedly influenced this article. I would like to thank Carmen Barceló for her comments on the first version of this article. My thanks are due to Salvador Peña for his useful suggestions and, together with Miguel Vega, for the clarification of various points referring to the numismatics of the period of 'Abd al-Raḥmān III.

2 This is the name by which the city founded by 'Abd al-Raḥmān III is referred to on the coins minted there. The same name also appears in literary sources, together with the form al-Madīna al-Zahrā'. For more details see Labarta and Barceló, Las fuentes árabes 93–106. I shall return to the subject of the name of the city later.

 | DOI 10.1163/9789004333154_046

buildings of the city.[3] The hall forms part of a collection of buildings including a pavilion just opposite – which appears to be a replica of the hall on a smaller scale[4] – located in the so-called High or Upper Garden and surrounded by pools. To one side of this garden there extends another, known as the Lower Garden.

The building of Madīnat al-Zahrā' was begun around the year 329/940–1, shortly after the battle of Simancas-Ahandega against the Christians. In this battle the disloyalty of some of the commanders of the *jund* [troops] and some of the lords of the frontier regions led to a Muslim defeat in which the life of the caliph himself was put in danger; as a result ʿAbd al-Raḥmān III's copy of the Quran fell into the hands of the Christians. There were other consequences:

> Al-Nāṣir was overwhelmed by his defeat in this campaign, unparalleled in all his history and, very displeased by his misfortune, his thoughts were confused and he was not just with himself; for which reason he was advised to assuage his worries by indulging in his greatest pleasure, building. They say that he devoted himself obsessively to it, founding al-Zahrā' below Cordoba, relieving his mind with the comfort and majesty of his buildings, and forgetting all else, for from that time on he ceased going to war in person.[5]

P. Chalmeta, in a study devoted to the repercussions of the Simancas-Ahandega episode, confirms that from then on the caliph

> did not trust his troops. The enemy was within, and it is possibly not so far-fetched to consider Madīnat al-Zahrā' not as a city-palace but rather as a stronghold or fortress, at least in part. If ʿAbd al-Raḥmān abandoned his palace (*qaṣr*) in Cordoba it was not because he enjoyed building, nor because it was too small. The real reason is very different from the 'official' reason: he no longer felt safe within his capital. This concern and mistrust is reflected in the extraordinary thickness of the double wall of carved stone blocks which defended the new city; and, above all, in the unusually massive thickness of the wall surrounding the Caliph's royal palace.

3 There is a brief and succinct presentation in Vallejo Triano, Madīnat al-Zahrā', capital y sede. See also the same author's Madīnat al-Zahrā': El triunfo 27–40 (English version Madīnat al-Zahrā': The triumph 27–39) and El proyecto urbanístico 69–81.

4 The panels of *ataurique* on the base of the wall which decorate the hall can also be found in the pavilion, although the latter still needs more detailed study.

5 Ibn Ḥayyān, *Crónica*, trans. Viguera and Corriente 327–8.

> Indeed, Madīnat al-Zahrāʾ is a fortified city, protected by walls whose strength was far greater than that of any fortress or castle ... I repeat, the thickness of the walls of the Caliph's city is not due merely to a desire for monumentalism, but for strategic reasons in the defense of what is considered to be the last bastion and stronghold of the dynasty ... They had before them the recent example of the Fatimids saving themselves from the rebellion of 'the man of the donkey' thanks to the creation of their palace-refuge of Mahdīya.[6]

But if this was perhaps the initial reason for its construction, it does not mean that the city did not later acquire other functions and meanings. In the case of the Hall of ʿAbd al-Raḥmān III, it seems to have been built between the years 342/953–4 and 345/956–7 and it was in those years that the extraordinarily complicated vegetal designs covering its walls were developed. The construction of the hall, as Antonio Vallejo Triano has shown, implied an important reworking of the original plan of the city.

2 The Hall of ʿAbd al-Raḥmān III and its Decorative Vegetal Motifs

The building of the hall coincides with the coming to power of the Fatimid Caliph al-Muʿizz (r. 341–65/953–75), who continued the construction of Ṣabra-Manṣūriyya begun in 335/946–7 by his father al-Manṣūr,[7] who himself had succeeded in putting down the rebellion of the Berber leader Abū Yazīd.[8] The latter, known as the 'man of the donkey' (I come back to him later), had been on the point of putting an end to a dynasty which had come to power by encouraging eschatological beliefs. Although toward the end of the reign of al-Muʿizz the idea that the arrival of the *mahdī* or Messiah was imminent had begun to wane, there still remained the Shiʿite doctrine that the Fatimid caliph possessed the charismatic powers of the Prophet: he could work miracles, he was infallible, and he was endowed with supernatural knowledge.[9] For a Sunni

6 Chalmeta, Simancas y Alhandega 397–8.

7 The Fatimid palatine city was circular in shape, following the model of ʿAbbasid Baghdad, in contrast with the rectangular shape of Madīnat al-Zahrāʾ, although a later source indicates that the original form of the palatine city of ʿAbd al-Raḥmān III was also circular (*mudawwar*), according to witnesses reported by an author from the East, al-Dhahabī (d. 748/1348), *Siyar aʿlām al-nubalāʾ* 265–9.

8 On these events, see Halm, *Empire* 298–325, and Brett, *Rise* 165–75.

9 Halm, *Empire* 350.

caliph such as ʿAbd al-Raḥmān III it was not easy to try to surpass his rival from the politico-religious point of view.[10] In this chapter I propose a possible way in which he did it: by assimilating his city to paradise.

Christian Ewert's studies on the vegetal motifs[11] covering the walls of the Hall of ʿAbd al-Raḥmān III point out, among other things, two aspects: 1) the enormous variety of forms found in this vegetal decoration, for it has been possible to list almost one thousand seven hundred different elements and motifs; and 2) the abundance of asymmetric compositions, in which those responsible for the decoration show a matchless sense of ornamental balance dictated by a central axis. The following description given by Ewert reflects the basic structure of this decoration, and gives us an idea of some of the motifs:

> Plaques of very soft limestone, a few centimeters thick, form a veneer replacing the favorite material for architectural decoration in al-Andalus, which is stucco. Wide borders suggest the effect of tapestries. The *ataurique* generally springs from the stalk or central trunk, which acts as an axis for symmetry. The pattern is extremely dense. The elements, well-defined by their sharp outlines, perfectly fill the spaces between the thick stems. They leave practically no background … The basic elements are leaves, very often in the form of a half palmette or calyx, fruits and flowers. They give rise to combinations of two half-palmettes, composite palmettes made up of three or more elements and occasionally with an asymmetric upper part … and, finally, to asymmetric combinations whose twisted axis distorts and warps what is basically a symmetrical concept … Another double decorative element, very heavily condensed, is that formed from two ring-shaped pearls. In this case, too, the occurrence of multiplication appears to have practically no limit. There is perfect harmony in a combination of four pearls arranged geometrically in a square which, for example, supports a totally asymmetric upper part with a wavy acanthus leaf.[12]

M. Acién Almansa has raised the question of the meaning and purpose of these decorative panels in a study[13] in which he starts by pointing out that the uniqueness of the hall does not lie in its architectural design (the hall of

10 For some of the ways in which ʿAbd al-Raḥmān III tried to do so, see Fierro, Espacio 168–77.

11 In this work I will not consider the sources of the decorative motifs.

12 Ewert, Elementos 41–58.

13 Acién Almansa, Materiales e hipótesis 177–95.

the upper terrace of Madīnat al-Zahrā' has the same layout) nor in the richness of the materials from which it was built (marble flooring is found in other parts of the city). Its uniqueness lies in the exuberant wall decoration and, in particular, in the panels of *ataurique* on the lower parts of the building's walls; similar panels are also found in the pavilion opposite the hall – the one which is a smaller-scale copy of the hall itself. The 'heavenly symbolism' of the whole and the unity of the design of the hall and the Upper Garden as a celestial palace and paradise have already been made clear by Antonio Vallejo Triano.[14] But what was the meaning of the wall decoration of the Hall of ʿAbd al-Raḥmān III?

Acién quotes the functional opinion proposed by D.F. Ruggles, for whom the repeated use of vegetation, which has generally been considered a reference to paradise, may also reflect a political meaning related to the garden and the ordering of a cultivated space. Indeed, Ruggles points out, there is no explicit textual reference to any relationship of the gardens of al-Andalus with paradise.[15] Acién, for his part, explains that

> even if the allusion to paradise may be considered as implicit in the work of many researchers, with respect to the specific meaning of the panels of the hall of al-Nāṣir I have only found it noted once in the commentary of L. Golvin on a marble slab, which does not come exactly from the hall itself, but from the adjoining bath room.[16]

Acién recalls that F. Hernández Giménez showed that these panels indicate "the imposition of an idea and absolute control over its execution," and that the surprising thing is that "the idea imposed and its control were exercised over more than two hundred square meters, distributed over at least sixty-five panels; and insufficient stress has been laid ... on the fact that they are all different from each other ..." Furthermore, the theoretical symmetrical center line traced by the decorative elements "is no such thing, *since the two sides do not present a mirror image*" [the italics are mine]; and in addition "what is represented is different vegetal elements on each panel."[17] Acién goes on to say that "underlying existing studies there is the general interpretation of identifying the extensive presence of *ataurique* with paradise," so that

14 Acién Almansa, El urbanismo musulmán, refers back to A. Vallejo Triano. See the latter's article Madīnat al-Zahrā', in Cabrera (ed.), *Abdarrahman III* 231–44.

15 See Ruggles, *Gardens* 219.

16 See Golvin, Note sur un décor 188.

17 Acién Almansa, Materiales e hipótesis 185.

> *all the decoration of the hall appears to repeat in the interior what exists outside, and the flora of the panels seem to have the same meaning as the real vegetation in the garden, which in its turn is the likeness of that of paradise* [the italics are mine]. The huge variety of vegetable forms would thus have a meaning, although it is not altogether clear why it has been split into panels of different sizes, in spite of the obvious subordination of the latter to the architectural whole.[18]

Acién therefore presents other hypotheses, such as possible relationships with courtly ceremonies, so that the different panels might have the function of indicating the respective positions of the people and groups present,[19] and with astrology, specifically with certain passages of the *Picatrix*. Acién's proposals are worthy of consideration, particularly the latter.[20] As was shown in a recent study, dynasties are normally legitimized based on multiple meanings that often intertwine and sometimes converge,[21] so that it is rarely possible to offer one single interpretation.

3 The Gardens of Paradise in the Light of the Quran 55:46–78

But it seems to me that the heavenly symbolism of ʿAbd al-Raḥmān III's hall and the gardens has not been established as it should be, and that this symbolism has not aroused greater interest; for the 'palace/garden' link with paradise is thought of as a general and vague reference, an indissoluble part of palace-building activities in the Muslim world[22] and, therefore, not very enlightening. I do not dwell on matters which are already familiar: as, for example, that it

18 Ibid., 186.

19 This is taking the hall to be a reception hall. For more on receptions in the era of the caliphs, see Barceló, El califa patente 51–71, repr. 155–75, and Barceló, *El sol que salió por Occidente* 137–62; English translation Barceló, The manifest caliph 425–56.

20 In my article Bāṭinism 87–112, I refer to this theory as in it I propose a new authorship and dating of the *Picatrix* that establish a precise link between the composition of the work and the reign of ʿAbd al-Raḥmān III.

21 See the study on Almohad coins carried out by Vega Martín, Peña Martín and Feria García, *El mensaje*.

22 The form in which the religious image of the celestial garden was often translated into secular paradises created in the palaces of Muslim governors has been the object of several studies: see especially Brookes, *Gardens of paradise*; Lehrmann, *Earthly paradise*; MacDougall and Ettinghausen (eds.), *The Islamic garden*; and more recently Blair and Bloom (eds.), *Images*.

was reasonable enough for the idea of the garden as paradise to emerge among the Arabs, inhabitants of a land where water, trees, and shade were exceptions among rocks, arid wastes, and scorched vegetation. Nor is it any wonder that the pleasures of paradise should be seen as those which are to be enjoyed in shady gardens, and related to food, drink, sexual union, and sociability, all of this taking place in paradise on a larger scale and free of imperfections. Gardens are desired and desirable, and so are usually surrounded by walls to control access to them, making them exclusive places dedicated to relaxation and physical and spiritual renewal:

> Exploring the topic of images of paradise in Islamic art raises a paradox: the closest parallel to the religious image of the heavenly garden is the secular paradise of the Islamic palace. Two interpretations are possible. The heaven of Islamic belief may represent the idea of a better life held by individuals living in arid and economically precarious societies; for them, a lush and well-watered garden represents all that the natural environment lacks. Alternatively, the builders of Islamic palaces may have had in mind the image of Heaven revealed in the Koran and created their earthly paradises following this concept. Both may be true, for the secular paradise of the Islamic palace can be traced back to pre-Islamic roots and is a reflection of the religious image. Palace courtyards with playing fountains and running streams have a long tradition in the Middle East and Mediterranean regions, while they also invoke the numerous Koranic descriptions of the heavenly garden.[23]

The texts to which I now refer help us to define more precisely this 'heavenly' interpretation and to give it specific meanings, showing its advantages over other possible interpretations (although without necessarily eliminating them): it explains not only the variety but also the asymmetry of the wall decorations of the hall; it gives a reason for a series of stories which arose around the subject of Madīnat al-Zahrā'; it allows us to give a new interpretation to the 'green and manganese' decoration of the ceramics produced there; suggests yet another aspect of the name by which the city was known; and may also help us to understand the reason behind one of the doctrines attributed to Mundhir b. Saʿīd al-Ballūṭī, the *qāḍī* of 'Abd al-Raḥmān III from 339/950 to the death of the caliph. The silence of Arab sources on this heavenly symbolism may be related, as we shall see, to the anecdote of how this same Mundhir b. Saʿīd censured 'Abd al-Raḥmān III's building activity.

---

23 Denny, Paradise attained 106.

It is very well known that in the Muslim conception of paradise there are abundant references to gardens, fruit, water, pavilions, and *ḥūrīs*,[24] all elements present in the Quran. Here is just a brief selection of verses on the subject (in the translation by A.J. Arberry)* not forgetting that garden or gardens are mentioned more than 130 times in the Holy Book of Islam:

> Give thou good tidings to those who believe and do deeds of righteousness, that for them await gardens underneath which rivers flow; whensoever they are provided with fruits therefrom they shall say, 'This is that wherewithal we were provided before'; that they shall be given in perfect semblance ... (Q 2:25)
>
> And Paradise shall be brought forward to the godfearing, not afar (Q 50:31; also in 26:90 and 81:13)
>
> The Companions of the Right (O Companions of the Right) mid thornless lote-trees and serried acacias, and spreading shade and outpoured waters, and fruits abounding, unfailing, unforbidden, and upraised couches (Q 56:28–34).
>
> Surely the godfearing shall dwell amid gardens and a river in a sure abode, in the presence of a King Omnipotent (*ʿinda malīk muqtadir*) (Q 54:54–5).

But for the specific 'heavenly' interpretation that I propose for the Hall of ʿAbd al-Raḥmān III with its gardens the following verses of the Quran are central:

> But such as fears the Station of his Lord,
> for them shall be two gardens –
> O which of your Lord's bounties will you and you deny?[25]
> abounding in branches – ...
> therein two fountains of running water – ...
> therein of every fruit two kinds –...

24 On this, see the following studies: El-Saleh, *La vie future*; Smith and Haddad, *Death and resurrection*; Blair and Bloom (eds.), *Images*; al-Azmeh, Rhetoric for the senses. [See also M. Jarrar's and N. Rustomji's contributions to this publication.]

* [Arberry (trans.), *The Koran*. Unless otherwise indicated, I cite this translation throughout this text.]

25 This phrase is repeated after practically each of the lines which follow. I have omitted it, indicating its presence by ellipses.

> reclining upon couches lined with brocade,
> the fruits of the gardens nigh to gather – …
> therein maidens restraining their glances,
> untouched before them by any man or jinn – …
> lovely as rubies, beautiful as coral – …
> Shall the recompense of goodness be other than goodness? …
> And besides these shall be two gardens – …
> green, green pastures [in the translation by Abdullah Yusuf Ali: Dark-green in colour (from plentiful watering)[26]] – …
> therein two fountains of gushing water – …
> therein fruits,
> and palm-trees, and pomegranates – …
> therein maidens good and comely – …
> houris, cloistered in cool pavilions – …
> untouched before them by man or jinn – …
> reclining upon green cushions and lovely druggets – … (Q 55:46–78).

In these verses a distinction is drawn between four gardens of paradise, although the actual number should not be taken too literally, since the important point is that there is a hierarchy among them.

4 The 'Upper' Gardens of Paradise: Variety and Asymmetry

There are two gardens which have a certain superiority relative to the other two. They are characterized as having within them *min kull fākihatin zawjāni*, a phrase which A. Arberry translates as 'therein of every fruit two kinds.' Although some exegetes have understood this simply in the sense that there will be two of each kind of fruit, one of the oldest commentators, al-Ṭabarī (d. 310/923), followed by others, specifies that *min kulli nawʿin min al-fākihati ḍarbāni*, means "of each type of fruit there will be two varieties."[27] If these fruits of paradise,

26 http://wikilivres.info/wiki/The_Holy_Qur%27an/Al-Rahman.

27 Al-Ṭabarī, *Jāmiʿ al-bayān* xxvii, 86. For his part, the Andalusian al-Qurṭubī (d. 671/1272) interprets the phrase in the sense that each fruit will be of two types, and both will be sweet. He goes on to quote the companion of the Prophet, Ibn ʿAbbās, saying that there is no tree in this world, be it sweet or sour, which is not to be found in paradise, including the colocynth, although in the next world this will be sweet. He adds that each fruit will be of two varieties, ripe and dried, although the latter will be every bit as sweet and good as the other. He ends by saying that the difference between the two upper and the two

which come in pairs but which are different, together with the plants or trees from which they proceed, were to be represented, perhaps one way of doing this might be a type of vegetation characterized by the asymmetry shown in the wall decorations of the hall? This makes sense of the fact, pointed out by Acién, that the two parts of the panels are not mirror images.

These fruits of paradise will be 'within easy reach': anyone in the Hall of 'Abd al-Raḥmān III could touch the panels with his hand, for they were on the wall. Acién points out that "all the decoration of the hall appears to repeat in the interior what exists outside, and the flora of the panels seem to have the same meaning as the real vegetation in the garden, which in its turn is the likeness of that of paradise."* But in the gardens of Madīnat al-Zahrā' each vegetable species could not produce, as it could in paradise, two different varieties of the same fruit at the same time. For this reason, what the asymmetrical decoration of the Hall of 'Abd al-Raḥmān III really did was to invert the sense proposed by Acién: its vegetal motifs were those which really constituted a 'likeness' of the flora of paradise, while the flora of the Upper Garden of the city could not go outside the bounds imposed by nature and it should therefore be 'seen' according to the heavenly model represented in the hall.

The image or images of paradise that Muslims have and have had throughout history are not based exclusively on the Quran: many other sources have contributed to them, and have been collected in different literary genres such as, among others, the compilations of the traditions of the Prophet and his companions and successors, theological treatises, and works of eschatology. A search in these texts gives a clue to help us outline the ways in which attempts are made to represent or suggest paradise in specific cases. We are fortunate enough to have available a text composed by an Andalusī author who lived in the first half of the third/ninth century; the text contains a minutely detailed description of paradise. I refer to the work of 'Abd al-Malik b. Ḥabīb (d. 238/853) entitled *Kitāb Waṣf al-firdaws* (Book on the description of paradise).[28] This is a most important text which has already been used

lower gardens will be that the latter will only have one type of each fruit, while the former will have two: see al-Qurṭubī, *al-Jāmiʿ li-aḥkām* xvii, 162–3. My thanks to Luis Molina for the information he has provided on the works of Quranic exegesis concerning this verse, based on the materials collected on the CD-ROM *Maktabat al-tafsīr wa-ʿulūm al-Qurʾān* [Amman: Markaz al-Turāth lil-Barmajiyyāt].

* [Acién, Materiales e hipótesis 186.]

28 The Arabic text was published in Beirut, 1407/1987, in an edition which I reviewed in *Sharq al-Andalus* 7 (1990), 243–4. The Arabic text has been translated into Spanish: Ibn Ḥabīb, *Kitāb Waṣf al-firdaws*, intro., trans. and study Monferrer Sala.

to obtain a better understanding of the iconography of the mosaics of the Umayyad Mosque of Damascus which, as is well known, has been interpreted as a vision of paradise.[29] Let us look at some of the descriptions it contains (the number which accompanies them corresponds to those of the paragraphs into which the editor divided the Arabic text, a division which has been followed by Monferrer Sala in his translation [on which the following is based]):

> (24)...ʿAbd al-Malik said: 'When the day of resurrection comes and the heavens and the earth are replaced, just as God has said, God will all at once draw up paradise, and then all the gardens that lie therein shall be laid out until they fill the abyss which occupied the space where the heavens were before they were replaced. Between it and the throne shall there be no sky, save only the throne which is [already] there now and which, in due time, shall be the sky of paradise. Thus spoke the Most High: "And paradise shall be brought forward for the godfearing" [Q 26:90]...The land shall be replaced by a land of silver [Q 3:133] and its highest terraces [shall climb] to the throne, which shall be the whole of its sky.'
>
> (25)...The Prophet...has said: 'In paradise there is a palace into which only a prophet, a [true: *ṣiddīq*, my addition] believer, a martyr or a just *imām* will enter.'[30]
>
> [The latter is identified as ʿUmar b. al-Khaṭṭāb. In other words this palace was reserved for prophets, martyrs, and the first two caliphs, Abū Bakr al-Ṣiddīq and ʿUmar, although by extension it is supposed that just and well-guided caliphs will also enter. My addition].
>
> (29)...The Prophet...has said: 'In paradise there are rooms from whose interior one can see what is outside, and from outside one can see what is inside, so fine and beautiful are they....'
>
> (41) Concerning that which God, the Most High, has said, And surely the world to come is greater in ranks, greater in preferment [Q 17:21] and [also on what] the Most High has said,...those in truth are the believers; they have degrees with their Lord, and forgiveness, and generous provision [Q 8:4], ʿAbd al-Malik said: 'The degrees indicate ranks and merits. The degrees of paradise indicate the merit and the rank through which God considers some superior to others in so far as they have obeyed [His laws] in this world...The people of each degree, rank and merit are companions. It is not that they are companions when they eat, drink or

29 Flood, *The Great Mosque* 28–9.

30 This is a reference to Q 4:69. See also Ibn Ḥabīb, *Kitāb Waṣf al-firdaws*, number 50.

live together, but when they are grouped together [according to] similar merit…'

(55) 'Abd al-Malik said: '… As to the garden of paradise, *al-firdaws* is vineyards and grapes. It is on a high hill of paradise from which spring the rivers of paradise. The Prophet… said: Ask God for *al-firdaws*, it is the very center of paradise, the highest garden from which flow the rivers of paradise; the people of paradise [there] shall hear the noise [*aṭīṭ*] of the throne.'

(90)… There the leaves of paradise are according to the types of fruit and the kinds of birds; in paradise there is no [dwelling place] which is not covered by boughs, even with the varieties of fruit and of birds. If a community were beneath one of their leaves, it would cover [them all] with shade. The flowers [form] gardens, the leaves are always fresh…

(92)… God has not created a [single] flower (*zahra*) nor a [single] color which is not found there, with the exception of the color black. In paradise there is no dwelling place which is not covered by its branches, which produce adornments and tunics, and from its stem two springs flow…*

(103) 'The branches of the trees of paradise are of gold, the leaves of sapphires and beryls, the palms are like the former. Their leaves are like the most beautiful tunics that were [ever] seen, their fruits are smoother than butter and sweeter than honey, on each of the trees there is [every] kind of fruit. Each species has a different flavor. When anyone desires any [particular one of all the fruits from all these] species, the branches on which the desired fruit grows bow down so that he may take it with his [own] hand, just as he wishes. [Whether] he wishes to be standing, seated or reclining, and [even] if he so wishes he may open his mouth so that [the fruit] may enter. Once he has taken any [fruit], God… will create another better and finer than the one before.'

(242) '… The fruits of this world have their season, and then they finish, whereas those of paradise are never exhausted; the fruits of this world have guardians, whereas those of paradise do not.' Concerning the saying of the Most High, "whose fruits shall be within a hand's reach," al-Ḥasan commented: 'They shall reach them, whether they are standing, or seated or reclining, as they wish.' As to what the Most High said, "their fruits, within reach, may easily be picked," he [al-Ḥasan] stated: 'They shall be

---

* [For the issue of colors and their meanings in Muslim eschatology, see S. Günther's contribution to this publication.]

within reach, picking them however they wish, whatever may be [the fruit] they may choose [to pick].' Concerning the saying of the Most High, "whensoever they are provided with fruits therefrom they shall say, 'This is that wherewithal we were provided before'; that they shall be given in perfect semblance" [Q 2:25], the best, with nothing bad within it, and like the first in taste and quality, with nothing bad within it.[31]

In the examples quoted (and they are only a small sample of the contents of Ibn Ḥabīb's book), there are clear correspondences with the topographical situation of Madīnat al-Zahrāʾ and with some of its characteristics. We have the layout of paradise as gardens (with earth of silver: the idea of whiteness[32] and brilliance) which stretch from the sky, where the Throne of God is located, downwards in steps or terraces. There is a garden which is the exact center of paradise, situated on a hill. The vegetation is lush, varied and dense.[33] There are always fruits within reach of the hands of those who want them. In paradise there is a palace for prophets, martyrs, and just *imāms*. And there are rooms from whose interior one may see what is outside and from outside what is within (a mirror image between the flowers in the garden and the plant decoration of the hall). In paradise believers are not mixed, there is a hierarchy according to rank and merit.[34]

In the texts referring to Madīnat al-Zahrāʾ frequent reference is made to *al-saṭḥ al-ʿalī*, which Labarta and Barceló translate as 'upper level,' pointing out that it is not clear whether the phrase alludes to "a topographic or architectural upper level. Here are located the reception halls and an open space."[35] The root *s-ṭ-ḥ* appears only once in the Quran, in chapter 88, verse 20. After describing hell and paradise (verses 1–16), the following verses mention the divine omnipotence, asking men to think about how God has raised the heavens "how the mountains were hoisted, how the earth was outstretched (*suṭiḥat*)." May the expression *saṭḥ* be seen as a reference to this Quranic verse? Is the term not being used, perhaps, to denote the part of the city where the ground

---

31 Ibn Ḥabīb, *Kitāb Waṣf al-firdaws*.

32 This idea of whiteness is reflected in the legendary story of the slave al-Zahrāʾ whose wish for a city bearing her name may have motivated the construction of Madīnat al-Zahrāʾ: on this subject, see Marín, *Mujeres en al-Andalus* 79–80, with references.

33 To what extent may the use of the so-called 'florid Kufic' script in the inscriptions of ʿAbd al-Raḥmān III (see Martínez Núñez, Sentido de la epigrafía 408–17) also be related to celestial symbolism?

34 See also Ibn Ḥabīb, *Kitāb Waṣf al-firdaws*, numbers 37, 41, 178.

35 Labarta and Barceló, Las fuentes árabes 101.

was leveled on the side of the hill? But C. Barceló reminds me that the term *saṭḥ* is also used in the description of the Alcázar (royal palace) of Cordoba, so that its use in Madīnat al-Zahrāʾ would have no particular relevance. Similarly, Juan Pedro Monferrer tells me that this term does not appear in the *Kitāb Waṣf al-firdaws*.

5 The 'Flashes of Lightning' and the 'Stewards' of Paradise

We saw earlier how in the wall decorations of the Hall of ʿAbd al-Raḥmān III there appear 'pearls.' In the Quranic description of paradise there are frequent references to jewels and pearls (Q 22:23; 37:49; 52:24; 56:23). The same thing happens in Muslim tradition, where it is said, for example, that the inhabitants of paradise will be given food consisting of ground up gold and pearls, and where there are references to palaces made of pearls or of one gigantic pearl of enormous size.[36] There is a famous description of what some authors identify as one of the rooms of Madīnat al-Zahrāʾ[37] where a pearl is in fact mentioned, and which I reproduce here in the version found in the *Dhikr bilād al-Andalus*:

> In the Alcázar [ʿAbd al-Raḥmān III] built a room called *Majlis al-khilāfa* whose walls and ceiling were of gold and thick marble, of the purest colour and of different types. In the centre of this prodigious hall was the pearl given to him by Leo, King of Constantinople, and its tiles were of gold and silver. In the middle of the hall was a great pool full of mercury, and on every side of the room there were four doors with arches of ivory and ebony decorated with gold and different precious stones resting on columns of coloured marble and pure crystal. As the sun came through these doors it bathed the ceiling and the walls of the hall with its light; and they reflected the rays, creating a dazzling brilliance (*nūr yaʾkhudhu l-abṣār*). The sovereign, when he wanted to frighten his guests, would make a sign to one of his slaves, who would stir the mercury, whereupon the hall would be filled with a flashing light which would overwhelm the hearts of those present (*nūr ka-lamaʿān al-barq yaʾkhudhu bi-jamīʿ al-qulūb*), for it seemed to them that the room was going round while

36 See Flood, *The Great Mosque* 27–8. Also Ibn Ḥabīb, *Kitāb Waṣf al-firdaws*, numbers 28, 38, 40.

37 Labarta and Barceló, Las fuentes árabes 102, however, think this actually dealt with a hall in the Alcázar in Cordoba. For the location of the hall in Madīnat al-Zahrāʾ, see Molina, Sobre el estanque.

> the mercury was in movement. Some say that the hall revolved so that it would always face the sun, but others say that it was fixed around the pool. Never before in Islam or before had anybody done anything similar, but to him it was possible because of the large quantities of mercury he had at his disposal.[38]

The elements seen in this account may be interpreted as a way of imitating central aspects of the description of paradise. One of these is the number of doors: paradise also has eight doors.[39] Another is the construction in gold and silver.[40] Another is the flashing light, which is one of the characteristics that are repeated when describing what each believer will find as he enters paradise:

> (128) … he shall enter, finding rows of cushions, doors [perfectly] aligned and carpets spread [everywhere], and he shall look at the foundations of the building, for behold it has been built on rocks of pearls [with a mixture] of yellow, green, red and white color; then he shall raise his eyes to the ceiling, and were it not for the fact that God has given him the ability [to resist], a light would destroy his sight, for it is like a flash of lightning (*barq*) …
>
> (47) … if any of [the dwellers] in paradise raise his eyes, he will be almost blinded by a dazzling light, and he will exclaim: 'What is this? For surely I do not believe that there are flashes of lightning in paradise …'[41]

The description of the hall referring to the tank or pool of mercury has generally been considered by researchers as legendary, pointing out possible literary precedents[42] and noting how it appears in late sources. But this description also mentions the tiles of gold and silver. There is indeed documentary evidence of the existence of tiles glazed in honey color and white in the excavations

---

38 Molina (ed. and trans.), *Dhikr bilād al-Andalus*, Arabic text 164, translation 174. In the appendix references are given to other sources (none earlier than the twelfth century) which tell the same story. See also references in Labarta and Barceló, Las fuentes árabes 102.

39 ʿAbd al-Malik Ibn Ḥabīb, *Kitāb Waṣf al-firdaws*, numbers 14, 17.

40 Ibid., numbers 7, 32.

41 Ibid.

42 See Rubiera, *La arquitectura* 84–5, for an account of the palace of the Egyptian governor Khumarāwayh b. Ṭulūn (second half of the third/tenth century). But in this account the function and characteristics of the pool of mercury have nothing to do with those of the hall in al-Andalus.

of Madīnat al-Zahrā'.[43] Although the description may be invented,[44] its origin may well be the fact that it was known that the Hall of ʿAbd al-Raḥmān III referred specifically to paradise, so that those later authors who circulated the story accumulated elements belonging to the same reference.

The same may be the case with the account of the Christian embassy to Madīnat al-Zahrā' told by the mystic Muḥyī l-Dīn b. ʿArabī and analyzed by F. de la Granja, in which the following story is told:

> When they [the ambassadors] arrived at the gate of Madīnat al-Zahrā', the ground was carpeted with brocade, from the gate of the city to the throne, all in the same impressive way. In special places they had set chamberlains, who looked like kings, dressed in brocade and silk, seated in ornate chairs.
>
> When they saw a chamberlain, they hastened to prostrate themselves before him, believing that he was the Caliph. But they said: 'Lift up your heads: this is only one of his slaves.'[45]

F. de la Granja has already indicated the literary precedents, both popular and classical, of this story. But it is also a story which is told about paradise: the believer will arrive in paradise and will confuse the angels and other servants of God, surrounded by splendor and light, with God Himself, so that they will go down on bended knee to adore them until they are told of their error.[46]

6 The Dark Green Gardens of Paradise

We have seen that in chapter 55 of the Quran there are two gardens mentioned which are located below the two 'upper' gardens, which seems to indicate that they would be destined for those who are not worthy of a reward so high as that enjoyed in the first two gardens. These 'lower' gardens are dark green (*mudhāmmatāni*), a color which al-Ṭabarī explains by the fact that "they appear black because of the intensity of their greenness" (*muswaddatāni min*

43 Communicated personally by Antonio Vallejo Triano, to whom I am grateful for the information; I also thank Manuel Acién Almansa.

44 See the critical opinion of al-Maqqarī in *Nafḥ al-ṭīb* i, 527–8 (I owe this reference to Carmen Barceló).

45 De la Granja, A propósito 393.

46 Ibn Ḥabīb, *Kitāb Waṣf al-firdaws*, numbers 129, 245.

shiddati khuḍratihimā)* – in other words, they, too, will have abundant vegetation, with two fountains, and in them there will be fruit trees, palm trees and pomegranates. For his part ʿAbd al-Malik b. Ḥabīb explains the Quranic term as "green, which, due to their weight, tend to become black."[47]

It is known that the founding of Madīnat al-Zahrā' was linked to the production of a special type of ceramics which is known as 'green and manganese': against a white background there are different motifs in green edged with black. Vegetal motifs are the most dominant among them.[48] This type of ceramic, in which open forms are most common (consequently it has been considered as tableware), seems to have been a frequent gift from the caliph. M. Barceló has linked the white background to the color of the Umayyads,[49] a connection with which Escudero agrees:

> the basic tricolor scheme employed in its decoration appears to be a symbol, or emblem, of the Andalusī Umayyads: white as the color of the dynasty, green as the color of the Prophet... and black as the synthesis of power, of Quranic austerity and the dignity of the Caliph's throne. A striking point, in this connection, is the frequent use of the term *al-mulk*, which proclaims 'the Caliphal identity, the legitimate Caliphal line of the Umayyad dynasty,' and floral elements like the palmette, which also carries clear symbolic connotations.[50]

But as well as these possible references, this green color with a black border may also be connected to the dark green gardens mentioned in Q 55. And we must not forget that the color green is the archetypal color of the Islamic paradise (Q 18:31; 55:76; 76:21), as well as of the martyrs.[51]

---

* [Al-Ṭabarī, *Jāmiʿ al-bayān* xxvii, 86.]

47 Ibn Ḥabīb, *Kitāb Waṣf al-firdaws* number 99, see also number 229, to the end.

48 See Escudero Aranda, La cerámica decorada 127–64. An update on what is known about these ceramics can be found in Bazzana, A., La ceramique verde 349–58 and Fuertes Santos, *La cerámica califal* 150–2.

49 Barceló, *Al-Mulk* 291–9, repr. in *El sol que salió por Occidente* 187–94.

50 Escudero Aranda, La cerámica califal 402, with references to Roselló Bordoy, La céramique verte 105–8.

51 See Ibn Ḥabīb, *Kitāb Waṣf al-firdaws*, numbers 162, 166, 240, 245. There is a well-known tradition that the breath of life (*nasam*) of martyrs is in the belly of green birds, that of believers is in the belly of white birds, and the breath of life of the people in hell is in the belly of black birds: see Lucini, *La escatología musulmana* 537. In the *Kitāb Waṣf al-firdaws*, number 303 we find the following variation: "when your brothers fell victim at Uḥud, their spirits were placed in green birds which drink their fill from the rivers

7 Umayyads and Fatimids in the Time of the Construction of the Hall of ʿAbd al-Raḥmān III

As we have seen, the Hall of ʿAbd al-Raḥmān III was not built until the years 342/953–4 and 345/956–7, and its construction implied an important remodeling of the original plan of the city.

At about this time, in the year 344/955, the caliph also carried out a reorganization of the administration,[52] which consisted of the creation of four 'departments,' each under the management of a different vizier: one department was responsible for inter-administration correspondence; the second, for correspondence with the frontier regions; the third, for the transmission of orders and decrees; and the fourth, for supervision of the complaints from and the affairs related to the caliph's subjects. This reform took place in the same year in which the Fatimids attacked the port of Almeria, wreaking great destruction. If this attack was seen as the prelude to a large-scale Fatimid invasion, it may have prompted the caliph to strengthen his control over the territory under his command by means of this administrative reform. But even as early as the overthrow of the 'man of the donkey' in 336/947, the threat presented by the Fatimid caliphate had acquired a new dimension. But first let us look briefly at this 'man of the donkey.'[53]

The Zanāta Berber (from the branch of the Ifran) Abū Yazīd Makhlad b. Kaydād was a Khārijite, and hence in favor of equality between Berbers and Arabs, of the right to reject and depose unjust rulers, and of the duty to name only the best and most pious of Muslims as the *imām* of the community, even if he were a black slave; thus he denied that the family of the Prophet had any special charisma. Toward the year 332/944, the Zanāta troops of the 'man of the donkey,' as he was called because of his mount (a symbol of humility), began to win military victories against the Fatimids in North Africa, even conquering Kairouan, where coins were minted in the name of Abū Yazīd. The Mālikī faction in the city, while against his doctrines, saw in him a way of freeing themselves from the Shiʿites, who were considered a greater threat. Abū Yazīd, for example, failed to capture either Mahdiyya, the fortress city built by the Fatimids at the beginning of their reign, or Susa.

---

of paradise, eat their fruits, and dwell in lanterns in the shadow of the throne…" [For al-Ghazālī's statements on the issue of the souls of the martyrs residing in the green birds of paradise, see S. Günther's contribution to this publication.]

52 See Ibn ʿIdhārī, *al-Bayān al-mughrib* 220.

53 See the bibliographic references in note 8.

At about the same time, in 333/944–5, according to [the early eighth/fourteenth-century Andalusian historian] Ibn ʿIdhārī, there appeared in Lisbon a man who said that he was a member of the family of the Prophet, and that his mother Maryam was a descendant of Fāṭima. He claimed to be a prophet, and declared that the angel Gabriel visited him. He gave his followers a series of rules and laws, among which was to shave their heads (a practice which is generally attributed to the Khārijites). Nothing else is known of this individual. ʿAbd al-Raḥmān III had already had to face messianic movements, no doubt exacerbated by the Fatimid example, for in the year 315/927 he had intervened to overthrow another false prophet, a Berber named Ḥamīm b. Mann Allāh al-Muftarī who had appeared on the outskirts of Tetuan.[54] Both the Fatimid caliph and his Umayyad counterpart, then, had to face heretical rebels.

When the Fatimid caliph Ismāʿīl al-Manṣūr (335–41/946–53), who gained his name precisely as a result of his victory over the 'man of the donkey,' acceded to the throne it was still by no means clear that this victory was going to be possible: but in the year 335/946 he managed to overthrow Abū Yazīd and put him to flight. This latter had sent embassies to Cordoba to recognize the Umayyad caliph, with the aim of gaining his military support in his fight against the Fatimids.[55] But the Andalusī caliph took too long to decide what to do, and when the Umayyad fleet arrived at the coast of Ifrīqiya, Abū Yazīd had been defeated (336/947).

This defeat was converted into a proof of the legitimacy of the Fatimid dynasty and the truth of their doctrine. Abū Yazīd was presented by the Fatimids as the Dajjāl, the Antichrist who would cause great havoc before the appearance of the Messiah or *mahdī*, who would overthrow him. By being identified with the eschatological figure of the Dajjāl, Abū Yazīd was no longer simply a rival who proposed a different version of Islam and was fighting for political power. He was the Great Enemy, whose overthrow would open the way to the consummation of divine destiny. By defeating him, the caliph al-Manṣūr became in his turn a messianic figure, he was the one who had triumphed over evil in order to inaugurate a new era in which the Fatimid dynasty would rule until the end of time.[56]

It was against this background that al-Manṣūr introduced certain innovations. We have already mentioned that he promoted the building of Ṣabra-Manṣūriyya, with its characteristic circular form, in imitation of ʿAbbasid Baghdad (and in contrast to the rectangular form of Madīnat al-Zahrāʾ,

54 Fierro, *La heterodoxia* 128–9, 143.
55 Viguera, Los Fatimíes de Ifrīqiya 29–37.
56 Brett, *Rise* 170–1.

although see my comments in note 7). But the most visible innovation was the reform of the coinage, with the appearance on the coins of three concentric circles around a central field with a horizontal inscription. Later, his successor al-Muʿizz introduced more radical changes both in the design and in the Shiʿite content of the inscription. The horizontal field disappeared, being replaced by a central point surrounded by three concentric circular bands containing an inscription which read: "There is no god but Allāh, one alone, without partner; and Muḥammad is the Messenger of Allāh; and ʿAlī b. Abī Ṭālib is the heir of the Messenger and the most excellent deputy (*wazīr*) and the husband of the Radiant and Pure (*al-Zahrāʾ al-batūl*)." On the reverse it said, among other things: "the servant of God Maʿadd Abū Tamīm, the *imām* al-Muʿizz li-dīn Allāh, Prince of the Faithful, Reviver of the *sunna* of Muḥammad, Lord of the messengers [sent by God], and heir to the glory of the well guided *imāms*." This assertive Shiʿite wording (ʿAlī as heir to the Prophet and his most excellent deputy, and the mention of his wife Fāṭima as the Radiant and Pure) only lasted two years (from 341–3/952–5); it was replaced by more moderate phraseology from 343/954–5 until the end of the reign of al-Muʿizz in which it only said: " ʿAlī is the most excellent heir and a deputy of the greatest of those among the messengers [of God]."[57]

If the victory over Abū Yazīd represented the truth and legitimacy of the Fatimids, what repercussions did the same victory have on the Umayyad legitimacy? The false prophet in Lisbon (about whom we know so little) may have served to demonstrate that the Umayyads were also vanquishing evil. But I believe that the remodeling of Madīnat al-Zahrāʾ, and more particularly the heavenly symbolism of the hall and gardens, was the main way in which ʿAbd al-Raḥmān III decided to counteract the benefits obtained by the Fatimids with their victory over the 'man of the donkey.'

One aspect of this remodeling was the transfer, in 336/947 (the same year in which Abū Yazīd, the Antichrist of the Fatimids, was overthrown), of the mint from Cordoba to Madīnat al-Zahrāʾ.[58] In fact, thanks to this move we can be absolutely certain that at the time this was the name of the city of ʿAbd

57 Walker, *Exploring an Islamic empire* 97, where we read: "Without an explanation of them in the other sources, whether these overt proclamations of Shiʿi belief had special significance remains unclear. What is most obvious in them is none the less completely in line with Fatimid doctrine both before and after their use on the coinage. Therefore, the main unanswered question is why al-Muʿizz decided to add them and also why he dropped them after such a brief run of only two years." No relation is established with what was happening in the Umayyad zone.

58 See Canto, Ceca de al-Andalus 111–9 (English translation: *Sikkat al-Andalus* 329–45).

al-Raḥmān III, since on the coins produced there the name of Madīnat al-Zahrāʾ appears.[59] Given that the mention of Fāṭima on the Fatimid coins with the text *al-Zahrāʾ al-batūl* came later (in the time of al-Muʿizz), did al-Muʿizz decide to introduce this text because the Umayyad caliph was calling his city by a name which could be understood as a reference to the daughter of the Prophet? In any case, the decision of ʿAbd al-Raḥmān III to call his city by a name which evoked Fāṭima must have been motivated precisely by her role in legitimizing the Fatimids (although the name by which the dynasty is known was not used by them until very late):[60] for example, in the official sermon accompanying the Friday prayer in Fatimid territory mention was made of the Prophet "Muḥammad and his family, ʿAlī, the Prince of the Faithful, his sons al-Ḥasan and al-Ḥusayn, and the radiant one (*zahrāʾ*)."[61]

The transfer of the mint from Cordoba to Madīnat al-Zahrāʾ also implied the introduction of innovations in the Umayyad coinage, for the legend on the reverse was arranged in three lines (this pattern lasted until 350/961), as against the four of the previous period (321–36/933–47).[62] Was this an imitation of the reform of the Fatimid coinage on the basis of the three concentric circles introduced by al-Manṣūr?

The series of coins produced by the mint in Madīnat al-Zahrāʾ are characterized by great variety and rich decoration. The decorative motifs are not only geometric but also based on a great variety of shapes: the issues of the period 336–41/947–52 are particularly notable for the appearance of this varied vegetal and floral ornamentation. During the period 316–29/928–40, the decorative signs were particularly simple, mostly of geometric shapes. In the period 330–5/941–6, a fixed decorative element was introduced on the back of the silver coins, it had the systematic repetition of an eight petaled flower. The extraordinary decorative development which took place in the years 336–41/947–952 (and here I echo A. Canto) coincides with the transfer of the mint from Cordoba to Madīnat al-Zahrāʾ. The issues of the years 336–7/947–9 are those which show the greatest decorative variety, and from the last year onwards we observe a slight decrease in the variety, which becomes more noticeable in the last years of the caliphate of ʿAbd al-Raḥmān III, when coins were decorated

59 The Oriental traveler and Fatimid spy Ibn Ḥawqal, who arrived in al-Andalus in the year 337/948, refers to the Palatine city by the name of al-Zahrāʾ, but it is not clear in his text if the form was 'Madīnat al-Zahrāʾ' or 'al-Madīna al-Zahrāʾ': *Kitāb Ṣūrat al-arḍ* 77–8; for the Spanish translation see Ibn Ḥawqal, *Configuración de mundo*, trans. Romaní Suay 64–5.

60 On this subject see my study On al-fāṭimi and al-fāṭimiyyūn 144–7.

61 Halm, *Empire* 124, 272.

62 The following section is based on the study by Canto mentioned in note 57.

with geometric themes or carry no decoration at all. It is clear that this rich vegetal and floral ornamentation of the coinage corresponds with the decorative program of the Hall of ʿAbd al-Raḥmān III: although the construction of the latter can be dated later than the changes effected in the coinage, both phenomena are closely linked.

Al-Muʿizz came to power in 341/953, and a year later (in 342/953) the Midrarid governor of Sijilmasa, who until then had pledged obedience to the Umayyad caliph of al-Andalus, pronounced himself caliph with the title of al-Shākir li-llāh.[63] According to [the well known fifth/eleventh-century scholar] Ibn Ḥazm, in letters sent by ʿAbd al-Raḥmān III from Madīnat al-Zahrāʾ which he himself saw, the Umayyad caliph called himself *al-qāʾim li-llāh*,[64] a title which is not mentioned in the chronicles and which has clear messianic overtones, having been used particularly by the Shiʿites. The fact that a Sunni caliph such as ʿAbd al-Raḥmān III decided to adopt it and use it reveals another aspect of this long rivalry between Umayyads and Fatimids, expressed via symbols of legitimacy. The adoption of this name may well have taken place after the defeat of the 'man of the donkey' appeared to confirm and reinforce the messianic role of the Fatimid dynasty.

8 Al-Madīna al-Zahrāʾ, the Shining or Dazzling City

One of the most remarkable characteristics of paradise is its brilliance, of which we have already seen evidence in talk of 'bolts of lightning.' Let us look at some other examples taken from ʿAbd al-Malik b. Ḥabīb:

> (45) … The Prophet said …: "The people in paradise will see the people in the higher ranks in the same way a shining star (*al-kawkab al-durrī*) is seen in the confines of the firmament."
>
> (46) … "The people in paradise will see each other in paradise as the Eastern Star is seen from the Western Star …"
>
> (150) … "He who dwells above contemplates all those who are below him; his light illuminates everything, just as the sun lights the Earth when it rises [in the morning].

---

63 Halm, *Empire* 397–8.

64 Ibn Ḥazm, *Naqṭ al-ʿarūs* iv, 49 (in the edition of Seybold, trans. Seco de Lucena 151–2/68, this title appears as *al-qāʾim bi-llāh*). In iv, 63, Ibn Ḥazm however uses the title *al-qāʾim bi-amr Allāh*. For more information see Fierro, Sobre la adopción 38–9.

> (229) ... his appearance shall be that of a brilliant light (*nūr sāṭiʿ*), whose rays shall be like the rays of the sun when it rises [in the morning] and like the shining star (*al-kawkab al-durrī*) and the brilliant day; the palaces shall be high ... and of sapphire, which will radiate its light (*yazharu nūruhā*); if it were not for the fact that [God] has taken it to His service, his eyesight would be blinded by the intensity of its brilliance and the eye of its jewels ..."[65]

We have already mentioned that the name of Madīnat al-Zahrāʾ by which the city of ʿAbd al-Raḥmān III is known may have been yet another example of that rivalry with the Fatimid dynasty of which we have just seen several examples. Indeed, in the Fatimid legitimacy, as the very name of the dynasty implies, the figure of the daughter of the Prophet, Fāṭima, occupies a central place; she is known by the name 'al-Zahrā''.[66] Be that as it may, the root *z-h-r* had been used to name other Umayyad buildings.[67]

But if Madīnat al-Zahrāʾ was built as an embodiment of paradise on earth, could its name not also be related to this idea of brilliance? The anecdote of the pool of mercury and the roofs of gold and silver would point in this direction. And we might also add what is known about the public illumination of the city.[68] The verses of Ibn Zaydūn about Madīnat al-Zahrāʾ, in which the city is compared to paradise, draw attention to its brilliance: "those royal palaces whose apartments shone, and where shaded receptions seemed like sunrise" (although this a cliché in describing palaces, remember the line 'What castles are those? They are high and bright ...'*), but in the same verses he mentions a building known as al-Kawkab (the star).[69]

65 Ibn Ḥabīb, *Kitāb Waṣf al-firdaws*, see also numbers 10, 33, 45, 47, 48, 229, 248.

66 See references included in my article Espacio 175.

67 See Rubiera, *La arquitectura* 122–4 and 177–8.

68 See Escudero, La cerámica califal 405, referring to Valdés, *Kalifale Lampen* 208–16. But A. Vallejo Triano tells me this is a rather contrived interpretation of the use of the lamps found in Madīnat al-Zahrāʾ.

* This is a reference to a famous Spanish poem (known as the 'romance' of Abenámar) in which a Christian asks the 'Moor' Abenámar about the palaces of Granada.

69 See Rubiera, *La arquitectura* 129; Pérès, *La poésie andalouse* 124–5 (my thanks to Carmen Barceló for the latter reference).

9 The Censure of Mundhir b. Saʿīd

One of the best-known anecdotes about the caliphate of ʿAbd al-Raḥmān III is that which tells of the censure of the *qāḍī* and preacher of Cordoba, Mundhir b. Saʿīd al-Ballūṭī (d. 355/966), toward the caliph for having failed to attend Friday prayer for some time because he was too busily occupied in the construction of Madīnat al-Zahrā'.[70] Mundhir had been appointed as *qāḍī* in 339/950 (as preacher some years before) and occupied the position until his death, in the times of the caliph al-Ḥakam II. It was thus during his term as *qāḍī* that the Hall of ʿAbd al-Raḥmān III was built. Mundhir's censure consisted of two parts, both of which were expressed using Quranic quotes. In the first instance, he quoted Q 26:128–35: "What, do you build on every prominence a sign, sporting, and do you take to you castles, haply to dwell forever? When you assault, you assault like tyrants! … Indeed, I fear for you the chastisement of a dreadful day." This quote appears to be a reproach for building Madīnat al-Zahrā', but in the anecdote it is presented as a warning lest the building keep the caliph away from his religious duties. In the second place, the *qāḍī* quotes Q 43:33–5 when he visits the hall of Madīnat al-Zahrā' (according to some sources, when he saw a dome covered in precious metals):

> And were it not that mankind would be one nation, We would have appointed for those who disbelieve in the All-merciful roofs of silver to their houses, and stairs whereon to mount, and doors to their houses, and couches whereon to recline, and ornaments; surely all this is but the enjoyment of the present life, and the world to come with thy Lord is for the godfearing.

In this case, it seems clear that the *qāḍī* was trying to send the message that he found the luxury and extravagance in which the caliph had indulged to be unacceptable; and it may also be understood that part of the censure was because the caliph was showing off in this world the luxury reserved for the righteous in the next.

I have indicated elsewhere[71] that an official preacher within the Sunni community is effective if it may be said of him that this official appointment has not tied his hands and feet – in other words, if he is allowed to censure the ruler. This censure is not only *not* a threat to the ruler, however daring it may

70 Sources quoting this censure (with variations) are collected by de Felipe, *Identidad y onomástica* 210–2.

71 See Fierro, La política religiosa 119–56.

appear, on the contrary, it strengthens that ruler. The religious authority of the Sunni caliph is based on his guaranteeing and protecting Islamic religious law (*sharīʿa*), which is interpreted by experts in religious knowledge (scholars, or *ʿulamāʾ*); the application of this law extends to the person of the caliph himself. A Sunni caliph will therefore be strengthened if the scholar he has named as official preacher dedicates part of his sermons to reminding the caliph of the rules to be obeyed, and to reproaching him when he fails to follow these rules. Only a good, just, and pious caliph would allow such exhortations and censures, and the fact that these take place closes the circle: the caliph is good, just, and pious. The censure of the Sunni ruler at the same time lends him legitimacy, in contrast to what happens among the Shiʿites, as there can never be censure of an *imām* who is infallible.

But even so, the censure is not pronounced without consequences. We do not know if Mundhir's censure had any effect on the quality of the materials used in the building of Madīnat al-Zahrāʾ, but it may well have. In the version of the story which mentions a dome of precious metals, the caliph is said to have ordered it to be rebuilt in a more simple way. We know that Mundhir b. Saʿīd criticized the elimination of the name of ʿAlī and material relative to him in some works composed in al-Andalus during the fourth/tenth century, and apparently his disapproval put a stop to a practice which arose from the Umayyad hatred of the fourth orthodox caliph (the cousin and son-in-law of the Prophet, of whom the Fatimids declared themselves to be descendants and heirs), a practice which could not be acceptable within the Sunni community.[72] Under al-Ḥakam II it was the mosque of Cordoba (the same one his predecessor ʿAbd al-Raḥmān had stopped attending) which was the object of sumptuous decoration. I refer to the famous mosaics of the *miḥrāb*, in which once again we can see celestial symbolism, with its roots in the building traditions of the Umayyads of Damascus,[73] but this time it was not associated to a city but to a religious building. Perhaps, as happened with the Fatimids when they had to discard the messianic propaganda of the early days of the dynasty, the second Umayyad caliph also had to dilute his promise of paradise on earth, taking it back to its eschatological dimension.[74]

One of the theological doctrines attributed to [the Andalusian legal expert and theologian] Mundhir b. Saʿīd [d. 355/966] deals with the difference

---

72 Ibid.

73 See references in Fierro, En torno a la decoración. At that time I was inclined to think that it was ʿAbd al-Raḥmān III who conceived the decoration of the *miḥrāb*.

74 Symptomatic of this would be the abandonment of florid Kufic script in the period of al-Ḥakam II: see Martínez Núñez, Sentido de la epigrafía 416.

between the earthly paradise in which Adam and Eve lived, and the other eternal paradise (*jannat al-khuld*) since the *qāḍī*

> thought that paradise and heaven have indeed already been created, except that paradise is not the same as that in which Adam and his wife were installed by God. He based this opinion on various reasons, one of which was that, if it had been eternal paradise itself, they would not have eaten of the tree in the hopes of living for ever. He also said that in the eternal paradise there is no room for lies and, nonetheless, the devil lied there. Finally he said that whoever enters paradise never leaves it, yet Adam and his wife left paradise.[75]

His contemporary, the scholar Wahb b. Masarra (d. 346/957),[76] would have shared this opinion. This is a doctrine which had not aroused any particular concern among Muslims[77] and perhaps it may reflect the debate about the identification of Madīnat al-Zahrā' with paradise that I have set out here. The comparison of a palace with eternal paradise (*jannat al-khuld*) had already been made in al-Andalus by ʿUbaydīs b. Maḥmūd when talking of one of the constructions of Ibn al-Shāliya:

> The palace of the Emir Abū Marwān
> is copied from eternal paradise,
> wrought with great magnificence:
> it has halls held up by columns,
> all made of marble mounted in purest gold.[78]

This comparison was still being made later with the construction of Almanzor: "Votre palais d'al-ʿAmiriya est comme le Paradis de Riḍwān."[79]

75 See Fierro, *Heterodoxia* 141, quoting the translation by M. Asín Palacios.

76 Fierro, *Heterodoxia* 139, note 52.

77 See van Ess, *Theologie und Gesellschaft* iv, 550–4 (for reference to the doctrine of Mundhir b. Saʿīd, 553).

78 Ibn Ḥayyān, *Muqtabis*, ed. Antuña 11. The Spanish translation [on which this is based] is by Terés, ʿUbaydīs ibn Maḥmūd 113.

79 Blachère, Un pionnier 30. Riḍwān is the guardian of paradise: see *EI*², s.v.

10 Conclusion

As I have said before, ʿAbd al-Raḥmān III found it difficult to try to compete with a rival, the Fatimid caliph, who assumed a type of authority that the Umayyad, as a Sunni caliph, could never hope to have. What he could do was emphasize certain aspects which formed part of the Sunni tradition. One of these is the caliph's assurance of salvation for his subjects.[80] And if he does so, is it not as if paradise already existed in this world, especially where the caliph had his residence?

The ensemble of the hall and gardens that ʿAbd al-Raḥmān III decided to build on the terraced site of Madīnat al-Zahrāʾ may, therefore, have the following message: with the proclamation of the caliphate in al-Andalus, it is as if God had extended the gardens of paradise down to earth. These gardens had different levels or grades, and the highest grade is that where the caliph dwells; and above him is only God. It is as if the caliph, the just *imām*, were living now in those two upper gardens mentioned in chapter 55 of the Quran. And so the decoration of the hall suggests those fruits which come in pairs, but which are not the same.

The other two gardens are below it. These two lower gardens are characterized by the almost black green of their vegetation. The production of ceramics in 'green and manganese' in Madīnat al-Zahrāʾ symbolized the fact that the caliph assured those who had not been chosen to reside in the upper level of the possibility of gaining access to the other gardens. The Quranic verse 76:20 says of paradise: "when thou seest them then thou seest bliss and a great kingdom" (*wa-idhā raʾayta thamma raʾayta naʿīman wa-mulkan kabīran*). The ceramics produced in Madīnat al-Zahrāʾ, with their vegetal decorations and their *al-mulk* text, proclaimed that this "bliss and a great kingdom,"[81] promised to the faithful in the next life, was linked to a city shining like paradise, and to the caliph who built it, ʿAbd al-Raḥmān III.

80 See Crone and Hinds, *God's caliph*.

81 The term *mulk* is generally thought to refer to the power of the caliph. The term has a negative sense, according to the *ḥadīth* which says that the true *khilāfa* of the Prophet lasted only 30 years, during the reign of the orthodox caliphs, and that the later caliphate was merely earthly royalty (*mulk*) acquired by usurpation. See this argument in a contemporary text on the reign of ʿAbd al-Raḥmān III in Madelung, A treatise on the imamate 76.

Bibliography

Acién Almansa, M., Madīnat al-Zahrā' en el urbanismo musulmán, in *Cuadernos de Madīnat al-Zahrā'* 1 (1998), 11–26.

———, Materiales e hipótesis para una interpretación del salón de 'Abd al-Rahman al-Nasir, in A. Vallejo Triano (ed.), *Madīnat al-Zahrā': El salón de 'Abd al-Rahman III*, Cordoba 1995, 179–95.

Arberry, A.J. (trans.), *The Koran*, Oxford 1982.

al-Azmeh, A., Rhetoric for the senses: A consideration of Muslim paradise narratives, in *JAL* 26 (1995), 215–31.

Barceló, M., El califa patente: El ceremonial omeya de Córdoba o la escenificación del poder, in *Estructuras y formas de poder en la historia*, Salamanca 1991, 51–71, repr. in *Madīnat al-Zahrā': El salón de 'Abd al-Rahman III*, Cordoba 1995, 155–75.

———, The manifest caliph: Umayyad ceremony in Córdoba, or the staging of power, in M. Marín (ed.), *The formation of al-Andalus: Part 1: History and society*, Aldershot UK 1998, 425–56.

———, *Al-Mulk*, el verde y el blanco: La vajilla califal omeya de Madīnat al-Zahrā', in A. Malpica Cuello (ed.), *La cerámica altomedieval en el si de al-Andalus*, Granada 1993, 291–9.

———, *El sol que salió por Occidente: Estudios sobre el estado omeya en al-Andalus*, Jaén 1997.

Bazzana, A., La ceramique verde e morado califale à Valence: Problèmes morphologiques et stylistiques, in *IV Congresso internacional: A cerāmica medieval no Mediterrāneo Occidental*, Lisbon 1987, 349–58.

Blachère, R., Un pionnier de la culture arabe orientale en Espagne au Xe siècle: Ṣā'id de Bagdad, in *Hespéris* X (1930), 16–36.

Blair, S.S. and J.M. Bloom (eds.), *Images of paradise in Islamic art*, Hanover NH 1991.

Brett, M., *The rise of the Fatimids: The world of the Mediterranean and the Middle East in the tenth century CE*, Leiden 2001.

Brookes, J., *Gardens of paradise: The history and design of the great Islamic gardens*, New York 1987.

Canto, A., De la ceca de al-Andalus a la de Madīnat al-Zahrā', in *Cuadernos de Madīnat al-Zahrā'* 3 (1991), 111–9.

———, From the *sikkat al-Andalus* to the mint of Madīnat al-Zahrā', in M. Marín (ed.), *The formation of al-Andalus: Part 1: History and society*, Aldershot UK 1998, 329–45.

Chalmeta, P., Simancas y Alhandega, in *Hispania* 36 (1976), 359–444.

Crone, P. and M. Hinds, *God's caliph: Religious authority in the first centuries of Islam*, Cambridge 1986.

al-Dhahabī, Abū 'Abdallāh Muḥammad, *Siyar a'lām al-nubalā'*, 23 vols., Beirut 1985.

Denny, W.B., Paradise attained: The Islamic palace, in S.S. Blair and J.M. Bloom (eds.), *Images of paradise in Islamic art*, Hanover NH 1991, 106–109.

Escudero Aranda, J., La cerámica califal de Madīnat al-Zahrāʾ, in *El esplendor de los omeyas cordobeses: La civilización musulmana de Europa Occidental: Exposición en Madīnat al-Zahrāʾ, 3 de mayo a 30 de septiembre de 2001*, Granada 2001, 398–407.

———, La cerámica decorada en 'verde y manganeso' de Madīnat al-Zahrāʾ, in *Cuadernos de Madīnat al-Zahrāʾ* 2 (1988–90), 127–64.

El-Saleh, S., *La vie future selon le Coran*, Paris 1971.

Ewert, C., Elementos de la decoración vegetal del salón Rico de Madīnat al-Zahrāʾ: Los tableros parietales, in A. Vallejo Triano (ed.), *Madīnat al-Zahrāʾ: El salón de ʿAbd al-Raḥmān III*, Cordoba 1995, 41–58.

Felipe, H. de, *Identidad y onomástica de los beréberes de al-Andalus*, Madrid 1997.

Fierro, M., Bāṭinism in al-Andalus: Maslama b. Qāsim al-Qurṭubī (d. 353/964), author of the *Rutbat al-ḥakīm* and the *Ghāyat al-ḥakīm* (*Picatrix*), in *SI* 84 (1996), 87–112.

———, Espacio sunní, espacio šīʿí, in *El esplendor de los omeyas cordobeses: La civilización musulmana de Europa Occidental: Exposición en Madīnat al-Zahrāʾ, 3 de mayo a 30 de septiembre de 2001*, Granada 2001, 168–77.

———, On al-fāṭimī and al-fāṭimiyyūn, in *JSAI* 20 (1996), 130–61.

———, *La heterodoxia en al-Andalus durante el período omeya*, Madrid 1987.

———, La política religiosa de ʿAbd al-Raḥmān III, in *Al-Qanṭara* 25 (2004), 119–56.

———, Sobre la adopción del título califal por ʿAbd al-Raḥmān III, in *Sharq al-Andalus* 4 (1989), 33–42.

———, En torno a la decoración con mosaicos de las mezquitas omeyas, in *Homenaje al Prof. Jacinto Bosch Vila*, i, Granada 1991, 131–44.

Flood, F.B., *The Great Mosque of Damascus: Studies on the making of an Umayyad visual culture*, Leiden 2001.

Fuertes Santos, M.C., *La cerámica califal del yacimiento de Cercadilla, Córdoba*, Sevilla 2002.

Golvin, L., Note sur un décor de marbre trouvé à Madinat al-Zahrāʾ, in *Al-Andalus* 25 (1960), 188.

Granja, F. de la, A propósito de una embajada cristiana en la corte de ʿAbd al-Raḥmān III, in *Al-Andalus* 39 (1974), 391–406.

Halm, H., *The empire of the Mahdi: The rise of the Fatimids*, trans. M. Bonner, Leiden 1996.

Ibn Ḥabīb, ʿAbd al-Malik, *Kitāb Waṣf al-firdaws* (*La descripción del paraíso*), intro., trans. and study J.P. Monferrer Sala, Granada 1997.

Ibn Ḥawqal, Abū l-Qāsim Muḥammad, *Configuración de mundo* (*fragmentos alusivos al Magreb y España*), trans. M.J. Romaní Suay, Valencia 1971.

———, *Kitāb Ṣūrat al-arḍ*, ed. J. Kramers, Leiden 1873.

Ibn Ḥayyān, Ibn Khalaf, *Crónica del califa ʿAbderraḥmān III an-Nāṣir entre los años 912 y 942 (al-Muqtabis V)*, trans. M.J. Viguera and F. Corriente, Zaragoza 1981.
———, *Muqtabis*, ed. M.M. Antuña, Paris 1937.
Ibn Ḥazm, ʿAlī b. Aḥmad, *Naqṭ al-ʿarūs*, in *Rasāʾil Ibn Ḥazm al-Andalusī*, ed. I. ʿAbbās, 4 vols., Beirut 1980–1.
———, *Naqṭ al-ʿarūs*, trans. L. Seco de Lucena, Valencia 1974.
Ibn ʿIdhārī al-Marākkushī, Abū l-ʿAbbās, *al-Bayān al-mughrib*, ed. G.S. Colin and E. Lévi-Provençal, 2 vols., Leiden 1948–51.
Labarta, A. and C. Barceló, Las fuentes árabes sobre al-Zahrāʾ: Estado de la cuestión, in *Cuadernos de Madīnat al-Zahrāʾ* 1 (1987), 93–106.
Lehrmann, J., *Earthly paradise: Garden and courtyard in Islam*, Berkeley and Los Angeles 1980.
Lucini, M., *La escatología musulmana en al-Andalus*: El Kitāb al-dajīra fī ʿilm al-dār al ājira, *atribuido a Ibn al-ʿArabī*, PhD dissertation, Universidad Autónoma de Madrid 1989.
MacDougall, E. and R. Ettinghausen (eds.), *The Islamic garden*, Washington, DC 1976.
Madelung, W., A treatise on the imamate of the Fatimid caliph al-Manṣūr bi-Allāh, in C. Robinson (ed.), *Texts, documents and artefacts: Islamic studies in honour of D.S. Richards*, Leiden and Boston 2003, 69–77.
Marín, M., *Mujeres en al-Andalus*, Madrid 2000.
Martínez Núñez, M.A., Sentido de la epigrafía omeya de al-Andalus, in *El esplendor de los omeyas cordobeses: La civilización musulmana de Europa Occidental: Exposición en Madīnat al-Zahrāʾ, 3 de mayo a 30 de septiembre de 2001*, Granada 2001, 408–17.
al-Maqqarī, Aḥmad b. Muḥammad, *Nafḥ al-ṭīb*, ed. I. ʿAbbās, 8 vols., Beirut 1968.
Molina, L. (ed. and trans.), *Dhikr bilād al-Andalus*, 2 vols., Madrid 1983.
———, Sobre el estanque de mercurio de Medina Azahara, in *Al-Qanṭara* 25 (2004), 329–34.
Pérès, H., *La poésie andalouse en arabe classique au XIe siècle: Ses aspects généraux, ses principaux thèmes et sa valeur documentaire*, Paris 1953².
al-Qurṭubī, Abū ʿAbdallāh, *al-Jāmiʿ li-aḥkām al-Qurʾān*, 20 vols. in 10, Beirut 1995.
Roselló Bordoy, G., La céramique verte et brune en al-Andalus du X au XIII siècles, in *Le vert et le brun: De Kairouan a Avignon, céramiques du X au XV siècle*, Marseille 1995, 105–8.
Rubiera, M.J., *La arquitectura en la literatura árabe*, Madrid 1981.
Ruggles, D.F., *Gardens, landscape, and vision in the palaces of Islamic Spain*, Philadelphia 2000.
Smith, J.L. and Y.Y. Haddad, *The Islamic understanding of death and resurrection*, Albany, NY 1981.
al-Ṭabarī, Muḥammad b. Jarīr, *Jāmiʿ al-bayān fī tafsīr al-Qurʾān*, 30 vols., Būlāq 1905–11 (1323–29).

Terés, E., ʿUbaydīs ibn Maḥmūd y Lubb ibn al-Šāliya, poetas de Šumuntān (Jaén), in *Al-Andalus* 41 (1976), 87–119.

Valdés, F., Kalifale Lampen, in *Madrider Mitteilungen* 25 (1984), 208–16.

Vallejo Triano, A., Madīnat al-Zahrāʾ, in E. Cabrera (ed.), *Abdarrahman III y su época*, Córdoba 1991, 231–44.

———, Madīnat al-Zahrāʾ, capital y sede del Califato omeya andalusí, in *El esplendor de los omeyas cordobeses: La civilización musulmana de Europa Occidental: Exposición en Madīnat al-Zahrāʾ, 3 de mayo a 30 de septiembre de 2001*, Granada 2001, 386–97.

———, Madīnat al-Zahrāʾ: The triumph of the Islamic state, in J.D. Dodds (ed.), *Al-Andalus: The art of Islamic Spain*, New York 1992, 27–39.

———, Madīnat al-Zahrāʾ: El triunfo del estado islámico, in J.D. Dodds (ed.), *Al-Andalus: Las artes islámicas en España*, Madrid 1992, 27–40.

———, El proyecto urbanístico del estado califal: Madīnat al-Zahrāʾ, in R. López Guzmán (ed.), *La arquitectura del Islam occidental*, Barcelona 1995, 69–81.

van Ess, J., *Theologie und Gesellschaft im 2. und 3. Jahrhundert Hidschra: Eine Geschichte des religiösen Denkens im frühen Islam*, iv, Berlin and New York 1997.

Vega Martín, M., S. Peña Martín, and M. Feria García, *El mensaje de las monedas almohades: Numismática, traducción y pensamiento*, Cuenca 2002.

Viguera, M.J., Los Fatimíes de Ifrīqiya en el Kitāb al-ḥulla de Ibn al-Abbār de Valencia, in *Sharq al-Andalus* 2 (1985), 29–37.

Walker, P.E., *Exploring an Islamic empire: Fatimid history and its sources*, London 2002.

Internet Sources

http://www.abc.es/hemeroteca/historico-28-02-2005/abc/Cultura/medina-azahara-la-ciudad-mas-grande-jamas-levantada-en-occidente_20900171890.html (accessed 9 December 2009).

http://wikilivres.info/wiki/The_Holy_Qur%27an/Al-Rahman (accessed 11 January 2010).

CHAPTER 46

The *Chār Muḥammad* Inscription, *Shafāʿa*, and the Mamluk Qubbat al-Manṣūriyya

Tehnyat Majeed

In medieval Cairo, living with the dead was a fact of life. Likewise, it could be said that Cairo was a dedicated necropolis where the living and the dead were in perpetual communion, continually negotiating mercy and salvation. An exchange of this nature was predicated on two sets of belief: first, that certain pious individuals after death had a great power of blessing or *baraka* which the living could obtain through remembrance, prayers, and by visiting their graves; and second, that the prayers of the living influenced the afterlife of the dead, to the extent that when performed with utmost sincerity, prayers could wash away the sins of the dead.[1] Not surprisingly then, a cult of the dead manifested itself around the numerous memorial buildings dotting the urban landscape of medieval Cairo where the practice of visiting graves (*ziyārat al-qubūr*) had emerged over time. In fact, a whole genre of literature on the *ziyārat al-qubūr* had developed, serving as guidebooks for the proper veneration of the dead.[2] Overall, these funerary devotional trends account for the preservation of Cairo's medieval cemeteries and burial structures.[3]

---

1 In a *ḥadīth* cited by al-Bukhārī on the *isnād* of Adam, Shuʿba, and ʿAbd al-ʿAziz b. Ṣuhayb, Anas b. Mālik notes how the deceased is remembered with his final abode in the afterlife. He relates: "They passed by a *janāza* (bier) and they said good things about [the deceased], whereupon the Prophet said, 'It has become incumbent (*wajabat*)'; and then they passed by another (*janāza*) and said bad things about [the deceased], whereupon the Prophet said, 'It has become incumbent.' ʿUmar asked, 'What has become incumbent?' The Prophet answered, 'Of this one, you said good things, so paradise became incumbent for him; and of that one, you said bad things, so hell became incumbent on him; you are the witnesses of God on earth.'" (Zaman, Death, funeral processions 46). Taylor observes that while in the Quran intercessory power is conditional upon God's will, there is confidence in the traditions about the intercession of the Prophet and "theologians promise that even great sins may be forgiven" except the sin of unbelief which will not be pardoned (Taylor, Some aspects of Islamic eschatology 64).

2 See Taylor, *In the vicinity of the righteous*. This monograph focuses primarily on the Qarāfa cemetery.

3 See Massignon, Le cité des morts au Caire.

© KONINKLIJKE BRILL NV, LEIDEN, 2017 | DOI 10.1163/9789004333154_047

While funerary architecture in Cairo is not a novelty of the Mamluk period and several significant tombs and shrines survive from the Fatimid and Ayyubid times, the high number of extant tomb chambers commissioned by Mamluk rulers and *amīr*s indicates that death and funerary concerns were a major preoccupation of the Mamluk elite during their lifetime. The Ayyubids[4] were the forerunners who established the trend of dynastic mausolea in Cairo,[5] but their architectural preference for institutions of learning was more dominant as they transformed the Fatimid hub of grand palatial monuments that had once signaled power and authority in the heart of Cairo, into a center for religious learning and education. Inspired by Ayyubid monumental patronage, the Mamluk fervently added to the city's principal axis not only charitable educational and religious foundations, but several tomb chambers as well. In a built landscape of grand Fatimid gateways, caliphal and vizieral mosques and commemorative *mashhad*s (martyria), and against the backdrop of the sprawling Ayyubid citadel, Mamluk architectural patronage effectively combined dynastic, religious and social functions with the funerary.[6] The multi-functional complex that invariably included a burial chamber for the patron was highly characteristic of Mamluk monumental architecture. As an integrated component of larger architectural complexes, the tomb was placed, most often, at the forefront along the main street or at street corners. This pivotal positioning of the mausoleum was aimed strategically to gain as much blessing or *baraka* as possible from passers-by. A number of architectural features were designed for this benefit. For example, the windows of the mausoleum on the interior were built as deep niches with large ornamental iron grills opening onto the street. Quran readers would sit in these window niches and recite during the day so that the attention of pedestrians was drawn to the tomb chamber. Moreover, in order to ensure that the tomb chamber was immediately recognizable from a distance, a lofty dome would frequently surmount it. These stone domes raised on high drums served as insignias and showed a wide range of carved

4 The later Ayyubids built *madrasas* dedicated to religious education in what was previously the Fatimid imperial center. Sultan al-Ṣāliḥ Najm al-Dīn Ayyūb (648/1250) rescued the decaying Bayn al-Qaṣrayn which had been neglected during Ṣalāḥ al-Dīn's reign, by founding a *madrasa* (648/1250) following the earlier example of his father's Dār al-Ḥadīth al-Kāmiliyya on the western side of the Bayn al-Qaṣrayn (Korn, The façade of aṣ-Ṣāliḥ Ayyūb's *madrasa* 114).

5 Three dynastic tomb chambers from the Ayyubid period survive in Cairo. These are the tomb structures of *imām* Shāfiʿī (608/1211) and that of the ʿAbbasid caliphs (c. 640/1242–3) in the southern cemetery (al-Qarāfa al-Ṣughrā), and the tomb of al-Ṣāliḥ Najm al-Dīn Ayyūb in the Fatimid city center.

6 Al-Harithy observes that Mamluk monuments were built to serve public communal needs (al-Harithy, The concept of space 83).

decorations from simple ribs and zigzags to complicated geometric interlacing stars and intricate arabesque patterns. In this way, *qubba*, which literally means "dome" became synonymous with the mausoleum. Not only do these countless *qubba*s reflect the Mamluk fascination with the afterlife, but their physical dominance of Cairo's skyline also attested to the increasing architectural attention they received.

In a general sense, while such funerary monuments reflect man's desire to be remembered, in the case of Mamluk Cairo there is a pervading sense that the dead continue to play a vital role in the affairs of the living. In the very heart of Islamic Cairo stands a funerary edifice whose layout, decoration and function provide some insight into this intersection of the spiritual and material worlds in the Mamluk conception of the afterlife. The monument in question is the acclaimed architectural *tour de force* of its period – the Qubbat al-Manṣūriyya commissioned in 683–4/1284–5 by the Bahri Mamluk Sultan al-Malik al-Manṣūr Qalāwūn [Fig. 46.1].[7] A square domed structure measuring roughly 21 m × 23 m, the Qubbat al-Manṣūriyya was part of a larger *waqf* endowment comprising a *madrasa* (college) and a *māristān* (hospital) on a site called the Bayn al-Qaṣrayn (between the two palaces) where the Fatimid royal palaces originally stood. Al-Harithy observes that Qalāwūn's architectural complex was a watershed in Mamluk architecture as it "consolidated the tradition of its predecessors and initiated new approaches to architectural and urban design."[8] The entire complex, built within a record thirteen months, presented an outstanding and innovative spectacle of eclectic architectural traditions. It stood like a trophy, with references not only to the Islamic monumental tradition, but also to buildings in Norman Sicily and those of the Crusaders in Palestine, all by imitating certain architectural features and by incorporating spolia. Hillenbrand astutely observed that "the entire Mediterranean world had been systematically trawled for ideas so as to make this foundation a monument truly representative of its time."[9] Situated on the main axis of the city, the magnificent stone façade of Qalāwūn's architectural ensemble departed from earlier examples of Cairene monuments, especially in its articulation of a series of pointed arched panels with double windows crowned by an oculus

---

7 By late fourteenth century, the Qubbat al-Manṣūriyya included the tombs of al-Malik Ṣayf al-Dīn Qalāwūn (d. 689/1290), of his son al-Malik al-Nāṣir Muḥammad b. Qalāwūn (d. 741/1341), and of his grandson al-Malik al-Ṣāliḥ ʿImād al-Dīn Ismāʿīl b. Muḥammad b. Qalāwūn (d. 746/1345) (al-Maqrīzī, *al-Khiṭaṭ* iv, 516).

8 Al-Harithy, The concept of space 76.

9 Hillenbrand, *Islamic architecture* 330.

in the center.[10] On the ground plan, we see that the central axis along with the inner walls of both the tomb chamber and the *madrasa* were skewed about 10 degrees south for correct orientation toward Mecca, even though on the exterior the structure followed the original street alignment [Fig. 46.2]. A decorated arched portal of modest dimensions provided access into the complex of buildings. It led into a wide corridor that connected the mausoleum on the right side with the *madrasa* on the left. At the further end of the corridor, before approaching the *māristān*, a short passage on the right with another elaborate portal led into the *qāʿa*, a small rectangular arcaded courtyard that preceded the tomb chamber. Al-Maqrīzī writes that the royal attendants (*ṭawāshiya*) gathered in this space which also provided accommodation for those attendants who were on regular duty in the *qubba*.[11] Here, Mamluk officials would have congregated before they made their ceremonial entry into Qalāwūn's mausoleum. Centered within the squarish interior of the mausoleum, the cenotaph was placed right under the large dome. Later during his reign, Sultan al-Nāṣir Muḥammad (d. 741/1341) formed an enclosed private space (*maqṣūra*) by adding a wooden screen (*mashrabiyya*) around his father's cenotaph. This *maqṣūra* was reserved for Mamluk officials. The richly ornamented prayer niche (*miḥrāb*) of rather large dimensions on the *qibla* side is considered a masterpiece of gilding and intricate patterning of mother-of-pearl, glass mosaics, and marble decoration. Complementing the *miḥrāb*, the interior walls are lavishly decorated with floral, arabesque, and geometric patterns and a majestic gilded inscription frieze. Such grandeur set the mausoleum as a stage for dynastic and religious ceremonials. In addition to hosting official events, the *qubba*'s deed stipulated the space for congregational prayers, Sufi gatherings, and for the teaching of the four schools of law (*madhāhib*).[12]

A unique feature of the Qubbat al-Manṣūriyya is its interior layout. Unlike any other Cairene mausoleum, the central square domed plan of the Qubbat al-Manṣūriyya is articulated by an inner octagonal setting of four piers and four columns[13] which along with parts of the decorative scheme, such as the

---

10 The paired arch-windows with the bull's eye is said to have been inspired by examples in Norman Sicily. Hillenbrand, *Islamic architecture* 326; Behrens-Abouseif, *Islamic architecture* 97.

11 Al-Maqrīzī, *al-Khiṭaṭ* iv, 516.

12 Al-Maqrīzī informs us that the *waqf* deed assigned an *imām* to lead the five daily prayers for the attendants, Quran reciters, and regular staff of the *qubba*. In its heyday, he adds, the best jurists were employed to instruct in the *qubba* (al-Maqrīzī, *al-Khiṭaṭ* iv, 518).

13 These then form eight arches that carry the drum that in turn supports the dome which is 11.60 m in diameter. All in all, the dome rises 31 m above the pavement. The rose granite

marble paneling, are considered to be direct references to the octagonal-shaped Qubbat al-Ṣakhra or the monument better known as the Dome of the Rock in Jerusalem built by the Umayyad caliph ʿAbd al-Malik, in 72/691–2 [Figs. 46.3a, 46.3b].[14] Although we do not know of any Mamluk historical source that compares these two monuments in an architectural or decorative context, we know that the Mamluks were acutely aware of Jerusalem's holy significance and the reverence attached to it by their immediate predecessors, the Ayyubids.[15] Contemporary architectural historians of the Mamluk period explain that in imitating aspects of Umayyad architecture, the Mamluk ruler was staking his claim as "spiritual heir to the glory of the Umayyads."[16] Other reasons may, however, also account for this conscious archaism on the part of Sultan Qalāwūn and his successors,[17] if the archetypal Dome of the Rock in any way inspired his mausoleum. We know that Qalāwūn, as well as his son al-Nāṣir Muḥammad,[18] sponsored new commissions and restorations that re-emphasized the sacred character of Jerusalem – sacredness epitomized by the structures of the *ḥaram al-sharīf*, in particular, that of the Dome of the Rock and al-Aqṣā Mosque.[19]

---

columns, according to Creswell, were most probably pillaged from some ancient edifice (Creswell, *Muslim architecture* 192).

14 Ibid.; Saladin, *Manual* 117–8; Herz, *Die Baugruppe* 19; Meinecke, Das Mausoleum des Qalāʾūn.

15 The books on *Faḍāʾil al-Quds* (The merits of Jerusalem) were in higher circulation during the Mamluk period than ever previously (Goitein, Al-Ḳuds).

16 Meinecke, Mamluk architecture 169–79. Flood extends this claim to include most of Qalāwūnid architecture because of its conscious appropriation of Umayyad prototypes in the effort to "transpose cultural context" and search for "images of legitimacy" (Flood, Umayyad survivals 73). It has been noted that many early Bahri Mamluk funerary monuments in Cairo employed glass mosaic designs, marble paneling, and gilded acanthus scroll friezes that were derived from the Umayyad decorative repertoire. But, as Walker perceptively notes, this Umayyad derivation was also inspired by the fact that much of the original Umayyad decoration in Jerusalem and Damascus was restored by Mamluk patrons who therefore would have hired the same craftsmen to work on their monuments (Walker, Commemorating the sacred spaces 34).

17 Although the complex was built during Qalāwūn's lifetime, the minaret and some of the decorative ornaments within the interior were added during his son Sultan al-Nāṣir Muḥammad's reign.

18 A historical inscription dated 718/1318 and rendered in gold on a sky-blue ground around the building of the Dome of the Rock carries a dedication to al-Nāṣir Muḥammad b. Qalāwūn (Tritton, Three inscriptions from Jerusalem 538).

19 Qalāwūn's earlier patronage involved a number of commissions and restorations in the holy cities of Mecca, Medina, and Jerusalem (Meinecke, *Die mamlukische Architektur*).

In addition to the stylistic parallels found in the ornamental repertoire of the two monuments that evoke such historical connections, I would like to draw attention to a set of enigmatic inscriptions in the Qubbat al-Manṣūriyya that may actually resonate with some of the more metaphysical and religious meanings that were associated with the Dome of the Rock.[20] These are the eight large marble mosaic panels[21] in square Kufic[22] writing carrying the name of the Prophet Muḥammad, installed on the four walls within the interior of the tomb chamber [Figs. 46.2, 46.4]. The unconventional formation of the name of Muḥammad and its repetitive rotations make a compositional design that could easily be mistaken for a non-epigraphic geometric pattern. This particular setting of the Prophet's name composed four times as a rotating symmetry within a single square became a very popular epigraphic motif known as the *chār Muḥammad* (four Muḥammads) that was later found on several monuments in various parts of the Islamic world.[23] The Qubbat al-Manṣūriyya *chār*

In 681/1282–3, a few years before he ordered his mausoleum in Cairo, Qalāwūn had built a *ribāṭ* (convent) in Jerusalem (Northrup, *From slave to sultan* 60). Little confirms that Qalāwūn was amongst the six Bahri sultans noted to have made extensive improvements to the buildings of Jerusalem and Hebron and also to have constructed new edifices (Little, Relations between Jerusalem and Egypt 74). The Bahri Mamluks invested in the revivification of the *ḥaram al-sharīf*: Sultan Baybārs (r. 658–76/1260–77) renovated the mosaics on the exterior façades of the Dome of the Rock, added a *miḥrāb* to the Dome of the Chain, Qalāwūn (r. 678–89/1279–90) repaired the roof of al-Aqṣā Mosque, and amongst the numerous refurbishments carried out by his son Sultan al-Nāṣir Muḥammad (r. 708–741/1309–40) was the re-gilding of the dome of al-Aqṣā and the Dome of the Rock (Drori, Jerusalem during the Mamluk period 198). According to Northrup, Qalāwūn's repairs and building works in Jerusalem, Medina, and Hebron were not only to assert his authority over the holy shrines of Islam but also to win popular support (Northrup, *From slave to sultan* 85–6).

20 We must note here that amongst Qalāwūn's numerous grand titles embellishing the exterior main façade of his complex in Cairo is the dignified epithet, *ṣāḥib al-qiblatayn* (possessor of the two *qiblas*) which publicly declares that he possessed not only Mecca, the present *qibla* but also the first *qibla* – the ancestral spiritual center of Jerusalem. For the complete inscription, see van Berchem, *Matériaux* 126).

21 The inscription is rendered in a technique called "opus sectile" which creates the design by an ordered arrangement of finely cut colored marble tesserae on a grid pattern (Meinecke, Das Mausoleum des Qalā'ūn 51).

22 Square Kufic or *kūfī murabbʿa* as known in nineteenth-century Egypt was a highly stylized form of writing predominantly found on Islamic architecture. It is a style of writing inscriptions that originated on buildings in the eastern Islamic lands sometime during the fifth/eleventh century.

23 Persian in origin, the inception of the term *chār Muḥammad* is unknown, but the term has found common currency in Islamic epigraphy. Similar epigraphic designs with the

Muḥammad is the earliest surviving example of this epigraphic type in Cairo. Within the formal vocabulary of square Kufic writing, the text composed of *chār Muḥammad* constitutes positive space, while the area surrounding and defining it that maintains the integrity of the inscription represents negative space [Fig. 46.5]. Each *Muḥammad* makes up a quarter of the whole design, representing a 90 degree symmetrical rotation in each subsequent turn. The four initial *mīms* of each *Muḥammad* are focal to the composition as they emerge from a common centered point of origin. The medial *mīms* are in parallel alignment with the initial ones, serving also as major points of reference for the text. Without these knotted *mīms*, the straight lines of the *ḥāʾ* and *dāl* are meaningless. From the initial *mīm*, the letters *ḥāʾ*, *mīm*, and *dāl* follow in twists and turns to create a design that delineates the outer periphery of the larger square. Fixed at the center and rotating clockwise, this composition is called a "pin-wheel." The intrinsic quality of symmetry and harmony created by the play of positive and negative space maintains effectively the visual and formal equilibrium of the inscription.

In the Qubbat al-Manṣūriyya, the *chār Muḥammad* inscription occurs in two vertically arranged schemes: as a double sequence (123 cm × 60 cm) in panels on the lateral walls [Fig. 46.6a] and in a triple square sequence (215 cm × 74 cm) on the axial walls flanking the *miḥrāb* and the main entrance door [Fig. 46.6b].[24] The geometric concept of the circle within the square that governs the design of the *chār Muḥammad* type is also the ordering principle of the plan of the Qubbat al-Manṣūriyya [Figs. 46.7a, 46.7b]. This fundamental correspondence between the design of the *chār Muḥammad* inscription and the plan of the *qubba* represents the fractal[25] relationship inherent in much traditional

name of ʿAlī called *chār ʿAlī* survive in Iran from at least the fourth/tenth century in a funerary structure commissioned by the Buyid ʿAḍud al-Dawla (Ghouchani, *Angular Kufic* 4). According to Herzfeld, *chār ʿAlī* was a generally used term for square Kufic epigraphy in Iran and Iraq (Herzfeld and Sarre, *Archäologische Reise* ii, 157). I have, therefore, retained the use of the Persian term *chār Muḥammad* in the context of the Qubbat al-Manṣūriyya because this inscriptional type, a widespread leitmotiv in the Islamic world, is best known by this term. We have, as yet, no knowledge about the term used to refer to this specific type of inscription during the Mamluk period.

24 The double type of *chār Muḥammad* became quite popular in funerary and religious buildings in Cairo after its appearance within Qalāwūn's tomb chamber; by contrast, there are no other surviving specimens of the triple sequence in the Islamic world.

25 A "fractal" is a self-similar pattern. Salingaros, who expounds that human interaction with space draws upon the "fractal" properties in architecture, defines a fractal as "a structure in which there is substructure (i.e. complexity) at every level of magnification" (Salingaros, Architecture, patterns, and mathematics 80). Thus, a fractal pattern replicates itself at

architecture where the fundamental geometry shaping the basic plan of the structure generates subsequent divisions and elements proportionately, creating harmony between the whole and its parts.[26] This geometric concept of the circle within the square, like a *mandala*, symbolically represents the unity of the material (square) with the cosmic (circle) – an appropriate metaphor in the funerary context. But, what about the content of the *chār Muḥammad* – what was its significance and relevance to the meaning and function of the Qubbat al-Manṣūriyya?

In popular piety, the name of the Prophet Muḥammad came to offer *baraka*, as the Quran itself affirms Muḥammad to be a source of *raḥma*.[27] Thus, inscriptions that pay tribute to Muḥammad solicit his *baraka* which in the burial chamber was specially invoked for the deceased. By the seventh/thirteenth century, the commemoration of the Prophet Muḥammad in religious spaces had taken several forms following a tradition that became established quite early under the Umayyads.[28] In the funerary context and particularly in tomb

---

different scales retaining the integrity of a fundamental design and its proportions. The "fractal relationship" implies that the observer, at some level of consciousness, experiences the geometric similarities between the layout of the interior and that of the sub structural elements, such as the inscriptions and ornamental motifs.

26 Recognizing the predominance of geometry in Mamluk aesthetic culture, Walls explores the intrinsic relationship between architectural plans, structural elements, and geometric concepts in his architectural analysis of the Ashrafiyya Madrasa (886/1482) in Jerusalem. Similarly, Fernándes-Puertas in his study of the Nasrid Alhambra palace discovered the presence of a harmonious proportional system in ground plans, elevations, structural elements, and decoration (Walls, *Geometry*; Fernándes-Puertas, *The Alhambra*). Kessler points out that the most striking feature on entering a Mamluk tomb chamber is its conscious symmetrical arrangement of elements within the interior (Kessler, Funerary architecture within the city; Fernándes, The foundation of Baybars al-Jashankir 32).

27 "*Wa-mā arsalnāka illā raḥmatan lil-ʿālamīna.*" (We sent thee not, but as a Mercy for all creatures) (Q 21:107). All translations from the Quran in this paper are quoted according to Ali (trans.), *Holy Qurʾān.*

28 Architectural forms as well as certain objects within religious spaces were held to be direct references to the Prophet. For instance, Whelan maintains that the architectural form of the *miḥrāb* replaced the *ʿanaza* – the spear of the Prophet – as the device to indicate the direction of the Kaʿba. And by extension, since the Prophet's role as *imām* was also connected to his *ʿanaza*, with the *miḥrāb* taking over this function, the space in front of it then became a reference to the Prophet himself. (Whelan, The origins of the *Miḥrāb Mujawwaf* 214–5). Flood contends that a similar signification was attached to a stone disc in the *miḥrāb* of the cave below the Dome of the Rock in Jerusalem (Flood, The commemoration of the Prophet 329). And we know that the pulpit (*minbar*) was another item that held specific associations with the Prophet Muḥammad. Within al-Aqṣā Mosque,

chambers, epigraphic dedications to the Prophet directly refer to his role as *shāfiʿ* or intercessor.[29] Though the Quran categorically states that God alone has the power of intercession, it allows for the right to intercede by another, if God so permits.[30] By the end of the fifth/eleventh century, the role of the Prophet as *shāfiʿ* for his *umma* (community) on the day of the resurrection was well-developed in classical *ḥadīth* literature and thereafter remained in vogue in popular Muslim culture. The presence of the *chār Muḥammad* in tombs reinforces the likelihood of its symbolic function as an 'icon' for intercession. Eschatological tradition developed formulas such as the *ṣalawāt sharīfa*, i.e., blessings in the Quran on the Prophet that were recited in the hope of securing his intercession:[31] "*Inna allāha wa-malāʾikatahu yuṣallūna ʿalā l-nabīyyi yā ayyuhā alladhīna amānū ṣallū ʿalayhi wa-ṣallimū taslīman.*" (Allāh and His Angels send blessings on the Prophet: O ye that believe! Send ye blessings on him, and salute him with all respect) (Q 33:56).[32]

In mystical texts, such as *al-Futuḥāt al-makkiyya* (*The Meccan Illuminations*) of Ibn ʿArabī (560–638/1165–1240), we find a great emphasis on the practice of *dhikr* blessing the Prophet through concentrated visualization so that a disciple may be graced by the presence of the Prophet and receive his *baraka*. It was believed that when blessings are made with sincerity and full immersion, they

---

the archaic Kufic inscription commemorating the Prophet that flanked the *miḥrāb* on one side shows an early development of architectural inscriptions with the name of Muḥammad (Flood, The commemoration of the Prophet 321; Le Strange, *Palestine* 100).

29 Even during his lifetime, the Prophet, as related by his wife ʿĀʾisha, would often go at night to the cemetery of Baqīʿ al-Gharqad to pray and intercede on behalf of the dead (Wensinck, Shafāʿa 177–9).

30 Q 6:51, 70; 32:4; and 39:43–4 declare God's sole right to intercession. While Q 10:3; 19:87 (cited below); 20:19; 21:28; and 53:26 state the privilege of intercession to another, as God permits. *"Lā yamlikūna al-shafāʿata illā man ittakhadha ʿinda al-raḥmāni ʿahdan"* (None shall have the power of intercession, but such a one as has received permission [or promise] from [Allāh] Most Gracious).

31 Schimmel, The Prophet in popular Muslim piety 377. "The *ṣalawāt* has developed in popular piety to the most important formula besides the *shahāda* [the Muslim creed] and the *basmala* [the formula "In the name of God, the Merciful, the Compassionate"], and many people will not begin their work unless they have uttered the *durūd* [invocation of God's blessing on the Prophet], which is often used also as a *dhikr* [remembrance of God] formula. It is believed that the Prophet is present in meetings devoted to the recitation of blessings for him ..." (Schimmel, The Prophet in popular Muslim piety 377).

32 Incidentally, this verse occurs in the original text of the Umayyad ʿAbd al-Malik's first/seventh-century inscription in the Dome of the Rock. For the complete transcription, see Kessler, ʿAbd al-Malik's inscription 4.

had the power to draw the Prophet to appear to the devotee.[33] To Ibn ʿArabī, however, it was the Prophet's universal and cosmological status as *al-insān al-kāmil*, the 'Perfect Man' that had to be invoked to mediate between the spiritual and the corporeal worlds. It was on the basis of a *ḥadīth* that mentions the conferral on Muḥammad of the *jawāmiʿ al-kalim* (all-comprehensive words) that Ibn Arabī interpreted the divine attributes whose actualization through Muḥammad indicated "why he will be the master of humanity of the Day of Ressurection."[34] In this framework, the Prophet's role as *shāfiʿ* is submerged within his eschatological position as *al-insān al-kāmil* (the perfect human being). Similarly, another mystic and adherent of Ibn ʿArabī, ʿAbd al-Karīm al-Jīlī (766–810/1365–1408) in his *Qāb qawsayn wa-l-multaqā l-nāmūsayn* (A distance of two bow-lengths and the meeting point of the two realms), counseled his disciples (as his spiritual master had) to combine prayers for God's forgiveness with imagining and visualizing the Prophet whom he considered "the reality of all realities."[35] In the same work, al-Jīlī presents a visual image of the Prophet's relationship to the cosmos:

> All of Reality may be conceived as a single circle divided in two, between the true, necessary, eternal existence and the created, possible, originated existence. Each half of the circle is a bow's length. The line dividing them is the string of the bow, used by each bow. The division of this line is the "distance of two bow-lengths."[36]

Just as al-Jīlī's single circle of reality draws a nuanced picture of the Prophet's spiritual status through the use of simple concrete terms, our *chār Muḥammad*

---

33 Hoffman, Annihilation in the Messenger of God 353.

34 Ibn ʿArabī, *al-Futūḥāt al-Makkiyya* i, 134–5, 144–5, in Hoffman, Annihilation in the Messenger of God 353. Hoffman further recalls that the Sufi *maqām* (rank) of *fanāʾ fī l-rasūl* (annihilation in the Prophet) was associated with visualization practices.

35 Hoffman, Annihilation in the Messenger of God 352, 358. Concerning the Prophet, al-Jīlī writes: "He hears you and sees you whenever you mention him, for he is described by the attributes of God, and God sits with those who remember Him. If you cannot do this and you have visited his tomb, recall its image in your mind. Whenever you do *dhikr* or bless him, be as if you were standing at his tomb, in all honor and respect, until his spiritual substance (*ruḥāniyyatuhu*) appears to you. If you have not visited his tomb, continue to bless him, and imagine him hearing you, and be entirely respectful, so your blessings will reach him" (Hoffman, Annihilation in the Messenger of God 357, note 28; al-Jīlī, *Qāb qawsayn* published in al-Nabhānī, *Jawāhir al-biḥār* iv, 236).

36 Hoffman's exposition on al-Jīlī's text *Qāb qawsayn* provides a visual image of this cosmological status of the Prophet (Hoffman, Annihilation in the Messenger of God 358).

panels in the Qubbat al-Manṣūriyya, as simplified abstract devices, may have been installed to visually evoke the posthumous realities and blessings associated with the Prophet. It is evident that such an enigmatic motif as that of the *chār Muḥammad* panels contained many layers of interpretation. Did the four repetitions of the name of the Prophet rotating on a central point within a single unit of the *chār Muḥammad* symbolically represent the universality of his message that extended in the four cardinal directions of the terrestrial sphere, or did it refer to the more mystical and cosmological dimensions of unity and integration inherent in the "reality of all realities?" No single interpretation takes precedence over another.

If the *qubba*'s *chār Muḥammad* panels refer to the Prophet's role as *shāfiʿ*, these could also have served as a graphic synecdoche of the *miʿrāj al-nabī* (the Prophet's ascension), since the ascension texts inform us that the Prophet Muḥammad received the gift of intercession at the time of the *miʿrāj*.[37] And the reference to the *miʿrāj* brings us to the monument that had come to commemorate this miraculous nocturnal event, the Dome of the Rock in Jerusalem – the monument to which the Qubbat al-Manṣūriyya alludes. According to Muslim belief, the archangel Gabriel brought the Prophet from Mecca to the site of the Dome of the Rock in Jerusalem[38] and there, before the actual ascension to the heavens, Muḥammad performed the ritual prayer with a number of other prophets.[39] After passing through the sixth heaven and

37 The *miʿrāj al-nabī* has continued to inspire and intrigue generations of Muslims throughout the centuries and the story of the *miʿrāj* is found not only in classical exegetical literature, but it also became a popular theme in Arabic literary, mystical, oral, and pictorial traditions (Schrieke et al., Miʿradj 97–105). Al-Jīlī also mentions the *miʿrāj* vis-à-vis Muḥammad's station as the "reality of realities" (Hoffman, Annihilation in the Messenger of God 358). See now also Gruber and Colby (eds.), *The Prophet's ascension*; as well as S. Günther's and M. Jarrar's contributions to the present publication.

38 On his arrival to Jerusalem, Ibn Baṭṭūṭa's first remarks were about the holiness of the city after Mecca and Medina and then he added that the rock in Jerusalem had been the site of the ascension of the Prophet (Ibn Baṭṭūṭa, *Travels* 77–8). Particularly well-developed in eighth/fourteenth-century Mamluk Egypt was also the position of Jerusalem in the category of Islamic sacred topography, after Mecca and Medina. For example, Shoshan recounts that in one section of the text *al-Rawḍ al-fāʾiq fī l-mawāʿiẓ wa-l-raqāʾiq* (The superior meadows of preaching and sermons) attributed to Shuʿayb al-Hurayfish, he mentions an anachronistic *ḥadīth* that on *laylat al-qadr* "the angels carry four banners (*liwaʾ*), one of which they place on Muḥammad's grave, one on Tūr Sīnīn, a third one on the Meccan *ḥaram* and the fourth in Jerusalem (Bayt al-Maqdis)" (Shoshan, Popular Sufi sermons 109).

39 Also inferred to be the site in Jerusalem from the verse Q 17:1 "Glory be to Him who transported His servant by night from the *masjid al-ḥarām* to the *masjid al-aqṣā* which We have surrounded with blessing, in order to show him one of our signs." While the *isrāʾ* signals

reaching the *sidrat al-muntahā* – the lote-tree of the boundary, at the threshold of the throne of God, the Prophet Muḥammad was given the privilege of *shafāʿa* or intercession. The *Ṣaḥīḥ* of Muslim cites a *ḥadīth* that during his audience with God, the Prophet was given three things: "the five ritual prayers, the seals of the *Sūrat al-Baqara*, and the forgiveness of the errors of one who dies a member of his community [while] not ascribing partners to God at all."[40] The ascension literature, we are told, circulated widely in the popular imagination amongst *ḥadīth* transmitters, mystics, storytellers, scholars, and theologians.[41] Thus, Muḥammad's role as *shāfiʿ*, the *miʿrāj*, and the Dome of the Rock are all interconnected in the medieval Islamic eschatological view. All three of these aspects that can be seen through the *chār Muḥammad* motif in Qalāwūn's *qubba* relate to the apocalyptic scenes of the *qiyāma* (resurrection), as well as to the intervening time between death and resurrection. Firstly, Muḥammad is sought for his *shafāʿa* by his community. Secondly, the *miʿrāj* event suggests his closeness to God above all other messengers and provides descriptions of paradise and hellfire.[42] And thirdly, according to medieval imagery, the Rock in Jerusalem is the gathering place of the first resurrection when the angel Isrāfīl blows his trumpet.[43] Jerusalem set the stage for the events of the last days and

---

a journey from one earthly coordinate to another and is symbolic of a soul's lateral development on the material plane, the *miʿrāj*'s upward movement signifies the soul's vertical integration with unity. Thus, in the Sufi tradition, the *miʿrāj* episode was an important reference to the stages in the soul's evolution.

40 Muslim, *Ṣaḥīḥ, Kitāb al-Īmān, Bāb fī dhikr sidrat al-muntahā*, no. 1, in Colby, *Narrating Muḥammad's night journey* 84. In fact, Colby observes that al-Tirmidhī's *ḥadīth* of "this eschatological scene continues with an additional anecdote attributed to Anas b. Mālik in which God explicitly invites Muḥammad to advance intercessory petitions." As reported by al-Tirmidhī: "Muḥammad states: 'I fall to the ground in prostration, and God inspires me to eulogize and praise. I am told, Raise your head! Ask and be given! Intercede and receive intercession! Speak and have your speech heard!'" (al-Tirmidhī, *Sunan, Kitāb Tafsīr al-Qurʾān, Bāb Tafsīr Sūrat Banī Isrāʾīl*, no. 20, in Colby, *Narrating Muḥammad's night journey* 89).

41 Colby, *Narrating Muḥammad's night journey* 166, 171.

42 Based on the resurrection literature, Bencheikh observes that the accounts of the *miʿrāj* and the *qiyāma* are clearly related (Bencheikh, Miʿradj in Arabic literature 101). The scenes of the afterlife that the Prophet witnessed during his nocturnal journey were meant to influence the actions of individuals. In the sequence of his heavenly itinerary as related in the ascension texts, hell was shown to the Prophet after his visit to paradise, which psychologically would have left a vivid memory of the horrific images of hellfire.

43 Schimmel, *Deciphering the signs of God* 2–3. Grabar observes that, "Jerusalem was the main locus for events preparing the establishment of divine rule on earth" (Grabar, *The shape of the holy* 48).

the decorative program of paradisal images of the Dome of the Rock symbolically suggested that it was at the epicenter of the events of the resurrection and divine judgment.[44] The eschatological landscape of Jerusalem was further marked by the Valley of Jehenna toward the east side of the town, and by the Mosque of Ascension that anticipated the return of Jesus which fit into the Muslim 'Last Days' messianic belief in the second coming of Jesus. The *chār Muḥammad* motif, in essence, bridged this temporal and geographical space between Jerusalem's eschatological monument, the Dome of the Rock, and the funerary chamber – the Qubbat al-Manṣūriyya in Cairo.

While the eschatological meanings of Jerusalem were deeply embedded in the medieval psyche, paradisal associations of Cairo were also fairly well-established by this period. During his sojourn in Cairo Ibn Baṭṭūṭa recounts not only the blessed sanctity of al-Qarāfa cemetery, "for it is part of the mount al-Muqaṭṭam, of which God has promised that it shall be one of the gardens of paradise,"[45] but also lists the Nile River as one of the two inner streams flowing through paradise.[46] And it is in the ascension literature that we are informed about the Nile's heavenly connection as it was one of the rivers seen by the Prophet as originating at the foot of the *sidrat al-muntahā*.[47]

Therefore, even though Cairo was not the stage for the apocalypse, its associations with the paradisal world, as recorded by Ibn Baṭṭūṭa, reflects the prevalent medieval notion of the city's heavenly connections. And the countless mausolea within the city and its surroundings were a constant reminder of eschatological realities, in particular, that of paradise and its attainment through the intercession of the Prophet in the present and in the hereafter.

Apart from the presence of the *chār Muḥammad* panels, it is evident from the *waqf* stipulations of the Qubbat al-Manṣūriyya that in appointing an *imām* to conduct the five daily prayers, and *faqīh*s to teach the four *madhāhib*, and

---

44 Rosen-Ayalon, *The early Islamic monuments*. While the Temple Mount on which the Dome of the Rock stands was held by the Jews to be the site of the Last Days and the Resurrection, a *ḥadīth* cited on the authority of two companions of the Prophet, 'Ubāda b. al-Ṣāmit and Rāfiʿ b. Khudayj corroborated that the Rock in Jerusalem was the *maqām* for the throne of God on the *yawm al-qiyāma* (Livne-Kafri, Fadā'il Bayt al-Maqdis 64, note 16).

45 The famous seventh/thirteenth-century Andalusian *faqīh* and *muḥaddith*, al-Qurṭubī, who traveled to Egypt and settled in Upper Egypt till his death, affirmed the Qarāfa's special virtue (Ibn Baṭṭūṭa, *Travels* 45–6).

46 Ibn Baṭṭūṭa, *Travels* 48–9.

47 Séguy, *The miraculous journey* 13, plate 31. A ninth/fifteenth-century illustrated *Miʿrājnāme* produced in Timurid Herat clearly depicts this particular scene at the *sidrat al-muntahā*. The manuscript seems to have been aimed at a larger audience as it is written in both Arabic and in eastern Turkish, Uighur script (Séguy, *The miraculous journey* 7).

in designating Quran readers to sit in the window niches to recite the scripture day and night in the *qubba*, Qalāwūn was unequivocally concerned with accumulating and negotiating as much *baraka*[48] as possible.[49] But maintaining his earthly status after death was of equal concern to him. We infer this from the fact that he chose an old palatial site on the main artery of the city instead of the blessed grounds of the Qarāfa cemetery where he would have been in closer proximity to the numerous graves of saints and pious figures, and especially in the shade of the venerated shrine of *imām* Shāfiʿī.[50] With the positioning of Qalāwūn's complex in the city center opposite the tomb of Sultan al-Ṣāliḥ Najm al-Dīn Ayyūb,[51] Qalāwūn not only affirmed loyal ties to his Ayyubid overlord, but he also stated his preference for more royal company in the afterlife.[52] Moreover, two incidents documented by al-Maqrīzī clearly illustrate that after his death Qalāwūn was not only memorialized as a dynastic patriarch under his immediate successors, but that his image was reinvented as a pious ruler who also served as an intermediary between the two worlds.

---

48 Meri surmises that *baraka* had come to be understood as a quality of intercession and its manifestation required a spiritual and devotional interaction with a concrete physical object, as well as a performance of ritual acts around this object of veneration. For instance, even though the divine word itself held *baraka*, Meri provides the example of the ʿUthmanic codex as an object used to solicit *baraka* especially in threatening circumstances of apocalyptic proportions (Meri, Aspects of *baraka* 46–69).

49 Such pious acts were considered to intercede on behalf of the patron. According to popular belief, even the Quran will "intercede for those who have studied and recited it devoutly, and this hope is often expressed in prayers written at the end of manuscripts of it" (Schimmel, Shafāʿa: In popular piety 179).

50 We know that Qalāwūn had his wife Fāṭima Khātūn's mausoleum (682–3/1283–4) built in the Qarāfa al-Ṣughrā, close to the shrines of the saints Sayyida Ruqayya and Sayyida ʿĀtika.

51 In fact, the mausoleum of al-Ṣāliḥ Najm al-Dīn Ayyūb built after his death in 648/1250 by his widow Shajar al-Durr, is the earliest surviving funerary structure in the heart of Fatimid Cairo. Qalāwūn, following this example, attached his own mausoleum to the religious and charitable institution that he had commissioned. This set a precedence for the Mamluk elite who constructed burial chambers and fit them within public institutions (al-Harithy, The concept of space 83). The physical connection between the two funerary monuments was highly significant, as we are informed that Qalāwūn questioned his architect al-Shujāʿī about why the *madrasa* and not the *qubba* was placed directly opposite the *qubba* of al-Ṣāliḥ (Northrup, *From slave to sultan* 119).

52 In effect, Qalāwūn's *nisba* al-Ṣāliḥī boldly inscribed in *thulth* script on the exterior foundation text of his complex also reflects this spirit of reinforcing loyal ties with, and presenting himself as rightful heir to his dynastic predecessor and Ayyubid master. For the Arabic text of this inscription, see van Berchem, *Matériaux* 126.

It might seem that the presence of the *chār Muḥammad* panels, which can be considered the 'marks of Muḥammad,' extended part of the Prophet's mediatory role between the material and the spiritual to Qalāwūn as well, once the Mamluk ruler was buried in his *qubba*. First, the grand oath-taking ceremony – the *bay'a* of Mamluk officials promoted in Egypt or nominated to Syria – was held at the Qubbat al-Manṣūriyya[53] during which the Mamluk *amīr* would pledge his allegiance at the grave of Sultan Qalāwūn.[54] And the second episode relates to Qalāwūn's son and successor al-Ashraf Khalīl who, in order to fulfill his father's aborted mission of conquering Acre, visited and prayed at his father's grave for success before setting off to battle. On his triumphal return, al-Ashraf Khalīl went directly to the Qubbat al-Manṣūriyya where, along with a host of Mamluk officials and elites, he held a brief ceremony in gratitude for this victory.[55] Thus, through the device of the *qubba* and the presence of specific inscriptional motifs, Qalāwūn, too, became a mediator between this world and the other world.[56]

As for integrating his *qubba* into the larger *madrasa* and *māristān* complex, in doing so Qalāwūn not only ensured its preservation and maintenance, but could also hope to secure recompense in the hereafter, for charitable endowments constituted *ṣadaqa jāriya*.[57] Unlike the *madrasa* and *māristān* which

---

53 Both Qalāwūn's mausoleum and his throne hall in the citadel are referred to as Qubbat al-Manṣūriyya. See Rabbat, Mamluk throne halls 203, for descriptions about the activities taking place in Qalāwūn's official throne hall. Such throne halls were also referred to as *īwān*, for example that built by al-Nāṣir Muḥammad on the citadel. After his demise, Qalāwūn's eponymous tomb chamber assumed a dynastic ceremonial character, and a link between his funerary monument and the administrative center at the citadel was established by virtue of the official processions that started at the citadel and culminated in ceremonies held within Qalāwūn's mausoleum (al-Maqrīzī, *al-Khiṭaṭ* iv, 516–24).

54 During Qalāwūn's reign, this official ceremony was enacted at the grave of Sultan Najm al-Dīn Ayyūb and was shifted to the Qubbat al-Manṣūriyya after Qalāwūn's burial (al-Maqrīzī, *al-Khiṭaṭ* iv, 519–20).

55 Afterwards, al-Ashraf Khalīl dedicated three estates in Acre to the endowment of the Qubbat al-Manṣūriyya.

56 As Wensinck observes, even though the *ḥadīth* literature makes Muḥammad the prime intercessor, "Islam was not content to make Muḥammad the sole conveyor of intercession. At his side, we find angels, prophets, martyrs and even simple believers…" (Wensinck, Shafā'a 178).

57 According to a *ḥadīth*, the worldly affairs of a man come to an end at death but three things will outlast him: first, *'ilm* (useful knowledge), second, *walad ṣāliḥ* (a just and pious descendant) who will pray for him, and lastly, *ṣadaqa jāriya 'ala yadayhi* (everlasting charity which flows from his hands) (Pahlitzsch, The concern for spiritual salvation 337. The author refers to Muslim, *Kitāb al-Waṣīyya* no. 14; Abū Dāwūd, *Kitāb al-Sunan,*

were religious and philanthropic enterprises and legal *waqf* properties, the mausoleum was a personal memorial which in spirit did not really qualify as *waqf*.[58] On its own, the Qubbat al-Manṣūriyya's life might have been really short, and even if, as an independent edifice it was preserved for a time, Qalāwūn's regal status would have been, eventually, lost to memory. By placing his mausoleum within this larger *waqf* endowment and stipulating liturgical functions within it, and adorning it with religious references, such as Quranic inscriptions and in particular, the eight *chār Muḥammad* panels that evoked connections with the *miʿrāj* and the iconic Dome of the Rock, Qalāwūn believed he would ensure longevity for the tomb, and for his own person,[59] and hoped that he might attain perpetual remembrance, eternal glory, God's benevolence, and thus, ultimately, salvation.

Bibliography

Ali, Y.A. (trans.), *The holy Qur'ān: English translation of "The Meanings and Commentary,"* Medina 1992.

Behrens-Abouseif, D., *Islamic architecture in Cairo: An introduction*, Leiden and New York 1989.

Bencheikh, J.E., Miʿradj in Arabic literature, in *EI*², vii, 100–3.

Colby. F.S., *Narrating Muḥammad's night journey: Tracing the development of the Ibn ʿAbbās ascension discourse*, Albany, NY 2008.

Creswell, K.A.C., *The Muslim architecture of Egypt: Ayyūbids and early Baḥrite Mamlūks A.D. 1171–1326*, Oxford 1952–9.

Kitāb al-Waṣīyya no. 14, al-Tirmidhī, *Kitāb al-Aḥkām* no. 26). In this way the *waqf* best embodies *ṣadaqa jāriya* as mentioned in the *ḥadīth*, for which recompense is in the hereafter. Moreover, one could consider that both al-Ashraf Khalīl and al-Nāṣir Muḥammad were Qalāwūn's *walad ṣāliḥ* (pious descendants) as they heeded the Quranic exhortation to secure their father a just reward: "*Khudh min amwālihim ṣadaqatan tuṭahhiruhum wa-tuzakkīhim bihā wa-ṣalli ʿalayhim inna ṣalātaka sakanun lahum wa-llāhu samīʿun ʿalīm.*" (Of their goods, take alms, that so thou mightiest purify and sanctify them; and pray on their behalf. Verily thy prayers are a source of security for them. And Allah is One who heareth and knoweth) (Q 9:103).

58 It would have particularly benefited and thus appeased both the religious elite, the *ʿulamāʾ*, and the general public, the *ʿāmma* – the two sections of society that could have raised objections to the building of a royal mausoleum. At its core, the concept of *waqf* endowment in Islam is firmly based on the religious precept of charity.

59 Pahlitzsch observes that the founding of a public endowment ensured the memory of the patron at an "institutional level" (Pahlitzsch, The concern for spiritual salvation 347).

Drori, J., Jerusalem during the Mamluk period (1250–1517), in *The Jerusalem Cathedra* 1 (1981), 190–213.
Fernándes, L., The foundation of Baybars al-Jashankir: Its waqf, history, and architecture, in *Muqarnas* 4 (1987), 21–42.
Fernándes-Puertas, A., *The Alhambra I: From the ninth century to Yusuf I (1354)*, plates by O. Jones, foreword by G. Goodwin, London 1997.
Flood, F.B., Light in stone: The commemoration of the Prophet in Umayyad architecture, in J. Johns (ed.), *Bayt al-Maqdis: Jerusalem and early Islam*, Oxford 1999, 311–59.
———, Umayyad survivals and Mamluk revivals: Qalawunid architecture and the Great Mosque of Damascus, in *Muqarnas* 14 (1997), 57–79.
Ghouchānī, A., *Angular Kufic on old mosques of Iṣfahān*, Tehran 1985.
Goitein, S.D., al-Ḳuds, in *EI*², v, 322–39.
Grabar, O., *The shape of the holy: Early Islamic Jerusalem*, Princeton, NJ 1996.
Gruber, C. and F.S. Colby (eds.), *The Prophet's ascension: Cross-cultural encounters with the Islamic Miʿraj tales*, Bloomington, IN 2010.
al-Harithy, H., The concept of space in Mamluk architecture, in *Muqarnas* 18 (2001), 73–93.
Herz, M., *Die Baugruppe des Sultans Qalāūn in Kairo*, Hamburg 1919.
Herzfeld, E. and F. von Sarre, *Archäologische Reise im Euphrat- und Tigris-Gebiet*, 4 vols., Berlin 1911–20.
Hillenbrand, R., *Islamic architecture*, Cairo 2000.
Hoffman, V.J., Annihilation in the Messenger of God: The development of a Sufi practice, in *IJMES* 31.3 (1999), 351–69.
Ibn ʿArabī, Muḥyī l-Dīn, *al-Futūḥāt al-Makkiyya*, i, Beirut 1966.
Ibn Baṭṭūṭa, Abū ʿAbdallāh Muḥammad, *Travels of Ibn Baṭṭūṭa, A.D. 1325–1354*, ed. and trans. H.A.R. Gibb, translated with revisions and notes from the Arabic text edited by C. Defremery and B.R. Sanguinetti, Cambridge 1958.
Kessler, C., ʿAbd al-Malik's inscription in the Dome of the Rock: A reconsideration, in *JRAS* 102 (1970), 2–14.
———, Funerary architecture within the city, in Ministry of Culture of the Arab Republic of Egypt (ed.), *Colloque international sur l'histoire du Caire, 27 mars–5 avril*, Cairo 1972, 257–67.
Korn, L., The façade of aṣ-Ṣāliḥ Ayyūb's *madrasa* and the style of Ayyubid architecture in Cairo, in U. Vermeulen and J.V. Steenbergen (eds.), *Egypt and Syria in the Fatimid, Ayyubid and Mamluk eras III*, Leuven 2001, 123–38.
Landay, J.M., *Dome of the Rock: Three faiths of Jerusalem*, New York 1972.
Little, D.P., Relations between Jerusalem and Egypt during the Mamluk period according to literary and documentary sources, in G. Baer and A. Cohen (eds.), *Egypt and Palestine: A millennium of association (868–1948)*, New York 1984, 73–93.
Livne-Kafri, O., Faḍāʾil Bayt al-Maqdis ('The merits of Jerusalem'): Two additional notes, in *QSA* 19 (2001), 61–70.

al-Maqrīzī, Aḥmad, *al-Mawāʿiẓ wa-l-iʿtibār fī dhikr al-khiṭaṭ wa-l-āthār fī Miṣr wa-l-Qāhira*, ed. A.F. Sayyid, 5 vols., London 2002–4.

Massignon, L., La cité des morts au Caire, Qarāfa – Darb al-Ahmar, in BIFAO 57.19 (1958), 25–79.

Meinecke, M., Mamluk architecture: Regional architectural traditions: Evolution and interrelations, in *Damaszener Mitteilungen* 2 (1985), 163–75.

———, *Die mamlukische Architektur in Ägypten und Syrien: 648/1250 bis 923/1517*, Glückstadt 1992.

———, Das Mausoleum des Qalā'ūn in Kairo: Untersuchungen zur Genese der mamlukischen Architekturdekoration, in *Mitteilungen des deutschen archäologischen Instituts Abteilung Kairo* (MDIK) 27.1 (1971), 47–80.

Meri, J.W., Aspects of *baraka* (blessings) and ritual devotion among medieval Muslims and Jews, in *Medieval Encounters* 5.1 (1999), 46–69.

al-Nabhānī, Y., *Jawāhir al-biḥār fī faḍā'il al-nabī l-mukhtār*, Cairo 1966.

Northrup, L.S., *From slave to sultan: The career of al-Manṣūr Qalāwūn and the consolidation of Mamluk rule in Egypt and Syria (678–689 A.H./1279–1290 A.D.)*, Stuttgart 1998.

Pahlitzsch, J., The concern for spiritual salvation and memoria in Islamic public endowments in Jerusalem (XII–XVI C.) as compared to the concepts of Christendom, in U. Vermeulen and J.V. Steenbergen (eds.), *Egypt and Syria in the Fatimid, Ayyubid and Mamluk eras III*, Leuven 2001, 329–44.

Rabbat, N., Mamluk throne halls: "Qubba" or "iwan"?, in *Ars Orientalis* 23 (1993), 201–18.

Rosen-Ayalon, M., *The early Islamic monuments of al-Ḥaram al-Sharīf: An iconographical study*, Jerusalem 1989.

Saladin, H., *Manual d'art musulman*, i, *L'Architecture*, Paris 1907.

Salingaros, N.A., Architecture, patterns, and mathematics, in *Nexus Network Journal* 1 (1999), 75–85.

Schimmel, A., *Deciphering the signs of God: A phenomenological approach to Islam*, Albany, NY 1994.

———, et al., Muḥammad: The Prophet in popular Muslim piety, in *EI*², vii, 376–7.

———, et al., Shafāʿa: In popular piety, in *EI*², ix, 179.

Schrieke, B. et al., Miʿradj, in *EI*², vii, 97–105.

Séguy, M.-R., *The miraculous journey of Mahomet: Miraj Nameh, Bibliotheque Nationale (Paris manuscript supplement Turc 190)*, New York 1977.

Shoshan, B., Popular Sufi sermons in late Mamluk Egypt, in D.J. Wassertein and A. Ayalon (eds.), *Mamluks & Ottomans*, London 2006, 106–13.

Strange, le G., *Palestine under the Moslems: A description of Syria and the Holy Land from A.D. 650 to 1500, translated from the works of the mediaeval Arab geographers*, London 1890.

Taylor, C.S., *In the vicinity of the righteous*: Ziyāra *and the veneration of Muslim saints in late medieval Egypt*, Leiden 1999.

Taylor, J.B., Some aspects of Islamic eschatology, in *Religious Studies* 4.1 (1968), 57–76.
Tritton, A.S., Three inscriptions from Jerusalem, in BSOAS 20 (1957), 537–9.
van Berchem, M., *Matériaux pour un corpus inscriptionum arabicarum: Première partie Egypte*, Cairo 1894.
Walker, B.J., Commemorating the sacred spaces of the past: The Mamluks and the Umayyad Mosque at Damascus, in *Near Eastern Archaeology* 67 (2004), 26–39.
Walls, A.G., *Geometry and architecture in Islamic Jerusalem: A study of the Ashrafiyya*, London 1990.
Wensinck, A.J. et al., Shafāʿa, in EI², ix, 177–9.
Whelan, E., The origins of the *Miḥrāb Mujawwaf*: A reinterpretation, in IJMES 18 (1986), 205–23.
Zaman, M.Q., Death, funeral processions, and the articulation of religious authority in early Islam, in SI 93 (2001), 27–58.

FIGURE 46.1 *Complex of Sultan al-Manṣūr Qalāwūn, Cairo, 683–4/1284–5, Exterior façade.*
COURTESY: B. O'KANE, PHOTO TAKEN OCTOBER 2007.

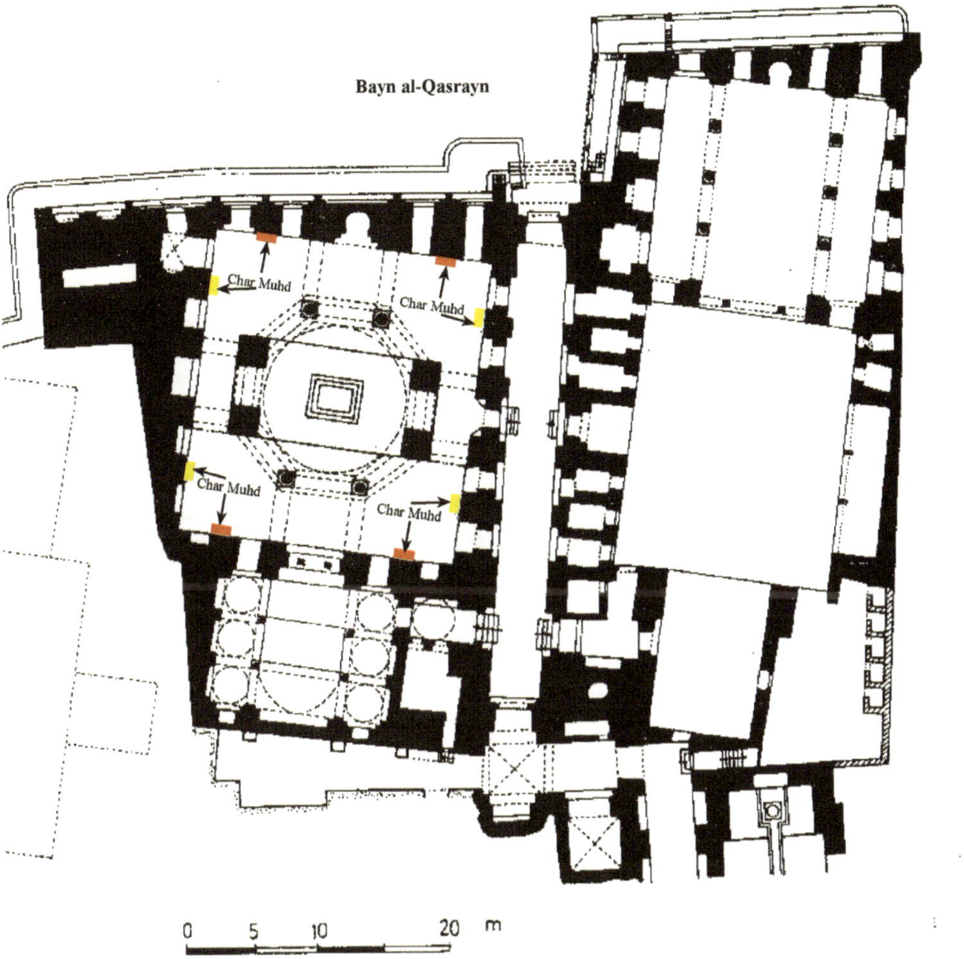

FIGURE 46.2 *Complex of Sultan Qalāwūn, ground plan (Creswell's plan in Behrens-Abouseif,* Islamic architecture *97, Fig. 20); Plan has been slightly modified by locating the* Chār Muḥammad *Panels on it.*

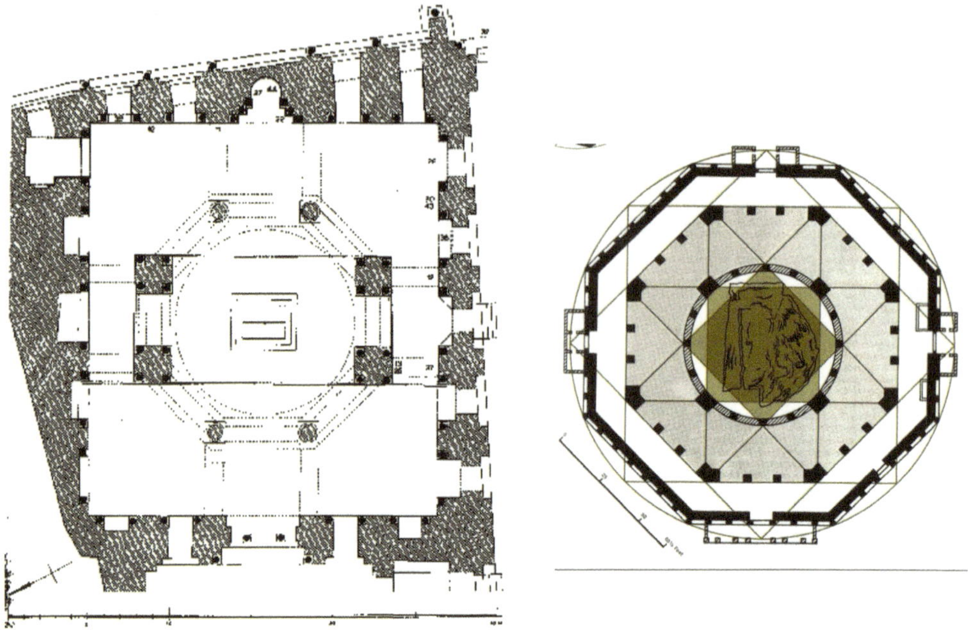

FIGURE 46.3 *Comparison of the 8-sided layouts.*
a. Qubbat al-Manṣūriyya, plan (Meinecke, Das Mausoleum des Qalāʾūn 49, Abb. 1).
b. Dome of the Rock, Plan (Landay, Dome of the Rock *70).*

FIGURE 46.4 *Qubbat al-Manṣūriyya, interior with* Chār Muḥammad *panel.*
COURTESY: B. O'KANE, PHOTO TAKEN OCTOBER 2007.

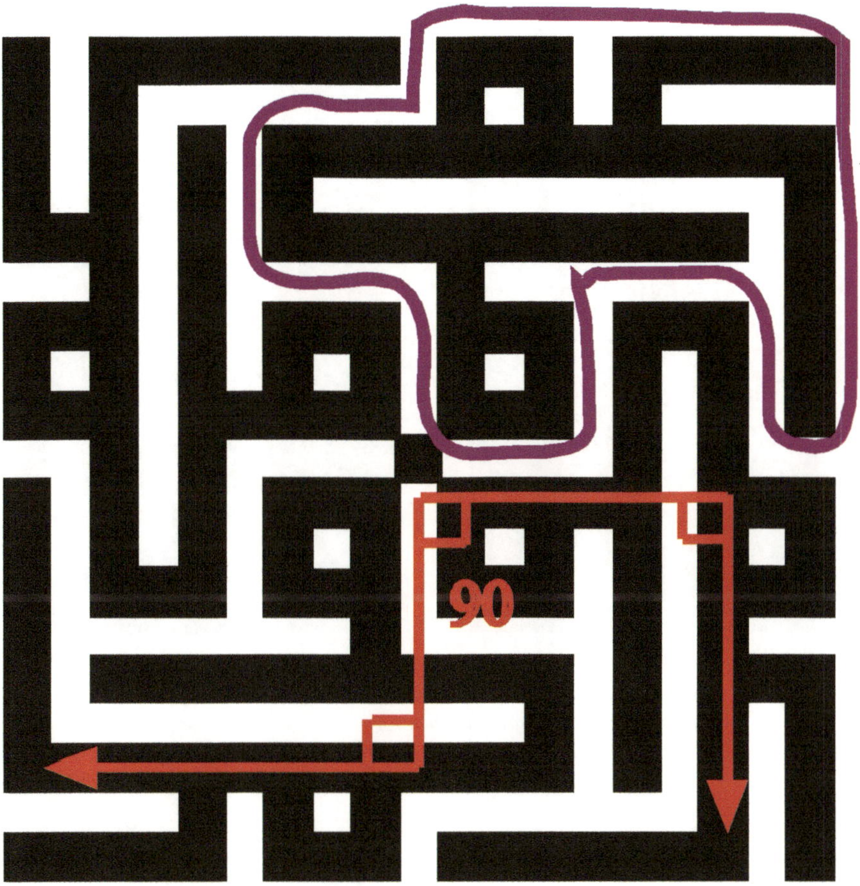

FIGURE 46.5 Chār Muḥammad *design.*

FIGURE 46.6 *Qubbat al-Manṣūriyya* Chār Muḥammad *Inscription.*
a. Double Chār Muḥammad *panel.*
b. Triple Chār Muḥammad *panel.*
COURTESY: B. O'KANE, PHOTO TAKEN OCTOBER 2007.

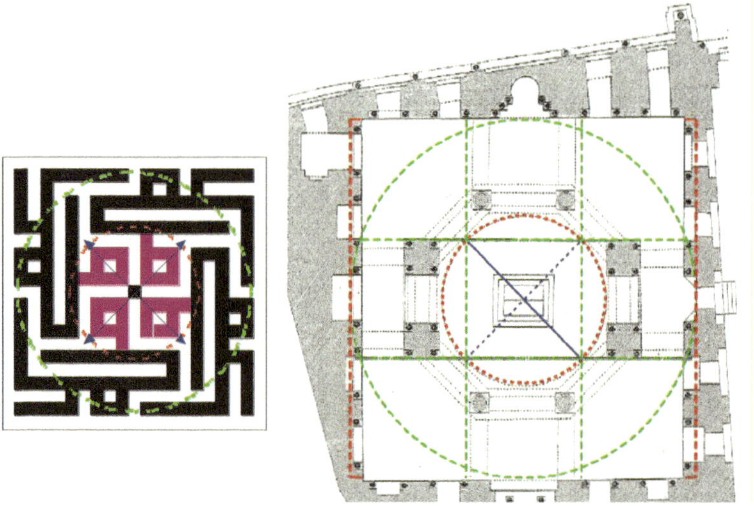

FIGURE 46.7 *Geometric correspondence: Circle within square.*
a. Plan, Qubbat al-Manṣūriyya (Meinecke, Das Mausoleum des Qalā'ūn 49, Abb. 1); plan has been modified with overdrawing.
b. Chār Muḥammad *design.*

CHAPTER 47

Visualizing Encounters on the Road to Paradise

*Karin Rührdanz**

The mystery of the "other world" created as great a challenge to Muslim artists as to artists in other cultures. In medieval and early modern times, imagination focused on this most important concept, and we may take it for granted that people expected it to be visualized, at least to be hinted at in religious spaces as well as in their everyday environment. The banishment of the figure from crucial spaces of worship, however, deprived the Muslim artists, and their patrons, of an important means of expression. For centuries, it left decorative writing as the only way to make well defined religious statements: A calligraphic inscription quoting relevant passages of the Quran, for instance, could evoke paradise directly. On the other hand, secular art extensively used figures throughout most periods. It did not flinch at all from taking figures and depicted elements out of their pre- and non-Islamic contexts, shaking off former religious connotations. Such happened, for instance, in early Islamic times with animal figures connected to Zoroastrian beliefs, and later with the round halo that became an accentuating device encircling the heads of humans and animals alike. While secular art had the complete range of themes and pictorial means at its disposal (including inscriptions), would inscriptions alone do the work for religious art?

Probably they did, and we have to regard the complicated geometrical framework surrounding inscriptions, and the intrinsic vegetal ornament they are embedded in, as pure ornament that enhanced the beauty of the whole. It is in the nature of ornament to lend its support to an idea expressed more explicitly by other means.[1] The concept of paradise (*janna*) as a garden, however, makes it equally probable that vegetal decoration is often meant as a metaphor for paradise.[2] Much depends upon the context. On the wall of a mosque, lavish vegetal decoration invites such an interpretation. As the main motif on

* The author would like to thank the Oriental Department of the Berlin State Library, the David Collection Copenhagen, the Los Angeles County Museum of Art, and the Harvard Art Museums for the permission to publish miniatures in their collections and for providing the photographs.

1 For a discussion of the functions of ornament, see Grabar, *Mediation of ornament*.

2 For a concise exploration of the subject, see Blair and Bloom, *Images of paradise*.

 | DOI 10.1163/9789004333154_048

a ceramic plate it would be much less convincing. However, even when the function of an object or building, the evidence of inscriptions, or particularities of the vegetal decoration itself justify its interpretation as a depiction of paradise, it could be nothing more than an nonspecific allusion to the promise of paradise and its beauty.

Figurative, especially narrative representation may equally invite multilayered interpretation. Figures, however, evoke a more specific context, often a particular event. Since most pictures of paradise, or from the roads to paradise, have come to us as manuscript illustrations their subjects are easily recognized. Besides, figurative representation allows us to address specific elements of the concept and follow the artist's imagination in much more detail. Furthermore, subject selection and iconography are open to a partisan approach that reflects sectarian beliefs and political contexts. This only became possible with the development of book illustration from the sixth/twelfth century, and with the subsequent widening of the scope of illustrated texts that eventually led to the inclusion of eschatological subjects. It obviously remained a phenomenon restricted to the Persianate world. Thus, the material dealt with here belongs to the late eighth to eleventh/fourteenth to seventeenth centuries and originates in Iran, Central Asia, and the Ottoman Empire.

Supported by normative Sunni theology which defended a literal understanding of relevant Quranic passages,[3] storytelling elaborated on the relevant Quranic verses in response to the insatiable hunger of the public for details about the other world and the events that already had happened there or would occur with the approach of the end of this world.[4] On the one hand, artists could easily rely on this common knowledge for their depictions. On the other hand, the doctrine of the fundamental difference between the two worlds[5] made the visualization of the other world impossible – or so one should assume. If objects mentioned in Quranic descriptions should not be imagined as being similar to objects known to people in this world – how to depict them? It seems, however, that this never posed a serious problem to artists as long as society (or a part of society) recognized figural representation as a means to visualize imagination.[6] Transferring the imaginative approach developed for the depiction of this world onto the representation of the hereafter probably implied the simultaneous transfer of the perception that the

---

3 Gardet, Dj̱anna 449.

4 For a detailed account, see Smith and Haddad, *Islamic understanding* 1–97.

5 Gardet, Dj̱anna 449.

6 In Christian discourse, a similar argumentation was turned to work in favor of pictorial representation, see Louth, 'Truly visible things' 22–3.

picture constitutes transformed reality. In this article we look at the other world from three aspects:

1. As the place humankind started from;[7]
2. As it was observed by privileged visitors during their lifetime;
3. As the ultimate abode of humankind.

Paradise as the dwelling place of Adam caught the attention of Persian painters early in the ninth/fifteenth century. Comprehensive historical works usually started with creation and the pre-Islamic prophets. This placed the focus on Adam, the first human being and first prophet. Paradise is reduced to the role of a setting where both decisive moments in Adam's life happened: his elevation by God's order that the angels should recognize his superiority and adore him, and his fall, his and his wife's expulsion from paradise. As a subject for illustration the adoration by the angels appears first in ninth/fifteenth-century historical texts as well as in the more popular stories of prophets.[8] From the tenth/sixteenth century it became a standard subject of the illustrative cycle of *Majālis al-ʿushshāq* manuscripts, a collection of Sufi biographies compiled about 1500.[9] The "Assemblies of Lovers" often portray Adam, who lays naked amidst lush vegetation and is surrounded by prostrating angels, as a vulnerable human being who was distinguished above all by God's grace. Such a depiction does not build upon Quranic wording but rather reflects a mystical approach to the relationship between God and human as would be expected in the *Majālis al-ʿushshāq*. A different iconography was chosen by painters in Central Asia when illustrating the same text in the eleventh/seventeenth century. They placed Adam – fully dressed and haloed, but without royal attributes – in the

7 Whether the garden of Eden where Adam lived should be identified with the paradise awaiting the true believer at the end of the world, was not completely agreed upon, see Gardet, Djanna 449–50. See also A. Lane's contribution in this publication.

8 Topkapi Saray Museum Istanbul, B. 282, fol. 16a, see Karatay, *Farsça kataloğu* 51–3, no. 138. This compilation of histories by Ḥāfiẓ-i Abrū contains illustrations only at the beginning where it deals with the prophets up to Muḥammad. The odd distribution of illustrations points not only to the importance of that part of history, but also to the existence of illustrated "Histories of the Prophets" as models, as, in fact, attested by a fragmentary manuscript, dated 1424, in a private collection. For a color illustration depicting the angels prostrating in front of Adam from the manuscript first mentioned, see Gray, *Arts of the book in Central Asia* 163, plate XLIII.

9 Uluç, Majālis al-ʿUshshāq, illustrations of the subject: figs. 2, 5; Uluç, *Sixteenth-century Shiraz manuscripts* 183–223, relevant illustrations 200–1, figs. 142–3; Gladiss, *Freunde Gottes*, Taf. 1, 3.

heavens on, or in, a golden cloud (Fig. 47.1).[10] Nearer to the common literary descriptions are pictures showing Adam enthroned, sometimes together with his wife, as the illustrations of the "Adoration" in the *Qiṣaṣ al-anbiyāʾ* (*Stories of the Prophets*) always do.[11] This iconographic solution follows the generic theme "King enthroned and served by attendants" and conveys Adam's extraordinary position by using royal imagery.

God's wrath upon Adam and his wife became a subject for illustration in the tenth/sixteenth century, and more so in manuscripts from the Ottoman Empire than from Iran.[12] When the period of Adam's prophethood is visually represented by a single illustration it happens to be the expulsion rather than the adoration. What was it that made sin and its punishment more important than the elevation of the human being? In any case, it does not seem to be a phenomenon specific to normative Sunnism because the relevant manuscripts include texts with ʿAlīd overtones produced under Ottoman rule in Baghdad,[13] and the earliest expulsion miniature (see below) is from Safavid Iran. One may think about an antithesis to the mystic interpretation of Adam's relationship with God,[14] particularly to Qizilbash ideology. Normative Sunnism as well as Imamism insisted on the importance of the individual's record in contrast to Qizilbash teaching which denied resurrection and judgment.[15]

Some representations of the expulsion from paradise allow us a closer look at paradise itself. While somewhat richer vegetation and the inclusion of palatial structures again show the adaptation of royal iconography to this subject, the presence of a peacock and snake (or dragon) introduces a specific element (Fig. 47.2). Both animals had roles in organizing the fall of Adam and his wife.[16] Consequently, in several pictures they were expelled together with the humans who used them as their mounts. As far as we know, this iconographic idea derives from early Safavid Iran where it constituted part of a royal "Book of

10 For a dispersed leaf (about 1600) in the Los Angeles County Museum of Art, no. 73.5.584, see http:// collectionsonline.lacma.org/mwebcgi/mweb.exe?request=image;hex=M73_5_584 .jpg. For a dispersed leaf from a *Majālis al-ʿushshāq* illustrated by the painter Farhad about 1650, see Soudavar, *Art of the Persian courts* 220–1, no. 85.

11 Milstein, Rührdanz, and Schmitz, *Stories of the prophets* 106–8, pls. XIII, 27, 57.

12 For illustrations in the stories of the prophets, see ibid., 108–9, pls. 2, 40, 48.

13 Milstein, *Miniature painting in Ottoman Baghdad*, pls. 10, 17.

14 Pedersen, Ādam 178.

15 Babayan, Safavid synthesis 1–2.

16 On the involvement of the peacock and snake, see, for instance, al-Thaʿlabī, *Islamische Erzählungen von Propheten und Gottesmännern* 39–41.

omens," a *Fālnāme*.[17] Thus, the paradise of the beginning is not a place without destructive elements. In dramatizing the fall of man Shiʿa concepts of retribution, as expressed in Ṭahmāsp's repentance,[18] may have been responsible for shaping the iconography of this crucial moment.

Expelled from, but promised return to, paradise after the destruction of this world, human beings had no chance to find out what they were to expect. Getting an impression of paradise while living was a rare privilege God granted to very few people. The Prophet Muḥammad was one of them. He got a glimpse of paradise and hell during his journey through the heavens.[19] The different stations on his journey were seldom depicted, however. Muḥammad's whole experience of the *miʿrāj* was condensed into one symbolic representation that shows him mounted on Burāq and surrounded by angels crossing the heavens. *Miʿrāj* pictures frequently illustrate romantic poems, too, where they are inserted near the beginning in connection with praise of the Prophet. Praising Muḥammad, the poets often explicitly dwell on the *miʿrāj*.[20] In part, the exclusive selection of this biographical moment for poetical description and subsequent illustration may be because it aligns well with the romantic mood of many *mathnawīs*.

Taking the many explicitly mystical poems and the mystical overtones of several romantic poems into account, it becomes more clear why the stations of the journey are not the picture of choice, but a generic representation of the mounted Prophet surrounded by angels is. The latter symbolizes the mystic journey of the individual to God better than a painting could, particularly one that tries to match the literal understanding of the details of the *miʿrāj*. There is, however, reason to believe that the *miʿrāj* picture also alluded to man's destiny at the end of time. As we see, it definitely developed into a symbol of resurrection, judgment, and paradise in the course of the tenth/sixteenth century.

Isolated depictions of the *miʿrāj* are known from the eighth and ninth/late fourteenth and early fifteenth centuries.[21] Starting with small miniatures that

---

17 This leaf (S86.0251) from a dispersed *Fālnāme* painted about 1550, is now in the Sackler Gallery, Washington, DC, see Lowry, *A jeweler's eye* 128–9, no. 33; Lowry and Beach, *Checklist of the Vever Collection* 138–44; Farhad, *Falnama* 98–9, no. 13. For a similar treatment of the subject in a *Qiṣaṣ al-anbiyāʾ* manuscript, see Farhad, *Falnama* 212–3, no. 65.

18 Newman, *Safavid Iran* 32.

19 Schrieke et al., Miʿrādj; Scherberger, *Miʿrāǧnāme* 11–26. See also S. Günther's contribution in this publication.

20 Mayel-Heravi, Quelques *meʿrāǧiyye* en persan 199–201; Schimmel, *Und Muhammad ist Sein Prophet* 145–54.

21 The early eighth/fourteenth-century depiction of Muḥammad on Burāq about to start his journey is not included here because it appears in a sequence of historical events

show little more than the haloed figure of the Prophet on Burāq (Fig. 47.3), the representations develop into glittering scenes with flying angels among fiery clouds, and with gold and jewels showered on the Prophet.[22] Then, with the rise of the Safavids, ʿAlī, represented as a lion, enters the scene and is usually depicted looking at the Prophet Muḥammad from above (Fig. 47.4).[23] The incorporation of the lion not only alludes to ʿAlī's proximity to God and to his role in the early days of Islam as a courageous warrior, but also to his role at the end of the world.[24] This becomes clear when one of the angels is shown with the seven-armed trumpet that reveals him as Isrāfīl.[25] In another case from late eleventh/seventeenth-century Bukhara, an angel shows a tablet to Muḥammad as he arrives at the throne of God – most probably a reminder of the eventual review of the record of each human at judgment day (Fig. 47.5).[26] It is difficult to determine whether such iconographic developments reflect a simultaneous growth of eschatological meaning charged upon the *miʿrāj* picture or whether the charge had been the same from the beginning and only became more explicitly visualized later.

Different stages of the journey to heaven were depicted in connection with the complete description of the *miʿrāj*. The few fragments preserved of a late eighth/fourteenth-century *Miʿrājnāme* refer only to some moments of the journey,[27] whereas a later manuscript produced in Herat during the reign of Shāh Rukh b. Tīmūr allows us to follow the complete *miʿrāj* as told in this

illustrating the world history composed by Rashīd al-Dīn, Edinburgh University Library, Arab 20, see Rice, *The illustrations of the "World History"* 110–1, no. 36.

Early pictures of the *miʿrāj* are found in two early Timurid anthologies, H. 796 (fol. 4b) of the Topkapi Saray Museum Istanbul, dated 1407, see Stchoukine, La peinture á Yazd, plate VII; and Add. 27261 (fol. 6a) of the British Library London, dated 1410–1, see Uluç, *Sixteenth-century Shiraz manuscripts* 396, fig. 299. To the earliest examples one may add now the copy of Niẓāmī's *Makhzan al-asrār*, dated 1388, in the David Collection Copenhagen, see Sotheby's *Art of the Islamic world* 52–3, lot 30.

22 For two elaborate *miʿrāj* pictures in poetical works, Or. 2265 (fol. 195a) of the BL, dated 1539–43, see Welch, *Persian painting* 95–7, plate 33, and 46.12 (fol. 275a) of the Freer Gallery of Art Washington, see Simpson, *Sultan Ibrahim Mirza's Haft Awrang* 210, fig. 126.

23 Shani, The lion image 305–92.

24 Ibid., 347–9.

25 Ibid., 349–50, pls. 14–5.

26 The illustration belongs to a copy of Jāmī's *Yūsuf-u Zulaykhā*, dated 1683–4, in the David Collection, Copenhagen (43/2000, fol. 10a) and is signed by the Janid court painter Bihzād.

27 Interestingly, they show Muḥammad carried on Jibrāʾīl's back. This may indicate that the story was divided into two parts, in which Burāq is related to the *isrāʾ* only, the journey from Mecca to Jerusalem. For the album paintings, see Ettinghausen, Persian ascension miniatures; Gruber, Ilkhanid *Miʿrajnama*.

Chaghatay translation.[28] Dealing with his delicate task the artist employed three different types of iconographic approaches. In a first series describing the journey through the heavens and comprising more than half of the sixty pictures, one element is usually singled out to respond to the text. It may be a prophet (or prophets), an amazing angel or a strange tree. Other elements of the description are neglected and the figures stand out against a deep blue background filled with golden clouds. These fiery golden clouds are the "wild cards" of the painter. When Muḥammad reaches the point nearest the throne of God he is completely enclosed in such clouds, which fill the picture space. In this way the artist conveys an impression of the most exalted moment while sparing himself the trouble of visualizing single elements of this enigmatic environment.

Another approach is used for the fifteen miniatures that illustrate the treatment of sinners in hell. Set against an appropriately black background, action takes place amidst golden flames. Although monstrous figures sometimes take part, the dirty work of the torture is done mostly by human-like figures (*zabāniya*) who are very engaged in their task. The painter took pains to show different moments in the application of punishment and a variety of postures. As is often observed, the pictures of hell are vivid and rich with ideas about how to torture people.

Before Muḥammad reaches hell he is allowed to see paradise. This vision is given only five images. We must concede to the artist, however, that he made the best of the short text that did not have many descriptive elements. For the first miniature that shows *kawthar*, the river in paradise, he fell back on familiar elements: palace architecture with domed buildings, a stream in front, and fine vessels – only the arrangement was made specific.[29] When the Prophet entered paradise, however, the report mentions only the walking, playing, and camel-riding *ḥūrī*s. For the appropriate background of their activities the painter used the image of an ideal garden, with trees and bushes in full blossom. At one point (fol. 47b) he introduced an element that did not exist in the description: three streams of different color crossing the green plain.[30] One guesses that, here, he refers to the streams of water, milk, wine, and honey of Sura 47,[31] most probably omitting the wine. Apart from this element, the garden could also be an earthly abode reserved for privileged people. This supports the idea that the

28 Bibliothèque nationale de France, suppl. turc 190, see Seguy, *Miraculous journey*. For translations of the text, see Scherberger, *Miʿrāǧnāme* 48–115; Thackston, The Paris Miʿrājnāme.

29 Seguy, *Miraculous journey*, plate 39.

30 Ibid., plate 40.

31 Paret (trans.), *Der Koran* 358.

garden image is always open to multilayered interpretation. It also reflects the artistic problem of how to outdo the royal garden when representing paradise. Clearly, it is easier to allude to paradise while illustrating an earthly garden than to depict paradise itself.

Before we leave the subject of visitors to paradise I would like to mention one other person who enjoyed similar grace. This is Idrīs, a somewhat enigmatic figure, commonly counted among the pre-Islamic prophets.[32] His vision of paradise and hell and his stay in the former place offered another opportunity for illustrators of the "Stories of the prophets" to depict these realms.[33] However, the juxtaposition of paradise and hell in one miniature results in extremely simplified iconography: two angels in front of a green hill represent paradise, and a demon clubbing sinners in fire represents hell.[34] When Idrīs is depicted spreading wisdom and teaching crafts to his children in paradise, this takes place in a colorful garden beside an ornamented pavilion.[35] From its balcony two angels are watching. They feature as the distinctive element in a setting which otherwise could equally well accommodate a princely gathering.

If we look for illustrated manuscripts describing the events at the end of times, one text in Turkish, the *Aḥwāl-i qiyāma* (The circumstances of resurrection), stands out as a vehicle for such pictures. Two manuscripts of the *Aḥwāl-i qiyāma* and, at least seventeen leaves of a dispersed copy are preserved.[36] To this we can add large paintings from Persian and Ottoman *Fālnāme*s (Books of omens)[37] that come with sparse text that only hints at the subject.

At the end of time, resurrection is preceded by destruction. To my knowledge, the illustrative cycle of the *Aḥwāl-i qiyāma* is the only one containing pictures that refer to the reversal of natural processes. Some supernatural actors

32 Vajda, Idrīs; Alexander, Jewish tradition in early Islam.

33 Milstein, Rührdanz, and Schmitz, *Stories of the prophets* 111–3.

34 Ibid., plate XXV.

35 Ibid., plates 3, 58.

36 For Ms. or. oct. 1596 of the Staatsbibliothek in Berlin, see Stchoukine et al., *Illuminierte islamische Handschriften* 229–37. For M. Hafid Efendi 139 in the Süleymaniye Library, Istanbul, see Bağci et al., *Osmanlı resim sanatı* 198–9; And, *Osmanlı tasvir sanatları* 85, 307–9. Dispersed leaves from another manuscript are in the Keir collection (IV.9–21), see Robinson et al., *Islamic painting* 227–8, and in the Free Library Philadelphia (Lewis Ms. O.-T7), Milstein, *Miniature painting in Ottoman Baghdad* 95–6, pls. 1–2.

37 In general about the early illustrated *Fālnāmes*, see Milstein, Rührdanz, and Schmitz, *Stories of the prophets* 65–69, 83–85; Farhad, *Falnama*. For the *Fālnāme* at Sächsische Landesbibliothek Dresden E. 445, see Rührdanz, Miniaturen des Dresdener ‚Fālnāmeh'; for H. 1703 at the Topkapi Saray Museum, see Sevin, A sixteenth-century Turkish artist; for a late copy see Huizenga, *Een fal-nama*.

of the last days, however, are represented in other contexts, too, for example the Dajjāl (the Antichrist), the Beast of the Earth, and the angel Isrāfīl.

A colorful and somewhat enigmatic image of the Dajjāl comes from the *Fālnāme* produced for Shāh Ṭahmāsp (Fig. 47.6).[38] The rider on the mule may be seen as mimicking his opposite: ʿAlī on Duldul, and while he does not look very strange, his retinue certainly does. Human figures with horns mix with people who resemble jesters – or dervishes? And their making music must probably be understood as additional proof of their wickedness at a time when Ṭahmāsp had denounced it.[39] In contrast, the Ottoman illustration of the killing of the Dajjāl by Jesus[40] renders this event as the rather common "hero killing monster" trope.

The Beast of the Earth became a favorite of *Fālnāme* artists. Three pictures from different *Fālnāme* manuscripts all follow the same model: an upright standing figure with the sparkled body of a demon and a human head and wings directly confronts us. It holds a rod in one hand and a ring in the other. The beast is placed in context in the Dresden *Fālnāme*[41] where believers are shown on one side, the damned people falling down on the other, while smaller demons with animal heads watch near the lower border. It becomes more fanciful in Topkapi Saray Museum *Fālnāme* H. 1702, and the humans have disappeared from the picture.[42] In H. 1703 the beast stands alone and is transformed with even more ornamentation. It comes with a leafy dress, without crown, but with golden horns and canine teeth.[43] In this case, we can easily follow the iconographic development the subject experienced over the rather short period of about 30 years from a Persian model[44] to an undisputedly Ottoman creation. The reduction of the composition that eventually led to the complete loss of the visualized context reflects the usual transformation Persian models underwent. Nevertheless, the subject remained understandable for the Ottoman patron. Beyond the typical, however, is the ornamental re-drawing of the beast, in which it is changed from a powerful demon into a decorative

---

38 Los Angeles County Museum of Art, M.85.237.72, see http://collectionsonline.lacma.org/mwebcgi/mweb.exe?request=image;hex=M85_237_72.jpg; Farhad, *Falnama* 184–5, no. 53. The *Fālnāme* H. 1702 at the Topkapi Saray Museum also contains a representation of the Dajjāl (fol. 48b), see Farhad, *Falnama* 288.

39 Monshi, *History* 203; Horn, *Denkwürdigkeiten* 48–9.

40 For an illustration, see Stchoukine et al., *Illuminierte islamische Handschriften*, Taf. 12.

41 Fol. 27b = p. 48, see Rührdanz, *Türkische Miniaturmalerei*, plate 11.

42 Fol. 47b, see And, *Minyatürlerle Osmanlı-İslâm mitologyası* 284; Farhad, *Falnama* 188.

43 Fol. 22b, Farhad, *Falnama* 186–7, no. 54.

44 The miniature in the Dresden *Fālnāme* is most probably of Ottoman origin, too, but closer to an assumed Persian model.

piece resembling the surface decoration on ceramics and wooden panels. One wonders whether this beast should be taken seriously. Or, did the artist merely amuse himself with the elaborate popular stories?

Another important actor during the events leading to the end of the world had been depicted much earlier in a completely different context. This is Isrāfīl, the angel who, on God's order, will announce the resurrection. In most cases, when Isrāfīl is represented in the chapters on angels in cosmographies from the late seventh/thirteenth century, he is shown holding or blowing the trumpet, thus referring to his extraordinary mission.[45] In later Persian and Turkish adaptations of the "Wonders of creation" the trumpet becomes a seven-armed one, but the angel is almost always shown as an isolated figure.[46] Probably because of the impact of this established iconography in the respective *Aḥwāl-i qiyāma* illustrations Isrāfīl is still depicted in isolation[47] although the text would favor more elaborate compositions.

We find Isrāfīl incorporated in extended compositions in the large judgment scenes on *Fālnāme* (Book of omens) leaves. On the painting from the *Fālnāme* of Ṭahmāsp,[48] he is one of three angels present at the moment the records of people are weighed (Fig. 47.7). In the lower half, a group of true believers kneels together with several groups of sinners whose sins are obvious through different iconographic idiosyncrasies. Center stage is taken by the angel Jibrāʾīl (or Mīkaʾīl) with the scales and by ʿAlī who seems to deliver the verdict after consultation with the Prophet Muḥammad. Eleven haloed figures on the top together with a lone halo complete the "fourteen immaculate ones." Here we have an example of a distinctively Shiʿi interpretation of the events of the last judgment.

The painting in the Dresden *Fālnāme*[49] closely adheres to this model, with interesting modifications, however. In the center, flanked by Muḥammad on the right and Isrāfīl on the left, we see again the angel with the scales and ʿAlī b. Abī Ṭālib. On the top, the painter knowingly or unknowingly distorted the

45 For an early example, still showing Isrāfīl blowing a simple trumpet, compare a leaf from Qazwini's *Ajāʾib al-makhlūqāt*, Freer Gallery of Art Washington, 54.51, see Ettinghausen, *Arab painting* 178.

46 Compare leaf 14.599 at the Museum of Fine Arts Boston, see Blair and Bloom, *Images of paradise* 10, no. 16a.

47 From the Ms. M. Hafid Efendi 139 (fol. 22a) in the Süleymaniye Library Istanbul, see Bağci et al., *Osmanlı resim sanatı* 199, fig. 161; among the leaves in the Keir Collection no. IV.18, see Robinson, *Islamic painting*, color plate 28.

48 Harvard University Art Museums, 1999.302, see Farhad, *Falnama* 190–1, no. 55.

49 Fol. 19b = p. 64, see Rührdanz, Die Miniaturen des Dresdener ‚Fālnāmeh', Abb. 4; Farhad, *Falnama* 66.

composition: There he placed seven haloed figures (none of them veiled), one lone halo, and part of a building from which two angels look out. Since haloed unveiled figures usually represent pre-Islamic prophets, we now get a glance of paradise with prophets and angels (although the floating halo is somewhat disturbing). The iconographic modification seems to transform the Shiʿi claim into a Sunni pro-ʿAlīd interpretation which was acceptable in Ottoman lands in the later tenth/sixteenth century.

Another change was introduced at the bottom of the painting in the Dresden *Fālnāme* where a horrible oversized demon and other monsters deal with the sinners in a sea of fire. The Turkish *Fālnāme* H. 1703 does not contain a picture of the judgment or paradise, but one of hell (fol. 21b) that shows two demons, and people tortured and perishing. The pictorial material again underlines the familiar observation: Thinking of hell must have occupied people much more than thinking of paradise, and they were encouraged to do so by explicit pictures no less than by drastic rhetoric.[50] This is even more evident in the illustrations of the *Aḥwāl-i qiyāma.*

Before focusing on hell and paradise in these Ottoman manuscripts, an *Aḥwāl-i qiyāma* picture, which seems to be inspired by the above described judgment scene, should be mentioned. There we have angels including Jibrāʾīl with the scales, the Prophet Muḥammad, and sinners taken away and tortured by demons.[51] Any ʿAlīd elements have disappeared, as one would expect in a manuscript from this time: the artist has gone to great lengths to incorporate the first three caliphs, Abū Bakr, ʿUmar, and ʿUthmān together with other champions of Sunni Islam into illustrations featuring the Prophet Muḥammad. Those three caliphs accompany him, for instance, when the Prophet appears after resurrection![52]

In the sequence of events leading to the judgment in the *Aḥwāl-i qiyāma*, scenes of fearful and hopeful expectations alternate with depictions of sudden attacks by demons and monsters.

When the people have moved to the gathering place (*maḥshar*) where they have to wait for a thousand years they experience a taste of punishment or reward: the believers will not suffer from the heat of the sun while the sinners will.[53] Later it rains scrolls on the crowd (Fig. 47.8).[54] The white scrolls are for

---

50 See for example N. Christie's contribution to the present publication.

51 Compare the description of IV.13 in the Keir Collection, see Robinson, *Islamic painting* 228.

52 For an illustration, see Stchoukine et al., *Illuminierte islamische Handschriften*, Taf. 53.

53 And, *Osmanlı tasvir sanatları* 309.

54 Ibid., 308.

the good people, the black ones for the lost ones, including unbelievers and Muslims who sinned.

Depicting these two events the painter of the Istanbul manuscript transferred the mixed crowd into an unspecified but promising land by using a shining golden background. Replacing the gold with two shades of pale blue in the Berlin *Aḥwāl-i qiyāma* the artist may have intended to evoke the character of this no-man's land through the color of the sky.[55] That the resurrected people appear already neatly divided into "good" and "bad" could also point to a more rigid, narrow-minded approach to peoples' chances of salvation. The picture of paradise that is preserved in three versions[56] seems to speak to an interpretive shift, too. Of two illustrations showing happy couples walking and playing among large trees and rich pavilions in the more elaborate one in the Istanbul *Aḥwāl-i qiyāma* they are also drinking wine. Four streams – one of them reddish in color – diagonally cross the space. Visualizing the paradisal environment strictly according to common descriptions, this picture focuses on the reward and enjoyment of the believer. In contrast, the respective miniature in the Berlin manuscript (Fig. 47.9) represents paradise in a sparse composition as a place for men only whose pleasure is to worship, not to enjoy a leisurely life.

Bibliography

Alexander, Ph.S., Jewish tradition in early Islam: The case of Enoch/Idrīs, in G.R. Hawting, J.A. Mojaddedi and A. Samely (eds.), *Studies in Islamic and middle eastern texts and traditions in memory of Norman Calder*, Oxford, New York 2000, 11–29.

And, M., *Minyatürlerle Osmanlı-İslām mitologyası*, Istanbul 1998.

———, *Osmanlı tasvir sanatları*, Istanbul 2002.

Babayan, K., The Safavid synthesis: From Qizilbash Islam to Imamite Shi'ism, in *Iranian Studies* 27 (1994), 135–61.

Bağci, S. et al., *Osmanlı resim sanatı*, Istanbul 2006.

Blair, S.S. and J.M. Bloom, *Images of paradise in Islamic art*, Hanover NH 1991.

Ettinghausen, R., *Arab painting*, Geneva 1962.

55 This choice also provided him with a less expensive alternative to the gold.

56 For the Istanbul manuscript, see And, *Osmanlı tasvir sanatları* 85; Bağci et al., *Osmanlı resim sanatı* 198, fig. 160; for a dispersed leaf in the Free Library, see Milstein, *Miniature painting in Ottoman Baghdad*, plate 2.

———, Persian ascension miniatures of the fourteenth century, (repr.) in R. Ettinghausen, *Islamic art and archaeology collected papers*, ed. M. Rosen-Ayalon, Berlin 1984, 244–267.
Farhad, M. with S. Bağci, *Falnama: The book of omens*, Washington, DC 2009.
Gardet, L., Djanna, in *EI*², ii, 447–52.
Gladiss, A. v., *Die Freunde Gottes: Die Bilderwelt einer persischen Luxushandschrift*, Berlin 2005.
Grabar, O., *The mediation of ornament*, Princeton, NJ 1992.
Gray, B. (ed.), *The arts of the book in Central Asia 14th – 16th centuries*, Paris and London 1979.
Gruber, Ch., The Ilkhanid *Miʿrajnama* as an illustrated Sunni prayer manual, in Ch. Gruber and F. Colby (eds.), *The prophet's ascension: Cross-cultural encounters with the Islamic miʿraj tales*, Bloomington and Indianapolis 2010, 27–49.
Horn, P. (trans.), *Die Denkwürdigkeiten Schah Tahmasp's des Ersten von Persien*, Straßburg 1891.
Huizenga, D., *Een fal-nama: Een voorstudie van het manuscript in het Museum voor Volkenkunde te Rotterdam [A fal-nama: A preliminary study of the manuscript in the Museum voor Volkenkunde in Rotterdam]*, PhD dissertation, University at Groningen 1996.
Karatay F.E., *Topkapı Sarayı Müzesi Kütüphanesi Farsça kataloğu*, Istanbul 1961.
Louth, A., 'Truly visible things are manifest images of invisible things': Dionysios the Areopagite on knowing the invisible, in G. de Nie, K.F. Morrison, and M. Mostert (eds.), *Seeing the invisible in late antiquity and the early middle ages*, Turnhout 2005, 15–24.
Lowry, G.D., *A jeweler's eye*, Washington, DC 1988.
——— and M.C. Beach, *An annotated and illustrated checklist of the Vever Collection*, Washington 1988.
Mayel-Heravi, N., Quelques *meʿrāğiyye* en persan, in M.A. Amir-Moezzi (dir.), *Le Voyage initiatique en terre d'Islam: Ascensions célestes et itinéraires spirituels*, Leuven and Paris 1996, 199–203.
Milstein, R., *Miniature painting in Ottoman Baghdad*, Costa Mesa, CA 1990.
———, K. Rührdanz and B. Schmitz, *Stories of the prophets: Illustrated manuscripts of Qiṣaṣ al-Anbiyāʾ*, Costa Mesa, CA 1999.
Monshi, E.B., *History of Shah ʿAbbas the Great*, trans. R.M. Savory, Boulder, CO 1978.
Newman, A.J., *Safavid Iran: Rebirth of a Persian empire*, London and New York 2006.
Paret, R. (trans.), *Der Koran*, Stuttgart, Berlin and Cologne 1989⁵.
Pedersen, J., Ādam, in *EI*², i, 176–8.
Rice, D.T., *The illustrations of the "World History" of Rashīd al-Dīn*, ed. B. Gray, Edinburgh 1976.
Robinson, B.W. et al., *Islamic painting and the arts of the book*, London 1976.
Rührdanz, K., Die Miniaturen des Dresdener ‚Fālnāmeh', in *Persica* 12 (1987), 1–56.

———, *Türkische Miniaturmalerei*, Leipzig 1988.

Scherberger, M., *Das Miʿrāğnāme: Die Himmel- und Höllenfahrt des Propheten Muhammad in der osttürkischen Überlieferung*, Würzburg 2003.

Schimmel, A., *Und Muhammad ist Sein Prophet: Die Verehrung des Propheten in der islamischen Frömmigkeit*, Düsseldorf and Cologne 1981.

Schrieke, B.J. et al., Miʿrādj̲, in EI², vii, 97–105.

Seguy, M.-R., *The miraculous journey of Mahomet: Mirāj Nāmeh*, New York 1977.

Sevin, N., A sixteenth-century Turkish artist whose miniatures were attributed to Kalender Paşa, in *IVᵉ Congrès International d'Art Turc 1971*, Aix-en-Provence 1976, 209–16.

Shani, R.Y., The lion image in Safavid *Miʿraj* paintings, in A. Daneshvari (ed.), *A survey of Persian art*, xviii, *Islamic Period*, Costa Mesa, CA 2005, 265–426.

Simpson, M.S., *Sultan Ibrahim Mirza's Haft Awrang: A princely manuscript from sixteenth-century Iran*, New Haven, CT and London 1999.

Smith, J.I. and Y.Y. Haddad, *The Islamic understanding of death and resurrection*, Oxford and New York 2002.

Soudavar, A., *Art of the Persian courts*, New York 1992.

Sotheby's, *Art of the Islamic world*, London, 9 April 2008.

Stchoukine, I. et al., *Illuminierte islamische Handschriften*, Wiesbaden 1971.

———, La peinture à Yazd au début du XVᵉ siècle, in *Syria* 43 (1966), 99–104.

Thackston, W.M., The Paris Miʿrājnāme, in *Journal of Turkish Studies* 18 (1994), 263–99.

al-Thaʿlabī, Aḥmad b. Muḥammad, *Islamische Erzählungen von Propheten und Gottesmännern: Qiṣaṣ al-anbiyāʾ oder ʿArāʾis al-majālis von Abū Isḥāq Aḥmad b. Muḥammad b. Ibrāhīm at-Thaʿlabī*, übers., komm. H. Busse, Wiesbaden 2006.

Uluç, L., The Majālis al-ʿUshshāq: Written in Herat, copied in Shiraz, read in Istanbul, in I.C. Schick (ed.), *M. Uğur Derman armağanı*, Istanbul 2000, 569–602.

———, *Turkman governors, Shiraz artisans and Ottoman collectors: Sixteenth-century Shiraz manuscripts*, Istanbul 2006.

Vajda, G., Idrīs, in EI², iii, 1030–31.

Welch, St.C., *Persian painting: Five royal Safavid manuscripts of the sixteenth century*, New York 1976.

Internet Sources

http://collectionsonline.lacma.org (accessed 1 May 2010).

FIGURE 47.1 *Angels adoring Adam, page from a dispersed manuscript of the* Majālis al-ʿushshāq, *Bukhara, ca. 1600. Los Angeles County Museum of Art, M.73.5.584.*

FIGURE 47.2 *Expulsion from paradise*, Qiṣaṣ al-anbiyāʾ, *Istanbul?, 1577. Staatsbibliothek zu Berlin, Diez A Fol. 3, fol. 13b.*

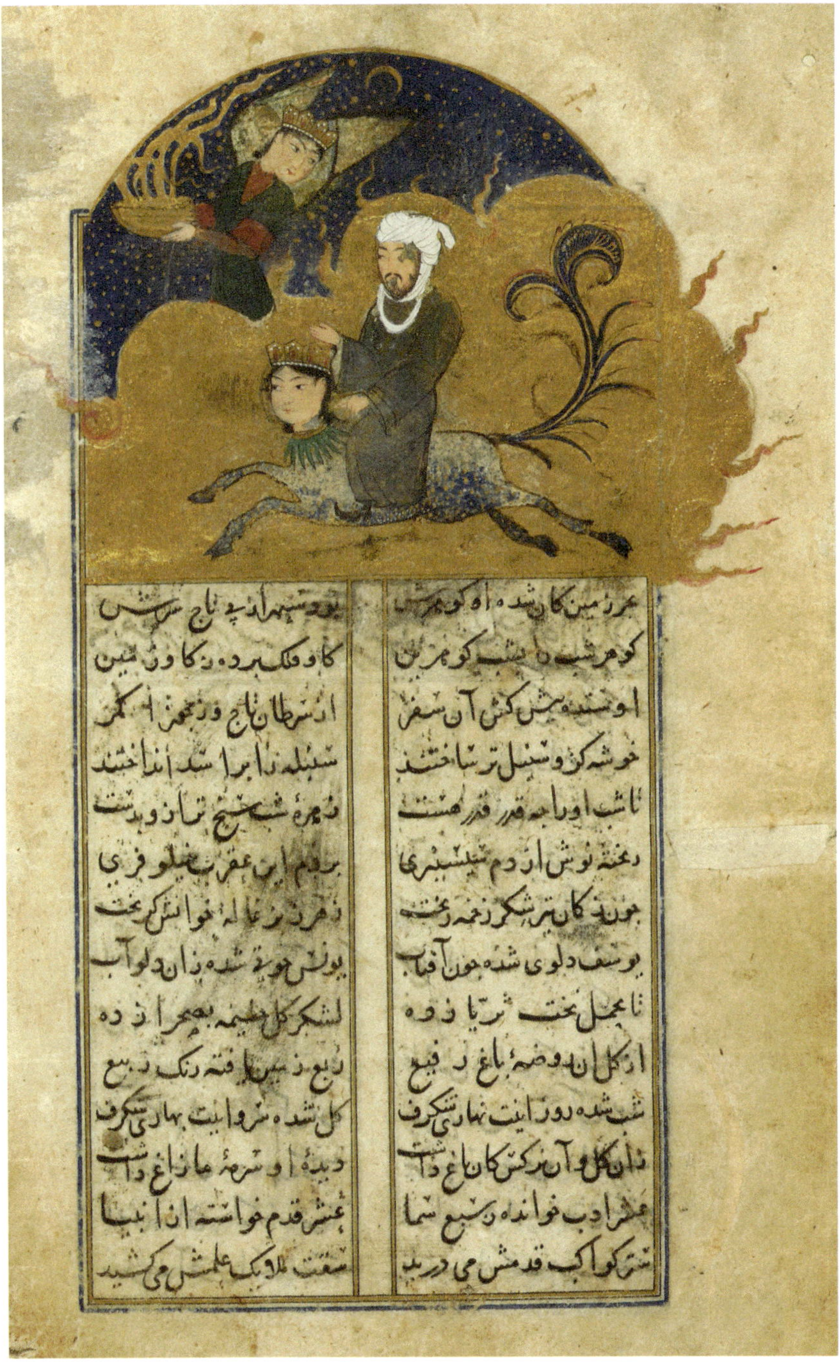

FIGURE 47.3 Miʿrāj, *Niẓāmī*, Makhzan al-asrār, *Baghdad?, 1388. David Collection Copenhagen, Ms. 20/2008, fol. 4b.*
PHOTOGRAPH BY PERNILLE KLEMP.

FIGURE 47.4 Miʿrāj, Qiṣaṣ al-anbiyāʾ, *Istanbul?, 1577. Staatsbibliothek zu Berlin, Diez A Fol. 3, fol. 226b.*

FIGURE 47.5 Miʿrāj, *Jāmī,* Yūsuf-u Zulaykhā, *Bukhara, 1683. David Collection Copenhagen, Ms. 43/2000, fol. 10a.*
PHOTOGRAPH BY PERNILLE KLEMP.

FIGURE 47.6 *Entry of the Dajjāl (Antichrist) into Jerusalem, page from a dispersed* Fālnāme *manuscript, Qazwin?, ca. 1560. Los Angeles County Museum of Art, M.85.237.72.*

FIGURE 47.7 *Last Judgment, page from a dispersed* Fālnāme *manuscript, Qazwin?, ca. 1560. Arthur M. Sackler Museum, 1999.302.*

FIGURE 47.8 *Records raining from the sky,* Aḥwāl-i qiyāma, *Istanbul, early seventeenth century. Staatsbibliothek zu Berlin, Ms. or. Oct. 1596, 34b.*

FIGURE 47.9 *In paradise,* Aḥwāl-i qiyāma, *Istanbul, early seventeenth century. Staatsbibliothek zu Berlin, Ms. or. Oct. 1596, 41a.*

CHAPTER 48

Images of Paradise in Popular Shiʿite Iconography

Ulrich Marzolph

In the visual expression of the Muslim world, paradise is the pivotal notion of bounty and happiness untroubled by the concerns and worries of human existence. As such, it is the ultimate reward for the true believer.[1] Meanwhile, Shiʿite Muslim imagery in general is dominated by the event of martyrdom, in particular the martyrdom of the Prophet's grandson Ḥusayn and his followers at Karbala.[2] Undoubtedly, Shiʿite imagery has undergone a certain development over the centuries. Today, few images could represent the modern Iranian interpretation of Shiʿite identity more specifically than, say, the depiction of Yazīd b. Muʿāwiya's troops parading Ḥusayn's severed head at Karbala, such as shown in a drawing illustrating the scene in a nineteenth-century lithographed edition of Sarbāz Burūjirdī's martyrological book *Asrār al-shahāda* (The spiritual realities of martyrdom)[3] or Iranian artist Maḥmūd Farshchiyān's famous modern painting of Ḥusayn's wounded horse returning to the wailing women at the camp without its master, a large version of which was temporarily installed in 2008 at the street crossing north of Tehran's Lālah Park.[4] Considering the impact of Ḥusayn's fate as the quintessential expression of martyrdom for Shiʿite Islam, there is little surprise that the Shiʿite imagery of paradise, in both learned and popular contexts, is no exception to the above mentioned rule: martyrdom is a direct way to paradise, and paradise is the ultimate reward for the martyr.[5]

The two areas of popular Shiʿite Islamic imagery I wish to consider briefly in the following both illustrate this belief in different, though ultimately connected ways. First, I discuss the depiction of paradise as part of the cumulative representation of the battle of Karbala (in 61/680) produced in the Qajar

1 Blair and Bloom, *Images of paradise*.

2 Aghaei, *Martyrs*; Newid, *Der schiitische Islam*; Varzi, *Warring souls*; Flaskerud, *Visualizing belief and piety*; see also Chelkowski and Dabashi, *Staging a revolution* 44–65.

3 Marzolph, *Narrative illustration* 101, fig. 37; see also Marzolph, Pictorial representation.

4 See Puin, *Islamische Plakate* ii, 458–60, and iii, 860, no. G-16.

5 On historical and contemporary notions of martyrdom in Islam see, e.g., Khosrokhavar, *L'Islamisme*; Khosrokhavar, *Les nouveaux martyrs*; Mayeur-Jaouen, *Saints et héros*; Neuwirth, Blut und Mythos.

 | DOI 10.1163/9789004333154_049

period. My examples include the tilework installed on commemorative buildings such as the Ḥusayniyyah-yi Mushīr, erected in 1876 by the wealthy philanthropist Mīrzā ʿAbd al-Ḥasan Mushīr al-Mulk (Fig. 48.1), or the Imāmzādah-yi Ibrāhīm in Shiraz[6] and the large canvasses that used to serve as prompts for professional storytellers performing in the streets and marketplaces well into the twentieth century.[7] Second, I discuss images of paradise incorporated into modern murals, many of which have been installed in recent years on the windowless walls of large buildings in the Tehran cityscape.[8] The extent to which any of these areas may or may not be adequately termed "popular" is open for discussion. The depictions of the battle of Karbala, on the one side, may be regarded as "popular" since they satisfy the demand of large gatherings of people from various strata of society commemorating the tragedy of Karbala by listening to, watching or actively partaking in live performances, whether recited or acted on stage. The murals, on the other side, might be regarded as a kind of "intentional folklore" (often termed "propaganda") insofar as they have been installed by state-subsidized institutions such as the powerful Bunyād-i shahīd (The Martyr's Foundation). Their aim is to keep alive and firmly root the memory of recent martyrs within present and future society, predominantly the memory of those men that lost their lives during the so-called "imposed" war of defense against the neighboring country of Iraq, as model characters of true Shiʿite behavior.

In the images of the battle of Karbala prepared in the Qajar period, both the scenes on tilework and on canvas depict a number of the battle's well-known scenes, such as Ḥusayn lamenting the death of his son ʿAlī Akbar, Ḥusayn bidding the women farewell while holding his son ʿAlī Aṣghar, and Ḥusayn attacking the enemy. In addition, the depictions regularly feature a vision of the hereafter. While in the tilework images considered here, this vision is placed in an arching area above the battle scenes, in the images on canvas it is regularly put on the image's upper side. The images on canvas concentrate on the battle scenes that are usually displayed around a central image of Ḥusayn attacking the enemy, and depict the image of the hereafter, sometimes in a truncated version, showing hell below and paradise above, separated by the *pul-i ṣirāṭ*, the narrow bridge that the dead must cross in order to be directed to either

6 Humāyūnī, *Ḥusayniyyah-yi Mushīr*; Ansari, *Malerei* 254, no. 54; Fontana, *Ahl al-Bayt*, fig. 58; And, *Ritüelden drama* 310; Chelkowski and Dabashi, *Staging a revolution* 62–3; Chelkowski, Patronage and piety 95; Newid, *Der schiitische Islam* 250; see also Mīrzāʾī Mihr, *Naqqāshīhā*.

7 Sayf, *Naqqāshī*; Ardalān, *Murshidān*; see also Floor, *Theater*, particularly 119–23.

8 Marzolph, The martyr's way to paradise; Chehabi and Christia, The art of state persuasion; Gruber, Mural arts; Karimi, Tehran's post Iran-Iraq war murals.

hell or paradise according to their respective merits. Full versions of this scene, such as those depicted on tilework or single images on canvas, include an array of dead people clad in white shrouds and waiting for their deeds to be evaluated. Paradise is here placed at the upper left or the upper right side of the image, relying on a small but fairly regular set of components (Fig. 48.2).[9]

In the lower center of the image representing paradise there is a small water basin, sometimes with a gushing fountain. This basin represents *kawthar*, the paradisal spring or well of water. Behind the water basin there is a tree in whose top branches we see a large bird with a female head wearing a crown. A legend sometimes identifies the bird as *murgh-i silm*, "the bird of peace." The surrounding landscape depicts a green lawn framed by groups of trees. In the distance there are, at times, also outlines of man-made structures such as a pathway, a bridge or a pavilion. While paradise is thus portrayed as the ideal garden, the image is dominated by two human characters placed in the foreground. The person seated on one side of the basin can reliably be identified as the Prophet Muḥammad by the halo around his head and, sometimes, the green turban he wears. By presenting a small vessel with water from the basin, Muḥammad welcomes a second person to paradise. This person stands on the opposite side of the basin and is clad in full armor, at times still wearing his sword. In his analysis of the tilework images of the Ḥusayniyya-yi Mushīr in Shiraz, Ṣādiq Humāyūnī identifies this person as ʿAlī, the Prophet's son-in-law and the first Shiʿite *imām*.[10] Even though this assumption is tempting, in Shiʿite iconography ʿAlī is usually depicted with his sword, known as *dhū l-fiqār*. Historically, this sword is known to have two cutting edges (*shafratān*) on both the upper and the lower side.[11] In popular Shiʿite iconography it is represented as a sword whose blade branches into two separate points. No other warrior is ever depicted bearing this sword, and thus it has become an unambiguous iconographic marker for ʿAlī. Meanwhile, the sword of the warrior to whom the Prophet Muḥammad hands the water does not have such an iconographic marker. In fact, the figure does not betray any particular characteristics at all. On the contrary, his dress is the same as that worn by the caliph's troops. A legend sometimes supplied on the images clearly identifies this person as Ḥurr, Ḥurr-i shahīd (The martyr Ḥurr) or Janāb-i Ḥurr (Our master Ḥurr). Surprising as the presence in paradise of a warrior from the enemy's party might be at first sight, the historical events perfectly justify this identification.[12]

---

9 For the following analysis see, particularly, Sayf, *Naqqāshī*, nos. 25, 30, 51, 63, and 65.

10 Humāyūnī, *Ḥusayniyyah-yi Mushīr* 43.

11 Halm, *Schia* 16, n. 20.

12 Kister, al-Ḥurr. Al-Ḥurr's (like al-Ḥusayn's) name is given in Arabic with and in Persian without the definite article.

Ḥurr, whose full name in Arabic is al-Ḥurr b. Yazīd al-Riyāhī, played a special role in the battle of Karbala. He was an army commander originally sent by order of Yazīd b. Muʿāwiya (d. 64/683), the second Umayyad caliph, to prevent Ḥusayn and his followers from reaching their eventual destination, the city of Kufa. According to Shiʿite legend, Ḥurr soon recognized Ḥusayn's rightful position and pitied him for the outrageous treatment he received from the caliph's troops. Consequently, Ḥurr switched sides, joined Ḥusayn's companions in their fight against the caliph's troops and died as a martyr at Karbala. Considering his story, Ḥurr thus is not just a randomly selected exemplary character but the quintessential martyr. Even though at first he was loyal to the caliph, he acknowledged Ḥusayn's justified claim to lead the Islamic community. Consequently, he became one of Ḥusayn's followers and died a martyr's death serving the just cause. His presence in paradise is the model of a true Shiʿite believer's destiny, since Ḥurr represents a *shahīd* in the double sense of the word: He is both a witness to Ḥusayn's martyrdom and a martyr himself, whose self-sacrifice for the Shiʿite and, in fact, for the Islamic community is endorsed by the Prophet Muḥammad. Furthermore, Ḥurr's martyrdom is particularly noteworthy because it is linked to his meritorious conversion to the Shiʿi branch of Islam shortly before his death.

The images from the Qajar period form part of the visual memory of Shiʿite culture, and their impact extends well into the present. In this manner, they also lie at the basis of the visual interpretation of paradise on murals in contemporary Iran, where after the revolution of 1979 a specific Shiʿite identity was cultivated. Murals have been a regular phenomenon in Tehran since the 1980s, and even though the agenda guiding their installation continues to develop with changing political trends, new murals appear occasionally. Direct depictions of paradise are not frequent on the Tehran murals, even though paradise was promised to Iranian soldiers slain on the front as their immediate reward, and many fighters wore the plastic key to paradise on a string around their neck.

It is probably not by coincidence that the most prominent depiction of paradise in a modern mural has been installed on the wall of the courtyard bordering the headquarters of the Foundation of Martyrs in central Tehran (Fig. 48.3). In its older version, the mural depicted an anonymous martyr who, after taking off his boots and putting aside his machine-gun, stood at the entrance to paradise, wrapped in a white shroud. The depersonalized image was supplied with a caption reading *shahīd avval kasī-st ki bi-bihisht vārid mīshavad*, "The martyr is the first one to enter paradise." This dictum is attributed to Ruhollah Khomeini (d. 1989), the charismatic leader of the revolution, and is quoted fairly often on Tehran murals. The mural's previous version was originally executed in a style reminiscent of traditional miniature painting. Since its colors were fading away, it was eventually replaced by a new image in bright colors.

The new image essentially depicts the same scene. Meanwhile, it emphasizes even further the lack of individuality of the person depicted and reduces the martyr's presence in the scene to a pair of worn boots placed in front of a field of red tulips. Yet, the martyr's body is still there. His bare feet are dangling below his swaying white shroud that is enveloped by a huge pair of white wings. His head is barely discernible in the center of the image where a hand holds his head while a second one loosens the red ribbon qualifying him as a martyr ready to sacrifice his life. The general applicability of the mural's message is further validated by a quotation from the *maqām-i muʿazzam-i rahbarī*, the Supreme Leadership of the Islamic Republic, stressing the fact that society will never forget the martyrs.

An emotionally moving martyr mural from the 1990s, replaced in 2002 by a mural relating to the fate of the Palestinian people, used to be on a building adjacent to the Mudarris freeway leading from the crowded business districts of southern Tehran to the quiet middle and upper-class residential areas in the north.[13] It showed a little girl wearing a black *chādur* and holding a red rose in her hand. The girl was mourning her dead father lying in front of her with the words: *Bābā-yi shahīdam – hīch gulī khushbūtar az yād-i to nīst*, "My martyr father – no rose smells sweeter than your memory!" While the mural's Tehran version did not specify the martyr's name, another version in the city of Sirjan gave his name as Jamshīd-e Zardusht. The lack of individuality in the mural in Tehran elevated the martyr's fate to a normative level whose appeal would arise from its general applicability. In addition, the image was supplied with a number of stars containing invocations addressed to the group of five persons (*panj tan*)[14] representing the holy family revered by Shiʿite Islam: Muḥammad, his daughter Fāṭima (here called by her cognomen al-Zahrāʾ, "the Luminous"), ʿAlī, and their sons Ḥasan and Ḥusayn. To this was added the hidden twelfth *imām*, al-Mahdī, who in the Shiʿite worldview is the only rightful ruler of the world. The upper right corner contained what looked like a crack in the sky that allowed a glimpse of paradise, the future home of all martyrs. Though the exact components of this image of paradise were difficult to identify, one could make out a cypress tree to the left, another tree with large white blossoms on the right, and a bird amidst a landscape that appeared to be an abode of peace. In its particular composition, this mural raised the anonymous martyr's individual fate to a Shiʿite believer's obligation, and the little girl's personal grief became a general appeal to applaud the martyr's dedication.

In a similar manner, other Tehran murals join in the call for martyrdom by emphasizing that it leads to paradise. Many of the murals have been refur-

13 Marzolph, The martyr's way to paradise 95; Bombardier, La peinture murale iranienne.

14 See Fontana, *Ahl al-Bayt*; Newid, *Der schiitische Islam* 189–204.

bished over the past few years, as authorities obviously took into account the fact that straightforward didactic or homiletic messages did not appeal to the general audience, much less the younger generation. Even so, images of paradise continue to appear in a number of new murals. One such mural has been installed on the wall bordering the courtyard of the Najmiyya Hospital on Tehran's Jumhūrī Avenue (Fig. 48.4).[15] At first sight this mural is a fairly surrealistic image dominated by a large wall that suggests the separation of two worlds. The world to this side of the wall appears to be the world we live in, since a spiral staircase starts in the courtyard right at the bottom of the image. The staircase leads up and over the wall, where its single steps gradually disintegrate and then fade altogether. The world on the wall's other side is only visible on the mural's left side, where spectators are permitted a glimpse into a scene of fertile fields and green trees. This world, however, is unreal and probably beyond human comprehension, since the trees are floating in the air, and the whole scene is mirrored upside down. Regarding the composition of this part of the image there is no doubt that the scene depicted on the wall's other side is paradise. This interpretation is further corroborated by the two popular symbols of the martyr's soul that have been integrated into the image. On the right, we see a group of white doves flying toward the other side of the wall, while on the left, a swaying fold of the wall has generated a line of balls floating in the air. These balls, once fully matured, open up to reveal white butterflies that also head for the Promised Land. In this manner, the mural revalidates the Shiʿite concept of martyrdom by reducing it to a set of symbols that have been propagated on and through the Tehran murals for many years, such as the white dove or the butterfly as a symbol of the martyr's soul. The essential message is thus retained, even though in terms of artistic representation it has been adapted to modern requirements.

In spring 2009, another new mural was installed on a building next to the Tehran Mudarris freeway. This mural, replacing the previously installed image of the Palestinian suicide bomber Rīm Ṣāliḥ al-Riyāshī,[16] is exceptional because it was executed in a style reminiscent of traditional Persian manuscript illustration (Fig. 48.5).[17] It is installed on a windowless wall facing the freeway, the wall being separated into two equally large halves by an emergency staircase. The dominant, and in fact only, background color is a blue so pure and untainted that it risks outdoing the impression of a blue cloudless sky against the backdrop of the natural color of Tehran's sky that is often veiled by heavy pollution. The same is true for the lower side of the image,

15 See Marzolph, The martyr's fading body.
16 Gruber, Mural arts 34.
17 For a detailed discussion of this mural, see Gruber, Images of Muhammad.

which ends in a darkish green of lawn and bushes merging with the heavily watered vegetation that covers the concrete structure framing the freeway. If one follows the artist's presumed original intention, both the sky and ground sections of the image intend to continue their natural surrounding, suggesting that the scene takes place in a manner known as *trompe l'œil*. Numerous other murals in a similar, though often more realistic manner have been installed in Tehran in recent years; these include, to give but one example, a mural on the eastern side of the Maydān-i Vanak on Valī-yi ʿAṣr street to the north of the city center.[18] Though this image does not intend to illustrate paradise, it incorporates a somewhat paradisal vision in that it depicts two fathers with their sons on their shoulders wandering off into a landscape of lush green hills that form a visual break in the concrete jungle of urban Tehran.

In contrast to realistic images such as the one on Maydān-i Vanak, the mural to the side of the Mudarris freeway depicts a scene that even without specialist knowledge can easily be identified as depicting the Prophet Muḥammad's *miʿrāj*, or voyage to the heavens. The Prophet is riding his fabulous steed Burāq on the mural's upper right side. He is clad in a green cloak and his head is surrounded by a halo of flames. The mural's left side suggests fragments of tilework on the upper side of an imaginary building together with the heads (and, in one case, the upper side of the body) of heavenly beings. The inscription on the tilework spells the phrases of the Islamic profession of faith, namely *lā ilāha illā llāh*, "There is no god but God," and *Muḥammad rasūl Allāh*, "Muḥammad is God's messenger." A third inscription placed above the prophet's head on the mural's upper right side reads in large letters *ʿAlī valī Allāh*, " ʿAlī is God's close friend," thus adding the specific Shiʿite component of the *shahāda*.[19] Except for the dominant sky, the landscape is almost devoid of other physical phenomena but for the lower right foreground that depicts a heavenly being plucking a branch from a small tree heavily loaded with large white blossoms. Moreover, there is a link between the mural's overall fictional atmosphere and contemporary reality. Stretching out his arms to take the branch is a man dressed in ordinary clothes who might well be taken for a living person, such as someone passing by on the adjacent street. What makes this image of paradise so exceptional is the fact that its components are exact, although isolated and rearranged copies from illustrations in a ninth/fifteenth-century manuscript of the *Miʿrājnāma* (The book of the ascension) that is today preserved in the Paris National Library.[20]

---

18 Karimi, Tehran's post Iran-Iraq war murals 57, fig. 5.

19 See Eliash, On the genesis and development.

20 Séguy, *Miraculous journey* 41, plate 40; Gruber, *El Libro de la Ascensión* 160, fol. 49r; Sims, Marshak, and Grube, *Peerless images* 169, fig. 83 (image mirrored sideways).

Whatever the artist's intention in executing this mural might have been, it is a new attraction that fits into the recent strategy of the Tehran murals, a strategy in which the formerly prominent life-like and somewhat gruesome realistic depiction of actual martyrs has been abondoned in favor of a mythical and transcendent vision of the hereafter as the martyr's ultimate goal.

Whether we consider the depictions on tilework or canvas from the Qajar period or those on contemporary murals in Tehran, it is clear that the dominant image of paradise in popular Shiʿite iconography is inseparably linked with martyrdom. While the characteristics of paradise as a true believer's ultimate destination are outlined in rather vague terms – allusions to general images of bounty and peace such as a lush vegetation – the message of the images is unambiguously clear: self-sacrifice in the service of a just cause remains the pivotal concept of the current interpretation of Shiʿite Islam in Iran and the gate through which the true believers have to pass in order to attain the Promised Land.

Bibliography

Aghaei, K.S., *The martyrs of Karbala: Shiʿi symbols and rituals in modern Iran*, Seattle and London 2004.

And, M., *Ritüelden drama: Kerbelā, muharrem, taʿziye*, Istanbul 2007².

Ansari, F.M., *Die Malerei der Qadjaren*, PhD dissertation, Tübingen 1986.

Ardalān, H., *Murshidān-i pardah-khvān-i Īrān*, Tehran 1386/2007.

Blair, S.S. and J.M. Bloom (eds.), *Images of paradise in Islamic art*, Hanover NH 1991.

Bombardier, A., La peinture murale iranienne, genèse et evolution, in D. Bernardi and N. Étienne (eds.), *External tour – Jerusalem: Standing on the beach with a gun in my hand*, Geneva 2011, 112–9.

Chehabi, H.E. and F. Christia, The art of state persuasion: Iran's post-revolutionary murals, in *Persica* 22 (2008), 1–13.

Chelkowski, P., Patronage and piety, in L.S. Diba with M. Ekhteyar (eds.), *Royal Persian paintings: The Qajar epoch, 1785–1925*, London and New York 1998, 90–9.

——— and H. Dabashi, *Staging a revolution: The art of persuasion in the Islamic Republic of Iran*, New York 1999.

Eliash, J., On the genesis and development of the Twelver-Shîʾî three-tenet Shahâda, in *Der Islam* 47 (1971), 265–72.

Flaskerud, I., *Visualizing belief and piety in Iranian Shiism*, London and New York 2010.

Floor, W., *The history of theater in Iran*, Washington, DC 2005.

Fontana, M.V., *Iconografia dell' Ahl al-bayt: Immagini di arte persiana dal XII al XX secolo*, Naples 1994.

Gruber, C., Images of Muhammad in and out of modernity: The curious case of a 2008 mural in Tehran, in C. Gruber and S. Haugbolle (eds.), *Visual culture in the modern Middle East*, Bloomington IN, 2013, 2–31.
———, *El "Libro de la Ascensión" (Miʿrajnama) timúrida: Estudio de textos e imágenes en un contexto panasiático*, Valencia 2008.
———, The message is on the wall: Mural arts in post-revolutionary Iran, in *Persica* 22 (2008), 15–46.
Halm, H., *Die Schia*, Darmstadt 1988.
Humāyūnī, Ṣ., *Ḥusayniyyah-yi Mushīr*, Tehran 2535/1976 (1371²/1992).
Karimi, P., Imagining warfare, imaging welfare: Tehran's post Iran-Iraq war murals and their legacy, in *Persica* 22 (2008), 47–63.
Khosrokhavar, F., *L'Islamisme et la mort: Le martyre révolutionnaire en Iran*, Paris 1995.
———, *Les nouveaux martyrs d'Allah*, Paris 2002.
Kister, M.J., al-Ḥurr b. Yazīd, in *EI*², iii, 588.
Marzolph, U., The martyr's fading body: Propaganda vs. beautification in the Tehran cityscape, in C. Gruber and S. Haugbolle (eds.), *Visual culture in the modern Middle East*, Bloomington IN 2013, 164–185.
———, The martyr's way to paradise: Shiite mural art in the urban context, in R. Bendix and J. Bendix (eds.), *Sleepers, moles and martyrs: Secret identifications, societal integration, and the differing meanings of freedom*, Copenhagen 2004, 87–98.
———, *Narrative illustration in Persian lithographed books*, Leiden 2001.
———, The pictorial representation of Shiite themes in lithographed books of the Qajar period, in P. Khosronejad (ed.), *The art and material culture of Iranian Shiʿism: Iconography and religious devotion in Shiʿi Islam*, London 2012, 74–103.
Mayeur-Jaouen, C. (ed.), *Saints et héros du Moyen-Orient contemporain*, Paris 2002.
Mīrzāʾī-Mihr, ʿA.A., *Naqqāshīhā-yi buqāʿ-i mutabarrikah dar Īrān*, Tehran 1386/2007.
Neuwirth, A., Blut und Mythos in der islamischen Kultur, in C. von Braun and C. Wulf (eds.), *Mythen des Blutes*, Frankfurt 2007, 62–89.
Newid, M.A., *Der schiitische Islam in Bildern: Rituale und Heilige*, Munich 2006.
Puin, E., *Islamische Plakate: Kalligraphie und Malerei im Dienste des Glaubens*, 3 vols., Dortmund 2008.
Sayf, H., *Naqqāshī-ye qahvah-khānah*, Tehran 1369/1990.
Seguy, M.-R., *The miraculous journey of Mahomet*, New York 1977.
Sims, E. with B.I. Marshak, and E.J. Grube, *Peerless images: Persian painting and its sources*, New Haven, CT and London 2002.
Varzi, R., *Warring souls: Youth, media, and martyrdom in post-revolutionary Iran*, Durham 2006.

FIGURE 48.1 *Tilework on the Ḥusayniyyah-yi Mushīr in Shiraz; from Humāyūnī,* Ḥusayniyyah-yi Mushīr, *folding page between 18 and 19.*

FIGURE 48.2 *Painting on canvas, from Sayf,* Naqqāshī *127, no 30.*

FIGURE 48.3 *Mural on the courtyard adjacent to the headquarters of the Bunyād-i shahīd, Tehran.*
© U. MARZOLPH, 2010.

FIGURE 48.4 *Mural on the courtyard of the Najmiyyah Hospital, Tehran.*
© U. MARZOLPH, 2010.

FIGURE 48.5 *Mural on a building next to Mudarris Freeway, Tehran.*
© U. MARZOLPH, 2010.

CHAPTER 49

Where is Paradise on Earth? Visual Arts in the Arab World and the Construction of a Mythic Past

Silvia Naef

Among the numerous definitions that the dictionary indicates for "paradise," there is "any place or condition that fulfils all one's desires or aspirations."[1] This is the meaning of the word that we apply in this article. The starting point of our reflection will be Pierre Nora's notion of *lieu de mémoire* as well as Jean Baudrillard's concepts of simulacrum and hyperreality; in this article, we examine the validity of these concepts for a specific type of pictorial representations produced in the Arab world that idealize times and traditions long gone by, conferring upon them timeless, quasi "Edenic" meanings.

For Nora, *lieux de mémoire* are places consecrated to remembering things past that, as he puts it, are at risk of being forgotten.[2] Nora considers that there is, in the present time, an acceleration of history, and that as a consequence of it, modern societies have lost the living memory that characterized traditional societies, a memory transmitted by the elders to the younger generations, a collective memory that has disappeared along with peasant societies.

The acceleration of time has given rise to a separation of what Nora names "real memory" (living memory) and "history," by which he designates the way modern societies organize a past that would otherwise fall into oblivion. Acceleration leads to quick forgetting, compensated by the compulsive and insistent attempt to keep memory alive through constant and repeated acts of remembrance – the *lieux de mémoire* – and the creation of archives – where every minor trace is preserved, supposedly for future generations, regardless of the fact that nobody will ever be able to consult them. To exemplify this, Nora quotes the French social security archives with their miles of files that no human being will be able to explore in their entirety, or oral history, which requires 36 hours of recording to document each hour, and therefore no one will be able to watch the material in detail.[3] This desperate (and useless) attempt at preserving the smallest traces of a fading past reminds us of the 1:1 map of

1 Barber (ed.), *Canadian English*, s. v.
2 Nora, Between memory and history.
3 Ibid., 9–10.

© KONINKLIJKE BRILL NV, LEIDEN, 2017 | DOI 10.1163/9789004333154_050

the Empire imagined by Jorge Luis Borges. In Borges' short story, a civil servant of an imaginary Empire tries to design a "perfect" map which would reproduce every single inch of the country in its real size: it is, obviously, an impossible endeavor that shows the absurdity of this intention of total preservation.[4]

1 Modernization, Acceleration of History and the Visual Arts in the Arab World

What Pierre Nora describes for France, which quickly, over the last few decades, changed from a rural to a modern, post-industrial society, is also true, although in a different way, of Arab societies. Modernization and change, which started in the main urban centers in the nineteenth century, have affected the Arab world, especially during the decades after World War II. This was when most countries became independent and tried to catch up with industrialization, even if the process is still far from being accomplished and excludes large parts of the population, especially in rural areas.

The replacement of inherited modes of art production by Western conceptions is strongly tied to this process. To understand the importance of this movement, we have to go back briefly to a moment that is essential in the history of modern art in the Arab world and beyond. In the wake of modernization, Western art – which already had had some impact on the production of what would commonly be called "Islamic art"[5] at the Ottoman court or in Iran – was introduced through the creation of art schools in the Western tradition by the authorities or by influential members of those societies that were close to the ruling families: 1883 in Istanbul, 1908 in Cairo, and 1911 in Tehran. The model or ideal for these schools, a typical top-down process, was the Parisian Fine Arts Academy, *École des Beaux-Arts*. The introduction of an institutionalized art education was part of an all-encompassing modernization process in which local art traditions (we might say "Islamic art") started

4 "In that Empire, the Art of Cartography attained such Perfection that the map of a single Province occupied the entirety of a City, and the map of the Empire, the entirety of a Province. In time, those Unconscionable Maps no longer satisfied, and the Cartographers Guilds struck a Map of the Empire whose size was that of the Empire, and which coincided point for point with it. Suarez Miranda, *Viajes de varones prudentes*, Libro IV, Cap. XLV, Lérida, 1658." Borges, *Collected fictions* 325.

5 Since the 1970s, when Oleg Grabar posed the question of how problematic the definition "Islamic art" was, the discussion has been ongoing. However, scholars still use it, since there is no other viable and satisfying option to define art production in the "central Islamic lands" from the seventh to the eighteenth century CE.

to be considered as inferior to the nineteenth-century Western academic tradition.[6] Therefore, just as this was the case for the army or the school system, art also had to be introduced according to the Western norm in order to catch up with "civilization"; the idea of a progress of humanity toward a better future was integrated into their own narrative by the local elites. This notion was expressed vividly, a few decades later, in January 1923, by one of the main modernizers in the region, the Turkish leader Mustafa Kemal (d. 1938): "A nation that ignores painting, a nation that ignores statues, and a nation that does not know the laws of positive science does not deserve to take its place on the road to progress."[7]

We can define the first period of an art practice along schemes imported from the West as a period of *adoption*, where the focus was on acquiring themes and techniques mostly unknown before.

This radical change affected only the profane field. Religious art, a term by which we might designate in the Islamic context any object, representation or building used for ritual practices, was spared this change and continued to be conceived along customary patterns, with the exception of architecture in some rare and recent cases.[8] Until the present day, mosque decoration mostly refers to ancient examples: in new buildings, calligraphic panels and decorations are mere reproductions of old patterns and styles. In modern art, religious themes were generally avoided, although a few artists using calligraphic symbols sometimes refer to a religious – mainly Sufi – experience or sense. In his 1989 series of lithographs, *Mesnevi*, the Turkish artist Ergin İnan (b. 1943) uses religious symbols and Arabic script. However, it reflects more a "breaking of taboos" – as Kiymet Giray suggests – than a desire to represent spiritual experience.[9] Religious paintings can rather be found in the work of some artists with a Christian background, like Saliba Douaihy (Ṣalībā al-Duwayhī) (1915?–1994) in Lebanon or Marguerite Nakhla (1908–1977) in Egypt, who both produced modern religious art, mostly for churches.[10] Typically, paradise or related subjects, represented symbolically in Islamic art,[11] have not been a theme for modern art.

6 On this topic, cf. Naef, Peindre pour être moderne.
7 Quoted in Kreiser, Public monuments in Turkey and Egypt 114.
8 For modern mosque architecture, see Holod and Khan, *The mosque and the modern world*.
9 Giray, *Ergin İnan* 188.
10 On Douaihy, cf. al-Duwayhī, *al-Madā wa-l-rūḥ*. On Nakhla, see Marcos, Moussa, and Ramzy, *Marguerite Nakhla*.
11 Blair and Bloom (eds.), *Images of paradise in Islamic art*.

Starting from the 1950s, a period of optimistic and often socialistic modernization and industrialization seized countries like Egypt, Iraq, and, in the 1960s, Algeria and, although the goal of mass consumption was not achieved, the disappearance or transformation of traditional ways of life did take place. The freshly independent countries were striving to build new societies, with local, non-alienated identities, modern but rooted in what was deemed to be the national past. In the visual arts, this period coincided with a "back to our roots" movement, which aimed at introducing elements taken from local traditions – referred to later on as heritage (*turāth*) – in an art form whose reference was exclusively modern Western art: no one contemplated the return to previously existing practices.

The somehow old-fashioned visual arts of the earlier adoption period, which could be defined to a certain extent – according to Gayatri Spivak – as a case of "mimicry of the colonized," were to be replaced by what was considered to be "authentic," meaning that it belonged to the cultural capital of the country before it was submitted to colonial rule and its influences. A new period of *adaptation* to what were deemed "local traditions" started.

Art production in the Arab world was, in the middle of the twentieth century, almost entirely figurative; abstraction started to be accepted only in the 1960s, although it had been known to many artists earlier on. One reason for this were the then prevailing socialist ideas that considered abstraction a form of "bourgeois decadence" since it could not express "revolutionary" values and educate the populace. In this worldview, not only could abstract art not reflect the "reality" of the popular classes, but it was often identified with the United States, not entirely wrongly. As Frances Stonor Saunders shows in her book *The cultural cold war*, the United States sponsored this type of art as being "the very antithesis to socialist realism" and "an explicitly *American* intervention in the modernist canon" and made of it the symbol of freedom of expression and modernity.[12] In the Arab world, art, in the view of many artists of the time, had to be made "by the people and for the people" and help to build a new and better society; it had to convey a message; abstract art was therefore not suitable. "Art for art's sake" was a slogan mostly rejected by artists in a period of social and economic upheaval. Nevertheless, most painters preferred to represent "the people" in a form of idealized settings, mostly rural. Modern life, urban landscapes, and industrial work were nearly absent. If we add that most of the time, these artists belonged to the modernizing elites, their reference to a folkloric image of land and people in order to represent the "authentic" appears to be even more of a conscious choice.

---

12 Saunders, *The cultural cold war* 254. Emphasis in the original.

FIGURE 49.1 *Sayyid 'Abd al-Rasūl,* Composition, *1961.*

Sayyid 'Abd al-Rasūl's (1917–1995) *Composition* (1961) (Fig. 49.1) exemplifies this. It shows a group of women and young girls on their way to the well, in what is supposed to be a typical scene of the Egyptian countryside. The women, whose faces and position remind us partly of Pharaonic representations, are expressionless, in spite of the fact that their features are individually delineated. Their colorful dresses have a high aesthetic value, as do the patterns on them. There is no hint of the painfulness of their job, even with the bending woman in the front. Water carrying appears as a picturesque activity, demanding no effort. At the same time, this composition is an example of what "authenticity" is meant to be: village women, in traditional dress, performing a centuries-old daily life ritual, seemingly untouched by modernization and Westernization. Their garments are a timeless variation on the theme of the Egyptian peasant's clothing: the different motifs and colors show the ability of local craftsmen. The reference to old Egyptian representational modes situates the work in a continuous "Egyptianness" and allows the identification with it.

In her article "The Painter's Landscape," Françoise Cachin shows how landscapes became a *lieu de mémoire* in nineteenth-century France at a time when industrialization changed not only daily life but also people's attitude toward

FIGURE 49.2
Mamdūḥ Qashlān, Local Features *70, 1979.*

the countryside.[13] Following Cachin, landscapes in their Impressionist interpretation have become the quintessential expression of France as such, as the still ongoing success of exhibitions of this school shows. For French audiences, France as shown in these paintings has turned into France itself, especially after World War I, when the genre of landscape painting disappeared from artistic practice.[14]

In the Arab world, landscape painting played only a secondary role in this post World War II period.[15] However, a phenomenon similar to that observed in France by Cachin can be retraced there, where the place held by French landscape painting is taken by idealized genre scenes and architectural depictions. In this sense, the break that occurred with academic art by the introduction of modern styles after World War II was merely a stylistic one, the subjects varied only slightly compared to the previous period. Modernity and its materializations are largely absent, regardless of the fact that these representations pretend to contemporaneity. Temporality, symbolized by items of our time, is not evoked: and as Cachin notes for Millet's peasants, whose "silhouettes … are those of the *eternal* French peasant,"[16] the pictorial rendering of the popular classes is timeless: timelessness, happiness, harmony of places, faces, and practices long forgotten but sublimated by their distance in time. Any reference to conflict, poverty, and illness is also nonexistent.

In Mamdūḥ Qashlān's (b. 1929) *Local features 70* (Fig. 49.2) a village scene shows men sitting, discussing, and drinking coffee and a group of women chatting and standing. In the background, we can make out houses and a tree. In

13 Cachin, The painter's landscape 296.

14 Cachin, The painter's landscape 337–8.

15 As Kirsten Scheid has shown, landscape painting had become the embodiment of the nation in Lebanon in the first half of the century. Scheid, *Painters, picture-makers, and Lebanon* 223–95, and especially 288–92.

16 Cachin, The painter's landscape 318. Our emphasis.

contrast to the liveliness and movement that characterize a village square, the whole composition is static and gives a sense of irreality. It would be difficult to situate this painting in a precise period: no element gives us a hint in this direction.

2 Visual Arts in a Hyperreal World

An important shift in ways of producing visual works occurred in the 1990s. With the rupture constituted by the first Gulf War in 1991, which marks the end of pan-Arab nationalism as a strong cross-border ideology, art production and discourses on art came to be less dominated by the idea of Arabness. *Globalization* had an impact on the regional scene: The co-optation of some artists of Middle Eastern and Arab origins into the world art market and the adoption by many of them of new concepts and techniques like installations and video art, initiated a partial shift in art production in the region, but this production is rather oriented toward international audiences. On the regional scene, which, for different reasons, has expanded since the 1990s, themes and techniques remained more conservative, painting and sculpture constituted the prevailing techniques.[17] A part of this production is still dedicated to idealized urban and rural representations, although many other subjects can be found as well.

This might be surprising, considering the changes that happened in the last decade. On the one side, it can be explained by a pictorial tradition that, in spite of the stylistic break that happened after World War II, has thematically kept its ties with genre painting, derived from the academic and Orientalist tradition, where only popular themes are considered "picturesque" enough to deserve representation. Another reading might be more fruitful, starting from the idea expressed by Jean Baudrillard in *Simulacra and Simulation*. For Baudrillard, simulacra play an essential role in our society. By simulacra he means representations of things that do not necessarily exist, in contrast to the past, when images were produced and used in order to represent the "real." Nowadays, the image, the simulated thing, the *simulacrum*, can exist without the real, it has become completely independent of it and exists as such: "Simulation is no longer . . . a referential being, or a substance. It is the generation by models of a real without origin or reality: a hyperreal. . . . The era of simulation is inaugurated by a liquidation of all referentials."[18] The signs of the

17 See Naef, Entre mondialisation 81–92.

18 Baudrillard, *Simulacra and simulation* 1–2.

real, i.e., a fake representation of what the real is supposed to be, have replaced the real, the image has replaced what it is supposed to represent. What counts is not the represented object, but the representation itself. With the disappearing of a concrete reality, replaced by what he calls "hyperreality," a virtual or better reality, our societies develop nostalgia, a will to preserve everything past, but in a "better" and "cleaner" form.

For Baudrillard, Disneyland is the quintessential expression of this, Disneyland which he considers to be "the real America" hiding the fact that the "real" does not exist anymore.[19] This development can be observed in the Arab world as well. For Deeba Haider for instance, the whole city of Dubai is an illustration of this. For her, Dubai has become an attraction park, where fake prevails over reality: shopping malls are simulating cities in other parts of the world,[20] functional elements of traditional architecture are used as purely decorative features,[21] buildings have to follow precise rules in order to make the environment look more "traditional."[22] We could add that the Dubai Museum, with its puppets representing and performing the activities the inhabitants of Dubai used to perform daily only a few decades ago, or the reconstituted traditional home presented in the courtyard, also reconstructs history and daily life in a largely sublimated and expurgated form, giving an *aesthetical* view of it (Fig. 49.3).

The construction of a simulated reality as an improved form of the existing urban structures is not limited to newly created entities: Historical cities of the region also show such examples. In her book about changing consumer cultures in Egypt, Mona Abaza describes Cairo's new shopping mall culture, which aims to replace the old and dirty city by a cleaner, more modern and comfortable way to shop. Located near Madinat Nasr, the new chic area outside Cairo, and only twenty minutes from the international airport, City Stars Mall opened in 2005 and offers a replica of the Khān al-Khalīlī Sūq, "displaying the identical jewelers, handicrafts and items that are sold in the old popular bazaar."[23] The illusion is perfect: the old is reproduced in its forms and functions (traditional shops) but this gated character transforms it into a clean and safe heaven for local shoppers and tourists; it is air-conditioned, free of poor people, pickpockets, and other "dangers" that exist in "real" life. Saree Makdisi

---

19 Ibid., 12.

20 Haider, Transformation of Dubai 655.

21 Ibid., 657.

22 Ibid., 656.

23 Abaza, *Changing consumer cultures* 30–1.

FIGURE 49.3 *Dubai Museum: Reconstruction of a traditional home in the courtyard.* PHOTO: S. NAEF, 2008.

observes the same phenomenon in the rebuilt city center of Beirut, reconstructed not as it was, but as

> it ought to have looked and felt: … [the] discourse of authenticity functions in a strictly visual register, so that what it means by *authenticity* is actually the look – the spectacle – of authenticity, rather than authenticity as such. … the authentic is what *looks like* it is authentic, …[24]

Aesthetization of past traditions and objects, stressing their "authenticity" can also be found in movies produced in the last two decades, as Nacer Khemir's (b. 1948) movies (*Les baliseurs du désert*, 1984; *Le collier perdu de la colombe*, 1991; *Bab 'Aziz, Le prince qui contemplait son âme*, 2006) or Moufida Tlatli's (b. 1947) *La saison des hommes* (2000). Shot on the Djerba island, *The Season of Men*, intended as a drama of separation and social injustice, pictures a traditional

24 Makdisi, Beirut, A city without history? 212. Emphasis in the original.

society where men-women relations are problematic and critically inspected, whereas architecture, handicraft production (weaving), and rituals performed among women are presented throughout as beautiful and harmonious. Even in a movie with a feminist agenda, nostalgia might prevail.

In painting, this timeless aesthetization, oblivious of history and other contingencies is even more striking. As in the movies mentioned, traditional architecture is often the main theme, as in this composition by the Syrian artist Hammoud Chantout (Ḥammūd Shantūt) (b. 1956), exhibited in 2001, showing a traditional house with its balcony and green plants (Fig. 49.4). Chantout has done many paintings on the theme of traditional architecture, illustrating houses in Syrian towns or villages, but also in invented locations, where the building becomes the subject of the composition.[25] The mere concentration on architectural details, the absence of human beings and of action, reinforces the effect of stillness and timelessness. It appeals to the new taste of the urban bourgeoisie for vernacular architecture (even when relatively recent) and visual traditions, which expresses itself in the Syrian case in the recent transformation of the old city of Damascus from a dwelling area for lower income classes to a trendy spot for its wealthier inhabitants, as the important number of restored houses, turned into elegant shops and cafés, demonstrates.

The replacement of reality by an improved fake version, which characterizes modern societies, including the Middle East, leads to a nostalgia for what becomes, very often, a form of idealized past. The heritage of the past is no longer seen as such, but used in order to create a present with no disturbing elements, where life seems to be spent in happiness and peace, in a generalized "Buddha Bar" atmosphere of relaxation and harmony.

In this view, the past can only be considered in an "improved" shape and appears as a time when families were still together, work was done mostly by hand, and the rhythm of life was much slower and less stressful. There is a romanticization of the representation not only of past life in the village, as some kind of ideal community, but as a form of life that modernization, and the subsequent introduction of machines, with their noise and accelerated rhythm (along with the appearance of new concepts and ideologies) has destroyed.

These representations of a past which never existed in such a form, of a tradition purified of everything that could trouble it, appears when it has become no more than a pale remembering. Paintings and films have parallels with the history museum in Dubai: they remind people of what they have lost, and what is gone forever. In consequence, the specific type of figurative painting which has been described here is indebted not only to traditions of representation,

25 See http://chantout.com/galo5.htm.

FIGURE 49.4 *Hammoud Chantout,* Traditional House, *undated, exhibited at al-Sayed Gallery, Damascus, November 2001.*
PHOTO: S. NAEF, 2001.

but is a way of recalling a vanished memory, of preserving what the acceleration of history has condemned to oblivion. Painting as a *lieu de mémoire*, as the embodiment of times gone, is a refuge, a protection from the uprooting induced by modernity, and is appreciated by a new bourgeoisie that has abandoned traditional ways of life, but wants to keep them as remembrance, a credential of authenticity. A past from which contradictory and conflicting images have been removed, now becomes an ideal reference, a time of a supposed perfection erased by modernization, a secular "paradise on earth."

Bibliography

Abaza, M., *Changing consumer cultures of modern Egypt: Cairo's urban reshaping*, Leiden and Boston 2006.

Barber, K. (ed.), *Collins Canadian English dictionary*, Toronto 2004.

Baudrillard, J., *Simulacra and simulation*, trans. S.A. Glaser, Ann Arbor 1994 [French: *Simulacres et simulation*, Paris 1981].

Blair, S. and J.M. Bloom, (eds.), *Images of paradise in Islamic art*, Hanover NH 1991.
Borges, J.L., *Collected fictions*, trans. A. Hurley, London and New York 1999.
Cachin, F., The painter's landscape, in P. Nora (ed.), *Rethinking France: Les lieux de mémoire*, trans. D.P. Jordan, Chicago and London 2006, 295–342 [French: Le paysage du peintre, in P. Nora (ed.), *Les lieux de mémoire*, 3 vols., i, Paris 1997, 957–96].
al-Duwayhī, Ṣ., *al-Madā wa-l-rūḥ, Maʿriḍ min "buyūtinā," Mahrajānāt Ihdin, 14 Aylūl 1999* n.p., n.d., Joseph D. Raïdy Printing Press (exhibition catalogue).
Giray, K., *Ergin İnan*, Istanbul 2001.
Haider, D., The transformation of Dubai: Turning culture into a theme park, in J. Dakhlia et al. (eds.), *Créations artistiques contemporaines en pays d'Islam: Des arts en tension*, Paris 2006, 650–61.
Holod, R. and H.-U. Khah, *The mosque and the modern world: Architects, patrons and designs since the 1950s*, London 1997.
Kreiser, K., Public monuments in Turkey and Egypt, 1840–1916, in *Muqarnas* 14 (1997), 103–17.
Makdisi, S., Beirut, a city without history? in U. Makdisi and P.A. Silverstein (eds.), *Memory and violence in the Middle East and North Africa*, Bloomington IN and Indianapolis 2006, 201–14.
Marcos, Fr. M.A., H. Moussa, and C.M. Ramzy, *Marguerite Nakhla: Legacy to modern Egyptian art*, Scarborough (Canada) 2009.
Naef, S., Entre mondialisation du champ artistique et recherche identitaire – Les arts plastiques contemporains dans la Méditerranée orientale, in J. Dakhlia et al. (eds.), *Créations artistiques contemporaines en pays d'Islam: Des arts en tension*, Paris 2006, 71–95.
———, Peindre pour être moderne? Remarques sur l'adoption de l'art occidental dans l'Orient arabe, in B. Heyberger and S. Naef (eds.), *La multiplication des images en pays d'Islam – De l'estampe à la télévision – (17ᵉ–21ᵉ siècles)*, Istanbul and Würzburg 2003, 189–207.
Nora, P., General introduction: Between memory and history, in P. Nora (ed.), *Realms of memory: Rethinking the French past*, trans. A. Goldhammer, New York 1996, 1–20.
Saunders, F.S., *The cultural cold war: The CIA and the world of art and letters*, New York 1999.
Scheid, K., *Painters, picture-makers, and Lebanon: Ambiguous identities in an unsettled state*, PhD dissertation, Princeton, NJ 2005.

Internet Source

http://chantout.com/gal05.htm (accessed 16 August 2016).

PART 10

Heavens and the Hereafter in Scholarship and Natural Sciences

CHAPTER 50

The Configuration of the Heavens in Islamic Astronomy

Ingrid Hehmeyer

1 Preamble

The account of the Prophet Muḥammad's night journey (*isrāʾ*) and his subsequent ascension to heaven (*miʿrāj*) includes a description of how Muḥammad was transported through seven heavens, from the first or lowest that is closest to Earth, to the seventh or highest. According to some prophetic traditions and *ḥadīth*-derived literature, on this occasion Muḥammad visited paradise. However, there is no consensus with regard to its location, which is given variously as in the first heaven or in the seventh, or even beyond the seven heavens.[1] The sevenfold layering of the celestial sphere can also be found in several verses of the Quran.[2] The concept itself originates in pre-Islamic times and is often traced back to the Greeks' understanding of the configuration of the heavens. But astronomy predates the era of the Greeks. From early times onwards humans have been engaged with the skies, the traces of which can be found in the mythologies of many cultures. In order to appreciate, therefore, the significance of the seven heavens it is necessary to look at the evidence from the first written records of astronomy, which takes us back to ancient Mesopotamia.

2 The Mesopotamians' Understanding of the Heavens

In the minds of the Mesopotamians, Heaven and Earth were created by the gods with an underlying order and regularity. This concept is expressed in various creation myths.[3] Besides prominent stars and constellations, the Mesopotamians recognized seven planets. The latter included the Sun and the Moon, in addition to what we refer to today as the five planets visible to the

1 For details see Roberto Tottoli's contribution to the present publication.

2 Q 2:29; 17:44; 23:17; 41:12; 65:12; 67:3; 78:12.

3 See Horowitz, *Cosmic geography* 107–50.

 | DOI 10.1163/9789004333154_051

naked-eye observer, viz.: Mercury, Venus, Mars, Jupiter, and Saturn. Together the seven planets were called *bibbu* in Akkadian, meaning "wild sheep," which relates to their seemingly erratic motion across the background of the fixed stars. These appear to maintain fixed positions relative to one another and to move always according to the same set pattern, as though mounted on a sphere rotating uniformly within a period of approximately one day. The fixed stars were therefore compared with domesticated animals.[4] What is reflected in this view of the sky is how fundamental a role agriculture in general and animal husbandry in particular played for Mesopotamian civilization.

A second significant aspect of the Mesopotamians' conception of the heavens relates to their perception of certain stars and constellations and, in particular, the planets as celestial manifestations of gods and goddesses. The changing astronomical patterns such as planetary alignments, the appearance of a planet within a prominent constellation and, most dramatically, a lunar or solar eclipse, were perceived as communications from the deities, who placed such signs in the heavens for humans to see. It is important to note that people did not necessarily believe there was any causative relationship between these signs and future events on Earth. They were merely indicators of what the gods had in store for humans. Reading and interpreting the signs offered the possibility of taking appropriate action, thereby modifying the potential outcome. The concept of determinism was not inherent. But we get a clear sense of correlation between divine, celestial, and terrestrial realms.[5]

The need to interpret the signs led to the systematic observation of the skies and record-keeping.[6] In due course, the experts – scholar-scribes – started to apply mathematics to their study of the heavens and to quantify celestial phenomena, such as future planetary movements and positions. The use of mathematical models for reliable numerical prediction in astronomy implies the comprehension of underlying patterns of regularities. This was a breakthrough for the development of scientific inquiry in the ancient world. Building on

---

4 Ibid., 153.

5 The details are best summarized in Rochberg-Halton, Scientific inquiry 26–30, and Steele, *Brief introduction* 30–7. There is an extensive corpus of specialized literature on the subject, in particular Rochberg, *Heavenly writing*, and – with a slightly different interpretation – Koch-Westenholz, *Mesopotamian astrology*. Both works include comprehensive bibliographies.

6 There is thus a close connection in ancient Mesopotamia between what according to modern terminology would be called astronomy, which involves the study of the movements and positions of the heavenly bodies, and astrology, which interprets these movements and positions as predictions for mundane events. Unlike today, they were not regarded as separate in ancient Mesopotamia; see Rochberg, *Heavenly writing* 102.

achievements from the third and second millennia BCE, astronomy flourished in Mesopotamia during the first millennium BCE.[7]

To give just one example, we may consider the Mesopotamian lunisolar calendar. The first evening sighting of the crescent Moon marked the beginning of a month. The length of the lunar month is approximately 29½ days (on average, half of the lunar months comprise 29, the other half 30 days). A lunar year of twelve months has 354 days (six times 29 days plus six times 30 days) and is therefore eleven days shorter than the solar year of 365 days. This means that the lunar year starts eleven days earlier each year and thus moves through the seasons. One of the purposes of the calendar was the provision of a framework for tax collection, which depended on the time of harvest during the solar year. In order to keep the lunar calendar and the solar year synchronized, an intercalary month was inserted every few years, at irregular intervals. Originally, it was the king's decision when such a month should be added. This was certainly not the best solution and could result in great irregularities. For instance, the king might have been reluctant to insert a month because it delayed tax collection. At the same time, the New Year celebrations in spring were the most significant social event of the year. The method adopted by the civil authorities from about 500 BCE onwards, but possibly originating in the eighth century BCE, involved seven intercalations in 19 years – a fixed cycle that predicted the beginning of a new month and a new year, and that regulated the calendar in general through mathematics. The intercalation no longer depended on observation or whim. This method also had a high degree of accuracy, because it corresponded to the underlying pattern of the regular lunar motion.[8]

We find varying traditions in ancient Mesopotamia that deal with the concept of the universe. However, they all agree that Heaven and Earth consist of a series of superimposed layers. For instance, two texts dating to the first millennium BCE, but likely with origins in the second millennium, describe the heavens as divided into three layers. The lowest one, closest to Earth, is specified as the visible sky that carries the stars. The domain of the gods of Heaven lies above it, with the lesser deities residing in the middle layer and the Heaven-god Anu, one of the major deities, in the third or highest layer. The three heavens are matched in one of the texts by three layers of Earth: the

7 See Britton and Walker, Astronomy 51–66, and Steele, *Brief introduction* 48–65, for examples of significant developments. Neugebauer, *Mathematical astronomy* i, 347–555, presents a comprehensive study of mathematical astronomy in ancient Mesopotamia.

8 Hunger and Pingree, *Astral sciences* 199–200; Britton and Walker, Astronomy 45–6, 52–5; Steele, *Brief introduction* 21–4. For details of the New Year festival, see Dalley, Influence 76–7.

visible Earth where humans live, below it the middle layer consisting of the subterranean waters, and finally the underworld of the dead.[9]

But there is also evidence of an earlier tradition of seven heavens and seven earths, preserved in several Sumerian texts.[10] Interestingly, all of them are incantations. It has been suggested that the number seven does not necessarily have to be understood in the literal sense of its numerical equivalent, but could rather be interpreted in a metaphorical way. One possible reading of "seven heavens" is "all of heaven" or "all heavens" which refers to Heaven in its entirety, without making reference to a specified number of layers.[11] The same applies to "seven earths."[12]

3 The Geocentric Model of the Greek Cosmos

The earliest attestation to the influence of the Mesopotamian astronomical tradition on the Greeks has been traced to around the eighth century BCE and Homer's *Iliad*. The account of how Hephaestus made Achilles' shield (Book 18) includes a description of its astronomical decorations,[13] and it has been pointed out that they bear a close resemblance to astronomical concepts found in earlier texts from Mesopotamia.[14] Alexander's conquest of Mesopotamia in the second half of the fourth century BCE brought the Greeks in direct contact with Mesopotamian astral sciences. They became the foundation for astronomical thought and practice by the Greek intellectuals who themselves eventually made great contributions, advances, and refinements to astronomy. Until the fourth century BCE, however, their main interest was to develop a philosophical approach to explaining the universe, relying on evidence of the senses and reason, rather than a mathematical approach. Unfortunately, hardly any of

---

9 The two tablets are KAR 307 and AO 8196, see Horowitz, *Cosmic geography* 3–19. Throughout the book, the author provides a wealth of detail from other texts. Of particular interest is chapter 11 that deals with the geography of the heavens. Of course, there are abundant variations on the theme of the heavens and the earths.

10 Horowitz, *Cosmic geography* 208–20.

11 Ibid., 218–9.

12 The symbolic meaning of "seven" is clearly expressed in some texts from Assyrian times from which we learn that an Assyrian king could claim the supreme title "king of the universe" after completing seven victorious campaigns. In these text examples, "seven" has the meaning of "universe," see Dalley, Influence 76. Conrad, Seven 43, note 1, provides further references to the symbolic usage of the number seven in the ancient world.

13 Homer, *Iliad* 349–53.

14 Pingree, Legacies 129.

the original writings of the Greek philosophers from before the fourth century are extant, and the first author whose comprehensive theories of the universe have survived is Aristotle (d. 322 BCE). One needs to bear in mind, though, that Aristotle's ideas are based on the works of his predecessors.

3.1 *Aristotle*

Aristotle addressed the topic of the universe in particular in his *Metaphysics* Λ and *On the heavens*, amongst other writings.[15] He saw a fundamental difference between the terrestrial and the celestial realm. Aristotle explained the universe as a great sphere that consisted of two parts, an upper and a lower region, divided by a sphere on which our closest celestial neighbor, the Moon, was located. The sublunary or terrestrial region included everything beneath the Moon. Terrestrial matter was made up of four elements: earth, water, air, and fire. The Earth, consisting (mainly) of elementary earth, had its natural place at the center of the sublunary region. It was surrounded by a shell of water – the seas. This, in turn, was encompassed by a shell of air – the atmosphere – and, finally, a shell of fire. Like the preceding ones, it was spherical and concentric with the Earth. Aristotle emphasized that in the sublunary region things were subject to impermanence and change, which included generation, growth, diminution, and decay.

From the Moon outwards, in the heavenly region, everything was perfect and unchanging. Here, matter was made up of a fifth, more precious element, the ether. The universe was finite, with its boundary marked by the sphere of the fixed stars. By contrast, the seven planets were each embedded on a separate sphere. These spheres were arranged concentrically and the planets orbited the Earth in the most perfect geometric figure, the circle.[16] From the Moon to the fixed stars, this resulted in seven planetary layers of the heavenly region (Fig. 50.1), a perfect example of seven being a number of totality, consummation, and wholeness.

---

15 For detailed references to Aristotle's works in which the following ideas can be found, see Dicks, *Early Greek astronomy* 194–219.

16 Aristotle's model was, in fact, slightly more complex. Refining a model first devised by his predecessor Eudoxus, Aristotle explained the intricacy of each planet's motion by a set of nested concentric spheres, with the planet itself being situated on the innermost one and each of these nested spheres carrying out one component of planetary motion, which was thus a combination of uniform circular motions. In addition, Aristotle inserted sets of spheres in between the innermost sphere carrying a planet and the outermost sphere belonging to the next planet placed below it, so as to counteract transmission of their respective movements.

Aristotle's geocentric model of the cosmos was widely accepted by philosophers and educated people in ancient Greece and beyond. It was straightforward and seemed to confirm the evidence of the senses. Night after night we can observe how the stars rise in the east, move through the skies and eventually set in the west, with the same groupings of stars or constellations reappearing in the same relative position, while we feel the Earth firmly at rest beneath our feet.[17] It is therefore not surprising that Aristotle's cosmology, reflecting perfection and symmetry, constituted the most influential model for nearly 2000 years.

Unfortunately, it did not work in detail. It was the planets, moving individually among the fixed stars, which caused problems. The Greek noun *planes*, meaning a "wanderer," "roamer," "vagabond," conveys a sense of random motion and reflects the Greek intellectuals' puzzlement with regard to the planets. One obvious problem was related to the observation that they vary in brightness. It strongly suggested that their distance from Earth increased and decreased considerably. Yet on a circular planetary orbit this would be impossible, because by definition the distance from the center is constant.

3.2 *Ptolemy*

It was the second-century CE Greek astronomer Ptolemy who – while preserving the underlying concept of the seven planetary spheres – readdressed the issue of planetary motion. Ptolemy took a mathematical approach and provided geometric models to explain and predict the movements of the planets. Ptolemy's main work dealing with astronomy, the *Almagest*, equipped mathematical astronomers with diagrams, formulas, and tables to calculate future planetary positions in longitude and latitude.[18] The predictions were much more accurate than those based on models presented by Ptolemy's predecessors. But as long as circular orbits and a geocentric (Earth-centered) model of the cosmos were used, mathematically derived forecasts and astronomical phenomena would never match exactly. Notwithstanding, Ptolemy's *Almagest*

17 By contrast, post-Copernican astronomy presents the notion that Earth is spinning on its axis, while at the same time racing through space at high speed.

18 Ptolemy's great contribution is a presentation of models for planetary movement that allowed the description of anomalistic motion while retaining the principle of uniform circular motion. The authoritative English translation of the *Almagest* was prepared by Toomer (trans. and annot.), *Ptolemy's Almagest*. See Pederson, *Survey*, and Neugebauer, *Mathematical astronomy* i, 21–261, for detailed commentaries on the work.

became enormously influential for the mathematical astronomers in the Islamic world.[19]

4 The Concept of the Seven Planetary Spheres in the Mithras Cult of the Ancient Roman World

We encounter the seven heavenly layers again in an entirely different context, in the Roman Mithras cult. Originally, the god Mithra (*sic*) was a deity in the early Zoroastrian pantheon of the Iranian-speaking peoples of the mid-first millennium BCE. Roman contact with the East brought knowledge of the deity's attributes to Italy, where there was a fundamental transformation of the beliefs. For the Iranians, Mithra "personifies the sanctity of contracts and thereby becomes the just judge who … judges the souls of men according to their deeds," while for the Romans, "Mithras is a saviour god who releases the human soul from the trammels of a purely mundane existence which is under the severe and hostile control of the Zodiac and the planets, the agents of an unseeing Fate."[20]

As in other cultures, planets were perceived of as errant and vagabond, and therefore potentially dangerous. Sacrifice was one way to propitiate these forces, and at the same time Mithras' slaying of the ceremonial bull was understood as an act that would ultimately offer immortality of the soul. Ritual sacrifice became a dominant element of Roman Mithraic ceremonies.[21]

Romanized Mithraism grew into an attractive alternative to the worship of the official Roman deities. In the almost complete absence of written sources, reconstruction of the practices of the cult relies on examination and interpretation of the archaeological record.[22] In the context of this paper, three well-preserved Mithras sanctuaries (Mithraea, sing. Mithraeum) dating to the mid-second to the mid-third centuries CE in Ostia, the port of ancient Rome, are of particular significance. Half-circles in the floor mosaics of the

19 For the seven celestial spheres in Islamic philosophy, see Michael Marmura's contribution to the present publication, especially the sections on al-Fārābī and Ibn Sīnā.

20 Zaehner, *Dawn and twilight of Zoroastrianism* 99.

21 It should be acknowledged here that explanations of origin and development of Mithraism vary widely. For a comprehensive survey of the different theories, see Jacobs, *Mithrasmysterien* 9–55.

22 Needless to say, there is no general consensus among the authors and a range of opinions can be found not only regarding detailed connotations, but also general concepts of the cult.

Mithraeum of the Seven Spheres divide the aisle into seven sections, a concept that is also found in the Mithraeum of the Seven Doors, while the mosaics in the Mithraeum of Felicissimus depict the seven planets.[23]

The interpretation of these artistic features takes us to the liturgical activity which seems to have included a ceremonial procession of (initiated) cult participants, and it has been suggested that as part of it

> the participants made a symbolic passage through the seven planetary spheres of salvation.... In the Mithraeum of Felicissimus the signs of the seven grades of initiation, which correspond to the seven planetary spheres, could represent the seven steps of salvation as one proceeded from the rear of the sanctuary to the front.[24]

5 Astronomy in the Islamic World

The foundations of astronomy and the study of the configuration of the heavens had thus been laid long before Islam. These included the concept of the seven planetary spheres. While one might assume that Muslim astronomers would have rejected pre-Islamic astronomy because it represented the pagan past, this was not the case. Most of the Muslim scholars treated the scientific works of their predecessors with great respect and studied them thoroughly, either the original texts in the languages in which they had been composed or after they had been translated into Arabic.[25] An extraordinary intellectual open-mindedness is expressed by the ninth-century scientist and philosopher Abū Yūsuf Yaʿqūb b. Isḥāq al-Kindī: "We must not be ashamed of deeming truth good and of acquiring truth from wherever it comes, even if it comes from races remote from us and nations different from us."[26] Al-Kindī's commitment

---

23 Groh, Ostian Mithraeum 11; Stewardson and Saunders, Mithraic liturgy 73; Laeuchli, *Mithraism* pls. 1, 21–8.

24 Stewardson and Saunders, Mithraic liturgy 73.

25 The religious debate over the appropriateness of studying the "ancient sciences" has been examined by Goldziher, Attitude 185–215. He draws the conclusion that "the theoretical protests and desiderata of one-sided theologians in Islam were scarcely able to interfere with developments in the real world." (Goldziher, Attitude 209) More recently, Ragep, Freeing astronomy, re-addresses the issue and provides a fresh approach to the complex relationship between the religion of Islam and science in general, and the study of astronomy in particular.

26 Al-Kindī, *Fī l-falsafa al-ūlā* (On first philosophy), chapter 1, translated in Marmura, *Islamic philosophy* 394.

to learning, whatever its source, included specifically the heritage from ancient, pre-Islamic civilizations. In astronomy this means, first and foremost, the works of the Greeks. It would be wrong, though, to state that science in the Islamic world is Greek science translated into Arabic.[27] From the beginning there was much more involved than mere translation. Based on a thorough study of the ancient texts, scholars in the Islamic world made their own original contributions to furthering scientific knowledge (Fig. 50.2).

5.1 *Astronomy and the Religion of Islam*[28]

The reason that astronomy became a prominent scientific discipline in the Islamic world is directly related to the religion of Islam and some of its core requirements. In Islam, more than in any other religion in human history, the appropriate performance of various religious rituals is determined with the help of astronomy. This includes – first – the use of crescent visibility and the lunar calendar for the regulation of the religious year. The first sighting of the crescent Moon that marks the beginning of a month is fairly simple, as long as one knows to look west shortly after sunset. Professional astronomers took up the cause to try and find a mathematical method to determine the beginning of a new month for calendar predictions. But they failed in their efforts. Even today, with the use of computers, the beginning and the end of a month based on the actual first sighting of the crescent Moon cannot be predicted with certainty, which becomes particularly apparent every year at the beginning and the end of Ramadan, the month of daylight fasting. This is to a large extent due to non-quantifiable atmospheric conditions. For instance, pollution may increase the glow in the sky from the setting Sun such that the first sliver of the crescent Moon is not visible.

The second religious requirement that posed a challenge for the astronomers involved the orientation of the *qibla*, the local direction of the Kaʿba in Mecca that Muslim believers face for prayer, wherever they are. It became an important issue with the rapid spread of Islam. The prayer wall of a mosque must

27 This is the fallacious assessment of Islamic medicine in particular and Islamic science in general which is expressed by Ullmann, *Islamic medicine* xi.

28 See King, Religion 245–62, and King, Islamic society 128–84, for the astronomical details. The notion of "science in the service of religion," a phrase originally coined by King, has been challenged by Ragep, Freeing astronomy 50–1, who argues that "Muslim ritual could have survived perfectly well without the astronomers" and "that this 'service to religion' was really religion's service to the astronomers, both Muslim and non-Muslim, providing on the one hand a degree of social legitimation and on the other a set of interesting mathematical problems to solve."

be oriented toward Mecca, and this has major repercussions for the layout of the entire building. The *qibla* is a function of longitude and latitude of a given locality and Mecca. The long distances across the Islamic world, together with the curvature of the Earth, present a complex problem that can only be solved with the help of spherical trigonometry. Scientists were also successful in reducing the three-dimensional problem to two dimensions, which allowed them to resolve the issue through plane trigonometry. The calculations involved in solving the *qibla* problem gave rise to a level of sophistication in trigonometry that was unknown in the Greek and Indian methods previously used. The resulting advances indicate that the discipline of trigonometry, both plane and spherical, should be considered "essentially a creation of Arabic-writing scientists."[29]

The third issue was the determination of the specific times of the daily prayers. Since the eighth century CE, the daytime prayers were defined on the basis of shadow length – or, more specifically, shadow increase – that is, by using the sundial principle.

- At astronomical midday the Sun has arrived at its highest position in the sky, and the shadow cast by any vertical object, which serves as the gnomon (the rod of a sundial), has reached its minimum. The absolute length of this minimum varies over the course of the year, following the Sun's changing altitude in the sky.
- The time of the *ẓuhr*, or noon prayer, begins when the shadow of the object has increased over its shortest length by an observable amount, that is, after the sun has noticeably started its downward path. This definition was even more specific in some medieval Muslim circles (al-Andalus and the Maghrib) where the noon prayer began as soon as the shadow increase equaled one quarter of the height of the vertical object.
- The *ʿaṣr*, or afternoon prayer, begins when the shadow increase over its mid-day minimum has reached the length of the object's height.

In the same way as the astronomers tackled crescent visibility and the *qibla* problem, they developed complex mathematical approaches in spherical astronomy to pre-determine the exact time when a prayer should begin. One of the results was the successful computation of prayer tables. Based on the astronomers' firm understanding of the changing solar altitude throughout the year – and the principle of the apparent daily rotation of the celestial sphere in general – the tables were calculated for a specific geographical latitude, for

29 Kennedy, The Arabic heritage 40.

instance the latitude of Baghdad or Cairo, and listed the shadow lengths of a gnomon for the individual daytime prayers.[30]

5.2 *Planetary Theories*

The questions addressed by the astronomers and the solutions found reflect scientific sophistication, and the fact that the requirements of the religion of Islam stimulated this work underscores the fact that the scholars were exploring new directions of astronomical inquiry and had to find answers to a set of problems not considered by the Greeks. In the same innovative spirit, astronomers soon started to tackle topics outside the religious sphere. Once again, it was the motion of the planets, the seven wanderers, which caused them to ponder.

A radical critique of Ptolemy's theory of planetary motion was written by the eleventh-century Iraqi scientist Ibn al-Haytham (d. ca. 1040) under the title *al-Shukūk ʿalā Baṭlamyūs* (Doubts on Ptolemy). In this work, the author identified sixteen problems in Ptolemy's controversial elaborations,[31] and because of the serious shortcomings of Ptolemaic theory, Ibn al-Haytham called for a new approach in astronomy, the aim of which was to rectify the mistakes made and to develop alternative theoretical underpinnings.

One of the astronomers who recognized the necessity to reform astronomy and establish non-Ptolemaic planetary models was the thirteenth-century Iranian astronomer Naṣīr al-Dīn al-Ṭūsī (d. 1274). It was Ptolemy's fundamentally flawed theory of planetary latitudes that evoked al-Ṭūsī's criticism. He developed a new mathematical model, known today as the "Ṭūsī couple," and then applied this device in his work *al-Tadhkira fī ʿilm al-hayʾa* (Memorandum on the science of astronomy, written around 1260) to provide a fresh explanation of the latitudinal motion of the planets.[32] Three hundred years after Naṣīr

30 Similarly, the time of night could be obtained from the altitudes of certain fixed stars.

31 Even though Ptolemy accepted the rule of uniform circular motion of the planets, he introduced an off-center point of a circle – the equant – around which he "uniformized" planetary motion, see Cohen, *New physics* 28–33. The equant was the most controversial issue in Ptolemy's theory of planetary motion. It seemed to violate the principle of uniform circular motion and while it may have made sense as part of a mathematical model, it contradicted the physical reality, as Ibn al-Haytham points out very clearly (*al-Shukūk* 26–7). See Pines, Critique 548–9, for a discussion of Ibn al-Haytham's criticism of the equant. Dallal, *Islam* 68–71, has recently re-examined Ibn al-Haytham's objections to Ptolemy's models.

32 Ragep (ed., trans. and comm.), *Memoir* i, 194–9. The Ṭūsī couple managed to reduce latitudinal planetary motion to a combination of uniform circular motions. It was physically admissible; Ptolemy's awkward equant was no longer required.

al-Dīn al-Ṭūsī, the Polish astronomer Copernicus (1473–1543), who was equally dissatisfied with Ptolemy's model of planetary motion, used the Ṭūsī couple in his heliocentric cosmology. In his *De revolutionibus* (1543) Copernicus in fact reproduced al-Ṭūsī's diagram, nearly identical with al-Ṭūsī's own version in the *Tadhkira*, regrettably without citing his source.[33]

6 Conclusion

Even though religious requirements stimulated astronomical research, the rich and sophisticated contributions to astronomy in the Islamic world were not made within the sphere of religion, but as part of the discourse of *ʿilm al-hayʾa*, the science of the configuration (of the heavens), a term that designated astronomy proper from the tenth century onwards.[34] This is despite the fact that many of the astronomers were also renowned religious scholars, with al-Ṭūsī being a prominent example.[35] The increasingly mathematical approach to the heavens as an object of astronomical inquiry was best expressed by al-Ṭūsī's student and later associate, the Persian astronomer (and polymath, who also wrote several works on religious topics) Quṭb al-Dīn al-Shīrāzī (d. 1311). He extrapolated from Ptolemy's *Almagest*[36] and stated in a succinct summary: "Astronomy is the noblest of the sciences.... [I]ts proofs are secure – being of number and geometry – about which there can be no doubt, unlike the proofs in physics and theology."[37] His point of view was shared by the Central Asian astronomer ʿAlāʾ al-Dīn ʿAlī al-Qūshjī (d. 1474):

> The upshot is that that which is stated in the science of astronomy (*ʿilm al-hayʾa*) does not depend upon physical (*ṭabīʿiyya*) and theological (*ilāhiyya*) premises (*muqaddamāt*). The common practice by authors of introducing their books with them is by way of following the philosophers; this, however, is not something necessary, and it is indeed possible

---

33 Copernicus, *Manuscript* fol. 75. The issue was discussed in detail by Swerdlow and Neugebauer, *Mathematical astronomy* i, 41–8.

34 See Saliba, Medieval Arabic thought 137–49 and 163, for the conceptual and linguistic designation of astronomy proper with the distinct term *ʿilm al-hayʾa*.

35 Saliba, *Islamic science* 188–90.

36 Book I.1, see Toomer (trans. and annot.), *Ptolemy's Almagest* 35–6.

37 Al-Shīrāzī, preface to *Nihāyat al-idrāk fī dirāyat al-aflāk* (The highest intelligence in the knowledge of the celestial spheres), translated in Ragep, Freeing astronomy 58. This book is one of two comprehensive works on astronomy by al-Shīrāzī.

> to establish [this science] without basing it upon them. For of what is stated in [this science]: (1) some things are geometrical premises, which are not open to doubt.[38]

Such an attitude was fundamental to enable great astronomical advances in understanding and explaining the heavens, and meant that the astronomers of the Islamic world could go far beyond the level of knowledge of their ancient predecessors and standard Aristotelian ideas of the seven heavenly spheres. Their concern was with the natural configuration of the heavens of this world, not with the spiritual heaven.

Bibliography

Britton, J. and C. Walker, Astronomy and astrology in Mesopotamia, in C. Walker (ed.), *Astronomy before the telescope*, London 1996, 42–67.

Cohen, I.B., *The birth of a new physics*, New York and London 1960, 1985 (rev. ed.).

Conrad, L.I., Seven and the *tasbīʿ*: On the implications of numerical symbolism for the study of medieval Islamic history, in *JESHO* 31 (1988), 42–73.

Copernicus, N., *Complete works*, i, *The manuscript of Nicholas Copernicus'* On the revolutions, *Facsimile*, London, Warsaw and Kracow 1972.

Dallal, A., *Islam, science, and the challenge of history*, New Haven, CT and London 2010.

Dalley, S., The influence of Mesopotamia upon Israel and the Bible, in S. Dalley (ed.), *The legacy of Mesopotamia*, Oxford 1998, 57–83.

Dicks, D.R., *Early Greek astronomy to Aristotle*, Bristol 1970.

Goldziher, I., Stellung der alten islamischen Orthodoxie zu den antiken Wissenschaften, in *Abhandlungen der Königlich-Preussischen Akademie der Wissenschaften, Philosophisch-historische Klasse* 8 (1915), 1–46, repr. in English translation: The attitude of orthodox Islam toward the "ancient sciences," in M.L. Swartz (ed. and trans.), *Studies on Islam*, New York and Oxford 1981, 185–215.

Gregory, A., *Eureka! The birth of science*, Duxford 2001.

Groh, D., The Ostian mithraeum, in S. Laeuchli (ed.), *Mithraism in Ostia* (Garrett Theological Studies, 1), Evanston IN 1967, 9–21.

Homer, *The Iliad*, trans. E.V. Rieu, Melbourne, London, and Baltimore 1950, repr. 1954.

Horowitz, W., *Mesopotamian cosmic geography*, Winona Lake IN 1998.

38 Al-Qūshjī, *Sharḥ tajrīd al-ʿaqāʾid* (Commentary on the epitome of belief), translated in Ragep, Freeing astronomy 68. The book is a commentary on al-Ṭūsī's theological work *Tajrīd al-ʿaqāʾid*.

Hunger, H. and D. Pingree, *Astral sciences in Mesopotamia* (HO 1.44), Leiden, Boston, and Cologne 1999.

Ibn al-Haytham, *al-Shukūk ʿalā Baṭlamyūs* (*Dubitationes in Ptolemaeum*), ed. A. Sabra and N. Shehaby, Cairo 1971.

Jacobs, B., *Die Herkunft und Entstehung der römischen Mithrasmysterien: Überlegungen zur Rolle des Stifters und zu den astronomischen Hintergründen der Kultlegende* (Xenia: Konstanzer Althistorische Vorträge und Forschungen, 43), Konstanz, Germany 1999.

Kennedy, E.S., The Arabic heritage in the exact sciences, in *al-Abḥāth* 23 (1970), 327–44, repr. in E.S. Kennedy, *Studies in the Islamic exact sciences*, Beirut 1983, 30–47.

King, D.A., Astronomy and Islamic society: Qibla, gnomonics and timekeeping, in R. Rashed (ed.), *Encyclopedia of the history of Arabic science*, i, London and New York 1996, 128–84.

———, Science in the service of religion: The case of Islam, in *Impact of science on society* 159 (1990), 245–62.

Koch-Westenholz, U., *Mesopotamian astrology: An introduction to Babylonian and Assyrian celestial divination* (The Carsten Niebuhr Institute Publications, 19), Copenhagen 1995.

Laeuchli, S. (ed.), *Mithraism in Ostia* (Garrett Theological Studies, 1), Evanston IN 1967.

Marmura, M., *Probing in Islamic philosophy: Studies in the philosophies of Ibn Sīnā, al-Ghazālī and other major Muslim thinkers*, Binghamton NY 2005.

Neugebauer, O., *A history of ancient mathematical astronomy*, 3 vols., Berlin, Heidelberg, and New York 1975.

Pedersen, O., *A survey of the Almagest*, Odense, Denmark 1974.

Pines, S., Ibn al-Haytham's critique of Ptolemy, in *Actes du dixième congrès international d'histoire des sciences* (*Ithaca 1962*), i, Paris 1964, 547–50.

Pingree, D.E., Legacies in astronomy and celestial omens, in S. Dalley (ed.), *The legacy of Mesopotamia*, Oxford 1998, 125–37.

Ragep, F.J., Freeing astronomy from philosophy: An aspect of Islamic influence on science, in *Osiris* 16 (2001), 49–71.

——— (ed., trans. and comm.), *Naṣīr al-Dīn al-Ṭūsī's* Memoir on astronomy (*al-Tadhkira fī ʿilm al-hayʾa*), 2 vols., New York 1993.

Rochberg-Halton, F., Astrology, astronomy, and the birth of scientific inquiry, in *Bulletin of the Canadian Society for Mesopotamian Studies* 19 (1990), 25–33.

———, *The heavenly writing: Divination, horoscopy, and astronomy in Mesopotamian culture*, Cambridge 2004.

Saliba, G., Astronomy and astrology in medieval Arabic thought, in R. Rashed and J. Biard (eds.), *Les doctrines de la science de l'antiquité à l'âge classique*, Leuven 1999, 131–64.

———, *Islamic science and the making of the European Renaissance*, Cambridge and London 2007.
Steele, J.M., *A brief introduction to astronomy in the Middle East*, London, San Francisco, and Beirut 2008.
Stewardson, J. and E. Saunders, Reflections on the Mithraic liturgy, in S. Laeuchli (ed.), *Mithraism in Ostia* (Garrett Theological Studies, 1), Evanston IN 1967, 67–84.
Swerdlow, N.M. and O. Neugebauer, *Mathematical astronomy in Copernicus's* De revolutionibus, 2 vols. (Studies in the History of Mathematics and Physical Sciences, 10), New York 1984.
Toomer, G.J. (trans. and annot.), *Ptolemy's Almagest*, London 1984.
Ullmann, M., *Islamic medicine*, Edinburgh 1978, repr. 1997.
Zaehner, R.C., *The dawn and twilight of Zoroastrianism*, London 1961.

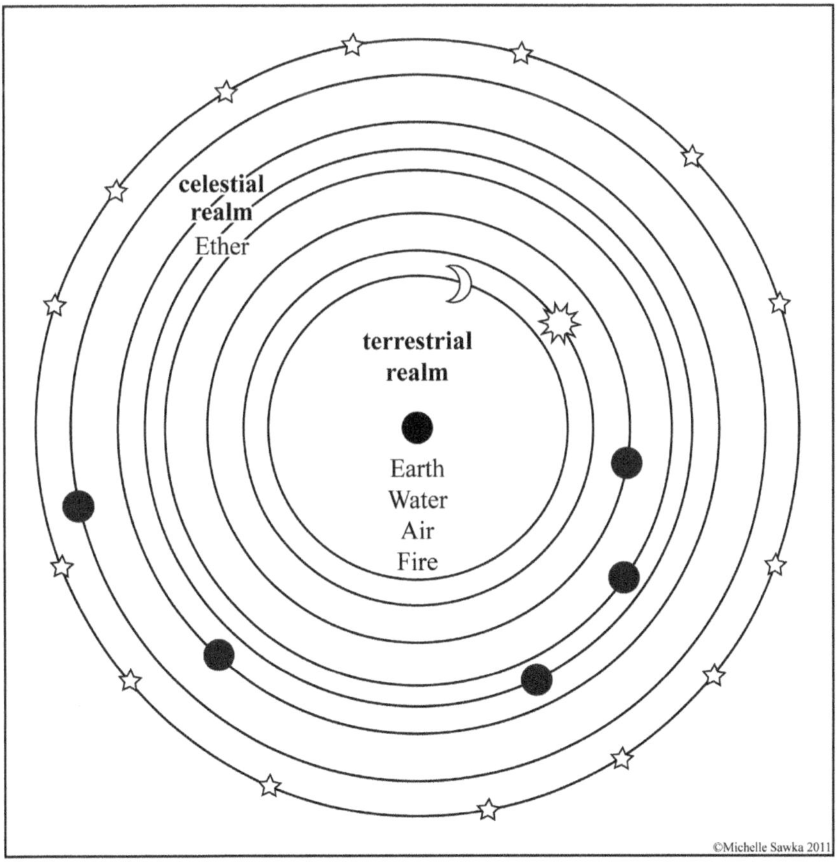

FIGURE 50.1 *Aristotle's Earth-centered cosmos (not drawn to scale, and with the set of nested spheres omitted) (based on Gregory,* Eureka *Figs. 9 and 12).*

FIGURE 50.2 *The constellation of Sagittarius the Archer as seen in the night sky. Ink and color on paper, from* Kitāb Ṣuwar al-kawākib al-thābita (*Book of the figures of the fixed stars*) *by ʿAbd al-Raḥmān al-Ṣūfī* (*d. 986*), *Iran, seventeenth century.*
WITH PERMISSION OF THE ROYAL ONTARIO MUSEUM © ROM (971.292.13).

CHAPTER 51

The Quadrants of *Sharīʿa*: The Here and Hereafter as Constitutive of Islamic Law

*Anver M. Emon**

The relationship between law and morality is a topic of considerable debate in Anglo-American legal philosophy. That debate is often identified with the exchange between H.L.A. Hart and Lord Patrick Devlin in the latter half of the twentieth century. The debate started when a 1957 committee recommended that consensual sexual activity between men in private should be decriminalized. This recommendation met with sharp criticism from Lord Devlin. As Peter Cane states,

> Although Devlin did not express it as straightforwardly as he might have, his basic point was that the criminal law was not (just) for the protection of individuals but also for the protection of society – 'the institutions and the community of ideas, political and moral, without which people cannot live together.'[1]

* The Islamic legal research herein was inspired by my work with Professor Denise Spellberg, of the University of Texas at Austin, a mentor, colleague, and friend, to whom I owe many thanks. The author also wishes to thank Sebastian Günther and Todd Lawson for their generous support and encouragement of this article, as well as Meghan Clark and Aleatha Cox for their assistance in editing the article. This article benefited greatly from all of the above; all errors and limitations that remain are the author's responsibility. The quadrants model offered herein was first presented at a graduate seminar at the Faculty of Law on Law, Religion, and the Public Sphere, which I co-taught with Jennifer Nedelsky. The debate around the quadrants model, from both the students in that seminar and from Professor Nedelsky helped make this a better article. The initial inspiration for this article came from a grant awarded to myself and my colleague Robert Gibbs from Canada's Social Science and Humanities Research Council, and which supported our research on the nature of legal reasoning in Islamic and Jewish law. The author gratefully acknowledges the support of the SSHRC.

1 Cane, Taking law seriously 22, quoting Patrick Devlin, *The enforcement of morals* (Oxford 1965), 22.

 | DOI 10.1163/9789004333154_052

Hart rejected Devlin's assertion, and instead argued that the scope of the criminal law was defined by the harm principle, which seeks to prevent harm to others.[2] He outright repudiated the view that legal enforcement of widely held moral norms is justified. This is a deeply contested debate, and one that remains a topic of considerable scholarship.[3] This is not the place to address the nuances of that debate. But that issue in contemporary legal philosophy certainly forms a backdrop to this essay.

The distinction between law and morality seems to be in the minds of many who write about Islamic law and explain its scope of regulation to an audience unfamiliar with the tradition.[4] In doing so, though, they rely on that distinction to illustrate the limits and inefficiency of the Islamic legal tradition. For instance, Wael Hallaq argues that the meaning of 'law' is so substantially founded upon assumptions about the state and its institutional powers that any characterization of *sharīʿa* as "law" will render it a failed system. As evidence, he refers to the "routine and widespread pronouncement, usually used to introduce Islamic law to the uninitiated, namely, that the Sharīʿa does not distinguish between law and morality."[5] For Hallaq, the view that *sharīʿa* suffers no distinction between law and morality is relied upon as one of the factors that "rendered [the *sharīʿa*] inefficient and paralyzed."[6] In Islamist circles, the unity between law and morality in the *sharīʿa*, however, is applauded as yet further evidence of the moral superiority of Islam over other legal systems; these systems, they say, have stripped law of moral content.[7] Between these two views of Islamic law lies a third, which emphasizes that all rules in Islamic law are categorized pursuant to the *al-aḥkām al-khamsa*, or the five categories of legal value: obligatory (*wājib*), recommended (*mustaḥabb*), permitted (*ḥalāl*), reprehensible (*makrūh*), and prohibited (*ḥarām/maḥẓūr*). This typology of rules is used to show that Islamic law has its own approach to distinguishing between 'law' and 'morality': the obligatory and prohibited are "law" in the modern sense, while the recommended and reprehensible categories are extra-legal, falling into the realm of morality.[8]

---

2 Cane, Taking law seriously 22.

3 For other views on the debate, see Dworkin, Enforcement of morals 986–1005.

4 Kamali, *Shari'ah law* 43–4; Coulson, *Conflicts and tensions* 77–95, who begins his discussion by reference to Hart's discussion of law and morality, where he responds to Devlin.

5 Hallaq, *Sharīʿa* 2.

6 Ibid.

7 Abu-Saud, *Concept of Islam* 118–20; Moaddel and Talattof, *Contemporary debates in Islam* 197–206 (presenting Sayyid Qutb's Islam and culture, excerpted from his *Milestones*).

8 Kamali, *Principles* 44–6; Kamali, *Shari'ah law* 44; Hallaq, *Sharīʿa* 84–5. Hallaq disagrees with this latter argument, and suggests that Muslim jurists did not distinguish between law and

Hallaq's apprehension and critique of characterizing Islamic law in terms of the law/morality distinction both challenges the assumptions underlying the meaning of "law," and runs the risk of isolating Islamic law from compelling philosophical debates about law, its limits, and its coercive power. The Hart/Devlin debate concerned whether and to what extent particular substantive moral norms could be relied upon in the UK legal system, which has its own history and institutional design. Elsewhere, I have written about how pre-modern Muslim jurists were cognizant about the public good (*ḥuqūq Allāh*) and individual interests (*ḥuqūq al-ʿibād*) as they used reason to reach legal outcomes about substantive doctrine.[9] In both cases, conceptual dichotomies operate to categorize different types of interests and aspirations that animate the development of law.

Conceptual dichotomies, whether law/morality or *ḥuqūq Allāh/ḥuqūq al-ʿibād*, provide analytic modes of understanding and appreciating the dynamics of the law. And however useful they may be, when employing them, we must remain mindful about how such conceptual dichotomies carry more intellectual baggage than may be duly disclosed. For instance, in Hart and Devlin's debate, at issue was not so much what is law and what is morality, but rather whether the state can legislate general rules of criminal law based on a particular moral outlook. The intelligibility of their debate depends, therefore, on a variety of unstated preconditions, not all of which were historically present in the formative period of Islamic law. Such preconditions might include:

- The existence of a state with centralized legislative and enforcement power;
- A morally pluralistic polity in which all are given equal status;
- A democratically formed state in which the will of the people is accounted for in a legislative process.

Not all of these preconditions map onto the Islamic historical tradition, legal or otherwise. Consequently the stakes for Hart and Devlin may not be easily translatable for the purpose of analyzing pre-modern Islamic law and legal theory. That does not mean that the underlying interests captured by "law" and "morality" cannot be defined or articulated in different ways that take into account the differences posed by competing legal systems. Nor are we constrained by conceptual dichotomies that are borrowed from other traditions. As noted above, the pre-modern Islamic conceptual dichotomy of *ḥuqūq*

---

morality. Instead, he queries the modern division between law and morality, which he suggests is neither normative nor natural in the course of human history.

9 Emon, *Ḥuqūq Allāh* and *ḥuqūq al-ʿibād*.

Allāh and *ḥuqūq al-ʿibād* offers one site of examination. Another site, which is the topic of this essay, concerns the role of the here and hereafter in legal reasoning.

Imagine for a moment each Islamic doctrinal rule occupying a position on an x-y graph. The horizontal x axis reflects the impact and significance of a given doctrinal rule on individuals living in society together. The vertical y axis reflects the relationship of the doctrinal rule to the will of God. Any doctrinal rule, therefore, is plotted on the x-y graph in light of considerations about the social significance of a given rule of law (the here = *al-dunya* in Quranic parlance), and its eschatological implications for the believer (the hereafter = *al-ākhira*). The more the doctrinal rules reflect social considerations, the higher the x value and the lower the y value (although greater than zero). The more the doctrinal rules reflect a concern about God's will and eschatological concerns, the higher the y value and the lower the x value. Ideally, every rule should be plotted in quadrant I, where the x and y values are both positive.

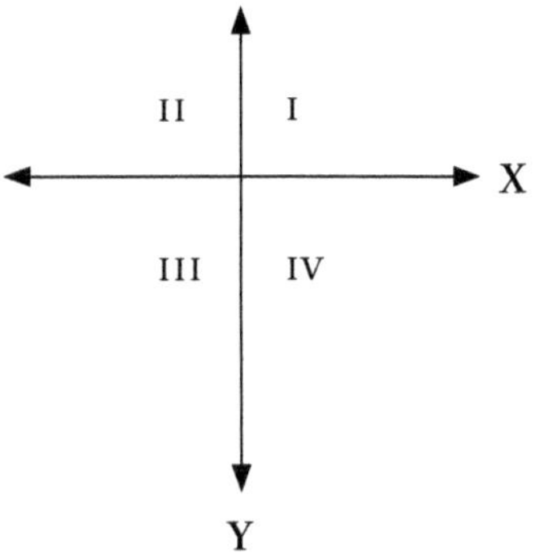

Problems in justification and legitimacy may arise when a doctrinal rule is plotted in quadrants II, III, or IV. For instance, a rule that aspires to fulfill God's will but comes at a certain social cost might have a negative X-value and a positive Y-value, and thus be plotted in quadrant II. A rule that has a positive social value but seems to violate God's desires will have a positive X-value but negative Y-value, and thus fall in quadrant IV. A rule that adversely impacts the social well-being and violates God's will falls into quadrant III. Being mindful of these quadrants, we can imagine a Muslim jurist taking into account both the 'here' and 'hereafter' when considering how to evaluate a particular doctrinal rule, with the goal of ensuring that every doctrinal rule is plotted in quadrant I. In other words, to the extent this collection of essays concerns paradise as a destination, Islamic law in general and the quadrants model in particular emphasize the signs along the way. Rather than being about paradise as eschatological destination, this chapter focuses on law in order to reflect on the challenges of the journey itself.

To illustrate and justify the explanatory power of this proposed quadrant model of analysis, this essay addresses different doctrinal issues in the history of Islamic law. In particular, the legal issues discussed revolve around the dog in Islamic law. The dog was a subject of legal debate that moved between concerns about the here and the hereafter. Those concerns were framed in terms of, for example, ritual requirements for prayer, the regulation of the domestic household, and the management of agricultural professions. Although this study focuses on traditions concerning dogs, it is not meant to offer a scholarly treatment of the dog in the Islamic tradition.[10] Rather this study introduces a conceptual model of analysis, using debates about the dog, to grasp and appreciate how the here and hereafter contribute to Muslim jurists' reasoning about the law.

1 Why the Dog?

The vast number of doctrinal rules about the dog, arguably, are built upon a particular tradition concerning a dog that licked water from a bowl. A *ḥadīth*, narrated by the companion of the Prophet Muḥammad, Abū Hurayra (d. ca. 58 or 59/678),[11] reads: "The messenger of God… said 'If a dog licks your container, wash it seven times.'"[12] A second version of this *ḥadīth* stipulates different numbers for the required washings;[13] and a third version requires one

10 For studies on the dog in the Islamic tradition, see Abou El Fadl, Lord of the essence 316–30; Abou El Fadl, Dogs in the Islamic tradition 498–500.

11 The fact that Abū Hurayra narrated this *ḥadīth* is a point of initial interest. It is relatively well known that Abū Hurayra was fond of cats. His name suggests his favoritism toward that animal (i.e., father of a female kitten). It is reported that he received his *kunya*, Abū Hurayra, because he found a kitten and carried it in his sleeve. On the other hand, other sources suggest that he may have also owned a farm dog. Al-Dhahabī, *Siyar aʿlām* ii, 579; al-Nawawī, *Sharḥ ṣaḥīḥ Muslim* ix–x, 478, 483.

12 Al-Nawawī, *Sharḥ ṣaḥīḥ Muslim* iii–iv, 174.

13 The Ḥanafīs rely on a version of the Abū Hurayra *ḥadīth* on dogs and water in which the Prophet is reported to have required either three, five, or seven washings. Al-Sarakhsī, *Kitāb al-Mabsūṭ* i–ii, 48; al-Kāsānī, *Badāʾiʿ al-ṣanāʾiʿ* i, 374; al-Shawkānī, *Nayl al-awṭār* i–ii, 34; Ibn Ḥajar al-ʿAsqalānī, *Fatḥ al-bārī* i, 332; al-Mubārakfūrī, *Tuḥfat al-aḥwadhī* 253–4.

to dump the contents of the container prior to washing it seven times.[14] A fourth version reads as follows: "The messenger of God ... said: 'Concerning the purity of your container (*ṭuhūrinā' aḥadikum*), if a dog licks from it, wash it seven times.'"[15] Furthermore, some versions of this *ḥadīth* pose the additional requirement of sprinkling sand or earth in one of the washings.[16] The use of sand or earth as a cleansing agent both recognizes the purity of the earth for purification purposes,[17] and renders the dog's impurity something that goes beyond a concern about conventional dirt per se.

At the core of the tradition is a concern about the implication of the dog for the purity of the water in the bowl. The implication of this concern can extend far and wide, based on the multitude of ways impurity can both transfer to other objects and affect human behavior. For instance:

- Can a Muslim use the water a dog licks to perform ritual ablutions?
- How large must the container of water be before concerns about wasting water used for purification arise?
- If the dog is impure, can it be bought and sold in the market?

The potential impact this single tradition could have on a multitude of issues prompted the jurist Ibn Ḥajar al-ʿAsqalānī (d. 853/1449) to write: "The discussions on this *ḥadīth*, and the issues that arise from it, are so widespread that one could write an entire book [about them]."[18] The wide array of legal issues the dog raises permits us to examine whether and how the proposed quadrants model of the *sharīʿa* offers a better approach to understanding the nature of Islamic legal analysis, in contrast to the more dominant model of jurisprudence that posits an analytic dichotomy between law and morality.

---

14 Al-Nawawī, *Sharḥ ṣaḥīḥ Muslim* iii–iv, 174. Those who oppose the implications of this addition (i.e., *iraqqa*) argue that one of the members of the *isnād*, ʿAlī b. Mushīr (d. 189/804), was not a reliable transmitter. However, al-Dhahabī considers him trustworthy. Al-Dhahabī, *Siyar aʿlām* viii, 484. See also al-Ziriklī, *al-Aʿlām* v, 22.

15 Al-Nawawī, *Sharḥ ṣaḥīḥ Muslim* iii–iv, 175. As will be indicated below, seven is not the only number mentioned on this matter. The Ḥanafīs adopt traditions which require three, five, or seven washings. The significance of the number is reflected in how jurists contend with its apparent arbitrariness, which will be discussed below. On the relationship between arbitrariness and rules, see Atiyah and Summers, *Form and substance* 13.

16 Al-Nawawī, *Sharḥ ṣaḥīḥ Muslim* iii–iv, 175–6. There is a debate as to whether one dusts prior to the seven washings, in the first wash, in the last wash, or somewhere in between. See also Ibn Ḥajar al-ʿAsqalānī, *Fatḥ al-bārī* i, 331.

17 Wensinck, Tayammum.

18 Ibn Ḥajar al-ʿAsqalānī, *Fatḥ al-bārī* i, 333.

2 The Dilemma of the Dog: Limiting the Dangers of the Logical Extreme

For Muslim jurists, a source text, such as a *ḥadīth*, can be applied to diverse situations, not all of which are expressly provided for in the *ḥadīth* text. Jurists can analogize (cf. *qiyās*) between express circumstances in the *ḥadīth* and the circumstances of a new situation. In doing so, they engage in an act of legal reasoning that seeks to extend the application of a rule to a similar case that warrants the legal extension.

However, the ability to extend a ruling by analogy depends on whether the *ḥadīth* espousing the initial rule, with its relevant factual circumstances, has a discernible rationale that explains and justifies the legal outcome. Without such a ratio, the *ḥadīth* may not be extended so easily to new and different situations, given that an analogy with a rational nexus between the given rule and the new circumstance cannot be rendered. But if a *ratio* is read into the law, such as "those dogs are impure," the *ratio* could have considerable consequences on social well being.

If jurists render all dogs impure, the consequence of applying the dog-water *ḥadīth* generally and absolutely might lead to considerable waste, whether of water or any other item a dog might touch or lick. This concern led Mālik b. Anas (d. 179/796) to consider it a grave sin for someone to discard something, which was the sustenance of God and was meant to be of benefit, because a dog licked it.[19] To require such waste arguably creates perverse incentives against animals, and could even incite violence against them. Traditions from the Prophet about killing dogs, discussed below, play into and further inflame this incentive.[20]

Jurists, well aware of the social costs that might arise if the dog-water *ḥadīth* were read and applied too broadly, developed different strategies to limit its application. Some jurists believed the tradition was a matter of "worshipful obedience" (*taʿabbud*), because it relates to the believer's commitment to obey God and seek the fulfillment of His will. Jurists such as al-Shāfiʿī held that the dog is impure in its essence. But if the dog is impure in its essence, it could contaminate anything it has contact with. For al-Shāfiʿī, though, this possibility

19 Saḥnūn, *al-Mudawwana* i, 5. See also Ibn Ḥazm, *al-Muḥallā* i, 121.

20 There are various animal rights groups in the Muslim world protesting against governments that engage in seasonal killings of stray dogs. See for example, http://www.esmaegypt.org/. The Fatimid caliph al-Ḥākim bi-Amr Allāh is well known for having decreed the execution of dogs on two separate occasions, presumably because their barking annoyed him. Canard, Ḥākim Bi-Amr Allāh.

is limited because of the absence of any *ratio* explaining the number of washings. For jurists like al-Shāfiʿī, the *ḥadīth* on the dog and water proved perplexing because of the apparent arbitrariness of the number of requisite washings. There seems to be no rationale justifying the number of washings, nor is there a necessary rational connection between the number of washings required and the kind of impurity presumed to be in the water or on the bowl. Indeed, if anything, the required number of washings was simply a directive to be obeyed dutifully. Consequently, while al-Shāfiʿī considered the dog impure, he read the *ḥadīth* as requiring strict, worshipful obedience (*taʿabbud*). In other words, the *ḥadīth* must be adhered to, but can be extended in very limited circumstances, given the lack of an underlying rationale. For this reason, al-Shāfiʿī remarked that it is inappropriate to use the dog-water *ḥadīth* to govern other cases when different impurities fall into water.[21] Hence, although al-Shāfiʿī considered the dog impure, the legal effect of its impurity is limited to instances involving only a dog. If a dog is part of the legal question, the dog-water tradition will govern, even in situations beyond the impurity of water. But other instances of impurity, in which a dog is not involved, cannot be governed by reference to the dog-water *ḥadīth*.

A second interpretive strategy was to read the *ḥadīth* as being less about the dog per se and more about the removal of impurities (*najāsa*). On this basis, these jurists extended the rule to apply to other types of impurity, thereby expanding the precedential effect of the dog-water *ḥadīth*. But in doing so, they had to contend with countervailing issues as well, such as waste. For instance, suppose a dog touches one's clothes or eats solid food from a bowl. Technically these circumstances are not addressed in Abū Hurayra's tradition as noted above. But if we believe the *ḥadīth* relies on the *ratio* of impurity, we may want to extend its application to these new situations. Yet if we extend its application, how far must we go before countervailing considerations, such as waste and limited resources, factor into the analysis?

For example, the Ḥanafī jurist al-Kāsānī (d. 587/1191) suggested that focusing on the dog itself actually blurs the larger issues at stake. Suppose a dog, after being immersed in water, emerges and shakes the water off its body near a group of people. If the water lands on someone's clothes, does that mean the clothing is impure? If we assume the dog is impure in its essence, then anything it touches becomes impure. But if we separate the impurity from the

21 Al-Shāfiʿī, *Umm* i, 20. Al-Shāfiʿī held that the dog-water tradition can be extended to other situations, depending on how one understands what it means to wash. Yet he explicitly considers the dog-water tradition a matter of worshipful obedience. See also al-Māwardī, *al-Ḥāwī l-kabīr* i, 308.

essence of the dog, we can put a break on the slippery slope of imputing pollution to all the dog touches. In other words, we can shift our focus to the impact of the purported impurity on the object of concern. In the example above, al-Kāsānī argues that the issue of impurity has less to do with the dog and more to do with the amount of water that splashes on the clothes. If the amount of water that hits the clothes exceeds the volume and size of a coin (i.e., dirham), the clothes are considered ritually impure and the wearer cannot perform ritual prayers. Anything less entails no impurity.[22]

Similarly, the Mālikī jurist Ibn Rushd al-Jadd (d. 520/1126) held that the tradition applies to the impurities that must be removed. For Ibn Rushd al-Jadd, the reference to the requisite seven washings evokes concerns over the health consequences associated with dogs lapping water, specifically dogs with rabies.[23] He noted that the Prophet said during an illness, "pour over me seven waterskins (*qirab*) whose tying ribbons are untied, so that I can attend to the people."[24] Here, the number seven is associated with medical care, and not any particular impurity. He wrote:

> It is necessary to be cautious of the dog's drinking or eating, and of using the vessel prior to washing it, out of fear that the dog has rabies. It is in the case of rabies, which appears in [the dog's] saliva looking like poison harmful to the body, that the Prophet's command, namely to wash the vessel from which the dog laps seven times to guard against illness, becomes applicable ...[25]

---

22 Al-Kāsānī, *Badāʾiʿ al-ṣanāʾiʿ* i, 414–5.

23 Ibn Rushd al-Jadd, *al-Muqaddimāt* i, 90. Not all Mālikīs would have agreed. Abū Bakr b. al-ʿArabī (d. 543/1148) said: "[In this case] the number [of washings] is mentioned, and a dusting is included with it. This [process] establishes that it is pure out of worship (*ʿibādatan*), [since] there is no requisite number or use of dust for washing out an impurity." Ibn al-ʿArabī, *ʿĀriḍat al-aḥwadhī* ii, 134.

24 Ibn Rushd al-Jadd, *al-Muqaddimāt* i, 90–1.

25 Ibid. This same sort of rationale exists in rules regulating dog ownership in cities across the United States. For instance, Austin, Texas City Ordinance contains a provision prohibiting the ownership of dogs that have not been vaccinated for rabies. Austin City Ordinance s3–3–25(A) provides: "No person shall own, keep or harbor within the city any dog or cat over the age of four months unless such dog or cat has a current rabies vaccination. The dog or cat shall be revaccinated before the expiration of the first and each subsequent current vaccination as provided by state law." Further, the City has gone so far as to authorize the city's Health Authority to sponsor rabies-vaccination clinics. Austin City, 3–3–26.

For Ibn Rushd al-Jadd, the number offers an insight into the rationale of the rule. He was unconvinced that the rule is simply about worshipful obedience; if it were, then the rule could not be extended or analogized to other situations since it lacks a *ratio legis* (*ʿilla*) that provides an objective basis for reasoned analysis. While it may be tempting to consider the *ḥadīth* as a rule of worshipful obedience that cannot be extended to other situations, the social reality of impurity, whether associated with the dog or not, would seem to require sufficient flexibility in the norm to extend to new situations.[26] This is not to suggest, though, that Ibn Rushd al-Jadd disregarded any limits to extending the rule. He was mindful of concerns about waste. So while he generally held that all carnivorous animals (including dogs) contaminate what they lick, whether water or food,[27] he devised two important exceptions. First, if the water lapped is large in quantity, then it is not rendered impure. The larger the quantity, the more likely it is that the impurity dissipates throughout the water, thus rendering the whole amount suitable for ritual purification. Second, one can only discard food licked by an animal if one is absolutely certain the food is polluted. But in this case, certitude is contingent upon an ancillary inquiry into whether the animal is domesticated or not. If the animal is wild or undomesticated, we can be certain the food is polluted. Otherwise, certainty cannot be established. For Ibn Rushd al-Jadd, the domesticity of the dog operates as a limiting factor on the extension of the *ḥadīth* to situations that might raise the specter of waste.[28] By shifting the focus of inquiry to issues such as the nature

---

26 Ibn Rushd al-Jadd was not compelled by those who argued that the dog-water tradition is purely about worshipful obedience or purely about impurity. He was critical of those who reduced the issue purely to a matter of removing impurity because they could not explain the specific number of washings stipulated in the tradition. But those who view the dog-water tradition as a rule of worshipful obedience seem to preclude concerns about impurity that seem present on the face of the tradition. Taking a middle road between these two positions, Ibn Rushd al-Jadd argued that whatever number of washings purifies the object, those are justified on the basis of removing the impurity. Any additional washing that occurs because of the *ḥadīth* is purely worshipful obedience, and nothing else. Ibn Rushd al-Jadd, *al-Muqaddimāt* i, 90.

27 Ibid., i, 87–8.

28 Ibn Rushd al-Jadd addressed the issue of domesticity of dogs by reference to a different *ḥadīth* concerning cats. In this tradition, a man named Abū Qatāda came upon his wife Kabasha while she was filling a container with water so that her husband could ritually purify himself before making prayers. A cat approached her, wanting to drink the water. Kabasha tilted the container so that the cat could lap water from it. Her husband later remarked: "The messenger of God … said 'The cat is not impure. Rather it is among those

of impurity, quantity, and domesticity, jurists such as al-Kāsānī and Ibn Rushd al-Jadd utilized complex legal reasoning to alleviate the potential burdens of assuming that the dog is impure.

Importantly, the two different readings of the tradition offer two significant reflections on the axes of analysis that operate within Islamic legal analysis. First, the view that the *ḥadīth* is *taʿabbud,* or worship-centric, emphasizes the eschatological significance implicit in any instance of Islamic legal reasoning. One cannot ignore the importance of obedience to God (and hence of eschatology) as part of the Islamic legal calculus. Consequently, the quadrants model of analysis accounts for the eschatology of legal analysis along the vertical y axis, which is meant to capture those modes of behavior that are directed solely for the pleasure of God. Second, the view that the dog-water *ḥadīth* is concerned with impurity but not to the point of waste, reflects the way in which the law cannot ignore, and indeed must account for, the social well-being of individuals living in an organized society. As such, we can account for the social ramifications of the dog-water *ḥadīth* on a different axis, the horizontal x axis. The x axis allows us to measure how a particular legal outcome will influence and impact human experience in its variety.

Using the quadrants model of Islamic reasoning, we begin at an initial starting point where both the x and y values are zero (0, 0), namely at the intersection of the x and y axes on the graph illustrated at the beginning of this essay. We then calculate whether a given act, in light of relevant sources, constitutes a matter along the x axis, the y axis, or both. In most cases, we will find that both axes matter, to varying degrees. Indeed, the debate among jurists may very well be captured by reference to how they emphasize the content of one

---

who mix with you (*min al-ṭawāfīn ʿalaykum aw al-ṭawāfāt*)," or in other words, it is a domestic animal. Mālik b. Anas, *Muwaṭṭāʾ* i, 22. By reference to this *ḥadīth*, Ibn Rushd al-Jadd argued that "those carnivorous animals that do not mix with us in our homes carry impurities." Ibn Rushd al-Jadd, *al-Muqaddimāt* i, 87. By implication, carnivorous animals such as dogs that mix with us in our homes do not necessarily pollute all that they touch or lick. Ibn Rushd al-Ḥafīd, *Bidāyat al-mujtahid* i, 30. Interestingly, Ibn Rushd al-Jadd noted that not all Mālikīs agree with this position. One group, following Ibn Wahb (d. 197/813) ignored the argument concerning the domesticity of dogs. Ibn Rushd al-Jadd, *al-Muqaddimāt* i, 88–9. But others such as Ibn al-Mājishūn (d. 211/827) held that rural dogs (*badawī*) pose no danger of pollution if domesticated, but urban dogs (*ḥaḍarī*) do. Ibn Rushd al-Jadd, *al-Muqaddimāt* i, 89. Of course, there is some inconsistency in holding that a domestic predatory animal does not necessarily pollute food, but does pollute a small amount of water. The answer to this may rest on other *ḥadīths* that involve animals drinking from large ponds.

axis over another. To illustrate how these axes operate in juristic reasoning to help plot doctrinal rules in one or another quadrant, we explore various rulings concerning the dog and its impurity. Throughout, we examine the extent and degree to which the jurist's reasoning reflects concerns along the x and y axes, and how those concerns are balanced to influence how each doctrinal rule is plotted in one or another quadrant.

3 The Axes of Analysis: From the Heavenly to the Earthly

If dogs are impure and polluting, one might wonder why jurists would tolerate the existence of dogs at all. If canines carry impurities and endanger the well-being (spiritual and otherwise) of Muslims, why not simply order the execution of all dogs? This option is not entirely far-fetched, in large part because of a tradition in which the Prophet expressly commanded killing all dogs. After issuing the command, he then exempted from its application hunting dogs, herding dogs, and farming dogs.[29] Some versions of the tradition include other exemptions. Other versions contain no exceptions whatsoever. In yet different versions, after the Prophet commanded the killing of dogs, he subsequently dispatched people to kill the dogs in the area around Medina.[30] A review of these traditions and later doctrinal rules suggests that jurists read different normative sources (e.g., *ḥadīth*) together to create a general rule to kill canines, with exceptions for limited classes of dogs.

The Prophet's motive in killing all dogs relates to a story that states that angels do not enter homes when dogs are present. We learn from the Prophet's wife ʿĀʾisha that the angel Gabriel promised to visit the Prophet Muḥammad at a given hour. That hour came but Gabriel did not. The Prophet, disturbed by Gabriel's absence, paced the room of ʿĀʾisha's house, holding a stick in one hand while slapping it into the other. At one point, the Prophet noticed to his surprise a puppy under the bed. He called out: "ʿĀʾisha when did this dog enter here?" ʿĀʾisha did not know, but immediately removed the dog from the premises upon the Prophet's request. Upon doing so, Gabriel arrived. The Prophet said to him: "You promised [to meet with] me so I waited. But you did not show

29 Al-Nawawī, *Sharḥ ṣaḥīḥ Muslim* iii–iv, 176. The last category of dogs, agricultural dogs, is not found in all versions of the tradition. There are other traditions, attributed to Abū Hurayra in which this particular dog is included among those that could be owned. Al-Nawawī, *Sharḥ ṣaḥīḥ Muslim* ix–x, 479.

30 Al-Nawawī, *Sharḥ ṣaḥīḥ Muslim* ix–x, 478; Abū Bakr b. al-ʿArabī, *Aḥkām al-Qurʾān* ii, 545–6.

up." Gabriel responded: "The dog that was in your house prevented me from entering. We [angels] do not enter a house which has a dog or picture in it."[31] Upon learning this, the Prophet commanded all dogs to be killed.[32]

The theological significance associated with angels is certainly great. In the Islamic tradition the angel Gabriel is considered to be the conduit of God's revelation to the Prophet. Further, for angels to visit people in their homes might reasonably be considered a blessing. For a dog to block angels from entering one's home defines the dog as antithetical to these sacred and pure representatives of the divine. For many Muslim jurists, this episode explains why the Prophet commanded the execution of all dogs.[33] Therefore, if we consider how to plot this rule, we can reasonably assert that the rule concerns one's closeness to God, something which is facilitated by one's closeness to God's representative. Consequently, given the above context, when the Prophet ordered all dogs killed, he may have infused his directive with a high y value and possibly an x value of zero.

With the command issued, various people went into the Medina countryside to fulfill the Prophet's order. The problem was that when the rule was put into effect the Prophet learned of its negative social implications. Two men came to the Prophet with a question. Their conversation is related by the Quranic exegete al-Qurṭubī (d. 671/1272):

> Oh Messenger of God, our people hunt with dogs and falcons. The dogs obtain [for us] cows, donkeys, and gazelles. From the dogs, we are able to sacrifice them [(i.e., the prey) for consumption]. But you [ordered] the killing of dogs; hence we cannot consume such food. Further, God has

---

31 Al-Nawawī, *Sharḥ ṣaḥīḥ Muslim* xiii–xiv, 307–9. See also Ibn Ḥanbal, *Musnad* vi, 163; Ibn Ḥajar al-ʿAsqalānī, *Fatḥ al-bārī* x, 380–1; al-Mubārakfūrī, *Tuḥfat al-aḥwadhī* viii, 72–3. Incidentally, al-Mubārakfūrī wrote that the puppy in question belonged to the Prophet's grandsons, Ḥasan and Ḥusayn. In another version, after the dog is removed from the house, the Prophet sprinkles water over the area where the dog was found, which some considered as positive evidence of the dog's inherent impurity. But the Mālikīs thought the sprinkling was precautionary at most. As Ibn Ḥajar al-ʿAsqalānī wrote, "Regarding those who do not consider the dog's essence to be impure, its place is sprinkled with water out of caution, since sprinkling is the lawful method of purification where there is doubt." Ibn Ḥajar al-ʿAsqalānī, *Fatḥ al-bārī* x, 381. See also al-Nawawī, *Sharḥ ṣaḥīḥ Muslim* xiii–xiv, 308–10.

32 Abū Bakr b. al-ʿArabī, *Aḥkām al-Qurʾān* ii, 546; al-Shawkānī, *Nayl al-awṭār* i–ii, 38.

33 Al-Nawawī, *Sharḥ ṣaḥīḥ Muslim* xiii–xiv, 310; Ibn Ḥajar al-ʿAsqalānī, *Fatḥ al-bārī* x, 380; al-Mubārakfūrī, *Tuḥfat al-aḥwadhī* viii, 72.

> made impermissible improperly slaughtered animals. So what is permitted for us?[34]

In response to this question, wrote al-Qurṭubī,[35] the Prophet received the following Quranic revelation:

> They ask thee what is lawful to them (as food). Say: lawful unto you are (all) things good and pure: and what you have taught your trained animals [*al-jawāriḥ al-mukallibīn*] (to catch) in the manner directed by God: eat what they catch for you, but pronounce the name of God over it: and fear God; for God is swift in taking account (Q 5:4).[36]

With this verse, the Prophet permitted one to own dogs of prey, herding dogs, and farm dogs.[37] Although the Prophet may have considered the original directive to have a high y value and likely a zero x value, he could not ignore the negative x value, once he learned this new evidence. When the consequences showed themselves, the rule had to be reconsidered in light of the negative implications for society. Taking the consequences into account, we find that while the original rule had a high y value, it had a negative x value, given its implications, thus plotting it in quadrant I. To shift it from quadrant II to quadrant I, where the rule can have a positive x and y value, the Prophet offered exceptions to the general directive to kill all dogs, based on the Quranic verse. In doing so, he preserved the directive to kill dogs, with some exceptions, thereby controlling for the x value while upholding his commitment to the positive y value in the original rule.

To shift the value from a negative to a positive x value, the Prophet construed an exception from the Quranic verse that reversed the social impact of the initial, general directive. We can glean the significance of the Quranic verse that redeems some animals (but not others) with reference to the term *al-jawāriḥ al-mukallibīn*, which literally means trained predatory animal. The Ḥanafī jurist al-Jaṣṣāṣ (d. 370/981) concluded that 'trained predatory animal' refers to those animals that hunt on behalf of their owners. Such animals include, according to him, dogs, carnivorous animals, and birds of prey.[38]

---

34 Al-Qurṭubī, *al-Jāmiʿ* iii, 44.

35 Ibid.. See also Abū Bakr b. al-ʿArabī, *Aḥkām al-Qurʾān* ii, 546; al-Jaṣṣāṣ, *Aḥkām al-Qurʾān* ii, 393; al-Ṭabarī, *Tafsīr al-Ṭabarī* iii, 21.

36 Ali (trans.), *The glorious Kurʾan.*

37 Al-Qurṭubī, *al-Jāmiʿ* iii, 44.

38 Al-Jaṣṣāṣ, *Aḥkām al-Qurʾān* ii, 393. See also al-Qurṭubī, *al-Jāmiʿ* v–vi, 45.

Al-Zamakhsharī (d. 538/1144) understood this term to refer to animals that hunt or gather (*kawāsib*), including dogs, tigers, and falcons.[39]

Consequently, while the dog constitutes a spiritual danger, it is also an important companion that ensures the well-being of people. While the spiritual danger of dogs may have led the Prophet to order the killing of all dogs, the fact that dogs can positively contribute to other aspects of human existence could not be denied, neither in fact nor in law. Instead, the example above illustrates that Islamic legal reasoning does not exist in a historical or social vacuum. Rather it is an ongoing process that reflects a multitude of calculations along different axes of analysis.

4 Purity and Resource Management: Waste and Well-being

An especially relevant issue that arises from the dog-water debate concerns the water left over in the container after the dog laps it up or drinks from it. Some jurists questioned whether the water lapped up by dogs can nonetheless be used for ritual purification purposes. A strict reading of Abū Hurayra's *ḥadīth* suggests that any water in a container must be discarded. But does that mean water in a container of any size, regardless of how large? And if so, then what about water in a puddle, pond, or lake, from which animals often drink? Ritual purity may be important to commune with God in prayer, but at what cost to the well-being of peoples' everyday lives? Or, to put it in terms of the axes of analysis, to emphasize the imperative of ritual purity (the y value) with disregard to the social consequences of waste (the x value) would plot the legal outcome in quadrant II, with potentially devastating effects on social well-being. A dog may be considered impure; but that does not end the inquiry, given the consequences that may arise from this ruling. The dog may cause ritual impurity, but the spiritual importance of ritual (its positive y value) does not preclude delimiting the scope of the dog's impurity in other areas of human existence (along the x axis). Since the possibility exists that a rule requiring that one waste water in order to become ritually pure might be plotted in quadrant II (i.e., a positive y value, negative x value), we see that jurists contended with how to find a better balance so that both x and y values can remain positive, thus keeping the rule plotted in quadrant I.

39 Al-Zamakhsharī, *al-Kashshāf* i, 594. For Ibn Kathīr, it refers to trained dogs and falcons and any bird taught to hunt. It includes predatory dogs, cheetahs or panthers, falcons, and other animals like them. Ibn Kathīr, *Mukhtaṣar tafsīr Ibn Kathīr* i, 484.

To address this situation of potential waste, Muslim jurists considered traditions from both the Prophet and his companion ʿUmar b. al-Khaṭṭāb, traditions concerning large bodies of water from which animals drink. In a *ḥadīth*, the Prophet was asked about using water from a pond between Mecca and Medina, from which predatory animals would drink. The Prophet responded: "For them [i.e., the animals] is what they drink. What remains is for us to drink, and it is pure."[40] In the second tradition, ʿUmar was with a riding party when they arrived at a pond. A member of the party asked the caretakers of the pond whether predatory animals drink from it. ʿUmar interrupted: "Oh caretakers of the pond do not tell us. We are welcomed by the animals and the animals are welcomed by us."[41] Sunni jurists relied on these traditions to shift the analysis from the impurity of animals to concerns about waste. They were no doubt aware that the issue of impurity arises in these cases, but the rules on impurity are not alone dispositive of the issue. Despite any impurity associated with the dog, jurists seemed to incorporate resource management, waste, and social well-being into their analytic concerns.

To shift the frame of analysis to waste, jurists inquired about the amount of water in a container or the size of the container itself. For many Sunni jurists, if the amount of water lapped up by a dog is large, the water is not impure, despite his lapping it up.[42] Mālik b. Anas said: "Ritual purification with the excess water of a dog does not please me, where the water is of a small amount… But it is not a problem if the water is of a large quantity."[43] Even jurists who generally considered the dog impure in its essence relied on quantity to limit the application of the dog-water tradition. For instance, al-Nawawī stated: "If a dog laps [up water] from a large quantity of water such that his

40 Al-Sarakhsī, *Kitāb al-Mabsūṭ* i-ii, 48–9; Saḥnūn, *al-Mudawwana* i, 6; al-Māwardī, *al-Ḥāwī l-kabīr* i, 304.

41 Mālik b. Anas, *Muwaṭṭāʾ* i, 23; al-Kāsānī, *Badāʾiʿ al-ṣanāʾiʿ* i, 375.

42 Al-Kāsānī, *Badāʾiʿ al-ṣanāʾiʿ* i, 375. Notably, the Ẓāhirī jurist Ibn Ḥazm argues that any reliance upon the quantity of water at issue is an inappropriate extension of the rule. Responding to the Shāfiʿīs, he wrote: "Al-Shāfiʿī said 'If the water in the container is 500 *raṭls*, do not dump it if a dog licked from it.'" Ibn Ḥazm, however, would dump out the contents out of worshipful obedience, regardless of the quantity of water at issue. Ibn Ḥazm, *al-Muḥallā* i, 123, 155.

43 Saḥnūn, *al-Mudawwana* i, 6. Likewise, the Ḥanbalī jurist Ibn Taymiyya (d. 728/1328), relied on quantity as a central feature of his analysis. Relying on customary practices (*ʿādāt*), Ibn Taymiyya held that the container from which a dog licks is usually small. Consequently, the dog's saliva sticks to the water and the container. Hence one must dump the water and wash the container. But if the container is large, no impurity arises. Ibn Taymiyya, *Majmūʿ* xx, 521.

lapping [it up] does not reduce it to [less than] two *qulla*s, then its [lapping it up] does not render [the water] impure."[44] "*Qulla*" is meant to convey a particular quantity of measure. The exact quantity it denotes is not clear; however, some suggest that it refers to a large jar (*al-jarraḥ al-kabīra*) or small jug (*al-kuz al-ṣaghīr*).[45] If the water is greater than two *qulla*s, it remains pure;[46] but if it is less, the water is impure.[47] In such cases, the jurists balanced their concerns of impurity and waste, and were keen to plot any resulting ruling in quadrant I, where both x and y values are positive.[48]

5 From Demon Dogs to Dangerous Women: Piety, Prayer, and the Polity

One of the more colorful dog-related traditions involves the situation in which a dog, often a black dog, passes in front of a man praying. A tradition on this point reads as follows:

44 Al-Nawawī, *Sharḥ ṣaḥīḥ Muslim* iii–iv, 177. See also Ibn Ḥajar al-Haytamī, *al-Fatāwā* i, 61, who addressed the situation in which a dog drinks from a well containing a large amount of water. Although he did not rely on the two *qulla* threshold, he still invoked the quantity of water as a mediating factor in the overall purity of water licked by a dog.

45 Ibn Manẓūr, *Lisān al-ʿarab* xi, 288.

46 Notably, even if the amount of waters is two *qulla*s or more, it can still become impure if one of its qualities is changed by the introduction of any external impurity. According to al-Qaffāl, although the amount of water may be greater than two *qulla*s, if there is a change in one of the characteristics of the water (i.e., color, taste, smell), then it is impure. If there is no such change, then the water remains pure, even if an impure entity, such as a dog, makes contact with it. Al-Qaffāl, *Ḥilyat al-ʿulamāʾ* i, 80. See also the Ḥanbalī Ibn Qayyim al-Jawziyya, *Iʿlām al-muwaqqiʿīn* i, 483.

47 Al-Qaffāl, *Ḥilyat al-ʿulamāʾ* i, 80. There are two prevailing views among the Shāfiʿīs on what one must do with the water in this case. Some require the contents of the container to be dumped, and prohibit their use. Others hold that dumping the contents of the container is not obligatory (*wājib*) but rather preferred (*mustaḥabb*). Furthermore, the use of the water, in certain circumstances, may be permitted. Al-Māwardī, *al-Ḥāwī l-kabīr* i, 305; al-Qaffāl, *Ḥilyat al-ʿulamāʾ* i, 314. Nevertheless, al-Māwardī and al-Qaffāl preferred dumping the vessel's content. Al-Māwardī, *al-Ḥāwī l-kabīr* i, 304; al-Qaffāl, *Ḥilyat al-ʿulamāʾ* i, 314.

48 The Ismaʿili jurist al-Qāḍī l-Nuʿmān discussed the case in which an animal falls into a well and dies. "If something emanating from the animal changes one of the water's characteristics [i.e., color, taste, or smell], [the water] should be avoided until the change is removed, [so that] the water becomes wholesome and obviates [the impurities]... At that moment, it is pure." Al-Qāḍī l-Nuʿmān, *Daʿāʾim al-Islām* i, 112–3.

> According to Abū Dharr [al-Ghifārī (d. ca. 32/652–3)], the Prophet said: "If one of you prays, he [should] lay before him a [barrier],[49] such as the back half of a saddle. If there is nothing, like the back half of a saddle, in front of him, then a donkey, woman, or black dog [that passes in front of him] voids [*qaṭ*ʿ] his prayer."[50]

The implications of this tradition vis-à-vis the dog, let alone women, are enormous.[51] The fact that a dog can invalidate one's prayer emphasizes the eschatological danger of dogs, or in other words, the need to avoid dogs in order to maintain a connection to God (a positive y value).[52] Prayer is the moment when one is communicating with God; it is an intimate moment for the soul of the believer. Jurists were certainly concerned about a dog's ability to interfere with that relationship and the eschatological implications of dogs, or in other words, the dog's affect on the vertical y axis.

Yet jurists could not read this tradition solely in terms of its implication on y values. They had to devise a ruling from this tradition that did not, at the same time, adversely affect the x value associated with any rules governing prayer. So for instance, if we take the tradition at face value as applying to black dogs,

---

49 A *sutra* is generally an item that someone praying sets before him, "sticking it in the ground or laying it down if the ground be hard, in order that no living being or image may be the object next before him." Lane, *Arabic-English lexicon* i, 1304; See also Ibn Manẓūr, *Lisān al-ʿarab* vi, 169.

50 Al-Nawawī, *Sharḥ ṣaḥīḥ Muslim* iii–iv, 450. In another version narrated by Abū Hurayra, the color of the dog is not specified. Al-Nawawī, *Sharḥ ṣaḥīḥ Muslim* iii–iv, 451; Ibn Ḥanbal, *Musnad* v, 194, 197, 202, 208; Ibn Ḥazm, *Muḥallā* ii, 320–6; Ibn Qayyim al-Jawziyya, *Iʿlām al-muwaqqiʿīn* ii, 79–80; Abū Bakr b. al-ʿArabī, *ʿĀriḍat al-aḥwadhī* i, 133. Ibn al-ʿArabī remarks that al-Tirmidhī considered this tradition to be *ḥasan ṣaḥīḥ*, a designation that is perhaps unique to al-Tirmidhī. Abou El Fadl, *The authoritative and the authoritarian* 47–8.

51 Ibn Ḥazm, *al-Muḥallā* ii, 322. See also Abū Bakr b. al-ʿArabī, *ʿĀriḍat al-aḥwadhī* ii, 134. As one can imagine, the fact that women can negate a man's prayer in the same fashion as a dog or a donkey, raises serious concerns at the possible chauvinism implicit in this tradition. Interestingly, this possibility was not necessarily lost on the jurists themselves. This tradition raises gender concerns over the association between animals and women. Whether Islamic theology supports such an assertion, or whether this tradition is the result of chauvinist tendencies among the narrators requires a separate study. See Abou El Fadl, *The authoritative and the authoritarian* 71, note 60, who suggests that discourses on women prostrating to their husbands are "largely chauvinistic, and possibly immoral." For an important recent study on gender, ethics and Islam, see Ali, *Sexual ethics*.

52 Notably, there are some versions that do not specify black dogs, and rather consider all dogs equally capable of voiding one's prayer. See for example, Ibn Ḥazm, *Muḥallā* ii, 321; Ibn Ḥanbal, *Musnad* vi, 99.

we might ask whether this tradition adversely impacts rules that allow the limited ownership of dogs. Drawing upon the Prophet's exemption of certain dogs from the general command to execute all dogs, the Shāfiʿī jurist al-Nawawī recognized that, in some cases, people should be permitted to own dogs. Those cases are characterized in terms of an individuals' needs and necessities, those which ensure his well-being. Al-Nawawī wrote:

> Our companions [i.e., Shāfiʿī jurists] and others agree that it is prohibited to own dogs for reasons other than need (*ḥāja*), such as owning a dog for the pleasure of its appearance, or out of pride. This is prohibited, without debate. As for the need (*ḥāja*) for which it is permissible to own a dog, the prophetic tradition includes an exception for any one of three dogs: farming, herding, and hunting. This is permitted without debate.[53]

The reference to *ḥāja* is a crucial indication that what is at stake in the prophetic exception to canine execution is an acknowledgment that dogs play an important role in certain activities. Need does not include the joy of a dog's companionship; rather need captures the functional role of a dog in ensuring the success of certain industries in society – industries upon which all of society potentially depends.[54]

But when read alongside the black dog tradition, jurists addressed whether the dogs that can be owned for agricultural purposes must be any color other than black. On the one hand, the black dog is deemed to be an eschatological threat. For example, in most accounts of the black dog tradition, an additional section is added which explains the specification of the color. Abū Dharr al-Ghifārī is asked: "Oh Abū Dharr, what is the [difference] between black dogs, red dogs, and yellow dogs?" Abū Dharr responded: "I asked [that of] the messenger of God, just as you are asking me. He said: 'The black dog is a devil (*shayṭān*).'"[55] The black dog that voids prayer is no simple dog. It is an evil spirit, a demon dog of hell.[56]

---

53 Al-Nawawī, *Sharḥ ṣaḥīḥ Muslim* iii–iv, 177.

54 Ibid., iii–iv, 176–7; ix–x, 479–80.

55 Ibid., iii–iv, 450; Ibn Ḥanbal, *Musnad* v, 194, 197. See also Abū Bakr b. al-ʿArabī, *ʿĀriḍat al-aḥwadhī* ii, 133 for reference to the black dog.

56 Incidentally, the association of the dog (particularly the black dog) with the devil is not unique to the medieval Islamic world. European folklore abounds with numerous references to demons and devils in dog form. Quite often, such demon dogs take the form of a black dog. For example, in Cambridge, Essex, Suffolk, and Norfolk the black dog ghost is: "frequently one-eyed, haunts coasts, fens, roads, and churchyards, and is always ominous ... In the Isle of Man, there is a vague ghost, sometimes in the form of a black dog,

The Islamic legal tradition's association of the black dog with the devil only reemphasizes the dog's negative value. More than simply being a source of filth and impurity, it is arguably a locus of evil. On the other hand, this is not to deny the useful social purposes that dogs can serve. How must the jurist plot the ruling? To plot the rule in quadrant I, what sort of factors might the jurist take into account? There was, as one might expect, considerable disagreement, especially because limiting ownership of dogs to those that are not black may or may not put a severe burden on the interests of farmers and agricultural laborers. Al-Nawawī tells us, for instance, that some jurists prohibited owning black hunting dogs. Rather such dogs must be killed since they are devils.[57] But he also related that al-Shāfiʿī (d. 204/820), Mālik b. Anas, and the majority of scholars permit one to own black hunting dogs. Al-Nawawī then noted: "The intent of the tradition [about dogs as devils] is not to displace [black dogs] from the dog species entirely."[58] While the tradition on black dogs might appear inflexible and unforgiving, the juristic debate on canine exceptions suggests that the black dog tradition had more bark than bite. Despite the negative attitude toward black dogs, jurists could not ignore the fact that dogs, black or otherwise, cannot be classified in absolute terms, whether as a pure eschatological threat or as a pure social benefit. Yet in plotting rules of law in

---

that haunts roads; and in Guernsey, black dogs attack wayfarers during the Twelve Days of Christmas." Brown, The black dog 176. Ethel Rudkin, writing in 1938, begins her article on the black dog by noting that the "Black Dog walks in Lincolnshire still; and there are a number of living people who have seen him, heard him, and even felt him." Rudkin, The black dog 111. When the black dog appears, it may have two heads or none at all. Its eyes may be as big as saucers. Brown, The black dog 180–1. Rudkin's research also indicates that in the British town of Northrope, "there is a Black Dog that haunts the churchyard, known as Barguest." Rudkin, The black dog 117. Sometimes the black dog is not necessarily evil. Nevertheless, its common association with evil is undeniable, especially in the regions of Scandinavia and Germany. Brown, The black dog 188. It is perhaps not entirely surprising that the black dog would be considered a devil given certain natural circumstances. In her study of the devil in dog form in European folklore, Barbara Allen Woods provides a possible explanation for why black dogs in particular might be associated with evil. She writes: "There is nothing extraordinary or mythical about such an incident. On the contrary it is entirely natural that a dog should be out trotting the deserted streets and paths. It is not even beyond credulity that such an animal would appear black in the darkness, or that its eyes, if they were caught in a faint ray of light, would appear large and fiery ... Yet, any or all of these normal characteristics can seem positively uncanny, especially when observed under eerie circumstances or in an anxious state of mind." Woods, *The Devil in dog form* 33.

57 Al-Nawawī, *Sharḥ ṣaḥīḥ Muslim* ix–x, 480; xiii, 76.

58 Ibid.

light of these types of concerns, we can observe the reliance on competing axes of analysis.

Indeed, those axes pose significant challenges when considering the indirect implications of the dog-prayer tradition on the status of women. By juxtaposing women with the black dog, this tradition suggests that the dangers of the black dog's impurity and evil apply to women as well. In fact, some Muslim jurists, relying on this tradition, deemed a man's prayer void if a donkey, black dog, or woman passes in front of him while he prays.[59] Others, however, omit the donkey and women from the tradition, and instead held that only the dog negates one's prayer. They argued that if a woman or donkey passes in front of a man praying, his prayer is not void, although his concentration in prayer may be interrupted.[60] This reading dissociates women from dogs, but maintains the link between women and donkeys. Although the animal comparators shift, women remain equated with beasts of burden.

The implications of this tradition were certainly not lost on the jurists. For instance, Ibn Ḥazm reported that ʿĀ'isha complained about the implications of this *ḥadīth*. She said: "You [men] put us [women] in the position of dogs and donkeys. Only the following negate prayer: dogs, donkeys, and cats."[61] As mentioned above, some jurists even omit "women" from the tradition entirely. This exclusion is based on traditions from the Prophet's wife, ʿĀ'isha. It was reported that she was lying down in front of the Prophet while he was praying. If the tradition equating dogs and women were historically accurate, then the Prophet's prayer would have been invalidated by his wife's position in front of him as he prayed. But the Prophet continued to pray undisturbed. Only later when she decided to sit upright did the Prophet move, thus suggesting that his prayer was disturbed. This particular set of events prompted the Andalusian jurist, Ibn Ḥazm (d. 456/1064), to suggest that as long as ʿĀ'isha was lying down in front of the Prophet, no damage was done. But once she sat upright, she obstructed his prayer prompting him to move, and presumably restart his

---

59 Al-Nawawī, *Sharḥ ṣaḥīḥ Muslim* iii–iv, 450; Abū Bakr b. al-ʿArabī, *ʿĀriḍat al-aḥwadhī* ii, 133–4, noted that the Companions Abū Dharr al-Ghifārī, Ibn ʿUmar, Anas, and al-Ḥasan were of this opinion; Ibn Ḥazm, *Muḥallā* ii, 320, adopted the general reading of the tradition, however he made an exception for women who are lying down as if asleep, on the basis of narrations from the Prophet's wife, ʿĀ'isha. These traditions will be discussed below.

60 Al-Nawawī, *Sharḥ ṣaḥīḥ Muslim* iii–iv, 450; Abū Bakr b. al-ʿArabī, *ʿĀriḍat al-aḥwadhī* ii, 133.

61 Ibn Ḥazm, *Muḥallā* ii, 324. Another view of this tradition narrows its meaning to apply only to menstruating women. Abū Bakr b. al-ʿArabī challenged this position as being based on weak evidence. Abū Bakr b. al-ʿArabī, *ʿĀriḍat al-aḥwadhī* ii, 134; Ibn Ḥazm, *Muḥallā* ii, 324.

prayer.[62] The rationale for Ibn Ḥazm's distinction is less important here than the fact that it has nothing to do with ʿĀʾisha *as a woman*.

Another reading goes so far as to redeem the dog in order to undermine the social implications of the dog-prayer tradition entirely. That reading holds that nothing negates one's prayer. Instead, the black dog tradition relates to the loss of one's concentration. This argument hinges on the way in which the particular Arabic term *qaṭʿ* is interpreted. The word *qaṭʿ* means to cut or sever, and could connote the voidance of the prayer in this tradition. But many jurists argued that what is "cut" is not the prayer itself, but rather the concentration of the person praying.[63] At most, the tradition emphasizes the need to concentrate on prayer and take pains to avoid distractions in prayer when possible. Instead of rendering the animal or woman a roving eschatological danger that can invalidate one's prayer, the majority of jurists put the onus on the person praying to pray in an environment where he can concentrate. In doing so, they remained committed to understanding the tradition in terms of its eschatological significance (its y value), without creating negative social implications (its x value). Thus, they saw the *ḥadīth* as a warning that those who pray should concentrate when convening with their Lord. In this sense, they plotted the resulting rule using a positive y axis while delimiting its social impact almost entirely (i.e., a zero x value).

The multiple interpretations about the black dog tradition illustrate that, despite source-texts providing an apparently clear statement of a rule, the effect of any such rule must be mediated in light of everyday life. By invalidating prayers, dogs are in bad standing with those who are concerned with their eschatological well-being, presumably any Muslim who seeks to commune with God. For such otherworldly-minded people, the danger the dog poses may constitute sufficient justification for a hostile stand against the dog in worldly and mundane affairs. The relationship between the eschatological and the sociological seems evident from the debate among jurists about whether

62 Ibn Ḥazm, *al-Muḥallā* ii, 322.

63 Al-Nawawī, *Sharḥ ṣaḥīḥ Muslim* iii–iv, 450; Abū Bakr b. al-ʿArabī, *ʿĀriḍat al-aḥwadhī* ii, 134. According to al-Nawawī, some held the tradition to be abrogated by another that states: "Nothing negates one's prayer. Block whatever you can [from crossing]." Al-Nawawī, *Sharḥ ṣaḥīḥ Muslim* iii–iv, 450. Ibn al-ʿArabī held that prayers are not voided, given another tradition in which Ibn ʿAbbās narrated as follows: "I was sitting behind [someone] on a donkey when we came upon the Prophet as he and his companions were praying at Mina. We descended from the donkey and entered the prayer line. The donkey passed in front of them, but their prayer was not negated." According to Ibn al-ʿArabī this tradition has two possible explanations: first, nothing negates prayer; second, the prayer leader's *sutra* is a *sutra* for the entire congregation. Abū Bakr b. al-ʿArabī, *ʿĀriḍat al-aḥwadhī* ii, 132–3.

black dogs can be owned, or whether they should constitute a special category of dogs, one that is vulnerable to the prophetic command to kill all dogs. The social implications of the eschatological concern are also evident in the way jurists considered the juxtaposition of dogs and women. Not only might black dogs be vulnerable, women might also be ostracized out of concern for their eschatological threat. To avoid such adverse social implications for both dogs and women, the majority position returns to the context of eschatology by reading the black dog tradition as a comment on the responsibility of those who pray. In doing so, the locus of danger shifts from the dog and woman to the individual in prayer who is not fully focused on what he or she is doing. Between the minority and majority positions we find a focus on eschatology, a topic that may fit uneasily with modern conceptions of legal ordering. But as suggested in this study, the eschatological component in these traditions animates broad-ranging concerns about what the polluting dog might mean to Muslims working in the fields, drinking from ponds, or praying in crowded areas.

6 Conclusion

The dog-water tradition is one among many dog-related traditions that contribute to a process of legal reasoning that cannot rely on a neat divide between the "legal" and the "moral," without at the same time controlling for the institutional assumptions that give the law/morality dichotomy salience and significance. This essay relies on a quadrant model that posits two axes of analysis, the here and the hereafter, as elemental to Muslim jurists' reasoning about the law. These two axes invoke ideas that may echo sentiments associated with the law/morality distinction; but the two axes also control for the unstated assumptions that may give the law/morality conceptual dichotomy its significance and poignancy. Muslim jurists recognized that the pollution of dogs in matters of ritual not only implicates eschatological concerns; the pollution of dogs for ritual purposes could also have serious implications on mundane matters that have little or nothing to do with ritual practice, and thereby have limited eschatological significance. The dog may have been viewed as a source of impurity that might prevent one from communing with God in prayer; but that view did not end the inquiry. For many jurists, that view constituted the beginning of an analytic process that contended with the complexity of human needs and lived experience. That process could not ignore the interests associated with what might be considered in contemporary parlance 'moral,' – if not 'religious' and thereby private – nor could it ignore those interests that might be considered 'legal.' However, to rely upon the dichotomy between the 'legal' and the 'moral' imposes a modern bifurcation that does not adequately explain what Muslim jurists were doing when working with competing source-texts, whether Quranic verses or *ḥadīth* texts. Adopting the quadrants model of analysis allows us to appreciate that the legitimacy and authority of any doctrinal rule depends on how it is plotted in light of two axes of analysis, one which is concerned with the individual's relationship with God and the other that is concerned with individual experience and social well-being. In other words, the jurists plotted doctrinal rules in terms of interests that pertain to both the here and the hereafter. By plotting a doctrinal rule in terms of both the here and the hereafter, I do not mean to distinguish the Islamic model of analysis from other modes of legal interpretation. Indeed, the rationales for the various rules noted above are highly rational and reasonable; their rationality is clear when we appreciate and understand the frame of reference or background factor that makes juristic reasoning intelligible. The dichotomy between law and morality is certainly an important dichotomy as it pertains to contemporary legal theory in the modern state. But it does not fully capture the framework that animated Muslim jurists in the past, whose presumptions about political society, and its relationship to the law, were different from ours today. The quadrants model shows how Muslim jurists reasoned and reached doctrinal outcomes in light of concerns that are not easily captured by contemporary philosophies of law, although that does not mean such concerns are unintelligible or irrational. Each doctrinal rule arises from a complex process of legal reasoning amidst axes of analysis that reflect fundamental concerns that lie at the heart of the Islamic legal worldview.

But why offer the quadrants model at all? In a world coming to terms with the growing significance of religion in the public sphere,[64] we cannot ignore

64 The increased relevance of religion (and in particular Islam) to debates about liberal governance and the public sphere in North America and Europe is evident in increasing scholarly attention to the issue of religion and the public sphere. For important scholarship on the issue, see Casanova, *Public religions in the modern world*; Casanova, Public religions revisited. Increasingly universities in North America and Europe are initiating centers devoted to the study of religion in the public sphere. See for instance, the University of Toronto's *Religion in the public sphere* (http://www.chass.utoronto.ca/rps/); The Baldy Center for Law and Social Policy, at the State University of New York Buffalo sponsors working groups on Law and Religion and Law, Religion and Culture (http://www.law.buffalo.edu/BALDYCENTER/research.htm); The University of Exeter in the United Kingdom is the home of the European Muslim Research Centre (http://centres.exeter.ac.uk/emrc/). In terms of policy development, Quebec's Reasonable Accommodation Commission, led by Charles Taylor and Gérard Bouchard, illustrates that even

the imperative to grapple with the difficult challenge of living together amidst our differences. All too often, that challenge is met with political rhetoric and polemics, leading to public policies that not only perpetuate stereotypes, but also marginalize, if not demonize, those who are deemed different. This tendency was certainly evident in the 2005 debate in Ontario, Canada that concerned *sharīʿa*-based family law arbitration,[65] and it took center stage again in 2010 when the Swiss constitution was amended by a popular referendum to ban the erection of minarets for mosques in the country.[66]

Yet, this polemic is confirmed by stories of Muslims who adhere to an uncompromising, inflexible, and at times an oppressive version of *sharīʿa*. Such stories include, for instance, Muslim taxi drivers who refuse to drive blind passengers accompanied by seeing-eye dogs, on the basis that dogs are impure according to Islamic law.[67] Such cases are often described in liberal constitutional terms as examples of rights in conflict: the rights of the disabled versus the rights of the religious adherent.

Resolving such conflicts is no easy matter. But that difficulty is not unique to a liberal constitutional system of law and order; nor will it always find an amenable resolution in liberal, constitutional terms of analysis and reference. For instance, such stories may situate the conflict in terms of a distinction and division between the public and the private, the secular and religious, the church and the state, and the law and morality.

The quadrants model developed above offers additional analytic terms to characterize such conflicts. These terms, described above as axes of analysis, take into account the dynamics of Islamic legal reasoning, without precluding the possibility of dialogue between the animating principles of different legal systems. Furthermore, the quadrants model has an important consequence: it counters the tendency to place Islamic doctrinal rules in contemporary categories such as the 'religious' or even the 'cultural.' Too often such terms are code for the 'irrational,' and thereby place debates about Islamic law and its significance for Muslims outside the realm of conscientious reasoned deliberation about law, order, and good governance.[68] The quadrants model, therefore, offers a way of unpacking the significance of a given legal rule by emphasizing

---

governments are not immune from contending with the place of religion in the public sphere (for official website, see http://www.accommodements.qc.ca/index-en.html).

65 For a commentary on the tenor and tone of the debate, and its marginalizing implications, see Bakht, Muslim barbarians 67–82.

66 Caldwell, No minarets, please 9; Nurrohman, A lesson to draw 7.

67 Brothers, Cabbie refused ride to guide dog B2; Saleh, Dirty dogs i, 27.

68 Brown, *Regulating aversion* 152–4.

the competing interests at stake. It shifts the focus from debating about the authoritative hold of a given rule, to appreciating and accounting for the rational inputs that made the rule intelligible in a given period or era.

Bibliography

Abou El Fadl, Kh., *The authoritative and the authoritarian in Islamic discourses: A contemporary case study*, Austin 1997².

———, Dogs in the Islamic tradition, in B. Taylor (ed.), *The encyclopedia of religion and nature*, ii, Briston 2005, 498–500.

———, The lord of the essence: A fatwa on dogs, in Kh. Abou El Fadl, *The search for beauty in Islam: A conference of the books*, Oxford 2006, 316–30.

Abu-Saud, M., *Concept of Islam*, Indianapolis 1983.

Ali, K., *Sexual ethics and Islam: Feminist reflections on Qur'an, Hadith and jurisprudence*, Oxford 2006.

Ali, Y.A. (trans.), *The glorious Kur'an*, Riyadh 1938³.

Atiyah, P.S. and R.S. Summers, *Form and substance in Anglo-American law: A comparative study of legal reasoning, legal theory, and legal institutions*, Oxford 1991.

Bakht, N., Were Muslim barbarians really knocking on the gates of Ontario? The religious arbitration controversy, in *Ottawa Law Review* 2006 (2006), 67–82.

Brothers, P., Cabbie refused ride to guide dog; Rights issue stymies city; Blind woman's dog 'impure,' in *The Cincinnati (Ohio) Enquirer* (April 3, 1999), B2.

Brown, T., The black dog, in *Folklore* 69 (September 1958), 175–92.

Brown, W., *Regulating aversion: Tolerance in the age of identity and empire*, Princeton, NJ 2006.

Caldwell, Ch., No minarets, please, in *The Weekly Standard* 15.3 (December 14, 2009), 9.

Canard, M., Ḥākim Bi-Amr Allāh, in *EI²*, iii, 76–82.

Cane, P., Taking law seriously: Starting points of the Hart/Devlin debate, in *The Journal of Ethics* 10 (2006), 21–51.

Casanova, J., *Public religions in the modern world*, Chicago 1994.

———, Public religions revisited, in H. de Vries (ed.), *Religion: Beyond a concept*, New York 2008, 101–19.

Coulson, N.J., *Conflicts and tensions in Islamic jurisprudence*, Chicago 1969.

al-Dhahabī, Shams al-Dīn, *Siyar aʿlām al-nubalāʾ*, ed. S. al-Arnaʿūt and A. al-Būshī, Beirut 1986⁴.

Dworkin, R., Lord Devlin and the enforcement of morals, in *The Yale Law Journal* 75.6 (May 1966), 986–1005.

Emon, A.M., *Ḥuqūq Allah* and *ḥuqūq al-ʿibād*: A legal heuristic for a natural rights regime, in *Islamic Law and Society* 13.3 (2006), 325–91.

Hallaq, W., *Sharīʿa: Theory, practice, transformations*, Cambridge 2009.
Ibn al-ʿArabī, Abū Bakr, *Aḥkām al-Qurʾān*, Beirut n.d.
———, *ʿĀriḍat al-aḥwadhī bi-sharḥ ṣaḥīḥ al-Tirmidhī*, Beirut 1997.
Ibn Ḥajar al-ʿAsqalānī, *Fatḥ al-bārī bi-sharḥ ṣaḥīḥ al-Bukhārī*, ed. Q. Muḥibb al-Dīn al-Khaṭīb, Cairo 1407 AH.
Ibn Ḥajar al-Haytamī, A., *al-Fatāwā l-kubrā l-fiqhiyya*, ed. ʿA. al-Fākihī al-Makkī and ʿA. ʿAbd al-Raḥmān, Beirut 1997.
Ibn Ḥanbal, A., *Musnad al-imām Aḥmad b. Hanbal*, ed. S. al-Majzūb, Beirut 1993.
Ibn Ḥazm, *al-Muḥallā bi-l-athār*, ed. ʿA. Sulaymān al-Bandārī, Beirut n.d.
Ibn Kathīr, *Mukhtaṣar tafsīr Ibn Kathīr*, ed. M. al-ʿAban, Beirut 1981.
Ibn Manẓūr, *Lisān al-ʿarab*, ed. A. Shīrī, Beirut 1988.
Ibn Qayyim al-Jawziyya, *Iʿlām al-muwaqqiʿīn ʿan rabb al-ʿālamīn*, Cairo n.d.
Ibn Rushd al-Ḥafīd, *Bidāyat al-mujtahid wa-nihāyat al-muqtaṣid*, ed. M. al-Bābī al-Ḥalabī, Cairo 1981.
Ibn Rushd al-Jadd, *al-Muqaddimāt al-mumahhidāt*, ed. M. Ḥujjī, Beirut 1988.
Ibn Taymiyya, *Majmūʿ fatāwā*, ed. M. ʿAbd al-Raḥmān, n.p., n.d.
al-Jaṣṣāṣ, Abū Bakr, *Aḥkām al-Qurʾān*, Beirut n.d.
Kamali, M.H., *Principles of Islamic jurisprudence*, Cambridge 2003.
———, *Shariʿah law: An introduction*, Oxford 2008.
al-Kāsānī, *Badāʾiʿ al-ṣanāʾiʿ fī tartīb al-sharāʾiʿ*, Beirut 1997.
Lane, E.W., *Arabic-English lexicon*, Cambridge 1984.
Mālik b. Anas, *Muwaṭṭāʾ*, Cairo n.d.
al-Māwardī, Abū l-Ḥasan ʿA., *al-Ḥāwī l-kabīr: Sharḥ mukhtaṣar al-muznā*, Beirut 1994.
Moaddel, M. and K. Talatoff, *Contemporary debates in Islam: An anthology of modernist and fundamentalist thought*, New York 2000.
al-Mubārakfūrī, M. ʿAbd al-Raḥmān, *Tuḥfat al-ahwadhī bi-sharḥ jāmiʿ al-Tirmidhī*, Beirut n.d.
al-Nawawī, *Sharḥ ṣaḥīḥ Muslim*, Beirut 1996.
Nurrohman, B., A lesson to draw from the Swiss ban on minarets, in *The Jakarta Post* (15 December 2009), 7.
al-Qāḍī al-Nuʿmān, *Daʿāʾim al-Islām wa-dhikr al-ḥalāl wa-l-ḥarām wa-l-qaḍāyā wa-l-aḥkām*, ed. A. ʿAlī Asghar Fīdī, Cairo 1963.
al-Qaffāl, Abū Bakr M., *Ḥilyat al-ʿulamāʾ fī maʿrifat madhhab al-fuqahāʾ*, ed. Y. Darādkah, Amman 1988.
al-Qurṭubī, Abū Bakr, *al-Jāmiʿ li-aḥkām al-Qurʾān*, Beirut 1993.
Rudkin, E.H., The black dog, in *Folklore* 49 (June 1938), 111–31.
Saḥnūn, *al-Mudawwana al-kubrā*, Cairo n.d.
Saleh, L., Dirty dogs, taxi drivers and a clash of faith, in *The Daily Telegraph* (12 October 2006) i, 27.
al-Sarakhsī, Shams al-Dīn, *Kitāb al-Mabsūṭ*, Beirut 1993.

al-Shāfiʿī, M. Ibn Idrīs, *Kitāb al-Umm*, Beirut 1990.
al-Shawkānī, M. Ibn ʿAlī, *Nayl al-awṭār sharh minṭaqā al-akhbār*, Cairo n.d.
al-Ṭabarī, M., *Tafsīr al-Ṭabarī: Jāmiʿ al-bayān fī tafsīr al-Qurʾān*, ed. B. ʿAwwād Maʿruf and ʿA.F. al-Ḥarastānī, Beirut 1994.
Wensinck, A.J. [with A.K. Reinhart], Tayammum, in *EI*², x, 399–400.
Woods, B.A., *The Devil in dog form: A partial type-index of Devil legends*, Berkeley 1959.
al-Zamakhsharī, *al-Kashshāf ʿan ḥaqāʾiq al-tanzīl wa-ʿuyūn al-aqawīl fī wujūh al-taʾwīl*, Beirut n.d.
al-Ziriklī, *al-Aʿlām: Qāmūs tarājim li-ashhar al-rijāl wa-l-nisāʾ min al-ʿArab wa-l-mutaʿarribīn wa-l-mustashriqīn*, Beirut 1997.

CHAPTER 52

Perceptions of Paradise in the Writings of Julius Wellhausen, Mark Lidzbarski, and Hans Heinrich Schaeder

*Ludmila Hanisch**

In his book on Europe's interest in the Quran during the Protestant Reformation, Hartmut Bobzin observes, "The full range of reasons for the study of Islam, and of the Quran in particular, can only be understood in the context of the theological disputes related to the Reformation."[1] Here, in addition to proselytization efforts, familiarity with the enemy (who was standing at the gates of Vienna), commercial interests, and a policy of foreign alliances, Bobzin was referring to the significance the confrontation with the alien religion would have for the development of Christian doctrine.

In the seventeenth century, theologians held the Quran to be a grossly inferior imitation of the Bible, and even in the early eighteenth century, the phrase "Mohammedan doctrine" was used pejoratively to denote a non-canonical tenet. Following the Enlightenment and the ensuing Romanticism movement, a strictly theological motivation for study ceased, and independence from the quest for theological knowledge was generally emphasized. Attempts to criticize religion through references to non-Christian belief also fell into relative oblivion.[2]

Though the religious elements of Oriental studies did not completely disappear from the consciousness of academic specialists (who gradually focused more on linguistic problems and literary texts during the nineteenth century), they were increasingly relegated to the background in scholarly endeavors. Nonetheless, in the nineteenth century, Heinrich Ewald maintained the link, "... and it is indeed true that the Bible – apart from its theological essence – appertains to the Orient."[3] Even H.L. Fleischer, the staunch proponent of a

* Sadly, as this book was in preparation, we learned of the untimely passing of Dr. Ludmila Hanisch of Berlin.

1 Bobzin, *Zeitalter der Reformation* 8.

2 One result of Marchand's extensive study *German Orientalism* is that in the era under scrutiny, the findings of Orientalist research also influenced Christian theological discourse.

3 Ewald, Plan 10.

 | DOI 10.1163/9789004333154_053

philological approach towards the Middle East reminded his audience, "We old Orientalists are, in fact, all theologians manqué."[4]

In his history of Arabic studies, Johann Fück emphasized that an unprejudiced study of Islam came into existence only after German Orientalists ceased to be swayed by theological modes of thought.[5] However, the emphasis with which the dissociation from religious considerations was stressed reflected a self-conception that, at that point, had been only partially implemented at the institutional level.

A survey of Semitic studies at German universities reveals that at the beginning of the twentieth century one-third of the faculty members still taught in the faculty of theology. This revelation, coupled with the finding that Indic studies, too, were not outside the influence of theological developments at some universities, suggests the need to take another, deeper look at the link between theology and Orientalist research.[6] A review of the main fields of research and teaching at several Near and Middle Eastern Studies departments in Germany over the past decades indicates that it would be advisable to include local Christian theological traditions in the consideration of the history of German Orientalism.

Even the academic interaction with France – the "blessed oriental paradise" (Fleischer) where many individuals who later held professorships in Germany in the area of Orientalism attended university – did not always do away with the influence of different local theological traditions. It must be noted, though, that German academia never emulated its Continental neighbor's strict secularist standards. Furthermore, Germany – unlike France – never possessed colonial territories, the majority of whose inhabitants were Muslims.[7] A diachronic examination of the relationships between Orientalist studies and theology at specific universities would make it possible to clarify the special way in which they were interwoven until well into the twentieth century. For individual universities, investigations of the subject already exist.[8]

4 Schaeder quoted this sentence in his inaugural lecture in Leipzig entitled "Die Idee der orientalischen Religionsgeschichte" 13.

5 Fück, *Die arabischen Studien* 97, 124, 158, 181.

6 This has recently emerged in regard to Indology, see Sengupta, *From salon to discipline* and Rabault-Feuerhahn, *L'archive des origines* 92–9.

7 In France, there were no departments of theology except at the University of Strasbourg. For a recent study of the influence of colonial history on the study of Arabic in France, see Messaoudi, *Savants, conseillers, médiateurs*.

8 Preissler, Orientalische Studien; Schnurrer, *Lehrer der Hebräischen Litteratur*.

1 Scope and Focus of Analysis

At the time of its founding in 1737, Göttingen's Georg August University did not grant its theology department pre-eminence over other faculties, as was the tradition elsewhere. This fact suggests that a deeper study of this institution is in order.

In 1745, the appointment of Johann David Michaelis to an Old Testament studies professorship in the Faculty of Philosophy of Georg August University created an academic position unique in the German university landscape. Göttingen's differentiation between science and revelation (or conviction) actually took on concrete form at the institutional level, even before the Humboldtian university model – with its privileging of the Faculty of Philosophy – was put into practice in Berlin. It is said that thanks to his appointment to the Faculty of Philosophy, Michaelis – who left the pietistic atmosphere of the University of Halle for Göttingen – enjoyed a certain degree of autonomy in comparison with colleagues who worked in an atmosphere of the ecclesiastical dogma that prevailed in the Faculty of Theology.[9] Götz von Selle's rendition of the history of the Georg August University's foundation reveals the repeated emphasis placed on the efforts of the institution's founders to distinguish its course offerings from those at Halle.[10]

The focus here is the degree to which scholars' early experience with a particular religious socialization impacted their interest in Orientalist research. Exposure to religious training at a formative stage of life certainly may increase sensitivity with regard to the strength and extent of one's religious commitment. It must be noted that while experience of this type of scholar certainly does not preclude an inclination toward agnosticism or atheism, growing up in the household of a pastor or rabbi certainly has a justifiable reputation for decisively directing a child's intellectual development, frequently away from explicitly religious studies and pursuits.[11]

My analysis focuses on the presentation of Near Eastern religions by three scholars who taught Semitic and Oriental philology from the last third of the nineteenth to the middle of the twentieth century: Julius Wellhausen (1844–1918), Mark Lidzbarski (1868–1928), and Hans Heinrich Schaeder (1896–1957). They were selected because their teaching activities took place in an era when Orientalist studies in Germany were primarily engaged in philology and occasionally history; these studies also held that the Near East was scientifically

9 Loewenbrueck, *Judenfeindschaft im Zeitalter der Aufklärung* 88.

10 Selle, *Universität zu Göttingen 1737–1937*.

11 Snouck Hurgronje, *de Goeje* 7.

uninteresting,[12] despite increasingly intense interactions through voyages, commerce, and colonization.[13] The growing interest in the Near East caused an expansion in the number of Orientalist teaching institutions and supported what at first was less of a paradigm change than a diversification of the discipline into various special subjects. This era saw both the division of the courses offered into Semitic and Indo-European languages, and the creation of Assyriology as an independent subject in its own right.[14]

The three scholars selected here, who externally manifested detachment from their religious convictions, are representatives of a gradual phase of revolution. Their earlier religious or theological training inspired their work, helped shape their investigations, and doubtlessly influenced their research, which had apparently non-theological objectives. Their research did not necessarily require travel to the Near East or South Asia, and they appeared disinclined to do so. Only Mark Lidzbarski is known to have made such a trip – to Istanbul to study manuscripts.

2 Julius Wellhausen

With regard to Julius Wellhausen, the works of Rudolf Smend – probably the person most familiar with Wellhausen's life and output – serve as a reference. He called Wellhausen a "pioneer in three disciplines": The Old Testament scholar who dealt intensively with the history of Israel and came – via a detour through Arabic studies – to the New Testament.[15]

The son of an orthodox Protestant pastor, Julius Wellhausen studied theology in Göttingen. Among his teachers was the theologian Heinrich Ewald, who, in addition to Oriental languages, instructed him in the analysis of academic issues – which included Ewald's emphasis on the significance of the Bible for Near Eastern research. After several years as a professor of theology in Greifswald, Wellhausen no longer wanted to take part in the training of

12 Becker, Hartmann 231.

13 For a full presentation of the evolution of Orientalist research in Göttingen, it would be necessary to include Johann David Michaelis, Heinrich Ewald, and others. They, however, were part of an era in which there was not yet an assertion of independence from theology.

14 Renger, Altorientalistik. In this context, it should be pointed out that the Assyriologist Friedrich Delitzsch was searching for the geographic location of paradise, see Delitzsch, *Paradies*.

15 Smend, *Julius Wellhausen*.

pastors. He applied to the Ministry of Education and first received a position as an associate professor in the Faculty of Philosophy at Halle.[16] After a period in Marburg, he went to Göttingen where he was the last theologian to teach Old Testament studies in the Faculty of Philosophy. After his death, his work had a better reception among theologians than Orientalists; for the former, his output on the history of Israel was of greater interest than that pertaining to the Arabs.

Carl Heinrich Becker and Enno Littmann were among those Orientalists who especially appreciated Wellhausen. Becker had studied Wellhausen's Arabist work for his dissertation, and Enno Littmann, who briefly succeeded Wellhausen as professor at Göttingen, intended to write a biography of Wellhausen, but this never materialized. Thus, the most comprehensive study of Wellhausen the Arabist appeared about twenty-five years ago, authored by Kurt Rudolph, an expert in religious studies.[17] Wellhausen explained his interest in early Islamic history with the pregnant quote: "... to become acquainted with the wild stem onto which priests and prophets have grafted the rice of Jahve's Thora."[18] Through this wish to gain familiarity with the pristine form of ancient Israel, he went beyond the requirements of Biblical exegesis. For Wellhausen, the history of the ancient Arabs – and not their holy book – contained information about the ancient Hebrews. He considered Muḥammad first and foremost a statesman and called the Quran the prophet's most meagre accomplishment.[19]

Wellhausen, coming from a Protestant milieu, considered Islam's "catholicism" (universality/*jamāʿiyya*) as an attribute that was both conservative and compliant with the powers that be. In contrast, he favored the idea of a theocracy recognized and accepted by individual believers.[20] For him, the subjective feeling of affiliation with a religion was more important than the institutions stipulated by the orthodoxy. His ideal was a religiosity without priests and prophets.

Since he concentrated on early Islamic history, Wellhausen's comments on Islam's vision of the afterlife are sparse. In his famous historical work *Das arabische Reich und sein Sturz*, it is the opposition parties who strove for entrance to paradise. After Muḥammad's death, the Kharijites (*khawārij*) fought on the

16 Jepsen, Wellhausen in Greifswald 51–2.
17 Rudolph, Wellhausen als Arabist.
18 Wellhausen, *Muhammed in Medina* 5.
19 Smend, *Julius Wellhausen* 31; Wellhausen, Mohammedanism 561.
20 Wellhausen, Oppositionsparteien 12; Rudolph, Wellhausen als Arabist 38; Wellhausen, *Das arabische Reich* 310.

battlefield in order to gain access to heaven.[21] Around the middle of the eighth century, they redirected their endeavors toward a terrestrial kingdom, no longer sacrificing themselves in an effort to reach paradise.[22]

3 Mark Lidzbarski

Mark Lidzbarski is less well-known than Wellhausen. In 1917, when he was a professor at Greifswald, he was appointed to take over the chair of Semitic philology in Göttingen. In the correspondence of his peers, his name is always mentioned with great respect and his works are invariably characterized in a positive light. The Royal Society of Sciences in Göttingen supported his publications, even in economically difficult times. Lidzbarski's autobiography, *Auf rauhem Wege*, appeared anonymously and ends with the beginning of his years as a university student in Berlin. This book is reminiscent of the image of his preschool instruction that Ignaz Goldziher portrayed in his diary.[23]

Abraham Mordechai Lidzbarski was born the son of a Hasidic businessman in Płock – in the Russian part of Poland at the time, on the right bank of the Vistula River. In those days, the city had about 20,000 inhabitants, 25–36 percent of whom were Jewish. The majority were either *chassidim* (pious) or *mitnaggedim* (opponents) and were initially rivals in Poland, but from the middle of the nineteenth century, any tension between these rivals lost its significance when both groups united against the "enlightened" Jews of the *Haskalah*.[24] Lidzbarski attended a Chassidic school at the age of three and began studying the Talmud at age six. His descriptions evoke the image of an obscurantist environment that one might expect to find in the easternmost corner of Halychyna better known as Galicia, rather than in a small town on the bank of the Vistula between Posen and Warsaw.[25] Lidzbarski's teachers were all

---

21 Muḥammad's first supporters were organized like an army, Wellhausen, *Arab kingdom* 65.

22 Wellhausen, *Arab kingdom* 388. In Wellhausen, Oppositionsparteien 57 is the saying handed down by Mughīra (between 668 and 671), that he was not willing to spill Muslim blood and in this way forfeit his way into heaven.

23 Goldziher, *Tagebuch*; Lidzbarski, *Auf rauhem Wege*. In a review, Hans Heinrich Schaeder called the book a "documentation of the history of education of considerable significance," Schaeder, Review of M. Lidzbarski, Auf rauhem Wege, 817.

24 Guesnet, *Polnische Juden*; Wodziński, *Haskalah and Hasidim*.

25 His observation that few demands were made on the daughters of Jewish families in regard to religious training is noteworthy. They were permitted to attend Polish schools where they acquired some knowledge of modern foreign languages, *Auf rauhem Wege* 91–2.

Chassidim and he described the origin of this trend as the consolidation of Judaism in an unadorned form, the "deeper-minded nature" in all religions in which a revival is sought. The way out in this case was to turn to mysticism.[26] He later became acquainted with representatives of the Jewish *Haskalah*, the "free spirits" whose knowledge impressed him. Instead of pursuing a rabbinical career as his family wished, Lidzbarski strove to become an "astronomer."[27]

At the age of fifteen, he secretly took a ferryboat across the Vistula in order to learn something "worth knowing."[28] After attending a German grammar school in Posen, where he was fortuitously introduced to the Arabic language by Hartwig Hirschfeld, Lidzbarski studied Near Eastern languages at the Berlin University.[29] He pursued his goals despite a precarious financial situation. When still a student, he converted to Protestantism and from that point on used the name Mark Lidzbarski. He never revealed whether he had abandoned Judaism out of conviction or whether the atmosphere in the German Empire made a conversion most opportune. In any case, despite his conversion, he never described his original community with any disdain whatsoever. After receiving his PhD in Berlin, for which he was examined by Eduard Sachau and Eberhard Schrader, Lidzbarski completed his postdoctoral thesis in 1896 in Kiel.[30] In 1907, he was appointed the successor to Wilhelm Ahlwardt in Greifswald.

In the scholarly world, Lidzbarski was best known for his works on North Semitic epigraphy. He was intensely interested in the Mandaeans, an interest that colleagues emphasized in their recommendation that he be selected for the Greifswald professorship. They described "the elucidation of the dark Mandaean literature, which is particularly important for the history of religion" as being his "actual aim in life."[31]

---

26 Ibid., 82.

27 Ibid., 31, 146. The autobiography was discussed by Klanska, *Aus dem Schtetl in die Welt* 254 and 278–83.

28 Some decades before him, Julius Fürst had chosen a similar path. In 1820, at the age of fifteen, Fürst also left his hometown in Prussian territory and later worked in Leipzig. Vogel, Der Orientalist Julius Fürst 41.

29 Hartwig Hirschfeld (1854 Thorn/Province of Posen – 1934 Ramsgate/England). In 1889, Lidzbarski is listed as a student on the attendance list of the former Friedrich-Wilhelms University.

30 Promotionsakte Lidzbarski, Faculty of Philosophy, no. 315, sheet 437, archive of the Humboldt University of Berlin.

31 The document from the Greifswald Faculty of Philosophy's appointment commission is in I HA, Rep. 76 Va, Sect. 7, Tit. 4, Nr. 22, Vol. 17, sheet 163. GSTA – Stiftung Preußischer Kulturbesitz, Berlin-Dahlem.

Until today, specialists in the field view Lidzbarski's editions of Mandaean texts, which he worked on continually during his entire scholarly life, as being second in importance only to Nöldeke's *Mandäische Grammatik*.[32] This respect is due to his having organized these texts – which also contained liturgies – on a sound philological basis; the introductions in the editions are brief and contain mainly technical explanations. Lidzbarski stated that the reason for his occupation with this religious community was that Mandaeism is the only Gnostic sect from which literature has been preserved. He described its significance by saying: "I don't know whether many who delve into the Mandaean religion can visualize what an enormous revolution it represented in regard to everything that preceded it."[33]

Lidzbarski's research dealt with Jewish influences on Near Eastern Gnosticism, for which he primarily relied on philological evidence.[34] His investigations led him to postulate that the Mandaeans were of western origin, from the Palestinian-Syrian region, even though they later settled in Mesopotamia. His work *Alter und Heimat der mandäischen Religion*, which he wrote shortly before his death, displays the fervor he felt for this topic; it contained harsh criticism of the theologian Erik Peterson's lecture "Urchristentum und Mandäismus."[35]

According to Lidzbarski, the Mandaeans focused exclusively on the life beyond, resulting in their failure to keep a written history. They regarded paradise as dwellings (*Shkinas*) flooded with light that received the soul after a journey through the world of light.[36] Lidzbarski's research goals and methods must be sought in his liturgy editions since he made only a few comments about them in his other works. His compilations of Mandaean texts documented the

---

32 Nöldeke, *Mandäische Grammatik*.

33 Lidzbarski, Alter und Heimat 384. In 1870, the Arabist and dialectologist Albert Socin traveled to Kurna on the lower Euphrates, the region of the last remnants of those who are seen to be Mandaeans. He was not able, however, to implement his plan to make voice recordings.

34 Later research has confirmed this. See also Rudolph, *Die Mandäer* 253: "The obvious Jewish colouring of this religion permits postulation of its western (Palestinian-Syrian) roots. These ultimately date back to a Judaism that had become heretical and was moved into the maelstrom of this late-antique religion by the Gnostic movement, …"

35 Peterson, Urchristentum und Mandäismus.

36 For example, Lidzbarski, *Mandäische Liturgien* 86, 181–2, 204, etc. A central aspect of their ritual was baptism in flowing water that they believed came from the north. Lidzbarski dedicated *Mandäische Liturgien* to Wilhelm Bousset (1865–1920), who represented the Religionsgeschichtliche Schule (History of Religions School), which was not well regarded by the Göttingen theologians.

significance of Judaism for the Gnostic religious communities. He felt that the Mandaean religion and beliefs continued to have an impact on the cultures of the Near Eastern peoples and were not obliterated by later influences.

4 Hans Heinrich Schaeder

Hans Heinrich Schaeder focused his scholarly attention on another branch of pre-Christian Gnosticism: Manicheism. When Hans Heinrich was born, his father, Erich Schaeder, was an associate professor of Protestant theology in Göttingen. Hans Heinrich Schaeder completed his studies in Theology and Orientalism in Breslau, where Franz Praetorius served as his PhD supervisor.[37] Even as a young scholar, Schaeder had already made a name for himself with works on the history of religion in pre-Islamic Iran, for which he had been prepared by Josef Markwart, one of his teachers. In 1924, he took part in the discussion of the various influences on, and strata of, the syncretistic religious communities in the Near East with a long treatise entitled "Urform und Fortbildungen des manichäischen Systems."[38]

After earning his post-doctoral teaching degree in 1926, Schaeder undertook work in Königsberg and, following a brief period in Leipzig, he held a position in Berlin from 1931 to 1944. These academic posts indicate his stature as a scholar. He did not return to the city of his birth until after the Second World War in 1948, when he was appointed to the chair of Oriental Philology and Religious Studies, which, after 1945, was the title of the position that had been held by both Wellhausen and Lidzbarski. It was during this period that he converted to Catholicism. Schaeder held Wellhausen's work in high regard and took pleasure in the fact that he now sat in his esteemed predecessor's chair.[39]

37 On 16 May 1919, Arthur Schaade introduced Hans Heinrich Schaeder to the Orientalist Carl Heinrich Becker, who worked in the Ministry of Education at the time. Of Schaeder, he wrote: "He is a very unusually talented individual… I believe his future plans go in the direction of comparative religious history. I already have a tendency to see him as a 'coming man.'" Estate of Becker, C.H., Rep. 92, no. 3693, GSTA – Stiftung Preußischer Kulturbesitz, Berlin-Dahlem.

38 Schaeder, *Urform* 15–107. Lidzbarski criticized Schaeder's assumption that Mani introduced a writing reform in a brief article entitled "Warum schrieb Mānī aramäisch?".

39 Letter by Schaeder to H.S. Nyberg from 5 July 1946, 58. In his 1936 article "Orientforschung und abendländisches Geschichtsbild," Schaeder conferred a position of honor on Wellhausen as a representative of "profound Occidental solidarity in the perception of things Oriental" 388.

The history of religion in pre-Islamic Iran was a focal point of activity throughout his academic career. He held its tenets more highly than Islamic doctrine, which he viewed as "an Arab layer of the Near Eastern religions of redemption."[40] In regard to Manicheism, he sought to analyze the mutual influence of Greek thinking and oriental religion.[41] He clung firmly to his plan to write a *Handbook of Old Persian*, even though the issue was put on hold due to his manifold interests and tasks; in the end, this work never appeared.

According to Schaeder, Mani, the founder of the religion, grew up in the presence of the Mandaeans and included Iranian elements in his doctrine. This included the characteristic radical dualism between light and darkness, as well as the conflict between the empire of good and the empire of evil. The goal of the struggle is the liberation of light, which forms the main component of the eschatology. Through asceticism and abstinence, the human being can reach gnosis, or true, salvific knowledge; evil darkness flees and returns to the light. Mani, whom Schaeder considered to have finalized the Hellenistic-Oriental gnosis, promoted a unidirectional tendency toward such a mode of salvation.[42]

In his conception of Manicheism, the Jewish components of the history of Near Eastern religion are relegated to the background. This becomes clear when his works are compared with those of Lidzbarski. In 1929, Schaeder wrote about his preoccupation with the history of religion to the Swedish theologian and Iranist Nyberg, "It is strange to me: I increasingly recoil from the type of history of religion whose tone has been set in the last forty years and come ever closer to 'conservative' theological consideration, although I personally have absolutely no theological interests."[43] Schaeder understood the term "conservative theological consideration" to mean interest in the "spiritual content of the sources," whereas he felt the *religionsgeschichtliche Schule* only dealt with the "external trappings."

A year later, he assumed the Fleischer professorship in Leipzig and, despite his statement denying that he had any interest in theology, in his inaugural lecture entitled "Die Idee der orientalischen Religionsgeschichte," he promoted the Old Testament to the rank of a classical corpus for the analysis of Oriental religions. Furthermore, he postulated that a theological orientation would protect the Orientalists from "arcane research into antiquity," as well as animate

40 Schaeder, Arabien I. Vorislamisch 460.

41 Schaeder, *Urform* 16.

42 Ibid., 106.

43 Letter by Schaeder to H.S. Nyberg dated 5 April 1929, 5. Schaeder's works on the history of religion were compiled after his death by his student Carsten Colpe and were published in one volume with a lengthy epilogue: *Studien zur Orientalischen Religionsgeschichte*.

the dialogue between Christians and humanists.[44] He viewed the latter as a fertile evolution of the Greek heritage in the Occident, whereas the Orient was only a passive recipient of this heritage. To him, the history of Oriental religion meant a history of decline. The prophets had been able to maintain the balance between escape from the world and openness to it, but after Jesus, a process of disintegration set in, of which Mani and Muḥammad were emblematic.

5 Conclusion

This study of the aforementioned three Orientalists' perspectives on various Near Eastern religions has necessarily been offered in broad strokes. Nonetheless, it is evident that their own religious training and personal relationships to religion influenced their selection of the fields and topics with which they dealt so intensively. Eschatology and the end of days played a subordinate role in this process, and descriptions of the details of rituals and myths were equally negligible.

Even though all of these scholars clearly recognized the powerful effect religious ideas had on the development of Near Eastern history, their approaches differed in regard to the issue of the persistence and changeability of religious traditions. In this area, their respective interests in history was of greater influence.

Bibliography

Becker, C.-H., Martin Hartmann, in *Der Islam* 10 (1920), 228–33.

Bobzin, H., *Der Koran im Zeitalter der Reformation*, Stuttgart 1995.

Canus-Crede, H. (ed.), Letters by Schaeder to H.S. Nyberg, in *Iranistische Mitteilungen* 28, 2, 3, and 4 (1998).

Delitzsch, F., *Wo lag das Paradies? Eine biblisch-assyriologische Studie*, Leipzig 1881.

Ewald, H.A., Plan dieser Zeitschrift, in *Zeitschrift für die Kunde des Morgenlandes* 1 (1837), 3–13.

Fück, J.W., *Die arabischen Studien in Europa bis in den Anfang des 20. Jahrhunderts*, Leipzig 1955.

Goldziher, I., *Tagebuch*, Leiden 1978.

Guesnet, F., *Polnische Juden im 19. Jahrhundert: Lebensbedingungen, Rechtsnormen und Organisation im Wandel*, Cologne 1998.

44 Schaeder, Die Idee der orientalischen Religionsgeschichte 1–14.

Jepsen, A., Wellhausen in Greifswald – Ein Beitrag zur Biographie Wellhausens, in Ernst Moritz Arndt-Universität Greifswald (ed.), *Festschrift zur 500 Jahrfeier der Universität Greifswald*, Greifswald 1956, 47–56.

Klanska, M., *Aus dem Schtetl in die Welt 1772–1938: Ostjüdische Autobiographien in deutscher Sprache*, Vienna 1994.

Lidzbarski, M., Alter und Heimat der mandäischen Religion, in *Zeitschrift für die neutestamentliche Wissenschaft und die Kunde der alten Kirche* 27 (1928), 321–6, repr. in G. Widengren (ed.), *Der Mandäismus*, Darmstadt 1982, 381–8.

———, *Auf rauhem Wege*, Giessen 1937.

———, *Mandäische Liturgien*, Berlin 1920.

———, Warum schrieb Mānī aramäisch? in *OLZ* 30 (1927), col. 913–7.

Loewenbrueck, A.-R., *Judenfeindschaft im Zeitalter der Aufklärung: Eine Studie zur Vorgeschichte des modernen Antisemitismus am Beispiel des Göttinger Theologen und Orientalisten Johann David Michaelis (1717–1791)*, Frankfurt 1995.

Marchand, S.L., *German Orientalism in the age of empire: Religion, race, and scholarship*, Cambridge 2009.

Messaoudi, A., *Savants, conseillers, médiateurs: Les arabisants et la France coloniale (vers 1830–vers 1930)*, PhD dissertation, Université Paris I 2008.

Nöldeke, T., *Mandäische Grammatik*, Halle/Saale 1875.

Peterson, E., Urchristentum und Mandäismus, in *Zeitschrift für die neutestamentliche Wissenschaft und die Kunde der alten Kirche* 27 (1928), 55–91, repr. in G. Widengren (ed.), *Der Mandäismus*, Darmstadt 1982, 372–80.

Preissler, H., Orientalische Studien in Leipzig vor Reiske, in H.-G. Ebert and T. Hanstein (eds.), *Johann Jakob Reiske: Leben und Wirkung: Ein Leipziger Byzantinist und Begründer der Orientalistik im 18. Jahrhundert*, Leipzig 2005, 19–43.

Rabault-Feuerhahn, P., *L'archive des origines: Sanskrit, philologie, anthropologie dans l'Allemagne du XIXe siècle*, Paris 2008.

Renger, J., Altorientalistik, in J. Elvert and J. Nielsen-Sikora (eds.), *Kulturwissenschaften und Nationalsozialismus*, Stuttgart 2008, 469–502.

Rudolph, K., *Die Mandäer*, Göttingen 1960.

———, Wellhausen als Arabist, in *Sitzungsberichte der Sächsischen Akademie der Wissenschaften, Phil.-Hist. Klasse* 123.5 (1983), 1–56.

Schaeder, H.H., Arabien I. Vorislamisch, in *Religion in Geschichte und Gegenwart*, i, Tübingen 1927, col. 460–3.

———, Die Idee der orientalischen Religionsgeschichte (1930), in H.H. Schaeder, *Studien zur Orientalischen Religionsgeschichte*, ed. C. Colpe, Darmstadt 1968, 1–14.

———, Die Orientforschung und das abendländische Geschichtsbild, in *Die Welt als Geschichte* 2 (1936), 377–96, repr. in G. Schaeder (ed.), *Der Mensch in Orient und Okzident*, Munich 1960.

———, Review of M. Lidzbarski, Auf rauhem Wege, in *OLZ* 31 (1928), col. 815–7.

———, *Studien zur Orientalischen Religionsgeschichte*, ed. C. Colpe, Darmstadt 1968.

———, Urform und Fortbildungen des manichäischen Systems (1927), in H.H. Schaeder, *Studien zur Orientalischen Religionsgeschichte*, ed. C. Colpe, Darmstadt 1968, 15–107.

Schnurrer, Chr., *Biographische und literarische Nachrichten von ehemaligen Lehrern der Hebräischen Litteratur in Tübingen*, Ulm, Germany 1792.

Selle, G. von, *Die Georg-August-Universität zu Göttingen 1737–1937*, Göttingen 1937.

Sengupta, I., *From salon to discipline: State, university and Indology in Germany 1821–1914*, Würzburg 2005.

Smend, R., *Julius Wellhausen: Ein Bahnbrecher in drei Disziplinen*, Munich 2004.

Snouck Hurgronje, C., *Michaël Jan de Goeje*, Paris 1911.

Vogel, K., Der Orientalist Julius Fürst (1805–1873): Wissenschaftler, Publizist und engagierter Bürger, in S. Wendehorst (ed.), *Bausteine einer jüdischen Geschichte der Universität Leipzig*, Leipzig 2006, 41–60.

Wellhausen, J., *The Arab kingdom and its fall*, Calcutta 1927.

———, *Das arabische Reich und sein Sturz*, Berlin 1902.

———, Mohammedanism, in *Encyclopaedia Britannica*, xvi, Edinburgh 1883[9], 545–65.

———, *Muhammed in Medina: Das ist Vakidi's Kitab al-Maghazi in verkürzter deutscher Wiedergabe herausgegeben*, Berlin 1882.

———, Die religiös-politischen Oppositionsparteien im alten Islam, in *Abhandlungen der königlichen Gesellschaft der Wissenschaften zu Göttingen, Phil.-hist. Klasse: Neue Serie* 5 (1901), 1–99.

Wodziński, M., *Haskalah and Hasidim in the Kingdom of Poland: A history of conflict*, Oxford 2005.

PART 11

Paradise Meets Modernity – The Dynamics of Paradise Discourse in the Nineteenth, Twentieth, and Twenty-First Centuries

CHAPTER 53

Islam and Paradise are Sheltered under the Shade of Swords: Phallocentric Fantasies of Paradise in Nineteenth-Century Acehnese War Propaganda and their Lasting Legacy

*Edwin P. Wieringa**

1 No Sex Please, We're Muslims

The blurb on the dust jacket of John Esposito's *What Everyone Needs to Know about Islam* self-assuredly asserts that this Q&A book on Islam is "the first place to look for information," written by "one of America's leading authorities on Islam." This unabashed claim to expertise and learning aroused my curiosity, and prompted me to start my inquiry into concepts of paradise in Islam by consulting Esposito's guidebook. Though I did not expect a quick and easy answer, I was disconcerted to find that Esposito's opaque language makes it rather difficult to grasp what kind of supreme happiness Islam promises its adherents in the afterlife: "Quranic descriptions of heavenly bliss are life-affirming, emphasizing the beauty of creation and enjoyment of its pleasures within the limits set by God."[1] Joy within limits sounds rather dull and stern, and the exact nature of these joys remains anyone's guess. Esposito speaks nebulously about "the pleasures of heavenly gardens of bliss," and contrasts the "comprehensive and integrated" Islamic images of heaven with the "more sedate, celibate" paradise of Christianity.[2] "The Quran," Esposito tells us, "does not draw a distinction between enjoying the joys of beatific vision and those of the fruits of creation."[3]

It is not clear what exactly this means; it does not tell us much about the kind of enjoyment the Muslim celestial elect may experience. Does it involve

* Prof. Willem van der Molen and Nico van Rooijen, MA at the KITLV in Leiden kindly helped me with the illustrations of Abdullah Arif's *Nasib Atjeh*. I also would like to thank Dr. S. Suryadi for providing me with photos of manuscript Cod. Or. 8747c of Leiden University Library.

1 Esposito, *What everyone needs* 28.

2 Ibid., 29.

3 Ibid.

 | DOI 10.1163/9789004333154_054

having sex with *ḥūrīs*? Apparently not, because Esposito translates the term *ḥūrīs* as "beautiful companions," stating that

> [t]he Quran makes no reference to a sexual role for the houris, but *some* Western critics have rendered houris as meaning 'virgins' and seized upon one popular belief that has been used to motivate *some* Muslim suicide bombers. However, *many* Quranic commentators and *most* Muslims understand houris as virgins only in the sense of pure or purified souls.[4]

What does this overwrought rhetoric mean? Something like "No sex please, we're Muslims"?

In order to comprehend Esposito's stilted dense prose, we should bear in mind that the issue of *ḥūrīs* is a very sensitive one, given its use as a stock argument in polemics against Islam as essentially a primitive, sensual religion, engrossed in worldly pleasure. Apparently wishing to avoid the pitfall of stereotyping Islam as depraved, Esposito goes to the other extreme, turning the notion of the *ḥūrīs* into spiritualized creatures that have no sexual potential at all. As David Cook makes clear, however, such denial of the existence of sexual themes as intrinsic parts of Islamic visions of paradise is a gross distortion of the prevailing evidence: "It is impossible to find any classical Muslim exegete who understood the verses concerning the houris as anything other than references to women whose purpose was to provide sexual pleasure for the blessed in heaven."[5] Aziz al-Azmeh, too, writes that before Muslims came "under the influence of nineteenth century European Puritanism," Islamic discourse on paradise was essentially on "carnal pleasures and the sumptuosity of victuals and provisions."[6]

It is hardly surprising that over the last years, stories about the sexual motives of 'testosterone terrorists' have tantalized Western media. On account of the public debate caused by the sanguinary actions of so-called jihadists (or *mujāhidīn*, defenders of the faith, or literally, "strugglers"), even non-Muslims now seem to know that the Islamic heaven offers the champions of the faith unlimited pleasures of the flesh. The main reaction in the Euro-Atlantic world has been a mixture of disbelief, ridicule, and even scorn, reinforcing age-long clichés of Islamic backwardness and the 'sex-craved Arab.' Reputedly, Muslim

---

4 Ibid., emphasis added.

5 Cook, *Martyrdom* 33. Elsewhere, too, Cook takes issue with "the works of John Esposito, whose writings on the subject of jihad border between the scholarly and the apologetic," see Cook, *Understanding* 41.

6 Al-Azmeh, Rhetoric for the senses 216, 218.

suicide bombers choose death in the firm belief that they will be welcomed in paradise by seventy-two curvaceous celestial playmates.[7] It is a telling fact that one of the best-known controversial Danish Muḥammad cartoons (a satirical drawing depicting a Mullah, supposedly representing the Prophet Muḥammad greeting disheveled suicide bombers lined up on a cloud as if in heaven and imploring them to stop killing themselves because paradise has run out of virgins), which first appeared in the newspaper *Jyllands-Posten* in 2005, was immediately understood by the general observer.

Unbelievable though it may seem, in the so-called spiritual manual of the attackers of 9/11 the young Muslim warriors, in the last night before the assault, are instructed to be optimistic as 'marriage' is ahead.[8] A wedding with the heavenly brides will be their guaranteed ultimate reward: "Know that the Heavens have raised their most beautiful decoration for you, and that your heavenly brides are calling you: 'Come oh follower of God,' while wearing their most beautiful jewelry."[9] Obviously, this is not the kind of language that many postcolonial scholars in the West are comfortable with. For example, Hans Kippenberg, a noted scholar of comparative religious studies, comments that "[t]he topic of the wedding of the martyr with the heavenly brides intensifies the feeling of inconceivability that befalls Western observers regarding Muslim concepts of martyrdom."[10] Ill at ease with this outré rhetoric, he refers to the historian Malise Ruthven, who in Kippenberg's view "has tried to open a path to understanding" here, by arguing that according to al-Ghazālī (d. 505/1111), the sexual imagery of paradise should be seen as an inducement to righteousness. So, just like Esposito, Kippenberg rejects, offhand, a literal interpretation of the wedding trope, and instead opts for a more refined, deeper meaning of the text: "The state of spiritual fulfilment can only be described in terms of familiar experiences."[11]

The uneasiness with 'vulgar' matters (i.e., affairs related to sex or bodily functions, the word 'vulgar' tellingly can be traced back to the Latin *vulgaris*,

---

7 Whereas Smith and Haddad, *Islamic understanding* 165 describe the *ḥūrīs* as "buxom," al-Azmeh, Rhetoric for the senses 226 argues that the heavenly consorts in pre-modern texts answered to a "bookish medieval Arab-Islamic canon of feminine beauty." The shape of their breasts should be "the small breasts of pubescent girls in early adolescence," conjoined to a "very narrow waist and unnaturally huge buttocks," see al-Azmeh, Rhetoric for the senses 226.

8 Kippenberg, The spiritual manual 41.

9 Cited in ibid., 45.

10 Ibid.

11 Ibid. Kippenberg refers to Ruthven, *A fury* 102. On the meaning of *ḥūrīs* and heavenly marriage, see also S. Griffith's contribution to the present publication.

derived from *vulgus* 'common people') may perhaps be typical for the elite group of intellectuals everywhere, *sui generis*.[12] In his essay on pre-modern Muslim views concerning love and sex in paradise, Franz Rosenthal observes that only "[r]are thinkers came to the wise conclusion that the situation in Paradise cannot be understood and conveyed in human terms."[13] Conversely, he notes that "[o]rdinary people, like true believers, saw the delights of Paradise in human terms," and that nearly all traditional Islamic fantasies about paradise are male-designed.[14] Male fantasizing about "effortless eating, drinking and cohabiting" for all eternity reflects an era that predates political correctness.[15] In their reference book *The Islamic Understanding of Death and Resurrection*, Jane Idleman Smith and Yvonne Yazbeck Haddad notice a heavy emphasis in traditional literature on "the specifically physical pleasures encountered with the females of the Garden and the clear indication that if desired the believer can in fact have children," but remarkably few discussions on this can be found in modern works.[16]

Contemporary Muslim exegetes commonly avoid discussing the enthralling particulars in the abode of the blessed, instead they merely comment that the pleasures of the next world are "really beyond human comprehension,"[17] and I am in no position to say whether nowadays raging hormones and sexual frustration could really play a role in motivating some angry young men to blow themselves up in anticipation of an afterlife of eternal sexual gratification and other sensual pleasures. I lack the expertise to theorize about terrorism, and hence it is not my intention to join the chorus of commentators who now try to explain what makes Islamic suicide bombers tick.

---

12 As the sociologist of religion Martin Riesebrodt points out, there is "a plurality of understandings of religion that are specific to different groups and categories of people and in their interaction with each other." He provides the example of intellectuals who tend to prioritize theoretical discourse regarding worldviews, metaphysics, and doctrine, whereas bureaucrats and rulers will emphasize the aspects of authority, order, and morality. See Martin Riesebrodt, Religion 17. Common people, then, would seem to be primarily interested in more 'common' issues. Cf. the view held by the Arabic-writing Persian philosopher and historian Miskawayh (said to have died in 421/1030, aged then a hundred, see Arkoun, Miskawayh 143) that "the sensual view of Paradise is one held by ignorant degenerates and uncouth commoners," see al-Azmeh, Rhetoric for the senses 219.

13 Rosenthal, Reflections 7.

14 Ibid., 23 (citation); ibid., 22 (male fantasies).

15 I owe the pithy formulation of the three pleasures in paradise to Rosenthal, Reflections 8.

16 Smith and Haddad, *Islamic understanding* 167.

17 Ibid.

My scholarly interest in the current topical issue of the ubiquitous suicide *mujāhidīn* lies in the new perspective it may provide on popular nineteenth-century Acehnese poems dealing with the 'holy war' against Dutch imperial encroachment. The 'Aceh War,' which the Acehnese called the "Dutch War" (*Prang Beulanda*) or "Infidel War" (*Prang Kaphé*),[18] was a brutal colonial conflict in North Sumatra (Indonesia) that was instigated in 1873 by the Dutch and dragged on for several decades. According to the history books, this bloodshed ended in 1903, but even after the last Dutchman had left the area, violence continued well into the twenty-first century, and the lyrics of the old wartime poems are still recited today. The Acehnese war poems issuing from the colonial period served the purpose of propaganda. It was the idea of 'testosterone terrorists' – imaginary or not – which has led me to rethink the intention behind this kind of literature. In what follows, I argue that bellicose poems from the Aceh War are not only hyper-violent but also highly sexualized narratives, aimed to incite young men eager to enjoy marital bliss.[19] Far from being curiosa from a long-forgotten war, in post-independence discourse the songs of the holy war against the Dutch have become emblematic of a constructed primordial Acehnese identity, epitomized by proud defenders of Aceh, "the abode of Islam." These incendiary texts have thus outlived their original creators, long after the combat with the Dutch was written definitively in the history books.

2 Acehnese War Literature

The literature that arose during the Aceh War comprises two kinds of writing: first, descriptive accounts of events taking place in this war, and second, blatantly propagandistic texts urging the Acehnese to take up the religious duty of fighting the Dutch infidels (*kaphé*, from Arabic *kāfir*).[20] An example of the first category is the *Hikayat Prang di Sigli* (Song of the war in Sigli) by Teungku Nyak Ahmat (alias Uri b. Mahmut b. Jalalōdin b. Abdōsalam), which describes an attack on Sigli and the retributive bombardment by the Dutch.[21] Arguably better known in secondary literature (though still unpublished and little-examined) is the *Hikayat Prang Gōmpeuni* (Song of the war with the Dutch), a truly great epic composed by the illiterate oral performer

18 Alfian, Aceh 111.

19 For a recent approach to Acehnese war literature from a historical perspective, see Hadi, Exploring.

20 Drewes, *Two Achehnese poems* 50.

21 Voorhoeve, *Catalogue* 65–6.

Dōkarim (also known as Abdulkarim), which the Dutch Orientalist Christiaan Snouck Hurgronje (1857–1936) discovered *in statu nascendi* in 1891–2, during his stay in Aceh where he was engaged in secret service activities on behalf of the Dutch government. It was due to Snouck Hurgronje's initiative that the *Hikayat Prang Gōmpeuni*, which until then was only mnemonically stored, was recorded in writing.[22] Dōkarim was not an especially devout person, and he did not recite his poem before a public of belligerent seminarians and guerilla fighters, but before common villagers like himself, who enjoyed a lyrical celebration of heroic deeds against the hated colonial *gōmpeuni*, i.e., "company," referring to the Dutch East Indies Company, the time-honored term by which the Dutch were known. Though the message of the poem was unmistakably directed against the foreign *kāfir*s (infidels), Snouck Hurgronje deemed that the entrenched theme of hatred of the infidel was just "a matter of custom," and did not represent "deep-seated and unyielding fanaticism."[23] He was even convinced that "under certain circumstances" Dōkarim might be persuaded to recast his account into a "glorification of the *gōmpeuni*."[24] In a postscript Snouck Hurgronje added that this indeed might have become a reality, were it not for the fact that Dōkarim was put to death in September 1897 by Acehnese troops for acting as guide to the Dutch forces.[25]

Professional storytellers are crowd pleasers by default, but the writers of the texts of the second category, collectively known as *Hikayat Prang Sabi* or Song of the holy war, were moralists and theologians, who possessed rather different entertaining qualities. Flowing from the pen of clerics (*ʿulamāʾ*), who were well-versed in Islamic learning, *Hikayat Prang Sabi* texts were basically popular sermons on hell and heaven. The Acehnese scholar Imran Teuku Abdullah groups the *Hikayat Prang Sabi* category into the genre of *tambéh* (from Arabic *tanbīh*, "warning, reminding") literature, i.e., theological literature comparable to Malay *kitab* ("religious book"; from Arabic *kitāb*) literature.[26] Drawing on the Quran and prophetic traditions, *Hikayat Prang Sabi* texts severely criticized their audience for neglecting the duty to fight the *jihād*. The portrayal of the terrible consequences of inaction gave preachers the opportunity to stress the future pains of hell. However, these frightening hell diatribes were juxtaposed with luring promises of the delights of heaven that awaited those who heeded

---

22 Snouck Hurgronje, *The Achehnese* ii, 100–17; Voorhoeve, *Catalogue* 59–62.

23 Snouck Hurgronje, *The Achehnese* ii, 102. On its anti-Dutch character, see Wieringa, The dream.

24 Snouck Hurgronje, *The Achehnese* ii, 102.

25 Ibid.

26 Abdullah, *Hikayat* 22.

the call to fight for Aceh's freedom. Martyrs would eternally enjoy "effortless eating, drinking, and cohabiting" in paradise.

The historian Anthony Reid duly called the *Hikayat Prang Sabi* the most famous of the Acehnese exhortations to *jihād*, and correctly pointed out that the Aceh War inspired quite a few local poets at the time to try their hand at this genre. To quote Reid: "These poems, read aloud by one of their number, became the *most popular entertainment* for the *young men* gathered in the *meunasah* (communal hall)."[27] He does not comment further upon this statement, but I think that the youth of the men who took part in the poetry recitation groups may be key to our understanding of the popularity of this kind of literature.

3 A Classic Rags-to-Riches Story

In fact, the title 'Song of the holy war' is a blanket term that lumps together an impressive number of Acehnese narrative poems that strongly induce its listeners to wage *jihād* against the infidel Dutch intruders.[28] These texts elicited such an overwhelming response that the Dutch authorities felt compelled to confiscate as many manuscripts of the *Hikayat Prang Sabi* as possible. Many were burnt, but a rather large proportion of this type of war propaganda was taken as booty and is still preserved in (Dutch-created) public libraries.[29]

A rather simple sort of 'Song of the holy war' that was discovered in 1911 in the manuscript collection of a captured 'rebel' contains a most earthy fantasy of heaven that emphasizes three bodily pleasures, viz. indulgences in eating, drinking, and, yes, sex. It is a relatively short, undated anonymous poem of 115 lines, part of a larger Islamic story collection in a composite manuscript.[30] So it begins (lines 1–2):

---

27 Reid, *The contest* 252, emphasis added.

28 A certain Teungku Chik Pante Kulu (alias Teungku Syekh Muhammad Pante Kulu) has been credited with the authorship of "the" *Hikayat Prang Sabi*, which he is supposed to have written while aboard a ship between Jidda and Penang (see e.g., Hasjmy, *Apa sebab* and Hasjmy, Alam Aceh viii), but this claim would appear to be just legendary (see Voorhoeve, *Catalogue* 73). Indonesian authors, however, generally tend to consider this claim as an established fact. Sofyan, Teungku 1–30 provides a recent legendary life story.

29 The Jakarta, Leiden, and Amsterdam collections are described in Voorhoeve, *Catalogue*. See Durie, Poetry and worship 80–6 for a discussion of collections and collectors.

30 Damsté, Atjèhsche oorlogspapieren 789 provides a short description of this composite manuscript, which is kept in Leiden University Library, shelf-marked Cod. Or. 8693

La ilaha ilalah, balék kisah lagèe la'én
Muhamadun Rasulōlah, bit that éndah haba saidina

There is no god but God. We will change the narrative, and sing another song.
Muḥammad is the Prophet of God. The story of our Master [i.e., Muḥammad] is really very beautiful.

The reference to "our Master" in this paratextual comment embeds the narrative with fictional characters in a made-up story during the single most important period of Islamic history; it is situated in the formative and normative time period of the Prophet himself. This lends it greater authority, and makes a formidable truth-claim.

This narrative poem is about three poor men discussing their destitute condition; one of them informs his friends that he once heard an explication of a prophetic saying advanced by a cleric (*teungku*) to the effect that participating in the holy war would bring many rewards.[31] As he tells them (lines 9–10):

Barangsoe ureueng jipoh kaphé, teukeudi mate raya pahla
Takeudi cahit lam prang sabi, Tuhanku Rabi peu ampōn deèsa

Whosoever attacks an infidel, and kills him, receives rich rewards.
Should one become a martyr in the holy war, then our Lord will forgive his sins.

Martyrs will receive a most pleasurable life in the hereafter (lines 11–13):

Makanan mangat Tuhan yue bri, budiadari idang gata
Taduek mangat tilam[32] *mangat, le that nèkmat kheun ulama*
Pue bu nabsu tameuhajat, hasé si'asat hana lama

God will order [angels] to give you delicious food, and nymphs will serve it.
You will be seated most comfortably on cushions. According to the *'ulamā'*, the pleasures are manifold.
All your wishes will come true, within a second, without delay.

(Voorhoeve, *Catalogue* 76). Leiden Cod. Or. 8747c contains a transliteration with a draft Dutch translation by Henri Damsté (Voorhoeve, *Catalogue* 79).

31 As Snouck Hurgronje, *The Achehnese* i, 70 once put it, *teungku* is the title given to all "who either hold an office in connection with religion or distinguish themselves from the common herd by superior knowledge or more strict observance of religious law."

32 The text has *talam*, which must be a mistake.

In fact, this promise goes back to a canonical prophetic tradition on wish-fulfillment in paradise, but it is perhaps the anticipation of the doubt of the implied reader/listener that motivates an exclamation of astonishment here: "Is it really like that, brother?" (*nyo bit meunan, hé cèedara*, line 14).[33] However, the reassuring answer is: "I'm not kidding you, older brother!" (*bukon polèm lōn meuseunda*, line 15); "I'm not making things up! By God, I'm not just telling you something!" (*Bukon polèm lōn beurakah, walabilah, bukon pura*, line 16).[34]

The three men decide not to go home, but to go instead to the main road in order to kill Dutch infidels. Although one of them has two children, he sees no point in returning to his family as there does not seem to be a way out of his problems. He later prays for the ones he left behind, and argues that his children should be taken care of by their mother. The spirit of the three would-be *mujāhidīn* could be called desperate rather than devout (line 22):

> *Nibak hudéb bahlé maté, miseue bacé han sapeue na*
>
> It is better to die than to continue living [like this].[35] We are as poor as a *bacé* fish, having nothing at all.

The *bacé* is a kind of murrel, and because this fish is "bald" (i.e., "slippery"), it has become a byword in Acehnese language for utter poverty.[36]

Two of our *mujāhidīn* are cut down in a furious fight with the Dutch infidels, but the third one flees. He falls asleep under a tree, and in his dream he beholds the glories of paradise, where he meets a beautiful, fair-skinned maiden called Cut Putroe Ti or "Lady Princess," who is already waiting for him in her luxurious boudoir.[37] One could say that it is merely a 'peep show': Lady Princess points out that the killing of two infidels merely grants a quick look in heaven.

---

33 For this prophetic tradition, see al-Azmeh, Rhetoric for the senses 221.

34 For my interpretation of *beurakah* as "to make things up," see Kreemer, *Atjèhsch handwoordenboek* 32 and Djajadiningrat, *Atjèhsch-Nederlandsch woordenboek* i, 257 (under *brakah*).

35 This expression is cited in Djajadiningrat, *Atjèhsch-Nederlandsch woordenboek* i, 105 under *ba'* II, but without reference.

36 See Djajadiningrat, *Atjèhsch-Nederlandsch woordenboek* i, 150 under *batjé*. Damsté, Atjèhsche oorlogspapieren 789 and Damsté, Meer Atjèhsche oorlogspapieren, paraphrases the text as "We have no means of subsistence, not even a small fish to eat," which is not quite correct.

37 Her skin color is described as "white" (*kulét putéh*, line 75) and "fine" (*kulit haloih*, line 77). This is in accordance with traditional Arab-Islamic descriptions of the *ḥūrīs*' complexions as white and soft, see al-Azmeh, Rhetoric for the senses 227. The preoccupation with fair skin will be discussed in more detail further below.

Unlike his two friends, who were killed and thus became martyrs with an eternal entrance permit to paradise, the fleeing fighter had not yet completely fulfilled his side of the bargain with God. As he has not been killed himself, he is not allowed to stay with her. The Dame tells him (lines 101–102):

Bak malam nyoe troih meuriwang, bayeue utang ubak Rabi
Deungon ulōn han jeuet rakan . . .

Go back tonight; pay your debt to God.
You're not allowed to keep company with me . . .

The choice is up to him (lines 103–104):

Meuna meuhet meuduek sajan, kuriwang dilèe bak prang sabi
Meuna hajat teu keu kamèe, sinoe takeubah janji

If you want to stay with me forever, then first return to the holy war.
If you desire me, then fulfill your promise.

The *mujāhid* immediately returns to earth, exclaiming in the final line of this poem:

Adat lōn thee dumnoe balaih, beu dami Alah, han lōn lari

If I had known all this before, by God, I would never have run away!

Henri Damsté (1874–1955), a Dutch colonial official long stationed in Aceh and an expert of all things Acehnese, discussed this text in 1912, and opined that "to a certain extent" it would explain the disregard for death among the rebellious Acehnese.[38] The key question is, however, whether this rather lowbrow type of propaganda really served well to mobilize young Acehnese men under the banner of Islam. There would seem to be good reason for being skeptical about its inflammatory potential. To begin with, there is a thinly concealed disdain on the part of the anonymous poet for his *dramatis personae* from wretched life. For example, at the beginning of the narrative the hapless trio is not only portrayed as penniless but also as pretty brainless. After having established the sad fact that they are utterly poor, and that "it is better to die than

38 Damsté, Atjèhsche oorlogspapieren 791.

to continue living [like this]" (line 22, see above), the following conversation ensues (lines 23–26):

Bahkeu keunan lhèe geutanyoe, nibak meunoe meureuraba
Bak gata adoe bak muwaham, pakri tapham hé cèedara
Nibak ulōn hana lé pham, maléngkan curam nibak gata
Nibak ulōn tan lé piké, bahlé maté Lèm Mat Lila

Let's go there [i.e., to the main road where the Dutch infidels are], the three of us, instead of roaming around like this.
And what about you, brother, what do you think about it?
As far as I'm concerned, I've got no idea at all, but you know so much more.
And I don't have to think anymore, let me[39] just die!

The gang leader's enthusiastic approach to holy war and the acquiescence of his two friends, who reply with frank admissions of ignorance, places the would-be *mujāhidīn* in the role of dumb yokels – not exactly complimentary, or for that matter, helpful if this story was meant to urge its listeners to identify with the fictional warriors and take up arms themselves. Looking down on the luckless ones, the poet does not appear to possess the gift of imaginative sympathy. Furthermore, the fabulist has cast his poem in the cultivated, classical style of Acehnese *hikayat* literature, and does not deign to reproduce the daily speech of the hoi polloi: for example, one of the simpletons uses the difficult word *maléngkan* in the admission of stupidity (line 25, cited above), which is not even included in Djajadiningrat's standard dictionary, generally acknowledged to be the most authoritative and comprehensive dictionary of the Acehnese language (interestingly enough, mainly based upon material from *hikayat* literature). Assuming, for the sake of argument, that the poem was intended for poor, uneducated peasants, how many listeners would have known that *maléngkan* is a calque of Malay *melainkan* ("but; however")?[40]

This story belongs to the genre of *kisah* (from Arabic *qiṣṣa*, "narrative, tale, story"), and is hardly concerned with the divine will.[41] Nowhere do we read

39 This (third) man, called Lèm Mat Lila, speaks about himself in the third person here.

40 An anonymous referee suggested that Malay *melainkan* was perhaps taken over from Arabic wa-lākin ("but; however"), but appearances are deceiving and the words are not related. In fact, the Malay word *melainkan* is formed on the basis of *lain* ("other; different") with the affixes *me-* and *-kan*.

41 On the genre of *kisah*, see Abdullah, *Hikayat* 20–1.

that the main reason for Muslims to go out to fight the holy war is because God commands them to do so. Attention is focused mono-thematically upon the three pleasures, viz. food, drink, and sex, while the religious dimension of the afterlife is completely overlooked. The three "nice things" are a common theme in Arabic belles-lettres, so much so that the Arabist Geert Jan van Gelder speaks of the sequence of eating–drinking–love as a narrative formula.[42] In Acehnese literature, however, this formula remained foreign, and was only employed in texts belonging to the *Hikayat Prang Sabi* corpus. This short poem, then, promises a simple way to end all misery: kill and be killed, and paradise will be yours, the abode of pure bodily pleasures.

The original owner of the manuscript, who was a rebel in Dutch eyes, possessed several versions of *Hikayat Prang Sabi* texts, but this same man also liked to read the fairytale *Hikayat Putroe Gumbak Meuih* (Song of Princess Goldilocks).[43] In fact, the role of the number 'three' in the story of the three *mujāhidīn* already seems to indicate that we are dealing here with a folktale familiar from childhood.[44] The story has a classic rags-to-riches theme with a predictable three-phase storyline: at first, a 'nobody' is living in lowly, miserable circumstances, but one day, this unlikely hero suddenly embarks on a strange series of adventures that brings about a miraculous transformation of his fortunes. Eventually, he wins the hand of a beautiful princess, and lives happily ever after.[45] It would seem quite unlikely that talking down to the 'simple folk' in this crude way really would have worked to recruit enthusiastic fighters in the way of God.

And yet, *mirabile dictu*, sometimes this bizarre tale of the destitute *mujāhid* was reenacted in real life. After the war was officially over, the Dutch were still confronted with what they called "Aceh murder" (*Atjeh moord*), whereas the Acehnese spoke of "killing an infidel" (*poh kaphé*),[46] i.e., "the slaying of Europeans by Atjehnese, which became a private form of the *prang sabi*" (i.e., holy war).[47] As James Siegel succinctly phrases it: "Through the murder of a

42 Van Gelder, *God's banquet* 110.

43 Damsté, Atjèhsche oorlogspapieren 789. The Song of Princess Goldilocks was published in a scholarly edition by Amshoff, *Goudkruintje*.

44 There is abundant scholarship on the role of "three" in folktales, here I only mention Butzer and Jacob, *Metzler Lexikon* 69–70 with further references. Booker, *The seven basic plots* 229–33 devotes a special section to "the rule of three."

45 Booker, who categorizes all human storytelling into seven basic plots, discusses the rags-to-riches variety as his second plot, see Booker, *The seven basic plots* 51–68.

46 Alfian, Aceh 114.

47 Siegel, *The rope* 82.

kaffir (an unbeliever), an Atjehnese man hoped to gain paradise."[48] This phenomenon took place at least some 120 times between 1910 and 1937.[49] The 1939 report by former Resident Jongejans reads like a sober retelling of our simplistic *jihād* poem – needless to say, stripped of its seductive elements: "The murders are simply carried out. The perpetrator goes to a place where he knows he will find a European – a military encampment, a bivouac, a station. He waits. When a European passes he runs at him and does him in. He himself is usually captured or killed."[50] One captured man, who had unsuccessfully attempted to commit 'Aceh murder,' declared that he had wished to kill a Dutchman in order to get into heaven. His statement that he "preferred to die rather than to live like this"[51] is a remarkable echo of the fable of the penniless holy warriors (see line 22, cited above).

4 The Neglected Duty

However, there are other, more sophisticated Acehnese poems dealing with the holy war against the Dutch. Broadly speaking, two major categories of *Hikayat Prang Sabi* texts can be distinguished, viz. first, works with a strongly sermonizing character that draw upon citations from the Quran and *ḥadīth* literature. This version, which is rooted in scholastic discourse, mainly stresses the 'push factor' for going to war, and presents *jihād* as a religious duty that the Acehnese have hitherto neglected. This is the first and older version (henceforward *Hikayat Prang Sabi* I), out of which a more narrative version (called *Hikayat Prang Sabi* II) emerged; the latter pays greater attention to the 'pull factor' of *jihād* by elaborating upon its wonderful rewards.

Let us first look at the *Hikayat Prang Sabi* I. Here the emphasis is upon dire warnings against the harsh rule of the Dutch tyrant. This version harps on the common people's fear of the horrifying events said to happen during the Last Days, whereas the theme of heavenly rewards for martyrs in the holy war is dealt with only briefly. According to the Aceh-born but Leiden-trained philologist Teuku Iskandar, the language of the *Hikayat Prang Sabi* I is "stylistically

---

48 Ibid. Cf. the commentary of the Dutch pioneer of "psycho-anthropology," Van Wulfften Palthe, *Geestesstoornis* 18, who stated that the killing of an infidel by an Acehnese was a kind of suicide motivated by a desire to enter "Muhammadan heaven."

49 Siegel, *The rope* 84. See also Reid, *An Indonesian frontier* 339–40.

50 Cited in translation in Siegel, *The rope* 82.

51 Ibid., 83.

attractive," but "the composition as a whole is rather dull."[52] This insipidity, I think, may be traced back to its genesis, being heavily indebted to the Arabic tract *Naṣīḥat al-muslimīn* (*Advice to Muslims*) by the eighteenth-century Palembang theologian ʿAbd al-Ṣamad al-Palimbānī (born 1116/1704?).[53]

The latter scholar, who wrote all his books in Mecca or in nearby cooler Ṭāʾif, already enjoyed considerable fame as a learned divine during his lifetime, but after his death, allegedly at the incredible age of 124, he came to be ranked among the "friends of God" (see below).[54] It is said that ʿAbd al-Ṣamad died in 1244/1828 as a swashbuckling *mujāhid* in a war waged in northern Kedah (Malaysia), somewhere in a Malay Muslim district, which had been occupied by infidel troops from Siam (Thailand). There was no way to bury the remains of the martyrs because the Kedah forces were forced to retreat, so the location of ʿAbd al-Ṣamad's grave remains unknown.[55]

---

52 Iskandar, Hikayat 96. In 1928, Damsté published an edition of the *Hikayat Prang Sabi* I, based upon a manuscript of the Snouck Hurgronje collection, see Damsté, Hikajat. This manuscript is kept in Leiden University Library, shelf-marked Cod. Or. 8145, see Voorhoeve, *Catalogue* 74.

53 Snouck Hurgronje, *The Achehnese* ii, 119; Drewes, *Directions* 223; Voorhoeve, *Catalogue* 70–1. Hasan, The Tuḥfat 73 mentions the year 1772 as its date of composition.

54 Reliable historical data for his biography are scarce. Reconstructions of his bio- and bibliography can be found in Drewes, *Directions* 222–24; Quzwain, *Mengenal Allah* 7–31; Azra, *The origins* 112–7; and Kaptein, ʿAbd al-Ṣamad al-Palimbānī, 25–6. If we accept that he was born in 1704, this would mean that he began composing his works at an already advanced age, viz. in 1181/1764, when he allegedly wrote his first work (see Drewes, *Directions* 222; Hasan, The Tuḥfat 73). His final work was completed on 20 Ramadan 1203/14 June 1789 (see ʿAbd al-Ṣamad al-Palimbānī, *Sair al-sālikīn* ii, part 4, 267), when he would have been 85 years old.

55 Quzwain, *Mengenal Allah* 11; Azra, *The origins* 114. The portrayal of ʿAbd al-Ṣamad in the role of an active *mujāhid* greatly enhanced his status as an exemplary theologian who wielded both pen and sword. In this essay I am only concerned with the traditional perception of him as saintly figure, and debunking his biography does not serve my purpose here. Perhaps I should mention that modern-day researchers (see preceding note) are highly skeptical about his life data. They are more inclined to believe that he spent his entire studious life in Arabia, and probably also died there. The modernist Muslim scholar Azyumardi Azra makes the common sense remark that 124 years is "too old to go to the battlefield" (Azra, *The origins* 114). However, traditional conventions and modern expectations often clash in Islamic historiography (cf. Robinson, *Islamic historiography* 149–55). Traditional biographies of *ʿulamāʾ* border on hagiography, and two (closely related) stock elements are the production of abundant scholarly works and astounding longevity (cf. note 12 on the centenarian Miskawayh).

His fierce reputation as an old warhorse notwithstanding, 'Abd al-Ṣamad's writing on the doctrine of *jihād* is basically a dry legal work (*fiqh*) lacking any motivational aspects. Although this rather pedestrian theological treatise forms the original kernel of the *Hikayat Prang Sabi* I, authors and copyists of variants of the *Hikayat Prang Sabi* I saw to it that their adaptations were studded with vituperative outbursts against the Dutch aggressors by inserting prayers for the downfall of the *gōmpeuni* and other 'hate speech.' As the writing of versified exhortations to sacrifice one's life in the holy war against the Dutch was quite popular, there are numerous variants of the *Hikayat Prang Sabi* I.[56]

There is a long list of studies on 'influence' in the field of literary studies. The literary theorist Harold Bloom famously sees poets in perpetual conflict with their predecessors, an idea he first propounded in *The Anxiety of Influence: A Theory of Poetry* (1973), and which he further elaborated in a sequence of books in the 1970s and 1980s. In Bloom's view, influence became an obstacle to creativity. However, the Bloomian literary anxiety principle, which suggests that poets are hindered in their creative process because of the influence of their precursors, deals exclusively with the 'Great Works' of Western literature, and is totally inapplicable to pre-modern Acehnese literature. Manuscripts belonging to the *Hikayat Prang Sabi* corpus are marked by what a philologist would call extensive cross-contamination. For example, with regard to a certain author of local fame, viz. Teungku Nyak Ahmat, whom we already encountered (above) as the poet of a short account of a local skirmish, we know that he also composed, in 1894, a version of the *Hikayat Prang Sabi* I category, entitled *Nasihat ureueng muprang* (Advice to warriors); this has, not coincidentally, almost the same title as the *Naṣīḥat al-muslimīn*:[57]

Lōn meung peugèt nyoe hikayat, nasihat keu ureueung muprang
Ulōnteu cōk dalam kitab, basa Arab lheueh gob karang
Teuma di lōn lōn peu-Acèh, mangat sarèh soe nyang pandang
Hana bacut kureueng leubèh, hana alèh dōm geutimang
Nasihatōy Museulimin nama kitab, Abeudō Samat ureueng karang
Elia Allah karamat that, nanggroe teumpat di Palimbang

I wish to compose a *hikayat*, an admonition to warriors.
I draw on a theological book, originally written in Arabic.

56 Snouck Hurgronje, *The Achehnese* ii, 119–20.

57 Abdullah, *Hikayat* 70.

Now, I adapt it into Acehnese, so it may be pleasant for those who want to take a look at it.
I will not omit or add anything, everything is evenly balanced.
Naṣīḥat al-muslimīn [Advice to Muslims] is the title of the book, and ʿAbd al-Ṣamad its writer.
He is a friend of God, most holy, originating from Palembang.

However, Nyak Ahmat also borrowed heavily from another *Hikayat Prang Sabi* I version, viz. Teungku Tiro's Lessons on the holy war, of which he embellished the rhyme and meter.[58] Furthermore, whole sections of Nyak Ahmat's treatise agree line for line with yet another redaction of the *Hikayat Prang Sabi* I which was published by Damsté, in particular it matches the final part of the published version.[59]

Foregrounding the threat of future Dutch mastery over Aceh, *Hikayat Prang Sabi* I texts mainly stress a 'push factor' for going to war. For example, in the widely-read pamphlets of Teungku Tiro, which Snouck Hurgronje dubbed Lessons on the holy war, we find the following call to arms:[60]

Watèe jitueng nanggroe lé kaphé, dumteu saré wajéb tamuprang
H'an jeuet ta'iem peuseungab droe, duek lam nanggroe mita seunang
Bak watèe nyan jeuet peurelèe 'in, beu tayakin lagèe seumayang
Wajéb tapubuet jeueb kutika, meung h'an dèechateu hay abang
H'an sampureuna seumayang puasa, meung h'an tabungka tajak muprang
Paki meuseukin dum cut raya, tuha muda agam inōng
Nyang na dapat lawan kaphé, beu that bahlé hamba urang
Peureulèe 'in cit u atueuh, beu that bèk lheueh bak jih utang

When the country is seized by the infidel, we all have the duty to wage war.
Inaction is not permitted, taking it easy in one's country.
At such times *jihād* is a religious obligation incumbent on all Muslims individually (*farḍ al-ʿayn*), as sure as prayer.
It is invariably obligatory, and if you're careless, you're sinful, o brother.
Your prayers and fasting are less than perfect, if you don't immediately go to the battlefield.

58 Snouck Hurgronje, *The Achehnese* ii, 119; Voorhoeve, *Catalogue* 71.
59 Damsté, Hikajat; Voorhoeve, *Catalogue* 70–1.
60 Abdullah, *Hikayat* 46.

The poor and needy (*faqīr miskīn*), the large and the small, the old and the young, men and women:
Those who are able should fight the infidel, even the bondsmen.
For them, too, it is a personal obligation (*farḍ al-ʿayn*), even though they have not yet settled their debts.

In another variant of the *Hikayat Prang Sabi* I (published by Damsté) *jihād* is said to be obligatory in order to prevent the infidel rule of the *majusi* (Arabic *majūsī*, "Magian") or "fire-worshipers," which is a play on the Dutch word *maréchaussée*, the brutal anti-guerrilla unit of the colonial army.[61] This same text cites the well-known prophetic saying that "paradise is under the shade of the swords" as well as other passages from *ḥadīth* literature and the Quran in support of *jihād*, but the heavenly bonus for martyrs is left to the imagination of the audience.[62] We are merely informed that all sins will be forgiven, and that[63]

neubri ceruga janat adan, teumpat raman suka'an até
teuka keunan peue nyang mehuet, peue meukeusut cit hasé lé

[God] gives the Garden of Eden, a place of feasts and enjoyments.
All that one craves will be brought to that place: all wishes will immediately come true.

The poem mentions as a special reward seventy (*sic*) *ḥūrī*s in addition to an unmentioned number of servants (*kadam*, from Arabic *khadam*), but does not specify any external features of the heavenly personnel, rather it blandly states that the handmaidens of paradise are "very wonderful."[64] Nor is there an explicit answer to the question of the usefulness of so many beautiful virgins for a male resident of paradise.

---

61 Cf. Damsté, Hikajat 550. The pun is also explained in Kreemer, *Atjèhsch handwoordenboek* 170 (under *madjoesi*).

62 Damsté, Hikajat 560.

63 Damsté, Hikajat 562.

64 Seventy *ḥūrī*s, etc. in Damsté, Hikajat 562. In these texts the number of *ḥūrī*s allotted to the blessed is generally seventy, whereas conventionally *ḥadīth*s speak of seventy-two *ḥūrī*s, see Rosenthal, Reflections 16–7.

5 Heavenly Rewards

There is a strong correlation between the dramatic situation of actual warfare and the length of enthusiastic descriptions of paradise. For example, the earliest known Acehnese expositions of the *jihād*, a text from 1710 that pre-dates the Aceh War, contains only minimal references to paradise.[65] This rather short poem merely emphasizes *jihād* as a personal obligation (*farḍ al-ʿayn*).[66] By contrast, the *Hikayat Prang Sabi* II tells rather long and enticing stories of paradisal delight with relish. This second category of *Hikayat Prang Sabi* texts consists of a string of exemplary narratives. Starting with admonitions to wage the holy war, its composer has borrowed freely material from the earlier *Hikayat Prang Sabi* I version. After a rather theological introduction advocating the immediate necessity of holy war, the text strings together accounts of four battles of (legendary) Islamic history, viz.

(1) A story that is also known as *Hikayat Abeudō Wahét* was named after the fictional narrator, Abeudō Wahét (or Abdul Wahid in Malay spelling). This person is depicted as an Arab scholar, who tells his learned colleagues the story of a good-looking young noble, just fifteen years old, who takes part in the holy war against Byzantium. The story is mainly concerned with the latter's dream of Ainul Mardiah, the most beautiful of all virgins in paradise; it is also commonly known as *Kisah Ainul Mardiah* (Story of Ainul Mardiah). The boy dies a heroic death, and has an everlasting life of joy with Ainul Mardiah.

(2) A story of the *jihād* between Mecca against the Abyssinians, in which the Meccans are rescued by the miraculous intervention of birds dropping stones on the enemy. This story is associated with Q 105 (The Elephant), which is well-known in Arabic Islamic historical and exegetical tradition.[67]

(3) A story of a man who left his pregnant wife behind and joined the holy war on the advice of the Prophet; he prayed to God to protect their unborn child. After his return home, he finds his wife buried in the grave and their child alive and well, sitting besides its dead mother. Only then does the warrior realize that he had forgotten to include his wife in his prayers

---

65 See Siegel, *Shadow* 236 note 20 and Alfian, Aceh 113. The manuscript is kept in Leiden University Library, shelf-marked Cod.Or. 8163b; it is described briefly in Voorhoeve, *Catalogue* 79.

66 See Alfian, Aceh 113.

67 See Shahīd, People.

for safety, but it is too late. This rather macabre story is widely known; and though it originated in early Buddhist lore, the Islamicized version was incorporated in an Arabic anthology entitled *Rawḍat al-ʿulamā'* (The garden of scholars), a collection of moralistic anecdotes about pious people. It is through this that it entered Acehnese literature.[68]

(4) A story of an ugly black man who is rejected in disgust by earthly women, but who is killed in a holy war and immediately thronged with voluptuous virgins in paradise.

Both the first and last stories are adaptations of the rags-to-riches plot, which in my opinion offered the greatest appeal to a young male public. The archetypal hero of folk tales of this variety is invariably young, and "stories specially written for children have always relied on the Rags to Riches theme."[69] Acehnese listeners, like people around the world, loved to hear stories with happy fairy tale endings. The fable of the three *mujāhidīn* (discussed above), which deals with wish-fulfillment in a most simple and sentimental form, is based upon the "boy meets girl, boy gets girl, and he lives happily ever after" formula. The major theme in the *Hikayat Prang Sabi* II is that *ḥūrīs* waiting in heaven are infinitely preferable to earthly women. In the introductory words of the poem:

Hé adék cut muda seudang, beudoh rijang jak prang sabi
Bah lé tinggay dum sibarang, jak cok bintang ateueh keurusi
Keu inong jroh bèk lé ta syén, ta cok la'èn nyang juhari
Bah lé kedéh ta meukawén, nyang that candén budiadari[70]

Hey, younger brother, immediately go to holy war!
Leave everything behind, take the stars on the Throne.
It is useless to desire pretty women, go for the other beauties.
Let's marry there, with the beautiful *ḥūrīs*.

This version of the *Hikayat Prang Sabi* is much more explicit about the role of the otherworldly belles: the verb *meukawén* in the last line above, which I have neatly translated as "marry," is a common euphemism for "sexual intercourse."[71]

The theme of the *ḥūrīs* permeates the next story, viz. the *Story of Ainul Mardiah*, which deals with a fifteen-year-old boy who dreams of the gorgeous

68 See Van Ronkel, Maleische litteratuur 175–84.

69 Booker, *The seven basic plots* 53.

70 Alfian, *Sastra perang* 50–2.

71 Djajadiningrat, *Atjèhsch-Nederlandsch woordenboek* i, 681.

paradisal virgin Ainul Mardiah, and who is promised 'marital bliss' after he is slain in holy war. In my opinion it is not coincidental that the young hero is only fifteen years old. According to Islamic law, minors are exempt from the *jihād* obligation, because they are not of legal age (*mukallaf*, or responsible), and also based on the following tradition about Ibn 'Umar: "The Messenger of Allah inspected him on the Day of Uḥud, when he was a fourteen-year-old boy and did not allow him to fight. Then, on the Day of the Trench, when he was a fifteen-year-old boy, he inspected him and allowed him to fight."[72]

In this connection I would like to draw attention to the exclamation "Hey, younger brother," which appears in the quotation above from the *Hikayat Prang Sabi* II, with which the poet directly addresses his audience. This ecphonesis and such variants as "Oh younger brother" (*wahé adék*) or "Hey, dear" (*hay boh até*) are used so often in the text that their function as 'attention getter' seems to have become worn from overuse. Commenting upon his Dutch translation of the *Hikayat Prang Sabi* I, the Aceh specialist Henri Damsté stated that the phrase "Oh my brother" or the like is merely a stop-gap.[73] In order not to 'overburden' his translation, he therefore decided to decrease the number of references to those brothers. However, it is germane to note that the 'young brothers' in this poem are adolescent boys; this is indicated by the terms used in the last-quoted fragment above (*cut*, "young; little"; *muda*, "young; unripe"; *seudang*, "young, not yet an adult").

In other words, the intended public of this text was teenagers, young pubescent boys with active hormones. At this age, testosterone surges drastically transform the male brain and lead to higher than normal levels of aggression and risk-taking. It is a telling fact that most crimes in any given country are committed by young males, but idealism is also remarkably common during this stage of the maturation process: religious conversions are far more likely to occur in adolescence than in any other period of life.[74] Furthermore, as biologists have noted, "[s]usceptibility to peer influence is highly variable, but generally peaks at about fourteen, when most, if not all, adolescents are likely to behave like lemmings."[75] A *jihād* agitator could easily exploit the 'herd instinct' of his young audience by holding meetings in communal halls.[76]

72 Peters, *Islam and colonialism* 15–6.

73 See also Abdullah, *Hikayat* 73, 795–6, who regards the habitual mentioning of the addressees in traditional Acehnese literature as mere filler words.

74 Pridmore-Brown, Surges 4.

75 Ibid.

76 Cf. Jowett and O'Donnell, *Propaganda* 281.

Another ubiquitous phrase in the *Hikayat Prang Sabi* II is the imperative *tueng ibarat* or "take the example."[77] The battle stories that are told in the *Hikayat Prang Sabi* II are not meant simply for entertainment, but are *exemplae*, fictitious moral anecdotes illustrating the point of *jihād*. It is reported that the poem was chanted before men went off to attack the Dutch. The listeners are said to have been dressed in the white shrouds of warriors about to martyr themselves.[78] Hate can be a great motivator, but bearing in mind that the prospective martyrs were generally young men, the poet of the *Hikayat Prang Sabi* II cleverly employed the lure of sexual fantasy, knowing full well that the promise of unlimited eternal sexual pleasure would certainly excite a pubescent audience.

The third story about the married man who found his dead wife and living child in the grave may perhaps show that the composer of the *Hikayat Prang Sabi* II tried to cast his nets widely, but I still think that the group of young men over the age of fifteen must have been his main target. His shrewd psychological insight into the innermost feelings of this age group is in my opinion nowhere better demonstrated than in the final tale about an ugly black man called Said Saleumi.[79] In this story the poet skillfully exploits the anxieties – feelings of inferiority and inadequacy – that typically beset teenagers. After having repeated, once again, the assurance that seventy *ḥūrī*s will be God's gift to holy warriors in the hereafter, the narrator begins by telling his readers that the ill-favored Said Saleumi was so repulsive to women that he was unable to find a wife:

Soe na hajat syureuga tinggi, bèk lé lanti jak beu leugat
Tujoh ploh droe budiadari, keu eseutiri wahé sahbat
Rupa indah hana sakri, peunulang Rabbi di akhirat
Saboh haba 'ajib sikali, wahé akhi tueng ibarat
Haba jameun tréb ka lawi, yoh prang Nabi Sayidil Ummat
Sidroe ureueng hé syèedara, jeuheut rupa cit hitam that
Pakri parot bak-bak muka, lom ngon sukla meukeu kilat
Keu peurumoh galak raya, neu jak mita jeueb-jeueb teumpat
Han ji tém tueng inong nyangna, sabab rupa eit jeuheut that
Ho nyang neu jak han ji tém tueng, sigala ureueng bandum luwat
Tahe gante teujak teu dong, han ji tém tueng jeueb-jeueb teumpat
Uroe malam jak mencari, keu eseutiri galak neu that[80]

77 Cf. Siegel, *Shadow* 262–3.

78 Ibid., 262.

79 An alternative transliteration of his name would be Sa'id Salmi, as in Alfian, Aceh 116.

80 Alfian, *Sastra perang* 142.

Whosoever wishes the highest heaven should hurry up.
Oh my friends, seventy *ḥūrī*s will be your wives.
They will be incomparably beautiful, being a gift of the Lord in the hereafter.
Oh my brothers, take the example of this most wonderful story,
a story of yore from the time of the war of our Prophet, Commander of the Community.
Oh brothers, once there was a man who was ugly and very black.
There were scratches on his face, and his black skin was shiny.
What he craved was a wife, and he searched everywhere.
Women did not like him, because of his most ugly appearance.
There wasn't anyone, anywhere that wanted him, everyone felt disgusted.
He became nervous and confused as he was unwanted everywhere he went.
Day and night he searched for a wife, because that was what he wished for.

The contrast between the dark this-worldly situation of the ugly, pitch-black Said Saleumi and the otherworldly brilliance of paradise could hardly be greater. As Siegel comments on the signification of paradise in the preceding *Story of Ainul Mardiah*: "Practically everything mentioned, in fact – women, rivers, palaces – is described in terms of radiance."[81] The light versus dark opposition in the story of Said Saleumi is associated with life and death: the hero will eventually emerge from temporary darkness into the eternal world of light. I omit the details of this story; suffice it to say that Said Saleumi's fortunes completely turned around when he died as martyr in the holy war with the infidel Jews. The *ḥūrī*s immediately picked him up from the battlefield, and lovingly embraced their dearest 'husband.'

Rejection, humiliation, confusion, and even skin problems – probably most teenage boys would have had no difficulties identifying with the unfortunate Said Saleumi and his repulsive appearance. Girls rarely yearn for the touch of an unsightly boy. Henri Damsté ironically comments upon the story about the unlovely Said Saleumi that the struggle against the Dutch was "also" very suitable for unfortunate lovers.[82] However, rather than considering this as a mere side effect, I would argue more strongly that 'unfortunate lovers' must have constituted the text's implied audience, and that the recruitment of future 'testosterone terrorists' was its very raison d'être.

---

81 Siegel, *Shadow* 253.
82 Damsté, Atjèhsche Oorlogspapieren 782.

I hasten to add that my interpretation does not touch on the issue of the sacrificial desires of listeners. It is quite conceivable that socio-political causes may have been of primary importance for them; although the *Hikayat Prang Sabi* II does not fail to mention that the world was in disarray as a result of economic hardship and political chaos, the text concentrates far more intently on the promise of instant sexual gratification in paradise. The *Hikayat Prang Sabi* II aims at the 'weak spot' of the intended young male public.

6 The Project of Persuasion

Almost no documentary evidence is available on the communal practice of reading a tale of war. Scholars often refer to a well-known anecdote in traditional Malay literature; this anecdote states that on the eve of the Portuguese attack on Malacca in 1511, the Malay nobles gathered together in the royal audience hall in order to stage a public recitation of the *Hikayat Muhammad Hanafiyya* (Story of Muḥammad b. al-Ḥanafiyya) in order "to derive profit" from it (*berfaédah*, a verb based upon the Arabic loanword *fāʾida*, "profit, benefit; useful lesson, moral").[83] The latter text, which is a legendary tale about the life of a son of ʿAlī and a concubine from the tribe of the Banū Ḥanīfa, is strongly imbued with the Shiʿi spirit of martyrdom.[84] Its protagonist, who was ʿAlī's last surviving son after the tragedy at Karbala, is presented as a single-minded hero bent on taking vengeance for his two murdered half-brothers, al-Ḥasan and al-Ḥusayn. A Western Malayist once admitted that he had read this *hikayat* "with more interest than pleasure," as in his opinion the story is "a test of any reader's stamina with its disheartening theme of defeat after defeat, and its endless accounts of cruelty, deceit, killing and mutilation."[85] In 1511, however, Malay officers apparently considered this particularly gory story an ideal way to prepare for battle with the infidel Portuguese, so they modeled themselves on the example of the vindictive Muḥammad b. al-Ḥanafiyya and his brave troops. Although there is substantial scholarship on the public recitation of stories in many ritual contexts throughout insular Southeast Asia, we do not know whether the communal reading of a tale of war was a common practice

83 For an English translation of this episode, see Brown, *Sějarah Mělayu* 161–6.

84 For a text edition and commentary, see Brakel, *The Hikayat* and the companion volume Brakel, *The story*. On the choice of this particular text, see Wieringa, Amir Hamza; for Shiʿi influences upon early Islamic Malay literature, see Wieringa, Does traditional Islamic Malay literature.

85 Jones, Review article 122.

in pre-modern warfare. Nevertheless, the oft-quoted anecdote concerning the 1511 Malay vigil has been paradigmatic for interpreting the *Hikayat Prang Sabi*.[86]

The feverish production of war propaganda in the 1880s cannot be separated from the historical reality that the definitive end of the Acehnese Sultanate was sealed during this period.[87] But although the *ʿulamāʾ* frantically circulated *Hikayat Prang Sabi* texts, which emphasized "the helplessness of the *kāfir* and the successes in store for the Atjehnese when once they accepted the true disciplines of Islam," these desires remained wishful thinking.[88] Anthony Reid writes about this last ditch effort to turn the tables on the opponent: "As the war with the Dutch proceeded, … leadership of the resistance passed increasingly to the most intransigent ulama, for whom the idiom of Islamic martyrdom was the ingredient needed to inspire courage in the face of overwhelming odds."[89] This hypothesis would fit well with what is told about the 1511 episode in Malacca, when an Islamic *corps d'élite* listened to blood-and-thunder tales drawn from extremist Shiʿi martyrology while awaiting the imminent fall of the sultanate.[90]

I cannot deny this possibility, but I propose to look at the authorial intention of *Hikayat Prang Sabi* texts from another angle. As I see it, these stories are primarily religious propaganda, i.e., "efforts to move people to a religious change or direction."[91] In disseminating this kind of propaganda, the *ʿulamāʾ* were doing what they as preachers had always done best, viz. teaching about heaven and hell. Their call for an altered way of life was not only addressed to coreligionists, but also to nonmembers, to persuade them to convert. Reid provides the example of Teungku Chik di Tiro (d. 1308/1891), a stern theologian, who in response to Dutch attempts to enter into an agreement, wrote a letter to the Resident in September 1885 urging the Dutch to embrace Islam first: "As soon as you accept Islam by pronouncing the two articles of faith, then we can conclude a treaty."[92] In his letter we can detect the same rhetorical technique as in *Hikayat Prang Sabi* literature – he contrasts the two ultimate possibilities of punishment (hell) and reward (heaven). The theologian assured his foreign

86 See e.g., Alfian, Aceh 113.
87 Cf. Reid, *The contest* 252.
88 Ibid.
89 Reid, War, peace 4.
90 Incidentally, Reid does not draw a comparison to sixteenth-century Malacca.
91 Riesebrodt, *The promise* 149.
92 Letter to Resident K.F.H. van Langen, September 1885, cited in translation by Reid, War, peace 4. Muhammad A.R., Teungku Chik Ditiro 45–60 provides a modern-day hagiographic account of this 'national hero.'

opponent that if they converted to Islam the Dutch would be spared humiliation on the battlefield and eternal punishment in hell, and instead would be granted access to paradise with "whatever the heart desires in the way of food, drink, fruit or women."[93]

However, as noted by experts on propaganda and persuasion, messages have "greater impact when they are in line with existing opinions, beliefs, and dispositions" of the target audience.[94] In this case, the impact was zero. Teungku Chik di Tiro's non-believing addressee was Karel van Langen (1848–1915) who, as an expert on Acehnese language and culture, was of course well acquainted with the ardent theological phraseology of his day and age, but this experienced colonial civil servant did not convert to Islam.[95] The belief that God will not abandon his religion is something which Teungku Chik di Tiro shared with other preachers, but Acehnese talk of God was not backed by any concrete, tangible proof of its correctness. As Reid dryly comments, "[o]f course God did not deliver the kind of victory Teungku di Tiro expected, and a later generation had sullenly to accept the reality of Dutch rule."[96]

The propaganda texts from the Aceh War are classified in overviews of Acehnese literature as "original treatises," by which is meant that they are not based upon Malay or Arabic examples.[97] However, the conventional wisdom that these texts have a "genuine Acehnese character" must be discarded.[98] Even a cursory look at classical Arabic literature shows that Acehnese war propaganda was modeled on an Arabic (sub)genre known as "the merits of holy war" (*faḍāʾil al-jihād*).[99] This genre first emerged in the eighth century, and was quickly popularized in public recitations by storytellers from Islamic Spain to Persia, as it was intended to arouse the enthusiasm of the crowds and to recruit volunteers. During the sixth and seventh/twelfth and thirteenth centuries, i.e., during the Crusades, the genre reached its heyday, and the exhortatory stories

93 Reid, War, peace 4.

94 Jowett and O'Donnell, *Propaganda* 279.

95 A short biography of Karel van Langen can be found in Anonymous, Langen 530.

96 Reid, War, peace 4.

97 See Snouck Hurgronje, *The Acehnese* ii, 117–8, whose categorization is adopted in Voorhoeve, *Catalogue*.

98 *Pace* Snouck Hurgronje, *The Acehnese* ii, 118, who first made this assertion.

99 Arabic literature has a special genre of works on "the merits" (*faḍāʾil*) of all kinds of topics, see Sellheim, Faḍīla 728–9 and Walther, *Kleine Geschichte* 164, 239. For the subgenre on "the merits of the holy war," see Jarrar, The martyrdom; Christie, Motivating; and Dajani-Shakeel, Jihād.

on holy war acquired their definitive form, becoming close to popular folk literature.[100]

Comparison with medieval Arabic literature on the *jihād* makes clear that Acehnese *ʿulamāʾ* must have been among its most avid readers. The historian Niall Christie disentangles three "major motivational threads" running through the narrative of the *Kitāb al-Jihād* (Book of the holy war) of ʿAlī b. Ṭāhir al-Sulamī (d. 500/1106), which we also know from Acehnese examples, viz. provoking "listeners into action through playing on feelings of guilt or shame, frightening them with the probable consequences of inaction, and tempting them with earthly rewards."[101] Furthermore, in his case study on the genre of "the merits of holy war" the Arabist Maher Jarrar draws attention to the central theme of "the holy war as a sacred wedding," and discusses several *topoi*, which we can also detect in Acehnese war poems (e.g., the revelatory dream of the hero who has a vision of paradise; the hero's immediate passage to the *ḥūrī*s directly upon his heroic death; the comparison between the paradisal virgins and earthly women; and the ridiculing of flesh-and-blood females).[102]

The appearance of militant motivational literature inciting the Acehnese to wage *jihād* against the infidel, has been hailed in postcolonial Indonesian discourse as an expression of an age-old Acehnese 'fighting tradition' on behalf of Islam. However, this attempt at mythmaking conveniently overlooks the remarkable fact that the *ʿulamāʾ* had to do their utmost to constantly remind their flock of this so-called 'fighting tradition.' The theologians who wrote the Acehnese war propaganda were steeped in the world of Arabic letters, and they did not wear their learning lightly. James Siegel writes that the *Hikayat Prang Sabi* II is difficult for people with little knowledge of Malay and Arabic to understand.[103] I am inclined to view the quest of the young hero for Ainul Mardiah in paradise, ascending from one level to the next, as something of a learned inside joke. This golden fiancée, who outshines all nymphs in paradise, has an exotic appellation, which means nothing to uneducated Acehnese, but could easily be recognized by Arabists as *ʿayn al-marḍiyya*, which loosely translates to "source of satisfaction."[104]

---

100 Jarrar, The martyrdom.

101 Christie, Motivating 2. See also N. Christie's discussion of al-Sulamī's *Kitāb al-Jihād* and M. Jarrar's contribution in the present publication.

102 Jarrar, The martyrdom.

103 Siegel, *Shadow* 259–61.

104 Ibid., 253–9; he discusses Ainul Mardiah at length, but does not refer to the Arabic origin of this term.

Hikayat Prang Sabi texts stand in a long tradition of Islamic rhetoric on *jihād*. Evocation of the pleasures of the wedding night is a central theme, but another common feature of these stories of "the merits of holy war" is the assurance that the pain of death for one fighting in the way of God is no more than "the pain of a pinch."[105] This notion, which could already be found in medieval Arabic *jihād* propaganda, is transposed in Acehnese *Hikayat Prang Sabi* texts into the comparison that if a *mujāhid* is hit by a Dutch bullet, it will feel like the quenching of a terrible thirst or like a mother tickling the legs of her infant.[106] Apparently, present-day recruiters of radicals still use the same rhetorical devices. For example, a few years ago, an Islamic preacher told British teenage boys to train with Kalashnikov rifles as soldiers for Islam. If they died as religious martyrs, their rewards in paradise would include seventy-two virgins, and they would eat from the fruits of paradise. Furthermore, this *jihād* enthusiast asserted that "[e]ven if you are hit by a cruise missile, the pain will feel like that of a mosquito bite."[107]

7 A War That Will Not Go Away

The theme of an oppressed people's fight against foreign colonialists can be found in much of the so-called decolonized world, as a recurrent element in the master plots of ethnicity/race and nationhood. In post-independence Indonesia the 'heroes' Teuku Umar (1854–99) and Teungku Chik di Tiro (1836–91), as well as the 'heroines' Cut Nyak Dien (1850–1908), and Cut Nyak Meutia (1870–1910), who all participated in the Aceh War, were given a place in the Indonesian nationalist pantheon of heroes, and are categorized in Indonesian schoolbooks as "heroes of the struggle for Indonesian independence."[108] The Acehnese *jihād* could easily be represented as simply one chapter among many in the state-sanctioned myth of the 350-year struggle of 'the Indonesian people' against their Dutch oppressors.

In the postcolonial period the Acehnese War was not only described as the manifestation of the so-called 'fighting tradition' of the Acehnese people against Dutch colonialism, but also, and much more importantly, as an

105 Jarrar, The martyrdom 100.

106 Damsté, Atjèhsche oorlogspapieren 782.

107 News item "British martyrs 'promised 72 virgins," dated 23 January 2003, http://news.bbc.co.uk/2/hi/uk_news/england/2687797.stm.

108 See e.g. Ajisaka, *Mengenal*, from which I also took the years of birth and death of the heroes.

expression of a primordial Acehnese identity. In contradistinction to other Indonesian ethnicities, Acehnese were not only defined as Muslims, but as singularly pious, militant defenders of the faith. I will not go into the complexities of Aceh's bitter internecine power struggle with Jakarta in the era of independence, but will only briefly discuss, in a short coda, the postcolonial legacy of the *Hikayat Prang Sabi*.

Few Acehnese-language books were published before World War II, and while Dutch sponsorship favored European-style texts, under Dutch rule the publication of the *Hikayat Prang Sabi* was not permitted. By contrast, in the postcolonial period a veritable book industry was established; it produced a steady stream of publications on local culture and regional history, including reprints of the *Hikayat Prang Sabi*.[109] The official nationalist celebration of Acehnese identity emphasized Aceh's "specialness," highlighted the heroism of the Acehnese people, and in the process of the glorification of Aceh, made wildly exaggerated claims that the Acehnese were Muslim from earliest times, and had been staunch defenders of the faith ever since.[110]

The role of Ali Hasjmy (1914–98), the first post-independence governor of Aceh, and a prolific author of romanticized accounts of the Aceh War, can hardly be underestimated; he disseminated the popular view that the bravery of the Acehnese people who opposed the Dutch infidel was due to their inherent religious zeal. The *Hikayat Prang Sabi* is interpreted in Ali Hasjmy's work as a blueprint for the 'victory' of the Acehnese in their holy war against the Dutch; the Acehnese willingly sacrificed their lives, undeterred by death, knowing that they would be given entrance into heaven.[111] Ali Hasjmy's mythologized rewriting of the Aceh War as a heroic epic along the lines of the *Hikayat Prang Sabi* has meanwhile become "an authoritative foundational text."[112] This oversimplified and fanciful history is nowadays considered by leading Acehnese academics as emblematic of Acehnese identity. For example, Hasan Basri, currently professor of Quranic exegesis and Islamic thought at the State Islamic Institute Ar-Raniriy Nanggroe Aceh Darussalam, states that Acehnese identity and Islam are synonymous: "The Acehnese are known today for the great care they take over religion, for the fact that they can read the Qur'an fluently, for the way they obediently perform their religious duties, for having nobility

109 Aspinall, *Islam and nation* 36–7.

110 See ibid., 37.

111 Ali Hasjmy's best-known book is entitled *Why the Acehnese People were able to fight Dutch Aggression for Decades*, see Hasjmy, *Apa sebab*.

112 Clavé-Celik, The Acehnese women warriors.

of character, and for the way they shun immoral behaviour and crime."[113] He claims that even the few exceptional Acehnese who are only nominal Muslims "will still defend Islam to the death and will oppose those who do identify with the infidels."[114] The spirit of *jihād*, then, would seem to be inherently Acehnese.

This constructed image of Acehnese as proud *mujāhidīn* was likewise eagerly exploited by the Acehnese separatist movement. Whereas the official, Jakarta-approved discourse lauded Acehnese anti-colonialism as an exemplary contribution to the Indonesian independence struggle, the anti-Jakarta insurgents liked to cast the national Indonesian government in the role of the hated colonialist. Propaganda materials from the Free Aceh Movement (known by its Indonesian acronym GAM, Gerakan Aceh Merdeka) routinely spoke of the "Javanese colonial government" or the "neo-colonial Indonesian government." The *Hikayat Prang Sabi* became "a kind of anthem by Aceh Merdeka fighters, who would sing it at secret meetings and in exile. Sometimes they would replace phrases in the original, such as *Dutch infidels*, with modern equivalents such as *Javanese spies*."[115] Edward Aspinall, who has looked into the contents of GAM literature, concludes that "it is easy to find evidence of a cult of martyrdom that extends the old ideology."[116]

In the history of publishing the *Hikayat Prang Sabi* in an effort to popularize it, I would like to single out the influential role of Abdullah Arif (1922–70), who was a leading literary figure in post-independence Aceh. Siegel calls him the most prominent person to present the past to the Acehnese public, and rightly remarks that "Abdullah Arif wrote to instruct."[117] In the 1950s and 1960s he was able to play the role of broker in local politics, because of his good relations with rebel leaders as well as with the national government.[118] Already at an early age, he drew attention to himself as an advocate of the militants in a local conflict, known as the Cumbok War, which was fought between December 1945 and January 1946.[119] A radical group that sided with the Republic had declared holy war against the nobles, and Abdullah Arif, in support of the *mujāhidīn* in

113 Basri, Islam in Aceh 187. Hasan Basri is also the same person who wrote a most laudatory biography of Ali Hasjmy, see Basri, Teungku A. Hasjmy.
114 Basri, Islam in Aceh 187.
115 Aspinall, *Islam and nation* 98.
116 Ibid., 97.
117 Siegel, *Shadow* 270.
118 See Sjamsuddin, *The republican revolt* 146. For more biographical details, see Siegel, *Shadow* 267–70.
119 Sjamsuddin, *The republican revolt* 146.

this fratricidal war, published a version of the *Hikayat Prang Sabi* in his newly established series *Seumangat Atjeh* (*Spirit of Aceh*).[120]

The Acehnese historian Mohammad Isa Sulaiman, who has studied the four booklets from the series *Spirit of Aceh*, which were first published between October 1945 and January 1946, observes that Abdullah Arif drew heavily on *Hikayat Prang Sabi* rhetoric for his anti-Dutch propaganda.[121] Sulaiman cites *inter alia* the trope that a martyr in the holy war will not fall, but will be caught by Ainul Mardiah:[122]

> *Hadis pangoelèe Rasoeloellah*
> *Gata han reubah oh keunong beudé*
> *Meungkon lam leumoeng Ainoel Mardiah*
> *Han lom reubah he boh haté*
>
> According to a Prophetic tradition,
> you will not fall down when you're shot.
> Only into the arms of Ainul Mardiah
> you'll fall, my dears.

Abdullah Arif possessed his own printing press in Aceh's capital Kutaraja from 1945, but we do not have an overview of his publications. The research library of the KITLV in Leiden, arguably one of the world's best research libraries on Indonesia, has collected a total of eighteen works from his press, the last ones from around 1963, including a 1960s copy of a four-volume edition, in Arabic script, of a version of the *Hikayat Prang Sabi* II.[123] The first volume of the latter edition contains the story of Ainul Mardiah, which he had published immediately after World War II, in Roman script, in the series *Spirit of Aceh* (volume iv).[124]

---

120 Sulaiman, From autonomy 127. A copy of this book, kept in the library of the research institute KITLV in Leiden, has been made available in a digitalized version on the Aceh Books website, see http://www.acehbooks.org/pdf/ACEH_03452.pdf. The title page informs the reader that a part of the revenue would be donated to victims from the Cumbok War.

121 See Sulaiman, Islam et propagande 207–17.

122 Ibid., 214, unaltered orthography.

123 The KITLV even has three copies of this edition, with shelf numbers mm-22–N, hh-3244–N, and hh-5462–N. The latter copy was digitalized, and is available at http://www.acehbooks.org/pdf/ACEH_00304.pdf. Since 1 July 2014, the KITLV library and collections have been managed by Leiden University Library.

124 Voorhoeve, *Catalogue* 73.

The front covers of Abdullah Arif's publications have a forceful iconographic denotation of Acehnese identity. For example, in the case of the *Spirit of Aceh* the two defining aspects of what is believed to be the Acehnese spirit are graphically illustrated, viz. militancy and piety (Fig. 53.1).[125] Two crossed daggers are prominently placed at the forefront, thereby functioning as a gate for the royal mosque in Kutaraja. Here Islam is most dramatically pictured sheltered in the shade of the swords. The two weapons, which can be identified as *réncong*s, are highly symbolic: the word *réncong* has entered the dictionaries as "an Acehnese dagger with a curved handle (often used as a symbol of Aceh)."[126] The shape of this dagger is said to symbolize the Arabic lettering of the *basmala*, reinforcing once more the close connection constructed between Aceh, Islam, and warfare.[127] The symbolism of the Acehnese daggers is also employed in the printer's vignette (Fig. 53.2), in which a radiant book is situated above the royal mosque. The sickle-and-star framework rising above the two crossed swords is likewise a powerful Islamic symbol, while the name Abdullah Arif is written in Arabic script upon the crescent moon.[128] The year 1945 between the crossed daggers heralds the year Abdullah Arif established his printing press, and also the year of Indonesia's declaration of independence.

Abdullah Arif also published collections of traditional and modern *pantōn*, which is a genre of oral poetry. Whereas this kind of poetry is generally not politically motivated in cognate literatures in Indonesia, even in this sector we encounter expressions of constructed Acehnese identity. From her fieldwork experiences in the 1990s, Jacqueline Aquino Siapno relates that Acehnese lullabies in the form of *pantōn* are sung from one generation to the next, rhapsodizing the spirit of *jihād*. Among those that are still often sung, she quotes the following example:[129]

Doo-doo-da-i-dang
Seulayang blang kaputoh talou
Bebagah rayek banta seudang
Tajak muprang bela nanggrou

---

125 Abdullah Arif's *Nasib Atjeh* iii is available in digital form at http://www.acehbooks.org/pdf/ACEH_03222.pdf.

126 See e.g., Stevens and Schmidgall-Tellings, *Dictionary* 823.

127 See Barbara Leigh, The rencong. Illustrations and a detailed description can be found in Van Zonneveld, *Traditional weapons* 113–4. Extending the *sīn-mīm* ligature of the phrase *bi-smi* (*llāh*), forming a long line, is the most common way of calligraphic embellishment in manuscripts from Indonesia, see Gallop, Beautifying 196–9.

128 On comparable graphic symbolism in Malay religious books, cf. Wieringa, Some light 188–9.

129 Siapno, *Gender* 145, unaltered orthography.

Doo-doo-da-i-dang,
the string broke, the kite flew off.
Grow up quickly, little child,
help us to go to war, defend this country.

Another favorite evergreen is:[130]

La Ilaaha Illallah
Muhammad Rasul nabi geutanyou
Beuteugoh Iman aneuk meutuwah
Di jalan Allah meuprang bek lalou

There is no God but Allāh
and Muḥammad is his Prophet.
Make your faith strong, little child,
striving in the path of Allāh.

Through these songs, Acehnese children are taught to be good Muslims, to fight to defend their religion and country.

Abdullah Arif's 1958 compilation *Pantōn aneuk miet* or Poems for small children, which formed part of the series *Pantōn Aceh* (Acehnese poems), was brought out again in 2006, this time accompanied by translations into Indonesian and playful illustrations. The new publication was made possible by commercial sponsors, but also by such official organizations as the Indonesian Chamber of Commerce and Industry and the Indonesian Ministry of Culture and Tourism. An example of what they sponsored was the poem *Muda seudang* (Teenage boy):[131]

Sidroe aneuk muda seudang
Jijak lam prang lawan kaphé
Ji-ék guda ka jipasang
Cok geuliwang deungon beudé

A young boy in his teens
joins the war against the infidels,
keen to ride on a horse,
armed with sword and rifle.

130 Ibid., unaltered orthography.

131 Arif, *Pantôn aneuk miet* 21–2.

Cok ngon reuncōng dum alat prang
That guransang dalam haté
'Oh trōih keudéh lam mideuen prang
Ka jimeucang sallō'alé

He takes the *réncong* and all military equipment.
He is endowed with combativeness.
Upon arrival on the battlefield,
he wages the holy war.

Le that maté kaphé suang
Keunong cékyang ngon boh beudé
Aneuk muda that guransang
Kaphé jicang dum sagai bé

Many miserable infidels are killed,
shot by his rifle.
The young boy is combative,
slaughtering all infidels.

Padum lawét lam mideuen prang
Meutang-ilang lawan kaphé
Teuma syahid muda seudang
Di teungoh blang ka meugulé

After a long time on the battlefield,
fighting the infidels,
the young boy is made a martyr,
fallen on the field of battle.

Samlakoe jroh hana bimbang
Dum sibarang han ingat lé
Tinggai rumoh gampōng ngon blang
Tinggai ladang di binèh glé

The warrior is never worried,
nothing can obstruct him.
Leave your house, village and rice field!
Leave the village at the edge of the mountain!

Cut samlakoe woe bak Tuham
Syeuruga lapan citka hasé
Meunan janji lam Kuru'an
Ne'mat Tuhan hanjeuet kheun lé

The warrior returns home, back to God.
The eighth heaven is already waiting,
as promised in the Quran;
God's pleasures are indescribable.

Budiadari iréng sajan
Rupa jih ban cahya kandé
Tujōh plōh droe saban-saban
Nyan balasan bak prang kaphé

The *ḥūrīs* are coming out in throngs to
welcome him,
with lit up countenances, shining brightly.[132]
Seventy in number, all looking similar,
being the reward for waging the war against the infidels.

Another poem in this twenty-first-century collection is called *Di babah pintō syeuruga lapan* (At the threshold of the eighth heaven), which also deserves to be quoted in full:[133]

Di babah pintō syeuruga lapan
Saboh krueng sinan indah han sakri
Batèe di panté pudoe ngon intan
Lam krueng meukawan budiadari

At the threshold of the eighth heaven
flows a beautiful river,
and the stones at the beach are diamonds.
The *ḥūrīs* amuse themselves in this river.

---

132 The word *kandé* (Malay *kandil*, Arabic *qindīl*, English *candle*) denotes a big lamp.

133 Arif, *Pantôn aneuk miet* 23. The term "eighth heaven" should be understood as the highest abode in paradise.

Budiadari dum muda seudang
Jiteubiet u blang jidong meuriti
Jicok ngon kipah jimat bak jaroe
Jiprèh woe lakoe dalam prang sabi

The *ḥūrīs* are all pretty.
Going to the grassland, they form neat rows,
gracefully waving their fans,
while waiting for their husband in the holy war.

'Ohban saré troih teungku meutuah
Jipeuduek pantaih ateueh keurusi
Jimueng ulèe jisampōh darah
Alhamdulillah trōih ban janji

When the fortunate gentleman arrives,
they lovingly welcome him on his throne,
caressing his head, cleaning his wounds.
Praise be to God, for the promise is kept.

Janji Tuhanku dilèe mula
Masōk syeuruga soe tém prang sabi
Soe nyang tém poh sitrèe ceulaka
Biek beulaga kaphé hareubi[134]

At first, Our Lord made a promise:
the reward for entering the holy war is heaven.
Let's wipe out the wretched enemies,
those pitch-black infidel enemies!

Meutuah that muda bahlia
Jipōt lingka lé putroe ti
Nyankeu balaih lam syeuruga
Le that pahla bak prang sabi

134 The word *hareubi* originates from Arabic *ḥarbī*, denoting an infidel against whom any kind of warfare is permissible.

The young man is most fortunate:
the fair ladies cool his body with their fans.
Such are the rewards in heaven,
as the holy war merits many awards.

If there is such a thing as Islamophobia, these ditties would seem to provide a good reason for it. However, a sloganeering, Manichean debate along the lines of either "Islam is evil" or "Islam means peace" leads nowhere. In this context I would like to draw attention to the fact that church-goers who earnestly claim and preach that "Christianity is love," may enthusiastically sing the hymn *Onward, Christian Soldiers*, without noticing the inherent paradox in the least. As the argument commonly goes, this song's obvious martial associations should be interpreted figuratively. Originally written as a processional hymn in 1865 in England by the Anglican cleric Sabine Baring-Gould, *Onward, Christian Soldiers* was not inspired by any actual war, but by "a special day for children when peace and brotherhood were the theme for all the activities."[135] As it happens, the Salvation Army eagerly added Father Baring-Gould's children's anthem to its militant hymnody, but *Onward, Christian Soldiers* has also been one of the Ku Klux Klan's favorite marching tunes.[136] The song has great emotional power: it will bring "chill bumps to any dedicated Klansman," as it will to many traditional Christians.[137] Stirring up strong emotions, it reinforces among its singers "a sense of solidarity with the group, a 'we-ness'."[138] The lyric has also lent scriptural authority to the African American civil rights movement in the United States. The well-known Baptist minister (and preacher of nonviolence and passive resistance) Martin Luther King, Jr. (1929–68) once wrote about the feelings of joy, pride, and fulfillment when singing it vigorously together:

> The opening hymn was the old familiar 'Onward Christian Soldiers,' and when that mammoth audience stood to sing, the voices outside (the church building could not accommodate the large gatherings) swelling the chorus in the church, there was a mighty ring like the glad echo of heaven itself.... The enthusiasm of these thousands of people swept everything along like an onrushing tidal wave.[139]

---

135 Collins, *Stories* 147.
136 See Murdoch, *Origins* 101; and McVeigh, *The rise* 143.
137 Quarles, *The Ku Klux Klan* 64.
138 Jasper, The emotions of protest 183.
139 Cited in Jasper, The emotions of protest 183.

The point that I wish to make is that lyrics related to the *Hikayat Prang Sabi,* too, are linked to "the pleasures of protest," fostering solidarity within one's own group.[140] Of course, the *Hikayat Prang Sabi* will always be associated with *jihād,* but in contemporary Aceh this does not necessarily imply that this loaded term must always be interpreted only in a historical and literal sense, i.e., in its traditional meaning of fighting a war against the infidel. In the terminology of some Islamic theologians the "*jihād* of the sword" or "physical *jihād*" is only "the smaller *jihād,*" in contrast to the peaceful forms of "the greater *jihād,*" viz., the struggle against one's own evil or exerting oneself for the sake of Islam and the community of believers, e.g., by the *jihād* of the tongue or the *jihād* of the pen.[141] Jacqueline Siapno informs us that in Aceh, in recent years, *jihād* has also come to be understood in more irenic ways, viz. "fighting against injustice and poverty, state violence, struggling to overcome ignorance, in addition to normative piety (striving to practice Islam properly)."[142]

The massive tsunami that struck on 26 December 2004 killed around 180,000 people in Aceh, and destroyed substantial parts of its coastal areas. However, this disaster was also the catalyst for peace talks between the Indonesian government and the Free Aceh Movement, resulting in the signing of a peace agreement on 15 August 2005. A long and sad history of much violence has seen to it that the 'Song of the holy war' has become deeply ingrained into the collective thought of the Acehnese people, but, hopefully, with the passing of time, a figurative rather than a literal interpretation of the term *jihād* may finally develop into the dominant mode of understanding. Whereas literalist advocates of the "*jihād* of the sword" may claim that direct entrance into heavenly paradise is for those who strive for martyrdom in the path of God, "the greater *jihād*" at least ensures that hell on earth will not materialize.

Bibliography

ʿAbd al-Ṣamad al-Palimbānī, *Sair al-sālikīn,* 2 vols., Semarang n.d.

Abdullah, I.T., *Hikayat Meukuta Alam: Suntingan teks dan terjemahan beserta telaah struktur dan resepsi* [Hikayat Meukuta Alam: Text edition and translation with a study of its structure and reception], Jakarta 1991.

Ajisaka, A., *Mengenal pahlawan Indonesia* [Getting to know the heroes of Indonesia], Jakarta 2010.

140 Jasper, The emotions of protest 182.

141 Peters, Jihād 369–70; Alfian, Aceh 109–10.

142 Siapno, *Gender* 143.

Alfian, I., *Sastra perang: Sebuah pembicaraan mengenai Hikayat Perang Sabil* [War literature: A discussion on the Hikayat Perang Sabil], Jakarta 1992.

Alfian, T.I., Aceh and the Holy War (*Prang Sabil*), in A. Reid (ed.), *Verandah of violence: The background to the Aceh problem*, Singapore 2006, 109–20.

Amshoff, M.C.H., *Goudkruintje: Een Atjèhsche roman met vertolking en toelichting* [Goldilocks: An Acehnese romance, paraphrased and annotated], Leiden 1929.

Anonymous, Langen (Karel Frederik Hendrik van), in S. de Graaff and D.G. Stibbe (eds.), *Encyclopaedie van Nederlandsch-Indië*, ii, 's-Gravenhage and Leiden 1918, 530.

Arif, Abdullah, *Nasib Atjeh* [The fate of Aceh], Kutaradja 1958.

———, *Pantôn aneuk miet: Pantun anak-anak*, ii [Poems for small children: Poems for children], Jakarta 2006.

Arkoun, M., Miskawayh, in *EI*², vii, 143–4.

Aspinall, E., *Islam and nation: Separatist rebellion in Aceh, Indonesia*, Stanford 2009.

al-Azmeh, A., Rhetoric for the senses: A consideration of Muslim paradise narratives, in *JAL* 26.3 (1995), 215–31.

Azra, A., *The origins of Islamic reformism in Southeast Asia: Networks of Malay-Indonesian and Middle Eastern 'ulamā' in the seventeenth and eighteenth centuries*, Crows Nest, NSW Australia and Honolulu 2004.

Basri, H., Islam in Aceh: Institutions, scholarly traditions, and relations between ulama and umara, in A. Graf, S. Schröter, and E. Wieringa (eds.), *Aceh: History, politics and culture*, Singapore 2010, 180–200.

———, Teungku A. Hasjmy: pengembang tradisi keilmuan dan perekat ulama-umara [Teungku A. Hasjmy: promoter of scholarly tradition and connector between theologians and government officials], in L. Aunie (ed.), *Ensiklopedi pemikiran ulama Aceh*, Banda Aceh 2004, 465–508.

Booker, C., *The seven basic plots: Why we tell stories*, London and New York 2004.

Brakel, L.F., *The Hikayat Muhammad Hanafiyyah: A medieval Muslim-Malay romance*, The Hague 1975.

———, *The story of Muhammad Hanafiyyah: A medieval Muslim romance*, The Hague 1977.

Brown, C.C., *Sějarah Mělayu or Malay Annals*, Kuala Lumpur, 1970.

Butzer, G. and J. Jacob (eds.), *Metzler Lexikon literarischer Symbole*, Stuttgart and Weimar 2008.

Christie, N., Motivating listeners in the *Kitab al-Jihad* of 'Ali ibn Tahir al-Sulami (d. 1106), in *Crusades* 6 (2007), 1–14.

Clavé-Celik, E., The Acehnese women warriors between images of the past and reality of the present, in *Komunitas Tikar Pandan*, http://www.tikarpandan.org/ index.php?option=com_content&view=article&id=77%3Athe-acehnese-women-war

riors-between-image-of-the-past-and-reality-of-the-present&catid=54%3Aartikel &Itemid=69 (accessed 18 October 2010).

Collins, A., *Stories behind the hymns that inspire America*, Grand Rapids MI 2003.

Cook, D., *Martyrdom in Islam*, Cambridge 2007.

———, *Understanding jihad*, Berkeley, Los Angeles, and London 2005.

Dajani-Shakeel, H., Jihād in twelfth-century Arabic poetry: A moral and religious force to counter the crusades, in *MW* 66 (1976), 96–113.

Damsté, H.T., Atjèhsche oorlogspapieren [Acehnese war documents], in *Indische Gids* 34.1 (1912), 617–33; 776–92.

———, Hikajat Perang Sabi, in *Bijdragen tot de Taal-, Land- en Volkenkunde* 84 (1928), 545–609.

———, Meer Atjèhsche oorlogspapieren [More Acehnese war documents], in *Nieuwsblad voor het Gouvernement Atjeh en Onderhoorigheden* (27 January 1912).

Djajadiningrat, H., *Atjèhsch-Nederlandsch woordenboek* [Acehnese-Dutch dictionary], 2 vols., Batavia 1934.

Drewes, G.W.J., *Directions for travellers on the mystic path: Zakariyyā' al-Anṣārī's Kitāb Fatḥ al-Raḥmān and its Indonesian adaptations*, The Hague 1977.

———, *Two Achehnese poems: Hikajat Ranto and Hikajat Teungku di Meukè'*, The Hague 1980.

Durie, M., Poetry and worship: Manuscripts from Aceh, in A. Kumar and J.H. McGlynn (eds.), *Illuminations: The writing traditions of Indonesia*, Jakarta and Tokyo 1996, 79–100.

Esposito, J.L., *What everyone needs to know about Islam*, Cambridge 2002.

Gallop, A.T., Beautifying Jawi: Between calligraphy and palaeography, in A.H. Omar (ed.), *Malay images*, Tanjung Malim 2005, 194–233.

Hadi, A., Exploring Acehnese understandings of jihad: A study of the Hikayat prang sabi, in R.M. Feener, P. Daly, and A. Reid (eds.), *Mapping the Acehnese past*, Leiden 2011, 183–97.

Hasan, N., The Tuḥfat al-Rāghibīn: The work of Abdul Samad al-Palimbani or Muhammad Arsyad al-Banjari?, in *Bijdragen tot de Taal-, Land- en Volkenkunde* 163.1 (2007), 67–85.

Hasjmy, A., Alam Aceh yang indah adalah puisi [Acehnese world of beauty is poetry], in L.K. Ara, T. Ismail and Ks. Hasyim (eds.), *Seulawah: Antologi sastra Aceh sekilas pintas*, Jakarta 1995, vii–x.

———, *Apa sebab rakyat Aceh sanggup berperang puluhan tahun melawan agressi Belanda* [Why the Acehnese people were able to fight Dutch aggression for decades], Jakarta 1977.

Hillenbrand, C., *The crusades: Islamic perspectives*, Edinburgh 1999.

Iskandar, T., The Hikayat Prang Geudōng, in C.D. Grijns and S.O. Robson (eds.), *Cultural contact and textual interpretation*, Dordrecht and Cinnaminson, NJ 1986, 94–120.

Jarrar, M., The martyrdom of passionate lovers: Holy war as a sacred wedding, in A. Neuwirth et al. (eds.), *Myths, historical archetypes and symbolic figures in Arabic literatures*, Beirut 1999, 87–107.

Jasper, J.M., The emotions of protest, in J. Goodwin and J.M. Jasper (eds.), *The social movements reader: Cases and concepts*, Oxford 2009, 175–85.

Jones, R., Review article: Problems of editing Malay texts, in *Archipel* 20 (1980), 121–7.

Jowett, G.S. and V. O'Donnell, *Propaganda and persuasion*, London 2006.

Kaptein, N.J.G., 'Abd al-Ṣamad al-Palimbānī, in *EI*³, ii, 25–6.

Kippenberg, H.G., "'Consider that it is a raid on the path of God": The spiritual manual of the attackers of 9/11, in *Numen* 52 (2005), 29–58.

Kreemer, J., *Atjèhsch handwoordenboek* (*Atjèhsch-Nederlandsch*) [Acehnese dictionary (Acehnese-Dutch)], Leiden 1931.

Leigh, B., The rencong, in http://old.blades.free.fr/daggers/rencong/rencong_bl.htm (accessed 18 October 2010).

McVeigh, R., *The rise of the Ku Klux Klan: Right-wing movements and national politics*, Minneapolis, MN 2009.

Muhammad A.R., Teungku Chik Ditiro: Ulama, pejuang dan pahlawan nasional Indonesia [Teungku Chik Ditiro: Scholar, fighter, and Indonesian national hero], in L. Aunie (ed.), *Ensiklopedi pemikiran ulama Aceh*, Banda Aceh 2004, 45–60.

Murdoch, N.H., *Origins of the Salvation Army*, Knoxville TN 1994.

Peters, R., *Islam and colonialism: The doctrine of jihad in modern history*, The Hague, Paris, and New York 1979.

———, Jihād, in J.L. Esposito (ed.), *The Oxford Encyclopedia of the modern Islamic world*, ii, Oxford 1995, 369–373.

Pridmore-Brown, M., Surges, in *The Times Literary Supplement* 5609 (2010), 3–4.

Quarles, C.L., *The Ku Klux Klan and related American racialist and antisemitic organizations: A history and analysis*, Jefferson NC 1999.

Quzwain, M.C., *Mengenal Allah: Suatu studi mengenai ajaran tasawuf Syaikh 'Abdus-Samad al-Palimbani ulama Palembang abad ke-18 Masehi* [Knowing God: A study on the mystical teachings of Sheikh 'Abdus-Samad al-Palimbani, an 18th-century scholar from Palembang], Jakarta 1985.

Reid, A., *The contest for North Sumatra: Atjeh, the Netherlands and Britain 1858–1898*, Kuala Lumpur 1969.

———, *An Indonesian frontier: Acehnese and other stories of Sumatra*, Leiden 2005.

———, War, peace and the burden of history in Aceh, in *ARI Working Paper Series* 1 (2003).

Riesebrodt, M., *The promise of salvation: A theory of religion*, Chicago and London 2010.

———, "Religion": Just another modern Western construction?, in http://divinity.uchicago.edu/martycenter/publications/webforum/122003/riesebrodtessay.pdf (1st published 2003) (accessed 18 October 2010).
Robinson, C.F., *Islamic historiography*, Cambridge 2003.
Rosenthal, F., Reflections on love in paradise, in F. Rosenthal, *Muslim intellectual and social history: A collection of essays*, Aldershot UK 1990.
Ruthven, M., *A fury for God: The Islamist attack on America*, London 2002.
Sellheim, R., Faḍīla, in *EI*², ii, 728–9.
Shahīd, I., People of the Elephant, in *EQ*, iv, 44–6.
Siapno, J.A., *Gender, Islam, nationalism and the state in Aceh: The paradox of power, co-optation and resistance*, London and New York 2002.
Siegel, J.T., *The rope of God*, Berkeley and Los Angeles 1969.
———, *Shadow and sound: The historical thought of a Sumatran people*, Chicago and London 1979.
Sjamsuddin, N., *The republican revolt: A study of the Acehnese rebellion*, Singapore 1985.
Smith, J.I. and Y.Y. Haddad, *The Islamic understanding of death and resurrection*, Albany, NY 1981.
Snouck Hurgronje, C., *The Achehnese*, 2 vols., Leiden 1906.
Sofyan, N.C., Teungku Chik Pante Kulu: Ulama dan penyair motivator perang Aceh [Teungku Chik Pante Kulu: Scholar and motivating poet of the Aceh War], in L. Aunie (ed.), *Ensiklopedi pemikiran ulama Aceh*, Banda Aceh 2004, 1–30.
Stevens, A.M. and A. Schmidgall-Tellings (eds.), *A comprehensive Indonesian-English dictionary*, Athens, OH 2004.
Sulaiman, M.I., From autonomy to periphery: A critical evaluation of the Acehnese nationalist movement, in A. Reid (ed.), *Verandah of violence: The background to the Aceh problem*, Singapore 2006, 121–48.
———, Islam et propagande anti-néerlandaise: Abdullah Arief et le Seumangat Atjeh 1945–1946, in *Archipel* 30 (1985), 207–17.
Van Gelder, G.J., *God's banquet: Food in classical Arabic literature*, New York 2000.
Van Ronkel, Ph.S., Maleische litteratuur van verren oorsprong [Malay literature originating from afar], in *Mededeelingen der Koninklijke Akademie van Wetenschappen, Afdeeling Letterkunde* 53 (1921), 175–92.
Van Wulfften Palthe, P.M., Geestesstoornis en gemeenschapsstructuur [Mental disorder and community structure], offprint of *Geneeskundig Tijdschrift voor Nederlandsch-Indië* 76 (1936).
Van Zonneveld, A.G., *Traditional weapons of the Indonesian archipelago*, Leiden 2001.
Voorhoeve, P., *Catalogue of Acehnese manuscripts in the Library of Leiden University and other collections outside Aceh*, Leiden 1994.

Walther, W., *Kleine Geschichte der arabischen Literatur: Von der vorislamischen Zeit bis zur Gegenwart*, Munich 2004.

Wieringa, E.P., Amir Hamza, the all too human hero, in *Kajian Malaysia* 14 (1996), 183–93.

———, Does traditional Islamic Malay literature contain shi'itic elements? 'Alî and Fâtimah in Malay hikayat literature, in *Studia Islamika, Indonesian journal for Islamic studies* 3 (1996), 93–111.

———, The dream of the king and the holy war against the Dutch: The *kôteubah* of the Acehnese epic, *Hikayat Prang Gômpeuni*, in BSOAS 61 (1998), 298–308.

———, Some light on Ahmad al-Fatani's Nur al-mubin ("The Clear Light"), in J. van der Putten and M. Kilcline Cody (eds.), *Lost times and untold tales from the Malay world*, Singapore 2009, 186–97.

Internet Sources

http://news.bbc.co.uk/2/hi/uk_news/england/2687797.stm (accessed 18 October 2010).

www.acehbooks.org (accessed 18 October 2010).

FIGURE 53.1 *Advertisement for volume xii of the series* Spirit of Aceh. *Its title page features two crossed traditional Acehnese daggers, which symbolically function as a gate for the royal mosque in Kutaraja. From Abdullah Arif,* Nasib Atjeh [*The fate of Aceh*] *iii, Kutaradja 1958.* KITLV *Leiden, shelf mark mm-199-N.*

FIGURE 53.2 *Cover of Abdullah Arif's* Nasib Atjeh *[The fate of Aceh] iii, Kutaradja 1958. The vignette has a strongly Islamic design.* KITLV *Leiden, shelf mark mm-199-N.*

CHAPTER 54

Eschatology between Reason and Revelation: Death and Resurrection in Modern Islamic Theology

Umar Ryad

By the end of the nineteenth century, a great number of Muslim scholars tried to revitalize a new *kalām* (or Islamic theology) to address modern philosophical and scientific issues. Facing a multitude of religious and intellectual challenges under the Western colonial dominion, these new theologians were forced to reevaluate classical theological and philosophical ideas related to the existence of God, creation, good and evil, prophecy, and the afterlife. Most of them became convinced that classical *kalām* concepts had lost the logical basis of argumentation in the face of newer experimental and empirical methods of science.[1] As eschatology is the main domain of metaphysical postulations, modern Muslim theologians analyzed various classical eschatological subjects in response to these intellectual challenges.

In their 1981 work, *The Islamic Understanding of Death and Resurrection*, Jane I. Smith and Y.Y. Haddad succinctly studied and presented examples of ideas by modern Islamic thinkers and theologians on such subjects.[2] The authors correctly observe that unlike classical theologians, who were generally interested in using particular references in the religious sources to the *barzakh* state after death to illustrate specific points about the nature of God and His justice,[3] modern Muslim writers rather tend to address the heavy Western emphasis on rationalism. In fact, the great majority of contemporary Muslim writers have chosen not to discuss the afterlife at all, since they are satisfied with simply affirming the reality of the day of judgment and human accountability and see no need to provide details or interpretive discussion. According to Smith and Haddad, this is, in large part, because Muslim thinkers face a kind of "embarrassment with the elaborate traditional detail concerning life in the grave and in the abodes of recompense, called into question by modern

1 *Ozervarli*, Attempts to revitalize.
2 Smith and Haddad, *The Islamic understanding*.
3 Ibid., 33.

 | DOI 10.1163/9789004333154_055

rationalists."[4] In their view, modern Muslim thinkers conceive their main task as emphasizing in particular the work ethic that will help achieve material and technological parity with the West.[5] Unfortunately Smith and Haddad did not select their case studies from the above-mentioned revitalization trend of the new Islamic theology. They therefore ignore an important aspect of modern theological thought as reflected by those thinkers and their attempts to reinterpret the traditional viewpoints concerning eschatological subjects.

Smith and Haddad analyze modern Muslim thinkers under three categories, namely traditionalists, modernists, and spiritualists; this is plausible but not comprehensive or representative. It is true that contemporary traditionalist Muslim writers produce new material in modern Arabic about the traditional view of Islam on the afterlife with no additional interpretation. Modernists, by contrast, are much more concerned with interpretive analyses of life, the conciliation between science and the immediate life after death, the possibility of continuing human development, and the Quran's affirmation of ethical responsibility.[6] Representatives of the trend of Islamic spirituality, who flourished during the colonial period, were interested in popular European and American spiritual writings; they looked to these writings especially in their responses to Orientalist and missionary accusations that Islam's conception of the afterlife is sensual and material.[7]

Despite the fact that the two authors agree that the three categories are fluid and certainly not always mutually exclusive, they sometimes tend to quote obscure writers to reach specific general conclusions on what they categorize as "modernist thinkers and theologians." In the present chapter, I argue that any attempt to renew the discipline of *kalām* in modern times (including in discussions of eschatological issues) should not be regarded as entirely liberal, modernist or reformist. This is not an organized movement, but rather sporadic attempts – representatives of this trend inevitably tried to harmonize traditional Islamic tenets with the positivistic modern attitude toward nature and science. Thus theirs was an attempt to combine religious values with scientific discoveries and interpret revelation (sometimes) according to the scientific theories of the age.[8]

The present chapter investigates the interpretations of significant modern Muslim theologians and scholars on eschatological issues. I have not

---

4 Ibid., 99–100.

5 Ibid.

6 Ibid., 100.

7 Ibid., 101.

8 *Ozervarli*, Attempts to revitalize *104*.

undertaken an exhaustive study, nor do I provide a comprehensive overview of their thoughts on the subject. Rather, this exploration seeks to clarify their multifaceted views about eschatological issues within this new trend of modern theology by examining a few key texts. The present paper explores their methods of including, analyzing, criticizing or circumventing the classical theological treatment of death and the life hereafter. What are the contributions of these modern theologians to the concept of resurrection and divine judgment, the portents prior to or accompanying these events, and the nature of the hereafter? To what extent did they agree or differ with traditional Islamic views on death and the afterlife? How did they relate their understanding of modern scientific findings to the religious truth about eschatological subjects? To what extent did they make use of natural phenomena and rational clarifications in this modern theological discourse?

1 A Bridge between Medieval and Modern Theology: Shāh Walī Allāh's Eschatology

Smith and Haddad note that Indo-Pakistani Muslim scholars emphasize a kind of Darwinian evolutionism as a vindication of Islamic ideas.[9] Their study however was limited to a scant analysis of the ideas of people like Abū l-Aʿlā al-Mawdūdī (d. 1399/1979) and the Aḥmadiyya modernist Mawlānā Muḥammad ʿAlī (d. 1371/1951). They did not dwell upon the ideas of other significant Indo-Pakistani theologians who seriously reinvestigated classical eschatological themes in the modern context.

Take, for example, the role of the great theologian Shāh Walī Allāh (d. 1176/1762) in renewing religious concepts. His ideas serve as a bridge between medieval and modern developments.[10] As part of his philosophy of religion in general, Walī Allāh deemed eschatological issues in the Quran and *ḥadīth* as belonging to the realm of a metaphysical-psychological system, but he was not inclined to explain relevant statements allegorically.[11] Rather he argued that all topics related to the afterlife (such as the questioning in the grave, the weighing of one's deeds, the crossing of the Bridge, and the vision of God) can be understood by the human intellect.[12] His explanations were

9 Smith and Haddad, *The Islamic understanding* 101.

10 Rafiabadi, *Saints and saviours* 134; for more about him, see Hermansen, Shāh Walī Allāh's theory; Baljon, *A mystical interpretation*; Baljon, *Religion and thought*.

11 Halepota, *Philosophy* 258.

12 Jalbani, *Teachings* 193.

mostly based on his psychological views of psychic states and their representations in mental images.[13]

Walī Allāh interpreted the day of judgment as a matter related to the non-material life, which should be shaped according to the nature of the *ʿālam al-mithāl* (World of Similitudes).[14] Walī Allāh developed this doctrine, also known as the Realm of Images, which was in fact a product of medieval Muslim mysticism, as an attempt to rationalize certain dogmatic beliefs, particularly those of an eschatological nature. As an example of such rationalization, and to demonstrate that it did not begin in the eighteenth century, he cited al-Ghazālī (d. 505/1111). For example, al-Ghazālī explained the tradition about the "punishment in the grave" of a disbeliever being stung by ninety-nine serpents, each with seven heads, by stating that this number refers to the chief vices and their numerous subdivisions that destroy human happiness.[15] Through later Muslim theologians and mystics, such as Ibn ʿArabī (d. 638/1240), Quṭb al-Dīn al-Shirāzī (d. 710/1311), and Mullā Ṣadrā (d. 1050/1640), this doctrine became an integral part of Sufi spiritual culture.[16]

Walī Allāh was of the view that there existed a "subtle vapor" in the human body, known as *nasma*. By employing the humoral theory (which was used by Greek, Roman, and Islamic physicians in treating the human body, and which was still used by European physicians until the nineteenth century), he argued that this subtle vapor was the cause of the essence of the four humors of the human body, i.e., blood, phlegm, yellow bile, and black bile. It was like a white fog that prevailed over the whole body and was responsible for its functioning.[17] In Walī Allāh's view, physicians agreed that as soon as this vapor was in the body, man was alive; but as soon as it was separated from it, he was dead. According to him this subtle vapor was the spirit. One of its qualities was that it could taste without a tongue and hear without the use of ears. When a man died, his *nasma* became very weak because the four humors did not exist anymore, but it did not completely disappear. Providence helped the vapor to gain strength until it was able to see, hear, and speak. The *nasma* would therefore serve as a steed for the real soul in the world to come.[18]

Walī Allāh maintained that the separation of the *nasma* from the body was the cause of death, but its connection with the soul remained intact. As the

---

13 Halepota, *Philosophy* 259.
14 Cf. Lawson, Ahmad Ahsa'i.
15 Rahman, Dream 168–9.
16 Ibid., 168–80.
17 Jalbani, *Teachings* 194.
18 Ibid., 194–5.

body was a vehicle for the *nasma* in this world, similarly the *nasma* would be the vehicle for the soul in the hereafter. Walī Allāh compared the condition of the *nasma* in this world to that of an expert writer with his fingers cut off, who could retain the faculty of writing. The *nasma* after man's death retained, with its airy essence, almost all the faculties of the head and heart.[19]

In Walī Allāh's view, in that world of symbols and images individual qualities would vanish and only the specific form would remain, as reflected by man's intellectual and imaginative faculties surviving through and in the *nasma*. The World of Similitude was a world full of knowledge, and a clear exposition of *ʿālam al-arwāḥ* (the World of Spirits). Also, sciences of the World of Similitude would be revealed to man and he himself would become a representative of the World of Similitudes. In this world, the re-gathering of bodies and the infusion of souls in them was not the creation of a new life, but rather the completion of worldly life; and the relation between them was like that of cause and effect. However, due to its great transformation, the body that would be given to the human being on the day of judgment would not be exactly the same as it was before. The state of the human being would appear as something between the material and the non-material.[20]

The stage following man's death was the *ʿālam al-barzakh* (World of the Grave). It resembled, in Walī Allāh's view, dreams during sleep, which were the reflection of man's thoughts and knowledge during the day. In sleep, man's sense faculties cease functioning and freely make their appearance. His feeling of pain in his dreams emanate from his thoughts, which appear to him in a particular form. The only difference between the world of dreams and that of the grave was that from the former one wakes up, while from the latter one will not rise until the day of judgment. Walī Allāh concluded, "a man overcome by fierceness and cruelty in this world will see in his grave a wild beast like a lion or a wolf scratching him with its claws. The miser will see a serpent or a scorpion biting or stinging him."[21] However, if his actions were good, he would see angels with beautiful faces, carrying silken clothes and musk in their hands.[22] Walī Allāh did not accept any metaphorical interpretations of these facts and stated that man would have twofold pain or pleasure in his grave. One part of this was his apprehension of his good or bad actions, and the other was that angels would be inspired to appear to him in some beautiful or ugly and awful form. All man's actions that were undertaken with full presence of mind were

19 Ibid., 196–7.
20 Ibid., 201–3.
21 Ibid., 197–8.
22 Ibid., 198.

preserved in his *nasma* and when his body decays after death, they will appear to him in their true colors.[23]

This explanation reminds us of the views of Shihāb al-Dīn al-Suhrawardī (d. 587/1191) who affirmed the existence of a new realm between the spiritual and the physical after death, which he called *al-muthul al-muʿallaqa* (the Realm of "Suspended Images") or of *al-ashbāḥ al-mujarrada* ("Pure Figures"). In his view, the fully developed spiritual souls become pure lights, but those that have not fully developed through "illumination" and those pious souls who have faithfully followed the credal and practical prescriptions of religions will not rise to the status of pure spirits, but will ascend to the Realm of Suspended Images wherein they enjoy the quasi-physical delights of paradise. The vicious people, who are damned, will be assigned to the Realm of Pure Figures, but the figures they shall live with will be obnoxious and torturous.[24]

As for the divine *mīzān* (lit., the Balance) and the *ṣirāṭ* (the Bridge to paradise), Walī Allāh pointed out that all actions of man will be weighed in the Balance, and he will be made to pass over the Bridge. He described the Bridge as the straight path of the *sharīʿa* that will appear there in its material form. It was the sample of the rule or way of life placed in the nature of men; their differences in crossing this path will reflect their differences in following the rules of the *sharīʿa* in their lives. Those who followed the path of *sharīʿa* will pass the Bridge as fast as lightning. The Balance will appear in a form, which is not purely material, nor is it immaterial, but is a shape in between.[25]

Walī Allāh explained metaphorically some essential material concepts related to the hereafter. For instance, according to him the issue of *ḥisāb* (reckoning) refers to one of the manifestations of God's attribute of discernment, while the river of Kawthar (a fountain) given to the Prophet Muḥammad points to a manifestation of his guidance. Every prophet has his fountain, but that of the Prophet Muḥammad is the source of all of them. The reward of paradise is a manifestation of God's *jamālī* (amiable) attributes, while punishment in hell is a manifestation of His *jalālī* (majestic) attributes.[26]

Another important aspect was Walī Allāh's clarification of the mountain of *al-aʿrāf* (the heights), which he portrays as the in-between destination of persons who did not do any good, nor did they commit any evil acts. In Walī Allāh's thinking, the "inmates of al-Aʿrāf" will include those who did not receive

23 Ibid., 199–200.

24 Rahman, Dream 169–70. For more about Suhrawardī, see for example, Davidson, *Alfarabi, Avicenna, and Averroes* 175–7; Cf. Walbridge, *The leaven*; Ohlander, *Sufism*.

25 Jalbani, *Teachings* 203–5.

26 Ibid., 205–6.

the message of God, and those living on the mountain-tops, who, because of their ignorance could not derive any benefit from the message of Islam, nor could they understand the Quran and its arguments. It also includes people who were deficient in reason, such as children, lunatics, imbeciles, fools, and "rustics." Walī Allāh gave the example of a black slave-woman, who when asked by the Prophet about God, had pointed to up to heaven; the Prophet had said explicitly that she was a believer. Those to whom the message of Islam had not been conveyed or explained properly, those whose doubts had not been removed, would be lodged in al-Aʿrāf as well.[27]

According to Walī Allāh's eschatological interpretations, man's progress did not end with his life in paradise; there was still a higher and nobler stage. After his long stay there, his *nasma* would become weak, and would continue to shape itself in various forms according to the requirements of the soul, until it attained its ultimate aim by eventually changing into the divine or the angelic soul.[28] Walī Allāh stressed that belief in the hereafter provided human beings with a clear-cut purpose in life and enabled them to endeavor to improve their present life and look forward to a pleasant state in the life hereafter.[29]

2 Indo-Pakistani Modernist Theology

2.1 *Sayyid Aḥmad Khān's Naturalism*

Walī Allāh paved the way for many subsequent Indo-Pakistani Muslim theologians. One of the most significant contributions to modern theological thinking was made by Sayyid Aḥmad Khān (d. 1306/1898), whose new interpretation of Islamic tenets was based on his understanding of the laws of nature. In his naturalist approach, Khān considered the soul immortal, stressing that it would not perish with the death of the body. In support of his theory, he used the materialistic doctrine that nothing perishes in the world. The quantity of matter remains unchanged, it is only its form that is subject to change.[30]

Khān did not present a systematic analysis of eschatological concepts. However, he stressed that man's happiness was dependent on his ability to ensure that his human faculty of "godliness" gained the upper hand over his faculty of "iniquity." In his view, in the hereafter the punishment for sins consists of the misery of the soul on the day of judgment. Due to his sins, the

27 Ibid., 206–8.

28 Ibid., 208–11.

29 Halepota, *Philosophy* 261.

30 Dar, *Religious thought* 221.

sinner will inflict wretchedness upon his soul, especially at the moment of death. Only the sin of *shirk* ("associationism," viz. the worship of other gods besides God) leads to everlasting misery that the soul can never be freed from.[31] Khān maintained that the human soul will live on after death as immaterial and separate from its original body. According to him, scientific observations had proven that the soul exists, even though we cannot grasp its inner reality. The human soul, unlike that of animals, was privileged to be "put under obligation." It was "unlimited" and "undetermined" in its actions; man could cause his soul to develop and be happy or decline and be miserable.[32]

Khān explained the Quranic references to *qiyāma* (resurrection) as a sign of the radical change of the individual human soul at the time of death, when it will be separated from its body and enter a new form. In this regard, Khān reinterpreted Quranic teachings on evolution against the background of the absence of belief in the existence of an immortal soul among the Arabs during the time of the revelation.[33] In other words, the Quran did not teach that the earthly body will rise again in the literal sense. But in order to impress the reality of reward and punishment upon the minds of "those Arabs," it had to appeal to their imagination by stressing the idea of such a bodily resurrection.[34]

In Khān's view, all eschatological events were beyond man's comprehension. The major objective of the relevant Quranic texts was only to urge men to good deeds and discourage them from evil acts by showing them the long-term consequences of their deeds. The verses on paradise and hell were formulated in figurative language so that human beings would imagine the highest form of eternal bliss and repose. Such language was designed to awaken man's desire to obey commands and respect divine prohibition. Khān understood all the physical descriptions of the hereafter as metaphor. For example, the "blowing of the trumpet" referred to the radical change of everything at the end of time, and the "book of deeds" or the "weighing of the deeds on the scales" was a metonym for God's justice.[35]

Khān argued that as the body was only the instrument of the soul, the subject of reward and punishment was the soul, not the body. At the time of death, the soul would acquire a certain kind of physical medium, which would be distinct from the present body, and at resurrection there would be no new life but a continuation of one's old life. The real purpose of the Quran's reference to

31 Troll, *Sayyid Ahmad Khan* 209–10.
32 Ibid.
33 Ibid.
34 Ibid 211.
35 Ibid.

the reality of resurrection was merely to refute the beliefs of those who denied the existence of the soul and identified life with life on this earth only. The relevant verses of the Quran specifically address those who disbelieve in a life after death; the Quran does not describe the resurrection as a fact, but rather as the kind of life that will come to be.[36]

Khān considered anyone who believes in the one God, even if he does not believe in Muḥammad, as not actually a *kāfir* (unbeliever), but a *muwaḥḥid* (unitarian believer). As for the status of non-Muslims in the hereafter, Khān quoted al-Ghazālī's view, that there would be three categories of unbelieving people: 1) those who never heard about Muḥammad and his message; 2) those who met Muslims and have a perfect knowledge of Islam; and 3) those who heard about Muḥammad and his message but insufficiently. People belonging to the first and third categories will find salvation in the hereafter.[37]

Regarding the nature of paradise, Khān refused to believe that the words "garden," "streams," "houses made of gold," "silver and pearl bricks," "rivulets of milk," "honey," "wine," "delicious fruit," "beautiful damsels," and so on, were to be taken literally; for in this case they would contradict the Quran and *ḥadīth*. Man can only understand the nature of things that he experiences through his senses; even the things he can conceive in his imagination must be based, ultimately, on what he has already seen. Khān maintained that it was impossible to express the reality of super-sensuous things in language, even in divine language. The words used in the Quran are all metaphorical, referring to the physiological states of happiness and unhappiness that man will experience in the life after death. Khān quoted one *ḥadīth* in which a man asked the Prophet Muḥammad whether there would be horses in paradise. He replied, "You will have a red turquoise horse and you will be free to ride anywhere you like." Another asked, "Will there be camels also?" He replied, "Yes, and everything else which you will desire to have." This *ḥadīth* does not mean that there will be horses and camels; the Prophet wanted to point out that it would be a place of perfect happiness, however a man might interpret the shape of that happiness.[38] *Ru'yat Allāh* (vision of God) in the hereafter has to be seen as the fundamental and highest blessing of paradise. Paradise should be understood metaphorically as referring to the ability to see the Holy Essence openly, without a veil; and such a "spiritual disclosure" transcends mere rational affirmation.[39]

36 Dar, *Religious thought* 222–3.
37 Troll, *Sayyid Ahmad Khan* 212–3.
38 Dar, *Religious thought* 222–6.
39 Troll, *Sayyid Ahmad Khan* 211.

2.2 *Afterlife between Science and Religion: Shiblī l-Nuʿmānī's Rationalist Theology*

The Indian revivalist historian Shiblī l-Nuʿmānī (d. 1332/1914) contributed to the discussions about the need for a modern theology as well. In his view, there is no conflict between science and religion, since they have nothing to do with each other as their subject matter and scope are different. All matters related to the creation, whether dealing with the components of water or the speed of light, belong to science and are of no concern to religion. Questions concerning the existence of God, life after death, or punishment and reward, however, should only be discussed in the domain of religion and are not to be touched by science. In his new theology, al-Nuʿmānī championed rational interpretations by the Muʿtazilīs and Muslim philosophers, and was later influenced by the mystical rationalism of Jalāl al-Dīn al-Rūmī.[40] He had been a close friend of Sayyid Aḥmad Khān, but later set aside his ideas. He even harshly criticized Khān and his group as "third-rate" and "short-sighted" materialists.[41]

Al-Nuʿmānī was of the view that modern materialistic and naturalistic theories must be countered by mystical and philosophical contemplation of theological matters. For this reason, he argued that the issues of *kalām* had not really changed, and that any "part of the old *kalām* which is useless today was insufficient before also and will so remain always."[42] All theological issues concerning the affirmation of God, His unity, prophecy, and the Quran as the word of God, and the hereafter, were legitimate concerns; the rest was irrelevant.[43]

Al-Nuʿmānī was a severe critic of Ashʿarī theology which he described as "childish argumentations and unbounded speculations which have people believe in magic."[44] However, he excluded al-Ghazālī's theological thought by arguing that al-Ghazālī believed that "Ashʿarism is good for the common people."[45] Al-Nuʿmānī further argued that Islam is unique in its confirmation of the usual concept of reward and punishment in the hereafter as good for the common people. He strongly supported al-Ghazālī's view that reward and punishment are inalienable effects of good and bad deeds by saying that "hell is right inside you." Al-Nuʿmānī concluded "if you did not understand the meanings in this manner, then you did not get from the Quran anything except the

40 Murad, *Intellectual modernism* 5.
41 Ibid., 6.
42 Ibid., 14.
43 Ibid., 15.
44 Ibid., 21.
45 Ibid., 27.

crust, as the cattle get only the husk from the wheat."[46] In his mind, reward and punishment after death are in fact material expressions of spiritual things.[47]

Al-Nuʿmānī found in Rūmī's views a better and more convincing way of interpretation, and a clearer and more appealing presentation of faith. He preferred Rūmī's positive arguments on the question of resurrection and the imperishability of the soul. He was attracted by Rūmī's mystical interpretation of the plausibility of resurrection on the basis of the process of evolution in life, which al-Nuʿmānī saw as a Darwinian as well as a Quranic concept. According to this view, there is likely to come yet another, and better stage of life, in accordance with modern science that holds that matter and energy are indestructible. Body and soul will therefore only assume other forms.[48]

2.3 *Muḥammad Iqbāl's Reconstruction of Faith*

In his *Reconstruction of the Religious Thought in Islam*, the well-known poet and thinker Muḥammad Iqbāl (d. 1357/1938) analyzed these ideas further. In his comment on the verse "and everyone of them will come to Him singly on the Day of Judgment" (Q 19:95),[49] Iqbāl argued that the passage must be understood as a clear insight into the Islamic theory of salvation. Whatever the final fate of man, it does not mean the loss of individuality. He maintained that man's "unceasing reward" is his gradual growth in self-possession, in uniqueness, and intensity of activity as an ego. Iqbāl interprets the *barzakh* stage in the Quranic terminology as some kind of suspense between death and resurrection. Resurrection is not based, as in Christianity, on the evidence of the actual resurrection of a historic person. Islam, in Iqbāl's mind, seems to take resurrection as a universal phenomenon of life.[50]

In Iqbāl's philosophy, even the scene of "universal destruction" preceding the day of judgment cannot affect the perfect calmness of a full-grown human ego.[51] Life offers a scope for ego-activity, while death is the first test of the synthetic activity of the ego. There are no pleasurable and painful acts after death; there are only acts that sustain and dissolve the ego.[52]

---

46 Ibid., 45–6.

47 Ibid., 48–9.

48 Ibid., 52–3.

49 Quranic verses quoted from the translation of Yusuf Ali are available at http://www.islam101.com/quran/yusufAli/index.htm.

50 Iqbāl, *The reconstruction* 92.

51 Ibid., 93.

52 Ibid., 95.

Iqbāl defined the state of *barzakh* as not merely a passive state of expectation, but as one in which the ego catches a glimpse of fresh aspects of reality, and prepares to adjust itself to these aspects. The ego must continue to struggle until it is able to gather itself, and win resurrection. The resurrection is not an external event, but a continuation of a life process within the ego and nothing but a kind of stock-taking of the ego's past achievements and its future possibilities.[53] Iqbāl was aware of the difference of opinions among Muslim philosophers and theologians on the re-emergence of man's former physical state in the afterlife. He was impressed by the views of Shāh Walī Allāh, whom he considered the last great theologian of Islam. Iqbāl liked about Walī Allāh's interpretations the sense that resurrection involves at least some kind of physical medium suitable to the ego's new environment (discussed above).[54]

Iqbāl claimed that Quranic teachings confirm that the ego's re-emergence will bring him "sharp sight" (Q 50:22) whereby it will clearly see the self it built as "fate fastened around his neck." He clearly stated that paradise and hell were states, not localities. According to him, the descriptions of the hereafter in the Quran were visual representations of an inner fact, i.e., of a human character. Hell, in the words of the Quran, is "God's kindled fire which mounts above the hearts" "(It is) the Fire of (the Wrath of) Allah kindled (to a blaze). The which doth mount (Right) to the Hearts:" (Q 104:6–7) – the painful realization of one's failure as a man. Heaven is the joy of triumph over the forces of disintegration. There is no such thing as eternal damnation in Islam. Iqbāl's view about the "eternity" of hell resembles the view of Ibn al-Qayyim (see below). In his view, the word *khulūd* (eternity), is explained by the Quran itself as only referring to a period of time (Q 78:23). Time cannot be wholly irrelevant to the development of personality. Hell as conceived in the Quran is not a pit of everlasting torture inflicted by a vengeful God; it is a corrective experience, which makes a hardened ego once more sensitive to the living breeze of Divine Grace. In Iqbāl's definition heaven is no holiday, as life is one and continuous:

> [M]an marches always onward to receive ever fresh illuminations from an Infinite Reality, which every moment appears in a new glory. And the recipient of Divine illumination is not merely a passive recipient. Every act of a free ego creates a new situation, and thus offers further opportunities of creative unfolding.[55]

---

53 Ibid., 96.

54 Ibid., 97.

55 Ibid., 98.

3 Death and Resurrection in Islamic Reformist Theology

3.1 *Al-Afghānī's Critique of Sayyid Aḥmad Khān*

Sayyid Jamāl al-Dīn al-Afghānī (d. 1314/1897) was still living in India when the ideas of Sayyid Aḥmad Khān became widespread among highly-educated Muslims in that country. As a sharp reaction to Khān and his followers, he wrote a treatise in Persian under the title: *The Truth about the Neicheri (or Naturalists) Sect and an Explanation of the Neicheris*, which was later translated by his Egyptian student Muḥammad ʿAbduh under the name *An Answer to the Dahriyyīn (or Materialists)*. Whatever the political concerns behind al-Afghānī's treatise, in the present study we are mainly interested in his religious evaluation of Khān's eschatological interpretations.[56]

Al-Afghānī did not present a systematic theological or philosophical interpretation of eschatological concepts in Islam, but deemed that Khān's ideas demolished the "pillars of the castle of man's happiness." Al-Afghānī considered belief in the day of judgment as one of the motivating forces driving human beings to become trustworthy and truthful in life. In al-Afghānī's view, Khān and his Neicheri group propagated the belief that there is no life after death and that

> man is like a plant that grows in the spring and dries up in the summer, returning to the soil. The happy man is [one] who attains in this world animal appetites and pleasures. Because of this false opinion they gave currency to misfortunes of perfidy, treachery, deception, and embezzlement; they exhorted men to mean and vicious acts.[57]

In al-Afghānī's mind, because of their denial of these facts the Neicheris had believed communism, and held that all desirable things should be shared among people.[58]

Al-Afghānī maintained that the appearance of materialists and naturalists had undermined the great nations of the past. Former Greek and Persian civilizations vanished when those doctrines spread among their people, and their greatness and glory completely disappeared.[59] Al-Afghānī claimed that the superiority and greatness of the Muslim community remained until the fourth

---

56 About al-Afghānī's philosophy, see Keddie, *An Islamic response*. Cf. Ali, Sayyid Jamaluddin Afghani.

57 Keddie, *An Islamic response* 148.

58 Ibid., 149.

59 Ibid., 154–7.

century when the Neicheris, or materialists, appeared among them. According to al-Afghānī, in Egypt, for instance, they appeared under the name of Bāṭiniyya or those who know the hidden. He refers here to the Muslim groups throughout Islamic history that advocated the esoteric meaning in the scriptures and the law. The term *bāṭinī* served as a pejorative name for the Ismaʿilis, especially by their opponents.[60] For al-Afghānī, they first created doubt in the Muslims about their beliefs. For a period of time, they strove, secretly, to corrupt the manners of Muslims till one of the followers of the well-known Bāṭiniyya sect publicly declared that

> at the time of the Resurrection there will be no duties incumbent upon mankind, neither external nor internal ones. The Resurrection consists of the rising of the True Redeemer, and I am the True Redeemer. After this let everyone do whatever he wants since obligations have been removed.[61]

Throughout his response, al-Afghānī did not mention Khān and his group directly by name. He despised them for "collaborating" with the British who were teaching their people slavery instead of freedom and putting obstacles before their progress. When living in Paris, in 1884, he started to mention them directly by name. He believed that the British had planted them in the country in order to destroy religious belief among Muslims. Aḥmad Khān hovered around the English in order to obtain some advantage for himself and his group. He called himself a Neicheri and naturalist and began to seduce the "frivolous young men" in India. By crying "Nature, Nature," he attempted to convince people that Europe had progressed in civilization, power, and strength by rejecting religion and explaining things in terms of nature. Oriental materialists, such as Khān, were not like materialists of Europe; for whoever abandons religion in Western countries retains the zeal to guard his people from the attacks of foreigners. Khān and his followers invited their people not only to reject religion, but also to disparage their fatherland and made their people consider foreign domination insignificant.[62] They drew their swords to cut the throats of Muslims, while weeping for them and crying: "we kill you only out of compassion and pity for you, and seeking to improve you and make your lives comfortable."[63]

---

60 See, for example, Walker, Bāṭiniyya; Halm, *Kosmologie*.

61 Keddie, *An Islamic response* 157. On this event see the discussion by Velji, Apocalyptic rhetoric, in the present publication.

62 Keddie, *An Islamic response* 175–8.

63 Ibid., 179.

3.2 *Muḥammad Abduh's Renewed Theology*

The Egyptian Mufti Muḥammad ʿAbduh (d. 1323/1905) discussed eschatological issues in different places. In his formative years, he referred to four main Islamic interpretations of the state of the soul after death in his *Risālat al-wāridāt* (Treatise on thoughts that come to one's mind):[64] 1) the first group argued that the soul does not exist outside of the body, and will cease to exist after the body's death. 2) Another group believed that it will continue to exist and will remain in full possession of its faculties after its separation from the body. 3) The third group, the *ḥukamāʾ*, or philosophers, agreed with the previous group about the independent existence of the soul from the body, but they argued that the separation between the two is permanent. The soul remains dependent on God and finds its existence in *ʿālam al-taʿalluq wa-l-takhalluq*,[65] an Islamic theological term that refers to two aspects of the divine names: active and passive attributes of God. *Takhalluq* shows the multiplicity of the divine attributes as manifested in the phenomenal world, whereas the relationship between the active side and the passive one is called *taʿalluq*.[66] The relationship between God and the soul is "like the son of a king who desires to reach the rank (*martaba*) of his father but because of his inability he withdraws to some aspects in which his power becomes manifest."[67] Therefore, the more the soul progresses intellectually and morally, the more it will be rewarded. Its failure to fulfill its role leads to punishment and pain.[68] 4) The Sufis, as the fourth group, understand the fate of the soul after death in a way similar to that of the philosophers, but they couched their understanding in Sufi terminology. The philosophers believed that the status of the soul is determined by its rational and moral abilities, but in the Sufi terms, the status of the soul depends on its progress on the mystical path that leads toward mystical union with its creator.[69]

According to Scharbrodt, although ʿAbduh does not explicitly identify himself with any of these groups and their respective beliefs, he certainly follows a metaphorical understanding of individual eschatology as developed by philosophers and mystics. He understood Quranic descriptions of the afterlife

64 There are various discussions about the ascription of the treatise to Muḥammad ʿAbduh. Some authors argue that it was not his work because it covered very complex theological issues that ʿAbduh would not have been familiar with at the time (he was very young and had not yet received his diploma from al-Azhar). See Scharbrodt, The Salafiyya and Sufism 95–7.

65 Ibid., 108.

66 Sawai, *The divine names* 15–6.

67 Scharbrodt, The Salafiyya and Sufism 108.

68 Ibid.

69 Ibid.

symbolically – whether in rational terms like those used by the philosophers or in spiritual terms used by the mystics. In his view, the fate of the soul in the afterlife depends on its spiritual and intellectual progress. Reward and punishment are characterized as the consequence of the degree of perfection the soul achieves.[70]

In fact, ʿAbduh was cautious about raising these earlier discussions in his Quranic exegesis entitled *al-Manār* or in his theological writings. In his *Risālat al-tawḥīd* (Treatise of unity), ʿAbduh repeated the same typology, but did not give preference to any of them. Instead, he developed other views on the belief in the afterlife as part of man's need of a prophetic mission. In addition, he stressed that among the nations, both ancient and modern, there are many competing ideas about the return of the soul. These schools of thought differ with regard to the nature of future bliss and torment, the delight of the life beyond, and how to achieve happiness or avert eternal punishment. For him, the human soul is immortal and lives on after its separation from the body; and the final death is a kind of womb of hiddenness.[71] ʿAbduh went beyond the old theological "disputatious" territory "where many thoughts and ideas jostle together."[72] According to him, human minds are not always able to know God or the life to come by themselves. Though they share a common sense of submission to a power higher than their own and most people feel that there is another realm beyond this one, heathenism has disordered their thoughts and diverted them from the path of blessedness. A few people, those to whom God has given perfect reason and the light of perception despite their not having the boon of prophetic guidance and example, will reach a proper understanding of the nature of the life to come.[73]

Moreover, ʿAbduh claimed that the human universal sense of the other world was not a mental aberration. In his view, intelligence and intuition ensure that this life-span is not the sum total of man's existence, since "man takes off this body of flesh, as he does his clothes, and is alive still in another guise, though its nature be beyond our ken."[74]

ʿAbduh maintained that there are

> intuitive feelings [that] stimulate the spirits of men to search into this eternal world and to anticipate how it will be when it is reached, and

---

70 Ibid., 110.

71 ʿAbduh, *Theology of unity* 81–2. Cf. Vatikiotis, Muḥammad ʿAbduh 65.

72 ʿAbduh, *Theology of unity* 81.

73 Ibid., 74.

74 Ibid., 82.

> how too they are to come to it. The answer, both as to what and wither, is obscure and illusive. We are conscious of inadequacy in the development of our minds in face of the issues of this brief existence here. They do not suffice to give us the right directions or make good of our need for teaching and guidance. We must appeal to the gathered judgment of ages in assessing our thoughts and correcting our views.... We are still in unresolved certainty about this earthly life, yearning for a quiet assurance still far to seek.[75]

Human beings have no power whereby they are able to understand the hidden store of fate. Rational study or intuition could hardly determine the link between the two worlds, in ʿAbduh's view. The two worlds mingle within us alone. More investigation of "temporal sciences cannot attain to assurance about the realities of the future realm."[76]

In ʿAbduh's thinking, prophets were sent by God to tell people about their fate and what they should do in order to reach a good fate. Some people might ask why God did not place this knowledge or "supernatural mercy" in men as an instinctive capacity to guide them to action and to the path leading to the goal in the life beyond. In answer, ʿAbduh stated that such questions come from "intellectual pretension" and the "ignorance" of human nature. He argued that,

> not everybody is ready and able to cope naturally with every condition, but needs study and evidence as a basis on which he can deal with existence. Were man to operate in this instinctive way in respect of his needs, he would be like animals not like himself. Indeed, he would become a sort of animal, or even like the ant and the bee, or one of the angels who are not of this world of ours.[77]

3.3 *Rashīd Riḍā's Puritan Interpretation of Eschatology*

In various places in his reformist journal *al-Manār*, the Syrio-Egyptian reformist Muḥammad Rashīd Riḍā (d. 1354/1935) touched upon different issues related to the afterlife. Many readers of his journal raised questions in this regard, which he published in his *fatwā* section. One of the early examples was a question from Cairo concerning al-Ghazālī's section on the afterlife in his *Iḥyāʾ ʿulūm al-dīn* (*The Revitalization of the Religious Sciences*). Were issues like the questioning and punishment by two angels in the grave, the bridge (*al-ṣirāṭ*)

75 Ibid., 83.
76 Ibid.
77 Ibid., 85.

spanning hell, and intercession (*shafāʿa*) in the hereafter, considered proven by authentic traditions? If a Muslim does not believe in these things, would he be considered an unbeliever? In his answer, Riḍā noted that al-Ghazālī mentioned these concepts from an Ashʿarī point of view, but he did not declare that those who disagreed with this doctrine were unbelievers. In other works, al-Ghazālī was of the opinion that the faith of a believer would not be affected, even if he lived and died without knowing about such controversial issues in theology. Riḍā urged Muslims not to investigate the contents of these hidden matters deeply, but to believe only in what had been proven by definitive or decisive (*qaṭʿī*) texts.[78] Riḍā also discouraged his readers from seeking theological clarifications about far-fetched questions, such as the abode of souls after death. The same held true for the location of paradise and hell, which Riḍā evaluated as real things, whose locations were not known.[79]

Despite his faith in the issue of *ʿadhāb al-qabr* (the torments of the grave), Riḍā did not give it any priority from a theological point of view. Man should leave these issues to God's knowledge.[80] One should believe in the authentic traditions reported in this regard, but the reality of the questioning by the angels was not known. Those who interpret these traditions metaphorically or even deny them, were not to be regarded as unbelievers.[81] Riḍā maintained that one should follow the *salafī* path by believing in the conditions of the hereafter without delving into philosophical issues: "there is nothing more despicable than disputations about the conditions of the hereafter which cannot be supported by reason or sense."[82] It sufficed Riḍā to cite al-Ghazālī's comparison of those experiencing the punishments of the grave with the state of a sleeper who feels pain or a snake's bite in his dream, while other people around him do not see any effect of pain on him.[83]

Another interesting point arose with regard to the process of the human body decaying. When its constituent parts become mixed with other elements, and plants and trees absorb its substances, then other people come and eat such trees and plants, how will all of these elements be resurrected? In Riḍā's view, religion proves that there shall be life after death. People, composed of body and soul, will also be people in their second life, which is an advanced form of life for good people but a worse form of life for bad people. The bodily

---

78 Riḍā, *al-Manār* 5 (1903), 911–2. See also 13 (1910), 104; 28 (1927), 504–7; 32 (1932), 268–89.

79 Riḍā, *al-Manār* 10 (1907), 442–3. See also 19 (1916), 282; 30 (1929), 185–92.

80 Riḍā, *al-Manār* 5 (1903), 945–6.

81 Riḍā, *al-Manār* 6 (1903), 671.

82 Riḍā, *al-Manār* 8/7 (1905), 256–7.

83 See ʿAbduh and Riḍā, *Tafsīr al-manār* xi, 191–3.

and biological substances of man change regularly during his lifetime, while he remains the same in his morals and behavior. In that sense, the substance of a body during its second life in the hereafter will be the same as it was in its first life. To say that all substances that enter the human body will be resurrected as they were during the first life was, according to Riḍā, a form of futile and impossible philosophical reasoning or speculation. If it were true, the shape of each resurrected human body would appear on the day of resurrection in gigantic measures. In his view, the next life would not be on earth, because it was indicated in the Quran that "One day the earth will be changed to a different earth, and so will be the heavens" (Q 14:48). The world will be destroyed when the earth hits another cosmic body and all planets are dispersed and return to nebula form (Q 56:4–6; 82:1–2). The last resurrection will take place on another, larger planet or world; and from there the eternal souls will take their new substances.[84]

In his journal, Riḍā adopted Ibn al-Qayyim's view regarding the duration of the hellfire. Ibn al-Qayyim was of the view that the fire does not function as retribution, according to the classical doctrine; rather it serves a therapeutic function, to cleanse people of their sins, even the sins of unbelief (*kufr*) and associationism (*shirk*). According to him, hell would be of no profit to God because He would not gain anything from punishing human beings. Therefore, the eternal punishment of the wretched would not increase the blessedness of God's beloved, and certainly would be of no benefit to those who suffered it.[85]

When a group of Riḍā's readers blamed him for his defense of Ibn al-Qayyim's views, he strongly argued that there was no consensus among Muslim theologians regarding the perpetuity of hellfire. Riḍā stated that Ibn al-Qayyim mentioned all theological opinions without holding any of them as definite, rather he ascribed all knowledge of this issue to God Himself. Riḍā maintained that he did not discuss anything secret and all books presenting the different views on this issue were available to everyone. As for the verse "Allah forgiveth not that partners should be set up with Him; but He forgiveth anything else" (Q 4:48, 116), Riḍā stated that this confirms that the punishment of unbelievers is self-evident and inevitable, but it does not indicate its endlessness.

84 Riḍā, *al-Manār* 7 (1904), 54–6. For more about *al-Manār*'s analysis of this issue, see *al-Manār* 11 (1908), 448–51.

85 Ibn al-Qayyim depended on reports that cast doubt on the eternity of punishment in the hellfire. One example was a report from the Prophet's Companion Abū Hurayra conveying a message similar to that of ʿUmar: "There will come to Hell a day when no one will remain in it," Hoover, Islamic universalism 183. See Ibn al-Qayyim, *Ḥādī l-arwāḥ*. Cf. Abrahamov, The creation and duration 87–102; Perlmann, Ibn Qayyim 330–7.

He argued that profound research or investigation into these issues was not a threat to the belief of Muslims. Riḍā criticized Muslim preachers and traditional scholars who disseminated weak and inauthentic traditions related to the hereafter among common Muslims, such as one indicating that God would save six thousand persons from hellfire every night during the month of Ramadan. Those preachers usually presented such issues as fundamentals of the faith. Some would even go further by claiming that the number of saved people during Ramadan was larger than the number of Muslim inhabitants on earth, especially during the time of the Prophet. By means of such discussions, Riḍā did not intend to address "atheists," but his aim was to clarify such issues in the minds "Muslim doubters" who still believed that the world had an almighty, forgiving and compassionate God.[86]

An Englishman once asked Riḍā: "Will it be suitable for God, the Greatest, to punish the weak human being for committing sins which are actually the essence of his fragility?" In his answer, Riḍā made it clear that unbelief and the rejection of God's bounty on humans by committing sins was contrary to His laws and would damage one's inherent consciousness and contaminate his soul. Punishment in the afterlife would therefore be a natural effect of man's corruption on earth, just as any disease is a natural result of man's disobedience of the doctor's advice and health instructions. In that sense, the reason for punishment is an interior matter emanating from man's own acts.[87]

Riḍā did not reject entirely the signs preceding the day of judgment that were reported in authentic prophetic traditions. However, he interpreted some of these events according to the spirit of his age. He explained the appearance of *dajjālūn* (or imposters) by claiming prophecy as one of these signs that had already happened, as in the cases of the Bahā'iyya and Aḥmadiyya. The Prophet's foretelling about the shrinking of time (*taqārub al-zamān*) was another sign that was observed in his time in the form of modern means of transport, such as trains, cars, and planes. Likewise, the prophetic report about the increase in killing might refer to the Turkish aggression on the Arabs and the military machinery that killed more than ten million people during World War I. Regarding the sign of some people boasting about their ability to construct tall buildings, Riḍā asserted that this had already occurred in the shape of modern skyscrapers during the early twentieth century.[88] The same held true for the conversation between the dwellers of paradise and hellfire

---

86 Riḍā, *al-Manār* 22 (1921), 315–20. See also 22 (1921), 379–89 and 553–60. Riḍā re-evaluated the same issue in his Quran exegesis, see 'Abduh and Riḍā, *Tafsīr al-manār* viii, 58–86.

87 'Abduh and Riḍā, *Tafsīr al-manār* xi, 262–3.

88 Ibid., ix, 401–3.

(Q 7:44), which was supported by modern knowledge in Riḍā's view. He argued that the meaning of the verse might have been strange for early Muslims, but in the early twentieth century telecommunications prove that people from remote distances can communicate by telephone and telegraph. At the time of writing his Quranic exegesis Riḍā had also been told that people in the West were about to invent audio-visual instruments for the same purpose.[89]

Nevertheless, Riḍā maintained that the majority of traditions pointing to the signs of the hereafter were reports of meaning only; there was no agreement among the narrators on their literal wording. In his evaluation, throughout Islamic history many people, such as the *zanādiqa* (atheists or heretics) and the Umayyad and ʿAbbasid supporters of racial and social solidarity (*ahl al-ʿaṣabiyya*), had fabricated many of these traditions.[90] However, Riḍā did not doubt the core of authenticity of such traditions regarding the coming of the Dajjāl (or Antichrist), but he was skeptical about the details mentioned in these traditions. He believed that these details were nothing but interpolations of Israelite origin.[91]

In 1904 and in 1924 Riḍā received questions from two readers in Egypt concerning an anonymous nineteenth-century eschatological document (which is still circulating among some Muslims on the Internet nowadays) reported to have been the dream of a certain *shaykh* Aḥmad, a caretaker of the Prophet Muḥammad's tomb in Medina.[92] This *shaykh* Aḥmad claimed to have been told by the Prophet that "the Day of Judgment was at hand; it was his interlocutor's duty to spread the word. Various blessings would accrue to those who copied the message; damnation would befall all who chose to ignore it."[93] Riḍā saw the document for the first time among his father's papers, in Syria, when he was a child learning to read and write. Initially he was interested in it and believed in its authenticity. Later, Riḍā described this "will" of *shaykh* Aḥmad as a foolish lie, which naive common people would easily believe. The inventor of

89 Ibid., viii, 374–5.

90 Ibid., viii, 418–20.

91 Ibid., viii, 403–13. About the *isrāʾīliyāt*, see for example, Schützinger, *Ursprung*; Albayrak, *Qurʾanic narrative*; Albayrak, Isrāʾīliyyāt 39–65; Nettler, Early Islam 1–14.

92 See, for example, http://www.bdr130.net/vb/t792318.html; http://www.muslmh.com/vb/t148485.html; http://www.jarash-uni.com/vb/forum4/thread1281.html; cf. http://www.qaradawi.net/site/topics/printArticle.asp?cu_no=2&item_no=6158&version=1&template_id=232&parent_id=17; http://www.binbaz.org.sa/mat/17886.

93 Katz, Shaykh Aḥmad's dream 157–80. In his advice to the Dutch government, C.S. Hurgronje mentioned this will, which Indonesian pilgrims carried back home to the archipelago. He published his Dutch translation in *De Indische Gids* (July 1884). C. Snouck Hurgronje, *Adviezen* 3, 1902.

this document was from the common people, as the language was archaic and silly. Those who fabricated this continue to use the name of *shaykh* Aḥmad, as if he were the "eternal" caretaker of the Prophet's tomb without regard to the change of time and governments. Some visitors to Medina ask about this *shaykh*, but do not find anyone by this name.[94]

3.4 *Al-Qaraḍāwī's Popularization of Eschatology for Common Muslims*

In his well-known television program *al-Sharīʿa wa-l-ḥayāt* (Sharīʿa and life) on Al-Jazeera, the Egyptian Muslim reformist Yūsuf al-Qaraḍāwī (b. 1345/1926) has popularized the events related to the day of judgment. He agrees that the destruction of the world at the end of life will challenge all technological discoveries in modern time. He accepts minor and major signs of the Hour, and compares the resurrection of the body with the medical achievements of cloning. Medical and biological scientists are now able to clone new bodies from a tiny cell. The *ʿajab al-dhanab* (incorruptible coccyges or a small bone at the end of the spine), mentioned in some traditions, might refer to a cell, like those used in the process of cloning, which is the origin of this new life. In his opinion, the way of resurrection is beyond the perception of human beings; it is like electricity, which nobody sees, though its results are perceptible everywhere. The location of resurrection will be in a new world and under a new sky. Al-Qaraḍāwī does not reject the phenomenon mentioned in the traditions regarding the day of resurrection. For example, he asserts that everyone will read the roll of his deeds recorded by the "divine registration pen" or, also in his words, that taken by the "divine candid camera" that records all acts and sayings in audiovisual form.[95] This is exactly what classical theologians and philosophers meant by their views that man would not find his deeds, which perish, in the afterlife, but he will find their "pictures." The Quranic phrase "Read thine (own) record" (Q 17:14) would mean, in al-Qaraḍāwī's interpretation: Look at the recorded "tape" or the "pictures" of your acts. Therefore, early Muslim theologians claimed that the book would be read by everyone, including illiterate people; all people would thus watch their acts and rehearse their own sayings. Al-Qaraḍāwī described the *mīzān* (Scale) as a thermometer that will measure one's deeds like the temperature of water and air is measured, or as a counter measures electricity or air pressure.[96]

Like Riḍā, al-Qaraḍāwī accepted Ibn al-Qayyim's view on the eternity of hell. In al-Qaraḍāwī's understanding, Ibn al-Qayyim's view could be the most

---

94 Riḍā, *al-Manār* 7 (1904), 614–5; 25 (1924), 416–20.

95 Al-Qaraḍāwī, Yawm al-ḥisāb.

96 Ibid.

excellent answer to the philosophical "allegations" made by atheists and materialists against God's mercy. In the end, the perishing of hell is something related to God's will.[97]

In al-Qaraḍāwī's mind, people in the modern age might see the minor signs preceding the hereafter in the changing social and economic situation of the world. For example, it was reported in some prophetic traditions that the Hour will approach when markets will draw closer toward each other (*taqārub al-aswāq*). Al-Qaraḍāwī argues that Muslims in the past might not have been aware of such things, but they did not witness what we do nowadays. In the present age, people can see the interrelatedness of markets clearly; London, Hong Kong and New York are not physically close, but are tied through the virtual world of the Internet.[98]

As for the major signs of the Hour, al-Qaraḍāwī accepts the theory of the Indian Muslim scholar Mawlānā Abū l-Kalām Āzād (d. 1377/1958) who suggested that the figure of Dhū l-Qarnayn mentioned in the Quran was Cyrus the Great (d. 530 BCE) and that Gog and Magog were the Mongols who attacked the Persian and Indian civilizations, and then attempted to destroy the Muslim rule of Baghdad and Central Asia.[99] Meanwhile, al-Qaraḍāwī maintains a common Muslim belief that the Dajjāl (Antichrist) will appear in person and be killed by Jesus. Moreover, he rejects the metaphorical interpretation of the Muslim convert Muhammad Asad (Leopold Weiss) that the Antichrist was actually a reference to Western civilization.[100] Al-Qaraḍāwī was of the view that everyone will be addressed in his grave and on the day of judgment in the language they could understand, and not only in Arabic as some argued.[101] As for those living in remote areas who did not receive the message of Islam or who received it only in a distorted way, they would all be saved in the afterlife.[102]

3.5 *Rational Mysticism: The Case of Said Nursi*

In the tenth word of *Risale-i Nur* (Treatise of light), the outstanding Turkish scholar Said Nursi (d. 1379/1960) elucidated what he considered the "sacred supreme evidences" of the resurrection of the dead as related to the existence and unity of God, the function of prophethood, the importance of man, and

97 Al-Qaraḍāwī, ʿAlāmāt al-sāʿa.
98 Ibid.
99 Ibid., Cf. Nadwi, *Faith*.
100 Al-Qaraḍāwī, ʿAlāmāt al-sāʿa, see Asad's chapter on the Dajjāl in *Road* 282–311.
101 Al-Qaraḍāwī, al-Īmān.
102 Ibid.

the necessity of the Eternal Creator of this transitory world.[103] A full analysis of Nursi's ideas in this regard falls outside the scope of the present study, but a few examples of his views will suffice to place him in the context of the new *kalām* movement.

In his lengthy analysis, Nursi used metaphors, comparisons, and stories in simple and common language and a straightforward style in order to facilitate comprehension and to show what he saw as rationality, and the coherence of the truths of Islam: "the meaning of the stories is contained in the truths that conclude them; each story is like an allusion pointing to its concluding truth. Therefore, they are not mere fictitious tales, but veritable truths."[104]

Nursi based his arguments of such proofs on the meaning of certain of the divine beautiful names. In addition, he confirmed that belief in the hereafter is essential for human social life and brings numerous comprehensive spiritual benefits. For example, children, who comprise one fourth of the human race, in his view could endure an awesome and tragic death by ensuring them that their lost beloveds exist in paradise after death. With this idea, they gain spiritual strength in their weak and delicate bodies, and find hope that permits them to live joyfully, despite their vulnerable spiritual disposition. By thinking of paradise, the child might say, for example, "My little brother or friend has died and become a bird in paradise. He is playing there, and leading a life finer than ours." Otherwise, the death of children and adults all around them would negatively affect their inner faculties – spirit, heart, and intellect – and they would either be destroyed or become like wretched animals.[105] The belief in the resurrection also benefits old people, who might find some consolation, tranquility, and comfort while experiencing the painful and awesome despair that arises from the anticipation of death and separation. The same holds true for young men, who can restrain their turbulent feelings and tempestuous souls and passions from committing transgression, oppression, and destruction; otherwise they would bring humanity down to a lowly and bestial state.[106]

Nursi deduced his ultimate faith in the resurrection from the "light" of the prophethood of Muḥammad and the Quran. If they were to depart from the cosmos and vanish, the cosmos would "die" and "lose its sanity, and the globe would lose its sense and its head. Its dizzy, uncomprehending head would collide with a planet, and the end of the world would result."[107]

---

103 Nursi, *From the Risale-i Nur* i, 59–132.

104 Ibid., i, 59.

105 Ibid., i, 109–10.

106 Ibid., i, 110–1.

107 Ibid., i, 123.

Moreover, Nursi argued that the reality of resurrection emanated from the divine beautiful names. For instance, the hereafter, as a manifestation of the names *al-Ḥakīm* (Wise) and *al-ʿĀdil* (Just) was the gate to God's "wisdom and justice." According to this view, man cannot experience the true essence of His

> justice in this transient world; it is for this reason that matters are postponed for a supreme tribunal. For true justice requires that man, this apparently petty creature, should be rewarded and punished, not in accordance with his pettiness, but in accordance with the magnitude of his crime, the importance of his nature and the greatness of his function. Since this passing and transient world is far from manifesting such wisdom and justice for man, who is created for eternity, of necessity there will be an eternal hell and everlasting Paradise.[108]

In one of his comparisons, Nursi maintains that life resembles a flower, which for a short time smiles and looks at us, and then hides behind the veil of annihilation. It departs like a word leaving your mouth. By entrusting thousands of its fellows to men's ears, the word leaves behind meanings in men's minds. The flower, too, expresses its meaning and thus fulfills its function, and departs. But it departs and leaves its apparent form in the memory of everything that sees it, its inner essence in every seed. It is as if each memory and seed were a camera to record the adornment of the flower, or a means for its perpetuation. If such be the case with an object at the simplest level of life, it can be readily understood that man, the highest form of life and the possessor of an eternal soul, is closely tied to eternity.[109] In Nursi's understanding, there is no truer report, no firmer claim, no more apparent truth in the whole world than the reality of the afterlife: "the world is without doubt a field, and the resurrection a threshing-floor, a harvest. Paradise and hell are each storehouses for the grain."[110]

Nursi made another interesting comparison between the state of affairs in the hereafter and circumstances that have been formed and arranged by way of imitation and representation. Brief gatherings and dispersions are arranged in this life at great expense merely for the sake of taking pictures that can be shown in the cinema in the hereafter. So too, one of the reasons for our passage through individual and social life in this world, for a brief time, is to enable pictures to be taken and images formed, to enable the result of our deeds to be

108 Ibid., i, 87.

109 Ibid.

110 Ibid., i, 95.

registered and recorded, to be displayed on a day of accounting, and be shown at a vast gathering, to yield the fruit of supreme happiness. Nursi deduced this image and meaning from the Prophet's saying: "This world is the tillage for the hereafter."[111]

Finally, Nursi concluded that "the hundred and twenty-four thousand prophets" have unanimously reported, partly on the basis of direct vision and partly on the basis of absolute certainty, that the hereafter exists and that all beings will be taken to the hereafter as the Creator has firmly promised. Similarly, "the one hundred and twenty-four million saints" who confirm the reports of the prophets through unveiling and witnessing give testimony to the existence of the hereafter in the form of certain knowledge, and also bear testimony to the existence of the hereafter.[112]

4 Eschatology in Neo-Modernist Thinking

4.1 *Fazlur Rahman and Quranic Ethics*

Fazlur Rahman (d. 1408/1988) adopted a philosophy similar to his Indo-Pakistani predecessors. In his view, the Quran's underlying picture of the joy of paradise and the distress of hell reveals that there will come an hour (*sāʿa*) when every human being will be shaken into a unique self-awareness of his own deeds by starkly facing "his doings, not-doings and misdoings and accept the judgment upon them."[113] Fazlur Rahman noted that the Quranic concept of the end of life provides the vision necessary to drive one to *taqwā* (piety).[114]

Fazlur Rahman argued that the Quran refers to *al-ākhira* (the end) as the moment of truth (Q 79:34–5), when everybody will find his deepest self, fully excavated from the debris of extrinsic and immediate concerns.[115] The Quran's use of the term "weighing" was to be understood as sarcastic, as it addressed Meccan merchants that all deeds in the hereafter shall be "weighed," not in gold, silver or any other trade commodity. Fazlur Rahman blamed the Muʿtazilīs for their literal interpretation of this "weighing" and their development of a strict *quid pro quo* theory of retribution. Instead of accepting God's infinite mercy as

111 Ibid., i, 99.

112 Ibid., i, 131.

113 Rahman, *Major themes* 106.

114 Berry, *Islam and modernity* 64.

115 Rahman, *Major themes* 106.

real, they did grave violence to religion by trying to get around this and explain it away.[116]

Fazlur Rahman pointed out that the Quranic statement about the record of deeds, which will speak [and] will never be denied by their actors (Q 23:62), is an indication that what is in people's minds will be public such that people will not be able to hide their thoughts. The speaking of one's organs (Q 41:19–24) confirms that in a situation where one's mind becomes transparently public one's physical organs even begin to bear witness against oneself. Fazlur Rahman understood that the Quran required man to reach this state of mind and transparency of his heart in the course of this life, if he were to achieve success and not burn in hell.[117]

He pointed to the significance of the fact that the earth shall be given as an inheritance to those dwelling in the garden. The earth will not be destroyed, but transformed with a view to creating new forms of life and new levels of being.[118] Fazlur Rahman believed that the Quran makes it clear that the effect of punishment in hell is dependent upon the sensitivity of the guilty and therefore involves conscience. He argued that punishment is basically moral or spiritual, but the Quran, unlike Muslim philosophers, does not recognize a hereafter that will be peopled by disembodied souls. In philosophy and Sufism the term *nafs* came to mean soul as a substance separate from the body, but in the Quran it mostly means "himself," "herself," "themselves" or "inner person." Although the Quran does not affirm any purely spiritual heaven or hell, and the subject of reward and punishment is a person, its vivid portrayals of a blazing hell and garden are meant to convey these effects as real spiritual-physical feelings.[119] Fazlur Rahman claimed, however, that one has to consider the spiritual aspect of punishment and reward in the hereafter as primary. God's pleasure (*riḍwān*) will be the greatest success, while disbelievers and evildoers will earn His displeasure and alienation (*sakhṭ*) as their greatest punishment.[120] "The central endeavor of the Quran," Rahman wrote, "is for man to develop this keen insight here and now, when there is opportunity for action and progress for at the Hour of Judgment it will be too late to remedy the state of affairs; there one will be reaping, not sowing or nurturing."[121]

116 Ibid., 109.

117 Ibid., 109–10.

118 Berry, *Islam and modernity* 65.

119 Ibid., 112.

120 Ibid., 113.

121 Ibid., 120.

In their definition of reward and punishment in the hereafter as a continuation of the status of the human ego, Iqbāl and Fazlur Rahman indirectly reiterated the views of the famous Sufi Ibn ʿArabī (d. 638/1240), who maintained that the hereafter will be created eternally on the pattern of this world. The hereafter requires the creation of a world from this world but it will be sensible (not merely mental). In Ibn ʿArabī's words, by the mere existence of an idea, or imaginative impulse (*hamm*), of a violation, desire or appetite, all this shall become sensible.[122]

4.2 *Ḥasan Ḥanafī's Anthropological Understanding of Theology*

In his voluminous work *Min al-ʿaqīda ilā l-thawra* (From dogma to revolution), the Egyptian philosopher Ḥasan Ḥanafī (b. 1353/1935) described prophecy as the past and the evolution of humanity as part of history, whereas the hereafter represented its future.[123] Ḥanafī's point of departure for his philosophical analysis was that in the past such eschatological issues were dependent on imagination. He was, first of all, skeptical that the concept of *al-mubashsharūn bi-l-janna* (those who were given the glad tiding of entering paradise) might contradict this law.[124] Likewise, Ḥanafī criticized the concept of the *shafāʿa* (intercession). All reports relating that some believers will enter paradise without any judgment were in his view part of the "folklore fantasy" about heroism and were a response to the need of simple folk for a savior. The Prophet appeared in such reports as "a nation leader, a sheikh of a clan or the head of a community."[125] Intercession in that sense would make believers lax, believing they could "gain without effort," and this would therefore eliminate repentance (*tawba*) and man's motivation to save himself by means of own deeds in this life and by learning from trial and error.[126] Ḥanafī compared intercession in the hereafter with the idea of the Jews as the chosen people, and the doctrine of Jesus bearing the sins of believers.[127]

Ḥanafī defined the belief in death on three levels: 1) on the divine level as part of human belief in God's destiny, and an indication of the end of one's age on earth, 2) on the natural level by subjecting death to science, and 3) on the human level it defines death as the opposite of life and is part of the soul

122 Rahman, Dream 171.
123 Ḥanafī, *Min al-ʿaqīda* iv, 321.
124 Ibid., iv, 404–7.
125 Ibid., iv, 313–4.
126 Ibid., iv, 419.
127 Ibid., iv, 420.

abandoning the human body and taking another destination.[128] Ḥanafī criticized the classical theological representations of the angel of death, ʿAzrāʾīl, and his assistants taking the souls of those destined to die. In Ḥanafī's view, its personification is a suitable poetic image expressing man's anxiety about death; this was seen as more effective than merely putting it in a scientific description or a rational theorization of the event of death.[129] He also stated that theological discussions related to the interval of life in one's grave after death before resurrection, such as the return of souls to bodies afterward and the questioning of (dis)believers by the two angels, were beyond the arena of theological sciences and he criticized them as "folklore fantasy." Ḥanafī argued that those elements were probably remnants of ancient beliefs regarding life in the grave, as in the case of the pyramids, which were dwellings for dead bodies waiting for the return of their souls. They may also have resulted from a strong desire to defeat the idea of death and reduce the pain in the grave, while keeping the memory of the dead in the mind of his beloved.[130]

In Ḥanafī's understanding such beliefs were based on "weak traditions" which were not included in the earliest theological works. They were inserted in later theological books under a separate subject during times of social and cultural decay. The afterlife emerged as compensation for this life; and the focus came to be on the victory of soul after the defeat of the body and on a happy future instead of an agonizing present. Ḥanafī claimed that these reports were not *mutawātir* and did not offer any rational or theoretical certainty.[131] He understood that the logic behind such doctrines was the strength of self-censorship and fear of God, but "folklore fantasy" reduced the angels to a kind of police interrogation and torture like that of an intelligence service. Ḥanafī noted that the two angels, who will appear in the grave after death, are references to particular meanings and these were later personified in the figures of Munkar and Nakīr.[132] Pain in the grave after death was part of the "folklore imagination of darkness, silent and stagnant air, rotten smell, loneliness, isolation and cheerlessness. It expresses a real human experience in the present life which he overthrows upon the unseen world."[133]

Ḥanafī's tone is at times sarcastic about the narratives reported about the state of the dead in the grave. For example, in his discussion of the tradition

128 Ibid., iv, 428.

129 Ibid., iv, 437–40.

130 Ibid., iv, 440–61.

131 Ibid., iv, 461–2.

132 Ibid., iv, 463–5.

133 Ibid., iv, 477.

that the ground sympathized with Fāṭima, the mother of ʿAlī, because the Prophet was reported to have put his shirt on her body after her burial in order that the hellfire not touch her, Ḥanafī ironically inquired:

> Would this shirt remain till the Day of Resurrection? What is the intercession of such a shirt? [This is] like a policeman who put his badge on the wall and went away, while his soldiers were standing in front of it with no movement. It [the badge] would appear as an alternative and symbol of him in order to keep the order in his absence. Why Fāṭima, the mother of ʿAlī, and not Fāṭima his wife, or ʿAlī himself or his children?![134]

Ḥanafī described the metaphysical supposition of physical resurrection as based on the identity of the human being and his relation to the world. The human being is the microcosm, while the world appears as the macrocosm. The destruction and revival of this "tiny world," represented in the death of man, is related to the destruction of the larger world. Once the reconstruction of the larger world happens, the second individual state of human resurrection follows.[135] Ḥanafī claimed that the scenes of resurrection in theological works appear to be dynamic in order to reflect a sense of the continuation of life and the accidental nature of death. Therefore, resurrection is an emotional event that represents the moment of awakening as the opposite of the moment of death and silence.[136] He believed that later Muslim theologians depended on "Sufi imaginations" in their divisions and descriptions of the events on the day of resurrection.[137]

As for the idea of a merely spiritual resurrection, Ḥanafī argued that this was based on a dualistic imagination of the world in which the state of the body is devalued while the position of the soul is emphasized. The emphasis on the goodness of the soul over the evil nature of the body reflects a puritan image of the world. This dualism was, in Ḥanafī's mind, a "childish" conception of the world, since it was dependent solely on the concept of good and evil and reward and punishment. A mature and reasonable human being does good and avoids evil for its own sake, without expecting any reward or punishment. This view is also based on hatred and not love because the "other" will never be able to reach the same spiritual resurrection as the "self." Sufis deny the punishment of others because they love all human beings, while others desire to save

134 Ibid., iv, 472.
135 Ibid., iv, 487.
136 Ibid., iv, 508.
137 Ibid., iv, 504.

people by means of their own suffering. In that sense man appears as a hero who would save the world; he is the center of the world and the pivot of history. Bodily suffering then becomes pleasurable, as a means of reaching a greater rejoicing by refining the soul.[138] Ḥanafī maintained that the dualism between body and soul is a pessimistic, capitalist, and racial conception of the hereafter, one that stresses that there is no hope in this world, but man should seek his happiness in the outside world. It expresses the dialectics between victory and defeat and becomes more apparent when society is weak. Competition moves from earth to heaven and from this world to the hereafter.[139]

Ḥanafī analyzed the *ʿalāmāt* (signs) of the hereafter and the events on and after the day of judgment as part of what he continuously categorized as "folklore fantasy." In his view, these signs were inserted into Islamic theology in order to complete the doctrinal array so that Islamic dogma would be as significant as Jewish and Christian theology. Ḥanafī argued that the signs mentioned in the Quran do not tell exactly when the day of judgment will happen; they are merely scenes that combine human facts and cosmological events. He believed that the hour would certainly come, but its precise knowledge is only known to God. The purpose of the Quranic descriptions was not to tell the actual time of the judgment, but rather to urge people to prepare for it and to perceive well that their time will end.[140]

Ḥanafī concluded that the classical theological treatment of the concept of resurrection was nothing but a reflection of the burden of the unknown future of human beings in that time time by stressing a sense of confidence or fear for that future. For that reason classical texts preserve artistic images of it in order to give value judgments. The meanings of these portrayals expose the essence of human experience in the future. According to him these texts do not convey material realities, but reveal emotional realities that express the structure of human existence. It would be wrong to interpret them as quantitative realities. They should be understood as a means of cultivating human behavior and influencing it from the very beginning. In Ḥanafī's own words, eternity is pure human desire expressing man's ambition in bypassing his perishing. In believing in his eternity the human will continue to strive for his perfection.[141]

---

138 Ibid., iv, 526.
139 Ibid., iv, 527.
140 Ibid., iv, 551.
141 Ibid., iv, 605–7.

5 Conclusion

Modern Muslim scholars of the new renewal movement of theology considered classical Islamic notions about death and eschatology as an arena vulnerable to scientific, materialistic, and positivistic challenges. They therefore attempted to analyze classical eschatological subjects in modern philosophical and scientific terms.

Influenced by mystical and philosophical ideas, Indo-Pakistani modernist theologians agreed that "the physical body plays no role in the immediate life of an individual after death."[142] Shāh Walī Allāh used the idea of the *ʿālam al-mithāl* as developed by medieval Muslim mystics in order to rationalize traditional eschatological images. By employing what Fazlur Rahman called a "philosophy of mediationism," Walī Allāh's eschatological thought is pervaded by the idea of synthesis, wherein contradictions in reality are resolved by establishing proper and binding relationships.[143] Khān followed the same path by harmonizing this doctrine with the idea of naturalism. In addition, the pioneers of this approach were sometimes critical of classical views on eschatology. Shiblī l-Nuʿmānī's critique of Ashʿarī theology came as a result of his argument that mystical ideas should be taken as "useful" parts of authentic theology. In rationalizing these theological parts with modern science, these scholars were not concerned with the consequences of events in the afterlife, but were attempting to reconcile the traditional dogma on eschatology with the findings of modern science and nature.

The reformist approach stressed the ethical values of eschatological tenets for Muslim life. However, there were certainly common points between their writings and those of classical and medieval traditionalists in their understanding of the life after death. Although ʿAbduh, Riḍā, and al-Qaraḍāwī were cautious in interpreting Islamic eschatological narratives, their views were still compatible with the affirmations of traditional Islamic theology. Riḍā and al-Qaraḍāwī in particular made use of their "worldviews" to explain the signs of the hereafter: Riḍā applied *taqārub al-zamān* (closeness of time) to modern means of transport, such as trains, cars, and planes, while Qaradāwī saw *taqārub al-aswāq* (closeness of markets) in the interrelatedness of the international markets in London, Hong Kong and New York and on the Internet. Moreover, their defense of Ibn al-Qayyim's views on hellfire represented their strenuous appeal for a response to modern challenges by returning to "authentic" and "pure" Islam. Nursi's rational mysticism (or what one can call "mystical

142 Smith and Haddad, *The Islamic understanding* 104.

143 Rahman, Dream 179.

reformism") went beyond the description of classical narratives or theological-philosophical analysis by stressing the "reality" of the other world on the basis of his understanding of cosmic symbolism – what he believed to be the "power" of God's beautiful names in the universe.

Neo-modernist Islamic theology is bold, but is only known or influential among elite intellectual groups. In their critiques, neo-modernists were not concerned with the reconciliation between the validity of Islamic traditional eschatological dogmas and the findings of modernity. In his anthropological understanding of theology, for example, Ḥasan Ḥanafī explained eschatology as a projection from "outside" Muslim societies and not as something that emerged from the "inside" real Islamic objectives. He was clearly influenced by Western scientists of religion and philosophers, such as Ludwig Feuerbach, who claimed that the conceptions of "god" are nothing but projections of humans' own values, and the idea of "heaven" or "eternal life" is simply a projection of human longing for immortality.[144]

Bibliography

ʿAbduh, M., *Theology of unity*, trans. I. Masaʾad and K. Cragg, London 1966.

——— and R. Riḍā., *Tafsīr al-manār*, 12 vols., Beirut 1999.

Abrahamov, B., The creation and duration of paradise and hell in Islamic theology, in *Der Islam* 79 (2002), 87–102.

Albayrak, I., *Qurʾanic narrative and Israʾiliyyat in Western scholarship and in classical exegesis*, PhD dissertation, University of Leeds.

———, Isrāʾīliyyāt and classical exegetes' comments on the calf with a hollow sound Q.20:83–98/7:147–155 with special reference to Ibn ʿAtiyya, in *JSS* 47.1 (2002), 39–65.

Ali, S.J., Sayyid Jamaluddin Afghani and his refutation of modern Western materialists, in H.N. Rafiabadi (ed.), *Challenges to religions and Islam: A study of Muslim movements, personalities, issues and trends*, ii, New Delhi 2007, 843–54.

Asad, M., *The road to Mecca*, Louisville KY 2005.

Baljon, J.M.S. (trans.), *A mystical interpretation of prophetic tales by an Indian Muslim: Shāh Walī Allāh's taʾwīl al-aḥādīth*, Leiden 1973.

———, *Religion and thought of Shāh Walī Allāh Dihlawī, 1703–1762*, Leiden 1986.

Berry, D.L., *Islam and modernity through the writings of Islamic modernist Fazlur Rahman*, Lewiston NY 2003.

Dar, B.A., *Religious thought of Sayyid Ahmad Khan*, Lahore 1971.

144 See, for example, Feuerbach, *The essence* 222f.

Davidson, H.A., *Alfarabi, Avicenna, and Averroes on intellect: Their cosmologies, theories of the active intellect, and theories of human intellect*, New York 1992.

Feuerbach, L., *The essence of Christianity*, trans. M. Evans, New York 1855.

Halepota, A.J., *Philosophy of Shah Waliullah*, Lahore n.d.

Halm, H., *Kosmologie und Heilslehre der frühen Ismāʿīlīya*, Wiesbaden 1978.

Ḥanafī, H., *Min al-ʿaqīda ilā l-thawra*, 5 vols., Cairo 1988.

Hermansen, M.K., Shāh Walī Allāh's theory of the subtle spiritual centers (laṭā'if): A Sufi model of personhood and self-transformation, in JNES 47 (1988), 1–25.

Hoover, J., Islamic universalism: Ibn Qayyim al-Jawziyya's Salafi deliberations on the duration of hell-fire, in *MW* 99 (2009), 181–201.

Ibn al-Qayyim a-Jawziyya, Shams al-Dīn, *Ḥādī l-arwāḥ ilā bilād al-afrāḥ aw waṣf al-janna wa-naʿīm ahlihā*, ed. B.M. ʿUyūn, Damascus 2002.

Iqbāl, M., *The reconstruction of religious thought in Islam*, ed. M. Saeed Sheikh, Lahore 1986.

Jalbani, G.N., *Teachings of Shāh Walīyullāh of Delhi*, New Delhi 1997.

Katz, J.G., Shaykh Aḥmad's dream: A 19th-century eschatological vision, in *SI* 79 (1994), 157–80.

Keddie, N., *An Islamic response to imperialism*, Berkeley 1983.

Lawson, T., Shaykh Ahmad al-Ahsa'i and the world of images, in D. Hermann and S. Mervin (eds.), Shi'i trends and dynamics in modern times, Würzburg 2010, 19–31.

Murad, M.A., *Intellectual modernism of Shibli Nu'mani*, New Delhi 1996.

Nadwi, S.A.H.A., *Faith versus materialism: The message of Surat al-Kahf*, Lucknow 1973, repr. Malaysia 2005.

Nettler, R.L., Early Islam, modern Islam and Judaism: The Isra'iliyyat in modern Islamic thought, in R.L. Nettler and S. Taji-Faruki (eds.), *Studies in Muslim-Jewish relations: Muslim-Jewish encounters; intellectual traditions and modern polities*, Oxford 1998, 1–14.

Nursi, S., *From the Risale-i Nur collection: The words*, trans. Ş. Vahide, 1992, available at www.nurpublishers.com (accessed 23 January 2010).

Ohlander, E.S., *Sufism in an age of transition: ʿUmar al-Suhrawardī and the rise of the Islamic mystical brotherhoods*, Leiden 2008.

Ozervarli, M.S., Attempts to revitalize *kalam* in the late 19th and early 20th centuries, in *MW* 89 (1999), 89–105

al-Qaraḍāwī Y., ʿAlāmāt al-saʿa, in al-Sharīʿa wa-l-ḥayāt, 17 May 2004, http://www.qaradawi.net/site/topics/article.asp?cu_no=2&item_no=3305&version=1&template_id=105 (accessed 6 December 2009).

———, al-Īmān bi-l-yawm al-ākhir, in *al-Sharīʿa wa-l-ḥayāt*, 26 May 2004, http://www.qaradawi.net/site/topics/article.asp?cu_no=2&item_no=3314&version=1&template_id=105&parent_id=1 (accessed 6 December 2009).

———, Yawm al-ḥisāb, in *al-Sharīʿa wa-l-ḥayāt*, 19 May 2004, http://www.qaradawi.net/site/topics/article.asp?cu_no=2&item_no=3306&version=1&template_id=105&parent_id=1 (accessed 5 December 2009).

Perlmann, M., Ibn Qayyim and the Devil, in R. Ciasca (ed.), *Studi Orientalistici in onore di Giorgio Levi della Vida*, ii, Rome 1956, 330–37.

Rafiabadi, H.N., *Saints and saviours of Islam*, New Delhi 2005.

Rahman, F., Dream, imagination and *ʿalam al-mithāl*, in *Islamic Studies* 3 (1964), 167–80.

———, *Major themes of the Quran*, Chicago 2009.

Riḍā, M.R., *al-Manār*, 35 vols., Cairo 1898–1935.

Robson, J., Is The Moslem hell eternal?, in *MW* 28 (1938), 386–93.

Sawai, M., *The divine names in Ibn ʿArabi's theory of oneness of existence*, MA thesis, American University in Cairo 2014.

Scharbrodt, O., The Salafiyya and Sufism: Muhammad ʿAbduh and his *Risālat al-Wāridāt* (Treatise on mystical inspirations), in *BSOAS* 70 (2007), 90–115.

Schützinger, H., *Ursprung und Entwicklung der arabischen Abraham-Nimrod Legende*, Bonn 1961.

Smith, J.I. and Y.Y. Haddad, *The Islamic understanding of death and resurrection*, Albany, NY 1981.

Snouck Hurgronje, C., *Ambtelijke adviezen van C. Snouck Hurgronje 1889–1936* [Official advices of Snouck Hurgronje 1889–1936], ed. E. Gobée and C. Adriaanse, The Hague 1957.

Troll, C.W., *Sayyid Ahmad Khan: A reinterpretation of Muslim theology*, New Delhi 1978.

Vatikiotis, J., Muḥammad ʿAbduh and the quest for a Muslim humanism, in *Arabica* 4 (1957), 57–72.

Walbridge, J., *The leaven of the ancients: Suhrawardi and the heritage of the Greeks*, Albany, NY 1999.

Walker, P.E., Bāṭiniyya, in *EI*³, online version, http://referenceworks.brillonline.com/entries/ encyclopaedia-of-islam-3/ba-t-iniyya-COM_22745 (accessed 28 November 2014).

Internet Sources

http://www.islam101.com/quran/yusufAli/index.htm (accessed 6 December 2009).

http://www.bdr130.net/vb/t792318.html; http://www.muslmh.com/vb/t148485.html (accessed 15 September 2010).

http://www.jarash-uni.com/vb/forum4/thread1281.html (accessed 15 September 2010).

http://www.qaradawi.net/site/topics/printArticle.asp?cu_no=2&item_no=6158&version=1&template_id=232&parent_id=17 (accessed 15 September 2010).

http://www.binbaz.org.sa/mat/17886 (accessed 15 September 2010).

CHAPTER 55

Between Science Fiction and Sermon: Eschatological Writings Inspired by Said Nursi

*Martin Riexinger**

Because studies on modern Islam tend to focus on political and legal aspects, eschatology has been neglected for quite some time. The fact that authors like Ghulām Aḥmad Parwēz (Pakistan, 1903–86),[1] Maḥmūd Muḥammad Ṭāhā (Sudan, 1909 or 1911–85),[2] or Ḥasan Ḥanafī (Egypt, b. 1935), the advocate of the "Islamic Left" in Egypt,[3] reformulate salvation as an inner-worldly concept seems to correspond to this politically focused approach to modern Islam. However, this should not distract from the persistence of more conservative interpretations in which the individual afterlife and traditional eschatological concepts play a dominant role. Jane I. Smith and Yvonne Y. Haddad have taken a first step toward filling the gap in research on such concepts by collecting references to the Intermediate World and the hereafter in nineteenth and twentieth-century Arab publications.[4] More recently, interest in modern Islamic eschatology has been boosted by the discovery of the importance

* *General notes*: In the summary of the sources, "Allah" is used when the authors use the word "Allâh," whereas *tanrı* is translated as "God." The English equivalents of religious terms that are generally capitalized in Turkish religious writings are capitalized. Content and URLs of all websites referred to were last checked on 26 April 2010.

Acknowledgments: Most of the material for this article was collected during my work for the research project "Nurculuk – fundamentalistische Theologie in der Türkei" (Nurculuk – fundamentalist theology in Turkey) under the supervision of Jens Peter Laut and funded by the Deutsche Forschungsgemeinschaft (German Research Council, DFG).

1 Parwēz, *Islam* 194–202.

2 The author interprets concepts like the *barzakh* as stages in a progressive development of mankind in which Muḥammad's prophethood does not figure as the climax: Ṭāhā, *Risāla* 211.

3 Riexinger, Nasserism 72, 79. In this case, the inner-worldly reinterpretation of eschatology reflects the influence of Latin American liberation theology on the author.

4 Smith and Haddad, *Islamic understanding* 99–146. Unfortunately, this work is more a collection of material than an analysis of concepts; Smith and Haddad do not discuss the ideas of the authors with regard to their general theological outlook nor do they endeavor to assess the impact and relevance of these concepts.

 | DOI 10.1163/9789004333154_056

of apocalyptic motives in jihadist ideology,[5] and radical currents in *imāmī* Shiʿism.[6] However, it would be a mistake to associate the interest in the hereafter exclusively with militancy, as life after death and the "last things" have been dealt with by a number of Turkish authors inspired by the ideas of Said Nursi, a figure with a rather irenic outlook.[7]

1 Said Nursi and the Nurcu Movement[8]

Nurcus (*Nurcular*, "disciples of [the divine] light"), is a term coined to describe the followers of Said Nursi, who was a Kurdish scholar born in the mid or late 1870s in the village of Nurs in eastern Anatolia.[9] After finishing his studies by traveling from scholar to scholar and from *medrese* to *medrese* as was the norm at the time in the region "East of Sivas," and while still at an early age he gained fame in his home region as someone skilled in religious disputations, and thereby attracted the interest of the state authorities. This earned him an invitation to the library of Tahir Paşa, the governor of Van. There, for several months he studied privately and dedicated himself to the study of the natural and social sciences. This experience convinced him that Islamic scholars should interpret the Quran in accordance with modern scientific findings, and that traditional religious studies should be combined with the teaching of secular subjects.

In 1908, Said Nursi traveled to Istanbul hoping to gain imperial support for his plans for a university designed to fit this purpose. While his efforts were of no avail, the trip thrust him into the life of the capital when sultan Abdülhamit II was deposed by the Committee for Union and Progress (İttihad ve Terakki Cemiyeti, commonly known in the West as the Young Turks). Although he initially lent his support to the Committee for Union and Progress, he was arrested for allegedly participating in the "counter-revolution" of 31 March 1909. After his acquittal, he withdrew to Van and gathered a group of disciples around

5 Cook, *Contemporary*; Damir-Geilsdorf, Ende; Reichmuth, Second Intifada.

6 Ourghi, *Schiitischer Messianismus*; Ourghi, Licht.

7 On the other hand, not all radicals are inclined to eschatological speculation. Mawdūdī, *Sīrat* i, 456, for example, urges the utmost caution with regard to traditions referring to the *mahdī*.

8 This biographical account is based on the somewhat hagiographic publications of Nurcu authors: Badıllı, *Bediüzzaman*; Şahiner, *Son şahitler*; Şahiner, *Bilinmeyen taraflarıyla*. An English-language biography based on these books was written by the British convert Şükran Vahide, who is married to the high ranking Nurcu Mehmed Fırıncı: Vahide, *Islam*.

9 The movement is often referred to as Nurculuk. However, unlike Nurcu, the term is considered derogatory by many followers of Said Nursi.

him. In the pre-war years he published his first books, which were mostly dedicated to what he considered the reconciliation of Islam with modern science and the defense of religion against the threat of materialism. During World War I, Said Nursi led a volunteer regiment formed by his disciples and in 1916 he was captured by the Russian army. After his release – or his escape – from captivity in northern Russia following the Bolshevik Revolution, he returned to Istanbul, where he began teaching and publishing again.

Said Nursi stayed in the capital when the National Liberation War began. In 1923, he went to Ankara at the invitation of the new Republican government. Apparently, Mustafa Kemal had expected him to legitimize the new republican government, but, on realizing the government's secularist tendencies, Said Nursi did not comply with his wishes. In 1924, Said Nursi withdrew to Van for a second time. After the suppression of the 1925 Kurdish revolt led by Sheikh Said, Said Nursi was rounded up with many religious scholars and tribal leaders although he had remained aloof from the insurrection.

He spent the next twenty-six years either banished or in prison in several places in western Anatolia and, in one case, in the Black Sea region. In Barla, a small mountain village in the province of Isparta to which he was confined from 1926 to 1935, the surveillance was loose enough to allow him to teach. His lectures were written down and copied by his disciples, and were dispersed countrywide through a network of followers. Together with his earlier publications, the collection of these oral discourses became known as the *Risâle-i Nûr*. These discourses consist mainly of interpretations of Quranic verses or discussions of theological or ethical problems. In spite of persecution by the Kemalist regime, Said Nursi restricted himself to the moral condemnation of the rulers and the "godless" lifestyle they propagated, as he objected to indulging in politics. During this period, he won the support of several religious young men who, in the following decades, formed the leadership of the Nurcu movement.

In 1951 Said Nursi was finally released from banishment by Prime Minister Adnan Menderes, who had won the first free multi-party elections the year before. Said Nursi could now propagate his ideas without major restrictions; he received permission to publish the *Risâle-i Nûr* in the Latin alphabet. In return for the relaxation of restrictions imposed on him and his disciples, Said Nursi lent support to Menderes' politics, in particular to his alignment with the United States against the Soviet Union. Said Nursi died on 23 March 1960, two months before the first military coup that led to the execution of Menderes and the first round of new persecutions of the Nurcus.

Because Said Nursi had not designated a successor, throughout the 1960s his followers were only loosely organized. Matters of common concern were handled by a council of his early associates. Some of the leaders were responsible for the dissemination of Said Nursi's teachings through recitation and elucidations in lecture circles that had sprung up throughout the country.[10] Others were responsible for the publication of the *Risâle-i Nûr*. Politically, most Nurcus lent their support to Süleyman Demirel's Justice Party (Adalet Partisi), the successor of Menderes' Demokrat Parti. Only a tiny minority turned to Turkey's first Islamist party, the National Order Party (Millî Nizâm Partisi) founded in 1969. To this day, the majority of the Nurcus criticize both Turkish and foreign Islamists for their anti-democratic ideology, their hierarchical forms of organization, their authoritarianism, and their tolerance of violence.

The publishing activities of the Nurcus were originally restricted to the dissemination of the *Risâle-i Nûr*. In the late 1960s, however, they began to enlarge their program. In Istanbul, they started the political daily *Yeni Asya* (New Asia, 1973) and the monthly review *Köprü* (The bridge, 1976). In the latter, and in many tracts published by the *Yeni Asya* publishing house, Nurcu authors addressed religious, ethical, and political issues on the basis of their interpretation of Said Nursi's teachings. One author even went so far as to write a novel for this purpose (see below). However, the expansion of publishing activities was resented by a number of leaders, who insisted that the movement should concentrate on disseminating the *Risâle-i Nûr* in reading circles and teaching sessions (*sohbet, ders*). The expansion of publishing activities was not the only issue to cause friction among the Nurcus. Some of the younger members were unwilling to subordinate themselves to the authority of Said Nursi's inner circle and they set up publishing enterprises of their own.

The 1980 military coup furthered the fragmentation of the Nurcu movement. Whereas the direct military intervention of 1960 and the threat of intervention (*muhtıra*) of 1971 were intended to reinstall undiluted Kemalism, the junta of Kenan Evren sought support from religious circles in its struggle against the Left. Although some Nurcus eagerly grasped this extended hand, the *Yeni Asya* group kept aloof. However, these politically motivated conflicts, and the animosity between certain leading figures, should not distract from the fact that, in other non-political matters there are no substantial differences between the various Nurcu factions.

The most important development among the Nurcus since the 1980s has been the increase in media use for the propagation of their ideas. In the course of this process, authors and lecturers who did not necessarily have a high status according to the old, albeit informal, system of initiation gained importance.

10 On Nurcu community life: Spuler-Stegemann, Organisationsstruktur; Yavuz, *Nur* study circles. These circles can be considered similar to Sufi models, adapted to new purposes under the restrictive conditions of the Kemalist regime: Zarcone, Transformation.

To a certain extent, this unintentionally weakened the old Nurcu structure based on the controlled reading circles.[11]

2 Said Nursi's Teachings

2.1 *General*

Said Nursi's works are characterized by their opaque style. Whereas his followers admire his language for its force, rhythm, and imagery, his detractors denounce it as "bad Turkish" because of the many indisputable grammatical errors or even as a symptom of his alleged mental derangement.[12] For the most part, Said Nursi did not follow the conventions of scholarly religious writings. Instead of theoretical concepts in abstract terms, he used parables and metaphors suitable for convincing laypeople.

Although the reconciliation of Islam with modern science was the most important stimulus of Said Nursi's activities, his overall theological outlook was conservative. He accepted modern astronomy and reinterpreted Quranic verses and *ḥadīth*s that reflect geocentric concepts or even support the mythological *sunna* cosmology, like the idea that the Earth rests on the horn of a bull standing on a whale.[13] In this respect, he followed the same line as modernist thinkers. With regard to other issues to which modernists attach particular importance, Said Nursi consciously opposed their solutions. For example, he objected to the concept of independent causality, and defended the idea that God sustains, at every moment, a generally regular succession of events. On the basis of this assumption, he defended the possibility of miracles. Nevertheless, he offered numerous rational explanations for many of the miracles reported in the Quran. Another outcome of his rejection of the idea of independent causality was his strong objection to the concept of self-organizing matter resulting in life. Although he never explicitly referred to the theory of evolution, his target was unmistakable. In the 1970s, the Nurcus took up his objections again, and bolstered their attempts to refute Darwinism with translations of American Protestant creationist literature. The Islamic brand of creationism that resulted from this synthesis is now popular throughout the Islamic world, perhaps even more so in the diaspora. Indeed, it may be considered the

---

11 On these aspects: Yavuz, *Nur* study circles 305–12; with particular emphasis on groups active in Europe: Şahinöz, *Nurculuk* 97–146, 156–60; Riexinger, *Schöpfungsordnung*.

12 Dursun, *Müslümanlık*.

13 Nursi, *Lem'alar* 93; Heinen, *Islamic cosmology*.

Nurcus' most important contribution to current ideological discussions in the Islamic world.[14]

Another major, but more traditional, aspect of Said Nursi's teachings consists of elements from later intellectual Sufism, in particular speculations based on the concept of macrocosm and microcosm,[15] and the notion of plural worlds.[16] According to him, everything that exists is animate to a certain degree.[17] One central aspect is the idea that the cosmos has two ontologically different manifestations:

> [The] cosmos has two sides, like the two sides of a mirror: *mülk* and *melekûtiyet*. The side of *mülk* is the realm where contradictions struggle (*ezdadın cevelangâhıdır*). It is the place where aspects like beautiful-ugly, good-bad, small-large clash. For its sake means and causes have been set up, so that the hand of power (*dest-i kudret*) does not manifest itself visibly in particulars as required by (His) Greatness and Aloofness (*azamet, izzet*). However they have not been given real power to effect (*hakikî tesir verilmemiş*) as required by (His) Oneness (*vahdet*).
>
> By contrast, the side of *melekûtiyet* is absolutely transparent (*mutlaka şeffafedir*); and it is not disturbed by specification (*teşahhusat*). This side is directly oriented toward the Creator. There is no order, sequence (of events). Causality cannot intrude (*illiyet, mâlûliyet giremez*). There are no deviations. No impediments interfere. (On this side) the atom becomes the brother of the sun.[18]

Another theme in Said Nursi's writings is the search for modern scientific discoveries and technical inventions that were anticipated in the Quran. This apologetic exegetical approach called *tafsīr ʿilmī*; it emerged in late nineteenth-century Egypt and gained popularity throughout the Islamic world.[19] In Turkey, some of Said Nursi's followers became its most ardent advocates.

---

14 Riexinger, Islamic opposition 488–498; Riexinger, Turkey.

15 Nursi, *Ishārat* 27; Nursi, *Sözler* 871; Nursi, *Mektûbât* 428.

16 Nursi, *Sözler* 839; Radtke, Sufism 349–53.

17 Nursi: *Khuṭba* 105; Nursi, *Mathnawī* 254; Nursi, *Sünuhât* 35. Remarkably, the same idea can be found in the writings of the German materialist authors who were popular among secular Ottoman intellectuals: Büchner, *Kraft und Stoff*; Haeckel, *Welträthsel* 258f. Whether Said Nursi was aware of this and considered it proof of the scientific character of his ideas is impossible to say.

18 Nursi, *Sünuhât* 33.

19 Baljon, *Modern Muslim* 88–94, 125f.; Jansen, *Interpretation* 40–54; Riexinger, *Ṣanāʾullāh* 406f.

Said Nursi's teachings on science and religion are closely related to his ethical and political views. A major part of his later works is devoted to coming to terms with the fact that Islamic norms are no longer generally binding. But instead of calling for the implementation of the *sharīʿa* with state support, he urged his followers to act according to Islamic norms out of conviction. For this purpose, he stressed, man has to know where he comes from and where he will go when he dies. Hence both eschatology and the affirmation of creation play a central role in his thought. The idea that it is impossible to lead an ethical life without the acceptance of the Creator is the reason for his revulsion toward both Kemalism and communism. And the notion that Christians and Muslims should oppose the forces of unbelief reinforced his favorable attitude to Christians, an attitude that he had already revealed before World War I.

2.2 *Eschatology*

Said Nursi's teachings defy the notion that Islamic discourses in the twentieth century are marked by a shift from religion to ideology. The *memento mori*[20] and the affirmation of the resurrection are central elements in Said Nursi's writings and sayings because he thought that the awareness of what will come is a prerequisite for an ethical life. Hence it comes as no surprise that eschatological themes figure prominently in the *Risâle-i Nûr*. However, in most instances he simply affirms traditional doctrines, as for example the *berzah* (Arabic: *barzakh*, cf. Q 23:100; 25:53; 55:20)[21] or the record of deeds.[22] Nevertheless, it is remarkable that he tries to underscore the veracity of the traditional concepts by claiming that he himself has seen them in visions and dreams.[23] In other cases, he endeavors to explain elements of eschatology in the light of modern science (as he understood it) or current events.

In some cases, Said Nursi mixes the affirmation of eschatology with *tafsīr ʿilmī* (scientific exegesis). For example, he says that the Small Hell (*Cehennem-i Suğrâ*) already exists, as this has been proven by the findings of modern geology. Based on the observation that the temperature of the earth increases by

---

20 Among the most frequently quoted passages from his works is a statement that appears in two sermons, in which he refers to a school playground with pretty teenage girls, whom he saw from his cell in the Eskişehir jail. He declares that their physical beauty is futile because in fifty years time they would either already lie in a grave or have become ugly and disrespected. Here the *memento mori* is combined with the criticism of the visibility of the female body encouraged by the Kemalists: Nursi, *Sözler* 178, 186, 191.

21 Nursi, *Sözler* 416, 692f., 878, 894f.; Nursi, *Mektûbât* 12–4: for martyrs, the Intermediate World will be free of hardship; Nursi, *Lemʿalar* 282–6.

22 Nursi, *Mektûbât* 221.

23 Nursi, *Sözler* 407–9: On the bridge the resurrected will have to cross before the judgment.

one degree centigrade every 33 meters one drills down, Said Nursi concluded that the center of the planet is 200,000° C. Thus he attempted to prove the veracity of the *ḥadīth* according to which hell's fire is one thousand times hotter than fire on Earth. However, in the end (*ahiret*), the inhabitants of the Earth, and those already smoldering in the Small Hell, will be delivered to the place of judgment. Those who are damned will end up in the Great Hell located inside the Earth's orbit. However, it is still invisible because its fire is hidden and lightless. With regard to the Great Hell, Said Nursi does not embellish his vision with reference to scientific theories or findings.[24] In light of new technical inventions, he proposed one new explanation for the Intermediate World (*berzah*), which was taken up again decades later. According to him, it can be compared to a cinema in which all past events are displayed.[25]

Other reflections on eschatology are connected with his ideas about society and politics. His irenic approach to the non-Muslims in this world motivated him to find an agreeable solution for their destiny in the hereafter. He did not dare to overrule the Quranic warning that they will end up in hell, but he argued that the morally excellent non-Muslims will be accommodated in a deluxe section of hell that resembles paradise in all major aspects. Until now, some Nurcus subscribe to this position.[26]

One of his treatises serves to endow the struggle against communism with an apocalyptic dimension. He identified the Dajjāl with a threat from the north, and he justified this association by referring to a *ḥadīth* according to which "the first day of the Dajjāl" will last a year, the second one a month, the third one a year, and the fourth one a day. During his captivity in Russia, he observed that near the North Pole days and nights last longer. If a railway train or a car traveled ahead of the sunset in such northern regions it would be possible to see the sun for a week. For Said Nursi, this served as decisive proof that the Dajjāl will come from the north. He added that this assumption is corroborated by two further universally accepted prophecies in the *ḥadīth*: first, Ya'jūj and Ma'jūj (Gog and Magog) will invade the civilized world from the north, and second, the Jews will be among the followers of the Dajjāl, which fits in with the fact that "Trotsky's committee" brought Lenin to power.[27] The identification of Ya'jūj and Ma'jūj with a threat – usually of nomadic people – from the northern steppes can be traced back to classical commentaries. In recent decades Arab authors, too, have reinterpreted these figures in a way that

24 Nursi, *Mektûbât* 14f.

25 Nursi, *Lem'alar* 524.

26 Nursi, *Ishārat* 81f.; Paksu, *Meseleler* i, 124–6: Hence Edison is admitted, Darwin not.

27 Nursi, *Şualar* 506–9, 513; on Ya'jūj and Ma'jūj also Nursi, *Sikke* 189.

reflects current political conflicts: They identify Ya'jūj and Ma'jūj as Israel with reference to the assertion that the eastern European Jews are descendants of the Khazars; this was brought forward by Koestler in his *The Thirteenth Tribe*.[28] Furthermore, Said Nursi claimed that the *ḥadīth* according to which one eye of the Dajjāl is blind should be reinterpreted to mean that one eye possesses special powers of a spiritualist nature, like a magnetism that enables its holder to control and steer (*teshir edici manyetizma*), as he himself claims to have seen "in a spiritual world" (*bir mânevi âlemde*).[29] In a similar way, Said Nursi connected the *ḥadīth* according to which there will be a time when nobody says "Allah, Allah" anymore, with the forced turkification of the call to prayer in 1932.[30] With regard to the beast of the Earth (*dābbat al-arḍ*; Q 27:82; 34:14) and the rising of the sun in the West, Said Nursi conceded that he was unable to find an explanation that is totally convincing. However, he speculated that the beast of the Earth might not be a single animal but a certain kind or herd (*tâife*) that afflicts mankind by devouring men's bones like bark beetle larvae chew trees.[31]

3 Fethullah Gülen: Affirmation without Explanation

At present, Fethullah Gülen (b. 1938 or 1941) is by far the most prominent figure to emerge from the ranks of the Nurcu movement. In fact, whether or not Gülen describes himself as a follower of Said Nursi depends on whether he considers it politically opportune to do so under prevailing circumstances. Gülen hails from the province of Erzurum in the east of Turkey, where he received a traditional religious education in underground *medreses*. After military service he worked for the Directorate of Religious Affairs as a preacher (*vaiz*). In this capacity, he was sent to two of Turkey's most westernized cities, Izmir and Edirne. In Izmir, where he served in the 1970s, he attracted conservative students with his sermons against materialism, and it was here that he began to form an independent movement. His disciples published the magazine *Sızıntı* (The leak [through which truth trickles]) and recordings of his sermons. Their ranks were filled with the help of summer camps that they organized for pupils. Because he supported the 1980 coup, and especially the government of Turgut Özal, he was treated favorably by the state authorities

28 Van Donzel and Ott, Yād̲jûd̲j wa-Mād̲jūdj; Cook, *Contemporary* 205–8.

29 Nursi, *Sözler* 513f.

30 Ibid., 499.

31 Ibid., 510f.

in the 1980s and early 1990s. Thus his followers were able to set up educational institutions, media outlets (especially the daily newspaper *Zaman*), and commercial enterprises in Turkey and abroad. Hence Gülen may be considered one of the most influential figures in Turkey even though he left the country for the United States after falling afoul of the army in 1999.[32]

Whereas these various activities of the Gülen movement reveal their willingness to make use of the most modern devices and strategies available, Gülen's religious writings are fairly conventional with regard to form and content. Like Said Nursi, he uses many examples and parables. Although he occasionally introduces modern scientific vocabulary of Turkish or Western origin, his language is characterized by a large number of Arabic and Persian words and hence appears quite Ottoman.[33] Major subjects of his writings are moral issues, in particular the defense of the traditional gender order, the glorification of the Ottoman past, and the struggle against materialism. However, he shuns direct reference to current Turkish politics.

One of his tracts is devoted to *Ölüm Ötesi Hayat* (Life beyond death).[34] However, the title is somewhat misleading because Gülen pays little attention to the description of the afterlife. Instead he focuses on demonstrating the possibility and necessity of the physical resurrection and punishment "on the basis of the Quran and reason." As expected, he is motivated by the observation that for "several centuries" the belief in the hereafter was subjected to the doubt and abuse of atheists, materialists and "denialists" (*inkârcı*).[35]

According to Gülen, it is unthinkable that someone's life could be "straight" (*müstakîm*) if he is not aware that his acts will be judged. Hence Allah warns humans that all their deeds will be recorded by angels. Those who believe in resurrection will therefore possess a remedy against the craziness of youth and

32 The bulk of the literature on the Gülen movement can be divided into uncritical apologetics and hysterical conspiracy theories by left-wing nationalists; a critical biography remains a desideratum. Two generally positive presentations do, however, take objections against Gülen into account: Hermann, Fethullah Gülen; Yavuz, *Islamic political identity* 179–205; a denunciation of Gülen as opportunist by an "old school" Nurcu: Şahinöz, Nurculuk 97–120; on Gülen's educational activities and the media associated with him: Agai, *Netzwerk*. Gülen's date of birth is controversial. Whereas 1941 is given in official documents, he himself claims to have been born on 10 November 1938, i.e., the day of Atatürk's death.

33 For example, he occasionally uses the word Hüdâ (from Pers. *khodā*) for God, which is nowadays quite uncommon in Turkey: Gülen, *Ölüm* 4.

34 The translation was chosen consciously because Gülen did not opt for the temporal *sonra* but for *öte*, which is used to express a local relation or an alternative.

35 Gülen, *Ölüm* i.

the desperation of old age and infirmity.[36] The belief in resurrection thus guarantees peace of mind (*huzur*) for the individual, which is a precondition for social stability.[37]

According to Gülen, the Lord (*Cenab-ı Hak*) has explained the possibility of resurrection to mankind in several ways. First, the Quran summons humans to observe the world so that they will recognize His infinite powers that keep the heavens in their place without pillars and resurrect vegetation every spring. Hence men have to ask themselves whether it is easier (for God) to create heaven, or to create them (Q 79:27). In fact, there is no difference between the first creation and the second one.[38] Another argument that he puts forward to bolster his claim is the universal wisdom that he says characterizes the universe (*kâinât*). This assumption is based on an expansion of the macrocosm-microcosm concept. According to Gülen, the universe is a "big person" (*büyük bir insan*, i.e., *insān akbar*). Hence no detail in the "macroworld, normoworld and microworld" is meaningless. This includes man's existence and also his sense of and longing for eternal life.[39] Because man is a manifestation of the mystery of the perfect order (*ahsen-i takvîm sırrının mazharı*, Q 95:4), resurrection and the Great Judgment are absolutely necessary in order to evaluate his deeds in this world.[40] Furthermore, he argues, one must consider that natural laws can explain only the events themselves but not why and for what purpose they occur. But everything has an objective and a purpose such as the creation of the human who longs for eternity (*ebed*).[41] Moreover, the necessity of resurrection can be concluded from the grace, pity, and generosity of the Lord.[42] In

36 Ibid., 1f., 10.

37 Ibid., 3, 6f., 13f.; on *huzur*, a central term in Turkish Islamic discourse: Glaßen, ‚Huzur'.

38 Gülen, *Ölüm* 23–31; spring was used by Said Nursi as metaphor for resurrection. In this context Gülen clings to the concept of a compact heaven, which contradicts modern theories of physics to which he refers elsewhere. Such inconsistencies are typical of this type of literature, see p. 1256. Furthermore, the passage includes an affirmation of the creation of man from clay and argil (29). This reflects Gülen's strong opposition to the theory of evolution.

39 Gülen, *Ölüm* 33–5. The three worlds to which Gülen refers are terms used in popular presentations of modern physics. The "normoworld" as opposed to the macroworld (astronomical phenomena) and the microworld (particles), is the one to which the human senses are adapted. According to Gülen, they show remarkable signs of correspondence: 59f.; similar, but without the terms: İsmail, *Ölüm* 18f.

40 Gülen, *Ölüm* 38.

41 Ibid., 34f., 66f.

42 Ibid., 41–9.

addition, the beauty of this world demands to be continued[43] and the graces (*nimetler*) of the True Lord (*Cenab-i Hakk*) in this world are hints of those to be received in the hereafter.[44] Finally, Gülen adds a list of Greek, Islamic, and Western philosophers who affirmed the belief in resurrection, at least in a collective form (Spinoza),[45] and he stresses that the basic teachings of the Old and New Testament correspond to those of the Quran.[46]

In the concluding chapter he states: "We believe in the truth of resurrection as reported in the Quran and *ḥadīth*s and leave the aspect of the question that is not our concern to the knowledge of the Lord." He considers the images of hell and paradise in the Quran to be entirely sufficient to motivate the pious and to warn those who might be led astray.[47]

Only in a few instances does Gülen offer explanations for eschatological events. For example, from the *ḥādith* according to which men will be resurrected naked and uncircumcised, he concludes that men will be resurrected with their souls and as "reproductions" (*eşbah*) of their bodies that consist of their original atoms/particles (*zerrat-ı asliye*).[48] The return of the moon, which is now commonly accepted to have been born of the Earth, to its mother might result in an atomic explosion that brings about the resurrection. However, comets or tests of nuclear bombs could lead to the same result.[49] The existence of DNA in human sperm (sic! the ovum does not seem to matter) and in all living beings is proof that all information in the universe is preserved. On the day of the resurrection this information will be used to reproduce all living beings.[50] In a second elaboration on spring as an anticipation of resurrection, Gülen tries to underscore this example by referring to photosynthesis.[51] His reluctance to indulge in more far-reaching speculations on the hereafter is remarkable because it contrasts with his approach to other exegetic issues discussed below.[52]

---

43 Ibid., 50f.

44 Ibid., 52–4.

45 Ibid., 75–80.

46 Ibid., 81–3.

47 Ibid., 85.

48 Ibid., 16–9; this traditional theory is upheld by other modern authors, too: Mawdūdī, *Sīrat* ii, 374.

49 Gülen, *Ölüm* 20f.

50 Ibid., 55–7.

51 Ibid., 63f.

52 However this is not uncommon in modern eschatological writings. For Arab examples see Smith and Haddad, *Islamic understanding* 131.

4 Hekimoğlu İsmail: On End of Time and the Human Transition

Hekimoğlu İsmail is the pen name of Ömer Okçu (b. 1932) who, unlike Gülen, did not receive a thorough religious education. After high school he went to the United States to study electrical engineering. But instead of seeking employment in that profession after his return, he began working as a freelance writer. In 1967, he published *Minyeli Abdullah* (ʿAbdallāh from al-Minya), arguably the first Turkish-Islamic thesis novel. He has been a prolific writer ever since. In addition to further novels, stories, and poems, İsmail has written a popular explanation of the main biographical facts and doctrines of Said Nursi (in response to 100 questions), and several collections of essays on religious and ethical questions. At present, he is closely associated with Gülen, and contributes columns on religious issues to the daily newspaper *Zaman* on a regular basis.[53]

Hekimoğlu İsmail deals with eschatological issues in his introduction to Said Nursi's life and doctrines.[54] According to İsmail, the signs of the coming of the day of resurrection described in the Quran will be caused by the suspension of those forces holding the universe together. But how are people supposed to be resurrected when ultimately the Earth breaks apart, magma surges out, gravitational forces cease to exist, and everything is dismantled into single atoms? Hekimoğlu İsmail explains this thus: At the beginning of the universe, God filled the void with atoms and ether. From these two components He created molecules, stars, and planets. When everything is dismantled in the end, God can easily create everything, including humans, anew in a second creation. Hence humans will not vanish in a void but will undergo a transition to another state as they did before when they died in the world of souls and were resurrected in a womb at the same time.[55]

When Hekimoğlu İsmail explains why hellfire can inflict unimaginable pain on humans without burning them, he argues that, according to God's order, this happens in human bodies at 37°C. Nevertheless, the Creator can decree that this process should take place at much higher temperatures. Moreover, He

53 http://www.hekimogluismail.com.

54 In 2004 he published the booklet *Ölüm yokluk mu?* (Does death mean void?) in which he writes about the general structure and harmony of the universe but says remarkably little about the afterlife. The only aspect to which he refers continually is God's infinite power, which can be observed in every detail of creation. This is supposed to prove that God can resurrect men *and* create an infinite hereafter. The necessity of the latter is justified with moral arguments. However, Hekimoğlu İsmail does not describe any details.

55 İsmail, *100 Soruda* 169f.; cf. Q 29:16–23.

could arrange for this not to burn the body and for the fire never to cease, just as the sun has been burning non-stop since time immemorial. Referring to firemen who wear protective suits made from asbestos, he asks why Allah should not create a protective device as He did when Abraham opposed Nimrod. At this point, however, İsmail turns from technicalities to morals, stressing that everyone should forge their own armor to protect themselves from hellfire by obeying the divine commandments.[56]

5 Muhammet Bozdağ: An Apocalyptic and Success Counselor

The most extensive book on eschatology was written by Muhammed Bozdağ (b. 1967), who has no formal religious education in the state education system nor does he play an important role in the leadership of a Nurcu organization. Bozdağ studied public administration. After completing his PhD he joined the Department of Laws and Ordinances of the Turkish National Assembly, where he has since risen to the rank of vice director. In the mid-1990s, he started to promote the popular concept of *kişisel gelişim* ("personal growth/development") in writings, public lectures, and on the Internet.[57] This concept is an Islamic adaptation of popular Western counseling literature that promises a combination of worldly success and spiritual satisfaction.[58] At first glance, this overly optimistic literature contrasts with Bozdağ's grim visions of doom. However, the Western models that he copied for this purpose did, in fact, leave their trace in his eschatological writings, too. Remarkably, his audience does not seem to be restricted to Nurcus, or to religious conservatives in general. Photographs of his lecture audiences show that not all of his female admirers cover their hair. This would be disapproved of in more religiously observant circles.[59]

Bozdağ reveals his eschatological ideas in his book *Sonsuzluk Yolculuğu* (The voyage toward infinity), in which he attempts to answer the question: "Where do we come from and where will we go?"[60] Hence the last things are treated as part of an all-encompassing cosmological model. The language of the book is marked by a dichotomy: on the one hand, he uses the common Arabic terms for traditional religious concepts, while in all other instances he clearly prefers

---

56 İsmail, *100 Soruda* 180–2.

57 Bozdağ, *Sonsuzluk* 4; http://www.yetenek.com/articles.asp?tid=1&cid=50.

58 Bozdağ, *Sonsuzluk* 12: "Ruhsal gelişimle omuz omuza giden kişisel gelişimi anlamlı buluyorum."

59 http://yetenek.com/articles_detail.asp?id=54.

60 Bozdağ, *Sonsuzluk* 13.

Turkish neologisms for Arabic or Persian terms. For example, he uses *evren* (universe) and *sonsuzluk* (infinity) where Gülen would prefer *kâinât* or *ebed*. By employing a "purified" Turkish instead of the "Ottoman" preferred by elder religious authors, he stresses his scientific credentials. His choice is typical of younger religious authors who place Islamic concepts on an equal footing with secular theories or ideologies by complying with the linguistic norms of Turkish secularism.[61] The book was published by Nesil Yayınları, the most important publishing house of Nurcus not affiliated with Fethullah Gülen. The first edition sold 110,000 copies, a second, revised edition was published in 2010 by Yakamoz Yayınları, a commercial publishing house.

The book begins with a description of the Big Bang as proof of the *creatio ex nihilo* and the illusory character of matter. However, the author claims that the void (*yokluk*) from which space/time (*uzay/zaman*) was created, was already made of light. Matter, as we experience it, is nothing more than a specific state of waves, and hence light. He claims that this insight fits Q 24:35: "God is the light of the heavens and the earth."[62] Furthermore, he maintains that Allah created parallel universes in which the speed of waves is not necessarily restricted to the speed of light in our universe. According to Bozdağ, parallel universes correspond to the concept of plural worlds as formulated by the Sufi masters.[63] In their dreams humans can access the other worlds/parallel universes because virtual (*sanal*) versions of the universes exist in fictional worlds (*hayal âlemleri*) already described by the Sufi masters.[64] This is because the souls of angels, humans, and *jinn* are free from the restrictions imposed on their bodies by the four dimensions.[65] Bozdağ, too, considers man to be a microcosm but he does not elaborate much on this subject. Like Said Nursi, he ascribes consciousness to particles.[66]

According to Bozdağ, Adam and Eve were created in the *Elest Yurdu*, the "Realm of *a lastu* (*bi-rabbikum*)," which alludes to Q 7:172 where Adam's offspring acknowledge God as their lord. This realm must be conceived of as "one of the imaginary dimensions in the heavens" (*Elest yurdunu, göklerdeki hayalî boyutlardan biri olarak değerlendireceğiz*).[67] Only after they were taken in by

61 Seufert, *Politischer Islam* 382.

62 Bozdağ, *Sonsuzluk* 17–22; the translation follows Arberry (trans.), *Koran interpreted*.

63 Bozdağ, *Sonsuzluk* 24–8.

64 Ibid., 28–31.

65 Ibid., 38–40.

66 Ibid., 48f. Similar ideas can be found in New Age literature, the reception of which will be dealt with below: Hanegraaff, *New Age* 157.

67 Bozdağ, *Sonsuzluk* 55.

Iblīs did they descend to our universe. Because their forefathers originated in another universe, where they were endowed with a soul, humans possess spiritual and intellectual capabilities that are unknown to animals. Above all they possess individuality. However: "Our brain cells have not heard, felt or seen concrete (*somut*) sound, rain, mountain or wind. Because (in the *elest yurdu*) there are no physical concretions (*cisimsel somutluklar*), the concepts were abstract (*soyut*) and had the value of a potential basis (*potansiyel temelleri itibarileydi*)."[68] Moreover, the memory of the experiences of their forefathers is retained in the human genes.[69] Bozdağ claims that an awareness of the origins and purpose of creation will pave the way for real success because gratitude toward God helps one to lead an ethical life,[70] which will yield rewards in this world: The orderly joys of marriage help to contain the potentially destructive force of sexuality,[71] and fulfilling the prescribed rites bestows peace of mind (*huzur*).[72]

Bozdağ's elaborations on eschatology begin with the assertion that death cannot be conceived of as a void because it means the separation of the body from the soul. The latter will continue to exist, and although dying is a process that affects only the body, the soul must taste the pain of death (Q 3:185; 21:35; 29:57).[73] He claims that this can be proven by accounts of near-death experiences, and he points out that even atheist scientists have been transformed into believers by what they have seen under such circumstances. Muslims who have undergone such a condition, however, are able to identify that what they experienced was none other than the transition to the Intermediate World (*berzah*). The fact that many accounts of near-death experiences resemble visions of space travel is considered by Bozdağ to be proof of his assertion that the soul will migrate to another dimension after death.[74]

Bozdağ's vision of this transition is not free of contradiction. Some pages later he ascribes to the "cause- and matterless" soul a longing to free itself from its physical garment. In accordance with the traditional concept of the "small death," Bozdağ asserts that the soul will remain close to the body until

68 Ibid., 55, 61–76, 79–87, quote: 86.

69 Ibid., 94f.

70 Ibid., 106–15.

71 Ibid., 115–20.

72 Ibid., 124–8; on this typically Turkish concept: Glaßen, ,Huzur'.

73 Bozdağ, *Sonsuzluk* 132, 134f.

74 Ibid., 135–9; on the development and variety of the concept of *barzakh*: Rebstock, Grabesleben. The Egyptian ʿAbd al-Razzāq Nawfal, an author of apologetic tracts, had referred to such reports in the 1960s: Smith and Haddad, *Islamic understanding* 121; another example is provided by Mawdūdī, *Sīrat* ii, 379.

the funeral, where most of the dead will see their loved ones for the last time. However, some very pious people will be granted the privilege of remaining in contact with their families. For example it was reported that an old woman known for her honesty had died before she could return a needle she had borrowed from her neighbors. With the permission of Allah she was able to talk to her son in a dream so that he could return the needle. Martyrs and friends of God (*velis*) may even be allowed to visit this world for a long time. Due to the connection the dead may keep with this world, Bozdağ sees no harm in visiting graves and praying for the dead, all the more so as those who oppose this practice erect mausoleums for Marx (*sic*), Lenin, and Mao, thereby encouraging the religious veneration of humans. Here, eschatology provides him with an opportunity for a covert attack on the Kemalist veneration of Atatürk. However, Bozdağ warns against excessive practices: Those who light candles at graves or put stones on them disregard the Creator and embarrass the friends of Allah. And those who ask the dead (or "a living secretary", i.e., contemporary religious authorities) for favors associate someone with God.[75] Although Bozdağ affirms the traditional concept of the afterlife in the grave, he passes over two prominent aspects of these teachings: the examination and the punishment in the grave, from which only exceptional figures like prophets, *velis*, and martyrs are exempt.[76]

The next stage that Bozdağ refers to is *berzah*. According to him, every place in the material world is a space bridge (*uzay köprüsü*) permitting access to the Intermediate World and other worlds of conception (*hayâl âlemleri*) because information related to the material universe is elevated to the status of waves and creates images in the world of conception. Hence a person who liberates the vision of his soul may see the troops of Mehmet Fatih storming the walls of Istanbul. One could say that the history of matter has been recorded in the world of conception and that it preserves the old positions of matter whenever they change. Hence the spiritual dimension of objects that have passed from their material surrounding can be contemplated, and the eternal world

---

75 Bozdağ, *Sonsuzluk* 145–8; on traditional views on the "small death": Eklund, *Life* 9f., 23f., 53; Rebstock, Grabesleben 374, 378; on classical concepts regarding the communication of the dead with the living: Smith and Haddad, *Islamic understanding* 50f. The criticism of the veneration of Atatürk via the criticism of communist personality cults can also be found in the writings of Harun Yahya, *Yahudîlik* 485–509, who is dealt with below. That Marx lies in a normal grave with a bust on Highgate Cemetery is apparently unknown to Bozdağ.

76 Eklund, *Life* 6f., 30–8, 45–53; Smith and Haddad, *Islamic understanding* 40–7; Rebstock, Grabesleben 374.

is visible to those residing in the Intermediate World. Thus, one should imagine this realm as a movie depicting one's own complete life. Moreover, it is possible that a personal universe will be created for everyone. In this realm, humans will not be recognized on the basis of their outward forms but by the feelings that are spread by their souls. Everyone will be endowed with luminous armor, the strength of which will depend on their deeds in this life. Hence the Intermediate World will either provide a foretaste of the joys of paradise or the torments of hell. In order to get an idea of the Intermediate World, one should imagine a movie that transcends the restrictions imposed by the four dimensions and addresses all the human senses.[77] But whereas communication of the inhabitants of the Intermediate World with the material world is a special favor, the awareness of the acts of those left behind is the norm because the verbal expression of every human takes two forms. On the one hand, the human produces physical waves that are perceived as sound in this world. On the other hand, a "form" (*form*) emanates from his soul, which can also be perceived via telepathy. This form is first sensed by the angels accompanying each human being. "Every soul is a virtual radio transmitter; it transmits its feelings, thoughts and wishes in the form of waves to a spiritual dimension (*dalgalar halinde ruhsal boyuta aktarır*)." This continuing connection with the material universe is a benefit to those who are held in pleasant memory by their fellow men. For example, someone who has dedicated a *waqf* to the poor will perceive it when someone utters "may Allah be pleased." If people pray at the graves of their deceased relatives they may also be able to perceive this "form." The author claims that this is confirmed by some people who report that in such an instance they heard voices supplicating the living to pray for them. Hence Bozdağ once again exhorts his readers to pray at the gravesites lest they be forgotten by their relatives. For his concept of *berzah* Bozdağ does not refer to modern concepts and Western authorities. Instead he relates visions ascribed to the early Muslim ascetics Mālik b. Dīnār (d. ca. 131/748–9) and Ḥasan al-Baṣrī (d. 110/728) without, however, mentioning the sources.[78] In this context it is

---

77 Bozdağ, *Sonsuzluk* 148–51; *ʿālam al-khayāl* or *ʿālam al-mithāl* are often used as more specific synonyms for the *barzakh* or as types of different *barāzikh*: Eklund, *Life* 169–74; Gardet, ʿĀlam.

78 Bozdağ, *Sonsuzluk* 151–4; on the conceptualization of the *barzakh* as an ontologically different realm and the classical formulation of this idea: Eklund, *Life* 93–146; on classical ideas of the continuing perception of the dead: Smith and Haddad, *Islamic understanding* 51; further reports on visions of the *barzakh*: Rebstock, Grabesleben 372 no. 2; on Mālik b. Dīnār, an important role model for early Sufis: Gramlich, *Alte Vorbilder* 59–121, on the dead exhorting the living: 75f.

interesting that the cover of the book shows seagulls heading toward the sky. This could be seen as an allusion to a *ḥadīth* according to which the souls of the dead before resurrection are compared to birds, although Bozdağ does not refer to this tradition in the text.[79]

In the chapter on the fourth stage, resurrection, Bozdağ offers several explanations for eschatological signs common to the Sunni tradition. This stage is preceded by a phase of decay, which will not come as a surprise to those who know that, like humans, the universe undergoes various phases of life. He maintains that in society, decay is already apparent. People are becoming more and more isolated from each other, and an orderly family life has become rare: in Turkey, which has been affected by globalization, 744,000 couples have divorced in the last five years. Millions died during the communist revolutions and the wars in Chechnya and Bosnia. Worldwide, 850 million people suffer from hunger, and although the advance of technology makes ever more sophisticated gadgets available, people have lost a sense of gratitude to the Creator who makes these developments possible. The number of earthquakes is on the rise, the same applies to storms, the latter being a result of global warming.

For the signs of moral decay Bozdağ refers to the canonical *ḥadīth* collections and later compilations; with regard to natural disasters, he quotes various reports from the Turkish daily newspaper *Milliyet*.[80] He also refers to a common Islamic eschatological sign. He explains the rising of the sun in the West, believed to be alluded to in the Quran, as a planetary catastrophe similar to events that have recently occurred or which have been detected by current research. The rising of the sun in the West alludes to a change in the direction of the Earth's rotation. If the rotation of our planet slowed to the velocity of an airplane, all the objects on its surface would be whirled around and the usual order of rainfall would cease. As proof, he refers to El Niño and the tsunami on 26 December 2004; he claims that these have disrupted the Earth's rotation. As an alternative explanation he suggests that the poles might shift, as this has happened at least 400 times during the last 330 million years. We can conclude that he has confused the magnetic poles with the poles of the rotation axis from his claim that the weakening of the magnetic field, which has recently been observed, proves his assertion.[81]

Another sign that the end of the world is imminent is the struggle between good and evil or between the builders and destroyers (*iyilik-kötülük kavgası/ yapıcılar ve yıkıcılar*). The leaders of the destroyers are intellectual leaders

79 Eklund, *Life* 101f.; Nursi, *Sözler* 677.

80 Bozdağ, *Sonsuzluk* 155–64.

81 Ibid., 164–6.

like Comte, Darwin, and Marx, who claimed that the universe is uncreated, that the soul does not exist, and that there is no reality beyond matter. In various Christian and Muslim countries, their followers, such as Hitler, Lenin, and Saddam Hussein, seized power and suppressed the people. Here again, we may assume that Bozdağ's readers will interpret his words as an attack on Kemalism; that is, he has singled out Comte as a thinker whose ideas were a major source of inspiration for Atatürk, and Darwin was another thinker whose theory inspired the founder of the Turkish Republic. However, according to Bozdağ the awareness of the Creator is threatened not only in the political field. He declares science fiction and fantasy films such as *Star Trek* (see below) to be unacceptable because they cast doubt on the wisdom of the Creator. Furthermore, he warns that if the seeds of hatred between Muslims and Christians are sown, they might result in armed conflicts.[82] On the other hand, he also considers positive developments in the religious sphere as signs of imminent doom: Although most Christians still cling to the belief in the Trinity, some have recently come close to accepting the true nature of Jesus. Hence they might be willing to accept that Jesus will reappear among the Muslims.[83]

Bozdağ himself even suggests a date for doomsday. In a dream, he experienced an earthquake and tumbling rocks. Suddenly he saw his soul leaving his body and floating above charred ruins toward an unknown place. The next day he read in *Hürriyet* that the British astronomer Duncan Shell had calculated that parts of the comet Tuttle will hit the Earth on 14 August 2126. This would fit with the *ḥadīth* according to which mankind will continue to exist until roughly 1,500 years after the Prophet's death. When he began to write the book, Bozdağ asked asteroid expert Brian G. Marsden for confirmation. In his e-mail, the astronomer replied that such a collision was highly unlikely and, if the Earth were to be hit, then it would be by a hitherto unknown celestial body. Obviously unacquainted with the irony of British academics, Bozdağ mistook Marsden's reply to mean that the likelihood that the Earth will be hit by an asteroid is high. As an alternative cause of the end of life on Earth, Bozdağ cites the radiation of an exploding neutron star. However, doomsday does not necessarily have to come from space: As predicted by Professor King, if current developments like global warming continue for another sixty years, the end of mankind will be unavoidable.[84] Frightening as these conjectures may

---

82 Ibid., 169–71.

83 Ibid., 171–6.

84 Ibid., 177–80. His knowledge is based on reports in *Hürriyet* and *Milliyet* that rely on the German tabloid *Bild*. With regard to the *ḥadīth*, he refers to a Turkish translation of

be, Bozdağ has to address the fact that he can only explain the end of life on Earth, not the end of the cosmos as a whole. In order to explain this aspect in accordance with traditional cosmological and eschatological motives, he juggles with scientific terminology of which he has only a limited understanding. As can be seen in Q 39:68, the end of the world will come when God orders the angel Isrāfīl to blow the trumpet. According to Bozdağ, this means that the energy balance of the universe will break down due to the withdrawal of dark energy that is responsible for the expansion of the universe. In order to understand what will happen then, one has to imagine what will happen when all energy is withdrawn from the electrons. All particles will suddenly leave their places. According to Bozdağ this fits the Quranic prediction that the moon will come to a standstill and merge with the sun, that the stars will be extinguished, and the mountains leveled (Q 56:4–6; 73:14, 18; 75:7–10; 77:8–11; 88:1–3; 99:1–2). This vision of a total dissolution of matter is quite abstract; thus in the depiction of the judgment he returns to more earthly dangers like earthquakes and the moon burning.[85]

In his description of the resurrection and doomsday, Bozdağ adheres to more conventional elements that are much less challenging to notions derived from everyday experience like the march to the place of judgment. In accordance with the majority of classical sources, he asserts that animals will accompany men on the march and that they will be present at the judgment. But in light of more recent biological knowledge, Bozdağ stresses that all living beings that have ever existed will participate, so that people will be able to see dinosaurs. Like Gülen and Hekimoğlu İsmail, Bozdağ claims that this is possible because the genetic code of all creatures has been recorded in divine memory. Hence, their atoms (*zerreler*, i.e., the theological, not the physical ones) will be pieced together anew on the occasion of the resurrection. As proof of the possibility of transporting atoms to a designated position, he refers to the experiment of Austrian physicists who allegedly managed to transfer particles in 2004. The experiment in question, regarding quantum entanglement, was indeed presented in the media as the first step toward transporting things by "beaming" (familiar to *Star Trek* fans) them, although scientists stressed that they were

---

ʿAlāmāt al-qiyāma by al-Barzanjī who quotes Jalāl al-Dīn al-Suyūṭī's *al-Kashf fī mujāzawat ḥazīn al-umma al-alfa alladhī dallat ʿalayhi al-āthār*.

85 Bozdağ, *Sonsuzluk* 181–4; the concept that the world could come to an end (*Ol ve öl*) when the forces keeping the cosmos together collapse can be found earlier in articles for Nurcu magazines: Anonymous, Kainatin sonu.

only transferring quantum states of photons and not matter.[86] For evildoers, the millennial march to the place of judgment will lead through a waterless plain; the period of waiting for the judgment is depicted as a material torment again, following traditional imagery.[87] But when his narrative addresses the record of deeds, Bozdağ adapts the traditional imagery to technological progress. Sins and virtuous acts are no longer put down in a book, but in a recording device unparalleled by anything we know. Everyone will be shown everything they ever did and said in word and image.[88] The Bridge, "thin as a hair and sharp as a sword," is again depicted according to the tradition. The speed with which it will be crossed, and whether one will succeed in crossing the passage at all, is determined by the amount of good and bad deeds of the person in question. The fact that Bozdağ emphasizes that people will be punished for the mistreatment of animals reflects an empathy for animals which is a trait typical in Nurcu thought with a well-known Quran and *ḥadīth* basis.[89]

For Bozdağ, punishment in hell is a logical consequence of the purpose of creation: "The universe has been created for the sake of praise and remembrance. Hence everybody will glorify Allah in his or her own particular language." Referring to Jalāl al-Dīn Rūmī (d. 672/1273), Bozdağ calls hell the place of worship of the deniers. He asserts that according to Ibn al-ʿArabī (d. 638/1240), four categories of men will end up there: (a) the deniers of the Creator, (b) leaders who elevate themselves to a god-like status, (c) those who associate causes, natural laws, humans or idols with the Creator, and (d) those who outwardly pretend to believe although they deny the existence of God. Bozdağ singles out group (c) because "those founders of destructive ideologies … [are the reason] thousands of young people were entrapped by their ideas and spilt blood. They passed away without preparing themselves for infinity." Every day they had millions of opportunities to repent and to begin to pray.[90] Those doomed

---

86 Bozdağ, *Sonsuzluk* 190–4; on the presence of animals in classical sources: Smith and Haddad, *Islamic understanding* 76f.; also see Nursi, *Sözler* 408. He stresses that wild beasts and snakes become tame. The idea that cloning proves the possibility of resurrection seems to be popular in the Islamic world: Nadwī, *Istinsākh*.

87 Bozdağ, *Sonsuzluk* 194–201; al-Ghazālī, *Iḥyāʾ* iv, 513–6; Gardet, Ḳiyāma; Gardet, *Grands problèmes* 274.

88 Bozdağ, *Sonsuzluk* 201–3.

89 Ibid., 203–5; cf.: al-Ghazālī, *Iḥyāʾ* iv, 524–6; Gardet, *Grand problèmes* 320f.; Smith and Haddad, *Islamic understanding* 78f.; on Said Nursi's empathy for animals: Şahiner, *Son şahitler* i, 418.

90 Bozdağ, *Sonsuzluk* 209–13; his references to the two great Sufi teachers are, however, questionable. Jalāl al-Dīn Rūmī states that the inhabitants of hell (*ahl-i dūzakh*) are happier in hell than they were in this world, in spite of their torments, because they are now aware of

to hell will be punished with a new kind of pain. While only the brain senses pain in this world, in hell every single cell will be tormented. In addition to physical pain, sinners will suffer from utter loneliness. The worst punishment, however, will be seeing those who have entered paradise. According to Bozdağ, Allah will distinguish between different types of sinners. The author expects a mild punishment for those who have not heard of Islam, but he does not take up Said Nursi's idea of a deluxe section for righteous non-believers.[91]

Whereas Hekimoğlu İsmail's vision of the hereafter does not differ fundamentally from this world, Bozdağ's does. According to his concept, the world will be created anew in totally different forms of matter and light.[92] Bozdağ claims that Allah will create eight paradises (*cennet*) with different "light levels." *Firdevs* will be the one closest to the throne, but, as it is possible to make the transition from one space/time system to the other, people will also be able to wander from one paradise to the other. Although Bozdağ gives quite concrete details of *what* will happen, he concedes that he is unable to explain *how* it will come about. He goes on to assert that, in addition to the common paradise, where all of the rewarded will interact, every individual will be endowed with a personal paradise. These personal paradises will differ in size and richness depending on the good deeds the person in question has done during his worldly life. And they will also make up for the hardship that the person had to endure.[93] The inhabitants of paradise will find themselves in a world that differs in one fundamental aspect from this world – a reference to Said Nursi's concept of the ontological difference between the two sides of creation: "The greatest difference between this world and Paradise is the separation between wisdom and power (*hikmet-kudret ayrımı*). The Creator creates this-worldly phenomena, and in order to prevent us from bewilderment, He

---

God (*az ḥaqq bā khabar*): Jalāl al-Dīn Rūmī, *Fīhī mā fīhi* 229/*Fîhi mâ-fîh* 199. The four categories Ibn ʿArabī mentions are (a) the arrogant (*al-mutakabbirūn*), (b) the associationists/idol worshipers (*al-mushrikūn*), (c) the deniers of God's attributes (*al-muʿaṭṭilūn*), and (d) the hypocrites (*al-munāfiqūn*). This short explanation of categories does not contain a reference to "destructive ideologies": Ibn ʿArabī, *Futūḥāt* iv, 393–4.

91 Bozdağ, *Sonsuzluk* 214f.; the idea of a hierarchy of "hells" is a traditional element: Thomassen, Islamic hell 408.

92 Bozdağ, *Sonsuzluk* 187.

93 Ibid., 222–6. The idea that paradise consists of levels that reflect different levels of piety and religious achievement as such could already be found in pre-modern eschatological literature: Rustomji, *Garden* 115–7. The idea of a hierarchy of paradises can also be found in the writings of the mid-twentieth-century Egyptian author ʿAbd al-Razzāq Nawfal: Smith and Haddad, *Islamic understanding* 136–7; on the *barāzikh* in the writings of al-Shaʿrānī: Eklund, *Life* 169.

hides His power behind the curtain of causes."[94] Whereas in this world God voluntarily abstains from certain actions, He will fulfill every wish of those who enter paradise. In addition, they will become spiritual beings, devoid of matter (*canlılığın genelleşmesi*). Furthermore, the inhabitants will experience objects, which are regarded as inanimate in this world, as living because an angel will be assigned to each one of them. According to Bozdağ, this was recently demonstrated by "Professor" Masaru Emoto, a Japanese esotericist, who claims to have proven the effect of human emotions on the formation of ice crystals.[95] Moreover, Bozdağ asserts that the senses will lose their restrictions so that it will be possible to see those colors whose light spectrum cannot be perceived in this world.[96] In addition to being freed from the restriction of causality, the inhabitants of paradise will be free from restrictions of place. Like the angels or Khiḍr, they will be capable of multi-locality (*çok mekanlılık*) and hence able to enjoy the company of their loved ones whenever they like while promenading above the clouds at the same time. Moreover, they will be able to assume any size they want. According to Bozdağ, certain experiences in this world already allow one to get an idea of these phenomena. For example, if something happens to her child in Japan, a mother will know about it via telepathy. The possibility of such an interconnection results from the fact that when the universe began it was compressed to 10^{-33} cm: "Although the universe expands, we are one whole and hence we are at every place in the universe," whereas, according to the crude materialism of Newtonian physics, "I am here and you are there." From this statement Bozdağ proceeds to an at least questionable application of Heisenberg's uncertainty principle to bodies definitely larger than subatomic particles. According to Bozdağ, everybody is simply in one place with a higher probability and in others with a lower probability. This also serves to explain reports about *veli*s who were seen at different places at the same time or who suddenly disappeared.[97] Moreover, everything in paradise will be living, but not in a wild way. Instead, all beings will be conscious, virtuous, dignified,

94 Bozdağ, *Sonsuzluk* 226f.

95 Ibid., 227–9.

96 Ibid., 230–3.

97 Ibid., 233–6; on the topos of bi- or multi-locality in *karāmāt* legends: Gramlich, *Wunder* 212–8, 280–7; on the sudden appearance of Khiḍr: Franke, *Begegnung* 18f. Bozdağ's polemics against Newtonian determinism are based on Davies and Gribbin, *Matter myth* 24–56. Moreover, the defamation of Newton and problematic speculations allegedly based on quantum physics are a common theme in New Age literature: Bochinger, „*New Age*" 427–9; Hanegraaff, *New Age* 145, 322–4; so, too, is the idea of cosmic interrelation: Hanegraaff, *New Age* 296.

honest, friendly, and of splendid purity as well as unique value.[98] For the sensual pleasures awaiting the inhabitants of paradise, Bozdağ finds a new explanation, too. First, it will be a compensation for emotional and sexual pleasure, which one should reasonably forgo in this world: How many beautiful women have fallen in love then become crazy and end up as drug addicts, because their marriages falter! "Who nurtures his soul from paradise for him love (*aşk*) will flourish there." Men will find pleasure in their union with the *ḥūrīs*. However, they will experience something completely different from sexual intercourse in this world, that is, from genital penetration. In the other world, all the cells of the two bodies will permeate each other. Women will either become *ḥūrīs* or their overseers (*hurilerin sultanları konumunda*).[99]

Those who enter paradise will pass their time with endless visits to friends. They will flow in the rhythm of the unknown music of the heavens, the winds, and nature in paradise. Everything will be filled with pleasant smells. Yet, even in paradise, people will not cease to ask questions. They will be curious and ask who grants them all these unbelievable favors and they will long to see Him. Finally the heavens will open up, the souls will stand still and freeze (*durup dondunuz*) and so will the time of paradise. Even the years in paradise cannot be compared to the moment when each servant in paradise (*cennetlik kulu*) will experience the presence of divine beauty (*İlahî Cemal*) according to their consciousness, rank, and judgment. This vision (*görüş*) will transform those who have undergone it into the most sought-after beauties in paradise. And this transformation is a reciprocal process: Because paradise and its inhabitants love each other, paradise, too, will increase in beauty.

> Infinity awaits us; it did not matter that we had to endure hardship, that we were freezing, that we could not enjoy ourselves for twenty years or so on this bitter road toward indescribable expanses; may those who did good deeds and gave priority to their ritual duties as believers enjoy infinity![100]

In the final chapter, Bozdağ switches back from the climax of his vision of the hereafter to everyday life. It is here that he admonishes his readers to collect the treasure and to plant a seedling for the hereafter with every single action.[101]

---

98 Bozdağ, *Sonsuzluk* 237–9.

99 Ibid., 240f.

100 Ibid., 243f.

101 Ibid., 247–50.

Remarkably, Bozdağ does not include the major features of traditional eschatology in his reformulation of eschatological concepts, namely the advent of the apocalyptical figures of the *mahdī*, Dajjāl, and the beast of the Earth, and the second coming of Jesus. These aspects are the focus of the attention of another author, Harun Yahya.

6 Harun Yahya (Adnan Oktar): The Eschatological Visions of a Fellow Traveler of the Nurcus

Eschatological motives form an important part of the writings of Adnan Oktar, a former student of architecture and philosophy (without a religious education), who is known under the pen name Harun Yahya (b. 1956). In the 1980s, he began to address students and pupils from Istanbul's upper class in sermons on the collapse of the theory of evolution, Judeo-Masonic conspiracies, and the imminent end of the world. These sermons were supplemented by books and tracts that consisted to a large extent of photocopied press clippings. Until the 1990s, Yahya was a figure on the fringe of the Islamic religious camp in Turkey and, as late as 1996, even the most knowledgeable observer of Islamic groups did not give his group much chance of survival.[102] However, at the end of the 1990s his fame increased considerably because he was one of the first Islamic activists to realize the opportunities the Internet provides for propagating one's agenda. Thus he has gained prominence in Turkey and abroad for his polemics against the theory of evolution on his various websites. He now commands considerable financial means and a staff of collaborators who write the dozens of books published under his name. Furthermore, he organizes conferences with non-Muslim opponents of the theory of evolution and with religious dignitaries. His emissaries are sent to Islamic conventions worldwide in order to propagate his ideas.[103] Although he has never been affiliated to any of the different currents of the Nurcu movement, he often refers to Said Nursi in his writings.

The first publication with which Harun Yahya attracted attention was the booklet *Is AIDS the Beast of Earth discussed in the Quran?* published in 1987.[104] After some pages containing a selection of press clippings related to AIDS, he comes forward with his first piece of evidence: a correlation between

102 Çakır, *Ayet* 246.

103 Riexinger, Propagating 104–8; Solberg, *Mahdi* 1–13, 194–200.

104 Chapters were published in advance in the Nurcu magazine *Zafer*, the *Millî Gazete*, the organ of the Islamist Refah Partisi, and the center right daily *Tercüman*; Dayıoğlu, AIDS.

the numbers of Quranic verses related to punishment for a sinful life and the decades of the twentieth century in which AIDS appeared. Verses 70–1 of Sura 22 warn those who deny God, and the first case of AIDS can be traced back to 1971! Q 7:80–4 reports the punishment inflicted on the *qawm Lūṭ*, and it was in the 1980s that homosexuals were punished with AIDS. The cross sum of Q 27:82 is 19, and 1982 is the year in which the number of AIDS infections began to explode.[105] With regard to the more detailed descriptions of the beast in the *ḥadīth*, Yahya argues that it is impossible to interpret them literally. Based on the dimensions indicated in some traditions, the beast's head would reach far beyond the Earth's atmosphere.[106] However, other traditions ascribe a human face to this creature and say that it walks on four feet. Furthermore, it is predicted that it will appear "beyond Mecca" but that it will be seen for the first time in the West. According to Yahya, these are unmistakable predictions of AIDS, which according to scientists in Europe and America was transmitted to humans from guenon monkeys in Africa, hence from beyond Mecca. The enormous speed ascribed to the beast refers to the quick rise in the number of those afflicted with AIDS.[107] Furthermore, Yahya declares that the leopard-like skin mentioned in some reports on the beast is a reference to Kaposi's sarcoma concomitant with AIDS.[108] Moreover, he stresses that, according to some *ḥadīth*s, the beast will first afflict the *qawm Lūṭ* (people of Lot, taken here to be a synonym for homosexuals), a prediction that has turned out to be true, because AIDS spread among homosexuals, and, as predicted, it does indeed brand the unbelievers.[109] As the chief evidence for his interpretations of the traditions on the beast, he refers to Said Nursi's comparison of the beast to a herd of animals devouring men from within,[110] to his equating the Dajjāl with dangerous ideological tendencies,[111] and to his demand that those verses and traditions, the literal sense of which contradicts established findings of science, be interpreted allegorically.[112]

Yahya's thesis did not meet with the approval of the Nurcus. Gülen declared that the beast would not appear unless the number of those believing in God

105 Yahya, *AIDS* 24–6, 31; Schönig, AIDS 216.

106 Yahya, *AIDS* 45–51.

107 Yahya, *AIDS* 54–64.

108 Ibid., 72f.; Schönig, AIDS 215.

109 Yahya, *AIDS* 76–82, 87–90. The association of AIDS with homosexuals is underscored by clippings from the secular press: 12–21.

110 Ibid., 29f., 40f., 91–6.

111 Ibid., 44.

112 Ibid., 49f.

declined dramatically. Moreover, he asserts that, when this time comes, philosophy and technology will have made so much progress that man will consider himself the true Creator. Hence, he concludes that if there was a development that could be associated with the advent of the beast then it should be sought in the field of reproductive medicine instead. A further objection Gülen raises is based on a *ḥadīth* transmitted by Abū Dāwūd. According to this tradition, there is no illness against which God has not sent a remedy. Hence, in earlier times the plague virus (sic) should have been considered the beast. Gülen concludes that AIDS may be considered one of the phenomena that constitute the beast, but the disease should not be identified with this eschatological sign – all the more so as there will be no more belief in God and everything will move backward after it appears.[113]

In 1989, Harun Yahya devoted the book *Mehdi ve Altınçağ* (The Mahdī and the golden age) to the imminent advent of the *mahdī*.[114] Like his treatise on AIDS,[115] this book is characterized by the ample use of pre-modern eschatological literature. For example, Yahya declares that the existence of such a figure cannot be doubted because of the *tawātur* traditions, as proven by Aḥmad Sirhindī (d. 1034/1624) in his *Maktūbāt*, al-Barzanjī (d. 1103/1691) in his *ʿAlāmāt al-qiyāma*,[116] and the Indian scholar Ṣiddīq Ḥasan Khān (1834–90) in his *Kitāb al-Burhān fī ʿalāmat al-mahdī ākhir al-zamān*.[117] In an updated version that can be found on the Internet he refers to medieval Muslim authorities such as Ibn ʿArabī, Ibn Ḥajar, and Jāsim al-Muhalhil as authorities who prove that the signs of the imminent advent of the *mahdī* are oppression and injustice on Earth. Furthermore Harun Yahya cites those authors in order to demonstrate that the *mahdī* will fight the Dajjāl and be a contemporary of Jesus who will return to Earth.[118]

Harun Yahya asserts that the period after the advent of the *mahdī* will be a golden age of abundance. Genetic modification and the use of new techniques of cultivation in desert areas will provide food in unforeseen quantities.[119] The *mahdī*'s generosity will end inflation and economic hardship. Moreover,

---

113 Gülen, *Asr* ii, 48ff.; Gülen, *İnanç* ii, 133ff. Gülen does not refer to Harun Yahya by name.

114 A short version is already contained in his voluminous book dedicated to anti-Semitic and anti-Masonic conspiracy theories: Yahya, *Yahudîlik* 514–56.

115 Sources are listed in Schönig, AIDS 214.

116 Cook, Messianism.

117 Yahya, *Mehdi* 4–8, 36–9; the scholarship of Ṣiddīq Ḥasan Khān is not tainted by any modernist influences: Preckel, *Islamische Bildungsnetzwerke*, Riexinger, *Ṣanāʾullāh* 128–35.

118 http://www.harunyahya.org/imani/mehdiyet/altin.html.

119 Yahya, *Mehdi* 16–25; http://www.harunyahya.org/imani/mehdiyet/altin5.html.

astonishing advancements in technology will transform people's lives.[120] He contrasts this vision with a bleak picture of the present. With headlines from newspapers he creates the impression that gambling, the consumption of alcohol, tobacco, and illegal drugs, crime, divorce, suicide, and prostitution are increasing relentlessly.[121]

Referring to a saying of *imām* ʿAlī (d. 40/661) reported by Ṣiddīq Ḥasan Khān, he asserts that death, hunger, strife, and catastrophes/discord (*fitneler*, Arabic: sing. *fitna*), the loss of traditions (*sünnetler*), the widespread appearance of innovations (*bid'atlerin ortaya çıkması*), and the neglect of *al-amr bi-l-maʿrūf wa-l-nahy ʿan al-munkar* are signs of the imminent coming of the *mahdī*. He considers this prophecy to be fulfilled by the various wars taking place at the time.[122] Furthermore, he quotes a prediction found in al-Barzanjī's treatise according to which an upheaval (*ayaklanma*) will take place in Shawwāl, and he talks about a war in Dhū l-Qaʿda, and a war in Dhū l-Ḥijja. He draws attention to the fact that the first demonstration against the Shah took place in September 1976/Shawwāl 1396, whereas the Iran-Iraq war started in September 1980/Dhū l-Qaʿda 1400.[123] He refers to another tradition reported by Ṣiddīq Ḥasan Khān according to which Ṭāliqān is in a pitiful state but that there are rich deposits of gold and silver, and that people with a proper knowledge of Allah will help the *mahdī*. He identifies Ṭāliqān as Afghanistan, which possesses natural resources in abundance and was in a pitiful state under Soviet occupation.[124] The prediction that the flow of the Euphrates will be interrupted is identified with the Keban Dam, a part of Turkey's irrigation system,[125] and the occupation of the *ḥaram* in Mecca by Saudi militants in 1979 is equated to prophecies regarding a violation of the sanctity of the Kaʿba.[126] Before the second Gulf War he identified the prophecies regarding a fire to be seen in the East, which burns people and goods, with the burning of a Romanian tanker in the Bosporus in 1979,[127] whereas in a revised version he identifies the fire

120 Yahya, *Mehdi* 25–9.

121 Ibid., 44–6.

122 Ibid., 48.

123 Ibid., 50f.; in the more recent online version photos of famines in Africa and Kurdish victims of the Ḥalabja gas attack are used to underline this assertion: http://www.harunyahya.org/imani/mehdiyet/altini.html.

124 Yahya, *Mehdi* 52f.

125 Ibid., 54f.; *Yahudîlik*, 531f.; the interruption of the Euphrates by the Turkish South Anatolia Project (GAP) is an important element in recent Arab apocalyptic writings: Cook, *Contemporary* 51.

126 Yahya, *Mehdi* 60f.; Yahya, *Yahudîlik* 535.

127 Yahya, *Mehdi* 62–9; Yahya, *Yahudîlik* 524–30.

with the oil pits set on fire by the Iraqi army during its flight from Kuwait in 1991.[128] As an example of the afflictions to which the Muslims are exposed he draws attention to Turkish atheists speaking out publicly,[129] and in a revised version he cites the alleged teaching of Darwinism from primary school to university in Turkey. Hence he equates contemporary Muslims, who have to cope with the propaganda of materialist ideologies, to the *ahl al-kahf*, who had to struggle in a hostile environment.[130] Furthermore, he refers to one *ḥadīth* listed by Ṣiddīq Ḥasan Khān according to which a "great event" will take place before the advent of the *mahdī*. However, he asserts that, contrary to common assumption, this will not happen in Medina. Instead, he argues, *madīna* may refer to any city, and all details (black stones, the killing of a woman, the extension over two kilometers) demonstrate that it must be equated with the violent May Day demonstration in Istanbul in 1977.[131] Last but not least, the *mahdī* will appear in a period without a caliph.[132]

But signs are not to be discovered through the analysis of political events alone. A list of apocalyptic signs also contains natural and major man-made disasters like the Chernobyl nuclear meltdown and the Bhopal gas leak.[133] As predicted, both a solar and lunar eclipse occurred during the months of Ramaḍān in 1981 and 1982, and Halley's Comet, which reappeared in 1986, is to be identified with the predicted star born in the East.[134] He identifies a "sign emerging from the sun" with a giant eruption on the solar surface, and the splitting of heaven referred to in the Quran (Q 77:9; 82:1; 84:1) with the shrinking ozone layer.[135]

According to a *ḥadīth* reported by Mālik the world will last seven days, but the days of God are like a thousand years for humans. Seven thousand years does not refer to human history as a whole, but to the time that will have passed after a landmark event in human history, such as the Great Flood. Harun Yahya objects to the claim that the *umma* will exist for 1,400 years. He prefers the time

128 http://www.harunyahya.org/imani/mehdiyet/altini.html.

129 Yahya, *Mehdi* 47; Yahya, *Yahudîlik* 545, here he also includes the increase in drug abuse (552–4).

130 Yahya, *Mehdi* 68f.

131 Ibid., 70–4.

132 Ibid., 84.

133 Ibid., 75; in the online version jihadist attacks figure prominently: http://www.harunyahya.org/imani/mehdiyet/altini.html.

134 Yahya, *Mehdi* 56–9; Yahya, *Yahudîlik* 536–9; http://www.harunyahya.org/imani/mehdiyet/altini.html; Halley's Comet also appears as an eschatological sign in Arab eschatological tracts of the same period: Cook, *Contemporary* 55, 75.

135 Yahya, *Mehdi* 78f.

frame of 1,500 to 1,600 years suggested by Aḥmad Sirhindī, but he considers the year 1,400 as the beginning of the end of time marked by the appearance of the *mahdī*.[136]

Whereas Harun Yahya identifies many eschatological signs with current events, he is much less explicit with regard to the person of the *mahdī*. He mainly restricts himself to listing his characteristics, and events that will help to identify him.[137] The conquest of Istanbul ascribed to the *mahdī* is described not as a military event but as a spiritual event without bloodshed.[138] Among the opponents of the *mahdī*, the Sufyānī, who will kill indiscriminately in al-Shām, is singled out and identified. Harun Yahya equates him to Ḥāfiẓ al-Asad because he delivered his country into the clutches of communism and killed 30,000 Muslims in Hama in 1982.[139] The Dajjāl and most of his followers are Jews, who lead people astray with the help of materialism, the consumption of pork and alcohol, homosexuality, and sexual perversion (*cinsi sapkınlık*) in general.[140] Another group of opponents referred to are the "reactionaries" (*gericiler*). With this term, which is usually used by Kemalists to denounce religious groups, Harun Yahya refers to those who impose excessive religious demands, and hence overemphasize formalities, forbid the arts and music, humiliate women, and oppose technology. Even with the end of the world in sight, Harun Yahya seems to consider it necessary to demonstrate his loyalty to the state.[141] Furthermore, he equates contemporary Muslims, who will witness the advent of the *mahdī*, to the *ahl al-kahf*, who also had to defend themselves against the onslaught of the anti-religious ideas of their time and their proponents.[142] Finally, he refers to Said Nursi, who remarked that the Naqshbandī Khalīd Baghdādī is the renewer (*müceddid*) of the thirteenth century and the *Risâle-i Nûr* – not himself as a person – will play this role in the fourteenth century. According to Harun Yahya, this bolsters his own claim that the *mahdī* will appear at the beginning of the fifteenth century.[143] In addition, he presents Said Nursi's prediction of the imminent renewal of the Muslim

136 Ibid., 36–9.

137 Ibid., 85–184.

138 Ibid., 104–11.

139 Ibid., 120–2; on this figure which is derived from pro-Umayyad eschatological predictions transformed into a black legend: Madelung, Sufyānī; Madelung, al-Sufyānī; Cook, *Studies* 122–36.

140 Yahya, *Mehdi* 195.

141 Ibid., 124–7.

142 Ibid., 150–6.

143 Ibid., 170f.; on Khālid al-Baghdādī and his importance for Naqshbandīs in the Ottoman Empire: Abu Manneh, Naqshbandiyya-Mujaddidiyya.

world in his "Damascus Sermon" (1913) as another allusion to the advent of the *mahdī*, although this figure is not mentioned in that tract.[144]

As in the case of the *mahdī*, Harun Yahya's treatment of Jesus is limited mainly to listing his characteristics.[145] His book on AIDS as the beast of Earth has been integrated (as a chapter) into the treatise on the *mahdī*. The last issue he deals with is the smoke from which Sura 44 takes its name. According to Harun Yahya, it has to be identified with the radioactive fallout after the core meltdown in Chernobyl in 1986.[146]

In a more recent version of the tract, Yahya also quotes *imāmī* Shiʿi sources like *Biḥār al-anwār* (Seas of light) by Muḥammad Bāqir al-Majlisī (d. 1110/1698) and al-Ṭabrisī's (d. 548/1153) Quranic commentary *Majmaʿ al-bayān li-ʿulūm al-Qurʾān* (Collection of the explanation of the sciences of the Quran), (Abū l-Naḍr) al-ʿAyyāshī (d. ca. 320/932), (Muḥammad b. al-Ḥasan) al-Ṭūsī (d. 460/1067), and a certain al-Qummī (most likely ʿAlī b. Ibrāhīm, d. fourth/tenth century). Given that page references are lacking, one may conclude that he has used material compiled by another author.[147] Furthermore, he has included poems in praise of the *mahdī* by the well known Islamist poet Sezai Karakoç (b. 1933) and other less well-known authors.[148]

The end of the world, the resurrection, and the judgment are apparently much less interesting for Harun Yahya than are the *mahdī* and the Dajjāl. Although he devoted the tract *Ölüm – Kıyamet – Cehennem* (Death, resurrection, and hell) to these issues, unlike the writings discussed above, it consists merely of affirmations of traditional beliefs and admonitions.[149]

7 Concluding Remarks

7.1 *Eschatology in the Context of Debates on Science and Religion*

References to concepts and terms of modern physics are a remarkable trait of Bozdağ's eschatology. Although this ingredient is absent from the eschatological writings of the other authors discussed here, it is a central element of Nurcu thought and Turkish Islamic discourse in general. Examples from other

144 Yahya, *Mehdi* 174f.

145 Ibid., 187–208.

146 Ibid., 290–6.

147 http://www.harunyahya.org/imani/mehdiyet/altin12.html.

148 http://www.harunyahya.org/imani/mehdiyet/altin6.html.

149 http://www.harunyahya.org/imani/OKiyametC.html; the first two and the last chapter are dedicated to the refutation of Darwinism and the affirmation of creation.

regions can easily be found, and a systematic analysis of the phenomenon promises to be rewarding.

In the particular Turkish case, this development can be traced back to the debate brought about by the Young Turks' enthusiastic reception of Ludwig Büchner's "Vulgärmaterialismus" and Ernst Haeckel's monism during the first years of the twentieth century.[150] As early as 1906, Ahmet Hilmî countered their materialist positions by remarking that it is impossible to differentiate strictly between matter and energy.[151] A more extensive elaboration of the argument was brought forward in 1928. İsmail Fenni (since 1935 Ertuğrul), a retired civil servant with a broad but autodidactic knowledge of Islamic and Western thought, published a polemic against Büchner's *Kraft und Stoff*, which – although already totally forgotten in Germany – still informed the mindset of most Turkish secular intellectuals. In order to undermine the foundations of materialism, he referred to French philosophers and scientists, stressing that the discovery of radioactivity had shown that matter was not eternal.[152] One and a half decades later, this theme was adopted by Mustafa Şekip Tunç (1886–1958), a psychiatrist and follower of Bergsonian philosophy, in Necip Fazıl Kısakürek's (1905–83) monthly *Büyük Doğu* (The great east), the first magazine with an Islamic agenda that was allowed to be published in the Turkish Republic. He went a decisive step further than Hilmî and Ertuğrul, both of whom had merely correctly demonstrated that materialism is based on an outdated concept of matter. By contrast, Tunç began to use the theory of relativity for far-reaching speculations that included eschatology. In his view, black holes prove that matter will finally disappear.[153] Around the same time, the reformulation of the macrocosm-microcosm concept mentioned above also made its first appearance in *Büyük Doğu*.[154]

The Nurcus, however, do not seem to have been interested in such speculations, at least initially. Said Nursi had no knowledge of modern physics

150 Hanioğlu, Blueprints.

151 Hilmî, *Meslek-i zalâleti* 64f. He was probably not aware of Einstein's special theory of relativity that had been published just one year before, but did know of George Poincaré's reflections on the equality of energy and matter published in 1900.

152 Fenni, *Mâddiyûn* 305–9.

153 Tunç, Madde ve ruh 2; Tunç, Madde ve ruh 4; Tunç, Madde ve ruh 5; Tunç, Madde ve ruh 6; Elbi, Kâinat ve aynştayn 1; Elbi, Kâinat ve aynştayn 2; in the 1920s, Tunç contributed to the review *Dergâh*, which opposed the positivist ideology underlying Kemalism and propagated the vitalism of Bergson instead: Ülken, *Türkiye'de çağdaş düşünce* 368–75; Çınar, Dergâh; İrem, Değişim siyaseti 107–10; on the *Büyük Doğu*: Cantek, Büyük Doğu; Koçak, Büyük Doğu.

154 Uzdilek, Atom ve yıldızlar 7.

and stuck to the nineteenth-century concepts with which he had become acquainted during his self-directed studies. Hence, he claimed that velocity can be increased infinitely, and for his explanation of the *miʿrāj* he relied on the concept of space filled with ether.[155] Things changed in the early 1970s when Gülen introduced the Big Bang theory as an argument in his campaign against the theory of evolution, which was, as he maintained, based on the conception of the eternity of matter.[156] Other authors go one step further. When they attack the alleged epistemological foundations of modernism, they claim that the theory of relativity and quantum physics have undermined "Newtonian" epistemology, which ascribes an exact position to each body, whereas neither simultaneity independent of an observer nor definite causes exist, and all phenomena are interconnected.[157]

Gülen also adopted far-reaching speculations that had been propagated by Haluk Nurbaki (1924–97), a physician, right-wing politician, and contributor to *Büyük Doğu*. In order to prove the existence of angels and *jinn*, Nurbaki formulated some arguments in favor of plural worlds that Bozdağ recycles for his eschatological concepts. Nurbaki asserts that the theory of relativity provides proof of the concept of plural worlds, because time is a dimension that does not differ from the other three that we perceive as space. Hence we must assume that further worlds exist, and we cannot perceive them because they consist of other dimensions. In these other worlds, time, movement, and velocity differ from those we experience here on Earth. The author cites the worlds of angels and souls, and hell as examples.[158] Furthermore, Nurbaki claims that he was able to calculate the speed of the angels' movements on the basis of Q 70:4. According to this verse, angels and spirits return to their Lord in one day, which equals 50,000 human years, which comprise 18,250,000 days. On the basis of this speculation, Nurbaki concludes that they move at 18,250,000 times the speed of light. Hence it is normally impossible to perceive them with human senses. But according to the experiments of Professor Feinberg, tachyons can intrude punctually into the physical world although they are subject to a different current of time. Therefore, it is possible that angels bring about effects

155 Nursi, *Sözler* 515, 775, 779.

156 Gülen, *Yaratılış* 94.

157 Bouguenaya-Mermer, Fizik; Bouguenaya-Mermer, *Bilimin* 46f. The author is a physicist from a secular Algerian family who married a Nurcu she met during her studies in Durham, England. Her argument is taken up by Bozdağ, *Sonsuzluk* 41.

158 Nurbaki, *Verses* 69; for a biography cf.: http://www.davetci.com/d_biyografi/biyografi_hnurbaki.htm.

in our world.[159] Gülen follows Nurbaki with regard to most points, but he adds further elements from modern physics or earlier concepts. For example, he claims that angels consist of either ether or anti-matter. Although he maintains that they move faster than light, he calls them quanta.[160]

The idea of plural worlds has also been associated with black holes, as we can see in this anonymous contribution to a Nurcu magazine:

> Hence entering a black hole can be explained as entering the eternal world (*beka âlemi*). If we could enter a black hole unharmed and leave it again, we would experience the end of this voyage as a homecoming after millions of years. Because of these particular characteristics, astrophysicists of the California Technology Institute describe black holes as "time tunnels" or gates to another world. The doctrine "matter does not disappear" has been torn down by (the discovery of) the black hole.… Today such subjects are not discussed in religious gatherings (*sohbetler*) but at the most modern centers for astronomical research.[161]

Another author even identifies black holes with hell: No light escapes from them, yet their temperature is enormous, hence they are the black flame that never dies which is mentioned in the *ḥadīth*.[162]

Clearly these references to modern physics are not motivated by the desire to furnish explanations for natural phenomena, but rather by the intention of the authors to defend key elements of their worldview. An unmistakable indicator of the paramount importance of this ideological motif is the abundance of decontextualized terms and contradictory arguments. On the one hand, the authors refer to the uncertainty principle, but, on the other hand, they assert that God appears as the one who arranges the atoms (*zerre*) in perfect order in definite places.[163] Furthermore, they invoke the theory of relativity to undermine materialism, but do not take into account that, according to the space-time concept, time cannot be "sliced" into moments. Hence the theory of relativity is totally at odds with the atomistic concept of time to which both the Nurcus and Harun Yahya cling, and which is a central part of Bozdağ's vision of the afterlife. Apparently, they select arguments with an exclusive criterion to bolster a specific position. A surprising aspect of this apologetic approach is

---

159 Nurbaki, *Verses* 155; Nurbaki, Kâinatlar.

160 Gülen, *İnançın gölgesinde* i, 144–6.

161 Anonymous, Yıldızların ölümü; similarly: Keha, Var yok; Karabaşoğlu, Bilim 150.

162 Yıldırım, Cehennem; cf. Davies and Gribbin, *Matter myth* 266–73.

163 Bozdağ, *Sonsuzluk* 47.

the striking heterogeneity of the sources. They include such diverse material as scientific literature, science fiction novels, TV serials, and spurious reports in tabloids.

In addition to these contradictions, the appropriation of catchwords from modern science is marked by blatant double standards. Most authors discussed in this contribution strongly object to the theory of evolution; they assert that the evidence put forward is insufficient.[164] Yet when a physicist declares that theoretically tachyons might be conceived of, this is regarded as convincing proof of the existence of angels and *jinn*.

7.2 *"New Age" and Parapsychology as a Source of Inspiration for a "Modernized" Eschatology*

With his references to New Age concepts, Bozdağ introduced a new element that relates to the issues discussed earlier. He refers extensively to the contentious attacks of the physicists Fred Hoyle and Peter Davies on a "materialist" and determinist vision of the universe.[165] Hence, for anyone who is unaware of the controversial status of these ideas in the scientific community, the reference to Hoyle and Davies' concepts fits in well with the criticism of materialism supported by modern physics. Furthermore, Bozdağ's references to New Age literature are a link to his writings on personal development, which rely on the writings of Dana Zohar and Ian Marshall, who derived their management concepts from "quantum metaphysics."[166] With his interest in New Age ideas, Bozdağ is not an exception among Turkish-Islamic authors. The positive reception of New Age authors (in the broad sense) such as Fritjof Capra and Jeremy Rifkin as "crown witnesses" against materialism has been noted on a number of occasions.[167] And among the Nurcus it is also apparent in other contexts. Some authors, including Bozdağ, express their discontent with modern medicine and propose holistic alternatives.[168] However, to date the reception of New Age

164 On Harun Yahya: Riexinger, Propagating; Riexinger, Turkey; Gülen, *Yaratılış*; Bozdağ, *Sonsuzluk* 45f., 90–2. He goes one step further than other Islamic creationists by buttressing the argument from design in accordance with his metaphysical premise: beings are either beyond the limits of space/time (*ezeli*) or they have been created in space time by someone's will and power.

165 Bozdağ, *Sonsuzluk* 20, 41, 52.

166 Bozdağ, *Ruhsal zeka* 19; on Zohar and Marshall: Hammer, *Claiming knowledge* 292, 297–302. On "quantum metaphysics" in general: Hammer, *Claiming knowledge* 208, 274–303, 310–9; Bochinger, *„New Age"* 429–35; Hanegraaff, *New Age* 129–31.

167 Seufert, *Politischer Islam* 346; on "parascientificity" as a characteristic of religious movements in modernity see also Lambert, Religion in modernity 311–3, 323.

168 Mirzaoğlu, *Gözle görülmeyen* 158; Bozdağ, *İsteme* 65.

concepts has not been studied in detail. Because the same is true for the reception of these ideological elements in other parts of the Islamic world, it would be premature to conclude that their integration into an Islamic worldview is a specifically Turkish phenomenon. However, there are particular factors in Turkey that facilitate the accessibility of such concepts:

1. The lack of religious censorship and the orientation of considerable sections of the metropolitan population toward Western fashions, including parareligious ideas and fads.[169]
2. Turkey lacks a strong Salafī movement, thus concepts of post-Ibn ʿArabī Sufism have continued to influence Islamic thought there. Since both traditions have a common root in hermeticism,[170] this may have facilitated the adaptation of modern reformulations of concepts like the macrocosm and microcosm. In addition, the eclectic nature of New Age literature makes it possible to assimilate single elements (e.g., reincarnation, pantheism, and the idea of an albeit teleological cosmic evolution) into one's own concepts, and to discard others.

Bozdağ's description of the Intermediate World reveals the influence of themes derived from parapsychology. In fact, this is not a new phenomenon because spiritualism has met with a favorable response from Muslim authors in various regions since the late nineteenth century.[171] As mentioned earlier, the reference to spiritualism was primarily used by İsmail Fenni to prove the existence of an eternal, sublime soul. Later, when Gülen and other authors were confronting the "denialists" they claimed that paranormal events scientifically proved the existence of angels, *jinn*, Satan, and the soul.[172] However, spiritualism does not appear to have been used to provide a detailed "scientific" explanation of life after death. Two of Bozdağ's proofs of eschatological concepts that are based on parapsychological notions have parallels in works by Arab authors written decades earlier: the existence of the *barzakh* and the communication of

169 On New Age belief and whether it can be considered a religion, this depends on whether one considers common rituals and persisting communities part of the definition: Zinser, New Age.

170 Hanegraaff, *New Age* 386–401, 419f.

171 Ibid., 435–41.

172 Gülen, *Prizma* ii, 102–5, 209; Gülen, *İnançın gölgesinde* i, 154ff., Mirzaoğlu, *Gözle görülmeyen* 13, 167; Arslan, *Şeytan* 18.

the dead with the living.[173] But because Bozdağ does not usually refer to Arab sources in the original, these parallels must be considered the same way we consider other independent speculations.

It is a truism that eschatological ideas reveal the aspects of present-day society that their proponents consider deficient. Hence, the writings of Bozdağ and Harun Yahya relate explanations of eschatological verses and traditions to current events and the denunciation of moral decay like crime, AIDS, sexual perversion, reproductive technologies, drug abuse, the loss of faith, and the fact that "true" Islam does not enjoy the status it deserves, in the same way many modern Arab eschatological writings explain them.[174] In the tracts in question, natural disasters are described as eschatological signs.[175] Cook argues that the choice of these "lesser signs" is motivated by the assumption that they might appear immediately convincing.[176] However, Harun Yahya is aware that this choice poses a problem, because the signs are quite unspecific. Therefore he asserts that only the concentration of such events within a short period corroborates their significance.[177]

Further parallels between the Turkish examples presented here and Arab apocalyptic writing stand out. Like Harun Yahya, some Arab authors describe the reign of the *mahdī* as an age of brotherhood and harmony that will result from the encompassing dominance of Islam. Cook rightly draws attention to the parallels with secular utopias, in particular with communism.[178] Like Bozdağ, Arab authors adapt (albeit totally different) elements from science fiction to their scenarios.[179] Another element that can be observed is the depersonalization of the eschatological personnel.[180] However, in Shiʿi tracts the connection to the sources is stronger and the speculation far less wide-ranging,

173 Smith and Haddad, *Islamic understanding* 113–26; Although not specifically eschatological, Bozdağ's belief in telekinesis is also derived from parapsychology: Bozdağ, *Sonsuzluk* 50.

174 Smith and Haddad, *Islamic understanding* 106, 128–30; Cook, *Contemporary* 51–3.

175 Cook, *Contemporary* 51.

176 Ibid., 49f.

177 Yahya, *Mehdi* 41.

178 Cook, *Contemporary* 145–9. This similarity is also acknowledged by Shiʿi authors who cite Western utopian thought as proof of the coming reign of the *mahdī*: Ourghi, *Schiitischer Messianismus* 161f.

179 Cook, *Contemporary* esp. 77–83. The interest of Islamic authors in science fiction is dealt with by Szyska, Utopian writing.

180 Damir-Geilsdorf, Ende 263.

most probably because the strength of the clerical hierarchy has been able to prevent such excesses.[181]

Yet significant differences cannot be ignored. In terms of the central elements of recent apocalyptical writing in the Arab world, Cook singles out anti-Semitic conspiracy theories[182] and the adaptation of apocalyptic interpretations of the Bible, either those of Christian fundamentalists or those arrived at independently.[183] Neither element figures prominently in the writings of Harun Yahya and Bozdağ on eschatology, although Harun Yahya is a conspiracy theorist par excellence. Though he integrated a short version of his ideas on the *mahdī* into his anti-Semitic and anti-Masonic tract, with the exception of the assertion that the Dajjāl will be a Jew, his treatment of eschatology is almost totally devoid of conspiracy theories. Bozdağ is not interested in Jews at all; his examples of the oppression of Muslims come not from Palestine but from the Balkans and the Caucasus.

The most striking difference between the writings of the Turkish authors discussed here and modern radical Islamist apocalyptics in the Arab world relates to the absence of conspiracy themes. Although violence plays an eminent role in all eschatological concepts, it is evaluated very differently.[184] Whereas, for Bozdağ, war as such is an evil that marks the end of time, Arab apocalyptic tracts invoke a nuclear war as deliverance that rids Palestine of Jews yet leaves Muslims miraculously unharmed.[185] In the most extreme cases, the victory over the Jews and their annihilation has become so dominant that the end of the world no longer matters.[186] Whereas Arab apocalyptic writers associate the *mahdī* with warfare, and, for example, identify the victory over Rome as the subjugation of the West,[187] Harun Yahya tries to reinterpret the *mahdī*'s conquests as spiritual victories. Although the technological superiority of the West is a cause of envy for Turkish and Arab authors, this envy causes hatred in the Arab case, whereas for Bozdağ it is a stimulus for selective emulation.[188] Technology as such forms the basis of the golden age according to Harun Yahya, whereas for Maḥmūd Dāwūd the golden age will be brought

181 Ourghi, *Schiitischer Messianismus* 237.

182 Cook, *Contemporary* 15, 35–49, 61–71.

183 Cook, *Contemporary* 15, 18–35, 165; in the Shiʿi case, references to Nostradamus deserve a mention: Ourghi, *Schiitischer Messianismus* 159f.

184 Cook, *Contemporary* 208–13.

185 Ibid., 75–7.

186 Damir-Geilsdorf, Ende 268f., 276.

187 Cook, *Contemporary* 129–45; Damir-Geilsdorf, Ende 271f.

188 Bozdağ, *Ruhsal*.

about by the forced transfer of technology from the West to the Islamic world after military victory.[189]

It would be tempting to interpret these findings as corroboration of the thesis popular in Turkey that there is a distinctive "Turkish Muslimness" (*Türk Müslümanlığı*) marked by moderation and a clear inclination toward aesthetics.[190] However, such an evaluation is rendered impossible when we take into account elements like the conspiracy theories of Harun Yahya or Fethullah Gülen's strong affinity with Turkish militarism in other contexts.[191] Nevertheless, the recent Turkish eschatological literature provides enough material to modify Cook's damning analysis of apocalyptic authors as odd figures.[192] Bozdağ, at least, does not fit this description. His language is not sloppy at all. On the contrary, many readers have complained that it is too elaborate and scientific.[193] His writings on "personal growth" contrast with his apocalyptical visions because they are intended to guarantee the optimal functioning of the individual in this world. Hence, the idea that the end of the world is near does not necessarily compel those who believe in it to engage in incalculable and violent acts of desperation. The easiness with which Bozdağ writes about both worldly success and the afterlife shows that preoccupation with the things to come may cause other believers to become effective accountants busy preparing impeccable balance sheets for both their employer and their Lord.

Bibliography

Abu-Rabiʿ, I. (ed.), *Islam at the crossroads: On the life and thought of Bediuzzaman Said Nursi*, Albany, NY 2003.

Agai, B., *Zwischen Netzwerk und Diskurs: Das Bildungsnetzwerk um Fethullah Gülen (geb. 1938): Die flexible Umsetzung modernen islamischen Gedankenguts*, Schenefeld, Germany 2004.

Anonymous, Yıldızların ölümü, in *Köprü* 25 (November 1978), 25–8.

Anonymous, Kainatin sonu, in *Köprü* 27 (May 1979), 20–4.

Arberry A.J. (trans.), *The Koran interpreted*, Oxford 1986.

Arslan, A., *Şeytan ve cinler*, Istanbul 2004.

189 Cook, *Contemporary* 145–9.

190 For a elaborate version of this argument: Yavuz, Turkish Islam; a critical evaluation: Özdalga, Hidden Arab; and Riexinger, *Schöpfungsordnung*.

191 Riexinger, *Schöpfungsordnung*.

192 Cook, *Contemporary* 2–4.

193 Private e-mail communication.

Badıllı, A., *Bediüzzaman Said-i Nursi: Tarihçe-i hayatı*, Istanbul 1990.

Baljon, J.M.S., *Modern Muslim Koran interpretation (1880–1960)*, Leiden 1961.

Bochinger, C., *„New Age" und moderne Religion: Religionswissenschaftliche Analysen*, Gütersloh, Germany 1995².

Bouguenaya-Mermer, Y., *Bilimin marifetullah boyutları: Kur'ânî bir metodoloji arayışı*, Istanbul 1998.

———, Fizik ve ötesi, in *Köprü* 104 (February 1986), 5–8.

Bozdağ, M., *İstemenin esrarı*, Istanbul 2007.

———, *Ruhsal zeka* (SQ), Istanbul 2007.

———, *Sonsuzluk yolculuğu*, Istanbul 2005.

Büchner, L., *Kraft und Stoff oder Grundzüge der natürlichen Weltordnung nebst einer darauf gebauten Moral oder Sittenlehre*, Leipzig 1904.

Büyük Doğu, weekly (with interruptions), 1943–78.

Çakır, R., *Ayet ve slogan: Türkiye'de İslami oluşumlar*, Istanbul 1995⁸.

Cantek, L., Büyük Doğu, in A. Çiğdem, (ed.), *Muhafazakârlık*, Istanbul 2003, 645–55.

Çiğdem, A. (ed.), *Muhafazakârlık*, Istanbul 2003.

Çınar, M., Dergâh dergisi, in A. Çiğdem (ed.), *Muhafazakârlık*, Istanbul 2003, 85–91.

Cook, D., *Contemporary Muslim apocalyptic literature*, Syracuse, NY 2005.

———, Messianism in the mid-11th/17th century as exemplified by al-Barzanjī (1040–1103/1630–1691), in *JSAI* 33 (2007), 261–78.

———, *Studies in Muslim apocalyptic*, Princeton, NJ 2002.

Damir-Geilsdorf, S., Das Ende eine politische Wende? Gegenwärtige muslimische Erinnerungen an die Zukunft, in *Orient* 44 (2003), 257–79.

Davies, P. and J. Gribbin, *The matter myth: Beyond chaos and complexity*, London 1991.

Dayıoğlu, B., AIDS: Son mu, başlangıç mı?, in *Köprü* 112 (October 1986) 29–32.

Dursun, T., *Müslümanlık ve Nurculuk*, Istanbul 2004⁴.

Eklund, R., *Life between death and resurrection according to Islam*, Uppsala 1941.

Elbi, S., Kâinat ve aynştayn 1, in *Büyük Doğu* (5 June 1959), 12.

———, Kâinat ve aynştayn 2, in *Büyük Doğu* (19 June 1959), 12.

Fenni, İ., *Mâddiyûn mezhebi izmihlâli*, Istanbul 1928.

Franke, P., *Begegnung mit Khidr: Quellenstudien zum Imaginären im traditionellen Islam*, Stuttgart 2000.

Gardet, L., *Les grands problèmes de la théologie Musulmane (Essai de la théologie comparée): Dieu et la destinée de l'homme*, Paris 1967.

Gardet, L., ʿĀlam 2: ʿĀlam al-d̲j̲abarūt, ʿālam al-malakūt, ʿālam al-mit̲h̲āl, in *EI*², i, 350f.

———, Ḳiyāma, in *EI*², v, 235a–8b.

al-Ghazālī, A.Ḥ., *Iḥyāʾ ʿulūm al-dīn*, Cairo n.d.

Glaßen, E., ‚Huzur': Trägheit, Seelenruhe, soziale Harmonie: Zur osmanischen Mentalitätsgeschichte, in J.-L. Bacqué-Grammont (ed.), *Türkische Miszellen: Robert Anhegger Festschrift/armağanı/mélanges*, Istanbul 1987, 145–66.

Gramlich, R., *Alte Vorbilder des Sufitums*, i, *Scheiche des Westens*, Wiesbaden 1995.
———, *Die Wunder der Freunde Gottes: Theologien und Erscheinungsformen des islamischen Heiligenwunders*, Wiesbaden 1987.
Gülen, F., *Asrın getirdiği tereddütler*, Istanbul 2003.
———, *İnançın gölgesinde*, Istanbul 2003.
———, *Ölüm ötesi hayat*, Istanbul 2002.
———, *Prizma*, Istanbul 2003.
———, *Yaratılış gerçeği ve evrim*, Istanbul 2003.
Haeckel, E., *Die Welträthsel: Gemeinverständliche Studien über monistische Philosophie*, Bonn 1899.
Hammer, O., *Claiming knowledge: Strategies of epistemology from theosophy to the new age*, Leiden 2001.
Hanegraaff, W.J., *New age religion and western culture: Esotericism in the mirror of secular thought*, Leiden 1996.
Hanioğlu, Ş., Blueprints for a future society: Late Ottoman materialists on science, religion and art, in E. Özdalga (ed.): *Ottoman society: The intellectual legacy*, London and New York, 28–116.
Heinen, A., *Islamic cosmology: A study of as-Suyūṭī's al-Hay'a as-sanīya fī l-hay'a as-sunnīya*, Wiesbaden 1982.
Hermann, R., Fethullah Gülen – eine muslimische Alternative zur Refah-Partei?, in *Orient* 37 (1996), 619–45.
Hilmî, A., *Huzur, akl ve fende maddiyun meslek-i zalâleti*, Istanbul 1914/15.
Hoyle, F., *The intelligent universe*, London 1983.
Ibn ʿArabī, M., *al-Futūḥāt al-Makkiyya*, ed. U. Yaḥyā, Cairo 1975.
İrem, N., Bir değişim siyaseti olarak Türkiye'de Cumhuriyetçi muhâfazakârlık: Temel kavramlar üzerine değerlendirmeler, in A. Çiğdem (ed.), *Muhafazakârlık*, Istanbul 2003, 105–17.
İsmail, H., *100 Soruda Bediüzzaman Said Nursi, Risale-i Nur külliyatı ve Risale-i Nur talebeleri*, Istanbul 1994.
İsmail, H., *Ölüm yokluk mudur?*, Istanbul 2001^{18}.
Jalāl al-Dīn Rūmī, *Fīhi mā fīhi*, ed. B. Forūzanfarr, Tehran 1979^{6}.
———, *Fîhi mâ-fîh*, ed. and trans. A. Gölpınarlı, Ankara 1959.
Jansen, J., *The interpretation of the Koran in modern Egypt*, Leiden 1974.
Karabaşoğlu, M., Bilim Rabbini tanısa, in M. Karabaşoğlu, Y. Bouguenaya-Mermer and S. Demirci (eds.): *Bilimin öteki yüzü*, Istanbul 1991, 147–62.
———, Text and community: An analysis of the *Risale-i Nur* movement, in I. Abu-Rabiʿ (ed.), *Islam at the crossroads: On the life and thought of Bediuzzaman Said Nursi*, Albany, NY 2003, 263–96.
Keha, E., Var yok, yok da var edilemez mi?, in Â. Tatlı (ed.), *Merak ettiklerimiz*, Istanbul 1990, 25–9.

Koçak, C., Türk milliyetçiliğin İslâm'la buluşması: Büyük Doğu, in T. Bora (ed.), *Milliyetçilik*, Istanbul 2002, 601–17.
Köprü, monthly, 1976–1993.
Koestler, A., *The thirteenth tribe: The Khazar empire and its heritage*, London 1976.
Lambert, Y., Religion in modernity as a new axial age: Secularization or new religious forms, in *Sociology of Religion* 60 (1999), 303–33.
Madelung, W., al-Sufyānī, in *EI*², xii, 754f.
———, The Sufyānī between tradition and history, in *SI* 63 (1986), 5–48.
Mawdūdī, A., *Sīrat-i sarwar-i ʿālam*, 2 vols., Lahore 1997.
Mirzaoğlu, D., *Gözle görülmeyen metafizik âlem ve ışınsal varlık cinler*, Istanbul 2004.
Nadwī, S., *al-Istinsākh al-jīnī yuṣaddiq al-maʿād al-jasadī*, Bangalore n.d.
Nurbaki, H., Kâinatlar, ışınlar, varlıklar, in *Zafer* 71 (November 1982), 12f.
———, *Verses from the Holy Qurʾān and the facts of science*, Delhi 2002.
Nursi, S., *Ishārat al-iʿjāz fī maẓann al-ījāz*, Istanbul 1999.
———, *al-Khuṭba al-shaʾmiyya*, Istanbul 2001.
———, *Lem'alar*, Istanbul 2002.
———, *al-Mathnawī al-ʿarabī al-nūrī*, Istanbul 1999.
———, *Mektûbât*, Istanbul 2002.
———, *Muhâkemât*, Istanbul 2001.
———, *Sikke-i tasdik-i gaybî*, Istanbul 2002.
———, *Sözler*, Istanbul 2004.
———, *Şualar*, Istanbul 2001.
———, *Sünuhât*, Istanbul.
Ourghi, M., „Ein Licht umgab mich …" – Die eschatologischen Visionen des iranischen Präsidenten Mahmūd Ahmadīnežād, in *WI* 49 (2009), 163–80.
———, *Schiitischer Messianismus und Mahdī-Glaube in der Neuzeit*, Würzburg 2008.
Özdalga, E., The hidden Arab: A critical reading of the notion 'Turkish Islam', in *MES* 42 (2006), 551–70.
Paksu, M., *Meseleler ve çözümleri*, 2 vols., Istanbul 2000.
Parwēz, G.A., *Islam a challenge to Religion*, Lahore 1968.
Preckel, C., *Islamische Bildungsnetzwerke und Gelehrtenkultur im Indien des 19. Jahrhunderts: Muḥammad Ṣiddīq Ḥasan Ḫân (st. 1890) und die Entstehung der Ahl-e ḥadīṯ-Bewegung in Bhopal*, Bochum (electronic thesis) 2008.
Radtke, B., Sufism in the eighteenth century: An attempt at a provisional appraisal, in *WI* 36 (1996), 326–64.
Rebstock, U., Das Grabesleben: Eine islamische Konstruktion zwischen Himmel und Hölle, in R. Brunner et al. (eds.): *Islamstudien ohne Ende: Festschrift für Werner Ende zum 65. Geburtstag*, Würzburg 2003, 371–82.
Reichmuth, S., The second Intifada and the "Day of Wrath": Safar al-Hawālī and his anti-Semitic reading of Biblical prophecy, in *WI* 46 (2006), 331–51.

Riexinger, M., Islamic opposition to the Darwinian theory of evolution, in O. Hammer and J.R. Lewis (eds.), *Handbook of religion and the authority of science*, Leiden 2011, 483–510.

———, Nasserism revitalized: A critical reading of Ḥasan Ḥanafī's projects "The Islamic Left" and "Occidentalism" (and their uncritical reading), in WI 47 (2007), 63–118.

———, Propagating Islamic creationism on the internet, in *Masaryk University Journal of Law and Technology* 2.2 (2008), 99–112.

———, *Ṣanā'ullāh Amritsarī (1867–1948) und die Ahl-i Ḥadīṯ im Punjab unter britischer Herrschaft*, Würzburg 2004.

———, Turkey?, in S. Blancke, H. Hjermitslev and P. Kjærgaard (eds.), *Creationism in Europe*, Baltimore 2014, 180–98.

———, *Die verinnerlichte Schöpfungsordnung: Weltbild und normative Konzepte in den Schriften Said Nursis und der Nur Cemaati*, Habilitationsschrift, Göttingen, forthcoming.

Rustomji, N., *The garden and the fire: Heaven and hell in Islamic culture*, New York 2009.

Şahiner, N., *Bilinmeyen taraflarıyla Bediüzzaman Said Nursi*, Istanbul 2005.

———, *Son şahitler anlatıyor*, 4 vols., Istanbul 1993.

Şahinöz, C., *Die Nurculuk Bewegung: Entstehung, Organisation und Vernetzung*, Istanbul 2009.

Schönig, H., AIDS als das Tier (*dābba*) der islamischen Eschatologie: Zur Argumentation einer türkischen Schrift, in WI 30 (1990), 211–18.

Seufert, G., *Politischer Islam in der Türkei: Islamismus als symbolische Repräsentation einer sich modernisierenden muslimischen Gesellschaft*, Stuttgart 1997.

Smith, J.I. and Y.Y. Haddad, *The Islamic understanding of death and resurrection*, Oxford 2002.

Solberg, A., *The Mahdi wears Armani: An analysis of the Harun Yahya Enterprise*, Huddinge, Sweden 2013.

Spuler, U., *Nurculuk*, Bonn 1973.

Spuler-Stegemann, U., Zur Organisationsstruktur der Nurculuk-Bewegung, in A. Noth and H. Roemer (eds.), *Studien zur Geschichte und Kultur des Vorderen Orients: Festschrift für Bertold Spuler zum siebzigsten Geburtstag*, Leiden 1981, 423–42.

Stenberg, L., *The Islamization of science: Four Muslim positions developing an Islamic modernity*, Lund, Sweden 1996.

Szyska, C., On Utopian writing in Nasserist prison and laicist Turkey, in WI 35 (1995), 95–125.

Ṭāhā, M.M., al-Risāla al-ṣalāt, in M.M. Ṭāhā, *Naḥwa mashrūʿ mustaqbalī lil-Islām: Thalātha min al-aʿmāl al-asāsiyya lil-mufakkir Maḥmūd Muḥammad Ṭāhā*, Beirut and Kuwait 2002, 199–266.

Thomassen, E., Islamic hell, in *Numen* 56 (2009), 401–16.

Tunç, M.Ş., Madde ve ruh 2: Bugünün atomu, in *Büyük Doğu* 26 (7 April 1944), 4, 16.
———, Madde ve ruh 4: (Aynştayn) ve kâinat yapısı, in *Büyük Doğu* 28 (21 April 1944), 4f.
———, Madde ve ruh 5: (Aynştayn) bize ne kazandırdı?, in *Büyük Doğu* 29 (28 April 1944), 4.
———, Madde ve ruh 6: Dünyamızın sonu, *Büyük Doğu* 30 (5 May 1944), 4.
Ülken, H.Z., *Türkiye'de çağdaş düşünce tarihi*, Istanbul 1979².
Uzdilek, S.M., Atom ve yıldızlar, in *Büyük Doğu* (2 November 1945), 7.
Vahide, Ş., *Islam in modern Turkey: An intellectual biography of Bediuzzaman Said Nursi*, Syracuse, NY 2005.
van Donzel, E. and C. Ott, Yādjûdj wa-Mādjūdj, in *EI*², xi, 231–4.
Yahya, H., AIDS *Kur'an'da bahsi geçen Dabbet-ül Arz mı?*, Istanbul n.d.
———, *Mehdi ve altın çağ*, Istanbul 1989.
———, *Yahudîlik ve Masonluk*, Istanbul 1987.
Yavuz, H., Is there a Turkish Islam? Emergence of convergence and consensus, in *Journal of Muslim Minority Affairs* 24 (2004), 213–32.
———, *Islamic political identity in Turkey*, Oxford 2003.
———, *Nur* study circles (*dershanes*) and the formation of a new religious consciousness in Turkey, in I. Abu-Rabiʿ (ed.), *Islam at the crossroads: On the life and thought of Bediuzzaman Said Nursi*, Albany, NY 2003, 297–316.
Yıldırım, S., Cehennem nerede?, in *Yeni Nesil* (26 March 1991).
Zafer, monthly, 1976–.
Zarcone, T., The transformation of the Sufi orders (*tarikat*) in the Turkish Republic and the question of crypto-Sufism, in J.L. Warner (ed.), *Cultural horizons: A festschrift in honor of Talat S. Halman*, Syracuse, NY and Istanbul 2001, 198–209.
Zinser, H., Ist das New Age eine Religion? Oder brauchen wir einen neuen Religionsbegriff?, in U. Bianchi (ed.), *The notion of "religion" in comparative research: Selected proceedings of the XVI I AHR Congress*, Rome 1994, 633–40.

Internet Sources

http://www.davetci.com/d_biyografi/biyografi_hnurbaki.htm (accessed 26 April 2010).
http://www.harunyahya.org/imani/mehdiyet/altin.html (accessed 26 April 2010).
http://www.harunyahya.org/imani/mehdiyet/altin1.html (accessed 26 April 2010).
http://www.harunyahya.org/imani/mehdiyet/altin12.html (accessed 26 April 2010).
http://www.harunyahya.org/imani/mehdiyet/altin6.html (accessed 26 April 2010).
http://www.harunyahya.org/imani/mehdiyet/altin5.html (accessed 26 April 2010).
http://www.harunyahya.org/imani/OKiyametC.html (accessed 26 April 2010).
http://www.hekimogluismail.com (accessed 26 April 2010).
http://www.yetenek.com/articles.asp?tid=1&cid=50 (accessed 26 April 2010).
http://yetenek.com/articles_detail.asp?id=54 (accessed 26 April 2010).

CHAPTER 56

Notions of Paradise and Martyrdom in Contemporary Palestinian Thought

Liza M. Franke

And say not of those slain in God's way, "they are dead"; rather they are living, but you are not aware.
Q 2:154[1]

∵

This Quranic verse communicated by Muḥammad in the seventh century CE has not lost its importance in contemporary Palestinian thought as regards the notion of the garden/paradise.[2] It is frequently quoted or referred to in print media just as it is frequently cited in fragments or in full in day to day oral discourse. In the context of modern-day martyrdom operations and those who seek martyrdom through them, the *istishhādiyyūn*, special importance is ascribed to the concepts of afterlife and salvation.[3] Martyrdom operations (*ʿamaliyyāt istishhādiyya*) are justified by these themes, which often clearly

1 All translations from the Quran in this paper are based on Arberry (trans.), *The Koran interpreted*.

2 According to Smith and Haddad, Women in the afterlife 40, in Arabic the Quranic term for this concept is *al-janna*, which can be translated literally as "the garden" (in contrast to *al-nār* with its literal translation "the fire," i.e., hell, the netherworld, Hades). However, throughout this paper I use the literal translation or the original Arabic term or the term paradise, being aware that this and other translations such as heaven or the hereafter may be comprehended according to cultural presuppositions and thus may differ from the meaning inherent in the Quranic term.

3 I use the term "martyr" and related expressions to refer to those Palestinians who have been killed by the Israeli military. In doing so, I do not intend to present any moral or religious evaluation of the people or their actions, rather I try to adhere as closely as possible to the emic turn of phrase as prevalent among the majority of the inhabitants of the Palestinian territories. For the Arabic equivalents of this and related terms, cf. the subchapter "The road to paradise: Martyrdom as means to an end?" below.

 | DOI 10.1163/9789004333154_057

depict visions of the eschatological garden. Here, corporeal death is likely to be perceived as a *rite de passage* in the sense that inexistence leads one to become real not only in the afterlife but also in the here and now, thus it reflects a symbol of non-death.

Although the notion of the garden more often than not appears in the context of martyrdom operations it is also mentioned more generally in everyday life. Phrases such as: "How shall we live under these circumstances?[4] *In shāʾ Allāh,* life will be more pleasant in the garden" can be heard frequently and may lead to the assumption that the eschatological garden symbolizes more than a realm of refuge from ordinary difficulties.

Because of the fact that scholarly work dealing with the above-mentioned topics in general is quite scarce and similar material for modern and contemporary times is even more meager, I base my analysis primarily on interview material that I have gathered during field trips to the West Bank and Gaza Strip. Thus, I examine notions of *al-janna* and martyrdom and where and how they prevail in contemporary Palestinian thought and discourse in relation to martyrdom operations.

1 Description of Interview Situation and Interview Partners

The subject of the garden/*al-janna* is ever present in contemporary Palestinian thought and discourse. In the context of death and its relation to an afterlife, ideas and images of the garden dominate. The imagination of what the dead can expect and what s/he will receive upon entering the mysterious space is rich in religious beliefs and convictions, some of which can be found in the Quran while others are conveyed through the *ḥadīth.* In what follows I refer to extracts from interviews I conducted with those Palestinians who identified themselves as believing in God and the garden. I argue that lived martyrdom and text traditions are tightly knotted together. Examples from my interviews and written testaments or eulogies and glorifying texts about Palestinian martyrs corroborate my findings.

The analysis presented in this paper is part of my PhD thesis, *At the door of paradise: Discourses of female self-sacrifice, martyrdom and resistance in Palestine* and thus presents preliminary observations. The interviews are part of my PhD project and deal with the overall topic of intentional acts of martyrdom (*istishhādiyyāt*) by women: how these women are perceived, talked about (or not, if it is considered taboo to discuss them), how they are glorified and

4 I.e., the Israeli military occupation of the West Bank and its control of the Gaza Strip.

mourned, and/or exploited and used for propaganda. Martyrdom and notions of the garden also play a role here. These are indicative of how Palestinians deal with death – especially the death of women (or female self-sacrificing martyrs), the afterlife, how they arrange their current life, and what practices of bereavement are specific for women and how these are included in their discourses.[5] In addition, the subject of the *ḥūr* (virgins in paradise, singular *ḥawrāʾ*) is part of the discourse, especially in terms of motivating factors and paradisal expectations for women.[6]

I begin by offering an insight into the fieldwork I conducted in 2006 and 2007. The meetings with my interview partners took place in the West Bank and the Gaza Strip. For the majority, Arabic was the language in which the interviews took place. Interview partners were not chosen randomly, but according to their involvement with or knowledge of the *istishhādiyyāt* and their corresponding *ʿamaliyyāt istishhādiyya* (martyrdom operations). In other words, my aim was to collect the interpretations, perceptions, and attitudes of the interviewees regarding the research topic. Almost every Palestinian has an opinion on this issue and the people I met and interacted with were thus valuable "data sources." The interview partners can be subdivided into the following groups: family members of the *istishhādiyyāt*; members of militant (resistance) organizations; academics; journalists; women; and students. Their age ranges from approximately 15 to 60 and their educational background likewise ranges from primary school to university.[7] Had another geographical region been the focus, it might have been striking that *none* of my interview partners were illiterate. However, in the Palestinian context where most people receive at least a basic education, it is not surprising that even people from rural areas are literate.[8] Not all of the people I spoke with came from precarious financial backgrounds but the majority were from the lower middle class. Among my interview partners were refugees living in one of the refugee camps either in the West Bank (where there are nineteen official refugee camps, i.e., registered with UNRWA,[9] which provide aid to these registered refugees) or Gaza (where there are eight

5 Abu-Lughod, Islam and the gendered discourses 189.

6 On the subject of the *ḥūr* in *ḥadīth* and Quran see the enlightening article by Smith and Haddad, Women in the afterlife 39–55. Cf. also Smith, Reflections on aspects of immortality 85–99.

7 I do not know the exact age of every interview partner, the above age range is a rough estimation.

8 Cf. on the educational system in Palestine, Jebril, *Reflections on higher education in Palestine*; Abu Lughod, Palestinian higher education 75–95.

9 UNRWA is the abbreviation for the United Nations Relief and Work Agency for Palestine Refugees (website: http://www.unrwa.org).

official refugee camps). The others, who are not refugees, live in Palestinian cities spread across the West Bank and Gaza. This meant that I had to calculate the travel distance and the time I would need to arrive at the meeting point where the interviews were planned. Most interviews took place in the homes of the interviewees. Thus these interviews occasionally had to be postponed if checkpoints were closed or "flying checkpoints"[10] blocked the road or the car broke down or there were long queues at the checkpoints so that by the time we would have passed the checkpoint, it would have been too dark to continue as the roads can be dangerous at night – either because of road damage or Israeli military patrols and/or shooting (either between Palestinians and Israelis, or among Israelis or Palestinians) in the respective area.

2 The Road to Paradise: Martyrdom as Means to an End?

While the notions of *gender* and *martyrdom* have so far been looked at separately in scholarship on the Middle East, they can also be used as one term consisting of both words: *gendered martyrdom*. This concept, which I have applied in my research so far, links a certain form of death or dying – namely martyrdom – with the social category gender. In focusing on the specificity of male or female martyrdom it is possible to attribute the implicit meaning to the notion that male martyrdom is different (or similar) to female martyrdom. In either case this conflict in meaning (i.e., male vs. female) is noteworthy as it issues in the conceptual tool *gendered martyrdom*. Martyrdom (including martyrdom "operations") in the Palestinian context takes place either as sacrifice within the scope of the notion *fī sabīl Allāh* (i.e., in the way of God) or in the context of the homeland. It is linked to the nation, resistance, trauma, narratives of suffering and objects of commemoration, collective mourning, and the celebration of funerals.

A good amount of the discussion in contemporary Palestinian thought relates to the idea that death can also mean a release (i.e., from current situations which are perceived to be unbearable) and with the reinterpretation of the tragic death (i.e., death that results from being killed by the Israeli army or self-inflicted death as in acts of martyrdom) of the *shahīd* into the positively connoted heroic death of the freedom fighter. Hence the current political and social realities have to be taken into consideration. These result from previous

10 "Deliberate checkpoints and roadblocks are permanent or semi-permanent, while hasty checkpoints and roadblocks are temporary, and established with less planning and preparation," Edwards, Suicide attacks 126.

circumstances and chains of events. Chief among them are commemorational events, which also have a trans-national character (i.e., they concern and unite all Palestinians) such as the *nakba* (catastrophe, i.e., the Palestinian exodus in 1948), the expulsion of the Palestinians, the war of 1967, and the first and the second Intifada.

In the Palestinian context it is necessary to differentiate between the notions of *shahīd* – martyr and *istishhādī* – male self-sacrificing martyr. Although both terms are used to denote someone who sacrificed his/her life as a martyr there exist historical and cultural differences that have to be taken into consideration. In contemporary Palestinian thought the concept of martyrdom draws on the earliest accounts of martyrdom in Islam in general and on more modern notions of martyrdom as part of its history and rationale in particular. Thus, it is culturally embedded and enriched – beginning in Mandatory Palestine until today. Both types of martyrs (the *shahīd*, or martyr and the *istishhādī*, or male self-sacrificing martyr) can be found in Palestine today. However, they are connoted differently and thus the way one or the other is glorified varies. Still, overlapping similarities can be identified. In the material from the Quran and *ḥadīth* the classical concept of martyrdom in Islam is conveyed. The following examples illustrate how this knowledge from the past is still important and alive in the contemporary Palestinian context.

Martyrdom in modern-day Palestine is first granted to the *shuhadāʾ* (martyrs/witnesses). This refers to any Palestinians who die by the weapons of an Israeli soldier. It also comprises fatal injuries suffered not only by militant Palestinians but also by civilians and bystanders. Here, martyrdom is characterized more by passivity although active militants with guns in their hands ready to shoot back are also called *shuhadāʾ*.

Second, martyrdom is nowadays usually also granted to those who die by actively attacking those perceived to be the enemy. In the Palestinian context these are Israeli military personnel and often Israeli civilians (especially since, for the most part, the latter are not considered civilians but soldiers, because in Israel military service is a gender-comprehensive duty – all citizens of Israel must serve in the military). The one actively (consciously with the religious *niyya*) seeking martyrdom is called *istishhādī* or *istishhādiyya*. In Arabic this term generally describes one who commits a martyrdom operation. In the Palestinian context, this term is mostly used in a positive sense. Yet, in English several terms exist and most of them have negative connotations; this is the reason I use – according to the self-designated Palestinian/Arabic word "*istishhādī*" or "*istishhādiyya*" – the term "self-sacrificing martyr" or "active martyr," since my aim in this paper is to analyze Palestinian voices and opinions. In this context I consider this term to be the most suitable to analyze notions of martyrdom and paradise in contemporary Palestinian thought, as it is a close translation of the Arabic word and includes the semantic aspect of self-inflicted death resulting in martyrdom. It combines both aspects of the operation and its actor – the active, to be precise the intentional/deliberate aspect and the passive, namely the sacrifice of life and body for the freedom of the land of Palestine, which is perceived to be indispensable. The term leaves the judgment to the listener, whereas the expressions *suicide bomber* or *suicide attacker* (*intiḥāriyyūn/āt*) carry a decidedly negative connotation with them. The contrasting terms *martyr* or *hero* (*shahīd/istishhādiyyūn/āt*) do the opposite by evoking a positive association that sometimes results in sentiments of understanding, sympathy, and compassion. Thus, the expression *self-sacrificing martyr* is an especially useful translation of the Arabic term *istishhādiyyūn/āt*, which already comprises the active character of the martyrdom due to the form of its root system (for the corresponding verb it would be form X: *istafʿala*).[11]

By carrying out a martyrdom operation, the self-sacrificing martyr consciously and deliberately chooses martyrdom and thus the promised afterlife[12] over life in this world. S/he achieves the status of martyrdom, which guarantees immediate admission to the garden. This latter type simultaneously evokes a more secular meaning in the sense of "heroism" (cf. *ḥamāsa*) that relates to the active character of this form of martyrdom.

According to my interviewees in Palestine, both the *shahīd* and the *istishhādī* are conceived of as true martyrs. The bodies of both types of martyr are not washed after death or covered with a shroud but buried in the clothes they were wearing when they died. It is said that a sweet scent of musk exudes from their bodies which are somehow preserved and do not putrefy. Their deaths should not be mourned but celebrated. As is written in Q 2:154, those killed in the way of God are not dead but alive, even though "you do not understand it." With martyrdom comes the often criticized and deplored enthusiastic behavior of

11 Hans Wehr translates *istishhād* also as "death of a martyr; death of a hero, heroic death; martyrdom." The passive verb form *ustushhida* then means: "to be martyred, die as a martyr, to die in battle, be killed in action." Cf. Wehr, *Arabic-English dictionary* 571–2.

12 In Muslim thought death is clearly understood as the continuation of life after the death of the body: "belief in the life after death is concomitant with belief in the Existence of God ... Failing belief in the life after death there is no faith at all." Islam is then considered to be the religion of the middle position, i.e., tying together this world and the next (*dīn* and *dunyā*). However, the afterlife concerns merely the soul and not the body, as "Islam in no sense espouses any idea of the possibility of transmigration from one physical body to another." Smith and Haddad, *The Islamic understanding* 106; 112.

the bereaved, who seem to celebrate the death of their martyred family member. I use the word "seem" here deliberately because this "joy" is often only the first reaction and grief comes later, after the guests, neighbors, and sometimes even foreigners have left. Consequently, martyrdom – especially self-sacrificing martyrdom – opens up a new space as it can be understood as a "shortcut" to paradise and a lethal action that results in a state of non-death – both in the hereafter, since the martyr immediately enters the garden, and in the here and now, because the self-sacrificing martyr is glorified and kept alive through posters, songs, and other acts of commemoration.

3 Discourse and Dissent Regarding the Garden

In terms of the "life" the *shuhadāʾ* can expect, the issue of the *ḥūr* almost always arises. These are said to be vestals or maidens – some 72 black-eyed females – awaiting the male *shahīd* upon his entry in the garden. This in itself is already complicated and raises questions as to whether the *ḥūr* trigger the *shahīd* to be reckless, intending to be killed by the Israeli army or whether they motivate him to conduct a martyrdom operation. Things become even more complicated in relation to female martyrs (*shahīdāt* and *istishhādiyyāt*). Are they also received by *ḥūr?* If so, what would either of them gain? In the interviews and in other conversations during my field research in Palestine the rewards that the *shuhadāʾ* are promised by God were not much of an issue. It seemed to me that this is something very clear and not something that requires further debate. The treatment of the *shuhadāʾ*, the funeral ceremonies and the expression of personal sentiments, however, provided material for various discussions. It is, for instance, highly contested whether the *istishhādiyyūn/āt* will enter the garden as martyrs or not. Some religious figures and political leaders and others are not convinced that the *istishhādiyyūn/āt* can be regarded as martyrs at all. For them and from a religious point of view, these actions may still constitute suicide, which then cannot be rewarded. However, these dissenting voices are comparatively weak and do not reflect the prevailing Palestinian opinion.

Due to the fact that female Palestinian self-sacrificing, intentional martyrs are quite a recent phenomenon, the opinions regarding their status in the garden vary greatly. Though it is mostly assumed that they enter the garden as martyrs, it is not clear what will await them in the afterlife: will they enter the garden as brides ready to be married off to someone they know, or will they turn themselves into one of the *ḥūr*. The issue of this modern phenomenon of female martyrs has not been treated in the classical written sources and is thus subject to vigorous debate.

During the second of my journeys to Gaza, I had the chance to meet a female politician who is a member of parliament representing Hamas. As a Palestinian woman living in Gaza, in the spotlight as a result of her political career and her membership in Hamas, Huda Naeem[13] is a unique figure. I was, therefore, more than delighted to have the chance to meet her; we met in Gaza's parliament building, which was destroyed in the military action "Operation Cast Lead" (which began 27 December 2008) by Israel in the Gaza Strip. She stated that the *ḥūr* have received more attention in popular discourse since martyrdom operations have become almost a habit in the Palestinian struggle for independence: "In any case, with or without the promise of the *ḥūr* upon entering the garden, the resistance is most important to us and martyrdom will continue to be a daily part of our life until the liberation of our land." She further opined that female martyrs also receive a glorious status in the garden: they will marry and the *ḥūr* will welcome them likewise: "but in a more friendship-like manner and not in the sexually connoted way as they are said to receive male martyrs."

Another interview partner, a military leader of the Islamic Jihad, a teacher and the mentor of Mīrfat Āmīn Mas'ūd, the ninth active female or intentional martyr in the Palestinian context, said about the subject of the *ḥūr* in relation to martyrdom operations:

> This is an important religious aspect and written in the Quran. The *ḥūr* are promised to the martyr be it male or female. The female martyr will join the *ḥūr* and become part of them. Martyrdom is very important to us as Muslims and to us as Palestinians it means more than just to die and to enter the garden. It means to us that our struggle is not in vain and that others should follow the martyrs to free Palestine.

4 Martyrdom and the Afterlife in Written Eulogies

Many issues that are not broached in everyday oral discourse are present in written glorifications, gray literature, posters, popular music, and songs. The subject of one example here indicates that the blood of the self-sacrificing martyrs will nourish the land of Palestine, which will be viable for new life. This is a theme going back to pre-Islamic concepts of nature and fertility. These and other subjects are brought up in the encomiums of the Palestinian

13 Huda Naeem and Professor Jameela Shanti are among the six women who were elected to parliament as members of Hamas after its victory in the parliamentary elections in January 2006.

istishhādiyyāt by their anonymous authors, as I demonstrate by referring to glorifying material.[14]

4.1 *Āyāt al-Akhras*[15]

The text glorifying the third female self-sacrificing martyr since the outbreak of the second Intifada clearly states the joyous sentiments that were the first reactions among family members and others in the refugee camp. Instead of referring to the death as an event of sadness, it is mentioned as a wedding ceremony. Āyāt is portrayed as a bride united with the land/husband Palestine by freeing it from the occupation – or at least taking a step in this direction. The motif of the "Palestinian wedding" is regularly repeated and not only remains in the text-based sphere but enters the social realm and characterizes death processions and burial rites.

In the first passage, the author reports what happened among the inhabitants of the refugee camp after Āyāt's martyrdom operation became publicly known. It was written that after receiving the message they went out on the streets to share the joyful celebrations of the "successful" completion of her act. Subsequently, in the second paragraph, which has her name, Āyāt al-Akhras, in captions, the symbol of the wedding occurs for the first time. It deals with the marriage topos in a prose-like style, and is therefore of particular significance:

> The joyful ululations were mixed with crying. For today is her wedding, even though she does not wear the white dress and even though there was no bridal procession to her groom, who has waited for this procession for the past one and a half years. Instead she was wearing a military uniform and a Palestinian *kūfiyya*. And she was adorned with her red and proud blood which transformed her ceremony into a Palestinian wedding. Such a wedding fills the hearts of each mother of the martyred or injured with calmness and joy. Actually her wedding ceremony should

---

14 This material consists mainly of written eulogies and encomiums, which glorify the *istishhādiyyāt*. These are usually written by members of the militant resistance organizations and distributed online (the websites are unstable since the operators frequently change the domain) or as leaflets passed out during demonstrations, commemorations or funerals. Other sources are audiovisual, such as video-testaments or glorifying songs. In some cases I was able to obtain the written testaments of the *istishhādiyyāt*.

15 Āyāt al-Akhras carried out a martyrdom operation on 29 March 2002. Born in Jerusalem, she was the third *istishhādiyya* and the youngest who, at the age of sixteen, joined the active militant resistance. The operation took place under the auspices of the al-Aqṣā Brigades at the Kiryat HaYovel supermarket in Jerusalem and killed two people, a seventeen-year-old Israeli girl and a fifty-five-year-old Israeli security guard.

> have taken place last July, completely normal like any other girl in this world. But she wanted to be wedded to her ["]bridegroom["] [the earth/land of Palestine] exclusively in the "blood-suit," by which only someone like her could consummate the marriage, [she did this] to create pride among her people by successfully killing and injuring dozens of Zionist occupiers in a successful and heroic operation. An operation, which has been conducted by a girl in the heart of Zionism.

Āyāt al-Akhras was planning to be married in the summer of 2002, yet she refused to be like just any girl, for she was wedded in her blood-soaked uniform. Instead of a wedding dress, she wore a military uniform and the Palestinian *kūfiyya* – a nationalistic symbol in the Palestinian context that is usually associated with Yasser Arafat, who has entered the social discourse as a legend. Yasser Arafat, too, always wore a military uniform and the *kūfiyya* in public. During his lifetime he became the embodiment of the Palestinian National Movement. He united the Palestinians to stand as a collective for the "Palestinian cause." Hence Āyāt al-Akhras's deliberately chosen clothing could be regarded as a symbol in the struggle for national existence and accordingly as an imitation and performance of the powerful role of a strong political personality. Instead of flowers and gold, she adorned herself with her red and proud blood, which transformed the act into a Palestinian "wedding," and transformed her into a Palestinian bride.

In this context, it is useful to mention the work of Angelika Neuwirth, who referred to the relationship between the symbol of the land of "Palestine" and the wedding of the martyr (who should be distinguished from the suicide bombers as martyrs) with this land in the poetry of Maḥmūd Darwīsh (1941–2008), a well-known Palestinian poet.[16] This reference can also be found in the encomium to Āyāt al-Akhras – given that she is characterized as the bride of Palestine, who remains an example and role model for every Palestinian girl and every Palestinian boy – an illustration of the strong presence of symbolic language in the discourse of martyrs. In doing so, the *istishhādiyya* is awarded the same function and honor as male martyrs: Āyāt al-Akhras unites with the land of Palestine, which is imagined to be female although or precisely because she is a woman. Her blood will nourish the land, which thereby is able to produce more children, and thus contribute to the persistence of the resistance until the final liberation of Palestine.

As soon as the message of the martyrdom operation traversed the narrow alleys of the refugee camp, Āyāt's mother realized what had happened and

---

16 Neuwirth, Embaló, and Pannewick, *Kulturelle Selbstbehauptung der Palästinenser*; Neuwirth, From sacrilege to sacrifice 271–4.

sobbed: "I think Āyāt has left us and she will never return. She turned into a Palestinian bride. She insisted on revenging ʿĪsā Faraḥ and Sāʾid ʿĪd. They were both neighbors of ours and died in their houses which were hit by rockets."

Āyāt is literally absorbed into the narrative of "fighting for the Palestinian cause." Her unconditional commitment gives her action a fanatical aspect. This is in line with the depersonification effect resulting from the phrase "Palestinian bride," which is a symbol and a myth at the same time. An explanation of the fanaticism is given in the next section, which is headed "The industry of death." Figurative verbalization is used in order to substantiate the claim. An exalted style and pretended objectivity (by means of factual description and witness statements) are some of the methods applied here. "It is said that Āyāt dreamt of becoming like the other martyrs whose names she can recite, but her female nature is the biggest obstacle." The fact that she was a woman and not a man could, in her eyes, only be overcome when the operation carried out by Wafāʾ Idrīs, the first Palestinian *istishhādiyya*, became well-known. Wafāʾ and her heroic attack became a symbol and an example for the following *istishhādiyyāt*.

"The pieces of chocolate" is the title of the penultimate passage in which Āyāt's sister Samāḥ is given the floor. She recounts the last moments of Āyāt's life, moments that she shared with her sister. On this last day Āyāt seemed to be very happy and gave her sister some pieces of chocolate and asked her: "Pray for me and ask God for success for me." Although Samāḥ feared her sister might want to carry out a martyrdom operation she was at the same time convinced that Āyāt would never be able to do so. Yet, "she congratulated her on her decision and said that she deserved it [i.e., the status of a martyr] for her courage: I promise to follow you and walk on the path of martyrdom. We are all a martyrdom project." Āyāt's sister encouraged her although she was not sure what to think of her behavior and how to deal with it. However, Samāḥ seemed to believe in the concept of martyrdom and thought that it could be a sustainable method and means for ending the current situation of living under alien military occupation.

In the last paragraph, "My bride is not for me," her fiancé Shādī has his say and recalls how he met and fell in love with Āyāt. He looks at the situation in a sober way, but not unemotionally. Just prior to the martyrdom operation he imagined their married life and how they would raise their firstborn son to become a fighter and free the Aqṣā from the chains of the occupation. "He saw that the girl would not marry him, but become a Palestinian bride after she blew herself up in the heart of Zionism." Again, the myth and symbol of the Palestinian bride is evoked. He also mentions paradise in the next sentence: "Our plan was to get married after the completion of her general secondary examinations this year, but God Almighty had other plans for us. Maybe we will meet again in paradise, as she wrote to me in her last letter." He continues talking about a recurring situation when he and Āyāt dreamt of their future life together:

> She dreamt of security for her children. This is why she was so concerned about the Zionist aggressors. Her dreams about martyrdom have disrupted her dreams about the future. And she stole from me my dream of marriage to seek refuge in martyrdom and the pictures of those killed by the enemy and our spilled blood, which will carry us to paradise. And we promised to do it together.

He concludes his elaboration: "I wish we had sacrificed ourselves together. And I congratulate her on her martyrdom. I ask God to let me follow her soon." In the very last sentence of this encomium, the metaphor of the wedding is referred to again and Āyāt is praised in an exalted way, namely that:

> The Palestinian bride, Āyāt al-Akhras, remains an example and a role model for every Palestinian girl and every Palestinian boy searching for security among the ruins of the massacres of Sharon while the offender pays with his blood and his future as a price for this security.

The aggressors and defenders are identified very clearly. As has been mentioned above, this final message reminds everyone of the responsibility Āyāt and every other Palestinian – male or female – has, to live a peaceful and secure life. Hence, the encomium is a rational appeal not to imitate passive Arab armies and inactive Arab leaders but to follow the shining, chatoyant, and glorious example of the heroic martyrs.

4.2 *Wafāʾ Idrīs*[17]

In comparing the encomium of Āyāt al-Akhras with that of Wafāʾ Idrīs,[18] we can see striking differences in the linguistic levels of the texts. In the case of

17 The first "modern" martyrdom operation by a woman in Palestine was carried out by Wafāʾ Idrīs, a twenty-eight-year-old paramedic working for the Red Crescent. She lived in the al-Amʿarī refugee camp in Ramallah. The explosion took place on 27 January 2002, in the center of Jerusalem on Jaffa Road in front of a shoe shop. One eighty-one-year-old Israeli man was killed and more than 100 people were injured. The al-Aqṣā Martyrs Brigades claimed responsibility for this attack immediately after it was conducted. Cf. also the insightful article on Wafāʾ Idrīs by Pannewick, Wafa Idris 110–3.

18 Cf. Katāʾib shuhadāʾ al-Aqṣā, Idrīs, Wafāʾ.

Wafāʾ Idrīs the author not only uses sacred elements of language, which are also present in the everyday speech of Palestinians, but also employs short sentences, rhythm, poetic-rhyming, and a figurative style.[19] Simple syntax mixed with uncomplex vocabulary and an exalted style are added. This encomium is suited for recitation, as the text – with its particular linguistic style (ornamental, poetic) and a way of reasoning which on closer examination is neither coherent nor unchallengeable – tries to convince its audience of the necessity of martyrdom operations. For instance, it argues, "that death is the embodiment of love for the land and humans," or "that the Arab rulers prefer to be [cowardly] sheep, instead of fighting and dying."

Both Wafāʾ Idrīs and Āyāt al-Akhras are described in the texts as brave heroes who lift the resistance to another level. They are the ones who defy the incompetent Arab rulers and show the Palestinian people that the land of Palestine is worthy of martyrdom operations. In contrast to their male counterparts who in the encomiums are not accredited with explicitly male attributes – rather their death is considered a duty for the deliverance of the Palestinian homeland – women often acquire male attributes. Wafāʾ Idrīs is even praised as a

> woman, who is worth a thousand men and who evokes memories of her [female] predecessors, the pious companions [of the Prophet] who accompanied the advance of the armies to new worlds, who embraced a new religion due to their fair-mindedness and their mercy and their heroism.

Furthermore, it is said that Wafāʾ Idrīs

> preferred to be a symbol of the fact that honor as well as death are a part of life. She is an Arab legend, an eternal legend, a legend which will be storied with its characters made of light in order to exemplify [the fact] that the Arab woman has not only been created for make-up, *rīmīl* [i.e.,

19 Nicholson, *History* 74, notes on the issue of unmetered prose in historical perspective: "… the oldest form of poetical speech in Arabia was rhyme without metre (Sajʿ), or, as we should say, 'rhymed prose', although the fact of Muhammad's adversaries calling him a poet because he used it in the Koran shows the light in which it was regarded even after the invention and elaboration of metre. Later on, as we shall see, Sajʿ became a merely rhetorical ornament, the distinguishing mark of all eloquence whether spoken or written, but originally it had a deeper, almost religious, significance as the special form adopted by poets, soothsayers, and the like in their supernatural revelations and for conveying to the vulgar every kind of mysterious and esoteric lore."

> lipstick from Rimmel, a London-based cosmetics company], and rouge. Rather, she has been created to tell the daughters of her sex as well as the other sex that love is also death.

Thus, here death is elevated and equated with love, which is not manifest in life but rather precisely in death. In the poetry of Maḥmūd Darwīsh death is given a special position: "This praise of death, which violates the central social convention that violent death is to be perceived as a loss and a paralysing blow to every relevant social interaction of the relatives, signalises an inversion of values."[20] This understanding is justified in the glorifying texts, especially in reference to myths. Indeed, the analysis by Neuwirth can be seamlessly woven into the encomiums of the *istishhādiyyāt*, yet it has to be acknowledged that Maḥmūd Darwīsh has unambiguously distanced himself, especially since the second Intifada, from the modern understanding of martyrdom which is propagated, for example, by the al-Aqṣā Brigades.[21]

According to the author of the encomium, Wafā' Idrīs said that

> spring only blossoms if one waters it with blood. For Palestine is the only country of the world in which the olives, the oranges and roses grow without water [but with blood]... Further on she said that the seeds of the earth would sprout spikes if they are watered with blood. In an unwritten statement she called upon all peoples of her homeland to be like the sand of the path, the clay of the earth and the scent of the linden trees after the rain.

The reference to blood also occurs in the encomium to Āyāt al-Akhras and thus proves that the myth of blood plays a decisive role in the encomiums. Blood has already been given particular attention in early history: it symbolized not only life but also death and to date connotes something either positively or negatively. In numerous myths blood is contextualized figuratively, ritually, in writing, or verbally. According to Neuwirth the myth of blood in Islamic culture, particularly in the context of figurations of martyrs, is subject to strong transformations.[22] In the Quran, this topic is elaborated on in the context of the role of blood as sacrifice. From an Islamic perspective, the significance of blood differs in Sunni and Shiʿi Islam. For the latter, blood is important for its "expiatory value" or impact. In Sunni tradition, the opinion that the martyr symbolizes a self-sacrifice developed only gradually: "Only the modern martyr

20 Neuwirth, From sacrilege to sacrifice 270.

21 Ibid., 274–8.

22 Neuwirth, Blut und Mythos 62–90.

spills his blood as sacrifice. He reconstructs the order through a substitutional *rite de passage* as 'groom of the homeland' by straightening up the dignity of society."[23] The martyr as the groom of the homeland makes the land Palestine female in the sense that through his blood Palestine nurtures the Palestinians and thus cares like a mother for its offspring and offers them security. The land of Palestine/homeland is frequently portrayed as female, when the nation is signified as a mother, lover or bride of the struggle. In other words the male/female agency of the martyr effectuates the future whereas the (female) land of Palestine seems to be a more passive recipient of the martyr's blood and action.

The anthropological concept of a *rite de passage* is here understood according to the anthropologist Arnold van Gennep.[24] Instead of remaining in a liminal status – in a state between growing up and the socially accepted position as a husband/father and wife/mother respectively – the martyrs' adolescent death is understood and interpreted as a wedding. The myth of blood serves in this context as an integral part of the wedding (and its consummation). This construct(ion) or *rite de passage* appears repeatedly throughout the encomiums. Thus, blood has a meaningful function here, not as a symbol of injury or of death but rather as a life-giving element.

The *istishhādiyyāt* are credited with a similarly powerful function, which is nonetheless ostensibly limited to external glorification, i.e., propaganda machinery, which is produced by the dispatching organizations: *istishhādiyyāt* are not necessarily glorified in everyday life. Hence these women are twice singled out or separated from society and seldom included in prevailing social structures anymore: as martyrs they receive a higher status in the discourse and by accentuating their femininity they are even elevated beyond the male martyr.

4.3 *Mīrfat Amīn Mas'ūd*[25]

In her last will, which Mīrfat reads in front of a video camera – she reads it very fast without pausing noticeably to breathe – she calls upon her parents (especially her beloved mother) "to be patient and strong and to consider her a martyr with God." Many comforting references to God are made as well as to paradise – here, a special level in paradise is mentioned, namely *al-firdaws*, the

23 Ibid., 83–4. In this context the martyr who is glorified most notably in poetry is a contrast to the "suicide bombers," too.

24 Van Gennep, *Les rites de passage*.

25 Mīrfat Amīn Mas'ūd was an eighteen-year-old woman from the Jabāliyya refugee camp in northern Gaza who carried out her martyrdom operation in Bayt Ḥānūn on 6 November 2006. The al-Quds Brigades claimed responsibility for the attack in which six people were killed.

highest level and one which martyrs enter immediately – the place where she and her parents "will meet again if it is God's will." She furthermore addresses her family asking them to forgive her mistakes: "pray to God for He will forgive my sins and you, please forgive me." Although she expresses her strong love for each family member she simultaneously states that "my desire to meet God and the Prophet and to spill my blood for my land is much greater than my love for you." With this statement her ambitious behavior and religious belief and understanding become apparent. Her strong emotional involvement, her political comprehension and awareness of the national issue are made explicit.

Her speech continues in a very personal tone. The tone is as beseeching as it is self-confident and intriguing. Martyrdom, resistance, and faithful support from society are some of the subjects she addresses in her testament. Other issues are revenge, the occupation, the land, the Prophet, and the sacrifice of the body. Mīrfat is positive about her choice to carry out a martyrdom operation, which she considers an act of revenge – an act of revenge "through the will of God."

References to God occur continuously in everyday life in Palestine and complete any kind of sentence, be it joking or serious. In the will and testament they fulfill yet another function: to give hope to her family members and fellow Palestinians. The last paragraph, in which she explicitly appeals to her family and even more explicitly to her parents, consists of three exhortations: the first concerns her grave. "It should be built according to the Sunna." The second is the "request *not* to distribute coffee or candies to the congratulatory and cheering crowd" (neighbors and others) after the martyrdom operation has been successfully completed and thus announced. Mīrfat concludes her appeal by focusing on Islam: her family should "stick to the holy Quran and the Sunna of the Prophet and ask God for forgiveness for me."

In her very last sentence Mīrfat Amīn Masʿūd bids farewell by saying: "And see you soon in paradise! [I am] your martyr daughter, through the will of God, who is alive with God." She seems certain that she will enter paradise by means of her action and that a family reunion will take place in this space beyond the earthly dimension.

4.4 *Hanādī Taysīr Jarādāt*[26]

"The heroic *istishhādiyya* Hanādī Taysīr ʿAbd al-Malik Jarādāt" is the title of another example: the encomium of Hanādī Jarādāt and her *waṣiyya* which

26 She was a lawyer from Jenin, the most northern city in the West Bank, who carried out a martyrdom operation on 4 October 2003. Her operation is counted as the sixth which was conducted by women. It took place in the Maxim Restaurant in Haifa, killed nineteen

is attached to the end of the publication. Her case received great attention from the local and international media because, as a highly educated working woman, she seemed to stand out from the masses of the otherwise poor and desperate self-sacrificers.[27]

Hanādī is dubbed as *al-istishhādiyya ʿarūs Ḥayfā*. Her action is linked to the motif of the "Palestinian wedding," as her martyrdom operation which took place in Haifa[28] transformed her into a bride, the "bride of Haifa." Here the writer of the encomium claims the authority for wedding Hanādī to the land. This is not an automatic process that takes place after a martyrdom operation has been carried out by a woman (in other encomiums this is not necessarily the case, as neither a bridal status is attributed to the woman nor is a particular space – land, city, etc. –always further specified) and thus this example is all the more striking and thought-provoking. Due to the fact that Hanādī sacrificed herself in Haifa – an Israeli city approximately 60 km from Jenin, the city where Hanādī came from – and because of her professional background and the high death toll of her action, her case became well-known in and outside Palestine. The composer of the encomium crowns her as a bride, which implies that by sacrificing her body she is united with the city of Haifa, which is here considered to be still Palestinian. His explicit statement reapplies the much older icon of the Palestinian wedding (formerly attributed to male fighters) to a female combatant who exercised a rather modern form of resistance in the Palestinian context. This symbol not only stands for joyful celebrations of armed actions but also for nationalist consciousness of revolutionary agency: Palestine, the land which the combatant embraces, to which s/he is wedded,

---

people and injured fifty. The al-Quds Brigades claimed responsibility for this action. This was the second time a martyrdom operation was carried out by a woman under the aegis of the al-Quds Brigades (Hiba Darāghma was the first on 19 May 2003; Mīrfat Amīn Masʿūd was the third and until now the last *istishhādiyya* who was trained and supervised by them).

27 Although it is true that her career and professional/educational background might suggest a rather prosperous future, it is not true that most martyrdom operations were carried out by poor, desperate people in otherwise futile situations. Cf. the studies on the financial and educational background of "suicide bombers": Moghadam, Palestinian suicide terrorism 65–92; Gambetta, Making sense of suicide missions.

28 The present-day city of Haifa is located in northern Israel and is the third largest city after Jerusalem and Tel Aviv. Haifa is a submontane seaport of Carmel and has industrial importance. It is also the only Israeli city with public transport running on the Sabbath. Many Arabs live and work in this city and form a huge Palestinian community. Though religiously unimportant (compared to the holy city of Jerusalem) many Palestinians living outside Israel have relatives living in Haifa.

is the main focus of the glorification – it is the reason for and reward of the martyrdom operation.

The salient features in Hanādī's case continue as her *waṣiyya* is also rather noteworthy. It consists of two parts – something I have not come across in the other testaments. The first one is short and general and the second describes in detail and on a very personal level her stance toward the operation. The former is a short paragraph with several key words such as *al-ṣahāyina* (the Zionists), *mustawṭin* (settler), *shahāda* (the creed/blood testimony/martyrdom). Her language is stereotypical and consists of declamatory elements. She concluded, or to be more precise, signed this testament with the words: "your daughter Hanādī Taysīr Jarādāt, daughter of the al-Quds Brigades." The latter is her long and elaborate last will. Here, Hanādī expresses her feelings and viewpoints in an extremely personal and emotional manner. The poignant style is mixed with a factual, almost business-like mode of writing – this is probably the result of her training in the law, which she received at university. This part of the testament is peppered with flowery religious phrases and quotations from the Quran. The combination of emotional and factual writing in the *waṣiyya* mirrors the facts on the ground of the conflict and the results or influence these have in the emotional realm. Literally, the reality is being imprinted (or imprints itself) on the emotional/psychological perception. It is precisely this loaded and highly fraught mixture that is reflected in Hanādī's testament – as of course is the case in the others – which gives these compositions a unique position among the various discursive possibilities: her very personal voice is heard and available to a larger public audience.

First she explicitly addresses her beloved father and next her mother. In both paragraphs she is convinced that she will be with God in *janna*. And if it is God's will she will meet her brother Fādī, her cousin Ṣāliḥ and her fiancé ʿAbd al-Raḥīm there. The subject of paradise and the afterlife plays an important role in the entire *waṣiyya*; this is also apparent in the Quranic quotations, such as Q 3:169 and Q 4:74.

She makes clear, as do the other testaments, her strong concern for justice and fairness, and her consciousness of what "the process of leaving this world willingly" means to her and to those she left behind. Hanādī concludes her testament with the following request, that "her parents should always bless and be benevolent toward her. And [the certainty] that they will meet each other again in paradise."

In the *waṣiyya* of Mīrfat Amīn Maʿsūd a similar phrase served as a concluding remark. The hopeful tone in this last sentence is evidence of her knowledge that a *shahīd* (or *istishhādiyya*), according to the Islamic religious tradition – the Sunna, collected in various volumes of *ḥadīth* – is allowed and able to grant access to paradise for a certain number of his/her relatives. The tone could also be interpreted as a beseeching remark that expresses the fear of the *istishhādiyya*; however, I read it as a rather hopeful statement that helps her remain convinced and steadfast.

In the encomiums of the *istishhādiyyāt* myths emerge as sources of norms, which serve to bestow meaning (*Sinnstiftung*) in the interpretation of daily life and events. Thus, the authors weave together elements endowed with meaning from different fields. Old religious motives are reorganized and coordinated with ideological elements of modernity in the environment of existing Palestinian myths and images. In relation to the encomiums the image of the Palestinian wedding is recurrent. To date, this figure has not lost its deeply symbolic impact – even though reinterpretations and thus meaningful shifts have taken place. Since the beginning of the twentieth century the victims of the struggles for independence – anti-colonialist and anti-Zionist – have been conceived as bridegrooms. Especially in the field of narrative and heroic discourses, the fighter is glorified; the would-be martyr is a bridegroom. These discourses become manifest in poetry, ritual practice, and songs.[29] The wedding symbolizes the shifting social status of the fighter as a *rite de passage*. The young combatant unites with the land of Palestine, which is connoted or construed as feminine, and spills his blood for this earth, which then becomes viable for new life. Indeed this motive transforms itself, it is subjected to changes in time and space and adapts to political and social realities; nevertheless this symbolism remains meaningful – especially in reference to the self-sacrificing martyrs whose obsequies are celebrated as wedding receptions. The same is true for *istishhādiyyāt*; both male and female martyrs unite with the land of Palestine by means of their blood. Moreover, Palestine is often imagined as the earthly paradise, the land where milk and honey flows and the place to live and die for. Many of the statements that I collected during my field research referred to and employed exactly this metaphor, namely that Palestine can be associated or substituted for paradise. This is true for diaspora Palestinians, returnees, and those living in Palestine: Palestine symbolizes the home and the destination/destiny for its inhabitants who will continuously revere its soil and its meaning beyond mere dust.

In some cases the defining motif of the "Palestinian wedding" prevails while in others the subject of the *ḥūr* preponderates. Yet again, in other cases the erotically charged themes are not the focus. Instead nationalist motifs occur:

29 Neuwirth, Embaló, and Pannewick, *Kulturelle Selbstbehauptung der Palästinenser* 14–22.

Mīrfat Mas'ūd[30] states in her testament that she prefers to give her blood for her land and to become a martyr by the will of God, who will reunite her with her family in paradise, instead of living under the intolerable and ugly occupation. She also calls upon the *mujāhidūn* around the world to take the way of resistance blessed by God. And sometimes, as is stated in the encomium of Wafā' Idrīs, secular references to life and death dominate the tone: "she preferred to be a symbol, that honor as well as death are part of life ... that life is also death and that death is the embodiment of love for homeland/earth and mankind. Death is the new life which recreates the Palestinian people."

Martyrdom in present-day Palestine is reminiscent of an act in a social drama. This idea is based on Victor Turner's concept that culture is a performative process and a social drama is the means for solving conflicts in society.[31] Christian Szyska also applies this approach to his analysis of Islamic written narratives concerned with martyrdom.[32] Turner's theoretical method can also be helpful to understand what happens in Palestinian society. The disastrous death of the martyr or self-sacrificing martyr with his mournful victims is transformed by social dynamics into a heroic death that is the result of a glorious act. The commemoration and re-enactment of the respective death in the form of posters, video-clips, and songs keep the dead alive and memorable for society. The martyrdom operation as a *rite de passage* then represents an initiated act of non-death with a continued living potential in the here and now as

30 She carried out her martyrdom operation in Bayt Ḥānūn on 6 November 2006. The al-Quds Brigades claimed responsibility for the attack in which six people were killed.

31 Cf. Turner, *From ritual to theatre*; Turner, *Drama, fields and metaphors* and Turner, *The anthropology of performance*. The social drama consists of four phases: (1) *Breach* of regular norm-governed social relations; (2) *Crisis*, during which there is a tendency for the breach to widen. Each public crisis has what I now call lamina characteristics, since it is a threshold (*limen*) between more or less stable phases of the social process, but it is not usually a sacred limen, surrounded by taboos and thrust away from the centers of public life. On the contrary it takes its menacing stance in the forum itself, and, as it were, dares the representatives of order to grapple with it; (3) *Redressive* action ranging from personal advice and informal mediation or arbitration to formal juridical and legal machinery, and, to resolve certain kinds of crisis or legitimate other modes of resolution, to the performance of public ritual. Redress, too, has its liminal features for it is "be-twixt and between," and, as such, famishes a distanced replication and critique of the events leading up to and composing the "crisis." This replication may be in the rational idiom of the judicial process, or in THC metaphorical and symbolic idiom of a ritual process; (4) The final phase consists either of the *reintegration* of the disturbed social group, or of the social recognition and legitimation of irreparable schism between the contesting parties. Cf. Turner, *Drama, fields, and metaphors* 37–42.

32 Szyska, Martyrdom 29–45.

well as in the afterlife: "[i]n Islam, human beings are created to survive, not to vanish. Death is a return to God."[33]

5 Conclusion

As has been demonstrated, contemporary martyrdom and the text tradition cannot be analyzed independently from each other. In the justification for martyrdom operations and the promised rewards in the garden several elements are involved. These range from religious concepts of martyrdom dating back to the early years of Islam, via modern societal notions of honor, pride, and shame, to nationalist elements of active political participation/resistance as well as sacrifices for freedom and liberation. The very present and important state of hope prevailing in Palestinian society is tied to notions of the garden, be it in terms of what the martyr can expect or in terms of the reasons it is important to continue living: in the garden the *ṣumūd* (steadfastness) will be rewarded.

Thus, concerning the sex-martyrdom debate, as As'ad Abu Khalil clarifies:

> It is not the 72 black-eyed virgins dancing in the heads in the would-be Islamic martyrs that should concern the West. Even if one succeeds in bringing about a radical change in the sexual life of Middle East men, the violent conflict will continue because the root cause of suicidal bombings is not sexual frustration, it is despair and deprivation. If prosperity and hope prevail in the Middle East, even the most charismatic warrior-preachers will not be able to find willing recruits.[34]

Bibliography

Abu Khalil, A., Sex and the suicide bomber (7 November 2001), available at: http://archive.salon.com/sex/feature/2001/11/07/islam/index1.html (last accessed 1 March 2011).

Abu Lughod, I., Palestinian higher education: National identity, liberation, and globalization, in *Boundary* 2, 27.1 (2000), 75–95.

Abu-Lughod, L., Islam and the gendered discourses of death, in *IJMES* 25.2 (1993), 187–205.

---

33 Gilanshah, Islamic customs 139.

34 Abu Khalil, Sex and the suicide bomber.

Arberry, A.J. (trans.), *The Koran interpreted*, New York 1996.

Boje, D.M., *Victor Turner's postmodern theory of social drama: Implications for organization studies*, PhD dissertation, New Mexico State University 2003.

Edwards, J.P., The law and rules of engagement against suicide attacks, in Centre of Excellence Defence Against Terrorism (ed.), *Suicide as a weapon*, Amsterdam 2007, 120–49.

Gambetta, D. (ed.), Making sense of suicide missions, New York 2005.

Gilanshah, F., Islamic customs regarding death, in D.-P. Irish et al. (eds.), *Ethnic variations in dying, death and grief: Diversity in universality*, Philadelphia and London 1993, 137–45.

Jebril, M.A.S., *Reflections on higher education in Palestine: Barriers to academia and intellectual dialogue in the Palestinian-Israeli context*, Oxford 2006.

Katā'ib shuhadā' al-Aqṣā: Idrīs, Wafā', available at: http://www.kataebaqsa.org/arabic/modules.php?name=News&file=article&sid= 72 (last accessed 1 July 2010, website recently shut down).

Moghadam, A., Palestinian suicide terrorism in the second Intifada, in *Studies in Conflict and Terrorism* 26 (2003), 65–92.

Neuwirth, A., Blut und Mythos in der islamischen Kultur, in C. von Braun and C. Wulf (eds.). *Mythen des Blutes*, Frankfurt and New York 2007, 62–90.

———, From sacrilege to sacrifice: Observations on violent death in classical and modern Arabic poetry, in F. Pannewick (ed.), *Martyrdom in literature: Visions of death and meaningful suffering in Europe and the Middle East from antiquity to modernity*, Wiesbaden 2004, 259–82.

———, B. Embaló, and F. Pannewick, *Kulturelle Selbstbehauptung der Palästinenser. Survey der Modernen Palästinensischen Dichtung*, Würzburg 2001.

Nicholson, R.A., *A literary history of the Arabs*, London 1907.

Pannewick, F., Wafa Idris – eine Selbstmordattentäterin zwischen Nationalheldin und Heiliger, in S. Weigel (ed.), *Märtyrer-Portraits: Von Opfertod, Blutzeugen und heiligen Kriegern*, Munich 2007, 110–3.

Smith, J.I., Reflections on aspects of immortality in Islam, in *The Harvard Theological Review* 70.1–2 (1977), 85–98.

——— and Y.Y. Haddad, *The Islamic understanding of death and resurrection*, Oxford 2002.

——— and Y.Y. Haddad, Women in the afterlife: The Islamic view as seen from Qur'an and tradition, in *Journal of the American Academy of Religion* 43.1 (1975), 39–55.

Szyska, C., Martyrdom: A drama of foundation and transition, in F. Pannewick (ed.), *Martyrdom in literature: Death and meaningful suffering in Europe and the Middle East from antiquity to modernity*, Wiesbaden 2004, 29–45.

Turner, V., *The anthropology of performance*, New York 1986.

———, *Dramas, fields, and metaphors: Symbolic action in human society*, Ithaca, NY and London 1974.
———, *From ritual to theatre: The human seriousness of play*, New York 1982.
Van Gennep, A., *Les rites de passage*, Paris 1909.
Wehr, H., *Arabic-English dictionary*, Urbana, IN 1994[4].

Internet Sources

http://www.unrwa.org (last accessed 1 March 2011).

CHAPTER 57

Crisis and the Secular Rhetoric of Islamic Paradise

Ruth Mas

Man is created with a restless anxiety.

Q 70:19

•••

Hyperboles are for young men to use; they show vehemence of character; and this is why angry people use them more than other people.

ARISTOTLE[1]

∵

Islam is in crisis: The shrillest of political clichés. Such is the rhetoric of many a scholar well versed in the tradition of Islam and insistent on its reform. Yet, Islam's crisis is not Islam's crisis but a crisis of the credibility and authority of religion now propelled down the anticipatory path of History by the drive of secularist politics. This generalized crisis forms the litany of modernity: holy wars, holy terrors, myths shattered, revolutions, hostile utopias, godly defenders, ungodly offenders, *jihād*, peace, martyrs, violence, assassins, new inquisitions, suicide terrorism, suicide bombers, veils, beards, minarets…: tired, overused, circular, sequential refrains growing weary of their urgency to overtake unsullied futures. However, despite (or perhaps due to) the upheavals of the twentieth century, the rhetoric of the crisis of Islam has tired and is running out of patience with its own repetitions; the secular search for new turning points is in its last breath and demanding renewal.[2] And so now, the turn to *janna*, i.e., *janna is the instrument of terror*. With this turn, Islamic

1 Aristotle, *Rhetoric* 96.

2 See Ferris, *Silent urns* 206, note 19, where he states, "Yet, in an age when crisis of one thing or another abounds, we are merely perpetuating the crisis that modernity uses to announce its arrival. In this case, it would be more accurate to speak not of the crisis of modernity but of its crises."

 | DOI 10.1163/9789004333154_058

paradise has been aligned with the faltering time of the secular in order to revive the rhetoric of crisis which claims that there is a "rejection of modernity [by Islam] in favor of a return to a sacred past."[3] Such rhetoric invokes sacred time in terms of how it is advanced by Islamic terrorists who usher in the divine time of Islam. Accordingly, the time of modernity is set against a traditional Islamic past resistant to the temporal extremes of Islam's anticipated future. Underpinning the long narrative of this rhetoric is now a highly bankrupted notion of history as progress that strategically reorients and distorts other understandings of time. *Janna* has thus entered a new era in its earthly narrative, but as "the instrument of terror" it is not yet a cliché. It is only an overstatement and hence still capable of projecting an eschatology of Islamic violence that must be overcome by a resurgent and timely sense of support for the modern.

It is with this in mind that we conduct the present examination of Nadia Tazi's (b. 1953) discourse about *janna* in order to address the way in which she renders Islamic paradise into a rhetoric of crisis. Like many Franco-Maghribi scholars seeking the reform of the Islamic tradition, Tazi's singular faith in modern secularity is premised on an ongoing preoccupation with "the great crisis of the Muslim world."[4] Tazi has worked extensively on the topics of gender and embodiment and as the editor of *La virilité en Islam*, has taken on the male "Islamist," a principal actor in this crisis whose agency has made of *janna* a prevailing mechanism of horror. She characterizes him (and by extension Islamism) as securing political disarray by conflating his paradisal aspirations with sexual desire. The social and political assault that concerns Tazi is founded on the androcentric order of Islamist power whose sexual and gendered politics enacts violence upon women. Tazi bases her argument on how Islamists contravene Islam's classical intellectual and religious tradition and she interprets their hermeneutics as a regression that brings the Islamic tradition into crisis.

For Tazi, this renders the desire for *janna* indefensible because it dangerously establishes the sovereignty of the male Muslim subject. The desire for *janna* does nothing but undo the limits of modernity that secure the boundaries between the political and the religious, paradise and the world, Islam and Islamism. She writes, "*Jannah* apparently becomes less inherently unfathomable when seen as expediting an otherwise untenable clash of two different realities, by becoming an instrument of terror."[5] Tazi does not simply assimilate

---

3 Lewis, *Crisis of Islam* 120.

4 Tazi and Benslama, Présentation 6.

5 Tazi, Jannah 29.

the instrumentalization of *janna* to violence. She ascribes to *janna* a dialectical mechanism that accelerates the binaries that modernity has set as a condition for its existence. The dyad set up by Tazi in the preceding statement is indicative of a difficulty within her thinking that I treat in this essay, namely a rhetoric of crisis that demands amplification and hyperbole as the operating features of Muslim agency.

Tazi first approached this topic in the late 1990s when the colonially sedimented violence that ravaged and rampantly shed blood in Algeria was also threatening the suburbs of Paris. The perverse paradox this violence has produced has made European modernity the antidote to Islam frequently touted by Muslim reformers from the Maghrib and France. In addition, these reformers have mostly remained silent on the question of *janna*. This raises several questions: Why has it been so difficult for some Muslim intellectuals to address one of the greatest resources of Islamic sensibility and imaginary – *janna* – and a theological staple of the religious and cultural heritage of Islam? What is significant about Tazi's breaching of this silence? And, if, as Michel Foucault tells us in *The Order of Things*, discourse proceeds out of silence, the silence of undifferentiated existence,[6] then what is it that is being differentiated in this discourse of Islamic paradise?

In *The Archeology of Knowledge*, Foucault treats the question of differentiation in terms of a crisis at the core of modernist thinking about transcendence and the unity (*un*differentiation) that is usually assumed as its essential characteristic. He states,

> But the major benefit, of course, is that it conceals the crisis in which we have been involved for so long, and which is constantly growing more serious: a crisis that concerns that transcendental reflection with which philosophy since Kant has identified itself; which concerns that theme of the origin, that promise of the return, by which we avoid the difference of our present; which concerns an anthropological thought that orders all these questions around the question of man's being, and allows us to avoid an analysis of practice; which concerns all humanist ideologies; which, above all, concerns *the status of the subject. It is this discussion that you would like to suppress*, and from which you would like to divert attention…[7]

6 Foucault, *Order of things* xx.

7 Foucault, *Archeology of knowledge* 225, emphasis added.

The question of differentiation for Foucault is located in the crisis that issued from the secularizing enlightenment as a result of the limits it recognized in our thinking about transcendence, i.e., the return to the origin or the very transcendence of *janna*. And, those limits permit us to differentiate ourselves (in distinction to the unification of transcendence) as subjects in history – the difference of our present to which Foucault refers. The issue for Foucault is how such differentiation demands a debate about the name and nature of crisis, a debate that raises the issue of the secular in relationship to transcendental – i.e., undifferentiated – reflection.

Literary critic Paul de Man takes up this issue in terms of how the rhetoric of crisis functions as a strategy of differentiation, a strategy which is particularly relevant to how Tazi positions Muslims in modernity. While not addressing the foundational questions raised by Foucault and Kant, he nevertheless is interested in the form that such rhetoric takes and by which it operates. In a well-known essay entitled "Criticism and crisis," de Man states, "We must ask ourselves if there is not a recurrent epistemological structure that characterizes all statements made in the mood and the rhetoric of crisis."[8] De Man alerts us to the ordering that occurs in the rhetoric of crisis and how it masquerades as knowledge when in fact it is a rhetoric passed off as knowledge without historical actuality. The rhetoric of crisis is thus productive of an epistemology that can only dissimulate knowledge. If we consider de Man's analysis, Tazi's coupling of "crisis" with "Islam" prompts us to pose the following questions: what is the structure that recurs in the reformulation of crisis as *janna* and "terror"? And, how does it sustain the historicist and present forms in which the catastrophic rhetoric about Islam and Muslims is framed? In what follows, the architecture of this most recent coupling in the rhetoric of crisis (from the Greek *krisis* and its cognate *krinein*, i.e., to separate) is examined as disclosing a method of discrimination, *differentiation*, and disjointing by which certain historical schemes are put into place and certain subjects are replaced.

Crucial then to the differentiation produced by the logic of crisis, is the question of the status of the subject to which Foucault alerts us. In other words, the place allotted to the Muslim subject and its assumed historical development within modernity depends on how Muslims are separated from the unity of transcendence to which they ascribe themselves, and from the tradition through which they have been shaped. We are interested here in the notion of subjectivity produced by the rhetorical coupling of *janna* with "terror" within modern structures of secularist differentiation. As we have seen in the quotation from Foucault above, what originates from post-Kantian idealist

8 De Man, Criticism and crisis 14.

projects is the desire to reinstate or recuperate a unifying subject after the modernist separations produced by Kant's examination of the limits of human understanding. For Kant, human understanding of transcendental reason is recognition of its own epistemological limitation viz. transcendence. A consequence of Kant's claim is that the subject is no longer understood as "being" but instead as "becoming" in its movement toward greater understanding. This consequence has been normatively accepted as the marker of progressive secular enlightenment, so that it produces a demand that Muslim subjects ultimately disassociate their knowledge and experience of Allah from any transcendental reference. Many of those seeking the reform of Islam take this demand for granted and pay little attention to the fact that this type of modern subject has been derived from a post-Christian context.

In pursuing the reform of Islam, Tazi resorts to the notion of "hyperbology," coined and developed by French philosopher Philippe Lacoue-Labarthe, to locate the agency of Muslims in modernity. Tazi works with a certain reading of Lacoue-Labarthe's concept of hyperbology of the subject that we differ with here because it entrenches this notion within a rhetoric of crisis, something which Lacoue-Labarthe does not do. The collection of his essays translated into English under the title *Typography: Mimesis, Philosophy and Politics*, tells us that, since Kant, efforts to absolutize the subject, "ha[ve] fallen prey to a certain *precipitation*... a certain panic."[9] Tazi turns to hyperbology as a means of explaining how this panic is present in the excessive representation of Islamic subjectivity that allows *janna* to be instrumentalized as terror. But, in doing so, Tazi emphasizes only one aspect of Lacoue-Labarthe's argument. In what follows, I take up the full consequences of Lacoue-Labarthe's argument in order to raise the question of how these consequences afford another reading of the crisis Tazi invokes. Before doing so however, I follow the path that brings Tazi to Lacoue-Labarthe, specifically, the path that runs through psychoanalysis and its language of desire and excess, as well as her dialectical account of subjectivity.

Tazi's attempt to put the experience of Muslim subjects into the political discourse of our modern epoch occurs in a recently published volume entitled *Islam and Psychoanalysis* of the *S-Journal of the Jan van Eyck Circle for Lacanian Ideology Critique*. In the introduction to the volume, editors Sigi Jöttkandt and Joan Copjec evoke terms that call for the urgent questioning of Islam "in this incisive moment in its history" and its relationship to modern modalities of rational inquiry. Urgency, the urgency of interrogation, is the rhetorical device

9 Lacoue-Labarthe, *Typography* 142.

in which the quickening of time instantiates the crisis of Islam. Of interest here is how it retreats behind the insipidness and predictability of a secularist rationality that leaves its political projects unchallenged. In the introduction, we read:

> ... the questions we have wanted to ask about the precise relation of secular male authority to religious authority in the Islamic world. But how can we pose these questions in the language of psychoanalysis in which some of us think? ... You will find it has a lot to say on these matters of the separateness and incommensurability of individual subjects and cultures and the problem of judgment ... The special issue of S – together with that of our sister journal Umbr(a) – on the topic of Islam could therefore not be more urgent ...[10]

Tazi's laconically titled "Jannah" within this volume interrogates Islam (both its tradition of classical interpretation and its present context) by assigning "gender" as the standard that determines our modern categories of emancipatory progress. The emergence of a gendered Islamic subject will inevitably be the object of the psychoanalytic demystification of Islam that Tazi takes up. She does so in accordance with the "hopes" of the volume to "seize Islam as an unseen, averted knowledge through which the stubborn and enigmatic imperative, 'Be psychoanalytic!' might be taken up."[11] The rhetoric of the crisis of Islam is here precipitated by a symptomatic imperative directed at Islam through its subjects – its gendered subjects.

For Tazi, what *janna* brings to our thinking about modernity and Islam lies in establishing the proper boundaries between Islam and Islamism. She asks, "Where does Paradise begin? Where does the world end? Where is the boundary between the political and the religious? And, in the modern context, where does Islam end and Islamism begin?"[12] The ability to separate the two is insisted upon in order to purge the gendered pathology that Tazi claims is specific to Islamism, and introduces the differentiations so crucial to the secular reform of Islam. Tazi establishes these separations within the rhetoric of modern dialectics that interpolates (what Tazi refers to as) the speculative tradition of Islam into a linear progressive history. She states,

---

10 Jöttkandt and Copjec, *Islam and psychoanalysis* 3.

11 Ibid., 4.

12 Tazi, Jannah 35, note 5.

> Tell me what *Jannah* is to you, and I will tell you who you are and what you desire. I will know if you are a libertine, a scholar, a philosopher or a mystic. Without seeking to appraise your spiritual understanding or moral fortitude, I will know the extent of your understanding, the nature of your intellectual and religious affinities and the historical tradition upon which you draw. Last but not least, if you are a man I will know how you view women and the sexual order in general. And from all that I will be able to divine where you stand in relation to modernity.[13]

This excerpt precipitates what throughout the rest of the article becomes a virtuosic display of Tazi's command of the primary sources that make up the tradition of Islam. Her reading renders *janna* the pivot to thinking of temporality and politics as constitutive of the dialectics of theology and philosophy out of which the gendered subject is produced. Moreover, it does so by placing the consummate modern subject, here "I," in the position to *limit janna* epistemologically: "I will tell you … I will know … I will know the extent … I will know how you view … I will be able to *divine*." This "I" establishes itself as the repetition of the modern predication of limits of transcendent epistemology – the foundational move of the rhetoric of the crisis of Islam. This founding repetition of modernist limits secures Tazi's faith in the singularity of modern secularity, as well as her platform ("I") from which she evaluates the proper confines of Islamic notions of transcendence. What proceeds from the reiterative rhetoric of her discriminating interrogation are questions that all presume the sense of limit to *janna* on which crisis feeds.

Tazi's iteration of the thinking and discriminating "I" serves to normalize it by rhetorically reproducing it as the inheritor of the enlightenment's doctrine of critical reason. To do so she cultivates the subject of the teleological narrative of modernity into a subject that is full of its own consciousness as the agent of that narrative. Tazi's rhetoric of Islam in crisis sets itself against this self-recognition by posing the danger of the "lethargy" of contemporary paradisal visions for the vitalism of the Islamic subject's rational inquiry. That lethargy, Tazi contends, brings the tradition of Islam to its point of conflict with a progressive epistemology:

> Islamism sweepingly disavows the intelligibility, rooted in both philosophy and mysticism, which identifies the real, the true and the invisible. Its great leap backwards begins with the repudiation of the *zâhir* (the apparent) and the *bâtin* (the esoteric) two fundamental states without

13 Ibid., 28.

> which the eschatology – and hence the road to the Hereafter – lose their sense. It would be no exaggeration to say that this literalist and juridist reduction eliminates Islam's most brilliant speculative legacy… The lazier the thinking, the more ostentatious the channels through which it is presented.[14]

So described, Islamism is an attack on knowledge and a betrayal of the classical tradition of Islamic thought, which reverses its trajectory and veers it off its modernist path through retrograde hermeneutics and the political degeneration caused by religious law. This postulating of a specific form of the Islamic tradition – Islamism, a form among forms, and one that she has not nuanced – is necessary to Tazi's separation of Islam from Islamism. Islamism is *the freezing point of thought* as Tazi so provocatively describes it, an obscurantist sacrality which paralyzes reflection, eschews the acculturated propriety and reasonable judgment of classical Islamic thought, and prevents its advance into modernity.[15] In this way, Tazi produces two possibilities for Islamic subjectivity. First, there is the Islamist male subject that is responsible for impeding Islamic thought through the misplacement of agency and the anesthetization of rationality. Or, there is the idealized subject of a rational Islam and/or a subjective, highly personalized, and highly privatized mystical state. (Despite an unfaltering obligation to the enlightenment however, this humanistic subject does not primarily concern himself with – i.e., does not think through – communal adherence to Islam nor the political and social possibilities made possible by such an adherence.)

Instead of reason, what activates the masculine subject of Islam put forward by Tazi is the Islamist desire for and guarantee of infinite satiation. She writes, "the Islamist doxa – true to the dogma – promises to the righteous, sex, sex and more sex, *ad infinitum*."[16] To this end, in Tazi's reading, the tradition's promised *ḥūrī* of *janna* surfaces from the allegorical and imaginal dimensions of

14 Ibid., 32.

15 Other scholars specialized in the psychology of Islamic masculinity, such as Durre S. Ahmed, may not find Tazi's definition of Islamism sufficiently nuanced. Ahmed's conceptualiztion of the psychology of Islamic fundamentalism, in *Masculinity, rationality and religion*, with regards to the "psycho-philosophical aspects of modernity" is elaborated as variegated. Furthermore, her analysis contradicts the lack of rationality that is imputed here to Islamism.

16 Tazi, Jannah 29. Readers may take note of the contribution of Baum to masculinity studies (Chasing horses), in which he critiques the Orientalist exploitation of the image of Arab Islamic masculinity as encased in cultural and physical impotence in the sexualization and exoticization of images of Palestinian masculinity and feminity.

the fountains, gardens, valleys, and rivers, resplendent with the most sensual of Arabian finery, into the figure of desire distorted by the modern caprices of Islamists. Tazi writes:

> There are none of the descriptions, the details, the admiration which once revealed her; she has become a mere shadow, a pure promise of flesh.... Her evanescent contours shaped entirely for male sexual pleasure, like the body glorious she exists for no other reason than to serve as a vehicle (for the desires of the righteous) or a rattle to be brandished during ideological disputes.[17]

The *ḥūrī* performs two intimately related roles: For Tazi, she is the misplaced masculinist teleology of virginity and object of suicide bombers' desire, and, the dissymmetric reflection of Islamist male power within which Muslim women are caught and reduced to mechanical and disembodied dimensions.[18] Hence, Tazi has the *ḥūrī* intercede between the inertia of male agency and its mechanics for female subjugation.

The *ḥūrī* is the model for which limits will surely need to be established! And they are – modernist, feminist ones in which the spectral *ḥūrī* points Tazi to the violent and ideological dimensions of Islam that must be dissected from modernity's project of freedom and emancipation, a project to which Tazi is clearly committed. Speaking of the androcentric order of Islamists whose sexual identity subjects women, Tazi states: "We must substitute the identity-based terminologies with the ideas and experiences of liberty... Remember that the political question involves the emancipation of both sexes, who are inextricably bound together in the domestic arena."[19] This figuring of the *ḥūrī* allows Tazi to displace the violence of politics on to the perversion of sexual politics and to critically differentiate between a liberated subject and the now revived extreme, puritanical, patriarchal, fantastical, combative, austere masculine subject of Islam who is guilty of conflating the sacred with the

17 Tazi, Jannah 30–1.

18 Ibid. Tazi seems unsure as to where to ascribe the catatonics of mechanicity. In an earlier essay, she defines the subject of virility as a macho: "Il n'y a rien d'étonnant à ce qu'il soit depeint comme un automate qui émet et reçoit des signaux pouvant anticiper ou annuler la pensée. Un être machinique qui est lui-même machine par la famille, le milieu, l'État, la loi communautaire, la nation; qui gendarme la vie, commes d'autres la mettent en musique ou l'extasient." Later on in the same article she refers to them as "des automates" that "s'adonnent a 'l'art de la mort.'" Tazi, Le désert perpétuel 33, 43.

19 Tazi, Jannah 42.

profanity of politics. In this way, Tazi correlates her critique of Muslim virility to the unsecularized limits of *janna*, which she defines as "articulat[ing] the eschatological anticipation enshrined in totalitarian slogans, a sectarian messianism and a pathological view of the masculine and the feminine which is quite specific to Islamism."[20] Tazi's commitment to the secular promise of redemption is repeated throughout her work, for example, when she states that the masculine subjectivity of Islamists and fundamentalism are the "virile foundation of Islam," or that "virility has . . . not been secularized."[21] The epistemological value that *janna* bears for Tazi is dependent on a secular corrective to gender inequality that directs the path of the modern subject away from the wayward masculinity that makes *janna* the crisis point of Islam.

---

20 Ibid., 29.

21 Tazi and Benslama, Présentation, 6. Tazi, Le désert perpétuel 30. Over the last two decades, scholarly concern with questions of gender and power has increasingly investigated the relationship of men to patriarchal privilege. What has emerged is an understanding of the definition, performance, and constitutedness of masculinity as varying over culture and time, across social, political, ethnic, biological, sexual, and economic lines, and as susceptible to hegemonic and subordinate constructions. While the Middle East and North Africa have attracted much consideration with regards to questions of women, gender, and the regulation of femininity, scant attention has been paid to masculinity in Islamic cultures. A more recent and welcome exception is Lahoucine Ouzgane's edited volume, *Islamic masculinities*, which grapples with enabling a thorough and clear examination of the issue of Islamic masculinity "without fuelling Eurocentric, anti-Arab, and anti-Islamic bigotry." (2) The volume explores the transformation of traditional and spiritual Islamic ideals of femininity and masculinity, and of the social and familial ties by the nation building aspirations of modern states deemed Islamic. Ouzgane's aims are pointed in his insistence that any examination of Islamic masculinity is necessarily and specifically a product of and constructed within different locales and particular political settings, something that seems to escape Tazi's analysis. Her identification of Islamic masculinity with suicide bombers should invite the reader to examine the specific and volatile nationalist setting of Israel and Palestine as discussed by scholars such as Massad in Conceiving the masculine, Peteet in Male gender, and Rothenberg in *Spirits of Palestine*. Their analysis of the ways in which Muslim masculinity is bundled with notions of state, territory, the politics of diaspora and return, and with notions of martyrdom, family honor, and the male as family provider, to name just a few of its imbrications, sheds serious doubt on Tazi's singular focus on virility as the favored modality of Islamic masculinity in modernity. Additionally, in Chasing horses, Baum makes clear how there really can be no discussion of masculinity without femininity, a point which I take up further on in this essay, at the same time as he demonstrates the further legal, administrative, and military imbrications of Palestinitian Muslim masculinity and feminity with Israeli masculinity and femininity. Their analysis points to the epistemological danger of short-circuiting Islamic masculinity with the category of suicide-bomber.

Tazi is thus able to mandate a reading of the history of the social and political organization of Islamic community in terms of the accumulation and surplus of the determinative virility of its male subjects: Islamic history begins with the word made virile, which is sedimented throughout successive caliphates, and which then abandons the "sovereignty of the desert" and "the chivalry of the great age" only to be laced with the arcaneness of the discourse of the seraglio.[22] To illustrate this process, Tazi provides us with an escalating list of what she terms modern "codes of virility": "veils, beards, minarets, mass movements, spectacular atrocities."[23] Inscribed within this inflated teleology (note how she unfortunately anchors virility in an absent feminine) is the "bestial destiny" of its contemporary embodiment. Such a culmination is presented by Tazi as an excess of worldly virility that is channeled into transcendence and then resubstantiated immanently as "holy predation," her description of the operation of male Islamist agency. She qualifies: "*virility* – [is] a quality I should distinguish from masculinity right at the outset, in that it always (and not only in the hereafter) masks hubris, hyperbole and excess."[24] Tazi has us understand

22 Tazi, Jannah 33–4. Here, Tazi abandons her previous discussions in "Le désert perpétuel," of the configurations of power of the modern nation state in Islamic countries and the structural subjectification of males within their despotic regimes, whose virility serves to "sully the Islamic tradition," and "betray the Muhammadan gesture." Tazi understands the relationships between men and women as caught within a microphysics of power and not simply in terms of the facile stratification of state-male-female. This much more nuanced discussion does not locate virility within a determined pattern of Islamic history and tradition, as she does in "Jannah." However, by locating its points of origin in the desert culture of Arab society through a reading of Ibn Khaldūn, Tazi produces a model of progress that is set up to fail in Islamic societies and states. This type of reading is fraught with the usual mythical trope – with all its ethno-fraught presuppositions – of "desert culture" as part of the founding myth of Islam.

23 Tazi, Jannah 33.

24 Ibid., 29. Tazi has previously attributed this to the failure of modernity, which she describes as "the antidote to virility" (Tazi, Le desert perpétuel 41) and which does not produce the values that it expounds in a uniform manner: "Il reste que la modernité pour fétichisée qu'elle soit dans les idées de liberté et dans la technique – s'avère segmentaire, elle n'agit pas au coeur du théologiqo-politique et de ses puissances symboliques." Indeed for Tazi, on page 43 of this same essay, modernity is even responsible for the nationalization of virility: "Les ideologies modernes ont surtout reterritorialisés la virilité sur la nation." It is not clear what Tazi would define as its opposite, though she does seem to be proposing that a rationalist Islamic male subjectivity is one that is stripped of (Arab) virility. For a less "apocalyptic" examination of Arab virility see Goldziher, Murruwa and din. In this article, Goldziher examines the classical notions of masculinity that developed in Islam and in the Greco-Latin world in terms of, for example, the virtue of *hilm*,

that the "supermasculine" vision implanted by the "divine optics" of Islamism is the militant constitution of unifying sovereignty and domination that establishes itself beyond limits and worldly law. Islamist virility is here equated with the kind of machismo celebrated by fascists – that of an unsatiated narcissism that feeds upon itself. This enables Tazi to generate a crisis of rhetoric that *inflates and compounds a reasoning of the unreasonable* that is out of step with and defiant of its modern constitution and confinement.

The vocabulary of desire and excess that Tazi introduces, is, however, polished by a Lacanian etiquette that would give many feminist scholars serious pause, and structures the crisis that lies in Tazi's representation of Muslim subjectivity. In an article directed at scholars of religion, Sîan Hawthorne, for example, eloquently and succinctly articulates the critique by many feminist scholars of the priority that Lacan attributes to masculinity. She states,

> [T]he masculine privilege that Lacan grants to the Symbolic register of language ... [is] a problematic gendered prioritization that renders all that is symbolically designated 'feminine' mute and absent and thus disenfranchised with respect to the sovereignty of language ... Language requires that the individual take up a masculine speaking position which necessarily implies that language itself is aligned with masculinity, indeed *is* masculinity par excellence: visible, concrete, definitive and divided corporeal entanglements and loyalties.[25]

---

i.e., forbearance, patience, and gentleness, which he actually indicates is something of a synonym for "*islām*" as an opposite of *jahl*. More recent discussions stemming from the field of masculinity studies, from scholars such as Roded in *Women in Islam* and which are concerned with the image of the prophet Muḥammad, also identify the pre-Islamic tradition of narrating military exploits (*ayyām al-ʿarab*) that shaped Islamic literature and produced other models of masculinity. Roded's discussion, in *Women in Islamic biographical collections*, of honorable lineage (*nasab*), as a virtue valued by men also complicates the idea of masculinity presented to us by Tazi.

25 Hawthorne, (M)Other in the text 167–8. Hawthorne provides an astute reading of the implications of Lacanian theories of ontology, language, and identity to the study of gender and religion. Elizabeth Grosz's *Jacques Lacan: A feminist introduction* is indicative of how extensive the body of feminist scholarship treating Lacanian psychoanalytic theory by scholars such as Luce Irigaray and Julia Kristeva. Irigaray's discussion of mimesis in *Speculum of the other women* can be read as a civilizing performance intending to correct Lacan's "erasure of the feminine" and could even be read constructively with Philippe Lacoue-Labarthe's treatment of Lacan and mimesis, which we address in the rest of this essay. Julia Kristeva, however, has positioned a more radical critique of Lacan in essays such as "Within the Microcosm of "the talking cure,'" which Hawthorne makes productive. On page 175 she advocates for Kristeva's model for a more "dynamic interrelation

In the readings of Lacan elucidated by Hawthorne and other feminist scholars, male desire is the desire for a totality that is constituted discursively and that culminates in jouissance. And female subjectivity comes into existence only negatively through language such that women are discursively subjected and undefined in their own right. This relates to Lacan's controversial proposal, "The woman does not exist," before he became the "the later Lacan" who attempted to formulate another type of jouissance that does not retreat into a phallic function. Jouissance, a term developed by Lacan (which in its sexual form is phallic and unrelated to the Other) is described by Dylan Evans as the pleasure followed by pain that is beyond language and experienced by the (male) subject when it has exceeded the limits put on its capacity to experience pleasure. In Lacanian language, jouissance is "the path towards death" – or, the structure that puts into place the parameters of death.[26]

Tazi's debt to Lacan is illustrated by her description of *janna* as the promise of never ending sex. This promise is made by Islamic doxa and dogma to its virtuous adherents who "pass straight from *jouissance* to the beatific vision just as they pass through death, with its overtones of martyrdom, this world to the next in a kind of permanent ecstasy."[27] In this way, *janna* shapes what Tazi considers the exaggerated desire, the desire in excess of Muslim men and its accumulation, which surpasses even jouissance. It is unclear where Tazi positions herself on this Lacanian scale or whether she is providing a corrective to its lack in her account of Islamic masculinity gone wrong. However, her adoption of Lacan's masculinist myopia and its exaggerated emphasis on the masculine subject ultimately results in the loss of the Muslim subject within her discussion. Where exactly is the speaking position of Muslim women in Tazi's discourse? Have Muslim subjects, male and female, here determined anything other than the rhetoric of Islam in crisis? Her discussion of Islamic male subjectivity effectively reinscribes the unrepresentability of women, Muslim women, even further by sustaining the analytic irresponsibility of Lacan on the backs of Muslim men. The latter are thus held accountable for what is already the discursive violence against women, which is in turn conflated with political violence and never empirically considered, verified or discussed.

To this point we can turn to the way in which Tazi's psychoanalytic project of demystifying Islam abjures the very tools of psychoanalysis to which Tazi

between the semiotic and symbolic elements of language" in Kristeva's *Revolution in poetic language* 22ff. Cf. Sian Hawthorne, Rethinking subjectivity in the gender oriented study of religions.

26 Evans, *Dictionary of Lacanian psychoanalysis* 91–2.

27 Tazi, Jannah 29.

gives such privileged status. This essay is, after all, where she takes up Jöttkandt and Copjec's imperative "Be psychoanalytic!" as a means of "seizing" Islam. Tazi could argue that other research has not developed notions surrounding the social phenomena of Muslim male subjectivity, i.e., virility. And yet, can one not question her recourse to the generalizing language of psychoanalysis here, framed by a rhetoric of escalating excess within which Islamic history and subjectivity has risen? In other words, should one not be suspicious of the unaccountability of a psychoanalytic approach in which it is theory that renders *social* phenomena comprehensible instead of the attentive subjective practice to which it lays claim – the very same caution Freud expresses in his *Civilization and its Discontents*?[28] What if we forgo such concerns and take Tazi on her own terms – would it be unfair to ask her, as a scholar publishing in a journal dedicated to Lacanian critique, what notion of Lacanian subjectivity she is drawing upon or developing? After all, how are we to understand Jöttkandt and Copjec's acquiescence – "Fine; put psychoanalysis on the spot. But then allow it to answer." – ? Or does psychoanalysis have a rhetorical function in which it puts itself into crisis ("on the spot") for the purposes of being able to speak?

The role of psychoanalysis and more specifically, how the question of excess in relation to the subject structures Lacan's treatment of jouissance, is importantly developed by Lacoue-Labarthe in both an early text on Lacan, *The Title of the Letter*, and his later development of what he calls hyperbology. While *The Title of the Letter* offers a critique of Lacan's unacknowledged indebtedness to Hegel's dialectical presentation of the subject, Lacoue-Labarthe's notion of hyperbology goes beyond this critique by arguing for an issue that remains undeveloped in both Lacan and Hegel, namely, the question of the difference that excess conceals. Lacoue-Labarthe's account of this difference is pertinent because it recasts Tazi's dependence on jouissance and hyperbology as the basis of her critique of Islamist virile subjectivity, as well as her congruent use of these two terms. This questioning establishes the important focus on dialectics in Lacoue-Labarthe's notion of hyperbology, specifically, the fact that the latter counters how, in response to the limitations of Kant's critical philosophy at the beginning of the nineteenth century, German idealism developed a dialectical account of the subject, that is, a subject understood as the effect of what it is mediated through rather than a subject whose unity is based on a

---

28 Cf. "Paradise and its Discontents: Eschatological Thought in Isma'ili, Hekmati, Shaykhi, Babi and Bahai Thought." This panel, organized and chaired by Todd Lawson at *ISIS-International Society for Iranian Studies*, 2008 Toronto is an example of "subaltern" readings and workings of a paradise discourse in Islam.

transcendental claim. Lacoue-Labarthe focuses on how Hegel uses dialectics to rescue the possibility of a unified subject after Kant. According to Lacoue-Labarthe, Hegel's unified subject belongs to a project whose goal is to establish the identity of the subject in the relation of the particular to the universal – an identity that results from the subject's infinite rediscovery of itself through its self-consciousness in the world. Here, Hegel responds to the fact that in Kant the subject can have no transcendent ground, a condition that, for Hegel, produces a deficiency for the subject. For Lacoue-Labarthe, the question of the excess of subjectivity first takes into account how Hegel seizes upon this deficiency as the opening for a dialectical development of the subject within history.

Lacoue-Labarthe's notion of hyperbology thus intervenes in an understanding of how, for Hegel, the subject is implicated in the dialectical move of recognizing itself in what it is not, a move that is also referred to as a speculative moment because it involves the subject recognizing itself as mirrored in something other than itself. In this way, the transcendent or unifying moment for the subject can be restored and integrated through its dialectical journey in time. Hegel's position is in opposition to Kant for whom the difference between transcendental reason and the understanding of the subject must be maintained. Hegel will thus attempt to recuperate this difference through the time of history. In other words, the impasse in which Kant preserves the transcendent as separate, has now, in Hegel, been displaced into a historical process as differentiation, which becomes the dynamic that sustains the subject through history and time. Lacoue-Labarthe asks, however, whether difference is really accounted for in the dialectical movement that Hegel proposes. Hegel only understands difference as playing a mediating role and thus never exists as pure difference. For Lacoue-Labarthe such a pure difference occurs as an excess that Hegelian dialectic cannot account for. This is the problem that Lacoue-Labarthe finds unresolved in Lacan's account of jouissance and from which he disassociates himself. It also marks an important difference which Tazi does not take up in her use of hyperbology.

The distance Lacoue-Labarthe takes from Lacan is evident in his earlier study, *The Title of the Letter*, which he co-authored with Jean-Luc Nancy. This volume provides an introduction to the modern problem of the subject in terms that allow us to grasp the relationship between Tazi's use of the language of jouissance and excess, and her subsequent turn to hyperbology to explain the significance of *janna* to terror. Lacoue-Labarthe's investigation in *The Title of the Letter* specifically addresses a seminal essay by Lacan, "The Agency of the Letter in the Unconscious or Reason since Freud" in order to argue that Lacan reinscribes a foundational subject into a metaphysics of truth, the very foundationalism that Kant and Hegel sought to avoid. Despite Lacan's claims to the contrary, and despite his attempts to prevent the relationship between subject and alterity from being wholly assimilated into a dialectical movement, Lacoue-Labarthe insists that Lacan is still founding the subject through dialectics i.e., the dialectical mediation that Lacan sought to suspend is still at work. His reading of Lacan brings into focus this reinscription through the latter's understanding of the subject as desire, more specifically, as jouissance: "[w]hen it is a question of desire, it is Hegel who intervenes in the text, albeit anonymously."[29] What then, does he mean when he states that Hegel intervenes in Lacan's text, or better still, how does Hegel intervene? Lacan, he argues, reads the subject according to a Hegelian dialectic in which the self is sustained in relationship to the other by desire, i.e., desire locates jouissance in dialectics. This signifies that the subject is maintained dialectically in its relationship to the Other, and that this relationship is the basis of desire. (Here, the Other in Lacan produces the dialectic of desire in the same way the absolute produces mediation in Hegel.) There is not enough space to take up in detail Lacoue-Labarthe's investigation of this aspect of Lacan's thinking. What interests us instead are the important consequences of Lacoue-Labarthe's critique of Lacan's account of jouissance for Tazi's treatment of the subject.

The focus of Lacoue-Labarthe's critique lies on Lacan's claim that the structure of jouissance suspends dialectics by refusing a synthesis or moment of completion. Because Lacan argues that desire is meaningful for the subject as long as it is not fulfilled, the dialectics of desire can never be completed. Lacan writes, "*jouissance* must be refused, so that it can be reached on the inverted ladder of the Law of desire."[30] In this dense remark, Lacan's conception of the Other is formulated in opposition to Hegel for whom alterity is always mediated and endlessly assimilated. However, Lacoue-Labarthe points out that since the failure of desire to complete itself in jouissance is an effect of alterity, then the Other nevertheless maintains a dialectical relationship to the subject, albeit negatively. In this way, the Other always keeps desire alive for Lacan by preventing any transcendent or absolute jouissance. He states, "And this alterity ... commands the structure, if you will, of *jouissance*: '... jouissance fulfilled has indeed the positive significance that self-consciousness has become objective to *itself*; but equally, it has the negative one of having sublated *itself*.'"[31]

29 Lacoue-Labarthe, *Title of the letter* 121.

30 Cited by Lacoue-Labarthe, *Title of the letter* 122.

31 Ibid., 123–4. The passage that Lacoue-Labarthe cites is from Hegel's *Phenomenology of spirit*. The fact that this contains a modified translation of Hegel is evident in his use of "jouissance" (and "sublated") where Hegel actually states *Befriedigung* which in the

That Other is always understood as something which does not accomplish jouissance but which is dialectical because it mediates jouissance and at the same time distances it. Lacoue-Labarthe refers to this as a diversion from, but not a suspension of, Hegel's dialectical account of the subject:

> Lacan's diversion of Hegel first consists in turning the dialectic of desire into a negative discourse. Lacanian dialectic thus governs a constant disappropriation of the subject against the background of absence and division by the Other, whereas Hegelian dialectic governs its process of appropriation against the background of presence and the reduction of alterity.[32]

Lacoue-Labarthe contends that the Hegelian dialectic of consciousness has been appropriated by Lacan for the psychoanalytic subject, if only in order to negate and disappropriate it. Thus, the same principle of negativity is at work in Hegel and Lacan. The only difference is that in Hegel it is turned toward the absolute, whereas in Lacan it is turned toward the Other. "Or, more precisely, it is the same process of alienation or negativity which can no longer 'simply' be understood in reference to the Absolute, but rather to the Other."[33] Despite Lacan's attempt to suspend the dialectic, this dialectic nevertheless remains an end "of reintegration and agreement."[34] As such, jouissance-as-excess does not bring an end to dialectics but rather refolds the subject within the dialectics whose purpose is thus maintained.

In two essays from a volume entitled *Typography*, Lacoue-Labarthe develops the question of this excess by examining how hyperbology is at work within it. Linking the development of the question of dialectics to the problem of mimesis in speculative thinking, Lacoue-Labarthe asks,

> But as regards "Plato," what happens here? Is the infinitization of the *mise-en-abyme*, its "hyperbolic" character, enough to compensate for the

English translation by A.V. Miller appears as "satisfaction." The quotation is drawn from this sentence, which in the German original reads as follows: "Um der Selbständigkeit des Gegenstandes willen kann es daher zur Befriedigung nur gelangen, indem dieser selbst die Negation an ihm vollzieht; und er muß diese Negation seiner selbst an sich vollziehen, denn er ist *an sich* das Negative, und muß für das Andere sein, was er ist." Hegel, *Phänomenologie* 144.

32 Lacoue-Labarthe, *Title of the letter* 124.

33 Ibid., 122.

34 Ibid., 124. Here, Lacoue-Labarthe is quoting Lacan's own terminology.

> appropriation of mimesis, for its onto-ideo-logical reduction? Is the use of *a* mimetic means enough to conjure mimesis? Can this means be the means of all means? Is it essentially a question, in mimesis, of *reflection*?[35]

Here, Lacoue-Labarthe addresses a central problem in philosophy since Plato: the idea that there is only one thing that is the same in itself. With Plato, identity, mimesis, and analogy thus become the means by which sameness is reintegrated as a relation between two things in history.[36] The subject emerges within this history through what Lacoue-Labarthe calls a "*speculative* apparatus," a notion that produces a *mise-en-abyme* – the mirror image, in which the subject contemplates, reflects, interiorizes itself, and sees itself as infinitely mirrored in its own absence. Implicit to this apparatus is the setting up of a dialectic between absence and presence, whereby the present subject (or the presence of the subject) is constantly mediated through its absence, which in turn becomes the sign of its presence. In "The Caesura of the Speculative," (the essay from which Tazi has drawn in her use of hyperbology), Lacoue-Labarthe explains that when the image takes the place of something absent, this establishes a dialectical logic, a speculative dialectics, which sets in motion the "absolutization or that paradoxical infinitization of the Subject within which philosophy will find its completion."[37] Contained within this process is the possibility of the "limit" which will demarcate the moment in which "the speculative (de)constitutes itself," and, in Lacoue-Labarthe's terms, "dismantles itself, deconstructs itself in the same movement by which it erects itself…"[38] It is the possibility of this limit that will enable Lacoue-Labarthe to disrupt the repetitive reinscription of dialectics and provide a resolution to the accumulating excess within its function.

To do so, Lacoue-Labarthe recasts the dialectical logic of mimesis as "hyperbology" and describes it in terms of the excess of both presence and loss produced in its mirror-imaging.[39] This reflection of the subject within the speculative moment allows the subject to exceed itself through its own reflection. And yet, for Lacoue-Labarthe, the condition of the subject's excess is also its loss in so far as it will always be less than what it could be without its reflection. Hence, the subject's excess is always the condition of its own finitude,

---

35 Lacoue-Labarthe, *Typography* 95.

36 For a discussion of the nature and function of historical understanding with respect to mimesis and its origin, see Ferris, *Theory and the evasion* 1–36.

37 Lacoue-Labarthe, *Typography* 217.

38 Ibid., 212.

39 Ibid., 221.

which Lacoue-Labarthe understands as a moment of (dis)appropriation that brings the subject face to face with its own finitude. He states,

> I should emphasize, however, that only the "hyperbologic" is undoubtedly capable of accounting for the scheme of the "double turning about" ... according to which the very excess of the speculative switches into the very excess of submission to finitude (a scheme in which the "categorical" turning about of the divine corresponds to the *volte-face*, as Beaufret says, of man toward the earth, his pious infidelity, and his extended wandering "under the unthinkable," which fundamentally define the Kantian age to which we belong).[40]

For Lacoue-Labarthe dialectics is inevitable and it is false to assume that he believes dialectics can be overcome with something external to itself – there is no outside to dialectics. While this is fundamentally the critique he levels at Lacan, for whom the "other" functions as external to a dialectics maintained by the subject's desire, Lacoue-Labarthe is still left with the problem of what to do with the latter's excess. To resolve this, he turns to what "dislocates [the speculative] *from within*." Lacoue-Labarthe conceives of this as an "immobilization," and "suspension" produced by a moment that cannot be mediated by anything else and which arrests and distorts the ability of dialectics to exhaust and fully integrate itself.[41] This is described by Lacoue-Labarthe in the following way:

> [T]his dialectical starting device, constantly reengaged, always lacks a principle of resolution. Everything happens, therefore, as though we were dealing with (and with nothing more than) a kind of immobilized attenuation of a dialectical process that marks time in an interminable oscillation between the two poles of an opposition, always infinitely distant from each Other. The act of suspension is this: quite simply, the incessant repetition of the engaging of the dialectical process in the – never changing – form of *the closer it is, the more distant it is; the more dissimilar it is, the more adequate it is; the more interior it is, the more exterior it is*. In short, the maximum of appropriation (for the perpetual comparison here originates in a movement of passing to the limit, the proceeds necessarily from a logic of excess – of the superlative) is the maximum of disappropriation, and conversely.[42]

40 Ibid., 232.
41 Ibid., 227.
42 Ibid., 230.

Lacoue-Labarthe does not place suspension outside of dialectics, nor does this suspension bring dialectics to an end. Suspension occurs with and is internal to dialectics; dialectics carries suspension along with itself as a condition of its movement. It is therefore not a stasis but an incessant repetition of an unmediatizable moment that suspends dialectics as a movement that cannot overcome the difference it produces. This suspension creates *endless separation*, or an excess of separation within the dialectical movement. He describes this as the *mise-en-abyme* in which the speculative reflection incessantly divides reflection from reflection to the point of its distortion. For Lacoue-Labarthe the subject's apprehension of itself has to be translated into the moment of its articulation; this moment is what he will call the "caesura." Here, he follows the German poet Friedrich Hölderlin, who in his discussion of tragedy, defines the "caesura" as "the pure word, the counter-rhythmic intrusion." On the basis of this remark, Lacoue-Labarthe describes Hölderlin as having "*caesuraed the speculative*." With the "caesura" Lacoue-Labarthe introduces an element within the dialectical practice besides what it mediates: the moment of speculative distortion, which is the non-articulation/interruption that always accompanies articulation.

The consequences of Lacoue-Labarthe's reading for Tazi begin with the fact that she limits herself to the mediating function of hyperbology without taking into account the *internalized* interruption out of which excess is produced. In this respect, she adheres to the diversion Lacoue-Labarthe criticizes in Lacan's account of jouissance – an adherence that she carries over into her understanding of Lacoue-Labarthe's concept of hyperbology and which then makes *janna* into the accomplishment of desire/jouissance. This is evident in the following description that she provides for *janna*: "Surpassing any form of representation or comparison, it can be thought of only as 'the end,' in every sense of the word: the end of thought itself, if not a transcendental idea of the conditions under which the end is possible, as a release expedited by faith."[43]

Here, Tazi has formulated *janna* as a liberation or escape from dialectics by means of desire. These are the grounds on which Tazi will place hyperbology as the impulse of male Islamist violence and then make *janna* resolve the dialectical problem of endless or excessive reinscription.

To do so, Tazi first establishes the death drive through jouissance that is produced out of hyperbology, "A violence, in other words, which scandalously promises a hyperbolic continuity between this world and the next, between the most mortal of deaths and eternal life."[44] For Tazi, hyperbole, or the

43 Tazi, Jannah 28.

44 Ibid., 29.

hyperbolic, is *janna* and unites life and death within the expansion of force that she attributes to the irrational subject of virility through its desire and excess: "The hyperbole of *Jannah* is already etched into the shattered face of our century, underpinned by death, as if the afterlife were utterly suffused with extreme violence."[45] In stating that "the expression of virility [is] the pursuit of sovereignty, hyperbolism . . . ," Tazi posits the Islamist subject as the conduit for "hyperbology," a concept that elaborates her Lacanian gloss of jouissance.[46] This subject is trapped within the hyperbological dialectics of excessive desire,[47] to which, she argues, he is compelled to put an end:

> In all the countless dramas affecting the Islamic world . . . we can interpret the Islamist position based upon the devastating aporiae of virilist hyperbology and its counter-effects. There comes a time when, caught in the asymptote of the virile, *dialectics cease to function* and, in response to political tragedies, we allow relationships to be invested by fascist impulses. Fed by a vicious circle of impotencies and humiliations, the game of double bind becomes the consuming male passion; the means whereby he, wounded, is able to wound life in return.[48]

To interrupt the amalgamating properties of a modern dialectics is to put it into crisis and Tazi leaves no rhetorical way out except for the Islamist position to fold back into fascism with the suspension of dialectics. Tazi's assertion of dialectics over male violence here makes her investment in dialectics clear: Once violence is eliminated, all that is left is functioning dialectics. Virilist hyperbology, which leads to the cessation of dialectics, is a threat to the dialectically based position Tazi wishes to affirm. The disparity in her use of Lacoue-Labarthe is produced by the fact that she does not take into account the limit that exists within dialectics and which prevents it from ever ceasing. Instead, she protects dialectics the same way Lacan protects dialectics by always locating the Other on the outside: For Tazi, *janna* operates like the unattainable Other in Lacan. The excess that commands and leads to *janna* or Lacan's jouissance, thus breaks through dialectics. Tazi is here surpassing even Lacan for whom the subject does not accomplish the desire. Let us recall that Lacoue-Labarthe sees the limit within dialectics in terms of the empty articulation (the caesura) that resides inside it; this empty articulation is the excess dialectics

45 Ibid.
46 Ibid., 37.
47 Ibid., 39.
48 Ibid., 41, emphasis added.

can never eliminate. For Tazi, despite the appeal to Lacan and hyperbology, that limit is relocated in *janna* by desire. Tazi is thus strongly suggesting that hyperbology, as, for example, the explosion of the desire of the suicide bomber into *janna*, destroys the dialectic, i.e., dialectics are thus suspended from the "outside." By pushing the question of hyperbology beyond excess and into its destruction, Tazi also overreads Lacoue-Labarthe for whom the suspension of dialectics does not ever cease its functioning.

To best approach how Tazi overstates Lacoue-Labarthe's notion of hyperbology, one must turn to her description of an "endless hyperbological circle," and ask, what does she expose by qualifying dialectics with circularity? Firstly, we now know from Tazi's argument that "The Muslim man's relationship with the carnal... puts him in a *double bind*."[49] In relationship to this, Tazi is also referring to the Islamist subject's lack of escape from the irrelevance of the transcendental to the material world of politics. In another moment in the text Tazi discusses the implications of his insistence on bringing the otherworldly dimensions to politics, that is to say, in the name of sacred law, "Affixing itself to the Law is the element of history, a political provision bringing with it a second *double bind*. In deferring to despotic power, this fundamentally separates Islamic society from the classical Greek tradition with which it appears to be allied."[50] Islamic society's lack of conformity to modernity lies in its refusal to fall in line with classical Greek thinking. To deviate from this legacy is to guarantee the political tyranny that is supposedly absent from a Greek inspired West. The rhetoric of Islam in crisis here preserves the singularity of linear progress from a prescribed point of origin and then throughout a defined history. The crisis of modernity is thus the crisis of an Islam caught in a vicious circle spun out of the dialectics of the modern only to chase and be chased by consuming violence.

The circular causality that for Tazi is contained in hyperbology takes place within political contradictions, oppositions, and conditions that build up into irrational excess and feed and fortify the Islamist male ego.[51] Tazi contends,

> The hyperbological complications hem him in on all sides, affecting his points of references, his formal roles and his abilities, without his machismo ever letting up on its demands for satiation... For all this, and unremitting in their submission to hyperbolic and disjunctive logics,

49 Ibid., 36.

50 Ibid., 39.

51 Ibid., 40. "[T]he antinomies and crazy excesses of hyperbology. In all of this there is a circular causality linking the sovereign and his subjects..."

> macho values are all the more resilient now that they are focused upon the domestic arena. The newspapers are full of stories relating how these constraints and dyschronic developments torment society. *What a wretched picture all of this reveals, of a masculinity and gender politics pushing the world into reverse.*[52]

Tazi has displaced the question of the excess that resides within virilist hyperbology, where the virile is set into a hyperbological state of an unceasing cycle of alternation. Therefore, what Tazi has omitted from Lacoue-Labarthe's dialectics of hyperbology is the problem of the excess of separation, which does not equal never-ending cycling. Positing an endless cycle to hyperbology is a move that remains consonant with Lacan, where endless desire is the interminable oscillation between subject and object. In leaving out the excess of separation, what she takes from Lacoue-Labarthe instead is a movement of alternation that she refers to as establishing endless cycling. In other words, in confusing endless separation with the excess of separation Tazi has stopped short of Lacoue-Labarthe's hyperbology. To repeat: for Lacoue-Labarthe the excess remains within the dialectics and is present in the caesura that is inherent to its operation and which interrupts the rhythm of its endless repetition in the form of "the closer it is the more distant it is" etc. This difference is crucial and because of it Lacoue-Labarthe could rephrase Tazi's argument as follows: *The excess of the speculative, jouissance, switches into the very excess of submission to finitude and not submission to Allah or janna.* This means that instead of an endless hyperbological circle that undoes the dialectics of belief in *janna*, Lacoue-Labarthe speaks of the caesura of the speculative as bringing to a halt, or disarticulating, the process of alternations: "It prevents the racing oscillation, *crazed panic* and an orientation towards this or that pole."[53] In other words, Lacoue-Labarthe posits hyperbology as containing the excess of oscillation between finitude and infinite *within it*, which is disarticulated not by *janna* and not by the finite on the other hand, but by an empty moment which is the caesura.

Lacoue-Labarthe's reading of the caesura comes out of his treatment of tragedy in Hölderlin and, accordingly, is suggestive of how Tazi engages with the discussion of religion and sacrifice. Caught by his "speculative desire for the infinite and the divine," the tragic figure in Hölderlin turns toward the infinite. And yet, that movement increases his distance with and estrangement from the divine so that instead of *janna* or a finite moment, he is met with the excess

52 Ibid., 41, emphasis added.

53 Lacoue-Labarthe, *Typography* 235.

of his own finitude.[54] For Lacoue-Labarthe, hyperbology is the effect of this impossibility in so far as it is about the intolerability of a limitless separation from the divine as a condition of the subject's desired unification with it.[55] The moment of tragedy lies in the subject's attempt to unite with the divine and escape from its speculative desire through death. This escape is what Lacoue-Labarthe refers to as the moment of sacrifice, "Tragedy, then, is the catharsis of the speculative. Which means also the catharsis of the religious itself and of the sacrifice."[56] His description of religious sacrifice is one that Tazi would support in her discussion of the desire of suicide bombers. Speaking of the death of the tragic figure, he says,

> He is destroyed not by directly provoking the punishment, but by calling up the old ritual of the scapegoat victim. He is destroyed, in short, by his belief in … religious "mechanisms," which are in fact, though with regard to a different concept of religion, "sacrilegious" mechanisms, because they presuppose the transgression of the human limit, the appropriation of a divine position …[57]

The moment of death, the moment of tragedy, is what Lacoue-Labarthe calls the "catharsis of the speculative." This is the moment of "*jouissance*" in Tazi's discussion of terror, but it is also where she stops and thereby avoids how Lacoue-Labarthe introduces the hyperbologic precisely to arrest its culmination in death.

The issues raised by Tazi's reading of Lacoue-Labarthe (and Lacan) have more at stake than whether she is working accurately with his concepts or not. They have to do with the type of subject positions that are produced for Muslims and what room they are assigned within modernity. In this regard, scholars dedicated to examining and mapping the existence of Islamist movements in the Middle East and Europe, the very context from which Tazi is writing, as well as the historical and political contexts which have given rise to them will take issue with how Tazi paints Islamism, Islamists, and Islamic "brothers" with violent literalism and juridistic hermeneutics. The important empirical, political, sociological, and anthropological differentiations within and between them, and their striated intersections and divergences are instead brought into crisis within a dialectics of the modern. By extension, one

54 Ibid., 232.
55 Martis, *Representation* 103.
56 Lacoue-Labarthe, *Typography* 232.
57 Ibid., 233.

wonders how she would nuance her argument for the experience of "liberty" and the "emancipation" of women to take into account the scholarship dedicated, for example, to examining the increased production of public piety by Muslim women responding to the now globalized label of oppressed[58] – or the growing research attesting to the functioning of Islamist movements within democratic political models and the mobilization and promotion of the role of women within these movements.[59] Even more acute is her silencing of the ways in which women's participation in Islamist movements have upset normative and liberal notions of freedom, agency, and resistance. Do we not have here a withdrawal from the rationalist tools of modernity at the very moment in which one asserts their primacy? Is this assertion of a rational-less "I" not overriding the very subjects that it claims are oppressed? All that is yielded by this rhetoric of the crisis of Islam is the fact that what remains in crisis is the means of modern rationalist referentiality by which crisis is incessantly identified and not the referent itself.

What puts modernity into crisis for Tazi is the subjectivity of Islamists, which is disproportionate or excessive to the forward succession of time. This view is solidly anchored in modernist secular understandings of temporality in which the unruliness of Islamist agency threatens to reverse the secular advance of modernity into the *arrhythmia* of Islam.[60] This account is also reinforced by a faith in the synthesizing movement of dialectical modernity borrowed from Hegel, developed by Marx and others. There have been many critiques of the way in which this tradition of thinking about history as dialectical ensures political progress, one of which is the kind that is here generalizing the rhetoric of crisis of Islam.[61] Lacoue-Labarthe is one of these critics who nevertheless formulates his response in terms of a non-dialectical moment within dialectics. It is on this point that we should return to Lacoue-Labarthe for whom the caesura *disarticulates the temporal succession of dialectics*. The caesura, Lacoue-Labarthe contends, impedes,

> the racing oscillation, *crazed panic*, and an orientation toward this or that pole. The disarticulation represents the active neutrality of the interval

58 Deeb, *Enchanted modern*.

59 Peter, *Islamic movements*; Burgat, *Face to face*; and Burgat, *The Islamic movement*.

60 Mas, Islam in secular time.

61 The most notable among them is probably the one leveled by Michel Foucault in *Archeology of knowledge* in which he began to develop his account of history in relation to Nietzsche's notion of genealogy, which eschewed linear causes and effects in favor of disruptions and change in order to determine the conditions and possibilities of discourse.

> between [entre-deux]. This is undoubtedly why it is not by chance that the caesura is, on each occasion, the empty moment – the absence of "moment" – of Tiresia's intervention: of the intrusion of the prophetic word...[62]

Lacoue-Labarthe's response to Tazi would be that the caesura is the absence of the intrusion of *janna*, i.e., it is where *janna* does not intrude. And by intrusion he refers to the problem that is established when the prophetic word is already true. Because the prophetic word for Lacoue-Labarthe is the absent moment out of which time unfolds, there is no time in its moment. It, "*janna*," is spoken from immanence and therefore awaits its referent, or that which makes it true and actualized in the world. Tazi would surely agree that the establishment of its truth is made retroactively, by the backwards glance of death, and hence its truth belongs to its promise. In other words, in order to be a prophecy, *janna* can only make the promise of fully actualized truth, which is the promise of its reference. As such, it articulates the place for that referent but, as it does so, it makes that referent dependent upon a finite moment – a finite moment that is empty. This is where Tazi departs from Lacoue-Labarthe's hyperbology. If the prophetic word is the promise that the word is empty, it still has to rely on the word to make that promise; that is its paradox, which means that the achievement of temporal significance lies in its promise of the transcendent. The prophetic word here is Lacoue-Labarthe's disarticulation of progressive temporality; its caesura suspends the forward rhythm of dialectical articulation. As opposed to Tazi, whose commitment to dialectics makes her stop at the acceleration of the reinscription of dialectics, Lacoue-Labarthe sees acceleration as simply the repetition of reinscription rather than the articulation of meaning. In contrast, through the caesura (the excess of articulation) and its interruptive function, Lacoue-Labarthe allows for the introduction of another temporal cycle of reinscription that is dislodged from and dislocates the successive movement of dialectics. The caesura on which this other temporal cycle is based protects *janna* from instrumentalization. In this way, Lacoue-Labarthe has formulated the caesura so that it cannot be appropriated by crisis toward a purpose, which in this case means toward the type of political project that would systematize the tradition of Islam and its subjects into the predetermined demands of a secular modernity.

•••

62 Lacoue-Labarthe, *Typography* 235.

Such secularizing readings proceed by making the strands of rationalism and spirituality that it picks and chooses to be representative of an "authentic" Islamic tradition conform to the historical moment of the Enlightenment, the complexity of which it also reduces. This means that the political aspirations of this kind of reading of the Islamic tradition also produce a particular reading of the modernist limits on transcendence, and more specifically on transcendent epistemology. The political urge advancing these readings takes the Islamic traditions of eschatology and turns them into a figure of Islamic apocalypse, one that is easily glossed with images of violence emerging from the Middle East. This figure justifies at the same time as it replicates secularizing govermentality and power, and it does so explicitly by putting itself forward as the stop-gap to the advent of an ever present Islamic apocalypse, where *janna* is its favored agent. Thus, the vast, dynamic eschatological fabric of the Islamic tradition, replete as it is with complex and subtle imagery of the afterlife that shapes the experience, culture, practices, daily life, beliefs, and theories of its practitioners and scholars, is dealt a remarkably reductive blow. This blow is leveled both on the level of culture and politics. If the richness of the eschatological aspect of the Islamic imaginary has heretofore been largely unexplored and understudied, the prospects of it productively shaping a society that supports reciprocal multilateral politics and interdependence are increasingly grim. This is especially true if the tradition of Islamic paradise and the hereafter is forcibly strained through the political sieve of the secularizing modern nation state and, above all, because of the way in which the latter is also beholden to and enforces very facile notions of the secular.

By now, it is a banal fact that a progressive view of time authorizes and couples both a temporal model of history and the advance of time with the material evidence of civilizational and political progress. And so is the fact that in doing so, this progressive view of time is meant to disinvolve other traditions of temporality and the transcendental notions to which they adhere while duplicitously hanging on to "their own." After all, the modern politicization of the secular is only enabled by the *constancy* of a specific notion of the religious as transcendence. The question for the secular govermentality of civic and social organization is which notion that can be. In other words, which notion is going to fuel the political administration of the secular and for whom? In the context of the secular nation state that already begrudges its dependency on notions of religion, especially transcendental ones, Islamic notions of transcendence (*janna* etc.) are ripe for exclusion. The reasons seem almost self-evident in so far as it is necessarily conjoined to the material world, such a notion of Islamic transcendence does not provide or replicate the model of civilizational and political progress already established by the modern nation state. To identify

Islamic notions of transcendence as apocalyptic, or, simply put, to couple notions of *janna* with the apocalypse (where the desire for the former invokes the latter) appears to be yet another example of the ploys of political exclusion. And it is; but this rejection is not simply authorized by the foreignness of the notion of *janna*. It operates by denying it any functional link of its own to the material and even secular world. This means that *janna* is only understood transcendentally, which only allows it to perform according to the predetermined duality of immanence and transcendence that has evolved out of the Christian world and the secularizing political apparatus that it subsequently instituted.[63] As such, *janna*, confined as it is to the transcendental realm is only in dialectical relationship to the secular material world so as to enable the necessary continuity of its own exclusion, one which puts into play the secular politics of socio-political organization. The problem in a modern context is also that by keeping the notion of *janna* safely ensconced in transcendence, it has narrowed its possibilities to such an extent that any account of *janna* can only be brought about by apocalyptic ambitions. It seems that the Islamic notion of *janna* (let alone heaven on earth) can only be terrifying.

The threat of Islamic apocalypse encased in a dialectic between the religious and the secular, is thus meant to synthesize the transcendent aims of religion out of the realm of secularizing governance. Not only does this beg the questions of why religious ideals are or should only be understood transcendentally, it also raises the question of what actually constitutes Islamic apocalypse. As Todd Lawson has noted, the Greek origins of the meaning of apocalypse do not yield the connotations of mass destruction, catastrophe or annihilation brought on by the end of the world (or misplaced notions of *janna*) traditionally evoked by contemporary notions of apocalypse. Apocalypse simply means revelation. Lawson's rich and sophisticated reading demonstrates how apocalypse, or the event of revelation, establishes a narrative framework in the Quran that discloses new ethical knowledge. A central feature of this disclosure appears in the form of conceptual dualities, oppositions and their parallel symmetries that narratively set up the unity of God (*tawḥīd*) as the origin and standard of virtue and social responsibility.[64] This is not a rehearsal of secular and modernistic dialectics between the two poles of religious and secular where the asymmetrical synthesis of the two is meant to eliminate through assimilation the disfavored pole in order to shore up the worldly force

---

63 For a reading that emphasizes the physical reality of Islamic paradise see Bouhdiba, *Sexuality in Islam*. In the present publication, see also Marmura's reading of the descriptions of physical paradise in Islamic philosophy.

64 Lawson, Le Coran.

of the other. Instead, the inviolable notion of *tawḥīd* is constantly highlighted in terms of its semantic opposites that give it a "symmetrical counterweight," which in turn posit the origin of that symmetry in God's very unity.[65] In other words, this duality exists for the sole purpose of establishing the oneness (*tawḥīd*) of God, what Lawson has termed the 'apocalyptic reversal' of dualities and oppositions.[66] Lawson describes this process within the narrative structure of the Quran: "Thus the Qur'an demonstrates through the orchestration of an equally vast number of interlocking and mutually reinforcing symmetries a heretofore undetected sacred and luminous order of enlightenment and plan."[67] Contained within this statement is evidence of Lawson's meticulous study of the ways in which the apocalypse of the Quran confounds its overall linear narrative, one that resists its cavalier absorption by the modernist dualities that produce progressive notions of time. Instead, the Quran is punctuated by the temporal markers of the Day (*al-yawm*), and the Hour (*al-sāʿa*), which "is simultaneously a time of self-awareness and of social responsibility,"[68] i.e., a reminder of the chaos (one of the principle semantic oppositions of *tawḥīd*) that is the ethical duty of all humans to ward off. Within the foundational text of the Islamic tradition, apocalypse can thus be understood as keeping apocalypse at bay.

Crucial to Lawson's analysis of apocalyptic temporality is the way it generates a new epistemology. The apocalypse as the revelation of new knowledge inaugurates the historical period of the Islamic age that supercedes the *jāhilī* age of ignorance by semantically positing Islam "as the polar opposite of *jahl* [so that] it comes to be understood precisely as 'enlightenment' rather than mere submission."[69] It is precisely this "modernity," as Lawson puts it, that not only "challenged the entrenched social and cultural mores of [Muḥammad's] time and place,"[70] it also continues to challenge the mores of contemporary modernity. Contrary to the claims of secular critics of the Islamic tradition and

65 Lawson, Coherent chaos 185. See also Lawson, Duality 26. His analysis of symmetry is here supplemented with a discussion of typological figuration, a very important element to the discussion of apocalyptic temporality. Unfortunately space does not allow me to pursue it at this time.

66 Lawson, Duality 32.

67 Lawson, Coherent chaos, 189–90; Lawson, Duality 27, 33.

68 Lawson, Le Coran 53. Quotations are from the English original, Lawson, The Qur'an and the apocalyptic imagination, available at http://toddlawson.ca/pdf/lawson_quran_apocalyptic_imagination.pdf.

69 Lawson, Duality 32.

70 Lawson, Le Coran 52.

its people, it does so by apocalyptically positing Islam as that which "stand[s] for the opposite of barbarity, savagery, brutality and vainglory as well as standing for the opposite of ignorance and polytheism."[71]

•••

In considering the stakes of apocalyptic orientation of the Quran toward the transformation of human behavior away from *jahl*, the last word should be given to Michael Marmura, an eminent scholar of classical Islamic thought beloved by all. His insistence that the integrity of the classical Islamic philosophical tradition lay in the ability of Muslim philosophers to develop their rationalism on Islamic grounds has marked his life's work, his colleagues, and all of us who studied under him. Marmura's discussion in this volume of al-Fārābī's (d. 339/950) ideal of the "virtuous" city (*al-madīna al-fāḍila*) fundamentally compels us to be attentive to the ways in which political justice cannot be restrained by the motivations that produce pre-modern/modern dichotomies and the rationalism that upholds them. His words withstand the vagaries of the politics of time:

> Alfarabi discusses those "cities" or political entities that are not virtuous and which he terms "ignorant." These are ignorant because they follow erroneous concepts of what constitutes true happiness. They consist of "the indispensable," "the vile," "the timocratic," "the despotic," and "the democratic." They mistakenly identify sheer survival, wealth, pleasure, honor, power or freedom, with true happiness. Those belonging to such political entities and who follow their erroneous concepts of happiness do not survive death. With death they disintegrate and become part of the process of generation and corruption. Then there are immoral political states where both the leaders and the citizens know what true happiness is, but deliberately forsake it for pleasure, power and so on. In the hereafter their souls live in eternal torment, ever seeking celestial happiness, but never attaining it. There are also "erring cities" where the leadership alone has knowledge of true happiness but deliberately forsakes it. The leaders alone are eternally punished, whereas the rest of the citizens, like those of the ignorant cities, have no afterlife.[72]

---

71 Lawson, Coherent chaos 189.

72 Marmura in the present publication.

Bibliography

Ahmed, D.S., *Masculinity, rationality, and religion: A feminist perspective*, Lahore 2001.

Aristotle, *The rhetoric*, trans. W.R. Roberts, New York 2005.

Baum, R.K., Chasing horses, eating Arabs, in L. Ouzgane (ed.), *Islamic masculinities*, New York 2006, 105–22.

Bouhdiba, A., *Sexuality in Islam*, London 2012.

Burgat, F., *Face to face with political Islam*, London 2003.

———, *The Islamic movement in North Africa*, trans. W. Dowell, Austin TX 1997.

Crownfield, D. (ed.), *Body/text in Julia Kristeva: Religion, women and psychoanalysis*, Albany, NY 1992.

Deeb, L., *An enchanted modern: Gender and public piety in Shiʿi Lebanon*, Princeton, NJ 2006.

de Man, P., Criticism and crisis, in P. de Man, *Blindness and insight*, Minneapolis, MN 1983, 3–19.

Evans, D., *An introductory dictionary of Lacanian psychoanalysis*, London 1996, 2001.

Ferris, D., *Silent urns: Romanticism, Hellenism, modernity*, Palo Alto, CA 2000.

———, *Theory and the evasion of history*, Baltimore, MD 1993.

Foucault, M., *The archeology of knowledge*, New York 2005.

———, *The order of things: An archeology of the human sciences*, New York 1970, repr. 1994.

Goldziher, I., Murruwa and din, in I. Goldziher, *Muslim studies*, trans. C.R. Barber and S.M. Stern, London 1967, 11–44.

Grosz, E., *Jacques Lacan: A feminist introduction*, New York 1990.

Hawthorne, S., Is there a (m)other in the text? Post-theistic Sikh ontology and the question of the phallus, in *Method & Theory in the Study of Religion* 23.2 (2011), 160–76.

———, Rethinking subjectivity in the gender oriented study of religions: Kristeva and the "subject-in-process," in U. King and T. Beattie (eds.), *Gender, religion, diversity: Cross-cultural perspectives*, London 2004, 40–50.

Hegel, F.W.J., *The difference between Fichte's and Schelling's system of philosophy*, trans. H.S. Harris, Albany, NY 1977.

———, *Phänomenologie des Geistes*, Frankfurt a. M. 1970.

———, *Phenomenology of spirit*, trans. A.V. Miller, Oxford 1977.

Jacobs, C., *In the language of Walter Benjamin*, Baltimore 1999.

Jöttkandt, S. and J. Copjec (eds.), *Islam and psychoanalysis*, Special Issue of the *S-Journal of the Jan van Eyck Circle for Lacanian Ideology Critique* 2 (2009).

Kristeva, J., *Revolution in poetic language*, trans. M. Walker, New York, 1984.

———, Within the microcosm of "the talking cure," trans. T. Gora and M. Waller, in J.H. Smith and W. Kerrigan (eds.), *Interpreting Lacan*, New Haven, CT 1983, 33–48.

Lacan, J., The agency of the letter in the unconscious or reason since Freud, in J. Lacan, *Écrits: A selection*, trans. A. Sheridan, New York 1982, 146–78.
Lacoue-Labarthe, P., *Typography: Mimesis, philosophy and politics*, Cambridge 1989.
——— and J.L. Nancy, *The title of the letter: A reading of Lacan*, Albany, NY 1992.
Lawson, T. Coherent chaos and chaotic cosmos: The Qur'an and the symmetry of truth, in P. Gemeinhardt and A. Zgoll (eds.), *Weltkonstruktionen: Religiöse Weltdeutung zwischen Chaos und Kosmos vom Alten Orient bis zum Islam*, Tübingen 2010, 177–93.
———, Le Coran et l'imaginaire apocalyptique, trans. G. Rivier, in *Religions et Histoire* 34 (2010), 48–53.
———, Duality, opposition and typology in the Qur'an: The apocalyptic substrate, in *JQS* 10.2 (2008), 23–49.
Lemaire, A., *Jacques Lacan*, trans. D. Macey, London 1977.
Lewis, B., *The crisis of Islam: Holy war and unholy terror*, New York 2003, 2004.
Martis, J., *Philippe Lacoue-Labarthe: Representation and the loss of the subject*, New York 2005.
Mas, R., On the apocalyptic tones of Islam in secular time, in A. Mandair and M. Dressler (eds.), *Secularism and religion making*, Oxford, 2011, 87–103.
Massad, J., Conceiving the masculine: Gender and Palestinian nationalism, in *Middle East Journal* 49.3 (1995), 467–84.
Minsky, R. (ed.), *Psychoanalysis and gender*, New York 1996.
Ouzgane, L. (ed.), *Islamic masculinities*, New York 2006.
Peteet, J., Male gender and rituals of resistance in the Palestinian intifada: A cultural politics of violence, in *American Ethnologist* 21.1 (1994), 31–49.
Peter, F. and R. Ortega (eds.), *Islamic movements of Europe*, London 2012.
Roded, R., *Women in Islam and the Middle East*, London 1999.
———, *Women in Islamic biographical collections from Ibn Sa'd to Who's Who*, Boulder, CO 1994.
Rothenberg, C., *Spirits f Palestine: Gender, society, and stories of the jinn*, New York 2004.
Tazi, N., Le désert perpétuel: Visages de la virilité au Maghreb, in N. Tazi and F. Benslama (eds.), *La virilité en Islam*, Paris 1998, 25–57.
———, Jannah, in S. Jöttkandt and J. Copjec (eds.), *Islam and psychoanalysis*, Special Issue of the *S-Journal of the Jan van Eyck Circle for Lacanian Ideology Critique* 2 (2009), 28–42.
——— and F. Benslama, Présentation, in N. Tazi and F. Benslama (eds.), *La virilité en Islam*, Paris 1998, 5–6.

Internet Sources

http://toddlawson.ca/pdf/lawson_quran_apocalyptic_imagination.pdf (accessed 28 January 2015).

Bibliographical Appendix

Eschatology and the Hereafter in Islam

This bibliography of primary and secondary sources is of principal importance for research on Islamic eschatology and concepts of the hereafter. It incorporates data provided in individual contributions to the present two volumes, but significantly expands on this by adding titles of primary and secondary sources in major European languages as well as in Arabic, Persian, and Turkish.

Obviously, an appendix cannot hope to achieve comprehensiveness, given the steadily growing bulk of relevant publications, Eastern and Western, and the problems of their accessibility, especially when these publications are not part of Western library systems. For these reasons, and in accordance with the thematic foci of studies included in the two volumes at hand, efforts have been made to achieve a near-complete coverage of the most pertinent publications in major European languages, while the bibliographical material in non-European languages – and here especially those in Persian and Turkish – had to remain selective in character. Thus, the latter two sections should be seen as helpful bibliographical starting points for scholars who wish to work on eschatological themes in those languages. With regard to completeness, this bibliographic appendix should be seen as a work in progress. A bibliography of Islamic exchatology, the editors have come to learn, is a topic that deserves a separate, discrete, and no doubt substantial volume.

For valuable bibliographic assistance, the Editors gratefully acknowledge the research of Mehmet Bilekli (Göttingen), Yoones Dehghani Farsani (Göttingen), Serdar Güneş (Frankfurt am Main), Dr. Mahmoud Haggag (Cairo), Christian Mauder (Göttingen), Ali Rida Khalil Rizek (Göttingen) and Dr. Omid Ghaemmaghami (Binghamton).

1 Arabic Sources

1.1 *Primary Sources*[1] – المراجع التراثيّة

الآجرّي، أبو بكر محمّد بن الحسين بن عبد الله: التصديق بالنظر إلى الله تعالى في الآخرة، تحقيق: سمير بن أمين الزهيري، بيروت: مؤسّسة الرسالة، ١٤٠٨/١٩٨٨.

آل كاشف الغطاء، محمّد الحسين: الفردوس الأعلى، تبريز: مطبعة رضائي، ١٩٥٣.

1 غالبًا، ثمّة غيرُ طبعةٍ لعناوين الكتب المذكورة، لا سيّما كتب التراث. وطلبًا للاختصار، اقتصرنا عند ذكر أكثر الكتب على إيراد طبعةٍ واحدةٍ فقط. ولن يجد القارئ التاريخ الهجريّ لصدور الطبعات إلّا إذا كان مذكورًا في الكتاب نفسه. وقد رتّبت العناوين بحيث تظهر على النحو التالي: المؤلّف: عنوان الكتاب، المحقّق، مكان الإصدار: دار النشر، سنة الإصدار.

 | DOI 10.1163/9789004333154_059

الآملي، حيدر: كتاب جامع الأسرار ومنبع الأنوار، به انضمام رسالة نقد النقود في معرفة الوجود، با تصحيحات ودو مقدمه وفهرستاى هنرى كربين وعثمان اسماعيل يحيى، تهران: قسمت ايران شناسى، انستيتو ايران وفرانسه پژوهشهاى علمى، ١٩٦٩.

ابن أبي الدنيا، أبو بكرعبد الله بن محمّد البغدادي الأموي القرشي: الأهوال، تحقيق: مجدي فتحي السيّد، القاهرة: مكتبة آل ياسر، ١٤١٣/١٩٩٣.

ابن أبي الدنيا، أبو بكرعبد الله بن محمّد البغدادي الأموي القرشي: صفة الجنّة وما أعدّ الله لأهلها من النعيم، تحقيق: عبد الرحيم أحمد عبد الرحيم العساسلة، القاهرة: مؤسّسة الرسالة، دار البشير، ١٤١٧/١٩٩٧.

ابن أبي الدنيا، أبو بكرعبد الله بن محمّد البغدادي الأموي القرشي: صفة النار، تحقيق: محمّد خير رمضان يوسف، بيروت: دار ابن حزم، ١٤١٧/١٩٩٧.

ابن أبي الدنيا، أبو بكرعبد الله بن محمّد البغدادي الأموي القرشي: كتاب الموت وكتاب القبور، تحقيق: ليه كينبيرغ، حيفا: جامعة حيفا، قسم الآداب واللغات، ١٩٨٣.

ابن أبي الدنيا، أبو بكرعبد الله بن محمّد البغدادي الأموي القرشي: من عاش بعد الموت، بيروت: عالم الكتب، ١٤٠٦/١٩٨٦؛ تحقيق: أبو معاذ أيمن بن عارف الدمشقي، القاهرة: مكتبة السنّة، ١٤١٣/١٩٩٣.

ابن أبي شيبة العبسي، محمّد بن عثمان: العرش وما روي فيه، تحقيق: محمّد بن حمد الحمّود، الكويت: مكتبة المعلا، ١٤٠٦/١٩٨٦.

ابن إسحاق الشيباني، أبو عليّ حنبل: الفتن، بيروت: دار البشائر الإسلاميّة، ١٤١٩/١٩٩٨.

ابن بابويه، أبو جعفر محمّد بن عليّ القمّي (الشيخ الصدوق): الاعتقادات، تحقيق: عصام عبد السيّد، بيروت: دار المفيد، ١٤١٤/١٩٩٣.

ابن بابويه، أبو جعفر محمّد بن عليّ القمّي (الشيخ الصدوق): كمال الدين وتمام النعمة، تحقيق: عليّ أكبر الغفّاري، مجلّدان، قم: مؤسّسة النشر الإسلامي التابعة لجماعة المدرّسين بقم المشرّفة، ١٤٠٥/١٩٨٤.

ابن تيمية، أحمد بن عبد الحليم بن عبد السلام: الردّ على من قال بفناء الجنّة والنار وبيان الأقوال في ذلك، تحقيق: محمّد السمهري، الرياض: دار بلنسية، ١٤١٥/١٩٩٥.

ابن حبيب الأندلسي، عبد الملك: أشراط الساعة وذهاب الأخيار وبقاء الأشرار، دراسة وتحقيق: عبد الله عبد المؤمن الغمّاري الحسيني، الرياض: مكتبة أضواء السلف، ١٤٢٥/٢٠٠٥.

ابن حبيب الأندلسي، عبد الملك: وصف الفردوس، تحقيق: عبد اللطيف حسن عبد الرحمن، بيروت: دار الكتب العلميّة، ١٤٠٧/١٩٨٧.

ابن حجر الهيثمي، أبو العبّاس أحمد بن محمّد: القول المختصر في علامات المهديّ المنتظر، تحقيق: مصطفى عاشور، القاهرة: مكتبة القرآن، ١٤٠٧/١٩٨٦.

ابن حزم الأندلسي، أبو محمّد عليّ بن أحمد بن سعيد: رسالة في حكم من قال إنّ أرواح أهل الشقاء معذّبة إلى يوم الدين، تحقيق: إحسان عبّاس، بيروت: المؤسّسة العربية للدراسات والنشر، ١٩٨٧.

ابن رجب الحنبلي، عبد الرحمن: أهوال القبور وأحوال أهلها إلى النشور، تحقيق: محمّد السعيد، بيروت: دار الكتاب العربي، ١٤١٤/١٩٩٤.

ابن رجب الحنبلي، عبد الرحمن: الحكم الجديرة بالإذاعة من قول النبيّ صلّى الله عليه وسلّم «بُعثت بالسيف بين يديّ الساعة» (مجموع رسائل الحافظ ابن رجب الحنبلي)، تحقيق: أبو مصعب طلعت ابن فؤاد الحلواني، القاهرة: دار الفاروق الحديثة، ١٤٢٢/٢٠٠٢.

ابن رجب الحنبلي، عبد الرحمن: التخويف من النار والتعريف بحال أهل البوار، دمشق: دار البيان، ١٣٩٩/١٩٧٩؛ دمشق: مكتبة دار البيان، ١٤٠٨/١٩٨٨.

ابن سينا، أبو عليّ الحسين بن عبد الله بن الحسن: الرسالة الأضحويّة في أمر المعاد، تحقيق: سليمان دنيا، القاهرة: دار الفكر العربي، ١٣٦٨/١٩٤٩.

ابن سينا، أبو عليّ الحسين بن عبد الله بن الحسن: المبدأ والمعاد، تهران: دانشگاه تهران، ١٣٦٣ ش. /١٩٨٤.

ابن طاووس، رضيّ الدين أبو القاسم عليّ بن موسى: الملاحم والفتن في ظهور الغائب المنتظر، قم: طليعة النور، ١٤٢٥/٢٠٠٤-٢٠٠٥.

ابن عربي، محيي الدين: عنقاء مغرب في ختم الأولياء وشمس المغرب، بيروت: دار الكتب العلميّة، ١٤٢٦/٢٠٠٥-٢٠٠٦.

ابن عربي، محيي الدين: الفتوحات المكّيّة، القاهرة: الهيئة المصريّة العامّة للكتّاب، ١٩٧٢.

ابن الفارض، عمر: ديوان ابن الفارض، بيروت: دار الكتب العلميّة، ١٤١٠/١٩٨٩-١٩٩٠.

ابن قيّم الجوزيّة، محمّد بن أبي بكر بن أيّوب: الروح، تحقيق: بسّام عليّ سلامة العلّوش الرياض: دار ابن تيمية، ١٤٠٦/١٩٨٦.

ابن قيّم الجوزيّة، محمّد بن أبي بكر بن أيّوب: حادي الأرواح إلى بلاد الأفراح، بيروت: مكتبة دار التراث، دار ابن كثير، ١٤١١/١٩٩١.

ابن قيّم الجوزيّة، محمّد بن أبي بكر بن أيّوب: زاد المعاد في هدي خير العباد محمّد، تحقيق: شعيب الأرناؤوط وعبد القادر الأرناؤوط، بيروت، ١٤١٨/١٩٩٨.

ابن كثير القرشي، عماد الدين أبو الفداء إسماعيل: أهوال يوم القيامة، دمشق: دار اليمامة، ١٤٢١/٢٠٠١.

ابن كثير القرشي، عماد الدين أبو الفداء إسماعيل: علامات يوم القيامة، القاهرة: دار الكتب العلميّة، ١٤٢٣/٢٠٠٢.

ابن كثير القرشي، عماد الدين أبو الفداء إسماعيل: النهاية في الفتن والملاحم، تحقيق: أحمد أبو ملحم وعليّ نجيب عطوي، القاهرة: دار الريّان للتراث، ١٤٠٨/١٩٨٨؛ تحقيق: محمّد عبد القادر عطا، القاهرة: دار التقوى للتراث، ١٤٢٢/٢٠٠٢.

ابن ماجة، محمّد بن يزيد بن ماجة الربعي القزويني: سنن ابن ماجة (كتاب الجنائز، كتاب الفتن)، تحقيق: محمّد فؤاد عبد الباقي، القاهرة: دار إحياء الكتب العربية (لا تاريخ).

ابن النفيس، علاء الدين عليّ بن أبي الحزم القرشي: الرسالة الكامليّة في السيرة النبويّة، تعليق وتحقيق: عبد المنعم محمّد عمر، القاهرة: وزارة الأوقاف المصريّة، المجلس الأعلى للشؤون الإسلاميّة، ١٤٠٧/١٩٨٧.

أبو حاتم الرازي، أحمد بن حمدان: كتاب الزينة في الكلمات الإسلاميّة العربيّة، تحقيق: حسين بن فيض الله الهمداني، صنعاء: مركز الدراسات والبحوث اليمني، ١٤١٥/١٩٩٤.

أبو داود، سليمان بن الأشعث (أبو داود السجستاني): سنن أبي داود (كتاب الجنائز، كتاب الفتن والملاحم)، تحقيق: عزّت عبيد الدعاس، بيروت: دار الكتب العلميّة، ١٣٨٩/١٩٦٩.

أبو العلاء المعرّي، أحمد بن عبد الله بن سليمان القضاعي التنوخي: رسالة الغفران، ومعها نصّ محقّق من رسالة ابن القارح، تحقيق: عائشة عبد الرحمن (بنت الشاطئ)، القاهرة: دار المعارف، ١٣٩٧/١٩٧٧.

أبو نعيم الأصفهاني، أحمد بن عبد الله: صفة الجنّة، تحقيق: عليّ رضا عبد الله، دمشق: دار المأمون للتراث، ١٤٠٧/١٩٨٦.

الأحسائي، أحمد بن زين الدين: أسرار الإمام المهديّ، تحقيق: عبد الرسول زين الدين، بيروت: دار المحجّة البيضاء، ١٤٢٥/٢٠٠٥.

الأحسائي، أحمد بن زين الدين: كتاب الرجعة، بيروت: دار العالميّة، ١٤١٤/١٩٩٣.

الأحسائي، أحمد بن زين الدين: جوامع الكلم، ٩ مجلّدات، البصرة: مطبعة الغدير، ١٣٤٠/٢٠٠٩.

الأحسائي، أحمد بن زين الدين: شرح العرشيّة، ٣ مجلّدات، تحقيق: صالح أحمد الدباب، بيروت: مؤسّسة شمس هجر، ١٤٢٦/٢٠٠٥.

أحمد بن حنبل: الردّ على الزنادقة والجهميّة، تحقيق: دغش بن شبيب العجمي، الكويت: غراس، ١٤٢٦/٢٠٠٥.

الأسترآبادي، محمّد مؤمن: الرجعة، تحقيق: فارس حسّون كريم، قم: مهر، ١٤١٥/١٩٩٤.

أطفيّش، محمّد بن يوسف: الجُنّة في وصف الجنّة، القاهرة: المطبعة السلفيّة، ١٣٢٥/١٩٢٧.

إقبال، محمّد: ديوان محمّد إقبال، الأعمال الكاملة (ومنها رسالة الغفران أو جاويد نامه)، تحقيق: سيّد عبد الماجد الغوري، بيروت: دار ابن كثير، ١٤٢٨/٢٠٠٧.

البحراني، ميثم بن عليّ بن ميثم: النجاة في القيامة في تحقيق أمر القيامة، قم: مجمع الفكر الإسلامي، ١٤١٧/١٩٩٦.

البحراني، هاشم بن سليمان: تبصرة الوليّ في مَن رأى القائم المهديّ، قم: مؤسّسة المعارف الإسلاميّة، ١٤١١/١٩٩٠-١٩٩١.
البخاري، محمّد بن إسماعيل: الجامع المسند الصحيح المختصر من أمور رسول الله وسننه وأيّامه (صحيح البخاري) (كتاب الفتن)، بيروت: دار الفكر، ١٤٢٢/٢٠٠١.
البرسي الحلّي، رجب بن محمّد بن رجب: مشارق أنوار اليقين في حقائق أسرار أمير المؤمنين، تحقيق: عبد الغفّار أشرف المازندراني، بيروت: دار القارئ، ١٤٢٧/٢٠٠٦.
البغدادي، أبو منصور عبد القاهر بن طاهر التميمي: أصول الدين، إستنابول (إسطنبول): مدرسة الإلهيّات بدار الفنون التركيّة، ١٣٤٦/١٩٢٨.
البيهقي، أبو بكر أحمد بن الحسين بن عليّ: إثبات عذاب القبر، تحقيق: شرف محمود القضاة، عمّان: دار الفرقان، ١٤٠٣/١٩٨٣.
البيهقي، أبو بكر أحمد بن الحسين بن عليّ: البعث والنشور، تحقيق: عامر أحمد حيدر، بيروت: مركز الخدمات والأبحاث الثقافية، ١٤٠٦/١٩٨٦.
بهاء الدين العاملي، محمّد بن الحسين (الشيخ البهائي): كشكول البهائي، بيروت: مؤسّسة الأعلمي للمطبوعات، ١٤٠٣/١٩٨٢-١٩٨٣.
الترمذي، محمّد بن عيسى: الجامع الصحيح (سنن الترمذي) (كتاب الفتن عن رسول الله صلّى الله عليه وسلّم، كتاب صفة القيامة والرقائق والورع عن رسول الله صلّى الله عليه وسلّم، كتاب صفة الجنّة عن رسول الله صلّى الله عليه وسلّم، كتاب صفة جهنّم)، بيروت: دار الفكر، (لا تاريخ).
الجزائري، نعمة الله: كتاب رياض الأبرار في مناقب الأئمّة الأطهار، الجزء الثالث: أحوال الإمام المهديّ، بيروت: مؤسّسة التاريخ العربيّ، ١٤٢٧/٢٠٠٦.
جعفر ابن منصور اليمن، جعفر بن الحسن: كتاب الكشف، تحقيق: مصطفى غالب، بيروت: دار الأندلس، ١٤١٦/١٩٩٥.
الجنيد، أبو القاسم ابن محمّد النهاوندي البغدادي: رسائل الجنيد، دمشق: دار اقرأ، ١٤٢٥/٢٠٠٥.
الجيلاني، عبد القادر: الفتح الربّاني والفيض الرحماني، القاهرة: مكتبة الثقافة الدينيّة، ١٤٢٦/٢٠٠٥-٢٠٠٦.
الجيلي، عبد الكريم بن إبراهيم: الإنسان الكامل في معرفة الأوائل والأواخر، القاهرة: مكتبة الثقافة الدينيّة، ٢٠٠٤.
الجيلي، عبد الكريم بن إبراهيم: كشف الغايات في شرح ما اكتنفت عليه التجلّيات: متن التجلّيات الإلهيّة للشيخ الأكبر محيي الدين ابن عربي، بيروت: دار الكتب العلميّة، ٢٠٠٨.
الجيلي، عبد الكريم بن إبراهيم: المناظر الإلهيّة، لقاهرة: دار المنار، ١٩٨٧.
الحرّ العاملي، محمّد بن الحسن بن عليّ: إثبات الهداة بالنصوص والمعجزات، ٥ مجلّدات، بيروت: مؤسّسة الأعلمي للمطبوعات، ١٤٢٥/٢٠٠٤.

الحرّ العاملي، محمّد بن الحسن بن عليّ: الإيقاظ من الهجعة بالبرهان على الرجعة، تهران: انتشارات نويد، ١٣٦٢ ش./١٩٨٣-١٩٨٤.

الحلّاج، حسين بن منصور: الأعمال الكاملة، بيروت: شركة رياض الريّس للكتب والنشر، ٢٠٠٢.

الحميدي، محمّد بن أبي نصر: التذكرة، ومعه كتاب مراتب الجزاء يوم القيامة، تحقيق: أبو عبد الرحمن ابن عقيل الظاهري، الرياض: دار العلوم، ١٤٠١/١٩٨١.

الخطيب التبريزي، أبو زكريا يحيى بن عليّ: مشكاة المصابيح، تحقيق: محمّد ناصر الدين الألباني، بيروت: المكتب الإسلامي، الطبعة الثانية، ١٣٩٩/١٩٧٩.

الذهبي، شمس الدين محمّد بن أحمد بن عثمان: إثبات الشفاعة، تحقيق: إبراهيم باجس عبد المجيد، الرياض: أضواء السلف، ١٤٢٠/١٩٩٩.

الرازي، فخر الدين: مفاتيح الغيب أو التفسير الكبير، بيروت: دار إحياء التراث العربي، ١٤٢١/٢٠٠٠.

الرشتي، السيّد كاظم: شرح الخطبة التطنجيّة، ٣ مجلّدات، الكويت: جامع الإمام الصادق، ١٤٢١/٢٠٠١.

السجستاني، أبو يعقوب إسحاق بن أحمد: كتاب الافتخار، تحقيق: إسماعيل قربان حسين پوناوالا، بيروت: دار الغرب الإسلامي، ٢٠٠٠.

السخاوي، شمس الدين أبو الخير محمّد بن عبد الرحمن: القناعة في ما يحسن الإحاطة به من أشراط الساعة، تحقيق: محمّد بن عبد الوهّاب العقيل، الرياض: دار أضواء السلف، ١٤٢٢/٢٠٠٢.

السفاريني، محمّد بن أحمد بن سالم بن سليمان: البحور الزاخرة في علوم الآخرة، تحقيق: محمّد إبراهيم شلبي شومان، الكويت: شركة غراس للنشر والتوزيع، ١٤٢٨/٢٠٠٧.

السفاريني، محمّد بن أحمد بن سالم بن سليمان: لوامع الأنوار البهيّة وسواطع الأسرار الأثريّة لشرح الدرّة المضيّة في عقد الفرقة المرضيّة، دمشق: مؤسّسة الخافقين، ١٤٠٢/١٩٨٢.

السفاريني، محمّد بن أحمد بن سالم بن سليمان: أهوال يوم القيامة وعلاماتها الكبرى، بيروت: مؤسّسة الكتب الثقافيّة، ١٤٠٦/١٩٨٦.

السلمي، يوسف بن يحيى بن عليّ المقدسي الشافعي: عقد الدرر في أخبار المنتظر، تحقيق: مهيب صالح عبد الرحمن البوريني، الزرقا (الأردن): مكتبة المنار، ١٤١٠/١٩٨٩.

السهروردي، شهاب الدين يحيى (شيخ الإشراق): مجموعة في الحكمة الإلهيّة، تحقيق: هنري كوربين، إسطنبول: مطبعة المعارف، ١٩٤٥.

السهروردي، عمر بن محمّد: عوارف المعارف، تحقيق: عبد الحليم محمود بن الشريف، [القاهرة: دار الكتب الحديثة، ١٩٧١].

السيوطي، جلال الدين عبد الرحمن بن أبي بكر: البدور السافرة في أحوال الآخرة، تحقيق: محمّد حسن إسماعيل، بيروت: دار الكتب العلميّة، ١٤١٦/١٩٩٦.

السيوطي، جلال الدين عبد الرحمن بن أبي بكر: بشرى الكئيب بلقاء الحبيب، القاهرة: مكتبة القرآن، ١٤٠٦/١٩٨٦.

السيوطي، جلال الدين عبد الرحمن بن أبي بكر: التعظيم والمنّة في أنّ أبوي النبيّ في الجنّة، دمشق: دار البيان، ١٣٩٩/١٩٧٩.

السيوطي، جلال الدين عبد الرحمن بن أبي بكر: الحبائك في أخبار الملائك، تحقيق: أبو هاجر محمّد السعيد بن بسيوني زغلول، بيروت: دار الكتب العلميّة، ١٤٠٥/١٩٨٥.

السيوطي، جلال الدين عبد الرحمن بن أبي بكر: دُرر الكلم وغُرر الحكم، تقديم وتحقيق: فايز عبد النبيّ القيسي، الإمارات العربية المتحدة: جامعة الإمارات، قسم اللغة العربيّة وآدابها، كلّيّة العلوم الإنسانيّة والاجتماعية (لا تاريخ).

السيوطي، جلال الدين عبد الرحمن بن أبي بكر: شرح الصدور بشرح حال الموتى والقبور، تحقيق: يوسف عليّ بدوي، دمشق: دار ابن كثير، ١٤٠٤/١٩٨٨؛ تحقيق: عبد المجيد طعمة حلبي، بيروت: دار المعرفة، ١٤١٧/١٩٩٦.

السيوطي، جلال الدين عبد الرحمن بن أبي بكر: العرف الورديّ في أخبار المهديّ، تحقيق: أبو يعلى البيضاوي، بيروت: دار الكتب العلميّة، ١٤٢٧/٢٠٠٦.

السيوطي، جلال الدين عبد الرحمن بن أبي بكر: كشف الصلصلة عن وصف الزلزلة، تحقيق: محمّد كمال الدين عزّ الدين، القاهرة: مكتبة عالم الكتب، ١٤٠٧/١٩٨٧.

السيوطي، جلال الدين عبد الرحمن بن أبي بكر: نزول المسيح آخر الزمان أو الإعلام في نزول عيسى عليه السلام، تحقيق: محمّد عبد القادر عطا، بيروت: دار الكتب العلميّة، ١٤٠٥/١٩٨٥.

شبّر، عبد الله: حقّ اليقين في معرفة أصول الدين، بيروت: مؤسّسة الأعلمي للمطبوعات، ١٤١٨/١٩٩٧.

شهرزوري، محمّد بن محمود: شرح حكمة الإشراق، تحقيق: حسين ضيائي، تهران: پژوهشگاه علوم انسانى ومطالعات فرهنگى، ٢٠٠١.

الشيرازي، صدر الدين محمّد (ملّا صدرا): المبدأ والمعاد في الحكمة المتعالية، تحقيق: محمّد ذبيحي وجعفر شاه نظري، بيروت: منشورات الجمل، ١٤٣٣/٢٠١٢.

الشيرازي، صدر الدين محمّد (ملّا صدرا): الحكمة المتعالية في الأسفار العقليّة الأربعة، تهران: بنياد حكمت إسلامى صدرا، ١٣٨٣/٢٠٠٤.

الشيرازي، صدر الدين محمّد (ملّا صدرا): إيقاظ النائمين، طهران: الجمعية الإسلاميّة للحكمة والفلسفة في إيران (لا تاريخ).

الشيرازي، قطب الدين: شرح حكمة الإشراق، تحقيق: محمّد موسوي، مجلّدان، تهران: مؤسسهٔ انتشارات حكمت، ١٤٣٠/٢٠٠٩.
الطبري، أبو جعفر محمّد بن جرير: تفسير الطبري، جامع البيان عن تأويل القرآن، تحقيق: محمود محمّد شاكر، القاهرة: دار المعارف، ١٣٧٣/١٩٥٤.
الطوسي، محمّد بن الحسن: كتاب الغيبة، تحقيق: عبد الله الطهراني وعليّ أحمد ناصح، قم: مؤسّسة المعارف الإسلاميّة، ١٤١١/١٩٩٠.
العزّ بن عبد السلام، عبد العزيز بن عبد السلام السلمي: بيان أحوال الناس يوم القيامة، تحقيق: إياد خالد الطبّاع، دمشق: دار الفكر المعاصر، ١٤٢٦/٢٠٠٥.
الغزالي، أبو حامد: إحياء علوم الدين (وفيه كتاب الموت وأحوال القيامة)، تحقيق: مكتب الدراسات والبحث العلمي بدار المنهاج، جدّة: دار المنهاج، ١٤٣٢/٢٠١١.
الغزالي، أبو حامد: الدرّة الفاخرة في كشف علوم الآخرة، تحقيق: موفّق فوزي الجبر، دمشق: دار الحكمة، ١٤١٥/١٩٩٥.
القاضي، عبد الرحيم بن أحمد: دقائق الأخبار في ذكر الجنّة والنار، بيروت: دار الكتب العلميّة، ١٤٠٤/١٩٨٤.
القاضي، عبد الرحيم بن أحمد: كتاب أحوال القيامة، لايبزغ: بروكهوس، ١٨٧٢.
القرطبي، أبو عبد الله محمّد بن أحمد: التذكرة في أحوال الموتى وأمور الآخرة، القاهرة: مطبعة الحلبي، ١٤٠٠/١٩٨٠؛ تحقيق: السيّد الجميلي، بيروت: دار ابن زيدون، ١٤٠٦/١٩٨٦.
القرطبي، أبو عبد الله محمّد بن أحمد: الجامع لأحكام القرآن، بيروت: مؤسّسة الرسالة، ١٤٢٧/٢٠٠٧.
القشيري، عبد الكريم بن هوازن: كتاب المعراج، القاهرة: دار الكتب الحديثة، ١٣٨٤/١٩٦٤.
الكاشاني، محمّد محسن بن مرتضى (الفيض الكاشاني): تسهيل السبيل بالحجّة في انتخاب كشف المحجّة لثمرة المهجة، تحقيق: حامد الخفّاف، بيروت: مؤسّسة آل البيت لإحياء التراث، ١٤١٣/١٩٩٣.
الكاشاني، محمّد محسن بن مرتضى (الفيض الكاشاني): علم اليقين في أصول الدين، تحقيق: محسن بيدارفر، مجلّدان، قم: منشورات بيدار، ١٤١٨/١٩٩٧–١٩٩٨.
الكاشاني، محمّد محسن بن مرتضى (الفيض الكاشاني): نوادر الأخبار في ما يتعلّق بأصول الدين، تحقيق: مهدي الأنصاري القمّي، تهران: مؤسسهٔ مطالعات وتحقيقات فرهنگی، ١٣٧٠ ش./١٩٩١–١٩٩٢.
كرماني، محمّد كريم خان: فصل الخطاب، [كرمان: مطبعة السعادة]، ١٣٥٢/١٩٧٣.
الكليني، محمّد بن يعقوب: الكافي، تحقيق: عليّ أكبر الغفاري، ٨ مجلدات، تهران: دار الكتب الإسلاميّة، ١٣٦٢ ش. /١٩٨٣–١٩٨٤.

المجلسي، محمّد باقر: بحار الأنوار الجامعة لدرر أخبار الأئمّة الأطهار، ١١٠ مجلّدات، بيروت: دار إحياء التراث العربيّ، ١٤٠٣/١٩٨٣.

المجلسي، محمّد باقر: زاد المعاد، بيروت: مؤسّسة الأعلمي للمطبوعات، ١٤٢٣/٢٠٠٣.

المجلسي، محمّد باقر: العقائد، تحقيق: حسين درگاهی، (لا مكان): مؤسّسة الهدى، ١٣٧٨ ش. /١٩٩٩–٢٠٠٠.

المحاسبي، أبو عبد الله الحارث بن أسد: آداب النفوس، ويليه كتاب التوهّم (توهّم حال أهل النار، وتوهّم حال أهل الجنّة)، تحقيق: عبد القادر أحمد عطا، بيروت: مؤسّسة الكتب الثقافية، ١٤١١/١٩٩١.

المحاسبي، أبو عبد الله الحارث بن أسد: كتاب التوهّم، تحقيق وترجمة أندريه رومان، باريس: كلنكسيك، ١٩٧٨.

المرتضى، عليّ بن الحسين (الشريف المرتضى): مسألة وجيزة في الغيبة، في: نفائس المخطوطات، المجلّد ٤، ص. ٩–١٣، تحقيق: محمّد حسين آل ياسين، بغداد: دار المعارف، ١٣٧٤/١٩٥٥.

المرتضى، عليّ بن الحسين (الشريف المرتضى): المقنع في الغيبة والزيادة المكمّلة له، تحقيق: محمّد عليّ الحكيم، بيروت: مؤسّسة آل البيت لإحياء التراث، ١٤١٩/١٩٩٨.

مركز الدراسات التخصّصيّة في الإمام المهديّ: الإمام المهديّ في مصادر علماء الشيعة من القرن الثالث إلى القرن الحادي عشر، ٣ مجلّدات، النجف: مركز الدراسات التخصّصيّة في الإمام المهديّ، ١٤٣٠/٢٠٠٨–٢٠٠٩.

مسلم بن الحجّاج القشيري، أبو الحسين النيسابوري: المسند الصحيح المختصر من السنن بنقل العدل عن العدل عن رسول الله (صحيح مسلم) (كتاب صفة القيامة والجنّة والنار وكتاب الجنّة وصفة نعيمها وأهلها)، بيروت: دار الفكر، ١٤٢٤/٢٠٠٣.

المفيد، محمّد بن محمّد بن النعمان (الشيخ المفيد): الإرشاد في معرفة حجج الله على العباد، مجلّدان، بيروت: دار المفيد، ١٤١٤/١٩٩٣.

المفيد، محمّد بن محمّد بن النعمان (الشيخ المفيد): المسائل العشر في الغيبة، تحقيق: فارس الحسّون، قمّ: دليل ما، ١٤٢٦/٢٠٠٥.

مقاتل بن سليمان: تفسير مقاتل، تحقيق: أحمد فريد، بيروت: دار الكتب العلميّة، ١٤٢٤/٢٠٠٣.

المقدسي، ضياء الدين أبو عبد الله محمّد الحنبلي: صفة الجنّة، الرياض: دار بلنسية، ١٤٢٣/٢٠٠٢.

المقدسي، مرعي بن يوسف الحنبلي: البرهان في إثبات حقيقة الميزان، تحقيق: سليمان بن صالح الخزي، القاهرة: مطبعة المدني، ١٤٠٨/١٩٨٨.

مقيبل المالكي، محمّد بن أحمد: حسن البراعة في تعدّد الشفاعة، تحقيق: إبراهيم رمضان، بيروت: دار الفكر اللبناني، ١٤١٢/١٩٩٢.

المنذري، عبد العظيم بن عبد القوي: الترغيب والترهيب، بيروت: دار الكتب العلميّة، ١٤١٦/١٩٩٦.

النسائي، أحمد بن شعيب: سنن النسائي (كتاب الجنائز)، بيروت: المكتبة العلميّة، (لا تاريخ).

النعماني، محمّد بن إبراهيم بن جعفر (ابن أبي زينب): الغيبة، قم: أنوار الهدى، ١٤٢٢/٢٠٠١-٢٠٠٢.

نعيم ابن حمّاد المروزي، أبو عبد الله نعيم بن حمّاد بن معاوية: كتاب الفتن، تحقيق: مجدي بن منصور الشوري، بيروت: دار الكتب العلميّة، ١٤١٨/١٩٩٧.

النوري، ميرزا حسين الطبرسي: جنّة المأوى في ذكر من فاز بلقاء الحجّة، تحقيق: محسن عاقل، بيروت: دار المحجّة البيضاء، ١٩٩٢.

النوري، ميرزا حسين الطبرسي: كشف الأستار عن وجه الغائب عن الأبصار، قم: مطبعة الخيّام، ١٤٠٠/١٩٧٩-١٩٨٠.

النيلي النجفي، بهاء الدين عليّ بن عبد الكريم بن عبد الحميد: سرور أهل الإيمان في علامات ظهور صاحب الزمان، تحقيق: قيس العطّار، قم: دليل ما، ١٤٢٦/٢٠٠٥-٢٠٠٦.

النيلي النجفي، بهاء الدين عليّ بن عبد الكريم بن عبد الحميد: السلطان المفرّج عن أهل الإيمان في مَن رأى صاحب الزمان، تحقيق: قيس العطّار، قم: دليل ما، ١٤٢٦/٢٠٠٥-٢٠٠٦.

النيلي النجفي، بهاء الدين عليّ بن عبد الكريم بن عبد الحميد: منتخب الأنوار المضيئة في ذكر القائم الحجّة عليه السلام، قم: مؤسّسة الإمام الهادي، ١٤٢٠/٢٠٠٠.

الهيئة العلميّة في مؤسّسة المعارف الإسلاميّة: معجم أحاديث الإمام المهديّ، ٨ مجلّدات، قم: مؤسّسة المعارف الإسلاميّة، ١٤٢٨/٢٠٠٧-٢٠٠٨.

1.2 *Secondary Sources* – المراجع الحديثة

آل درويش، عبد الله حسن: مهديّ الأمم عجّل الله تعالى فرجه الشريف، بيروت: دار الأولياء، ٢٠١١.

آل قطيط، هشام: المهديّ قادم، خرائط ووثائق وسيناريوهات مرتقبة، بيروت: مؤسّسة البلاغة، ٢٠٠٧.

آل مبارك، ماهر بن صالح: الرسالة في الفتن والملاحم وأشراط الساعة، القاهرة: مكتبة الحرمين للعلوم النافعة، ١٤٠٩/١٩٨٩.

آل ياسين، محمّد حسن: المهديّ المنتظر بين التصوّر والتصديق، بيروت: دار مكتبة الحياة، ١٤١٣/١٩٩٢.

ابن أبي العينين، أبو عبد الله أحمد بن إبراهيم: تحذير ذوي الفطن من عبث الخائضين في أشراط الساعة والملاحم والفتن، ومعه سلّ الهنديّ على تعسّف من ضعّف أحاديث المهديّ، جدّة: مكتبة السلف الصالح ومصر: مكتبة ابن عبّاس (سمنود)، ١٤٢٤/٢٠٠٣.

أبو المعاش، سعيد: الإمام المهديّ في القرآن والسنّة، مشهد: مؤسّسة الطبع والنشر التابعة للآستانة الرضويّة المقدّسة، ١٤٢٥/٢٠٠٤-٢٠٠٥.
إسماعيل، لبنى طه: الفرصة قادمة لتغيير العالم، الاتّجاه الحضاري والإداري والاقتصادي المتوقّع في عصر ظهور الإمام المهديّ، بيروت: دار المرتضى، ٢٠١١.
الأشقر، عمر سليمان: الجنّة والنار، مصر: دار النفائس والأردن: دار السلام، ٢٠٠٨.
الأشقر، عمر سليمان: اليوم الآخر، الكويت: مكتبة الفلاح، ١٤٠٨/١٩٨٨.
أصفهاني، محمّد تقي موسوي: مكيال المكارم في فوائد الدعاء للقائم، مجلّدان، تحقيق: عليّ عاشور، بيروت: مؤسّسة الأعلمي للمطبوعات، ١٤٢٢/٢٠٠١.
أكبرنژاد، محمّد تقي: موسوعة توقيعات الإمام المهديّ، بيروت: دار الرسول الأكرم، ٢٠٠٧.
الألباني، محمّد ناصر الدين: قصّة المسيح الدجّال ونزول عيسى عليه السلام وقتله إيّاه، عمّان: المكتبة الإسلاميّة، ١٤٢١/٢٠٠٠.
الألباني، محمّد ناصر الدين: الفتن وأشراط الساعة، الرياض: دار المعارف، ١٤٢٦/٢٠٠٥.
أمين، محمّد بشار محمّد: أحاديث أشراط الساعة الكبرى، دراسة وتحليل (رسالة دكتوراه)، بغداد: جامعة بغداد: كلّيّة العلوم الإسلاميّة، ١٩٩٦.
أيّوب، سعيد: المسيح الدجّال، القاهرة: دار الفتح العربي، ١٤١١/١٩٩١.
بالي، وحيد عبد السلام: وصف الجنّة ووصف النار، القاهرة: دار الاعتصام، ١٤٠٩/١٩٨٩.
بدري، عليّ: غرائب الأخبار في ظهور الحجّة المختار، بيروت: دار الأميرة، ٢٠١١.
بدري، عليّ: عوالم البيان في مهديّ القرآن عجّل الله تعالى فرجه، بيروت: دار الأميرة، ٢٠١١.
البرّاك، مبارك: الضعيف والموضوع من أخبار الفتن والملاحم وأشراط الساعة، القاهرة: دار السلام، ١٤١٦/١٩٩٦.
البرّاك، مبارك: العقلانيّون ومشكلتهم مع أحاديث الفتن، الإسكندريّة: دار الإيمان، ١٤٢٠/١٩٩٩.
البستوي، عبد العليم عبد العظيم: مجموعة الأحاديث الواردة في المهديّ في ميزان الجرح والتعديل، جزءان، بيروت: دار ابن حزم، ١٤٢٠/١٩٩٩.
البستوي، عبد العليم: المهديّ المنتظر في ضوء الأحاديث والآثار الصحيحة، بيروت: دار ابن حزم، ١٤٢٠/١٩٩٩.
بهجت، أحمد: مسرور ومقرور، لا-رواية تبدأ أحداثها بعد الموت، القاهرة: دار الريّان للتراث، ١٤٠٧/١٩٨٧.
بيّومي، محمّد: المهديّ المنتظر وأدعياء المهديّة، القاهرة: مكتبة الإيمان، ١٤١٦/١٩٩٥.
التويجري: حمّود بن عبد الله: إتحاف الجماعة بما جاء في الفتن والملاحم وأشراط الساعة، الرياض: دار الصميعي، ١٤١٤/١٩٩٣.

التويجري، حمّود بن عبد الله: الاحتجاج بالأثر على من أنكر المهديّ، الرياض: الرئاسة العامّة لإدارات البحوث العلميّة والإفتاء والدعوة والإرشاد، ١٤٠٣/١٩٨٣.

الجاسم، محمود بن خليفة: أوّل مشاهد يوم القيامة النفخ في الصور، الكويت: مكتبة ابن تيمية، ١٤٠٨/١٩٨٨.

جبر، محمّد سلامة: أحوال الآخرة وأهوالها، الكويت: دار الإستانبولي، ١٤١٠/١٩٩٠.

الجديع، ناصر بن عبد الرحمن: الشفاعة عند أهل السنّة والردّ على المخالفين فيها، دمشق: دار أطلس، ١٤١٦/١٩٩٦.

الجزائري، أبو بكر: اللقطات في بعض ما ظهر للسّاعة من علامات، القاهرة: مكتبة الكلّيّات الأزهريّة، ١٤٠٤/١٩٨٤.

جعفر، خليل مهدي: الإمام المهديّ في الأديان، بيروت: دار المحجّة البيضاء، ٢٠٠٨.

جمال الدين، أمين محمّد: القول المبين في الأشراط الصغرى ليوم الدين، القاهرة: المكتبة التوفيقيّة، ١٤١٨/١٩٩٧.

الجهرمي، علي: رعاية الإمام المهديّ للمراجع والعلماء الأعلام، بيروت: منشورات دار الياسين، ١٤١٤/١٩٩٣.

حازمي، عجب الله بن علي: دراسات عقديّة في الحياة البرزخيّة، بيروت: دار ابن حزم، ١٤٢٤/٢٠٠٤.

الحائري العاملي، إسماعيل إبراهيم: أحداث آخر الزمان في روايات أهل البيت، بيروت: دار المحجّة البيضاء، ٢٠٠٦.

الحائري اليزدي، الحاج الشيخ علي: إلزام الناصب في إثبات حجّة الغائب، مجلّدان، بيروت: مؤسّسة الأعلمي للمطبوعات، ١٤٢٢/٢٠٠٢.

حجاب، محمّد فريد: المهديّ المنتظر بين العقيدة الدينية والمضمون السياسي، الجزائر: المؤسّسة الوطنيّة للكتّاب، ١٩٨٤.

حسّان، محمّد: أحداث النهاية ونهاية العالم، المنصورة (مصر): مكتبة فيّاض، ١٤٢٨/٢٠٠٧.

حسن، سعد محمّد: المهديّة في الإسلام، القاهرة: دار الكتّاب العربي، ١٣٧٣/١٩٥٣.

حسن، محمّد صدّيق: يقظة أولي الاعتبار ممّا ورد في ذكر النار وأصحاب النار، القاهرة: دار الأنصار، ١٣٩٨/١٩٨٧.

الحسيني الصدر، عليّ: محاضرات في الرجعة، قم: دليل ما، ١٤٢٧هـ. /٢٠٠٦.

الحلو، محمّد عليّ: الغيبة والانتظار، النجف: مركز الدراسات التخصّصيّة في الإمام المهديّ، ١٤٢٤/٢٠٠٣-٢٠٠٤.

الحمد، محمّد بن إبراهيم: الإيمان باليوم الآخر، الرياض: دار ابن خزيمة، ١٤٢٣/٢٠٠٢.

حمدان، محمّد فهمي: نبوءات نبيّ الإسلام في علامات الساعة الكبرى والصغرى، الدجّالون قديمًا وحديثًا والفتن الدامية بين المسلين، بيروت: دار الكتب العلميّة، ١٤٢٧/٢٠٠٦.

الحمش، عداب محمود: المهديّ المنتظر في روايات أهل السنة والشيعة الإماميّة، عمّان: دار الفتح، ١٤٢٢/٢٠٠١.

خاقاني، محمّد كاظم: المهديّ المنتظر، بيروت: دار صاحب الأمر، ٢٠٠٤.

الخطيب، عبد الكريم: المهديّ المنتظر ومن ينتظرونه، القاهرة: دار الفكر العربي، ١٤٠٠/١٩٨٠.

خليفة، محمّد عبد الظاهر: الحياة البرزخيّة من الموت إلى البعث، القاهرة: دار الاعتصام، ١٤٢٩/٢٠٠٨.

الداني، عثمان بن سعيد: السنن الواردة في الفتن وغوائلها والساعة وأشراطها، تحقيق: رضاء الدين بن محمّد المباركفوري، الرياض: دار العاصمة، ١٤١٦/١٩٩٥.

داود، محمّد عيسى: احذروا، المسيح الدجّال يغزو العالم من مثلّث برمودا، القاهرة: مؤسّسة دار المختار الإسلامي، ١٤١١/١٩٩١.

داود، محمّد عيسى: المهديّ المنتظر على الأبواب، المحلّة الكبرى (مصر): دار المصطفى للطباعة والكمبيوتر، ١٤٢٤/٢٠٠٣.

الدحدوح، سلمان نصيف: يوم القيامة أسماؤه وصفاته، بيروت: دار البشائر، ١٤١٩/١٩٩٨.

الدخيل الله، صالح بن محمّد: أحاديث أشراط الساعة الصغرى، المدينة المنورة: الجامعة الإسلاميّة، ١٤١٠/١٩٩٠.

دستغيب، عبد الحسين: الدار الآخرة، بيروت: دار المحجّة البيضاء، ٢٠٠٩.

الدسوقي، فاروق: موسوعة أشراط الساعة والقيامة الصغرى على الأبواب، ١٠ أجزاء، القاهرة: مكتبة مدبولي والإسكندريّة: دار الدعوة، ١٤٢٠/١٩٩٩.

الراشد، صلاح صالح: رواية على أبواب الملحمة من جلسات العلّامة عليم الدين، الكويت: شركة فرانشايز الراشد، ٢٠٠٩.

الرحباوي، عبد القادر: اليوم الآخر، القاهرة: دار السلام، ٢٠٠٧.

الرضوي، محمّد حسين: المهديّ الموعود في القرآن الكريم، بيروت: دار الهادي، ٢٠٠١.

الزبيدي، ماجد ناصر: أروع القصص في من رأى المهديّ في غيبته الكبرى، بيروت: دار المحجّة البيضاء، ١٤٢٦/٢٠٠٥.

الزبيدي، ماجد ناصر: الإمام المهديّ المنتظر من قبل الميلاد إلى ما بعد الظهور، بيروت: منشورات الفجر، ٢٠٠٨.

الزبيدي، ماجد ناصر: كيف تلتقي بالإمام المهديّ، بيروت: دار المحجّة البيضاء، ١٤٣٠/٢٠٠٩.

الزرفي، عامر: أبحاث حول المهدويّة، قم: مؤسّسة الإمام المهديّ الموعود الثقافيّة، ٢٠١١.

زغلول، محمّد السعيد: موسوعة أطراف الحديث، بيروت: دار الكتب العلميّة، ١٤١٠/١٩٨٩.

زهر الدين، نايف: الحياة بعد الموت: حقيقة أم خيال؟، بيروت: رياض الريّس للكتب والنشر، ٢٠٠٨.

زين الدين، عبد الرسول: معجم بلدان عصر الظهور، بيروت: منشورات الفجر، ٢٠٠٩.

السالم، فهد: أسرار الساعة، القاهرة: مكتبة مدبولي الصغير، ١٤١٩/١٩٩٨.

سرور، رفاعي: علامات الساعة، الإسكندرية: دار الفرقان للتراث، ١٤٢٢/٢٠٠١.

سعيد، ناطق: سقيفة الغيبة، بيروت: دار المحجّة البيضاء، ٢٠١٢.

سليمان، رانيا: عجائب الأسرار للإمام عليّ بن أبي طالب عن علامات آخر الزمان، بيروت: منشورات مؤسّسة الخرسان للمطبوعات، ٢٠٠٥.

سليمان، كامل: يوم الخلاص في ظلّ القائم المهديّ عليه السلام، بيروت: دار الكتاب اللبناني، ١٩٧٩.

السند، محمّد: الإمام المهدي والظواهر القرآنية، النجف: مركز الدراسات التخصّصية في الإمام المهديّ، ١٤٣١/٢٠١٠–٢٠١١.

السند، محمّد: دعوة السفارة في الغيبة الكبرى ويليه فقه علائم الظهور، قم: محبين، ١٤٢٧/٢٠٠٦.

السويدان، طارق: قصّة النهاية، الموت والآخرة وأشراط الساعة، الرياض: مؤسّسة قرطبة للإنتاج الفني، ١٤٢٦/٢٠٠٥.

الشاهرودي، جواد السيّد حسين الحسينيّ آل عليّ: الإمام المهديّ وظهوره، بيروت: مؤسّسة النعمان، ١٤١٢/١٩٩٢.

شاهين، مهدي عبد الرازق: كتب الفتن والمهديّ والملاحم في سنن أبي داود، بغداد: دراسة ماجستير، جامعة النهرين (جامعة صدّام سابقًا)، ١٩٩٥.

شبّوط، إبراهيم: المهديّة في عصر الغيبة، بيروت: مؤسّسة الأعلمي للمطبوعات، ٢٠٠٦.

الشعراوي، محمّد متولّي: الدار الآخرة، القاهرة: المكتبة العصرية، ١٤٢٦/٢٠٠٥.

الشفت، أسد الله بن محمّد باقر الموسوي: كتاب الغيبة في الإمام الثاني عشر القائم الحجّة، مجلّدان، بيروت: مؤسّسة العروة الوثقى، ١٤٢٨/٢٠٠٧.

شقر، عليّ محسن: يوم القيامة: أسماء يوم القيامة ومعانيها وخصائصها وصفاتها، بيروت: دار المرتضى، ٢٠٠٨.

الشلبي، مصطفى أبو النصر: صحيح أشراط الساعة ووصف ليوم البعث وأهوال القيامة، بيروت: دار ابن حزم، ١٤٢٣/٢٠٠٣.

الشلبي، مصطفى أبو النصر: صحيح أشراط الساعة، جدّة: مكتبة السوادي، ١٤١٦/١٩٩٥.

الشناوي، عبد العزيز: النساء أكثر أهل النار، القاهرة: دار الإيمان، ١٤١٦/١٩٩٦.

الشيباني، محمّد بن إبراهيم: من أشراط الساعة الكبرى خراب الكعبة، الكويت: مكتبة ابن تيمية، ١٤٠٧/١٩٨٧.

الشيخ، عزّ الدين بن حسين: أشراط الساعة الصغرى والكبرى، الرياض: دار الهديان، ١٤١٧/١٩٩٩.

الشيرازي، حسن الحسين: كلمة الإمام المهديّ، بيروت:دار العلوم، ١٤٢٧/٢٠٠٦.

الصابوني، محمّد علي: المهديّ وأشراط الساعة، الجزائر: شركة الشهاب، ١٩٩٠.

صالح، محمّد أديب: القيامة مشاهدها وعظاتها في السنّة النبويّة، المجلّد الأوّل، بيروت: المكتب الإسلامي، ١٤١٥/١٩٩٤.

الصائغ، مجيد: شياطين ما قبل ظهور الإمام المهديّ، بيروت: مؤسّسة البلاغ، ٢٠٠٩.

صبري، يوسف: الخطر المحدق من نحو المشرق، القاهرة: مكتبة عالم الفكر والقانون، ١٤٠٨/١٩٨٧.

الصدر، صدر الدين: المهديّ، بيروت:دار الزهراء، ١٣٩٨/١٩٧٨.

الصدر، محمّد: تاريخ ما بعد الظهور، بيروت:دار المعارف، (لا تاريخ).

الصدر، محمّد باقر: بحث حول المهديّ، بيروت:دار التعارف، ١٩٦٦.

الصفّار النجفي، سالم: موسوعة الإمام المهديّ المنتظر: من المهد إلى يوم القيامة، بيروت:دار نظير عبّود، ٢٠٠٨.

الصوّاف، محمّد محمود: القيامة رأي العين، القاهرة: مكتبة السنة، ١٤١٣/١٩٩٣.

الطامي، محمّد: تحذير الرجال من فتنة الدجّال، تحقيق: محمّد الجهاني، القاهرة: المركز العربي الحديث، ١٤٠٩/١٩٨٩.

الطعمي، محيي الدين: تطريز الديباج بحقائق الإسراء والمعراج، بيروت: دار ومكتبة الهلال، ١٤١٥/١٩٩٤.

الطعمي، محيي الدين: موسوعة الإسراء والمعراج، بيروت:دار ومكتبة الهلال، ١٤١٤/١٩٩٤.

طلبة، منى محمّد: أدب الرحلة إلى العالم الآخر، القاهرة: جامعة عين شمس، أطروحة دكتوراه غير منشورة، ١٩٩٨.

طلبة، منى محمّد: الرمز في الأدب الأخرويّ - رحلة في المعراج، القاهرة: في مجلّة الإبداع، ١٩٩٧.

الطنطاوي، عليّ أحمد عبد العال: الحياة بعد الموت، جزءان في مجلّد واحد، بيروت:دار الكتب العلميّة، ١٤٣٠/٢٠٠٩.

الطنطاوي، عليّ أحمد عبد العال: أهوال القبور وما بعد الموت، القاهرة: دار البشير ودار الجيل، (لا تاريخ).

الطنطاوي، عليّ أحمد عبد العال: الحياة بعد الموت: كتاب فيه ذكر الحياة والموت، والجنّة والترغيب فيها، والنار والترهيب منها والقبر وعذابه، من القرآن الكريم والسنة النبوية الشريفة والآثار، بيروت: منشورات محمّد عليّ بيضون، دار الكتب العلميّة، ١٤٢٥/٢٠٠٤.

عاشور، عليّ: سرّ المهديّ في علم عليّ، بيروت: مؤسّسة التاريخ العربي، ٢٠٠٨.

عاشور، عليّ: ظهور المهديّ المنتظر وعدالة دولته، بيروت: دار الصفوة، ٢٠٠٨.

عاشور، عليّ: موسوعة أهل البيت، المجلد ١٩: سيرة الإمام المهديّ المنتظر، بيروت: دار نظير عبّود، ١٤٢٧/٢٠٠٦.

العبّاد، عبد المحسن بن حمد: الردّ على من كذّب بالأحاديث الصحيحة الواردة في المهديّ، الرياض: دار الفضيلة، ١٤٢٤/٢٠٠٤.

العبّاد، عبد المحسن بن حمد: عقيدة أهل السنّة والأثر في المهديّ المنتظر، الرياض: دار الفضيلة، ١٤٢٥/٢٠٠٤.

عبد الحكيم، منصور: بلاد الشام، أرض الأنبياء والملاحم وأشراط الساعة، القاهرة: دار الكتاب العربي، ١٤٢٦/٢٠٠٥.

عبد المطّلب، رفعت فوزي: أحاديث الإسراء والمعراج - دراسة توثيقيّة، القاهرة: مكتبة الخانجي، ١٤٠٣/١٩٨٢.

عبد المقصود، عبد المعطي: المهديّ المنتظر في الميزان، الإسكندريّة: دار نشر الثقافة، (لا تاريخ).

عبد المنان، عكاشة: عذاب القبر في الميزان، القاهرة: دار الاعتصام، ١٤١٣/١٩٩٢.

عتريسي، جعفر حسن: مخاض عصر الظهور، راية اليمان الداعي لقائم آل محمّد، بيروت: مركز الأبحاث والفكر الإسلامي، مؤسّسة البلاغة، ٢٠٠٨.

عتريسي، جعفر حسن: موسوعة بقيّة الله الأعظم الإمام المهديّ، ٣ مجلّدات، بيروت: دار الهادي، ٢٠٠٦.

العجيري، عبد الله بن صالح: معالم ومنارات في تنزيل نصوص الفتن والملاحم وأشراط الساعة على الوقائع والحوادث، الظهران (السعوديّة): الدرر السنيّة، ١٤٣٣/٢٠١٢.

العدوي، مصطفى: الصحيح المسند من أحاديث الفتن والملاحم وأشراط الساعة، الرياض: دار الهجرة للنشر، ١٤١٢/١٩٩١.

عطا، عبد القادر أحمد: المهديّ المنتظر بين الحقيقة والخرافة، القاهرة: دار العلوم، ١٩٧٩.

العظمة، نذير: المعراج والرمز الصوفي، بيروت: دار الباحث، ١٤٠٢/١٩٨٢.

العقيل، سعود بن عبد العزيز: الآثار الواردة عن السلف في الإيمان باليوم الآخر في تفسير الطبري، رسالة دكتوراه، الرياض: جامعة الإمام محمّد بن سعود، قسم العقيدة والمذاهب المعاصرة، كلّيّة أصول الدين ٢٠٠٢.

عقيل، محسن: الإمام المهديّ وعلامات ظهوره عند الإمام الصادق، بيروت: دار المحجّة البيضاء، ٢٠٠٩.

عقيل، محسن: موسوعة الإمام المهديّ: الجامع المعتبر لأحاديث الإمام المنتظر عند السنّة والشيعة، بيروت: دار المحجّة البيضاء، ٢٠١١.

عقيل، محسن: من أروع ما قاله الإمام المهديّ المنتظر، بيروت: دار المحجّة البيضاء، ٢٠٠٩.

علويّة، توفيق حسن: يأجوج ومأجوج في عصر الظهور، بيروت: دار الصفوة، ٢٠٠٧.

العلي، إبراهيم: الأرض المقدّسة بين الماضي والحاضر والمستقبل، لندن: منشورات فلسطين المسلمة، ١٩٩٦.

عليّ، جواد: المهديّ المنتظر عند الشيعة الاثني عشريّة، ترجمة أبو العيد دودو، كولونيا: منشورات الجمل، ٢٠٠٥.

عليّ، محمّد أحمد: الطريق الهادي إلى حقيقة المهديّ، عمّان: مكتبة الرسالة الحديثة، ١٤٢٩/٢٠٠٨.

علي، محمود عطيّة محمّد: فقد جاء أشراطها، الدمّام: الدمّام للنشر، ١٤١٧/١٩٩٧.

عمارة، محمّد عمارة: قصّة النهاية وعلامات الساعة الصغرى والكبرى، بيروت: دار ابن حزم، ١٤٢٣/٢٠٠٢.

عواجي، غالب بن عليّ: الحياة الآخرة ما بين البعث إلى دخول الجنّة أو النار، القاهرة: دار لينة، ١٤١٧/١٩٩٦.

الغامدي، خالد بن ناصر: أشراط الساعة في مسند الإمام أحمد وزوائد الصحيحين، بيروت: دار ابن حزم، ١٤٢٠/١٩٩٩.

الغريفي، السيّد عبد الله: الإمام المنتظر، قراءة في الإشكاليّات، بيروت: دار السلام، ١٤٣٣/٢٠١٢.

الغفيلي، عبد الله بن سليمان: أشراط الساعة، الرياض: وزارة الشؤون الإسلاميّة والأوقاف والدعوة والإرشاد، ١٤٢٢/٢٠٠١.

الغماري المغربي، أبو الفضل عبد الله بن الصدّيق: إبراز الوهم المكنون من كلام ابن خلدون، المسمّى المرشد المبدي في فساد طعن ابن خلدون في أحاديث المهديّ، دمشق: مطبعة الترقّي، ١٣٤٧/١٩٢٩.

الغماري المغربي، أبو الفضل عبد الله بن الصدّيق: عقيدة أهل الإسلام في نزول عيسى عليه السلام، القاهرة: عالم الكتاب، ١٩٩٩.

الغماري المغربي، أبو الفضل عبد الله بن الصدّيق: مطابقة المخترعات العصريّة لما أخبر به سيّد البريّة، القاهرة: مكتبة القاهرة، دار الطباعة المحمّديّة بالأزهر، ١٣٩١/١٩٧١.

الغماري المغربي، أبو الفضل عبد الله بن الصدّيق: المهديّ المنتظر، القاهرة: مكتبة القاهرة، ١٣٩٨/١٩٧٨.

فقيه، شبّر: نهاية الكون في الفكر القرآني الفلسفي: رؤية أبستيمولوجيّة معرفيّة مقارنة في نشأة الكون ونهايته، بيروت: دار البحار، ٢٠٠٩.

فقيه، فارس: كرامات الإمام المهديّ، بيروت: دار المحجّة البيضاء، ٢٠٠٣.

فقيه، فارس: لقاءات العلماء بالإمام الحجّة، بيروت: دار المحجّة البيضاء، ٢٠٠٣.

القبانجي، محمّد: التقويم المهدويّ، بيروت: مؤسّسة الأعلمي للمطبوعات، ٢٠١٢.

القزويني، محمّد كاظم: الإمام المهديّ من المهد إلى الظهور، بيروت: مؤسّسة النور للمطبوعات، ١٤١٤/١٩٩٥.

قطب، سيّد: مشاهد القيامة في القرآن، القاهرة: دار الشروق، ١٤٢٣/٢٠٠٢.

القنوجي [خان]، محمّد صدّيق حسن: الإذاعة لما كان وما يكون بين يديّ الساعة، بهوپال (الهند): المطبع الصدّيقي، ١٢٩٣/١٨٧٦.

الكاظمي، صلاح: ويسألونك عن القائم عليه السلام، بيروت: دار المحجّة البيضاء، ١٤٣٢/٢٠١١.

كامل، مرفت: المنهج الشرعي في مواجهة الفتن، الرياض: دار الوطن، ١٤٢٠/٢٠٠٠.

كبرى، نجم الدين: منهاج السالكين ومعراج الطالبين، كرج (إيران): نجم كبرى، ١٣٨٨ ش./٢٠٠٩–٢٠١٠.

الكشميري الهندي، محمّد أنور شاه بن معظم شاه: التصريح بما تواتر في نزول المسيح، تحقيق: عبد الفتاح أبو غدّة، حلب: مكتب المطبوعات الإسلاميّة، ١٤٠٢/١٩٨٢.

الكلبايكاني، لطف الله الصافي: منتخب الأثر في الإمام الثاني عشر، تهران: مركز نشر كتاب: ١٣٧٣/١٩٥٤.

الكليب، عبد الملك عليّ: أهوال القيامة، الكويت: مكتبة الصحابة الإسلاميّة، ١٤٠٠/١٩٧٩.

كمال، هشام: عصر المسيح الدجّال -الحقائق والوثائق، القاهرة: مركز الحضارة العربيّة، ٢٠٠٠.

الكوثري، محمّد زاهد: نظرة عابرة في مزاعم من ينكر نزول عيسى قبل الآخرة، القاهرة: مكتبة القدسي، ١٤٠٠/١٩٨٠.

الكوراني، حسين: حول رؤية الإمام المنتظر، بيروت، ١٤١٧/١٩٩٨.

الكوراني، عليّ: آداب عصر الغيبة، بيروت، ١٤٢٦/٢٠٠٥.

الكوراني، عليّ: المعجم الموضوعيّ لأحاديث الإمام المهديّ، بيروت: دار المرتضى، ١٤٣٠/٢٠٠٩.

مبروك، ليلى: علامات الساعة الصغرى والكبرى، القاهرة: المختار الإسلامي، ١٤٠٦/١٩٨٦.

المحامي، محمّد كامل حسن: الجنّة في القرآن الكريم، بيروت: المكتب العالميّ للطباعة والنشر، ١٤٠٨/١٩٨٨.

محمّد، حسين نجيب: يوم القيامة ونسبيّة الزمن بين العلم والقرآن الكريم، بيروت: دار الهادي، ٢٠٠٤.
محمّد، عليّ عليّ: لمعة البيان في أحداث آخر الزمان، أشراط الساعة الصغرى والكبرى، عمّان: دار الإسراء، ١٤١٤/١٩٩٤.
محمود، إبراهيم: جغرافية الملذّات - الجنس في الجنّة، بيروت: رياض الريّس للكتب والنشر، ١٤١٩/١٩٩٨.
محمود، مصطفى: زيارة للجنّة والنار، القاهرة: دار أخبار اليوم، ١٩٩٦.
المصباح، الكاظم: دولة الإمام المهديّ وعصر الظهور، بيروت: دار الكتّاب العربي، ١٤٢٨/٢٠٠٧.
مصطفى، أسامة نعيم: أشراط الساعة في ظهور المهديّ المنتظر - المسيح الدجّال - عيسى عليه السلام - يأجوج ومأجوج، عمّان: دار عالم الثقافة، ٢٠٠٢.
المطيري، عبد المحسن بن زين: اليوم الآخر في القرآن والسنّة، بيروت: دار البشائر الإسلاميّة، ١٤٢٣/٢٠٠٢.
مربونجر المكّي، محمّد نور الدين: من هو المهديّ المنتظر؟ القاهرة: دار الحقيقة للإعلام، ١٩٩٣.
المشعلي، عبد الله سليمان: مختصر الأخبار المشاعة في الفتن والملاحم والمهديّ والساعة، الرياض: مطابع الرياض، ١٩٧١.
المشوخي، إبراهيم: المهديّ المنتظر، الزرقا (الأردن): مكتبة المنار، ١٤٠٥/١٩٨٥.
معرفي، عبد الله: المهدويّة الخاتمة فوق زيف الدعاوى وتضليل الأدعياء، مجلّدان، قم: باقيات، ١٤٣٥/٢٠١٤.
المقدّم، محمّد بن أحمد بن إسماعيل: المهديّ، الإسكندريّة: الدار العالميّة للنشر، ١٤٢٤/٢٠٠٤.
المقدّم، محمّد بن أحمد بن اسماعيل: فقه أشراط الساعة، الإسكندريّة: الدار العالميّة للنشر، ١٤٢٤/٢٠٠٣.
منيني، إبراهيم بن مصطفى: المهديّ المنتظر عليه السلام والمعمّرون من البشر، بيروت: دار المحجّة البيضاء، ٢٠١١.
الموسوي، جلال: الأربعون في المهديّ وقصّة الجزيرة الخضراء، بيروت، الدار الإسلاميّة، ١٤٢٣/٢٠٠٢.
الموسوي الزنجاني النجفي، إبراهيم: عقائد الإماميّة الاثني عشريّة، ٣ مجلّدات، قم: انتشارات حضرت مهدى، ١٤٠٢/١٩٨٢.
الموسوي، عبّاس عليّ: الإمام المهديّ عدالة السماء، بيروت: دار الرسول الأكرم، ١٤٣٣/٢٠١٢.
الموسوي، محسن النوري: اللقاء المهدويّ، بيروت: دار الكتّاب العربي، ١٤٢٩/٢٠٠٨.
موسوي، محمود عبد اللطيف: كيف ومتى يظهر الإمام المهديّ؟، بيروت: الأيّام، ٢٠٠٨.

موسوي، ناظم: الاستعداد لظهور الإمام المهديّ عجّل الله تعالى فرجه الشريف، بيروت: دار المحجّة البيضاء، ٢٠١١.
الندوي، محمّد ولي الله عبد الرحمن: نبوءات الرسول - ما تحقّق منها وما سيتحقّق، القاهرة: دار السلام، ١٩٩٩.
هاني، إدريس: الإمام المهدي: حقيقة تاريخيّة أم فرضيّة فلسفيّة - حوار غير مكتمل مع أحمد الكاتب، بيروت: دار المحجّة البيضاء، ٢٠١١.
هرّاس، محمّد خليل: فصل المقال في رفع عيسى حيًّا ونزوله وقتله الدجّال، القاهرة: مكتبة السنّة، ١٤٠٩/١٩٨٩.
الوابل، يوسف بن عبد الله بن يوسف: أشراط الساعة، الدمّام: دار ابن الجوزي، ١٤١٥/١٩٩٥.
الوادعي، أبو عبد الرحمن مقبل بن هادي: الشفاعة، الكويت: دار الأرقم، ١٤٠٣/١٩٨٣.
وائلي، مرتضى: جيش الإمام المهديّ وحزب الله في القرآن وروايات أهل البيت، بيروت: مؤسّسة الهدى الإسلاميّة، ٢٠٠٩.
ولينكود، أبو أنس صديق: صحيح الفتن وأشراط الساعة من الكتاب والسنّة، الرياض: فهرسة الرياض، ١٤٢٤/٢٠٠٣.

2 Persian Sources

2.1 *Primary Sources*

آیتی، عبد المجید: قرآن مجید (ترجمهٔ فارسی)، تهران: سروش. واحد احیای هنرهای اسلامی، ۱۳۷۱ ش./ ۱۹۹۲–۱۹۹۳ م.
أبوالفتوح رازی، حسین بن علی: روض الجنان و روح الجنان فی تفسیر القرآن مشهور به تفسیر شیخ ابوالفتوح رازی، ۲۰ جلد، مشهد: مؤسسة الدراسات الإسلامية في الروضة الرضوية المقدسة، ۱۴۰۸ هـ./ ۱۹۸۷–۱۹۸۸ م.
اسفراینی، نورالدین عبدالرحمن بن محمّد: کاشف الأسرار. به انضمام پاسخ به چند پرسش. رساله در روش سلوک و خلوت نشینی. به اهتمام دکتر هرمان لندلت، تهران: انتشارات مؤسّسهٔ مطالعات اسلامی دانشگاه مکگیل شعبهٔ تهران، با همکاری مرکز بین المللی گفتگوی تمدّنها، ۱۳۸۳ ش./ ۲۰۰۴–۲۰۰۵ م.
انصاری، عبدالله: مناجات نامهٔ خواجه عبدالله انصاری، [تهران]: دوستان، ۱۳۸۷ ش./ ۲۰۰۸–۲۰۰۹ م.
باباافضل: مصنفات افضل الدین محمّد مرقی کاشانی، به تصحیح مجتبی مینوی و یحیی مهدوی، تهران: انتشارات خوارزمی، ۱۳۶۶ ش./ ۱۹۸۷ م.

بهاءالله [میرزا حسین علی نوری]: کتاب ایقان، هوفهایم: مؤسّسهٔ ملّی مطبوعات بهائی آلمان، ۱۹۹۸ م.

بیرجندی قائنی، محمدباقر: بغية الطالب في من رأى الإمام الغائب، مشهد: انتشارات خراسان ۱۳۲٤ هـ./ ۱۹۲۳-۱۹۲٤ م.

جامی، نورالدین عبدالرحمن بن احمد: هفت اورنگ، تهران: کتابفروشی سعدی، ۱۳۳۷ ش./ ۱۹۵۸ م.

حافظ شیرازی، خواجه شمس الدین محمد: دیوان حافظ. بر اساس هشت نسخهٔ کامل کهن مؤرخ به سالهای ۸۱۳ تا ۸۲۷ هجری قمری، تهران: نشر صدوق، ۱۳۷٦ ش./ ۱۹۹۷ م.

خادمی شیرازی، محمد: تحفهٔ امام مهدی. مجموعهٔ سخنان و توقیعات و ادعیهٔ حضرت بقیة الله، تهران: موعود عصر، ۱۳۸۳ ش./ ۲۰۰٤-۲۰۰۵ م.

دهدار شیرازی، محمد بن محمود: شرح خطبة البیان امام علی بن ابی طالب علیه السلام، تهران: انتشارات صائب، ۱۳۷۹ ش./ ۲۰۰۰ م.

رشتی، سید کاظم: مقامات العارفین. در حقیقت بدء و عود و احوال خلق و توحید و معرفت خداوند، تارنما: http://www.alabrar.info.

رومی، جلال الدین: غزلیات شمس التبریزی، [تهران]: [بنگاه مطبوعاتی صفی علی شاه]، [۱۹۵٦ م.].

رومی، جلال الدین: کتاب مثنوی معنوی، تهران: کتابخانه و مطبعهٔ بروحیم، ۱۳۱٤-۱۳۱۷ ش./ ۱۹۳۵-۱۹۳۸ م.

سبزواری، محمد بن محمد میرلوحی: کفایة المهتدي في معرفة المهدي، ویرایش آیت الله حاج سید مصطفی شریعت موسوی اصفهانی، قم: انتشارات دار التفسیر، ۱۳۸٤ ش./ ۲۰۰۵-۲۰۰٦ م.

سجستانی، أبویعقوب: کشف المحجوب. رساله در آئین اسماعیلی از قرن چهارم هجری با مقدمه به زبان فرانسه به قلم هانری کوربن، پاریس: انجمن ایرانشناسی فرانسه در ایران: ۱۹۸۸ م.

سمنانی، علاء الدوله: دیوان کامل اشعار فارسی و عربی شیخ علاء الدوله سمنانی عارف بزرگ قرن هفتم و هشتم هجری، تهران: شرکت مؤلفان و مترجمان ایران، ۱۳٦٤ ش./ ۱۹۸۵-۱۹۸٦ م.

سمنانی، علاء الدوله: چهل مجلس علاء الدوله سمنانی، تهران: شرکت مؤلفان و مترجمان ایران، ۱۳۵۸ ش./ ۱۹۷۹ م.

سمنانی، علاء الدوله: مصنّفات فارسی علاء الدوله سمنانی، به اهتمام نجیب مایل هروی، تهران: شرکت انتشارات علمی و فرهنگی، ۱۳٦۹ ش./ ۱۹۹۰ م.

شبستری، محمود بن عبدالکریم: گلشن راز. از آثار حضرت شیخ محمود شبستری، با تصحیح و مقدمه و حواشی و تعلیقات جواد نوربخش، [تهران]: خانقاه نعمت اللهی، [۱۹۷٦ م.].

شیرازی، روزبهان بن ابی النصر بقلی: چهار رسالهٔ چاپ نشده از روزبهان بقلی شیرازی. متن عربی به همراه تفسیر و مقدمهٔ فرانسوی از پل بلانفا، تهران: معین، ۱۳۷۷ ش./ ۱۹۹۸ م.

شیرازی، روزبهان بن ابی النصر بقلی: شرح شطحیات. تصحیح و مقدمهٔ هانری کوربن، پاریس: انستیتو ایرانشناسی دانشگاه پاریس، ۱۳۴۴ ش./ ۱۹۶۶ م.

شیرازی، روزبهان بن ابی النصر بقلی: عبهر العاشقین، [تهران]: یلدا قلم، ۱۳۸۰ ش./ ۲۰۰۱ م.

شیرازی، قطب الدین: درّة التاج لغرّة الدباج، تصحیح محمّد مشکوة، ۵ جلد، تهران: انتشارات حمکت، ۱۳۸۵ ش./ ۲۰۰۶ م.

طوسی، نصیرالدین: روضهٔ تسلیم (تصوّرات). تصحیح و پیشگفتار از سید جلال حسینی بدخشانی. بامقدّمهٔ هرمان لندلت، تهران: مرکز پژوهشی میراث مکتوب باهمکاری مؤسّسهٔ مطالعات اسماعیلی در لندن، ۲۰۱۴ م.

عبدالبهاء [عبّاس افندی]: النور الأبهی في مفاوضات عبد البهاء؛ لیدن: بریل، ۱۹۰۸ م.

عراقی میثمی، محمود: دارالسلام در احوالات حضرت مهدی و علائم ظهور و کسانی که در خواب یا بیداری به محضر آن حضرت مبارک شرفیاب شده‌اند، ویرایش ابوالحسن حسینی، قم: نگین، ۱۳۸۰ ش./ ۲۰۰۱–۲۰۰۲ م.

عراقی میثمی، محمود: رؤیای نور. شامل داستانهایی جالب و شنیدنی از کتاب دارالسلام، ویرایش رضا استادی، قم: محدث، ۱۳۸۲ ش./ ۲۰۰۳ م.

فردوسی، حکیم ابوالقاسم: شاهنامه، تهران: مؤسّسهٔ انتشارات و چاپ امیرکبیر، ۱۳۶۴ ش./ ۱۹۶۴ م.

عطار نیشابوری، فریدالدین: دیوان غزلیات و ترجیعات و قصائد فریدالدین عطار نیشابوری، تهران: کتابخانهٔ سنائی، ۱۳۳۵- ۱۳۳۶ ش./ ۱۹۵۶–۱۹۵۷ م.

عطار نیشابوری، فریدالدین: منطق الطیر، تهران: کتابفروشی تهران، ۱۳۴۱ ش./ ۱۹۶۲ م.

عین القضاة همدانی، عبدالله بن محمد: تمهیدات، تهران: چاپخانهٔ دانشگاه تهران، ۱۳۴۱ ش./ ۱۹۶۳ م.

غزالی، ابوحامد محمد بن محمد: کیمیای سعادت، تهران: شرکت علمی و فرهنگی، ۱۳۸۴ ش./ ۲۰۰۴ م.

کاشانی، کمال الدین عبدالرزّاق: مجموعهٔ رسائل و مصنفات، تهران: میراث مکتوب، ۱۳۷۵ ش./ ۲۰۰۰ م.

کرمانی، محمدکریم خان: رسالهٔ ناصریه در تحقیق معاد جسمانی، کرمان: چاپخانهٔ سعادت، ۱۳۷۵ ش./ ۱۹۹۶–۱۹۹۷ م.

کرمانی، نعمت الله ولی: دیوان شاه نعمت الله ولی ماهانی کرمانی، [تهران]: کتابفروشی محمد علمی، ۱۳۷۲ ش./ ۱۹۹۳ م.

لاهیجی، شمس الدین محمد: مفاتیح الإعجاز في شرح گلشن راز، با مقدمهٔ کامل به قلم کیوان سمیعی، تهران: کتابفروشی محمودی، ۱۳۳۷ ش./ ۱۹۵۸ م.

مجلسي، محمد باقر: حقّ اليقين در اصول و فروع اعتقادات، اصفهان: کانون پژوهش، ۱۳۸۰ ش./ ۲۰۰۱–۲۰۰۲ م.

مجلسی، محمد باقر: کتاب رجعت. چهارده حدیث از ولادت امام زمان تا رجعت ائمه، ویرایش حسن موسوی، قم: دلیل ما، ۱۳۸۲ ش./ ۲۰۰۳ م.

مجلسی، محمد باقر: مهدی موعود، ترجمهٔ علی دوانی، تهران: دار الکتب الإسلامية، ۱۳۸٤ ش./ ۲۰۰۵–۲۰۰٦ م.

مجلسی، محمد باقر: مهدی موعود. ترجمهٔ جلد سیزدهم بحار الأنوار، ۲ جلد، ترجمهٔ حسن بن محمد ولی ارومیه ای، قم: انتشارات مسجد مقدّس جمکران، ۱٤۱۸ هـ./ ۱۹۹۷ م.

میبدی، ابوالفضل رشید الدین: کشف الأسرار وعدة الأبرار، تهران: [دانشگاه تهران]، [۱۳۳۱–۱۳۳۹ ش./ ۱۹۵۲–۱۹٦۱ م.].

ناصرخسرو، زاد المسافرین، تصحیح و تحقیق محمد عمادی حائری، تهران: میراث مکتوب، ۱۳۸٤ ش./ ۲۰۰۵ م.

نسفی، عزیز الدین بن محمد: کشف الحقایق، به اهتمام و تعلیق احمد مهدوی دامغانی، تهران: بنگاه ترجمه و نشر کتاب، ۱۳۵۹ ش./ ۱۹۸۰ م.

نورعلی شاه، محمّد علي بن عبد الحسین: جنات الوصال، به کوشش جواد نوربخش، تهران: چاپخانهٔ فردوسی، ۱۳٤۸ ش./ ۱۹۷۰ م.

نهاوندی، علی اکبر: برکات حضرت ولی عصر. حکایات عبقري الحسان في أحوال مولانا صاحب الزمان، ویرایش سید جواد معلّم، مشهد: انتشارات تکسوار حجاز، ۱۳۸۲ ش./ ۲۰۰۳ م.

هجویری، علي بن عثمان: کشف المحجوب، تصحیح و ژوکوفسکی با مقدمهٔ قاسم انصاری، تهران: کتابخانهٔ طهوری، ۱۳۵۸ ش./ ۱۹۷۹ م.

همدانی، علی بن محمد: چهل اسرار یا غزلیات میر سید علی همدانی، [تهران]: انتشارات وحید، ۱۳٤۷ ش./ ۱۹٦۸ م.

2.2 *Secondary Sources*

آشتیانی، جلال الدین: معاد جسمانی. شرح بر زاد المسافر ملا صدرا، تهران: انجمن اسلامی حکمت و فلسفهٔ ایران، ۱۳۵۹ ش./ ۱۹۸۰ م.

ابطحی، حسن: ملاقات با امام زمان علیه السلام، مشهد: کانون بحث و انتقاد دینی، ۱٤۰٦ هـ./ ۱۹۸٦ م.

ابرقويي، روح الله: سیاحت در قیامت. شرح حوادث و وقایع روز محشر و احوال مردم در آن روز از دیدگاه قرآن و روایات، قم: انتشارات دلشاد، ۱۳۸٤ ش./۲۰۰۵–۲۰۰٦ م.

امامی‌جمعه، سید مهدی: عین‌القضات در آینهٔ هرمینوتیک مدرن، مجلهٔ دانشکدهٔ ادبیات و علوم انسانی دانشگاه اصفهان، ۳۹ (۱۳۸۳ ش./ ۲۰۰٤ م.): صص. ۲۱–۳٤ .

امینی، ابراهیم: دادگستر جهان، [قم]: انتشارات شفق، ۱۳٦۷ ش./۱۹۸۸–۱۹۸۹ م.

امینی گلستانی، محمد: سیمای جهان در عصر امام زمان: اجتماعی، اقتصادی، آموزش و پرورش، نظامی و قضایی، قم: انتشارات مسجد مقدس جمکران، ۱۳۸۵ ش./ ۲۰۰٦ م.

باقرزاده بابلی، عبدالرحمن: توجهات ولی عصر به علماء و مراجع تقلید، قم: لاهیجی، ۱۳۷۹ ش./ ۲۰۰۰ م.

باقی اصفهانی، علی رضا: عنایات حضرت مهدی به علماء و طلاب، قم: انتشارات نصایح، ۱۳۷۹ ش./ ۲۰۰۰ م.

بنیاد فرهنگی حضرت مهدی موعود و پایگاه اطّلاع‌رسانی سراسری اسلامی (پارسا): کتابشناسی، قم: کیمیا، ۱۳۸۲ ش./ ۲۰۰٤ م.

بنیاد فرهنگی حضرت مهدی موعود: امام مهدی در آینهٔ قلم. کارنامهٔ منابع پیرامون امام مهدی و مهدویت، قم: پایگاه اطّلاع رسانی اسلامی مرجع، ۱۳۸۸ ش./ ۲۰۰۹–۲۰۱۰ م.

پویان، مرتضی: معاد جسمانی در حکمت متعالیه. اثبات معاد جسمانی از نگرگاه صدرالمتألهین و نقد دلایل مخالفان، قم: بوستان کتاب قم، ۱۳۸۸ ش./ ۲۰۰۹ م.

تونه‌ای، مجتبی: موعودنامه. فرهنگ الفبایی مهدویت. پیرامون حضرت مهدی، غیبت، انتظار، ظهور و ...، قم: عصر ظهور، ۱۳۸۸ ش./ ۲۰۰۹–۲۰۱۰ م.

جعفری، جواد: دیدار در عصر غیبت، قم: مؤسسهٔ آیندهٔ روشن، ۱۳۸۹ ش./ ۲۰۱۰–۲۰۱۱ م.

جلالی، غلام رضا: فلسفهٔ غیبت در منابع کلامی شیعی، در: چشم به راه مهدی: تألیف جمعی از نویسندگان مجلهٔ حوزه، صص. ٤۰۵-٤۳۹، قم: دفتر تبلیغات اسلامی، ۱۳۷۵ ش./ ۱۹۹٦–۱۹۹۷ م.

جوادی آملی، عبدالله: یاد معاد، مرکز نشر فرهنگی رجاء، ۱۳۷۰ ش./ ۱۹۹۱ م.

حسنی، نرگس: عادات‌ستیزی آثار عین‌القضات همدانی، مجلهٔ علوم انسانی دانشگاه الزهراء، ٦۱–٦۲ (۱۳۸۵ ش./ ۲۰۰٦–۲۰۰۷ م.): صص. ۷۱–۱۰۰.

حسنی، نرگس: سیمای محمّد در آثار عین‌القضات همدانی، مجلهٔ ادبیات عرفانی، ۲ (۱۳۸۹ ش./ ۲۰۱۰ م.): صص. ۲۵–٤۸.

حسنی، نرگس: سیمای ابلیس در آثار عین‌القضات همدانی، مجلهٔ مطالعات عرفانی، ٦ (١٣٨٦ شـ./ ٢٠٠٧ مـ.): صص. ٥-٣٤.

خادمی شیرازی، محمد: جهان بعد از ظهور یا فروغ بی نهایت، [تهران؟]: با همکاری مؤسسهٔ الغدیر، ١٣٧٠ شـ./ ١٩٩١ مـ.

خادمی شیرازی، محمد: نشانه‌های ظهور او، قم: انتشارات مسجد مقدس جمکران، ١٣٨٥ شـ./ ٢٠٠٦-٢٠٠٧ مـ.

خادمی شیرازی، محمد: یاد مهدی، قم: انتشارات مسجد مقدس جمکران، ١٣٨٦ شـ./ ٢٠٠٧-٢٠٠٨ مـ.

خرازی طهرانی، محسن: قیامت. بررسی مستند در اثبات معاد، قم: انتشارات قیام، ١٣٧١ شـ./ ١٩٩٢ مـ.

خرّمشاهی، بهاءالدین: دانشنامهٔ قرآن و قرآن‌پژوهشی، تهران: انتشارات ناهید، ١٣٨١ شـ./ ٢٠٠٢ مـ.

خمینی، روح الله: معاد از دیدگاه امام خمینی (س)، ویرایش فروغ السادات رحیمپور، [تهران]: مؤسسهٔ تنظیم و نشر آثار امام خمینی، ١٣٧٨ شـ./ ١٩٩٩ مـ.

دستغیب، عبد الحسین: بحثهای اصول عقاید. بخش معاد، [تهران]: کانون انتشارات جیبی، بی تا.

دیوانی، امیر: حیات جاودانه: پژوهشی در قلمرو معادشناسی، قم: انتشارات معاونت امور اساتید و دروس معارف اسلامی، ١٣٧٦ شـ./ ١٩٩٧ مـ.

رحمتی شهرضا، محمّد: هزار و یک نکته پیرامون امام زمان علیه السلام، قم: انتشارات مسجد مقدّس جمکران، ١٣٨٧ شـ./ ٢٠٠٨ مـ.

رضوانی، علی اصغر: موعودشناسی و پاسخ به شبهات، ویرایش: احمد سعیدی، قم: انتشارات مسجد مقدس جمکران، ١٣٨٦ شـ./ ٢٠٠٧-٢٠٠٨ مـ.

سبزواری، هادی بن مهدی: معاد در فلسفه و کلام اسلامی. همراه با ترجمه و شرح معاد منظومه، ترجمهٔ مهدی نجفی افرا، تهران: انتشارات جامی، ١٣٨٣ شـ./ ٢٠٠٤-٢٠٠٥ مـ.

سیف، عبدالرضا: زندگی جاوید در مثنوی‌های عرفانی. حدیقة الحقیقة سنایی غزنوی، مثنوی معنوی مولوی، و بوستان سعدی، تهران: دانشگاه تهران، ١٣٨٩ شـ./ ٢٠١٠-٢٠١١ مـ.

شریعتی سبزواری، محمد باقر: معاد در نگاه عقل و دین، قم: مرکز انتشارات دفتر تبلیغات اسلامی، ١٣٨٠ شـ./ ٢٠٠١ مـ.

صمدی، قنبرعلی: بررسی مسألهٔ دیدار با امام زمان در عصر غیبت کبری. مقاله‌ای چاپ شده در کتاب دیدار انتظار خورشید. مجموعهٔ مقالات همایش در انتظار خورشید، صص. ١٧٧-٢٦١، قم: انتشارات مرکز جهانی علوم اسلامی، ١٣٨٥ شـ./ ٢٠٠٦ مـ.

طاهری، حبیب: سیمای آفتاب. سیری در زندگی حضرت مهدی، قم: انتشارات مشهور، ۱۳۷۸ ش./ ۱۹۹۹ م.
طبرسی نوری، میرزا حسین: نجم ثاقب در احوال امام غایب، ۲ جلد، قم: انتشارات مسجد مقدس جمکران، ۱۳۸۷ ش./ ۲۰۰۸ م.
طبسی، نجم الدین: چشم‌اندازی از حکومت مهدی، [تهران]: سازمان تبلیغات اسلامی، ۱۳۷۳ ش./ ۱۹۹۵ م.
عرفانی‌مزدک، فرهاد: غروب آخرین سپیده: داستان قتل عین‌القضات همدانی، مجلهٔ چیستا ۲۲۰ (۱۳۸٤ ش./ ۲۰۰۵ م.): صص. ۷٦۲–۷٦۹.
عسکری راد، حسن: شبی در برزخ، قم: مرکز انتشارات دفتر تبلیغات اسلامی حوزهٔ علمیهٔ قم، ۱۳۷۷ ش./ ۱۹۸۸–۱۹۸۹ م.
عطایی کوزانی، علی: رمز و راز پنهانی: آسیب‌شناسی زمینه‌های ظهور، قم: انتشارات مسجد مقدس جمکران، ۱۳۹۰ ش./ ۲۰۱۱–۲۰۱۲ م.
علیپور، حسین: جلوه‌های پنهانی امام عصر، قم: انتشارات مسجد مقدس جمکران، ۱۳۸۰ ش./ ۲۰۰۱ م.
فتحی، زهرا: پژوهشی در اندیشه‌های عرفانی عین‌القضات همدانی، تهران: انتشارات ترفند، ۱۳۸٤ ش./ ۲۰۰۵ م.
فرمنش، رحیم: احوال و آثار عین‌القضات، تهران: چاپ آفتاب، ۱۳۳۸ ش./ ۱۹۵۹ م.
فلسفیان، عبدالمجید: علی علیه السلام و پایان تاریخ: آخرین امام در نگاه اولین امام، قم: انتشارات مسجد مقدس جمکران، ۱۳۷۹ ش./ ۲۰۰۰ م.
قربانی، زین العادین: به سوی جهان ابدی، قم: انتشارات مؤسسهٔ مطبوعات طباطبائی، ۱۳۸۵ ش./ ۱۹٦۵ م.
قزوینی خراسانی، مجتبی: بیان الفرقان در بیان اصول اعتقادی شیعه، ویراستار: نقی افشاری، قزوین: حدیث امروز، ۱۳۸۷ ش./ ۲۰۰۸–۲۰۰۹ م.
قمی، عباس بن محمد رضا: منازل الآخرة. پیرامون مرگ و جهان پس از مرگ، قم: مؤسسهٔ در راه حق، ۱۳۷۱ ش./ ۱۹۹۲–۱۹۹۳ م.
کمره‌ای، میرزا خلیل: دوازدهمین امام و فلسفهٔ غیبت مهدی، [تهران]: عباس کسائی اردستانی (چاپخانهٔ حیدری)، بی تا.
کورانی عاملی، علی: دانشنامهٔ امام مهدی، تارنما: http://www.alameli.net/books/index.php?book=76&part=1 .
کیاشمشکی، ابوالفضل: راز رستاخیز و کاوشهای عقل نظری، قم: آیات عشق، ۱۳۷۳ ش. / ۲۰۰٤ م.

گلپایگانی، لطف الله: امامت و مهدویت، ۲ جلد، قم: دفتر انتشارات اسلامی، ۱۳۶۵ شـ. /۱۹۸۶ مـ.

گلپایگانی، لطف الله: پاسخ ده پرسش پیرامون امامت و اوصاف حضرت مهدی، قم: انتشارات سپهر، ۱۳۷۵ شـ. / ۱۹۹۶–۱۹۹۷ مـ.

گلپایگانی، محمودی: علائم آخرالزمان: پیرامون ایران و طهران، تهران: مؤسسۀ انتشارات لاهوت، ۱۳۸۲ شـ. / ۲۰۰۳ مـ.

گویا، عبدالعلی: علی (ع) و خطبۀ تطنجیه، تهران: انتشارات زراره، ۱۳۷۹ شـ. / ۲۰۰۰–۲۰۰۱ مـ.

لاهیجی، عبدالرزّاق: رسالۀ نوریّه در عالم مثال، تحقیق: جلال الدین آشتیانی، مشهد: دانشگاه مشهد، ۱۳۵۱ شـ. / ۱۹۷۲ مـ.

مایل هروی، نجیب: خاصّیات آینگی، تهران: نشر نی، ۱۳۸۶ شـ. / ۱۹۹۵ مـ.

مهدی اشتهاردی، محمد: حضرت مهدی: فروغ تابان ولایت، قم: انتشارات مسجد مقدس جمکران، ۱۳۸۶ شـ. / ۲۰۰۷ مـ.

مهدی اشتهاردی، محمد: ده گردنۀ قیامت: بوشهر، موعود اسلام، ۱۳۸۳ شـ. / ۲۰۰۵ مـ.

مرکز فرهنگ و معارف قرآن: پرسمان قرآنی معاد، قم: بوستان کتاب، ۱۳۸٤ شـ. / ۲۰۰۵ مـ.

معظمی، مجتبی: دلبری برگزیده ام. تحقیقی دربارۀ مهدویت و انسان کامل در اشعار حافظ، تهران: مرکز فرهنگ آبا، ۱۳۷۵ شـ. / ۱۹۹۶ مـ.

مکارم شیرازی، ناصر: معاد و جهان پس از مرگ، قم: انتشارات مطبوعات هدف، [۱۳۷٦ شـ. / ۱۹۹۸مـ.].

موسوی اندانی، محمد: روزی دیگر. برزخ و معاد از دیدگاه قرآن و روایات، اصفهان: بوستان فدک، ۱۳۸٤ شـ. / ۲۰۰۵–۲۰۰٦ مـ.

موسوی، محبّ الاسلام: محبوب عالم یا موعود امم. هفده گفتار دربارۀ حضرت ولی عصر صاحب الزمان، تهران: انتشارات منیر، ۱۳۸۲ شـ. / ۲۰۰۳–۲۰۰٤ مـ.

مهدیپور، علی اکبر: کتابنامۀ حضرت مهدی، ۲ جلد، قم: مؤسسۀ چاپ الهادی، ۱۳۷۵ شـ. / ۱۹۹٦ مـ.

نظری منفرد، علی: معاد. روز رستاخیز، تهران: دارالفکر، ۱۳۸۳ شـ. / ۲۰۰٤ مـ.

نوری طبرسی، إسماعیل بن أحمد: کفایة الموحّدین في عقاید الدین، ۲ جلد، قم: شرکت معارف اسلامیه، ۱۳۸۲ شـ. / ۱۹٦۳ مـ.

هاشمی، آصف: بهشتیان و دوزخیان در آینۀ قرآن: قم: زائر، بـ بی تا.

3 Turkish Sources

3.1 *Primary and Secondary Sources*

Abuzerova, Ülker, Ahiret İnancının Ontolojik Açıdan Temellendirilmesi, in *Bakı Devlet Üniversitesi İlahiyyat Fakültesi'nin Elmi Mecmuasi = Bakü Devlet Üniversitesi İlahiyat Fakültesi'nin İlmi Mecmuası* 10 (2008), 178–93.

Akgül, Muhittin, Nûzûl-i Îsâ Meselesinin Tefsir Geleneğine Yansımaları, in *Harran Üniversitesi İlahiyat Fakültesi Dergisi* 11.16 (2006), 43–75.

Altay, Ali Rıza, *Ahirete Giden Yol (Keşf'us-Sutur)*, Istanbul: Sönmez Neşriyat, 1969.

Altıntaş, Ramazan, İslamî Anlayışa Göre "el-Hayâtü'd-Dünyâ" Kavramını Yorumlama Biçimleri, in *Cumhuriyet Üniversitesi İlahiyat Fakültesi Dergisi* 7.1 (2003), 129–59.

Altundağ, Mustafa, Kur'an'da Müşkil Bir Mesele: Cehennem Azabının Ebediliği, in *Bakı Devlet Üniversitesi İlahiyyat Fakültesi'nin Elmi Mecmuasi = Bakü Devlet Üniversitesi İlahiyat Fakültesi'nin İlmi Mecmuası* 7 (2007), 41–88.

Araz, Mehtap, *Ahir Zaman Garipleri*, Istanbul: Sinan Yayınevi, 1996.

Asımgil, Sevim, *Cennet ve Cehennem*, Istanbul: İpek Yayın Dağıtım, 2008.

Aslanbaba, Ramazan, *Ahirete İman*, Istanbul: Sırlar Matbaası, 1961.

Ateş, Süleyman, Cennet Kimsenin Tekelinde Değildir, in *İslâmî Araştırmalar* 3.1 (1989), 8–24.

———, Cennet Tekelcisi mi?, in *İslâmî Araştırmalar* 4.1 (1990), 29–37.

Aydın, Ali Arslan, Ahirete ve Öldükten Sonra Dirilmeye İman [1], in *Diyanet İlmi Dergi* 8.86–87 (1969), 216–21.

———, Ahirette ve Öldükten Sonra Dirilmeye İman [2], in *Diyanet İlmi Dergi* 8.88–89 (1969), 278–80.

Aydın, Mahmut, İsa-Mesih'in Ölümden Dirilmesi Hakikat mi Mitoloji mi? İsa'nın Ölümden Dirilişi ve Taraftarlarına Görülmesiyle İlgili Rivayetlerin Tarihsel Açıdan Değerlendirilmesi, in *Ondokuz Mayıs Üniversitesi İlahiyat Fakültesi Dergisi* 24–25 (2007), 87–116.

Bebek, Adil, Mâtüridî'nin Kelâm Sisteminde Âhiret İnancı, in *Marmara Üniversitesi İlahiyat Fakültesi Dergisi* 19 (2000), 5–41.

Bebek, Ali, Cennet Meyveleri Örneğinde Âhiret Hayatına Kelâmî Bir Bakış, in *Fırat Üniversitesi İlahiyat Fakültesi Dergisi* 10.2 (2005), 1–8.

Bozgeyik, Burhan, *Öldükten Sonra Neler Olacak*, Istanbul: Tuğra Neşriyat, 2011.

Buladı, Kerim, *Kur'ân'ın İnsan Tasavvuru: Kıyamet Süresi Tefsiri*, Istanbul: Pınar Yayınları, 2007.

Bursalı, Mustafa Necati, *Ölüm, Kabir ve Kıyamet*, Istanbul: Erhan Yayıncılık, 1996.

Candan, Ergun, *Kıyamet Alametleri*, Istanbul: Sınır Ötesi Yayınları, 2000.

———, *Ölümden Sonra Neler Oluyor?*, Istanbul: Sınır Ötesi Yayınları, 2007.

Cilacı, Osman, *İlahi Dinlerde Cennet İnancı: Mukayeseli Bir Araştırma*, Istanbul: Beyan Yayınları, 1995.

Çelik, Ahmet, *Cennet ve Cehennem'in Sonsuzluğu*, Erzurum: Kültür Eğitim Vakfı Yayınevi, 2002.

———, Kur'ân'a Göre Ahiret İnancının Bireysel ve Toplumsal Yönü, in *Atatürk Üniversitesi İlahiyat Fakültesi Dergisi* 16 (2001), 173–95.

Çelik, İsa, Türk Tasavvuf Düşüncesinde Ölüm, in *Atatürk Üniversitesi Türkiyat Araştırmaları Enstitüsü Dergisi* 40 (2009), 119–46.

Çolak, Ali, Ölmek Üzere Olan Kişiye ve Mezardaki Ölüye Yapılan Telkin ile İlgili Rivayetler, in *Çukurova Üniversitesi İlahiyat Fakültesi Dergisi* 4.2 (2005), 202–24.

Coşkun, Ahmet, Kur'an-ı Kerim'in Dünya ve Ahirete Bakışı, in *Erciyes Üniversitesi İlahiyat Fakültesi Dergisi* 4 (1987), 267–84.

Dartma, Bahattin, Hz. Âdem'in Dışlandığı Cennetin Dünyası Meselesi, in *Din Bilimleri Akademik Araştırma Dergisi* 9.2 (2009), 11–22.

Demirci, Mehmet, Mutasavviflara Göre Ölüm, in *İslâmî Araştırmalar Dergisi* 1.3 (1986), 89–105.

———, Zâhidlik Nedir, Dünyâ Âhiret Dengesi Nasıl Kurulur?, in *Dokuz Eylül Üniversitesi İlahiyat Fakültesi Dergisi* 4 (1987), 105–28.

Egemen, Bedi Ziya, Ölüm Üzerine, in *Ankara Üniversitesi İlahiyat Fakültesi Dergisi* 11.1 (1963), 31–5.

Elik, Hasan, Kur'an'daki Allah Tasavvuru Açısından Şefâat'e Bakış, in *Din Eğitimi Araştırmaları Dergisi* 16 (2005), 29–48.

Erdoğan, Hüseyin Suudi, *Ölüm ve Ötesi: Kabir – Kıyamet – Ahiret*, Istanbul: Çelik Yayınevi, 1999.

Erdoğan, Naim, *Kıyamet, Âhiret, Ölüm ve Sonrası*, Istanbul: Huzur Yayınevi, 2007.

Eren, Ali, *Ecel, Kıyamet, Âhiret*, Istanbul: Merve Yayınları, 1993.

Eren, Sıddık Naci, *Ölüm, Kıyamet ve Ahiret*, Istanbul: Demir Kitabevi Yayınları, 1995.

Ersöz, Veyis, *Ayet ve Hadisler Işığında Ölüm ve Sonrası*, Istanbul: Kardelen Yayınları, 2009.

Erten, Mevlüt, Kuran'da Ölüm Panoraması (Kıyamet Süresi 26–30: Ayetlerine Yeni Bir Bakış), in *Gümüşhane Üniversitesi İlahiyat Fakültesi Dergisi* 15.1 (2011), 193–214.

Eyyüb, Said, *Deccal Komplosu: Üç Büyük Dini Kaynaaklarına Göre Deccal'ın Üç Bin Yıllık Tarihi*, Istanbul: Sır Yayıncılık, 2000.

Faiz, Ahmet, *Kıyamet ve Ahiret*, Konya: Uysal Kitabevi, 1993.

Faruk Yavuz, Ömer, Kur'an Perspektifinde Dünya-Ahiret Bütünlüğü, in *Din Bilimleri Akademik Araştırma Dergisi* 6.3 (2006), 159–98.

Gölpınarlı, Abdülbakî, *100 Soruda Tasavvuf*, Istanbul: Gerçek Yayınevi, ^{4}1985.

———, *Mevlânâ Celâleddin: Hayatı, Felsefesi, Eserleri, Eserlerinden Seçmeler*, Istanbul: İnkılâp Kitabevi, ^{4}1985.

———, *Mevlânâ'dan sonra Mevlevîlîk*, Istanbul: İnkılâp Kitabevi, 1953.

———, *Yunus Emre: Hayati ve Bütün Şiirleri*, Istanbul: Altin Kitaplar Yayinevi, 1981.

———, *Yunus Emre ve Tasavvuf*, Istanbul: Remzı Kitabevi, 1961.

Görener, İbrahim, Ademin Cennet'ten Yeryüzüne İnişi, in *Bilimname* 8.18 (2010–1), 39–54.

Gülen, M. Fethullah, *Ölüm Ötesi Hayat*, Istanbul: Nil Yayınları, 2005.

Güllüce, Veysel, Kur'ân'da Cennet Çocukları için Kullanılan Vildan ve Gılman Kelimeler, in *EKEV Akademi Dergisi: Sosyal Bilimler* 10.27 (2006), 65–80.

Güngör, Mevlüt, Kur'an Bağlamında İslâm Öncesi Mekke Toplumundaki Tanrı ve Ahiret İnancı, in *Dinî Araştırmalar* 8.23 (2005), 13–28.

Gürkan, Salime Leyla, Yahudi ve İslâm Kutsal Metinlerinde İnsan'ın Yaratılışı ve Cennet'ten Düşüş, in *İslâm Araştırmaları Dergisi* 9 (2003), 1–48.

Hatip, Abdulaziz, *Dünya Ötesi Yolculuk*, Istanbul: Gençlik Yayınları, 1994.

Haznedaroğlu, Ömer Faruk, *Ölüm, Kabir, Kıyamet, Mahşer*, Istanbul: Medine Yayıncılık, 2001.

Hekimoğlu, İsmail, *Ahiret Gününe İman*, Istanbul: Timaş Yayınları, 2005.

———, *Ölüm Yokluk mudur?*, Istanbul: Timaş Yayınları, 2011.

Hilmi, Ömer Faruk, *Ölüm Kabir Kıyamet ve Âhiret: Cennet ve Cehennem*, Istanbul: Sultan Yayınevi, 2012.

Hökelekli, Hayati, Ölüm ve Ölüm Ötesi Psikolojisi, in *Uludağ Üniversitesi İlahiyat Fakültesi Dergisi* 2.3 (1991), 151–65.

———, Ölümle İlgili Tutumlar ve Dinî Davranış, in *İslâmî Araştırmalar Dergisi* 5.2 (1991), 83–91.

———, Ölümle İlgili Tutumların Dinî Davranışla İlişkisi Üzerine Bir Araştırma, in *Uludağ Üniversitesi İlahiyat Fakültesi Dergisi* 4.4 (1992), 57–85.

İmamoğlu, Vahit, Uyku ve Ölümün Tabiatıyla İlgili Çağdaş Müslüman Yorumlarda Nefs ve Ruh Anlayışı, in *Atatürk Üniversitesi İlahiyat Fakültesi Dergisi* 13 (1997), 231–45.

Kara, Ömer, Kur'ân'da "Âdem Cenneti", in *EKEV Akademi Dergisi: Sosyal Bilimler* 1.3 (1998), 77–111.

Karaca, Faruk, *Ölüm Psikolojisi*, Istanbul: Beyan Yayınları, 2000.

Karakaş, Vehbi, *Kıyamet Yaklaşıyor*, Istanbul: Tüdav Basım Yayın, 1995.

Karaman, Hayrettin, *Ebediyet Yolcusunu Uğurlarken*, Ankara: Türkiye Diyanet Vakfı Yayınları, ^{3}1988.

Karlık, Halil, İslam'ın Dünya ve Ahiret Anlayışı, in *Diyanet İlmi Dergi* (*Özel Sayı*) 25.4 (1989), 373–7.

Kemal, Osmanbey, *Ruh Aleminde Bir Seyahat*, Istanbul: Kıtsan Basım Yayın, 1995.

Kesler, M. Fatih, Kur'ân-ı Kerim ve Hadislerde Şefaat İnancı, in *Tasavvuf: İlmî ve Akademik Araştırma Dergisi* 5.13 (2004), 119–53.

Köşk, Said, *Ayetlerle Ölüm ve Diriliş*, Istanbul: Kahraman Yayınları, 1993.

———, *Kur'an'da Kıyamet Sahneleri*, Istanbul: Kahraman Yayınları, 1998.

Kotku, Mehmet Zahid, *Cennet Yolları* (*Hadislerle İlim*), Istanbul: Seha Neşriyat, 1985.

Küçüker, Ali, *İman Nurları: Ahiret Sırları*, Istanbul: Bahar Yayınları, 1987.

Murat, Mustafa, *Kur'an ve Sünnet ışığında Ahiret Yolculuğu: Ölüm, Kabir ve Kıyamet Alametleri*, Istanbul: Beka Yayınları, 2011.
Musaoğlu, Ahmet, *Kıyamet: Ölüm Yeniden Doğuş İçin*, Istanbul: Okul Yayınları, 2004.
Mutlu, İsmail, *Bediüzzaman'ın Görüşleri Işığında Ölüm – Cenaze – Kabir*, Istanbul: Mutlu Yayıncılık, 1993.
———, *Kıyamet Alametleri: Bediüzzaman'ın Yorumları Işığında Kıyamet Alametleri*, Istanbul: Mutlu Yayıncılık, 1996.
Nasih, Abdülhay, *Ölüm Ötesi Hayat*, Izmir: Nil Yayınları, 1993.
Oğuz, Ihsan Muhammed, *Dünya ve Ahiret Hayatı*, Istanbul: Oğuz Yayınları, 1994.
Okuyan, Mehmet, *Kur'ân-ı Kerîm'e Göre Kabir Azabı Var Mı?*, Samsun: Etüt Yayınları, 2007.
Oral, Osman, *100 Soruda Ahiret Hayatı*, Istanbul: Işık Yayınları, 2003.
———, *Ahiret Gününe İnanıyorum*, Istanbul: Muştu Yayınları, 2010.
Özarslan, Selim, Ahiret İnancının İnsanın Anlam Arayışına Müspet Katkısı, in *Fırat Üniversitesi İlahiyat Fakültesi Dergisi* 5 (2000), 295–307.
Özbek, Yusuf, *Hadislerde Cehennem*, Istanbul: Ocak Yayınları, 2006.
Özdamar, Mustafa, *Huvel Bâkî: Ölümü Herkes Tadacak*, Istanbul: Kırk Kandil Yayınları, 1996.
Özhazar, Hüseyin, *Ahiret Bilinci*, Istanbul: Çıra Yayınları, 2007.
Öztürk, Mustafa, Adem, Cennet ve Düşüş, in *Milel ve Nihal: Inanç, kültür ve mitoloji araştırmaları dergisi* 1.2 (2004), 151–86.
———, İblis'in Trajik Hikayesi: Allah, Şeytan, İnsan ve Kötülüğe Dair, in *Çukurova Üniversitesi İlahiyat Fakültesi Dergisi* 5.1 (2005), 39–65.
———, Kur'an'ın Cennet Betimlemelerinde Yerel ve Tarihsel Motifler, in *İslâmiyât Dergisi* 4.1 (2001), 145–62.
———, Kur'an'ın Değer Sisteminde Dünya ve Dünyevi Hayatın Anlamı, in *Tasavvuf: İlmî ve Akademik Araştırma Dergisi* 7.16 (2006), 65–86.
———, Kur'an'da Uhrevi Azap Figürleri, in *İslâmiyât Dergisi* 5.1 (2002), 233–59.
Öztürk, Yener, Şefaat İnancının Naklî ve Aklî Açıdan İmkânı, in *EKEV Akademi Dergisi: Sosyal Bilimler* 9.23 (2005), 103–22.
Paçacı, Mehmet, *Kur'an'da ve Kitab-ı Mukaddes'te Ahiret İnancı*, Istanbul: Nûn Yayınları, 1994.
———, *Kutsal Kitaplarda Ölümötesi*, Istanbul: Ankara Okulu Yayınları, 2001.
Paksu, Mehmed, *Ölüm ve Sonrası*, Istanbul: Nesil Yayınları, 1997.
Sâdık, Dânâ, *Ahiret Hazırlığı*, Istanbul: Erkam Yayınları, 1991.
Safvet, Senih, *Ölüm ve Diriliş*, Istanbul: Işık Yayınları, 2004.
Saka, Şevki, Müminler Cehennem'e Girer mi?, in *Ankara Üniversitesi İlahiyat Fakültesi Dergisi* 41.1 (2000), 29–42.
Salih, Subhi, *Ölümden Sonra Diriliş: Âyet ve Hadislerle Cennet-Cehennem*, Istanbul: Kayıhan Yayınları, 2004.

Samedoğlu, Yusuf, *Kıyamet Günü*, Istanbul: Ötüken Neşriyat, 1995.

Sarıtoprak, Zeki, Deccâl: İslâmiyet'te Deccâl, in Türkiye Diyanet Vakfı (ed.), *İslam Ansiklopedisi*, ix, Istanbul: Türkiye Diyanet Vakfı Yayın Matbaacılık ve Ticaret İşletmesi, 1994, 69–72.

———, *İslâm inancı açısından Nüzûl-i Îsâ meselesi*, Istanbul: Nil Yayınları, 1997.

———, *İslama ve Diğer Dinlere Göre Deccal*, Istanbul: Nesil Yayınları, 1999.

Sarmış, İbrahim, *Hz. İsa ve Mesih İnancı*, Istanbul: Ekin Yayınları, 2007.

Sayar, Süleyman, Cehennem, in Ahmet Cevizci (ed.), *Felsefe Ansiklopedisi*, iii, Istanbul: Ebabil Yayıncılık, 2004, 109–25.

Seyhan, Ahmet Emin, *Hadislerde Kıyamet Alametleri, Envaru'l-Aşıkin Örneğinden*, Isparta 2006.

Smith, I. Jane, Uyku ve Ölümün Tabiatıyla İlgili Çağdaş Müslüman Yorumlarda Nefs ve Ruh Anlayışı, trans. Vahit İmamoğlu, in *Atatürk Üniversitesi İlahiyat Fakültesi Dergisi* 13 (1997), 231–46

Soysaldı, Mehmet, Kuran-ı Kerim'e Göre Ahiret İnancı, in *Fırat Üniversitesi İlahiyat Fakültesi Dergisi* 1 (1996), 43–67.

Sunar, Cavit, *Kıyamet – Cennet – Cehennem*, Ankara: Kılıç Kitabevi, 1979.

Şah Yasdıman, Hakkı, İslami Literatürde İsrailiyyat İzleri: Cennet'in Kaybı, in *Dokuz Eylül Üniversitesi İlahiyat Fakültesi Dergisi* 2.34 (2011), 37–64.

Şener, Abdullah Naim, *Kıyâmet Alâmetleri*, Istanbul: Dilek Matbaası, 1984.

Şensoy, Yusuf, *Ahirete Açılan Kapı Kabir*, Istanbul: Furkan Yayınları, 1996.

Şentürk, Habil, Ölüm Gerçeği ve Allah İnancı, in *Dokuz Eylül Üniversitesi İlahiyat Fakültesi Dergisi* 1.1 (1983), 303–12.

Tamor, Ahmet, *Dünya ve Ahiret*, Adapazarı: Erkam Yayınları, 1998.

Taşdemir, Ahmet, Müslüman Çocukların Ahiretteki Durumları, in *Kelam Araştırmaları Dergisi* 11.1 (2013), 501–9.

Taştekin, Osman, *Kıyâmet ve Âhiretle İlgili Kavramların Öğretimi*, Samsun: Palmiya Kitapları, 2002.

Tavaslı, Yusuf, *Ölüm Öncesi ve Sonrası Kıyamet ve Ahiret: Âyet ve Hadisler Işığında Cennet ve Cehennem*, Istanbul: Tavaslı Yayınları, 2009.

Tekin, Mehmet, *Kur'an'ı Kerim'e Göre Cennet ve Cehennem*, Kayseri: Emel Matbaacılık, 1982.

Tekin, Serkan, *Kur'an'da Kıyamet Alametleri*, Istanbul: Liman Kitaplar, 2006.

Topaloğlu, Bekir, Âhiret, in Türkiye Diyanet Vakfı (ed.), *İslam Ansiklopedisi*, i, Istanbul: Türkiye Diyanet Vakfı Yayın Matbaacılık ve Ticaret İşletmesi, 1988, 543–8.

———, Cennet, in Türkiye Diyanet Vakfı (ed.), *İslam Ansiklopedisi*, vii, Istanbul: Türkiye Diyanet Vakfı Yayın Matbaacılık ve Ticaret İşletmesi, 1993, 376–86.

Toprak, Süleyman, *Ölümden Sonraki Hayat: Kabir Hayatı*, Istanbul: Esra Yayınları, 1997.

Tunçbilek, Hasan Hüseyin, Cennet ve Cehennem Halen Mevcut mu?, in *Dicle Üniversitesi İlahiyat Fakültesi Dergisi* 7.2 (2005), 53–62.

———, İslâm Düşüncesinde Cehennemin ve Cehennem Azabının Ebediyeti ve Fenası Problemi, in *Çukurova Üniversitesi İlahiyat Fakültesi Dergisi* 6.1 (2006), 15–33.

Uludağ, Süleyman, Ölüm ve Ötesi, in *Köprü Dergisi* 76 (2001), 50–61.

Ülkü, Kübra, *Kıyamet Alametleri ve Ahir Zaman Fitneleri*, Istanbul: Yasin Yayınevi, 2009.

Ünal, Mustafa, Ölüm Sonrası Hayata Bir Tür Giriş Töreni Olarak "Telkin" Uygulamasına Fenomenolojik Bir Bakış, in *Erciyes Üniversitesi İlahiyat Fakültesi Dergisi* 10 (1998), 163–8.

Ünverdi, Mustafa, Kuranda Ahiret İnancı Bağlamında Adana ve Hatay Bölgesindeki Tenasüh ve Reenkarnasyon İnançlarının Değerlendirilmesi, in *Çukurova Üniversitesi İlahiyat Fakültesi Dergisi* 4.2 (2004), 277–300.

Yahya, Harun, *Kıyamet Günü*, Istanbul: Vural Yayıncılık, 2005.

———, *Mehdi ve Altın Çağ: İslam Ahlakının Dünya Hakimiyeti*, Istanbul: Vural Yayıncılık, 1989.

Yalçın, Cavit, *Ölüm, Kıyamet, Cehennem*, Istanbul: Vural Yayıncılık, 2005.

Yar, Erkan, Diriliş Kuramları ve Gerçeklik Bağlamında Kur'an'ın Ahiret Hakkındaki Anlatımları, in *Dinî Araştırmalar* 9.25 (2006), 43–60.

Yargıcı, Said A., Kur'an Ölümden Niçin Bahsediyor?, in *Köprü Dergisi* 76 (2001), 26–31.

Yavuz, Ömer Faruk, *Kur'an ve Kıyamet*, Istanbul: Marifet Yayınları, 1997.

Yavuz, Yusuf Şevki, Kıyâmet Alâmetleri, in Türkiye Diyanet Vakfı (ed.), *İslam Ansiklopedisi*, xxv, Istanbul: Türkiye Diyanet Vakfı Yayın Matbaacılık ve Ticaret İşletmesi, 2002, 522–5.

Yazıcı, Olcay, *Büyük Gün: Hazret-i İsa'nın Dönüşü*, Istanbul: Marifet Yayınları, 2001.

Yıldız, Murat, *Ölüm Kaygısı ve Dindarlık*, Izmir: İzmir İlahiyat Vakfı Yayınları, 2006.

Yılmaz, Ali, Kur'ân-ı Kerîm'de "Yevm/Gün" Kavramıyla Zikredilen Âhiret İsimleri, in *Atatürk Üniversitesi İlahiyat Fakültesi Dergisi* 16 (2001), 141–71.

Yunal, Abbas, *Ah Şu Ölüm Dedikleri*, Konya: Uysal Kitabevi, 1997.

Yüksel, Emrullah, İslâm'da Şefaat Yetkisi, in *İstanbul Üniversitesi İlahiyat Fakültesi Dergisi* 5 (2002), 17–31.

———, Mutlak Adâletin Tecelli Edeceği İnancı (Âhiret), in *İstanbul Üniversitesi İlahiyat Fakültesi Dergisi* 3 (2001), 17–29.

3.2 *Turkish Translations of Arabic Sources*

Berzenci, Muhammed b. Resul el-Hüseyni. *Kıyamet Alametleri*, trans. Naim Erdoğan, Istanbul: Pamuk Yayınları, 1977.

Birgivi, İmam Muhammed, *Cennet Bahçeleri*, trans. Mehmed Emre, Istanbul: Çile Yayınları, 1976.

Çelebi, Mahmud, *Cennetteki Hayat*, trans. İsmet Ersöz, Istanbul: Sultan Yayınevi, 1976.

Gazâli, İmam *Ölüm ve Sonrası: Kabir, Kıyamet, Ahiret*, trans. Hüseyin Okur, Istanbul: Semerkand Yayınları, 2004.

İbn Kesîr, *Ölüm Ötesi Tarihi*, trans. Mehmet Keskin, Istanbul: Çağrı Yayınları, 2001.

İbn Miskeveyh, Ölüm Korkusu, Mahiyeti ve Nefsin Ölümden Sonraki Durumu, trans. İbrahim Aslan, in *Ankara Üniversitesi İlahiyat Fakültesi Dergisi* 52.2 (2011), 327–32.

İbnu'l-Kayyîm el-Cevziye, *Cennetin Tasviri*, trans. İsmail Hakkı Sezer, Konya: Uysal Kitabevi, 1994.

Kutub, Seyyid, *Kur'ân'da Kıyamet Sahneleri (Cennet-Cehennem)*, trans. Süleyman Ateş, Istanbul: Hilal Yayınları, 1969.

Suyuti, İmam, *Kıyamet Alametleri Ölüm ve Diriliş*, trans. Abdullah Aydın, Istanbul: Seda Yayınları, 2000.

Suyûti, İmam Cemaleddin, *Kabir Alemi*, trans. Bahaeddin Sağlam, Istanbul: Kahraman Yayınları, 2012.

Şe'ranî, İmam, *Ölüm, Kıyâmet, Âhiret ve Âhir Zaman Alametleri*, trans. Halil Günaydın, Istanbul: Bedir Yayınları, 2011.

4 Sources in European Languages

Abdel Haleem, M., Life and beyond in the Qur'an, in C. Lewis and D. Cohn-Sherbok (eds.), *Beyond death*, London 1995, 66–79.

Abdesselem, M., Mawt, in EI², vi, 910–1.

Abel, A., al-Dadjdjāl, in EI², ii, 76–7.

Abrahamov, B., The creation and duration of paradise and hell in Islamic theology, in *Der Islam* 79 (2002), 87–102.

Abu-Deeb, K., *The imagination unbound:* Al-adab al-ʿaja'ibi *and the literature of the fantastic in the Arabic tradition*, London 2007 (including a critical edition of *Kitāb al-ʿAẓama (The book of greatness)*, 67–163).

Abu-Lughod, L., Islam and the gendered discourses of death, in IJMES 25.2 (1993), 187–205.

Adhami, S., The conversion of the Japanese emperor to Islam: A study of Central Asian eschatology, in *Central Asiatic Journal* 43.1 (1999), 1–9.

Afsaruddin, A., Garden, in EQ, ii, 282–7.

———, *Striving in the path of God: Jihad and martyrdom in Islamic thought*, Oxford 2013.

Aghaei, K.S., *The martyrs of Karbala: Shiʿi symbols and rituals in modern Iran*, Seattle and London 2004.

Ağır, A. and T. Okçuoğlu, The art of eternal rest: Ottoman mausoleums and tombstones, in A. Fabris (ed.), *Tra quattro paradisi: Esperienze, ideologie e riti reltivi all morte tra Oriente e Occidente*, Venice 2013, 129–47.

Aguade, J., *Messianismus zur Zeit der frühen ʿAbbāsiden: Das "Kitāb al-fitan" des Nuʿaim b. Ḥammād*, PhD dissertation, University of Tübigen 1979.

Ahmad, B., An observation on Mullā Ṣadrā's ideas of the posthumous existence and its relev[a]nce in the recent study on near death experience, in World Congress on Mulla Sadra (ed.), *Islam-West philosophical dialogue: The papers presented at the World Congress on Mulla Sadra (May, 1999, Tehran)*, x, *Eschatology, exegesis, hadith*, Tehran 2005, 247–56.

Ahmed, Ahmed al-, *Untersuchungen zu al-Qurṭubīs (st. 1273) «Memorandum über die Verhältnisse der Toten und die Angelegenheiten des Jenseits»: Ein Beitrag zur Erforschung der islamischen eschatologischen Literatur und der islamischen Jenseitsvorstellungen*, Cologne 2007.

Aijaz, I., Belief, providence and eschatology: Some philosophical problems in Islamic theism, in *Philosophy Compass* 3 (2008), 231–53.

Akintola, I., The soul in Islamic eschatology, in World Congress on Mulla Sadra (ed.), *Islam-West philosophical dialogue: The papers presented at the World Congress on Mulla Sadra (May, 1999, Tehran)*, x, *Eschatology, exegesis, hadith*, Tehran 2005, 285–94.

Alexander, P.S., Jewish tradition in early Islam: The case of Enoch/Idrīs, in G.R. Hawting, J.A. Mojaddedi and A. Samely (eds.), *Studies in Islamic and middle eastern texts and traditions in memory of Norman Calder*, Oxford and New York 2000, 11–29.

Algar, H., Burial in Islam, in *EIr*, iv, 563–5.

———, Dajjāl, in *EIr*, vi, 603–6.

———, Eblīs, in *EIr*, vii, 656–61.

——— (trans.), *Najm al-Dīn Rāzī: The path of God's bondsmen from origin to return: A Sufi compendium*, Delmar 1982.

Allen, T., *Imagining paradise in Islamic art*, Occidental, CA, 1995. (Online publication, http://sonic.net/~tallen/palmtree/ip.html, accessed 18 February 2010).

Almond, I., Two versions of Islam and the apocalypse: The persistence of eschatology in Schlegel, Baudrillard and Zizek, in *Journal for Cultural Research* 13.3–4 (2009), 309–21.

Amanat, A., Apocalyptic anxieties and millennial hopes in the salvation religions of the Middle East, in A. Amanat and M.T. Bernhardsson (eds.), *Imagining the end: Visions of apocalypse from the ancient Middle East to modern America*, London and New York 2002, 1–22.

———, The resurgence of the apocalyptic in modern Islam, in S.J. Stein (ed.), *The encyclopedia of apocalypticism*, iii, *Apocalypticism in the modern period and the contemporary age*, New York 1999, 230–64.

Amir-Moezzi, M.A., Aspects de la figure du sauveur dans l'eschtologie chiite duodécimaine, in J.-C. Attias et al. (eds.), *Messianismes: Variations sur une figure juive*, Geneva 2000, 213–28.

———, Cosmogony and cosmology v. In Twelver Shiʿism, in *EIr*, vi, 317–22.

———, *The divine guide in early Shīʿism*, trans D. Streight, Albany, NY 1994.

———, Eschatologie et initiation dans le Shiʿisme Imamite, in A. Shishmanian and D. Shishmanian (eds.), *Ascension et hypostases initiatiques de l'âme: Mystique et eschatologie à travers les traditions religieuses*, i, Paris 2006, 447–56.

———, Eschatology iii. In Imami Shiʿism, in *EIr*, vi, 575–81.

———, Fin du temps et retour à l'origine, in M. Garcia-Arenal (ed.), *Mahdisme et millénarisme en Islam*, Aix-en-Provence 2001, 53–72.

———, *Le guide divine dans le shīʿisme originel: Aux sources de l'ésotérisme en Islam*, Lagrasse 1992.

———, Islam in Iran vii: The concept of mahdi in Twelver Shiʿism, in *EIr*, xiv, 136–43.

———, Remarques sur la divinité de l'imām (aspects de l'imamologie duodécimaine i), in *Arabica* 45 (1998), 193–216.

———, Seul l'homme de Dieu est humain: Theologie et anthropologie mystique à travers l'exégèse imamite ancienne (aspects de l'imamologie duodécimaine iv), in *Arabica* 45 (1998), 193–214.

———, *The spirituality of Shiʿi Islam: Beliefs and practices*, London 2011.

——— (ed.), *Le voyage initiatique en terre d'Islam: Ascensions célestes et itinéraires spirituels*, Leuven et al. 1996.

Amri, N., *Les saints en Islam, les messagers de l'espérance: Sainteté et eschatologie au Maghreb aux XIVe et XVe siècles*, Paris 2008.

——— and D. Gril (eds.), *Saint et sainteté dans le christianisme et l'islam: Le regard des sciences de l'homme*, Paris 2007.

Anawati, G.C., Un cas typique de l'ésotérisme avicennien: Sa doctrine de la résurrection des corps, in *La Revue du Caire* 27 (1951), 68–94; repr. in G.C. Anawati, *Etudes de philosophie musulmane*, Paris 1974, 263–89.

Anthony, S., The Mahdī and the treasures of al-Ṭālaqān, in *Arabica* 59 (2012), 459–83.

Aquinas, T., *On the unity of the intellect against the Averroists*, trans. B. Zedler, Wisconsin 1968.

Ara, M., *Eschatology in the Indo-Iranian traditions: The genesis and transformation of a doctrine*, New York 2008.

Aries, W.D., Eschatologisch orientierte Verantwortung angesichts von Tod und Gericht aus muslimischer Perspektive, in H. Bedford-Strohm (ed.), *«… und das Leben der zukünftigen Welt»: Von Auferstehung und Jüngstem Gericht*, Neukirchen-Vluyn 2007, 109–13.

Arjomand, S.A., The consolation of theology: Absence of the imam and the transition from chiliasm to law in Shiʿism, in *Journal of Religion* 76.4 (1996), 548–71.

———, Islam in Iran. VI. The concept of Mahdi in Sunni Islam, in *EIr*, xiv, 134–6.

———, Islamic apocalypticism in the classical period, in B. McGinn (ed.), *The encyclopedia of apocalypticism*, ii, New York 1998, 238–83.

———, Messianism, millennialism and revolution in early Islamic history, in A. Amanat and M. Bernhardsson (eds.), *Imagining the end: Visions of apocalypse from the ancient Middle East to modern America*, London 2002, 106–25.

———, Millennial beliefs, hierocratic authority and revolution in Shi'ite Iran, in S. Amir Arjomand (ed.), *The political dimensions of religion*, Albany, NY 1993, 219–42.

———, *The shadow of God and the hidden Imam*, Chicago 1984.

Arkoun, M. et al. (eds.), *L'étrange et le merveilleux dans l'Islam médiéval: Actes du colloque tenu au Collège de France à Paris, en mars 1974*, Paris 1978.

Arnaldez, R., Khalk, in EI², iv, 980–8.

———, Ḳidam, in EI², v, 95–9.

———, Maʿād, in EI², v, 892–4.

———, Rudjūʿ, in EI², viii, 587–8.

———, Suḳrāṭ, in EI², ix, 806.

Arnold, T. (trans.), *Der Koran, Oder insgemein so genannte Alcoran des Mohammeds: Unmittelbahr aus dem Arabischen Original in das Englische übersetzt, und mit beygefügten, aus den bewährtesten Commentatoribus genommenen Erklärungs-Noten, Wie auch einer Vorläuffigen Einleitung versehen / Von George Sale... Aufs treulichste wieder ins Teutsche verdollmetscht Von Theodor Arnold*, Lemgo 1746.

Asín Palacios, M., *La escatología musulmana en la Divina Comedia*, Madrid 1919, 1984².

———, *Islam and the Divine Comedy*, trans. H. Sutherland, London 1968.

Attema, D.S., *De Mohammedaansche opvattingen omtrent het tijdstip van den jongsten dag en zijn voorteekenen*, Amsterdam 1942.

Auffarth, C., *Irdische Wege und himmlischer Lohn: Kreuzzug, Jerusalem und Fegefeuer in religionswissenschaftlicher Perspektive*, Göttingen 2002.

Awn, P.J., *Satan's tragedy and redemption: Iblîs in Sufi psychology*, Leiden 1983.

Ayoub, M., Divine preordination and human hope: A study of the concept of *badāʾ* in Imāmī Shīʿī tradition, in *JAOS* 106.4 (1986), 623–32.

———, *Redemptive suffering in Islām: A study of the devotional aspects of ʿĀshūrāʾ in Twelver Shīʿism*, The Hague 1978.

al-Azmeh, A., Rhetoric for the senses: A consideration of Muslim paradise narratives, in *JAL* 26 (1995), 215–31.

———, Rhétorique des sens: une réflexion sur les récits du paradis musulman, in *Cahiers Intersignes* 11–12 (1998), 75–90.

Bacharach, J.L., *Laqab* for a future caliph: The case of the ʿAbbāsid al-Mahdī, in *JAOS* 113 (1993), 271–4.

Badakhchani, S. (trans.), *Paradise of submission: A medieval treatise on Ismaili thought: A new Persian edition and English translation of Naṣīr al-Dīn al-Ṭūsī's* Rawḍa-yi taslīm, London 2005.

———, *Shiʿi interpretations of Islam: Three treatises on theology and eschatology*, London 2010.

Badawi, ʿA., *Le problème de la mort dans la philosophie existentielle*, Cairo 1964.

Baker, P.L., Fabrics fit for angels, in K. Dévényi and A. Fodor (eds.), *Proceedings of the colloquium on paradise and hell in Islam, Keszthely, 7–14 July 2002*, Budapest 2008 (= *The Arabist* 28–29 (2008)), 1–18.

Baljon, J.M.S., *Modern Muslim Koran interpretation (1880–1960)*, Leiden 1961.

———, *A mystical interpretation of prophetic tales by an Indian Muslim: Shāh Walī Allāh's* Taʾwīl al-aḥādīth, Leiden 1973.

———, *Religion and thought of Shāh Walī Allāh Dihlawī, 1703–1762*, Leiden 1986.

Ballanfant, P., *Le dévoilement des secrets et les apparitions des lumières: Journal spirituel du maître de Shîrâz*, Paris 1996.

——— and Abu Muhammad ibn Abi Nasr Fasʾi Shirazi Ruzbehan Baqli, *Quatre traités inédits de Ruzbehān Baqlī Shīrāzī*, Tehran and Leuven 1998.

Bamberger, B., A Messianic document of the seventh century, in *Hebrew Union College Annual* 15 (1940), 425–31.

Bar-Asher, M., Exegesis ii. In Shiʿism, in *EIr*, ix, 116–9.

———, *Scripture and exegesis in early Imāmī Shiism*, Leiden, Boston and Cologne 1999.

Barceló, M., El califa patente: El ceremonial omeya de Córdoba o la escenificación del poder, in R. Pastor (ed.), *Estructuras y formas de poder en la historia*, Salamanca 1991, 51–71, repr. in A. Vallejo Triano (ed.), *Madīnat al-Zahrāʾ: El salón de ʿAbd al-Rahman III*, Cordoba 1995, 155–75.

———, *Al-Mulk*, el verde y el blanco: La vajilla califal omeya de Madīnat al-Zahrāʾ, in A. Malpica Cuello (ed.), *La cerámica altomedieval en el si de al-Andalus*, Granada 1993, 291–9.

———, *El sol que salió por Occidente: Estudios sobre el estado omeya en al-Andalus*, Jaén 1997.

Barrucand, M., Gärten und gestaltete Landschaft als irdisches Paradies: Gärten im westlichen Islam, in *Der Islam* 65 (1988), 244–67.

Bashear, S., Apocalyptic and other materials on early Muslim-Byzantine wars: A review of Arabic sources, in *JRAS (Third Series)* 1.2 (1991), 173–207.

———, Muslim apocalypses and the hour: A case study in traditional reinterpretation, in *IOS* 13 (1993), 75–99.

———, Riding beasts on divine missions, in *JSS* 37 (1991), 37–75.

Bashier, S., *Ibn al-ʿArabī's* barzakh: *The concept of the limit and the relationship between God and the world*, New York 2004.

Bashir, S., After the messiah: The Nurbakhshiyya in late Timurid and early Safavid times, in A. Newman (ed.), *Society and culture in the early modern Middle East: Studies on Iran in the Safavid period*, Leiden 2003, 295–313.

———, Deciphering the cosmos from creation to apocalypse: The Hurufiyya movement and Medieval Islamic esotericism, in A. Amanat and M. Bernhardsson (eds.),

Imagining the end: Visions of apocalypse from the ancient Middle East to contemporary America, London 2002, 168–84.
———, Enshrining divinity: The death and memorialization of Fażlallāh Astarābādī in Ḥurūfī thought, *MW* 90 (2000), 289–308.
———, Eternity, in *EQ*, ii, 54–5.
———, *Fazlallah Astarabadi and the Hurufis*, Oxford 2005.
———, The Imam's return: Messianic leadership in late medieval Shiʿism, in L.S. Walbridge (ed.), *The most learned of the Shiʿa: The institution of the Marjaʿ Taqlid*, New York 2001, 21–33.
———, *Messianic hopes and mystical visions: The Nūrbakhshīya between medieval and modern Islam*, Columbia 2003.
Bauer, T., Islamische Totenbücher, in S. Leder, H. Kilpatrick, B. Martel-Thoumian and H. Schönig (eds), *Studies in Arabic and Islam: Proceedings of the 19th congress, Union Européenne des Arabisants et Islamisants, Halle 1998*, Leuven 2002, 421–36.
Beaumont, D., Simile, in *EQ*, v, 13–8.
Beck, E., Eine christliche Parallele zu den Paradiesesjungfrauen des Korans?, in *Orientalia Christiana Periodica* 14 (1948), 398–405.
———, Les Houris du Coran et Ephrem le Syrien, in *MIDEO* 6 (1959–1961), 405–8.
Behrens-Abouseif, D., Cups and vessels, in *EQ*, i, 489–91.
Beltz, W., *Sehnsucht nach dem Paradies: Mythologie des Korans*, Berlin 1979.
Bencheikh, J.E., Miʿradj in Arabic literature, in EI^2, vii, 100–3.
———, *Le voyage nocturne de Mahomet*, Paris 1988.
Bennett, A., Reincarnation, sect unity, and identity among the Druze, in *Ethnology* 45 (2006), 87–104.
Berkey, J.P., *Popular preaching and religious authority in the medieval Islamic Near East*, Seattle 2001.
Bernardini, M., Hašt Behešt (2), in *EIr*, xii, 49–51.
Bernardo, A.S., Dante's Divine Comedy: The view from God's eye, in W. De Sua and G. Rizzo (eds.), *A Dante symposium: In commemoration of the 700th anniversary of the poet's birth (1265–1965)*, Chapel Hill, NC 1965, 45–58.
——— and A.L. Pellegrini, *A critical study guide to Dante's Divine Comedy*, Totowa, NJ and Los Angeles 1968.
Berthels, E.P., Die paradiesischen Jungfrauen (Ḥūrīs) im Islam, in *Islamica* 1 (1925), 263–88.
Bevan, A.A., Mohammed's ascension into heaven, in *Beihefte zur Zeitschrift für Alttestamentliche Wissenschaft* 27 (1914), 51–61.
Bijlefeld, W.A., Eschatology: Some Muslim and Christian data, in *Islam and Christian-Muslim Relations* 15 (2004), 35–54.
Bjorling, J., *Reincarnation: A bibliography*, New York and London 1996.
Blair, S.S., Ascending to heaven: Fourteenth-century illustrations of the Prophet's *miʿraǧ*, in K. Dévényi and A. Fodor (eds.), *Proceedings of the colloquium on paradise*

and hell in Islam, Keszthely, 7–14 July 2002, Budapest 2008 (= *The Arabist* 28–29 (2008)), 19–26.

——— and J.M. Bloom (eds.), *Images of paradise in Islamic art*, Hannover 1991.

Blichfeldt, J., *Early Mahdism: Politics and religion in the formative period of Islam*, Leiden 1985.

Blochet, E, *Le Messianisme dans l'heterodoxie musulman*, Paris 1903.

Bloom, J.M., Paradise as a garden, the Garden as garden, in K. Dévényi and A. Fodor (eds.), *Proceedings of the colloquium on paradise and hell in Islam, Keszthely, 7–14 July 2002*, Budapest 2008 (= *The Arabist* 28–29 (2008)), 37–54.

Börner, K.H., *Auf der Suche nach dem irdischen Paradies: Zur Ikonographie der geographischen Utopie*, Frankfurt am Main 1984.

Borrmans, M., Resurrection, in *EQ*, iv, 434–43.

Bosworth, C.E., Zaḳḳūm, in *EI*², xi, 425–6.

Böwering, G., The concept of time in Islam, in *Proceedings of the American Philosophical Society* 141.1 (1997), 55–66.

———, Ibn ʿArabi's concept of time, in J.C. Bürgel and A. Giese (eds.), *Gott ist schön und Er liebt die Schönheit: Festschrift für Annemarie Schimmel zum 7. April 1992 dargebracht von Schülern, Freunden und Kollegen. God is beautiful and loves beauty: Festschrift for Annemarie Schimmel presented by students, friends and collegues* [sic] *on April 7, 1992*, Bern 1994, 71–91.

———, Ideas of time in Persian Sufism, in *Iran: Journal of the British Institute of Persian Studies* 30 (1992), 77–89.

———, Ideas of time in Persian Sufism, in L. Lewisohn (ed.) *The heritage of Sufism: Classical Persian Sufism from its origins to Rumi (700–1300)*, repr. Oxford 1999, 199–233.

———, Miʿrāj, in *ER*, ix, 6058–62.

———, *The mystical vision of existence in classical Islam: The Qur'ānic hermeneutics of the Sūfī Sahl al-Tustarī (d. 283/896)*, Berlin and New York 1980.

———, The scriptural "senses" in medieval Ṣūfī Qur'ān exegesis, in J.D. McAuliffe, B.D. Walfish, and J.W. Goering (eds.), *With reference for the word: Medieval scriptural exegesis in Judaism, Christianity, and Islam* (2003), 346–65.

———, Time, in *EQ*, v, 278–90.

Boyce, M., Apocalyptic i. In Zoroastrianism, in *EIr*, ii, 154–60.

———, Death i. Among Zoroastrians, in *EIr*, vii, 179–81.

Branca, P., « Ogni anima gusterà la morte »: Tanatologia musulmana, in A. Fabris (ed.), *Tra quattro paradisi: Esperienze, ideologie e riti reltivi all morte tra Oriente e Occidente*, Venice 2013, 16–35.

Brandes, W. and F. Schmieder, *Millenium Studies – Endzeiten: Eschatologie in monotheistischen Weltreligionen*, Berlin 2008.

Brinner, W.M., People of the heights, in *EQ*, iv, 46–8.

Brookes, J., *Gardens of paradise: The history and design of the great Islamic gardens*, New York 1987.
Brown, K., *Time, perpetuity, and eternity: Mir Damad's theory of perpetual creation and the threefold division of existence: An analysis of "Kitab al-Qabasat: The Book of Blazing Brands"*, PhD dissertation, University of California, Los Angeles 2006.
Brown, N.O., The apocalyse of Islam, in *Social Text* 8 (1983–84), 155–71.
Brunner, R., Le charisme des songeurs: Ḥusayn al-Nūrī al-Ṭabrisī et la fonction des rêves dans le shiʿisme duodécimain, in M.A. Amir-Moezzi, M.M. Bar-Asher, and S. Hopkins (eds.), *Le shīʿisme imāmite quarante ans après: Hommage à Etan Kohlberg*, Turnhout 2009, 95–115.'
Bürgel, J.C., Sana'is Jenseitsreise der Gottesknechte als Poesia docta, in *Der Islam* 60 (1983), 78–90.
Busse, H., Jerusalem in the story of Muhammad's night journey and ascension, in *JSAI* 14 (1991), 1–40.
———, Messianismus und Eschatologie im Islam, in W. Breuning (ed.), *Der Messias*, Neukirchen-Vluyn 1993, 273–91.
———, ʿOmar b. al-Ḫaṭṭāb in Jerusalem, in *JSAI* 5 (1984), 73–119.
———, The sanctity of Jerusalem in Islam, in *Judaism* 17 (1968), 441–68.
Calmard, J., ʿAzādārī, in *EIr*, iii, 174–7.
Campo, J.E., Burial, in *EQ*, i, 263–5.
Canova, G., Animals in Islamic paradise and hell, in *Eurasian Studies* 4.2 (2005), 189–204.
———, Animals in Islamic paradise and hell, in K. Dévényi and A. Fodor (eds.), *Proceedings of the colloquium on paradise and hell in Islam, Keszthely, 7–14 July 2002*, Budapest 2008 (= *The Arabist* 28–29 (2008)), 55–82.
Canto, A., De la ceca de al-Andalus a la de Madīnat al-Zahrā', in *Cuadernos de Madīnat al-Zahrā'* 3 (1991), 111–9.
Casanova, P., *Mohammad et la fin du monde: Étude critique sur l'Islam primitive*, Paris 1911–3.
Cerulli, E., *Il "Libro della scala" e la questione delle fonti arabo-spagnole della Divina Commedia*, Vatican City 1949.
Çevik, M., Farabi's utopia and its eschatological relations, in *İslam Araştırmaları: Journal of Islamic Research* 3.2 (2010), 173–8.
Chabbi, J., Jinn, in *EQ*, iii, 43–9.
Chalmeta, P., Simancas y Alhandega, in *Hispania* 36 (1976), 359–444.
Chittick. W.C., Death and the world of imagination: Ibn al-ʿArabi's eschatology, in *MW* 78 (1988), 51–82.
———, The disclosure of the intervening image: Ibn ʿArabī on death, in *Discourse: Journal for theoretical studies in media and culture* 24.1 (2002), 51–62.

———, Eschatology, in S.H. Nasr (ed.), *Islamic spirituality: Foundations*, New York 1987, 378–409.

———, *The heart of Islamic philosophy: The quest for self-knowledge in the teachings of Afḍal al-Dīn Kāshānī*, Oxford 2001.

———, Ibn al-ʿArabī's hermeneutics of mercy, in S. Katz (ed.), *Mysticism and sacred scripture*, New York 2000, 153–68.

———, *Imaginal worlds: Ibn al-ʿArabī and the problem of religious diversity*, Albany, NY 1994.

———, Muslim eschatology, in J.L. Walls (ed.), *Oxford handbook of eschatology*, Oxford 2008, 132–50.

———, Rumi's view of death, in *Alserat* 13.2 (1987), 30–51.

———, *In Search of the lost heart: Explorations in Islamic thought*, New York 2012, esp. 233–59.

———, *The self-disclosure of God: Principles of Ibn al-ʿArabī's cosmology*, Albany, NY 1998.

———, 'Your sight today is piercing': Death and the afterlife in Islam, in H. Obayashi (ed.), *Death and afterlife: perspectives of world religions*, New York 1992, 125–39.

———, *The Sufi path of knowledge: Ibn al-ʿArabī's metaphysics of imagination*, Albany, NY 1989.

———, *The Sufi path of love: The spiritual teachings of Rumi*, Albany, NY 1983.

———, Worship, in T. Winter (ed.), *The Cambridge companion to classical Islamic theology*, Cambridge 2008, 218–36.

Chodkiewicz, M., *Le sceau des saints: Prophétie et sainteté dans la doctrine d'Ibn Arabî*, Paris 1986.

———, *Un océan sans rivage: Ibn Arabî, le livre et la loi*, Paris 1992.

Christie, N., *The Book of the jihad of ʿAli ibn Tahir al-Sulami (d. 1106): Text, translation and commentary*, Aldershot 2013.

———, Jerusalem in the *Kitab al-Jihad* of ʿAli ibn Tahir al-Sulami, in *Medieval Encounters* 13 (2007), 209–21.

———, Motivating listeners in the *Kitab al-Jihad* of ʿAli ibn Tahir al-Sulami (d. 1106), in *Crusades* 6 (2007), 1–14.

———, Religious campaign or war of conquest? Muslim views of the motives of the First Crusade, in N. Christie and M. Yazigi (eds.), *Noble ideals and bloody realities: Warfare in the middle ages* (History of Warfare, 37), Leiden 2006, 57–72.

Cohn, N., *The pursuit of the millennium*, London 1957.

Colby, F.S., *Constructing an Islamic ascension narrative: The interplay of official and popular culture in pseudo-Ibn ʿAbbas*, PhD Dissertation, Duke University 2002.

———, *Narrating Muḥammad's night journey: Tracing the development of the Ibn ʿAbbās ascension discourse*, Albany, NY 2008.

Collins, J.J., *The apocalyptic imagination: An introduction to Jewish apocalyptic literature*, Grand Rapids, MI 1998².

———, Introduction: Towards the morphology of a genre, in J.J. Collins (ed.), *Apocalypse: The morphology of a genre* (Semeia 14), Missoula, MT 1979, 1–20.

Conrad, L.I., Portents of the hour, in *Der Islam* (forthcoming).

———, Seven and the *Tasbīʿ*: On the implications of numerical symbolism for the study of medieval Islamic history, in *JESHO* 31 (1988), 42–73.

Cook, D., Apocalyptic events connected to the Mongol invasions, in A.I. Baumgarten (ed.), *Apocalyptic time*, Leiden 2000, 41–68.

———, *Apostasy revisited* (forthcoming).

———, *Contemporary Muslim apocalyptic literature*, Syracuse and New York 2005.

———, An early Muslim Daniel apocalypse, in *Arabica* 49.1 (2002), 55–96.

———, *Martyrdom in Islam*, Cambridge 2007.

———, Messianism in the mid-11th/17th century as exemplified by al-Barzanjī (1040–1103/1630–1691), in *JSAI* 33 (2007), 261–78.

———, *Modern Muslim apocalyptic literature*, i, *The Sunnī Arabic material* (forthcoming).

———, Moral apocalyptic in Islam, in *SI* 86 (1997), 37–69.

———, Muslim apocalyptic and *jihād*, in *JSAI* 20 (1996), 66–104.

———, Muslim fears of the year 2000, in *Middle East Quarterly* 5 (1998), 51–62.

———, *Studies in Muslim apocalyptic*, Princeton, NJ 2002.

———, *Understanding jihad*, Berkeley, Los Angeles and London 2005.

Cook, D.W., A survey of Muslim material on comets and meteors, in *Journal for the History of Astronomy* 30 (1999), 131–60.

Cook, M., An early Muslim apocalyptic chronicle, in *JNES* 52 (1993), 25–9.

———, Eschatology, history and the dating of traditions, in *Princeton Papers in Near Eastern Studies* 1 (1992), 23–48.

———, The Heraclian dynasty in Muslim eschatology, in *Qanṭara* 13 (1992), 3–24.

Corbin, H., *Avicenne et le récit visionnaire*, Paris 1954.

———, *Cyclical time and Ismaili gnosis*, trans. L. Sherrard, London 1983.

———, *L'homme et son ange*, Paris 1983.

———, *L'imagination créatrice dans le soufisme d'Ibn ʿArabī*, Paris 1976.

———, *En Islam iranien: Aspects spirituels et philosophiques*, 4 vols., Paris 1971–2.

———, *The man of light in Iranian Sufis*, trans. N. Pearson, Boulder, CO 1987.

———, De la philosophie prophétique en islam shîʿite, in *Eranos-Jahrbuch* 31 (1962), 49–116.

———, *Spiritual body and celestial earth*, trans. N. Pearson, Princeton, NJ 2014.

———, *Temple and contemplation*, trans. P. Sherrard and L. Sherrard, London and New York 1986.

———, *Terre céleste et corps de résurrection: De l'Iran mazdéen à l'Iran shî 'ite*, Paris 1960.

———, Le thème de la résurrection chez Mollâ Ṣadrâ Shîrâzî (1050/1640) commentateur de Sohrawardî (587/1191), in E.E. Urbach (ed.), *Studies in mysticism and religion presented to Gershom G. Scholem on his seventieth birthday by pupils, colleagues and friends*, Jerusalem 1967, 71–115.

———, *The visionary dream in Islamic spirituality*, in G. von Grunebaume and R. Caillois (eds.), *The dream and human society*, Berkeley and Los Angeles 1966, 381–408.

Crone, P., *The nativist prophets of early Islamic Iran: Rural revolt and local Zoroastrianism*, Cambridge 2012.

Cuypers, M., Une lecture rhétorique et intertextuelle de la sourate al-Ikhlāṣ, in *MIDEO* 25–26 (2004), 141–75.

———, Pour une exégèse contextuelle du Coran, in *Islamochristiana* 33 (2007), 23–49.

———, Semitic rhetoric as a key to the question of the *naẓm* of the Qur'anic text, in *JQS* 13 (2011), 1–24.

———, La sourate 55 (al-Raḥmān) et le Psautier, in *Luqmān* 19 (2002), 71–106.

———, Structures rhétoriques dans le Coran: Une analyse structurelle de la sourate 'Joseph' et de quelques sourates brèves, in *MIDEO* 22 (1995), 1007–95.

———, Structures rhétoriques de la sourate 74 (al-Mudaththir), in *Luqmān* 13 (1997), 37–74.

———, Structures rhétoriques des sourates 81 à 84, in *AI* 37 (2003), 91–136.

———, Structures rhétoriques des sourates 85 à 90, in *AI* 35 (2001), 27–99.

———, Structures rhétoriques des sourates 92 à 98, in *AI* 34 (2000), 95–138.

———, Structures rhétoriques des sourates 99 à 104, in *AI* 33 (1999), 31–62.

———, Structures rhétoriques des sourates 105 à 114, in *MIDEO* 23 (1997), 157–96.

Daftary, F., Cyclical time and sacred history in medieval Ismaili thought. (Online publication, http://iis.ac.uk/view_article.asp?ContentID=109987&l=en, accessed 20 January 2011).

———, Ḥamid-al-Din Kermāni, in *EIr*, xi, 639–41.

———, Ḥasan II, 'Alā Ḏekrehe'l-Salām, in *EIr*, xii, 24–5.

———, Ḥasan-i Ṣabbāḥ and the origins of the Nizārī Ismaʿili movement, in F. Daftary (ed.), *Medieval Ismaʿili history and thought*, Cambridge 1996, 181–204.

———, Hidden imams and mahdis in Ismaili history, in B. Craig (ed.), *Ismaili and Fatimid studies in honor of Paul E. Walker*, Chicago 2010, 1–22.

———, *The Ismāʿīlīs: Their history and doctrines*, Cambridge 1990, 2007[2] (rev. ed.).

Daiber, H., Shaḳāwa, in *EI*[2], ix, 246–7.

Dajani-Shakeel, H., Jihād in twelfth-century Arabic poetry: A moral and religious force to counter the crusades, in *MW* 66 (1976), 96–113.

Dakake, M., The soul as *Barzakh*: Substantial motion and Mullā Ṣadrā's theory of human becoming, in *MW* 94.1 (2004), 107–30.
Dan, J., Messianic movements in the period of the crusades, in D.V. Arbel and A.A. Orlov (eds.), *With letters of light: Studies in the Dead Sea scrolls, early Jewish apocalypticism, magic, and mysticism in honor of Rachel Elior*, New York 2011, 285–98.
Dar al-Taqwa, *The soul's journey after death: An abridgement of Ibn Al-Qayyim's Kitab ar-Ruh*, com. L. Mabrouk, London 1987.
Darmesteter, J., L'apocalypse persane de Daniel, in *Mélanges Renier* 73 (1887), 405–20.
———, *Le Mahdi depuis les origines de l'Islam jusqu'à nous jours*, Paris 1885.
———, *The mahdi: Past and present*, trans. A. Ballin, London 1885.
Davidson, H.A., *Alfarabi, Avicenna, and Averroes on intellect: Their cosmologies, theories of the active intellect, and theories of human intellect*, New York 1992.
Day, K.K., Ibn Sina and Mulla Sadra's arguments against *tanasukh* in the afterlife of souls, in *Papers of the Sadra Islamic Philosophy Research Institute* (2006). (Online publication, http://www.mullasadra.org/new_site/english/Paper%20Bank/Anthropology/Kennedy%20day%20@.htm, accessed 26 October 2011).
De Smet, D., La doctrine avicennienne des deux faces de l'âme et ses raciness ismaéliennes, in *SI* 93 (2001), 77–89.
———, The sacredness of nature in Shiʿi Ismaʿili Islam, in A. Vanderjagt et al. (eds.), *The book of nature in antiquity and middle ages*, Leuven 2005, 85–96.
Dehbashi, M., *Transubstantial motion and the natural world*, London 2010.
Denny, W.B., Paradise attained: The Islamic palace, in S.S. Blair and J.M. Bloom (eds.), *Images of paradise in Islamic art*, Hanover, NH 1991, 106–9.
Dévényi, K. and A. Fodor (eds.), *Proceedings of the colloquium on paradise and hell in Islam, Keszthely, 7–14 July 2002*, Budapest 2008 (= *The Arabist* 28–29 (2008)).
Donner. F.M., The death of Abu Talib, in J.H. Marks and R.M. Good (eds.), *Love and death in the ancient Near East: Essays in honor of Marvin H. Pope*, Gilford, CT, 1987, 237–45.
———, *Muhammad and the believers: At the origins of Islam*, Cambridge 2010.
———, Piety and eschatology in early Kharijite poetry, in M. al-Saʿafin (ed.), *Fī miḥrāb al-maʿrifa: Festschrift for Ihsan ʿAbbas*, Beirut 1997, 3–19 [English section].
———, The sources of Islamic conceptions of war, in J. Kelsay and J.T. Johnson (eds.), *Just war and Jihad: Historical and theoretical perspectives on war and peace in western and Islamic traditions*, New York 1991, 31–69.
———, *Was early Islam an apocalyptic movement?* (forthcoming).
Dorraj, M., Symbolic and utilitarian political value of a tradition: Martyrdom in the Iranian political culture, in *Review of Politics* 59.3 (1997), 489–521.
Eichler, P.A., *Die Dschinn, Teufel und Engel im Koran*, Leipzig 1928.
Eklund, R., *Life between death and resurrection according to Islam*, Uppsala 1941.

Elad, A., The Caliph Abū al-ʿAbbās al-Saffāh, the first ʿAbbāsid *Mahdī*, in E. Fleischer (ed.), *Masat Moshe: Mekharim te-yarbut Yisrael mugashim le-Moshe Gil* (1998), 9–55 (in Hebrew).

———, *Medieval Jerusalem and Islamic worship: Holy places, ceremonies, pilgrimage*, Leiden 1995.

———, Why did ʿAbd al-Malik build the Dome of the Rock?, in J. Raby and J. John (eds.), *Bayt al-Maqdis: ʿAbd al-Malik's Jerusalem*, Oxford 1992, 33–58.

Elahi, O., *Knowing the spirit*, trans. J.W. Morris, New York 2007.

El-Bizri, N., Uneasy interrogations following Levinas, in *Studia Phænomenologica* 6 (2006), 293–315.

Eliade, M., Cosmogonic myth and "sacred history," in M. Eliade, *The quest: History and meaning in religion*, Chicago and London 1969, 72–87.

Eliash, J., On the genesis and development of the Twelver-Shîʿî three-tenet Shahâda, in *Der Islam* 47 (1971), 265–72.

Ellwood, R., *Tales of lights and shadows: The mythology of the afterlife*, New York 2010.

El-Ṣaleḥ, S., *La vie future selon le Coran*, Paris 1971.

El-Shakry, H., Revolutionary eschatology: Islam and the end of time in al-Ṭāhir Waṭṭār's "al-Zilzāl," in *JAL* 42.2–3 (2011), 120–47.

El-Zein, A., Water of paradise, in *EQ*, v, 466–7.

Ernst, C.W., From hagiography to martyrology: Conflicting testimonies to a Sufi martyr of the Delhi sultanate, in *History of Religions* 24.4 (1985), 308–27.

———, *How to read the Qurʾan: A new guide with select translations*, Chapel Hill, NC 2011.

———, *Rūzbihān Baqlī: Mysticism and the rhetoric of sainthood in Persian Sufism*, Richmond, UK 1996.

———, *Words of ecstasy in Sufism*, Albany, NY 1985.

Evrin, S., *Eschatology in Islam*, trans. S. Huri, Istanbul 1960.

Fadel, M.H., Chastisement and punishment, in *EQ*, i, 294–8.

Fahd, T., Djafr, in *EI*², ii, 375–7.

———, Ḥurūf, ʿilm al-, in *EI*², iii, 595–6.

———, Malḥama, in *EI*², vi, 247.

———, Nār, in *EI*², vii, 957–60.

——— and H. Daiber, Ruʾyā, in *EI*², viii, 645–9.

Falaturi, A., Tod – Gericht – Auferstehung in koranischer Sicht, in A. Falaturi (ed.), *Zukunftshoffnung und Heilserwartung in den monotheistischen Religionen*, Freiburg 1983, 121–38.

Farrin, R.K., *Structure and Qurʾanic interpretation: A study of symmetry and coherence in Islam's holy text*, Ashland, OR 2014.

Feldmeier, R. and M. Winet (eds.), *Gottesgedanken: Erkenntnis, Eschatologie und Ethik in Religionen der Spätantike und des frühen Mittelalters*, Tübingen 2016.

Filiu, J.-P., *L'apocalypse dans l'Islam*, Paris 2008.
———, *Apocalypse in Islam*, trans. M.B. de Bevoise, Berkeley 2011.
Fleischer, C.H., The lawgiver as messiah: The making of the imperial image in the reign of Süleyman, in G. Veinstein (ed.), *Soliman le magnifique et son temps: Actes du Colloque de Paris… mars 1990. Süleymân the Magnificent and his time: Acts of the Parisian Conference… March 1990*, Paris 1992, 159–77.
———, Mahdi and millenium: Messianic dimensions in the development of Ottoman imperial ideology, in K. Çiçek (ed.), *The great Ottoman-Turkish civilization*, iii, Ankara 2000, 42–54.
Fleischer, E., *Medieval Jerusalem and Islamic worship: Holy places, ceremonies, pilgrimage*, Leiden 1995.
Flori, J., *L'islam et la fin des temps: l'interprétation prophétique des invasions musulmanes dans la chrétienté médiévale*, Paris 2007.
Flügel, G., Schaʿrânî und sein Werk über die muhammedanische Glaubenslehre, in *ZDMG* 20 (1866), 1–48, esp. 20–49 (hell and hereafter).
Fodor, A., Malḥamat Daniyal, in Gy. Kaldy-Nagy (ed.), *The Muslim east: Studies in honor of Julius Germanus*, Budapest 1974, 85–160.
Frankfurter, D., Tabitha in the Apocalypse of Elijah, in *JTS* 41 (1990), 13–25.
Freitag, R., *Seelenwanderung in der islamischen Häresie*, Berlin 1985.
Friedman, Y., Ḵaṣībī, in *EIr*, xvi.1, 68–70.
Gambetta, D. (ed.), *Making sense of suicide missions*, New York 2005.
Garciá-Arenal, M., *Messianism and puritanical reform: Mahdīs of the Muslim west*, Leiden 2006.
Gardet, L., ʿĀlam 2: ʿĀlam al-djabarūt, ʿālam al-malakūt, ʿālam al-mithāl, in *EI*², i, 350–2.
———, *Dieu et la destinée de l'homme*, Paris 1967.
———, Djahannam, in *EI*², ii, 381–2.
———, Djanna, in *EI*², ii, 447–52.
———, *Les grands problèmes de la théologie Musulmane (Essai de la théologie comparée): Dieu et la destinée de l'homme*, Paris 1967.
———, Ḥisāb, in *EI*², iii, 465–6.
———, *Introduction à la théologie musulmane: Essai de théologie compare*, Paris 1948.
———, Ḳiyāma, in *EI*², v, 235–8.
Gätje, H., Eschatologie, in H. Gätje, *Koran und Koranexegese*, Zurich 1971, 230–47.
Geddes, M., The messiah in South Arabia, in *MW* 57 (1967), 311–20.
Ghaemmaghami, O., *The invention of tradition: Encounters with the hidden imam in early and pre-modern Twelver Shīʿī Islam*, Leiden (forthcoming).
Gianotti, T.J., *al-Ghazālī's unspeakable doctrine of the soul: Unveiling the esoteric psychology and eschatology of the Iḥyāʾ*, Leiden, Boston, and Cologne 2001.
Gignoux, P., Hamēstagān, in *EIr*, xi, 637–8.
———, Hell i. In Zoroastrianism, in *EIr*, xii, 154–6.

Gilanshah, F., Islamic customs regarding death, in D.-P. Irish et al. (eds.), *Ethnic variations in dying, death and grief: Diversity in universality*, Philadelphia and London 1993, 137–45.

Gilliot, C., Coran 17, *Isrāʾ*, 1 dans la recherche occidentale: De la critique des traditions au Coran comme texte, in M.A. Amir-Moezzi (ed.), *Le voyage initiatique en terre d'Islam: Ascensions célestes et itinéraires spirituels*, Leuven and Paris 1996, 1–26.

Gimaret, D., Ruʾyat Allāh, in *EI*², viii, 649.

Gimaret, G., Saḳar, in *EI*², viii, 881.

Gimaret, D., J. Jolivet and G. Monnot (trans.), *Livre des religions et des sectes*, 2 vols., Leuven 1986–93.

Goitein, S.D., al-Ḳuds, in *EI*², v, 322–39.

Goldziher, I., ʿIjādat al-marīḍ, in *Zeitschrift für Assyriologie* 32 (1918/19), 185–200.

———, *Zur Charakteristik Ǵelâl ud-dîn us-Sujûṭî's und seiner literarischen Thätigkeit*, Vienna 1871.

Golombek, L., Garden vi. In Persian art, in *EIr*, x, 310–3.

Grabar, O., *The shape of the holy: Early Islamic Jerusalem*, Princeton, NJ 1996.

Gramlich, R., *Die Wunder der Freunde Gottes: Theologien und Erscheinungsformen des islamischen Heiligenwunders*, Wiesbaden 1987.

Griffel, F., Divine actions, creation, and human fate after death in 9th/15th-century Imāmī Shiʿite theology, in *JAOS* 125 (2005), 67–78.

Gril, D., *Le dévoilement des effets du voyage*, Combas 1994.

———, *Saint et sainteté dans le christianisme et l'islam: Le regard des sciences de l'homme*, Paris 2007.

Gruber, C.J., *El "Libro de la Ascensión"* (*Miʿrajnama*) *timúrida: Estudio de textos e imágenes en un contexto panasiático*, Valencia 2008.

———, Meʿrāj ii. Illustrations, in *EIr*, online version (http://www.iranicaonline.org/articles/meraj-ii-illustrations, accessed 16 April 2014).

——— and F.S. Colby (eds.), *The Prophet's ascension: Cross-cultural encounters with the Islamic miʿraj tales*, Bloomignton, IN 2010.

———, *The Prophet Muḥammad's ascension* (miʿrāj) *in Islamic art and literature, ca. 1300–1600*, PhD Dissertation, University of Pennsylvania 2005.

Grünbaum, M., Die beiden Welten bei den arabisch-persischen und bei den jüdischen Autoren, in *ZDMG* 42 (1888), 258–95.

Guijarro, A., *Los signos del fin de los tiempos según el Islam*, Madrid 2007.

Günther, S., Day, times of, in *EQ*, i, 499–504.

———, *« Die Menschen schlafen; und wenn sie sterben, erwachen sie »*: Eschatologische Vorstellungen im Koran, in R. Feldmeier and M. Winet (eds.), *Gottesgedanken: Erkenntnis, Eschatologie und Ethik in Religionen der Spätantike und des frühen Mittelalters*, Tübingen 2016, 113–22.

———, Eschatology, in M. Abdel Haleem and M. Shah (eds.), *The Oxford handbook of Qur'anic studies*, Oxford 2017 (forthcoming).

———, « *Gepriesen sei der, der seinen Diener bei Nacht reisen ließ* » (Koran 17:1): Paradiesvorstellungen und Himmelsreisen im Islam – Grundfesten des Glaubens und literarische Topoi, in E. Hornung and A. Schweizer (eds.), *Jenseitsreisen: ERANOS 2009 und 2010*, Basel 2011, 15–56.

———, Tag und Tageszeiten im Qur'ān, in *Hallesche Beiträge zur Orientwissenschaft* 25 (1998), 46–67.

Gwynne, R.W., Hell and hellfire, in EQ, ii, 414–9.

Haase, L., Garten und Paradies im Islam, in H.-C. Goßmann (ed.), *Begegnungen zwischen Christentum und Islam: Festschrift für Hans-Jürgen Brandt*, Ammersbek, Germany 1994, 11–34.

Hagemann, L., Eschatologie im Islam, in A.-T. Khoury and P. Hünermann (eds.), *Weiterleben – nach dem Tode? Die Antwort der Weltreligionen*, Freiburg im Breisgau 1985, 103–20.

———, Die „letzten Dinge" in der Sicht des Korans: Sterben und Weiterleben in islamischer Deutung, in K. Kremer (ed.) *Unsterblichkeit und Eschatologie im Denken des Nikolaus von Kues: Akten des Symposions in Trier vom 19. bis 21. Oktober 1995*, Trier, Germany 1996, 119–32.

Hajjaji-Jarrah, S.M., Āyat al-Nūr: A metaphor for where we come from, what we are and where we are going, in T. Lawson (ed.), *Reason and inspiration in Islam: Theology, philosophy and mysticism in Muslim thought*, London and New York 2005, 169–81.

Hajnal, I., The events of paradise: Facts and eschatological doctrines in the medieval Ismāʿīlī history, in K. Dévényi and A. Fodor (eds.), *Proceedings of the colloquium on paradise and hell in Islam, Keszthely, 7–14 July 2002*, Budapest 2008 (= *The Arabist* 28–29 (2008)), 83–104.

Halevi, L., *Muhammad's grave: Death rites and the making of Islamic society*, New York 2007.

Halm, H., Abū Ḥātem Rāzī, in *EIr*, i, 315.

———, The cosmology of pre-Fatimid Ismāʿīliyya, in F. Daftary (ed.), *Mediaeval Ismaʿili history and thought*, Cambridge 1996, 75–83.

———, Dawr (A. pl. ādwar), in EI², xii, 206–7.

———, *The empire of the Mahdi: The rise of the Fatimids*, trans. M. Bonner, Leiden 1996.

———, *Kosmologie und Heilslehre der frühen Ismāʿīlīya: Eine Studie zur islamischen Gnosis*, Wiesbaden 1978.

———, Der Schöpfungsmythos der Nusairier und die Tradition der Gulat, in ZDMG *Supplement IV: XX. Deutscher Orientalistentag* (1977), 219–20.

Hamblin, W.J. and D.C. Peterson, Eschatology, in *Oxford encyclopedia of the modern Islamic world*, i, New York 1995, 440–2.

Hamza, F., *To hell and back: The Prophet's intercession and the making of temporary hell-fire in Sunni orthodoxy*, Leiden (forthcoming).

Hanaway, W.L.Jr., Paradise on earth, in E.B. MacDougall and R. Ettinghausen (eds.), *The Islamic garden*, Washington, DC, 1976, 3–67.

Hartmann, R., *Die Himmelsreise Muhammeds und ihre Bedeutung in der Religion des Islam*, Leipzig 1930.

Hasan, N., The ruḥfat al-rāghibīn: The work of Abdul Samad al-Palimbani or Muhammad Arsyad al-Banjari?, in *Bijdragen tot de Taal-, Land- en Volkenkunde* 163.1 (2007), 67–85.

Hassan, F., *Prophecy and the fundamentalist quest: an integrative study of Christian and Muslim apocalyptic religion*, Jefferson, NC, 2008.

Hasson, I., Last judgment, in *EQ*, iii, 136–45.

———, Muslim literature in praise of Jerusalem, in *Jerusalem Cathedra* 1 (1984), 168–84.

Hegedus, G., Where is paradise? Eschatology in early medieval Judaic and Islamic thought, in *Dionysius* 25 (2007), 153–76.

Heijer, H. den, *Malḥamat Daniyāl* and Christian Arabic literature, in *Orientalia Christiana Analecta* 218 (1982), 223–32.

Heinen, A., *Islamic cosmology: A study of as-Suyūṭī's* al-Hay'a as-sanīya fī l-hay'a as-sunnīya, Beirut 1982.

Hell, J., Baliyya, in *EI*², i, 997.

Hellholm, D. (ed.), *Apocalypticism in the Mediterranean world and the Near East: Proceedings of the International Colloquium on Apocalypticism, Uppsala, August 12–17, 1979*, Tübingen 1983.

Hermansen, M., Eschatology, in T. Winter (ed.), *The Cambridge companion to classical Islamic theology*, Cambridge 2008, 308–24.

———, Shāh Walī Allāh's theory of the subtle spiritual centers (laṭā'if): A Sufi model of personhood and self-transformation, in JNES 47 (1988), 1–25.

Hodgson, M., *The order of assassins: The struggle of the early Nizārī Ismāʿīlīs against the Islamic world*, The Hague 1955, repr. Philadelphia 2005.

Hoffman, V.J., Annihilation in the messenger of God: The development of a Sufi practice, in *IJMES* 31.3 (1999), 351–69.

Hollenberg, D., *Interpretation after the end of days: The Fāṭimid-Ismāʿīlī ta'wīl (interpretation) of Jaʿfar b. Manṣūr al-Yaman (d. ca. 960)*, PhD dissertation, University of Pennsylvania 2006.

Homerin, T.E., Echoes of a thirsty owl: Death and afterlife in pre-Islamic Arabic poetry, in *JNES* 44.3 (1985), 165–84.

———, Soul, in *EQ*, v, 80–4.

Hoover, J., Islamic universalism: Ibn Qayyim al-Jawziyya's Salafī deliberations on the duration of hell-fire, in *MW* 99.1 (2009), 181–201.

Hornung, E., Im Reich des Osiris, in E. Hornung and A. Schweizer (eds.), *Jenseitsreisen: ERANOS 2009 und 2010*, Basel 2011, 211–43.
——— and A. Schweizer (eds.), *Jenseitsreisen: ERANOS 2009 und 2010*, Basel 2011.
Horten, M., Das Weltgebäude, in *Die religiöse Gedankenwelt des Volkes im heutigen Islam*, Halle/Saale 1917, 10–128.
Horovitz, J., Das koranische Paradies, in *Scripta Universitatis atque Bibliothecae Hierosolymitanarum* 1 (1923), 1–16, repr. in R. Paret (ed.), *Der Koran*, Darmstadt 1975, 53–73.
———, Mohammeds Himmelfahrt, in *Der Islam* 9 (1919), 159–83.
———, Die Paradiesischen Jungfrauen im Koran, in *Islamica* 1 (1925), 543.
Horsch-Al-Saad, S., *Tod im Kampf: Figurationen des Märtyrers in frühen sunnitischen Schriften*, Würzburg 2011.
Hoyland, R.G., *Seeing Islam as others saw it: A survey and evaluation of Christian, Jewish, and Zoroastrian writings on early Islam*, Princeton, NJ 1997.
Hübsch, H., *Paradies und Hölle: Jenseitsvorstellungen im Islam*, Düsseldorf 2003.
Hunsberger, A. (ed.), *Pearls of Persia: The philosophical poetry of Nāṣir-i Khusraw*, London 2013.
Hussain, A., Death, in J.L. Esposito (ed.), *The Oxford encyclopedia of the Islamic world*, ii, New York 2009, 47–9.
Hussain, J., *The occultation of the twelfth imam*, Cambridge 1982.
Ibn ʿArabī, M, *De la mort à la résurrection: Chapitres 61 à 65 des ouvertures spirituelles Mekkoises*, trans. M. Gloton, Beirut 2009.
Ibn Qayyim al-Jawziyya, Shams al-Dīn Muḥammad ibn Abī Bakr, *Provisions for the hereafter*, trans. I.M. At-Tamimi, Riyadh 2003 [abridged English trans. of Ibn Qayyim al-Jawziyya's *Zād al-maʿād*].
Ibrahim, T., Tanāsukh, in *Islam: Entsiklopedicheskiy slovar'*, Moscow 1991, 223–4.
Irshai, O., Dating the eschaton, in A. Baumgarten (ed.), *Apocalyptic time*, Leiden 2000, 113–53.
Izutsu, T., Creation and the timeless order of things: A study in the mystical philosophy of ʿAyn Al-Qudat, in *Philosophical Forum* 4 (1972), 124–40.
———, The paradox of light and darkness in the garden of mystery as speculation of Shabastarī, in J.P. Strelka (ed.), *Anagogic qualities of literature*, London 1971, 287–307.
Jacob, G., *Altarabisches Beduinenleben: Nach den Quellen geschildert*, Berlin 1897, repr. Hildesheim 1967, esp. 139–44.
Jaffer, T., Bodies, souls and resurrection in Avicenna's *ar-Risāla al-Aḍḥawīya fī amr al-maʿād*, in D. Reisman et al. (eds.), *Before and after Avicenna: Proceedings of the first conference of the Avicenna study group*, Leiden 2003, 163–74.
Jafri, S.H.M, *Origins and early development of Shiʿa Islam*, London 1979.
Jambet, C., *L'Acte d'être: La philosophie de la révélation chez Mollâ Sadrâ*, Paris 2002.

———, *La grande résurrection d'Alamūt: Les formes de la liberté dans le shi'isme ismaélien*, Paris 1990.

———, *Mort et résurrection en islam: L'au-delà selon Mullâ Sadrâ*, Paris 2008.

———, *Se rendre immortel, suivi du* Traité de la résurrection *de Mollâ Sadrâ Shîrâzî*, Paris 2000.

Jarrar, M., Heaven and sky, in *EQ*, ii, 410–2.

———, Houris, in *EQ*, ii, 456–7.

———, The martyrdom of passionate lovers: Holy war as a sacred wedding, in A. Neuwirth et al. (eds.), *Myths, historical archetypes and symbolic figures in Arabic literatures*, Beirut 1999, 87–107.

Jenkinson, E., The Muslim antichrist, in *MW* 20 (1930), 50–5.

Jones, A., Heaven and hell in the Qur'ān, in K. Dévényi and A. Fodor (eds.), *Proceedings of the colloquium on paradise and hell in Islam, Keszthely, 7–14 July 2002*, Budapest 2008 (= *The Arabist* 28–29 (2008)), 105–22.

Jonker, G., The many facets of Islam: Death, dying and disposal between orthodox rule and historical convention, in C. Murray Parkes (ed.), *Death and bereavement across cultures*, London 1997, 147–65.

Kamada, S., Metempsychosis (*tanāsukh*) in Mullā Ṣadrā's thought, in *Orient* 30–31 (1995), 119–32.

———, Transmigration of soul (*tanāsukh*) in Shaykh al-Mufīd and Mullā Ṣadrā, in *Orient* 44 (2009), 105–19.

Kanga, M.F., Astwihād, in *EIr*, ii, 873.

Kani, C.Y., The extent of Islamic eschatological thought about soul and its influence on a person's attitude to death, in World Congress on Mulla Sadra (ed.), *Islam-West philosophical dialogue: The papers presented at the World Congress on Mulla Sadra (May, 1999, Tehran)*, x, *Eschatology, exegesis, hadith*, Tehran 2005, 257–64.

Kaplony, A., *The Ḥaram of Jerusalem 324–1099: Temple, Friday mosque, area of spiritual power*, Stuttgart 2002.

———, Jerusalem's sacred esplanade 635/638–1099: The Mosque of Jerusalem (Masjid Bayt al-Maqdis), in O. Grabar and B.Z. Kedar (eds.), *Where heaven and earth meet: Jerusalem's sacred esplanade*, Jerusalem and Austin 2009, 100–31.

Kappler, C. et al., *Apocalypses et voyages dans l'au-delà*, Paris 1987.

Kaptein, L., *Apocalypse and the antichrist dajjal in Islam: Ajmed Bijan's eschatology revisited*, Asch, The Netherlands 2011.

Kaptein, N.J.G., 'Abd al-Ṣamad al-Palimbānī, in *EI*², ii, 25–6.

Karimi, P., Imagining warfare, imaging welfare: Tehran's post Iran-Iraq war murals and their legacy, in *Persica* 22 (2008), 47–63.

Katz, J.G., Shaykh Aḥmad's dream: A 19th-century eschatological vision, in *SI* 79 (1994), 157–80.

Kessler, C., 'Abd al-Malik's inscription in the Dome of the Rock: A reconsideration, in *JRAS* 102 (1970), 2–14.

Khaksar, M., Reincarnation as perceived by the "People of the Truth," in *Iran and the Caucasus* 13 (2009), 117–23.

Khaled-Rubi, G., *Die Reise ins Jenseits: Über den Tod und das Leben danach*, Düsseldorf 2012.

Khalil, M.H. (ed.), *Between heaven and hell: Islam, salvation, and the fate of others*, Oxford 2013.

———, *Islam and the fate of others: The salvation question*, New York 2012.

Khosrokhavar, F., *L'Islamisme et la mort: Le martyre révolutionnaire en Iran*, Paris 1995.

———, *Les nouveaux martyrs d'Allah*, Paris 2002.

Khoury, A.T. and P. Heine, *Im Garten Allahs: Der Islam*, Freiburg 1996.

Kinberg, L., Interaction between this world and the afterworld in early Islamic tradition, in *Oriens* 29 (1986), 285–308.

———, Paradise, in *EQ*, iv, 12–20.

King, D.A., Astronomy and Islamic society: Qibla, gnomonics and timekeeping, in R. Rashed (ed.), *Encyclopedia of the history of Arabic science*, i, London and New York 1996, 128–84.

———, Saʿīr, in *EI*², viii, 872.

Kippenberg, H.G., "Consider that it is a raid on the path of God": The spiritual manual of the attackers of 9/11, in *Numen* 52 (2005), 29–58.

———, Die Geschichte der mittelpersischen apokalyptischen Traditionen, *SIr* 7 (1978), 49–80.

Kister, M.J., 'A booth like the booth of Moses ...': A study of an early Hadīth, in *BSOAS* 25 (1962), 150–5.

———, A comment on the antiquity of traditions praising Jerusalem, in *Jerusalem Cathedra* 1 (1981), 185–6.

Klausner, J.G., Eschatology, in M. Berenbau and F. Skolnik (eds.), *Encyclopaedia Judaica*, vi, Detroit 2006², 489–500.

Klobe, T., Islamic paradise in a Christian text: The ceiling of the Cappella Palatina in Palermo, Sicily, in K. Dévényi and A. Fodor (eds.), *Proceedings of the colloquium on paradise and hell in Islam, Keszthely, 7–14 July 2002*, Budapest 2008 (= *The Arabist* 28–29 (2008)), 123–36.

Klopfer, H. (ed. and trans.), *Das arabische Traumbuch des Ibn Sirin: Aus dem arabischen Arabischen übersetzt und kommentiert*, Munich 1998.

Klorman, E.B.-Z., Jewish and Muslim messianism in Yemen, in *IJMES* 22 (1990), 201–28.

Koç, T., Body-mind relationship with regard to life after death according to Mullā Ṣadrā, in World Congress on Mulla Sadra (ed.), *Islam-West philosophical dialogue: The papers presented at the World Congress on Mulla Sadra (May, 1999, Tehran)*, x, *Eschatology*, exegesis, hadith, Tehran 2005, 213–28.

Kohlberg, E., Radjʿa, in *EI*², viii, 371–3.

———, Taqiyya in Shīʿī theology and religion, in H. Kippenberg and G. Stroumsa (eds.), *Secrecy and concealment: Studies in the history of Mediterranean and near eastern religions*, Leiden 1995, 345–80.

———, The term "Rāfida" in Imāmī Shīʿī usage, in *JAOS* 99.4 (1979), 677–9.

Krauss, H., *Das Paradies: Eine kleine Kulturgeschichte*, Munich 2004.

Kunitzsch, P., *The Arabs and the stars: Texts and traditions on the fixed stars, and their influence in medieval Europe*, Northampton 1989.

Künstlinger, D., Die Namen und Freuden des kuranischen Paradieses, in *BSOS* 6 (1930–2), 617–32.

al-Kutubi, E., *Mulla Sadra and eschatology: Evolution of being*, NewYork 2014.

Lambden, S., Eschatology iv. In Babism and Bahaism, in *EIr*, vii, 581–2.

Landay, J.M., *Dome of the Rock: Three faiths of Jerusalem*, New York 1972.

Landolt, H. (ed.), *Creation and resurrection: An early Muslim perspective on divine unity and cosmology*, London 2014.

———, Khwāja Naṣīr al-Dīn al-Ṭūsī (597/1201–672/1274): Ismāʿīlism and Ishrāqī philosophy, in H. Landolt, *Recherches en spiritualité iranienne*, Tehran 2005, 13–30.

——— (trans. and ann.), *Nûruddîn Abdurrahmân-i Isfarâyinî: Le révélateur des mystères: Kâshif al-asrâr*, Lagrasse, France 1986.

———, Suhrawardī between philosophy, Sufism and Ismailism: A re-appraisal, repr. in H. Landolt, *Recherches en spiritualité iranienne*, Tehran 2005, 107–18.

———, Suhrawardi's "Tales of Initation," in *JAOS* 102.3 (1987), 475–86.

Lange, C., The eschatology of punishment, in C. Lange, *Justice, punishment, and medieval Muslim imagination*, Cambridge 2008, 99–175.

———, (ed.), *Locating hell in Islamic traditions*, Leiden 2016.

———, Islamische Höllenvorstellungen: Genese – Struktur – Funktion, in E. Hornung and A. Schweizer (eds.), *Jenseitsreisen: ERANOS 2009 und 2010*, Basel 2011, 169–209.

———, *Paradise and hell in Islamic traditions*, Cambridge 2016.

———, Where on earth is hell? State punishment and eschatology in the Islamic middle period, in C. Lange and M. Fierro (eds.), *Public violence in Islamic societies: Power, discipline, and the construction of the public sphere, 7th–19th centuries CE*, Edinburgh 2009, 156–78.

Lanternari, V., *The religions of the oppressed: A study of modern messianic cults*, trans. L. Sergio, New York 1963.

Lari, M., *Resurrection, judgement and the hereafter*, trans. H. Algar, Qum 1412/1992.

Laut, J.P, Hells in Central Asian Turkic Buddhism and early Turkic Islam, in A. Fabris (ed.), *Tra quattro paradisi: Esperienze, ideologie e riti reltivi all morte tra Oriente e Occidente*, Venice 2013, 16–35.

Lawson, T., A 14th Century Shíʿi Gnostic: Rajab Bursí and his *Masháriq al-Anwár*, in *Ishraq: Islamic Philosophy Yearbook* 1 (2010), 422–38.

———, Apocalypse, in G. Bowering et al. (eds.), *Princeton encyclopedia of Islamic political thought*, Princeton, NJ 2012, 38–9.

———, Coincidentia oppositorum in the Qayyum al-Asma: The terms "point" (*nuqta*), "pole" (*qutb*), "center" (*markaz*) and the Khutbat al-tatanjiya, in *Occasional Papers in Shaykhi, Babi and Baha'i Studies* 5.1 (2001). (Online publication, http://www.h-net.org/~bahai/bhpapers/vol5/tatanj/tatanj.htm, accessed 20 January 2011).

———, Le Coran et l'imaginaire apocalyptique, trans. G. Rivier, in *Religions et Histoire* 34 (2010), 48–53.

———, Divine wrath and divine mercy in Islam: Their reflection in the Qurʾān and Quranic images of water, in R. Kratz and H. Spieckermann (eds.), *Divine wrath and divine mercy in the world of antiquity*, Tübingen 2008, 248–67.

———, Duality, opposition and typology in the Qur'an: The apocalyptic substrate, in *JQS* 10.2 (2008), 23–49.

———, *Gnostic apocalypse and Islam: Qur'an, exegesis, messianism, and the literary origins of the Babi religion*, London and New York 2011.

———, Hermeneutics, in *EIr*, xii, 235–9.

———, Martyrdom, in J.L. Esposito (ed.), *The Oxford encyclopedia of the modern Islamic world*, iii, Oxford 1995, 54–9.

———, The Qur'an and epic, in *JQS* 16.1 (2014), 58–92.

——— (ed.), *Reason and inspiration in Islam: Theology, philosophy and mysticism in Muslim thought*, London and New York 2005.

Lazarus-Yafeh, H., The sanctity of Jerusalem in the Islamic tradition, in H. Lazarus-Yafeh (ed.), *Some religious aspects of Islam*, Leiden 1981, 58–71.

Le Goff, J., *La naissance du purgatoire*, Paris 1981.

Leaman, O., Death, in O. Leaman (ed.), *The Qur'an: An encyclopedia*, New York 2006, 170–8.

——— and H. Landolt, Wudjūd (a.), in *EI*², xi, 216–7.

Leemhuis, F., Apocalypse, in *EQ*, i, 111–4.

Lehrmann, J., *Earthly paradise: Garden and courtyard in Islam*, Berkeley and Los Angeles 1980.

Leisten, T., Die Gärten des Islam: Das islamische Paradies als Idealbild des Gartens, in H. Forkl et al. (eds.), *Die Gärten des Islam*, Stuttgart 1993, 47–55.

Leszynsky, R., *Mohammedanische Traditionen über das jüngste Gericht: Eine vergleichende Studie zur jüdisch-christlichen und mohammedanischen Eschatologie*, PhD dissertation, University of Heidelberg 1909.

Levi, I., Une apocalypse judeo-arabe, in *Revue des études juives* 67 (1914), 178–82.

Lewinstein, K., Gog and Magog, in *EQ*, ii, 331–3.

Lewis, B., An apocalyptic vision of Islamic history, in *BSOAS* 13 (1950), 308–39.

———, *The crisis of Islam: Holy war and unholy terror*, New York 2003.

Lewisohn, L., *Beyond faith and infidelity: The Sufi poetry and teachings of Mahmud Shabistari*, Richmond 1995.

———, In quest of annihilation: Imaginalization and mystical death in the *Tamhīdāt* of ʿAyn al-Quḍāt Hamadhānī, L. Lewisohn (ed.), *The heritage of Sufism*, i, Oxford 1999, 285–336.

———, *The wisdom of Sufism*, Oxford 2001.

Livne-Kafri, O., *Faḍāʾil bayt al-maqdis* ('The merits of Jerusalem'): Two additional notes, in *QSA* 19 (2001), 61–70.

———, Jerusalem in early Islam: The eschatological aspect, in *Arabica* 53.3 (2006), 382–403.

Lory, P., La vision de Dieu dans l'onirocritique musulmane médiévale, in T. Lawson (ed.), *Reason and inspiration in Islam: Theology, philosophy and mysticism in Muslim thought,* London and New York 2005, 356–63.

Lucini, M., *La escatología musulmana en al-Andalus*: El Kitāb al-dajīra fī ʿilm al-dār al ājira, *atribuido a Ibn al-ʿArabī*, PhD dissertation, Universidad Autónoma de Madrid 1989.

Lumbard, J., *Love and remembrance: The life and teachings of Aḥmad al-Ghazālī*, Albany, NY 2015.

Maalouf, A., *The crusades through Arab eyes*, trans. J. Rothschild, London 1984.

MacCulloch, J.A., Eschatology, in *ERE*, v, 373–91.

Macdonald, J, The angel of death in late Islamic tradition, in *Islamic Studies* 3 (1964), 485–519.

———, The creation of man and angels in the eschatological literature, in *Islamic Studies* 3 (1964), 285–308.

———, The day of resurrection, in *Islamic Studies* 5 (1966), 29–197.

———, Paradise, in *Islamic Studies* 5 (1966), 331–83.

———, The preliminaries to the resurrection and judgement, in *Islamic Studies* 4 (1965), 137–79.

———, The twilight of the dead, in *Islamic Studies* 4 (1965), 55–102.

MacDougall, E. and R. Ettinghausen (eds.), *The Islamic garden*, Washington, DC 1976.

MacEoin, D.M., Hierarchy, authority and eschatology in early Bâbî thought, in P. Smith (ed.), *Studies in Bâbî and Bahâʾî History*, iii, *In Iran*, Los Angeles 1986, 95–155.

———, *The messiah of Shiraz: Studies in early and middle Babism*, Boston 2009.

MacGregor, G., *Images of afterlife: Beliefs from antiquity to modern times*, New York 1992.

Macler, F., L'apocalypse arabe de Daniel, in *Revue de l'histoire des religions* 49 (1904), 265–305.

Madelung, W., Apocalyptic prophecies in Ḥimṣ in the Umayyad age, in *JSS* 31 (1986), 141–85.

———, Cosmogony and cosmology vi. In Ismaʿilism, in *EIr*, vi, 322–6.

———, *Der Imām al-Qāsim ibn Ibrāhīm und die Glaubenslehre der Zaiditen*, Berlin 1965.
———, Das Imamat in der frühen ismailitischen Lehre, in *Der Islam* 37 (1961), 43–135.
———, Ismāʿīliyya, in *EI*², iv, 198–206.
———, Ḳāʾim Āl Muḥammad, in *EI*², iv, 456–7.
———, Khaṭṭābiyya, in *EI*², iv, 1132–3.
———, al-Mahdī, in *EI*², v, 1230–8.
———, Malāʾika, in *EI*², vi, 216–9.
———, Murdjiʾa, in *EI*², vii, 605–7.
———, al-Sufyānī, in *EI*², xii, 754–6.
———, A treatise on the imamate of the Fatimid Caliph al-Manṣūr bi-Allāh, in C. Robinson (ed.), *Texts, documents and artefacts: Islamic studies in honour of D.S. Richards*, Leiden and Boston 2003, 69–77.
Maḥmūd, S.B., *Doomsday and life after death: A systematic study of the complex realities of life*, Islamabad 2006.
Malandra, W.W., Garōdmān, in *EIr*, x, 317–8.
Malick, F., *The destiny of Islam in the endtimes: Understanding God's heart for the Muslim people*, Shippensburg, PA, 2007.
Marcotte, R., L'eschatologie d'Abū al-ʿAbbās al-Lawkarī (mort après 503/1109): Le *Bayān al-ḥaqq* et le *Sharḥ-e Qaṣīda-ye asrār al-ḥikma*, in *MIDEO* 29 (2012), 1–25.
———, Resurrection (*maʿād*) in the Persian *Ḥayāt al-Nufūs* of Ismāʿīl Ibn Muḥammad Rīzī: The Avicennan background, in D.C. Reisman (ed.), *Interpreting Avicenna: Science and philosophy in medieval Islam*, Leiden 2004, 213–35.
———, Suhrawardi's realm of the imaginal, in *Ishrâq: Islamic Philosophy Yearbook* 2 (2011), 68–79.
Marmura, M.E., Soul: Islamic concepts, in *ER*, xii, 8566–71.
Maróth, M., Paradise and hell in Muslim philosophy, in K. Dévényi and A. Fodor (eds.), *Proceedings of the colloquium on paradise and hell in Islam, Keszthely, 7–14 July 2002*, Budapest 2008 (= *The Arabist* 28–29 (2008)), 137–46.
Marzolph, U., The martyr's fading body: Propaganda vs. beautification in the Tehran cityscape, in C. Gruber and S. Haugbolle (eds.), *Visual culture in the modern Middle East: Rhetoric of the image*, Bloomington, IN (2013), 164–85.
———, The martyr's way to paradise: Shiite mural art in the urban context, in R. Bendix and J. Bendix (eds.), *Sleepers, moles and martyrs: Secret identifications, societal integration, and the differing meanings of freedom*, Copenhagen 2004, 87–98.
Mas, R., On the apocalyptic tones of Islam in secular time, in A. Mandair and M. Dressler (eds.), *Secularism and religion making*, Oxford 2011, 87–103.
Massignon, L., La cité des morts au Caire, Qarāfa – Darb al-Ahmar, in *BIFAO* 57.19 (1958), 25–79.

———, *La passion de Husayn ibn Mansûr Hallâj: Martyr mystique de l'Islam, exécuté à Bagdad le 26 Mars 922: Étude d'histoire religieuse*, 4 vols., Paris 1922, repr. Paris 1975.

———, *The passion of al-Hallaj: Mystic and martyr of Islam*, ed. and trans. H. Mason, 4 vols., Princeton, NJ 1994.

Mavani, H., *Doctrine of the imamate in twelver Shi'ism: Traditional, theological, philosophical, and mystical perspectives*, PhD dissertation, McGill University 2005.

Mayel-Heravi, N., Quelques *me'rāǧiyye* en persan, in M.A. Amir-Moezzi (ed.), *Le Voyage initiatique en terre d'Islam: Ascensions célestes et itinéraires spirituels*, Leuven and Paris 1996, 199–203.

McDannell, C. and B. Lang, *Heaven: A history*, New Haven and London 2001².

McIntosh, C., *Gardens of the gods: Myth, magic and meaning*, London and New York 2005, esp. 35–45.

Meier, F., Ein Prophetenwort gegen die Totenbeweinung, in *Der Islam* 50 (1973), 207–29.

———, The ultimate origin and the hereafter in Islam, in G.L. Tikku (ed.), *Islam and its cultural divergence: Studies in honor of Gustave E. von Grunebaum*, Urbana, IL 1971, 96–112.

Meisami, J.S., Allegorical gardens in the Persian poetic tradition: Nezami, Rumi, and Hafez, in *IJMES* 17 (1985), 229–60.

———, Palaces and paradises: Palace descriptions in medieval Persian poetry, in O. Grabar and C. Robinson (eds.), *Islamic art and literature*, Princeton, NJ 2001, 21–54.

Mernissi, F., *Women in Moslem paradise*, New Delhi 1986.

Meyer, J., *Die Hölle im Islam*, PhD dissertation, Basel University 1901.

Mez, A., *Die Renaissance des Islâms*, Heidelberg 1922, esp. 308–14.

Michot, J.R., *La destinée de l'homme selon Avicenne*, Lovanii 1986.

———, L'eschatologie d'Avicenne selon F.D. al-Rāzī, in *Revue Philosophique de Louvain* 87 (1989), 235–63.

Michot, Y., A Mamlūk theologian's commentary on Avicenna's *Risāla Aḍḥawiyya*: Being a translation of a part of the *Dar' al-Ta'āruḍ* of Ibn Taymiyya, with introduction, annotation, and appendices, in *Oxford Journal of Islamic Studies* 14 (2003), 149–203 (part 1), 309–63 (part 2).

Miller, F.P., A.F. Vandome, and J. McBrewster, *Islamic view of the last judgement*, Saarbrücken, Germany 2009.

Miller, S., *After death: How people around the world map the journey after life*, New York 1997.

Milstein, R., Paradise as a parable, in K. Dévényi and A. Fodor (eds.), *Proceedings of the colloquium on paradise and hell in Islam, Keszthely, 7–14 July 2002*, Budapest 2008 (= *The Arabist* 28–29 (2008)), 147–62.

Mir-Kasimov, O., Les dérivés de la racine *rḥm*: Homme, femme et connaissance dans le *Jāvdān-nāma* de Faḍlallāh Astarābādī, in *JA* 295.1 (2007), 9–34.

———, Jāvdān-nāma, in *EIr*, xiv, 6035.

———, Notes sur deux textes Ḥurūfī: Le *Jāvdān-nāma* de Faḍlallāh Astarābādī et l'un de ses commentaires, le *Maḥram-nāma* de Sayyid Isḥāq, in *SIr* 35.2 (2006), 203–35.
———, Some specific features of the Ḥurūfī Interpretation of the Qurʾānic and Biblical episodes related to Moses, in *JQS* 10.1 (2008), 21–49.
———, *Words of power: Ḥurūfī teachings between Shiʿism and Sufism in medieval Islam, the original doctrine of Faḍl Allāh Astarābādī*, London 2015.
Mirza, N., *Reincarnation and Islam*, Adyar 1927.
Miskin, T. el-, The miʿrāj controversy: Dante, Palacios and Islamic eschatology, in *International Journal of Islamic and Arabic Studies* 4 (1987), 45–53.
Moghadam, A., Palestinian suicide terrorism in the second Intifada, in *Studies in Conflict and Terrorism* 26 (2003), 65–92.
Mohammed, O.N., *Averroes' doctrine of immortality: A matter of controversy*, Waterloo 1984.
Monnot, G., Ṣalāt, in *EI*², viii, 925–34.
Moore, C., W.J. Mitchell and W. Turnbull Jr., *The poetics of gardens*, Cambridge 1993.
Morabia, A., L'antéchrist: s'este-il manifesté du vivant du l'envoyé d'Allah?, in *JA* 267 (1979), 81–94.
———, Lawn, in *EI*², v, 698–707.
Moreman, C.M., *Beyond the threshhold: Afterlife beliefs and experiences in world religions*, Plymouth UK 2008.
Morris, J.W. (trans. and ann.), *The wisdom of the throne: An introduction to the philosophy of Mullā Ṣadrā*, Princeton, NJ 1981.
Muharijani, A., Twelve-Imām Shiʿite theological and philosophical thought, in S.H. Nasr and O. Leaman (eds.), *History of Islamic philosophy*, i, London 1996, 119–43.
Muṭahharī, M., *Das ewige Leben*, Tehran 1982.
Nabielek, R., Weintrauben statt Jungfrauen als paradiesische Freude, in *DAVO-Nachrichten* 17 (2003), 37–45.
Nagel, T., *Der Koran: Einführung, Texte, Erläuterungen*, Munich 1983.
Nasr, S.H. et al. (eds.), *Expectation of the millennium: Shīʿism in history*, Albany, NY 1989.
———, *An introduction to Islamic cosmological doctrines*, Cambridge 1964.
———, et al. (eds.), *The study Quran: A new translation and commentary*, New York 2015.
Netton, I.R., Nafs, in *EI*², vii, 880–4.
———, The perils of allegory: Medieval Islam and the angel of the grave, in I.R. Netton (ed.), *Studies in honour of Clifford Edmund Bosworth*, i, *Hunter of the East*, Leiden 2000, 417–27.
Neuwirth, A., Blut und Mythos in der islamischen Kultur, in C. von Braun and C. Wulf (eds.), *Mythen des Blutes*, Frankfurt 2007, 62–89.
———, Die Autopsie des Mondes: Vom kosmischen Körper zum kalligraphischen Prophetenbild, in R. Feldmeier and M. Winet (eds.), *Gottesgedanken: Erkenntnis,*

Eschatologie und Ethik in Religionen der Spätantike und des frühen Mittelalters, Tübingen 2016, 123–32.

———, From sacrilege to sacrifice: Observations on violent death in classical and modern Arabic poetry, in F. Pannewick (ed.), *Martyrdom in literature: Visions of death and meaningful suffering in Europe and the Middle East from antiquity to modernity*, Wiesbaden 2004, 259–82.

———, *Der Koran: Frühmekkanische Suren*, Berlin 2011.

———, Symmetrie und Paarbildung in der Koranischen Eschatologie: Philologisch-Stilistisches zu Surat ar-Rahman, in *MFOB* 50.1 (1984), 443–75.

Newman, A.J., al-Jaḥīm, in I.R. Netton (ed.), *The encyclopedia of Islamic civilisation and religion*, London and New York 2008, 324.

Nicholson, R.A. (ed. and trans.), *The Mathnawí of Jalálu'ddín Rúmí*, 8 vols., London 1925–40.

Nomoto, S., An early Ismāʿīlī-Shīʿī thought on the messianic figure (the Qāʾim) according to al-Rāzī (d. ca. 322/933–4), in *Orient: Reports of the Society for Near Eastern Studies in Japan* 45 (2009), 19–39.

———, An introduction to Abū Ḥātim al-Rāzī's *Kitāb al-Iṣlāḥ*, in Ḥ. Mīnūchihr and M. Muḥaqqiq (eds.), *Kitāb al-Iṣlāḥ by Abū l-Ḥātim Aḥmad ibn Ḥamdān al-Rāzī*, Tehran 1998, 1–34.

O'Leary, S., *Arguing the apocalypse: A theory of millennial rhetoric*, New York 1994.

Omar, K., *Tod im Islam und Sterben in der Türkei*, Franfurt am Main 2004.

Omidsalar, M., Hell ii. Islamic period, in *EIr*, online version (http://www.iranicaonline.org/articles/hell-ii-islamic-period, accessed 16 April 2014).

O'Shaughnessy, T., *Muhammad's thoughts on death: A thematic study of the Qur'anic data*, Leiden 1969.

———, The seven names for hell in the Qurʾān, in *BSOAS* 24 (1961), 444–69.

Ott, C., Das Paradies in den Erzählungen aus Tausendundeiner Nacht, in A. Müller and H. Roder (eds.), *1001 Nacht – Wege ins Paradies*, Mainz 2006, 11–8.

Ourghi, M., „Ein Licht umgab mich …" – Die eschatologischen Visionen des iranischen Präsidenten Mahmūd Ahmadīnežād, in *WI* 49 (2009), 163–80.

———, Eschatologie im zwölferschiitischen Islam, in P. Bukovec and B. Kolkmann-Klamt (eds.), *Jenseitsvorstellungen im Orient. Kongressakten der 2. Tagung der RVO (3./4. Juni 2011, Tübingen)*, Hamburg (2014), 503–18.

———, *Schiitischer Messianismus und Mahdi-Glaube in der Neuzeit*, Würzburg 2008.

Pahlitzsch, J., The concern for spiritual salvation and memoria in Islamic public endowments in Jerusalem (XII–XVI C.) as compared to the concepts of Christendom, in U. Vermeulen and J.V. Steenbergen (eds.), *Egypt and Syria in the Fatimid, Ayyubid and Mamluk eras III*, Leuven 2001, 329–44.

Pannewick, F., Wafa Idris – eine Selbstmordattentäterin zwischen Nationalheldin und Heiliger, in S. Weigel (ed.), *Märtyrer-Portraits: Von Opfertod, Blutzeugen und heiligen Kriegern*, Munich 2007, 110–3.

Panzac, D., Wabāʾ, in *EI*², xi, 2–4.
Papan-Matin, F., *Beyond death: The mystical teachings of ʿAyn al-Quḍāt al-Hamadhānī*, Leiden 2010.
Paret, R., al-Aʿrāf, in *EI*², I, 603–4.
———, al-Burāḳ, in *EI*², i, 1310–1.
———, Die 'ferne Gebetsstätte' in Sure 17, 1, in *Der Islam* 34 (1959), 150–2.
Pedani, M.P, L'idea della morte nel mondo ottomano, in A. Fabris (ed.), *Tra quattro paradisi: Esperienze, ideologie e riti reltivi all morte tra Oriente e Occidente*, Venice 2013, 107–28.
Peerwani, L.-P. (trans.), *Spiritual psychology: The fourth intellectual journey in transcendent philosophy: Volumes VIII & IX of the Asfar* [of Mullā Ṣadrā], London 2008.
Pellat, Ch., Ghayba, in *EI*², ii, 1026.
Pera, R., *Ibn Qaiyim al-Ǧauzīya und die Frage nach dem Vergehen des Höllenfeuers: Vita, Opera, eine Argumentationsanalyse anhand seines Werks* ḥādī l-arwāḥ ilā bilād al-afrāḥ, Berlin 2014.
Perlmann, M., Ibn Qayyim and the Devil, in R. Ciasca (ed.), *Studi Orientalistici in onore di Giorgio Levi della Vida*, ii, Rome 1956, 330–7.
Peters, R., *Islam and colonialism: The doctrine of jihad in modern history*, The Hague, Paris, and New York 1979.
———, Jihād, in J.L. Esposito (ed.), *The Oxford encyclopedia of the modern Islamic world*, ii, Oxford 1995, 369–73.
Peterson, D.C., Creation, in *EQ*, i, 472–80.
Petruccioli, A. (ed.), *Gardens in the time of the great Muslim empires: Papers from a conference at Harvard University and the Massachusetts Institute of Technology*, Cambridge and Leiden 1997.
Pielow, D., *Der Stachel des Bösen: Vorstellungen über den Bösen und das Böse im Islam*, Würzburg 2008.
Pines, S., Ibn al-Haytham's critique of Ptolemy, in H. Guerlac (ed.), *Actes du dixième congrès international d'histoire des sciences (Ithaca 1962)*, i, Paris 1964, 547–50.
Poonawala, I.K., Apocalyptic ii. In Muslim Iran, in *EIr*, ii, 154–60.
Piotrovskiy, M.B., Jahannam, in *Islam: Entsiklopedicheskiy slovar'*, Moscow 1991, 63.
———, Janna, in *Islam: Entsiklopedicheskiy slovar'*, Moscow 1991, 59–60.
———, *Koranicheskie skazaniya* [*The Quranic stories*], Moscow 1991.
Poston, L., The second coming of ʿIsa: An exploration of Islamic premillennialism, in *MW* 100 (2010), 100–16.
Qāḍī, ʿAbd-ar-Raḥīm Ibn-Aḥmad al-: *Das Totenbuch des Islam: die Lehren des Propheten Mohammed über das Leben nach dem Tode*, Freiburg im Breisgau 1993.
Qāḍī, Wadād, al-, *The primordial covenant and human history in the Qurʾān*, Beirut 2006.
Rafiabadi, H.N., *Saints and saviours of Islam*, New Delhi 2005.
Rahman, F., Dreams, imagination, and ʿĀlam al-Mithāl, in *Islamic Studies* (1964), 167–80.

———, Eschatology, in B.S. Turner (ed.), *Islam: Critical concepts in sociology*, i, *Islam as religion and law*, London and New York 2003, 148–61.

Raven, W., A *Kitāb al-ʿaẓama*: On cosmology, hell and paradise, in F. de Jong (ed.), *Miscellanea arabica et islamica*, Leuven 1993, 135–42.

———, Riḍwān, in *EI*², viii, 519.

Rebstock, U., Das Grabesleben: Eine islamische Konstruktion zwischen Himmel und Hölle, in R. Brunner et al. (eds.), *Islamstudien ohne Ende: Festschrift für Werner Ende zum 65. Geburtstag*, Würzburg 2003, 371–82.

Reineccius, C. (ed.), *Eduardi Pocockii lingvarum orientalium in academia Oxoniensi qvandam professoris notæ miscellaneæ philologico-biblicæ, qvibus Porta Mosis sive præfationum R. Mosis Maimonidis in libros Mischnajoth Commentariis præmissarum & à Pocockio ex Arabico Latine versarum fascis olim stipata prodiit*, Leipzig 1705.

Reinhart, A.K., *Before revelation: The boundaries of Muslim moral thought*, New York 1995.

———, The here and the hereafter in Islamic religious thought, in S.S. Blair and J. Bloom (eds.), *Images of paradise in Islamic art*, Hanover, NH 1991, 15–24.

Riesebrodt, M., *The promise of salvation: A theory of religion*, Chicago and London 2010.

Ringgren, H., Resurrection, in *ER*, vii, 7762–8.

Rippin, A., Colors, in *EQ*, i, 361–5.

———, The commerce of eschatology, in S. Wild (ed.), *The Qurʾān as text*, Leiden 1996, 125–36.

———, Devil, in *EQ*, i, 524–7.

———, Shayṭān, in *EI*², ix, 406–9.

———, Sidrat al-Muntahā, in *EI*², ix, 550.

Ritter, H., *Das Meer der Seele: Mensch, Welt und Gott in den Geschichten des Fariduddin ʿAttar*, Leiden 1978, repr. Leiden 1995.

———, *The ocean of the soul: Men, the world and God in the stories of Farīd al-Dīn ʿAṭṭār*, trans. J. O'Kane, with the editorial assistance of B. Radtke, Leiden and Boston 2003.

Robinson, B.W., Miʿrādj, in *EI*², xii, 97–105.

Robinson, C., Seeing paradise: Metaphor and vision in Taifa palace architecture, in *Gesta* 36.2 (1988), 145–55.

Robson, J., Is the Moslem hell eternal?, in *MW* 28 (1938), 386–93.

Rosenthal, F., History and the Qurʾān, in *EQ*, ii, 428–42.

———, *Knowledge triumphant*, Leiden 1970.

———, Reflections on love in paradise, in J.H. Marks and R.M. Good (eds.), *Love & death in the ancient Near East: Essays in the honor of Marvin H. Pope*, Guilford, CT, 1987, 247–54, repr. in F. Rosenthal, *Muslim intellectual and social history: A collection of essays*, Aldershot 1990.

Rubin, U., Apocalypse and authority in Islamic tradition: The emergence of the twelve leaders, in *Qanṭara* 18 (1997), 11–41.

———, Pre-existence and light: Aspects of the concept of Nur Muhammad, in IOS 5 (1975), 62–119, repr. in U. Rubin, *Muhammad the Prophet and Arabia*, Farnham 2011.

Rudolph, U., al-Waʿd wa ʾl-Waʿīd, in EI², xi, 6–7.

Rueter, W.M., *Aljamiado narratives of Muhammad's ascension to heaven: The Moriscos and the miʿraj*, Ann Arbor, MI 2009.

Ruggles, D.F., *Gardens, landscape and vision in the palaces of Islamic Spain*, University Park, PA 2003.

Rüling, J.B., *Beiträge zur Eschatologie: Der Islam*, Leipzig 1895.

Russell, J.R., Burial iii. In Zoroastrianism, in *EIr*, iv, 561–3.

Rustom, M., Deliverance, in M. Iqbal (ed.), *The integrated encyclopedia of the Qurʾān*, Sherwood Park (forthcoming).

———, Eschatology in the Quran, in M. Dakake and D. Madigan (eds.), *The Routledge companion to the Quran*, New York (forthcoming).

———, The nature and significance of Mullā Ṣadrā's Qurʾānic writings, in *Journal of Islamic Philosophy* 6 (2010), 109–30.

———, Psychology, eschatology, and imagination in Mullā Ṣadrā Shīrāzī's commentary on the *ḥadīth* of awakening, in *Islam and Science* 5.1 (2007), 9–22.

———, *The triumph of mercy: Philosophy and scripture in Mullā Ṣadrā*, Albany, NY 2012.

Rustomji, N., American visions of the Houri, in MW 97.1 (2007), 79–92.

———, *The garden and the fire: Heaven and hell in Islamic culture*, New York 2009.

Ryan, P., The descending scroll: A study of the notion of revelation as apocalypse in the Bible and in the Qurʾān, in *Ghana Bulletin of Theology* 4 (1975), 24–39.

Sachedina, A., *Islamic messianism: The idea of the mahdī in twelver Shīʿism*, Albany, NY 1981.

———, Messianism, in J.L. Esposito (ed.), *Oxford encyclopedia of the modern Islamic world*, iii, New York 1995, 95–9.

Sadan, J., Khamr, in EI², iv, 997–8.

Saleh, W., Death and dying in the Qur'an, in *American Journal of Islamic Studies: Texts and Society* 25.3 (2008), 97–111.

———, The etymological fallacy and Quranic studies: Muhammad, paradise, and late antiquity, in A. Neuwirth et al. (eds.), *The Qurʾān in context: Historical and literary investigations into the Qurʾānic milieu*, Leiden 2010, 649–98.

———, The woman as a locus of apocalyptic anxiety, in A. Neuwirth et al. (eds.), *Myths, historical archetypes and symbolic figures in Arabic literature*, Beirut 1999, 123–45.

Sarhill, N. et al., The terminally ill Muslim: Death and dying from the Muslim perspective, in *American Journal of Hospice and Palliative Medicine* 18.4 (2001), 251–5.

Schacht, J., Ḳatl, in EI², ix (1997), 767–72.

Scheiner, J., Wenn Jesus nach Damaksus kommt: Islamische Vorstellungen zum Ende der Welt, in R. Feldmeier and M. Winet (eds.), *Gottesgedanken: Erkenntnis,*

Eschatologie und Ethik in Religionen der Spätantike und des frühen Mittelalters, Tübingen 2016, 105–11.

Scherberger, M., The Chagatay *Miʿrājnāma* attributed to Ḥakīm Süleymān Ata: A misisonary text from the twelfth or thirteenth century preserved in modern manuscripts, in C. Gruber and F. Colby (eds.), *The Prophet's ascension: Cross-cultural encounters with the Islamic* miʿrāj *tales*, Bloomington, IN 2010, 78–96.

———, *Das Miʿrāğname: Die Himmel- und Höllenfahrt des Propheten Muhammad in der osttürkischen Überlieferung*, Würzburg 2003.

Schimmel, A., The celestial garden, in E.B. Macdougal and R. Ettinghausen (eds.), *The Islamic garden*, Washington, DC 1976, 13–39.

———, Creation and judgment in the Koran and the mystic-poetical interpretation, in A. Schimmel and A. Falaturi (eds.), *We believe in one God*, New York 1979, 148–80.

———, Karbala and the Imam Husayn in Persian and Indo-Muslim literature, in *al-Serat* 12 (1986). (Electronic publication, http://www.al-islam.org/al-serat/Karbala-Schimmel.htm, accessed 18 February 2010).

———, *Mystical dimensions of Islam*, Chapel Hill, NC 1975.

———, Some aspects of mystical prayer in Islam, in *WI New series* 2.2 (1952), 112–25.

———, *Die Träume des Kalifen. Träume und ihre Deutung in der islamischen Kultur*, Munich 1998, esp. 198–229 (Dreaming about the hereafter).

Schmidtke, S., Destiny, in *EQ*, i, 522–4.

———, The doctrine of the transmigration of soul according to Shihāb al-Dīn al-Suhrawardī (killed 587/1191) and his followers, in *SIr* 28 (1999), 237–54.

———, Pairs and pairing, in *EQ*, iv, 1–9.

Schoeler, G., *Abū l-ʿAlāʾ al-Maʿarrī, Paradies und Hölle: Die Jenseitsreise aus dem « Sendschreiben über die Vergebung »*, Munich 2002.

Schönig, H., AIDS als das Tier (*dābba*) der islamischen Eschatologie: Zur Argumentation einer türkischen Schrift, in *WI* 30 (1990), 211–8.

Schrieke, B., Die Himmelsreise Mohammeds, in *Der Islam* 6 (1916), 1–30.

——— et al., Miʿrādj, in *EI*², vii, 97–105.

Schützinger, H., *Ursprung und Entwicklung der arabischen Abraham-Nimrod Legende*, Bonn 1961.

Sells, M., Ascension, in *EQ*, i, 176–81.

———, Ibn ʿArabī's garden among the flames: A reevaluation, in *History of Religions* 23.4 (1984), 287–315.

———, Spirit, in *EQ*, v, 114–7.

Shaked, S., Eschatology i. In Zoroatsrianism and Zoroastrian influence, in *EIr* viii, 565–9.

Shaki, M., Dūzak, in *EIr*, vii, 613–5.

Shani, R.Y., The lion image in Safavid *miʿraj* paintings, in A. Daneshvari (ed.), *A survey of Persian art*, xviii, *Islamic period*, Costa Mesa, CA 2005, 265–426.

Shoemaker, S.J., *The death of a prophet: The end of Muhammad's life and the beginnings of Islam*, Philadelphia 2012.

Slyper, A., The eschatological conflict between Judaism and Islam, in *Midstream* 54.6 (2008), 27–32.

Smirnov, A.V., Happiness as self-realization: Two Islamic approaches, in *Bulletin of Peoples' Friendship University of Russia* 1 (2014), 94–100.

———, *Velikij šejch sufizma: Opyt paradigmal'nogo analiza filosofii Ibn Arabi*, Moscow 1993.

Smith, J.I., Concourse between the living and the dead in Islamic eschatological literature, in *History of Religions* 19 (1980), 224–36.

———, Eschatology, in *EQ*, ii, 44–54.

———, Reflections on aspects of immortality in Islam, in *Harvard Theological Review* 70.1–2 (1977), 85–98.

——— and Y.Y. Haddad, *The Islamic understanding of death and resurrection*, Oxford and New York et al. 2002.

——— and Y.Y. Haddad, Women in the afterlife: The Islamic view as seen from Qur'ān and tradition, in *Journal of the American Academy of Religion* 43.1 (1975), 39–50.

Smith, M., On the history of *ΑΠΟΚΑΛΥΠΤΩ* and *ΑΠΟΚΑΛΥΨΙΣ*, in D. Hellholm (ed.), *Apocalypticism in the Mediterranean world and the near east*, Tübingen 1989, 9–20.

Smoor, P., Elegies and other poems on death by Ibn al-Rūmī, in *JAL* 27 (1996), 49–84.

Snouck Hurgronje, C., Der Mahdi, in C. Snouck Hurgronje (ed.), *Verspreide geschriften*, i, Bonn and Leipzig 1923–7, 145–82.

Stager, L.E., Jerusalem and the garden of Eden, in *Eretz-Israel* 26 (1999), 183–94.

———, Jerusalem as Eden, in *Biblical Archaeology Review* 26.3 (2000), 36–47.

Stehly, R., Un probleme de théologie islamique: La definition des fautes graves (*kabā'ir*), in *REI* 45 (1977), 165–81.

Stetkevych, S.P., Intoxication and immortality: Wine and associated imagery in al-Maʿarrī's garden, in J.W. Wright and E.K. Rowson (eds.), *Homoeroticism in classical Arabic literature*, New York 1997, 210–32.

Stieglecker, H., Die Eschatologie, in H. Stieglecker, *Die Glaubenslehren des Islam*, Munich 1962, 730–808.

Stowasser, B., The apocalypse in the teachings of Said Nursi, in Ibrahim M. Abu-Rabiʿ (ed.), *Islam at the crossroads: On the life and thought of Bediuzzaman Said Nursi*, Albany, NY 2003, 229–36.

———, The end is near: Minor and major signs of the hour in Islamic texts and contexts, in A. Amanat and J. Collins (eds.), *Apocalypse and violence*, New Haven, NH 2002, 45–68.

Subtelny, M.E., The Jews at the edge of the world in a Timurid-era *Miʿrājnāma*: The Islamic ascension narrative as missionary text, in C. Gruber and F. Colby (eds.),

The Prophet's ascension: Cross-cultural encounters with the Islamic miʿrāj *tales*, Bloomington, IN 2010, 50–77.

Suermann, H., Muḥammad in Christian and Jewish apocalyptic expectations, in *Islam and Christian-Muslim Relations* 5 (1994), 15–21.

———, Notes concernant l'apocalypse copte de Daniel et la chute des Omayades, in *Parole de l'Orient* 11 (1983), 329–48.

Sunderman, W., Eschatology ii. Manichean eschatology, in *EIr*, viii, 569–75.

Szombathy, Z., Come hell or high water: Afterlife as a poetic convention in medieval Arabic literature, in K. Dévényi and A. Fodor (eds.), *Proceedings of the colloquium on paradise and hell in Islam, Keszthely, 7–14 July 2002*, Budapest 2008 (= *The Arabist* 28–29 (2008)), 163–78.

Szyska, C., Martyrdom: A drama of foundation and transition, in F. Pannewick (ed.), *Martyrdom in literature: Death and meaningful suffering in Europe and the Middle East from antiquity to modernity*, Wiesbaden 2004, 29–45.

Tafażżoli, A., Āsmān, in *EIr*, ii, 770–1.

———, Činwad Puhl, in *EIr*, v, 594–5.

Tamari, S., *Iconotextual studies in the Muslim vision of paradise*, Wiesbaden 1999.

Tamer, G., *Zeit und Gott: Hellenistische Zeitvorstellungen in der altarabischen Dichtung und im Koran*, Berlin and New York 2008.

Taylor, C.D., *In the vicinity of the righteous: Ziyara and the veneration of Muslim saints in late medieval Egypt*, Leiden 1999.

Taylor, J.B., Some aspects of Islamic eschatology, in *Religious Studies* 4.1 (1968), 57–76.

Thackston, W.M., The Paris Miʿrājnāme, in *Journal of Turkish Studies* 18 (1994), 263–99.

Thomassen, E., Islamic hell, in *Numen* 56 (2009), 401–16.

Tlili, S., The meaning of the Qur'anic word 'dābba': 'Animals' or 'nonhuman animals'?, in *JQS* 12.1–2 (2010), 167–87.

Toelle, H., Fire, in *EQ*, ii, 210–3.

Tottoli, R., "Due fiumi sono credenti e due miscredenti ...": Una geografia fluviale sacra in un detto di Muḥammad?, in M. Bernardini, G.M. D'Erme, and N.L. Tornesello (eds.), *Scritti in onore di Giovanni M. D'Erme*, Naples 2005, 1221–35.

———, Muslim eschatological literature and western studies, in *Der Islam* 83 (2006), 452–77.

———, The Qur'an, Qur'anic exegesis and Muslim traditions: The case of *zamharīr* (Q. 76:13) among hell's punishments, in *JQS* 10 (2009), 142–52.

———, Tours of hell and punishments of sinners in *miʿrāj* narratives: Use and meaning of eschatology, in C.C. Gruber and F. Colby (eds.), *The Prophet's ascension: Cross-cultural encounters with the Islamic* miʿraj *tales*, Bloomington, IN 2010, 11–26.

———, Two *Kitāb al-Miʿrāj* in the manuscripts collection of the Paul Kahle Library of the University of Turin, in P.G. Borbone, A. Mengozzi, and M. Tosco (eds.), *Loquentes linguis: Studi linguistici e orientali in onore di Fabrizio A. Pennacchietti*, Wiesbaden 2006, 703–10.

———, What will be the fate of the sinners in hell? The categories of the damned in some Muslim popular literature, in K. Dévényi and A. Fodor (eds.), *Proceedings of the colloquium on paradise and hell in Islam, Keszthely, 7–14 July 2002*, Budapest 2008 (= *The Arabist* 28–29 (2008)), 179–96.

Tritton, A.S,. Baʿth, in EI², i, 1092–3.

———, Dunyā, in EI², ii, 626.

Tubach, J., A. Drost-Abgarjan and S. Vashalomidze (eds.), *Sehnsucht nach dem Paradies: Paradiesvorstellungen in Judentum, Christentum, Manichäismus und Islam: Beiträge des Leucorea-Kolloquiums zu Ehren von Walther Beltz*, Wiesbaden 2010.

Turner, C., The "tradition of Mufaḍḍal" and the doctrine of the *Rajʿa*: Evidence of *ghuluww* in the eschatology of Twelver Shiʿism?, in *Iran: Journal of the British Institute of Persian Studies* 44 (2006), 175–95.

Ünal, A., *The resurrection and the afterlife*, New Jersey 2005.

Vahman, F., *Arda Wiraz Namag: The Iranian Divina Commedia*, London 1986.

Vajda, G., Idrīs, in EI², iii, 1030–1.

———, A propos de la perpétuité de la rétribution d'outre-tombe en théologie musulmane, in *SIs* 11 (1959), 29–38.

Vakily, A., Some notes on Shaykh Aḥmad Sirhindī and the problem of the mystical significance of paradise, in T. Lawson (ed.), *Reason and inspiration in Islam: Theology, philosophy and mysticism in Muslim thought*, London and New York 2005, 407–17.

van Bladel, K., Heavenly cords and prophetic authority in the Quran and its late antique context, in BSOAS 70.2 (2007), 223–46.

van den Bergh, S., Abad, in EI², i, 2.

van Donzel, E. and A. Schmidt, *Gog and Magog in early Eastern Christian and Islamic sources: Sallam's quest for Alexander's wall*, Leiden 2010.

van Donzel, E. and C. Ott, Yādjûdj wa-Mādjūdj, in EI², xi, 231–4.

van Ess, J., Das begrenzte Paradies, in P. Salmon (ed.), *Mélanges d'islamologie: Volume dédié à la mémoire de Armand Abel*, Leiden 1974, 108–27.

———, *Dschihad gestern und heute*, Berlin 2012.

———, *Theologie und Gesellschaft im 2. und 3. Jahrhundert Hidschra: Eine Geschichte des religiösen Denkens im frühen Islam*, 6 vols., Berlin 1991–7.

———, Vision and ascension: *Sūrat al-Najm* and its relationship with Muḥammad's *miʿrāj*, in JQS 1 (1999), 47–62.

van Lit, L.W.C., *Eschatology and the world of image in Suhrawardi and his commentators*, PhD dissertation, University of Utrecht 2014.

———, Ghiyāth al-Dīn Dashtakī on the world of image (*ʿālam al-mithāl*): The place of his *Ishrāq Hayākil al-nūr* in the commentary tradition on Suhrawardī, in *Ishrâq: Islamic Philosophy Yearbook* 5 (2014), 116–36.

van Reeth, J., Le vignoble du paradis et le chemin qui y mène; la thèse de C. Luxenberg et les sources du Coran, in *Arabica* 53 (2006), 511–24.

Varzi, R., *Warring souls: Youth, media, and martyrdom in post-revolutionary Iran*, Durham 2006.

Vasram, N. and A. Toussi, *Mahdi in the Qur'an according to Shi'ite Qur'an commentators*, Qum 1387/2008.

Vuckovic, B.O., *Heavenly journeys, earthly concerns: The legacy of the mi'rāj in the formation of Islam*, New York and London 2005.

Waardenburg, J., Death and the dead, in *EQ*, i, 505–11.

Waldman, M.R., Eschatology: Islamic eschatology, in *ER*, iv, 2836–40.

———, Islamic eschatology, in *ER*, v, 152–6.

Walker, P., The doctrine of metempsychosis in Islam, in W. Hallaq and D. Little (eds.), *Islamic studies presented to Charles J. Adams*, Leiden 1991, 219–38.

———, Eternal cosmos and the womb of history: Time in early Ismaili thought, in *IJMES* 9 (1978), 355–66.

———, Ismaili eschatology, in G. Howarth and O. Leaman (eds.), *Encyclopedia of death and dying*, London 2001, 378–9.

Walls, J.L. (ed.), *The Oxford handbook of eschatology*, New York 2008.

Wan, S., Ibn Sina and Abu al-Barakat al-Baghdadi on the origination of the soul and the invalidation of its transmigration, in *Islam and Science* 52 (2007), 151–64.

Wanes, D., Tree(s), in *EQ*, v, 358–62.

Webb, G., Angel, in *EQ*, i, 84–92.

Welch, A.T., Death and dying in the Qur'an, in F.E. Reynolds and E.H. Waugh (eds.), *Religious encounters with Death: Insights from the history and anthropology of religions*, University Park, PA 1977, 183–99.

Wendell, C., The denizens of paradise, in H.W. Mason et al. (eds.), *Humaniora Islamica*, ii, The Hague 1974, 29–59.

Wensinck, A.J., Ḥawḍ, in *EI*², iii, 286.

———, Iblīs, in *EI*², iii, 668–9.

———, Isrāfīl, in *EI*², iv, 211.

———, Khaṭīʾa, in *EI*², iv, 1106–9.

———, Munkar wa-Nakīr, in *EI*², vii, 576–7.

———, Tasnīm, in *EI*², x, 360.

——— and A.S. Tritton, ʿAḏhāb al-Ḳabr in *EI*², i, 186–7.

——— and Ch. Pellat, Ḥūr, in *EI*², iii, 581–2.

Werbick, J., S. Kalisch and K. von Stosch (eds.), *Glaubensgewissheit und Gewalt: Eschatologische Erkundungen in Islam und Christentum*, Paderborn 2011.

Wheeler, B., *Mecca and Eden: Rituals, relics, and territory in Islam*, Chicago 2006.

Widengren, G., *The ascension of the Apostle and the heavenly book*, Uppsala and Wiesbaden 1950.

———, *Muḥammad, the Apostle of God, and his ascension*, Uppsala and Wiesbaden 1955.
Wild, S., Hell, in O. Leaman (ed.), *The Qur'an: An encyclopedia*, London 2006, 259–63.
———, Virgins of paradise and the Luxenberg hypothesis, in A. Neuwirth, N. Sinai, and M. Marx (eds.), *The Qur'ān in context: Historical and literary investigations into the Qur'ānic milieu*, Leiden 2009, 627–47.
Wisnovsky, R., Heavenly book, in *EQ*, ii, 412–4.
Wolff, M. (ed.), *Aḥwāl al-qiyāma: Muhammedanische Eschatologie*, Leipzig 1872, repr. Hildesheim, Zurich, and New York 2004.
Woods, B.A., *The Devil in dog form: A partial type-index of devil legends*, Berkeley 1959.
Wyatt, N., *Space and time in the religious life of the Near East*, Sheffield 2001.
Yücesoy, H., *Messianic beliefs and imperial politics in medieval Islam: The ʿAbbasid caliphate in the early ninth century*, Columbia, SC 2009.
Yusuf, H., Death, dying, and the afterlife in the Quran, in S. Nasr et al. (eds.), *The study Quran: A new translation and commentary*, New York 2015, 1819–55.
Zahniser, M.A.H, Parable, in *EQ*, iv, 9–12.
Zaki, M.M., Barzakh, in *EQ*, i, 204–7.
Zaman, M.Q., Death, funeral processions, and the articulation of religious authority in early Islam, in *SI* 93 (2001), 27–58.
———, Early ʿAbbāsid response to apocalyptic propaganda, in *IQ* 32 (1988), 236–44.
———, Muḥammad al-Nafs al-Zakkiya's mahdism, in *Hamdard Islamicus* 13 (1990), 59–65.

Indices

Notes on the Indices

In the indices that follow, the "al-", ayn (ʿ), and hamza (ʾ) are disregarded in the sort order. Information that appears in hard brackets is explanatory and has been added by the editors.

The Index of Proper Names is organized according to the name by which a figure is most commonly known, with cross references as necessary. It includes all mortal figures, including prophets. Groups of people (e.g., Sabians, Muʿtazilīs), angels, and other "beings" (e.g., God, Khiḍr) appear in the Index of Topics and Keywords. When texts are mentioned in relation to a figure, these are cited in the index by the original titles only.

The Index of Geographical Names and Toponyms includes earthly places. Otherworldly locations (e.g., rivers in paradise, Qāf mountain) appear in the Index of Topics and Keywords.

The Index of Book Titles and Other Texts includes all books and texts, with their translations, followed by the author (wherever possible).

The Index of Scriptural References includes all references to specific Quranic verses (with Sura number followed by a colon and the verse number) and Biblical verses. When a discussion concerns a whole chapter rather than a specific chapter and verse, this is cited under the appropriate chapter number followed by an en-dash. More general discussions of topics in the Quran and Bible appear in the Index of Topics and Keywords.

The Ḥadīth Index includes specific *ḥadīth* and *ḥadīth qudsī* (those quoted and those discussed as topics), while discussions related to the science of *ḥadīth* (e.g., categories of, criticism of, literature on) appear in the Index of Topics and Keywords under *ḥadīth*.

Index of Proper Names

Aaron (prophet, Hārūn) 51, 118, 202, 206
Abaza, Mona 1075
ʿAbdallāh b. ʿAbd al-Muṭallib 109 n. 52
Abdel Haleem, Muhammad 16
"Life and Beyond in the Qur'an" (1995) 9
Abdi, Murtuza Husain (fl. second half of the fourteenth/twentieth century) 743, 752
ʿAḇdīshōʿ bar Berīkā (d. 1318) – *Paradise of Eden* 806
ʿAbd al-Jabbār (d. 415/1025) 480
ʿAbd al-Malik (Umayyad) 1014
ʿAbd al-Raḥīm b. Aḥmad al-Qāḍī (fl. probably fifth–sixth/eleventh–twelfth centuries) 186, 861
Daqāʾiq al-akhbār fī dhikr al-janna wa-l-nār 188, 347–48, 819, 842
ʿAbd al-Raḥmān III 25, 979–80, 982, 992, 997–1002, 1005
ʿAbd al-Raḥmān Jāmī. *See* Jāmī, ʿAbd al-Rahmān
ʿAbd al-Raḥmān al-Ṣūfī (d. 986) – *Kitāb Ṣuwar al-kawākib al-thābita* 1098 fig.50.2
ʿAbduh, Muḥammad (d. 1323/1905) 1199, 1203, 1218
al-Manār 1202
Risālat al-tawḥīd 1202
Risālat al-wāridāt 1201
Abdülhamit II, 1223
Abdullah Arif (1922–70) 1171–73
Di babah pintō syeuruga lapan 1176
Nasib Atjeh 1186 fig.53.2
Pantōn Aceh 1174
ʿAbd al-Wāḥid b. Zayd (d. 177/793?) 281–83
ʿAbīd b. al-Abraṣ 149
Abraham (prophet, Ibrāhīm) 33, 42, 51–52, 190, 203–4, 402, 436, 517, 594, 658, 678 n. 9, 740, 853, 1235
Abū ʿAlī l-Daqqāq (d. 405/1015 or 412/1021) 274 n. 19
Abū ʿAlī l-Fārisī (d. 377/987) – *al-Ḥujja* 854
Abū ʿAlī Rudābar 594
Abū Bakr 118, 192 n. 24, 437 n. 25, 570, 880
Abū Bakr b. al-ʿArabī (d. 543/1148) 1107 n. 23
Abū Bakr al-Shiblī (d. 334/946) 568, 577, 580
Abū Bakr al-Ṣiddīq 989, 1043
Abū l-Dardāʾ (d. ca. 32/652) 240
Abū Dharr al-Ghifārī (d. ca. 32/652–3) 1116–17
Abū Dhuʾayb 149
Abū Ḥanīfa (d. 150/767) 171, 192 n. 25
Abū l-Ḥasan al-Ashʿarī. *See* al-Ashʿarī, Abū l-Ḥasan
Abū l-Ḥasan al-Bakrī (fl. sixth/twelfth century?) – *Ḥadīth al-miʿrāj* 878–79
Abū l-Ḥasan Nūrī (d. 205/907) 568
Abū Hāshim (d. 321/933) 480, 483
Abū Hurayra 330–31, 333–34, 411
Abu-Jaber, Diana – *Crescent* (2003) 953
Abū Jahl 570
Abū l-Kalām Āzād, Mawlānā (d. 1377/1958) 1209
Abu Khalil, As'ad 1287
Abū l-Khaṭṭāb b. Diḥya (d. 635/1236) 876
Abū Lahab 570
Abū Mijlaz (d. 106/724) 390, 400–2
Abū Muḥammad ʿAbdān (d. 286/899) 629
Abū Naḍra (d. 106/724) 390
Abū Nuʿaym al-Iṣfahānī (d. 430/1038) 821, 823–29, 831, 833, 843–44, 873
Ḥilyat al-awliyāʾ wa-ṭabaqāt al-aṣfiyāʾ 385–87, 820 n. 12
Ṣifat al-janna 347, 817
Abū Nuwās (d. 198 or 200/813 or 815) 300
Abū Saʿīd, Shaykh 580 n. 9
Abū Saʿīd b. Abī l-Khayr (d. 440/1049) 580, 582, 586–87, 589
Abū Saʿīd al-Khudrī (d. ca. 74/693) 275, 864
Abū Sufyān 410
Abū Tammām 856
Abū ʿUbayda 350
Abū Yaḥyā l-Nāqid (d. 285/898) 280
Abū Yaʿlā l-Mawṣilī = Aḥmad b. ʿAlī l-Tamīmī (d. 307/919) 823
Abū Yazīd (Berber leader) 981
Abū Yazīd al-Bisṭāmī. *See* al-Bisṭāmī, Abū Yazīd

Abū Yazīd Makhlad b. Kaydād 996–98
Acién Almansa, M. 982–84, 988
Adam 16, 35–37, 43–45, 51, 69, 110, 325, 402, 518, 561, 569 n. 15, 571, 573, 658, 678 n. 9, 710, 740, 796–98, 801, 863–64, 876, 1004
  creation of 183–84, 278, 327, 745
  and Eve, creation of 321, 431, 715, 869 n. 37, 1236
  fall of/expulsion from paradise 592–93, 798, 869 n. 37, 953, 1035–36
  and forbidden tree 720
  form of 711 n. 23, 713–14, 716, 721, 723, 725, 727
  as locus of manifestation of divine Word 724, 729
  lost paradise/Eden of 70, 136, 137 n. 5, 141, 186, 607, 659, 711 n. 24, 798, 1035
  primordial 511, 517
  sons/progeny/descendants 52, 112, 334, 497, 702–3, 725, 945
ʿAdī b. Zayd (d. ca. 600 CE) 853
ʿAḍud al-Dawla (Buyid) 1015 n. 23
Aeneas 110
al-Afghānī, Sayyid Jamāl al-Dīn (d. 1314/1897) 1200
  The Truth about the Neicheri (or Naturalists) Sect and an Explanation of the Neicheris / An Answer to the Dahriyyīn (or Materialists) 1199
Afsaruddin, Asma 17
Agathodaimon 506
Ahlwardt, Wilhelm 1133
Aḥmad b. Ayyūb b. Mānūs 738 n. 16
Aḥmad b. Ḥābiṭ (or, Khābiṭ or Ḥā'iṭ, d. 232/847) 738
Ahmed, Waleed 23
al-Aḥsā'ī, Aḥmad (d. 1241/1826) 716 n. 35
  Kitāb al-Rajʿa 607 n. 10
al-Aḥsā'ī, Ibn Abī Jumhūr (d. soon after 906/1501) 634 n. 171, 737 n. 11
ʿĀ'isha bt. Abī Bakr (d. 58/678) 325, 1110, 1119–20
al-Akhras, Āyāt 1275–80
al-Akhṭal (d. 92/710) 854
al-Albānī, Muḥammad Nāṣir al-Dīn (d. 1999) 333
  Ṣaḥīḥ al-targhīb wa-l-tarhīb 845
Albertus Magnus 908, 914
Alexander the Great [al-Iskandar/Dhū l-Qarnayn] 922–23, 1086
Alexandrin, Elizabeth 21
Alfarabi. *See* al-Fārābī
Alfonso the Wise (1221–84) 893, 899, 902
Algar, Hamid – *Najm al-Dīn Rāzī: The Path of God's Bondsmen from Origin to Return* (1982) 8
Ali, Tariq – *Shadows of the Pomegranate Tree* (1993) 953, 954 n. 7
Ali, Yusuf 257
ʿAlī Akbar and ʿAlī Aṣghar 1057
ʿAlī b. Abī Ṭālib (d. 40/661) 211 n. 66, 513, 581, 588, 616 n. 67, 619, 630, 632, 853, 880, 913, 916, 998, 1038, 1041–42, 1058
  as master of *ta'wīl* 677
  walāya of 680–81, 683
ʿAlī l-Jārim 957
ʿAlī l-Riḍā (d. 203/818) 616, 625
Alpago (d. 1522) – *Epistolla Sulla Vita Futura* 457 n. 51
Alphonse Mingana 781
ʿAlqama 144
Alvaro, Paulo (d. ca. 862) 894
al-ʿĀmilī al-Iṣfahānī (d. 1138/1726) 617
Āmina bt. Wahb (Prophet Muḥammad's mother) 109 n. 52
al-ʿĀmirī, Abū Manṣūr (d. 381/992) 62
Amīr Khusraw (d. 725/1325) – *Hasht bihisht* 349
Amir-Moezzi, Mohammad Ali 9, 606–7, 619, 681 n. 22
  Le Guide divin dans le shīʿisme originel: Aux sources de l'ésotérisme en Islam (1992) 9
  Le Voyage initiatique en terre d'Islam: Ascensions célestes et itinéraires spirituels (1996) 9
ʿAmr b. Dīnār (d. 126/743) 384–85, 391, 395
ʿAmr b. Kulthūm (fl. sixth century CE) 854
al-Āmulī, Ḥaydar (d. after 787/1385) 287, 516–17, 626 n. 117
Anas b. Mālik (d. most probably 91–3/709–11) 861, 878
Anaxagoras 664
Andrae, Tor (1885–1947) 6, 783–87, 794, 799, 801

ʿAntara (fl. sixth century CE) 138 n. 9, 147, 150–53, 854
Aquinas, St. Thomas 352, 897, 906, 908, 914–15, 918
Arafat, Yasser 1276
Arberry, A. 237, 392, 987
Aristophanes (ca. 450–388 BCE) 259–60
The Birds 253 n. 13
Aristotle (d. 322 BCE) 320, 427, 436, 446 n. 7, 447–48, 450, 522, 664, 897, 903 n. 29, 914
On the heavens 1087
Metaphysics Λ, 1087
Organon 451
Arnold, Theodor 5
Asad, Muhammad (b. Leopold Weiss, d. 1992) 107, 209, 747, 1209
al-Asad, Ḥāfiẓ 1252
al-Aṣamm (d. 200/816) 169
al-Aṣbahānī, Abū l-Qāsim al-Jawzī (d. 535/1140) – *Kitāb al-Targhīb wa-l-tarhīb* (known as *Qawām al-sunna*) 842 n. 120
Aʿshā Qays 853
al-Ashʿarī, Abū l-Ḥasan (d. 324/935–6) 371, 479, 738, 856
Kitāb al-Lumaʿ 471–72, 909
al-Ashʿarī, Abū Mūsā 867
al-Ashraf Khalīl 1024
ʿĀshūr, Raḍwā (b. 1946) 25, 957, 959–60, 962, 965–67, 973–74
Thulāthiyyat Gharnāṭa; The Granada Trilogy (1994–8) 953–54, 973
ʿĀṣim 174
Asín Palacios, Miguel 195 n. 36, 893, 900, 911, 915 n. 58, 916 n. 59
La Escatologia musulmana en la Divina Comedia (Muslim Eschatology and the Divine Comedy) 892
Aspinall, Edward 1171
Astarābādī, Faḍlallāh (d. 796/1394) 701
Jāwidān-nāma-yi kabīr 22, 702
Astarābādī, Sayyid Isḥāq – *Hidāyat-nāma* 708 n. 20
ʿAṭāʾ b. Abī Rabāḥ (d. 114/732) 384–85, 395
Aṭafayyish, Muḥammad b. Yūsuf (d. 1332/1914) 354
Atatürk, Mustafa Kemal (d. 1938) 1070, 1224, 1238, 1241
Attar, Samar 24
ʿAṭṭār, Farīd al-Dīn (d. ca. 617/1220–1) 489, 581, 916
Asrār-nāme (Book of secrets) 281
Manṭiq al-ṭayr (*Conference of the Birds*) 21, 200 n. 46, 579, 582–84, 586, 591–92, 595, 599
Augustine, St. 915
Avempace. *See* Ibn Bājja
Averroes. *See* Ibn Rushd
Avicenna. *See* Ibn Sīnā
Aws b. Ḥajar 147
al-Aylī, Yūnus (d. 159/775) 273 n. 15
Ayoub, Mahmoud – *Redemptive Suffering in Islam: A Study of the Devotional Aspects of Ashura in Twelver Shīʿism* (1978) 8
al-ʿAyyāshī, Abū l-Naḍr (d. ca. 320/932) 1253
al-ʿAyyāshī, Muḥammad (d. end third/ninth–beginning fourth/tenth century) 621
al-ʿAzīz (d. 386/996) [Fatimid caliph] 260
ʿAzīz-i Nasafī (seventh/thirteenth century) 518
al-Azmeh, Aziz 342, 560–61, 1144
al-Azraqī (d. ca. 250/864) – *Akhbār Makka* 357 n. 80

Bābā Ṭāhir (d. after 446/1055) 580 n. 9
Bābur, Sultan (888–937/1483–1530) 956 n. 13
Bacon, Francis (d. 1626) 98 n. 17
Bacon, Roger 116 n. 85, 915
Badakhchani, S.J. 22, 628, 684 n. 31
Badawi, Abd el-Rahman 488
al-Baghawī (d. 516/1122) 872
Baghdādī, Khalīd 1252
al-Baghdādī, Majd al-Dīn (d. 633/1219) 581
Bahāʾ-ī Walad (d. 628/1230) 286–87
al-Baḥrānī (d. 1107/1695–96 or 1109/1697–98) 607 n. 11
Bakhtin, Mikhail 818
Ballanfat, Paul – *Le dévoilement des secrets et les apparitions des lumières: Journal spirituel du maître de Shîrâz* (1996) 9
al-Ballūṭī, Mundhir b. Saʿīd (d. 355/966) 985, 1002–3
al-Baqlī. *See* Rūzbihān al-Baqlī
Barceló, C. 991–92, 995
al-Barghūtī, Murīd (1944–) 955

al-Barqī, Aḥmad (d. ca. 280/893–4) – *Kitāb al-Maḥāsin* 608
al-Barzanjī, Zayn al-ʿĀbidīn (d. 1103/1691) 876
ʿAlāmāt al-qiyāma 1249–50
Bashshār b. Burd (d. 168/784) 852–53
Basri, Hasan 1170
al-Baṭalyawsī (d. 521/1127) – *Sharḥ al-mukhtār min Luzūmiyyāt Abī l-ʿAlāʾ* 850
Baudrillard, Jean 1068, 1075
Simulacra and Simulation 1074
Baur, F.Ch. 103
Bausani, A. 596
al-Bayāḍī (d. 877/1472–3) – *al-Ṣirāṭ* 608 n. 15
Baybārs, Sultan (r. 658–76/1260–77) 1014 n. 19
al-Bayḍāwī (d. ca. 685/1286) 224, 228 n. 21, 230 n. 23, 232–33, 236, 239, 241–43, 246
Anwār al-tanzīl wa-asrār al-taʾwīl 223, 228, 244–45, 248
al-Bayḍāwī, ʿAbdallāh (d. 716/1316) 18, 469, 477, 481
Ṭawāliʿ al-anwār 470, 479
al-Bayhaqī, Abū Bakr (d. 458/1066) 187 n. 15, 823, 863
Beck, Dom Edmund (1902–91) 785–86, 794, 800
Becker, Carl Heinrich 102, 1131
Bell, Richard 58, 102
Beltz, Walter 341 n. 1
Sehnsucht nach dem Paradies: Mythologie des Korans (1979) 7–8
Bencheikh, J.E. 1021 n. 42
Bernardo, Aldo 913
Bernard of Clairvaux, Saint 904–5, 918
Bijlefeld, Willem – "Eschatology" (2004) 10
Birkeland, Harris 102
al-Bisṭāmī, Abū Yazīd (d. 261/874 or 264/877–8) 283, 567, 580, 582, 586, 589
al-Biṭrūjī (d. 1185–86) 905 n. 32
Bloom, Harold 892 n. 4, 915
The Anxiety of Influence: A Theory of Poetry (1973) 1157
Bobzin, Hartmut 1127
Boethius 909
De Consolatione Philosophiae (*On the Consolation of Philosophy*) 902–3
Bonaventura of Siena 893, 899, 918
Boniface VIII (pope) 897
Borges, Jorge Luis 1069
Botha, P.J. 799
Böwering, Gerhard – *The Mystical Vision of Existence in Classical Islam: The Qurʾānic Hermeneutics of the Ṣūfī Sahl at-Tustarī (d. 283/896)* (1980) 8
Boym, S. 955
Bozdağ, Muhammed (b. 1967) 1236–45, 1253, 1256–61
Sonsuzluk Yolculuğu 1235
Brett, M. 677
Brock, Sebastian 797
Brockelmann, Carl 222 n. 3, 806 n. 1
Brown, Jonathan 313 n. 6, 822 n. 23
Brunetto Latini (1220–94) 899, 902, 913, 915
Büchner, Ludwig – *Kraft und Stoff* 1254
Buhl, Frants 6
al-Bukhārī (d. 256/870) 191, 193, 211, 313, 822, 825, 861, 871
Ṣaḥīḥ al-Bukhārī (= *al-Jāmiʿ al-ṣaḥīḥ*) 182, 189, 196, 261
Bultmann, Rudolf Karl 344
Bürgel, J.Ch. 586
al-Bursī, Rajab (d. ca. 843/1411) 619
Burūjirdī, Sarbāz – *Asrār al-shahāda* 1056
Burzōye (or Barzūya, Barzawayhi) 925
al-Būṣīrī – *Burda* 35

Cachin, Françoise – "The Painter's Landscape," 1072–73
Cane, Peter 1099
Cantarino, Vicente 903
Canto, A. 999
Cantor, Paul A. 914
Casanova, Paul 11
Mohammed et la fin du monde (1911–13) 6, 102
Cavalcanti, Guido (1257–1300) 909, 913, 915
Chalmeta, P. 980
Charkhī, Yaʿqūb (d. 851/1447) – *Risāla-yi abdāliyya* 695
Charlemagne 896, 908
Chittick, William 3–4, 6
Imaginal Worlds (1994) 9
Sufi Path of Knowledge (1989) 8
Chodkiewicz, Michel
Le sceau des saints: Prophétie et sainteté dans la doctrine d'Ibn Arabî (1986) 8

Un océan sans rivage: Ibn Arabî, le livre et la loi (1992) 8
Christie, Niall 19, 1168
Colby, Frederick 875, 877, 885
Coleridge, Samuel Taylor 428
Collins, John 98, 111
Dead Sea Scrolls 93
Comte 1241
Conrad III of Germany 895–96
Cook, David 11, 1144, 1259–61
Studies in Muslim Apocalyptic (2002) 10
Copernicus (1473–1543) – *De revolutionibus* (1543) 1094
Corbin, Henry 7–9, 20, 94 n. 2, 487–88, 498–502, 510–11, 516, 631, 633, 686 n. 40, 687
En Islam iranien 7, 491 n. 22
Terre céleste et corps de résurrection: De l'Iran mazdéen à l'Iran shî'ite (1960) 7
Cosquin, Emmanuel 924
Crone, Patricia 68
Csapo, Eric 343
Cut Nyak Dien (1850–1908) 1169
Cut Nyak Meutia (1870–1910) 1169
Cyrus the Great (d. 530 BCE) 1209

Daftary, Farhad 521, 676, 683
al-Ḍaḥḥāk b. Muzāḥim (d. 105/723) 167, 231–32, 248, 257
Dakake, Maria 11
"The Soul as *barzakh:* Substantial Motion and Mullā Ṣadrā's Theory of Human Becoming" (2004) 10
Damsté, Henri (1874–1955) 1152, 1158–59, 1162, 1164
Dante 893, 901, 903, 907, 913
Divine Comedy 24, 892, 894, 898–900, 904, 906, 912, 914–19
Inferno 898
Paradiso 895–96, 902, 906, 908
Purgatorio 902, 912, 914
al-Dārānī, Abū Sulaymān (d. 235/850) 283
al-Dāraquṭnī (d. 385/995) 821
al-Dārimī (d. 255/869) 872
Sunan 313
Darwin 1241
Darwīsh, Maḥmūd (1941–2008) 1276, 1280
Dāvar-Panāh (d. 1384 SH/2005) 622
da Vinci, Leonardo 116 n. 85
Dāwūd, Maḥmūd 1260–61
Ḍayf, Shawqī 850
al-Daylamī, Abū l-Ḥasan ʿAlī b. Muḥammad (fourth/tenth century) – *Kitāb ʿAṭf al-alif al-māʾlūf ʿalā l-lām al-maʿṭūf* 707 n. 17
Dean, Deborah 818
de Blunes, Miguel Angel 953
de Chardin, Teilhard 511–12
Decius (emperor) 433
de la Granja, F. 994
de Man, Paul 1293
Demirel, Süleyman 1225
Democritus 664
Derrida, Jean Jacques 972
Descartes 500
DeSmet, D. 652, 659
Deszcz, Justyna 968
Devitt, Amy J. 818
Devlin, Lord Patrick 1099–1100, 1101
al-Dhahabī (d. 748/1348 or 753/1352–3) 823
Dhū l-Nūn al-Miṣrī (d. 246/861) 567, 573
Diogenes 664
Dodd, C.H. 771
Dōkarim (also known as Abdulkarim) – *Hikayat Prang Gōmpeuni* 1147–48
Donner, Fred 9, 11, 13, 23
"Piety and Eschatology in Early Kharijite Poetry" (1997) 9
Was Early Islam an Apocalyptic Movement? 9
Doufikar-Aerts, Faustina 923
Dubler, C.E. 934
Duff, David 818
Duke Godfrey 895–96, 908

Eklund, Ragnar – *Life Between Death and Resurrection According to Islam* (1941) 6
Eliade, Mircea (1907–86) 186, 342
Elijah 110
Emon, Anver M. 26
Empedocles 903 n. 29
Emre, Yunus (d. 720/1320–1) – *Divan* 349 n. 38
Ephraem the Syrian (c. 306–373) 23, 783, 785
Hymns on Paradise 84–85
Madrāshê 'On paradise' 794, 796, 799–800, 802
Ernst, Carl 598
Words of Ecstasy (1985) 9

El-Ṣaleḥ, Ṣoubḥī 247–48
La vie future selon le Coran 223, 246
Escudero Aranda, J. 995
Esposito, John 1145
What Everyone Needs to Know about Islam 1143
Evans, Dylan 1302
Eve 22, 43, 69, 141, 186, 431, 723, 797–98, 1004
face/form of 713–17
Evren, Kenan 1225
Ewald, Heinrich 103, 1127, 1130
Ewert, Christian 982
Ezekiel (570–582) (Catholicos) 774, 777
Ezekiel (prophet) 106, 359

Faḍl b. al-Ḥadabī (or al-Faḍl al-Ḥadathī, d. 257/871) 738
al-Fanārī, Muḥammad b. Ḥamza (d. 834/1431) 534
al-Fārābī, Abū Naṣr (d. 339/950) 20, 204 n. 53, 351, 445, 451, 454, 457, 462, 468, 477, 735, 1319
Kitāb Ārā' ahl al-madīna al-fāḍila 460
Kitāb al-Jam' 493
Maqāla fī l-jam' bayn ra'yay Aflāṭūn wa-Arisṭū 501 n. 43
Farrūkh, Muṣṭafā 954 n. 6
Farshchiyān, Maḥmūd 1056
Fāṭima (daughter of Muḥammad) 276, 998–99, 1001
Fāṭima (mother of 'Alī) 1216
Faṭima b. Waliyya 910
Fenni, İsmail (since 1935 Ertuğrul) 1254, 1258
Fernándes-Puertas, A. 1017 n. 26
Feuerbach, Ludwig 1219
Fierro, Maribel 25
Firdawsī (d. 411/1020) – *Shāhnāma* 585
Fleischer, H.L. 1127
Föllmer, Katja 21
Foucault, Michel 312, 1293
The Archeology of Knowledge 1292, 1314 n. 61
The Order of Things 1292
Francis of Assisi, Saint (Francesco Bernardone 1182–1226) 906, 915, 918
Franke, Liza M. 28
Frederick II of Hohenstaufen (1215–50) 897–99, 913, 918
Freud, Sigmund 972
Civilization and its Discontents 1303
Frye, Northrop 95 n. 4, 111, 341 n. 3
Fück, Johann 1128

Gala, Antonio – *La pasión turca* (1993) 953
Galen 320–21
Gandhi, Indira (1917–1984) 968
Gardet, Louis
Dieu et la destinée de l'homme (1967) 7
Introduction à la théologie musulmane: Essai de théologie comparée (1948) 7
Gätje, Helmut 8
Koran und Koranexegese (1971) 7
Gautier, L. 901 n. 26
La perle précieuse 566 n. 2
Geiger, Abraham (1833) 68
Geissinger, Aisha 18
George I (661–680) (Catholicos) 776
Ghaemmaghami, Omid 21
al-Ghayṭī, Najm al-Dīn (d. 984/1576) 876
al-Ghazālī, Abū Ḥāmid (d. 505/1111) 41, 187, 200–201, 203, 205–6, 286, 351, 462, 468, 475, 477, 509, 520 n. 96, 580, 582, 588, 597 n. 103, 856, 901, 919, 1145, 1190, 1196
al-Durra al-fākhira (*The Precious Pearl*) 17, 182, 195–96, 199–200, 202–4, 206–8, 211, 347, 566 n. 2, 901 n. 26, 937
Iḥyā' 'ulūm al-dīn (*The Revitalization of the Religious Sciences*) 196, 206, 352, 1203
Kitāb al-Ṣabr (Book of steadfastness), of *Iḥyā' 'ulūm al-dīn* 423
al-Maḍnūn bih 'alā ghayr ahlih 422
Masā'il al-maḍnūn 19, 423
Mishkāt al-anwār (*The Niche of Light*) 586, 595
Mīzān al-'amal 352
Risālat al-ṭayr 586
Tahāfut al-falāsifa (*The Incoherence of the Philosophers*) 422
al-Ghazālī, Aḥmad (d. 520/1126) 569 n. 15, 573, 582, 586, 588
Kitāb Sawāniḥ 707 n. 17
Ghulām Aḥmad Parwēz (1903–86) 1222
Ghulām Khalīl (d. 275/888) 192 n. 25
Gilliot, C. 376
Gimaret, Daniel 8, 474
Livre des religions et des sects (1986–93) [with J. Jolivet, G. Monnot] 8

Giménez, F. Hernández 983
Giray, Kiymet 1070
Goethe – *West-Eastern Divan* 435
Goldziher, Ignaz 5, 221, 1132, 1300 n. 24
"Zur Charakteristik Ǵel.l ud-dîn us-Sujûṭî's und seiner literarischen Thätigkeit" (1871) 5
Golvin, L. 983
Goodman, Lenn 499 n. 36
Grabar, Oleg 1069 n. 5
Granara, William 961, 964
Gregory IX (pope) 898
Griffith, Sidney H. 23
Gril, Denis
Le dévoilement des effets du voyage (1994) 9
Saint et sainteté dans le christianisme et l'islam: Le regard des sciences de l'homme (2007) 10
Grimme, Hubert 58, 783
Grotzfeld, Heinz and Sophia 924
Guichard, Pierre 959
Guido da Montefeltro 896
Guiscard, Robert 895–96, 908
Gülen, Fethullah (b. 1938 or 1941) 28, 1232, 1234, 1236, 1242, 1248–49, 1255–56, 1258, 1261
Ölüm Ötesi Hayat 1231
Sızıntı 1230
Gully, Adrian 959
Günther, Sebastian 17, 835 n. 85, 836 n. 86
"*«Gepriesen sei der, der seinen Diener bei Nacht reisen ließ»* (Koran 17:1): Paradiesvorstellungen und Himmelsreisen im Islam – Grundfesten des Glaubens und literarische Topoi" (2011) 10–11

Haddad, Yvonne Y. 8, 1188–89, 1222
The Islamic Understanding of Death and Resurrection [with Jane Smith] 1146, 1187
Haeckel, Ernst 1254
Ḥāfiẓ-i Abrū 1035 n. 8
Ḥafṣ (d. 180/796) 173–74
Haider, Deeba 1075
Ḥājjī Bektāsh (d. 669/1270) 691 n. 7
Ḥājj Niʿmat Allāh Jayḥūnābādī Mukrī (1871–1919) – *Furqān al-akhbār* 691
al-Ḥakam II 1002–3
al-Ḥallāj, Manṣūr (d. 309/922) 6, 569 n. 15, 580–81, 589–90, 597–98, 741–42, 856
Hallaq, Wael 1100–1101
Halm, H. 649, 677
Hamadānī / al-Hamadhānī, ʿAyn al-Quḍāt (d. 525/1131) 520 n. 96, 576–77
Tamhīdāt 21, 568–69, 573
Zubdat al-ḥaqāʾiq 568 n. 12, 570
al-Hamadhānī, Badīʿ al-Zamān (d. 398/1008) – *al-Maqāma al-majāʿiyya* 263–64
Hämeen-Anttila, Jaakko 17
Ḥamīm b. Mann Allāh al-Muftarī 997
al-Hammūʾī, Saʿd al-Dīn (d. 650/1252–53) 581
Hamza, Feras 19
Ḥamza b. ʿAbd al-Muṭṭalib 171
Ḥanafī, Ḥasan (b. 1353/1935) 27, 1215–17, 1219, 1222
Min al-ʿaqīda ilā l-thawra 1214
Hanisch, Ludmila 27
Hanson, P.D. 96, 101
Ḥanẓala al-Kātib 273 n. 13
al-Harithy 1012
Hart, H.L.A. 1099–1101
Hārūn al-Rashīd 926
Ḥasan *ʿalā dhikrihi l-salām* 683–87
al-Ḥasan b. ʿAlī 349 n. 38, 1165
al-Ḥasan al-Baṣrī (d. 110/728) 168, 226, 231, 240–41, 243–45, 246, 248, 397–98, 567 n. 3, 831, 1239
al-Ḥasan b. Hānīʿ 856
Ḥasan II (d. 561/1166) [Ismaʿili *imām*] 632 n. 163
Ḥasan-i Ṣabbāḥ 632 n. 163
Hasjmy, Ali (1914–98) 1170
Ḥassān b. Thābit (d. ca. 40/659) 259, 854
Havely, Nick 906
Hawthorne, Sîan 1301–2
al-Haythamī, Aḥmad b. Muḥammad Ibn Ḥajar (d. 974/1567). *See* Ibn Ḥajar al-Haytamī
Heath, P. 288
Hegazi, Mahmoud 24
Hegel 1303–6, 1314
Hehmeyer, Ingrid 26
Heidegger, Martin 487–88
Heinen, Anton 355
Islamic cosmology 935 n. 17

Hermes 506
Herodotus 254
Hillenbrand, R. 1012
Hilmî, Ahmet 1254
Hippocrates 320
Hirschfeld, Hartwig 1133
Hishām b. al-Ḥakam (d. 179/795–6) 495 n. 27, 523, 743 n. 36
Hitler 1241
Hodgson, Marshall 124, 684 n. 31, 684 n. 32, 686 n. 40
Hölderlin, Friedrich 1309, 1312
Holmes, George 909
Homer – *Iliad* 1086
Horovitz, Josef 58, 74, 86
"Das Koranische Paradies" (1923) 68
al-Hujwīrī, ʿAlī b. ʿUthmān al-Jullābī (d. 465–9/1072–7) – *Kashf al-maḥjūb* 567, 695
Ḥunayn b. Isḥāq (d. 260/873) 204 n. 53
Hunke, Sigrid 910
al-Hurayfish, Shuʿayb – *al-Rawḍ al-fāʾiq fī l-mawāʿiẓ wa-l-raqāʾiq* 1020 n. 38
Ḥurr/Ḥurr-i shahīd or Janāb-i Ḥurr = al-Ḥurr b. Yazīd al-Riyāḥī 1058–59
al-Ḥusayn b. ʿAlī 276, 349 n. 38, 597, 626, 632, 1056–57, 1059, 1165
al-Ḥuṭayʾa (d. after 41/661) 853

Ibn ʿAbbās, ʿAbdallāh (d. 68/687–8) 62, 163, 166–69, 171, 226, 232, 235, 238, 246, 248, 345, 383, 385, 387–88, 391–94, 619, 829, 879, 987 n. 27
Ibn ʿAbd al-Barr (d. 463/1071) 350
Ibn ʿAbd Rabbih (d. 328/940) – *al-ʿIqd al-farīd* 357 n. 80
Ibn Abī l-Dunyā (d. 281/894) 346–47, 821, 823–29, 831, 833, 843–44, 873
Ṣifat al-janna 817
Ibn Abī Shayba (d. 235/849) 872
Muṣannaf 313, 375
Ibn ʿAdī l-Jurjānī (d. 363/974) 821
Ibn al-ʿAdīm (d. 660/1262) – *al-Inṣāf* 850
Ibn ʿAdī = Yaḥyā b. ʿAdī (d. 363/974) 351
Ibn ʿArabī (d. 638/1240) 4, 6, 8–10, 108, 187 n. 15, 287, 516, 521, 534–35, 539, 541, 548, 707 n. 15, 892, 901, 910, 916, 919, 994, 1019, 1190, 1214, 1243, 1249
Fuṣūṣ al-ḥikam 502 n. 47, 538
al-Futūḥāt al-Makkiyya 522, 538, 549, 900, 1018
al-Isrāʾ ilā maqām al-asrā 900
Tarjumān al-ashwāq 900
Ibn ʿAsākir (d. 571/1175) 863
Ibn al-Ashʿath (ca. 82/701) 384
Ibn ʿAṭāʾ = Abū l-ʿAbbās Aḥmad b. Muḥammad al-Adamī (d. 309/922) 235
Ibn Bājja (also known as Ibn al-Ṣāʾigh) (d. 532/1138) 20, 445, 461–66
Ittiṣāl al-ʿaql bi-l-insān 461
Risālat al-ittiṣāl 462
Tadbīr al-mutawaḥḥid 462
Ibn Bashshār al-Sulamī (or Abū Bashshār) 166
Ibn Baṭṭūṭa 1020 n. 38, 1022
Ibn Durayd (d. 321/933) 144 n. 20
Ibn Fāriḍ (d. 632/1235) 255 n. 20
Ibn Fūrak – *Mujarrad* 471–72
Ibn Gabriol = Solomon ben Gabriol 903
Ibn Ḥabīb = ʿAbd al-Malik b. Ḥabīb (d. 238/853) 346, 819, 822, 825, 843, 873, 991, 995
Kitāb Waṣf al-firdaws 285, 304, 821, 825–826, 988, 992
Ibn Ḥajar al-ʿAsqalānī (d. 853/1449) 1104, 1111 n. 31, 1249
al-Kāfī l-shāfī fī takhrīj aḥādīth al-Kashshāf 247
Ibn Ḥajar al-Haytamī (d. 974/1567) 32–33, 872
al-Fatāwā al-ḥadīthiyya 16, 31
Ibn Ḥanbal, Aḥmad (d. 241/855) 278, 374 n. 13, 827
Ibn al-Ḥārith = Saʿīd b. al-Ḥārith 418–19
Ibn Ḥawqal 999 n. 59
Ibn Ḥawshāb = Shahr b. Ḥawshāb (d. between 100/718 and 112/720) 230
Ibn al-Haytham, Abū ʿAlī l-Ḥasan (d. 430/1040) 916
al-Shukūk ʿalā Baṭlamyūs 1093
Ibn Ḥazm (d. 456/1064) 352, 738 n. 16, 910, 916, 1000, 1114 n. 42, 1119–20
Ṭūq al-ḥamāma (*The Dove's Necklace*) 899–900
Ibn Ḥibbān (d. 354/965) 872
Kitāb al-Thiqāt 823
Ibn Hishām = ʿAbd al-Malik b. Hishām (d. 218/833) 182, 191–92, 211, 275, 862, 864
Sīra 877
Ibn ʿIdhārī 997

Ibn Isḥāq = Muḥammad b. Isḥāq (d. 150/767–8) 109 n. 52, 167, 171, 176, 191–92, 211, 275, 956
Sīrat al-nabī or *al-Sīra al-nabawiyya* 182
Ibn al-Jawzī (d. 654/1257) – *Mirʾāt al-zamān* 850
Ibn al-Jawzī al-Tamīmī (d. 597/1201) 823, 872
Ibn Jubayr = Saʿīd b. Jubayr (d. 95/713) 384–85
Ibn al-Juḥām (d. ca. 328/939) – *Mā nazala min al-Qurʾān fī ahl al-bayt* 610 n. 25
Ibn Kathīr (d. 774/1373) 194, 821, 823, 825–32, 838
Nihāya 873
al-Nihāya fī l-fitan wa-l-malāḥim 817 n. 1
Ibn Khaldūn (d. 808/1406) 470, 942
Ibn al-Khurshub = Salama b. al-Khurshub 152
Ibn Maʿīn = Yaḥyā b. Maʿīn (d. 233/847) 827
Ibn Māja (d. 273/887) 404, 872
Sunan 841 n. 116
Ibn al-Mājishūn (d. 211/827) 1108 n. 28
Ibn al-Malāḥimī = Rukn al-Dīn b. al-Malāḥimī (d. 536/1141) – *Tuḥfat al-mutakallimīn fī l-radd ʿalā l-falāsifa* 423
Ibn Manẓūr (630–711/1312–1233) – *Lisān al-ʿarab* 226 n. 14
Ibn Masarra (883–931) 900 n. 22, 916
Ibn Masʿūd, ʿAbdallāh (d. 32/652–3) 167–68, 395, 695
Ibn Miskawayh (d. 421/1030) 352
Ibn al-Mubārak, ʿAbdallāh (d. 181/797) – *Kitāb al-Jihād* 418
Ibn al-Muqaffaʿ, ʿAbdallāh (d. 139/756) 925
Ibn al-Nadīm 925
Ibn al-Nafīs (d. 687/1288) – *al-Risāla al-Kāmiliyya fī l-sīra al-nabawiyya* 195
Ibn al-Qāriḥ 851, 854–55
Risāla 856
Ibn al-Qaṭṭān al-Fāsī (d. 628/1231) 559 n. 12
Ibn Qayyim al-Jawziyya (d. 751/1350) 186, 350, 534, 750, 821, 823, 825–26, 828–30, 832, 873, 1198, 1205, 1208, 1218
Ḥādī l-arwāḥ ilā bilād al-afrāḥ 347, 817, 820 n. 13, 838
Ibn Qutayba 925
Ibn Quzmān (d. 1160) 900, 916
Ibn Rawāḥa = ʿAbdallāh b. Rawāḥa 416
Ibn al-Rāwandī (early third/ninth to mid-fourth/tenth century) 856
Kitāb Faḍīḥat al-Muʿtazila 223 n. 6
Ibn al-Rūmī 856
Ibn Rushd (d. 595/1198) 61, 204 n. 53, 286, 461, 897, 901, 903 n. 29, 908, 911–15, 918
Ibn Rushd al-Jadd (d. 520/1126) 1107–9
Ibn Sabʿīn = Abū Muḥammad ʿAbd al-Ḥaqq b. Sabʿīn (1217–69)
al-Ajwiba ʿan al-asʾila al-Ṣiqilliyya 898
Asrār al-ḥikma al-mashriqiyya 898
Ibn Saʿd (d. 230/845) 864
Kitāb al-Ṭabaqāt 862
Ibn al-Ṣalāḥ (d. 643/1245) 832 n. 74
ʿUlūm al-ḥadīth (known as *Muqaddimat Ibn al-Ṣalāḥ*) 824
Ibn Salām = ʿAbdallāh b. Salām (d. 43/663) – *Kitāb al-ʿAjāʾib wa-l-gharāʾib* 883
Ibn Shihāb al-Zuhrī (d. 124/742) 273 n. 15, 861, 863–64
Ibn Shuhayd (d. 426/1035) 916
al-Tawābiʿ wa-l-zawābiʿ 856
Ibn Sīnā (Avicenna, d. 428/1037) 20, 204 n. 53, 286, 351, 422, 425, 445, 455–59, 466, 468, 474–75, 479, 482, 485, 571, 582, 591 n. 68, 596, 652–53, 664–65, 672, 707 n. 15, 727 n. 61, 736, 903, 911, 913, 916, 918
Dānishnāme-yi ʿalāʾī 455 n. 43
Fī ithbāt al-nubuwwāt 520 n. 96
al-Ishārāt wa-l-tanbīhāt 455 n. 43, 460
Kitāb al-Inṣāf 653
al-Mabdaʾ wa-l-Maʿād, Metaphysics of the Healing (*al-Ilāhiyyāt min al-shifāʾ*) 459–61
Metaphysics of *The Healing* 492
al-Najāt 455 n. 43
al-Qānūn fī l-ṭibb (*The canon of medicine*) 455 n. 43
al-Risāla al-Aḍḥawiyya fī l-maʿād 457, 459, 473, 477–78, 498–99
Risālat al-ṭayr 200, 586
al-Shifāʾ (*The healing*) 455 n. 43, 481
Ibn Sīrīn = Muḥammad b. Sīrīn (d. 110/728) 330–31
Muntakhab fī khulāṣat al-kalām fī taʾwīl al-aḥlām 437–38
Ibn Taymiyya (d. 728/1328) 534, 750, 1114 n. 43
Ibn Ṭufayl (d. 581/1185) 461, 916, 919
Ḥayy Ibn Yaqẓān 24, 893, 903–8
Ibn Zaydūn (1003–71) 900, 916, 1001

Ibrahim, Tawfiq 10
Idrīs (prophet) 51
Idrīs, Wafā' 1277–80, 1286
al-Ījī, 'Aḍud al-Dīn (d. 756/1355) 469, 475–77, 480, 483
Kitāb al-Mawāqif fī 'ilm al-kalām 470–71, 479, 481–82
'Ikrima (d. 105/723–4) 165, 235, 246, 383, 387, 829
Ilāhī, Nūr 'Alī (d. 1394/1974) 22
Imran Teuku Abdullah 1148
Imru' al-Qays (d. ca. 550 CE) 146, 259
Mu'allaqa 256
İnan, Ergin (b. 1943) – *Mesnevi* [lithographs] 1070
Iqbāl, Muḥammad (d. 1357/1938) 6, 1198, 1214
Bāl-i Jibrīl 954 n. 7
Reconstruction of the Religious Thought in Islam 1197
Irigaray, Luce 1301 n. 25
al-Iṣfahānī, Abū l-Shaykh (d. 396/1006) – *Kitāb al-'Aẓama* 874
Ishmael (prophet) 51
Ishō'yahb I (582–596) (Catholicos) 775, 777–78
İsmail, Hekimoğlu (pen name of Ömer Okçu, b. 1932) 1242
Minyeli Abdullah 1234
Ivanow, W.A. (1886–1970) 690–91
al-Iznīqī, Mūsā b. Ḥājjī Ḥusayn (d. 833/1430) 880

Jābir b. 'Abdallāh (d. 78/697) 167–68, 171, 385–87
Jacob (prophet, Ya'qūb) 358 n. 83, 763
Jacob of Serugh (c. 451–521) 798, 800, 802
Ja'far b. Abī Ṭālib 415
Ja'far b. Manṣūr al-Yaman (d. ca. 346/957) 651
Kitāb al-Kashf 629, 676–77, 679, 683
Ja'far al-Ṣādiq (d. 148/765) 278, 612 n. 56, 613, 615, 743 n. 36
Jafri, Syed Husain Mohammad – *Origins and Early Development of Shi'a Islam* (1979) 8
Jalāl al-Dīn Rūmī. *See* Rūmī, Jalāl al-Dīn
Jambet, Christian 9, 487 n. 3, 519, 685, 687
La Grande résurrection d'Alamût: Les formes de la liberté dans le shi'isme ismaélien (1996) 9
L'Acte d'être: La philosophie de la révélation chez Mollâ Sadrâ (2002) 9
Jāmī, 'Abd al-Raḥmān (d. 898/1492) 217 fig.9.1, 692
Jarādāt, Hanādī Taysīr 1282–84
Jarrar, Maher 18, 1168
al-Jaṣṣāṣ (d. 370/981) 1112
al-Jawharī, Abū 'Abdallāh (d. 401/1010–1) – *Mā nazala min al-Quran fī ṣāḥib al-zamān* 609 n. 18
Jeffrey, Arthur 781–782
Jesus Christ (prophet, 'Īsā) 37, 51–52, 103, 201, 203, 206, 271, 327, 402, 517, 617 n. 69, 618, 620 n. 84, 658, 675, 678 n. 9, 703 n. 7, 724, 731, 747–48, 762, 779, 791, 801, 1137, 1214, 1253
as Alpha and Omega 511–12
resurrection/second coming of 110, 626 n. 118, 763–64, 771, 1022, 1241, 1247, 1249
al-Jīlī, 'Abd al-Karīm (766–810/1365–1408) – *Qāb qawsayn wa-l-multaqā l-nāmūsayn* 1019
Job (prophet, Ayyūb) 202, 205, 747
John (prophet, Yaḥyā) 51, 110, 202
John of Patmos 97
Jolivet, Jean 8
Jonah 110
Jones, Alan 257
Joseph (d. 576) (Catholicos) 777
Joseph (prophet, Yūsuf) 52, 110, 202, 205, 710, 728
Jöttkandt, Sigi and Joan Copjec 1294, 1303
al-Jubbā'ī (d. 303/915–6) 480, 738
al-Ju'fī, Mufaḍḍal b. 'Umar (d. late second/eighth century) 615, 618
Islamic Messianism 612
al-Junayd (d. 298/911) 580, 588–89, 591, 597
al-Jurjānī (d. 816/1413) 470
al-Juwaynī, Abū l-Ma'ālī (d. 478/1085) 422, 580

al-Kalbī (d. 204/819 or 206/821) 164
al-Kāmil Muḥammad (1218–38) [sultan of Egypt] 898
Kant 1293–94, 1303–5
Karakoç, Sezai (b. 1933) 1253
al-Kāsānī (d. 587/1191) 1106–7, 1109
Kāshānī, 'Abd al-Razzāq (d. 736/1335) 538 n. 18
al-Kātib, 'Abdallāh b. 'Abd al-'Azīz 925
Kessler, C. 1017 n. 26

Khadīja (d. 620 CE) 853
Khālid b. Abī Bakr 822–23
Khālid b. Maʿdān (d. 103/721) 389, 403
Khālid b. Yazīd b. Abī Mālik 827
Khalil, Mohammad Hassan 22
Between Heaven and Hell: Islam, Salvation, and the Fate of Others (2013) 10
Khān, Sayyid Aḥmad (d. 1306/1898) 1193–96, 1199–1200, 1218
Khān, Ṣiddīq Ḥasan (1834–90) 1251
Kitāb al-Burhān fī ʿalāmat al-mahdī ākhir al-zamān 1249
al-Khansāʾ (poetess) 852
Kharaqānī, Abū l-Ḥasan (d. 425/1033) 572 n. 24, 582
al-Kharrāz, Abū Muḥammad 282
al-Kharrāz = Abū Saʿīd Aḥmad b. ʿĪsā (d. 286/899) – *Kitāb al-Sirr* 236 n. 37
al-Khaṭīb al-Baghdādī 832 n. 74
al-Khayyāṭ, Abū l-Ḥusayn ʿAbd al-Raḥīm (ca. 220–300/835–913) – *Kitāb al-Intiṣār* 223–24
Khemir, Nacer (b. 1948) – *Les baliseurs du désert* (1984); *Le collier perdu de la colombe* (1991); *Bab ʿAziz, Le prince qui contemplait son âme* (2006) 1076
Khismatulin, Alexey A. 22
Khomeini, Ruhollah (d. 1989) 956, 1059
Khusraw I. Anushirwān 925
Kinberg, L. 103–4
al-Kindī, Abū Yūsuf Yaʿqūb b. Isḥāq (d. ca. 256/870) 20, 204 n. 53, 351, 445, 448, 466, 1090
A Discourse on the soul: Summary of the book[s] of Aristotle and Plato and the rest of the philosophers 447
Fī annahu tūjad jawāhir lā ajsām (*That there exist substances that are not bodies*) 447
Fī l-falsafa al-ūlā (On first philosophy) 446
Risāla fī l-ḥīla li-dafʿ al-aḥzān 448
Risāla fī kammiyyat kutub Arisṭāṭālīs wa-mā yuḥtaju ilayhi fī taḥṣīl al-falsafa 450
King, Martin Luther, Jr. (1929–68) 1178
Kipling, R. 917
Kippenberg, Hans 1145
al-Kirmānī, Ḥamīd al-Dīn (d. ca. 411/1020–1) 631, 651, 655 n. 26, 659, 664 n. 21, 666, 736
Kashf al-maḥjūb 653–54
Rāḥat al-ʿaql 650
Risālat al-bāhira 653, 656
al-Kisāʾī (d. 189/805) 852
Kısakürek, Necip Fazıl (1905–83) – *Büyük Doğu* 1254
Kristeva, Julia 1301 n. 25
Krüger, Paul 806 n. 1
al-Kubrā, Najm al-Dīn (d. ca. 617/1220) 581, 593
Kudsieh, Suha 25
al-Kūfī, Furāt b. Ibrāhīm (d. early fourth/tenth century) 624
al-Kulaynī, Muḥammad b. Yaʿqūb (d. 329/941) – *Uṣūl al-kāfī* 513

Labarta, A. 991
Labīd (d. ca. 31/661) 71, 86–87, 145 n. 24, 146, 852–53
Lacan, J. 1301–2, 1303–6, 1308–13
Lacoue-Labarthe, Philippe 28, 1303–15
The Title of the Letter 1303
Typography: Mimesis, Philosophy and Politics 1294, 1306
La Fontaine (1668–94) – *Fables* 899
Landolt, Hermann 9, 20, 680
Lane, Andrew J. 17
Lane, E.W. 60
Lange, Christian 10, 18
Locating Hell in Islamic Traditions (2016) 10
Paradise and Hell in Islamic Traditions 10
"Where on Earth is Hell? State Punishment and Eschatology in the Islamic Middle Period" (2009) 10
Lasater, Alice – *Spain To England* 911
Lawson, Todd 11, 16, 1317–18
"Divine Wrath and Divine Mercy in Islam: Their Reflection in the Qurʾān and Quranic Images of Water" (2008) 11
"Duality, Opposition and Typology in the Qur'an: The Apocalyptic Substrate" (2008) 11
Gnostic Apocalypse and Islam: Qur'an, Exegesis, Messianism, and the Literary Origins of the Babi Religion (2011) 11
"The Qurʾān and Epic" (2014) 11

Lazarus-Yafeh, Hava 195 n. 36
Leach, Edmund 343
Leibniz 116 n. 85
Lenin 1241
Leucippus 664
Lévi-Strauss, Claude 343–44, 512 n. 75
Lidzbarski, Mark (1868–1928) 1129–30, 1133–34, 1136
Alter und Heimat der mandäischen Religion 1134
Auf rauhem Wege 1132
Littmann, Enno 924, 1131
Lot 147, 1248
Louis VII (of France) 895
Lüling, Günter 782 n. 7
Lull, Raymond 900
Luxenberg, Christoph 83 n. 45, 272, 782–83, 785, 799

al-Maʿarrī, Abū l-ʿAlāʾ (d. 449/1057) 432, 853–54, 916
Risālat al-ghufrān 24, 195, 850–51, 855–56
MacDonald, John 348
Madelung, Wilferd 19
al-Mahdī (*imām*) 1060
Maḥmūd of Ghazna (d. 421/1030) 589, 593
Maimonides 5
Majeed, Tehnyat 25
al-Majlisī, Muḥammad Bāqir (d. 1110/1698) 743 n. 36
Biḥār al-anwār (Seas of light) 614, 1253
Makdisi, Saree 1075
al-Mālījī (fl. 450–52/1058–60) 651
Mālik b. Anas (d. 179/796) 171, 1105, 1114, 1118
Mālik b. Dīnār (d. ca. 131/748–9) 1239
al-Mālikī, Muḥammad b. Aḥmad – *Kitāb Miʿrāj al-nabī* 880
al-Malik al-Nāṣir Muḥammad b. Qalāwūn (d. 741/1341) 1012 n. 7
al-Malik al-Ṣāliḥ ʿImād al-Dīn Ismāʿīl b. Muḥammad b. Qalāwūn (d. 746/1345) 1012 n. 7
al-Malik Ṣayf al-Dīn Qalāwūn (d. 689/1290) [Bahri Mamluk] 1012
Malouf, Amin – *Leo Africanus* 1986, 953
Maʿmar (d. 209/824–5) 164
Maʿmar b. Rāshid (d. 154/770) 396
al-Maʾmūn (r. 197–218/813–33) 357
al-Manṣūr, Ismāʿīl (335–41/946–53) 997
al-Manṣūr [Fatimid] 981, 999
al-Manṣūr al-Ṣanādīqī 855
al-Maqdisī, Ḍiyāʾ al-Dīn (d. 643/1245) 873
Ṣifat al-janna 817 n. 1
al-Maqrīzī 1013, 1023
Mar Abā (540–552) (Catholicos) 773–74, 777
Marʿī b. Yūsuf al-Karmī (d. 1033/1624) 25, 933–34
Bahjat al-nāẓirīn wa-āyāt al-mustadillīn 931–32, 935–37, 939–42
Markwart, Josef 1135
Marmura, Michael E. 20, 1319
Marquet, Yves 488
Martin, Raymond 900
Marx 1241, 1314
Mary (Maryam, mother of Jesus) 51–52, 110 n. 57, 910
Marzolph, Ulrich 26
Mas, Ruth 28
Masrūq b. al-Ajdaʿ (d. 63/682–3) 167
Massignon, Louis – *La passion de Husayn ibn Mansûr Hallâj: Martyr mystique de l'Islam, exécuté à Bagdad le 26 Mars 922: Étude d'histoire religieuse* 6
Mas'ūd, Mīrfat Āmīn 1274, 1281–82, 1284–85
al-Mawdūdī, Abū l-Aʿlā (1903–79) 210, 1189
al-Maymūnī (Ibrāhim b. Muḥammad b. ʿĪsā, d. 1079/1669) 938 n. 25
Meier, Fritz 11, 286, 344
"The Ultimate Origin and the Hereafter in Islam" (1971) 7
Menderes, Adnan 1224–25
Menocal, Maria Rosa 917–18
Meyrink, Gustav – *The Green Face* 435
Michaelis, Johann David 1129
Michot, Y. 474
Milton, John (d. 1674) 915
Areopagitica 36
Paradise Lost 37
Minorsky, V.F. (1877–1966) 690
Mīr Dāmād (d. 1041/1631–32) 488
Mir-Kasimov, Orkhan 22
Mirza, Nadarbek K. (fl. first half of fourteenth/twentieth century) 741, 750, 752
Reincarnation and Islam 739–40
Mīrzā ʿAbd al-Ḥasan Mushīr al-Mulk 1057
Miskawayh (d. 421/1030) 1146 n. 12

Mitchell, W.J.T. 555
Moazzen, Maryam 21
Monferrer, Juan Pedro 992
Monnot, Guy 8
More, Henry 500
Morewedge, Parviz 663
Morris, James Winston 681 n. 22
Mullā Ṣadrā: The Wisdom of the Throne (1981) 8
Moses (prophet, Mūsā) 32, 51–52, 65, 108, 110, 118, 264, 393, 402, 434, 517, 658, 678 n. 9, 695, 748, 792
Mourtada-Sabbah, Nada 959
Mowinckel, Sigmund 758
al-Mu'ayyad fī l-Dīn al-Shīrāzī (d. 471/1078) 651, 658–59
al-Majālis al-Mu'ayyadiyya 649–50, 656
al-Mubārak 222 n. 3
al-Mubārakfūrī 1111 n. 31
al-Mubarrad (d. 286/900) 350, 852
al-Muhalhil, Jāsim 1249
Muḥammad (prophet) 32, 34, 55, 110, 118, 169, 183, 206, 266, 315, 331, 402, 437, 489, 513, 515–17, 561, 570–71, 587–88, 658, 678 n. 9, 740, 767, 782–83, 787, 803, 913, 918, 956, 998, 1059–60, 1131, 1137, 1192, 1195, 1267, 1282
on believers and unbelievers, states of 165, 167
biography of 102, 188, 275, 862
on Burāq 1037 n. 21, 1038
as Chosen One (*muṣṭafā*) 566
creation/conception of 109 n. 52, 274
cycle of 631
on divine names 510
on Eden 240
and events of judgment/end of time 605, 616, 1042–43
family of 657
images of 1038 n. 27, 1058, 1300 n. 24
intercession of 19, 26, 197, 836, 840, 1010 n. 1, 1018–22
light of 274 n. 19, 569, 576, 1210
and Muslim community in afterlife 836, 843
name of, in design/architecture 1015, 1017
night journey (*isrā'*) and ascension to heaven (*mi'rāj*) 26, 121, 192, 217 fig.9.1, 273, 709–10, 712, 724, 728, 802, 836 n. 86, 858–59, 863, 875, 877, 884, 892–94, 900, 916, 918, 1020, 1062, 1083
as Perfect Man 35, 1019
prophetic mission/message of 34, 51, 209, 677
revelation/descent of Quran to 435, 518
as source of *raḥma* 1017
supremacy/role of 44, 201–2, 208
and vision of hereafter 189, 191, 193, 721, 861, 864, 869, 876–80, 1037, 1039, 1083
"was given three things ..." 1021
Muḥammad 'Alī, Mawlānā (d. 1371/1951) 1189
Muḥammad b. 'Alī b. al-Ḥusayn [al-Bāqir] (d. between 114/732 and 118/736) 615, 821
Muḥammad b. al-Ḥanafiyya (16–81/637–701) 822
Muḥammad b. Isḥāq. *See* Ibn Isḥāq
Muḥammad b. Ismā'īl 631
Muḥammad b. Yusūf al-Ṣāliḥī al-Shāmī (d. 942/1536) – *Khulāṣat al-faḍl al-fā'iq fī mi'rāj khayr al-khalā'iq* 876–77
al-Muḥāsibī, 'Abdallāh Ḥārith (d. 243/857) 284–85
Kitāb al-Tawahhum 283, 304, 566 n. 2
al-Muḥibbī (d. 1111/1699) 933
Muir, William 6
al-Mu'izz (r. 341–65/953–75) 981, 998, 1000
Mujāhid b. Jabr al-Makkī (died between 100/718 and 104/722) 165, 235, 238, 246, 248, 384–85, 395, 399, 831
Mullā Ṣadrā. *See* Ṣadr al-Dīn al-Shīrāzī
al-Mundhirī, Abū Muḥammad Zakī l-Dīn (d. 656/1258) 313 n. 6
Mukhtaṣar Ṣaḥīḥ Muslim 315, 333–34
al-Targhīb wa-l-tarhīb 819, 842–44
Munshī, Ḥasan Ṣalāḥ 684 n. 31
Muqātil b. Sulaymān (d. ca. 150/767) 19, 163, 167–68, 172, 175, 278, 373, 375–80, 396, 398–99
Muṣ'ab b. 'Umayr 171
Mūsā l-Kāẓim (d. 183/799) 612 n. 56, 625, 690
Muslim b. al-Ḥajjāj (d. 261/875) 18, 313 n. 6, 384–85, 825, 861, 871–72
Ṣaḥīḥ Muslim 819, 841–42
Ṣaḥīḥ Muslim (Kitāb al-Janna wa-ṣifat na'īmihā wa-ahlihā) 311–15, 317–21, 323, 325, 332, 334, 336

al-Mutanabbī 856
al-Mutanakhkhil 149

al-Nābigha al-Dhubyānī 853
Nābighat Banī Ja'da 853
Naeem, Huda 1274
Naef, Silvia 26
Nāfi' (d. 66/685) 387–88, 391–94
Nagel, Tilman 15, 343
  "Der Prophet und die Weltgeschichte" in Der Koran (2002) 10
al-Najafī, Sharaf al-Dīn 'Alī l-Ḥusaynī l-Astarābādī (fl. tenth/sixteenth century) 610 n. 25, 621
al-Najāshī (d. 450/1058–9) – *Rijāl al-Najāshī* 609 n. 18
Nakhla, Marguerite (1908–1977) 1070
al-Nasafī (d. ca. 331/942) 649
Nāṣir-i Khusraw (d. after 465/1072) 498, 517, 631, 651, 666
al-Nāṣir Muḥammad (d. 741/1341) 1013–14
Nasr, Seyyed Hossein 499
al-Nawawī (d. 676/1277) 314, 328–29, 1114, 1117–18
al-Naẓẓām (d. 231/845) 738
Nehru, Jawaharlal (1889–1964) 968
Nell, Victor 288
Neuwirth, Angelika 16, 1280
  Der Koran: Frühmekkanische Suren (2011) 10
  "Symmetrie und Paarbildung in der Koranischen Eschatologie" (1984) 8
Newton, Isaac (d. 1727) 98 n. 17
Nicholson, Reynold A. 6
  The Mystics of Islam 909
al-Nīlī (d. after 803/1400–1) – *Muntakhab* 609 n. 18
al-Nisābūrī (d. 508/1114–5) – *Rawḍat* 608 n. 15
Niẓām al-Mulk (d. 485/1092) 580 n. 5, 580 n. 9, 581, 597 n. 103
Noah (prophet, Nūḥ) 52, 202, 206, 253 n. 13, 517, 658, 678 n. 9
Nöldeke, Theodor 6
  Mandäische Grammatik 1134
Nomoto, Shin 682 n. 26
Nora, Pierre 1068–69
Nu'aym b. Ḥammād – *Kitāb al-Fitan* 937
Nu'mān b. Mālik b. Tha'laba 416
Nūr 'Alī Ilāhī/Ostād Elāhī (1895–1974) 690 n. 6, 691, 695–96
Nurbaki, Haluk (1924–97) 1255–56
Nūr al-Dīn (d. 569/1174) 408
Nūr al-Dīn al-Karakī = al-Muḥaqqiq al-Thānī (d. 549/1533) 610 n. 25
Nūrī, Ismā'īl Ṭabarsī (d. 1321/1903) 613 n. 59
Nursi, Said (d. 1379/1960) 27–28, 1210–12, 1223, 1225–30, 1234, 1244, 1248, 1254
  Köprü 1225
  Risale-i Nur 1209, 1224–25, 1228, 1252
  Yeni Asya 1225
Nyberg, Henrik S. 6, 1136

Obank, Margaret 807
Oktar, Adnan (pen name Harun Yahya, b. 1956) 1247–49, 1251–53, 1256, 1259–60
  Mehdi ve Altınçağ 1249
  Ölüm – Kıyamet – Cehennem 1253
O'Meara, Simon 20
O'Shaughnessy, T. – *Muhammad's Thoughts on Death* (1969) 7
Ott, Claudia 24
Ovid 894, 910
Özal, Turgut 1230

Padwick, Constance 107
al-Palimbānī, 'Abd al-Ṣamad (b. 1116/1704?) 1157
  Naṣīḥat al-muslimīn (*Advice to Muslims*) 1156–57
Paul (apostle, missionary) 97, 271, 675
Peter (of Gospel) 97
Peterson, Erik 1134
Pharoah 34, 393
Pielow, Dorothee 19
Piotrovskiy, Michail B. 10
Plato 351, 496, 506, 664, 735, 903 n. 29, 1307
  Republic 185 n. 7, 454, 463
Plotinus (d. 270 CE) 522, 653
  Enneads 351, 495
  Theology of Aristotle 503 n. 54, 522–23
Plutarch 260
Pocock, Edward (d. 1691) – *Porta Mosis* 5
Praetorius, Franz 1135
pseudo-Callisthenes 24, 922

Ptolemy 905 n. 32, 1093–94
Almagest 1088, 1094
Tetrabiblos 357
Pythagoras 448–49

al-Qāḍī, ʿAbd al-Raḥīm (d. ca. sixth/twelfth century) – *Daqāʾiq al-akhbār fī dhikr al-janna wa-l-nār* (The meticulous accounts referring to paradise and hell) 5–6, 19, 296, 304
al-Qāḍī ʿIyāḍ (d. 544/1149) 314, 327–28, 334
al-Qāḍī l-Nuʿmān (d. 363/974) 1115 n. 48
Sharḥ al-akhbār 625 n. 115
al-Qaffāl 1115 n. 46
Qalāwūn, Sultan al-Malik al-Manṣūr (d. 689/1290) 25–26, 1014, 1015 n. 20, 1021, 1023–24
al-Qaraḍāwī, Yūsuf (b. 1345/1926) 1209, 1218
al-Sharīʿa wa-l-ḥayāt 1208
Qashlān, Mamdūḥ (b. 1929) – *Local features 70* 1073
al-Qasrī, Khālid 385
Qatāda b. Diʿāma al-Sadūsī (d. 117/735) 164–65, 167, 231, 235, 238, 246, 389, 396, 399, 829–30
al-Qayṣarī, Dāwūd (d. 751/1350) 516, 538–39
al-Qazwīnī 25, 935, 941
ʿAjāʾib al-makhlūqāt 932–33, 936, 938–39
Qian, Ailin 18
al-Qummī, ʿAlī b. Ibrāhīm (d. after 307/919) 616, 618, 743 n. 36, 1253
al-Qummī, Saʿd b. ʿAbdallāh al-Ashʿarī (d. 299/911–2 or 301/913–4) – *Kitāb al-Maqālāt* 608 n. 14
al-Qūnawī, Ṣadr al-Dīn (d. 673/1274) 534
al-Qurṭubī (d. 671/1272) 163, 170, 175–76, 303, 861, 987 n. 27, 1111–12
al-Tadhkira fī aḥwāl al-mawtā 347, 873–74
al-Qushayrī, Abū l-Qāsim ʿAbd al-Karīm b. Hawāzin (d. 465/1072) 274 n. 19, 582 n. 19, 875
Kitāb al-Miʿrāj 877
Laṭāʾif al-ishārāt 222 n. 4
al-Qūshjī, ʿAlāʾ al-Dīn ʿAlī (d. 1474) 1094
Quṭb, Sayyid (1906–66) 209–10
Qu Yuan (ca. 339–278 BCE) – *Summons of the soul* 265–66

al-Rabīʿa (d. 136/753) 165, 167
Rābiʿa al-ʿAdawiyya (d. 185/801) 41, 267–68, 282, 567 n. 3, 589, 593, 596, 911
Raḍawī, Muḥammad Taqī Mudarris 663
Rahman, Fazlur (d. 1408/1988) 499 n. 36, 1212–14, 1218
al-Rāʿī, Shaybān (d. 158/774–5) 569 n. 14
al-Rāzī, Abū Ḥātim (d. ca. 322/934) 589, 626 n. 118, 649–50, 682 n. 26
al-Rāzī, Fakhr al-Dīn (d. 606/1209) 163, 168–71, 174, 176, 178–79, 350 n. 41, 353, 745–48
Muḥaṣṣal 471
Uṣūl al-dīn 471
Rebstock, Ulrich – "Das Grabesleben" (2002) 10
Reid, Anthony 1149, 1166–67
Reinhart, Kevin – "The Here and the Hereafter in Islamic Religious Thought" (1991) 9
Reynald, or Reneward ("Rainouart au tinel") 896
Reynolds, Gabriel 68
Riḍā, Muḥammad Rashīd (d. 1354/1935) 1204–8, 1218
al-Manār 1203
Riexinger, Martin 27
al-Rijāʾ-Chāchī, Aḥmad (d. 516/1122) 587
Rippin, A. 221, 222 n. 4
Ritter, H. 286, 584
al-Riyāshī, Rīm Ṣāliḥ, 1061
Robson, J. 223
Roland 896, 908
Roman, A. – *Une vision humaine des fins dernières* 566 n. 2
Rosenthal, Franz 113 n. 71, 1146
Rudolph, Kurt 1131
Ruggles, D.F. 983
Rührdanz, Karin 26
Rüling, Josef Bernhard – *Beiträge zur Eschatologie des Islam* (1895) 6
Rūmī, Jalāl al-Dīn (d. 672/1273) 354, 489, 584, 695, 741–42, 906, 916, 1196–97, 1243
Mathnawī-yi maʿnawī 6, 267, 587, 692–93
al-Rummānī, ʿAlī b. ʿĪsā (296–384/908–994) 222 n. 3

Rushdie, Salman (b. 1947) 25, 967, 970–74
The Moor's Last Sigh (1995) 953–54, 956, 966
The Satanic Verses 956
Rustom, Mohammed 20
The Triumph of Mercy: Philosophy and Scripture in Mulla Sadra (2012) 10
Rustomji, Nerina 18, 865
The Garden and the Fire: Heaven and Hell in Islamic Culture (2009) 10
Ruthven, Malise 1145
Rūzbihān al-Baqlī = Abū Muḥammad Rūzbihān b. Abī Naṣr al-Baqlī (d. 606/1209) 9, 18, 224, 227, 228 n. 20, 232, 235, 239, 241–43, 245
ʿArāʾis al-bayān fī ḥaqāʾāiq al-Qurʾān 222
Kitāb ʿAbhar al-ʿāshiqīn 707 n. 17
Ryad, Umar 27

Sachau, Eduard 1133
Sachedina, Abdulaziz 606–7, 613
Islamic Messianism: The Idea of Mahdī in Twelver Shīʿism (1981) 8
Saddam Hussein 1241
Ṣādiq Humāyūnī 1058
Ṣadr al-Dīn al-Shīrāzī = Mullā Ṣadrā (ca. 979/1571–2 to 1045/1635–6 or to 1050/1640–1) 6, 9–10, 20, 211, 287, 487–88, 495, 498, 500–2, 505, 507–8, 511–12, 521–22, 528–29, 534–35, 539–41, 545–46, 739, 1190
al-Asfār al-arbaʿa al-ʿaqliyya 490, 503, 516, 519, 535–36, 542, 544, 547
Glosses (*Taʿlīqāt* or *Taʿālīq*) 501
Le livre de la sagesse orientale 501
al-Mabdaʾ wa-l-maʿād 535
Mafātīḥ al-ghayb 672
Risāla fī l-ḥashr 490, 517
Risāla fī l-ḥudūth 518
Tafsīr āyat al-kursī 536 n. 10
Tafsīr sūrat al-fātiḥa 542–43
Taʿlīqāt 491 n. 22, 509
al-Ṣadūq Ibn Bābūya, Shaykh (d. 381/991) 736 n. 7
al-Ṣaffār al-Qummī (d. 290/902–3) – *Baṣāʾir al-darajāt* 608
Sala, Monferrer 989
Ṣalāḥ al-Dīn al-Ayyūbī (Saladin, d. 589/1193) 408, 897, 912–13, 916, 918
Sale, George 5
Saleh, Walid A. 25, 68
Saliba Douaihy (Ṣalībā al-Duwayhī) (1915?–1994) 1070
Ṣāliḥ b. Musarrih (d. 76/695) 276
al-Ṣāliḥ Najm al-Dīn Ayyūb (648/1250) 1011 n. 4, 1011 n. 5, 1023
al-Samarqandī, Abū l-Layth (d. 373/983) 347
Kitāb Ḥaqāʾiq al-daqāʾiq (Book of the true natures of the subtleties) 348–49
Qurrat al-ʿuyūn [attrib.] 349 n. 36
Tanbīh al-ghāfilīn 349 n. 36
Sanāʾī (d. 525/1131) 584
al-Ṣanʿānī, ʿAbd al-Razzāq (d. 211/827) 19, 163–64, 374, 872
Muṣannaf 313, 346, 373, 381, 385–87, 403–4
Sargon Boulus 23, 807–809
Poetry and Other Mysteries 808
Saunders, Frances Stonor – *The cultural cold war* 1071
Schacht, Joseph 821
Schaeder, Hans Heinrich (1896–1957) 1129, 1135–36
Scharbrodt, O. 1201
Schimmel, Annemarie 9, 56–58, 341 n. 2, 354, 599, 742
"Creation and Judgment in the Koran and in the Mystico-Poetical Interpretation" (1979) 7
Mystical Dimensions of Islam (1975) 7
Schrader, Eberhard 1133
Schuon, Frithjof 511
Scot, Michael 897, 913, 918
Scott, John A. 909–10
Sells, M.A. 151 n. 33
al-Shaʿbī (d. 104/722) 399
Shāfiʿī (*imām*) (608/1211) 1011 n. 5, 1023
al-Shāfiʿī (d. 204/820) 171, 1105–6, 1118
Shāfiʿī-Kadkanī, M. 587
Shah, Idries 906
Shāh ʿAbbās I 522
Shahin, Sultan – *New Age Islam* 743
al-Shahrastānī, Muḥammad b. ʿAbd al-Karīm (d. 548/1153–4) 635 n. 174, 738 n. 16
Kitāb al-Milal wa-l-niḥal 8

al-Shahrazūrī, Shams al-Dīn (d. in or after 687/1288) 505–7, 737
Shāh Rukh b. Tīmūr 1038
Shāh Walī Allāh (d. 1176/1762) 27, 1189–93, 1198, 1218
al-Shalmaghānī 856
Shantout, Hammoud (Ḥammūd Shantūt) (b. 1956) 1077–78
al-Sharīf al-Murtaḍā (d. 436/1044) 607 n. 11
Shawqī, Aḥmad 957
al-Shaykh al-Mufīd, Muḥammad al-Baghdādī (d. 413/1022) 633, 736
Kitāb al-Irshād 608
Shiblī l-Nuʿmānī (d. 1332/1914) 1196–97, 1218
al-Shīrāzī, al-Mu'ayyad fī l-Dīn (d. 471/1078) 21
al-Shīrāzī, Quṭb al-Dīn (d. 710/1311 or 716/1316) 522, 1094, 1190
Commentary (*Sharḥ*) 501
Shoemaker, Stephen J. 102–3
The Death of a Prophet: The End of Muhammad's Life and the Beginnings of Islam (2012) 11
Shuʿayb (prophet) 202, 204
al-Shubbar, ʿAbdallāh (d. 1242/1826–7) 613 n. 59
Siapno, Jacqueline Aquino 1173, 1179
Sībawayhi (d. ca. 180/796) 852
Siegel, James 1154, 1164, 1168, 1171
Sigier of Brabant 908, 914
al-Sijistānī, Abū Yaʿqūb (d. ca. 361/971–2) 21, 649–51, 654, 659, 666
Ithbāt al-nubuwwa 630–31
Kashf al-maḥjūb 498, 517, 522
Kitāb al-Iftikhār 653, 655–56
Kitāb Ithbāt al-nubuwwāt 652
Kitāb al-Yanābīʿ 652–53, 655–56
al-Simnānī, ʿAlāʾ al-Dawla (d. 736/1336) – *al-ʿUrwa li-ahl al-khalwa wa-l-jalwa* 695
Sinai, N. – *Philosophie der Erleuchtung* 501 n. 42
al-Ṣinhājī, Muḥammad (d. ca. 798/1393) 934
Kanz al-asrār wa-lawāqiḥ al-afkār 936
Sirhindī, Aḥmad (d. 1034/1624) 598, 1252
Maktūbāt 1249
Sleiman, Jean Benjamin 23, 810, 812
Smend, Rudolf 1130
Smirnov, Andrey 10
Smith, Huston 741
Smith, J.I. 200, 1188–89, 1222
The Islamic Understanding of Death and Resurrection [with Y. Haddad, 1981] 8
Snouck Hurgronje, Christiaan (1857–1936) 6, 102, 1148, 1158
Socin, Albert 1134 n. 33
Solomon (prophet, Sulaymān) 203, 206, 588
Soucek, Priscilla 359
Southern, Richard William 891–93, 895, 911–12, 917
Speyer, Heinrich (1931) 68
Spivak, Gayatri 1071
Sprenger, Aloys 6
Starkie, W.J.M. 260
Stetkevych, Suzanne 71, 109 n. 52, 137 n. 5
Stieglecker, Hermann – *Die Glaubenslehren des Islam* (1962) 7
al-Suddī (d. 128/745) 167, 402
Sufyān al-Thawrī (d. 161/778) 171, 231, 246
al-Suhrawardī, Shihāb al-Dīn Yaḥyā (d. 587/1191) 20, 94 n. 2, 200 n. 46, 502, 505–6, 512, 522, 528–29, 583, 586, 595–96, 689 n. 3, 707 n. 15, 723 n. 50, 916, 1192
Hayākil al-nūr 516
Ḥikmat al-ishrāq 491 n. 22
Kitāb Ḥikmat al-ishrāq 501, 509
Kitāb Ḥikmat al-ishrāq = *Wisdom of Oriental Illumination* 493
Sulaiman, Mohammad Isa 1172
al-Sulamī, Abū ʿAbd al-Raḥmān Muḥammad b. al-Ḥusayn (325 or 330–412/937 or 942–1021) 17, 224, 227, 228 n. 20, 232, 238, 243–45
ʿArāʾis al-bayān 241–42
Ḥaqāʾiq al-tafsīr 222
Ziyādāt ḥaqāʾiq al-tafsīr 222
al-Sulamī, Abū Marwān ʿAbd al-Malik b. Ḥabīb b. Sulaymān (d. 238/853) – *Waṣf al-firdaws* (The description of paradise) 817
al-Sulamī, ʿAlī b. Ṭāhir (d. 500/1106) 19, 411–21
Kitāb al-Jihād (The Book of the Jihād) 407, 1168
Sulaymān (r. 1076–1105/1666–94) [Safavid Shāh] 349
Sultan Isḥāq 690–91, 693
al-Ṣūrī (d. ca. 487/1094) 651
Sutherland, Harold 892

al-Suyūṭī, Jalāl al-Dīn (d. 911/1505) 314, 328, 561, 872
al-Durar al-ḥisān fī l-baʿth wa-naʿīm al-jinān [attrib.] 819, 842
al-Hayʾa al-saniyya 937
al-Kashf ʿan mujāwazat hādhihī l-umma al-alf 941 n. 28
al-Laʾālī l-maṣnūʿa fī l-aḥādīth al-mawḍūʿa 864
Szyska, Christian 1286

al-Ṭabarī, ʿAlī b. Rabban (third/ninth century) 204 n. 53
al-Ṭabarī, Muḥammad b. Jarīr (d. 310/923) 163–68, 172–73, 175–78, 186, 257, 380, 388–89, 393, 395, 397, 400, 745–46, 829–30, 863, 871, 956, 987, 994
Jāmiʿ al-bayān 832
Ṭabarsī, Ḥusayn Nūrī (d. 1320/1902) 614
al-Ṭabrisī (d. 548/1153) 221
Majmaʿ al-bayān li-ʿulūm al-Qurʾān 1253
al-Taftāzānī, Saʿd al-Dīn (d. 793/1390) 469, 471–72, 474–80, 483
Sharḥ al-ʿaqāʾid al-Nasafiyya 470 n. 9
Sharḥ al-maqāṣid 20, 470–71, 473, 481–82, 485
Ṭāhā, Maḥmūd Muḥammad (1909 or 1911–85) 1222
Ṭahmāsp 1037
Ṭalq b. Ḥabīb (d. between 90/708 and 100/718) 384–87
Tamcke, Martin 23
Tamīm b. Muqbil (d. after 37/657) 853
Ṭarafa (fl. ca. sixth century CE) 854
Taylor, J.B. – "Some Aspects of Islamic Eschatology" (1968) 7
al-Ṭayyibī, Shams al-Dīn Aḥmad b. Yaʿqūb 663 n. 8
Tazi, Nadia (b. 1953) 28, 1291–92, 1294, 1295–1304, 1307, 1309–12, 1315
Islam and Psychoanalysis 1294
Teuku Iskandar 1155
Teuku Umar (1854–99) 1169
Teungku Chik di Tiro (d. 1308/1891) 1166–67, 1169
Teungku Chik Pante Kulu (alias Teungku Syekh Muhammad Pante Kulu) – *Hikayat Prang Sabi* 1149 n. 28
Teungku Nyak Ahmat (alias Uri b. Mahmut b. Jalalōdin b. Abdōsalam)
Hikayat Prang di Sigli 1147
Nasihat ureueng muprang 1157–58
Thābit b. Qurra (d. 288/901) 499
Thaʿlab (d. 291/904) 852
al-Thaʿlabī, Aḥmad (d. 427/1035) – *al-Kashf wa-l-bayān ʿan tafsīr al-Qurʾān* 931, 936
Thales 664
Thomas (of Gospel) 97
al-Ṭihrānī – *al-Dharīʿa* 609 n. 18
Tillich, Paul 779
Tīmūr (d. 807/1405) 469–70
al-Tirmidhī (d. 279/892) 303, 313 n. 9, 404, 872
al-Jāmiʿ al-ṣaḥīḥ, 819, 822, 841–842
Tlatli, Moufida (b. 1947) – *La saison des hommes* (2000) 1076
Tottoli, Roberto 24, 347, 932, 935
Triano, Antonio Vallejo 981, 983
Ṭughril Beg, Sultan (d. 455/1063) 580 n. 9
Tunç, Mustafa Şekip (1886–1958) 1254
Turner, Colin 613
Turner, Victor 1286
al-Ṭūsī, Muḥammad b. al-Ḥasan (d. 460/1067) 17, 221, 224, 226–27, 228 n. 21, 230 n. 23, 231–32, 234–35, 238, 241, 243–44, 246, 1253
al-Tibyān fī tafsīr al-Qurʾān (The explanation in Quranic exegesis) 222
al-Ṭūsī, Naṣīr al-Dīn (d. 672/1274) 22, 455 n. 42, 460, 502, 511 n. 72, 631, 665–66, 669–71
Āghāz wa-anjām (*The Beginning and the End*) 662–63, 672
Akhlāq-i Muḥtashamī (The Muḥtashamid ethics) 662
Akhlāq-i Nāṣirī (*The Nasirean Ethics*) 662
Awṣāf al-ashrāf (Attributes of the nobles) 662
al-Dustūr wa-daʿwat al-muʾminīn lil-ḥuḍūr 663
Jabr wa-ikhtiyār (*Free Will and Predestination*) 663
Maṭlūb al-muʾminīn (*Desideratum of the Faithful*) 662, 672

Mujārāt 663
Rawḍa-yi taslīm (*The Paradise of Submission*) 662–63, 667, 672
Risāla dar niʿmat-hā, khushī-hā wa-ladhdhat-hā (*Treatise on Comfort, Happiness and Joyfulness*) 662–63
Sayr wa-sulūk (*Contemplation and Action*) 662–63
al-Tadhkira fī ʿilm al-hayʾa 1093–94
Tawallā wa-tabarrā (*Solidarity and Dissociation*) 662, 672
al-Tustarī, Sahl b. ʿAbdallāh (d. 283/896) 188, 567, 569 n. 14, 569 n. 15
al-Tuṭīlī 900, 916

ʿUbaydīs b. Maḥmūd 1004
al-Ujhurī, Abū l-Irshād (d. 1066/1656) 877
ʿUmar b. ʿAbd al-ʿAzīz 384–85
ʿUmar b. al-Khaṭṭāb 382, 410, 437 n. 25, 570, 869, 880, 989, 1043
Urban (pope) 895
ʿUthmān b. ʿAffān 880, 1043
ʿUzair (Ezra) 434

van Ess, Josef 376, 474
Theologie und Gesellschaft 9, 272
van Gelder, Geert Jan 1154
van Gennep, Arnold 1281
van Langen, Karel (1848–1915) 1167
van Reeth, Jan M.F. 789
van Steenberghen, Abbé F. 914
Velji, Jamel A. 22
Versteegh, C.H.M. 376–77
Virgil 904
Aeneid 902–3
von Hees, Syrinx 933–34, 939
von Selle, Götz 1129
Vossler, Karl 909
Medieval Culture: An Introduction to Dante and His Times 912

Wahb b. Masarra (d. 346/957) 1004
al-Wāḥidī (d. 468/1076) 163, 167–68, 173, 931 n. 1
Waldman, Marilyn Robinson 3, 9, 665
al-Walīd b. ʿAbd al-Malik 384
al-Walīd b. Yazīd (d. 126/743) 276, 856
Walker, P. 649, 677, 735–37, 739
Walls, A.G. 1017 n. 26
Wansbrough, J. 57, 81 n. 41
al-Wardanī, ʿAlī b. Salīm (1861–1915) 954 n. 6
Watt, Montgomery 102, 195 n. 36
Welch, A.T. – "Death and Dying in the Qurʾān" (1977) 7
Wellhausen, Julius (1844–1918) 1129–30
Das arabische Reich und sein Sturz 1131
Whelan, E. 1017 n. 28
Widengren, Geo – *Muhammad, the Apostle of God, and his Ascension* (1955) 7
Wieringa, Edwin P. 27
Wild, Stefan 72
William, Count of Orange (Guillaume au Curb Nes) 896
Winter, Michael 933
Wolff, Moritz 348
Muhammedanische Eschatologie (1872) 5
Würtz, Thomas 20

Yahya, Harun 28
Yazīd b. Muʿāwiya (d. 39/680) 854, 1056, 1059
Yūsuf Ibn ʿAṭīya (Quzmān) – *Sīrat al-malik Iskandar Dhū l-Qarnayn* 922–23

al-Zajjāj (ca. 230–311/844–923) 233 n. 32, 351
Zakī, Aḥmad (1867–1934) 954 n. 6
Zakzouk, Mahmoud 16
al-Zamakhsharī, Abū l-Qāsim Maḥmūd b. ʿUmar (d. 538/1144) 17, 163, 168, 173, 188, 226–29, 231, 233–34, 236–40, 243–44, 745, 1113
Kashshāf ʿan ḥaqāʾiq ghawāmiḍ al-tanzīl wa-ʿuyūn al-aqāwīl fī wujūh al-taʾwīl 221–24, 230 n. 23, 241, 245–48
Zangī, ʿImād al-Dīn (d. 541/1146) 408
Zarrinkoob, A. 588
Zaydān, Jurjī 957
Zayd b. Ḥāritha 275, 862, 876
Zayd b. Thābit 415, 781
al-Zaylaʿī, Jamāl al-Dīn Abū Muḥammad ʿAbdallāh b. Yūsuf (d. 762/1360–1) – *Risāla fī takhrīj aḥādīth al-kashshāf wa-mā fīhi min qiṣaṣ wa-āthār* 247
Zechariah (prophet, Zakariyya) 51
Ziai, H. and J. Walbridge – *The philosophy of illumination* 501 n. 42
Zuhayr 853, 855

Index of Geographical Names and Toponyms

Aceh 1152, 1173, 1179
Acre 897, 899, 1024
Afghanistan 469, 1250
Africa 1248
Agra 974
al-Aḥsāʾ 855
Alamut 521, 586–97, 650 n. 4, 662, 672, 683, 685
Alcázar (royal palace) (Cordoba) 992
Algeria 1071, 1292
Alhambra (al-Ḥamrāʾ) Palace 971, 974, 1017 n. 26
 garden(s) of 953
Almanzor 1004
Almeria 996
Anagni cathedral 116, 117 ill.
Anatolia 1223–24
al-Andalus 25, 285, 287, 953–54, 956, 959–60, 966–67, 971, 973–74, 982, 1005, 1092
 fall of 962
 myth of 955
 reign of Petty Kings (*mulūk al-ṭawāʾif*) 957
Ankara 1224
al-Aqṣā Mosque ('Furthest Mosque') 188, 435, 1014
Arabia/Arabian Peninsula 58, 72, 144–45, 254, 256, 259, 273, 801, 827 n. 42
 southern 781
Ashrafiyya Madrasa (Jerusalem) 1017 n. 26
Austria 910
al-Azhar Library (Cairo) 875

Babri Mosque (Uttar Pradesh) 956, 970
Babylon 110, 506
Badr, battle of (2/624) 17, 118, 163–64, 178
 those slain in/martyrs of 167–71, 175
Baghdad 264, 451, 580, 662, 807, 810, 852, 926, 962, 997, 1036, 1093, 1209
Basra 277, 281, 283, 389, 926
Bayn al-Qaṣrayn (Fatimid palace) 1011 n. 4, 1012
Bayt Lihyā, Mosque of 407
Beirut 807, 809, 899, 962, 1076
Berlin 807, 1129, 1133, 1135
Biʾr Maʿūna 170–71, 175
Black Sea region 1224
Bombay 966–69, 971–72
Bosnia 1240
Breslau 1135
Bukhara 1038
Bunyād-i shahīd (Martyr's Foundation) 1057
 mural 1066 fig.48.3

Cairo 262, 942, 956, 971, 1010–12, 1016, 1022, 1069, 1093
Catalonia 903
Central Asia 26, 1034, 1209
Ceuta, Morocco 898
Chechnya 1240
China 258, 923–24
City Stars Mall (Cairo) 1075
Constantinople 259
Cordoba 899, 954 n. 7, 979–80, 997–98, 1003

Damascus 407–8, 965, 1077
Dār al-Ḥadīth al-Kāmiliyya (of Ayyubids) 1011 n. 4
Delhi 974
Derb Bou Hajj (Morocco) 557
Derb al-Keddan (Morocco) 557
Derb Masmouda (Morocco) 558
Dome of the Rock (Jerusalem) 25, 345, 357–60, 894 n. 6, 1014–15, 1020–22, 1025, 1030 fig.46.3
Dubai 1075, 1077
Dubai Museum 1075–76

East Africa 258–59
École des Beaux-Arts (Parisian Fine Arts Academy) 1069
Edessa 790
Edirne 1230
Egypt 32, 110, 138, 262, 273, 470, 506, 955, 957, 964–66, 971, 1024, 1071, 1200
 ancient 436
 Upper 959
Ephesus 433
Erzurum 1230
Euphrates (al-Furāt) River 318, 928

Europe 893, 897, 899–900, 903, 915–17, 1122 n. 64, 1200

Fez, Morocco 21, 556–57, 559
Florence 893, 899, 907, 914–15
Foundation of Martyrs (central Tehran) 1059
France 895, 900, 910, 1069, 1072–73, 1128, 1292

Gaza Strip 28, 1268–70, 1274
Germany 897, 910, 1117 n. 56, 1128
Gezira (Morocco) 558
Göttingen 1130–32, 1135
Göttingen University 1129
Granada 899, 954, 956, 961, 966, 972–74
  fall of (897/1494) 953, 957
  Muslims of 958, 960
Great Britain 810, 956, 968
Greece 26, 254, 259, 506, 1088
Greifswald 1130, 1132–33

al-Habbaniyya (Iraq) 808
Haifa 1283
Halle, University of 1129, 1131
al-Ḥamrāʾ. *See* Alhambra (al-Ḥamrāʾ) Palace
Hebron 1014 n. 19
Herat (Afghanistan) 1038
Hijaz 32, 469
Ḥusayniyyah-yi Mushīr 1057–58
  tilework of 1065 fig.48.1

Iberian Peninsula 899. *See also* al-Andalus
Ibn al-Shāliya (al-Andalus) 1004
Imāmzādah-yi Ibrāhīm (Shiraz) 1057
India 258, 262, 506, 924, 955–56, 966–68, 970–71, 973
Indonesia 27
Iran 26, 258, 469, 583, 691, 1015 n. 23, 1034, 1036, 1069
  pre-Islamic 1135–36
Iraq 23, 256, 273, 380, 615, 807–9, 965, 1015 n. 23, 1071
Isfahan 349
Israel 1299 n. 21
Istanbul 1069, 1130, 1223–25
Italy 894–95, 897, 899, 904, 910, 914, 1089
Izmir 1230

Jaffa 898
Jenin 1283
Jerusalem 193, 345, 357, 407, 892, 894 n. 6, 895, 897–98, 912, 1014, 1020–21, 1038 n. 27
  New Jerusalem (of Revelation) 316 n. 22

Kaʿba 178, 190, 782 n. 7, 1017 n. 28, 1091, 1250
Kairouan 996
Karbala, battle of (61/680) 26, 276, 1056–57, 1059, 1165
Khurasan 579, 583
Khwārazm 469
Kirkuk 807
Königsberg 1135
Kufa 606, 1059
Kutaraja (capital of Aceh) 1172–73

Lālah Park (Tehran) 1056
Lebanon 962
Leipzig 1135
Levant 418
Lisbon 997

Madinat Nasr (Cairo) 1075
Madīnat al-Zahrāʾ (al-Andalus) 25, 979–81, 985, 988, 991–92, 994–95, 997, 999–1001, 1005
  construction of 1002–3
  gardens of 980, 983, 991
  Hall of ʿAbd al-Raḥmān III 979, 981–84, 986, 988, 992, 994, 996, 1000, 1002, 1005
Maghrib 1092, 1292. *See also* North Africa
Mahdiyya (Fatimid palace) 981, 996
Malacca 1165–66
Malaga 956
Marburg 1131
Mashhad 662
Masjid al-Kūfa 624
Maydān-i Vanak (Tehran) 1062
Mecca 34, 59, 178, 191, 273, 357 n. 80, 435, 606, 782 n. 7, 827 n. 42, 853, 894 n. 6, 900, 1013, 1014 n. 19, 1020 n. 38, 1038 n. 27, 1091–92, 1156, 1160, 1248
  Sacred Mosque 188
Medina 34, 172, 179, 273, 385, 607, 1014 n. 19, 1020 n. 38, 1110, 1208
Mesopotamia 26, 781, 790, 1083–86, 1134
Middle East 1128, 1270, 1299 n. 21
Mudarris freeway mural (Tehran) 1061–62
al-Muqaṭṭam (Cairo) 1022

Murcia 900
Mu'ta, battle of (8/629) 416

Najmiyya Hospital (Tehran) 1061
National Library (Dār al-Kutub) (Cairo) 875
Near East 254. *See also* Middle East
Nile River 318, 1022
Nishapur 579–80
North Africa 683, 996, 1299 n. 21
North America 1122 n. 64

Ostia 1089
Oued Chorfa [Morocco] 557

Palestine 781, 956, 1012, 1271–72, 1279–83, 1286, 1299 n. 21
  as land/husband 1275–76
  loss of 954, 962
Paris 1292
Persia 506, 683, 923, 1167. *See also* Iran
Płock, Poland 1132
Provence 900, 918

Qalqaliyine (Morocco) 557
al-Qarāfa cemetery (Cairo) 1022–23
al-Qarāfa al-Ṣughrā (Cairo) 1011 n. 5
Qubbat al-Manṣūriyya (Cairo) 25, 1012–13, 1015–17, 1020, 1022, 1024–25, 1030 fig.46.3, 1030 fig.46.4, 1032 fig.46.6
Qum 633 n. 165

Rahbat Zebib (Morocco) 558
Ravenna, Italy 893
Rayy 633 n. 165
Rome 26, 110
Russia 1224

Ṣabra-Manṣūriyya (Fatimid city near Kairouan) 981, 997
Samarqand 469–70
Samarra 262
Scandinavia 1117 n. 56
Seville 900, 902
Shiraz 1057
Sicily 895, 897–99, 903, 910, 918
  under Normans 1012
Sidi al-Aouad (Morocco) 558
Sidon 899
Sijilmasa 1000
Simancas-Ahandega, battle of 980
Sinai 781, 962
Sirjan 1060
Southeast Asia 258
Soviet Union 1224
Spain 262, 899, 902, 904, 910, 918, 965, 970, 1167. *See also* al-Andalus
Sultan Ḥasan Mosque (Cairo) 933
Sultan Qalāwūn, Complex of 1028 fig.46.1, 1029 fig.46.2
Susa 996
Syria 256, 262, 273, 277, 407, 781, 790, 1024

Taftāzān 469
Ṭā'if 1156
Tarsus 899
Tehran 26, 1057, 1059–63, 1069
Temple Mount (Jerusalem) 191, 345, 357, 359, 1022 n. 44
Tetuan 997
Tigris (al-Dijla) River 926, 928
Toledo 899
Transjordan 781
Tripoli 899
Ṭūl Karm, Palestine 931
Turkey 1231
Ṭūs 662
Tyre 899

Uḥud, battle of (3/625) 17, 164, 170–71, 410, 416
  martyrs of 166–67, 170, 175
Umayyad Mosque (Damascus) 407–8, 989
United States 807, 809, 1071, 1178, 1224, 1231, 1234
  idealization of 811
  migration to 807–10

Valencia 959, 962
Van 1223–24

West Bank (Palestine) 28, 1268–70

Yemen 855

Index of Book Titles and Other Texts

Aeneid, Virgil 902
Āghāz wa-anjām (*The Beginning and the End*), Naṣīr al-Dīn al-Ṭūsī 662–63, 672
Aḥwāl-i qiyāma (The circumstances of resurrection) 1040, 1042–44
in paradise 1055 fig.47.9
records raining from the sky 1054 fig.47.8
ʿAjāʾib al-makhlūqāt, al-Qazwīnī 932–33, 936, 938–39
al-Ajwiba ʿan al-asʾila al-Ṣiqilliyya (The responses to the Sicilian questions), Ibn Sabʿīn 898
Akhbār Makka, al-Azraqī 357 n. 80
Akhlāq-i Muḥtashamī (The Muḥtashamid ethics), Naṣīr al-Dīn al-Ṭūsī 662
Akhlāq-i Nāṣirī (*The Nasirean Ethics*), Naṣīr al-Dīn al-Ṭūsī 662
ʿAlāmāt al-qiyāma, al-Barzanjī 1249
Alf layla wa-layla (*A Thousand and One Nights*) 25, 286, 435, 587, 923–27
Almagest, Ptolemy 357, 1088, 1094
Alter und Heimat der mandäischen Religion, Mark Lidzbarski 1134
Anwār al-tanzīl wa-asrār al-taʾwīl (The lights of revelation and the secrets of interpretation), al-Bayḍāwī 223, 228, 244–45, 248
Anxiety of Influence: A Theory of Poetry (1973), Harold Bloom 1157
Apocalypse of Peter 312 n. 5
Apocalypse of St. John (or *The Apocalypse of Jesus Christ*) 95–97
Arabian Nights. See Alf layla wa-layla
ʿArāʾis al-bayān fī ḥaqāʾiq al-Qurʾān (The brides of explanation on the truths of the Quran), Rūzbihān al-Baqlī 222, 241–42
Archeology of Knowledge, Michel Foucault 1292, 1314 n. 61
Ardā Wīrāz Nāmag 251–52, 255 n. 20, 267, 312 n. 5, 585
Areopagitica, John Milton 36
Asfār = *al-Ḥikma al-mutaʿāliya fī l-asfār al-ʿaqliyya al-arbaʿa* (*The Four Journeys*), Mullā Ṣadrā 490, 503, 516, 519, 535–36, 542, 544, 547
Asrār al-ḥikma al-mashriqiyya (The Mysteries of Illuministic Philosophy), Ibn Sabʿīn 898
Asrār-nāme (Book of secrets), ʿAṭṭār 281
Asrār al-shahāda (The spiritual realities of martyrdom), Sarbāz Burūjirdī 1056
Asrār al-tawḥīd (Secrets of oneness) 580 n. 9
Auf rauhem Wege, Mark Lidzbarski 1132
Awṣāf al-ashrāf (Attributes of the nobles), Naṣīr al-Dīn al-Ṭūsī 662

Bahjat al-nāẓirīn wa-āyāt al-mustadillīn (The delight of onlookers and the signs for investigators), Marʿī b. Yūsuf al-Karmī 25, 931–32, 935–36, 939–42
Bāl-i Jibrīl (*Gabriel's Wing*), Muḥammad Iqbāl 954 n. 7
Baṣāʾir al-darajāt, al-Ṣaffār al-Qummī 608
Beiträge zur Eschatologie des Islam (1895), Josef Bernhard Rüling 6
Between Heaven and Hell: Islam, Salvation, and the Fate of Others (2013), Mohammad Khalil 10
Biḥār al-anwār (Seas of light), Muḥammad Bāqir al-Majlisī 614, 1253
The Birds, Aristophanes 253 n. 13
The Book of the Ladder (or *al-Miʿrāj*) 899
Bundahishn 356
Burda, al-Būṣīrī 35
Burda, Kaʿb b. Zubayr 109 n. 52
Büyük Doğu (The great east), Necip Fazıl Kısakürek 1254

Civilization and its Discontents, Sigmund Freud 1303
Commentary (*Sharḥ*), Quṭb al-Dīn al-Shīrāzī 501
Composition (1961), Sayyid ʿAbd al-Rasūl 1072
"Creation and Judgment in the Koran and in the Mystico-Poetical Interpretation" (1979), Annemarie Schimmel 7
Crescent (2003), Diana Abu-Jaber 953
Cultural cold war, Frances Stonor Saunders 1071

Dānishnāme-yi ʿalāʾī (The book of sciences dedicated to ʿAlāʾ al-Dawla), Ibn Sīnā 455 n. 43
Daqāʾiq al-akhbār fī dhikr al-janna wa-l-nār (The meticulous accounts referring to paradise and hell), ʿAbd al-Raḥīm b. Aḥmad al-Qāḍī 5–6, 19, 296, 304, 347–48, 360, 819, 842
Das arabische Reich und sein Sturz, Julius Wellhausen 1131
"Das Grabesleben" (2002), Ulrich Rebstock 10
"Das Koranische Paradies" (1923), Josef Horovitz 68
Dead Sea Scrolls, John Collins 93
Death, Graves and the Hereafter in Islam: Muslim Perception of the Last Things in the Middle Ages and Today (2015) 11
"Death and Dying in the Qurʾān" (1977), A.T. Welch 7
The Death of a Prophet: The End of Muhammad's Life and the Beginnings of Islam (2012), Stephen J. Shoemaker 11
De Consolatione Philosophiae (*On the Consolation of Philosophy*), Boethius 902
Dēnkart 356
De revolutionibus (1543), Copernicus 1094
Der Koran: Frühmekkanische Suren (2011), Angelika Neuwirth 10
"Der Prophet und die Weltgeschichte" in *Der Koran* (2002), Tilman Nagel 10
Der Ursprung des Islams und das Christentum, Tor Andrae 783
al-Dharīʿa, al-Ṭihrānī 609 n. 18
Dhikr bilād al-Andalus 992
Di babah pintō syeuruga lapan (At the threshold of the eighth heaven), Abdullah Arif 1176
Die Glaubenslehren des Islam (1962), Hermann Stieglecker 7
Dieu et la destinée de l'homme (1967), L. Gardet 7
Discourse on the soul: Summary of the book[s] *of Aristotle and Plato and the rest of the philosophers*, al-Kindī 447
Divine Comedy, Dante 24, 904, 906, 912, 914
"Divine Wrath and Divine Mercy in Islam: Their Reflection in the Qurʾān and Quranic Images of Water" (2008), Todd Lawson 11
"Duality, Opposition and Typology in the Qurʾan: The Apocalyptic Substrate" (2008), Todd Lawson 11
al-Durar al-ḥisān fī l-baʿth wa-naʿīm al-jinān [The Comely Jewels on the Resurrection and the Bliss of Paradise], [attrib. to al-Ṣuyūṭī] 819, 842
al-Durra al-fākhira (*The Precious Pearl*), al-Ghazālī 17, 182, 195–96, 199–200, 202, 207–8, 211, 347, 566 n. 2, 937, 939
al-Dustūr wa-daʿwat al-muʾminīn lil-ḥuḍūr, Naṣīr al-Dīn al-Ṭūsī 663

Encyclopaedia Iranica 4
Encyclopaedia of Islam 4
Encyclopaedia of the Qurʾān 4, 65
Encyclopedia of Apocalypticism 98
En Islam iranien: Aspects spirituels et philosophiques (1971), Henry Corbin 7, 491 n. 22
Enneads, Plotinus 351, 495
Epistoles of the Brethren of Purity 506, 522
Epistolla Sulla Vita Futura, Alpago 457 n. 51
"Eschatology" (2004), Willem Bijlefeld 10

Fables, La Fontaine (1668–94) 899
Fālnāme ("Book of omens") 26, 1036–37, 1040–42
  Dresden manuscript 1041–43
  entry of Dajjāl (Antichrist) into Jerusalem 1052 fig.47.6
  last judgment 1053 fig.47.7
al-Fatāwā al-ḥadīthiyya (Rulings regarding prophetic traditions), Ibn Ḥajar al-Haytamī 16, 31
Fī annahu tūjad jawāhir lā ajsām (*That there exist substances that are not bodies*), al-Kindī 447
Fī l-falsafa al-ūlā (On first philosophy), al-Kindī 446
Fī ithbāt al-nubuwwāt, Ibn Sīnā 520 n. 96
Furqān al-akhbār, Ḥājj Niʿmat Allāh Jayḥūnābādī Mukrī 691
Fuṣūṣ al-ḥikam (*The Bezels of Wisdom*), Ibn ʿArabī 502 n. 47, 538
al-Futūḥāt al-Makkiyya (*The Meccan Openings/Revelations*), Ibn ʿArabī 522, 538, 549, 900, 1018

The Garden and the Fire: Heaven and Hell in Islamic Culture (2009), Nerina Rustomji 10
"«*Gepriesen sei der, der seinen Diener bei Nacht reisen ließ*» (Koran 17:1): Paradiesvorstellungen und Himmelsreisen im Islam – Grundfesten des Glaubens und literarische Topoi" (2011), Sebastian Günther 10–11
Gilgamesh Epic 253
Glosses (*Taʿlīqāt* or *Taʿālīq*), Mullā Ṣadrā 501
Gnostic Apocalypse and Islam: Qurʾan, Exegesis, Messianism, and the Literary Origins of the Babi Religion (2011), Todd Lawson 11
The Green Face, Gustav Meyrink 435

Ḥādī l-arwāḥ ilā bilād al-afrāḥ (The guide of souls to the land of delights / Urging souls forward toward the lands of happiness), Ibn Qayyim al-Jawziyya 347, 817, 820 n. 13, 831, 838
Ḥadīth al-miʿrāj, Abū l-Ḥasan al-Bakrī 878–79
Haft bāb-i Bābā Sayyidnā (Seven chapters of our master) 22, 676, 684–86
Ḥaqāʾiq al-tafsīr (The truths of exegesis), Abū ʿAbd al-Raḥmān Muḥammad b. al-Ḥusayn al-Sulamī 222
Hasht bihisht ("eight paradises"), Amīr Khusraw 349
Hayākil al-nūr, Shihāb al-Dīn al-Suhrawardī 516
al-Hayʾa al-saniyya, al-Suyūṭī 937
Ḥayy Ibn Yaqẓān, Ibn Ṭufayl 24, 893, 903–5
Hazār afsān (*A Thousand Tales*) 925
"The Here and the Hereafter in Islamic Religious Thought" (1991), Kevin Reinhart 9
Hidāyat-nāma, Sayyid Isḥāq Astarābādī 708 n. 20
Hikayat Abeudō Wahét 1160
Hikayat Muhammad Hanafiyya (Story of Muḥammad b. al-Ḥanafiyya) 1165
Hikayat Prang di Sigli (Song of the war in Sigli), Teungku Nyak Ahmat (alias Uri b. Mahmut b. Jalalōdin b. Abdōsalam) 1147
Hikayat Prang Gōmpeuni (Song of the war with the Dutch), Dōkarim (also known as Abdulkarim) 1147–48
Hikayat Prang Sabi (Song of the holy war) 1148–49, 1154–55, 1166, 1169–72, 1179
Hikayat Prang Sabi, Teungku Chik Pante Kulu (alias Teungku Syekh Muhammad Pante Kulu) 1149 n. 28
Hikayat Prang Sabi I 1155, 1157–59, 1162
Hikayat Prang Sabi II 1155, 1160–63, 1165, 1168, 1172
Hikayat Putroe Gumbak Meuih (Song of Princess Goldilocks) 1154
Ḥikmat al-ishrāq, al-Suhrawardī 491 n. 22
Ḥilyat al-awliyāʾ wa-ṭabaqāt al-aṣfiyāʾ, Abū Nuʿaym al-Iṣfahānī 385–86, 820 n. 12
al-Ḥujja (The proof, on Quranic readings), Abū ʿAlī l-Fārisī 854
Hymns on Paradise, Ephraem the Syrian 84

Iḥyāʾ ʿulūm al-dīn (*The Revitalization of the Religious Sciences*), al-Ghazālī 196, 206, 352, 1203
Iliad, Homer 1086
Imaginal Worlds (1994), William Chittick 9
al-Inṣāf (The just treatment), Ibn al-ʿAdīm 850
Introduction à la théologie musulmane: Essai de théologie comparée (1948), Louis Gardet 7
al-ʿIqd al-farīd, Ibn ʿAbd Rabbih 357 n. 80
al-Ishārāt wa-l-tanbīhāt (Pointers and remarks), Ibn Sīnā 455 n. 43, 460
Islam and Psychoanalysis, Nadia Tazi 1294
Islamic cosmology, Anton Heinen 935 n. 17
"Islamic Eschatology" (1987), Marilyn Robinson Waldman 3
Islamic Messianism, Mufaḍḍal b. ʿUmar al-Juʿfī 612
Islamic Messianism: The Idea of Mahdī in Twelver Shīʿism (1981), Abdulaziz Sachedina 8
Islamic Spirituality: Foundations (1987), Seyyed Hossein Nasr (ed.) 8
Islamic Understanding of Death and Resurrection (1981), Y. Y. Haddad and Jane Smith 8, 1146, 1187

al-Isrāʾ ilā maqām al-asrā (The nocturnal journey toward the station of the most magnanimous one), Ibn ʿArabī 900
Ittiṣāl al-ʿaql bi-l-insān (Treatise on the Conjunction of the Human Rational Soul with the Active Intellect), Ibn Bājja 461

Jabr wa-ikhtiyār (*Free Will and Predestination*), Naṣīr al-Dīn al-Ṭūsī 663
Jāmiʿ al-bayān, al-Ṭabarī 832
al-Jāmiʿ al-ṣaḥīḥ, al-Tirmidhī 819, 822, 841–842
Jātaka (of the Pali Buddhist Canonical tradition) 924
Jāwidān-nāma-yi kabīr (The great book of eternity), Faḍlallāh Astarābādī 22, 702

al-Kāfī l-shāfī fī takhrīj aḥādīth al-Kashshāf, Ibn Ḥajar al-ʿAsqalānī 247 n. 59
Kalīla wa-Dimna 587, 899, 925
Kanz al-asrār wa-lawāqiḥ al-afkār (Treasure of secrets and the harbingers of thoughts), Muḥammad al-Ṣinhājī 931, 936, 939
al-Kashf ʿan mujāwazat hādhihī l-umma al-alf, al-Suyūṭī 941 n. 28
Kashf al-maḥjūb, Abū Yaʿqūb al-Sijistānī 498, 517, 522
Kashf al-maḥjūb (Revealing the concealed), Ḥamīd al-Dīn al-Kirmānī 653–54
Kashf al-maḥjūb (Revelation of that which is veiled), al-Hujwīrī 567, 695
al-Kashf wa-l-bayān ʿan tafsīr al-Qurʾān (Investigation and explanation of the exegesis of the Quran), Aḥmad al-Thaʿlabī 931, 936
Kashshāf ʿan ḥaqāʾiq ghawāmiḍ al-tanzīl wa-ʿuyūn al-aqāwīl fī wujūh al-taʾwīl (The discoverer of the truths of the hidden things of revelation and the choicest statements concerning the aspects of interpretation), al-Zamakhsharī 221, 241, 245–48
Khulāṣat al-faḍl al-fāʾiq fī miʿrāj khayr al-khalāʾiq, Muḥammad b. Yusūf al-Ṣāliḥī al-Shāmī 876–77
Kisah Ainul Mardiah (Story of Ainul Mardiah) 1160–61, 1164
Kitāb ʿAbhar al-ʿāshiqīn, Rūzbihān al-Baqlī 707 n. 17
Kitāb al-ʿAjāʾib wa-l-gharāʾib (The marvels of unfamilar things), ʿAbdallāh b. Salām 883
Kitāb al-ʿĀlim wa-l-mutaʿallim 376
Kitāb Ārāʾ ahl al-madīna al-fāḍila [The book of opinions of the inhabitants of the virtuous city], al-Fārābī 460
Kitāb ʿAṭf al-alif al-māʾlūf ʿalā l-lām al-maʿṭūf, Abū l-Ḥasan ʿAlī b. Muḥammad al-Daylamī 707 n. 17
Kitāb al-ʿAẓama, Anonymous 883
Kitāb al-ʿAẓama (The book of the sublime), Abū l-Shaykh al-Iṣfahānī 874
Kitāb al-Burhān fī ʿalāmat al-mahdī ākhir al-zamān, Ṣiddīq Ḥasan Khān 1249
Kitāb Faḍīḥat al-Muʿtazila, Ibn al-Rāwandī 223 n. 6
Kitāb al-Fitan, Nuʿaym b. Ḥammād 937
Kitāb Ḥaqāʾiq al-daqāʾiq (Book of the true natures of the subtleties), Abū l-Layth al-Samarqandī 348–49
Kitāb Ḥikmat al-ishrāq (*Wisdom of Oriental Illumination*), al-Suhrawardī 493, 501, 509
Kitāb al-Iftikhār (The book of the boast), al-Sijistānī 653, 655–56
Kitāb al-Inṣāf (The book of impartial judgment), Ibn Sīnā 653
Kitāb al-Intiṣār (The book of triumph), Abū l-Ḥusayn ʿAbd al-Raḥīm al-Khayyāṭ, 223–24
Kitāb al-Irshād, Muḥammad al-Baghdādī = al-Shaykh al-Mufīd 608
Kitāb Ithbāt al-nubuwwāt (The book on the proof of prophecies), Abū Yaʿqūb al-Sijistānī 630–31, 652
Kitāb al-Jamʿ (*Harmonization of the Two Views*), al-Fārābī 493
Kitāb al-Jihād, ʿAbdallāh b. al-Mubārak 418
Kitāb al-Jihād (The Book of the Jihād), ʿAlī b. Ṭāhir al-Sulamī 407, 1168
Kitāb al-Kashf (Book of unveiling), Jaʿfar b. Manṣūr al-Yaman 22, 629, 676–77, 679, 683
Kitāb al-Lumaʿ (lit., The book of flashes), al-Ashʿarī 471–72, 909

Kitāb al-Maḥāsin, Aḥmad al-Barqī 608
Kitāb al-Maqālāt, Saʿd b. ʿAbdallāh al-Ashʿarī al-Qummī 608 n. 14
Kitāb al-Mawāqif fī ʿilm al-kalām, ʿAḍud al-Dīn al-Ījī 470–71, 479, 481–82
Kitāb al-Milal wa-l-niḥal, ʿAbd al-Karīm Shahrastānī 8
Kitāb al-Miʿrāj, al-Qushayrī 877
Kitāb Miʿrāj al-nabī, Muḥammad b. Aḥmad al-Mālikī 880
Kitāb al-Rajʿa, Aḥmad al-Aḥsāʾī 607 n. 10
Kitāb al-Ṣabr (Book of steadfastness), of *Iḥyāʾ ʿulūm al-dīn,* al-Ghazālī 423
Kitāb Sawāniḥ, Aḥmad al-Ghazālī 707 n. 17
Kitāb al-Sirr, al-Kharrāz 236 n. 37
Kitāb Ṣuwar al-kawākib al-thābita (Book of the figures of the fixed stars), ʿAbd al-Raḥmān al-Ṣūfī 1098 fig.50.2
Kitāb al-Ṭabaqāt, Ibn Saʿd 862
Kitāb al-Targhīb wa-l-tarhīb (known as *Qawām al-sunna*), Abū l-Qāsim al-Jawzī l-Aṣbahānī 842 n. 120
Kitāb al-Tawahhum (Imaginary representations), al-Muḥāsibī 283, 304, 566 n. 2
Kitāb al-Thiqāt, Ibn Ḥibbān 823
Kitāb Waṣf al-firdaws (Book on the description of paradise), Ibn Ḥabīb 285, 304, 821, 825–26, 829, 988, 992
Kitāb al-Yanābīʿ (The book of the wellsprings), Abū Yaʿqūb al-Sijistānī 652–53, 655–56
Köprü (The bridge, 1976), Said Nursi 1225
Koran und Koranexegese (1971), Helmut Gätje 7
Kraft und Stoff, Ludwig Büchner 1254

al-Laʾālī l-maṣnūʿa fī l-aḥādīth al-mawḍūʿa (The artificial pearls on the fabricated *ḥadīths*), al-Suyūṭī 864
La Escatologia musulmana en la Divina Comedia (Muslim Eschatology and the Divine Comedy), Miguel Asín Palacios 892
La Grande résurrection d'Alamût: Les formes de la liberté dans le shi'isme ismaélien (1996), Christian Jambet 9
La pasión turca, 1993, Antonio Gala 953
La passion de Husayn ibn Mansûr Hallâj: Martyr mystique de l'Islam, exécuté à Bagdad le 26 Mars 922: Étude d'histoire religieuse, Louis Massignon 6
La perle précieuse, L. Gautier 566 n. 2
Larger Sutra on Amitāyus 251–52
Laṭāʾif al-ishārāt, al-Qushayrī 222 n. 4
La vie future selon le Coran (The next life according to the Quran), Ṣoubḥī El-Ṣaleḥ 223, 246
Le dévoilement des effets du voyage (1994), Denis Gril 9
Le dévoilement des secrets et les apparitions des lumières: Journal spirituel du maître de Shîrâz (1996), Paul Ballanfat 9
Le Guide divin dans le shîʿisme originel: Aux sources de l'ésotérisme en Islam (1992), Mohammad A. Amir-Moezzi 9
Le livre de la sagesse orientale, Mullā Ṣadrā 501
Leo Africanus (1986), Amin Malouf 953
Le sceau des saints: Prophétie et sainteté dans la doctrine d'Ibn Arabî (1986), Michel Chodkiewicz 8
Le Voyage initiatique en terre d'Islam: Ascensions célestes et itinéraires spirituels (1996), Mohammad A. Amir-Moezzi 9
Liber scale Machemeti 893
"Life and Beyond in the Qurʾan" (1995), Muhammad Abdel Haleem 9
Life Between Death and Resurrection According to Islam (1941), Ragnar Eklund 6
Lisān al-ʿarab, Ibn Manẓūr 226 n. 14
Livre des religions et des sects (1986–93), D. Gimaret, J. Jolivet, G. Monnot 8
Local features 70, Mamdūḥ Qashlān 1073
Locating Hell in Islamic Traditions (2016), Christian Lange 10
L'Acte d'être: La philosophie de la révélation chez Mollâ Sadrâ (2002), Christian Jambet 9

al-Mabdaʾ wa-l-maʿād (lit., The beginning and the return), Ibn Sīnā 459–61
al-Mabdaʾ wa-l-maʿād (The origin and the return), Mullā Ṣadrā 535
al-Maḍnūn bih ʿalā ghayr ahlih, al-Ghazālī 422

Madrāshâ VII (On Paradise), Ephraem the Syrian 783–91, 794, 796, 799–800, 802
Mafātīḥ al-ghayb (Keys to the unseen), Mullā Ṣadrā 672
al-Majālis al-Mu'ayyadiyya (The Mu'ayyadian lectures), al-Mu'ayyad fī l-Dīn al-Shīrāzī 649–50, 656
Majālis al-ʿushshāq 26, 1035, 1047 fig.47.1
Majmaʿ al-bayān li-ʿulūm al-Qur'ān (Collection of the explanation of the sciences of the Quran), al-Ṭabrisī 1253
Maktūbāt, Aḥmad Sirhindī 1249
al-Manār, Muḥammad ʿAbduh 1202
al-Manār, Muḥammad Rashīd Riḍā 1203
Mā nazala min al-Qur'ān fī ahl al-bayt, Ibn al-Juḥām 610 n. 25
Mā nazala min al-Quran fī ṣāḥib al-zamān, Abū ʿAbdallāh al-Jawharī 609 n. 18
Mandäische Grammatik, Nöldeke 1134
Manṭiq al-ṭayr (*Conference of the Birds*), Farīd al-Dīn ʿAṭṭār 21, 200 n. 46, 579, 582–84, 591–92, 595, 599
Maqāla fī l-jamʿ bayn ra ʾyay Aflāṭūn wa-Arisṭū, al-Fārābī 501 n. 43
al-Maqāma al-majāʿiyya (*Maqāma* of the famine), Badīʿ al-Zamān al-Hamadhānī 263–64
Masā'il al-maḍnūn (Questions of the withheld science), al-Ghazālī 19, 423
Masā'il Nāfiʿ b. al-Azraq 388
Mathnawī-yi maʿnawī, Jalāl al-Dīn Rūmī 6, 267, 587, 692–93
Maṭlūb al-mu'minīn (*Desideratum of the Faithful*), Naṣīr al-Dīn al-Ṭūsī 662, 672
Medieval Culture: An Introduction to Dante and His Times, Karl Vossler 912
Mehdi ve Altınçağ (The Mahdī and the golden age), Adnan Oktar (Harun Yahya) 1249
Mesnevi, Ergin İnan (b. 1943) [lithographs] 1070
Metaphysics of the Healing (*al-Ilāhiyyāt min al-shifā'*), Ibn Sīnā 459–61, 492
Metaphysics Λ, Aristotle 1087
Min al-ʿaqīda ilā l-thawra (From dogma to revolution), Ḥasan Ḥanafī 1214
Miʿrāğ-nāmes 26
Miʿrāj, Jāmī, *Yūsuf-u Zulaykhā* 1051 fig.47.5
Miʿrāj, Niẓāmī, *Makhzan al-asrār* 1049 fig.47.3
Miʿrāj, *Qiṣaṣ al-anbiyā'*, 1050 fig.47.4
Miʿrāj al-nabī [attrib. to Ibn ʿAbbās] 879
Miʿrājnāma (The book of the ascension) 1038, 1062
al-Miʿrāj al-sharīf, Anonymous 880
Mir'āt al-zamān (The mirror of time), Ibn al-Jawzī 850
Mishkāt al-anwār (*The Niche of Light*), al-Ghazālī 586, 595
Mīzān al-ʿamal (The criterion of action), al-Ghazālī 352
Mohammed et la fin du monde (1911–13), Paul Casanova 6, 102
Moor's Last Sigh (1995), Salman Rushdie 953–54, 956, 966
Muʿallaqa, Imru' al-Qays 256
Muhammad, the Apostle of God, and his Ascension (1955), Geo Widengren 7
Muhammad's Thoughts on Death (1969), T. O'Shaughnessy 7
Muhammedanische Eschatologie, Moritz Wolff (1872) 5
Muḥaṣṣal, al-Rāzī 471
Mujārāt, Naṣīr al-Dīn al-Ṭūsī 663
Mujarrad, Ibn Fūrak 471–72
Mukhtaṣar Ṣaḥīḥ Muslim, al-Mundhirī 315, 333–34
Mullā Ṣadrā: The Wisdom of the Throne (1981), James Winston Morris 8
Muntakhab, al-Nīlī 609 n. 18
Muntakhab fī khulāṣat al-kalām fī ta ʾwīl al-aḥlām (Selection of the essentials of discussion about the interpretation of dreams), Ibn Sīrīn 437–38
Muṣannaf, ʿAbd al-Razzāq al-Ṣanʿānī 313, 346, 373, 381, 385–86, 403–4
Muṣannaf (Compilation), Ibn Abī Shayba 313, 375
Mystical Dimensions of Islam (1975), Annemarie Schimmel 7
Mystical Vision of Existence in Classical Islam: The Qur'ānic Hermeneutics of the Ṣūfī Sahl at-Tustarī (d. 283/896) (1980), Gerhard Böwering 8
Mystics of Islam, Reynold A. Nicholson 909

al-Najāt (The salvation), Ibn Sīnā 455 n. 43
Najm al-Dīn Rāzī: The Path of God's Bondsmen from Origin to Return (1982), Hamid Algar 8
Nasib Atjeh [The fate of Aceh], Abdullah Arif 1186 fig.53.2
Naṣīḥat al-muslimīn (*Advice to Muslims*), ʿAbd al-Ṣamad al-Palimbānī 1156–57
Nasihat ureueng muprang (Advice to warriors), Teungku Nyak Ahmat 1157–58
Nihāya, Ibn Kathīr 873
al-Nihāya fī l-fitan wa-l-malāḥim, Ibn Kathīr 817 n. 1
Notae miscellaneae, Edward Pocock 5

Ölüm – Kıyamet – Cehennem (Death, resurrection, and hell), Adnan Oktar (Harun Yahya) 1253
Ölüm Ötesi Hayat (Life beyond death), Fethullah Gülen 1231
One Thousand and One Nights. See Alf layla wa-layla
On the Heavens, Aristotle 1087
Order of Things, Michel Foucault 1292
Organon, Aristotle 451
Origins and Early Development of Shiʿa Islam (1979), Syed Husain Mohammad Jafri 8

"The Painter's Landscape," Françoise Cachin 1072
Pañcatantra 925
Pantōn Aceh (Acehnese poems), Abdullah Arif 1174
Paradise and Hell in Islamic Traditions (Cambridge), Christian Lange 10
Paradise Lost, John Milton 37
Paradise of Eden, ʿAḇdīshōʿ bar Berīkā 806
Paradiso, Dante 902, 906, 908
Philosophie der Erleuchtung, n. Sinai 501 n. 42
Philosophy of illumination, H. Ziai and J. Walbridge 501 n. 42
Picatrix 984
"Piety and Eschatology in Early Kharijite Poetry" (1997), Fred Donner 9
Poetry and Other Mysteries, Sargon Boulus 808
Porta Mosis, Edward Pocock 5
Purgatorio, Dante 902, 912, 914

Qāb qawsayn wa-l-multaqā l-nāmūsayn (A distance of two bow-lengths and the meeting point of the two realms), ʿAbd al-Karīm al-Jīlī 1019
al-Qānūn fī l-ṭibb (*The canon of medicine*), Ibn Sīnā 455 n. 43
Qiṣaṣ al-anbiyāʾ (*Stories of the Prophets*) 1036, 1048 fig.47.2
Qiṣṣat al-miʿrāj, Anonymous 881
"The Qurʾān and Epic" (2014), Todd Lawson 11

Rāḥat al-ʿaql (Peace of mind), Ḥamīd al-Dīn al-Kirmānī 650
Rawḍat, al-Nisābūrī 608 n. 15
Rawḍat al-ʿulamāʾ (The garden of scholars), Arabic anthology 1161
Rawḍa-yi taslīm (*The Paradise of Submission*), Naṣīr al-Dīn al-Ṭūsī 662–63, 667, 672
al-Rawḍ al-fāʾiq fī l-mawāʿiẓ wa-l-raqāʾiq (The superior meadows of preaching and sermons), Shuʿayb al-Hurayfish 1020 n. 38
Reconstruction of the Religious Thought in Islam, Muḥammad Iqbāl 1197
Redemptive Suffering in Islam: A Study of the Devotional Aspects of Ashura in Twelver Shiʿism (1978), Mahmoud Ayoub 8
Reincarnation and Islam, Nadarbek K. Mirza 739–40
Republic, Plato 185 n. 7, 454, 463
Rijāl al-Najāshī, al-Najāshī 609 n. 18
Risāla, Ibn al-Qāriḥ 856
al-Risāla al-Aḍḥawiyya fī l-maʿād (Epistle on the afterlife for the feast of sacrifice), Ibn Sīnā 457, 473, 477–78, 498–99
Risāla dar niʿmat-hā, khushī-hā wa-ladhdhat-hā (*Treatise on Comfort, Happiness and Joyfulness*), Naṣīr al-Dīn al-Ṭūsī 662–63
Risāla fī l-ḥashr (Treatise on resurrection), Mullā Ṣadrā 490, 517
Risāla fī l-ḥīla li-dafʿ al-aḥzān (*Epistle on the Device of Dispelling Sorrows*), al-Kindī 448

Risāla fī l-ḥudūth (On beginning in time), Mullā Ṣadrā 518
Risāla fī kammiyyat kutub Arisṭāṭālīs wa-mā yuḥtaju ilayhi fī taḥṣīl al-falsafa (On the Quantity of Aristotle's Books and what is Needed in Attaining Philosophy), al-Kindī 450
Risāla fī takhrīj aḥādīth al-kashshāf wa-mā fīhi min qiṣaṣ wa-āthār, al-Zaylaʿī 247 n. 59
al-Risāla al-Kāmiliyya fī l-sīra al-nabawiyya (The treatise of Kāmil on the Prophet's biography), Ibn al-Nafīs 195
Risālat al-bāhira (The treatise of dazzling brilliance), Ḥamīd al-Dīn al-Kirmānī 653
Risālat al-ghufrān (The epistle of forgiveness), Abū l-ʿAlāʾ al-Maʿarrī 24, 195, 850–51, 855–56
Risālat al-ittiṣāl (The treatise on conjunction), Ibn Bājja (known as Ibn al-Ṣāʾigh) 462
Risālat al-tawḥīd (Treatise of unity), Muḥammad ʿAbduh 1202
Risālat al-ṭayr, al-Ghazālī 586
Risālat al-ṭayr (Treatise of the birds), Ibn Sīnā 200, 586
Risālat al-wāridāt (Treatise on thoughts that come to one's mind), Muḥammad ʿAbduh 1201
Risāla-yi abdāliyya, Yaʿqūb Charkhī 695
Risale-i Nur (Treatise of light), Said Nursi 1209, 1224–25, 1228, 1252

Ṣaḥīḥ al-Bukhārī (= *al-Jāmiʿ al-ṣaḥīḥ*) (Compilation of authentic prophetic traditions), al-Bukhārī 182, 196, 261
Ṣaḥīḥ Muslim, Muslim b. al-Ḥajjāj 819, 841–42
Ṣaḥīḥ Muslim – Kitāb al-Janna wa-ṣifat naʿīmihā wa-ahlihā ("The chapter of the garden and the characteristics of its bounties and its inhabitants"), Muslim b. al-Ḥajjāj 311–15, 317–21, 323, 325, 332, 334, 336
Ṣaḥīḥ al-targhīb wa-l-tarhīb (The sound [traditions] of moral suasion and exhortation), Muḥammad Nāṣir al-Dīn al-Albānī 845
Saint et sainteté dans le christianisme et l'islam: Le regard des sciences de l'homme (2007), Denis Gril 10
Satanic Verses, Salman Rushdie 956
Sayr wa-sulūk (*Contemplation and Action*), Naṣīr al-Dīn al-Ṭūsī 662–63
Sehnsucht nach dem Paradies: Mythologie des Korans (1979), Walter Beltz 7–8
Seumangat Atjeh (*Spirit of Aceh*) 1172–73, 1185 fig.53.1
Shadows of the Pomegranate Tree (1993), Tariq Ali 953, 954 n. 7
Shāhnāma, Firdawsī 585
Sharḥ al-akhbār, al-Qāḍī l-Nuʿmān 625 n. 115
Sharḥ al-ʿaqāʾid al-Nasafiyya (Commentary on the creed of al-Nasafī), Saʿd al-Dīn al-Taftāzānī 470 n. 9
Sharḥ al-maqāṣid (Commentary on the main fields of [theological] investigation), Saʿd al-Dīn al-Taftāzānī 20, 470–71, 473, 485
Sharḥ al-mukhtār min Luzūmiyyāt Abī l-ʿAlāʾ (The explanation of selections from Abū l-ʿAlāʾ's "Luzūmiyyāt"), Ibn Sayyid al-Baṭalyawsī 850
al-Sharīʿa wa-l-ḥayāt (Sharīʿa and life), Yūsuf al-Qaraḍāwī (b. 1345/1926) 1208
al-Shifāʾ (*The healing*), Ibn Sīnā 455 n. 43, 481
al-Shukūk ʿalā Baṭlamyūs (Doubts on Ptolemy), Ibn al-Haytham 1093
Ṣifat al-janna, Abū Nuʿaym al-Iṣfahānī 347, 817
Ṣifat al-janna, al-Ḍiyāʾ al-Maqdisī 817
Ṣifat al-janna, Ibn Abī l-Dunyā 817
Simulacra and Simulation, Jean Baudrillard 1074
Sīra, Ibn Hishām 877
al-Ṣirāṭ, al-Bayāḍī 608 n. 15
Sīrat al-malik Iskandar Dhū l-Qarnayn, Yūsuf Ibn ʿAṭīya (Quzmān) 922–23, 930 fig.42.1
Sīrat al-nabī or *al-Sīra al-nabawiyya* (The biography of the Prophet), Ibn Isḥāq 182
Sızıntı (The leak [through which truth trickles]), Fethullah Gülen 1230

"Some Aspects of Islamic Eschatology" (1968), J.B. Taylor 7
Sonsuzluk Yolculuğu (The voyage toward infinity), Muhammed Bozdağ 1235
"The Soul as *barzakh:* Substantial Motion and Mullā Ṣadrā's Theory of Human Becoming" (2004), Maria M. Dakake 10
Spain To England, Alice Lasater 911
Studies in Muslim Apocalyptic (2002), David Cook 10
Sufi Path of Knowledge (1989), William Chittick 8
Summons of the soul [Chu kingdom poem], Qu Yuan 265–66
Sunan, al-Dārimī 313
Sunan, Ibn Māja 841 n. 116
"Symmetrie und Paarbildung in der Koranischen Eschatologie" (1984), Angelika Neuwirth 8
Synodicon orientale 773 n. 1

Tadbīr al-mutawaḥḥid (The governance of the solitary), Ibn Bājja 462
al-Tadhkira fī aḥwāl al-mawtā (Memoir about the conditions of the dead), al-Qurṭubī 347, 873–74
al-Tadhkira fī ʿilm al-hayʾa (Memorandum on the science of astronomy), Naṣīr al-Dīn al-Ṭūsī 1093–94
Tafsīr āyat al-kursī, Mullā Ṣadrā 536 n. 10
Tafsīr sūrat al-fātiḥa, Mullā Ṣadrā 542–43
Tahāfut al-falāsifa (*The Incoherence of the Philosophers*), al-Ghazālī 422
Taʿlīqāt, Mullā Ṣadrā 491 n. 22, 509
Tamhīdāt (Preambles), ʿAyn al-Quḍāt Hamadānī 21, 568–69, 573
Tanbīh al-ghāfilīn, Abū l-Layth al-Samarqandī 349 n. 36
Tanwīr al-miqbās, al-Fayrūzābādī (ed.) 163–64, 172, 175–76
al-Targhīb wa-l-tarhīb (The [moral] suasion and exhortation), al-Mundhirī 819, 842–43
Tarjumān al-ashwāq (The Interpreter of Longing), Ibn ʿArabī 900
al-Tawābiʿ wa-l-zawābiʿ (The familiar spirits and demons), Ibn Shuhayd 856
Ṭawāliʿ al-anwār, al-Bayḍāwī 470, 479
Tawallā wa-tabarrā (*Solidarity and Dissociation*), Naṣīr al-Dīn al-Ṭūsī 662, 672
Terre céleste et corps de résurrection: De l'Iran mazdéen à l'Iran shīʿite (1960), Henry Corbin 7
Tetrabiblos, Ptolemy 357
Theologie und Gesellschaft, Josef van Ess 9
Theology of Aristotle, Plotinus 503 n. 54, 522–23
Thulāthiyyat Gharnāṭa; The Granada Trilogy (1994–8), Raḍwā ʿĀshūr 953–54, 973
al-Tibyān fī tafsīr al-Qurʾān (The explanation in Quranic exegesis), Muḥammad b. al-Ḥasan al-Ṭūsī 222
Tipiṭaka (Buddhist collection of stories) 924
Title of the Letter, Philippe Lacoue-Labarthe 1303
The Triumph of Mercy: Philosophy and Scripture in Mulla Sadra (2012), Mohammed Rustom 10
Truth about the Neicheri (*or Naturalists*) *Sect and an Explanation of the Neicheris* /*An Answer to the Dahriyyīn* (*or Materialists*), Sayyid Jamāl al-Dīn al-Afghānī 1199
Tuḥfat al-mutakallimīn fī l-radd ʿalā l-falāsifa (Gift for the theologians in refutation of the philosophers), Rukn al-Dīn b. al-Malāḥimī 423
Ṭūq al-ḥamāma (*The Dove's Necklace*), Ibn Ḥazm 899–900
Typography: Mimesis, Philosophy and Politics, Philippe Lacoue-Labarthe 1294, 1306

"The Ultimate Origin and the Hereafter in Islam" (1971), Fritz Meier 7
ʿUlūm al-ḥadīth (known as *Muqaddimat Ibn al-Ṣalāḥ* – The introduction of Ibn al-Ṣalāḥ), Ibn al-Ṣalāḥ 824
Une vision humaine des fins dernières, A. Roman 566 n. 2
Un océan sans rivage: Ibn Arabî, le livre et la loi (1992), Michel Chodkiewicz 8
Upanishads 759
al-ʿUrwa li-ahl al-khalwa wa-l-jalwa (Relation of the people of seclusion and openness), ʿAlāʾ al-Dawla al-Simnānī 695
Uṣūl al-dīn, al-Rāzī 471

Uṣūl al-kāfī, Muḥammad b. Yaʿqūb al-Kulaynī 513

Was Early Islam an Apocalyptic Movement?, Fred Donner 9
Waṣf al-firdaws (The description of paradise), al-Sulamī 817
West-Eastern Divan, Goethe 435
What Everyone Needs to Know about Islam, John Esposito 1143
"Where on Earth is Hell? State Punishment and Eschatology in the Islamic Middle Period" (2009), Christian Lange 10
Words of Ecstasy (1985), Carl Ernst 9

Yeni Asya (New Asia, 1973), Said Nursi 1225

Ziyādāt ḥaqāʾiq al-tafsīr, Abū ʿAbd al-Raḥmān al-Sulamī 222
Zubdat al-ḥaqāʾiq, ʿAyn al-Quḍāt Hamadānī 568 n. 12, 570
"Zur Charakteristik Ǵelâl ud-dîn us-Sujûṭî's und seiner literarischen Thätigkeit" (1871), Ignaz Goldziher 5

Index of Scriptural References

Quran

Sura numbers are followed by a colon and verse number. Discussions about whole Suras are denoted by the number and en-dash.

1 (al-Fātiḥa)
- 1– 353, 396 n.76, 713
- 1:6 491, 503 n.52, 544, 546, 610
- 1:6–7 44

2 (al-Baqara)
- 2– 35, 182, 1021
- 2:2 610
- 2:3 65, 610, 730 n.67
- 2:8 629
- 2:8–9 678
- 2:12 678
- 2:22 142
- 2:24 155, 681
- 2:25 64, 185, 272 n.7, 279 n.46, 302, 312, 322 n.55, 336 n.115, 653, 656, 801, 866, 986, 991
- 2:28 183, 744, 745, 746, 747
- 2:29 515, 973 n.80, 1083 n.2
- 2:30 45
- 2:31 705, 708, 711
- 2:34 710
- 2:35 709, 711, 719, 723
- 2:35–6 186
- 2:35–7 35
- 2:37–8 43
- 2:38 51
- 2:44 44
- 2:55–6 746
- 2:62 52
- 2:63 62
- 2:65 752 n.59
- 2:66 142
- 2:72–3 746
- 2:87 454
- 2:111 137
- 2:118 45
- 2:133 621
- 2:138 203 n.52, 655
- 2:148 612
- 2:154 17, 162–64, 166–68, 170, 175, 748, 1267, 1272
- 2:155 50
- 2:156 693
- 2:158 63
- 2:165 630
- 2:167 386 n.49
- 2:190 46
- 2:196 40
- 2:210 621, 622, 630
- 2:221 183
- 2:243 747
- 2:248 118–19
- 2:249 143 n.19
- 2:255 108, 225, 228, 242, 431, 626 n.118
- 2:258 42
- 2:259 434, 476, 747
- 2:264–5 145
- 2:266 139
- 2:274 926 n.23
- 2:285 51
- 2:286 42

3 (Āl ʿImrān)
- 3– 967 n.55
- 3:2 626 n.118
- 3:3 52
- 3:5 559
- 3:7 724
- 3:15 155, 239, 302, 653, 801
- 3:18 610
- 3:27 744
- 3:67 967 n.55
- 3:82 52
- 3:83 39
- 3:98 162
- 3:103 40
- 3:113–5 52
- 3:131–3 480
- 3:133 55, 140 n.15, 707 n.16, 989
- 3:133–6 53
- 3:140 621
- 3:154 431
- 3:156 60

3 (Āl ʿImrān) (cont.)
3:157 174
3:157–8 17, 162, 172
3:158 173–74
3:169 17, 62, 162–64, 166, 168–70, 175–76, 1284
3:169–70 167
3:185 197 n.38, 1237
3:189 12, 181
3:192 19, 63, 376 n.16, 396–98, 403
3:193 185
3:194 50
3:198 40, 64
3:200 610
4 (al-Nisāʾ)
4:13 65
4:31 63
4:48 116, 1205
4:56 342, 694, 740 n.26
4:57 50, 156, 302, 801
4:69 50, 64, 169, 176, 183, 610, 989 n.30
4:74 1284
4:77 612
4:79 741
4:94 417 n.40
4:95 177
4:97 401 n.92
4:116 851
4:122 50
4:124 50, 53
4:145 169, 373 n.11
4:150–1 52
4:163 52
4:171 724, 801
5 (al-Māʾida)
5:3 612
5:4 1112
5:12 51
5:32 693
5:37 19, 383–84, 386 n.49, 387–88, 393 n.71, 397–98, 403
5:54 610
5:60 752 n.59
5:69 52
5:72 52
5:77 801
5:90 254
5:110 747
5:117–118 327 n.74
5:119 65
6 (al-Anʿām)
6– 210 n.65
6:6 139 n.13, 142
6:19 162
6:38 738 n.16
6:51 70, 1018 n.30
6:59 43
6:60 41
6:116 45
6:125 33 n.7
6:127 56, 64
6:128 379, 403
6:153 546
6:158 621
7 (al-Aʿrāf)
7– 399
7:12 717–19
7:12–25 718
7:14 750
7:22 141
7:23 429
7:32 63
7:36 540
7:37 401 n.92
7:40 199
7:42 42, 429
7:43 33, 58, 319 n.36
7:44 399, 1207
7:46 19, 403
7:46–9 399
7:46–49 737 n.15
7:49 64, 402
7:50 719
7:53 612
7:56 145 n.25
7:57 744
7:57–8 160
7:59 206
7:80–4 1248
7:84 148
7:87 851
7:97 431
7:100 34
7:128 34
7:137 34
7:143 108

7:156 52, 543
7:157–8 724
7:166 752 n.59
7:169–70 52, 210 n.65
7:172 16, 40, 100, 104, 111–12, 113 n.69, 114, 117, 119, 121, 497, 718 n.37, 745, 748 n.53, 1236
7:187 613, 617
8 (al-Anfāl)
8:4 831 n.72, 989
8:11 431
8:16 13
8:50 401 n.92
8:72 177–78
9 (al-Tawba)
9:3 612
9:19 177–78
9:20 177–78
9:21 41
9:26 119
9:33 612
9:35 13
9:40 119
9:72 40, 60, 63, 65, 240–41, 869 n.34
9:89 65
9:100 65, 139 n.11
9:103 1024 n.57
9:111 153
9:112 350
9:129 228 n.21
10 (Yūnus)
10:2 63, 186 n.10, 548
10:3 1018 n.30
10:5 224 n.7
10:20 56, 610
10:25 40
10:26 56, 224 n.7, 837
10:62 63
10:62–4 183
10:75–6 206
11 (Hūd)
11– 390
11:7 228 n.21, 243
11:8 628
11:80 610
11:86 610
11:97–8 767 n.15
11:98 391–93, 630
11:105–8 376 n.16, 379, 388
11:106 530, 566 n.2
11:106–7 389
11:107 19, 389–90, 403
11:107–8 530
12 (Yūsuf)
12– 436
12:2 273
12:4 710
12:4–102 205
12:24 727
12:53 429, 692
12:101 52, 710
12:107 183
12:108 546
13 (al-Raʿd)
13:4 926
13:12–3 146
13:17 160
13:18 56
13:22 430
13:23 50, 55, 63, 83, 866, 869 n.34
13:23–4 62, 709
13:24 401 n.91
13:29 829, 870
13:35 56, 64, 266, 481
13:39 724
14 (Ibrāhīm)
14:5 530, 620
14:16–7 566 n.2
14:24 707 n.16
14:24–5 853
14:26 719
14:32 142 n.17
14:48 64, 510, 530, 573, 1205
14:48–50 201
14:49 566 n.2
14:50 718–19
15 (al-Ḥijr)
15:17 721
15:17–8 717, 720
15:23 34
15:29 40
15:36 750
15:38 623
15:41 65
15:43–4 566 n.2, 714
15:44 185, 373 n.11, 374, 713 n.27

15 (al-Ḥijr) (cont.)
15:45 138, 266
15:45–8 140 n.15
15:46 64
15:47 61
15:48 64, 141
15:66 148
15:74 148 n.30
15:87 727
16 (al-Naḥl)
16:1 623
16:10 145
16:20–1 745 n.46
16:21 745
16:28–9 401 n.92
16:30 39
16:31 40
16:32 64, 401 n.91, 432
16:33 623, 633 n.169
16:65–9 59
16:77 41, 520
16:125 608
17 (al-Isrāʾ)
17– 894
17:1 188, 191, 273, 1020 n.39
17:13 566 n.2
17:14 1208
17:21 224 n.7, 247–48, 989
17:23 539, 540
17:40 402 n.93
17:42–3 228 n.21
17:44 973 n.80, 1083 n.2
17:60 192, 719
17:71 566 n.2, 715
17:72 730
17:73 610 n.25
17:81 610
17:95 62
18 (al-Kahf)
18– 57, 433–34
18:9–16 620 n.83
18:9–26 747
18:18 439 n.31
18:19 433
18:21 747 n.50
18:29 85
18:30 266
18:31 13, 59, 156, 236 n.38, 261 n.57, 261 n.59, 995
18:32–44 142
18:32ff. 57
18:33 143 n.19
18:37 742 n.32
18:39 56 n.6
18:40–2 143
18:51 721
18:65ff. 434
18:80–1 695
18:107 56, 64, 137, 239, 871
18:107–8 141
18:108 40, 65
18:110 515
19 (Maryam)
19– 110 n.57, 391, 394
19:40 34
19:58–61 52
19:61 240, 658
19:62 530
19:63 33
19:68–72 19, 391
19:71 392, 403
19:71–2 394–95
19:75 615
19:76 625
19:85 831 n.72
19:86 392, 393
19:87 1018 n.30
19:95 1197
19:96 42
20 (Ṭaha)
20:5 228 n.21, 548
20:19 611, 1018 n.30
20:55 746
20:102 203 n.52
20:102–104 183
20:108 681
20:111 626 n.118
20:113 611
20:117 429
20:117–21 141
20:120 43, 869 n.37
20:131 107
20:135 611
21 (al-Anbiyāʾ)
21– 393
21:12 628 n.125
21:28 1018 n.30
21:30 57

21:35 197 n.38, 432, 1237
21:48 206
21:83 205
21:84 747
21:89 34
21:98 391–93
21:98–102 393
21:101 393
21:102 392
21:104 40
21:105 62, 611, 831 n.72
21:107 202, 1017 n.26
22 (al-Ḥajj)
22:5 694
22:5–7 489 n.13
22:19–21 566 n.2
22:22 386 n.49
22:23 156 n.41, 236, 266, 992
22:31 199
22:35 156 n.41
22:45 611
22:47 510, 517, 530
22:56 56, 169
22:58 267
22:59 63
22:70–1 1248
23 (al-Mu'minūn)
23:11 33, 137, 239 n.46
23:14 489 n.13
23:17 973 n.80, 1083 n.2
23:50 103
23:62 1213
23:99–100 750
23:100 194, 530, 689, 696, 750, 1228
23:101–18 181 n.3
23:104 185
23:115–6 49
24 (al-Nūr)
24:30–1 558
24:35 107–8, 891, 1236
24:43 161
24:54 573
25 (al-Furqān)
25:8 142
25:10 142
25:11–4 566 n.2
25:13–4 439
25:15 40, 138, 185, 926
25:15–6 185, 566 n.2
25:16 65, 185
25:31 681
25:47 431
25:49 745 n.46
25:53 1228
25:59 225, 229, 231–32, 517
25:64–76 53
25:75 59 n.22, 139, 318 n.29
26 (al-Shuʿarāʾ)
26:35 901 n.25
26:40 901 n.25
26:57 138
26:78–89 751
26:83–5 33
26:90 986, 989
26:128–35 1002
26:134 138
26:147–8 138
26:173 148
26:193 454
27 (al-Naml)
27:15–9 206
27:58 148
27:60 137 n.6
27:60–1 143 n.19, 147
27:62 611
27:82 622 n.93, 769, 1230, 1248
27:83 634 n.171
27:87 529, 530, 531
28 (al-Qaṣaṣ)
28:5 34
28:13 65
28:23 393
28:58 34
28:61 50
28:82–5 52
28:85 471, 476, 625
28:88 480, 568, 693
29 (al-ʿAnkabūt)
29:10 611
29:16–23 1234 n.55
29:20 489 n.13, 531, 650
29:57 197 n.38, 750 n.56, 1237
29:58 40, 45, 59 n.22, 139, 262
29:64 186 n.10, 489, 530, 667, 685
30 (al-Rūm)
30– 100
30:3 612

30 (al-Rūm) (cont.)

30:13	55
30:15	138, 185, 831 n.72
30:19	625
30:22	203 n.52
30:23	428
30:24	146, 625
30:48–51	161
30:50	625
30:55–7	183

31 (Luqmān)

31:8	50, 56
31:18	107
31:28	519

32 (al-Sajda)

32–	183
32:4	1018 n.30
32:5	517
32:16	145 n.25
32:17	54, 65, 316, 563, 831 n.72
32:19	56, 138
32:19–21	184
32:20	386 n.49
32:21	628
32:29	612

33 (al-Aḥzāb)

33:21	630
33:26–7	34
33:35	60
33:55–7	751
33:56	1018
33:63	613

34 (Sabā)

34:14	622, 622 n.93, 1230
34:15	57, 866
34:28	62, 202
34:37	139, 262
34:51–3	625

35 (Fāṭir)

35:10	352 n.59, 720, 730, 853
35:13	42
35:24	738 n.16
35:27–8	205
35:28	203 n.52
35:33	156 n.41, 236, 239, 241
35:34	831 n.72
35:35	60, 63, 186 n.10, 430
35:56	17
35:150	402 n.93

36 (Yā Sīn)

36:33	745 n.46
36:36	231 n.28
36:52	623
36:55	56, 282, 830–31, 841 n.117
36:55–7	156
36:56	59, 60, 83, 233–36
36:65–6	566 n.2
36:77–86	450
36:78	478

37 (al-Ṣāffāt)

37:6	721
37:8	503, 721
37:8–10	717, 720
37:10	721
37:18–27	566 n.2
37:21	517
37:35–47	181 n.3
37:42–4	61
37:43	801
37:45	257, 298
37:47	255 n.20, 298
37:48	185, 302
37:48–9	272 n.7
37:49	64, 992
37:57	63
37:58–60	748
37:59	64
37:60–6	181 n.3
37:62	265
37:62–8	566 n.2
37:102	436
37:172	608 n.14

38 (Ṣad)

38:16	201
38:26	201
38:28	50
38:49	801
38:50–4	156
38:52	272 n.7, 302
38:53	201
38:56–8	403 n.96
38:69	503
38:79	750
38:81	623
38:87–88	625

39 (al-Zumar)

39–	377, 618, 620
39:3	540

39:6 431, 745
39:19 681
39:20 59 n.22, 139, 262
39:21 203 n.52
39:22 33 n.7
39:32 13
39:34 65
39:42 431
39:43–4 1018 n.30
39:50 73, 866
39:53 851
39:60 13
39:67 225 n.10, 232 n.31, 548
39:67–9 107, 510
39:67–70 93
39:68 148 n.31, 529–31, 1242
39:68–75 181 n.3
39:69 21, 618
39:70 50
39:71 55, 401 n.92
39:73 55, 62, 64, 349–50, 354, 401 n.91
39:73–4 709
39:73–5 55
39:75 62
40 (Ghāfir)
40:8 50
40:11 169, 746–47
40:19 558 n.5
40:27 201
40:39 56, 497, 530
40:40 267
40:45–50 767
40:46 169, 199, 530
40:67 489 n.13
40:84 628
41 (Fuṣṣilat)
41:10–11 716 n.36
41:12 1083 n.2
41:13 148 n.31
41:16 148 n.31
41:17 148 n.31
41:19–24 1213
41:21 727
41:28 56
41:30 56
41:31 655
41:32 64
41:52 45
41:53 2, 45, 109, 113, 162, 573, 610
42 (al-Shūrā)
42:7 56, 517
42:13 317
42:17–8 615
42:18 614
42:22 62, 65, 137, 138
42:30 50
42:47 50
42:49 12, 181
43 (al-Zukhruf)
43:4 724
43:11 744, 746
43:19 402 n.93
43:33–5 1002
43:35 261
43:51 139 n.13
43:66 613, 615
43:69 801
43:70 56, 64
43:70–3 157
43:71 59, 262
43:72 53, 56, 429
43:85 613
44 (al-Dukhān)
44– 1253
44:25–8 138
44:43 265, 722 n.46
44:44 61 n.28
44:51 54, 56, 186 n.10, 801
44:53 61 n.28, 236 n.38
44:54 279 n.46, 302, 323 n.60, 783 n.10, 787, 801, 831 n.69
44:56 197 n.38, 730, 748
44:57 62
45 (al-Jāthiyya)
45:14 530, 620
45:26 50
45:30 62, 65
46 (al-Aḥqāf)
46:15–6 54
46:16 42, 46, 50
47 (Muḥammad)
47– 1039
47:1 680
47:14 62
47:15 56, 58, 64, 139, 254, 255 n.22, 262, 264, 866
47:15ff. 59

47 (Muḥammad) (cont.)
47:16ff. 58
47:18 613
48 (al-Fatḥ)
48:4 119
48:5 65, 323 n.58
48:18 119
48:26 119
48:28 612
50 (Qāf)
50– 620
50:15 522, 650
50:16 40
50:22 1198
50:31 56, 986
50:31–5 429
50:34 64, 141 n.16
50:35 65, 531, 837
50:41 612, 620
50:42 620
50:44 476
51 (al-Dhāriyāt)
51:15 138
51:22–3 612
51:23 610
51:49 81
52 (al-Ṭūr)
52– 72, 75
52:7–8 630 n.145
52:17 54, 138, 801
52:17–20 157
52:17–28 60
52:20 61, 272 n.7, 302, 323 n.60, 783 n.10, 787, 801, 831 n.69
52:21 83
52:22 63, 263, 298
52:22–4 157
52:23 59, 61, 298
52:23–5 300
52:24 64, 299, 323 n.59, 714, 992
52:27 63
52:45 148 n.31
53 (al-Najm)
53:1 13, 711
53:1–18 273, 859
53:3–4 566
53:14 187, 611, 711, 870
53:14–5 866
53:14–6 503 n.52
53:15 711
53:21 27, 402 n.93
53:25 749
53:26 1018 n.30
53:47 489 n.13, 635 n.172
54 (al-Qamar)
54:1 613, 616
54:19–20 148
54:31 148
54:54 54, 139, 143 n.19
54:54–5 63, 986
54:55 186 n.10
55 (al-Raḥman)
55– 16, 25, 57, 71–72, 75, 77–80, 82, 89, 354–55, 994–95, 1005
55:1–4 87
55:1–36 81
55:17 749
55:20 1228
55:22 82
55:26–7 232 n.31
55:36–73 57
55:37 630
55:37–45 81
55:41 628
55:44 566 n.2
55:46 54, 56, 81, 238–39, 354, 866
55:46–59 137
55:46–60 60, 81
55:46–61 57, 81–82
55:46–75 354
55:46–76 81 n.41, 157
55:46–78 82, 984, 987
55:48 81
55:48–76 566 n.2
55:50 58, 81, 139 n.12
55:52 81
55:54 185, 261 n.57, 658
55:54 76, 831 n.73
55:56 83, 185, 272 n.7, 302
55:56 58, 70, 72, 74, 323 n.60
55:56–74 82
55:58 82, 83, 319 n.38
55:60 63
55:62 81, 185 n.9, 658, 866
55:62–76 137
55:62–77 57, 81

55:62–78 82
55:63 56, 437 n.26
55:66 58
55:70–6 272 n.7
55:71 83, 83 n.45
55:72 82, 284, 302, 323 n.61
55:73 83, 83 n.45
55:74 83
55:75 83
55:76 185, 995
55:84 83

56 (al-Wāqiʿa)
56– 57, 72, 252, 265
56:1 183
56:4–6 1205, 1242
56:8ff. 319 n.37
56:11–26 60
56:12–9 300
56:12–24 158
56:15 59, 262, 831 n.72
56:17 185, 299
56:17–8 323 n.59
56:18–9 301
56:18–21 319 n.39
56:19 300
56:20–1 263
56:21 59, 298
56:22 61, 783 n.10
56:22–3 302
56:22–4 323 n.60
56:23 64, 992
56:24 51
56:27–38 158
56:28–30 317 n.28
56:28–31 866
56:28–34 986
56:30 869 n.37
56:35 60, 278
56:35–7 272 n.7, 279 n.46, 302
56:47 478
56:52 265
56:54–5 393 n.70
56:61 60
56:62 489 n.13
56:88–94 185
56:89 138, 185, 256

57 (al-Ḥadīd)
57:3 12
57:5 181
57:6 12
57:12 54, 63, 65, 323 n.58
57:13 358
57:17 625
57:20 107
57:21 55, 140 n.15, 710, 729–30
57:26–7 317 n.27

58 (al-Mujādila)
58:7 41
58:13 264
58:22 41

59 (al-Ḥashr)
59– 34
59:22 563

60 (al-Mumtaḥana)
60:8 46

61 (al-Ṣaff)
61:6 206
61:8 611
61:9 612
61:11–3 627 n.120
61:12 65, 137 n.6

63 (al-Munāfiqūn)
63:11 750 n.56

64 (al-Taghābun)
64:8 619 n.77
64:9 65

65 (al-Ṭalāq)
65:12 1083 n.2

66 (al-Taḥrīm)
66:8 63
66:11 56

67 (al-Mulk)
67:2 51
67:3 185, 347, 1083 n.2
67:7–8 566 n.2

68 (al-Qalam)
68:16 622
68:17 56 n.6
68:34 62

69 (al-Ḥāqqa)
69:1–3 183
69:7 148
69:13–37 181 n.3
69:16 230 n.22
69:17 62, 225, 229, 231–32, 243, 248, 348 n.31, 356
69:18 233
69:22 55

69 (al-Ḥāqqa) (cont.)
69:24 185
69:30–2 566 n.2
69:31 373 n.11
70 (al-Maʿārij)
70– 72
70:1–35 181 n.3
70:3 530
70:3–4 510
70:4 517, 530, 694, 1255
70:19 1290
70:26 624
70:35 62
70:38 138
70:40 749
70:44 625
71 (Nūḥ)
71:14 740 n.25
71:17–8 744, 746 n.47
71:25 169
72 (al-Jinn)
72:8 720
72:8–9 717
72:24 625
72:25 630
73 (al-Muzzammil)
73:14 18, 1242
74 (al-Muddaththir)
74:8 622, 630
74:9–10 622
74:19–20 628
74:35 373 n.11
74:39–42 378
74:46 624
74:47 624
74:50–1 136 n.3
75 (al-Qiyāma)
75– 72
75:7–10 1242
75:19 516
75:20 39
75:22–3 63, 73
75:24–5 73
76 (al-Insān)
76– 183, 252–53, 256, 260, 264
76:4 184
76:6 58
76:7–9 54
76:7–22 60
76:11–4 236–39, 246
76:12–21 159
76:12–22 181 n.3
76:13–9 300
76:14 784, 784 n.17
76:15–6 260, 262
76:17 59, 301
76:17–8 239
76:18 866, 960 n.26
76:19 61, 64, 185, 299, 323 n.59
76:20 1005
76:20–2 184
76:21 59, 62, 236 n.38, 261 n.57, 995
76:22 59, 62–63
76:29 40
77 (al-Mursalāt)
77:8–11 1242
77:9 1251
77:41 54, 138, 866
78 (al-Nabāʾ)
78– 71, 73, 75–76, 679
78:2 630, 631
78:9–11 431
78:12 185, 347, 1083 n.2
78:14–6 161
78:17 629, 679
78:18 679
78:20 679
78:21 403
78:21–6 73
78:23 389, 1198
78:31 801
78:31–5 159
78:31–6 73
78:32 137 n.6
78:33 60, 272 n.7, 302
78:35 59
78:40 40
79 (al-Nāziʿāt)
79– 72
79:25 749
79:27 1232
79:34 530, 628
79:34–5 1212
79:37–9 73
79:39 56, 138 n.10
79:40 54

79:40–1 73
79:41 138
79:42 613
80 (ʿAbasa)
80– 72
80:30 137 n.6
80:38–9 72
80:40–2 73
81 (al-Takwīr)
81– 183
81:1–14 12, 183
81:13 56, 986
81:19–25 273
82 (al-Infiṭār)
82:1 1251
82:1–2 1205
82:13 138
82:13–14 169
82:14 13
82:19 631
83 (al-Muṭaffifīn)
83– 71, 257
83:7–8 497
83:18 666 n.25
83:22 76, 138
83:22–4 234–36, 244
83:23 59, 560
83:24 61
83:25 256 n.26
83:25–8 255
83:27 866
83:35 59
84 (al-Inshiqāq)
84:1 1251
84:6 491 n.21
84:19 740 n.25
85 (al-Burūj)
85:11 65
87 (al-Aʿlā)
87:13 747 n.50
87:17 50, 64
87:17–19 52
88 (al-Ghāshiya)
88– 71, 73, 76
88:1 59, 628
88:1–3 1242
88:2–7 73, 75
88:8–16 73, 75
88:8ff. 240 n.21
88:10 55
88:10–6 160
88:13 234–36, 244
88:20 991
89 (al-Fajr)
89:1 611
89:22 622, 630
89:23 566 n.2
89:27–30 63, 682
89:28 669
89:29 62
89:29–30 802
90 (al-Balad)
90:2 740 n.25
90:11 39
90:14 264
91 (al-Shams)
91:1 611
91:3 611
92 (al-Layl)
92:1 617
92:2 611, 617
92:14 628
92:20 40
93 (al-Ḍuḥā)
93:4 749
93:5 831 n.72
94 (al-Sharḥ)
94:4 622
95 (al-Tīn)
95– 675
95:3 611
95:4 1232
95:4–6 42
95:5 694
95:7–8 50
95:15 666 n.25
96 (al-ʿAlaq)
96:1–5 435 n.17
97 (al-Qadr)
97:5 612
98 (al-Bayyina)
98:5 611
98:8 63
99 (al-Zalzala)
99:1–2 1242
99:6 50
101 (al-Qāriʿa)
101:4 148

102 (al-Takāthur)
102:8 138
103 (al-ʿAṣr)
103:1 612
104 (al-Humaza)
104– 72, 375, 378 n.28
104:6–7 1198
105 (al-Fīl)
105– 1160
105:5 148
107 (al-Māʿūn)
107– 675
108 (al-Kawthar)
108– 959
108:1 830, 866, 871

Biblical References

Hebrew Bible

Amos
9:7–15 104 n.38
Dan.
7 104 n.38
10 97 n.15
12:1–2 627 n.119
Deut.
18:15 110
Eccles.
5:11 431
9:5 10, 763
Ezek.
1:10 230 n.24
10 106
40:31 359 n.91
40:34 359 n.91
40:37 359 n.91
40:41 359 n.91
47:1–12 358
Gen.
141 792
1 357 n.82
1:27 327 n.77
2 69
2:8 55, 187 n.14
2:8–24 321 n.52
2:10 59 n.21
2:15 187 n.14
2:20 36
2:21–3 431
3:17–19 36
3:24 36, 69 n.16
15:12 431 n.7
31:40 431 n.7
37:35 763
Hab.
2:5 208 n.61
Isa.
11–12 104 n.38
11:24–27 104 n.38
11:35 104 n.38
11:60–66 104 n.38
19:25b 110 n.55
28:15 208 n.61
28:18 208 n.61
40–55 762 n.7
64:4 316 n.21
Jer.
9:20 208 n.61
Job
3:13 431 n.7
Mic.
4–5 104 n.38
4:42 74
Prov.
6:9 431 n.7
20:13 431
Ps.
23:5 74
46:5 358
136 89

New Testament

1 Cor.
2:9 240 n.49, 316 n.21, 721 n.44
15:26 208 n.61
1 Thess.
4:16 618
1 Tim.
2.12 910
Heb.
9:27 747 n.52
John
3:3 699, 731 n.69
10:10 114

Luke
9:7–9 110
9:35 620 n.84
20:34–6 271
21:27 620 n.84
23:39–43 791
Mark
15:23 259
Matt.
16:18 201
24:31 618
24:36 626 n.118
Rev.
2:11 747
6–19 764
6:8 208 n.61
20–21 764
20:13–4 208 n.61
20:14 747
21:1 763 n.10
21:10ff. 316 n.22
21:22–3 237 n.42
22:5 237 n.42

Ḥadīth Index

ḥadīth
"Allah created me from light…" 569 n.14
"Avoid sitting on roadsides…" 559
"Concerning the purity of containers…" 1104
"During the *mi'rāj* Muḥammad saw…" 860 n.5
"Every newborn child…" 32
"God created Adam in his form…" 705, 716 n.33, 720–21, 727
"God will send down one…" 626 n.117
"He who knows himself…" 670–71
"If a dog licks your container…" 1103, 1105–6, 1113
"If the earth were to ever be without an *imām*…" 513–14
"I have prepared for my pious servants…" 563 n.31, 721
"I looked into paradise, and saw…" 333
"I saw in the Garden…" 803
"I saw my Lord in the most beautiful form…" 712, 714
"I was led into paradise…" 861
"Muḥammad and Gabriel did not abandon…" 860 n.5
"Muḥammad states: 'I fall to the ground…'" 1021 n.40
"Muḥammad was given three things…" 1021
"None will remain in the fire…" 540–41
"Paradise is encompassed by loathsome…" 315, 329
"Paradise is under the shade of the swords…" 1159
"Paradise lies at the feet of mothers…" 706, 714, 717, 732
"People are asleep…" 121, 211
"People of paradise will have sex with women…" 320 n.42
"Pour over me seven waterskins…" 1107
"Prayer (*ṣalāt*) is the heavenly ascension (*mi'rāj*) of the believer…" 729–30
"Prayer is the key to paradise…" 729
"Satan binds three knots…" 439
"Soul of the believer is a bird…" 199
"Spirits of the martyrs (*arwāḥ al-shuhadā'*) reside in the birds…" 199–200
"The cat is not impure…" 1108 n.28
"The first day of the Dajjāl…" 1229
"The fornication of the eye…" 558
"The Hour and I have been sent…" 605
"The look is a poisonous arrow…" 558
"There are rooms in paradise…" 560
"There will come to Hell a day…" 1205 n.85
"The Rock in Jerusalem was the *maqām* for the throne of God on the *yawm al-qiyāma*…" 1022 n.44
"The true dream is sent by God…" 436
"They passed by a *janāza*…" 1010 n.1
"This world is a prison…" 576 n.42
"This world is the tillage…" 1212
"When the elect of paradise…" 563 n.29
"While I was sleeping…" 437 n.24
"Whoever dies, his resurrection…" 423, 520
"Whoever enters the *walāya*…" 627 n.121
"Whoever loves to meet God…" 537 n.13
"Whoever loves us, the *ahl al-bayt*…" 627 n.121
"Whoever peers into a house…" 559
"Worldly affairs of a man come to an end at death but three things will outlast him…" 1024 n.57

ḥadīth (topics), 3, 14, 169, 171–72, 188, 196, 230, 247–48, 555–57, 605–6, 634, 749, 751, 827, 839, 878, 1110, 1114, 1148, 1155
on the beast 1248
on castle Muḥammad saw 860 n.5
on Dajjāl as blind in one eye 1230
on date of end of time 1241
on day of judgment, time as a white ram 342
on deeds of those entering paradise 837
on dogs 1103–5, 1115
on dream as part of prophecy 709
on escape from hell 382
on eschatology 347, 349 n.36, 381

on events before the *mahdī* 1251
on existence after death 12
on first called to paradise, those who thank God 825 n.35
on gates (eight) of paradise 345–47, 353–54, 359, 361, 843 n.122
on God sending remedies for illnesses 1249
on Gog and Magog invading 1229
on height/size of people of paradise 826–27, 841 n.117
on hell 285, 1229, 1256
on hereafter 33
on hierarchy of *abdāl* and *quṭb* 695
against hitting women 329 n.85
on horses in paradise 1195
on *ḥūr* for believers in paradise 303, 827–28
on intentions 411–12
on intercession of Muḥammad 327 n.74, 843 n.122, 1021 n.40
on *jihād*/holy war 1150
on language in paradise as Arabic 843 n.122
on *laylat al-qadr* "angels carry four banners…" 1020 n.38
on lowest rank in paradise 824 n.33, 825 n.35
on men as majority in paradise 330–31, 334
on men resurrected naked 1233
on most of the inmates of hell being women 322 n.57
on Muḥammad asking "his Lord to show him paradise and hell" 862
on Muḥammad first to enter paradise 843 n.122
on Muslims in paradise 843 n.122
on night journey and ascension 191, 861
on no one saying "Allah, Allah" 1230
on number of levels of paradise 825 n.36
on number of wives in paradise 826–28, 841 n.117
on paradise 285, 311, 319, 555, 560, 841, 859, 867
on people of the heights 413
on prayer invalidated by donkey, woman, or black dog… 1119
on questioning in the grave 424
on rivers in paradise 841, 843 n.121
on seeing God on day of judgment 381
Shiʿi 21, 606–7, 609, 620, 708 n.20
on *ṣirāṭ* being fine like a hair 427
on souls of dead compared to birds 1240
on souls of martyrs 167–68
on suicide 412
on visions of paradise 417–18
on wish fulfillment in paradise 1151
on women as smallest group in paradise 335
on world lasting seven days 1251
and worshipful obedience 1108

ḥadīth qudsī
"I have prepared for my righteous servants…" 316
on intercession of God as All-Merciful 546–47
"My mercy outweighs my wrath…" 354, 383, 538
"When I love him, I become for him ear, sight,…" 573 n.30

Index of Topics and Keywords

ʿAbbasid(s) 126, 582, 677, 1207
caliphs (c. 640/1242–3) 1011 n.5
period 163
poetry 298, 300
ablutions 346. *See also* washings
above, *vs.* below 778
Abrahamic. *See also* Christianity/Christians; Judaism/Jewish; monotheism
faiths 1, 93–94
genealogy 118
absence 104
and presence 1307
abstinence 907, 909
abstract (*mujarrad*) 704
Abyssinian(s) 1160
language 830
accident 453
accountability, human 1187
accounting, day of/final 702, 1212. *See also* reckoning (*ḥisāb*)
Acehnese
language and culture 1167
literature 1153, 1157, 1161
poetry 1147, 1149, 1155, 1168
Sultanate 1166
Aceh War (Dutch War, Infidel War) 1147, 1149, 1167, 1169–70
Achaemenid kings 259
actions 837
objects and modes of 361–63
worth of 840
active
vs. passive 1272
principle 494
actuality (*bi-l-fiʿl*) 656, 712–13, 730. *See also* potentiality
actualization 464
ʿĀd 148 n.31
adab 15, 824, 856
adaptation/adoption, period of 1070–71
ʿādat parast (tradition-worshiper) 571
adultery/adulterers 190–91, 329, 483
aesthetics 18, 272, 853, 1075, 1261
of the garden 296–97
aesthetization 1076–77
afflictions/infirmities 202, 205, 775, 1251. *See also* suffering; trials/tribulations
afterlife/afterworld 1–3, 94, 104, 120, 327, 336, 343, 535, 757, 1010, 1187, 1203, 1218, 1222, 1267, 1272 n.12, 1284
descriptions of 190, 315–17, 1201
existence in 287
in the grave 1238
Muḥammad and Muslim community in 836
reality/nature of 546, 1211
religious dimension of 1154
visions of 916, 918, 1131
age 324
agency 1297, 1314
male 1298, 1300
of martyrs (male *vs.* female) 1281
Muslim 1292, 1294
revolutionary 1283
agnosticism 1129. *See also* atheism/atheists
agriculture 144, 1084, 1103, 1118
cornfields [in Quran] 138–39, 143
dogs for 1110 n.29, 1117
harvest, time of 1085
Ahasver (of Jewish legend) 434
ahl (as a term) 541
ahl al-bayt 607 n.11, 626 n.118
Ahl-i Ḥaqq (Followers of the True/Real) 22, 690–93, 736 n.9
ahl al-kahf 1251–52. *See also* companions, of the cave
Aḥmadiyya 126, 1206
Ahriman (Avestan "Angra Mainyu" (Evil Spirit)) 723
Ahura Mazda (god of good) 761. *See also* deities/gods
AIDS 1248
Aingra Mainyu (god of evil) 761. *See also* deities/gods
Ainul Mardiah 1160, 1162, 1168, 1172
air 508
as element 456, 459, 473, 667 n.32, 717–18, 1087
ʿajāʾib (marvels of creations)
definition of 933–34

genre 25, 931, 934, 936–37, 939
al-makhlūqāt (of created beings), and *al-malakūt* (of divine realm) 941
Akhbārī (scholars) 633
ākhira (the last, end, hereafter) 50, 100, 103–4, 114, 343, 530, 627, 667, 852, 1102–3, 1121–22, 1212
ahl al-(people of) 852
al-dār al- (home) 56, 137
ʿulūm al- (knowledge of eschatology) 182, 194
Akkadian [loanwords] 256
ʿālam (world, dominion)
al-arwāḥ (of Spirits) 1191
al-ashbāḥ al-mujarrada (of immaterial shapes) 509
al-barzakh (of the grave) 1191
al-jabarūtī (might) 197
al-khayāl 1239 n.77
al-malākūtī (power) 197
al-mithāl (of similitudes/images) 494, 501, 1190, 1218, 1239 n.77
al-ṣuwar (of images) 689
Alamut (period) 662
Lord of 685
alcohol 254. *See also* wine
Alexander (romance) 24, 922–23
alienation 1306. *See also* marginalization
ʿāliya (high, lofty) 55
Aljamiado (literature) 882 n.77
Al-Jazeera 1208
Allah. *See* God
allegories 209–10, 288, 579, 596, 892, 900, 905, 908, 967
interpretations/meanings of 274, 477, 567, 584, 656, 665, 833
allusions 713
to paradise 983–84
alms/almsgiving 198, 345, 360, 362–64
amr (cause; command; revelation; period or dispensation) 100, 606
of God 622–23, 626 n.118, 629, 631, 653–54, 669
analogy 1105, 1307
analysis
axes of 1109–10, 1113, 1119, 1121–23
quadrant model of 1103, 1109–10, 1121–23
ʿanaza (spear, of Muḥammad) 1017 n.28
androcentricism 325, 331
anecdotes 585, 824, 1153, 1163
angel(s) 17, 45, 51, 55, 62, 100, 146, 189–90, 224, 227, 245, 324, 400–2, 437, 503, 507, 547, 562, 583, 595, 630, 670, 692–93, 710, 712, 717, 720, 737 n.15, 742, 764, 770, 776, 852, 945, 994, 1037–40, 1042–43, 1150, 1191, 1203, 1236, 1245, 1255–58
abode of 229–30
and adoration of Adam 1035–36, 1047 fig.47.1
archangels 189, 193
ʿAzrāʾīl 594, 1215
-Christology 782 n.7
of death 432, 529
and dogs 1110–11
Gabriel (Jibrāʾīl) 100, 189, 274–75, 378 n.28, 435, 724, 794 n.45, 862, 877–81, 883, 997, 1020, 1042–43, 1110–11
Isrāfīl 193, 529, 1021, 1038, 1041–42, 1242
malak, malāʾika 197–98, 229–30, 232–33
Mīkaʾīl (Michael) 1042
Munkar and Nakīr 424, 432, 572, 1215
number of 231, 243
recording deeds 1231
Riḍwān 879–81, 1004
rows or classes (*ṣufūf*) of 231–33
and throne 229, 232, 247–48
world of 935
animal(s) 149, 230, 263, 393, 456, 506–7, 514–15, 670, 692–93, 696, 719, 742, 907, 1036, 1084, 1119–20, 1194, 1203, 1237, 1242–43. *See also* birds
community/kingdom of 452, 738 n.16
figures of 1033
husbandry 1084
impurity of 1114
in paradise 834, 870, 880, 1195
passions 448, 458
predatory 1112
annihilation 1317
fanāʾ, 114, 205 n.54, 236 n.37, 472, 510, 585, 587, 591
of paradise and hell 481
of soul 594
anṣār (Medinan Helpers) 163
anthropocentric (view of paradise) 318
anthropology 474, 512 n.75, 656, 701
anthropomorphism 227, 246–47, 249, 705 n.10

anti-colonialism 1171, 1285
antiquity 3, 766
anti-sectarian (impulse) 372–73
anti-Zionists 1285
Anu (Heaven-god) 1085. *See also* deities/gods
apocalypse/apocalyptic 16–17, 94–96, 209–10, 675, 757, 769, 863, 884, 937, 941, 1318. *See also* eschatology(ies)
  battle 607
  Christian 101, 783
  definition of 98, 101
  events of 936
  features of Quran 11
  genre 99, 125
  history 942
  Islamic 124, 1260, 1316–17
  Jewish 69, 101
  literature 69, 121, 182, 195, 365
  movements/revolution 6, 111
  narratives 191, 341–42, 344, 1218
  nature of 122
  resignification 678, 683
  Shiʿa 687
  studies in/scholarship 94, 97–99
  Zoroastrian 101
apocalyptica 125
apocalypticism 97, 105, 686
aporia 86, 88
apostates 192, 956. *See also* heresy
  zanādiqa 855–56, 1207
appetites (lowly) 429
al-Aqṣā Brigades 1275 n.15, 1278 n.17, 1280
Arabic (language) 55–56, 259, 350, 355, 703 n.8, 806, 836, 894, 897, 925, 942, 1133, 1231, 1235
  ancient poetry 74, 81, 86, 88–89, 204 n.53
  contemporary poetry 154
  grammar 236
  literature 67, 114 n.75, 807, 850, 932–33, 954 n.6
  manuscripts 897
  morphology 77
  in paradise (*ḥadīth* on) 843 n.122
  philologists 81
  poetry/poets 67, 137 n.5, 299, 806–7, 809, 853–54, 912
  Quran in 272–73
  rasm 788
Arab(ic) 954, 962, 985, 1131
  culture 556, 897, 917
  identity ("Arabness") 1074
  and Islamic sources 902–3, 912, 915, 918
  nationalism 957
  -Ottoman East 941–43
  society 961, 1069, 1300 n.22
  writers/literati 954, 957, 962, 964
Aramaic 781
architecture/architectural (features) 15, 25, 349, 982, 1014 n.16, 1039, 1070, 1073
  arched panels 1012
  canopy, alcove (*ḥajala; ḥijāl*) 233–35
  cupolas 879
  designs/forms 982, 1017 n.28
  domes (*qubba*, pl. *qibāb*) 621 n.91, 1012–13, 1021, 1024
  funerary 1011, 1017
  Mamluk 1011–12
  of paradise 865, 868, 874, 878, 885
  qāʿa (small rectangular arcaded courtyard) 1013
  traditional 1016–17, 1075, 1077
  Umayyad 1014
archives 1068
Aristotelian
  category of substance 499
  classification 512
  metaphysics 545
  telos 489
  thought 522
  tradition 478
aromatics 253–54, 257–60, 266. *See also* fragrances
  camphor (*kāfūr*) 105, 252, 257–58, 259–60, 303
  musk (*misk*) 255–59, 277, 283, 295, 297, 303–5, 318, 562, 703, 711, 835, 861, 868, 882, 1272
arrogance/pride 43, 72, 1287. *See also* vices
art 3, 15, 26, 67, 1069, 1071
  academic 1073–74
  history, Islamic 555–56
  Islamic 985, 1069
  modern 1069–70
  murals 1057, 1059–63, 1067 fig.48.4, 1067 fig.48.5
  production 1069, 1074
  sculpture 1074

secular 1033
video 1074
Western 1069, 1071
artifice (*makr*) 703
artists 11, 1033–34
ascension/ascent 503, 512, 904
literature/texts 937, 1020–22
of Muḥammad 121, 192, 273–74, 709–10, 712, 724, 728–29, 802, 858–60, 863, 875–77, 892–94, 900, 917–18
spiritual 677
asceticism 117, 384, 853, 1136. *See also* piety
ascetic(s) 18, 272, 277, 281, 283, 346 n.23, 580
Ashʿarī(s) 274, 371 n.1, 482, 567, 581
doctrine of *kasb* 373 n.9
kalām 476 (*See also kalām* (discursive theology))
school/perspective 468–70, 480, 1204
theology 422, 474, 1196, 1218
assembly (*ḥashr*) 520, 521 n.102. *See also* gathering
Assyrians 808–9
astrology 901, 984, 1084 n.6. *See also* zodiac
astronomy/astronomers 26, 901, 905 n.32, 1083, 1085–86, 1090–91, 1093–94, 1226
ataurique 982–83
atheism/atheists 850, 855–56, 1129, 1206–7, 1209, 1231, 1251
atoms 507, 731, 1227, 1234, 1242
attributes 473, 571, 573, 1035
divine/of God (*ṣifāt*) 228 n.19, 236, 373 n.9, 453, 471, 477, 547, 703–4, 712, 729, 1019
aurality 100
samʿiyyāt (lit., things which are heard) 470
authenticity 1071–72, 1076, 1078
degree of 825 n.35
of *isnād*s/traditions 845
authoritarianism 345, 365, 1225
authority 676, 683–84, 687, 1003, 1005, 1122
of religion 1290
Ayyubids 1011, 1014
al-Azhar 470, 476, 485, 933
ʿAzrāʾīl 594, 1215. *See also* angel(s)

Babis 126
Babylonian (notions/texts) 355–56
backbiting 172, 329
Bahāʾiyya/Bahaʾis 126, 1206
balance 197, 201, 704, 946. *See also* scale(s)
banners (*rāya*) 202–4
banquets 16, 74, 86, 797–98
Banū Ādam 112
Banū ʿĀmir 170 n.35
Banū l-Nataʾyīdīr 34
Banū Qurayẓa 34
Banū Sulaym 170 n.35
baqāʾ (perpetuation/permanence) 472–73, 510, 587, 591, 594–95
al-taʿabbud 852
barzakh (isthmus, barrier, intermediate state between death and resurrection) 10, 14, 22, 100, 166, 175, 194, 196, 492, 498, 500, 510–11, 520, 522–23, 529–30, 591 n.68, 592, 655 n.26, 689, 692, 694, 696–99, 750, 1187, 1197–98, 1222 n.2, 1258
abode of 530–31
al-baḥrayn (between the two seas) 657 n.34
berzah 1228–29, 1237–39
impermeability of 769
basin (in paradise) 830
ḥawḍ 382, 472, 871
kawthar 1058
basmala 1018 n.31
bāṭil (wrong) 853
bāṭin (inner, hidden, esoteric, invisible) 571–72, 589, 628, 676–77, 685, 1296
Bāṭiniyya 328, 1200. *See also* Ismaʿili(s)/Ismaʿilism
battles, of Islam 176, 1160
Badr (2/624) 17, 118, 163–64, 167–71, 175, 178
Karbala (61/680) 26, 276, 1056–57, 1059, 1165
Muʾta (8/629) 416
of Simancas-Ahandega 980
Uḥud (3/625) 17, 164, 166–67, 170–71, 175, 410, 416
bayān
explanation, understanding 87, 516
revelation 100, 122
b-d-l 694
beast of the Earth (*dābbat al-arḍ*) 622, 1041, 1230, 1247–48

beatific vision 284, 287, 567–68, 942, 947, 1143, 1302
states (*aḥwāl*) of 286–87
beauty 300–302, 304, 721, 727, 853, 905, 919, 927, 1033, 1227
of creation/this world 43, 1233
jamāl (God's names/attributes of) 301, 538, 546–47, 569, 1246
nature of, in garden 295–96, 304–5
physical and spiritual 297, 299
Bedouins 125, 137 n.5, 144–45
behavior 453, 468, 843, 1104
commendable (*faḍāʾil al-aʿmāl* or *adab*) 824
moral 765, 839
Behemoth (*dābbat al-arḍ*) 622. *See also* beast of the Earth
being/Being 512, 542, 570. *See also* existence/being
act of (*l'acte d'être*) 488
divine 569
nature of 546
wujūd 535, 542
beings
akwān 236 n.37
organic 456
spiritual 197
being towards death 6, 20, 487, 488 n.12
being-towards-resurrection 20, 489, 510
Bektāshiyya (Sufi brotherhood) 691 n.7
belief 778–79, 838 n.100, 840, 850. *See also* faith
in day of judgment 1199
and disbelief 33 n.7, 593
in *al-ghayb* 65
in God's unity 837
in hell 191, 285
in hereafter 1210
īmān 51, 377–78, 380
in life in paradise/heaven 191, 285, 311, 665
in resurrection 311, 1232
sincere 198, 203
and works/deeds 52, 377 n.24, 837, 840
believers 34, 119, 145, 153, 170, 198, 266, 324, 332, 364, 432, 479, 497, 547, 618, 685, 767–68, 777, 831, 874, 947, 989, 991, 993, 995 n.51, 1041–42
arriving in paradise 203, 994
common (*vs.* martyrs) 190
definition of 472
fate of 377
and fighting 167, 172, 174
and infidels 622
male and female 267
muʾmin, status of 398
pious 165–66
reward and enjoyment of 1044
of the right hand (*aṣḥāb al-yamīn*) 319, 378
sinning 372, 378, 398
and vision of God in paradise 821
wives of 304
belles-lettres 15, 932
beloved 86, 151–52, 174, 563, 575, 728, 901, 927
betrayal 969
Bible 59, 69, 84, 97, 104–5, 123, 193, 210, 244, 317, 432, 775, 794, 1127, 1130
Genesis 58, 83 n.44
Gospel, of John 516
Gospels 153, 347, 626 n.118, 708 n.20, 763, 791
Isaiah (Book of) 675
New Testament 74, 95–96, 102, 110–11, 123, 126, 230 n.24, 316–17, 747, 1130, 1233
Old Testament/Hebrew 36, 105 n.45, 110, 121, 316–17, 347, 431, 763, 1130–31, 1136, 1233
Revelation (Book of) 97–98, 104, 116, 124–25, 237 n.42, 622, 747, 763–64, 769
Biblical
exegesis 1131
figures 205, 728
imagery 74
loanwords 256
psalms/texts/stories 89, 208, 253 n.13
scholarship 120
traditions 84, 315–16, 336
Big Bang 1236
Bildungsmythos 121
binary
discourse 107
juxtapositions 81–82
biography, of the Prophet (*sīra*) 17, 182, 188, 862
birds 588, 926, 990, 1058, 1060–61

green/white (in heaven) 164–65, 167–68, 171, 175, 187, 200, 995 n.51, 1061
hoopoe 585, 588, 593–94, 596
of peace (*murgh-i silm*) 1058
peacocks 592, 1036
of prey 1112
Sīmurgh 585, 595
birth 519, 759. *See also nash'a*
period before (*amwāt*) 745
second, or ultimate growth/arising (*al-nash'a al-ākhira*) 489, 650
second/new (*wilādat al-thāniya*) 699
spiritual (*al-nash'a al-rūḥāniyya*) 515
birth-decay-death 320, 322, 332
birth-life-death-rebirth 759, 763
blasphemy 210. *See also* apostates; heresy
blessed (people) 319, 437, 537, 561
death of 196
lives of, in paradise 224, 232 n.31, 233, 236, 239, 244–45, 796–97
blessings 475, 831, 1111
baraka 25, 1010–11, 1017–18, 1023
blind (people) 202, 204, 852
bliss/joy 170, 185 n.7, 234, 252, 268, 538, 1202
best, most beautiful (*ḥusnā*) 103
place of (*mafāz*) 74
blood (of martyrs) 1274, 1280, 1285
Boabdil (of Granada) 966, 969, 971
bodiliness 315–16, 333
bodily form 713, 718, 722, 725, 731
as locus of manifestation (*maẓhar*) 703, 722–23, 728
of mothers 716
bodily/physical
functions 1145
premises (i.e., *ṭabīʿiyya*) 1094
residue (*faḍl*) 479
return [to God] (*al-maʿād al-jismānī*) 490
vs. spiritual 61
suffering, as pleasurable 1217
body(ies) 12, 14, 18, 317, 321–22, 324–25, 336–37, 447 n.10, 453, 456, 509, 689
celestial 451–52, 459–60, 656
essential parts of (*al-ajzāʾ al-aṣliyya*) 478–79
evil nature of 1216
gendered 312, 314, 320, 324, 331, 337
jism 227–28, 495, 499
male 326
physical/material 492, 523, 750, 1218
private parts (*ʿawra*) 559
restoration/resurrection of 484, 1208
separation, and return of 425
and souls 199, 277, 907, 1191, 1197, 1204, 1217, 1237
and spirit (worlds of) 530
of women/female(s) 18, 322, 326, 336, 714
body-soul (*qālib-nafs*) 574
body-soul dyad 659
book, mother of (*umm al-kitāb*) 724
book(s) 113, 606, 825
illustrations 1022 n.47, 1034, 1061
qāʾim as 610
of records 936 (*See also* records (of deeds))
topically arranged (*muṣannaf*) 313 n.7, 871
borders, of heaven (*arjāʾ*) 229, 231–32, 243, 245
bourgeoisie 1078
boys/youth 301–2. *See also* males
Brahmanical 850
Brethren of Purity (Ikhwān al-Ṣafāʾ) 20, 489, 508, 512, 521
bridal chambers 797
bridegrooms 1285
brides 1273. *See also* marriage
bridge/path (*ṣirāṭ*) 283, 572, 609–10, 627, 946, 1057, 1189, 1203, 1243
British occupation (in Iraq) 808
brotherhood 582
brutality 1319
b-ʿ-th 750
Buddha 696, 740
Buddha-land 252, 267
Buddhism/Buddhists 580, 743, 759, 763
Mahāyāna 759
Pure Land 267
Theravāda 267, 759
buildings 1075
in paradise 868–69, 879
Burāq 435, 1037, 1038 n.27, 1062
burial(s) 171, 856. *See also* funerary
structures 1010
Buyid period 633
Byzantines 258

caesura 1309–10, 1312, 1314–15
calamities/cataclysmic events 67, 147–48, 632, 771. *See also* catastrophes
caliphate, in al-Andalus 1005
caliphs 1003
  first four 588, 878, 880
  first two 678
callers to prayer 171, 176
camphor (*kāfūr*) 105, 252, 257–60, 303
campsites, deserted (motif of) 86, 88, 90, 147
candelabra (in heaven) 164, 167–68
capitalist
  concept of hereafter 1217
  society 762
carpets (in paradise) 261, 305, 993
cartoons (of Muḥammad) 1145
castles (in paradise) 561–62, 864 n.18, 868, 878–81, 883, 1002. *See also* palaces
catastrophes 101, 149, 200, 769, 1317. *See also* calamities/cataclysmic events
catharsis 1313
catholicoi 776
Catholics/Catholicism 966, 1135. *See also* Christianity/Christians
causality 482, 1227, 1245
  circular 1311
  independent 1226
cause 513
  and effect 692
  first/First 473, 504
  God, as cause of universe 422
  God, as Causer of causes (*musabbib al-asbāb*) 544
cave, companions of (*aṣḥāb al-kahf*) 433–34, 620 n.83
celestial
  chair (of God) 936
  intellects 457, 462
  souls 457, 520
  spheres 449, 452, 473, 476, 494, 507, 904–5, 1083, 1092
  spirit 460
  symbolism 1003
  world/realm 451–52, 454–55, 1084, 1087
celibacy 803
Celts 260
cemeteries 1010. *See also* burial(s); funerary (matters)
cenotaph 1013
ceramics 262, 995
  green and manganese 995, 1005
certitude 837, 938
chahār bāgh (Persian fourfold garden) 261, 355
chaos 608, 1318
chār ʿAlī 1015 n.23
charitable
  foundations 1011, 1024 (*See also waqf* (endowment))
  people (*mutaṣaddiqūn*) 838
chār Muḥammad (four Muḥammads) 1015–22, 1024–25
  design 1031 fig.46.5
  inscriptions 25–26, 1032 fig.46.6
Chassidim 1133
chassidim (pious), *vs. mitnaggedim* (opponents) 1132
chastisement 540, 741. *See also* punishment
  cessation of, not eternal 537–39
chauvinism 1116 n.51
cherubim 36, 197. *See also* angel(s)
children 796, 962, 1193, 1210. *See also* infants, deceased
Children of Israel 51–52
Chinese
  Daoists 267
  medicine, traditional 258
  texts 18
Chinvat Bridge 770
Christianity/Christians 15, 23, 52, 55, 69, 73, 98–99, 255, 271, 280, 315, 317, 327, 352, 372 n.5, 374 n.13, 458, 468, 580, 590, 593, 659, 690, 725, 757, 759, 771, 778, 800, 812, 853, 899, 906, 908, 912–13, 917, 960, 964, 980, 1137, 1197, 1228, 1241, 1317
  apocalypse/eschatology of 101, 783
  Arabian 781, 801
  Aramaean 782
  doctrine/theology 27, 894, 1127
  early 103
  East-Syrian 773
  exegetes 798
  influence 923
  in Iraq 810–11
  and Islam/Muslims 24, 801
  Jacobite or Nestorian 782
  missionaries 675

and paradise 70, 83, 153, 787
Protestant 762, 1133
and Reformation 1127
scriptures 77
story of Ephesus 433–34
tradition/culture of 95 n.6, 699, 809
Christology 779
angel- 782 n.7
Chu kingdom (770–223 BCE) 265–66
church(es) 777, 1070
scholasticism 124
and state 1123
Church of the East 775–76, 779. *See also* Nestorian (Christianity)
circle, within square 1016–17, 1031 fig.46.7
circularity 1311
cities 926. *See also* urban
madā'in 881
civilization(s) 36, 87, 811, 954 n.7, 1070, 1200
Greek 1199
Indian 1209
Islamic 210, 809, 892–93, 911, 917, 934
material 83, 296
Persian 1199, 1209
pre-Islamic 1091
Western 1209
clay 36, 497
clerics (*'ulamā'*, *teungku*) 1148, 1150
clothing/garments 140–41, 153, 156, 184, 236, 252, 834
Egyptian peasant 1072
silk 13, 59, 62, 159, 261, 296, 703
clouds 144, 146, 160–61, 437, 945, 1036, 1038–39. *See also* rain
coins 151, 153, 998–1000
cold (*zamharīr*) 237
colonial (territories) 1128
colonization 1130
color(s) 17, 210, 463–64, 1072, 1245
black 205 n.54
Greek theories of 204 n.53
green 205, 437, 994
multicolored 206
of paradise 205
spiritual (*al-aṣbāgh al-rūḥāniyya*) 655
symbolic meaning of 203–4
of Umayyads 995
white 204–5
yellow/saffron 205–6
command (of God) 574, 623, 712, 1154
commander of the faithful 682
commanding right and forbidding wrong (*al-amr bi-l-ma'rūf wa-nahy 'an al-munkar*) 104, 252, 345, 360–61, 363–65, 559, 1250
commemoration 1270–71
commentaries 14, 833. *See also* exegeses; *tafsīr*
mystical 222 n.4, 246
on *Ṣaḥīḥ Muslim* 314
shurūḥ, of *ḥadīth* 937
traditional/orthodox 223–24
commerce 907, 1130
Committee for Union and Progress (İttihad ve Terakki Cemiyeti; Young Turks) 1223
common
people 584, 1146, 1155, 1196, 1207–8
sense 463
communal 767
division 331–32
eschatologies 767–68
communality 597
communication 106
communion (with God) 361–63
communism 1199, 1228–29, 1259
community(ies) 123, 757, 971, 974
of believers 769
ideal 1077
Islamic/Muslim 961, 1300
companions 76–77, 297, 302, 989
aṣḥāb 56, 541
of the cave/Seven Sleepers (*aṣḥāb al-kahf*) 433–34, 620 n.83
of Muḥammad 416, 1279
in paradise 297–98, 303, 305, 794 n.45, 986
compassion 838. *See also* mercy
composites (minerals, vegetables, animals) 507
compositions, assymetrical 982
compos mentis 739
concealment (*ghayba*) 606 n.7
conceptions, mental (*taṣawwur*) 494, 669
concubines 958. *See also* slaves
conscience 972, 1213
consciousness 432, 972, 1245–46, 1306
consensus (*ijmā'*) 825 n.37
consorts, in paradise 560. *See also* wives/spouses

conspiracy (theories) 1231 n.32, 1247, 1260–61
constellations 1083–84, 1088. *See also* astrology; astronomy/astronomers; planets; stars
contemplation 583
contingencies (*ittifāqiyyāt*) 515
contradictory (things) 667
conventions/devices 818
convents 777
convivencia 953, 967, 971
Corpus Coranicum 69
corruption 540, 760, 907, 912, 969–70, 1319
cosmogony 14, 100, 701
cosmographies 667 n.32, 934, 1042
cosmology 14, 19, 25, 34, 347, 422, 597, 656
 of Aristotle 1088
 creationist 650
 eight orbs (*aflāk*) of 357
 heliocentric 1094
 Islamic 692, 935–36
 Ismaʿili 652
 linear and cyclical 759
 mythological *sunna* 1226
 Near Eastern 356
 Neoplatonic emanative 451
 Ptolemaic 357
 Shiʿi 626, 635 n.172
 treatises 937
 Zoroastrian 761
cosmopolitanism 960, 974
cosmos 113, 548–49, 570, 572, 597, 757, 1227, 1242
 configuration/structure of 542, 547
 as geocentric 1088
 as unified whole 576
couches (in paradise) 17, 80, 156, 158–60, 185, 244, 562, 986–87. *See also* furnishings
 arīka, arāʾik 141, 233–35, 236–38
 sarīr, asirra, surūr 141, 226, 233, 235, 238
courage (*shajāʿa*) 352
covenant (*ʿahd, mithāq*) 94–95, 100, 109, 116, 121, 196
 day of 16, 111–12, 114–15, 117–18
 primordial 112–13, 718 n.37, 731, 945
craftsmen 261, 1072
creation 43, 78, 81–82, 87, 89, 117, 183, 231, 473–74, 652, 706, 720, 741, 937, 942, 1035, 1187, 1228, 1237
 act of 38, 78, 496, 502
 and Adam and Eve 278, 321, 869 n.37
 diversity of God's 203, 206
 ex nihilo 446, 450–51, 1236
 first and second 477, 744, 1232, 1234
 of humanity 49, 745
 myths 1083
 narrative in Quran 100
 new (*khalq jadīd*) 522, 650
 of paradise (and hell) 224 n.8, 278, 480, 836, 838, 872, 1004
 of Quran 207
 to reflect God's beauty 575
 types of 692
 wonders/marvels of 934, 936, 938, 943
 of world/heavens and earth 87, 224 n.8, 721, 871
creationists 1226, 1257 n.164
creeds 326, 371–72, 851
 and dogmatic literature (*ʿaqīda*) 192
 orthodox Shiʿi 273
 traditional Sunni 273, 423, 426
crisis
 of Islam 1290, 1295–96
 rhetoric of 1291–96, 1301
crusades/crusaders 19, 407–9, 895–97, 899, 907, 912, 965, 1012, 1167
culture 512 n.75, 899, 961, 1286
 local 1170
 material 105
 Western 95
Cumbok War 1171
cupolas 879. *See also* architecture; dome(s)
cups/vessels 255, 257, 260, 301, 1039
 beakers (sing. *ibrīq*) 260
 of crystal and gold/silver 252, 260–61
 tableware/dishes (in paradise) 18, 157, 159, 262
customary practices (*ʿādāt*) 1114 n.43
cycles 621, 736 n.9, 759
 Adamic 635 n.173
 of development of man 631
 of heavenly spheres 424
 of Ismaʿili history 685
 of prophecy 651, 653, 659, 724–25
 of reincarnation/successive lives 697, 744–46, 749
 of sacred history 628

daēnā/Daēnā 207
Dajjāl/Antichrist 997, 1041, 1207, 1247–49, 1252, 1260
  appearance of 764
  ḥadīth on 1229–30
  killing of (by Jesus) 1041
dajjālūn (imposters) 1206
damnation 120, 400, 411
damned 324–25, 401, 862, 1041, 1192, 1229
  descriptions of 858, 861, 864
  lives of, in hell 224
Daoists 267
dār (abode, dwelling, house) 837, 851
  dār/jannat al-khuld (eternal abode/garden) 103
  al-ḥaqīqa (of true reality) 530
  al-ḥayawān (of [true] life) 186 n.10
  al-jinān 186
  al-khuld (eternal) 56, 137, 658
  al-muqāma (eternal) 103, 137, 186 n.10
  al-qarār (of [true] dwelling) 497
  al-ṣafāʾ (of purity) 657, 659
  al-salām (of peace) 56, 64, 103, 137, 187
darkness 110, 144–45, 201, 570, 589
  and light 919
Darwinism 1226, 1251
daʿwa (Islamic religious call) 3, 657–59, 676, 679–81, 683
day of *a-last* 113, 115
dead 163–67, 169, 174, 749, 1010
  awakening of 67
  kingdom of 902
  shades of (*repaʾīm*) 763
  underworld of 1086
Dead Sea Scrolls 120, 123 n.102
deanthropomorphization (*tanzīh*) 249
death 3, 5, 7, 21, 32, 194, 337, 432, 479, 488, 519, 579, 590, 594, 744, 746, 779, 856, 873, 936, 945–47, 1024 n.57, 1152, 1189, 1191, 1194, 1214, 1313, 1319
  accounts/narratives of 182, 200
  after life in graves 746
  of blessed (people) 196
  classical Islamic notions of 1218
  corporeal/physical 423, 500, 521, 746, 749, 1268
  defining 743, 748
  dying (in the path of God) 162–63, 165, 168, 170–74, 176–77, 179, 267, 1162
  first (*al-mawta al-ūlā*) 747–49
  kinds of 197
  and life 14, 1164, 1279–80, 1310
  life/existence after 1, 39, 191, 429, 1196, 1204, 1218, 1223
  natural 170, 497–98
  pain of 1169, 1237
  and paradise virgins 276
  personified 208
  praise of 1280
  second 745, 766
  single 759
  small 1237
  and soul 198, 211, 591
  spiritual 747–49
  and statements in Quran 12, 432
  state of 428, 439
  as state of sleep 432
  while traveling 173
  of women 1269
debt (of martyrs) 172, 412
decay 337, 1087, 1240
  of human body 1204
deception (*shayd*) 703. *See also* falsehood; lying/liars
deconstruction 15
decorative (elements) 983, 1012, 1070. *See also* ornaments; patterns/designs
  asymmetrical 988
  green and manganese 985
  motifs 999
  on walls 983, 988, 992
  and writing 1033
decree (of God) 539, 545, 763, 966
deeds 120, 196, 398, 475, 851, 1239. *See also* good deeds
  bad/unjust 40, 854, 1196, 1243
  good and evil equal/balance out 737, 748
  record/book of 93, 946, 1208
defamation (*qadhf*) 483
deficiency 508
deities/gods 253, 761, 766, 1084–85
  false 745
  Mithra (Indo-Iranian) 185 n.9
  Roman 1089
delights 537, 671. *See also* joys
  of paradise 159, 184
democracy 1101
Demokrat Parti 1225

demonization 1123
demons 100, 438, 720, 722, 1041, 1043, 1117 n.56
Umm al-Layl (Mother of the Night) 438
denialists (*inkârcı*) 1231
deserts 149, 926–27
culture of 1300 n.22
descriptions of 136
designs. *See also* decorative (elements); motifs; ornaments; patterns/designs
vegetal 25, 981–84, 988, 995, 999–1000, 1005, 1033–34
despotism 329. *See also* authoritarianism
destiny 39, 42, 182, 211, 697, 1037, 1214. *See also* fate
acceptance of 417
eternal 484
in paradise or hell 479
destruction 100, 149, 1040
final 626
mass 1317
of paradise/heaven(s) 224 n.8, 232, 243, 245, 482, 971
of sinful communities 770
of the world/universal 114, 1197, 1208
determinism 1084
devils 429, 590, 617, 945, 1118. *See also* demons; *jinn*
dhāt (essence) 492
dhikr 121, 1019 n.35
blessing the Prophet 1018
remembrance of God 1018 n.31
dhimmīs 839
Dhū l-Qarnayn 922, 1209
dialectics 1217, 1305, 1308–9, 1311–12, 1315, 1317
of absence and presence 1307
of consciousness 1306
of desire 1305–6
of theology and philosophy 1296
dichotomies 1101
exoteric-esoteric (*ẓāhir-bāṭin*) 571
law/morality 1121–22
pre-modern/modern 1319
differentiation 1293, 1295, 1304
dimensions
of paradise 140 n.15, 866, 869–70, 874, 878, 880, 885
of throne (*ʿarsh*), of God 935
diminution 543, 1087
dīn (Islam; true religion) 207, 675
yawm al-dīn (doomsday) 100, 197
directions, four cardinal 1020
disbelievers/disbelief 13, 36, 119, 184, 627, 1190. *See also* unbelievers
discrimination 852, 1293
Disneyland 1075
disobedience 202, 472, 570, 666
to God 471–72
to one's parents 839
dissuasion (*tarhīb*) 824
distinction (*mubāyanat*) 666
diversity 953–54, 960, 968, 974
divine/divinity 14, 253 n.11, 596, 682, 779, 910, 919, 1084, 1312–13
archetypes (*al-muthul al-ilāhiyya*) 496
colors 652
essence 456, 711
favor 408
form (*ṣūrat-i khudāʾī*) 703
forms (*nashʾa al-ṣuwar al-malakūtiyya*) 657, 659
locus of 685–86
presence 70, 100, 104, 111, 163–65, 171, 178, 211, 426, 496, 571, 594
presence (*sakīna*) 16, 94–95, 100, 104, 106, 109, 113–14, 116–19, 123
secrets (*al-asrār al-ilāhiyya*) 938
shapes (*al-ashbāḥ al-rabbāniyya*) 529
source 97
tree (*al-shajara al-ilāhiyya*) 505
will 177, 1153 (*See also* will, of God/Lord)
world of 575, 905
doctrine
disagreements of 331
rules of 1110, 1122
dogs 1103
black 1115–19, 1121
classes of 1110, 1112, 1117
domesticity of 1108
as eschatological threat 1116–17
essence of 1107, 1111 n.31, 1114
impurity of 1104–5, 1109
killing of 1105, 1110–11, 1113, 1117, 1121
ownership of 1117–18
and water tradition/debate 1104, 1113, 1121
dome(s) 1011. *See also* architecture/ architectural (features); *qubba* (pl. *qibāb*)
covered in precious metals 1002–3

domination 548, 1301
dominion (*mulk*), of God 225–26, 228, 243, 245, 248
doomsday 481, 1241
  yawm al-dīn 100, 197
doubt 591
dreams 115, 428, 435, 457, 492, 671, 709–10, 730, 945, 1191, 1228
  interpretation of (*taʿbīr*) 437, 457 n.49, 710
  of Muḥammad 189, 437 n.25
  nightmare (figure) 438
drinks 157, 166, 168, 184–85, 239, 259, 264, 299, 666, 834–35, 985, 1149, 1154, 1167. *See also* milk (in paradise); wine
  four types of 58–59, 62
  in hell 947
  intoxicating 854–55
  non-intoxicating 301, 305
  in paradise/heaven 251–52, 255, 261, 266–68, 312, 319, 328
Druzes 736 n.9
dualism 21, 569, 576, 1136, 1216–17
dualities 57, 78, 82, 94, 105, 109, 121, 125, 576, 683, 758, 1317–18
dunyā (this world) 117, 343, 529–30, 555, 562, 667, 851, 1102–3, 1121–22
durūd (invocation of God's blessing on Muḥammad) 1018 n.31
Dutch East Indies Company 1148
dystopias 764

Earth 590, 697–98, 712, 1000, 1083, 1085, 1087–88, 1226, 1233, 1234
  -centered cosmos, of Aristotle 1097 fig.50.1
  curvature of 1092
  rotation of 1240
earthquakes 1240
earth(s) 530, 760–62, 991, 1213
  as element 456, 473, 667 n.32, 1087
  as element of Adam and Eve 717–18
  heart of (*bāṭin al-arḍ*) 973
  as locus of manifestation 718
  new life for 625–26
  purity of 1104
  seven 228, 945, 1086
East 107, 917, 968
eclipses 803, 1251
ecstasy 115, 595
Eden (*ʿadn*) 103, 137, 187, 240–41, 244, 793, 798, 866–67, 869 n.34, 927, 958, 966, 1068. *See also* expulsion, of Adam (and Eve)
  gardens of 36, 85, 156–57, 186 n.11, 187, 239–40, 357, 431–32, 794, 1035 n.7, 1159
  loss of 953
education 15, 958–59, 964, 967
effusions (*ifāḍāt*) 656
egalitarianism 331, 333, 760
ego 1197–98, 1214
  lower, passion of 728
Egyptian tradition (ancient) 200–1, 768
elderly 1210
elements 82, 507
  arkān 490
  four (earth, water, air, fire) 456, 473, 667 n.32, 717, 1087
  heat, cold, dry, moist 321
elites 1070–71
  spiritual 589
Elysium, clay of 497
emanation 452, 456–57, 465, 473, 502, 507, 521, 650, 656, 703, 705, 712
emancipation 1298
  of women 1314
emigration (*hijra*) 118, 178, 810
  emigrants (*muhājirūn*) 163, 178–79
  narratives 137 n.5
enantiodromia 94, 100, 104, 121
encomiums 1274, 1275 n.14, 1276, 1278–83, 1285–86
end 101, 1229, 1309
  of days 122, 1137
  of life 1208, 1241–42
  of time 12, 43, 181, 424, 605, 679, 760–61, 763, 765, 771
  of the world 6, 14, 95, 102, 114, 312, 607, 762, 873, 937, 942, 1034, 1042, 1240, 1247, 1261
enlightenment 22, 591, 1127, 1316, 1318
  secular 1293–94
entertainment 101, 1163
  of companions of the left (*aṣḥāb al-mash'ama*) 265
environmental disaster/global warming 762, 765, 768, 1240–41

ephemeral
  vs. eternal 778
  world 773–75, 779
Ephesus, Christian story of 433–34
Epicureans 898
epigraphy
  Islamic 1015 n.23
  North Semitic 1133
  types of 1016
episcopate 776
epistemology 626, 1293, 1296, 1318
  transcendent 1316
equality 811, 907, 996
erotic
  terms (in Quran) 153
  themes 150, 153
eroticism 85, 87, 141, 323
eschatology(ies)/eschatological 1, 3–7, 20, 89, 95, 101, 120, 123, 182, 194, 253, 345–46, 366, 423, 449, 471, 473–74, 536, 579, 597, 626, 664, 859, 861, 863, 885, 981, 1109, 1136–37, 1228–29, 1237–38, 1259, 1297
  amoral 765–66
  defined 13, 23
  events 72
  Ḥurūfī and Ismaʿili 22
  of Ibn Sīnā 455, 458–59
  individual 13–14, 767
  Islamic 3, 663 n.10, 693, 803, 902, 1199, 1218, 1316
  linear 760
  literature 17, 24, 365, 609, 817, 860, 862, 865, 873, 883, 934, 1249, 1261
  Mesopotamian 769
  modern Islamic 1222
  of Mullā Ṣadrā 501
  narratives 191, 341, 344, 1218
  other-worldly 760, 762–63, 767, 770
  in the Quran 21, 67, 566, 620, 649, 782, 858, 865, 1240
  realized 770, 803
  schools of 663
  and science 27
  secular 760, 765
  serial 758, 768
  symbols/symbolism 105, 676–77, 679, 683–85
  this-worldly 760, 762–63, 771
  threats 1118, 1120–21
  Twelver Shiʿi 606, 633–34
  types of 14, 757–58, 760, 764, 766, 768, 771
  works/texts/treatises of 295, 303–4, 566 n.2, 870, 936–37, 988, 1207
eschaton 3–4, 6, 9, 12, 614, 616, 629, 633 n.165, 664
esoteric/hidden
  bāṭin 589, 628, 676–77
  truths (*ḥaqāʾiq*) 629
esotericism 633
essence
  dhāt 492, 520
  of [divine] Oneness/God 236, 704–5
  doctrine of 456
  jawhar 570
  of Truth 905
essentialism 502
estimative imagination (*wahm*) 666, 669
eternal
  life (in paradise) 779
  paradise as 592, 1004
  youths 158, 712, 728
eternity/eternality 39, 41, 43, 141–42, 235, 331, 333, 342, 1232
  of God 227
  of hell 264, 371, 379–80, 396, 940, 1208
  of paradise/heaven 243, 319, 328, 336, 371, 380
  words for (*baqāʾ, al-taʾbīd, al-khulūd, abad/ebed, azal*) 235, 851, 1198
ether 1087, 1234, 1255–56
ethics 15, 36, 351–52, 427, 448–49, 597, 663, 855, 1218
  of the Bible 780
  Muslim religious 361
ethnicity/race 953, 965, 1169
evil 98, 110, 124, 429, 483, 542–43, 761, 1117 n.56
  deeds 46
  locus of 1118–19
evildoers 72, 74, 1243
evolution 499, 511–12, 1197, 1226, 1232 n.38, 1247, 1255, 1257
  Darwinian 1189
  of lower forms 727
  Quran on 1194
exegeses (*tafsīr*) 25, 68, 103, 162, 249, 311, 372, 388, 787, 831, 834, 842, 1202. *See also* commentaries

classical/traditional 221, 223, 242, 244, 403, 832
fundamentalist 288
Isma'ili 676
and lexical explanations 377
Meccan 395
modern 223
mystical 221, 223
rationalist 17, 221, 223
scientific (*'ilmī*) 1227–28
and *ṣifat al-janna* works 829
spiritual/metaphorical (*ta'wīl*) 22, 242, 457 n.49, 510, 516, 572, 612, 659, 666, 678–79, 681, 685, 708, 710
exegetes 51, 108, 154, 162–63, 165, 168, 171–72, 176–77, 188, 221, 246, 248, 256, 273, 277–80, 287, 350, 373–74, 380, 388, 390, 399, 401–2, 563, 622, 677, 740 n.25, 743 n.36, 745, 747, 749, 871, 956, 987, 1111, 1144, 1146
Christian 798
exile 271, 954, 956
existence/being (*wujūd*) 115, 456, 487, 491, 542, 547
chain of 514
first/earthly 468
of infinite quantity 446
Oneness of 576
of paradise and hellfire 468, 481, 485
primacy/fundamentality of (*aṣālat al-*) 488, 535
second 468
seven planes of 206
existential
flux (*al-fayḍ al-wujūdī*) 503
ipseity (*al-huwiyya al-wujūdiyya*) 502 n.47
existentialism 488, 499
existent(s)
vs. non-existent 668
states of 514
exoteric/apparent (*ẓāhir*) 676–77
expulsion, of Adam (and Eve), from garden 36–37, 70, 141, 480, 966, 969, 1035–36, 1048 fig.47.2
extravagance 1002

fables 899. *See also* anecdotes; parables; story(ies)
fabricators (*waḍḍāʿūn*) 939
facial features 713–15
fairness 303. *See also* equality; justice/equity
fairy tales 432–33, 435
faith 1, 39, 41, 181, 191, 200, 333, 429, 562, 570, 582, 776, 843, 938, 1206
articles of 210
definition of 838
and good works 280
īmān 178, 188, 398, 472, 837
sincerity/fidelity of 176, 205
verbal confession of (*bi-l-qawl*) 837
fall (of Adam/humankind) 136, 186, 956, 1035–37. *See also* expulsion
Ḥurūfī perspective of 717–20
falsehood 160, 477, 667–68, 670, 672
family 961, 967
holy (*panj tan*) [i.e., Muḥammad, Fāṭima, 'Alī, Ḥasan, Ḥusayn] 1060
fanatics/fanaticism 954–55, 962–63, 1148, 1277. *See also* fundamentalism
fantasies 968
of heaven/paradise 1146, 1149
sexual 1163
faqīh, pl. *fuqahā'* [jurists] 365, 454, 1022
fascism 1310
fasting 26, 198, 207, 364
fate 87, 458, 566–67, 757, 771, 852. *See also* destiny
of believers, *vs.* unbelievers 377–78
Fatimid(s) 25, 683, 981, 996–97, 999–1000, 1005
doctrines 659
hierarchy of 678–79
period 22, 650 n.4, 651, 654 n.22, 676, 1011
and rivalry with Umayyads 1000–1001
ta'wīl of 685 n.35
fatwās 32, 956, 1203
fawz ([great] triumph) 65
fear 590–91
of God 202, 206, 238, 773–74, 1215
of hell 267, 282, 286, 596
and hope 149
"sacred" 145–46
felicity 546. *See also* happiness; joy
femaleness 323–24, 332
feminine/femininity 322, 330, 333, 337, 1285, 1299

fertility 1274
figurative
art/painting 1071, 1077
representations of paradise 26
figures (of animals) 1033
films 1077
firdaws 56, 104, 137, 187, 282, 852, 866–67, 871, 925, 1281–82
al-akbar (greatest) 507
as closest to throne 1244
gardens, of paradise 244, 990
as highest paradise 103, 121, 592
jannāt al- (gardens of) 56, 239–40
fire 36, 166, 530, 666. *See also* hell/hellfire
crushing (*ḥuṭama*) 374–75, 378 n.28
depictions of 264
as element 456, 473, 667 n.32, 717–18, 1087
ḥadīth on 540–41, 1229
nār 56, 373–74
people/inhabitants of 35, 334, 399, 412, 540–41, 719
raging (*saʿīr*) 374, 411
scorching (*saqar*) 374
firmament
layers (*ṭabaqa, daraja, aflāk*) of 357
seven (*sabʿ shidād*) 347
fiṭra (innate, natural disposition) 32, 497, 539–40, 546, 724
fixity (*thubūt*) 548
flood 761, 1251
flowers 153, 982, 984, 988, 990
folklore 19, 1117 n.56, 1161, 1215, 1217
and image of land/people 1071
intentional (i.e., propaganda) 1057
food(s) 145, 237, 239, 244, 420, 507, 562, 665, 834–35, 985, 1149–50, 1154, 1167. *See also* fruits
eternal (*akluhum dāʾim*) 481–82
in hell 947
kinds of (dates, olives, pomegranates) 263
necessity for 726–27
in paradise/heaven 18, 59, 166, 185, 251–52, 263–64, 266–68, 298, 312, 319, 328, 807, 873, 881
unlawful 853
forbearance 202
force 852. *See also* violence
foreignness (*ajnabiyya*) 485
foremost (*sābiqūn*) 319
forgiveness 53, 104, 851, 989, 1021, 1150
from God 172–74, 176, 536, 838 n.100, 1019
forms (*ṣūra, ṣuwar*) 456, 478, 529, 689, 705, 726, 1191, 1239
of Adam (on form of God) 711 n.23
and bodies 731
of female body 714
imaginal (*khayāliyya; mithāliyya*) 492, 494, 503
perfect, i.e., its entelechy (*kamāliyya*) 492
primary (length, breadth, depth) 503
psychic (*nafsāniyya*) 510
spiritual 463, 508, 655
fortress 980–81. *See also* castles; palaces
fortunate/saved 401. *See also* blessed (people)
fountain(s)/springs 76, 80, 139, 144, 156, 158, 160, 260, 298, 438, 86-6, 960, 990, 995, 1058, 1298. *See also* rivers (in paradise); water
ʿayn, ʿuyūn 138, 143, 255
Kawthar 927, 1192
Salsabīl 104, 159, 239, 257, 265, 301
Tasnīm 256–57, 265
Zanjabīl 257
fragmentation 962
fragrances 263. *See also* aromatics
amber 303, 305, 562
of paradise 839
rayḥān 252, 256
frame story 924–25
Franks 408, 409, 411, 413, 418, 895
Free Aceh Movement (Gerakan Aceh Merdeka, GAM) 1171
freedom 454, 810–11, 907, 959, 1200, 1287, 1298, 1314
of expression 1071
fighters 1270
from hell 851
free people, *vs.* slaves 324
free will 373 n.9, 452, 465, 776, 904, 907, 913, 919
Fridays 184, 207, 318, 328
friends (of God) 1156, 1238. *See also* saints; *walāya*

fruit(s) 59, 80–81, 139–42, 147, 155–59, 175, 252, 430, 656–57, 703, 727, 786, 794–98, 802, 881, 926, 982, 986–87, 990–91, 1167, 1195
divine (*malakūtiyya*) 164–66, 657, 659
in dreams 438
grapes/grapevines 785–86, 799–800, 802, 926, 990
in heaven/paradise 167–68, 263, 276, 988
pomegranates 80, 158, 987, 995
of this world 990
trees 995
fundamentalism/fundamentalists 489, 971, 974
Hindu 968–69
Islamic 1297 n.15, 1299
funerals 1270
funerary (matters)
chambers 1022
monuments/architecture 1011–12, 1017
practices 171, 176
furnishings (in paradise) 76–77, 82–83, 234, 561. *See also* couches (in paradise); textiles
cushions 82–83, 185, 993
future 774–78, 1217, 1278, 1281
lives 759
-oriented 758, 770

Gabriel (archangel) 100, 189, 274–75, 378 n.28, 435, 724, 794 n.45, 862, 997, 1020, 1110–11
and Muḥammad enter paradise 877–81, 883
gardens (of paradise) 13, 16, 17, 40, 43, 63, 74, 139, 142, 153, 155, 160, 205, 224, 267, 302–3, 540, 703, 883, 985, 1195, 1213, 1298. *See also janna;* paradise
of abode/refuge/rest (*jannat al-maʾwā*) 56, 187, 414, 417
admission to 1272–74
beauty of 304
of bliss/comfort/happiness (*jannat al-naʿīm*) 52, 56, 61, 187, 414, 437
bustān; ḥadīqa 137, 237–39, 656
descriptions of 25, 190, 295–97, 348
of eternity (*jannat al-khuld*) 185, 187
females of 1146
firdaws 239–40, 244, 990
with flowing streams 51, 53–54, 60, 63, 65, 866, 986
ḥadīths on 345–47, 803
janna 4, 25, 136, 194, 239, 413–14, 764, 866, 926, 1268
names of 187
number of (two, four, or seven) 80–81, 158, 185 n.9, 238, 354, 986–87, 994, 1005
parameters/dimensions of 301
people/inhabitants of 325, 334, 548
physical (*al-janna al-jismāniyya*) 287
garden(s) 1039
aesthetics of 296–97
chahār bāgh (Persian fourfold) 261, 355
earthly 137 n.6, 141–42, 153, 1040
of Eden 36, 85, 156–57, 186 n.11, 187, 239–40, 357, 431–32, 794, 1035 n.7, 1159
of al-Ḥamrāʾ (Alhambra) Palace 953
lost primordial 69–70
as metaphor/motif 17, 187 n.14
upper and lower, in Madīnat al-Zahrāʾ, 980, 983, 1005
garments. *See* clothing/garments
gates
to the *ḥaram al-sharīf* 359
to hell (*jahannam*) 55, 202, 351, 374–75, 947
to hell, number of 346, 354, 373–74, 713–14, 868 n.29
gates (*bāb*, pl. *abwāb*) [of paradise] 19, 55, 140 n.15, 193 n.29, 274, 357–58, 560, 710, 793, 822–23, 827 n.42, 834 n.77, 836, 865–66, 873, 876, 878–80, 926
of charity (*al-ṣadaqa/mutaṣaddiqīn*) 346–47
ḥadīth on 843 n.122
of *jihād* (*al-jihād/al-mujāhidīn*) 346–47, 839
of the lush [garden?] (*al-rayyān*) 346
major (*bāb al-abwāb*) 502–3
number of (four, seven, eight) 185, 344–45, 348, 351 n.45, 353–55, 359, 361, 713, 867–68
of prayer (*al-ṣalāt/al-muṣallīn*) 346–47
of repentance (*al-tawba*) 608 n.14
of *shahāda* 364 n.103

gates (*bāb*, pl. *abwāb*) [of paradise] (cont.)
of those who seek (*al-ṭālibīn*), those who perform hijra (*al-muhājirīn*), those who keep connections (*al-wāṣilīn*), those who fast (*al-ṣā'imīn*) 347
gathering (*ḥashr*) 626
general, and specific (*al-ḥashr al-ʿāmm/al-khāṣṣ*) 634 n.171
place (*maḥshar*) 1043
Gehanna. *See* fire; hell
gems/jewels/precious metals 140–41, 156, 184, 417, 1001, 1038
bracelets, gold and silver 59, 238 n.43, 239 n.46, 261
corals, rubies, emeralds, chyrsolite, sapphires 61, 80, 83, 158, 296, 561–62, 712, 882, 990, 1001
pearls 61, 159, 238 n.43, 239 n.46, 279, 295, 299, 300–302, 305, 561, 703, 835, 868, 882, 982, 992
gender/gendered 18, 320–21, 323, 852, 1116 n.51, 1270, 1291, 1295, 1299 n.21
angels, as male 402
body(ies) 312, 314, 320, 324, 331, 337
equality 959
inequality 1299
Islamic subject 1295–96
martyrdom 1270
politics 1291, 1312
and religion 1301 n.25
social and spatial pattern 318
space 83
studies 15
vision 555–56
generation 489, 1087, 1319
and corruption 454, 495–96, 498, 656
generous/generosity 82
of God 164
people (*askhiyā'*) 345, 360, 364
genitals 558. *See also* sexuality
genre(s) 101, 275 n.27, 313 n.6, 818–19, 863, 1073–74
maqāma 263–64
narrative, tale, story (*kisah*, Ar. *qiṣṣa*) 1153
ṣifat al-janna 819, 821, 840–42, 844–45
of warning, reminding (*tambéh*, Ar. *tanbīh*) 1148
on *ziyārat al-qubūr* 1010
geography
divine 941
of paradise/hell 105, 185, 304, 870
of unseen 209
Georg August University 1129
German Empire 1133
ghayb (unseen/unknown) 55, 65, 104, 563
Ghaznavid sultans 580, 590
ghilmān (slave boys) 18, 297–99, 301, 305
ghulāt (sects) 22, 736, 752
girls. *See also* maidens/girls; virgins
kāʿib, pl., *kawāʿib* 60
maidservants (*jāriya, jāriyatun, jawārin*) 60–61, 298, 304–5, 828
globalization 1074, 1240
glorification 1281, 1284
glory 106–9, 117–18, 121, 798, 905
divine/of God 111, 248
motif 94–95, 100, 105–6, 118, 121
gnosis/gnostic(s) 286, 356 n.76, 489, 512, 909, 1134, 1136
approach 272, 277
intuitive knowledge (*maʿrifat*) 585, 668
Gnosticism, Near Eastern 1134–35
goblets. *See* cups/vessels
God 51, 123, 183, 200–1, 240, 243, 422, 437, 446 n.7, 571, 590, 620 n.86, 675, 686, 728, 1019 n.35, 1201–2, 1243, 1256, 1294. *See also* throne (of God)
acts of 453, 476
as All-Seeing (*al-Baṣīr*) 558–59
beauty (*jamāl*) of 301, 538, 546–47, 569, 1192
as Creator 453, 656
encounter/meeting with 703, 884
existence of 589, 1187, 1196, 1209
face of 39–40, 232 n.31, 274, 283, 286, 415, 480–82, 562–63, 570, 576, 592, 693
feet/hands of 232 n.31, 477, 510, 547–49
grace/forgiveness of 174, 710, 838 n.100
greatness/glory (*ʿaẓama*) of 225, 228, 245
as Just (*al-ʿĀdil*) 1211
majesty (*jalāl*) of 304, 538, 546, 569, 802, 934, 1192
mercy of 235, 547–49, 574, 940
names of 100, 235, 510, 516, 531, 537–38, 540, 548, 558, 703–4, 708 n.20, 1210–11, 1219

as necessarily existing (*al-wājib al-wujūd*) 468–69
as omnipotent 474, 991
pleasure (*riḍwān*) of 1213
power of 145, 147, 242, 248, 477
presence of 115, 420, 477, 589, 671–72
proximity/those nearest to (*muqarrabūn*) 252, 657
revelations of 837
taught Adam the names 705, 708, 710–12, 717, 720
throne as manifestation of 242
union with 902
unity of 177, 579, 592, 595, 597–98, 666, 730–31, 1196, 1209
vision of/beholding 224 n.8, 381, 561, 567–68, 577, 712, 714, 863, 905, 1189, 1195
in the way of God (*fī sabīl Allāh*) 166, 178–79, 1270
as Wise (*al-Ḥakīm*) 1211
wrath of 540, 542, 547

God-fearing (*muttaqūn*) 54, 72, 254, 345, 360, 362, 394, 480, 801. *See also* piety/pious
abode of (*dār al-*) 103

godliness, human faculty of 1193

gods. *See* deities/gods

Gog and Magog 764, 923, 1209, 1230

Golden Chain of Being 654

gold/silver 303, 305, 345, 562, 835, 992, 1038
in paradise/garden 295–97, 867–68, 882, 993, 1001, 1195

gōmpeuni 1157

good 98, 124, 542, 761, 765
vs. evil 36, 121, 268, 574, 576, 670, 761, 964, 1044, 1136, 1187, 1216, 1227, 1240

good deeds 39–42, 45, 49–54, 56, 65, 157, 267, 280, 282, 345, 420, 853–54, 1194, 1196, 1243–44
balance out bad deeds 399–400
doers of (*muḥsinūn*) 202

Gospels. *See* Bible

grace (of God) 1035, 1198
luṭf or *niʿma* 280–81
nimetler of the True Lord (*Cenab-i Hakk*) 1233

Granada, fall of (897/1494) 953, 957

grapes/grapevines 785–86, 799–800, 802, 926, 990
syrup (*ṭilāʾ*) 855

graves 7, 165–66, 171, 286, 313, 315, 471, 492, 625, 946
afterlife/second life in 745–46, 1215, 1238
life in (*barzakh*) 10, 14, 22
praying at 1239
punishment in 199, 1190–91, 1203, 1238
questioning of angels in 424, 1189, 1203, 1209, 1215, 1238
reward/pleasure in 169, 199, 1191
of saints 1023
torments/horrors of 38, 170, 324, 420, 572, 770, 817 n.1, 842, 1204
visiting (*ziyārat al-qubūr*) 1010, 1238
World of (*ʿālam al-barzakh*) 1191

Greco-Roman
culture 74
eschatological schemes 769
writings 101

greed 907

Greek(s) 258, 260–61, 895, 1083, 1086, 1091, 1093
apokalypsis 89
language 897
mythology 968
philosophy/philosophers 351, 664, 1087
sources 917
thought 891, 1311
traditions (ancient) 253
wisdom of 583

growth 1087
and personal development (*kişisel gelişim*) 1235

guidance 35, 40, 44, 625, 724, 775, 1192
of God (*hidāya, hudā, rushd*) 280, 352
prophetic 503, 1202

guilds 580

guilt/shame 779, 1168, 1213, 1287

Gulf War (1991) 1074

guzīdagān 654

ḥadd (degree/rank) 658

Hades 664, 747, 763, 968

ḥadīth 3, 14, 17–19, 181–82, 188, 196, 208, 224 n.7, 247–48, 277, 295, 380, 398, 555–57, 585, 596, 634, 693, 749, 751, 820, 827, 833, 839, 842, 845, 878, 885, 939, 1110, 1114, 1122, 1148, 1155, 1204, 1226
accepted (*ḥasan*) 821, 824, 841–42
aṣḥāb al-ḥadīth; ahl al-ḥadīth 372, 376 n.17

ḥadīth (cont.)
canonical 822, 824–25, 828, 861, 864
categories/classifications of 285, 821–23, 845–46, 1215
collections 862–63, 934–37, 988, 1240
criticism 832, 832 n.74
forged/false 824, 832 n.74, 833 n.75, 872
literature 119, 862, 865, 870–71, 875–76, 883, 1018, 1083, 1159
metaphorical readings of 328
scholars/scholarship 314 n.12, 824, 863
sciences of 820–21, 832 n.74
in *ṣifat al-janna* works 819, 834
social undertones 838
sound (*ṣaḥīḥ*) 821, 824–25
and theological issues 872
transmitters/transmission 820, 823, 825
weak (*ḍaʿīf*) 821–22, 824, 825 n.35, 841–42, 845, 1206, 1215
on *wurūd* 395
ḥajala; ḥijāl (canopy, alcove) 233–35
ḥājj. See pilgrimage
haloes 1033, 1042–43, 1062
on figure of Muḥammad 1038, 1058
Hamas 1274
Ḥanafīs 371 n.1, 581, 820 n.13, 1103 n.13. *See also madhāhib*
Ḥanbalīs 283, 371 n.1, 373 n.9, 819, 837, 933. *See also madhāhib*
handicrafts 1077
ḥanīfiyya (pre-Islamic Arabian monotheism) 853. *See also* monotheism
happiness 352, 905–6, 1073, 1202, 1319. *See also* delights; joys
everlasting 14
pursuit of celestial 454–55
temporal 898–99
ḥaqq 100, 117, 122
ḥāqqa (reality [of the hour]) 183
ḥaram al-sharīf 357–59, 1014
harmony 332, 548, 840, 1016–17, 1073, 1259
hatred 852
ḥayrat (astonishment, perplexity) 585, 587, 591
heart 594
purity of 268
role of 286
and soul, renunciation of (*istighnā'*) 585
heavenly
beings 1062
region 1087
sphere(s) 424, 729
heaven(s) 5, 21–22, 100, 252, 530, 549, 626, 710, 775, 1036, 1083, 1085–86, 1177–78. *See also* gardens (of paradise); paradise
abode in 763
in actu, vs. in potentia 649, 658
as anthropocentric 283–85
configuration of 1090, 1095
delights of 1148
destruction of 232, 243
and earth 225–29, 433, 451
earthly fantasy of 1149
eighth 711–12, 1176
gates of 274 (*See also* gates (*bāb*, pl. *abwāb*))
God-centered 288
and hell 266, 585 n.36, 1166
idea/concept of 1084, 1219
inhabitants/dwellers of 251, 253
light of 569
Quranic references to 223–24
rolled up/folded in God's right hand 232 n.31, 510, 548
seven 26, 185, 196, 198, 228–29, 274, 296, 347–49, 711, 861, 904, 973 n.80, 1083, 1086
split (on day of resurrection) 243
Hebrews 138, 1131
heedless 760
heights (*al-aʿrāf*), between heaven and hell 398, 400–401, 834 n.76, 1192
limbo of 737, 947
people of (*aṣḥāb al-*) 399–402, 413
hell/hellfire (*al-nār, jahannam, al-jaḥīm, laẓā*) 4–5, 7, 13–14, 20–22, 32, 39, 63, 73, 100, 103–5, 120, 123, 190, 197, 199, 229, 312–13, 315, 343–44, 377, 437, 468, 476–77, 549, 572, 626, 664–65, 669–70, 676, 696, 702, 763–64, 775, 842, 853, 902, 911, 936, 947, 1043, 1057, 1212, 1218, 1234, 1255–56. *See also* hell/hellfire
absolute (*dūzakh-i muṭlaq*) 672
Baghdad as 810
bridge over 381
crushing fire (*ḥuṭama*) 374–75, 378 n.28

description of 75–76, 144 n.21, 185, 201, 210, 409–11, 420, 595, 861, 871, 884, 1021
entry into 184
eternality of 264, 379–80, 396, 940, 1205, 1208
eternity of 371, 534–37, 1198
existence of 181, 940
exit from/getting out of 378–80, 382, 385–87, 392
fear of 267, 282
as female body 329
fuel for 393
gates of 55, 202, 346, 351, 354, 373–75, 713–14, 868 n.29, 947
images/motifs of 74, 420, 1039–40, 1233
journey to 251
levels of 852
Muḥammad's vision of/visit to 189, 859, 863, 875, 884, 1021 n.42
Muslim sinners in 388
people/inhabitants of 35, 156 n.42, 325, 376, 380, 389, 393–94, 400, 404, 548, 666, 703, 995 n.51, 1206
as pleasurable 541
punishment/torments in 34, 49, 324, 342, 397, 408, 415, 539, 831, 1213, 1239
as purgative 371, 380, 399
Quranic references to 223–24, 671
real 669, 671–72
saved from 413
seven 185, 375, 598
sinners/wicked in 67, 193
Small (*Cehennem-i Suğrâ*), and Great 1228–29
as temporary 19, 371–73, 380–81, 383, 385–86, 389, 392, 396–98, 403–4, 411, 534
women as denizens of 334
words for 374, 852

hereafter 4, 12, 34, 117, 174, 194, 324, 343, 447, 455, 458, 489, 664, 696, 702, 1189, 1196, 1211, 1222, 1297, 1316
ākhira 627, 667, 852, 1102–3, 1121–22
Ashʿarī understanding of 20
created eternally 1214
descriptions of 208, 271, 1198
existence of 1212
fear of 286
ishrāqī concept of 501
pleasurable life in 1150
representation of 1034
vision of 1057, 1063

heresiography 8
heresy 126, 900
heretics 590, 914
zanādiqa 855–56, 1207
heritage (*turāth*) 1071
hermeneutics 8, 800, 1313
hermeticism 1258
heroes 954, 961, 969–70, 973–74, 1041, 1161, 1164, 1168–69, 1217, 1270, 1279, 1286
heroism 67, 1214, 1272
heterotopia (Foucault's concept of) 312–13
hierarchy 298, 331, 570, 987
of angels 773
Ismaʿili 679
in paradise 991
of paradise 282, 579, 1244 n.93
sacrosanct (*ḥudūd-i qudsī*) 670
Hindi (language) 830
Hindus/Hinduism 740, 743, 759–60, 763, 956 n.13
historians (*al-muʾarrikhūn*) 939
historiography 14, 942
history 15, 89, 121, 937, 966, 1068, 1077–78, 1129, 1214, 1316
as cosmic 943
as cyclical/linear 628, 635, 685
of Granada 974
Indian 972
Islamic 1131
Ismaʿili 676
of Israel 1130–31
as progress 1291
regional 1170
sacred 681, 684
transformation/transcendence of 196–97
universal 942
holy land (*al-arḍ al-muqaddasa*) 189
Holy Spirit 686
holy war 1150, 1153–54, 1168, 1175, 1177. *See also jihād*; wars
against Dutch 1155
martyrs and tropes on 1172
merits of 1168

holy warriors 1163–64. *See also mujāhid, mujāhidūn*
homeland/nation 1270
homosexuality 1248, 1252
honey 58–59, 140, 254, 261, 264, 577, 665, 703, 795, 855, 866, 990, 1039, 1195, 1285. *See also* food(s)
honor 454, 1279, 1286–87, 1299 n.21
hope 96
  for paradise 267, 282, 593, 596
  as profane 145–46
horizons (*ufuq*) 503
horn (*ṣūr*) 529, 680. *See also* trumpet
hospices 777
hospital (*māristān*) 1012–13, 1024
hour (*al-sāʿa*) 4, 7, 12, 14, 100, 102, 114, 122, 183, 194, 196, 199, 605, 613–14, 617, 631, 937, 1212, 1318
  and appearance of *qāʾim* 605 n.3, 615
  one who establishes (*muqīm al-*) 616 n.67
house, oft-frequented (*bayt al-maʿmūr*) 710
Hūd, people of 138
al-Ḥudaybiya, oath-taking at (6/628) 118
ḥujjas 515–16, 679–80, 682–83
human 337
  agency 760
  -animal (*bashar*) soul 692
  appetites/irascibility 448
  body/bodiliness 258, 722–23, 725, 801
  constitution (*nashʾa*) 540
  existence, poles of 775
  face 706, 717, 722–23, 725
  form 22, 705–6, 727
  form/body, and manifestation of divine Word 710–11, 713, 724, 726, 730
  as mortal (*insān basharī*) 496
humanism 37
humanists 1137
humanity/humans 14, 44, 62, 80, 83, 120, 143 n.19, 147, 153, 185, 190, 230, 302, 321, 402, 452–53, 463, 490 n.17, 491, 507, 514–15, 531, 540, 670, 692–93, 714, 737 n.15, 742, 768, 776–77, 779, 796, 808, 969, 1033, 1077, 1209, 1236–37
  abode of 1035
  ascension to heaven 900
  Banū Ādam 112, 400
  and cycles of development/growth 499, 631
  duties of 39
  earthly 335
  existence of 36, 271, 572, 1217
  fall of 186, 1037 (*See also* expulsion)
  intellectual (or noetic, *ʿaqlī*) 495–96
  Muḥammad as master of 1019
  in need of guidance 724
  in perfection 512
  psychic (*nafsānī*) 495–96
  simple-minded 478–79, 1193
  single human mortals (*afrād al-bashar*) 496–97
  unity of 112, 726
humors 457
  four (blood, phlegm, yellow bile, black bile) 1190
ḥūr, ḥūr ʿīn (*ḥawrāʾ*, pl. *aḥwar*) (wide-eyed maidens) 18, 61, 83 n.45, 185 n.8, 297–99, 300, 302–5, 561, 783, 801, 852, 1269, 1273–74, 1285
  ḥawrāʾ ʿaynāʾ, 278
  ḥ-w-r 297
ḥūrīs 18, 32, 80, 83, 105, 147, 151, 153, 159, 281–83, 319 n.38, 323, 333–34, 336–37, 342, 577, 712, 714, 716, 785–86, 789–790, 800, 828, 879–81, 986, 1039, 1161, 1168, 1176–77, 1246, 1297, 1298
  buying/acquiring of 280
  as celestial bodies 287
  as companions 1144
  descriptions of 285, 286–87, 878 n.67
  faces of 728
  interpretation of 278
  in the Quran 787
  reality of 286
  as reward for pious 277–78
  seventy 1159, 1163–64
Ḥurūfīs 126
  definition of paradise 709, 712
  doctrines of 22, 701, 703, 705, 729
  texts of 706
hybridity 954, 960, 973–74
hymnody 782 n.7, 790
hyperbology 28, 1294, 1303–4, 1306–7, 1309–13, 1315
hyperreality 1068, 1074–75

hypocrisy 412, 855, 856
hypocrites/Hypocrites 169–70, 173–74, 176, 374 n.13, 497

iʿāda (restoration) 472–74, 476
Iblīs 36, 576, 624, 1237. *See also* Satan
iconography 989, 1034–37
  and approaches 1039–43
  Shiʿite 1058, 1063
idealism 1162, 1303
ideals 970
identity 478, 492, 595, 1216
  Arab 1074
  Muslim 960
  primordial Acehnese 1147, 1170, 1173
  religious 964
  Shiʿite 1056
ideology 365, 1228
  dimension of 818
  of mainstream Sunni Islam 840
idol worshipers 571, 590. *See also* pagans/paganism
Idrīs 1040
ignorance 465, 576, 626 n.117, 717, 1203, 1319
Ikhwān al-Ṣafā 506, 666. *See also* Brethren of Purity
ʿilliyyūn/ʿilliyyīn (exalted realms or creatures) 103, 592, 666
illuminations 109 n.52, 510, 595, 1192. *See also* light
Illuministic school 895, 900 n.22, 916
imagery/image(s) 182, 208, 225, 230 n.24, 457, 768, 785, 787, 799–800, 1021, 1075
  dualistic 144–45
  of grapes and grapevines 788–89, 796, 803
  of Ibn ʿArabī 547
  as metaphorical opposites 592
  of paradise/garden/hereafter 221, 236, 241, 295, 348, 801, 1022, 1040, 1061
  Quranic 264, 268
  realistic 1062
  realm of suspended (*al-muthul al-muʿallaqa*) 509, 1192
  royal 1036
imaginaire 862
imaginal
  body 523, 671
  reality 500
  world 509
imaginary (Islamic) 1316
imagination 460, 508–9, 522, 809, 968, 1033, 1195, 1214
  faculty of (*al-quwwa al-khayāliyya*) 453, 457, 463, 466, 494–95, 500, 671
  forms of 493
  mundus imaginalis 501
imamate 651–52, 685
  cyclical view of 633
  rank of 514
Imamism 1036
imāms 497, 503 n.52, 505, 512, 515, 521, 607, 622 n.92, 627, 654, 658, 677, 681–83, 692, 715, 855, 989, 996, 998, 1003
  appearance of 634
  chain of 651
  cosmic 569 n.15, 705 n.10
  on equal footing with God 618 n.75
  hidden 607 n.11, 684–85, 736
  immaculate ones, fourteen 1042
  infallible 597 n.103
  just 991
  knowledge of 680
  obedience (*ṭāʿa*) to 659
  seven/heptad of 490 n.17, 651
  Shiʿi concept of 708 n.20, 715 n.32
  twelfth 510–11, 609 n.16, 619 n.80
imbeciles/fools 1193
imitation 1211
  taqlīd 722–23, 729
immanence 361, 1317
immanent (activism and quietism) 361–65
immaterial
  shapes (*al-ashbāḥ al-mujarrada*), world of 509, 528, 1192
  soul (*nafs*, or *rūḥ*) 422–23, 425, 447, 451, 453, 475, 500, 586, 707 n.16, 1194
immortality 253–54, 299, 462
  of souls (*nafs*, or *rūḥ*) 181, 473, 1089, 1193–94, 1197
imperfection 497, 521, 570, 773
impurity 337, 1104, 1106–7, 1109, 1118, 1121
  ritual 319, 336
  rules on 1114–15
incarnation 855
  in animal bodies 752
  ḥulūl 737
independence 1170, 1173
Indians 855
individualism 964

individuality 464–66, 1060, 1197, 1237
individual(s) 1099, 1109, 1211
vs. communal 758, 768
grades of 546
interests (*ḥuqūq al-ʿibād*) 1101–2
induction (*istidlāl*) 938
industrialization 1069, 1071–72
indwelling (*ḥalla*) 453
infallibility 597 n.103, 981, 1003
infants, deceased 738–39, 748, 752. *See also* children
inferiority (female) 336
infidels 34, 894, 896, 1148, 1159, 1175
Dutch (*kaphé,* Ar. *kāfir*) 1147
killing of 1154
Muslims as 905, 908
infiniteness 81
inflation/economic hardship 1249
iniquity 1193
initiation 634, 1090
injustice 624, 1179, 1249
innate disposition (*fiṭra*) 539–40, 546
innovations (*bidʿa*) 332
inscriptions 998
calligraphic 1033
Kufic 1015–16, 1017 n.28
insecurity 581
inside (homeland/heaven), *vs.* outside (foreign/hell) 265–66
inspiration (*ilhām, waḥy*) 713, 752
installations 1074
intellect/Intellect 451, 456, 502–3, 504 n.55, 510, 512, 520, 521, 573, 582, 589, 650, 669, 686, 1189
acquired (*al-ʿaql al-mustafād*) 452, 463
Active 452–54, 462–65
ʿaql, pl. *ʿuqūl* 529, 669–70, 704
first/First 451–52, 456, 653–55
rational 593
realm/world of 506, 509, 652
spiritual 507
Universal 503 n.52, 649, 652, 656–57, 659
intellegibilia 508
intelligence 1202
intelligibles 463–64, 658
world of 653
intentions, right/good 412, 416
intercalations 1085
intercession (*shafāʿa*) 19, 236 n.37, 397, 851, 853, 946, 947, 1010 n.1, 1020, 1023 n.48, 1204, 1214
of advocates 498
on bridge 396
to get people out of hell 386–87
of God 1018 n.30
of messengers 196
of Muḥammad 26, 197, 371, 373, 398–99, 402–4, 426, 836, 840, 1010 n.1, 1018–22
of scholars 202
inter-communal
boundaries 312
debates 317
intermediary, between two worlds 1023–24
Internet 1247
inter-religious dialogue 10
intertexts 68
intertextual approach 16
intertextuality, intra-Quranic 70
intervention, divine 958, 965
Intifada, first and second 1271, 1280
intimacy 117
intolerance 973
intoxicants
alcohol 254 (*See also* wine)
narcotic (*mang*) 251
intra-communal
boundaries 312
debates 70, 314, 317
intrinsic (*bi-l-dhāt*), *vs.* accidental (*bi-l-ʿaraḍ*) 537
intuition(s) 457, 905, 1202–3
Iranian
import ware 76
lore 84
traditions 74
irjāʾ, 384 n.42, 385
irony 104
irreality 1074
Ishrāqī(s)/*ishrāqī* 493, 501–2, 505
philosophy 737
school, of Suhrawardī 20, 506
Islam 99, 120, 204, 659, 675, 759, 899, 918, 1091, 1093, 1173, 1178, 1259, 1318
and Acehnese 1170
catholicism, universality of (*jamāʿiyya*) 1131

conversion to 184, 193, 483, 884
in crisis 1296
enemies of 896, 912–13
eschatological vision of 3, 803
explanation/message of 556, 1193
five pillars of 198, 360, 364
and Greek thought 891
history of 102, 701–2
modern 1222
and modern science 1224, 1226
and Oriental Christianity 23
orthodox 210
personified 207
precedence (*sābiqa*) in accepting 179
radical 966
reform of 1291, 1294–95
renunciation of 483
those not reached by message of 739, 748, 752, 1195, 1244

islām 377, 677, 1300 n.24

Islamic
civilization/culture 809, 892–93, 911, 917, 934
history 941
law 1100, 1103
names 916 n.59
norms 1228
sciences (*tafsīr, ḥadīth*) 935
studies 4, 932
tenets, new interpretation of 1193
theology (*ʿilm al-kalām*) 468–70
tradition 1316

Islamicists 735

Islamic Jihad 1274

Islamism 1291, 1295, 1297, 1299, 1301, 1313

Islamist(s) 1225, 1298, 1313
movements 1313–14

islāmiyya, vs. jāhiliyya 115

Islamophobia 1178

Ismaʿili(s)/Ismaʿilism 20–21, 328, 506, 512, 517–18, 582–83, 650 n.4, 662, 676, 690, 701, 735, 856, 1200
of Alamut 596–97, 650 n.4, 672
eschatological texts 22
exegesis 676
gnosis 511
hierarchy 679
history, seven cycles of 685
imāms 855
mission (*daʿwa*), and *dāʿīs* 21, 498, 629, 650, 652, 656, 658, 677, 683
and Neoplatonism/Neoplatonist thought 649, 653, 654 n.22, 656
Nizārī 521
Ṭayyibī 511 n.72, 521

isnād (chain of transmitters) 331, 346 n.22, 821–23, 825, 827, 842, 862
citation of 821, 833
criticism 828, 844
reliability/value of 832, 846

isrāʾ (night journey). *See* night journey

Israelis 963, 1271

Israelites 206, 761, 767

Isrāfīl (angel) 193, 529, 1021, 1038, 1041–42, 1242

istithnāʾ (exception) 380, 390, 403

īwān (throne halls) 1024 n.53

jāhiliyya (age of ignorance) 115, 454 n.40, 1318–19

Jahmīs 207

janāza (bier) 1010 n.1. *See also* funerary (matters)

janna, pl. *jannāt* (garden/paradise/heaven) 4, 17, 25, 64, 70, 103, 121, 136–38, 186, 236–38, 239–41, 295, 343, 413, 563, 592, 656, 658, 852, 866, 867, 1268, 1284, 1290–91, 1295–96, 1299, 1309–12, 1315–17. *See also* gardens (of paradise); heaven(s); paradise
ʿadn (Eden) 852, 871
ahl al- (inhabitants/people of) 331, 376, 392, 872, 874
and crisis of Islam 1299
al-firdaws 56
jannatān (dual) 55–56, 81, 354
jannāt tajrī min taḥtihā l-anhār 139
al-khuld (of eternity) 138, 185, 187, 926
al-maʾwā (of abode/refuge/rest) 56, 138, 187, 414, 417, 877
al-naʿīm (of bliss/comfort/happiness) 56, 185, 187, 414
and sex 1302
those given glad tiding of entering (*al-mubashsharūn bi-l-janna*) 1214
and violence/terror 28, 1292–94, 1304
wa-l-nār (and fire) 194
wa-ʿuyūn 139

Jehenna, Valley of 1022
Jehovah's Witnesses 762
Jews 52, 55, 121, 255, 315, 317, 359, 374 n.13, 725, 800, 908, 966, 1022 n.44, 1132, 1214, 1229, 1252
  expulsion from al-Andalus 953
  as infidels 1164
Jibrā'īl 1042–43. *See also* angel(s); Gabriel
jihād 19, 165, 169–70, 176, 277, 345, 408–9, 414, 839, 842, 1155, 1168–69, 1290
  books on 418, 1160
  as duty 409–10, 1148–49, 1155, 1158–60
  against Franks 413
  military 173–74, 407, 411, 413 n.21, 417, 419
  neglect of 421
  reasons for 1163
  against self/greater *vs.* lesser 178–79, 412
  spirit of 1171, 1173
  those who perform 360, 362–65
  types of 1179
jinn 32, 80, 83, 100, 158, 185, 282, 302, 438, 717, 737 n.15, 852, 854, 945, 947, 987, 1236, 1255, 1257–58
j-n-n 55, 563
jouissance 1302–6, 1309–10, 1313
journeys 909
  to heaven (stations on) 1037–38
  heavenly 11, 770
  of Muḥammad 916, 919, 1037, 1039
  to/through heaven and hell 251, 285, 792, 893, 908, 916
  to truth/Mover of the Universe 904–5, 908
joys 905–6, 1143, 1273
  of paradise 790, 799, 1212, 1239
Judaism/Jewish 15, 69–70, 73, 83 n.44, 95 n.6, 99, 271, 659, 757, 771, 1133, 1135
  and apocalypse 101
  lore and Muslim tradition 193
  messianism 765
  missionaries 675
  paradise 83, 153
  Rabbinic tradition 356 n.76
  texts 77
judgment 5, 14, 49–50, 81, 87, 100, 121, 124, 181–82, 200, 224 n.8, 856, 946, 1036, 1189, 1206
  day of 14, 33, 35, 38–41, 43, 63, 112–13, 123, 169, 183, 194, 196–97, 201–3, 207, 264, 277, 312–13, 315, 419, 624, 676, 751, 767, 936, 1038, 1187, 1190, 1208, 1232
  hour of 1213
  imagery of 769
  last 72, 626, 764–65, 769–70
  place of 1229
  waiting for 1243
Jupiter 904. *See also* astronomy/astronomers; planets
jurisprudence 820
just (people) 72
  arbiter (*ḥakam ʿadl*) 838
justice/equity 43, 50, 246, 468, 606, 610
  ʿadāla 352
  divine/of God 16, 34, 737–38, 1187, 1194
  obligatory (*wājib*) 479–80
Justice Party (Adalet Partisi) 1225

Kaʿba 178, 190, 782 n.7, 1017 n.28, 1091, 1250
Kāfūr (fountain; spring) 256–57. *See also* fountain(s)/springs
kāʿib (pl. *kawāʿib*) (young girls) 60
kalām (discursive theology) 11, 27, 423–24, 458, 473–74, 482, 485, 1196
  analysis 15
  Islamic 1187–88
  movement 1210
  Muʿtazilī 474
kalām (Word, of God) 542
karma 740, 759–60
kashf (mystical knowledge; unveiling) 100, 122, 938, 941. *See also* unveiling(s)
kawthar (fountain, or river in paradise) 104–5, 830, 871, 927, 1039, 1192
Kemalism 1225, 1228, 1241
khānegāhs 580–81
Khārijīs (*khawārij*) 372, 376 n.17, 380, 383–84, 387, 389, 394, 996–97, 1131
Khazars 1230
Khiḍr 434, 569 n.14, 695, 1245
kh-l-d 141
kh-r-j 746
khurūj 620
khuṭba, of Ḥasan [Nizārī Ismaʿili] 683–84
kh-z-y 397, 403

knower (*ʿārif*, pl. *ʿārifūn*) [of God] 202, 227
knowing, modes of 450
knowledge 21, 36 n.10, 187–88, 198, 202, 451–52, 457, 466, 498, 961, 964, 1136, 1203, 1293–94, 1297
  of divine names 720
  divine/of God 242–43, 245, 248, 717, 1204
  of divine Word 719, 727
  ethical 1317
  of *ḥadīth* sciences 833 n.75
  of the hereafter 194, 197
  of the Hour (*ʿilm al-sāʿa*) 613 n.60
  ʿilm 225–28, 1024 n.57
  and love 582, 727
  maʿrifa (intuitive knowledge/gnosis of God) 235, 585, 668
  of one's self 456, 571, 723, 727, 732
  pure 652, 654–55
  revealed 450, 468
  search for 45
  of the soul (*maʿrifat al-nafs*) 519
  supernatural 981
  of truth 905
  of the world 938
Krishna 740
Kubrāwiyya order 581
Kufic writing/inscription 1015–16, 1017 n.28
kūfiyya 1275–76
Kurds 691
kursī (throne, celestial chair, footstool) 225–28, 242–43, 245, 548, 935, 944. *See also* throne

labor 298, 302, 305
Land-of-no-return 763
landscape 1058
language 113, 707, 722, 731, 919, 953, 1301
  descriptive and prescriptive 453
  of Ibn ʿArabī 547
  of questioning in grave/on day of judgment 708 n.20, 1209
  symbolic 595
last day (*al-yawm al-ākhir*) 72, 678–79, 759
  events of 67
Last Days 1022
Latin 897, 903
lawful 1112
law/morality (dichotomy) 27, 1101, 1121–23
law(s) 4, 15, 335, 606, 1099–1100, 1103–4
  of cause and effect 692
  compilations on 14
  criminal 1101
  medieval Islamic 335 n.112
  of reason 779
  revealed 465
  rules of 1118
legal
  philosophy 1100
  reasoning 27, 1121–23
  value, five categories of (*al-aḥkām al-khamsa*) 1100
  works (*fiqh*) 1157
legatees (*waṣī*, *awṣiyāʾ*) 517, 631, 654, 658
legitimacy 1014 n.16, 1102, 1122
letters (*ḥarf*, pl. *ḥurūf*) 701, 704, 706–7
  of divine writing 725
  isolated (*al-ḥurūf al-muqaṭṭaʿa*) 701, 715, 724
  kāf and *nūn* 720
liberal 1188
liberty/liberation 632, 1309, 1314. *See also* freedom
lieux de mémoire 1068, 1072, 1078
life
  after death 1, 191, 1196, 1204, 1218, 1223
  breath of (*nasam*) 995 n.51
  and death 14, 743, 748, 1164, 1310
  earthly 43, 768, 851–53, 1191
  following the resurrection 746
  Muslim vision of 489
  second, in the graves (*qubūr*) 745
lifelessness, two periods of 746–47
light 106, 144–45, 201, 237 n.42, 279–80, 303, 426, 502, 570, 621, 657, 761, 798, 902, 904, 907, 910, 1000, 1236
  Absolute 576
  vs. darkness 576, 968, 1136, 1164
  divine 563, 569, 588–89, 904–5, 909
  flashing 993
  of *imām* 618
  metaphors of 905
  Muḥammadan Light (*nūr muḥammadī*) 187–88, 274 n.19, 569, 576, 1210
  overflowing (*ifāḍa*/*istifāḍa*) 653
  primordial 569 n.15

lightning 161, 993, 1000, 1192
 barq; ṣaʿq 145–46, 529–30
Light verse 107, 122, 619, 901 n.25
likeness (*mithāl; mathal*) 54–56, 492. *See also* similitude
limbo 911, 913–14
 of the heights (*al-aʿrāf*) 737, 947
liminal
 location 271, 288
 status (of martyrs) 1281
lineage 324
literacy 1269
literal/literalist approach 272–73, 277, 285, 287, 656, 665
 meaning/interpretation 477–78, 677
 to Quran 669
 scholars (*ʿulamāʾ*) 567
literary
 criticism 819
 forms and devices 100, 907
 genres 817–18, 834, 841, 858, 870, 874–75, 937, 988
 motifs 884–85
 studies 1157
 texts, medieval Muslim 335 n.111
 theory 15
literature 15, 194, 335, 349, 893, 895, 902
 Aljamiado 882 n.77
 apocalyptic/eschatological 121, 182, 195, 365
 Arabian epic (*sīra shaʿbiyya*) 922
 Arabic/Islamic 17, 67, 114 n.75, 807, 850, 915, 932–33, 954 n.6
 Christian 357–58
 hikayat 1165
 Indian 924–25
 Malay *kitab* (religious book) 1148
 of merits of holy war (*faḍāʾil al-jihād*) 1167–68
 Middle Persian 925
 mythical 365
 Rabbinical 357
 revelatory 98
 and rhymed prose (*sajʿ*) 100, 263–64, 1279 n.19
 ṣifat al-janna genre 24
 social drama 1286 n.31
 Western 1157
litterateurs/literati 261, 954, 957, 962, 964
liturgies 791, 801, 803, 1134
 poetry set to music 790
loanwords (Persian) 137
locus amoenus (delightful place) 73
logic/logicians 450, 455
logos (*qurʾān*) 87
lote tree, of the boundary (*ṭūbā* or *sidrat al-muntahā*) 163, 165, 175, 187–88, 274, 276, 284, 503 n.52, 611, 710–11, 728, 730, 859, 861, 866, 870, 876, 881, 986, 1021–22
love 21, 25, 43, 576, 585, 590, 594, 727 n.61, 732, 899, 908, 919, 927
 and death 1280
 of God/divine 21, 353, 571, 575, 577, 589, 591, 593, 596–97, 904, 918
 motif of 150, 589, 596
 as obligation (*farḍ*) 575
 Platonic 900
 poems, women of (Laylā, ʿAbla, Buthayna, Rābiʿa al-ʿAdawiyya, Niẓām) 910
 poetry 900, 910, 916, 918
 as superior to knowledge 582
 as way to paradise 728
 as way to self-knowledge 727
lover(s)
 and Beloved 574, 577
 of God 205–6
lower
 classes 584
 forms 719, 727
 self (*nafs*) 721
 species 506
loyalty 965
luminosity 285, 299, 332
lunar
 calendar 1091
 month/year 1085
lunatics/insane (people) 1193
lust 907
luxuries/luxuriousness 140–41, 151, 205, 244, 266, 296, 430, 598, 1002
 in paradise 821, 835
luxurious growth 147, 149
lying/liars 190–91

maʿād (place of return) 4–5, 20, 104, 470–75, 484, 489, 519, 663 n.11
machismo 1301
macrocosm 1216, 1227, 1232, 1254, 1258

madhāhib (schools of law) 837, 1013, 1022
madīna 21, 556–57, 559
madrasas 580 n.5, 1011 n.4, 1012–13, 1024
madrāshê (of Ephraem the Syrian) 23
Magians (Ar. *majūsī*) or fire-worshipers 374 n.13, 1159
mahdī 434, 510–11, 513, 516–17, 606–7, 609, 618–20, 629–30, 651, 678 n.9, 679, 997, 1247
  arrival of 677–78, 680, 683, 765, 981, 1249–50, 1252–53
  -*qā'im* figure 683
  reign of 1259
  signs of 1250
  and warfare 1260
maidens/girls 80, 82–83, 157, 160, 185, 665, 947, 987, 1195. *See also* virgins
ma'iyya (propinquity, nearness) 113
majesty (*jalāl*), *vs.* generosity (*ikrām*) 82
maleness 323–24, 332. *See also* masculinity
male(s) 320–21, 1146, 1299 n.21
  agency of 1298, 1300
  bodies, earthly 322
  cupbearers (*suqāh, sāqin*) 298–99, 305
  eternal/immortal 158, 728
  inhabitants of paradise 318, 328
  Islamic subjectivity of 1300 n.24, 1302–3
  Islamists 1291, 1297–98, 1309
  martyrs, *vs.* female 1270, 1285
  servants (*wildān*) 18, 32, 64, 141, 153 n.39, 158 n.44, 297–99, 301–2, 305
  slave boys (*ghilmān*) 18, 297–99, 301, 305, 714
  young/youths 32, 279, 297, 299, 302, 716, 1149, 1162, 1210
Mālikī(s) 371 n.1
  madhhab 819, 837, 1108 n.28 (*See also* *madhāhib*)
Mamluk period 32, 163, 942, 1011, 1014
Mandaeans 1133–34
mandala 1017
Manicheans/Manicheism 850, 1135–37
manifestation, loci of (*maẓhar*, pl. *maẓāhir*) 705
  of complete divine alphabet [i.e., Adam] 724
  of the Divine Essence 690, 695
  of divine knowledge 717
  of divine Word 713, 731
  female form as 714
  most perfect place (*al-akmal*) 510
  supreme place (*al-a'ẓam*) 510, 516, 531
mansions 139, 865. *See also* castles; palaces
marginalization 958, 1123
market inspectors (*muḥtasibūn*) 171, 176
markets
  closeness of (*taqārub al-aswāq*) 1209, 1218
  of paradise 873
marriage 796
  and marital imagery 797, 799–801
Mars 904. *See also* astronomy/astronomers; planets
martyrdom operation (*'amaliyyāt istishhādī* or *istishhādiyya*) 1267, 1269, 1271, 1273, 1276–77, 1279, 1283–84
  as *rite de passage* 1286
martyrology
  Shi'i 1166
  Sufi 598
martyrs (*shahīd/shuhadā'*)/martyrdom 1, 14, 21, 26, 163–65, 177, 191, 202, 240–41, 277, 345, 360, 362–63, 414, 419, 465–66, 579, 597–98, 796, 842, 852, 896, 989, 991, 995, 1056, 1149–50, 1152, 1166, 1175, 1179, 1238, 1270–73, 1276, 1282, 1284, 1286–87, 1290, 1299 n.21, 1302
  in battle of Badr (2/624) 167–71, 175
  in battle of Uḥud (3/625) 166–67, 170, 175
  call for 1060
  categories/taxonomy of 171, 176
  for Christ 764
  cult of 1171
  debt of 172, 412
  discourse of 1276
  and *ḥūrīs* 276
  of Ḥurr 1059
  male *vs.* female 1270, 1285
  military 17, 162, 172, 175–76, 179, 415–16
  Muslim concept of 1145
  and paradise 190, 417, 839
  Shi'ite concept of 1061, 1063, 1165
  souls of 166–67, 171, 1061
  status of 169, 839
  of women (*istishhādiyyāt*) 28, 1268–69, 1280–81, 1285
marvels. *See 'ajā'ib* (marvels of creations)
Marxism/Leninism 760, 762

masculine (gender) 1299. *See also* male(s)
  and angels 402
masculinity 322, 330, 333, 337, 1297 n.16, 1299 n.21, 1300–1302, 1312
mashhads (martyria) 1011
mashriqī ishrāqī (oriental illuminationist) 501–2
master
  of creation (*sayyid al-khalq*) 623
  and disciple relationship 593
  of ontological hermeneutics (*ṣāḥib-i ta'wīl*) 677, 708
materialism 1224, 1230, 1245, 1252, 1254, 1256–57
materialists 1196, 1199–1200, 1209, 1231
material/materiality 473, 545, 1191
  character of paradise and hell 468
  culture/civilization 83, 296
  subtlety 508
  and this-worldly existence 497
  world 468, 698, 761
mathematicians 493
mathematics/mathematical approach 450, 1084–86, 1088, 1092, 1094
mathnawīs 584 n.31, 1037
matn 823
  criticism 825–28, 832, 845
matter 453, 478, 502, 1226
  as eternal 1255
  illusory character of 1236
  as passive 494
Māturīdīs 371 n.1
mausoleum, mausolea 1012–13, 1022, 1025
Mazdaism 719 n.41
mean, between extremes 427
meaning(s) (*maʿnā,* pl. *maʿānī*) 704
  of beatific vision 287
Meccan
  period 33, 67, 75
  suras/verses 59, 71–72, 120, 252, 254, 675
media 28, 1225
Medinan suras 59, 120
melancholy 590
melisma 114, 117
memory 463
Mercury 904. *See also* astronomy/astronomers; planets
mercy 20, 40, 104, 548, 573, 722, 1203
  as essential 542–43
  of God 44, 105, 144, 149, 160–61, 172, 174, 176, 353, 371, 435, 498, 536, 538–39, 549, 593–94, 665, 851, 947, 1209, 1212
  and salvation 1010
  sleep as 428, 434
merit (*faḍā'il*), works on 407
message (of God/Islam), those not reached by 739, 748, 752, 1192–93, 1195, 1244
messengers 51–52, 201–3, 345, 360, 362, 536, 635 n.173, 658, 665, 739
messiah/Messiah 52, 630–31, 655, 757, 762, 801, 981, 997
  false (*dajjāl*) 382
  Hebr. *māshīaḥ* 761
messianic
  figure 997, 1000
  movements 14, 767, 997
messianism 21, 649
  sectarian 1299
meta-discourse 89
meta-historical 519
metaphorical approach 475, 1201
metaphors 153, 210, 228, 233, 244, 295, 426, 799, 919, 955, 1017, 1194, 1210, 1226, 1285
  of paradise 806, 811, 1033
  of wedding 1278
metaphysical-psychological system 1189
metaphysics 450, 474, 476
  existential 488
  of truth 1304
metempsychosis 736, 748, 751–52. *See also* reincarnation
metensomatosis 498, 505
microcosm 1216, 1227, 1232, 1254, 1258
middle ages 3
migration
  to America 807–10
  of Assyrians 807
miḥna 332 n.97
miḥrāb 1016, 1017 n.28
Mīka'īl (Michael, archangel) 189, 1042–43. *See also* angel(s)
militancy/militants 1173, 1223, 1271
military 856
  campaigns/expeditions (*ghazā, ghazawāt*) 172, 178
  occupations 1277, 1282

milk (in paradise) 58–59, 105, 140, 254, 255 n.22, 261, 264, 577, 665, 703, 795, 866, 1039, 1195, 1285
millenarism 519, 764
mimesis 1306–7
minatures 1037, 1039–40, 1059
minerals 490 n.17, 507, 515, 670, 692, 719, 727, 742
minority 811
mint (of Umayyads) 999
miracles 495, 981, 1226
miʿrāj (ascension to heaven) 17, 26, 188, 273–74, 347, 917, 1020–21, 1025, 1062, 1083, 1255
  description of 1038
  genre 858–59
  literature on 24, 875, 884–85
  "Modern Standard" version of 879–80
  narrative of 191–93, 862–65, 878, 934
  picture 1037–38
  purpose of 877
  spiritual 792
  texts/works on 275–76, 881–83
mirror-image 983, 988, 991, 1307
misery 546
misguidance (*taḍlīl*) 477
mission, prophetic (man's need of) 1202. *See also* guidance
missionaries 1188
Mithraism 1089–90
mīzān (balance, scale) 19, 425, 472, 1192, 1208
ʾ-m-m 724
moderation 1261
modernism 1255
modernists 1188, 1226
modernity 28, 1071, 1073, 1078, 1219, 1285, 1291–95, 1297, 1299 n.21, 1300 n.24, 1311, 1313–15, 1318
  shopping malls 1075
  skyscrapers 1206
  technology 1250, 1260–61
  telecommunications 1207
modernization 26, 809, 1069, 1071–72, 1077–78
modesty 302
monasticism 776
Mongols 505, 582, 1209
monotheism/monotheistic faiths 70, 72, 93, 99, 125, 665, 692, 852–53
monotheists 327, 398, 497, 947
  muwaḥḥid 371, 374 n.13, 375–80, 403, 1195
monumentalism 981
monuments 1011
moon 109, 237, 264, 330, 332 n.96, 436, 473, 710, 904–5, 944, 1083, 1087, 1091, 1233, 1242. *See also* astronomy/astronomers; planets; stars
moral 1205
  vs. amoral 758
  deeds (*ṣāliḥa*) 253, 264
  eschatologies 765
  excellence 177–78
  questions 871–72
  restraint 326
  -social order 325
  threat 325–26
moralism 766
morality 253, 774, 840, 853, 1099–1100, 1104
mosaic panels 1015. *See also* architecture/architectural (features)
mosques
  al-Aqṣā Mosque ('Furthest Mosque') 188, 435, 1014
  of Ascension 1022
  caliphal/vizieral 1011
  decoration of 1070
mother(s) 53, 706, 715, 723, 732
  bodily form of 716
  ḥadīth: "Paradise lies at the feet of . . . ," 44, 706, 714, 717, 732
motifs 413, 432, 858, 865, 875, 878–80, 923–24, 1020, 1072
  nationalist 1285
  of Palestinian wedding 1275–76
  of permanent traveler 434
  of Riḍwān 881–83
motions (*ḥarakāt*) 446 n.6, 491, 515, 545
  of natural disposition (*jibilliyya*) 544
  substantial (*al-jawhariyya*) 499, 541
  upward 503
mountains 870, 1242
  Qāf 585, 635 n.173
mourning, collective 1270
Mughal Empire 954 n.7
  landmarks 969

muḥāḍara (presence) 568 n.8
mujaddid (renewer) 5
mujāhid, mujāhidūn 27, 412, 415, 418–19, 962, 1144, 1151–54, 1161, 1169, 1171, 1285
Mujassima (anthropomorphists) 226, 243
mülk and *melekûtiyet* 1227
multiplicity 446 n.7, 548
munkar (objectionable) 825–26
Munkar and Nakīr (angels) 424, 432, 572, 1215. *See also* angel(s)
murals 1057, 1059–63, 1067 fig.48.4, 1067 fig.48.5. *See also* art
murīd (committed one), and *murshid* (guide) 677
Murji'a/Murji'īs 376, 377, 380, 383–85, 387
mursal (traditions) 821–22, 825
music 114–15, 126, 562, 791, 1041
  and instruments 329
  melodies (*alḥān*) 703
  songs 1285
musicality 126
musicians (*qiyān*) 298
musk (*misk*) 255–59, 277, 283, 295, 297, 303–5, 318, 562, 703, 711, 835, 861, 868, 882, 1272
Muslim Brotherhood 963
Muslim(s) 49, 169, 359, 725, 964, 1228, 1241
  community 836
  debates 863
  defined as 1170
  expulsion from al-Andalus 953–54, 965
  of Granada 958, 960
  muslimūn (those who submit to the will of God) 202
  non-Sunni 327
  rank in paradise 838 n.100
  sinners 380, 383–84, 388–89, 391, 398–99, 403–4, 871, 1044
  status of Muḥammad and 843
mustawṭin (settler) 1284
Muʿtazila/Muʿtazilīs 22, 32, 207, 223 n.6, 224, 247, 274–75, 278 n.42, 314, 319 n.35, 337, 373 n.9, 387, 424, 468–69, 474, 479–80, 482–84, 567, 737, 838, 1196, 1212
  doctrine 328, 594 n.79
  heresy 245 n.53
m-w-t 744
mystical
  approach 14, 343
  guide 919
  interpretation 246
  path, and stages of 585, 587–88, 598
mysticism 3, 205–6, 236 n.37, 581, 596, 1133
  Islamic 200
  of love, Iranian 707, 731
  manuals on 15
  Persian 580
mystics 11, 18, 274, 436, 742, 908, 919, 1201
mythemes 361
mythologies 208, 1083
  Hellenic 801 n.74
  Iranian 595
  Sumerian 253
mythopoetic strategy 288
myth(s) 18, 104, 121, 321, 396 n.76, 1277, 1280–81, 1285, 1290
  of al-Andalus 955, 959–60, 966, 974
  of blood 1281
  definitions of 341 n.3, 342–43
  of *Enki and Ninhursag* 253
  functions of 365
  of Islam 1300 n.22
  Mullā Ṣadrā's use of 548
  paradise as 341
  structural study of 366

naʿīm (grace; bliss; delight) 103, 137–38
  al-dā'im (permanent) 852
nakba (lit., catastrophe; Palestinian exodus in 1948) 1271
names
  Adam taught angels 720, 725
  of all created beings 35–36, 45
  divine/of God 100, 106, 510, 516, 531, 537–38, 540, 558, 703–4, 1210–11, 1219
  God taught Adam 705, 708, 710–12, 717, 720
  of majesty, wrath, beauty (God's) 540, 542, 547
Naqshbandī (Sufis) 598
nār (hell/fire) 56, 376, 378, 381, 410–11, 852. *See also* hell/hellfire
narcotics (*mang*) 251
narrative(s) 125, 210, 858, 875, 877–78, 966, 972, 1034, 1150, 1286

apocalyptic/eschatological 191, 341–42, 344, 1218
formula (eating–drinking–love) 1154
miʿrāj (ascension to heaven) 191–93, 862–65, 878, 934
of paradise 273, 344, 835, 845
rags-to-riches theme 1154, 1161
structure of Quran 125, 1317–18
nashʾa (birth, origination, growth)
of divine forms (*al-ṣuwar al-malakūtiyya*) 657, 659
of human constitution 540
Quranic notion of 489
second (*ākhira*) 650
spiritual (*rūḥāniyya*) 515
nasīb 71, 81 n.41, 86–87, 136, 137 n.5, 145 n.24, 146, 149–50. *See also* poetry/poets
nasma (subtle vapor) 1190–93
nationalism 974, 1287
Arab 957
pan-Arab 1074
National Order Party (Millî Nizâm Partisi) (Islamist party) 1225
nation/nationhood 1169, 1276, 1281
nāṭiq, pl. *nuṭaqāʾ* (enunciators, speakers) 517, 678 n.9, 679, 682
speaking-prophet 629
natural
disasters 1240 (*See also* calamities/ cataclysmic events; catastrophes; environmental disaster/global warming)
resources 1250
sciences 3, 450, 1223
world/realm 493, 656
naturalism 1218
naturalists 493, 1199
nature 71, 76–77, 81, 85–87, 137 n.5, 143 n.19, 147, 152–53, 205, 490, 497, 503, 507, 512, 760, 1188, 1274
laws of 1193
original (*fiṭrat; khilqa*) 715–16, 724, 731
Quranic descriptions of 17, 136, 154
n-dh-r 394
necessary
being 481–82, 485
by choice (*ikhtiyāriyya*) *vs.* by nature (*iḍṭirāriyya*) 503 n.52
vs. possible 468
Necessary Existent 456
need (*ḥāja*) 1117
negativity 1306
Neicheri (group) 1199–1200
neo-modernists 1219
neo-Orientalism 123
Neoplatonism/Neoplatonic 448, 903
and Aristotelianism 504
concepts/thought 474, 489, 512, 652
mystics 286, 892
Neoplatonists 522, 692
philosophy of 21, 649–50
Nestorian (Christianity) 782. *See also* Christianity/Christians; Church of the East
New Age (concepts/literature) 1257–58
New Year (celebrations) 1085
n-h-r 58
night journey (*isrāʾ*), of Muḥammad 26, 188, 192, 273 n.15, 836 n.86, 858 n.1, 875, 892–94, 1020 n.39, 1083. *See also* ascension/ascent
Night of Power 122
nighttime 435, 438
niẓām (hierarchic order) 537
Nizārī(s) 736 n.4
Ismaʿilis 511 n.72, 581, 662, 683, 684 n.32
period 22, 632 n.163, 666, 676
noble 774–75
non-being 570
non-believers 378, 432, 1244. *See also* disbelievers/disbelief; unbelievers
non-existence 543
non-material 492, 1191. *See also* immaterial
non-Muslims 49, 302, 305
military expeditions against 408
morally excellent 1229
status of 1195
Normans 895, 897
nostalgia 955, 1075, 1077
Nuqṭawīs 736 n.4
Nurcus (Nurcular, disciples of [divine] light) 27, 1223, 1225
movement 1224, 1230, 1235, 1247–48, 1254, 1256
Nuṣayrīs (or Alawites) 635 n.173, 736 n.9
sources of 629 n.132, 631 n.157

oath-taking (*bayʿa*) 1024
obedience 472, 498, 570, 666, 687, 908
to God 169, 173, 183, 238, 411, 417, 421, 465, 471–72, 838, 1109
to law 364

obligation, personal (*farḍ al-ʿayn*) 1158–60
obligatory (*wājib*) 1100
justice/equity 479–80
Occident 892, 1137
occultation 631
ocean (divine) 592
oneness/Oneness (*waḥda/vahdet/tawḥīd*), of
God 122, 654, 666, 1227
of being 21
ontology 21, 535, 568, 571, 574
opposites 570, 593. *See also* dualism
opposition(s) 82, 94, 121, 515
oppression 110, 329, 760–62, 811, 1210, 1249
orators 287
Orient 892, 953, 1137
Orientalism 1128
Orientalist(s) 6, 27, 1128, 1131, 1188, 1297 n.16
studies 272, 1127, 1129
teaching institutions 1130
tradition 1074
origin, of soul 545
origination
direct (*ikhtirāʿ*) 494
immediately originated entities (*al-ibdāʿiyyāt*) 514–15
Ormazd (Avestan "Ahura Mazda," Lord of Wisdom) 723
ornaments 1015, 1033. *See also* decorative (elements); patterns/designs
floral 999–1000
motifs of 1016 n.25
orphans 198
"orthodox" theologians (*ahl al-sunna wa-l-jamāʿa*) 282
orthodoxy 126, 372, 1131
Osiris (god of the underworld) 766. *See also* deities/gods
Other 1305–6, 1308, 1310
other world 343–44, 758, 777, 811, 1033–34, 1219, 1311
other-worldly 758
beings 100
eschatologies 760, 762–63, 767, 770–71
existence 497
paradise 1164
realms 757, 764, 770
Ottomans/Ottoman Empire 25–26, 126, 810, 942, 1034, 1036
Ottoman Turkish 942
outside (foreign/hell), *vs.* inside (homeland/heaven) 265

pagans/paganism 84, 195, 315, 325, 806, 852, 908, 985, 1090
ideology/traditions 67–68
imagery 16, 70–71
Pahlavi (Persian) 925
pain 591. *See also* suffering
of death 1169, 1237
painters/painting 1070, 1074, 1077. *See also* art
Central Asian 1035
figurative 1077
landscape 1073
Persian 1035
pairi-daeza 925
palaces 282, 577, 665, 834–35, 853, 980–81, 984–85, 989, 991, 1001, 1004, 1039
Alhambra 953, 1017 n.26
Bayn al-Qaṣrayn (between the two palaces) 1011 n.4, 1012
celestial 983
Hasht bihisht buildings 355
of pearl, ruby and (green) chrysolite 240, 245
Palestinian National Movement 1276
Palestinians 1060
and bride/wedding (metaphor) 1276–78, 1283, 1285
expulsion of 1271
palimpsest 971–73
pan-Arab nationalism 1074
pantheism 1258
parables 136, 137 n.6, 141–44, 147, 153, 209–10, 1226, 1231
Plato, of the cave 463
paradise 2–3, 7, 14, 32, 39, 63, 73, 109, 117, 120, 123, 142, 147, 186, 197, 205, 297, 312–13, 315, 343, 410, 437, 451, 458, 476, 477, 572, 575, 657, 664–66, 676, 683, 696, 702, 715, 769, 795, 834, 861, 925, 936, 1057, 1143–44, 1160, 1272, 1284, 1291, 1316. *See also* gardens (of paradise); *janna*
admittance/access/entry to 51, 184, 315, 372, 413, 839, 853, 1284
allusion to 983–84
America as 810–11
animals in 834, 870, 880, 1195

and banquet of God (*mā'idat al-Raḥmān*) 284
as best, most beautiful (*ḥusnā*) 56, 103
brilliance/light of 1000–1001, 1134
celestial abodes of (seven) 185
common, *vs.* personal 1244
creation of 836, 872, 1004
definitions of 650, 1068
degrees/layers (*ṭabaqāt, darajāt*) of 41, 187, 247, 347, 852, 865, 989
descriptions of 24, 75–76, 84, 124–25, 137, 140, 142, 150–52, 160, 201, 210, 241, 244, 287, 317, 320, 409, 413, 420, 560, 706, 799, 821, 834, 840, 843, 865, 870–71, 873–74, 876, 883, 885, 947, 988, 993, 1021, 1034, 1056
as destination 449, 1102
destruction of 224 n.8, 245, 482, 971
dimensions of/space of 140 n.15, 317, 557, 561, 874
earthly 26, 357–58, 953–54, 967, 973–74, 985, 1001, 1004, 1078, 1285
eternality of 243, 319, 328, 336, 380, 592, 1004
existence of 181, 860, 863, 872, 884, 940
expulsion of Adam (and Eve) from 36–37, 70, 141, 480, 966, 969, 1035–36, 1048 fig.47.2
of al-Fārābī (Alfarabi) 454
at feet of mothers 44
as a female body 329
females/wives in 318, 326
figurative/visual representations of 26, 1059
figures in (guardian of, prophets, angels) 796, 878, 1043
as garden(s) 468, 592, 784, 883, 991, 1058
gates of 19, 55, 140 n.15, 193 n.29, 353, 355, 713, 793, 876, 993
geography/topography of 239, 286, 354, 562, 869
and hell 593–94, 630, 665, 668, 904, 1040, 1194, 1198
and hell, meriting both 398–400
hierarchy of 282, 579, 1244 n.93
hope for 267, 282, 286, 593, 596
Ḥurūfī views of 708, 712, 717–19, 732
images of 67, 70–71, 87, 712, 724, 729–30, 985, 988, 1057
intellectual rewards of 466, 649, 652–53, 659
joys of/delights in 34, 36, 38, 43, 49, 54, 252, 408, 419–20, 595
loss of/lost 23, 25, 37, 723, 810–11
majority Muslims 836
male inhabitants of 318, 328
and metaphors 23, 25, 809, 927
motifs/themes of 67, 420, 956
as myth 341
narratives of 344, 835, 845
nature of 561, 669, 866, 868, 870, 1195, 1246
notions/images of, in Abrahamic religions 74, 430, 1143
number of 349, 598, 874, 880–81, 1244
people/inhabitants of 50, 54, 59–61, 63, 237–38, 255, 284, 312, 317, 319, 322, 325, 332, 335, 380, 393, 399, 400, 412, 560, 703, 716, 747, 749, 834, 852, 873, 947, 990, 992, 1000, 1206, 1244–45
proceeding directly to 419–20
promise of 407, 415, 671, 1037
Quranic descriptions of 16, 71, 263, 266, 273, 311, 430, 714, 979 n.*, 1233
real, *vs.* relative 669–71
roads/ways to 45, 732, 850, 853, 856, 1034, 1056
rooms, chambers, mansions (*ghurfa*, pl. *ghuraf*) in 139, 317–18, 869
seat of honor (*maqʿad al-ṣidq*) in 103, 186 n.10
as secure dwelling/place (*maqām amīn*) 56, 103, 186 n.10
sensual images/rewards of 27, 784, 799, 918, 1146
signification of 1164
spiritual 666
structure of 863, 868, 873
symbolism of 979 n.*
Syriac descriptions of 800, 802
tour of/visit (of Muḥammad) to 190, 858–59, 862–65, 869, 875–81, 882 n.77, 883
visibility in 555–56, 559–61, 563
visions of 199, 859–60, 862, 881, 884–85, 989, 1040, 1060–62, 1168
water in (springs, rivers) 57, 318, 328, 712, 843, 928

paradise (cont.)
weather/climate in 237, 239, 244, 247, 264
words for (*jannat, bihisht, khuld, firdaws, dhāt al-qarār*) 103–4, 137 n.5, 592, 663 n.11, 672, 830, 852, 940, 943, 1033
paradox 1315
paralipsis 104
pardah (Persian, veil) 689
Parthians 258
particles 478, 1236, 1242
particulars 654
and universal 1304
passions 588, 593, 907
passivity 974, 1271
path, travelers on 506. *See also* journeys
patience 40, 168, 202, 206–7, 238, 907, 909
patriarchy/partriarchal 1299 n.21
society/social order 329 n.85, 335, 958–59
patrons 1033
patterns/designs. *See also* decorative (elements); ornaments
arabesques 1012–13
floral 1013
fractal 1016
geometric 999, 1012–13, 1015, 1033
of leaves 982, 990
multiplication 982
vegetal 25, 981–84, 988, 995, 999–1000, 1005, 1033–34
pavilions 983, 986, 1040
peace 562, 838
of mind (*huzur*) 1232, 1237
pen 575, 936, 944
people, of the right/left 702, 718 n.37
People of the Book 34, 52–53, 302. *See also* Christianity/Christians; Judaism/Jewish
perception 494–95
perfection 453, 491–92, 497–98, 503–4, 508, 513, 521, 537, 543, 594, 670, 692, 698, 773, 778, 905–6, 908, 1088, 1202
actualization of 507, 696
of existents 541
of the garden/paradise 295, 319, 322, 336
of God 938
human (striving for) 531, 649, 803
intellectual 458
of prophetic utterances 116
of the soul 449
spiritual 694, 739
perfect man
God as 597
al-insān al-kāmil; insān-i kāmil 513–14, 693, 1019
performances 126, 1057
Peripatetic (philosophy) 502 n.47, 505
perishability/perishable 141–42, 174
of earth 232 n.31
hālik 481–82
permitted (*ḥalāl*) 1100
persecution 101
Persian (language) 259, 703 n.8, 708 n.20, 942, 1231
Persian(s) 260–61
culture 925
poetry 894
world 1034
personality 1198. *See also* individualism
pessimism 956
Pharaoh 139 n.13, 168, 678–79, 767
philologists 854, 856
classical Arabic 81
philology/philological 790, 829, 831, 1128–29
philosopher-prophet 452–54
philosophy/philosophers 3–4, 11, 15, 327, 422–23, 448, 452–53, 477, 482, 506, 567, 893, 908, 912, 919, 941, 1094, 1201, 1213, 1292, 1307
approach/thought of 14–15, 343, 457
comparative 488
falāsifa 735
Greek 468, 586, 1233
Hellenistic 87
ḥukamā', 1201
Illuminationist (*ishrāqī*) 737
Isfahan school/Twelver Shiʿi 672
of law 1122
of mediationism 1218
Muslim/Islamic 20, 436, 446, 468–69, 484, 520, 664–65, 727 n.61, 895, 902, 913, 915, 918, 1196, 1198, 1233, 1319
mystical 706–7, 731
Neoplatonist 21, 649–50
Peripatetic 502 n.47, 505
prophetic 500

rationalist 589
Shiʿite 501–2
souls 460, 464
Sufi 739
-theological treatises 14
'three brothers' dilemma 738, 741
universal 505
Western 1233
phonemes 704–7, 726 n.57, 730
physicality 331
physicians 258
physics 474
picturesque 1074
piety/pious 1, 19, 44, 162, 165–66, 198, 345, 346 n.23, 360, 416–17, 419–20, 465–66, 594, 1173, 1179, 1314
caliphs/rulers 1003, 1023
ḥūrīs as reward for 277–78
popular 1017, 1018 n.31
taqwā, tuqā 24, 853, 1212
pilgrimage 198, 363–64, 470, 612, 853, 909
pilgrims 345, 360
place 474, 651, 1245
planetary
motion 1088, 1093–94
spheres 357, 1088, 1090
planets 696, 945, 1089
seven 1083–84, 1087–88, 1090
upper celestial bodies (*al-ajrām al-ʿulwiyya*) 656
plants 253, 490 n.17, 514–15, 670, 692, 719, 727, 742, 907, 988
Platonic
archetypes (*al-muthul al-Aflāṭūniyya*) 509
ethics 448
political philosophy 454
Platonism 501
pleasures 105, 166–67, 430, 454, 598, 764, 835, 907, 1154
bodily/physical 312, 477, 567, 1146, 1154
of God 1176
of paradise 277, 286, 342, 627, 985, 1246
of wedding night 1169
worldly 1144
plunder 420
pluralism 955, 1101
religious 743
plural worlds 1227, 1236, 1255–56
poetic (motifs, traditions) 15, 90
poeticity 81 n.41
poetics 114 n.75
poetry/poets 11, 18, 24, 27, 125, 138, 143–45, 149–50, 261, 410, 831, 852, 856, 900, 908–9, 918, 1280, 1281 n.23, 1285
ʿAbbasid 144, 298, 300
ancient Arabic 71, 74, 81, 86–89, 204 n.53
Arabic 67, 137 n.5, 299, 806–7, 809, 853–54, 912
contemporary Arabic 154
erotic 900
eschatological, in Syriac 799
Hellenistic 88
mystic 707 n.17, 902, 1037
nasīb 71, 81 n.41, 86, 87, 136, 137 n.5, 145 n.24, 146, 149–50
Palestinian 954 n.6, 962
pantōn (genre of oral poetry) 1173
Persian 586, 707 n.17
pre-Islamic 17, 77, 109 n.52, 136, 144, 298, 300
qaṣīda 71, 86–88, 136, 145 n.24, 299
and rhyme 79, 138
romantic 1037
Urdu 969
wartime 1147
pole (*quṭb*) 695
polemics 838, 1123, 1144, 1247
political philosophy 451, 454, 455, 462
politics 1229, 1311, 1317
of diaspora 1299 n.21
polygyny 323 n.61
polytheism 327, 851, 1319
polytheists 59, 169, 178, 302, 374 n.13, 376, 386, 397
pool (of mercury) 992–93, 1001
possible being/existing 469, 481–82, 485
postcolonial discourse (Indonesian) 1168
post-eternity 571
post-millennial 757
potentiality 730, 778
bi-l-quwwa 656, 712–13
poverty/the poor 203, 206, 325, 581, 760, 762, 796, 838, 906–7, 909, 946, 1073, 1151–53, 1159, 1179, 1239, 1283

power 454
 and gender 1299 n.21
 of God 145, 147, 242, 248
 and social status 332
praise/glorification 106, 230
prang sabi (holy war) 1154
prayer niche (*miḥrāb*) 1013
prayer(s) 26, 168, 183, 198, 207, 346, 360, 362–64, 732, 1010, 1020–22, 1092, 1107, 1120, 1157
 call to 1230
 congregational 1013
 for the dead 1238
 five 229, 1092
 of Muḥammad 1119
 and proximity to God 1116
 requirements for 1103
 ṣalāt 121, 319 n.41, 728–29
 as way to paradise 728
preachers 193 n.30, 409
predestinarians 373 n.9
predestined (by God) 191
pre-eternity 571
pre-Islamic ritual practices 254
preordination 196
presence 106, 1307
 divine/of God 16, 94–95, 100, 104, 106, 109, 113–19, 123, 420, 477, 589, 671–72
present, and future 778
price, of paradise (*thaman al-janna*) 837
priests 777–78
prime matter 452, 456
Prime Mover (of the Universe) 909
primordial
 Acehnese identity 1147, 1170
 covenant 100, 112–13, 718 n.37, 945
 creation (*al-fiṭra al-aṣliyya*) 497
 garden/paradise (of Adam) 186, 798
 letters/words 703, 711 n.23, 713, 720, 722, 725, 729
 pen 936
principles or basis (*aṣl*, pl. *uṣūl*) 491, 851
 of speech (*aṣl-i kalām*) 726
privacy 361, 363
prohibited (*ḥarām*/*maḥzūr*) 1100
Promised Land 16, 33, 1061, 1063
promises 81
 of paradise 418
 of rewards 409–10
 and threat (*al-waʿd wa-l-waʿīd*) 246, 472
proof (*ḥujja*) 608
propaganda 1269, 1281
 on *jihād* 1169
 religious 1166
 texts 1147, 1167, 1172
 types of 1152
prophecy(ies) 124, 364, 710, 1187, 1196, 1206, 1214, 1250, 1315
 cycles of 651, 653, 724–25
 of Muḥammad 315
 signs of 863
prophethood 635 n.173, 1209, 1222 n.2
prophetology 702, 715 n.32
prophet(s) 100, 114, 123, 145, 169, 171, 176, 199, 202–3, 240–41, 318, 345, 360, 362–63, 465–66, 490, 505, 517, 561, 607, 652, 658, 685, 692, 708, 722, 775, 839, 852, 904–5, 989, 991, 1020, 1039, 1137, 1203, 1212, 1238
 and day of judgment, proximity between 605 n.3
 false 997–98
 guidance of (*nabī hādin*) 503
 heavens/God shown to 712–13
 intercession of 547
 legislator (*nabī*) 631
 mission of 855
 Muḥammad as last 317
 Muḥammad meeting other 861
 payghambarān 654
 pre-Islamic 1035, 1040, 1043
 promise of 730
 revelations of 628, 709, 732
 status of 197
 stories of 1035, 1040
 as *ummī* 724, 731
prose, rhymed (*sajʿ*) 100, 263–64, 1279 n.19
proselytizing texts 884
prostration, mark of 382
Protestantism 762, 1133
proto-Shiʿism 376 n.17
proto-Twelver Shiʿi sources 628
proximity/closeness
 of ʿAlī (to God) 1038
 to God 106, 172, 235, 449, 451, 498, 692, 711, 1111
 of immaterial soul to God 466
 to realm of transcendent 362
psychical (*nafsī*) [conceptions] 669
psychoanalysis 1302–3

psychology/psychological 474, 536, 574
approach 484, 595, 1190
spiritual 21
public (*ʿāmma*) 1025 n.58
vs. private 1123
public good (*ḥuqūq Allāh*) 1101–2
pulpit (*minbar*) 1017 n.28
punishment 20, 39, 67, 124, 146, 191, 698, 1202, 1231
in afterlife 386
descriptions of 413–14, 475, 862
as distance 118
eternal 377, 672
hell 542, 1166–67, 1243
overwhelming [hour of] (*ghāshiya*) 183
Quranic verses on 1248
reasons for 1206
taste of 1043
temporary, cessation of 390–91, 534, 871
in the tomb (*ʿadhāb al-qabr*) 382
Pure Land Buddhism 267
purgatory 372 n.5, 904
hell/hellfire as purgative 371, 380, 399
purification
in hell 539
ritual 1108, 1113–14
of soul 571
purity 204, 255, 264, 299–300, 302, 337, 574, 795, 1246
of knowledge (*ṣafwat al-ʿilm*) 655
and reward 206
ritual 319 n.41
Pythagoreans 664

qāʿa (small rectangular arcaded courtyard) 1013
qadar (debate) 373 n.9
Qāf mountain 585, 635 n.173, 945
qāʾim (Ariser/Savior) 21, 510, 513, 609, 626, 631, 659, 678 n.9, 682, 708 n.20
advent/appearance of 613–14, 616–18, 622–25, 628–31, 650–52, 655 n.26, 681
conjoined with God 620
as the dawn (*fajr*) 611 n.38
death of 607 n.11
and disbelievers 621–22
followers of 625
al-mahdī 619
as messianic figure 606
names/epithets of 619
al-qiyāma (*qāʾim* of resurrection) 517, 627, 631–32, 685–86
and *qiyāma* 607, 609, 612, 616, 632
rise of 615, 628
Qajar (period) 26, 1056–57, 1063
images from 1059
Qarmatians 687, 855–56
qaṣīda 71, 86–88, 136, 145 n.24, 299. *See also* poetry/poets
qaṭʿī (definitive, decisive [texts]) 1204
qibla(s) 227, 403
orientation of 1091–92
qiyām (arising) 496
qiyāma (resurrection/rising) 4, 21, 194, 471, 474, 476, 628, 630–31, 683–85, 687, 715, 1021, 1194
declared (in 559/1164) 632 n.163
juzʾiyya (particular), *vs. kulliyya* (universal) 521 n.102
al-kubrā (major/Great) 517, 518 n.91, 519, 521, 530 n.115, 651
qayyim al- (one who causes *qiyāma*) 616 n.67
al-ṣughrā (minor) 518 n.91, 519
al-ʿuẓmā (supreme) 517–18
Qizilbash ideology 1036
quadrant model (of analysis) 1103, 1109–10, 1121–23
qubba (pl. *qibāb*) (dome) 621 n.91, 1012–13, 1021, 1024
al-Quds Brigade 1281 n.25, 1282 n.26, 1284
quiddity(ies) 488, 491, 502
Qumran community 74, 120
Quran 3, 14, 16–17, 23, 26, 33, 35, 39, 41, 49, 54, 94, 111, 124, 196, 295, 450, 515, 518, 658, 701, 708 n.20, 767, 769, 783, 819, 833, 842, 845, 883, 939, 956, 985–86, 988, 1023 n.48, 1122, 1127, 1131, 1148, 1155, 1176, 1193, 1198, 1210, 1226, 1233, 1282, 1284
and Adam 36
as an apocalypse 122
commentaries 21, 154, 181, 221, 241, 617, 829, 862, 937, 939, 1227
creation of 207
and dark-eyed *ḥūrīs* 799
on death 432
as *al-Dhikr* 113
and eschatological signs/symbols 11, 115, 676–77, 679, 683, 782, 858, 1240

Quran (cont.)
and eternal joy 13
on existence after death 12
al-Fātiḥa 266
foreign vocabulary of 781
inimitability (*iʿjāz*), doctrine of 350
inscriptions 1025
interpretation of 693, 833, 1224
on *jihād* 1159
on judgment 1217
literal meanings 479, 571, 669
Meccan suras/verses 59, 71–72, 120, 252, 254, 675
Medinan suras 59, 120
message of 67, 210
and metaphor 1195
narrative structure of 125–26, 1317–18
and nature 87, 136
on paradise 55, 59, 69, 71, 346, 829, 835, 841, 865
personified 94 n.1, 207
on primordial covenant 718 n.37
readers/reciters 100, 119, 171, 175–76, 191, 411, 1011, 1013 n.12, 1023
and reason 40, 42
Shiʿi secrets in 615
sources of language and imagery 801
and studies of apocalypse 99
style and terminology of 78, 781, 1197
and the Sunna 834
symbols in 22, 485, 634
translations of 5, 894
as word of God 1196
qurʾān (divine Word/instruction) 78
Quraysh 118
quṣṣāṣ (storytellers) 193 n.30, 842
quwwa (faculty)
al-kāmiliyya (perfecting) 653
al-khayāliyya (imaginative) 493, 671
al-muṣawwira (formative) 494

racial
concepts of hereafter 1217
and social solidarity (*ahl al-ʿaṣabiyya*) 1207
radicalism 955. *See also* fundamentalism
raḥīq (wine) 255–57
raiment 718, 797. *See also* clothing/garments
rain 144–47, 151, 161, 437, 945
as destructive 148
and thunder 17, 136, 143, 147–49, 437
Ramadan 1091
ranks 989
of paradise 839, 991
of people in paradise 1246
ratio 1105–6
legis (*ʿilla*) 1108
rationalism 1187, 1316, 1319
rationality 590, 1210, 1297
rationalization 1190
rational/rationalists 941
approach 633, 1203
faculty 453
Islam 1297
theologians 425
rawḍa (meadow) 103, 138, 185
reality 211, 809, 907, 909, 1019, 1062, 1075
of all realities (Muḥammad) 1019, 1020 n.37
replaced by fake version of 1077
realm(s). *See also* world(s)
of clear distinction (*kawn-i mubāyanat*) 667–68
of discord (*taḍādd*) 666
of Images 1190
of *a lastu* (*bi-rabbikum*) 1236
other-worldly 757, 764, 770
of punishment (*ʿiqāb*) and reward (*thawāb*) 671
of similitudes (*kawn-i mushābahat*) 667–68, 672
uppermost angelic (*al-malakūt al-aʿlā*) 652
reason 36–37, 40, 42, 45, 452, 775, 779, 856, 895, 904–5, 907–8, 1086, 1101, 1202, 1204
those deficient in 1193
reasoning
individual (*ahl al-raʾy*) 820 n.13
philosophical 1205
rebirth 12
recital (*ḥikāya*) 113
recitation, public 1165
reckoning (*ḥisāb*)
day of 157, 201, 842
final 425, 1192
individual 197
recommended (*mustaḥabb*) 1100

records (of deeds) 936, 1042, 1213, 1243
re-creation 279
recycling 759
reflection (*fikr*) 666
Reformation 1127
reformists/reformers 1188, 1292
refuge (*ma'wā*) 103, 137
gardens/abode of (*jannat al-*) 56, 187, 414, 417
reign, of Petty Kings (*mulūk al-ṭawā'if*) in al-Andalus 957
reincarnation (*tanāsukh*) 22, 739, 760, 1258
and controversy 743
cycle of 744–46, 749
doctrine of 740–42
-for-justice 737–39, 748
human-to-animal 752 n.59
Muʿtazilite 751–52
Quranic 740, 743
reincarnationists 743 n.36, 748
Muslim 746, 751
relations, with relatives 838–39
release (*mokṣa*) 740, 759
religion/religious 324, 668, 965, 969–70
abrogating Islam 607
defense of 1224
doctrines and teachings of 41, 691, 760, 824, 840, 1011
exoteric (*ẓāhir*) 628
false 696
goal of 536
history of 1136
imagery 811
instruction (*taʿlīm/amūkhtan/riyāẓat*) 654
law/rules 14, 453, 465–66, 597
new law for 629, 678 n.9
and politics 34
in public sphere 1122 n.64
revealed 46, 455
and sacrifice 1312
vs. secular 758
socialization 1129
stratification 302
religiosity 855–56
remembrance 1010
remorse (*nadam*) 483. *See also* repentance
réncongs (Acehnese dagger) 1173, 1175
renunciation 907, 909
repentance 20, 469, 482–84, 909
gate of (*bāb al-tawba*) 608 n.14
tawba 24, 483, 851, 854, 856, 1214
reprehensible (*makrūh*) 1100
representations 1074–75, 1077, 1211
reproduction 336
resignification, eschatological 679
resistance 1270, 1314
resurrection (*baʿth, qiyāma*) 7, 14, 19, 49, 100, 175, 182, 196, 200, 324, 437, 472, 492, 496, 626, 652, 654–55, 683, 744, 751, 778, 856, 1021 n.42, 1036, 1040, 1189, 1197–98, 1228, 1240
bodily/physical 181, 312, 336, 422, 450–51, 454–55, 458–59, 473, 475–76, 478–79, 484, 498, 509, 528–29, 586, 630, 664, 735, 1194, 1216, 1231
day of 21, 50, 63, 93, 112, 169, 173, 182, 187, 196, 199, 201, 229, 381, 433, 492, 607, 609, 622, 629–30, 683, 696, 699, 751, 947, 1233
descriptions/scenes of 349 n.36, 422, 618, 1216
to end all Resurrections (*qiyāmat al-qiyāmāt*) 632 n.163
kinds of 519
lesser/minor 521, 634
major/greater 423, 489, 507, 634
material circumstances of 425
metaphysics of 499
moment of 480
occurrence of 423–24
proclamation of (by Nizārī Ismaʿilis) 521
reality of 1195, 1211
spiritual 468–69, 475, 478–79, 666, 1216
terms for 469–71
waiting for 420
resurrector (*qā'im*). *See qā'im* (Ariser/Savior)
return (*rajʿa; maʿād*) 476, 607 n.11, 625, 736, 1292
chain of 496
day of 622
spiritual and bodily 490
Revelation, Book of 97–98, 104, 116, 124–25, 237 n.42, 622, 747, 763–64, 769
revelation(s) 14, 19, 40, 42, 89, 93–95, 107, 126, 272, 277, 435, 629, 654, 809, 1112, 1129, 1188, 1317

revelation(s) (cont.)
modes/occasions of (*asbāb al-nuzūl*) 96 n.10, 123
purpose of 536
Quranic historiography of 111
and revelatory literature 98
supernatural 99
tanzīl 94, 96, 100, 122, 516, 659, 676
types of 457
revenge 1282
revivification 147, 196
revolutions 1290
rewards 13, 18, 39, 49, 56, 60, 62, 83, 124, 159, 191, 206, 251–52, 296, 298, 303, 415, 840, 1043, 1150, 1155
for believers 272
for companions of the right hand (*aṣḥāb al-maymana*) 265
earthly/in this world 42, 415, 1168
eternal 671
in garden/paradise 27, 163–64, 650, 1287
heaven/paradise 1166–67
material/physical 64, 267–68, 460
as nearness [to God] 118
and punishment 7, 22, 33, 458, 465, 471, 630, 668, 768, 904, 1194, 1196–97, 1202, 1213–14, 1216
spiritual/moral 64, 458, 477
rhetoric 198, 199 n.42
of Islam in crisis 1302, 1311, 1314
persuasive (*targhīb*) 54
Semitic 125
rhetorical
allegory 285
and lexicographical works 15
rhyme 79, 138
ribāṭ (convent) 1014 n.19
rich (people) 203, 206, 411, 946
riches 420
Riḍwān (angel) 879–81, 1004
riḍwān (divine attribute of pleasure, approval, acceptance) 104
right
actions, belief, dogma 840
conduct 412, 413 n.21, 415, 419
path (*al-ṣirāṭ al-mustaqīm*) 680
vs. wrong 667
righteous (people) 205, 240–41, 252, 266, 465–66, 667, 737, 748, 761–62, 768, 770, 795, 839
ṣāliḥūn 202
righteousness 205, 1145
rights, in conflict 1123
riḥla 136
Rishī Sufi order (in Kashmir) 743
rite de passage 1281, 1285
rituals 597, 691, 854, 1285
rivers (in paradise) 167–68, 187, 241, 262, 318, 328, 437, 830, 834, 843 n.121, 865–66, 869, 879–81, 883, 928, 959, 990, 1176, 1298
Bāriq, at gate of paradise 166
brooklets 139–40, 143 n.19, 156
four 358
Jayḥān 318, 328, 928
al-Kawthar 876
nahr, pl. *anhār* 58–59, 105, 143
Nile 318
from ocean of Oneness 542
Sayḥān 318, 328
Shayḥān 928
r-k-d 149
romances, popular 912
Romans/Roman Empire 192, 258, 260
Romanticism 1127
romanticization 1077
roots (Quranic) 106
rūḥ (spirit)
al-amīn (faithful) 454
al-aʿẓam (mightiest/supreme) 188, 510
ruins (motif of) 86, 88
rulers
administration of 996
just (*imām ʿadl* or *sulṭān muqṣiṭ*) 838
Muslim (criticism of) 408, 412
pious 1023
Russian formalists 818

Sabians 52, 374 n.13
sacred 675–76
axis of 687
history 681, 684
sacredness 1014
sacrifice 253–54, 436, 1089, 1280–82, 1287, 1312–13
Safavid(s) 126, 487, 502, 513, 522, 1038
period 633, 1036
sage (*ḥakīm*) 503. *See also* wisdom
ṣaḥīḥ (sound) 828, 841–42
saints 199, 495, 692, 724, 796, 802, 1212
awliyāʾ, 654, 701, 708

graves of 1023
substitutes (*abdāl*) 236 n.37, 695
saj' (rhymed prose) 100, 263–64, 1279 n.19
Salafī
movement 1258
scholars 932–33
salafī (path) 1204
Saljuqs 163, 580–81, 597
Salsabīl (fountain; spring, in paradise) 104, 159, 239, 257, 265, 301
salvation/deliverance 14, 37, 44, 120, 181, 200, 209–10, 272, 335, 371–72, 382 n.34, 400, 404, 546, 649, 651, 656, 757, 766–67, 835, 840, 853, 856, 908, 913, 1044, 1195, 1197, 1222, 1267
assured by caliph 1005
as being spared hell 392
Biblical narrative of 89
guarantee of 402
najāt 392, 394
path to 536
seven steps of 1090
saṃsāra (cycle of birth, death, and reincarnation) 740, 759–60, 763
Sanskrit 925
Saracens 895, 912
Sasanians 258–59
Satan 35, 43, 141, 186, 436, 574, 703, 717–18, 764, 902, 913, 916, 1258. *See also* devils
and Adam/Eve's fall from paradise 720
and humans 721
Iblīs 569–71, 750
satanic, *vs.* divine 574
satisfaction 909
Saturn 904–5. *See also* astronomy/ astronomers; planets
saved 332, 650
savior 1214
scale(s) 201, 572, 1042–43. *See also* balance
scholars 171, 176, 537, 852
men of letters (*aṣḥāb qalam*) 24, 856
religious 202–4
'ulamā' 327, 580, 1003, 1025 n.58, 1166
schools 777
of [Islamic] law (*madhāhib*) 837, 1013, 1022
science 499, 705, 893, 915, 1070, 1129, 1196–97, 1214
modern 1218, 1228, 1257
of observation (*'ilm al-naẓar*) 938
and religion 1196, 1228
scientific approach/inquiry 14–15, 1084
scriptures 51, 112 n.64, 437, 536, 659, 787–88
apocryphal 800
esoteric/metaphorical meanings of 422, 1200
scrolls, raining (from sky) 1043
sculpture 1074. *See also* art
Scythians 260
seas 437, 1087
in paradise 869
seasons 109
seclusion (of *ḥūrīs*) 337
sects 324
sectarian movements 675
secular
art 1033
ideologies 762
vs. religious 760, 1123, 1317
and transcendental 1293
secularism 969–70, 1224
in India 966, 968
Turkish 1236
secularity 1291
secularization 26
self-awareness 598
self-disclosures, God's infinite 538
self-image/self-referential 93–94
self-knowledge 456, 571, 732
self-reflection 485
Semitic studies 1128
sense(s) 494, 1086, 1088, 1195, 1204, 1239, 1245
perceptions 667
realm/world of 653, 667
sensibilia 508
sensibles 582
sensible world 492
sensory 669
bridge (*jisr maḥsūs*) 544
data 564
powers 509
separation 1294–95
endless/limitless 1309, 1312–13
of *nasma* from body 1190–91
of the worlds 779
sermons, on heaven and hell 1148
servant(s) 261 n.58, 297, 299, 305, 420, 575, 835, 852, 994. *See also* girls
girls (*jāriya*) 304
in heaven (*kadam;* Ar. *khadam*) 1159
relationship with Lord 577

sex/sexual 61, 312, 319, 830, 853, 985, 1099, 1144, 1145, 1149, 1154, 1297
fantasies 1163
imagery 787, 799–800, 1145
pleasure/gratification 1144, 1165
relationships in paradise (*jimāʿ ahl al-janna*) 834 n.77
sexuality 84, 141, 300, 317, 323, 1237
shade 140, 144, 156, 159, 234, 237–38, 430, 866, 869, 985–86, 990
and fountains 138
Shāfiʿī (*madhhab*) 581, 819, 837. *See also* *madhāhib*
shahāda (testimony of faith) 346, 364, 377 n.23, 652, 731, 837, 1018 n.31, 1284
Shiʿi component of 1062
sharīʿa (religious/divinely revealed law) 208, 654, 683, 687, 851, 1003, 1100, 1104, 1123, 1192, 1228
shaykh murshid ([Sufi] shaykh) 503
Sheba
people of 57
Queen of (Bilqīs), Quranic tale of 588
Sheol 664, 763, 765, 767, 769, 796
Shiʿa/Shiʿis 8, 18, 274–75, 380, 503 n.52, 505, 588, 678, 683, 690, 695, 731, 735, 996, 998, 1000, 1003
apocalyptic 687
culture 26
history, dualistic vision of 681 n.22
imagery 1056
imāmī 596, 1223
Imams 9, 434
Islam, conversion to 1059
Ismaʿili ideas 579
literature 21, 860 n.5
orthodox creed 273
proto- 376 n.17, 628
traditions 162, 276, 569 n.15
Twelver Shiʿi community 511–13, 582, 663
vision of judgment 1042
worldview 8, 581
ships/watermills 437
shirk (associationism) 626 n.117, 1194, 1205
shopping malls 1075
shroud, white 1059–60. *See also* funerary
ṣiddīq, pl. *ṣiddīqūn* (righteous; those who affirm the revelation) 176, 202, 278
sides (*jawānib*) 229, 231–32
ṣifat al-janna (characteristics of paradise)
works 817, 820, 822–24, 827 n.42, 829–34, 839, 841, 872–74
compilers of 820–21, 826, 829, 831, 844
signs 109, 113, 343, 665
of day of resurrection/apocalypse 946, 1234, 1251
of God 136, 143, 147, 203, 428, 434
of hereafter 1217–18
of the hour/Hour 771, 942, 1208–9
of the *mahdī* 1250
portents (*ʿalāmāt/ashrāṭ*) 606
preceding day of judgment 1206–7
Sijjīn, clay of 497
silk 17, 239, 247, 252, 295–96, 299, 303, 305. *See also* textiles
ḥarīr 236–38, 239 n.46
sundus 236 n.38, 261 n.59
similes 150–51, 208–10, 426. *See also* metaphors
similitude (*mushābahat; mithāl*) 666
world of 494, 501, 1190, 1218, 1239 n.77
simulcrum 1068, 1074
sincerity 853, 1010, 1018
single (*mufrad*) 704
sin(s)/sinners 35, 53, 67, 172, 190, 325, 429, 472, 483, 566, 628, 770, 902, 1042–43, 1194
from among righteous community 768
of the dead 1010
descriptions of 862, 884
hell expunges 382
kinds of 471, 861, 1244
major/grave (*kabāʾir*) 351 n.46, 371–72, 380, 403, 412, 536
Muslim(s) 380, 383–84, 388–89, 391, 398–99, 403–4, 871, 1044
original 37, 70, 271, 280, 775
and punishment/torment 342, 410, 1036, 1039–40, 1244
ṣirāṭ
as bridge to paradise 1192
as path [of righteousness] (in *al-Fātiḥa*) 396 n.76
as path/bridge (over hell) 4, 19, 427, 472
Sisyphus 766
s-k-n 118
sky(ies) 490, 1084–85
slander 172

slaves/slavery 324, 828, 838, 958
sleep 19, 108, 111, 211, 428, 430–31
  and death 432, 439
  deprivation of 431, 436
  motif of long-lasting sleep 434
  temple/mystery sleep 436
Sleepers
  allegorical meanings of sleeping boys 434
  of the Cave 746
slipwares 262. *See also* ceramics; cups/vessels
s-l-m 104
smoke/vapor 459
sociability 985
social 839, 1211
  activism 101, 345, 361
  control 335
  fabric, of Muslim polity 941
  function/purpose 840, 1118
  hierarchies/stratification 298, 302, 332–33
  implications 1111–14, 1120
  issues 1250
  moral models 844
  responsibility 1317
  stability 365, 1232
  structure 512 n.75
  value 1102
social sciences 1223
society(ies) 1099, 1102, 1217, 1229
  Andalusian 960
  Islamic/Muslim 555, 564, 959, 962
  modern 1068, 1077
  traditional 1068, 1076–77
Sodom (and Gomorrah) 770–71
Sogdian (traders) 258
solidarity 1178–79
soteriology 548, 766
  Ḥurūfī 706
  Isma'ili 649
  in scripture 566
Soul 504 n.55, 512, 654–56, 686
  as passive/receptive 653–54
  realm of 652
  Universal 656
soul (*nafs*, or *rūḥ*) 2, 12–14, 113, 181 n.2, 197, 206, 265, 431, 436, 447 n.10, 452, 492, 494, 496, 499, 507, 529, 544, 571–73, 669, 704, 750 n.56, 1191, 1194, 1213, 1237, 1255, 1258
  after death 475, 659, 1194, 1201
  appetitive 465
  ascent of 545
  and birds 200
  and bodies 198, 448, 476–77, 664, 795–96, 802, 1194, 1201, 1214–15
  definitions of 664
  domineering/commanding (*ammāra*) 692
  evolution of 742
  existence of 665, 1195
  fate of human 458
  formation of 114
  fortunate ones 198–99
  goodness of 1216
  in hereafter 423
  imaginative 287
  of imbeciles and children 458, 460
  as immaterial 422–23, 425, 447, 451, 453, 475, 500, 586, 707 n.16, 1194
  immortality/imperishability of 181, 473, 1089, 1193–94, 1197
  jān 575–76
  material/corporeality 473, 515, 545
  mineral, plant, animal 692
  Neoplatonic theories of 448
  of non-philosophical masses 459–60, 462, 466
  origin of 545
  of outermost sphere 456
  particular (*al-anfus al-juzi'āt*) 507, 656
  rational 456–57, 459
  return to/of 1202, 1215
  separated from bodies after death 432, 464, 473, 505, 817 n.1
  as simple entity 448–49, 515
  states of 22
  substance/essence of 508, 545, 655
  unfortunate/wicked 198–99, 460
  Universal (*kullī*) 503 n.52, 507, 649–51, 653, 656
  world/realm of 509, 652, 1234
sound 722
  ṣaḥīḥ [legal category] 828, 841–42, 845
source (*ma'din*) 227
sovereignty 593, 1301
  divine 593
space 113, 569, 697, 761, 769 n.17
  of paradise 868
  positive and negative 1016

space bridge (*uzay köprüsü*) 1238
space/time (*uzay/zaman*) 1236
Spaniards 963–64
speaker-prophets (*nāṭiq*) 629, 678 n.9
species 515
speech 78, 713, 726–27, 731
  of God 563
spices, in paradise 18, 252, 254
  basil (*rayḥān*) 703
  cumin, fennel, anise, and thyme 259
  frankincense, myrrh, cassia, cinnamon and ladanum 254
  ginger (*zanjabīl*) 252, 257–60
  pepper, cinnamon, cloves, aromatic herbs 259
  saffron 277, 279–80, 283, 295, 297, 303–5, 703, 711, 835, 868
spirit(s) (*rūḥ, arwāḥ*) 235, 459, 499, 512, 529, 574, 664, 699, 761, 802, 1190
  deeds of 697
  holy (*al-qudus*) 454
spiritual (*nafsānī; malakūtī; rūḥāniyya*) 61
  extension (*spissitudo spiritualis*) 500
  vs. material 18, 268, 778
  matter (*hayūlā, mādda*) 500
  world/realm 208, 656
spiritualists (*rūḥāniyyūn*) 282, 1188
spirituality/spiritualism 1, 1258, 1316
spoils 408
spouses. *See* wives/spouses
spring (as metaphor of resurrection) 1232 n.38, 1233
springs. *See* fountain(s)/springs
ṣ-q-ʿ 148 n.31
stages (*darajāt*) 357, 653
stars 109, 330, 332 n.96, 436, 452, 494, 710–11, 721, 1000–1001, 1083, 1242
  fixed 357, 905, 1084, 1087–88
states (*aḥwāl*) (of beatific vision) 286–87
state/territory 1299 n.21
stations (*maqām*) 711
  of Adam 723
  on journey to heaven 1037–38
statues 1070. *See also* art
steadfastness (*ṣumūd*) 1287
stereotypes 1123
s-ṭ-ḥ 991
stoning (*rajm*) 382
story(ies) 277, 968, 1034
  adventure 1154
  frame 588
  on holy war 1167–68
  of the ʿIfrīt and the Maiden 924
  Judeo-Christian 16, 374, 431
  of Paradise, of Ephraem 792–94
  of Shahriyār and Shahrazād 924–25
storytellers (*quṣṣāṣ*, sing. *qāṣṣ*) 193 n.30, 833 n.75, 842, 1057, 1148
straight path 39–40, 42, 44, 491, 503 n.52, 546, 702
  ṣirāṭ mustaqīm 266, 427, 496, 544
streams (in paradise) 1044, 1195. *See also* rivers
  of different colors 1039
  running 139, 142–43, 155–56, 430, 665
streetscape 556–57
strife/discord (*fitneler*, Ar. *fitna*) 1250
structuralism 15, 344
structure (*hay'a*) 492
subject, and alterity 1305
subjectivity 1293
  excess of 1304
  female 28, 1302
  Islamic male 1300 n.24, 1302–3
  of Islamists 1314
  masculine 1299
  Muslim/Islamic 1294, 1301
sublunar realm 113, 1087
submission 1318
substances/essence (*jawhar*) 473, 570
  obscure (*ghāsiq*) 502
  of prophethood (*nubuwwa*) 426
  of the soul (*nafs*) 655
  subtle (*laṭīfa*) 574
substantiation (*tajawhur*) 492, 496
substitutes/substitution 694–95
  aʿwāḍ 236 n.37
  saints, intercessors (*abdāl*) as 236 n.37, 695
successor(s)
  generation (*tābiʿūn*) 235 n.34, 397, 820
  of Muḥammad, legitimacy of 437 n.25, 588
suffering 14, 205, 591, 594, 703, 793, 807, 852, 856, 1217. *See also* afflictions/infirmities; trials/tribulations
  narratives of 1270

Sufi(s) 22, 40, 222 n.4, 353, 422, 425, 434, 567, 579, 739, 743, 752, 855, 911, 918, 1070, 1201
  Bektāshiyya 691 n.7
  beliefs/ideals 581, 695
  gatherings 1013
  imagination 1216
  Kubrāwiyya order 581
  music and songs (*samāʿ*) 283
  Naqshbandīs 598
  orders 580–82
  orthodox 573
  Rishī order (in Kashmir) 743
  traditions 699
Sufism 4, 8, 513, 579, 583, 586, 731, 1213, 1258
  intellectual 1227
  Khurasani 580
  and *sharīʿa* 582
suicide 1, 412, 1273
  bombers 1144–45, 1146, 1298, 1299 n.21, 1311, 1313
  mujāhidīn 1147
Sumerian
  mythology 253
  texts 1086
Sunna 939, 1282
sunna (pl. *sunan*) 4, 6, 208, 313 n.8, 328, 386, 426, 606, 840, 843, 845, 998
Sunni(s) 314, 328, 371, 588
  eschatological literature 24
  groups 18
  Islam 819, 837
  orthodox (*ahl al-sunna wa-l-jamāʿa*) 273–75
  religious identity/view 372–73
  and Shiʿites (controversies between) 596
  theology 1034
  traditionist exegetes 390
Sunnism 372, 373 n.9, 398, 690
  classical 376 n.17, 381, 382 n.34, 404
  normative 1036
sun/Sun 109, 234, 254, 264, 436, 710, 904–5, 944, 1000, 1083, 1091–92, 1235, 1242
  heat of 1043
supernatural (world) 98, 209
sustenance (*rizq*) 166, 172, 175
sword, of ʿAlī (*dhū l-fiqār*) 1058
symbols/symbolism 104, 182, 190, 207, 211, 253, 343, 437, 457, 576, 984, 995, 1022, 1173, 1268, 1279, 1285–86
  apocalyptic/eschatological 105, 683–85
  function of (as icon) 1018
  heavenly/paradisal 25–26, 561, 983, 985, 998
  imagery/representation 210, 244, 547, 1037
  of legitimacy 1000
  of Palestinian wedding 1275–76
  of *qāʾim* 617
  Quranic 572, 666
  of struggle 1276–77
symmetry(ies) 77–78, 82, 94, 105 n.41, 109, 113, 122, 982, 1016, 1088, 1317, 1318
synchronic perspective 819
syncretism 580
  of religious communities 1135
synesthesia 121
synods 777, 779
synthesis, idea of 1218
Syriac 23, 781–82, 785, 807
  churches of Late Antiquity 801
  galyutha 89
  language 788, 800, 806
  literature 782, 797
  sources 272
Syrian Church 782
Syrian Renaissance 806
Syro-Aramaic reading 787

taʿbīr ([dream] interpretations) 437, 457 n.49, 710
table, heavenly (*māʾida*) 123
tablet(s) 187, 575, 686, 1038
  of Moses 708, 717
tafsīr (commentary, exegesis) 8, 100, 154, 677, 829 n.57, 833, 871, 931, 935–36. *See also* commentaries; exegeses
  al-aḥlām (of dreams) 19
  on eschatology 620
  ʿilmī (scientific exegesis) 1228
  Shiʿi 616
tajwīd (performance tradition) 100
ṭalab (pursuit) 585
tanāsukh (reincarnation, metempsychosis, transmigration) 500, 505, 735, 737, 745, 749, 752, 855. *See also* reincarnation; transmigration
targhīb (moral suasion) 54, 824, 832 n.74, 845

Tartarus 664, 763, 765–66, 769
Tasnīm (fountain; spring) 256–57, 265. *See also* fountain(s)/springs
tawḥīd (affirming unity [of God], the One) 200, 246, 377, 426, 585, 653, 711, 723, 1317–18. *See also* unity
  ahl al- 377–79, 380, 389–90
taʾwīl. See exegeses (*tafsīr*)
taxes 1085
taxonomy 365
taʾyīd (divine support) 649, 651, 654–55, 657, 659
  aṣḥāb al- (possessors of) 658
teaching
  master (*ustādh muʿallim*) 503
  sessions (*sohbet, ders*) 1225
technology 1250, 1260–61
telecommunications 1207
teleological approach 68
telepathy 1239, 1245
temperance (*ʿiffa*) 352
temples 507, 777
temporal 761, 769 n.17
  and material world 42
  vs. non-temporal 778
temporality 1073, 1314–16, 1318
terminology 23, 413, 462, 468, 474–75, 663 n.10, 691, 703 n.7, 832 n.74
  philosophical 473
  Sufi 1201
terrain (*arḍ*) 561
terrestrial (realm/worlds) 452, 456, 459, 462, 507, 1084, 1087
terrorism/terrorists 1144, 1146–47, 1164
test (*fitna*) 192
textiles
  brocade 13, 80, 83, 156, 158–59, 184–85, 236 n.38, 261, 295–96, 430, 435, 703, 712, 987, 994
  silk 13, 59, 62, 159, 261, 296, 703
Thamūd 138
theocracy 970, 1131
theodicy 675, 738, 940
theologians 468, 477, 482, 1187
  classical 1187
  Indo-Pakistani 1189, 1218
  Muslim 735, 1198, 1216
  mutakallimūn 454
  rational 274
theologoumenon 77
theology 3, 4, 820, 893, 1128, 1130, 1136, 1204
  approach of 14–15, 1189
  bi-lā kayf 373 n.9
  Christian 778, 1217
  doctrines of 1003
  Jewish 1217
  modern/new Islamic 1188–89, 1196, 1218
  Muslim/Islamic 12, 32, 34, 1116 n.51, 1217–18
  politics of 380–81
  (*ilāhiyya*) premises 1094
  questions/issues/discussions of 871, 873, 940, 1215, 1224
  treatises on 937, 988
theophany 107, 116, 531, 570 n.17
  divine self-manifestation (*tajallī*) 100, 108, 510
this-worldly 761, 765, 770, 1164
threats (of punishment) 409–10
throne (of God) 17, 55, 62, 108, 163–64, 167–68, 175, 187, 196, 224, 232, 236, 248, 296, 510, 562, 892, 904, 918, 936, 944, 989–91, 1021, 1038–39, 1244
  ʿarsh 225–29, 242–43, 245, 548, 574
  carried above angels 356
  creation of 226–27, 243
  expansion of 512, 531
  God sitting on 517
  light of and creation of Muḥammad 274
  as metaphor 245
  presence of God on 246–47
throne-chariot (*merkabah*) 106
thrones, people in garden on 252, 560
Throne verse 108, 122, 225, 227, 244, 248
tilework 1057–58, 1063
time 42, 112–15, 121, 504, 512, 569, 651, 697, 1316
  age (*ḥuqb*) 389 n.62, 403
  Aristotelian definition of 446
  blink of an eye (*ṭarfat ʿayn*) 561
  cyclical perception of 72
  eternal/sacred 342–43
  linear motion of 43
  moment (*ānan; waqt*) 122, 482
  months, twelve 229
  and motion 446
  new eon 758, 760–61
  in paradise 1246

shrinking/closeness of (*taqārub al-zamān*) 1206, 1218
solar year 1085
timelessness 1073, 1077
tolerance
of India 955–56
of Islam 953
tombs/shrines 856, 1011, 1025. *See also* funerary (matters)
chambers of 1013, 1017–18
topography 1020 n.38. *See also* rivers
meadows (*rawḍa*) 103, 138, 185
mountains 870, 1242
of paradise 865
wādīs 144
topos 120. *See also* motifs
Andalusian 974
Torah 153, 708 n.20, 792
paradise in 791
torments 671
endless 764
of the grave 842
as pleasure 62, 538, 540, 1202
torture 963, 1039, 1043
traditionalists 395–96, 403, 567, 939, 1188
traditionists [i.e., *ḥadīth* scholars] 392, 820
traditions
local 1071
Near Eastern 253–54, 348, 767
Shiʿi, from Jaʿfar al-Ṣādiq 513
sünnetler, loss of 1250
traditions, prophetic (*aḥādīth*/*khabar*, pl. *akhbār*). *See* Ḥadīth Index
tragedy 1312–13
transcendence 361, 1292, 1316–17
Islamic notions of 1296
and unity 1304
transcendent activism or quietism 361–64
translation 1091
movement (of ʿAbbasids) 320
transmigration (*tanāsukh*) 458, 498, 505–6, 659
Ḥurūfī theory 726 n.59
Platonic concept of 736 n.5
of souls 735
transmigrationists (*ahl-i tanāsukh*) 518 n.91
transmission, chains of (*isnāds*) 820
transmutation (*tabaddul*) 520
transport 1218
tree(s) 59, 144, 159, 241, 252, 656–57, 665, 719 n.42, 794, 796, 798, 800, 834 n.77, 853, 926, 985, 988, 1039, 1058, 1060–61. *See also* shade
acacias 986
cosmic 944
of eternity (*shajarat al-khuld*) 869 n.37
forbidden 43, 141, 719
of life 35–36, 798
in Light verse 107
palm 80, 870, 987, 995
in paradise 561, 830, 864 n.18, 865–66, 869, 879–80, 990
ṭūbā 103, 284, 821, 829–30, 870, 881
zaqqūm 105, 265, 722 n.46
triads, *vs.* dyads 455–56
trials/tribulations (of this life) 271, 429, 543, 764. *See also* afflictions/infirmities
tribalism 965
trompe l'oeil 1062
tropes 932
heroes killing monsters 1041
pagan poetic 90
troubadours 894, 897, 906, 908, 910
trumpet 93, 183, 193, 196, 277–78, 497, 529–30, 618, 622, 630, 944, 946, 1021, 1038, 1042, 1242
trust (in God) 907, 909
truth 160, 667–68, 670, 672, 853
Absolute 575
and falsehood 621, 679
God as 563
ḥaqq, ḥaqīqa, pl. *ḥaqāʾiq* 109, 122, 519, 576, 677, 685, 704, 713
qāʾim as 610
search for 45
truthful (people) 169
Turkish (language) 1236
Turkmen tribes 581
typological figuration 111–12, 115, 122, 125, 1318 n.65
typology(ies) 111, 679–81, 683, 1100, 1202
tyranny 101

Umayyads (of Andalus) 995, 1005
buildings of 1001
coinage 999–1000
and Fatimids 1000–1001
legitimacy of 997–99

Umayyads (of Damascus) 359, 1003, 1017, 1207
umma (community) 380, 726, 1018, 1251
division of 588
unbelievers/unbelief 165–66, 169, 173, 185, 302, 388, 395–97, 475, 479–80, 497, 570, 618, 678, 725, 750, 767–69, 1044, 1155, 1204, 1228, 1248. *See also* disbelievers/disbelief
children of 32
definition of 472
fate of 377–78
ingratitude (*kufr; kāfir,* pl. *kuffār*) of 104, 302, 376–77, 397, 422, 851, 1166, 1195, 1205
punishment of 1205
slain by 171
unconsciousness 431, 438, 972
underworld 763, 765–66, 769–70
unification 113, 463–64, 595, 652, 1313
union
between divine and human realms 797
with God 255 n.20
intellectual 463–64
ittiḥād 113, 510
jamʿ 521 n.102
perfection of 575 n.41
unitary reality 535
unity 331, 446 n.7, 591, 731, 840, 968, 1017, 1292–93
communal 967
of existence 742
individual 492
of, with God/divine 579, 592–93, 595, 597–98, 666, 730–31
universality (of Muḥammad's message) 1020
universals, and particulars 654
universe 1087, 1232
expansion of 1242
as manifestation of divine Word 722
organization of 720
parallel 1236
personal 1239
Prime Mover of 909
as uncreated 1241
unrighteous 737, 749
UNRWA 1269
unseen 41, 43, 318, 563
qāʾim as 610
unveiling(s) 95, 722. *See also kashf*
masters of 506, 632
mukāshafa 568 n.8
people of (*ahl al-kashf*) 537, 539
urban
character 76–77
culture, Arab-Muslim 559
design 1012
visuality, Arab-Muslim 564
urbanism, Muslim 557
usury/usurers 190–91
utopia(s) 69, 271, 341 n.3
apocalyptic vision of 942
perfect 764
secular 1259, 1290
ʿUzair (Ezra), legend of 434

vainglory 1319
Vedic religion 192
vegetation 988, 991, 995, 1005, 1036, 1063
seasonal 744–45
veil
on heights 399–400
ḥijāb, between God and worshippers 562
or curtain (*sitār*) 234
veiling 589
velis 1245. *See also* friends (of God); saints; *walāya*
Venus 904. *See also* astronomy/astronomers; planets
verses/signs (*āyāt*) 100
vicegerent, of God 36, 39, 45, 720
vices 351–52, 912
arrogance/pride 43, 72, 1287
defamation (*qadhf*) 483
greed, lust 907
victory, and defeat 1217
vines/vineyards 74, 143, 160, 926, 990. *See also* grapes/grapevines
violence 125, 329, 581, 590, 1105, 1179, 1225, 1260, 1290–92, 1309–10
cycle of 964
images of 1316
male Islamist 1309
of politics 1298
against women 959, 1291, 1302

virginity 82, 150–53, 342, 785, 803, 1298
virgins 28, 158, 430, 784–85, 796, 828, 831, 852, 1144, 1159. *See also* maidens/girls
in paradise 271–72, 275–77, 279, 1162, 1168
virility 1303, 1312
codes of 1300–1301
Muslim 1299
virtues 351–52, 760, 1317
generosity 345, 360, 364
and moral excellence (*faḍl, faḍīla*) 177, 179
patience 40, 168, 202, 206–7, 238, 907, 909
philosophical and theological 353
virtuous 1245
city (*al-madīna al-fāḍila*) 454, 1319
person (of "wrong"/unbelieving community) 768
visibility 557–58
of inhabited, built world 559
in world, *vs.* paradise 555–56
visible 563
form 705
vs. invisible 576
visio beatifica 7, 121, 274, 282–83, 285
visions 19, 21, 281, 493–94, 555, 558, 809, 1228
of beloved (*ṭayf al-khayāl*) 146
of God 246–47, 282, 559, 837–38
of next world 251
of paradise 298, 301, 336, 803, 808, 1246
of paradise and hell 255 n.20, 432
in sleep 435
visio smaragdina (outburst of green) 205
visiting graves (*ziyārat al-qubūr*) 1010, 1238
visuality 21
Muslim 555–56, 564
study of 556
visualization 209, 1034
vita angelica 773
void (*yokluk*) 1236
vulgar (matters) 1145

wahm (estimative imagination) 669
waḥy (revelation) 16, 86, 88–89, 658. *See also* revelation(s)
waiting (*intiẓār*) 634
wajd (ecstasy) 115
wakefulness 432, 439
walad ṣāliḥ (a just, pious descendant) 1024 n.57
walāya (friendship with God) 588, 682. *See also* saints
of ʿAlī 680–81, 683
doctrine of 516
walls 868, 881, 883. *See also* architecture/architectural (features)
around gardens 985
decoration 983, 988, 992
of paradise 880
waqf (endowment) 1012, 1022, 1025, 1239
wāqiʿa (hour of terror) 100, 123, 183
warriors 1157
war(s) 764, 855, 1149, 1165, 1173, 1260
of 1967, 1271
Aceh War (Dutch War, Infidel War) 1147, 1149, 1167, 1169–70
Cumbok War 1171
Gulf War (1991) 1074
Iran-Iraq 1057, 1250
World War I 1073, 1206
World War II 1073–74
washings 1103–4, 1107. *See also* ablutions
wasīla (highest place, seat) 836
waṣiyya [will] 1282, 1284
waste 1105–6, 1108–9, 1113–15
water 57–59, 105, 109, 139 n.13, 140, 142–43, 146, 151, 153, 160–61, 228 n.21, 254, 255 n.22, 261, 264, 665, 907, 985–86, 1039
amount of 1107, 1114–15
characteristics of 1115 n.46, 1115 n.48
as element 456, 473, 667 n.32, 717–18, 1087
flowing 703
fresh 508
source of 542
subterranean 1086
wāw al-thamāniya (of eight things) 350–51, 353
weak (*ḍaʿīf*) 821–22, 824, 845
wealth 198, 203, 206, 234–35, 252, 454, 907
love of 239
use of, in *jihād* 410
wedding
ceremony 1275, 1281
trope 1145
weighing, of actions/deeds (*mīzān-i aʿmāl*) 702, 1189

Weltanschauung 67
Western
colonization/colonizers 963, 966
media 1144
orientation 810
Westernization 1072
west/West 107, 265–66, 809, 892, 917, 925, 1188, 1311
wicked 765. *See also* damned
death of 196
souls of 199
wickedness 101. *See also* evil
will, of God/Lord 379, 423, 450, 477, 537, 1102, 1209, 1282, 1284
wind 148, 160–61, 228 n.21, 234, 239, 318, 562, 945
wine 85, 105, 140, 147, 158, 185, 251, 253–58, 260, 264, 305, 430, 665, 703, 785, 795, 866, 1039, 1044, 1195
khamr 257, 854–56
nabīdh (intoxicating drink, wine) 855
in paradise 18, 58–59, 74, 560
poetry, ʿAbbasid (*khamrīyya*) 300
qahwa (wine) 855
in Quran 263
Roman/Byzantine 259
wisdom 1040
of God 537, 938
ḥikma 352, 570
literature 922
witness/eyewitness 162
wives/spouses 62, 155–57, 185, 233, 280, 282, 284, 302–3, 319, 333, 335, 801, 834 n.77
earthly 305
heavenly 417, 420, 828
of *mujāhidīn* 419
pure 322, 336 n.115
two (*zawjatān*) 166
women/female(s) 18, 65, 83 n.45, 86, 151, 320–22, 419, 828, 839, 852–53, 882, 909–11, 915, 958, 961–62, 1071–72, 1116, 1144, 1167, 1268–69, 1279, 1281, 1299 n.21, 1314
in Arabic history 895
believing [Muslim] 60, 267, 331, 910, 1298
bodies of 18, 322, 326, 336, 714
clothed [yet] naked 326, 328
earthly 278–79, 303, 322–23, 333–34, 336–37, 1161, 1168
face, form of 714
of garden/in paradise 827, 1146
hell/paradise, as a female body 329
inferiority of 336
literati 959
martyrs 1270, 1273, 1275, 1285
as mothers 706
in paradise 318, 333, 789
as pure (*ṭayyibāt*) 278
status of 1119–21
subjectivity of 28, 1302
subjugation 1298
transmitters 325
violence against 959, 1291, 1302
wonders, of [God's] kingdom (*ʿajāʾib al-malakūt*) 938
word(s) (*kalima*) 713, 722
corrupt *vs.* pure 720
divine/of God 703–4, 706, 708, 710, 712–13, 717, 719, 724, 726
locus of manifestation of 709–10, 712
original 704, 706
works, importance of 382 n.34. *See also* good deeds
world(s)
in ascension 499
boundaries of 923
of conception (*hayâl âlemleri*) 1238
earthly (*dunyawī*) 197
as eternal 446 n.7
external, *vs.* internal 2
fictional worlds (*hayal âlemleri*) 1236
first (*ūlā*), and last 50
higher (*ʿulwī*) realm 939
intelligible 492
Intermediate 1222, 1258
of the kingdom (*malakūt*) 227
of light 1134
lowermost depths/realm 666, 939
and paradise 557, 579
plural 1227, 1236, 1255–56
present 758, 774–76, 778–79
sensible 492
of similitudes/likenesses (*amthāl*) 689, 697, 1191
of spiritual unveiling (*kashf*) 713
of symbols and images 575, 1191
of theophanic imagination (*mithāl, khayāl*) 702, 706, 707 n.16, 730

this world (*mudānāt*) 236
as transitory 39
True [of philosophers] 449
ultimate (*ukhrā*) 529
visibility of 563
worship 853
acts of 124, 329
God as object of 539
worshipful obedience (*taʿabbud*) 1105–6, 1108–9, 1114 n.42
wrath 548, 703, 722
as accidental 543
of God 543, 549, 665
w-r-d 391–93
wurūd 393, 395
wretched (people) 537. *See also* damned; wicked
wretchedness 546, 1194
writers 852
Western 809
writings 731
American/European spiritual 1188
wrongdoers 394–95, 668
wuʿʿāẓ (public preachers) 833 n.75

Yahweh 761
yawm (day) 1318. *See also* resurrection
al-ākhir (last) 471
al-faṣl (of separation) 517, 679
al-jamʿ (of union) 517
al-qiyāma (of resurrection) 519, 521, 605, 634 n.170
al-waqt al-maʿlūm (of the appointed time) 623
yearning (*ʿishq*), for existence 537
Young Turks 1254

zabāniya (human-like figures) 1039
ẓāhir (literal, apparent, exoteric) 334, 571, 589, 685, 1296
-bāṭin (esoteric) dichotomy 571
zamharīr (burning cold) 159 n.45, 237
z-m-h-r 237 n.40
zanādiqa (apostates; atheists; heretics) 855–56, 1207
Zanjabīl (fountain; spring) 257
zawjiyya (dyad of pure pairedness) 653
z-h-r 1001
zināʾ (unlawful sexual intercourse) 329
Zionism 1276–77, 1284
zodiac 228, 667 n.32, 1089. *See also* astrology
Zoroaster 696
Zoroastrianism 207, 348, 590, 659, 761, 770
Zoroastrian(s) 15, 255 n.22, 580, 1089
apocalypse 101, 765
beliefs 396 n.76, 1033
cosmology 761
sources 585 n.36
texts 633 n.165
zuhd (asceticism) 346 n.23, 872

If you have any questions regarding this title, please contact:

Koninklijke Brill BV
Plantijnstraat 2
2321 JC Leiden
Email: info@brill.com

Batch number: 08683593